International Handbook of Love

Claude-Hélène Mayer • Elisabeth Vanderheiden
Editors

International Handbook of Love

Transcultural and Transdisciplinary Perspectives

Editors
Claude-Hélène Mayer
Department of Industrial Psychology
and People Management
University of Johannesburg
Johannesburg, South Africa

Elisabeth Vanderheiden
Global Institute for Transcultural Research
Römerberg, Germany

Institut für therapeutische Kommunikation
und Sprachgebrauch
Europa Universität Viadrina
Frankfurt (Oder), Germany

ISBN 978-3-030-45995-6   ISBN 978-3-030-45996-3 (eBook)
https://doi.org/10.1007/978-3-030-45996-3

© Springer Nature Switzerland AG 2021

This work is subject to copyright. All rights are reserved by the Publisher, whether the whole or part of the material is concerned, specifically the rights of translation, reprinting, reuse of illustrations, recitation, broadcasting, reproduction on microfilms or in any other physical way, and transmission or information storage and retrieval, electronic adaptation, computer software, or by similar or dissimilar methodology now known or hereafter developed.

The use of general descriptive names, registered names, trademarks, service marks, etc. in this publication does not imply, even in the absence of a specific statement, that such names are exempt from the relevant protective laws and regulations and therefore free for general use.

The publisher, the authors, and the editors are safe to assume that the advice and information in this book are believed to be true and accurate at the date of publication. Neither the publisher nor the authors or the editors give a warranty, expressed or implied, with respect to the material contained herein or for any errors or omissions that may have been made. The publisher remains neutral with regard to jurisdictional claims in published maps and institutional affiliations.

Cover illustration: Sharon McCutcheon

This Springer imprint is published by the registered company Springer Nature Switzerland AG.
The registered company address is: Gewerbestrasse 11, 6330 Cham, Switzerland

Acknowledgments

Dear Human: You've got it all wrong. You didn't come here to master unconditional love.
This is where you came from and where you'll return. You came here to learn personal love. Universal love. Messy love. Sweaty Love. Crazy love.
Broken love. Whole love. Infused with divinity. Lived through the grace of stumbling. Demonstrated through the beauty of ... messing up. Often. You didn't come here to be perfect, you already are. You came here to be gorgeously human. Flawed and fabulous. And rising again into remembering.
Courtney A. Walsh

Writing an international multidisciplinary and culturally diverse handbook about love is a monumental project. It could only succeed because many internationally renowned authors were willing to share their expertise and perspectives with us and to contribute them to this book. We are very grateful for that.

We would like to thank some individuals in particular:

We would like to thank Professor Freddie Crous, Head of the Department of Industrial Psychology and People Management, University of Johannesburg. Freddie is the incorporated example of a loving leader and an extraordinary role model for many people. A few weeks ago, he said in our annual departmental meeting: "We must just love each other. We must just love each other." When ever have you personally heard a (male) leader in higher education or in any other organisation saying this openly and you felt you could just believe him?

We would also like to thank Mrs. Ruth Cotzee, our wonderful language editor who has worked with us on several projects already over the past few years. Ruth is a great example for passionate love when it comes to language, and she is always very patient with us and our ways of expressing ourselves.

Further, we would like to express our thanks to all the individuals who have participated in our research projects and studies on love and who have shared their knowledge, emotions and deep insights with us.

Finally, we would like to thank our publisher Springer International Publishing AG for continuous support and interest in our projects. Especially we would like to thank Shinjini Chatterjee and Ameena Jaafar, Nitesh Shrivastava and his team for their commitment and support with regard to this book project.

We dedicate this book to the children in our lives: Blanche, Lolo, Ecee, Till, Marie, Jan, Irma, Emilia, Julian and Annabelle.

Contents

Part I Introductory Chapters

1. Voicing the Stories of Love Across Cultures: An Introduction 3
   Claude-Hélène Mayer and Elisabeth Vanderheiden

2. The State of Ethnological Research on Love: A Critical Review ... 23
   William Jankowiak and Alex J. Nelson

3. Love's Ethnographic Record: Beyond the Love/Arranged
   Marriage Dichotomy and Other False Essentialisms 41
   Alex J. Nelson and William Jankowiak

4. Cultural Diversity of Romantic Love Experience 59
   Victor Karandashev

Part II Particular Facets and Manifestations of Love in Digital Social, Cultural and Political Contexts

5. Cyberspace: The Alternative Romantic Culture 83
   Aaron Ben-Ze'ev

6. Climbing, and Falling Off, Plato's Ladder of Love: The Emotions
   of Love and of Love's Undoing 101
   Warren Tenhouten

7. Towards the Performance of Embodied Cultures of Love 123
   Freddie Crous and Leigh Leo

8. "A Friend? A Single Soul Dwelling in Two Bodies."
   Friendship—a Special Kind of Love 135
   Elisabeth Vanderheiden

9   "Have a Friend with Benefits, Whom off and on I See."
    Friends with Benefits Relationships   155
    Elisabeth Vanderheiden

10 Building a Culture of Revolutionary Love: The Politics
    of Love in Radical Social Transformation   177
    Matt York

Part III   Love in Religious and Belief Systems

11 Devotion: "Being Shore to the Ocean"   195
    Thomas Ryan

12 *Ashk*: The Sufi Concept for Love   209
    Çiğdem Buğdaycı

13 Prema in kabIr's sAkhI: Indigenous Perspectives on Love   223
    Dharm P. S. Bhawuk

Part IV   Love Within the Framework of Family and Intergenerational Relations

14 Videography of Love and Marriage Order   245
    Elena Rozhdestvenskaya

15 Low-SES Parents' Love as Educational Involvement with Their
    Primary School Children: A Synthesis of Qualitative Research . . .   267
    Naomi Takashiro and Clifford H. Clarke

16 When a Mother's Love Is Not Enough: A Cross-Cultural Critical
    Review of Anxiety, Attachment, Maternal Ambivalence,
    Abandonment, and Infanticide   291
    Sergio A. Silverio, Catherine Wilkinson, Victoria Fallon,
    Alessandra Bramante, and Aleksandra A. Staneva

17 A Semi-Peripheral Myth of the "Good Mother": The History
    of Motherly Love in Hungary from a Global Perspective   317
    Gergely Csányi and Szabina Kerényi

18 Loving Like I Was Loved: Mother-Child Relationship
    from the Malay Muslims' Perspective   333
    Dini Farhana Baharudin, Melati Sumari, Suhailiza Md Hamdani,
    and Hazlina Abdullah

19 Sexuality, Love and Sexual Well-Being in Old Age   351
    Sofia von Humboldt, Isabel Leal, and Gail Low

20 "A Matter of Age?" Love Relationships Between Older Women
    and Younger Men: The So-called "Cougar" Phenomenon   369
    Elisabeth Vanderheiden

21	A Table for One: The Homosexual Single and the Absence of Romantic Love.. Aliraza Javaid	391
22	On Homosexual Love and Right to Same-Sex Marriage: Questioning the Paradox of #LoveWins Discourse............. Tinnaphop Sinsomboonthong	405
23	Love and Conflicts Between Identity-Forming Values........... Michael Kühler	423
24	The Importance of Family Members in Love Letters............ Paul C. Rosenblatt	439

Part V Love in the Context of Counselling, Psychotherapy and Psychiatry

25	Love at the Psychiatric Ward................................. Dominic Harion, Sarah Francesca Löw, Sascha Settegast, and Dominik Zink	457
26	Love from a Psychotherapeutic Perspective Including Case Studies: The Need for Effective Altruism..................... Hans-Jörg Lütgerhorst, Sabine Diekmeier, and Jörg Fengler	481
27	Coming Home to Self: Finding Self-Compassion and Self-Love in Psychotherapy... Aakriti Malik	503
28	How to Research Performances of Love with Timelines.......... Sharon Rose Brehm	521

Part VI Love in the Context of Globalisation

29	Correlates of Love Across Relationship Types and Cultural Regions.. Charles T. Hill and Collaborators	543
30	Love in a Time of Globalization: Intimacy Re-imagined Across Cultural Flows..................................... Bahira Trask	567
31	The Expression of Compassionate Love in the South African Cultural Diversity Context................................. Rudolf M. Oosthuizen	583
32	Love in the Context of Transnational Academic Exchanges: Promoting Mental Health and Wellbeing..................... Rashmi Singla and Ulrike de Ponte	599

| 33 | Living with Love in Today's World: Philosophical Reflections on Some of Its Complexities | 621 |

Ondřej Beran and Camilla Kronqvist

Part VII The Dark Side of Love

| 34 | Love in Unhappy Couples | 641 |

Paul C. Rosenblatt

| 35 | "A Silver Duck in the Dish Washing Water" or Love and Crime in the Context of Positive Victimology | 657 |

Claude-Hélène Mayer

| 36 | Free to Love: Experiences with Love for Women in Prison | 679 |

Estibaliz de Miguel-Calvo

| 37 | Hatred, Life Without Love, and the Descent into Hell | 699 |

Warren TenHouten

| 38 | When the Love Is Bad | 719 |

Patricia L. Grosse

Part VIII Love in Literature

| 39 | Cosmopolitan Love: The Actuality of Goethe's Passions | 735 |

Rainer Matthias Holm-Hadulla and Alexander Nicolai Wendt

| 40 | On the Discoursive Construction of the Spanish Hero in Intercultural Romances | 749 |

María-Isabel González-Cruz

| 41 | Passion Love, Masculine Rivalry and Arabic Poetry in Mauritania | 769 |

Corinne Fortier

| 42 | "How Do You Spell Love?"—"You Don't Spell It. You Feel It." | 789 |

Willie van Peer and Anna Chesnokova

| 43 | "There Are as Many Kinds of Love as There Are Hearts": Age-Gap Relationships in Literature and Cultural Attitudes | 807 |

Anna Chesnokova and Willie van Peer

| 44 | Imagining Love: Teen Romance Novels and American Teen Relational Capacity | 827 |

Estella Carolye Kuchta

Part IX Love in Workplaces and Business Contexts

| 45 | Compassionate Love in Leaders: Leadership Solutions in the Fourth Industrial Revolution | 845 |

Claude-Hélène Mayer

46	Love Is a Many-Splendoured Thing: Brand Love in a Consumer Culture Leona M. Ungerer	871

Part X Love in Different Cultural Contexts

47	Meaning-making Through Love Stories in Cultural Perspectives: Expressions, Rituals and Symbols Claude-Hélène Mayer	895
48	Forbidden Love: Controlling Partnerships Across Ethnoracial Boundaries Dan Rodríguez-García	923
49	The Triangular Theory of Love Scale Used in a South African Context: A Research Study Kathryn Anne Nel and Saraswathie Govender	943
50	Love in China (1950–Now) Pan Wang	955
51	Sustaining Love and Building Bicultural Marriages Between Japanese and Americans in Japan Clifford H. Clarke and Naomi Takashiro	975
52	Agape Love in Indigenous Women's Memoir: A Quest for Justice and Unity Helen Fordham	995
53	Sacrifice and the Agapic Love Gender Gap in South Korean Romantic Relationships Alex J. Nelson	1013
54	Contestations and Complexities of Love In Contemporary Cuba Heidi Härkönen	1029
55	"If Any Man Loveth Not His Father": Søren Kierkegaard's Psychology of Love James L. Kelley	1047
56	Focus on Cross-Cultural Models of Love Barbara Lewandowska-Tomaszczyk and P. A. Wilson	1063
57	Could Trump Be His Own Valentine? *On Narcissism and Selfless Self-Love* Jan Bransen	1087

Part XI Emic Perspectives on Love

58 Love, Dementia and Intimate Citizenship 1105
Catherine Barrett, Anne Tudor, John Quinn, and Glenys Petrie

59 Enlisting Positive Psychologies to Challenge Love Within SAD's Culture of Maladaptive Self-Beliefs 1121
Robert F. Mullen

60 "Different Race, Same Cultures": Developing Intercultural Identities 1141
Claude-Hélène Mayer and Lolo Jacques Mayer

List of Photographs and Photographers

Two People Holding Hands *Pablo Heimplatz* 1
Graffiti "Couple" *Jon Tyson*. 81
Malaysian Wedding *Aliff Hassan@Alex Hudson* 193
Sommer Romance *Carl Breisig* 243
Self Love *Claude-Hélène Mayer* 455
Newari Marriage Ceremony—Nhyākaḥmū *Rupak Shrestha*. 541
Trump *Pete Linforth*. 639
Reading Girl *Anuja Mary Tilj*. 733
Time to Rethink: Leading with Love *Elisabeth Vanderheiden*. . 843
"抛绣球" Ceremony or "Embroidered Balls Throwing" *JJ Ying* 893
Holding Your Hand *Jon Tyson*. 1103

Editors and Contributors

About the Editors

Claude-Hélène Mayer is a Full Professor in Industrial and Organisational Psychology at the Department of Industrial Psychology and People Management at the University of Johannesburg, an Adjunct Professor at the European University Viadrina in Frankfurt (Oder), Germany and a Senior Research Associate at Rhodes University, Grahamstown, South Africa. She holds a Ph.D. in Psychology (University of Pretoria, South Africa), a Ph.D. in Management (Rhodes University, South Africa), a Doctorate (Georg-August University, Germany) in Political Sciences (socio-cultural anthropology and intercultural didactics) and Master degrees in Ethnology, Intercultural Didactics and Socio-economics (Georg-August University, Germany) as well as in Crime Science, Investigation and Intelligence (University of Portsmouth, UK). Her Venia Legendi is in Psychology with a focus on work, organizational, and cultural psychology (Europa Universität Viadrina, Germany). She has published numerous monographs, text collections, accredited journal articles, and special issues on transcultural mental health and well-being, salutogenesis, transforming shame, transcultural conflict management and mediation, women in leadership in culturally diverse work contexts, coaching, culture and crime and psychobiography.

Elisabeth Vanderheiden (Second) is a pedagogue, theologian, intercultural mediator, managing director of the Catholic Adult Education Rhineland-Palatinate and the federal chairwoman of the Catholic Adult Education of Germany. She is the CEO of the Global Institute for Transcultural Research. Her publishing focus on basic education for adults, in particular on training for teachers and trainers in adult education, as well as vocational and civic education, text collections on intercultural opening processes and intercultural mediation. Her latest publications focused on shame as resource as well as mistakes, errors and failure and their hidden potentials in the context of culture and positive psychology. She lives in Germany and Florida.

Contributors

Hazlina Abdullah Faculty of Major Language Studies, Universiti Sains Islam Malaysia, Nilai, Malaysia

Catherine Barrett Museum of Love, St. Kilda, VIC, Australia

Ondřej Beran Centre for Ethics as Study in Human Value, University of Pardubice, Pardubice, Czech Republic

Aaron Ben-Ze'ev Department of Philosophy, University of Haifa, Haifa, Israel

Dharm P. S. Bhawuk Management and Culture and Community Psychology, University of Hawaii at Manoa, Honolulu, Hawaii, USA

Alessandra Bramante Policentro Donna Ambulatory, Milan, Italy

Jan Bransen Department of Philosophy of Behavioural Science, Radboud University, Nijmegen, The Netherlands

Sharon Rose Brehm Munich, Germany

Çiğdem Buğdaycı Amsterdam School for Cultural Analysis, University of Amsterdam, Amsterdam, The Netherlands

Anna Chesnokova Department of English Philology and Translation, Borys Grinchenko Kyiv University, Kyiv, Ukraine

Clifford H. Clarke School of Communications, University of Hawaii at Manoa, Honolulu, Hawaii

Freddie Crous Department of Industrial Psychology and People Management, University of Johannesburg, Johannesburg, South Africa

Gergely Csányi Centre for Social Sciences, Hungarian Academy of Sciences Centre of Excellence, Budapest, Hungary

Estibaliz de Miguel-Calvo Department of Sociology and Social Work. University of the Basque Country, Leioa, Spain

Sabine Diekmeier Institute for Cognitive Behavioral Therapy, Justus-Liebig-University of Gießen, Gießen, Germany

Victoria Fallon Department of Psychological Sciences, University of Liverpool, Liverpool, UK

Dini Farhana Baharudin Faculty of Leadership and Management, Universiti Sains Islam Malaysia, Nilai, Malaysia

Jörg Fengler Institute of Applied Psychology, Cologne, Germany

Helen Fordham Department of Media and Communications, University of Western Australia, Crawley, WA, Australia

Corinne Fortier French National Center of Scientific Research (CNRS), Social Anthropology Lab (Collège de France), Paris, France

María-Isabel González-Cruz Department of Modern Languages, University of Las Palmas de Gran Canaria, Las Palmas, Spain

Saraswathie Govender Department of Psychological Sciences, University of Limpopo, Polokwane, South Africa

Dominic Harion Luxembourg Centre for Educational Testing (LUCET), University of Luxembourg, Esch-sur-Alzette, Luxembourg

Heidi Härkönen Gender Studies, University of Helsinki, Helsinki, Finland

Charles T. Hill Department of Psychology, Whittier College, Whittier, CA, USA

Rainer Matthias Holm-Hadulla Department of Psychiatry, Psychosomatic Medicine, and Psychotherapy, Heidelberg University, Heidelberg, Germany

William Jankowiak Department of Anthropology, University of Nevada, Las Vegas, NV, USA

Aliraza Javaid University of East London, University Square, London, UK

Victor Karandashev Department of Psychology and Counselor Education, Aquinas College, Grand Rapids, MI, USA

James L. Kelley Norman, OK, USA

Szabina Kerényi Centre for Social Sciences, Hungarian Academy of Sciences Centre of Excellence, Budapest, Hungary

Camilla Kronqvist Åbo Akademi University, Turku, Finland

Estella Carolye Kuchta Langara College, Vancouver, BC, Canada

Michael Kühler Academy for Responsible Research, Teaching, and Innovation (ARRTI), Karlsruhe Institute of Technology (KIT), Karlsruhe, Germany
Münster University, Münster, Germany

Isabel Leal William James Center for Research, ISPA – Instituto Universitário, Lisboa, Portugal

Leigh Leo Department of Industrial Psychology and People Management, University of Johannesburg, Johannesburg, South Africa

Barbara Lewandowska-Tomaszczyk Department of Language and Communication, State University of Applied Sciences, Konin, Poland

Sarah Francesca Löw Trier, Germany

Gail Low Faculty of Nursing, Edmonton Clinical Health Academy (ECHA), University of Alberta, Edmonton, AB, Canada

Hans-Jörg Lütgerhorst Bochum, Germany

Aakriti Malik Middlemore Hospital, Auckland, New Zealand

Lolo Jacques Mayer Courtney House International School, Pretoria, South Africa

Suhailiza Md Hamdani Faculty of Leadership and Management, Universiti Sains Islam Malaysia, Nilai, Malaysia

Robert F. Mullen ReChanneling Inc, San Francisco, CA, USA

Kathryn Anne Nel Research, Administration and Development, University of Limpopo, Polokwane, South Africa

Alex J. Nelson Department of Anthropology, University of Nevada, Las Vegas, NV, USA

Rudolf M. Oosthuizen Department of Industrial and Organisational Psychology, University of South Africa, Pretoria, South Africa

Glenys Petrie Museum of Love, St. Kilda, VIC, Australia

Ulrike de Ponte Department of Natural Sciences and Cultural Studies, Applied University of Regensburg (OTH Regensburg), Regensburg, Germany

John Quinn Museum of Love, St. Kilda, VIC, Australia

Dan Rodríguez-García Department of Social and Cultural Anthropology, Autonomous University of Barcelona, Bellaterra, Spain

Paul C. Rosenblatt Department of Family Social Science, University of Minnesota, St. Paul, MN, USA

Elena Rozhdestvenskaya Faculty of Social Sciences, International Laboratory for Social Integration Studies, HSE University, Moscow, Russia
Institute of Sociology Russian Academy of Sciences, Moscow, Russia

Thomas Ryan Faculty of Theology and Philosophy, Australian Catholic University, NSW, Australia
Adjunct Associate Professor of the School of Philosophy and Theology University of Notre Dame, Fremantle, Australia

Sascha Settegast Department of Philosophy, Trier University, Trier, Germany

Sergio A. Silverio Department of Women & Children's Health, King's College London, London, UK

Rashmi Singla Department of People and Technology, Roskilde University, Denmark

Tinnaphop Sinsomboonthong Faculty of Sociology and Anthropology, Thammasat University, Bangkok, Thailand

Aleksandra A. Staneva School of Psychology, The University of Queensland, St. Lucia, Australia

Melati Sumari University of Malaya, Kuala Lumpur, Malaysia

Naomi Takashiro Department of Global Tourism, Kyoto University of Foreign Studies, Kyoto, Japan

Warren D. TenHouten Department of Sociology, University of California at Los Angeles, Los Angeles, CA, USA

Bahira Trask Department of Human Development and Family Sciences, University of Delaware, Newark, DE, USA

Anne Tudor Museum of Love, St. Kilda, VIC, Australia

Leona Ungerer Department of Industrial and Organisational Psychology, University of South Africa, Pretoria, South Africa

Willie van Peer Faculty of Languages and Literatures, Ludwig Maximilian University, Munich, Germany

Sofia von Humboldt William James Center for Research, ISPA – Instituto Universitário, Lisboa, Portugal

Pan Wang Department of Chinese and Asian Studies, University of New South Wales, Sydney, NSW, Australia

Alexander Nicolai Wendt Department of Experimental and Theoretical Psychology, Heidelberg University, Heidelberg, Germany

Catherine Wilkinson School of Education, Liverpool John Moores University, Liverpool, UK

Paul A. Wilson Department of English Language and Applied Linguistics, University of Lodz, Lodz, Poland

Matt York Department of Government and Politics, University College Cork, Cork, Ireland

Dominik Zink Department of German Studies, Trier University, Trier, Germany

Photographer's Biography

Aliff Hassan @ Alex Hudson is a Photographer, Kuala Lumpur, Malaysia

Pablo Heimplatz is a photographer and computer scientist, Hamburg, Germany

Carl Breisig is a student at State Academy of Fine Arts Stuttgart, Germany

Jon Tyson is a Pastor at church.nyc, author and photography New York City

Pete Linforth is a Digital Artist, United Kingdom

Rupak Shrestha is a PhD student from Nepal in the USA

Anuja Mary Tilj is a pharmacist and photographer from Kerala, India, living in Germany

J. J. Ying is a visual designer from China

Sharon McCutcheon is a photographer on Unsplash, sharing images since 2006

Part I
Introductory Chapters

Two people holding hands (Photo: Pablo Heimplatz)

Chapter 1
Voicing the Stories of Love Across Cultures: An Introduction

Claude-Hélène Mayer and Elisabeth Vanderheiden

> *Not all storms come to disrupt your life,*
> *Some come to clear your paths.*
> Paulo Coelho

Abstract This chapter builds the introductory part to the "Handbook on Love in Cultural and Transcultural Contexts". It provides a brief theoretical overview on the state of the art in love research and different cultural and transcultural perspectives and provides insight into the chapters presented in this book.

Keywords Love · Theories · Introduction · Culture · Transculture

1.1 Introduction

Love and its meanings vary across time, space and culture; they are socially and culturally constructed and need to be understood from a contextualised point of view (Beall & Sternberg, 1995; Karandashev, 2019, see Chap. 4; Swidler, 2013). Beall and Sternberg (1995) emphasise that love always needs to be contextualised to grasp its meaning and suggest that love should be viewed in connection with four contextual forces: (a) the beloved person, (b) the feelings which accompany love,

---

C.-H. Mayer (✉)
Department of Industrial Psychology and People Management, University of Johannesburg, Johannesburg, South Africa

Institut für therapeutische Kommunikation und Sprachgebrauch, Europa Universität Viadrina, Frankfurt (Oder), Germany
e-mail: claudemayer@gmx.net

E. Vanderheiden
Global Institute for Transcultural Research, Römerberg, Germany
e-mail: ev@keb-rheinland-pfalz.de

© Springer Nature Switzerland AG 2021
C.-H. Mayer, E. Vanderheiden (eds.), *International Handbook of Love*,
https://doi.org/10.1007/978-3-030-45996-3_1

(c) the thoughts that accompany love, and (d) the actions or the relations which a person has with the beloved.

Love is a concept which, in linguistic terms, strongly relates to "attachment, desire, preference, taking pleasure in something, and physical acts within Western contexts" (Gratzke, 2017, 4). Gratzke (2017) emphasises further that language plays an important role in expressing love, and that the way people experience love is connected to how they express it. Therefore, it is assumed that definitions of love, terms for and concepts of love, as well as feelings associated with love might differ across language groups. Although people may use similar words to express love, these words do not mean the same across cultures and language groups (Twamley, 2014). Therefore, to define and understand what love means from different cultural perspectives, a wide variety of in-depth, multi-method approaches needs to be explored.

In Western literature on love, researchers such as Barsade and O'Neill (2014) often distinguish between so-called "romantic" love and love in general, often referring to a humanistic, compassionate concept of love. While compassionate love is thereby usually associated with compassion, caring, and tenderness for others in general, it has also been researched in work settings (Barsade & O'Neill, 2014).

Several researchers (such as Jankowiak, 2008; Chaps. 2 and 3 of Jankowiak) have explored the concept of love in cultural contexts and from varying perspectives and within and across cultures. Malinowsky and Gratzke (2017) point out that interest in studies on love has risen during the past years and that "love matters", not only in relationship perspectives, but also in any kind of social interaction and organisation. Although it has been researched from various theoretical perspectives and methodological stances, there is nonetheless a void in the literature which brings transdisciplinary and transcultural views on love together, not focusing on mainly romantic love or Western views, but also taking different cultural, social, political and economic views on love into account and having researchers from various cultural standpoints speak out about love as a concept. According to Swidler (2013), love talk is present constantly in day-to-day interactions all over the world. The talk about love provides ideas on how humans shape their relationships, their expectations and behaviours which are influenced by culture. Therefore, love is a "perfect place to study love in action" and contradictory aspects of culture and love (Swidler, 2013, 2) need to be taken into account and verbalised.

Narrations and stories are part of human nature. These are present in daily acts and interactions and include feelings, thoughts and ideas of individuals to create identity for the self and others (Mayer & Flotman, 2017). Through narrative acts, self, society and socio-cultural acts are created within a dynamic interplay. McAdams et al. (2004) highlight that life narratives often include themes of interpersonal communion such as love and friendship.

According to Andrews et al. (2009), stories involve the narration of series of events in a plotted sequence which unfolds in time. Through narrations and stories, meaning is created (Hardy, 1968) and through narrations, humans make sense of their lives, and life becomes meaningful (Wood, 2001). Love narrations thereby seem to be particularly valuable in certain cultures. Further, it is assumed that every human being is able to tell stories about their life, their experiences and feelings (Leskela-Kärki, 2008).

Narrations of love highlight love as a spiritual and social act, emphasise dynamic and social life aspects and are narrated via stories or other textual material (Erol-Isik, 2015). According to Sternberg (1996), love is a story which is created through personal interaction with the environment. Thereby, individuals develop stories about love which they aim to fulfil in their lifetimes. At the same time, by telling their stories of love, they influence creation of ideas about love in others.

In this book, we aim to tell and give voice to many stories of love from diverse viewpoints to create new and original ideas about love in transdisciplinary and transcultural realms. We do not define love, culture and transculture upfront in this book, but rather invite each author to speak for themselves with regard to their personal point of view on how to define the concepts, relating to their contexts, constructing new worlds of love. We thereby refer to Hardy (1968) who emphasises that stories are a product of the mind—of the writer and the reader.

In the following section, we briefly introduce the chapters which can be found in this book.

1.2 The Contributions of this Book

This book is divided into 11 parts which provide various insights into love from different theoretical and methodological, as well as cultural perspectives. Here, we provide the reader with an overview of the contents of this volume to give guidance with regard to the theoretical, methodological and conceptual perspectives presented.

This volume presents a variety of cultural and transcultural perspectives on love by bringing together researchers from all over the world, from different age groups, cultures, scientific disciplines, theoretical, methodological and conceptual stances. The book thereby provides insights into the different concepts and meanings of love, and into transcultural spaces which open the topic for transdisciplinary research and practice.

Part I contains the introductory chapters to love.

The introduction, written by **Claude-Hélène Mayer** and **Elisabeth Vanderheiden**, gives a brief overview on the topic and the contents of the book.

William Jankowiak and **Alex Nelson** present a foundational insight into the state of ethnological research on love by providing a critical review of the literature with regard to social structures and the transformation of expectations and experiences of love. They also address how cultural constructions of love and the social structures that formed them give rise to social inequalities. In conclusion they present a singular view on how psychological and cultural perspectives form concepts of love.

The following chapter, also written by **Alex Nelson** and **William Jankowiak**, presents research findings regarding love and arranged marriage dichotomies and essentialist perspectives. The chapter provides different insights into love across cultures and histories from in-depth reviews of ethnographic literature. The authors focus specifically on love, arranged marriage, love's association with sexual exclusivity, the separation of love from material and sexual interest, and the belief that romantic love is a product of modernity. The authors close with questions which will lead future research forward.

In his chapter "Cultural Diversity of Romantic Love Experiences", **Victor Karandashev** presents a review of modern cross-cultural research on love. He identifies five different concepts of love with regard to its specific cultural accents and thereby provides valuable insights for multicultural couples, psychologists, counsellors, social workers, and other practitioners working with multicultural populations.

Part II of the book focuses in particular on facets and manifestations of love in digital, cultural and political contexts.

In this part of the book **Aaron Ben-Ze'ev** explores cyberspace as an alternative romantic culture. He argues that cyberspace enables participants to explore exciting romantic options without bearing significant costs in terms of resources and efforts, and without necessarily violating significant personal commitments. The new romantic culture, in which cyberspace has a prominent role, is both seductive and sustainable. Finally, the author proposes that a combination of offline and online interactions can be very fruitful for cultivating the romantic realm.

Warren Tenhouten provides a view on the concept of love from a social relationship and emotion theoretical perspective. Thereby the author emphasises and discusses six defined emotions which are key signals of emotions of troubled intimacy.

Freddie Crous and **Leigh Leo** speak of "The Embodied Psychology of Love" and explores the age-old question of whether humans are a loving species. The author refers in his theoretical foundations of this chapter to bipedalism and neoteny and describes how humans need to be nurtured for the sake of humankind's future well-being. The author further presents two performative instruments, namely the positivity projective and enactment technique and the rebirth sign formula designed by the eminent artist, Michelangelo Pistoletto (2018), which can be utilised to nurture the loving nature of humans.

Elisabeth Vanderheiden writes in her chapter about friendship: a very special kind of love which generally might lead to increased mental health and well-being. Friendships have special relationship characteristics since, in their essence, friendships are the only human relationships that do without legal regulations, official founding rites, and mutual obligations. What a friendship looks like, why and how long it works, is negotiated only between the participants. The author presents an overview on the international discourse on friendship which is highly vivid and responds to key questions of the debate on what friendship means in different cultures.

In the following chapter, **Elisabeth Vanderheiden** then focuses on "Friends with Benefits Relationships" which are defined as not as romantic as love relationships, but rather as friendships with sexual interaction. The author reviews the contemporary literature on friends with benefits relationships and reflects on these relationships within cultural and gendered contexts.

Matt York addresses this section of the book with his chapter on "Building a Culture of Revolutionary Love: The Politics of Love in Radical Social Transformation". This chapter positions love as a key concept in political theory and philosophy and for performing a central (counter-hegemonic) role in the revolutionary transformation of contemporary global capitalism. The author focuses on the works of anarchist/autonomist theorists Emma Goldman and Michael Hardt and explores how new love-based political subjectivities, practices, and group formations might present opportunities for a reimagining of the frame within which an alter-globalisation can occur. This could be done by drawing on and making links with contemporary ideas of love as a political concept for radical social transformation in the twenty-first century.

The following part of the book, **Part III**, deals with love in the context religious and belief systems.

Thomas Ryan builds on Robert Frost, examining devotion in terms of "loyalty and love or care for someone or something". The first half explores foundational consideration about love as devotion through clarifying language and various understandings of love. The author introduces "robust concern" (carefully understood) as a possible description for devotion and explores the various forms, benefits (and limits) of devotion which emerge together with its necessary relationship to the guidance of moral wisdom.

Çiğdem Buğdaycı presents the Turkish Sufi concept of love which has so far been disregarded. The author explains Sufi cosmology and the transcendental concept of love, which has the capacity to go beyond the division of the sacred and the profane. She argues that leaving out the Sufi concept of love has so far been ideological as the European cultural, economic expansion over the world suppressed and ignored Non-European elements. The author therefore explains the particularity of Sufi love, its parallels and disparities with that of *eros* and *agape* and discusses how and why Sufi love has historically been neglected with reference to the European colonialism as well as hostilities towards Sufism in the Islamic world. Finally, the concept of Sufi love is placed within the context of current academic and political discourses.

In the next chapter, **dharma prakAza zarmA bhAwuka** analyses ways in which the medieval mystic poet and saint, kabIr (1398–1448), used *prema* (love) in his *sAkhI* (teachings). The author presents excerpts from the collection of kabIr's teachings published by the centre in dAmAkheDA, rAypur, chattisgaDha, India and analyses those which are relevant to love, including the love of God and spiritual pathways. Implications for research on emotion for both indigenous and global psychology are discussed.

Part IV of the book focuses on love within the framework of family and intergenerational relations.

Elena Rozhdestvenskaya's chapter deals with the dramatisation of a collective utopia of love. Anchored in the Russian context, the author explores the concept of the so-called "exit marriage registration" as a relatively new and expanding wedding trend. In an empirical study, focus is placed on the media video product and on how the media sacralise the utopia of romantic love, which is monopolised by the professionals of this particular market of services. Videos about the wedding deliver the narcissistic joy of reflection and recognition, and thus create a modified reverse perspective on one's own life world. This chapter takes a closer look at the meaning of videos in weddings and love relationships.

Naomi Takashiro and **Clifford H. Clarke** explore parental love towards children through the parental involvement in their children's education. The authors focus on the involvement of parents from low socioeconomic backgrounds from international perspectives, through the conduct of a qualitative empirical study. Findings show that parents attempt to resolve children's problems by establishing relationships with teachers. Some parents also show unique cultural forms of love in motivation to compete, thereby fulfilling traditional roles of fathers, and practising religious beliefs. The authors show that parents with low socioeconomic status are dedicated to showing love in terms of their involvement with their children's education, despite the predicaments.

In the next chapter, **Sergio A. Silverio, Catherine Wilkinson, Victoria Fallon, Alessandra Bramante** and **Aleksandra A. Stanevanskaya** write about the situation "When a Mother's Love is Not Enough: A cross-cultural critical review of attachment, anxiety, abandonment, and infanticide". The authors refer to concepts of "good" and "bad" motherhood, the emotional investment between those who mother, and those who are mothered, and social expectations which reinforce motherhood as being underpinned by an innate psychological bond. The authors juxtapose historically placed demands on mothers with the intense societal scrutiny placed on modern mothers, rendering the meaning of a mother's love as ambiguous, and the traditional senses of motherhood being increasingly difficult to achieve. They further focus on aspects of maternal abandonment and even infanticide. While reflecting on these problematic issues, the authors recommend ways to navigate distress to avoid detrimental outcomes, not only by focusing on mothers themselves, but also by making society accountable to support mothers in providing their infants with the love they require.

The chapter written by **Gergely Csányi** and **Szabina Kerényi** focuses on the "good" and the "bad" mother. By using Foucault's theory of the soul, as well as the methodological insights of Fernand Braudel and world systems analysis, the authors demonstrate how the myth of the good and the bad mother was created by certain actors during the various cycles of the capitalist world system, and how these myths have been embedded in the logic of capitalist accumulation. The authors show how, on one hand, these myths have contributed to securing unpaid reproductive labour, care and love necessitated by accumulation, and how, on the other hand, the myths have supported a new market segment from the nineteenth century onwards by manipulating maternal conscience. Empirical evidence is offered by using examples from the Hungarian context and the socialist Soviet Union.

As a woman takes on the role of mothering, her identity grows and develops according to **Dini Farhana Baharudin, Melati Sumari, Suhailiza Md Hamdani** and **Hazlina Abdullah**, who focus on the mother–child relationship from the Malay Muslims' perspective. The authors examine the challenges of mothers in contemporary Malaysia with trends of globalisation and technological advances. They present qualitative findings based on interviews conducted with mothers and daughters. Gendered and cultural influences are discussed and the authors refer back to previous studies and the links between love and affection in childhood and positive well-being, happiness and conduct of relationships later in life.

Sofia von Humboldt, Isabel Leal, and **Gail Low** speak in their chapter about how age significantly influences older adults' perspectives of love and sexuality. They use the framework of sexual well-being while referring to the experience of adults regarding love, sexual desire and engagement in sexual activities, and highlight the void of research on cultural aspects in the literature on sexuality, love and sexual well-being in old age. They come to the conclusion that different factors influence sexual well-being and contribute to sexual un-wellness in terms of physical and mental health, psychological variables, culture, daily stress, relationship quality and duration, intercourse difficulties, general sexual dysfunctions, and sexual communication.

Elisabeth Vanderheiden also refers to age in her chapter. The author focuses on the exploration of the "cougar" phenomenon, of love relationships between older women and younger men. Although this phenomenon is still under-researched, interest in the topic has increased owing to prominent cases, such as those of Demi Moore and President Macron. This chapter explores the impact that age difference has on relationships, the issues that arise for the partners, and the opinions and prejudices that partners have to face.

Aliraza Javoid narrates in his chapter the sheer loneliness, solitude and invisibility that some single homosexuals embody in the midst of individualism and secularisation. The author critically reflects on gay love which is still often tabooed and stigmatised in social relationship contexts. Drawing on the works of Goffman, the author attempts to understand how homosexual singles are subjected to hostility, social disapproval and stigma, often resulting in the absence of same-sex love. Love is therefore often out of reach for many gay men because of the rise of fleeting sexual and fluid intimacy. The author suggests that gay men carry a "double stigma" emanating from embodying both a homosexual and a single identity. Javoid comes to the conclusion that a singlehood career (Lahad, 2017) evokes the absence of romantic love, leaving the homosexual single eating alone at a table for one.

Tinnaphop Sinsomboonthong also refers to homosexual love, however not with regard to loneliness and reduced romantic love relationships, but rather with reference to the right to same-sex marriages in Thailand. He mentions that the decriminalisation of homosexuality has become a global trend and that support for the legalisation of same-sex marriage in many countries can be found on social media. The author refers to the hashtag #LoveWins, on social media in June 2015 and speaks about the ongoing confrontation between advocates of the junta-backed legislation related to same-sex marriage laws, known as "Thailand's Civil Partnership Draft Bills", and its detractors. He emphasises that the hashtag has widely been employed by active Thai social media users for creating an LGBT-friendly atmosphere while attempting to neutralise the bi-polarised politics of the law. This chapter, as a ethnographical study, focuses on how #LoveWins is used by analysing its discursive implications in the hypertexts of the hashtag as articulated by

Thailand's social media users on Twitter during the Drafted-Bills period and the national elections in late 2018 to mid-2019.

Michael Kühler addresses love and conflict in the context of identity formation. He speaks about occurring value conflicts between individuals in love and the challenges associated with cultural and value-based differences. In this context, the chapter examines three influential philosophical theories of love and their relation to the lovers' identities. To resolve conflicts, these theories can be used. However, the author argues, that both love and identity need to be understood as something that can actively be shaped. While often individuals believe that love and identity "just happen", this chapter is a final speech to see love and identity as something that can be actively created.

In the following chapter **Paul Rosenblatt** analyses the love letters of ten couples who have lived and written love letters in the nineteenth or twentieth century in the United States or Europe. The author's findings suggest the possibility that in an escalating couple relationship in some cultural contexts the couple is not an isolated dyad. They may be connected to their families of origin and communicating that to their lover and perhaps quite possibly looking forward to a committed couple relationship in which family members of one or both of them will have a significant place. Culture intersects these matters in a number of ways. These ways the author explains in the text and thereby gives insights into love letters from the past, their intentions and cultural backgrounds.

Part V explores love in the context of counselling, psychotherapy and psychiatry.

Dominic Harion, Sarah F. Löw, Sascha Settegast and **Dominik Zink** explore love in exile and other extraordinary circumstances, such as love in a psychiatric ward. They use the framework of Comte-Sponville's important differentiation between several types of love and highlight that love always needs to be seen as a contextualised and systemic emotion. In their study of love in the context of a psychiatric ward, love is seen as a point between a dichotomy of selfishness and compassion.

Hans-Jörg Lütgerhorst, Sabine Diekmeier and **Jörg Fengler** discuss love from a psychotherapeutic perspective, distinguishing between erotic love and love for one's neighbour. While the former implies a serious rupture in the therapeutic alliance requiring immediate supervision and termination of psychotherapy in most cases, the latter in everyday language is used as a synonym for extended sympathy—presupposing empathy, compassion, care, reliability and effort-taking. The perception of a good therapeutic alliance and culture by the client complies with an ascription of competence to the therapist and an early improvement of complaints. The authors present selected case examples in which love plays a role within the therapeutic alliance which eventually leads to success in psychotherapy.

Aakriti Malik sees love as a deeply rooted emotion which can hold a great potential to unravel deep-seated trauma and a gamut of emotions in the context of psychopathology in psychotherapy. The chapter deals with love in the psychotherapeutic process, which can open up layers of past history around being loved. This history can determine a client's present belief systems around love, being loved or loving someone. The author further refers to concepts of self-love in psychotherapy and the importance of self-compassion as a successful psychotherapeutic approach. The chapter aims at understanding love through different theoretical perspectives, by its link with psychopathology and in how it presents itself with other emotions. Selected case examples regarding compassion-based therapy with clients are given with reference to Indian contexts.

This following chapter on "How to Research Performances of Love with Timelines", written by **Sharon Rose Brehm**, provides a methodological addition to ethnographic approaches to the study of love. It tackles the question of how one can investigate performances of love, not only in terms of narrations, but also with regard to bodily reactions. This chapter presents research on experiences of German-Russian couples using ethnographic and systemic psychotherapeutic methods. This chapter contributes to increasing the understanding of the experiences of bi-national couples.

Love in the context of globalisation is the key topic in **Part VI**.

Charles T. Hill and his **co-authors** present a cross-cultural study of intimate relationships, exploring correlates of love around the world. Structural equation modelling was used in the study, which identified factors associated with love across nine cultural regions, as well as across eight relationship types defined by men and women, married or unmarried, in opposite-sex or same-sex relationships. The findings presented in this chapter have implications for future research, self-reflection, and couples counselling in global and local contexts.

Bahira Trask explores love in the time of globalisation across cultures from a socially constructionism point of view. Trask examines the question of what is meant by love and intimate relationships in varying cultural and socioeconomic contexts, contexts that are rapidly transforming in response to social, political, economic and technological transformations. Responses to this question are found in the chapter at hand by taking intersectionalities such as class, race, nationality, sexualities, and geographic location into account.

"The Expression of Compassionate Love in Cultural Diversity Contexts" is the focus of **Rudolf M. Oosthuizen**'s chapter. He refers to compassionate love in the South African context in which government and citizens have called for compassion. In this conceptual chapter, the author presents different studies and outcomes of compassionate love, arguing that building personal relationships with culturally diverse out-group members is an important catalyst for positive cultural intergroup attitudes. The chapter provides a critical review of the way in which compassionate love holds promise as a positive pathway to prejudice reduction.

Rashmi Singla and **Ulrike de Ponte** narrate "Love in the Context of Transnational Academic Exchanges: Promoting Mental Health and Well-being". The authors explain that through the increase in educational and cultural exchange programmes, love and intimate relations in academic exchange in European settings increase. They provide case studies from two projects while using the theoretical framework of cultural psychology in combination with narrative psychology, intersectionality, digital emotional reflexivity and transnationalism.

From a philosophical viewpoint, **Ondřej Beran** and **Camilla Kronqvist** reflect on "Living with Love in Today's World" by elaborating on the minority observation which characterises love as making a difference to one's whole life (endowing it with meaning). The authors discuss the importance of the compartmentalisation of our lives and the interplay between life and love, responsibility and perseverance. These analyses relate to the phenomenon of environmental despair (first section) and high-functioning burnout (second section). The findings are anchored in deeper theoretical discourses.

Love and crime are topics discussed in **Part XII** of the book.

The first chapter in this part is written by **Paul C. Rosenblatt** and deals with the topic of "Love in Unhappy Couples". He argues that some unhappy couples feel love for one another and he tells the story of an unhappy couple with a long history of difficult marital interaction and who, despite their history, cannot exist apart from each other. He argues that some unhappy couples remain together because of love, even possibly a love that is unspoken and out of their awareness. The chapter offers a number of conceptual paths to understanding how strong negativity may be linked to love, noting that in some cultural contexts negativity may be a form of expressing love and not even be perceived as negativity.

Claude-Hélène Mayer researches crime in the context of love. Her chapter aims at providing an insight on the complex topic of love and crime research, focusing particularly on hate and love crimes, love, relationship crime in gendered and cultural contexts, and love and the desistance from crime. The author argues that positive criminology and positive victimology perspectives in the context of love and crime can help to overcome criminal acts from the point of view of the offender, as well as that of the victim. The chapter provides insights into 12-step and 16-step programmes as a potential positive psychology and positive victimology intervention tool for crime victims. It presents a case example of a female victim of criminal acts within the context of a divorce, and her process of rehabilitation and de-traumatisation through a 16-step programme.

The next chapter titled "Free to Love: Experiences with Love for Women in Prison" describes the relational dynamics of romantic relationships of incarcerated women, in the context of reflection on the agency of criminalised women. The author, **Estibaliz de Miguel Calvo**, presents women's experiences with love in prison as a means of redefining one's identity and one's decisions in the realm of emotions. Experiences involving love also constitute a way for the participants to articulate the meaning of prison life and redefine the self. Being in love in contemporary Western society is sociologically understood as a means of self-validation and experiencing freedom, which has a particular symbolic value for incarcerated women, who lack freedom. This chapter provides exciting new insight into the topic.

In his second chapter in this book, **Warren Tenhouten** explains that love and hate are often seen as opposites, but they are rather opponents. By using primary and basic emotion theory, the author explains why hatred is based on the three elementary emotions disgust, fear and anger and how love and hatred can be closely related.

Patricia L. Grosse does not focus on unhappy couples, but rather on "Bad Love". She highlights that some emotional states are set over and against love: they are false loves and masquerade as "the real thing", but deep down have their origin in violence and hatred, misogyny and rage. The author responds to questions, such as: what if these vicious states are kinds of love? What if they come from the same place from whence the purest of loves springs? What if they are, in fact, forms of "bad love"?

Part VIII of this book is about love in literature.

The authors **Rainer Matthias Holm-Hadulla** and **Alexander Nicolai Wendt** write in their chapter about "Cosmopolitan Love—the Actuality of Goethe's Passions". The authors explore the biography of Johann Wolfgang von Goethe who augmented his experience of love with his poetic abilities, but also enabled his poetry by experiencing love. This chapter depicts the life of Goethe and highlight different aspects in which love expresses itself. The authors further emphasise how Goethe was able to see love as the fabric that "holds the world together in its innermost core" (Faust I). The authors discuss Goethe's love in the context of Schelerian phenomenology of love.

María-Isabel González-Cruz's chapter explores the different strategies employed for the construction of the Spanish identity of male protagonists in a sample of romances published by Harlequin/Mills & Boon between 1955 and 2003. It deals with the construction of the Spanish hero in intercultural romances in popular culture and the concepts of identity and national character, the perceptions of Spaniards and the image of Spain throughout history. The roles of personal characterisation and language are highlighted, to understand the construction of the romantic Spanish hero in the literature.

Corinne Fortier presents a chapter on "Love, Gender, and Poetry. Mauritanian Poetry and Pre-Islamic Arabic Poetry: the Taste of 'Flowers of Evil'". The author analyses the pre-Islamic Arabic poetry of the sixth century which testifies love poetry's existence in the ancient Arab world. These poems are well-known among Moors and inspire the local poetic forms in Mauritania. In the Moorish society of Mauritania, the sphere of seduction and passion, very often poeticised, coexists in parallel with the marital sphere. This chapter analyses poetry in a specific cultural context with regard to a cross-cultural and gendered discourse.

Anna Chesnokova and **Willie van Peer** explore the topic of love stories in a global context and specifically the question of why people want to know and read about people's love stories. In their chapter, the authors propose two motifs for reading about love in fiction: a cognitive and an emotional one. The cognitive motif refers to people's curiosity about the love life of other humans. On the other hand, readers want to "feel" how it is to go through specific passages of love, to emotionally experience what it means to be loved, or to be rejected, to suffer or to be elated, to face the difficulties involved in love relations and how to overcome them. The chapter explains the transfer of love stories into everyday life.

In a second chapter, **Anna Chesnokova** and **Willie van Peer** speak about age gap relationships in literature and cultural stereotypes. In this chapter, the authors study love relations between either an older man and a considerably younger woman, or vice versa (an older woman and a considerably younger man) in two societies: Brazil and the Ukraine. They offer some examples of empirical methods with which to investigate short-term and longitudinal effects of confronting fictional love stories. The authors also report on a case study in which they examine how social views on intimate relationships involving a substantial age difference between partners were influenced by reading literary passages from canonical literature, focusing on age gap relationships.

Estella Carolye Kuchta writes about "Teen Romance Novels: Imagining Possible Futures for the North American Youth", referring to the challenge of the decreasing relational capacity of American youth with each generation because of unsupportive cultural practices. However, relational capacity hampered in early childhood, may be fostered by relationally focused literature in later childhood. The chapter deals with teen romance novels advancing relational capacity by stimulating pro-relational neurological pathways, and by providing templates that simulate social experience. The author argues that in a reading context, the emotionally engrossing and sensory literature supports relational development.

Part IX deals with love in workplaces and business contexts.

Claude-Hélène Mayer argues in her chapter that leaders need many competencies to drive diverse and transcultural workforces by building strong work relationships and positive intergroup relationships. She further points out that love, defined as a compassion (Schopenhauer), is a form of caring, a form of altruism which emphasises concern for the self and the other person's well-being and which is needed in contemporary globalising work environments. This chapter presents findings from a qualitative research study and shows that love is split into concepts of interpersonal, intra-personal, object-related and toxic or non-existent love in a work environment. The chapter gives new insights on how loving leaders can contribute to a sustainable and peaceful world.

Leona Ungerer studies brand love in a consumer culture, in which people make sense of their everyday existence according to meanings generated during the consumption process. Considering the importance of brands during the social meaning-making process, consumers often form strong attachments with brands and might "fall in love" with brands that meet their needs. The chapter looks at "brand love", provides a brief introduction to consumer culture and elaborates on the role of branding in this context. It concludes with suggestions on how brand love may be enhanced.

Part X explores love in different cultural contexts.

The meaning of love differs across social and cultural contexts according to a study which **Claude-Hélène Mayer** has conducted. These meanings are often constructed and reconstructed through narrations on love across the lifespan. This chapter presents love narrations from individuals in Japan, the US, South Africa, Israel and Germany. Based on this qualitative study, the aim of this chapter is to explore and compare love concepts and narrations of individuals of different cultural, gender, religious and language contexts. Findings provide new insight into concepts of love, feelings associated with love, expressions of love, rituals of love, love symbols and stories of love.

Kathryn Anne Nel and **Saraswathie Govender** use Sternberg's triangular theory of love which refers to the notions of intimacy, passion and commitment as a theoretical underpinning for what we define as "love". The authors decided to investigate how black undergraduate South African students self-report notions of love and discover if any of the participants scored highly in the three components, indicating consummate love. This chapter shows the outcomes of a quantitative approach utilising a cross-sectional survey design and a random sample of undergraduate students.

The chapter by **Pan Wang** explores love in China in three principal historical stages: The Maoist era, the opening-up and economic reform period, and the new millennium. The author reflects on love and its interlinkages with political, social, and economic matters in China from the 1950s. It also explains the challenges of love in contemporary China where love has appeared to fall into "crisis" owing to the growing level of single individuals resulting from the gender imbalance, rising marriage dissolution, strengthened love censorship and commercialised love practice.

The numbers of Japanese and non-Japanese marriages in Japan is increasing along with the inherent increase of intercultural conflict that contributes to increasing divorce rates. The authors **Clifford H. Clarke** and **Naomi Takashiro** in their chapter aim at discovering the cultural issues and identifying the intercultural competencies employed in sustaining loving relationships in Japan. Transforming bicultural misunderstandings into trusting relationships in bicultural businesses in Japan and the US through training, coaching, and counselling intervention models have been effective by utilising the theoretical frameworks and are applicable to the issues most frequently identified in bicultural marriages in Japan as well. The authors discuss the applicability of the models and how to use them with regard to bi-national couples in Japan.

Helen Fordham examines indigenous women's memoirs published during the 1980s which show how representations of love discursively reconstructed indigenous humanity, which had been excluded from official history. The memoirs illustrate the authors' self-love as they reclaim their identities from colonial categorisation and in expressing a hope that indigenous and non-indigenous Australians can find a way to coexist beyond the nation's racist past. In this way, the author also expresses an agape version of love. The author frames these discourses of love in the context of theories of power, justice and culture.

Alex Nelson speaks about the agapic love gender gap in South Korean romantic relationships and highlights how young women in East Asian societies stand out in ethnological studies of love by expressing less agapic (altruistic) attitudes towards their romantic partners than do their male counterparts. The author draws on 18 months of ethnographic fieldwork and examines South Korean cultural logics of sacrifice in the context of romantic love in order to shed light on the agapic love gender gap found in cross-cultural studies of love. Findings show that sacrifices should not compromise a person's major life goals or sense of self and should be reciprocated in ways perceived as fair. The chapter provides in-depth insight into this topic.

While love is something deeply personal, people's intimate experiences of love are simultaneously shaped by large-scale cultural and historical processes according to **Heidi Härkönen**. Drawing on long-term ethnographic research in Havana, Cuba, this chapter explores ordinary people's understandings and experiences of love in the midst of Cuba's contemporary political and economic changes. The findings indicate that these structural changes have created intensified complexities and contestations in individuals' love relationships in ways that are emblematic of the emergence of sharpened social inequalities in contemporary Cuba.

James L. Kelley presents a description of the philosopher Søren Kierkegaard and his psychology of love. For Kierkegaard, love is a self-relation that is grounded in a unified and transcendent principle beyond self and society. This chapter seeks, through a Kleinian psychobiography of Kierkegaard, to sketch an outline of a psychology of love beyond the paradigm of persons-in-relation, which is dominant in social science research today.

Barbara Lewandowska-Tomaszczyk and **Paul A. Wilson** focus on cross-cultural models of love in a comparison between the concept of "love" in English, and its Polish equivalent *miłość*, as well as the love cluster concepts as they are used in both languages. The authors make use of the GRID instrument—which is explained in the chapter—for analysis. Reference to figurative language, mainly metaphor and metonymy, is also discussed. The authors develop a typology of models of love as an emotion in both cultures and observe differences in the dimension of novelty as well as in the clustering structure in Polish and English love, which can be considered to be associated with a more collectivistic versus individualistic profile in these respective cultures.

In "Could Trump Be His Own Valentine?" **Jan Bransen** explores narcissism and selfless self-love, aiming to contribute to the philosophy of love by arguing for a conceptual distinction between two varieties of self-love. The author uses the example of Donald Trump by analysing a conceptual exploration of the different roles played by people in love relationships, roles that can best be identified and understood when we focus on reciprocal relations, for which the author uses, as an illustration, the relationship between Donald and Melania Trump.

Part XI of this book explores "Emic perspectives on love".

Catherine Barrett, Anne Tudor, John Quinn and **Glenys Petrie** explain "Love, Dementia and Intimate Citizenship" by exploring the meaning of love in the lives of people with dementia and the shift from romanticised notions of love, to love as caring. The chapter builds on Fromm's seminal work, *The Art of Love*, to show how love is a skill that can be developed and must be studied. It presents a framework called "small acts of love" to show the ways in which reciprocity is sought and love is enacted.

Robert Mullen writes about love in the context of social anxiety disorder, which affects more than 15 million US adults. This disorder usually disrupts the normal course of human motivational development, affecting physiological safety, belongingness and love. The chapter at hand provides insight into the symptomatic impairments that obstruct the ability of a person with social anxiety disorder to acquire seven of the eight basic types of interpersonal love: philia, eros, agape, storge, ludus, pragma and unhealthy philautia. The author stresses the need for innovative psychological and philosophical research to address the broader implications of healthy philautia's positive-self qualities, which could deliver the potential for self-love and societal concern to people with this disorder, opening the bridge to the procurement of all forms of interpersonal love.

Claude-Hélène Mayer and **Lolo Jacques Mayer** present a commentary on the topic "'Different Race, Same Cultures': Developing Intercultural Identities". The commentary describes the impact of intercultural narrations and auto-ethnographic experiences regarding intercultural identity development. This development occurs in the context of building successful intercultural encounters based on a loving view of the other person. The chapter refers to the importance of "seeing individuals as a whole, entire arts project", based on intersectionalities which need to be embraced with love to create intercultural understanding and identity development.

1.3 The Photographic Contribution to this Book

Ich gebe dem Moment Dauer.[1] Manuel Alvarez Bravo

Even if many people are not aware of it, people are above all visual beings. Unlike language or writing, which are both constructed forms of communication, people perceive images much more directly and intuitively. People think, dream, remember and narrate to each other in pictures what seems important to them. Visual signals can be processed by the human brain more directly and significantly faster than other signals. For example, the content of a photo can usually be captured in just about 0.1 s (DigitalPHOTO, 2018). At the same time, people are able to store image information on a larger scale and to reproduce it more easily after several days than, for example, a list of words (DigitalPHOTO, 2018). Images therefore play an important role in the perception and storage of experiences, memories and information. This process takes place as an individual and subjective process of interpretation, whereby it is influenced by a wide variety of socio-cultural factors and can be understood differently depending on the context (Lobinger, 2015; Niesyto & Marotzki, 2005; Schelske, 1997).

In addition to the high speed of communication, clarity, comprehensibility and memory rate, images enable interaction on a very subtle level and can thus directly articulate attitudes and feelings, questions or protest, demonstrate, teach, manipulate and lie. Increasing media consumption, the internet, but above all social media services such as Youtube, Pinterest and Instagram, lead to a change in information and communication behaviour. People prefer to receive information that, at first glance, stands out from the flood of information and can be absorbed and thoughtfully processed particularly quickly. All people have ideas of love, which are linked to certain images for them. These do not necessarily have to be images of romantic love; they can be images that express their loving connection to a parent, child or other beloved being, or the deep attachment to a place, a country or an idea. As the editors of this book, we were interested in how people in different cultural contexts

---

[1] I give the moment duration.

visualise love in pictures, and so we have organised an international photo competition for this book. We found this particularly interesting because, as the pedagogue Mollenhauer (1983) puts it, images conceal "the rules of social reality construction". He points out that form and content are united in pictorial aesthetics; in this way ambiguity and multi-perspectivity can be linked with one another and thus represent the reciprocal integration of individual and society, nature and culture (Mollenhauer, 1983, p. 134). However, images do not only reflect how people perceive or interpret reality. The process is double-sided, as the following quotation illustrates

> Pictures always give the impression of depicting something. They represent something they are not themselves. But if that something doesn't really exist, then pictures not only depict these unreal objects, they even produce them. These images do not reflect reality, but create reality. The creation of a picture becomes a twofold creative process: on the one hand in the design of the picture and on the other hand in the production of objects (Scheler, 2019, p. 7, translated by the author).

In this respect, in the context of the theme of this book—love in transcultural contexts—they may represent an attempt to create reality in a world where same-sex relationships or those between people with different skin colours are no longer subject to discrimination and restrictions. The selected photos reflect very different forms of affectionate relationships, and at the same time they show how this is expressed very specifically in certain cultural contexts through certain symbols and actions, but on the other hand how they seem to converge in the context of globalisation. The many pictures of graffiti express the *zeitgeist* in a very particular way.

Photos were contributed from Germany (Carl Breisig, Pablo Heimplatz and Anuja Mary Tilj, Elisabeth Vanderheiden), Germany and South Africa (Claude-Hélène Mayer) and from Nepal/USA (Rupak Shrestha) and the United Kingdom (Pete Linforth) reached us as well as from China (JJ Ying), from India (Anuja Mary Tilj, Malaysia (Aliff Hassan @Alex Hudson) and Australia/USA (Jon Tyson and Sharon McCutcheon).

Carl Breisig is dedicated to the theme of love from the LGBT perspective. Carl Breisig stages the homosexual love between two young men as a "homoerotic poem" (Part IV).

In addition to a painted picture with a rather symbolic character Claude-Hélène Mayer's photograph show above all spontaneous everyday scenes, which express interpersonal relationships in the captured interactions (Chaps. 1, 8, 16, 17, and 59).

Elisabeth Vanderheiden photographic contributions to this book is a representational snapshots with symbolic character. She is particularly interested in photographing complex topics and questions without intervening in an arranging way (Part IX).

Rupak Shrestha—originally from Nepal now a PhD student in the USA—contributed two photographs to this book, The first photograph (Chap. 3) is from the marriage ceremony of a Newar woman—who now lives in Minneapolis—in Patan, Nepal. During a Newari marriage ceremony, the bride's father gifts her a nhyākaḥmū (bronze mirror) which she is looking at in the photograph. This gift by her father along with a sinhaḥmū—a container shaped as a pinnacle to hold sinhaḥ (vermillion powder that signifies that she is married)—are the last gifts from her parents before she leaves for her husband's home.

Pete Linforth is a digital artist from the UK producing a wide variety of digital media from graphic design, photo manipulation, geometric design and more recently political images in support of the Climate Change agenda. Pete donates all of his work to the world through Pixabay and unsplash under the name TheDigitalArtist. He contributed the Trump photo (Part VII).

Jon Tyson is a pastor, and author and photography enthusiast living in New York City. He is originally from Australia and his community can be found at church.nyc. In his photographs he often picks up snapshots from street scenes, often graffiti, sometimes light installations, which often deal with love in its manifold manifestations as a motif (Part II and Part XI). Sharon McCutcheon, a photographer from New England, USA, sharing images on Unsplash since 2006, contributed the coverphoto for this book.

Pablo Heimplatz works as a full-time photographer and computer scientist in Hamburg, Germany. He contributed a photo from an Indian wedding ceremony to this book (Part I).

JJ Ying is a visual designer designer from China. He also co-hosted a design podcast called Anyway.FM. When he is not designing, he loves to take travel photographs. The photo he contributed (Part X) was taken in an old city in Shanxi, China. People in this photo were performing a very ancient and traditional custom called "抛绣球" or "Embroidered balls throwing". In old time, on a certain day girls stood on a high building with a beautiful handcrafted ball on their hands. And boys who love & claim to be ready to marry that girl will gather around the building. The girl then throw the ball to the boy she love the most to decide her life-time husband.

Anuja Mary Tilj is a pharmacist and photographer from Kerala, India, living in Germany now. She contributed a photo with a girl who hides under a blanket, devoting herself to reading her book.

Aliff Hassan @ Alex Hudson ist a photographer from Photographer from Kuala Lumpur, Malaysia. He contributed a photo from a Malaysian wedding ceremony (Part III).

References

Andrews, M., et al. (2009). *The uses of narrative: Explorations in sociology, psychology, and cultural studies.* New Brunswick, NJ: Transaction Publ.
Barsade, S. G., & O'Neill, O. A. (2014). What's love got to do with with? A longitudinal study of the culture of companionate love and employee and client outcomes in a long-term care setting. *Administrative Science Quarterly, 59,* 1–48. https://doi.org/10.1177/0001839214538636
Beall, A. E., & Sternberg, R. J. (1995). The social construction of love. *Journal of Social and Personal Relationships, 12*(3), 417–438.
DigitalPHOTO. (2018). *Die Macht der Bilder: Was Fotos in uns bewegen.* Retrieved 31 October 2019, from https://www.digitalphoto.de/news/macht-bilder-was-fotos-uns-bewegen-100341501.html
Erol-Isik, N. (2015). The role of narrative methods in sociology: Stories as a powerful tool to understand individual and society. *Journal of Sociological Research, 18*(1), 103–125.

Gratzke, M. (2017). Love is what people say it is: Performativity and narrativity in critical love studies. *Journal of Popular Romance Studies*. http://jprstudies.org/wp-content/uploads/2017/04/LIWPSII.4.2017.pdf

Hardy, B. (1968). Towards a poetics of fiction: An approach through narrative. *Novel: A Forum on Fiction, 2*(1), 5–14.

Jankowiak, W. R. (2008). *Intimacies. Love and sex across cultures*. New York: Columbia University Press.

Karandashev, V. (2019). Idealization and romantic beliefs in love. In V. Karandashev (Ed.), *Cross-cultural perspectives on the experience and expression of love* (pp. 83–98). Cham: Springer.

Leskela-Kärki, M. (2008). Narrating life stories in between the fictional and the autobiographical. *Qualitative Research, 8*(3), 325–332.

Lobinger, K. (2015). Visualität. In A. Hepp, F. Krotz, S. Lingenberg, & J. Wimmer (Eds.), *Handbuch Cultural Studies und Medienanalyse. Medien. Kultur. Kommunikation*. Wiesbaden: Springer VS. https://doi.org/10.1007/978-3-531-19021-1_10

Malinowsky, A., & Gratzke, M. (2017). *The materiality of love. Essays on affection and cultural practice*. New York: Routledge.

Mayer, C.-H., & Flotman, A.-P. (2017). Chapter 4: Constructing identity. Implications for reflexive HRM. In J. Mahadevan & C.-H. Mayer (Eds.), *Muslim minorities, workplace diversity and reflexive HRM* (pp. 61–76). London: Routledge.

McAdams, D. P., Anyidoho, N. A., Brown, C., Huang, Y. T., Kaplan, B., & Machado, M. A. (2004). Traits and stories: Links between dispositional and narrative features of personality. *Journal of Personality, 72*(4), 761–784.

Mollenhauer, K. (1983). *Vergessene Zusammenhänge. Über Kultur und Erziehung*. München: Juventa.

Niesyto, H., & Marotzki, W. (2005). Editorial: Visuelle Methoden in Der Forschung. MedienPädagogik: *Zeitschrift für Theorie Und Praxis Der Medienbildung 9*. Retrieved 31 October 2019, from https://doi.org/10.21240/mpaed/09/2005.06.08.X

Scheler, U. (2019). *Die photographische Wahrnehmung der Wirklichkeit*. Retrieved 31 October 2019, from http://www.uwescheler.de/Texte/E6Wahrn.pdf

Schelske, A. (1997). *Die kulturelle Bedeutung von Bildern. Soziologische und semiotische Überlegungen zur visuellen Kommunikation*. Wiesbaden: Springer Fachmedien.

Sternberg, R. J. (1996). Love stories. *Personal Relationship, 3*(1), 59–79.

Swidler, A. (2013). *Talk of love. How culture matters*. Chicago, IL: The University of Chicago Press.

Twamley, K. (2014). *Love, marriage and intimacy among Gujarati Indians: A suitable match*. Basingstoke: Palgrave McMillian.

Wood, J. T. (2001). The normalization of violence in heterosexual romantic relationships: Women's narratives of love and violence. *Journal of Social and Personal Relationships, 18*(2), 239–261.

Claude-Hélène Mayer is a Full Professor in Industrial and Organisational Psychology at the Department of Industrial Psychology and People Management at the University of Johannesburg, an Adjunct Professor at the European University Viadrina in Frankfurt (Oder), Germany and a Senior Research Associate at Rhodes University, Grahamstown, South Africa. She holds a Ph.D. in Psychology (University of Pretoria, South Africa), a Ph.D. in Management (Rhodes University, South Africa), a Doctorate (Georg-August University, Germany) in Political Sciences (socio-cultural anthropology and intercultural didactics) and Master degrees in Ethnology, Intercultural Didactics and Socio-economics (Georg-August University, Germany) as well as in Crime Science, Investigation and Intelligence (University of Portsmouth, UK). Her Venia Legendi is in Psychology with focus on work, organizational, and cultural psychology (Europa Universität Viadrina, Germany). She has published numerous monographs, text collections, accredited journal articles, and special issues on transcultural mental health and well-being, salutogenesis, transforming shame, transcultural conflict management and mediation, women in leadership in culturally diverse work contexts, coaching, culture and crime and psychobiography.

Elisabeth Vanderheiden (Second state examination) is a pedagogue, theologian, intercultural mediator, managing director of the Catholic Adult Education Rhineland-Palatinate, the President of the Catholic Adult Education of Germany and the CEO of the Global Institute for Trancultural Research. Her publishing centres on in the context of basic education for adults, in particular on trainings for teachers and trainers in adult education, as well as vocational, and civic education, text collections on intercultural opening processes and intercultural mediation. Her latest publications focus on shame as resource as well as mistakes, errors and failure and their hidden potentials in the context of culture and positive psychology.

Chapter 2
The State of Ethnological Research on Love: A Critical Review

William Jankowiak and Alex J. Nelson

Abstract Within anthropology and sociology three primary theoretical lenses have arisen for examining love in cultural and transcultural contexts: (1) The social-structural perspective that examines how features of a society's organization and beliefs give rise to particular conceptions of love and how changes to social structures further transform expectations and experiences of love; (2) The bio-social theory of love which merges social structural perspectives on cross-cultural variation with evolutionary psychological and cognitive perspectives aimed at explaining why certain aspects of love are culturally universal; and (3) The critical perspective of love that highlights how cultural constructions of love and the social structures that formed them give rise to social inequalities. After synthesizing these three perspectives we examine how they have influenced the findings of the latest ethnographic and empirical studies of love and its cross-cultural variability and continuity. We thereby compare the fruits each theoretical perspective has born as tools to interrogate love as both a psychological essence and cultural experience.

Keywords Love · Romantic love · Ethnography · Cross-cultural research · Social theory · Companionate marriage

2.1 Introduction

Almost every culture has either oral or written stories of individuals falling in and out of love (Lee, 2007; Pan, 2016; Ryang, 2006; Singer, 2009). However, historians remind us that with the exception of seventeenth century England (Sarsby, 1983), romantic love only recently became a primary criterion for selecting a marriage partner in state societies (Baily, 1988; Coontz, 2005). Marriage, with a few notable

W. Jankowiak (✉) · A. J. Nelson
Department of Anthropology, University of Nevada, Las Vegas, Las Vegas, NV, USA
e-mail: jankbill@unlv.nevada.edu; nelson26@unlv.nevada.edu

© Springer Nature Switzerland AG 2021
C.-H. Mayer, E. Vanderheiden (eds.), *International Handbook of Love*,
https://doi.org/10.1007/978-3-030-45996-3_2

exceptions, was more of an economic or social arrangement between families than an institution designed to fulfill personal satisfaction. Prior to the advent of professional ethnographic fieldwork, cultural evolutionary theorists argued the romantic love complex to be a product of capitalism (Engels, 1884) or of the French troubadours, enumerating the ways they saw "savages" and "barbarians" failing to live up to Victorian love ideals (Finck, 1899). Later thinkers noted that the Victorians themselves failed to meet these ideals and concluded love, as it was idealized, was mere fantasy, with influential thinkers like Sigmund Freud dismissing love as an expression of narcissism or a frustrated libido even while theorizing sexual love as a prototype of all man's happiness (Freud, 1961). Given the prevalence of these assumptions, social scientists neglected to seriously investigate whether romantic love could be present in non-state societies.

In effect, the conventional wisdom was love is a uniquely western creation and held little value in understanding "western" behavior, let alone premodern eras. By the 1980s a few anthropologists began to probe the possibility that love was more than a modern globalizing discourse with its own history. The finding that love was not atypical outside of marriage in many state and tribal societies and within marriage for numerous foraging groups raised questions about the claim that romantic love was Europe's contribution to world history (de Munck, 2019; Lindholm, 2002). As researchers focused on adolescence in arranged marriage societies, they found love crushes were not unusual (de Munck, 1996, 1998, 2019; Jankowiak, 1995c). Closer examination found that romantic love concepts share common attributes recognized as central to experiencing affects of love cross-culturally (Coppinger & Rosenblatt, 1968; Lindholm, 2002; Jankowiak & Fischer, 1992; Reddy, 2001; de Munck & Korotayev, 1999, 2007; Karandashev, 2017, 2019; see Chap. 4; Sternberg & Sternberg, 2019).

In this chapter, we discuss the significance of recent remarkable ethnographic findings and explore the development of the various theoretical approaches applied to understanding romantic love. These approaches differ in their assumptions, such as those regarding the question of romantic love's universality as a human experience. They range from the dismissive (sociology) to the skeptical (cultural history and socio-cultural anthropology), to the taken for granted (evolutionary psychology and biological anthropology). They also open new lines of inquiry, including using love as a lens for understanding social inequality, exploring the neurobiology of love, and exploring variations in romantic love's culturally constructed meanings. In reviewing these perspectives, we present a picture of the present state of ethnological knowledge of romantic love's cross-cultural variability and continuity. We conclude by identifying gaps in current research and suggesting new directions for future research.

2.2 Theoretical Approaches to Studying Love: An Overview

2.2.1 Comparative Approaches: Socio-Cultural and Evolutionary Perspectives on Love

The earliest anthropological studies to broadly theorize romantic love's cross-cultural variability focused on the frequency and conditions in which love was an official value in a given society (Collins & Gregor, 1995; Murdock, 1949). They drew upon databases of ethnographic material from studies in which romantic love was not an explicit subject of investigation and was often noted only in passing. The first such study was conducted by Jankowiak and Fischer (1992) and looked for virtually any sign of what they called "passionate love" which elsewhere is variously defined as romantic love, romantic passion, infatuation, or "being in love" (Jankowiak, 1995b, 6). They examined materials in the Standard Cross-Cultural Sample (SCCS) database drawing on a definition of love as "an intense attraction that involves the idealization of the other, within an erotic context, with the expectation of enduring for some time into the future," based in part on the work of Charles Lindholm (1988). Jankowiak and Fischer (1992) also drew on folklore and personal reports from ethnographers not in the SCCS to fill gaps in that ethnographic dataset and ultimately identified observations of romantic love's presence in 91 percent (151 of 166) of the cultures examined. This finding had two important repercussions. First, it challenged the notion that romantic love originated in Europe, spreading only through cultural diffusion. Secondly, it suggested that if romantic love was not a human universal, it is a near human universal (Jankowiak & Ramsey, 2000).

This second finding provided fertile soil to test variations in romantic love related behaviors across cultures. The evolutionary psychological theory of love proposes that romantic love consists of a "complex suite of adaptations" that encourage fathers to invest in their offspring by emotionally binding them to their mates (Buss, 2019, 42). The application of this theory to the study of love has given rise to a diversifying array of research programs designed to test whether humans' love behaviors appear to correspond to the evolutionary logic of love promoting behavior patterns that would have on average improved such individual's reproductive success in the context of pre-agricultural forager societies. The theory that romantic love may be an evolved set of predispositions has even inspired neurological studies that search for the biological mechanisms of love (for a synthesis of evolutionary perspectives on romantic love see Buss, 2019; Fisher, 2004, 2016; Cacioppo, 2019).

Charles Lindholm (1998) conducted his own cross-cultural archival study of romantic love's ethnological prevalence using the Human Area Relations Files (HRAF) for 248 cultures of which he identified 21 societies with "elaborated romantic love complexes" and drew on his analysis of their similarities and differences to identify potential preconditions to the cultural elaboration of romantic love complexes. Lindholm theorized that variations in a society's social structure, particularly those shaping gender relations and kinship, along with other factors such as degree of competitiveness within a society, the prevalence of personal property, and the harshness of ecological conditions, together contributed to the promotion (or suppression) of a romantic love ethos. Most of these conditions correspond to characteristics of modernity and may point to cultural and social structural aspects of modernity responsible for encouraging the spread of romantic love's institutionalization, as in the rise of courtship and love as a criterion for marriage.

While Jankowiak and Fischer's passionate love study and Lindholm's study of love and structure came to different conclusions as to the pervasiveness of romantic love, their findings are more complementary than contradictory. Lindholm is skeptical of romantic love's universality but admits there is insufficient ethnographic evidence to rule out the possibility of romantic love being a universal experience. Jankowiak and Fischer assume that romantic love can be suppressed by a given society's social structures. However, they do not take the next step of Lindholm to develop a theory of the conditions in which romantic love would be culturally emphasized. Where the two studies disagree is over whether romantic love necessarily has a sexual component. Lindholm points to the Pashtuns of Pakistan, where he conducted fieldwork, and to the courtly love espoused by fifteenth century French troubadours as examples of romantic love that is ideally chaste. Lindholm's theory of romantic love's cultural variation anticipated connections between social structure and romantic love's behavioral and ideological manifestations that would become the central focus of subsequent ethnographic research and theoretical treatises on love within regional, societal and subcultural contexts which have shown limited interest in cultural comparison (see the following section). This disinterest left the synthesis of evolutionary and socio-cultural theories to more evolutionary oriented anthropologists.

On the heels of these findings, Victor de Munck and his collaborators developed a series of studies to begin empirically answering an important question raised by Jankowiak, Fischer and Lindholm's ethnological comparisons: If romantic love is a human universal, what meanings do all cultures share in their conceptions of love? This cognitive approach combined ethnographic knowledge with survey measures to test whether participants in three cultures, the U.S., Russia and Lithuania endorsed meanings attributed to romantic love within the existing psychological, philosophical and anthropological literature (de Munck, Korotayev, de Munck, & Khaltourina, 2011; de Munck, Korotayev, & Khaltourina, 2009). They identified five candidates that could form a universal core of beliefs humans hold about the experience of being in love. These attributes were identified by positive responses to the following statements: "I will do anything for the person I love," "I constantly think about the person I am in love with," "romantic love is the supreme happiness of life," "my love makes my partner a stronger and better person", and "sexual attraction is necessary for love." While Lindholm had postulated core characteristics of love in his study based on available literature, de Munck's methods differed by not presuming all of the characterizations of love identified in past literature needed to be present, devising a method for determining which features were most and least cross-culturally variable.

Recently Jankowiak, Shen, Yao, Wang, and Volsche (2015) and Nelson and Yon (2019; see Chap. 53) expanded de Munck et al.'s research to East Asia. Their respective studies conducted in urban China and South Korea are the first studies to empirically probe underlying cognitive assumptions embedded in a non-western population's notions of romantic love. Although these studies found cultural variation, they also found urban Chinese and South Koreans are in good agreement with Euro-Americans concerning romantic love's five main cognitive attributes. The enlarged sample of cultures also suggest that love's most cross-culturally variable meanings are those negative attributions made to love, such as its propensity to promote irrational behavior (Nelson & Yon, 2019). However, because these studies have been conducted exclusively in highly urban industrialized state societies where love has been institutionalized in marriage (if only recently), they have not resolved Jankowiak and Lindholm's competing assumptions about whether romantic love necessarily involves an erotic component. Resolution of that debate will require further empirical studies in societies claiming chaste ideals of love.

Returning to archival ethnographic comparison and evolutionarily derived research questions, de Munck and his collaborators have endeavored to unite Lindholm's theory of social structural elaboration and suppression of romantic love with evolutionary explanations of romantic love's ultimate function and underlying logic of enhancing reproductive success in their hybrid bio-social model of love (de Munck, Korotayev, & McGreevey, 2016). Drawing on eHRAF data, de Munck and his colleagues investigated the ways a society's social organization and gender norms, such as women's relative status, freedom to choose a spouse, and post-marital residence norms are correlated with love's institutionalization as a basis for marriage. In effect, de Munck et al. documented one of the ways social organization mutes or enhances an individual's opportunities to experience love through differences in institutions of kinship. De Munck and his colleagues interpret their findings, such as the negative correlation between involvement of extended family in marriage with love's acceptance as a marriage criterion and the positive correlation of women's status and love's use as a marriage criterion, as supporting the evolutionary hypothesis that love's role in creating pair bonds is only evolutionarily necessary in social contexts where other familial bonds for providing childcare are less available (de Munck et al., 2016; de Munck & Korotayev, 1999, 2007).

Mainstream socio-cultural anthropologists and sociologists have fiercely opposed "socio-biological" explanations of contemporary human behavior. They criticize evolutionary explanations for being teleological, a criticism that could as easily be made of many cultural constructivist and critical explanations of human behavior. The disdain of mainstream cultural anthropology and sociology for evolutionary explanations, however, likely has more to do with the political implications of evolutionary research, which can and has been utilized in racist and sexist discourses that seek to naturalize inequalities or worse, propose eugenic programs of social change. In the field of love studies the notion that all humans have a propensity to fall in love is not attacked so much as it is considered irrelevant to the research questions and objectives of ethnographers and theorists seeking to understand the effects of the revolutionary social processes of urbanization, development, globalization, and modernity on love and its associated behavioral expressions and problems.

2.2.2 Dynamics of Love: Critical Approaches

The question driving most ethnographic, theoretical, and historical studies of romantic love is not how love differs between one cultural context or society and another or whether love is a purely cultural construct or an evolved tendency. Instead, they ask: why and how are people's experiences of love changing? Are these new ideals creating as many problems as they solve? And, where does the power to shape these changing ideals of love lie? In sociology at least, there is a degree of consensus as to the answers of these questions: Our experiences of love are changing because of a suite of processes described as modernity, or late modernity, including: urbanization, industrialization, consumerism, nuclearization of the family, globalization, expansion of women's access to education and employment (and hence decreased financial dependence on husbands and kin), the increased separation of sex from reproduction, and the popularization of psychotherapeutic ideologies (See Bauman, 2003; Beck & Beck-Gernshein, 1995, 2014; Cancian, 1987; Endleman, 1989; Giddens, 1992; Hatfield & Rapson, 1996; and Illouz, 1997, 1998, 2012). They also attribute demographic shifts in marriage practices to these processes, including later age at first marriage, increased rates of divorce, and decreased rates of marriage (Duncombe & Marsden, 1993; Farrer, 2015; Farrer & Sun, 2003). These processes and the demographic changes that resulted from them are in turn argued to have changed the nature of love and romantic relationships in the following ways: feminizing love by centering its expression increasingly on verbal communication (Cancian, 1987); making romantic relationships increasingly voluntary and in need of constant negotiation to be maintained (Giddens, 1992); individualizing love to the point that lovers have increasingly few institutional guide posts to direct their romantic pursuits (Bauman, 2003; Beck & Beck-Gernshein, 1995); commodifying love, which makes romantic expression increasingly dependent on consumption of entertainment and leisure experiences (Baily, 1988; Illouz, 1997); and expansion of the cultural toolkits for making sense of experiences of love and formulating strategies of action (Constable, 2003; Hewamanne, 2008; Kottman, 2017; Swidler, 2001).

These researchers and thinkers vary by whether they emphasize the positive or the problematic repercussions of these changes. Anthony Giddens (1992) and Paul Kottman (2017) paint relatively rosy pictures of these transformations in romantic relationships, emphasizing increased individual freedom from constraint. At the opposite end of the spectrum, Ulrich Beck, Elisabeth Beck-Gernshein (1995) and Eva Illouz (1997, 2012) highlight how these apparent increases in freedom have left individuals lost and confused as to how to negotiate a less clearly demarcated field for forming love relationships. They also highlight how structural inequalities, such as men's and women's differing biological fertility constraints, differential access to economic capital to participate and succeed in courtship, and rising standards provoked by the psychology of technologically enhanced matchmaking, leave many stuck on the sidelines of the game of love and blaming themselves or their would be partners rather than the social inequalities shaping their predicament thanks to acceptance of neoliberal ideologies of self-governance.

These critical approaches dominate the ethnographic research on love and help to justify funding for love's academic study by focusing on social problems surrounding romantic relationships. Like Lindholm's and de Munck's comparative studies, they emphasize social structures' roles in shaping romantic love. Critical studies of love also tend to highlight social change, comparing practices and ideologies across historical periods. And, though critically oriented ethnographies of love focus on a single society or sub group, by engaging theories of love's historical transformation in western societies, these studies of love in other cultural contexts are able to compare and contrast the effects of social transformations that are increasingly pervasive globally. Although we will argue in the chapter's conclusion that ethnographic studies of love would benefit from adoption of some standardized measures and methods that would enable direct cross-cultural comparison as a complement to their use of participant observation, the growth of ethnographic studies explicitly examining love means future ethnological studies will not have to rely solely on ethnographic side notes and mythology to understand the diversity of love ideologies and practices.

2.3 Emerging Themes in Love's Ethnographic Record

Ethnographic studies of romantic love are becoming a cottage industry, with a growing number of edited volumes providing opportunities for ethnographers who collected insights on love, but whose work had not centrally focused on that subject, to compile their findings. Beginning with Jankowiak's (1995a) landmark edited volume that first assembled the newly emergent theories and findings on love cross-culturally, anthropological and interdisciplinary edited volumes on love are expanding the literature to cover further topical cross-sections including: love and sex/eroticism (de Munck, 1996; Featherstone, 1999; Jankowiak, 2008), courtship and companionate marriage (Hirsch & Wardlow, 2006), love and globalization (Padilla, Hirsch, Munoz-Laboy, Sember, & Parker, 2007), love and infidelity (Hirsch et al., 2009), love and communication (Wyss, 2014), love and radicalism (Grossi & West, 2017) and love and feminism (Garcia-Andade, Gunnarsson, & Jonasdottir, 2018). Recently there has even been sufficient growth in love research for edited volumes to focus on love and intimacy within particular regions, including Africa (Cole & Thomas, 2009) and Japan (Alexy & Cook, 2019).

2.3.1 The Global Rise of Companionate Marriages

The potential weakness found in every cross-cultural survey arises from the absence of a cultural context in which to evaluate the tacit meanings often associated with a specific type of behavior. Without studies probing the meanings individuals bring to behavior, survey research will always be open to a concern with validity. Because in-depth ethnographic research provides a more nuanced documentation of tacit and overt behavior, anthropologists consider it to have high validity. To this end, cultural anthropologists were less concerned with understanding love as a private experience and more focused on describing how and why a culture embraced love as its new normative ideal (Cole & Thomas, 2009; Hirsch & Wardlow, 2006; Padilla et al., 2007). This is the message of Hirsch and Wardlow's (2006) important edited book *Modern Loves* that is the first to probe, in a variety of ethnographic settings, the emergence of companionate marriage as a cultural ideal. Companionate marriage is characterized by feeling an enriched satisfaction with being emotionally linked together and prioritizing the spousal relationship over those with other kin. From a historical perspective, this institutionalization of companionate love within marital relationships is relatively recent (Coontz, 2005). But this does not mean that couples did not experience an enriched emotional satisfaction with being together before this form's institutionalization. We suspect many did.

2.3.2 Companionate Love as a Marital Ideal

The contributors to Hirsch and Wardlow's (2006) edited volume are less interested in exploring the origins of companionate love as a cultural ideal than they are in probing the role of various forms of inequalities that enhance or undermine a companionate marriage. Yunxiang Yan (2003) and Jane Collier (1997) describe these processes unfolding in rural China and Spain where family based agricultural production shifted toward wage labor. This economic shift freed an individual from extended kinship obligations to develop a more independent self that is able to transfer one's loyalties and affective focus from natal kin to one's spouse. Similarly, Carla Freeman (2007) provides a solid analysis of how middle-class Barbadians' understanding of the meaning and value of marriage shifted away from "duties" to more personal forms of satisfaction. Rebhun (1999) discusses a similar generational change in Northwest Brazil where the expectation of marital satisfaction has shifted from respect to also include a desire for greater emotional exchange. Laura Ahearn (2001, 81) discovered youthful Majars of Nepal, unlike their parents' generation, materialized their thoughts about love through letter writing between spouses that revealed the value they placed on the formation of close martial ties. And, in Port Morsby (capital city of PNG), Rosi and Zimmer-Tamakoshi (1993) illustrate how these transitions to companionate marriages can be fraught with difficulty as young people strive to realize ideals of conjugal equality while respecting the wishes of kin who insist on pre-companionate marital customs of bride price even when grooms hail from regions lacking this custom. These studies illustrate the tensions faced by the first generations of lovers navigating new ideals that have yet to become broadly held cultural values with institutional support. They are a reminder that where the companionate marriage ideal departs from practices of the parental generation the ideal likely lacks structural and ideological supports and may be institutionalized in law but not in cultural practice.

2.3.3 Weak and Strong Institutional Support for Companionate Marital Love

A lack of institutional support does not necessarily make marriages based on companionate ideals more fragile. Shalini Grover's (2018) study of marriage among the scheduled classes of Delhi's poor found that despite the widespread folk belief that 99% of love marriages fail in India, such partnerships were often more stable, if not more satisfying, because the lack of affinal support for brides forced them to endure in the face of hardship while their peers in arranged marriages retained the right to seek refuge among their kin in the face of discord. Grover points to over utilization of affinal refuge as a major strain and potential detriment to Indian marriages. Jankowiak and Li (2017) identify a similar transformation amongst urban Chinese who placed stronger emphasis on developing and sustaining an emotional connection within the marriage (see also Jankowiak, 2013; Schneider, 2014; Wang, 2015). Concurring, Michiko Suzuki's (2010, 72) exploration of contemporary urban Japanese world-views discovered youth idealized the possibility that self-cultivation and self-improvement could be developed within a love marriage. In short, marriage was neither the tomb of love nor the death of individuality.

Although we now know romantic love not to be a product of the west, for many love's discursive power draws from its association with Euro-American modernity and may even be promoted as such by colonial agents. For example, Holly Wardlow (2006) finds in Papua New Guinea, Christian missionaries actively promote a companionship love ideal, which was embraced by Huli youth as a way to counter their parents' expectation that they would enter into an arranged marriage. Numerous other ethnographers have highlighted love discourses' use as a marker of identity in assertions of self as a "modern" individual (Faier, 2007; Hart, 2007; Lewinson, 2006; Marsden, 2007; Mody, 2008; Rosi & Zimmer-Tamakoshi, 1993; Shohet, 2017; Tran, 2018). Most of these ethnographers illustrate that the "modern" - "traditional" dichotomy is a discourse practice of personal distinction rather than an accurate historical account of how present and past marital relationships differ.

Companionate marriage ideologies are not only precipitated by capitalist markets, urbanization, and the diffusion of colonial ideologies. The companionate marriage ideal is also normative amongst the Lahu, a Tibeto-Burman language speaking population living in Yunnan, China (Du, 1995, 2002). Shanshan Du found Lahu couples conceptualized their marriages as permanent social and emotional unions. In daily life, they perform almost every activity together. The local metaphor of "chopsticks only come in pairs" aptly signifies the interdependency of bride and groom and the centrality of the marital relationship in the Lahu Family. Daniel Smith (2006) found that among the Igbo of Nigeria courtship rituals promoted some sense of companionate love that is thought to be "a preamble to a successful marriage" (Hirsch & Wardlow, 2006, 5). Unlike the Lahu, however, the majority of Igbo marriages were not able to sustain their feelings of emotional contentment, which was confined to the courtship stage and not expected to continue into the marriage where other considerations (e.g., sustainable income, child care, and so forth) became paramount. The ethnographic record of companionate love demonstrates there is no single source or cause of companionate marital ideals. By directing an analytical lens on marriage as an emotional relationship, these studies show marital expectations often extend beyond performance of social roles and ethical obligations.

2.3.4 Expanding Romantic Love: Beyond Monogamy and Heteronormativity

Recent ethnographies of love and marriage challenge us to expand our conceptualizations of romantic love and companionate marriage to incorporate attitudes often seen as antithetical to romantic love. In a northern Indian tribal region, Himika Bhattacharya (2017) found the Lahauli community conceptualized love as an idealized state of being that extended beyond their "joint" or polyandrous marriage (i.e., one woman with two or more husbands who are siblings) to include the wider community and the countryside they inhabit. The cosmological linkage between idealized love for their "joint" marriage, and of the wider settlement, is being undermined by the encroachment of Indian nationalist values that associate monogamy with modernity and "joint" marriages with backwardness, despite the hegemonic Indian marriage ideal being an arranged marriage (Grover, 2018; Mody, 2008). In both Battacharrya's ethnography and Lisa Wynn's (2018) account of love in Cairo we are also asked to broaden our conceptualization of love to account for its co-occurrence with violence. Wynn proposes that in these cases we attend to the ways in which "love and desire promise hope" to make sense of this contradiction between action and affect (Wynn, 2018, Loc, 4101). Perhaps this paradox is evidence of the extreme power of idealization, which Lindholm identifies as a core component of romantic love. Furthermore, Elizabeth Povinelli's (2006) critical review of societies who claim romantic love and companionate marriage as core values (the US, Canada, Australia) highlights the role the state exerts in limiting with whom such "love" unions are permissible. Povinelli points out how historically, governments have used the legal code to (violently) deny love marriages that crossed racial lines or failed to conform to heteronormativity (plural marriage might likewise be added). These accounts demand that we attune to the unexpected forms love can manifest cross-culturally, affirming our own experiences of love in strange ways, and challenging our notions of love in familiar cases.

The anthropological exploration of love within a variety of cultural settings provides a welcome correction to the exclusive focus on the structural conditions that influence behavior. Returning to probing the emotional sphere, we are reminded of the power of choice to uphold, challenge, or undermine social convention. In the domain of love, or dyadic intimacy, individuals often discover themselves. It is a discovery that can also result in individuals redefining their commitment to community values (Jankowiak & Paladino, 2008). For example, Jankowiak and Allen's (1995) investigation of a fundamentalist Mormon polygamous community found romantic love, as an unvoiced preference to form an intimate dyadic bond, presents a challenge to the community's plural love ideal where sister wives are expected not only to respect each other but also love one another. More recently, Jillian Deri's (2015) ethnographic account of American polyamorous communities asserts that jealousy, at least for some individuals, is not inevitable. Deri's informants argue that with the right attitude and sufficient communication it is possible for individuals to teach themselves to find satisfaction and contentment in knowing their partner is enjoying emotional or sexual gratification with someone else. However, the polyamourists' insistence that "it is possible to love more than one person at the same time" may need to be qualified. Other research finds sexually non-exclusive relationships tend to be organized around an emotional hierarchy whereby one lover is considered "primary" and the other is the "secondary" lover (Conley, Gusakova, & Piermonte, 2019; Jankowiak & Gerth, 2012). One might ask then whether the love for the primary and secondary lover is the same. That one can love more than one person is self-evident in cases such as parent-child relationships as Bhattachacharya's Himalayan polyandrous informant attested when asked if love is reduced when it is divided (Bhattacharya, 2017). However, Jankowiak and Gerth's (2012) American college student informants found the experience of being in love with two people simultaneously to be distressing and difficult to sustain. Furthermore, they often experienced these loves as qualitatively different, with the love for one being more companionate and that for the other more passionate.

American Polyamorists assert their difficulties with jealousy lies in their socialization (de Munck, 2019; Deri, 2015). This raises the question of whether more communally raised children are less jealous. There do seem to be societies that feature marital and extramarital love bonds where jealousy is relatively mild, as among the Mehinaku of Brazzilan Amazonia (Gregor, 1995). The Mehinaku also seemed to speak of experiencing companionate love for one partner and passionate love for another, comparing their relative strengths. As we discuss below, though many societies exhibit such dichotomies of marital companionate love and extramarital passionate love, usually the latter is a secret kept from the former (Padilla et al., 2007).

Despite the increasing number of countries legalizing gay marriage and the extensive literature on queer sexuality, there are only a few studies of queer love. The Hijiras of Hyderabad (transgender females) constructed their ideal companionate marriage around sexual and emotional intimacy rather than on reproduction (Reddy, 2006). Afro-Surinamese Mati same-sex relationships are also organized around sexual attraction along with deep emotional involvement (Wekker, 1996). Lisa Diamond (2008) has powerfully illustrated women's fluidity of sexual orientation and choice of love object at least among Americans. In Jakarta, Saskia Wieringa (2007) documents Indonesian lesbians' insistence that romantic love and erotic energy are two powerful forces in women's lives. Noelle Stout's (2014) study of queer men and women in Cuba reveals how profound financial inequalities can inspire love, or incentivize its performance, even between individuals asserting opposing sexual orientations.

Studies of romantic love outside heteronormative relationships point to both the potential for queer experiences to challenge heteronormatively constructed theorizations of romantic love while also highlighting the challenges faced by queer people's pursuits of intimacy. Victor de Munck's (2019) comparison of non-binary gay Americans' cultural models of love with those of cis-male and female heterosexuals found his informants to generally share the key qualities he identified as central to American constructions of love. However, unlike his heterosexual interviewees, de Munck's gay and lesbian informants reported access to fewer applicable cultural scripts to draw on in modeling their romantic relationships. They also faced stigma and discrimination in many cases for their partner choices and had to grapple with the complexities of their sexual identities and orientations in respect to the sexing of their partners' bodies, which could shift in the case of transgender partners who transition from male to female and vice versa (de Munck, 2019). Renata Grossi's (2014) study of love in Australia's legal discourses argues that love is seen as posing both a danger and a force for radical change in debates over equal rights within queer communities as love discourses can be used either to reinforce patriarchy and heteronormative gender norms or serve as a "radical and liberating force" that carries similar cultural weight and legitimacy to same-sex couples' claims to the right to marry (105).

Despite the burgeoning literature on love and companionate marriage, numerous empirical questions and information gaps remain. Anthropological research into the phenomenon that is companionate marriage has yet to explore whether some cultures are more successful than others in achieving their martial ideal. Moreover, most researchers have not sought to determine if the psychological factors (e.g., family violence, birth order effect, personality differences, and so forth) that are often used to account for successful marriage are also applicable in a nonwestern martial setting. Polyamorists' assertion that jealousy is culturally constructed is also in need of empirical investigation. Is it possible to have a society free of jealousy? Even the among Moso, whose custom of walking marriage lends no ideological support to claims to exclusivity in sexual and romantic liaisons, jealousy is reported to occur (Shih, 2010). This raises the question of whether jealousy is a cultural or an experiential universal (Brown, 1991).

2.4 Conclusion

The ethnographic record of love is having great success with the important work of challenging ethnocentric assumptions about the nature of romantic love. Psychologists and neurobiologists have made remarkable insights probing love's essence. But because most of these insights come from WERID people, we cannot, however, be certain of their universality. Moreover, most cultural anthropologists, albeit working in different cultures, continue to find comfort framing their analysis within a constructionist framework. This results in an excessively concentrated probing of the relationships between changes in a society's social organization and corresponding shifts in cultural meanings associated with love. In this way, the preference for institutional understanding has resulted in ignoring, or deeming irrelevant, the psychological research on love. Furthermore, without cross-cultural comparison the ability to illuminate causation rather than mere correlation and verify theories of changes in cultures of love remains limited despite the burgeoning ethnographic record we can now draw upon.

References

Ahearn, L. (2001). *Invitations to love: Literacy, love letters, and social change in Nepal*. Ann Arbor, MI: University of Michigan Press.
Alexy, A., & Cook, E. (Eds.). (2019). *Intimate Japan: Ethnographies of closeness and conflict*. Honolulu, HI: University of Hawaii Press.
Baily, B. (1988). *From front porch to back seat: Courtship in twentieth-century America*. Baltimore, MD: The Johns Hopkins University Press.
Bauman, Z. (2003). *Liquid love: On the frailty of human bonds*. Cambridge, MA: Polity Press.
Beck, U., & Beck-Gernsheim, E. (1995). *The normal chaos of love*. Oxford: Polity Press.
Beck, U., & Beck-Gernsheim, E. (2014). *Distant love*. Oxford: Polity Press.
Bhattacharya, H. (2017). *Narrating love and violence: Women contesting caste, tribe and state in Lahaul, India*. New Brunswick, NJ: Rutgers University Press.
Brown, D. E. (1991). *Human universals*. New York, NY: McGraw-Hill Education.
Buss, D. (2019). The evolution of love in humans. In R. J. Sternberg & K. Sternberg (Eds.), *The new psychology of love* (2nd ed., pp. 42–63). Cambridge: Cambridge University Press.
Cacioppo, S. (2019). Neuroimaging of love in the twenty-first century. In R. J. Sternberg & K. Sternberg (Eds.), *The new psychology of love* (2nd ed., pp. 64–83). Cambridge: Cambridge University Press.
Cancian, F. (1987). *Love in America: Gender and self-development*. Cambridge: Cambridge University Press.
Cole, J., & Thomas, L. (Eds.). (2009). *Love in Africa*. Chicago, IL: University of Chicago Press.
Collier, J. F. (1997). *From duty to desire: Remaking families in a Spanish village*. Princeton, NJ: Princeton University Press.
Collins, J., & Gregor, T. (1995). Boundaries of love. In W. Jankowiak (Ed.), *Romantic passion: A universal experience?* (pp. 72–92). New York, NY: Columbia University Press.
Conley, T., Gusakova, S., & Piermonte, P. (2019). Love is political: How power and bias influence our intimate lives. In R. J. Sternberg & K. Sternberg (Eds.), *The new psychology of love* (2nd ed., pp. 117–138). Cambridge: Cambridge University Press.

Constable, N. (2003). *Romance on a global stage: Pen pals, virtual realities, "mail order" marriages*. Berkeley, CA: University of California Press.

Coontz, S. (2005). *Marriage, a history: From obedience to intimacy or how love conquered marriage*. New York, NY: Viking.

Coppinger, R. M., & Rosenblatt, P. C. (1968). Romantic love and subsistence dependence of spouses. *Journal of Anthropological Research, 24*(3), 310–319.

de Munck, V. (1996). Love and marriage in a Sri Lankan Muslim community: Toward a reevaluation of Dravidian marriage practices. *American Ethnologist, 23*(4), 698–716.

de Munck, V. (Ed.). (1998). *Romantic love and sexual behavior: Perspectives from the social sciences*. Westport, CT: Praeger.

de Munck, V. (2019). *Romantic love in America: Cultural models of gay, straight and polyamorous relationship*. Lanham, MD: Lexington Press.

de Munck, V., & Korotayev, A. (1999). Sexual equality and romantic love: A reanalysis of Rosenblatt's study on the function of romantic love. *Cross-Cultural Research., 33*(3), 265–277.

de Munck, V., & Korotayev, A. (2007). Wife-husband intimacy and female status in cross-cultural perspective. *Journal of Cross-Cultural Research, 4*(7), 307–335.

de Munck, V., Korotayev, A., de Munck, J., & Khaltourina, D. (2011). Cross-cultural analysis of models of romantic love among U.S. residents, Russians, and Lithuanians. *Cross-Cultural Research, 45*(2), 128–154.

de Munck, V., Korotayev, A., & Khaltourina, D. (2009). A comparative study of the structure of love in the US and Russia: Finding a common core of characteristics and national and gender difference. *Ethnology, 45*(4), 337–357.

de Munck, V., Korotayev, A., & McGreevey, J. (2016). Romantic love and family organization: A case for romantic love as a biosocial universal. *Evolutionary Psychology, 14*(4), 1–13.

Deri, J. (2015). *Love's refraction: Jealousy and compersion in queer women's polyamorous relationships*. Toronto, ON: University of Toronto Press.

Diamond, L. (2008). *Sexual fluidity: Understanding women's love and desire*. Cambridge, MA: Harvard University Press.

Du, S. (1995). The aesthetic axis in the construction of emotions and decisions: Love-pact suicide among the Lahu Na of southwestern China. In C. Ellis, D. D. Franks, & M. G. Flaherty (Eds.), *Social perspectives on emotions* (Vol. 3, pp. 199–221). Greenwich, CT: Emerald Group.

Du, S. (2002). *Chopsticks only work in pairs: Gender unity and gender equality among the Lahu of Southwest China*. New York: Columbia University Press.

Duncombe, J., & Marsden, D. (1993). Love and intimacy: The gender division of emotion and 'emotion work: A neglected aspect of sociological discussion of heterosexual relationships. *Sociology, 27*(2), 221–241.

Endleman, R. (1989). *Love and sex in twelve cultures*. New York, NY: Psych.

Engels, F. (1884). *The origins of the family, private property and the state*. London: Penguin Books.

Faier, L. (2007). Filipina migrants in rural Japan and their professions of love. *American Ethnologist, 34*(1), 148–162.

Farrer, J. (2015). Love, sex and commitment: Rethinking premarital intimacy from marriage in urban China. In D. Davis & S. Friedman (Eds.), *Wives, husbands, and lovers: Marriage and sexuality in Hong Kong, Taiwan, and urban China* (pp. 62–96). Stanford, CA: Stanford University Press.

Farrer, J., & Sun, Z. (2003). Extramarital love in Shanghai. *The China Journal, 50*(2), 1–36.

Featherstone, M. (Ed.). (1999). *Love & eroticism*. London: Theory, Culture & Society.

Finck, H. (1899). *Primitive love and love-stories*. New York, NY: Charles Scribner.

Fisher, H. (2004). *Why we love: The nature and chemistry of romantic love*. New York, NY: Henry Holt.

Fisher, H. (2016). *Anatomy of love: The natural history of monogamy, adultery and divorce*. New York, NY: Norton.

Freeman, C. (2007). Neoliberalism and the marriage of reputation and respectability: Entrepreneurship and the Barbadian middle class. In M. Padilla, J. Hirsch, M. Munoz-Laboy, R. Sember, &

R. Parker (Eds.), *Love and globalization: Transformations in the contemporary world* (pp. 3–37). Nashville, TN: Vanderbilt University Press.

Freud, S. (1961). *Civilization and its discontents*. New York, NY: W. W. Norton.

Garcia-Andade, A., Gunnarsson, L., & Jonasdottir, A. G. (Eds.). (2018). *Feminism and the power of love: Interdisciplinary interventions*. New York, NY: Routledge.

Giddens, A. (1992). *The transformation of intimacy: Sexuality, love, and eroticism in modern societies*. Stanford, CA: Stanford University Press.

Gregor, T. (1995). Sexuality and the experience of love. In P. Abramson & S. Pinkerton (Eds.), *Sexual nature sexual culture*. Chicago, IL: The University of Chicago Press.

Grossi, R. (2014). *Looking for love in the legal discourse of marriage*. Canberra, AU: ANU Press.

Grossi, R., & West, D. (Eds.). (2017). *The radicalism of romantic love: Critical perspectives*. New York, NY: Routledge.

Grover, S. (2018). *Marriage, love, caste and kinship support: Lived experiences of the urban poor in India*. London: Routledge.

Hart, K. (2007). Love by arrangement: The ambiguity of 'spousal choice' in a Turkish village. *Journal of the Royal Anthropological Institute, 13*, 321–343.

Hatfield, E., & Rapson, R. (1996). *Love and sex: Cross-cultural perspective*. Lanham, MD: University Press of America.

Hewamanne, S. (2008). *Stitching identities in a free trade zone*. Philadelphia, PA: University of Pennsylvania Press.

Hirsch, J., & Wardlow, H. (Eds.). (2006). *Modern loves: The romantic courtship and companionate marriage*. Ann Arbor, MI: University of Michigan Press.

Hirsch, J., Wardlow, W., Smith, D. J., Phinney, H., Parikh, S., & Nathanson, C. (Eds.). (2009). *The secret: Love, marriage, and HIV*. Nashville, TN: Vanderbilt University Press.

Illouz, E. (1997). *Consuming the romantic utopia: Love and the cultural contradictions of capitalism*. Berkeley, CA: University of California Press.

Illouz, E. (1998). The lost innocence of love: Romance as a postmodern condition. *Theory, Culture and Society, 15*(3–4), 161–186.

Illouz, E. (2012). *Why love hurts: A sociological explanation*. Oxford: Polity Press.

Jankowiak, W. (Ed.). (1995a). *Romantic passion: A universal experience?* New York, NY: Columbia University Press.

Jankowiak, W. (1995b). Introduction. In W. Jankowiak (Ed.), *Romantic passion: A universal experience?* (pp. 1–22). New York, NY: Columbia University Press.

Jankowiak, W. (1995c). Romantic passion in the People's Republic of China. In W. Jankowiak (Ed.), *Romantic passion: A universal experience?* (pp. 166–184). New York, NY: Columbia University Press.

Jankowiak, W. (Ed.). (2008). *Intimacies: Between love and sex*. New York, NY: Columbia University Press.

Jankowiak, W. (2013). Chinese youth: Hot romance and cold calculation. In P. Link, R. P. Madsen, & P. G. Pickowicz (Eds.), *Restless China*. Lanham, MD: Rowman and Littlefield.

Jankowiak, W., & Allen, E. (1995). The balance of duty and desire in an American polygamous community. In W. Jankowiak (Ed.), *Romantic passion: A universal experience?* (pp. 166–186). New York: Columbia University Press.

Jankowiak, W., & Fischer, E. F. (1992). A cross-cultural perspective on romantic love. *Ethnology, 31*(2), 149–155.

Jankowiak, W., & Gerth, H. (2012). Can you love two people at the same time? A research report. *Anthropologica, 54*(1), 78–89.

Jankowiak, W., & Li, X. (2017). Emergent conjugal love, mutual affection, and female martial power. In S. Harrell & G. Santos (Eds.), *Transforming patriarchy: Chinese families in the twenty-first century* (pp. 146–162). Seattle, WA: Washington University Press.

Jankowiak, W., & Paladino, T. (2008). Desiring sex, longing for love: A tripartite conundrum. In W. Jankowiak (Ed.), *Intimacies: Love and sex across cultures* (pp. 1–32). New York: Columbia University Press.

Jankowiak, W., & Ramsey, A. (2000). Femme fatale and status fatale: A cross-cultural perspective. *Cross Cultural Research, 34*(1), 57–69.

Jankowiak, W., Shen, Y., Yao, S., Wang, C., & Volsche, S. (2015). Investigating love's universal attributes: A research report from China. *Cross-Cultural Research, 49*(4), 422–436.

Karandashev, V. (2017). *Romantic love in cultural contexts*. Cham: Springer.

Karandashev, V. (2019). *Cross-cultural perspectives on the experience and expression of love*. Cham: Springer.

Kottman, P. (2017). *Love as human freedom*. Stanford, CA: Stanford University Press.

Lee, H. (2007). *Revolution of the heart: A genealogy of love in China 1900–1950*. Stanford, CA: Stanford University Press.

Lewinson, A. (2006). Love in the city: Navigating multiple relationships in Dar Es Salaam, Tanzania. *City & Society, 18*(1), 90–115.

Lindholm, C. (1988). Lovers and leaders: A comparison of social and psychological models of romance and charisma. *Information (International Social Science Council), 27*(1), 2–45.

Lindholm, C. (1998). Love and structure. *Theory, Culture & Society, 15*(3–4), 243–263.

Lindholm, C. (2002). *Cultural & identity: The history, theory, and practice of psychological anthropology*. New York, NY: McGraw Hill.

Marsden, M. (2007). Love and elopement in northern Pakistan. *Journal of the Royal Anthropological Institute, 13*(1), 91–108.

Mody, P. (2008). *The intimate state: Love-marriage and the law in Delhi*. London, UK: Routledge.

Murdock, G. P. (1949). *Social structure*. New York, NY: Macmillan.

Nelson, A. J., & Yon, K. J. (2019). Core and peripheral features of the cross-cultural model of romantic love. *Cross-Cultural Research, 53*(5), 447–482. https://doi.org/10.1177/1069397118813306.

Padilla, M., Hirsch, J., Munoz-Laboy, M., Sember, R., & Parker, R. (Eds.). (2007). *Love and globalization: Transformations of intimacy in the contemporary world*. Nashville, TN: Vanderbilt University Press.

Pan, L. (2016). *When true love came to China*. Hong Kong: Hong Kong University Press.

Povinelli, E. A. (2006). *The empire of love: Toward a theory of intimacy, genealogy, and carnality*. Durham, NC: Duke University Press.

Rebhun, L. A. (1999). *The heart is unknown country: Love in the changing economy of northeast Brazil*. Stanford, CA: Stanford University Press.

Reddy, W. M. (2001). *The navigation of feeling: A framework for the history of emotions*. Cambridge: Cambridge University Press.

Reddy, G. (2006). The bonds of love: Companionate marriage and the desire for intimacy among Hirjas in Hyberabad, India. In J. Hirsch & H. Wardlow (Eds.), *Modern loves: The anthropology of romantic courtship & companionate marriage* (pp. 174–192). Ann Arbor, MI: University of Michigan Press.

Rosi, P., & Zimmer-Tamakoshi, L. (1993). Love and marriage among the educated elite in Port Morsby. In R. Marksbury (Ed.), *The business of marriage: Transformations in oceanic matrimony* (pp. 175–204). Pittsburgh, PA: University of Pittsburgh Press.

Ryang, S. (2006). *Love in modern Japan*. New York, NY: Routledge.

Sarsby, J. (1983). *Romantic love and society*. London: Penguin Books.

Schneider, M. (2014). *The ugly wife is a treasure at home: True stories of love and marriage in communist China*. Lincoln, NB: Potomac Books.

Shih, C. (2010). *Quest for harmony: The Moso traditions of sexual union and family life*. Stanford, CA: Stanford University Press.

Shohet, M. (2017). Troubling love: Gender, class, and sideshadowing the "happy family" in Vietnam. *Ethos, 45*(4), 555–576.

Singer, I. (2009). *The nature of love: Plato to Luther* (Vol. 1). Cambridge, MA: The MIT Press.

Smith, D. (2006). Love and the risk of HIV: Courtship, marriage, and infidelity in southeastern Nigeria. In J. Hirsch & H. Wardlow (Eds.), *Modern loves: The anthropology of romantic courtship & companionate marriage* (pp. 135–156). Ann Arbor, MI: University of Michigan Press.

Sternberg, R., & Sternberg, K. (Eds.). (2019). *The new psychology of love* (2nd ed.). Cambridge: Cambridge University Press.

Stout, N. (2014). *After love: Queer intimacy and erotic economies in post-soviet Cuba*. Durham, NC: Duke University Press.

Suzuki, M. (2010). *Becoming modern women: Love and female identity in prewar Japanese literature and culture*. Stanford, CA: Stanford University Press.

Swidler, A. (2001). *Talk of love: How culture matters*. Chicago, IL: University of Chicago Press.

Tran, A. (2018). The anxiety of romantic love in Ho Chi Minh City, Vietnam. *Journal of the Royal Anthropological Institute, 24*(3), 512–531.

Wang, P. (2015). *Love and marriage in globalizing China*. New York, NY: Routledge.

Wardlow, H. (2006). All's fair when love is war: Romantic passion and companionate marriage among the Huli of Papua New Guinea. In J. Hirsch & H. Wardlow (Eds.), *Modern loves: The romantic courtship and companionate marriage* (pp. 51–77). Ann Arbor, MI: University of Michigan Press.

Wekker, G. (1996). *The politics of passion: Women's sexual culture in the Afro-Surinamese diaspora*. New York, NY: Columbia University Press.

Wieringa, S. E. (2007). "If there is no felling. . .": The dilemma between silence and coming out in a working-class butch/femme community in Jakarta. In M. Padilla, J. Hirsch, M. Munoz-Laboy, R. Sember, & R. Parker (Eds.), *Love and globalization: Transformations in the contemporary world* (pp. 70–92). Nashville, TN: Vanderbilt University Press.

Wynn, L. L. (2018). *Love, sex, desire in modern Egypt: Navigating the margins of respectability*. Austin, TX: University of Texas Press.

Wyss, E. (Ed.). (2014). *Communication of love: Mediatized intimacy from love letters to SMS*. Blelefeld, DE: Transcript Veriag.

Yan, Y. (2003). *Private life under socialism: Love, intimacy, and family change in a Chinese village, 1949–1999*. Stanford, CA: Stanford University Press.

William Jankowiak is an internationally recognized authority on urban Chinese society, urban Mongols, Mormon fundamentalist polygyny, and love around the world. Professor Jankowiak is often invited to present the results of his research as well as called on by media to provide background information on various topics. His research has been featured in numerous media outlets, including The New York Times, Time magazine, NPR, History Channel, TLC, ABC Primetime, and NBC.

Alex J. Nelson earned his Ph.D. in Anthropology at the University of Nevada, Las Vegas and is writing an ethnography of romantic love in South Korea. His work explores how historical/inter-generational changes in Korean expectations and experiences of love and romantic relationships reflect changes in Korean gender relations and the social and economic structures shaping them. He is also a researcher with the Erotic Entrepreneurs Project (www.eroticentrepreneurs.com), an interdisciplinary participatory action study of the business practices and strategies of independent erotic escorts in USA.

Chapter 3
Love's Ethnographic Record: Beyond the Love/Arranged Marriage Dichotomy and Other False Essentialisms

Alex J. Nelson and William Jankowiak

Abstract Social scientists long ignored love as a topic for empirical research, presuming love to be a European contribution to world culture. Therefore, some researchers were surprised of and resistant to mounting evidence that most societies had a long history concerning love. However, across peoples and histories, love has carried different meanings and been put to different ends. We provide an in-depth review of current ethnographic research on love in the context of romantic relationships. We find that the ethnographic literature on romantic love challenges essentialisms within western love ideals, including: the division of love and arranged marriage, love's association with sexual exclusivity, the separation of love and material and sexual interest, and the belief that romantic love is a product of modernity. We conclude the chapter by identifying questions the growing ethnographic literature on love have left unanswered and point to the areas where further investigation is most needed.

Keywords Love · Romantic love · Marriage · Extra-marital sexual intimacy · Reciprocity · Modernity

3.1 Introduction

A principle objective of anthropology is to challenge cultural stereotypes and, through participant observation, bring to light the differences between what people do and what they claim to do. In this chapter we continue our review of the ethnographic literature on love (see Chap. 2) and highlight findings that illustrate the distance that can exist between practice and ideology in the realm of love. In so doing, we emphasize the challenges the ethnographic record poses to western essentialisms concerning romantic love. To continue assuming that western love

A. J. Nelson (✉) · W. Jankowiak
Department of Anthropology, University of Nevada, Las Vegas, Las Vegas, NV, USA
e-mail: nelson26@unlv.nevada.edu; jankbill@unlv.nevada.edu

ideals define the experience leads to the conclusion that romantic love does not exist (because no one lives up to its ideals), or that deviations from these ideals are not "true love," but mere infatuation or attachment. Understanding which features of love are cross-culturally variable and invariable is the necessary first step toward determining the essential features of the human experience of love.

This chapter covers three principle themes: love in arranged and non-monogamous relationships, love's entwinement with practical expectations of support, and love's association with modernity and communication. Within each theme we challenge key assumptions of love and highlight departures between love's ideology and practice. Love is popularly imagined to be synonymous with individuals' free choice of one another as lovers and with sexual fidelity to a single individual. Elopements and arranged marriages are imagined as opposed opposites. But where marriages are ideally arranged, elopements and courtship may precede arrangement as a strategy to guide or force parents' hands. Love is also regularly idealized as free of practical calculations, however lovers who fail to meet expectations of reciprocal support sow discontent and may be discarded. Furthermore, romantic love is imagined as a product of modernity. However, the ethnographic and historical record suggest that forms of romantic love long predate the modern era and some ethnographers suggest that where romantic love is absent, modernity does not ensure its manifestation.

3.2 The False Dichotomy of Love and Arranged Marriage

Arranged marriages came late to human history. Foraging societies prefer to allow individual choice in selecting a mate. But, this changed with the growth of farming communities that were organized around family and not individual interests. The paramount concern was family survival and not personal satisfaction or self-development. Within the arranged marriage normative order, there was always the possibility that individuals might follow private promptings and challenge family marital plans.

Although arranged marriages are popularly assumed to occur with little or no contact between the betrothed before the wedding, ethnographic investigations reveal the practice often differs significantly from the ideal. Victor de Munck (1996) discovered that in the Muslim Sri Lankan community where he conducted years of fieldwork, love was a precursor to many arranged marriages despite official prohibitions against courtship. De Munck found "the absence of sanctions against public interaction between opposite-sex cross-cousins and the obvious intent of the post-circumcision visits help direct the course of love toward someone from the culturally approved social category" (1996, 708).

In other words, institutions encouraged romance (despite its overall proscription) towards the very same partners one would likely have their marriage arranged to. These Sri Lankan arranged marriages were, in fact, romantic relationships that offspring had entered into earlier without parental permission. If parents refused to agree to the marriage, they threatened to run away or commit suicide. These threats were taken seriously. De Munck concluded that the Sri Lankan ideal marriage was neither an elopement nor an arranged marriage to a stranger but rather a "love-come-arranged marriage" (for similar responses in other societies see Ohara & Reynolds, 1970; Rubinstein, 1995; Schmitt et al., 2004). Among rural villages in Western Turkey, Kimberley Hart (2007) illustrates how ideologies of love and arranged marriage are fraught with contradictions as her informants simultaneously idealized marital choice while prohibiting public courtship, forcing couples to pursue their romances and marriages clandestinely or during the engagement process after having been initially introduced by arrangement. These studies challenge simple dichotomies between arranged and love marriages.

In India's Delhi, Perveez Mody (2008) describes love-come-arranged marriages as the ideal among her eloping interlocuters. However, due to differences of class, caste, or religion, these couples faced strong opposition, leading to kidnappings and other forms of violence from kin or the community in numerous cases. Mody describes how the state apparatuses for legal marriage works to exploit eloping couples and push them towards ideals of homogamy and submission to parental authority. For such couples, legal marriage is ideally a bargaining chip to help them overcome parental opposition. Like de Munck's Sri Lankan villagers, Delhi couples ideally turn their love marriages into arranged marriages to preserve their familial ties and the reputations of themselves and their kin, whose honor is threatened along with that of their entire community through the circumvention of parental authority. Among Delhi's poor of the scheduled classes, Shalini Grover (2018) found less severe reactions from kin, though those eloping couples unable to secure love-come-arranged marriages did greatly diminish their ability to count on support from their natal family in times of post-marital strife. This conundrum is paralleled in the Bedouin justification for disapproving of love marriages (Abu-Lughod, 1986, 210). Grover (2018) found that the arbitration organizations set up by a women's organization to settle marital disputes, much like the courts (Mody, 2008), strongly enforced norms of gender relations and the superiority of arranged marriage, disparaging love marriage couples as deserving of trouble for failing to marry properly. These two extensive studies of marriage in Delhi highlight the role of the state and non-government entities in managing love and marriage and how they uphold "traditional" gender and family ideologies despite their bureaucratic structure and official directives to uphold a marriage law that permits self-selected marriages and bans dowry exchange.

Further studies of love and marriage in South Asia shed light on the means by which love-come-arranged marriages are gaining popularity. Magnus Marsden's (2007) ethnographic account of love and marriage among the Chitralis of northern Pakistan illustrates that love marriages and arranged marriages form a continuum of practices rather than clearly distinct categories. He found eloping couples beseeched politically powerful intermediaries to convince their parents to convert their elopements to love-come-arranged marriages. Marsden points to public expression of sympathy for eloping couples as a method of signaling one's identity as "modern" among his informants. Yet while courtship and elopement are tied to notions of the modern, emblematic in Bollywood songs and films, Marsden (2007) describes the continued persistence of local and regional pre-modern love discourses (in the form of local love poetry) as forming a "synthesis" with globalized love discourses (104). Shireen Lateef (1993) documents the diversification of marital patterns from arranged, arranged-love, love, and bureau (overseas pen-pal) marriages among Indo-Fijians and how each follows the ideology of arranged marriage to a greater or lesser extent. She observes educated urban elites to be the only segment of the female population permitted to court, so long as they constrain their pursuits to relations with endogamous partners on the basis of religion, class, and race. Lateef finds these women's access to mixed-sex urban spaces through employment and education create opportunities for romances which their parents quickly arrange into marriages upon discovery.

Several themes emerge in these accounts of love-come-arranged marriages. First, opportunities for parent controlled courtship is weakened when cross-sex interaction can no longer be restricted. Second, homogamous and hypergamous couplings meet less parental resistance and, in cases of interreligious marriage, one party is usually expected to convert to the religion of the other. Third, although love as a basis for marriage is often conceptualized as a modern practice contrasted with tradition, this does not mean pre-modern notions of love were absent nor that these modern love marriages dispense with the gender roles of arranged marriages. The problems faced by eloping couples after marriage illustrates how courtship practices change more easily and rapidly than the norms of post-marital relations (see also Tran, 2018).

3.2.1 Spousal Love after (Arranged) Marriage

Marriages arranged without courtship do not necessarily preclude a cultural ideal of love between spouses after marriage. For example, in 1980s urban China, William Jankowiak (1993, 1995) discovered, in contrast to the pattern found in many "western" societies, urbanites tended to fall passionately in love *after*, rather than before, agreeing to marry. Thus, individuals usually began their self-arranged marriage discussions with a skeptical detachment and in cold calculation of each other's negative and positive marital attributes. Once an agreement was reached, however, individuals involved tend to fantasize about their future spouse and their forthcoming marriage with a passionate intensity. Mody (2008) noticed a similar pattern amongst New Delhians who also formed a passionate love bond after agreeing to an arranged marriage. Martha Inhorn, working amongst Cairo's middle class, observed a similar trend where intense love bonds developed after entering into an arranged marriage transaction. She documents how numerous urban Egyptians' who had developed deeply felt loving marriages chose not to follow the culturally prescribed expectation that couples divorce in the face of infertility (Inhorn, 2007).

3.3 Love in Plural and Extra-Marital Relationships

Although cross-cultural research finds that 75% of cultures do not approve of extramarital sex, such affairs appear common (Chamie, 2018). In cultures where it is more "tolerated," it remains imperative for married men to never publicly acknowledge their involvement in an illicit sexual liaison (Hirsch et al., 2009). An exception to this global norm is spousal exchange where partners are aware, accept, and render approval prior to the sexual transaction (Berndt, 1976; Jankowiak & Mixson, 2008; Jankowiak, Nell, & Buckmaster, 2002; Lipset, 1997; Stern & Condon, 1995).

It used to be assumed that males were the primary agents seeking sexual variety for its own sake. Closer investigation finds that there are other motives—principally the desire to form an intense love bond with another. In societies that tolerate polygamous marriage, it is not unusual for a husband to have more freedom in choosing his second wife on the basis of sentiment (see Lewinson, 2006). This is also observed in monogamous societies where the choice of a first spouse is constrained but individuals re-marrying after widowhood, divorce, or abandonment are able to choose their subsequent partners more freely (Grover, 2018; Jankowiak, 1993; Parry, 2001).

Within highly sexually restrictive cultures, where extramarital sex and romance is grounds for death or exile, love affairs none the less are carried out in institutionalized, yet secret, relationships, initially in adolescence but sometimes also into adulthood. Paul Manning (2015) describes such a custom of high-stakes secret extramarital romance among the late Khesurs, a tribal people of Georgia's mountain regions. Are Knudson (2009) describes similar practices in a Palas community of the Koshitan Mountainous region of Northern Pakistan. In both societies, marriages are arranged but men and women, particularly in their youth, engage in romantic dalliances under cover of darkness. Intermediaries who serve as matchmakers, taking on significant risks themselves should the couple be discovered, facilitate these meetings, in which the lovers spend the night together in ideally chaste embraces. As we discuss below, the passionate longing cultivated in these secret liaisons are immortalized in local poetry. Charles Lindholm (1995) notes from his observations of the Pashtuns, that it is difficult to gauge the extent to which these illicit love affairs truly were chaste in practice or whether asserting their chastity was more a necessary protective rhetoric to preserve a dangerous custom. However, chastity aside, the willingness of men and women to risk their lives to sustain these intense love bonds is testament to how rewarding the experience of love can be even when the bond's social recognition is a complete impossibility. They may also speak to the intimate power of shared secrets.

Alternatively, where polygyny is not culturally sanctioned, men with sufficient economic or erotic capital often seek sex and love in extramarital relationships (see Gregor, 1995; Harkonen, 2016, 2018; Hirsch et al., 2009; Osburg, 2013; Stark, 2017; Uretsky, 2016; Wynn, 2018). Concurring, Dales and Yamamato's (2019) investigation of Japanese marriage centers found couples who utilized their services were more concerned with reproduction than sexual fulfillment or the creation of an intimate love bond in their marriages. It was understood, albeit unvoiced, that the man, if interested, would seek a love bond elsewhere. Ho Swee Lin (2012), also studying Japan, documents that married Japanese women also seek love and sexual fulfillment outside of marriage where they "love like a man" (321). However, Ho demonstrates "loving like a man" involves more than simply seeking love and sex outside marriage, it also often requires suppressing one's expectations of and attachment to lovers. This detachment enables them to avoid disappointment when their male partners do not match their emotional investment in the relationship and to preserve their own marriages, which may be satisfactory beyond the absence of sexual and romantic intimacy. Japanese women, like their male counterparts, may also seek extramarital intimacy in the hands of professionals (Takeyama, 2016). These examples from Japan diverge from the cases of female plural relationships we describe in the next section in that, rather than seeking extra marital intimacy to meet needs for material care, these Japanese wives invest substantial material resources to make themselves more attractive through cosmetics and to engage in leisure activities with lovers or male sex workers for sexual and emotional fulfillment. Accounts of female sex tourism also observe women from several cultural contexts are willing to pay for extra-marital intimacy when they can afford to (Brennan, 2004, 2007; Stout, 2014).

The moral imperative embedded within an extramarital relationship is to maintain "the secret" or never mention the affair in front of a spouse (Hirsch et al., 2009). In these contexts, spouses often, albeit grudgingly, tolerate these affairs so long as they are respectfully hidden, denied, and discretely kept from the spouse (Harkonen, 2016; Hirsch et al., 2009; Ho, 2012; Lepani, 2012; Lewinson, 2006; Osburg, 2013; Wynn, 2018). In relatively sexually open cultures (e.g., Oceania and the Caribbean), the sexual double standard, where men's sexual transgression is more publicly tolerated while women are held in moral contempt for seeking an affair, persists but is lessened and requires negotiation. For example, in Cuba, expressions of jealousy, though common, have negative implications for both men and women (Harkonen, 2018; see also Chap. 54). In these cultures, a double standard appears to extend to the domain of love as well, with male jealous rage recieving less censure compared to female jealous anger.

Although advocates often claim that plural or group love is superior to monogamous love. Closer investigation suggests this seldom occurs. Instead there often appears to be an underlying dyadic love bond preference. For example, Polyamorous and swinger marriages involve the prior mutual negotiation of boundaries to determine how much information is shared between lovers about their other partners and whether and when outside relationships require approval or discussion between the couple that is preexisting (and often primary) (Deri, 2015; Jankowiak & Mixson, 2008). Both relationship types in the American context approach Anthony Giddens' (1992) ideal of the "pure relationship" in this way, with the couple negotiating boundaries to assure mutual utility (1). However, these are also emergent subcultures. Unlike most Americans, swingers and polyamorists appear to adopt more ideological conceptions of love that center on an internally consistent cultural logic or ideology (Swidler, 2001; Deri, 2015; de Munck, 2019).

The only cultures to seemingly do away with "the secret" do so within polygamous marriage systems where these plural relationships are institutionalized and where spousal exchanges take place in delimited ritualized contexts (Lipset, 1997). Even when love is an expectation in polygamous relationships, most ethnographic accounts report spouses are careful not to draw attention to their affection for one spouse in front of another (Jankowiak & Allen, 1995; Tiwari, 2008). However, Himika Bhattacharya (2017) is unclear on this point among the Lahaulis of Northern India. In this sense non-monogamous couples too keep the secret of multiple loves, even if it is a completely open secret. The secret seems a near universal strategy for dealing with jealousy, particularly when it threatens institutionalized ties in which children, extended families, and households are at stake. The secret thus gives these relationships the flexibility to sustain themselves in the face of desires that threaten its continuation. Yet whether jealousy is primarily a product of socialization, as the polyamorists assert, is unclear. As with all cases of nature vs nurture, the truth is probably somewhere in between.

3.4 Inseparable Spheres, Intimate Worlds: Sex and Materiality in Love

No topic on love has received more ethnographic attention in recent years than the relationship between love and material interests. In the United States love and financial considerations are ideally separated and incommensurable, forming "separate spheres and hostile worlds" (Zelizer, 2005, 21). America is not alone in idealizing the separation of the romantic from the material domains (see Eerdewijk, 2006; Mody, 2008; Shohet, 2017; Stark, 2017; Stout, 2014). But, the logic behind the conception of "hostile worlds" is not universally idealized and is nearly nonexistent in practice. In every society, whether acknowledged or denied, the spheres of love and pragmatic concerns are inextricably linked (see Durham, 2002; El-Dine, 2018; Faier, 2007; Grover, 2018; Harkonen, 2016, 2018, see also Chap. 54; Hoefinger, 2013; Lepani, 2012; Lewinson, 2006; Patico, 2009; Stark, 2017; Wynn, 2018). There are certainly situations where romantic love as an inauthentic discourse is evoked as a performance designed to attract and reassure a potential mate (Brennan, 2004, 2007). But the line between performance and sincere affection, including contexts of transactional sexual relationships, is frequently blurred (see Carrier-Moisan, 2017; Cheng, 2007, 2010; Faier, 2007; Harkonen, 2016; Hoefinger, 2013; Parrenas, 2011; Stark, 2017; Stout, 2014; Wijk, 2006).

3.4.1 Love, Exchange, and Gendered Respectability

Even when ideologies of affection entail expectations of material support, individuals must navigate discourses of gendered respectability to position themselves as moral subjects to themselves and to others (Cheng, 2010; Eerdewijk, 2006; Harkonen, 2016, 2018; Mody, 2008; Shohet, 2017; Stout, 2014; Wynn, 2018; Zigon, 2013). For example, although young women in Qatar idealize the separation of gifts and monetary aid from romantic love, they still expect and rely on such gifts and other forms of financial support from their lovers to support their families, enhance their beauty and status, and enjoy entertainment (Eerdewijk, 2006). Qatari women then evoke a discourse of evaluating men's breadwinner masculinity and suitability as a prospective husband on those grounds, distancing themselves from the implied need to reciprocate these gifts with what they believe unsuitable boyfriends desire, premarital sex (Eerdewijk, 2006). In this way both men and women negotiate intimate relationships through offers and counter offers of material, sexual, and emotional exchange that must be juggled in the management of one's reputation, less one's desire and character be reduced to that of the greedy "prostitute" or the lustful "dog".

Most societies prefer to forge intimacy within some form of an exchange relationship, in contrast to the Euro-American courtship heritage's fetishized ideal of spiritual love (i.e., a psychic union that transcends the body and denies self-interest) (Donner & Santos, 2016). In *Africa in Love* (Cole & Thomas, 2009) various contributors probed the relationship between material discourse and the presence or absence of love. Authors repeatedly pointed out that the Christian preference to spiritualize love does not make it a superior form of love. It only made it a different form of expression. Many cultures prefer that authentic emotionally grounded affection be voiced within a materialistic discourse. In effect, "emotions and materiality [can] be deeply intertwined" (Cole, 2009, 111), so that "affectionate connections and material resources" often overlap (Cole, 2009, 127). Amongst the African poor and middle class "material support is taken as evidence of emotional commitment" (Thomas & Cole, 2009, 24). Material support not only meets basic needs, it is also one solution to the problem of clearly expressing a highly subjective state like love. Particularly for men who have few resources, material provisioning can be a costly signal of one's affection, and its absence a sign of potential insincerity or duplicity (Stark, 2017).

Complementing the mountainous evidence that romantic love is often linked to material considerations are accounts of love's loss, denial, and suppression in the name of suitability. In Seoul, South Korea, Jean-Paul Baldacchino (2008) describes a young informant's exacerbation with a boyfriend whose affection she did not share and whom she saw as inadequate as she says: "I did not want to love him, he was too poor" (111–112). Neil Diamant (2000) recorded a similar sentiment in 1952 when a young Chinese woman readily acknowledged the simple reason behind her recurrent pattern of marriage and divorce: "I marry to eat, and when I have nothing to eat I divorce" (81). The distinction between partners who might be suitable lovers but unsuitable for marriage is prevalent when informal courtship or dating is permitted while concerns with upholding family status remain high (Lewinson, 2006; Mody, 2008; Wynn, 2018).

3.4.2 *"True" Love and Concerns of Romantic Purity and Sincerity*

The denial of love's relationship to erotic desire as a difficult to counterfeit litmus test of a beloved's devotion is also no more universal than the separation of love and pragmatic needs. The idea of a spiritualized love came late to China, arriving in the early twentieth century when Chinese writers (Lee, 1987, 2007) adopted a Freudian explanation for human behavior (Pan, 2016). For much of Imperial China's history love and sex were presumed to be intertwined, albeit unvoiced, but often present. Sonia Ryang (2006) found a similar orientation amongst the medieval Japanese elite. William Reddy (2012) also found evidence of the intertwinement of love and sex in Japan's Heian era, and again in medieval South Asia. In effect, there was no "sharp separation of sacred and the profane" (Reddy, 2012, 339), or between sex and love. They were considered to be two emotional states that are constantly flowing together. Ironically, though Giddens ascribes the harmony of love and sex as a product of late modernity, in Japan and India this harmony was premodern, disrupted instead by concerns with respectability in the modern era (Reddy, 2012; Ryang, 2006). For example, when Indian lovers elope, they do not assert that love justifies their sexual union, rather they claim respectability by asserting that their love is a spiritual, divine love, devoid of the connotations of lust (Mody, 2008). In such cases ideologies idealizing the separation of love from sex appear to reflect concerns for the purity of the community rather than the practices of actual lovers, illustrating that ideals of true love reflect cultural norms and discourses rather than actual practice or "nature."

Anne Rebhun (1999a, 1999b) points out that the arrival of an ideology of "true love" in Northeast Brazil did not eliminate other motivations for entering into a marriage. A concern with "interests" or economic well-being is considered to be a legitimate rationale for marrying. The problem arises when one partner thinks he is entering into a love marriage when from the other's perspective they understand they have an economic sexual exchange. And while this concern over feigned love interest for material gain is ethnographically more a male insecurity in interpreting women's behavior, adoption of love discourses for material gain is not the sole purview of women. In Staged Seduction, Akikio Takeyama (2016) describes young male hosts' adept manipulation of their middle-aged female clients' desires to be seen as unique, interesting, sexy and popular in Tokyo. In the Caribbean, Denise Brennan (2004, 2007) describes similar dynamics between European female tourists and Dominican men. Joan van Wijk (2006) recounts similar relations between female tourists and beach boys in Belize. And in Cuba, Noelle Stout

(2014) delves into the complexities of heterosexual men performing desire for both male and female tourists, as well as queer locals, to take advantage of the steep gap between the worth of tourists' tips and gifts and relatively miniscule wages available in Cuba. Sealing Cheng's (2010) ethnography of Filipina migrant sex workers' engagements with American soldiers in Army camp towns in South Korea illustrates how both men and women engage in discourses of love strategically, but that doing so instrumentally in one case does not preclude doing so out of felt emotion in other circumstances (see also Carrier-Moisan, 2017; Hoefinger, 2013; Parrenas, 2011). These ethnographies illustrate that the line between experience and performance, and the desire for love and material support, often form a continuum with most acts of loving reciprocation falling somewhere in the middle of a spectrum between desired outcome and the affect of loving desire.

Even in straightforward cases of courtship, in most societies sexual desire, loving attachment, and material interest are more deeply interwoven than acknowledged. Pierre Bourdieu (1984) theorizes that what we experience as attraction is in fact the product of recognizing one's class habitus (learned and shared tastes, aesthetics, comportment and competencies) in another. David Lipset's (2015) analysis of a contemporary American romantic courtship narrative finds agreement with Bourdieu's (1984) theorization. In effect, individuals fall "in love" with those who share their upbringing through subconscious recognition of their shared economic, cultural, social and erotic capital. Lipset illustrates ways in which the apparent ease felt between two individuals engaging in courtship leads them to feel they are experiencing fated love but which he argues is truly to "love one's fate" (2015, 168). This observation demystifies attraction, revealing how that inexplicable chemistry may in fact be the synergy experienced when interacting with someone of shared or complementary learned behaviors and mentality which gives the appearance of a love devoid of material considerations while in fact those material calculations are merely being calculated subconsciously through the affect of felt comfort.

To date, anthropology continues to place reciprocity at the center of its inquiry into practices of love (Venkatesan, Edwards, Willerslev, Povinelli, & Mody, 2011). Through this framework for theorizing love as it is practiced, anthropologists have conceptualized love as the reciprocation of sexual affection, material support, and emotional care. The idealization of love as a spiritualized state or "free gift" unbound by material or sexual interest exists only as a transcendental ideal rarely actualized in practice (Venkatesan et al., 2011). However, this framing raises the question of whether this unachievable ideal plays a necessary role in human experiences of love, or if it merely sets an unattainable standard achievable only in fantasy.

3.5 Communicating Love: Entangling Tradition and Modernity

Ethnographers have observed that it is not always possible or appropriate to express one's love directly. In a number of societies singing love songs has been found to be a primary method of courtship. Australian Aborigine Waipuddanya men sing magical love songs for help in securing a mate (Gioia, 2015, 9). Among the Lahu romantic songs are typically sung interactively between two lovers in semi-public settings (Du, 1995, 2002). If parents refuse to accept a person as a suitable mate, the courtship love song can readily be transformed into a fantasy love suicide pact where the doomed lovers create an imaginary blissful life in the next world that seems to legitimate the couple's deaths. This rationale is in part responsible for the Lahu's extremely high suicide rate. Among the Huli love songs are not sung to a potential lover, but rather something men sing to other men in homosocial settings. Their purpose is not to woo a woman but rather to signal their emotional interest with a woman who works in a brothel. Wardlow (2008) points out if he does marry such a woman she would never be the first wife but rather the third or fourth.

Even where directly singing to one's beloved is not orthodox courtship practice, the theme of love is ever present in folk and contemporary music and has drawn anthropological inquiry. Roland Berndt (1976) identifies a notion of sexual love apparent in the mytho-ritual song cycles of the Aborigines of north-east Arnhem Land in northern Australia, arguing that the songs created a "romantic atmosphere" and reveal what he describes as the "social-sacred," "sacred-ritual" and "personal faces" of (sexual) love (154). Antoinette Schimorelpennick's (1997) research in southern rural China found 9 out of 10 folksongs were about love (cited in Gioia 2015, 180). Colin Campbell (2006), in his analysis of romantic love in 1960s English pop music, argues that the 'romantic love complex' was not only a powerful part of intimate relationships, but a "force of cultural change" more broadly. Other forms of popular entertainment media, such as television, films, and perhaps now, video blogs and podcasts, offer opportunities to share and shape experiences and ideologies of romantic love. Janneke Verheijen's (2006) study of the impact of telenovelas in rural Guatemala, for instance, suggests that the messages in these romantic dramas have an "emancipating impact" that challenged villagers' traditional gender roles. However, even where romantic love is a pervasive theme in popular music and television, as in South Korea or India, these media may represent fantasy far more than reality. Baldacchino (2014) asserts that romantic melodramas serve both as cautionary tales and romantic inspiration for South Korean young women, particularly when they depict love transgressing social and moral norms. These studies of love's portrayal in popular culture raise questions of how popular media influences and reflects actual experiences and expectations of romantic love and whether the globalization of such media diffuses local conceptions across and beyond regions.

Letter and poetry writing (see Chap. 24) have also proven fruitful mediums of study for understanding romantic love, as have their twenty-first century counterpart, text messaging (see de Leon, 2017; Kotthoff, 2014). Lila Abu-Lughod's (1986) ethnography of Bedouin society skillfully illustrates how Bedouins deploy poetry to express sentiments of love and heart ache in a context and medium that avoids violating norms of honor and modesty, and in so doing highlights the agency of women's adherence to those virtues and the force of will and effort they exert in publicly adhering to them despite their actions' incongruity with their emotions and desires. Among the historical Khesurs of Georgia's mountain regions, Paul Manning (2015) demonstrates the connections between Khesur romantic liaisons, carried out in secret between young lovers, and their love poetry, which disguise the speaker and addressee, preserving the anonymity of both lovers.

Letter writing (Ahearn, 2001) and access to mobile phones (de Leon, 2017) also provide mediums for courtship and romantic discourse that circumvents familial authority where marriages are ideally arranged. However, the introduction of such technologies is not a certain harbinger of romantic discourse, as Lipset (2004) argues in his analysis of Murik young men's courtship stories, which omit the conventions of idealization, longing, and pursuit of a unique other. He further notes that while these communicative enhancements, along with increased physical mobility, increased the number of available partners, along with their ability to circumvent parental authority, love engagements were mute. This same mobility has also brought love to reckon with global inequalities, raising the stakes of romantic decisions by thrusting youth into the global political economy of love (see Padilla, Hirsch, Munoz-Laboy, Sember, & Parker, 2007; Beck & Beck-Gernsheim, 2014; Constable, 2003, 2005; Illouz, 2012; Groes & Fernandez, 2018).

3.6 Conclusion and Future Directions

As the above review illustrates (see Chap. 2), within romantic relationships, love's practice regularly diverges from culturally orthodox ideals. This gap between discourse and practice is why methods such as long-term ethnographic fieldwork and participant observation are essential tools for the study of love in cultural context. Cultural historiography and literary analysis into the private lives of past peoples is equally important for challenging widespread assumptions of romantic love's modern nativity. However, documenting ambiguity and variation from proscribed norms should not be the final and sole conclusion of empirical or interpretive study. The time is upon us to again take up the task of comparative inquiries to illuminate the cross-cultural patterns of love's variability, test our hypotheses of their causes, and discern the universal essence of love as a human experience.

A fruitful direction for future comparative research would be to combine anthropological and psychological approaches to explore cultural variation in the individual differences of love. Because researchers have rarely studied the relative frequency with which a person falls in and out of love, it is not clear whether passionate love is experienced with less frequency in those cultures that deny or disapprove of the emotional experience. The relative frequency with which members of a community experience romantic love may very well depend upon that culture's social structure, degree of social fluidity, and ideological orientation. Thus, a greater proportion of Americans compared to tribal Yanomamo or Murik peoples (Lipset, 2004) may experience the sensations associated with romantic love. We suspect this is the case. However, research amongst forgers like the Ache and Hadza reveal individuals falling into numerous intense, albeit short-lived love encounters. This suggests that romantic love may prove to be a relatively brief psychological experience that requires socially inspired ethical obligations to sustain a long-term bond. Such a study might also illuminate whether the cultural suppression or emphasis of love impacts actual frequency of experience, or merely its valuation. Such investigation will still require ethnographic grounding to illuminate the meanings and practices ascribed to love when it is said to occur. The research program begun by Victor de Munck and his colleagues is a step in this direction by comparing the intra and inter-cultural variations in ideals and experiences of romantic love empirically by researchers with long-term ethnographic insights into the contexts they are comparing (de Munck, Korotayev, de Munck, & Khaltourina, 2011). They asked what ideals and experiences are universally associated with romantic love to enable us to call these phenomena by the same name? These are intriguing questions that require further research. Until then, they remain only tantalizing hypotheses.

References

Abu-Lughod, L. (1986). *Veiled sentiments: Honor and poetry in a Bedouin society*. Berkeley, CA: University of California Press.
Ahearn, L. (2001). *Invitations to love: Literacy, love letters, and social change in Nepal*. Ann Arbor, MI: University of Michigan Press.
Baldacchino, J. P. (2008). Eros and modernity: Convulsions of the heart in modern Korea. *Asian Studies Review, 32*, 99–122.
Baldacchino, J. P. (2014). In sickness and in love?: Autumn in my heart and the embodiment of morality in Korean television drama. *Korea Journal, 54*(4), 5–28.
Beck, U., & Beck-Gernsheim, E. (2014). *Distant love*. Oxford: Polity Press.
Berndt, R. M. (1976). *Love songs of Arnhem Land*. Chicago, IL: The University of Chicago Press.
Bhattacharya, H. (2017). *Narrating love and violence: Women contesting caste, tribe and state in Lahaul, India*. New Brunswick, NJ: Rutgers University Press.
Bourdieu, P. (1984). *Distinction: A social critique of the judgement of taste*. Cambridge, MA: Harvard University Press.
Brennan, D. (2004). *What's love got to do with it?: Transnational desires and sex tourism in the Dominican Republic*. Durham, NC: Duke University Press.
Brennan, D. (2007). Love work in a tourist town: Dominican sex workers and resort workers perform at love. In M. Padilla, J. Hirsch, M. Munoz-Laboy, R. Sember, & R. Parker (Eds.), *Love and globalization: Transformations in the contemporary world* (pp. 203–225). Nashville, TN: Vanderbilt University Press.
Campbell, C. (2006). 'All you need is love': From romance to romanticism: The Beatles, romantic love and cultural change. *Etnofoor, 19*(1), 111–123.
Carrier-Moisan, M. E. (2017). "I have to feel something": Gringo love in the sexual economy of tourism in Natal, Brazil. *The Journal of Latin American and Caribbean Anthropology, 23*(1), 131–151.

Chamie, J. (2018). World agrees: Adultery, while prevalent, is wrong. *YaleGlobal Online*. Accessed July 1 2019, from https://yaleglobal.yale.edu/content/world-agrees-adultery-while-prevalent-wrong

Cheng, S. (2007). Romancing the club: Love dynamics between Filipina entertainers and GIs in U.S. military camp towns in South Korea. In M. Padilla, J. Hirsch, M. Munoz-Laboy, R. Sember, & R. Parker (Eds.), *Love and globalization: Transformations in the contemporary world* (pp. 226–251). Nashville, TN: Vanderbilt University Press.

Cheng, S. (2010). *On the move for love: Migrant entertainers and the U.S. military in South Korea*. Philadelphia, PA: University of Pennsylvania Press.

Cole, J. (2009). Love, money, and economies of intimacy in Tamatave, Madagascar. In J. Cole & T. Lynn (Eds.), *Love in Africa* (pp. 109–134). Chicago, IL: University of Chicago Press.

Cole, J., & Thomas, L. (Eds.). (2009). *Love in Africa*. Chicago, IL: University of Chicago Press.

Constable, N. (2003). *Romance on a global stage: Pen pals, virtual realities, "mail order" marriages*. Berkeley, CA: University of California Press.

Constable, N. (Ed.). (2005). *Cross-border marriages: Gender and mobility in transnational Asia*. Philadelphia, PA: University of Pennsylvania Press.

Dales, L., & Yamamato, B. (2019). Romantic and sexual intimacy before and beyond marriage. In A. Alexy & E. Cook (Eds.), *Intimate Japan: Ethnographies of closeness and conflict* (pp. 1740–2098). Honolulu, HI: University of Hawaii Press. Kindle Edition.

de Leon, L. (2017). Texting amor: Emerging intimacies in textually mediated romance among Tzotzil Mayan youth. *Ethos, 45*(4), 462–488.

de Munck, V. (1996). Love and marriage in a Sri Lankan Muslim community: Toward a reevaluation of Dravidian marriage practices. *American Ethnologist, 23*(4), 698–716.

de Munck, V., Korotayev, A., de Munck, J., & Khaltourina, D. (2011). Cross-cultural analysis of models of romantic love among U.S. residents, Russians, and Lithuanians. *Cross-Cultural Research, 45*(2), 128–154.

de Munck, V. (2019). *Romantic love in America: cultural models of gay, straight and polyamorous relationship*. Lanham, MD: Lexington Press.

Deri, J. (2015). *Love's refraction: Jealousy and compersion in queer women's polyamorous relationships*. Toronto, ON: University of Toronto Press.

Diamant, N. (2000). *Revolutionizing the family: Politics, love, and divorce in urban and rural China, 1949–1968*. Berkeley, CA: University of California Press.

Donner, H., & Santos, G. (2016). Love, marriage, and intimate citizenship in contemporary China and India: An introduction. *Modern Asian Studies, 50*(4), 1123–1146.

Du, S. (1995). The aesthetic axis in the construction of emotions and decisions: Love-pact suicide among the Lahu Na of southwestern China. In C. Ellis, D. D. Franks, & M. G. Flaherty (Eds.), *Social perspectives on emotions* (Vol. 3, pp. 199–221). Greenwich, CT: Emerald Group Publishing.

Du, S. (2002). *Chopsticks only work in pairs: Gender unity and gender equality among the Lahu of Southwest China*. New York: Columbia University Press.

Durham, D. (2002). Love and jealousy in the space of death. *Ethnos, 67*(2), 155–179.

Eerdewijk, A. V. (2006). What's love got to do with it?: The intimate relationships of Dakarois girls. *Etnofoor, 19*(1), 41–61.

El-Dine, S. (2018). Love, materiality, and masculinity in Jordan: "Doing" romance with limited resources. *Men and Masculinities, 21*(3), 423–442.

Faier, L. (2007). Filipina migrants in rural Japan and their professions of love. *American Ethnologist, 34*(1), 148–162.

Giddens, A. (1992). *The transformation of intimacy: Sexuality, love, and eroticism in modern societies*. Stanford, CA: Stanford University Press.

Gioia, T. (2015). *Love songs: The hidden history*. Oxford: Oxford University Press.

Gregor, T. (1995). Sexuality and the experience of love. In P. Abramson & S. Pinkerton (Eds.), *Sexual nature sexual culture*. Chicago, IL: The University of Chicago Press.

Groes, C., & Fernandez, N. T. (Eds.). (2018). *Intimate mobilities: Sexual economies, marriage and migration in a disparate world*. New York, NY: Berghahn.

Grover, S. (2018). *Marriage, love, caste and kinship support: Lived experiences of the urban poor in India*. London, UK: Routledge.

Harkonen, H. (2016). *Kinship, love, and life cycle in contemporary Havana, Cuba: To not die alone*. New York, NY: Palgrave Macmillan.

Harkonen, H. (2018). Money, love, and fragile reciprocity in contemporary Havana, Cuba. *The Journal of Latin American and Caribbean Anthropology, 24*, 370–387. https://doi.org/10.1111/jlca.12367

Hart, K. (2007). Love by arrangement: The ambiguity of 'spousal choice' in a Turkish village. *Journal of the Royal Anthropological Institute, 13*, 321–343.

Hirsch, J., Wardlow, W., Smith, D. J., Phinney, H., Parikh, S., & Nathanson, C. (Eds.). (2009). *The secret: Love, marriage, and HIV*. Nashville, TN: Vanderbilt University Press.

Ho, S. L. (2012). 'Playing like men': The extramarital experiences of women in contemporary Japan. *Ethnos, 77*(3), 321–343.

Hoefinger, H. (2013). *Sex, love and money in Cambodia: Professional girlfriends and transactional relationships*. London: Routledge.

Illouz, E. (2012). *Why love hurts: A sociological explanation*. Oxford, UK: Polity Press.

Inhorn, M. (2007). Loving your infertile Muslim spouse: Notes on the globalization of IVF and its romantic commitments in Sunni Egypt and Shia Lebanon. In M. Padilla, J. Hirsch, M. Munoz-Laboy, R. Sember, & R. Parker (Eds.), *Love and globalization: Transformations in the contemporary world* (pp. 139–162). Nashville, TN: Vanderbilt University Press.

Jankowiak, W. (1993). *Sex, death, and hierarchy in a Chinese city an anthropological account*. New York, NY: Columbia University Press.

Jankowiak, W. (1995). Romantic passion in the People's Republic of China. In W. Jankowiak (Ed.), *Romantic passion: A universal experience?* (pp. 166–184). New York, NY: Columbia University Press.

Jankowiak, W., & Allen, E. (1995). The balance of duty and desire in an American polygamous community. In W. Jankowiak (Ed.), *Romantic passion: A universal experience?* (pp. 166–186). New York: Columbia University Press.

Jankowiak, W., & Mixson, L. (2008). "I have his heart, swinging is just sex": The ritualization of sex and the rejuvenation of the love bond in an American spouse exchange community. In W. Jankowiak (Ed.), *Intimacies: Love and sex across cultures* (pp. 245–266). New York: Columbia University Press.

Jankowiak, W., Nell, M. D., & Buckmaster, A. (2002). Managing infidelity: A cross-cultural perspective. *Ethnology, 41*(1), 85–101.

Knudson, A. (2009). *Violence and belonging: Land, love and lethal conflict in the north-west frontier province of Pakistan*. Copenhagen: Nordic Institute of Asian Studies.

Kotthoff, H. (2014). Adolescent girls on the phone: The management of dating and social networks. In E. Wyss (Ed.), *Communication of love: Mediating intimacy from love letters to SMS* (pp. 111–150). Blelefeld, DE: Transcript Veriag.

Lateef, S. (1993). Indo-Fijian marriage in Suva: A little love, a little romance, and a visa. In R. Marksbury (Ed.), *The business of marriage: Transformations in oceanic matrimony* (pp. 205–230). Pittsburgh, PA: University of Pittsburgh Press.

Lee, L. O. (1987). *Voices from the Iron House: A study of Lu Xun*. Bloomington, IN: Indiana University Press.

Lee, H. (2007). *Revolution of the heart: A genealogy of love in China 1900–1950*. Stanford, CA: Stanford University Press.

Lepani, K. (2012). *Islands of love, islands of risk: Culture and HIV in the Trobriands*. Nashville, TN: Vanderbilt University Press.

Lewinson, A. (2006). Love in the city: Navigating multiple relationships in Dar es Salaam, Tanzania. *City & Society, 18*(1), 90–115.

Lindholm, C. (1995). Love as an experience of transcendence. In W. Jankowiak (Ed.), *Romantic Passion: A universal experience?* (pp. 57–71). New York: Columbia University Press.
Lipset, D. (1997). *Mangrove man: Dialogics of culture in the Sepik estuary.* Cambridge, UK: Cambridge University Press.
Lipset, D. (2004). Modernity without romance?: Masculinity and desire in courtship stories told by Papua New Guinean men. *American Ethnologist, 31*(2), 205–224.
Lipset, D. (2015). On the bridge: Class and the chronotrope of modern romance in an American love story. *Anthropology Quarterly, 88*(1), 163–186.
Manning, P. (2015). *Love stories: Language, private love, and public romance in Georgia.* Toronto, ON: University of Toronto Press.
Marsden, M. (2007). Love and elopement in northern Pakistan. *Journal of the Royal Anthropological Institute, 13*(1), 91–108.
Mody, P. (2008). *The intimate state: Love-marriage and the law in Delhi.* London: Routledge.
Ohara, K., & Reynolds, D. (1970). Love-pact suicide. *OMEGA – Journal of Death and Dying, 1*(3), 159–166.
Osburg, J. (2013). *Anxious wealth: Money and morality among China's new rich.* Stanford, CA: Stanford University Press.
Padilla, M., Hirsch, J., Munoz-Laboy, M., Sember, R., & Parker, R. (Eds.). (2007). *Love and globalization: Transformations of intimacy in the contemporary world.* Nashville, TN: Vanderbilt University Press.
Pan, L. (2016). *When true love came to China.* Hong Kong: Hong Kong University Press.
Parrenas, R. (2011). *Illicit flirtations: Labor, migration, and sex trafficking in Tokyo.* Stanford, CA: Stanford University Press.
Parry, J. (2001). 'Ankulu's errant wife: Sex, marriage and industry in contemporary Chhattisgarh. *Modern Asian Studies, 35*(4), 783–820.
Patico, J. (2009). For love, money, or normalcy: Meanings of strategy and sentiment in the Russian-American matchmaking industry. *Ethnos, 74*(3), 307–330.
Rebhun, L. A. (1999a). *The heart is unknown country: Love in the changing economy of Northeast Brazil.* Stanford, CA: Stanford University Press.
Rebhun, L. A. (1999b). For love and for money: Romance urbanizing Northeast Brazil. *City & Society, 11*(1–2), 145–164.
Reddy, W. M. (2012). *The making of romantic love: Longing and sexuality in Europe, South Asia & Japan, 900–1200 CE.* Chicago, IL: The University of Chicago Press.
Rubinstein, D. (1995). Love and suffering: Adolescent socialization and suicide in Micronesia. *The Contemporary Pacific, 7*(1), 21–53.
Ryang, S. (2006). *Love in modern Japan.* New York, NY: Routledge.
Schimorelpennick, A. (1997). *Chinese folk songs and folk singers: Shan'ge traditions in southern Jiangsu.* Leiden, NL: Chime Foundation.
Schmitt, D., Alcalay, L., Allensworth, M., Allik, J., Ault, I., Austers, I., et al. (2004). Patterns and universals of adult romantic attachment across 62 cultural regions: Are models of self and of other Pancultural constructs? *Journal of Cross-Cultural Psychology, 35*(4), 367–402.
Shohet, M. (2017). Troubling love: Gender, class, and sideshadowing the "happy family" in Vietnam. *Ethos, 45*(4), 555–576.
Stark, L. (2017). Cultural politics of love and provision among poor youth in urban Tanzania. *Ethnos, 82*(3), 569–591.
Stern, P. R., & Condon, R. G. (1995). A good spouse is hard to find: Marriage, spouse exchange, and infatuation among the copper inuit. In W. Jankowiak (Ed.), *Romantic passion: A universal experience?* (pp. 196–218). New York: Columbia University Press.
Stout, N. (2014). *After love: Queer intimacy and erotic economies in post-Soviet Cuba.* Durham, NC: Duke University Press.
Swidler, A. (2001). *Talk of love: How culture matters.* Chicago, IL: University of Chicago Press.
Takeyama, A. (2016). *Staged seduction: Selling dreams in a Tokyo host club.* Stanford, CA: Stanford University Press.

Thomas, L. M., & Cole, J. (2009). Introduction. In J. Cole & L. Thomas (Eds.), *Love in Africa* (pp. 1–30). Chicago, IL: University of Chicago Press.

Tiwari, G. (2008). Interplay of love, sex, and marriage in a polyandrous society in the high Himalayas of India. In W. Jankowiak (Ed.), *Intimacies: Between love and sex* (pp. 122–147). New York, NY: Columbia University Press.

Tran, A. (2018). The anxiety of romantic love in Ho Chi Minh City, Vietnam. *Journal of the Royal Anthropological Institute, 24*(3), 512–531.

Uretsky, E. (2016). *Occupational hazards: Business, sex, and HIV in post-Mao China*. Stanford, CA: Stanford University Press.

Venkatesan, S., Edwards, J., Willerslev, R., Povinelli, E., & Mody, P. (2011). The anthropological fixation with reciprocity leaves no room for love: 2009 meeting of the group for debates in anthropological theory. *Critique of Anthropology, 31*(3), 210–250.

Verheijen, J. (2006). Mass media and gender equality: The empowering message of romantic love in telanovelas. *Etnofoor, 19*(1), 23–39.

Wardlow, H. (2008). "She likes it best when she is on top": Intimacies and estrangements in Huli men's marital and extramarital relationships. In W. Jankowiak (Ed.), *Intimacies: Love and sex across cultures* (pp. 194–223). New York, NY: Columbia University Press.

Wijk, J. V. (2006). Romance tourism on Ambergris Caye, Belize: The entanglement of love and prostitution. *Etnofoor, 19*(1), 71–89.

Wynn, L. L. (2018). *Love, sex, desire in modern Egypt: Navigating the margins of respectability*. Austin, TX: University of Texas Press.

Zelizer, V. (2005). *The purchase of intimacy*. Princeton, NJ: Princeton University Press.

Zigon, J. (2013). On love: Remaking moral subjectivity in post-rehabilitation Russia. *American Ethnologist, 40*(1), 201–215.

Alex J. Nelson earned his Ph.D. in Anthropology at the University of Nevada, Las Vegas and is writing an ethnography of romantic love in South Korea. His work explores how historical/intergenerational changes in Korean expectations and experiences of love and romantic relationships reflect changes in Korean gender relations and the social and economic structures shaping them. He is also a researcher with the Erotic Entrepreneurs Project (www.eroticentrepreneurs.com), an interdisciplinary participatory action study of the business practices and strategies of independent erotic escorts in USA.

William Jankowiak is an internationally recognized authority on urban Chinese society, urban Mongols, Mormon fundamentalist polygyny, and love around the world. Professor Jankowiak is often invited to present the results of his research as well as called on by media to provide background information on various topics. His research has been featured in numerous media outlets, including The New York Times, Time magazine, NPR, History Channel, TLC, ABC Primetime, and NBC.

Chapter 4
Cultural Diversity of Romantic Love Experience

Victor Karandashev

Abstract This theoretical article presents the review of modern cross-cultural research on love. Despite the cross-cultural universality of love, its specific interpretation differs from culture to culture. This review of cross-cultural findings depicts the diversity of romantic love experience across cultures.

Love is the variety of emotions. Therefore, the cultural context of their emotional life has an impact on how people experience love. The diversity of emotional experience reflects on love beliefs, attitudes, and feelings. As for the specific experiences of love, the article presents the examples and discusses

1. Experience of passion in love, along with reviewing its cross-cultural similarities and differences;
2. Romantic experience in love, in the frame of romantic beliefs, attitudes, and idealization, romantic ideas of union, exclusivity, and jealousy;
3. Erotic and sexual experience of love, as well as their relations from different cultural views;
4. Joyful and powerful experience of love, along with describing the joy, satisfaction, and happiness that love brings;
5. Maladaptive experience of love, along with emotional instability, suffering, obsessive, and possessive feelings.

All these experiences of love have culturally specific accents in the minds of people from different cultures. The chapter summarizes the variety of theoretical and empirical findings from various disciplines, such as anthropology, psychology, sociology, and communication science.

The research findings on how people with different cultural background experience love should be valuable for multicultural couples, psychologists, counselors, social workers, and other practitioners working with multicultural population.

V. Karandashev (✉)
Department of Psychology and Counselor Education, Aquinas College, Grand Rapids, MI, USA
e-mail: vk001@aquinas.edu

Keywords Love · Passion · Romantic beliefs · Idealization · Jealousy · Erotic love · Sexual love · Joy and happiness of love · Obsessional love · Suffering from love · Lovesickness

The modern world becomes increasingly multicultural and intercultural. Instead of former geographical separation of cultures, the recent massive migration creates blended and mixed cultural communities. Yet, cultures reluctantly mix in such multicultural communities; the sameness preferences still work despite the multicultural opportunities. Many people prefer to stay in proximity and communicate with others of the same cultural identity. In the same vein, mono-cultural romantic relationships are still prevalent.

Nevertheless, the increasing tendency for intercultural romantic relationships is evidently noticeable. Such couples, however, encounter problems with understanding each other. Passionate love is usually understandable without words. Passion of love—being fueled by sexual drive—is a cross-cultural universal (Jankowiak, 1995). Yet, when a relationship evolves, the difficulties in understanding of partner' attitudes, thoughts, and emotions may arise. It seems that people—being egocentric and ethnocentric by nature—tend to underestimate the diversity of emotional experience.

The purpose of this chapter is to present a brief review of the modern cross-cultural research on romantic love and multiple references to the studies that scholars of love have conducted throughout recent decades about similarities and differences in this experience across cultures. Despite cross-cultural universality of love, its specific interpretation differs from culture to culture (see for review, Karandashev, 2017, 2019). An abundance of findings and sources provided in the text should promote the better appreciation of cultural diversity of love experience by academicians and practitioners. This knowledge should be helpful in the counseling of intercultural couples who are in romantic relationship and marriages.

Love is a variety of emotions and experiences. Therefore, the cultural context of their emotional life has an impact on how people experience love. Sociological, anthropological, and psychological research demonstrated that the labelling and description of emotions vary from culture to culture. Emotional experience are often presented in a different set of concepts (e.g., Hochschild, 1979; Kitayama, Markus, & Matsumoto, 1995; Lutz, 1988; Lynch, 1990; Mesquita & Frijda, 1992; Shaver, Wu, & Schwartz, 1992; Shweder, 1993; Soto, Levenson, & Ebling, 2005). Even though, basic human emotions are mostly universal, yet cultures substantially influence the attitudes toward emotions and the experience and expression of complex emotional realities (Karandashev, 2019). This diversity of emotional experience reflects on love beliefs, attitudes, and feelings.

This chapter reviews cross-cultural similarities and differences in the following experiences of romantic love (1) passion, (2) romantic beliefs and attitudes, (3) erotic and sexual feelings, (4) the joy, happiness, and empowerment of love, and (5) maladaptive features of romantic love, such as obsession, suffering, and the symptoms of lovesickness. All these experiences of love have specific accents in the minds of people from different cultures.

4.1 Experience of Passion in Love

4.1.1 Cross-cultural Similarities in the Experience of Passion

Researchers in anthropology, linguistics, sociology, and psychology consider passion as the most salient experience of people in love (see for review, Karandashev, 2017, 2019), as an emotion that is highly saturated with sexual feelings. Early research on love suggested that experience of passionate love is cross-culturally universal (Hatfield & Rapson, 1987).

Romantic lovers believe in the myth of passion, and they equate love with strong passion (De Roda, Martínez-Iñigo, De Paul, & Yela, 1999). Lovers assume that intense passionate feelings should last forever. Once passion fades, they think they do not love their partner anymore.

Passion of love characterizes the intensity of emotional experience. The conceptual metaphor "my heart is on fire" represents this intensity aspect of love (Kövecses, 1990) and it is typical in Western literary tradition and common sense. The similar metaphorical concepts are present in other languages supporting cross-cultural universality of this experience. These are some examples of such metaphorical expressions: in Chinese "ài shì dōng tiān lǐ de yī bǎ huǒ" ("love is fire in winter"), "ài shì huǒ néng shǐ bīng xuě róng huà" ("love is fire that melts the snow") (Chang & Li, 2006); in Turkish "O, aşk ateşi ile yanıyordu" ("he was burning with love fire"), in Albanian "I gjithe trupi me digjet nga zjarri i dashurise ("the whole body burned with the fire of love"), in German "Ich brenne vor Liebe" ("I am burning with the fire of love"), in Portuguese "O amor é um fogo que arde sem se ver" ("Love is a fire that burns without seeing itself"), in French "Mon coeur brule d'amour" ("my heart burns with love"), Russian "Любовь сжигает тебя" ("lubov sjigaet tebia, love burns you") (see Chap. 56).

Cross-cultural universality of these expressions is due to physiological basis of passion as the intensity characteristic of love. Since passion is a biologically rooted characteristic of emotion, then men and women—regardless of their culture—should experience it similar. The results of anthropological and psycholinguistic studies conducted in many countries are in support of this theory. For example, the comparative cross-cultural studies of people in the United States, Lithuania, and Russia (De Munck, Korotayev, de Munck, & Khaltourina, 2011) and in Brazil, Russia, and Central Africa (Pilishvili & Koyanongo, 2016) found that many participants viewed passion among the main emotions of love. Other study (in Japan, Farrer, Tsuchiya, & Bagrowicz, 2008) explored how Japanese feel being involved in tsukiau (dating) relationships. Self-reported narratives identified passion and the desire for sex (ecchi wo suru) as the main features of tsukiau relationship. Partners feel passion (netsujou), romance (koi), and love (ai)—the experiences usually associated with sex. (see also Chap. 51).

Many other studies investigated experience of passion measuring it with Passionate Love Scale (PAS), Eros subscale of Love Attitude Scale (LAS), and Passion subscale of Triangular Love Scale (TLS). The results of the studies on cultural differences of passion in love, which were obtained with those measures, are not convincing so far. Some researchers found the differences, however, majority did not. The methods, which studies employed, and relatively small samples, which they used, can explain such inconsistencies (see for details, Karandashev, 2019). Operational definitions also can play their role in the studies of passion: whether it is (a) beliefs in passion as an important feature/component of love, (2) personal attitudes to love or (3) real experience of passion.

4.1.2 Cross-cultural Differences in the Experience of Passion

Despite this universality, cultural variability in the attitudes to love is still present. For example, linguistic analysis of English and Chinese metaphors discovered the following cross-cultural differences in the attitudes to passion in love (see also Chap. 50). Western people appear to be passionate and romantic. They tend to express their love emotions passionately, openly, and directly: "I am burning with love‖", "My love is a red rose". English and American people understand love as brilliant, mighty, and powerful experience comparing it with the sun. The love-as-fire metaphor reflects "the extroverted characteristic of English speakers". "Westerners talked about love with great passion and bravery." (Lv & Zhang, 2012, p. 356).

Such degree of extroversion is not typical for Chinese culture. Their conceptual metaphor *love-as-silk* reflects "the more introverted character of speakers of Chinese. They talk about love indirectly and tactfully". They compare love with the moon since moon is indirect and gentle as love (Lv & Zhang, 2012, p. 356–357).

Empirical studies of the cultural attitudes are also in accord with this interpretation. The norms of Western cultures suggest that people have their rights to experience and express emotions as they are, while the norms of Eastern cultures encourage to moderate emotion (Pennebaker & Graybeal, 2001). These cultural norms are still gender specific, therefore, Chinese men experience the lowest intensity of emotion (compared to Chinese women and American men), while American women had the highest. Chinese masculine norms encourage men to moderate their emotions according to the cultural ideal; therefore, they employ *disengagement* emotion-regulation strategies. Different from this, American feminine norms encourage women to experience intense emotions naturally (Davis et al., 2012).

In the same vein, other researchers revealed cultural differences in the intensity of emotional experience (Lim, 2016). Multiple studies (see for review Lim, 2016) demonstrated that people in Western cultures experience high arousal emotions more than low arousal emotions and people in Eastern cultures experience low arousal emotions more than high arousal emotions. These differences are due to normative cultural influence. Western (individualist) cultures promoted high arousal emotions more than low arousal emotions. On the other side, Eastern (collectivist) cultures value low arousal emotions more than high arousal emotions. To explain these differences, Lim (2016) argues that according to typical Western values, people should influence others. High arousal emotions are very effective to reach this goal. On the other side, according to normative Eastern values, people should adjust and conform to other people. Low arousal emotions are better (than high arousal emotions) suited to achieve this goal (Lim, 2016). These cultural differences in emotional arousal should reflect on the arousal in passionate love.

4.2 Romantic Experience in Love

4.2.1 Romantic Beliefs in Love

Romantic love is a special type of love, which is characterized by a certain set of romantic beliefs. The key feature of romantic experience is idealization of a lover's unique qualities and considering a relationship with him/her as exceptionally perfect (De Munck et al., 2011; De Silva & De Silva, 1999; Fisher, 2004; Giddens, 1992; Gross, 1944; Hinkle & Sporakowski, 1975; Kephart, 1967; Knee, 1998; Knox & Sporakowski, 1968; Munro & Adams, 1978; Sprecher & Metts, 1989). Romantic attitudes include

1. Believing that a beloved is an ideal romantic match,
2. Thinking that the beloved is the best and unique individual,
3. Paying attention to the positive qualities of the beloved,
4. Overlooking his/her negative qualities,
5. Trusting to follow your heart,
6. Believing that love conquer all.

Such romantic love attitudes have their positive and negative sides (Karandashev, 2019). They are frequently opposed to pragmatic beliefs. Romantic love is irrational, while pragmatic love is rational, romantic love is idealistic, while pragmatic love is realistic, romantic love believes in predestined match and compatibility of lovers, while pragmatic love believes in the process of building a loving relationship, romantic love expresses love in emotions, while pragmatic love expresses love in actions.

4.2.2 Early Studies of Romantic Beliefs in Western Countries

Empirical studies of romantic beliefs in Western countries were active in 1960–1980s (Dion & Dion, 1973; Hinkle & Sporakowski, 1975; Kephart, 1967; Knox & Sporakowski, 1968; Munro & Adams, 1978; Sprecher & Metts, 1989). The results showed that, despite the ideals inspired by romantic novels and movies, many

Americans did not share the cultural stereotype of romantic love. Women believed in romantic love more, still expressing pragmatic orientation. Younger participants were more romantic than the older ones.

4.2.3 Studies of Romantic Beliefs in Africa and West Indies

Cross-cultural research of romantic beliefs started later—in 1980–1990s in Africa (Philbrick, 1988; Philbrick & Opolot, 1980; Philbrick & Stones, 1988a, 1988b; Stones, 1986, 1992; Stones & Philbrick, 1989, 1991; Vandewiele & Philbrick, 1983). The results revealed lower romantic idealism among participants in several African countries, compared to American and British samples. At the same time, cultural understanding of love for Africans was a well-balanced blend of the traditional indigenous conceptions of love and the Western ideals of romantic love.

Study of attitudes toward love in West Indies (the Caribbean islands) (Payne & Vandewiele, 1987) revealed that romantic beliefs of participants in those samples were similar to those in American and higher than in African samples. Women from Caribbean islands believed in romantic love more than men, and the younger participants more than the older ones.

Those results demonstrated that West Indians—due to greater exposure to Western ideas through the mass media, tourists, and visits to overseas relatives—assimilated Western notions of romantic idealism more than Africans did. Nevertheless, West Indians (like Africans) had a relatively low concern with conjugal intimacy. As the authors noted (Payne & Vandewiele, 1987), women might look to men for an emotional relationship. Nevertheless, kinship and community relationships were more important for them. On the other hand, many young West Indian men did not really know how to maintain a relationship with women, except in a sexual way. "Double standards" of sexual behavior for men and women was an important cultural factor of relationships in the Caribbean (Payne & Vandewiele, 1987), as well as in some other Latin American cultures (e.g., Berglund, Liljestrand, Marín, Salgado, & Zelaya, 1997; Eggleston, Jackson, & Hardee, 1999; Rani, Figueroa, & Ainsle, 2003). Men's infidelity was a widespread practice, while women's infidelity was unacceptable.

4.2.4 Studies of Romantic Attitudes in Japan, the USA, Germany, France, Russia, Turkey, China, India

Cross-cultural studies of romantic beliefs were also conducted in other countries: Japan, the United States, Germany, France, Russia, Turkey, China, India (Medora, Larson, Hortaçsu, & Dave, 2002; Simmons, vom Kolke, & Shimizu, 1986; Simmons, Wehner, & Kay, 1989; Sprecher et al., 1994; Sprecher & Toro-Morn,

2002). They found that Germans and Russians had the higher romantic attitudes than Americans, while Japanese had the lower romanticism in love. Chinese scored higher in that study. High romantic attitudes of Germans, French, and Russians might be explained by a strong European romantic cultural tradition. Americans, however, despite the Hollywood inspirational romantic movies, were still more friendship-oriented in their love attitudes. Nevertheless, American students believed in romantic love more than Turkish and Indian college students. Indians had the lowest score of romantic beliefs among these three cultural groups.

In Spanish society of 1990s, many people believed in romantic myths (Barrón, de Paúl, Martinez-Iñigo, & Yela, 1999), especially older people and those with fewer years of formal education, as well as religious people. Women in Spain, as well in many other cultural samples, were more romantic than men.

4.2.5 Gender Differences in Romantic Attitudes

As for gender differences, the findings of studies in 1980–1990s conducted in Western countries among university students (Hendrick & Hendrick, 1992; Sprecher & Metts, 1989; Sternberg & Barnes, 1985), revealed that men had more romantic beliefs than women. However, the studies conducted in other cultures (cited above) found the opposite differences: women demonstrated more romantic beliefs in love. Another interesting finding revealed in the study in the USA and Russia (De Munck, Korotayev, & Khaltourina, 2009) was that the strongest agreement in romantic beliefs was between cultures, rather than between genders. It seems that culture matters more than gender (see Chap. 20).

4.2.6 Romantic Idea of Exclusivity

The concept of romantic love holds *the ideas of exclusivity* and *commitment to a beloved*. There is only *one predestined beloved* and a *love relationship with him/her is perfect*. This belief is honest and sincere—at least, for the time being of a relationship. A lover believes that his/her love is *unique, exceptional*, and *exclusive*. The lover is *committed to a beloved* and to *a relationship*.

Such expectations of durability of love emotions are the commonly acknowledged features of romantic love (Lindholm, 1995, 1998; Marston, Hecht, Manke, McDaniel, & Reeder, 1998; Rosenblatt, 1967; Rubin, 1970; Sprecher & Metts, 1989; Sternberg, 1987).

The belief in a perfect love match with a predestined partner is enduring throughout centuries. This is what people call *a true love*—for life. Various cultural contexts have produced the similar idea of an exclusive and perfect love and embodied it in lexical expressions.

- *ananke* (star-crossed love, in classical Greek)—a binding force and unshakable destiny,
- *yuán fèn* (in Chinese)—a force that impels a predestined relationship,
- *koi no yokan* (in Japanese)—the feeling that the falling in love with someone is inevitable,
- *sarang* (in Korean) an unshakable lifelong form of love (Lomas, 2018).

The meeting—by lucky chance or by destiny—such a perfect beloved makes a perfect relationship and happiness: "They lived together happily ever after". European and American cultures, for instance, promote a romantic tendency to perceive the beloved and the relationship in such idealized ways. Many educated people, inspired by romantic novels, think that there should be one ideal and unique person who is a perfect match for them (Sastry, 1999).

The modern idea of exclusivity is less demanding, but still strives for an ideal. Three romantic myths (De Roda et al., 1999) adhere to it:

1. Romantic belief admits that to be in love with more than one person at the same time is impossible (*the myth of exclusiveness*).
2. Romantic belief suggests that the couple-relationship is natural and inherent to humans (*the couple myth*). People implicitly transfer this belief to animals (love doves, or swans).
3. Romantic belief advises that one who really loves should always be faithful to a beloved (*the myth of fidelity*). If one is not faithful, he or she does not really love.

The study of 1990s conducted in Spain showed that quite a substantial portion of Spanish population (from 55% to 95%, depending on a belief) agreed with these romantic ideas, especially women, older generation, and people with lower level of education (De Roda et al., 1999). It seems that in many cultures, there are romantic beliefs, which adore exclusive devotion and commitment to a partner and a relationship. These are culturally inspired idealistic beliefs.

The reality, however, might be different. Moreover, evolutionary theorists assert (e.g., Fisher, 2004) that love is fleeting and transient; therefore, long-term commitment is not a viable option from evolutionary standpoint, especially for men. The evolutionary view declares that men fall in love for a short period, necessary to conceive and support a little child. Once men are no longer needed for the survival of the child, they are predisposed to fall out of love with their current partner and to fall in love with a new one. The evolutionary need for biological diversity may also encourage women to have a diverse pool of partners in the long-term perspective.

It seems that people in earlier stages of biological and cultural evolution were inclined to be polygamous (e.g., D'Hondt & Vandewiele, 1983). Counteracting the evolution, it was a later cultural idea to encourage monogamy, commitment and long-term exclusive partnership.

Some modern scholars have attempted to revive the idea of open marriage (O'Neill & O'Neill, 1984)—a new life style for couples, and polyamory (Anapol, 2010)—as the love and intimacy with multiple partners. However, these ideas seem not widely accepted by people who prefer to pursue the ideal of exclusive commitment in love—in a short-term run or in a long-term run.

4.2.7 Romantic Idea of Union in Love

The Western model of romantic love as a *unity of two complementary parts* is depicted beautifully and tragically in *Romeo and Juliet* (Sánchez, 1995). The *unity metaphor* is widespread in English and Chinese lexicons (Chang & Li, 2006; Kövecses, 1988, 2005)—among other languages. Since Chinese and English belong to different cultural groups and did not have much communication with each other when metaphors developed, their comparison is especially interesting and illustrative for this commonality of cultural evolution. Both languages express the semantic concept of a *unity of two complementary parts* in many lexical forms (e.g., "We *are one*", "She is *my better half*", "They are *inseparable*", "We *belong together*", etc. (Chang & Li, 2006, p. 20; Kövecses, 1988, p. 18). Comparing lovers with a pair of birds (e.g., doves, swans) or other devoted animals are popular in many languages.

The metaphor of *love doves* (Kövecses, 1988, 1990) has stamped this cultural ideal in many cultures (see also Chap. 45). The idea of love as *a union of two*—either for a short-term, or for a long-term—has been an enduring cultural model in many societies for centuries.

The modern psychology, sociology, anthropology, and communication studies define love as a longing of lovers for an absorption (Berscheid & Walster, 1978), as a longing for union with another (Hatfield & Rapson, 1993), as a desire of union with the beloved (Fisher, 2004), as a longing for association (Reddy, 2012), as connection (Lomas, 2018). Generally, such *longing for unity* includes motivation for sexual, emotional, and mental unions and it is suitable for a variety of cultures. Studies in several cultural contexts—the USA, Lithuania, and Russia, (De Munck et al., 2011), Japan (see for review Farrer et al., 2008)—identified the feelings of unity, being together, and connectedness as the key features of romantic love.

The *notion of unity* implies the experience when *two* bodies and/or souls and/or minds feel like *one*. It is a sense of self-loss through the expansive merger with the beloved *other*. It is a quiet understanding and a fusion (Simenon, quoted in Garis, 1984). Such unity can be reached by fusion of equal partners, or merging one partner into another (via dominant embrace or submission).

Unity is multifaceted. Such experience of love is communicated in expressions reflecting the fusion in sexual act as the unity of two physical parts. In case of heterosexual love, complementarity of bodies is well designed by nature.

Other linguistic expressions convey the role of physical closeness in love in more general meaning (e.g., "I want *to hold you in my arms*"; "I wanna *hold your hand*"; "*Please don't* ever *let me go*"; "I want *to be with you* all my life." (Kövecses, 1988, p. 21).

There is a range of other mergers, which metaphors of *love as a union* imply. A variety of words articulates this idea (e.g., *ties, bonds, connections*), and many expressions (e.g., There are romantic *ties between* them; There's a *strong bond* between them; *There is something between* them) (Kövecses, 1988, p. 20). The *unity metaphor* denotes a perfect harmony and an idyllic state of being.

4.2.8 Romantic Jealousy

The cross-cultural universality of experience of romantic jealousy supports the ideals of unity and exclusivity in romantic love (see for review, Karandashev, 2017, 2019). However, such cultural factors as cultural conceptualization of jealousy, social conditions of living, gender norms, and gender equality play their role. Cross-cultural studies present many examples of cultural diversity in the experience of romantic jealousy. (e.g., Bhugra, 1993; De Silva & De Silva, 1999; Díaz-Vera & Caballero, 2013; Jankowiak, Bell, & Buckmaster, 2002; Kim & Hupka, 2002; Zhang, Ting-Toomey, Dorjee, & Lee, 2012).

4.3 Erotic and Sexual Experience of Love

4.3.1 Erotic Love

The Greek word *eros* (*érōs*) means aesthetic appreciation and yearning for beauty (Lomas, 2018): one loves person/partner as a beautiful individual. Romantic love with its idealization perceives everything through rose-tinted glasses, including *physical appearance* of the admired individual. The experience of *erotic love* is the *attraction of physical appearance*: face and hair, eyes and lips, expressive behavior, smile, and gestures, voice and speaking, shape of body, and body movement (Karandashev et al., 2016). Erotic love is also the admiration of the beautiful and exotic attire. Western and Eastern fashion traditions have presented many designs that created the cultural norms of romantic attraction. The *erotic love* can implicitly trigger sexual connotations, among the others.

4.3.2 Sexual Love

The experience of *sexual love* is in (a) explicit sexual desire—yearning, longing, sensual expectations, and (b) explicit sexual action—sexual hugging, kissing, petting, sensual self-fulfillment. In Western scholarly tradition, *sexual love* is often termed as *epithymia* (in Greek), or as *libido* (in Latin) (Larson, 1983; Tillich, 1954a, 1954b). *Epithymia* is the love encompassing physical attraction and sensual desire (Lomas, 2018). It is the hunger and thirst for closeness and union with the whole person (Tillich, 1954b).

The meaning of *epithymia* is recognizable in the lexicons of many languages (Lomas, 2018). For example, in Chilean Yagán, *mamihlapinatapei* means a look between two persons, which expresses unspoken mutual desire. In Tagalog, *kilig* describes the feelings of butterflies in the stomach associated with thinking or interaction with sexually desirable attractive person.

4.3.3 The Experiences of Relations Between Erotic and Sexual Love

The differences in the interpretation of relations between sex and love existed in traditional cultures for quite long time. Western Christian cultures viewed them as opposites, considering one as "bodily" and the other as "spiritual". Eastern Buddhist cultures did not think of relations between sex and love in such oppositional and dualistic perspective. People in those cultures regarded sexual desire and spiritual devotional love as naturally intertwined and indistinguishable (Reddy, 2012).

Erotic love and *sexual love* are the feelings of different kind, yet they are delicately intertwined. *Beautiful* is often *sexy*, but not necessarily. We can admire someone's physical appearance without a desire to get sex with him or her.

The cultural ideals of *erotic love* and *sexual love* have been enduring throughout history and across cultures. Recent anthropological studies in many cultural contexts found that sex and love are compatible to each other in the societies where both males and females have a possibility to give (or not give) love freely (De Munck & Korotayev, 1999). The cultural recognition of gender equality is important for sex and romantic love being connected to each other. The cultural changes in acknowledgement of gender equality, which recently evolved in some societies, lead people to agree on the importance of sexual attraction for cultivation of love. The recent ethnographic research (Jankowiak, 2013) and sexual surveys (Burger, 2012) demonstrated this, for example, in a new generation of Chinese people.

Recent studies from different cultural contexts (De Munck et al., 2011; Farrer et al., 2008; Fisher, 2004; Jankowiak, Shen, Yao, Wang, & Volsche, 2015) demonstrated that laypeople acknowledge *erotic feelings*, *physical attraction*, and *sexual desire* as the *core* experiences in passionate and romantic love. However, perception of the relations between love and sex may be personal, contextual, and cultural. (see also Chap. 29).

For example, in the USA, Hendrick and Hendrick (2002) conducted the study of how university students view the link between love and sex in their romantic relationships. Participants generated descriptive responses, which authors classified in 27 themes, which in turn were reduced into 17 items, which were psychometrically factorized into four major themes:

- Love is most important
- Sex demonstrates love,
- Love comes before sex, and

- Sex is declining.

Another example of the study on relations between love and sex is from Japan (Farrer et al., 2008). Interviewing young Japanese men and women involved in *tsukiau* (dating) relationships, authors found that many informants viewed passion and having sex *(ecchi wo suru)* as the essential constituents of such relationship. Once the commitment for a steady relationship was declared—through a formal "confession" *(kokuhaku)*—then, having sex was natural *(shizeri)*, normal *(jutsuu)*, or a matter of fact *(touzeri)*. Partners considered sexual intercourse as the key experience which differentiates being in a *tsukiau* relationship from being just a friend. Having sex was a way to facilitate verbal communication and a unique intimate way of physical communication.

For many, sex was driven by their hedonic desire of sexual pleasure. Having *ecchi* (sex) was an expression of physically sensing passion and the desire that lead to the development of the feelings of love *(koi* and *ai)*. Having sex deepened their passionate feelings *(jou)* and lead to the deeper form of love *(ai)*.

Some partners believed that they had an obligation to have sex. Problems with having sex was viewed as a valid motivation for dissatisfaction and a break-up of a *tsukiau* relationship.

4.4 Joyful and Powerful Experience of Love

4.4.1 Joy and Happiness of Love

Love is an enjoyable cluster of emotions and feelings. People dream about love and pursue it, hoping to achieve happiness in their love relationships. They generally assume that love will bring them joy, happiness, well-being, and personal fulfilment. Is it possible to reach in love? Does love bring happiness?

The folk models of love in conventionalized lexicons represent "This love makes me happy" as a typical related concept of English language (Kövecses, 1988). It is assumed that "if I am in love (and my love is returned), then I am happy." Happiness is a result of love ("This love has made me happy"). It is a consequence of being in love: "if I am in love, then I am happy" (Kövecses, 1988, p. 39).

People in other cultures, however, may have different emotional associations with love. For example, the study of early 1990s (Shaver et al., 1992) revealed that Americans and Italians viewed passionate love as associated with intensely pleasurable experiences and happiness, while Chinese had sad associations with passionate love. Chinese recalled fewer "happy-love" words, while produced more negative associations with love than did Americans. This might be because the culture of Chinese society of that time allowed less freedom in the choice of a romantic partner.

However, Chinese and Americans were surprisingly similar in their list of words about negative features of love. In both cultural samples, respondents mentioned being tied down, time consumption, pain, separation, unrequited love, loss, jealousy, betrayal/desertion, and conflict. Nevertheless, in a separate account participants mentioned the list of positive features of love similar in both cultures (Shaver et al., 1992).

Other researchers in the survey administered among Chinese students 20 years later (Jankowiak et al., 2015) did not find many negative associations related to love, as in the study of early 1990s (Shaver et al., 1992). Chinese students generated the lists of love words that contained many positive expressions of the love feelings of being happy and sweet-talking (see also Chaps. 2 and 3).

The results of other cross-cultural studies, e.g. in the samples of Lithuanians, Russians, Americans, and Chinese (De Munck et al., 2009, 2011; Jankowiak et al., 2015), show that *emotional fulfilment is a core experience of love* and *love is the supreme happiness of life*. Thus, the modern beliefs in love that brings happiness and well-being are present cross-culturally.

The happiness of love is a powerful and omnipotent emotion. Lovers believe in myth that *love conquers all* (De Roda et al., 1999). Chinese, Russian, Lithuanian, and American youth think that *my love makes their partner stronger and a better person* (De Munck et al., 2011; Jankowiak et al., 2015). Passion, however, is not the only quality of love experience that is necessary for this. Differences in social status, religion, culture, and age can surpass love and bring unhappiness (Murstein, 1974).

4.4.2 The Quality of Love Makes Differences

Researchers explored specific characteristics of relationships that make people happy. Empirical data obtained in Europe and the USA demonstrated that experience of romantic love and being in a relationship allow to predict feelings of happiness and well-being (Argyle, 2001; Crossley & Langridge, 2005; Demir, 2008; Dush & Amato, 2005; Khaleque & Rohner, 2004; Myers, 2000; Reis, Collins, & Berscheid, 2000; Sedikides, Oliver, & Campbell, 1994). People in love are significantly happier and more satisfied with their life.

The quality of a relationship certainly matters. Studies demonstrated that across diverse cultures, the quality of romantic and intimate relationship (as well as other close relationships) significantly influences people's experience of individual happiness and well-being (de Munck et al., 2009, 2011; Diener, Gohm, Suh, & Oishi, 2000; Fok & Cheng, 2018; Garcia, Pereira, & Bucher-Maluschke, 2018; Jankowiak et al., 2015).

In particular, happiness in America positively correlates with passionate, friendship love (S. Hendrick & Hendrick, 2002), intimacy (Vaillants, 2012), companionship and emotional security (Demir, 2008). Reciprocated, wholehearted love, as well as rational love, brings happiness. However, unrequited, obsessive, and irrational love does not lead to happiness, while people who are uncomfortable with intimacy and commitment are unhappy and discontented (Vaillants, 2012).

There is certain cross-cultural similarity in how love brings subjective well-being. For instance, the results of the study among American students in University of

Hawaii and in Korea University (Kim & Hatfield, 2004) found that passionate love was the strongest predictor of positive emotions, while companionate love was the strongest predictor of life satisfaction. No cultural differences were found in that study.

4.4.3 The Predictors of Happy Love Across Cultures

Other research, however, revealed not only cross-cultural similarities, but also the differences in love experience that is predictive for subjective well-being of people. The study conducted in three cultures—North American (the USA as an individualistic country), Eastern African (Mozambique as a collectivistic country), and South European (Portugal as a country in between the American and the Mozambican in the continuum of individualism-collectivism)—presented the complex relationships between attachment, love styles, and subjective well-being (Galinha, Oishi, Pereira, Wirtz, & Esteves, 2014).

In the USA, *storge* and *pragma* love styles, as well as *attachment security,* were the major predictors of subjective well-being. In Portugal, the results were partially similar to Americans, and partially to Mozambicans. The predictors of subjective well-being were *attachment security* and *storge* love style—similar to Americans, and *eros* love style—similar to Mozambicans. In Mozambique, *eros* love style was the major predictor of subjective well-being. Different degree of individualism-collectivism, gender equality-inequality, as well as American history and the Latin heritage of Portuguese and the Mozambican societies explain the similarity and differences of the results in these three cultures.

4.5 Maladaptive Experience of Love

4.5.1 Obsession in Love

Despite being enjoyable, fulfilling, and uplifting, the experience of love can be painful, disappointing, frustrating. Tormenting obsession, mental suffering, even love sickness can escort love.

Extreme passion of love can become obsession, accompanied by intrusive thoughts dominating a lover's mind, by the experience of overwhelming desire to possess an object of love. The obsessional love is experienced as something suffocating and urgent. An obsessive lover feels needy in a beloved, not being able to accept rejection or failure.

The tendency of lovers to engage in intrusive, sometimes obsessive thinking about a beloved is a common cross-cultural phenomenon (see for review, Fisher, 2004). In the USA, Tennov (1979/1998) conducted the extensive exploration of such experience of infatuation in love. The author named this kind of experience as *limerence*. In the Lithuania, Russia, the United States, (De Munck et al., 2009,

2011), and China (Jankowiak et al., 2015), many informants identified similar features of passionate obsessive love.

This maladaptive experience of love is also described in sociology, psychology, and relationship science as *mania* love style (Hendrick & Hendrick, 1986, 1989; Lee, 1973, 1976, 1977, 1988). This love style/attitude is characterized by very intense emotional involvement, feeling of dependency on a beloved, accompanied by obsessive and possessive thoughts. Multiple cross-cultural studies investigated this love style/attitude throughout years. The results obtained with Love Attitudes Scale (LAS, Hendrick & Hendrick, 1986), or the short form of LAS (Hendrick, Hendrick, & Dicke, 1998), revealed cross-cultural universality of this love experience in different cultural contexts The data about cross-cultural differences were controversial (see for review, Karandashev, 2019).

4.5.2 Suffering in Love

The folk wisdom of love in many cultures considers suffering as a natural part of love. Unattainable love, unrequited love, and separation of lovers are the typical examples of circumstances associated with feelings of emptiness, anxiety, or despair.

Psycholinguistic studies have revealed that *suffering* is a salient experience of love described in culturally specific contexts. The big cluster of words and expressions in North American lexicon refers to the suffering caused by experience of romantic love: *helpless, sad, hurt-hurts, lost, frustrated, vulnerable, jealous,* and *angry* (De Munck & Kronenfeld, 2016). In Catholic Latin American culture, the concept of love implies *suffering, self-abnegation,* and *self-sacrifice* (Hagene, 2008).

There are many Turkish conceptual metaphors of suffering in love, such as *pain/ suffering, ineffability, deadly force, sacrifice,* etc. (Aksan & Kantar, 2008). The large presence of this conceptual domain in Turkish metaphors of love can be due to the culturally accepted in Turkey traditional model of lovers as the passive sufferers. The metaphors resonate the Sufi conception of love as an encompassing force in the universe, yet unattainable. Accordingly, in Turkish culture love is deemed as a pleasant experience, but painful (Aksan & Kantar, 2008, p. 282). The main emotion reflecting how love is represented for Russians is suffering. People perceive love as an obstacle, a problem in itself (Pilishvili & Koyanongo, 2016).

4.5.3 Lovesickness

From early times of antiquity, the medical doctors of different epochs and cultures described the case studies of *lovesickness* as an actual psychological disorder with a specific etiology, pathogenesis, and treatment (see for references, Money, 1980; Tallis, 2004). The historical review of Dzaja (2008) presented several cases drawn from various periods and cultures. Hajal (1994) presented the diagnosis and treatment of lovesickness based an Islamic Medieval case study.

In modern medicine, *lovesickness* may still be present in the form of *somatoform disorder, bipolar disorder, erotomania, or addiction* (Dzaja, 2008). Manifestations of extreme passion, with irrational, intrusive, obsessive thinking about beloved, acute longing for reciprocation, may resemble the symptoms of a psychological disorder (Money, 1980; Tallis, 2004; Tennov, 1979/1998). The symptoms of lovesickness are rapid breathing, palpitations, agitation, fever, loss of appetite, headache, frenzy and intrusive thinking, despair and depression (Dzaja, 2008; Leonti & Casu, 2018).

Anthropologists observed such symptoms in various cultures. For example, people in South Indian Tamil community describe an individual who falls head-over-heels in desperate and wild love as suffering from *mayakkam*-dizziness, intoxication, confusion, and delusion (Trawick, 1990).

The study in Italy (Marazziti, Akiskal, Rossi, & Cassano, 1999; Marazziti & Canale, 2004) found that the experience of passionate love resembles the symptoms of obsessive-compulsive disorder and neuroticism. The biochemical similarities in brain and body were found for these conditions (Marazziti et al., 1999).

4.6 Conclusion

I believe that the research findings on how people with different cultural background experience love, which are presented in this chapter, will be valuable for multicultural couples, psychologists, counselors, social workers, and other practitioners working with multicultural population or in cross-cultural contexts.

References

Aksan, Y., & Kantar, D. (2008). No wellness feels better than this sickness: Love metaphors from a cross-cultural perspective. *Metaphor and Symbol, 23*(4), 262–291.
Anapol, D. (2010). *Polyamory in the 21st century: Love and intimacy with multiple partners*. Lanham, MD: Rowman & Littlefield.
Argyle, M. (2001). *The psychology of happiness*. London: Routledge.
Barrón, A., de Paúl, P., Martinez-Iñigo, D., & Yela, C. (1999). Beliefs and romantic myths in Spain. *The Spanish Journal of Psychology, 2*(1), 64–73.
Berglund, S., Liljestrand, J., Marín, F. D. M., Salgado, N., & Zelaya, E. (1997). The background of adolescent pregnancies in Nicaragua: A qualitative approach. *Social Science & Medicine, 44*(1), 1–12.
Berscheid, E., & Walster, E. (1978). *Interpersonal attraction* (2nd ed.). Reading, MA: Addison-Wesley. (Original work published 1969).
Bhugra, D. (1993). Cross-cultural aspects of jealousy. *International Review of Psychiatry, 5*(2–3), 271–280.
Burger, R. (2012). *Behind the red door: Sex in China*. London: Earnshaw.

Chang, D., & Li, Y. (2006). *Visual representations of Kövecses's conceptual metaphor "love is fire" in the Chinese comic old master Q'*. Bayreuth, Germany. Retrieved from http://citeseerx.ist.psu.edu/viewdoc/download?doi=10.1.1.507.7887&rep=rep1&type=pdf

Crossley, A., & Langridge, D. (2005). Perceived sources of happiness: A network analysis. *Journal of Happiness Studies, 6*, 107–135.

Davis, E., Greenberger, E., Charles, S., Chen, C., Zhao, L., & Dong, Q. (2012). Emotion experience and regulation in China and the United States: How do culture and gender shape emotion responding? *International Journal of Psychology, 47*(3), 230–239.

De Munck, V. C., & Korotayev, A. (1999). Sexual equality and romantic love: A reanalysis of Rosenblatt's study on the function of romantic love. *Cross-Cultural Research, 33*(3), 265–277.

De Munck, V. C., Korotayev, A., de Munck, J., & Khaltourina, D. (2011). Cross-cultural analysis of models of romantic love among US residents, Russians, and Lithuanians. *Cross-Cultural Research, 45*(2), 128–154.

De Munck, V., Korotayev, A., & Khaltourina, D. (2009). A comparative study of the structure of love in the US and Russia: Finding a common core of characteristics and national and gender differences. *Ethnology: An International Journal of Cultural and Social Anthropology, 48*(4), 337–357.

De Munck, V. C., & Kronenfeld, D. B. (2016). Romantic love in the United States: Applying cultural models theory and methods. *SAGE Open*, 1–17. https://doi.org/10.1177/2158244015622797

De Roda, A. B. L., Martínez-Iñigo, D., De Paul, P., & Yela, C. (1999). Romantic beliefs and myths in Spain. *The Spanish Journal of Psychology, 2*, 64–73.

De Silva, D., & De Silva, P. (1999). Morbid jealousy in an Asian country: A clinical exploration from Sri Lanka. *International Review of Psychiatry, 11*(2–3), 116–121.

Demir, M. (2008). Sweetheart, you really make me happy: Romantic relationship quality and personality as predictors of happiness among emerging adults. *Journal of Happiness Studies, 9*(2), 257–277.

D'Hondt, W., & Vandewiele, M. (1983). Attitudes of West African students toward love and marriage. *Psychological Reports, 53*(2), 615–621.

Díaz-Vera, J. E., & Caballero, R. (2013). Exploring the feeling-emotions continuum across cultures: Jealousy in English and Spanish. *Intercultural Pragmatics, 10*(2), 265–294.

Diener, E., Gohm, C., Suh, E., & Oishi, S. (2000). Similarity of the relations between marital status and subjective well-being across cultures. *Journal of Cross-Cultural Psychology, 31*, 419–436.

Dion, K. L., & Dion, K. K. (1973). Correlates of romantic love. *Journal of Consulting and Clinical Psychology, 41*(1), 51–56.

Dush, C. M. K., & Amato, P. R. (2005). Consequences of relationship status and quality for subjective well-being. *Journal of Social and Personal Relationships, 22*, 607–627.

Dzaja, N. (2008). Lovesickness: The most common form of heart disease. *University of West Ontario Medical Journal (UWOMJ), 78*(1), 66–69.

Eggleston, E., Jackson, J., & Hardee, K. (1999). Sexual attitudes and behavior among young adolescents in Jamaica. *International Family Planning Perspectives, 25*(2), 78–91.

Farrer, J., Tsuchiya, H., & Bagrowicz, B. (2008). Emotional expression in tsukiau dating relationships in Japan. *Journal of Social and Personal Relationships, 25*(1), 169–188.

Fisher, H. (2004). *Why we love: The nature and chemistry of romantic love*. New York, NY: Henry Holt.

Fok, H. K., & Cheng, S. T. (2018). Intimate relationships and happiness in Asia: A critical review. In M. Demir & N. Sümer (Eds.), *Close relationships and happiness across cultures* (pp. 55–67). Cham: Springer.

Galinha, I. C., Oishi, S., Pereira, C. R., Wirtz, D., & Esteves, F. (2014). Adult attachment, love styles, relationship experiences and subjective well-being: Cross-cultural and gender comparison between Americans, Portuguese, and Mozambicans. *Social Indicators Research, 119*(2), 823–852.

Garcia, A., Pereira, F. N., & Bucher-Maluschke, J. S. (2018). Close relationships and happiness in South America. In M. Demir & N. Sümer (Eds.), *Close relationships and happiness across cultures* (pp. 69–85). Cham: Springer.

Garis, L. (1984, April 22). Simenon's last case. *The New York Times,* 20.

Giddens, A. (1992). *The transformation of intimacy: Sexuality, love, and eroticism in modern societies.* Cambridge: Polity.

Gross, L. (1944). A belief pattern scale for measuring attitudes toward romanticism. *American Sociological Review, 9*(5), 463–472.

Hagene, T. (2008). *Negotiating love in post-revolutionary Nicaragua: The role of love in the reproduction of gender asymmetry.* Oxford, UK: Peter Lang.

Hajal, F. (1994). Diagnosis and treatment of lovesickness: An Islamic Medieval case study. *Psychiatric Services, 45*(7), 647–650.

Hatfield, E., & Rapson, R. L. (1987). Passionate love: New directions in research. In W. H. Jones & D. Perlman (Eds.), *Advances in personal relationships* (Vol. 1). Greenwich, CT: JAI.

Hatfield, E., & Rapson, R. L. (1993). *Love, sex, and intimacy: Their psychology, biology, and history.* New York, NY: HarperCollins.

Hendrick, C., & Hendrick, S. (1986). A theory and method of love. *Journal of Personality and Social Psychology, 50,* 392–402.

Hendrick, C., & Hendrick, S. (1989). Research on love: Does it measure up? *Journal of Personality and Social Psychology, 56,* 784–794.

Hendrick, S. S., & Hendrick, C. (1992). *Romantic love: An interdisciplinary analysis of the complex and elusive nature of love.* Newbury Park, CA: Sage.

Hendrick, S. S., & Hendrick, C. (2002). Linking romantic love with sex: Development of the perceptions of love and sex scale. *Journal of Social and Personal Relationships, 19*(3), 361–378.

Hendrick, C., Hendrick, S. S., & Dicke, A. (1998). The love attitudes scale: Short form. *Journal of Social and Personal Relationships, 15*(2), 147–159.

Hinkle, D. E., & Sporakowski, M. J. (1975). Attitudes toward love: A reexamination. *Journal of Marriage and the Family, 37*(4), 764–767.

Hochschild, A. (1979). Emotion work, feeling rules, and social structure. *American Journal of Sociology, 85*(3), 551–575.

Jankowiak, W. (Ed.). (1995). *Romantic passion: A universal experience?* New York, NY: Columbia University Press.

Jankowiak, W. (2013). From courtship to dating culture: China's emergent youth. In P. Link, R. Madsen, & P. Pickowitz (Eds.), *China at risk* (pp. 191–214). New York, NY: McGraw-Hill.

Jankowiak, W., Bell, M. D., & Buckmaster, A. (2002). Managing infidelity: A cross-cultural perspective. *Ethnology, 41*(1), 85.

Jankowiak, W., Shen, Y., Yao, S., Wang, C., & Volsche, S. (2015). Investigating love's universal attributes: A research report from China. *Cross-Cultural Research, 49*(4), 422–436.

Karandashev, V. (2017). *Romantic love in cultural contexts.* New York, NY: Springer.

Karandashev, V. (2019). *Cross-cultural perspectives on the experience and expression of love.* New York, NY: Springer.

Karandashev, V., Zarubko, E., Artemyeva, V., Neto, F., Surmanidze, L., & Feybesse, C. (2016). Sensory values in romantic attraction in four Europeans countries: Gender and cross-cultural comparison. *Cross-Cultural Research, 50*(5), 478–504. https://doi.org/10.1177/1069397116674446

Kephart, W. M. (1967). Some correlates of romantic love. *Journal of Marriage and the Family, 29*(3), 470–474.

Khaleque, A. R., & Rohner, N. (2004). Intimate adult relationships, quality of life and psychological adjustment. *Social Indicators Research, 69,* 351–360.

Kim, J., & Hatfield, E. (2004). Love types and subjective well-being: A cross-cultural study. *Social Behavior and Personality: An International Journal, 32*(2), 173–182.

Kim, H. J., & Hupka, R. B. (2002). Comparison of associative meaning of the concepts of anger, envy, fear, romantic jealousy, and sadness between English and Korean. *Cross-Cultural Research, 36*(3), 229–255.

Kitayama, S., Markus, H. R., & Matsumoto, H. (1995). Culture, self, and emotion: A cultural perspective on "self-conscious" emotions. In J. P. Tangney & K. W. Fischer (Eds.), *Self-conscious emotions: The psychology of shame, guilt, embarrassment, and pride* (pp. 439–464). New York, NY: Guilford Press.

Knee, R. (1998). Implicit theories of relationships: Assessment and prediction of romantic relationship initiation, coping, and longevity. *Journal of Personality and Social Psychology, 74*, 360–370.

Knox, D. H., & Sporakowski, M. J. (1968). College students attitudes toward love. *Journal of Marriage and the Family, 30*, 638–642.

Kövecses, Z. (1988). *The language of love: The semantics of passion in conversational English*. Lewisburg, PA: Bucknell University Press.

Kövecses, Z. (1990). *Emotion concepts*. New York, NY: Springer.

Kövecses, Z. (2005). *Metaphor in culture: Universality and variation*. Cambridge: Cambridge University Press.

Larson, D. R. (1983). Sexuality and Christian ethics. *A Report from Argentina Second Thoughts on Military Service Inside the Weimar Institute, 15*(1), 10–18.

Lee, J. (1973). *The colors of love: The exploration of the ways of loving*. Ontario: New Press.

Lee, J. (1976). *The colors of love*. Englewood Cliffs, NJ: Prentice-Hall.

Lee, J. A. (1977). A typology of styles of loving. *Personality and Social Psychology Bulletin, 3*(2), 173–182.

Lee, J. A. (1988). Love styles. In R. J. Sternberg & M. L. Barnes (Eds.), *The psychology of love*. Yale: Yale University Press.

Leonti, M., & Casu, L. (2018). Ethnopharmacology of love. *Frontiers in Pharmacology, 9*(567), 1–16. https://doi.org/10.3389/fphar.2018.00567

Lim, N. (2016). Cultural differences in emotion: Differences in emotional arousal level between the east and the west. *Integrative Medicine Research, 5*(2), 105–109.

Lindholm, C. (1995). Love as an experience of transcendence. In W. Jankowiak (Ed.), *Romantic passion: A universal experience?* (pp. 57–71). New York, NY: Columbia University Press.

Lindholm, C. (1998). The future of love. In V. C. De Munck (Ed.), *Romantic love and sexual desire behavior: Perspectives from social sciences* (pp. 17–32). Westport, CT: Praeger.

Lomas, T. (2018). The flavours of love: A cross-cultural lexical analysis. *Journal for the Theory of Social Behaviour, 48*, 134–152.

Lutz, C. (1988). *Unnatural emotions: Everyday sentiments on a Micronesian atoll and their challenge to Western theory*. Chicago, IL: University of Chicago Press.

Lv, Z., & Zhang, Y. (2012). Universality and variation of conceptual metaphor of love in Chinese and English. *Theory and Practice in Language Studies, 2*(2), 355–359.

Lynch, O. M. (Ed.). (1990). *Divine passions: The social construction of emotion in India*. Berkeley, CA: University of California Press.

Marazziti, D., Akiskal, H. S., Rossi, A., & Cassano, G. B. (1999). Alteration of the platelet serotonin transporter in romantic love. *Psychological Medicine, 29*(3), 741–745.

Marazziti, D., & Canale, D. (2004). Hormonal changes when falling in love. *Psychoneuroendocrinology, 29*(7), 931–936.

Marston, P. J., Hecht, M. L., Manke, M. L., McDaniel, S., & Reeder, H. (1998). The subjective experience of intimacy. Passion, and commitment in heterosexual loving relationships. *Personal Relationships, 5*, 15–30.

Medora, N. P., Larson, J. H., Hortaçsu, N., & Dave, P. (2002). Perceived attitudes towards romanticism: A cross-cultural study of American, Asian-Indian, and Turkish young adults. *Journal of Comparative Family Studies, 33*, 155–179.

Mesquita, B., & Frijda, N. H. (1992). Cultural variations in emotions: A review. *Psychological Bulletin, 112*, 179–204.

Money, J. (1980). *Love and love sickness*. Baltimore, MD: Johns Hopkins University Press.
Munro, B., & Adams, G. (1978). Correlates of romantic love revisited. *Journal of Psychology, 98*, 211–214.
Murstein, B. I. (1974). *Love, sex, and marriage through the ages*. New York, NY: Springer.
Myers, D. (2000). The funds, friends and faith of happy people. *American Psychologist, 55*, 56–67.
O'Neill, N., & O'Neill, G. (1984). *Open marriage: A new life style for couples*. Lanham, MD: Rowman & Littlefield.
Payne, M., & Vandewiele, M. (1987). Attitudes toward love in the Caribbean. *Psychological Reports, 60*(3), 715–721.
Pennebaker, J. W., & Graybeal, A. (2001). Patterns of natural language use: Disclosure, personality, and social integration. *Current Directions in Psychological Science, 10*(3), 90–93.
Philbrick, J. L. (1988). Love African style: A comparison of sex differences in love-attitudes of east African university students. *Psychological Reports, 63*(3), 913–914.
Philbrick, J. L., & Opolot, J. A. (1980). Love style: Comparison of African and American attitudes. *Psychological Reports, 1980*(46), 286.
Philbrick, J. L., & Stones, C. R. (1988a). Love-attitudes of white South African adolescents. *Psychological Reports, 62*(1), 17–18.
Philbrick, J. L., & Stones, C. R. (1988b). Love attitudes in black South Africa: A comparison of school and university students. *The Psychological Record, 38*(2), 249–251.
Pilishvili, T. S., Koyanongo E. (2016). The representation of love among Brazilians, Russians and central Africans: A comparative analysis. *Psychology in Russia: State of the Art, 9* (1). Retrieved April 11, 2019, from https://cyberleninka.ru/article/n/the-representation-of-love-among-brazilians-russians-and-central-africans-a-comparative-analysis
Rani, M., Figueroa, M. E., & Ainsle, R. (2003). The psychosocial context of young adult sexual behavior in Nicaragua: Looking through the gender lens. *International Family Planning Perspectives, 29*(4), 174–181.
Reddy, W. M. (2012). *The making of romantic love: Longing and sexuality in Europe, South Asia, and Japan, 900–1200 CE*. Chicago, IL: The University of Chicago Press.
Reis, H. T., Collins, W. A., & Berscheid, E. (2000). The relationship context of human behavior and development. *Psychological Bulletin, 126*, 844–872.
Rosenblatt, P. (1967). Marital residence and the functions of romantic love. *Ethnology, 6*, 471–480.
Rubin, Z. (1970). Measurement of romantic love. *Journal of Personality and Social Psychology, 16*, 265–273.
Sánchez, A. B. (1995). Metaphorical models of romantic love in Romeo and Juliet. *Journal of Pragmatics, 24*(6), 667–688.
Sastry, J. (1999). Household structure, satisfaction and distress in India and the United States: A comparative cultural examination. *Journal of Comparative Family Studies, 30*(1), 135–152.
Sedikides, C., Oliver, M. B., & Campbell, W. K. (1994). Perceived benefits and costs of romantic relationships for women and men: Implications for exchange theory. *Personal Relationships, 1*, 5–21.
Shaver, P. R., Wu, S., & Schwartz, J. C. (1992). Cross-cultural similarities and differences in emotion and its representation: A prototype approach. In M. S. Clark (Ed.), *Review of personality and social psychology* (pp. 175–212). Newbury Park, CA: Sage.
Shweder, R. (1993). The cultural psychology of the emotions. In M. Lewis & J. M. Haviland (Eds.), *The handbook of emotions* (pp. 417–431). New York, NY: Guilford Press.
Simmons, C. H., vom Kolke, A., & Shimizu, H. (1986). Attitudes toward romantic love among American, German, and Japanese students. *Journal of Social Psychology, 126*(3), 327–336.
Simmons, C. H., Wehner, E. A., & Kay, K. A. (1989). Differences in attitudes toward romantic love of French and American college students. *The Journal of Social Psychology, 129*(6), 793–799.
Soto, J. A., Levenson, R. W., & Ebling, R. (2005). Cultures of moderation and expression: Emotional experience, behavior, and physiology in Chinese Americans and Mexican Americans. *Emotion, 5*(2), 154–165.

Sprecher, S., Aron, A., Hatfield, E., Cortese, A., Potapova, E., & Levitskaya, A. (1994). Love: American style, Russian style, and Japanese style. *Personal Relationships, 1*, 349–369.

Sprecher, S., & Metts, S. (1989). Development of the romantic beliefs scale and examination of the effects of gender and gender-role orientation. *Journal of Social and Personal Relationships, 6*, 387–411.

Sprecher, S., & Toro-Morn, M. (2002). A study of men and women from different sides of earth to determine if men are from Mars and women are from Venus in their beliefs about love and romantic relationships. *Sex Roles, 46*(5–6), 131–147.

Sternberg, R. J. (1987). *The triangle of love*. New York, NY: Basic Books.

Sternberg, R. J., & Barnes, H. L. (1985). Real and ideal others in romantic relationships: Is four a crowd? *Journal of Personality and Social Psychology, 49*(6), 1586–1608.

Stones, C. R. (1986). Love styles revisited: A cross-national comparison with particular reference to South Africa. *Human Relations, 39*(4), 379–381.

Stones, C. R. (1992). Love attitudes of white South African and British university students. *The Journal of Social Psychology, 132*(5), 609–613.

Stones, C. R., & Philbrick, J. L. (1989). Attitudes toward love among Xhosa university students in South Africa. *The Journal of Social Psychology, 129*(4), 573–575.

Stones, C. R., & Philbrick, J. L. (1991). Attitudes toward love among members of a small fundamentalist community in South Africa. *The Journal of Social Psychology, 131*(2), 219–223.

Tallis, F. (2004). *Lovesick: Love as a mental illness*. New York, NY: Thunder's Mouth Press.

Tennov, D. (1979/1998). *Love and limerence: The experience of being in love*. Lanham, MD: Scarborough House.

Tillich, P. (1954a). Being and love. *Pastoral Psychology, 5*(3), 59–60.

Tillich, P. (1954b). *Love, power, and justice*. New York: Oxford University Press.

Trawick, M. (1990). *Notes on love in a Tamil family*. Berkeley, CA: University of California Press.

Vaillants, G. E. (2012). *Triumphs of experience: The men of the Harvard Grant study*. Cambridge, MA: Belknap Press.

Vandewiele, M., & Philbrick, J. L. (1983). Attitudes of Senegalese students toward love. *Psychological Reports, 52*(3), 915–918.

Zhang, R., Ting-Toomey, S., Dorjee, T., & Lee, P. S. (2012). Culture and self-construal as predictors of relational responses to emotional infidelity: China and the United States. *Chinese Journal of Communication, 5*(2), 137–159.

Victor Karandashev is Professor of Psychology at Aquinas College, Grand Rapids, Michigan, USA. He is a scholar with extensive international and cross-cultural experience and interests. He has conducted research on international psychology in several European countries, including universities in Norway, Sweden, Germany, Switzerland, and the UK. He was a visiting professor and a Fulbright Scholar in the U.S.A. He has presented his work related to international and cross-cultural psychology at many conferences. He co-edited three volumes of Teaching Psychology Around the World (2007, 2009, 2012). His major area of research interests is the study of love. He published several articles and chapters on the topic. His recent books Romantic love in cultural contexts (2017) and Cross-cultural perspectives on the experience and expression of love 2019) are among the most distinguished interdisciplinary contributions to the field.

Part II
Particular Facets and Manifestations of Love in Digital Social, Cultural and Political Contexts

Graffiti "Couple" (Photo: Jon Tyson)

Chapter 5
Cyberspace: The Alternative Romantic Culture

Aaron Ben-Ze'ev

Abstract Cyberspace provides an alternative culture to one's actual romantic setting. It enables participants to explore exciting romantic options without bearing significant costs in terms of resources and efforts, and without necessarily violating significant personal commitments. The new romantic culture, in which cyberspace has a prominent role, is both seductive and sustainable. Two major contributions of cyberspace to the romantic realm are facilitating finding a willing romantic partner, and creating more types of romantic relationships. Their impact upon the nature of romantic relations is examined. A major impact is making romantic relations more complex, diverse and flexible, and at the same time briefer and more superficial. The normative impact of cyberspace on the romantic culture is discussed, indicating the increasing violations of values and boundaries in our romantic behavior. Today's abundance of romantic and sexual options facilitates finding love, but obstructs keeping it for a long time. However, the need for love does not disappear among young people as well as people in their later life, or when love is mature. A combination of offline and online interactions can be very fruitful for cultivating the romantic realm.

Keywords Love · Cyberspace · Cyberlove · Diversity · Flexibility · Profundity

5.1 More and Different Romantic Options

Cyberspace constitutes one of today's most exciting social and cultural sites. This is also true of the romantic realm, in which seeking a romantic partner as well as conducting loving and sexual activities are very common. In fact, the most common way these days to meet a future spouse is online—and the popularity of this method is expected to soar in the near future. Studies indicate that the overall quality of

A. Ben-Ze'ev (✉)
Department of Philosophy, University of Haifa, Haifa, Israel
e-mail: abenzeev@univ.haifa.ac.il

relations started online is about the same, and sometimes even higher, than those began otherwise (Ortega & Hergovich, 2018; Rosenfeld & Thomas, 2012). Cyberspace does not merely help people find their romantic partner, but also enables some novel types of love, termed "cyberlove".

The new romantic culture, in which cyberspace has a prominent role, is extremely seductive for various reasons; two such main reasons are the abundance of available romantic options and the interactive nature of the romantic imagination in cyberspace. Whereas the first feature significantly increases the number of options for the common, offline type of relation, the second one adds other types of romantic relations that are easy to obtain. I begin by briefly describing a few major facets of cyberlove and cybersex, and then discuss the aforementioned two reasons for the intense appeal of this cyber use.

5.1.1 Cyberlove and Cybersex

Cyberlove is a romantic relationship that takes place mainly through a computer and application-mediated communication. Despite the fact that the partner is physically remote and sometimes somewhat anonymous, the emotion of love is experienced as fully and as intensely as in an offline relationship (Bergen, 2006; Jiang & Hancock, 2013; Kelmer, Rhoades, Stanley, & Markman, 2013; Stafford, 2005). Nevertheless, geographic proximity remains a strong driver of romantic interaction (Bruch & Newman, 2019).

In a broad sense, cybersex (or in slang, "cybering") refers to all types of sexually related activities offered in cyberspace, including mobile applications. People send provocative and erotic messages to each other with the purpose of bringing each other to orgasm as they masturbate together in real time. In cybersex, people describe body characteristics to one another, verbalize sexual actions and reactions, and make believe that the virtual happenings are real. Cybersex requires the articulation of sexual desire to an extent that would be most unusual in face-to-face encounters. In cyberspace, that which often remains unspoken must be put into words (Döring, 2002). When people are engaged in cybersex, they cannot actually kiss each other; nevertheless, the kiss they send is emotionally vivid, and its emotional impact is often similar to that of an actual kiss. Our active role in cyberspace makes this environment more enticing and exciting than that of daydreams, erotic novels, or X-rated movies. And it is this enhanced excitement that amplifies the temptation to engage in sexual activities (Ben-Ze'ev, 2004, 4–6).

Nevertheless, geographic proximity remains a strong driver of romantic interaction. The distinction between online relationships that are used as a way of finding an offline partner and online-only relationships is related to the more general distinction between considering the Internet as a cultural artifact—that is, a means of communication in an offline social world—and considering it as a culture of its own—that is, regarding cyberspace as a cultural space in its own right. Since the Internet is not a unified phenomenon, the two uses of the Net coexist (Ben-Ze'ev, 2004, 133; Slater, 2002).

5.1.2 Abundant Available Romantic Options

Cyberspace is an alternative, available culture providing us with ready access to a world of available options. It is easy and an inexpensive to reach desired partners, and simple to perform desired actions. It takes less effort to find romantic partners in cyberspace than at bars, shopping malls, or supermarkets. Thus, in the United States meeting online has become the most popular way couples meet, eclipsing meeting through friends for the first time around 2013. Traditional ways of meeting partners (through family, in church, in the neighborhood) have all been declining since World War II. Meeting through friends has been in decline since roughly 1995 (Rosenfeld, Thomas, & Hausen, 2019).

Cyberspace is also highly available in the sense that it is highly accessible (for the time being, more so in the West than in other parts of the world). Connections to cyberspace are everywhere—home, work, hotels, and even cafes—and logging in takes no time at all. Thanks to the exceptional accessibility and convenience of cyberspace, people feel comfortable about entering and remaining there. Little investment is required to step into this imaginative paradise. Millions of people eagerly await you on the Net every moment of the day for full-blown romantic relations, or merely sexual interactions. These people are available, willing, and easy to find. (It bears remembering, of course, that, as is true in offline life, most of those people will not suit or interest you and will not reply to your request to meet them.) Such overwhelming availability is associated with frequent novel changes, and this makes cyberspace intensely dynamic, unstable, and exciting (Ben-Ze'ev, 2004, 18–20).

The abundance of romantic options does not merely include future novel romantic options, but also previous romantic relationships. Past lovers never quite disappear from view on the internet and social networks, and if some remnant of the closeness we once felt with them remains, people can feel entitled to be with them again. The ghosts of past lovers remain just a click away and may prevent lovers from accepting their own current romantic lot.

Cyberspace increases one's romantic options, not only in the sense of being able to identify many candidates previously unknown to us, but also in the sense of significantly increasing the percentage in this group of those who are willing to start a relationship. There are, of course, cultural differences; overall, though, the direction is clear: greater usage of cyberspace in the initiation of romantic relationships. This is because of the egalitarian aspect of cyberspace. Interactions in this realm erase social constraints, particularly status differences. One does not have to be the product of many years of evolution, personal development, and luck in order to share the advantages enjoyed by handsome and rich people. In the virtual culture of cyberspace, these advantages are open to everyone.

The egalitarian aspect of cyberspace is also expressed in the fact that it is highly accessible for specific sectors of society that may have more difficulty finding a suitable partner. This is true of those who are physically disadvantaged, sick, older, younger, shy, unattractive, homosexual, bisexual, and transsexual. All of them—not to mention others—may find the Net an attractive place to initiate and maintain romantic and sexual relationships. Indeed, up to 70% of homosexual relationships start online (Ortega & Hergovich, 2018).

In many aspects, cyberspace seems to be an egalitarian medium—in theory, at least, everyone has access to it, and everyone is treated equally regardless of personal characteristics such as external appearance, gender, color, religion, race, age, disability, social status, and income level (Katz & Rice, 2002). On the Net, people connect because of what they have to say, and what is on their mind. While income level, education, and place of residence can clearly limit one's access to the Internet, decreases in costs of computers and advancements in the developing world's education and infrastructure make the Internet increasingly accessible. There are, however, other characteristics, such as creativity, intellect, interests, wit, a sense of humor, and the ability to respond quickly in a witty manner, that give an edge to those who possess such skills, and this makes the Internet less egalitarian.

Bruch and Newman (2018) discuss another aspect of inequality in online dating, namely, the hierarchy of desirability. They argue that in light of the high volume of partners and low threshold for sending a message, competition for potential partners' attention is likely fiercer online than offline. This may increase "the presence of a hierarchy of desirability online, and reduce people's willingness to respond to less desirable mates: When there are plenty of fish in the sea, one can afford to throw a few back" (Bruch & Newman, 2018).

Cyberspace can be likened to an enormous commune—a kind of mentally nude commune. People feel free to strip off their mental mask and unload their secret desires. Imagination, which paints cyberspace in exceptionally vivid colors, also helps people satisfy some of their profound desires. This does not mean, however, that personality differences or differences relating to gender, race, and age completely disappear, as such differences are connected to psychological, social, cultural, and physical differences that are not automatically eliminated by online communication (Ben-Ze'ev, 2004, 16–18).

5.1.3 Interactive Exciting Imagination

Imagination has a crucial role in generating emotions. This role has to do with the comparative nature of emotions: emotional comparison involves reference to a situation that is different from the present one. Emotional imagination does not merely refer to situations that are not present to our senses, but also to situations that do not exist now—most of which will never exist at all.

The important role of emotional imagination, and positive cognitive biases in particular, is clearly evident in the romantic realm. Contrary to the belief that lasting romantic satisfaction depends on an accurate understanding of the partners' real strengths and frailties, positive cognitive biases are quite valuable in making romantic relationships more satisfying and less distressing. Sustaining a sense of security often requires weaving an elaborate story that both embellishes a partner's virtues and overlooks, or at least minimizes, his or her faults (Ben-Ze'ev & Goussinsky, 2008, Chap. 5; Gilbert, 2007: 26, 98; Taylor, 1989).

Today, dreams are no longer the major tool for imagining a better situation. Cyberspace has taken up that role and run with it. In cyberspace, two lovers feel as if they are directly connected— as if their bodies do not interfere, allowing their hearts to be in direct communication. Online relationship as can be described as dreaming while awake and delight in these dreams.

Imaginative activity is hardly new, of course; people have always imagined themselves doing all sorts of things with all sorts of others in all sorts of places. The novelty of cyberspace lies in the magnitude of the imaginary aspect and, in particular, in its interactive nature. Such interactivity has made this psychological reality a social and cultural reality as well: imaginary actions have become common practice for many people. Cyberspace is similar to fictional space in the sense that in both cases the flight into virtual reality is not so much a denial of reality as a form of exploring and playing with it. One crucial difference between the two is the interactive nature of cyberspace. In cyberspace, people do not merely read or watch a romantic affair undertaken by others, but in a sense, they are actually participating in it. The active nature of cyberspace is also expressed in the fact that finding a partner online does not involve patiently waiting for her to cross one's path (a traditional offline method), but rather entails an active search through cyberspace for exactly what one seeks (Best & Delmege, 2012).

The above considerations have revolutionized the role of imagination in personal relationships and have promoted imagination from being a peripheral tool used at best by artists, and at worst by dreamers and others who—it was thought, had nothing better to do—to a central means of personal relationship for ordinary folks who have busy, involved lives, but prefer to interact online. Although some areas of cyberspace can be regarded as electronic bedrooms, in other areas different types of personal relationships flourish.

Cyberspace is virtual in the sense that imagination is intrinsic to that space. In many online relationships, you can imagine your cybermate in whatever way you wish to, and you can describe yourself as you want to be seen. In another important sense, however, cyberspace is not virtual: online relationships are conducted between actual, flesh-and-blood people. Although this relationship involves many imaginative aspects, the relationship itself is not imaginary. Cyberspace is a part of reality; it is, then, incorrect to regard it as the direct opposite of real space. Cyberspace is part of real space, and online relationships are real relationships (Ben-Ze'ev, 2004, 1–4).

The active personal role in cyberspace makes this environment more enchanting than that of sexual fantasies, erotic novels and movies; hence, the massive temptation to engage in cybersex. Since the line separating passive observation from full interaction is crossed in cybersex, it becomes easier to blur the line separating imagination from reality. The presence of interactive characteristics in the imaginary realm of an online relationship is a revolution in personal relationships, as it enables people to reap many of the benefits associated with offline relationships without a significant investment of resources. Cyberlove, which is a new kind of romantic relation, lacks some central features of offline love—but it may fulfill one's basic romantic needs at a dramatically lower cost (Benski & Fisher, 2014; Ben-Ze'ev, 2004, 1–6).

5.2 The Impact of Cyberspace on Romantic Relations

Cyberspace has had a tremendous impact on modern life in general and on the romantic realm in particular. Here, I focus on the impact of the aforementioned two reasons that cyberspace is such a bewitching romantic draw: the abundance of available romantic options and the interactive essence of the romantic imagination. Some immediate consequences of these features are an increase in the diversity and flexibility, and hence the complexity, of the romantic culture, and making romantic relations briefer and more superficial.

5.2.1 Increasing Diversity and Flexibility

Cyberspace significantly increases diversity and flexibility in one's romantic life. People are aware of more alluring romantic options, and staying in one's romantic place becomes harder. Indeed, cybersex provides more flexible boundaries than real-life sex. Survival in a diverse environment hinges on the ability to be flexible. Modern technology enables us to maintain remote relationships. It not only offers more options for meeting willing people; it also provides more comfortable and efficient ways to pursue several romantic relationships at the same time.

Human life concerns not only—or even mainly—the present, but rather, and to a significant extent, the realm of imagined possibilities, that is, opportunities which can be realized, or at least be imagined. The imaginary realm is much more central in cyberspace than in our offline environment. The realm of potential possibilities is promising, but risky as well. To guide our walk through this unknown territory we have created boundaries that eliminate those options that seem immoral or risky. In many circumstances, these boundaries may be suitable as general guidelines, but they cannot cover all the various circumstances. Hence, flexibility involving overstepping the boundaries seems inevitable (Ben-Ze'ev & Goussinsky, 2008: Chap. 5).

Quoidbach et al. (2014) argue that "emodiversity"—that is, the variety and abundance of the emotions that people experience—is an independent predictor of mental and physical health, such as decreased depression and fewer visits to doctors. They further claim that experiencing many different specific emotional states (e.g., anger, shame, and sadness) can have more survival value than experiencing fewer or more global states (e.g., feeling bad). Since the diversity of these specific emotions provides richer information about our environment, the individual is more able to deal with a given emotional situation. (Quoidbach et al., 2014).

Diversity in cyber society is increased in the sense of allowing people to meet strangers. In this regard, I suggest considering two major processes: (1) increasing the feasibility of meeting strangers, and (2) increasing the feasibility of meeting individuals who face a thinner market for potential partners, such as gays, lesbians, and middle-aged heterosexuals. Cyberspace increasingly allows people to meet and form relationships with perfects strangers, and hence increases the likelihood of interracial marriages in our societies, which is remarkably low (Ortega & Hergovich, 2018). On the other hand, cyberspace facilitates creating bonds between individuals who face a thin market. In the case of interracial marriages, the first process seems to have great impact, while in the case of individuals facing a thin market, the impact of the second process is strong. Consequently, a very high percentage of homosexual relations begin online. Indeed, partnership rate has increased during the Internet era (consistent with Internet efficiency of search) for same-sex couples, but the heterosexual partnership rate has remained flat (Rosenfeld & Thomas, 2012).

The diversity in cyber society does not add new emotions to the ones we experience in our offline environment. Such diversity, however, does change the circumstances in which our emotions are generated—there are a greater number of circumstances in which the emotions are generated in a faster and more intense manner. Thus, people often fall in love in a faster and in a more intense manner in online relations than in offline ones. One reason for this is the greater role of imagination in these relations. Another reason concerns the issue of self-disclosure, which is vital in romantic relations. The greater sense of security due to physical separation means that self-disclosure is also more prevalent in cyberspace. This in turn increases intimacy and, accordingly, the seductiveness of online relationships is further enhanced (Ben-Ze'ev, 2004, Chap. 4).

Davidson, Joinson, and Jones (2018) argue that there are several ways in which technology has shaped the ways in which relationships start, progress, maintained and end. Technology has vastly increased the volume of potential partners available to an individual, has transformed the pace and order in which a relationship develops, and has revised the way in which humans go about choosing a suitable partner (Davidson et al., 2018).

Diversity is generally good for us. Is it also good in the romantic realm? Does the abundance of romantic options enhance the "quantity" and quality of love in the world? It seems that indeed these days, "love is in the air," everywhere we look around. However, is this the love that people have dreamt about? Is it possible that the air is a bit polluted?

Thaler and Sunstein (2009) discuss the drive for incessant options arguing that there is a significant problem with the notion—popular in economics and ordinary life—that you can never be made worse off by having more choices because you can always turn some of them down. This principle, they argue, fails to take into account self-control, temptation, and the conflict between short-term desires and long-term welfare. Thaler and Sunstein criticize the wish to have more mainly because it tends to privilege many superficial, short-term desires and ignore our fewer, profound long-terms needs. Similarly, Barry Schwartz (2004) points out that maximizers' unending desire for more leads to general dissatisfaction and reduces their sense of well-being.

Oftentimes, it is, in fact, not good to have more or to be searching for more. And so, we hear: "More is less," "Less is more," "Too much of a good thing," and "Too many are not enough." In the romantic realm, these expressions refer to the current abundance of romantic options, which put people in an ongoing process of choosing, thereby hindering their ability to establish profound long-term love. Such circumstances often lead to frustration, sadness, and feelings of loneliness. The idea "Less is more" has a similar meaning. In focusing on fewer romantic partners, you can achieve greater profundity and meaningfulness. In this sense, less romantic quantity—that is, fewer romantic partners—is often associated with greater quality and romantic profundity. The expression "Too many are not enough" also refers to an imbalance preventing us from settling on what we have (Ben-Ze'ev, 2019, 152–154).

It is worthwhile to remember that terms like "more" and "less", and "too much" and "too little", are domain- and context-dependent. Aristotle believed that the most important aspect of an activity is not its quantity, but whether it is appropriate—that is, how suitable it is in the given circumstances. Finding the appropriate flexibility balance here is the key to romantic flourishing.

We can think of flexibility, which is the quality of bending without breaking, as the ability to make changes in a situation that is changing. Stability is very valuable in romantic relations, and in particular for achieving profundity in these relations. Interestingly, in our diverse and dynamic culture, it is through flexibility that our enduring romantic relationships remain stable. To understand this point, let us first consider the value of psychological flexibility in general health.

Kashdan and Rottenberg (2010) discuss the importance of psychological flexibility (and stability) for health. This flexibility spans a wide range of human abilities, such as adapting to situational demands, shifting behavioral priorities when needed, maintaining balance among important life areas, and being open and committed to behaviors that fit with deeply held values. These abilities capture the dynamic, fluctuating, and context-specific behaviors of people navigating the challenges of daily life. Rigidity, which indicates a lack of sensitivity to one's context, often points to psychopathology. Kashdan and Rottenberg (2010) claim that healthy people can manage themselves in the uncertain, unpredictable world around them, where novelty and change are the norm rather than the exception. With psychological flexibility, we can find ways to shape our automatic processes in better directions. In light of the more diverse nature of cyberspace, being able to add online interactions to our cultural repertoire may enhance people's health, if they do not neglect major offline interactions.

Psychological flexibility, which is essential to a flourishing life, is also crucial in the romantic realm. This is largely so because romantic flourishing presupposes general flourishing. And romantic flexibility echoes psychological flexibility:

adapting to situational demands, shifting priorities, and maintaining a balance between life, love, and sexual needs. Regarding romantic stability as well, flexibility, which involves bending some rigid rules, can prevent romantic relationships from breaking.

It is easier to draw clear romantic (and other) boundaries than to keep them. Although normative boundaries are supposed to guide our behavior, reality is rather complicated. In this regard, the distinction between guiding and specific rules is relevant. Guiding principles provide general directions, such as "Drive safely," rather than specific rules, like "Don't exceed 100 miles per hour." What constitutes safe driving can vary considerably, depending on different factors, such as driver competence and road conditions (Averill, Catlin, & Chon, 1990, 34). Similarly, what constitutes romantic flourishing varies considerably, depending on personal and contextual features. People use specific rules to help them cope with their chaotic romantic culture, but there is no golden rule to tell us what constitutes a flourishing, lasting romantic relationship.

Our romantic life is made more complicated by the many alternatives available to us. These alternatives concern not merely finding a new partner, but also reunion with a former one. This widespread state, which prevails more among young adults, can be described as "not together, but not completely broken up"; it reflects the presence of dynamic trajectories involving "a heterogeneous and multidirectional array of transitions" (Binstock & Thornton, 2003). Since ex-lovers have a privileged place in our heart, and as it has become simpler to find them, their contribution to the flexible nature of our romantic culture is significant.

Extreme romantic flexibility, in which we try every such alternative, is contrary to the values relating to who we are. However, extreme rigidity is likely to break us. Bending, which is a kind of compromise, is the flexibility that enables what is less than ideal to be maintained and enhanced for a long time. People who refuse to compromise their ideals often end up abandoning them. It is indeed better to bend than to break. But too much bending can break us as well (Ben-Ze'ev, 2019, 235–236).

Increasing flexibility will probably modify present social and cultural forms such as marriage and cohabitation, as well as current romantic practices relating to courtship, casual sex, committed romantic relationships, and romantic exclusivity. Catherine Hakim (2012) argues that as the Pill made premarital sex among young people much easier, the internet facilitates playfairs among older married people. Recent history teaches us that we can expect a further relaxation of social and moral norms. In light of the complex, diverse, and flexible nature of online relations, cyberspace has been a crucial factor in the relaxation of our norms.

5.2.2 Profundity and Superficiality

Something that is profound extends far below the surface and has a lasting effect. Profound emotional experiences have a lingering impact on our life and personality.

Profound activities, however, are not necessarily pleasant activities. Some writers and artists experience great agony in the process of creating their works. In such cases, profundity typically involves deep, meaningful satisfaction in overcoming difficulties while using one's most distinctive capacities.

In the romantic realm, we can distinguish between profound and superficial phenomena by paying attention to *romantic intensity,* on the one hand, and *romantic profundity,* on the other. Romantic intensity is a snapshot of a momentary peak of passionate, often sexual, desire. Romantic profundity goes beyond mere romantic intensity and refers to the lover's broader and more enduring attitude. External change is highly significant in generating romantic intensity; in romantic depth, familiarity, stability, and development are tremendously important. While romantic novelty is useful in preventing boredom, romantic familiarity is valuable in promoting flourishing (Ben-Ze'ev & Krebs, 2018).

The dynamic nature of cyberspace often upsets the delicate balance between change and stability in our lives, particularly in the romantic domain, as it significantly increases the role of change. Offline boundaries that delineate, for instance, place, time, social and moral behavior, are of less weight in cyberspace, and people often feel freer to do in cyberspace deeds that they would not do in offline reality. Cyberspace has a less unitary, stable structure. To be in cyberspace is to be in a perpetual state of searching, an endless chase that rarely settles into stability. Hence, online events often lack a stable narrative, with an expected beginning and ending. Such never-ending events, which are analogous to unfinished business, increase uncertainty and frustration, and hence, emotional intensity (Almog, 2002; Ben-Ze'ev, 2004, 223–227). As I argue below, despite the diverse and flexible nature of our cyber culture, many couples still enjoy a stable, enduring relationship. Nevertheless, it remains much easier these days to find love than to develop it over an extended period of time.

The technology associated with online relationships, and in particular the various mobile applications, make it easier, more convenient, and safer to increase flexibility and reduce exclusivity. The romantic environment in cyberspace perfectly aligns with our accelerated society, while making this society even more sexually efficient. Many people are too busy nowadays even to make superficial sexual contacts on a face-to-face basis. They let their mobile applications do the work. Modern technology continues to improve the methods available for both initiating and maintaining offline (as well as online) sexual and romantic relations (Ben-Ze'ev, 2019, 183–185).

In addition to the many websites offering potential partners, various mobile applications ease the initiation of a relationship. The popular application "Tinder" makes the selection process simple (selection is based mainly on external appearance) and easy (one sweeps the smartphone screen to the right to say "like" or to the left to say "pass"). Motivations for using this application vary; users are looking not merely for casual sex, but also for love, communication, validation of their self-worth, thrills or excitement, and to be trendy. Hence, "Tinder should not be seen as merely a fun, hookup app without any strings attached," but also as a new way "to initiate committed romantic relationships" (Sumter, Vandenbosch, & Ligtenberg,

2017). It seems that online dating sites are excellent tools for locating possible romantic candidates, but much less useful in establishing long-term profound love (Finkel, Eastwick, Karney, Reis, & Sprecher, 2012).

Falling in love in cyberspace is akin to love at first sight: we do not have all the required information and we fill in the gaps with idealized assumptions. As in love at first sight, the chat skips, in a sense, the usual process of information processing, and is directly "injected" into the brain evaluative centers. Thus, we can speak about "love at first chat." For example, one might detect in the first chat a sense of humor and wittiness, and instantly fall in love with the sender.

Our accelerated cyber culture is addicted to external change. Investing time in profound endeavors, including romantic relations, is not our first—or even second or third—choice of activity. Yet romantic depth requires serious time investment. Over the past few decades, spouses have spent less and less time together, with work taking more and more of the clock share. And stress, information overload, and multitasking have made the moments that spouses do spend with one another feel less good (Finkel, Hui, Carswell, & Larson, 2014).

Fast change is the hallmark of our throwaway and restless culture, which is based on overconsumption and excessive production of short-lived or disposable items. We are addicted to rapid novelty that takes place in constant flux (Bauman, 2003; Rosa, 2013). For many people, remaining in one place feels like treading water. There is no rest for lovers, and not because the road of love on which they are traveling is not good; it might be a bit boring, but it is still a valuable road— probably one of the best in the history of humanity. Yet the novel road not taken is seen to be more attractive, and there appear to be many roads from which to choose. Chasing after a short-term fantasy is often the problem, not the solution. Fantasies about what is or might be "out there" often prove to be a poor substitute for what we already have. It does not take too much to become enslaved by our own fantasies about the possible (Ben-Ze'ev, 2019).

The ease of establishing online relationships and the reduced investment that they require may make some of them superficial, alongside the superficial nature of our culture that emphasizes the value of immediate satisfaction. However, online relationships can also be used to establish romantic profundity. Both the internet and mobile applications provide an enjoyable and efficient means by which various people get to know each other intimately without the distractions of external factors, such as appearance, age, geographical distance, race, nationality, religion, or marital status. As indicated above, this is likely to increase the number of international, intercultural, and interreligious marriages, ultimately modifying global social norms—in the main, making them more flexible and often more superficial (Ortega & Hergovich, 2018). We can expect that as technology develops, the norms of romantic relationships will also morph to include cyberspace as a realm in which viable romantic love can be achieved. Online social networks have increased the number of people we are in touch with, but they cannot sustain the profundity of a traditional friendship.

Alongside greater romantic diversity and flexibility, there has been another, somewhat surprising, development in romantic relationships: the increasing presence of romantic profundity. No doubt about it—tempestuous romantic experiences are certainly valuable. However, our high-paced culture floods us with superficial excitement. Slow, profound, or older people often fall victim to this rapid pace; fast and superficial people have the edge. Social networks make connection between people faster and less profound, decreasing romantic profundity and increasing loneliness, which stems not from a lack of social connections, but from a lack of meaningful, profound connections. As we live longer and our society offers ever more superficial experiences, romantic profundity has taken on even greater value. These days, it is not more brief, exciting experiences that we need for a happiness upgrade, but rather the ability to establish and enhance long-term robust romantic relationships (Ben-Ze'ev, 2019).

5.2.3 Romantic Complexity

Are our romantic lives now more or less complex? The answer is not straightforward. On the one hand, the greater diversity and flexibility promoted by cyberspace make our romantic life more complex; on the other, the greater superficiality that is promoted by cyberspace takes the romantic life to be simpler.

In this regard, we can discuss two senses of romantic complexity: (a) holistic complexity, as when love is directed at the beloved as a complex, whole person; and (b) type complexity, as when one person's love is directed at various individuals. The first form of complexity, which is highly praised, underlies long-term profound love. The second form of complexity is more disputable. Polyamorous lovers practice it and maintain that such complexity does not damage, and can even enhance, the intensity and depth of their love overall.

Profound romantic love involves a comprehensive attitude that takes cognizance of the rich and complex nature of the beloved (Ortega y Gasset, 1941, 43, 76–77). The lover's comprehensive attitude is complex in its profundity, that is, it does not focus on simple narrow aspects of the beloved, but considers the beloved as a whole multifaceted being. Sexual desire is less comprehensive in this sense, as it typically focuses on the animate nature of a person's body in the here-and-now, rather than their wider character and history. In romantic love we see both the forest and the trees, whereas in sexual desire we focus upon one or several trees. The limited nature of sexual desire is manifested in the notion of a "one-night stand." One-night stands, although often meaningful and exciting, are inherently simple and limited (Ben-Ze'ev & Brunning, 2018; Förster, Epstude, & Özelsel, 2009).

Prime examples in our culture of complexity that involves dealing with many different romantic experiences are consensual non-monogamous relations such as open marriage and polyamory. The complexity of these relations creates the need for an order of priorities. Such a hierarchy is obvious in open sexual relationships, where a clear difference exists between the primary relation and the secondary one. Polyamory is a more complicated romantic framework, as the involvement of more people in the romantic framework is not limited to sexual activities—which is often the case in open marriages—but involves a comprehensive romantic attitude.

Romantic complexity in polyamory is often dealt with by adopting the primary-secondary model. Primary and secondary relationships differ with respect to time spent together, physical cohabitation, child-rearing, and finances. The secondary relation, which is more novel, often enjoys greater romantic intensity. The primary partner has more rights and obligations than those of the secondary one in these aspects—this is mainly due to the connection of the primary partner to the children. We might say, in this regard, that the primary partner has "more shares in the business". The secondary partner, who can be a primary partner in another relation, has the right to be treated with respect and attentiveness, though when conflicts arise, the primary partner usually has first priority—albeit not an absolute one. Thus, it is possible that over time, the secondary relation evolves into a primary (or co-primary) form, and sometimes the primary-secondary aspect is not present, or at least is unclear. Indeed, there are polyamorous relations lacking a strict hierarchy, thereby involving a more complex romantic framework.

While it is tempting to think that having more loving relations decreases conflicts and frustration in a simple way, polyamory is actually quite complex, requiring much time and effort to achieve the optimal arrangements for all concerned parties.

5.3 The Normative Impact of Cyberspace

The normative aspects of online relationships raise greater interest as such relationships become more popular and their moral implications ever more powerful. Thus, more and more people are seeking divorce on grounds of virtual infidelity: their spouses are having online affairs. The fact that their spouses never met their lovers does not seem to alleviate the experience of emotional and moral injury.

The extensive use of imagination in cyberspace raises interesting moral questions concerning the assumed reality of the imaginative environment and its implications for our actual one. If the imaginative environment were in no sense real to us, it would be of little relevance to moral discussions. Imagination, however, has a powerful impact precisely because it is considered to be in some sense real, and hence may have a harmful impact on our actions. The active role of the participant in an online relationship raises the question of whether electronic correspondence has already left the imaginary realm; if so, online fantasizing could be considered to constitute immoral behavior. Taking a stand on this issue depends on the degree of reality we attribute to such relationships. Although online affairs are similar in some ways to lustful fantasies, people treat such affairs as real, and, in this sense, their moral status becomes problematic (Ben-Ze'ev, 2004, Chap. 9).

Human communities need boundaries: living with others necessitates limiting our desires. However, globalization, in which cyberspace is a central arena of action, is essentially an act of crossing, fracturing, and breaking boundaries. The seductiveness of cyberspace and the effortlessness of becoming involved in online affairs also entail risks: people are easily carried away, and the risk of addiction is high. Like other types of addiction, cyberspace does not merely satisfy needs but creates new, often unfulfillable ones. This can lower the probability of being satisfied with one's romantic lot.

Once people get used to violating boundaries in the virtual space, normative boundaries in real space are likely to be treated with greater flexibility too. This, in turn, can weaken the safeguards against further violation. Indeed, it has been suggested that increasing development of technology may begin to change our existing attitudes both to monogamy and to human–robot relations (Davidson et al., 2018).

The flexible nature of boundaries in cyberspace is not necessarily immoral. On the contrary, adhering to strict boundaries in our romantic life can be immoral if such adherence does not take into account the specific, personal, and circumstantial aspects of the lover. Of course, greater flexibility has its own costs. Take, for example, cybersex, where romantic and sexual boundaries are much more flexible than in offline circumstances. This flexibility has not reduced the number of offline violations of boundaries but rather increased it. With the expanded use of the internet and particularly mobile applications, romantic and sexual cheating has increased. Moreover, even if the sexual cheating is limited to the online arena, partners can feel betrayed and traumatized (Schneider, Weiss, & Samenow, 2012).

As cybersex is often seen as less immoral—since it can be considered merely a process of talking that involves no actual physical encounter—some offline partners will tolerate or even support it (Ben-Ze'ev, 2004, 208–216). Letting your partner know about, and even watch, your sexual activity with another person is significant in the sense that the committed couple knowingly accepts that sexual exclusivity is not an absolute category that should never be violated. Sexual exclusivity is thus seen as a continuum, and, in some circumstances, certain points along that continuum can permissibly be violated in sexual relationships. The internet and mobile applications facilitate not merely pleasurable sexual activities, but deep romantic relationships as well. A one-night cyberstand is more available and easier to keep a secret than its non-cyber counterpart. However, cyberspace also offers an outlet for developing alternative emotional ties sometimes without completely ruining the primary offline relationship.

5.4 Conclusions and Recommendations

In our accelerated, cyber culture, more and more people are giving up the lengthy, and often unsuccessful, search for romantic profundity, and are instead settling for occasional, instantaneous sexual intensity. Many others, however, still yearn for romantic profundity—which produces the sweet fruits of romantic serenity and trust. Thus, most people, including the current generation of adolescents, continue to believe in the possibility of long-term love. A survey of young adults (ages 18–29) in the United States revealed that the vast majority holds highly optimistic views about marriage, with 86% expecting to have a marriage that lasts a lifetime (Arnett, 2012). Similarly, Match's eighth annual "Singles in America" study (2018) indicates that 69% of today's singles are seeking a serious romantic relationship (Ben-Ze'ev, 2019, 201–203).

The task of combining romantic intensity with profundity has never been so urgent. As the abundance of romantic opportunities is likely to reduce the number of people living without love, we may yet witness love's comeback.

Cyberspace has a significant impact on offline romantic activities, as it offers increased opportunities, greater self-disclosure, decreased vulnerability, lesser commitment, an increase in boundary violations, and reduced exclusivity. Cyberspace provides technical tools that considerably improve the chances of finding a suitable partner (Schwartz & Velotta, 2018). Cyberspace also facilitates the opportunity to conduct several romantic and sexual relationships at the same time.

Although cyberlove and cybersex are likely to become more popular, they cannot replace offline relationships. Nonetheless, they can complement them. Like the current romantic culture, cyberspace is multifaceted. Optimally, we will see more combinations of offline and online romantic relationships. The increased lure of the internet and mobile applications lower the likelihood that those with access to it will restrict themselves solely to offline relationships. However, since online relationships lack some basic romantic activities, such as touching and actual sex, satisfying offline relationships will continue to be considered an upgraded and more fulfilling relationship.

Learning to integrate cyberspace with actual space in the romantic domain is a major future task for our culture. Indeed, many marriages now begin online. In comparison to marriages that began through traditional offline venues, those that began online were found to be slightly less likely to result in a marital breakup and were associated with slightly higher marital satisfaction among those respondents who remained married. We should pay attention to the fact that the internet may be altering both the dynamics and the outcomes of marriage itself (Cacioppo, Cacioppo, Gonzaga, Ogburn, & VanderWeele, 2013).

Accurate outlooks on our future behavior require that research and practice take into account the above considerations concerning the complexity and flexibility of our evolving cyber culture, as well as the vital distinction between short-term superficial values and long-term profound ones.

A life of mere dreams is dangerous because of its disconnect from reality. Online romantic relationships are beneficial when they complement, rather than replace, offline relationships. Dreams, like cyberspace, are most valuable when they are bounded by reality. Combining offline and online relations is of vital importance for the flourishing of our future culture.

References

Almog, S. (2002). From Sterne and Borges to lost storytellers: Cyberspace, narrative, and law. *Fordham Intellectual Property, Media & Entertainment Law Journal, 13*, 1–34.

Arnett, J. J. (2012, December). *The Clark University poll of emerging adults.* http://www2.clarku.edu/clark-poll-emerging-adults/pdfs/clark-university-poll-emerging-adults-findings.pdf

Averill, J. R., Catlin, G., & Chon, K. K. (1990). *Rules of hope.* New York: Springer.

Bauman, Z. (2003). *Liquid love.* Cambridge: Polity Press.

Benski, T., & Fisher, E. (Eds.). (2014). *Internet and emotions.* New York: Routledge.

Ben-Ze'ev, A. (2019). *The arc of love: How our romantic lives change over time.* Chicago, IL: University of Chicago Press.

Ben-Ze'ev, A., & Brunning, L. (2018). How complex is your love? The case of romantic compromises and polyamory. *Journal for the Theory of Social Behaviour, 48*, 98–116.

Ben-Ze'ev, A., & Krebs, A. (2018). Love and time. In C. Grau & A. Smuts (Eds.), *The Oxford handbook of philosophy of love.* Oxford: Oxford University Press.

Ben-Ze'ev, A. (2004). *Love online.* Cambridge: Cambridge University Press.

Ben-Ze'ev, A., & Goussinsky, R. (2008). *In the name of love: Romantic ideology and its victims.* Oxford: Oxford University Press.

Bergen, K. M. (2006). *Women's narratives about commuter marriage.* Unpublished doctoral dissertation. University of Nebraska-Lincoln.

Best, K., & Delmege, S. (2012). The filtered encounter: Online dating and the problem of filtering through excessive information. *Social Semiotics, 22*, 237–258.

Binstock, G., & Thornton, A. (2003). Separations, reconciliations, and living apart in cohabiting and marital unions. *Journal of Marriage and Family, 65*, 432–443.

Bruch, E. E., & Newman, M. E. J. (2018). Aspirational pursuit of mates in online dating markets. *Science Advances, 4*(8), eaap9815.

Bruch, E. E., & Newman, M. E. J. (2019). Structure of online dating markets in US cities. *Sociological Science, 6*, 219–234.

Cacioppo, J. T., Cacioppo, S., Gonzaga, G. C., Ogburn, E. L., & VanderWeele, T. J. (2013). Marital satisfaction and break-ups differ across on-line and off-line meeting venues. *Proceedings of the Academy of Sciences, 110*, 1–6.

Davidson, B., Joinson, A., & Jones, S. (2018). Technologically enhanced dating: Augmented human relationships, robots, and fantasy. In Z. Papcharissi (Ed.), *A networked self and love* (pp. 129–155). New York: Routledge.

Döring, N. (2002). Studying online love and cyber romance. In B. Batinic, U.-D. Reips, & M. Bosnjak (Eds.), *Online Social Sciences* (pp. 333–356).

Finkel, E. J., Eastwick, P. W., Karney, B. R., Reis, H. T., & Sprecher, S. (2012). Online dating: A critical analysis from the perspective of psychological science. *Psychology Science in the Public Interest, 13*, 3–66.

Finkel, E. J., Hui, C. M., Carswell, K. L., & Larson, G. M. (2014). The suffocation of marriage: Climbing mount Maslow without enough oxygen. *Psychological Inquiry, 25*, 1–41.

Förster, J., Epstude, K., & Özelsel, A. (2009). Why love has wings and sex has not: How reminders of love and sex influence creative and analytic thinking. *Personality and Social Psychology Bulletin, 35*, 1479–1491.

Gilbert, D. (2007). *Stumbling on happiness.* New York: Vintage.

Hakim, C. (2012). *The new rules.* London: Gibson Square.

Jiang, L. C., & Hancock, J. T. (2013). Absence makes the communication grow fonder: Geographic separation, interpersonal media, and intimacy in dating relationships. *Journal of Communication, 63*, 556–577.

Kashdan, T. B., & Rottenberg, J. (2010). Psychological flexibility as a fundamental aspect of health. *Clinical Psychology Review, 30*, 865–878.

Katz, J. E., & Rice, R. E. (2002). Syntopia: Access, civic involvement, and social interaction on the net. In B. Wellman & C. Haythornthwaite (Eds.), *The internet in everyday life* (pp. 114–138). Malden: Blackwell.

Kelmer, G., Rhoades, G. K., Stanley, S. M., & Markman, H. J. (2013). Relationship quality, commitment, and stability in long-distance relationships. *Family Process, 52*, 257–270.

Ortega, J., & Hergovich, P. (2018). The strength of absent ties: Social integration via online dating. *arXiv preprint arXiv*.1709.10478.

Ortega y Gasset, J. (1941). *On love* (p. 1967). London: Jonathan Cape.

Quoidbach, J., Gruber, J., Mikolajczak, M., Kogan, A., Kotsou, I., & Norton, M. I. (2014). Emodiversity and the emotional ecosystem. *Journal of Experimental Psychology: General, 143*, 2057–2066.

Rosa, H. (2013). *Social acceleration*. New York: Columbia University Press.

Rosenfeld, M. J., & Thomas, R. J. (2012). Searching for a mate: The rise of the internet as a social intermediary. *American Sociological Review, 77*, 523–547.

Rosenfeld, M. J., Thomas, R. J., & Hausen, S. (2019). Disintermediating your friends: How online dating in the United States displaces other ways of meeting. *Proceedings of the National Academy of Sciences, 116*, 17753–17758.

Schneider, J. P., Weiss, R., & Samenow, C. (2012). Is it really cheating? Understanding the emotional reactions and clinical treatment of spouses and partners affected by cybersex infidelity. *Sexual Addiction & Compulsivity, 19*, 123–139.

Schwartz, B. (2004). *The paradox of choice*. New York: HarperCollins.

Schwartz, P., & Velotta, N. (2018). Online dating: Changing intimacy one swipe at a time? In J. Van Hook, S. M. McHale, & V. King (Eds.), *Families and technology* (pp. 57–88). Heidelberg: Springer.

Slater, D. (2002). Social relationships and identity online and offline. In L. A. Lievrouw & S. Livingstone (Eds.), *Handbook of new media: Social shaping and consequences of ICTs* (pp. 533–546). London: Sage.

Stafford, L. (2005). *Maintaining long-distance and cross-residential relationships*. Mahwah, NJ: Lawrence Erlbaum.

Sumter, S. R., Vandenbosch, L., & Ligtenberg, L. (2017). Love me Tinder: Untangling emerging adults' motivations for using the dating application Tinder. *Telematics and Informatics, 34*, 67–78.

Taylor, S. E. (1989). *Positive illusions: Creative self-deception and the healthy mind*. New York: Basic Books.

Thaler, R. H., & Sunstein, C. R. (2009). *Nudge*. London: Penguin Books.

Aaron Ben-Ze'ev is Professor of Philosophy at the University of Haifa, where he has served as Rector (2000–2004) and President (2004–2012). He is considered one of the world's leading experts in the study of emotions. Major books: The Subtlety of Emotions (MIT, 2000), Love Online (Cambridge, 2004), In The Name of Love (Oxford, 2008); The Arc of Love (Chicago, 2019).

Chapter 6
Climbing, and Falling Off, Plato's Ladder of Love: The Emotions of Love and of Love's Undoing

Warren Tenhouten

> [P]assions are susceptible of an entire union; and like colours, may be blended so perfectlytogether, that each of them may lose itself andcontribute only to vary that uniform impressionwhich arises from the whole. Some of the mostcurious phenomena of the human mind arederiv'd from this property of the passions.
> David Hume ([1739] 1978, 366)

Abstract Love is a state of mind, a social relationship, and a potent emotion. Love is examined as the emotion of two cross-cultural problems of life, temporality and social identity, the bases of communally-shared and equality-matched social-relations. It is proposed that there exist a set of primary emotions which combine in pairs to form secondary emotions. Love is defined as a mixture of joy–happiness and acceptance, the prototypical positively-valenced adaptive reactions to temporality and identity. As an individual loses a love relationship, the primary emotional foundations of love, joy–happiness and acceptance, can turn into their opposites, disgust–rejection and sadness, respectively. Potentially emerging from these four primary emotions are five secondary emotions that contain disgust and/or sadness. These secondary-level emotions are defined as ambivalence (acceptance & disgust–rejection), bittersweetness (joy–happiness & sadness), derisiveness (joy–happiness & disgust–rejection), resignation (acceptance & sadness/loss), and loneliness (sadness & disgust–rejection). These are hypothesized to be the key emotions of troubled intimacy, and are described as they occur during the process of the breakdown and dissolution of love-based social relationships.

Keywords Love · Emotion · Acceptance · Joy · Happiness · Derisiveness · Resignation · Loneliness

---

W. Tenhouten (✉)
Department of Sociology, University of California at Los Angeles, Los Angeles, CA, USA
e-mail: wtenhout@ucla.edu

6.1 Love as an Emotion

Love has been defined and described in innumerable ways. This chapter examines love as an emotion. It is proposed that love is not a basic emotion, like anger, fear, and joy, but instead is a mixture of two basic emotions. This account assumes that primary emotions exist, and requires their identification, so we begin with the contested notion of basic, or primary, emotions. Among emotions researchers, the preponderance of social constructivists and psychological constructivists do not accept the notion of basic emotions, and see all emotions as existing *sui generis*, as no more than social constructions emerging in languages, cultures, and societies. This position, taken to its limit, asserts that emotions are not natural kinds, and are therefore not proper objects for scientific investigating.

It is proposed, however, that there exists a set of basic, or primary, emotions, which can be combined in pairs to form secondary emotions (Plutchik, [1962] 1991, pp. 117–118) and in triples to form tertiary-level emotions (TenHouten, 2007, pp. 200–240; 2013, pp. 19–22). If this contention, that emotions mix together and form a hierarchical classification, is valid, it follows that, if love is not a primary emotion, then it must be a secondary or tertiary emotion. Thus, a classificatory definition of love requires prior identification of the primary emotions. Many theorists have attempted to do this, beginning with Plato (380 BCE), who proposed that fear, hope, joy, and sorrow are the most basic of the emotions. There can only be one correct solution to this problem, and it either has or has not been solved. This identification problem, this author asserts (TenHouten, 2007, 15; 2013, 15; 2017b), was solved, over half a century ago, by Robert Plutchik (1958, 1962).

Robert Plutchik (1958, 1962, 1980, 1983) presented a psychoevolutionary model of primary emotions, which claimed that for nearly all animal species, there are four fundamental problems of life—identity, temporality, hierarchy, and territoriality. These correspond to the four kinds of social communicative displays that MacLean (1990) in his ethogram found common to reptiles, primates, and humans—signature, courtship, challenge (and submission), and territorial. The author's Affect-spectrum theory (TenHouten, 1996, 2007, 2013, 2017a, 2017b) holds that these existential-problems/communicative-displays have evolved into four elementary social relationships: communal-sharing, equality-matching (egalitarian or equity-based relations), hierarchical-ranking, and market-pricing (socioeconomic exchanging). For each of these life problems, there can be an opportunity, or a potential misfortune or danger, so that each of these four dimensions can be associated with a negative or positive adaptive reaction. These reactions, Plutchik claimed, comprise *the* eight primary emotions: These subjective-experiences are: for identity, acceptance and disgust–rejection; for temporality, joy–happiness and sadness; for hierarchy, anger and fear; and for territoriality, anticipation and surprise. Plutchik's model, including his 'wheel' or circumplex, where distance between emotions indicates dissimilarity, is shown as Fig. 6.1.

Plutchik ([1962] 1991, pp. 117–118), with limited success, offered definitions of 23 of the 28 possible secondary emotions. A substantial revision of this classification is presented elsewhere (TenHouten, 2017b). While medieval and early modern

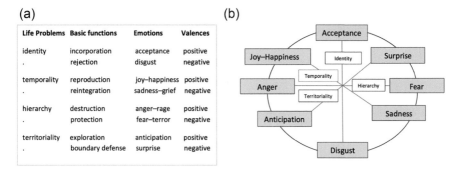

6.1 (**a**) Plutchik's model of the primary emotions. (**b**) Plutchik's circumplex or 'wheel' of the eight primary emotions

classifications of primary emotions often included love (St. Thomas Aquinas, 1265–1274; Descartes, 1647; Malebranche, 1674–1675; Locke, 1689; Hume, 1739), since the 1950s love has seldom been considered to be a primary emotion (with the notable exception of Shaver, Morgan, & Wu, 1996).

Plutchik ([1962] 1991, p. 117) defined love as a secondary emotion: "joy + acceptance = love, friendliness." This definition, which has been ignored by emotions researchers, and which was neither discussed nor followed up by Plutchik, is insightful, but problematic. First of all, "friendliness" is better seen as a personality trait, and as a pattern of behavior, rather than as an emotion. And second, "joy" can be expanded to include happiness. With these two modifications, a revised definition is obtained:

$$Love = joy\text{--}happiness\ \&\ acceptance.$$

While at first glance this equation might seem to be an oversimplification, it hardly reduces the meaning of love; it rather expands, and even ennobles, love's meaning, for we can now see love for what it most fundamentally is: the joyful acceptance of another person, together, if requited, with the joy of being accepted by this other. These two hypothesized constituent primary emotions of love are next briefly described.

6.1.1 Joy and Happiness

While joy is a foreground acute emotion concentrated in an intense moment, happiness is a background baseline feeling (Ben-Ze'ev, 2000, 450) (see Ben-Ze'ev's chapter in this book). From a psychological standpoint, those individuals who have a propensity to feel happy can be said to *be* happy. Of course, happiness can be felt by those who, on balance, are not happy persons (Haybron, 2008; Brogaard, 2015,

223). A warm, loving social relationship can provide moments of great joy, an inner joyfulness, and sustained happiness. Happiness, the most general positive emotional sentiment, derives from a favorable evaluation of significant aspects of life, or of one's overall situation (Averill & More, 2000). Happiness is a state of "feeling good—enjoying life and wanting the feeling to be maintained"; unhappiness, "feeling bad and wishing things were different" (Layard, 2005, 12). Joy and happiness need not have an object, and they are not necessarily linked to any particular course of action or social encounter. They can be considered aspects of the same basic or primary emotion.

Human beings are naturally predisposed to form close social bonds. This tendency doubtless has an evolutionary basis, for it has survival and reproductive benefits (Axelrod & Hamilton, 1981). Individuals living communally can share food, find mates, and contribute to their offspring's care. Adults able to form close attachments are most apt to reproduce, and long-term committed relationships increase the chances that offspring will reproduce in turn. A long and successful life is most likely for those who find membership in a group of familiar, cooperative individuals displaying and providing mutual care, nurturing, and support. Thus, evolutionary pressures have led humans to develop internal mechanisms guiding enduring social group membership, reflecting a basic need for social involvement and belonging to groups and collectivities.

Plutchik (1983) saw the problem of sexual reproduction (together with 'reintegration' following loss or death of a community member) as the positive and negative poles of his 'temporality' dimension. In humans, these two existential problems have been addressed by the emergence of the social institutions of the family, marriage and kinship rules, the clan, fictive kinship bonds created through neighborly social relationships, the community, and most generally the emergence of communally-shared, solidifying social bonds and social relationships (Axelrod & Hamilton, 1981; Fiske, 1991, pp. 258–285; Baumeister & Leary, 1995).

Positive experiences of communally-shared social relationships, in which close feelings are both received and given, are a generic cause of the experience of joy and happiness. A key to happiness is to have one close relationship and a network of good friends (Argyle, 2001) (see Vanderheiden on Friendship in this book). A supportive, intimate relationship is one of life's greatest joys. Communally-shared social relationships are a cause of joy and happiness, and many studies show that positively-valenced affective experiences increase individuals' perceived attractiveness and solidify social bonds (May & Hamilton, 1980).

A wide range of occasions signifying new relationships, and the formation of new social bonds, are marked by positive emotions and celebrated as joyous (Baumeister & Leary, 1995, 505). Enjoyment resulting from the sharing of hedonic stimuli with others is enhanced when others positively assess the shared stimuli, but diminished when these evaluations are negatively valenced. The positive experiences of communally-shared social relationships contribute to enjoyment and happy social experiences, which in turn contribute to feelings of love (Brogaard, 2015; Shaver & Hazen, 1988). But happiness is not just a matter of receiving supportive interactions, but also of giving. Very happy individuals are those with highly satisfying, close relationships, as they report more positive events and emotions in their daily lives, are satisfied with life, and experience a high level of subjective well-being (Diener & Seligman, 2002).

6.1.2 Acceptance

The experience of love is clearly linked to happiness, so much so that these states have been equated. Berit Brogaard (2015, 223) claims that, "Happiness is love: full stop." But love has a necessary second emotional ingredient, acceptance. While usually existing as a diffuse and global feeling about another or oneself, acceptance can also manifest as an acute emotional experience, a sudden recognition that one wishes to incorporate another person as a social intimate, or that another is making gestures indicating a wish for intimacy with oneself. Interpersonal relationships begin with subtle cues of acceptance, and of invitation, from, or to, potentially significant others, which might include a warm smile, posturing, inviting eye contact, and other forms of subtle gesturing. Such communicative displays and affect-laden conversations lie at the beginning of nearly every close romantic relationship (Rohner & Kaleque, 2005; Khaleque & Ali, 2017).

Child development involves a process of identity-formation through individuation. At the earliest developmental stages, the child incorporates the primary caretaker and the world, and thrives on the parents' displayed responsiveness and need-gratifying behaviors. Given a world perceived as accepting and benevolent, the child gradually experiences itself as a separate, autonomous self, and gradually differentiates itself from the primary caretaker and from the rest of the social world (Lear, 1991). Children who do not experience acceptance in the earliest stages of life can develop the belief that they are somehow bad, unacceptable, or undesirable (Bowlby, 1980; Rohner, 1975; Rohner & Kaleque, 2005). *The likely pathologies that follow include an inability to* develop self-love—the prerequisite for the capability of becoming lovable (Rousseau, [1762] 1979, book iv, 214), incapability for experiencing love of others (Zweig, 1968), the development of rejection sensitivity in close or intimate relationships (Gyurak & Ayduk, 2008), and difficulties in accepting responsibility for, and exerting control over, archaic drives and instincts (Lear, 1991, pp. 195–198).

The experience of acceptance is an inner psychological process, yet it is also intrinsically social-interactional. The incorporative function of acceptance is illustrated by the man in love who tells his lover that she fills his heart. The inclusion of acceptance as a component of love can be understood by noting that, in Plutchik's psychoevolutionary theory, acceptance is the positive emotional adaptive reaction to the existential problem of social identity and to relationships characterized by social equality. The linking of love and identity-as-equality was considered by David Holbrook (1972, 36), who observed that,

> love…is capable of growth by the discovery of the reality of self and the object of our love, of the problems of give-and-take…. It leads towards the capacity to give and meet in relation. It leads toward equality.

Jane Goldberg (1999, 251) asserts, "Unlike the unequal relationship between parent and child, true love between adults is love between equals." And Sheila Sullivan (1999, 281) sees in romantic love an "equality-in-difference" wherein "each recognizes the other as Subject," such that each is "capable of the 'co-feeling' which shares in mutuality without domination." When relationships are not hierarchically ordered, but are rather egalitarian, a commitment to collective goals is facilitated by the emergence of love, which serves to regulate self-interest by creating a spirit of community oriented to common goals, and stimulates the development of trust and loyalty.

While experiencing acceptance of and by a newfound love, it is not unusual for the smitten individual to project this spirit of acceptance onto the individual(s) he or she has 'left behind'. As observed by G. H. Mead ([1934] 1962, 31), the past is just as open to conceptual reconstruction as is the future. Thus, individuals who have 'fallen' in love are able to reconstruct their life narrative, seeing all that has happened before as preparation for the fateful moment of realization that they are in love. The past is neither denied nor hidden, but is treated as a mythic prehistory, for true history can now, at last, begin. At this juncture, a choice must be made, either to

> reorient…life around this new reality or choose to not be bothered because the new way… [has] so many uncertainties and so much uncharted territory (Cowan, 2016, 114).

To choose the path of love, to follow one's heart, involves commitment of the deepest part of one's being, and requires reflecting upon one's essential self through ruminating on past love-based relationships. One result can be that any and all feelings of remorse, resentment, sense of betrayal, and desire for revenge over past relationships can be let loose. What no longer has value cannot be hated, and hard feelings about these relationships gradually come to be recalled with a detached tenderness and understanding. The joyful immersion in a new relationship can contribute to an illusion, that the people 'left behind' will accept this new reality with equanimity, serenity, and peacefulness, which can lead to a jarring confrontation with reality, so that there will be no forgetting, forgiving, or accepting of being rejected (TenHouten, 2007, 55); it is possible that a terrible desire will arise in the mind of an abandoned partner, including a bitter feeling of resentment, a thirst for revenge, and the cultivation of hatred.

6.2 The Nature and Experience of Love

In the everyday world, people in general hardly share an understanding of love. On the contrary, many individuals are deeply unsure if love is fulfillment or escape, good or bad. Thomas Gould (1963, 2) asserted that, "most of us have hornets' nests instead of clear thoughts on the nature of love." It is, he added, "a thing too violent, too important to us, and it goes wrong too easily, for us to be able to achieve an easy understanding of it." William McDougall shared this understanding, as he commented, "In common speech, the word 'love' is used with amazing laxity." He explained that two ambiguities contribute to this conceptual morass. First, "common speech fails to distinguish clearly between the sentiments of love and the various emotional excitements which it calls 'love'." Second, there is a tendency in everyday discourse "to accept as essentially alike whatever things are given the same name," which creates a failure "to recognize the great variety of sentiments all of which may properly be called 'love'" (McDougall ([1923] 1947, 430).

Developing a love relationship is a highly problematic enterprise in part because individuals have no direct way to access the other's mind and to know the other's 'true' feelings. This is a reason why the process of falling in love requires trust. It is risky business, rendering us vulnerable. When one person confessed, "I love you" and the other replies, "I love you, too," is it tempting to infer that meaning has been fully shared. However, conceptualizations of what 'love' means can differ radically from one person to another, for there can be several "styles" of loving or "colors" of love, that can occur in either pure or mixed forms. One party might mean by love "*erôs*," a passionate or romantic love, whereas the other could mean "ludus," love as a game (Lee, 1976).

In order to understand love as it develops in the adult person, it is especially helpful to examine the process of falling in love, an aspect of romantic love which was notably manifested in eleventh- and twelfth-century European courtly life (Singer, 1984). Despite this suggestion that romantic love had such a specific beginning point, and found conceptual elaboration in the social movements of sentimentalism and romanticism (TenHouten, 2019), there is evidence that intense, passionate love is a human universal (Jankowiak & Fischer, 1992) (see Jankowiak's chapters in this book), not specific to Western civilization.

In the process of falling in love, there is an initial, 'magical' process of revelation which unfolds, but following this intense feeling, when one returns to the uninspiring routines of everyday life, to one's amazement the feeling persists, coming repeatedly to mind, creating sense of waiting and a desire fulfilled only when we are again united with the other. If this drive recurs over and over, and impresses itself on us, then we know that what we have experienced is no mere infatuation but rather a radical restructuring of our social world, compelling us to change every other relationship.

The emotions of arousal of erotic love involve joy as opposed to a lower-intensity sentiment of happiness, for this 'moment' involves a speeding up of mental and physiological activities and thereby creates the phenomenological experience of time moving slowly. Erotic love also involves a high level of acceptance, for one is at least temporarily seeing the other as nearly perfect, as flaws are glossed over, distorted, or not perceived at all. One so aroused feels a sense of anticipatory excitement and a neurochemical reaction experienced as a surge of pleasure. One might sweat, feel a tightening of the stomach, and experience an increased heart-rate and heavy breathing, in the midst of being delighted with the smell, touch, and sight of the other. The temporal compression involved in the experience of falling in love is captured, in Japanese culture, by the word *nin*, which refers to the world of peace and daily tranquility, and by the word *ten*, which denotes the extraordinary moment of love. "Thus, *nin* is already joy, and a day of *nin* corresponds to a year in a world without tranquility. But a day of *ten* corresponds to a thousand or ten thousand years of time" (Alberoni, 1983, p. 15). This immersion in love creates the mental experience of an eternalization of the present. All love involves happiness and acceptance, but in the process of falling in love the happiness is elevated to an *intense* joyfulness and one experiences a *total* acceptance of the other. Thus, the pure object of *erôs* appears in an instant, the instant universally described as a revelation, as a 'falling'. But falling in love is in reality not, as it is sometimes portrayed and misremembered, instantaneous, taking place 'at first sight'. The process of falling in love can indeed *begin* in such a temporally compressed moment of *nine* or *ten*, but it is also a sociorelational process taking some time to unfold, for it is no less than the creation of a new community, of a social movement built for two (Alberoni, 1983). This whole process is fascinating, and as Lionel Tiger (1999, p. 616) wryly observes, "lovers are engaged in nature's core construction work and spectators enjoy the show."

6.3 Ascending the Ladder of Love

In Plato's ([c. 385 BCE] 1989, p. 210a–b) *Symposium*, the 'ladder of love' is first approached by falling in love with the bodily beauty of another individual. In the unreformed love at the base of the ladder, *erôs* was seen as "a longing for the possibility of something...valuable and urgently needed" (Plato [c. 385 BCE] 1989, 483; see also Gould, 1963, Chap. 3, and Nussbaum, 1986, Chap. 6). Here we find a desire for sexual involvement with, and control of, an object viewed as physically beautiful in the hope that one's needy, insecure, and incomplete condition of self could be healed, or at least ameliorated. Feeling incomplete, the unreformed hope is to find their 'other half' in a love that would magically render them whole, secure, and complete. The next rung of the ladder is secured by realization that all bodies possess beauty, which diffuses one's passion and reduces its importance. As one ascends the ladder, love is still a desire for possession of an object, of an 'other half', but one also comes to seek the good so that one can flourish (Nussbaum, 2001, 487). Good resides in the other, although the other possesses qualities and features which are not part of that good. Yet another rung is reached by a realization that bodily beauty is eclipsed by the beauty of the other's soul, so that even a relatively unlovely body can house a spiritual loveliness and a noble nature, a perception which motivates contemplation of the beauty of laws and institutions. The next step requires a shift of attention from institutions to science, philosophy, and all other forms of knowledge, so that one is no longer thinking of a beautiful body but the beauty of lofty thought. Ascent to the highest rung is reached by apprehension of the very soul of beauty itself, the sanctuary of love and of the virtuous, reasoning mind.

Thus, love can release creative passions. The cure for the vulnerability which comes with passion is the development of a passion for understanding. This ideal, articulated by the priestess Diotima and summarized by Socrates in Plato's *Symposium*, had profound influence on Roman thought and Christian theology. The 'ladder' served as a metaphor for the lover's ascent from physical attraction to contemplation of beauty and the attainment of wisdom.

Thus, to reach a high position on the ladder of love, one must: (i) be able to distinguish between the whole person and the good within the person; (ii) recognize that this good is akin to other goods people pursue in their many projects and activities; and (iii) understand that the ultimate good in this love is to create good by one's own efforts. The creative desire of such love is beyond carnal desire, for it must also possess spiritual and intellectual depth. If these three criteria are satisfied, the result can be an appreciation of the fineness of the other's love and appreciation of his or her admirable character. And once it is clear that one's love is but one object in a vast sea of the fine, it is to the pursuit of the fine to which one can be dedicated. Of course, this consciousness of the other can also lead to the knowledge that the particular properties of one's love are not unique, and that comparable fineness might be found in any number of other potential partners. This enables one to approach the world with an evenhanded joy, incorporating knowledge in the quest for philosophical wisdom, the foundation of good laws, institutions, and cultural forms.

While some would simply bemoan the fact that passion over time fades, and that a 'honeymoon period' cannot last forever, a more enlightened view holds that attaining the higher rungs of the ladder is better from a social and moral perspective. It must be kept in mind, as Nussbaum (2001, 473) insists, that "love, while an emotion, is also a relationship." While love in its earliest, erotic, stage is linked to possession and control of the love object, as the ladder of love is ascended the focus gradually changes from one of possessiveness to companionship, commitment, and efforts to carry out actions beneficial to the object of love. There is no such thing as loving another because one has no choice. On the contrary, for love there must be a choice, for to love requires freely chosen actions, of "being with you, fighting for you, protecting you, [and] caring for you" (Cowan, 2016, 116). Engagement in a love relationship thus requires actively thinking about, and behaviorally accepting responsibility for, the welfare and best interests of the other (Lear, 1991, pp. 177–182).

6.4 Falling Off the Ladder: Emotions of Failing Love

As a love relationship begins to be devalued by one or both participants, the primary emotional foundations of love, joy–happiness and acceptance, are weakened substantially and can begin to turn into their opposites, resulting in emotions which can characterize the process by which a love relationship comes to be damaged and eventually destroyed. These emotions consist of the primary emotions that are the prototypical adaptive reactions to negative experiences of temporality and social identity, sadness and disgust–rejection, respectively. As a love relationship deteriorates, its component of joy–happiness comes to mix with sadness, creating a *bittersweet feeling*, and its acceptance–incorporation component mixes with feelings of disgust–rejection, resulting in a feeling of *ambivalence*. Feelings of bittersweetness and of ambivalence will occur even in the best of love relationships, but increases of frequency and intensity of these two emotions can also manifest as signs of trouble.

There are three additional secondary emotions which can signal the impending breakdown of a love relationship. First, as a love relationship deteriorates, it is not unusual for one party to treat the other with derision, which we can define as a secondary emotion, *derisiveness = joy–happiness & disgust–rejection*. Second, the party most committed to a love relationship, who is experiencing being 'left behind', will, however reluctantly, have to accept losing his or her other, which requires as an adaptive reaction the emotion of resignation, which can be defined as *resignation = acceptance & sadness*. And third, when the relationship is at an end, one or both parties are apt to be left alone, experiencing the pangs of being rejected, thrown away as an object of disgust, which is expressed in the secondary emotion of *loneliness = sadness & rejection–disgust*. We next further describe these emotions of troubled or failing love (see also Mullen in this book).

6.4.1 Disgust, Rejection

Darwin (1872, 253) was keenly interested in the emotion, disgust, which he defined as

> something revolting, primarily in relation to the sense of taste, as actually perceived or vividly imagined; and secondarily to anything which causes a similar feeling, through the sense of smell, touch and even eyesight.

One meaning of the English word, disgust, is 'bad taste'. Just as acceptance, on the functional level, is an emotional reaction of incorporation, disgust is "recruited to defend the self against psychic incorporation or any increase in intimacy with a repellent object" (Tomkins, 1963, 223). Consistent with this, Plutchik (1958, [1962] 1991, pp. 96–99) saw the basic function of disgust as rejection. Disgust as an emotional reaction commonly experienced by the perception of the close other's non-acceptable, norm-violating behavior, which can involve deceit, betrayal, or other perceived transgressions.

6.4.2 Sadness

All higher primates, including humans, are group-living creatures whose survival and well-being depend upon social relationships. When relationships fail, it becomes necessary to restructure one's community position. In the case of intimate, dyadic relationships, this can lead to an acute sense of sadness. In the classical romantic view of love, unhappiness was an essential component of love, which was often portrayed in artistic productions as a tragedy leading to the complete loss of one's love and of oneself. While joy–happiness is the positive emotional reaction to rewarding relationships, the corresponding negative emotion is sadness. Sadness is a natural, healthy reaction to a failed relationship, or to the loss or the death of a valued other (Plutchik, [1962] 1991, pp. 91–95; Bowlby, 1980; Sbarra, 2006). Loss of an object of attachment means loss of a source of joy, excitement, affection, security, and a reduced sense of well-being. If sadness is intense, the active struggle to cope is best described as *grief*, which can take the form of intense emotions compressed in time, or of a long-lasting sentiment (Lazarus, 1999, 656). The loss of a loved partner typically creates the highest level of sadness. Other triggers of sadness include loss of some aspect of self-attractiveness, vigor, sensory or motor capacity, intellectual power and memory, money and treasure, or even loss of one's homeland. There can be symbolic losses as well, such as a loss of honor, pride, self-esteem, and face (where sadness mixes with fear to form shame (TenHouten, 2017c)).

6.4.3 Bittersweetness

The emotion of bittersweetness has long been associated with love. As the Roman poet Ovid put it, "Grief twines with joy; bitter is mix't with sweet" (in his *Metamorphoses*, as cited by Burton, 1927, 493). And Burton ([1621] 1971, III, 2, iii, cited in Sullivan, 1999, 284) in turn opined that, "for the most part love is a plague, a torture, a hell, a bitter sweet passion." On numerous occasions in the everyday world, the opposite primary emotions, joy–happiness and sadness, occur together. These two emotions of temporality are oppositely valenced and also differ in their motor intensity. The expression of joy–happiness reveals a hypertonicity, whereas sadness, especially at the level of grief, is characterized by muscular hypotonicity (Dumas, 1905). An acceptable name for the combination of these two primary emotions can be derived from a metaphor of taste, as the emotion that comprises the combination of joy and sadness can be called "bittersweetness" (TenHouten, 2007, pp. 103–105). Several dictionaries define the adjective 'bittersweet' as an emotional mixture of joy or happiness and sadness. Darwin (1872, 206) described the phenomenon of individuals laughing until they cry, and laughing and crying simultaneously. He remarked:

> It is scarcely possible to point out any difference between the tear-stained face of a person after a paroxysm of laughter and after a bitter crying fit.

Instances where this emotion is elicited might include parents at a child's high-school or college graduation, who feel joyful concerning their offspring's successful 'coming of age', yet simultaneously sad that their offspring's childhood phase of life is over and they face the prospect of an 'empty nest'.

6.4.4 Ambivalence

Ambivalence is the coexistence within an individual of positive and negative feelings toward another individual, group, object, act, or condition. The broadest meaning of the term 'ambivalence' is "the experience of opposite emotions at once" (King & Napa, 1999, 38). More narrowly defined, ambivalence is the simultaneous occurrence of two specific, opposite emotions, acceptance/incorporation and disgust/rejection. Neurosurgeon Joseph Bogen (personal communication) provided an example of the simultaneous acceptance and rejection of another individual. Following corpus callosotomy, or 'split-brain' surgery, one of his patients would place his right arm around his wife, while simultaneously trying to push her away with his left hand. His left cerebral hemisphere was apparently accepting of her, but the right hemisphere considered the honeymoon long over. This dramatic example shows real ambivalence: the patient was literally of two minds concerning his spouse.

6.4.5 Derisiveness

Plutchik ([1962] 1991, 118) tentatively suggested that "disgust + joy = morbidness (?)." This is plausible insofar as a morbid individual finds pleasure in what others see as disgusting. But pleasure cannot be equated with joy–happiness, and morbidness is a pathology of character rather than emotion. An alternative definition is *derisiveness = joy–happiness & disgust* (TenHouten, 2017a, 82). When experiencing a feeling of derisiveness, an individual will enjoy reducing his or her targeted other's sense of self-worth. The behavior associated with this externally-focused emotion includes laughing at, making fun of, sneering at, ridiculing, and mocking. The derisive individual can find enjoyment and pleasure in treating another as an object of disgust. Derisiveness can range from a mild put-down or joke to a mean-spirited effort to harm, shame, or otherwise weaken the other's social identity. When combined with anger, derisiveness can assume a virulent form and cause the victim suffering and loss of self-esteem. This ruthlessness can be used, consciously or unconsciously, as a means of liberating the derisive individual from the no-longer tolerable confines of a deteriorating relationship. Or, it can be regularized as an ongoing program of cruelty to a no-longer valued or loved partner.

6.4.6 Resignation

A sense of resignation is the emotion that completes the winding down and dissolution of a love relationship. It is when resignation is called for, but does not occur, that love can stimulate feelings of depression, hatred, shame, resentment, a desire for revenge, and destructive behaviors such as stalking, assault, and murder can occur.

Plutchik ([1962] 1991, 118) defined "acceptance + sorrow = resignation, sentimentality." The inclusion of sentimentality is problematic, as it means being easily moved by sentiments in a general way; and sentiments, in turn, are defined as (i) views, opinions, general feelings, or self-indulgent emotions, and (ii) as sadness and nostalgia. Resignation includes passive acceptance, acquiescence, and submission, so that the primary emotion acceptance is clearly included in its meaning. It is thus proposed that resignation is the acceptance of a saddening loss of a valued social relationship or social situation.

Consistent with the definition *resignation = acceptance & sadness* (TenHouten, 2007, pp. 91–93), Ortony, Clore and Collins (1988, pp. 131–132) have linked resignation to acceptance, as they assert:

> The focus of resignation is not on the [undesirable] event in question...but...on a corresponding reluctant acceptance of the event's inevitability.

Ben-Ze'ev (2000, 481) notes that resignation is an affective state which might be closer to a mood than to an emotion; it is a negative mood with the potential to "turn into a nonaffective attitude of indifference." And as Lazarus (1999, 656, emphasis added) asserted:

> Sadness belongs at the low end of the dimension of engagement and involves resignation rather than struggle, and...the person has been moving toward acceptance of a disengagement from the lost commitment, therefore, sadness is a step toward resignation, which emerges from a difficult coping struggle in which the emotional outlook is often contradictory, fragile, and changing.

Expulsion from a dyad can trigger a wide range of emotional reactions, including embarrassment/shame, anger, aggressiveness, and possibly disappointment and misery. Such emotional reactions can range from non-existent, to mild, to intense, depending upon the other's value to the excluded individual. The excluded individual hopefully will eventually experience resignation, and acquiesce, to being rejected or left behind. In cases of an individual whose involvement is temporary, does not involve self-esteem, or who possess high levels of self-esteem, such resignation might not be experienced at all, as the emotional reaction might be one of straightforward acceptance. In established intimate dyads, in contrast, some sense of loss will in all probability experienced, which will involve some level of acceptance, sadness, and eventual resignation. An enormous body of social-psychological research concerns the process through which individuals first deny, feel angry about, bargain about, feel depressed about, and ultimately accept, and resign themselves to, the loss of a loved or cared-about other (Kübler-Ross, 1969). Because the two primary components of the secondary emotion resignation are of opposite valence, and dissimilar (being three positions apart in Plutchik's wheel), it is unsurprising that it has a contradiction-laden, unstable character, and can trigger pathological behavior.

6.4.7 Loneliness

While love is a joyful acceptance of and by another, its opposite combines the opposites of joy, sadness, and the opposite of acceptance, disgust. Plutchik ([1962] 1991, 118) rather defined the opposite of love as "sorrow + disgust = misery, remorse forlornness." On the functional level, misery represents the loss that attends being rejected by a close other. An individual can feel a strong sense of sadness, and remorse, upon realizing that they have been rejected as a friend, companion, lover, or mate. A feeling of forlornness is also apt to grip the mind of an individual experiencing the loss of a love-object. Thus, Plutchik's definition is not wrong, but the notion of 'loneliness' is a broader term for the normal, functional adaptive reaction to the loss of closeness of the other (Cacioppo & Patrick, 2008; Ernst & Cacioppo, 1998), which can begin as a feeling of being 'alone together', and culminate in the total loss of the other, as one faces rejection, being ignored, 'dumped', replaced, abandoned, divorced, or ostracized. Thus, when love has run its course, and its component primary emotions have become negatively valenced, the emotion *loneliness = sadness & rejection–disgust* will be experienced.

Thus, at the end of a love episode, the emotion of loneliness will be experienced. This is often a return to loneliness, because a sense of loneliness motivates the desire to find romantic love in the first place. Especially in troubled times, where a sense of community is being lost, religious life is abandoned,

> love is pursued for solace, as escape from an over-ordered world of alienation and loneliness... (Sullivan, 1999, 21).

Loneliness occurs in the absence of attachment figures, a sense of not belonging, and a deficiency, disruption, or loss of close social relations. To lose a love relationship is to experience a sudden contraction of one's social territory, and the experience of territory induces as an adaptive reaction of the primary emotion, surprise (Plutchik, [1962] 1991, pp. 99–102). The occurrence of a surprising state of loneliness, a collapse of one's social world, can create an intolerable mental pain, and can lead to the tertiary-level emotion of despair (TenHouten, 2017a, pp. 96–97), a state of misery, hopelessness, and gloom, and can even result in suicidality (Shneidman, 1993, pp. 51–57). For the individual for whom love has first been enjoyed, the experience of then being rejected "creates pain less final than death, but often just as cruel," as this pain "deadens a once warm and open heart" (Sullivan, 1999, 270).

6.5 Discussion

We have assumed that primary emotions exist as natural kinds and that they combine to form more complex emotions. The reasoning and evidence against and for these assumptions merits a brief discussion. The preponderance of cognitive-appraisal theorists (Scherer, Schorr, & Johnstone, 2001), psychological constructionists (Barrett, 2006; Barrett & Russell, 2015), and social constructionists (Boiger & Mesquita, 2012; Harré, 1986; Mesquita, Boiger, & De Leersnyder, 2016) reject the concept of primary emotions, suggesting that emotions exist only as psychological or cultural constructions. This view holds that processes classified under the vernacular category of emotions are not sufficiently similar to allow a unified theory of the emotions. Theories that explain a subset of emotions accordingly "will not adequately explain the whole range of human emotions" and even single affective states, such as joy and anger, will require multiple theories (Griffiths, 2004). Because affective states of mind such as sadness, joy, fear, and anger are not genuine 'natural kinds', it is held, emotion terms should accordingly be eliminated from scientific vocabulary. In this view, these emotions are not natural kinds primarily because they lack specific causal mechanisms in the brain, have permeable boundaries impacted by culture and language use, and therefore lack boundaries "carved in nature" (Barrett, 2006, p. 28).

However, emotions researchers with ecological, psychoevolutionary, and affective-neuroscientific orientations have adduced impressive evidence indicating that a small subset of emotions are primordial, elementary, basic, or primary, and are innate capabilities: (i) Fundamental emotions emerge in infancy while infants are still relying on subcortical behavioral mechanisms and before the onset of language (Izard, Woodburn, & Finlon, 2010); (ii) human babies born without cerebral hemispheres (anencephalic) cannot become intellectually developed but can grow up to be affectively vibrant if raised in nurturing and stimulating social environments (Shewmon, Holmes, & Byrne, 1999); (iii), the first emotions of the child unfold through epigenetic programs according to precise, universal timetables (LaFrenière, 2000; Sroufe, 1997), and (iv) persist throughout the life-span (Demos, 2007); and (v), deaf and blind children make facial expressions similar to those of non-impaired children (Eibl-Eibesfeldt, 1973; for a review, see Valente, Theurel, & Gentaz, 2018). This and a wealth of other evidence strongly suggests that the most basic emotions have evolved through natural selection across a wide variety of animal species (Darwin, 1872; MacLean, 1990; Panksepp & Biven, 2012). The basic emotions are neural, motivational, and expressive reactions that can occur rapidly in response to an environmental stimulus posing an opportunity or a threat (Izard, 2007; Panksepp, 2011). In humans, these primordial responses are cognitively elaborated, and are crucial to the process of sharing important information with conspecifics about pressing problems of life (MacLean, 1990; LaFrenière, 2000, pp. 42–43). They remain essential for humans' ability to meet universal survival needs, reproduce, engage the social world, and flourish. The conclusion that can be drawn is that basic or primary emotions do exist as natural kinds, that they can combine to form more complex emotions, and that, while constrained and structured by human neurobiology, they can be subjected to extensive sociocultural construction. The social construction of emotions does not at all require denial of the evolved biological nature of emotions, and it is the natural topic of the sociologies and anthropologies of emotions. Moreover, the neurobiological bases of the primary emotions further enable the development of interdisciplinary sciences of neurosociology, neuroanthropology, neuroeconomics, neurophenomenology, and beyond. This argument of course applies to the emotion of love.

6.6 Conclusions

It should be conceded that, while Plutchik's models of primary and secondary emotions have been treated with respect, his classification has neither been accepted or rejected by emotions researchers. Moreover, the emotion of acceptance–incorporation, the positive pole of the identity axis, has rarely been classified as primary beyond Plutchik. Love finds a wide range of meanings both across and within human cultures, and has been given elaborate social and cultural construction. But this social construction of love does not mean it exists only *sui generis*, for it rests on a foundation of two natural kinds, the primary emotions of joy–happiness and acceptance, both of which have a deep evolutionary history and require a highly elaborated process of cognitive appraisal based on complex brainwork not limited to specific dedicated mechanism but rather involving a complex network of connectivity structures that are also involved in other mental functions. Barrett (2006) argues that because emotions involve multiple brain structures, they cannot be natural kinds, but almost all structures in the brain participate in a multiplicity of functions involving connected structures. The social construction and linguistic elaboration of primary, secondary, and tertiary emotions is a locus of cultural creativity.

While the debate about the existence, or non-existence, of primary emotions continues unabated, less attention has focused upon the consequences of these two claims. If there are no primary emotions, and all emotions therefore exist *sui generis*, then there can be no hierarchical classification of the emotions. However, if as claimed, primary emotions do exist, then it becomes possible to classify the complex emotions formed from pairs and triples of the primary emotions. Plutchik recognized this implication of his model of primary emotions, and this recognition led him to develop an innovative, if not entirely successful, classification of secondary emotions.

If emotions do not mix or combine to form more complex emotions, then it makes little difference if primary emotions exist or not. This issue is of slight concern to affective neuroscientists, who typically focus on studies of single emotions that are not difficult to evoke in a laboratory setting. But for the social-psychology, sociology, and anthropology of emotions, the possibility of primary emotions mixing and combining makes a great deal of difference, because the emotions most interior to social life are indeed complex and embedded in social relations. This is certainly true of love: To define love is secondary does not render it less important than emotions that are primary, for it rather places love in a higher-level position, as a complex emotion accompanied by complex social processes requiring elaborated mechanisms of cognitive appraisal.

Factor related to the exercise of social power and to socioeconomic exchange processes can become involved as a love-based relationship deteriorates, which can evoke yet other emotions. As examples, failing close relationships can involve the dynamics of the secondary-level emotions of pride (an angry joy) and shame (a fearful sadness) (TenHouten, 2017c), and are sure to also involve emotions that have been classified as tertiary, possibly including jealousy (TenHouten, 1996), envy (TenHouten, 2007, pp. 205–214), resentment (TenHouten, 2018), discouragement (TenHouten, 2017a, pp. 82–86) or hatred. A natural elaboration of this essay would be consideration of the four tertiary-level emotions that contain three of our four primary emotions. Identification and description of these emotions is required for a full classification of the emotions of problematic intimacy, but is not included in this chapter. Love can involve many other complex affective states that are not easily classifiable as emotions, including the negative affects heartache, disillusionment, and insecurity, and positive affects such as contentment, admiration, and sanguinity. Thus, while love is itself complex, in both stable and unstable social relationships, the emotion of love will exist together with a myriad of additional emotional and affective states of mind, emerging as adaptive reactions to complex and dynamically changing sociorelational situations.

Love has been correctly described as a universal phenomenon (Karandashev, 2015) (see his chapter in this book). And indeed, insofar as love is a mixture of primary emotions, which are themselves universal across human cultures, then love itself should be universal. Of course, love finds many manifestations and 'colors', and its meanings proliferate as cultural innovations. Despite the continuing influence of anti-Enlightenment romanticism on our understanding of love (TenHouten, 2019), love, as an emotion, is rooted in biology, in the organization of the polarities of joy–happiness and sadness, and of incorporation–acceptance and disgust in the human brain. It is the common neurobiological infrastructure of the components of love that will preserves its unity, regardless of the endless emergence of new understandings of love in human culture.

While love is a mysterious, and highly romanticized, concept, it is also, in part, a specific emotion. As such, it is just as available for objective, scientific study as is any other emotion. It is hoped the present classificatory effort will provide a frame-of-reference useful for research on love in a context of social relationships that develop over time, having a beginning, flowering, then a 'falling' as love unravels. The present model, based on a larger theoretical formulation, Affect-Spectrum Theory (TenHouten, 2013, 2017b), links the opposite emotions joy/sadness and acceptance/disgust, which for Plutchik (1983) arise as adaptive reactions to the (valenced) existential problems of temporality and identity, which have in humans been generalized to the elementary social relationships of "communal sharing" (CS) and "equality matching" (EM), respectively (Fiske, 1991; TenHouten, 2017b). These social relations are essential element of social organization that are reflected in prototypical patterns of cultural behavior. Together with "authority ranking" and "market pricing" (Fiske, 1991; TenHouten, 2013, pp. 27–46), the four social-relations models, all of which have cognitive and affective aspects, comprise the elementary forms of culture (Gross & Rayner, 1985, pp. ix–xiv). Cross-cultural and subcultural variations in these models, especially in CS and EM, impacts the way love relationships are structured.

The classification of primary and secondary emotion used here is predicated on the assumptions that: (i) there exist primary or basic emotions, which include acceptance/disgust and joy/sadness; (ii) these primary emotions address fundamental problems of life, exists across all human cultures and societies, and are shared at least by the more complex of animal species; and (iii), in humans and other complex species, these irreducible, existential problems are addressed by specific elementary forms of sociality. The aim of this chapter was to define love as a secondary emotion, then explore consequences of this definition. Love involves not just emotion, but is also highly elaborated cognition, which on the phenomenological level might mean that it is newly emergent in humans. Love can take many forms and colors, but as an emotion it is pan-cultural. Rather than exploring cross-cultural varieties of cultural expression, we have focused on its infrastructure.

One use of an explicit definition of love, placed within a larger classification of emotions, is that it permits specification of what emotions emerge in the midst of falling out of love. This process is hypothesized to involve two primary emotions—sadness and disgust–rejection, and five secondary emotions— bittersweetness, ambivalence, derisiveness, resignation, and loneliness. Sadness and disgust, being basic emotions linked to many complex emotions, are not in themselves indicative of trouble in a love relationship. But the appearance of these five secondary emotions could potentially have diagnostic and therapeutic value, as the emergence of these emotions in a love-based relationship might well signal, and be used as empirical indicators of, troubled or destabilized intimacy and the waning of love. We have also discovered in this classificatory effort that the opposite situation of love is a forlorn sense of loneliness. While love and loneliness involve oppositely-valenced poles of the temporality/communal-sharing and identity/equality-matching sociorelational axes, they are not themselves 'opposites' in any sense beyond a 'dialectical' metaphor. Love, in everyday discourse, is typically 'opposed' not to loneliness but to hatred, a topic we explore in the next chapter.

References

Alberoni, F. (1983). *Falling in love* (L. Venuti, Trans.). New York: Random House.
Aquinas, T. [1265–1274] (1947–1948). *The summa theologica*, first complete American ed. New York: Benziger.
Argyle, M. (2001). *The psychology of happiness* (2nd ed.). New York: Routledge.
Averill, J. R., & More, T. A. (2000). Happiness. In M. Lewis & J. M. Haviland-Jones (Eds.), *Handbook of emotions* (2nd ed., pp. 663–676). New York: Guilford Press.
Axelrod, R., & Hamilton, W. D. (1981). The evolution of cooperation. *Science, 211*, 1390–1396.
Barrett, L. F. (2006). Are emotions natural kinds? *Perspectives on Psychological Science, 1*, 28–58.
Barrett, L. F., & Russell, J. A. (Eds.). (2015). *The psychological construction of emotion*. New York: Guilford Press.
Baumeister, R. F., & Leary, M. R. (1995). The need to belong: Desire for interpersonal attachment as a fundamental human motivation. *Psychological Bulletin, 117*, 497–529.
Ben-Ze'ev, A. (2000). *The subtlety of emotions*. Cambridge, MA: MIT Press.

Boiger, M., & Mesquita, B. (2012). The construction of emotions in interactions, relationships, and cultures. *Emotion Review, 4*, 221–229.
Bowlby, J. (1980). *Attachment and loss (Vol. III, Loss: Sadness and depression)*. New York: Basic Books.
Brogaard, B. (2015). *On romantic love: Simple truths about a complex emotion*. New York: Oaxford University Press.
Burton, R. [1611] (1927). *The anatomy of melancholy*. New York: Tudor.
Burton, R. [1611] (1971). *The anatomy of melancholy*. Oxford: Oxford University Press.
Cacioppo, J. T., & Patrick, W. (2008). *Loneliness: Human nature and the need for social connection*. New York: W. W. Norton.
Cowan, T. (2016). *Human heart, cosmic heart*. White River Junction, VT: Chelsea Green Publishing.
Darwin, C. (1872). *The expression of the emotions in man and the animals*. London: John Murray.
Demos, E. V. (2007). The dynamics of development. In J. P. Muller & J. Brent (Eds.), *Self-organizing complexity in psychological systems* (pp. 135–163). Lanham, MD: Jason Aronson.
Descartes, R. [1647] (1989). *The passions of the soul* (S. Voss, Trans.). Indianapolis, IN: Hackett Publishing.
Diener, E., & Seligman, M. E. P. (2002). Very happy people. *Psychological Science, 13*, 81–84.
Dumas, G. (1905). Le prejudice intellectualistic et al prejudice finalist dans les theories de l'expression. *Revue Philsophique, 60*, 561–582.
Eibl-Eibesfeldt, I. (1973). The expressive behavior of the deaf-and-blind born. In M. Von Cranach & I. Vine (Eds.), *Social communication and movement* (pp. 163–194).
Ernst, J. M., & Cacioppo, J. T. (1998). Lonely hearts: Psychological perspectives on loneliness. *Applied and Preventive Psychology, 8*, 1–22.
Fiske, A. P. (1991). *Structures of social life: The four elementary forms of human relations*. New York: Free Press.
Goldberg, J. G. (1999). *The dark side of love: The positive role of negative feelings*. New Brunswick, NJ: Transaction Publishers.
Gould, T. (1963). *Platonic love*. New York: Free Press of Glencoe.
Griffiths, P. E. (2004). Emotions as normative and natural kinds. *Philosophy of Science, 21*, 759–777.
Gross, J. L., & Rayner, S. (1985). *Measuring culture: Paradigm for the analysis of social organization*. New York: Columbia University Press.
Gyurak, A., & Ayduk, Ö. (2008). Resting respiratory sinus arrhythmia buffers against rejection sensitivity via emotion control. *Emotion, 8*, 458–467.
Harré, R. (Ed.). (1986). *The social construction of emotions*. New York: Basil Blackwell.
Haybron, D. (2008). *The pursuit of unhappiness: The elusive psychology of well-being*. New York: Oxford University Press.
Holbrook, D. (1972). *The masks of hate: The problem of false solutions in the culture of an acquisitive society*. Oxford: Pergamon Press.
Hume, D. [1739] (1978). *A treatise of human nature*, L. A. Selby-Bigge (Ed.). Oxford: Clarendon Press.
Izard, C. E. (2007). Basic emotions, natural kinds, emotion schemas, and a new paradigm. *Perspectives on Psychological Science, 2*, 260–268.
Izard, C. E., Woodburn, E. M., & Finlon, K. J. (2010). Extending emotion science to the study of discrete emotions in infants. *Emotion Review, 2*, 134–136.
Jankowiak, W. R., & Fischer, E. F. (1992). A cross-cultural perspective on romantic love. *Ethnology, 31*, 149–155.
Karandashev, V. (2015). A cultural perspective on romantic love. *Online Readings on Psychology and Culture, 5*, 1–21.
Khaleque, A., & Ali, S. (2017). A systematic review of meta-analyses of research on interpersonal acceptance-rejection theory: Constructs and measures: IPART theory meta-analyses. *Journal of Family Theory & Review, 9*, 441–458.

King, J. A., & Napa, C. K. (1999). Max Weber. In E. N. Zalta (Ed.), *The Stanford encyclopedia of philosophy*. Stanford, CA: Stanford University Press.

Kübler-Ross, E. (1969). *On death and dying*. New York: The Macmillan Company.

LaFrenière, P. (2000). *Emotional development: A biosocial perspective*. Belmont, CA: Wadsworth Thomson Learning.

Layard, R. (2005). *Happiness: Lessons from a new science*. New York: Penguin Books.

Lazarus, R. S. (1999). Hope: An emotion and a vital coping resource. *Social Research, 66*, 653–678.

Lear, J. (1991). *Love and its place in nature: A philosophical interpretation of Freudian psychoanalysis*. New York: Noonday Press.

Lee, J. A. (1976). *The colors of love: An exploration of the ways of loving*. Don Mills, Ontario, Canada: New Press.

Locke, J. [1689] (1995). *An essay concerning human understanding*. Amherst, NY: Prometheus Books.

MacLean, P. D. (1990). *The triune brain in evolution: Role in paleocerebral functions*. New York: Plenum Press.

Malebranche, N. [1674–1675] (1997). *The search after truth* (T. M. Lennon & P. J. Olscamp, Trans.). New York: Cambridge University Press.

May, J. L., & Hamilton, P. A. (1980). Effects of musically evoked affect on women's interpersonal attraction toward and perceptual judgment of physical attractiveness of men. *Motivation and Emotion, 4*, 217–228.

McDougall, W. [1923] (1947). *An outline of psychology* (11th ed.). London: Methuen.

Mead, G. H. [1934] (1962). *Mind, self, and society from the standpoint of a social behaviorist*. Chicago, IL: University of Chicago Press.

Mesquita, B., Boiger, M., & De Leersnyder, J. (2016). The cultural construction of emotions. *Current Opinion in Psychology, 8*, 31–36.

Nussbaum, M. C. (1986). *The fragility of goodness: Luck and ethics in Greek tragedy and philosophy*. Cambridge, UK: Cambridge University Press.

Nussbaum, M. C. (2001). *Upheavals of thought: The intelligence of emotions*. Cambridge, UK: Cambridge University Press.

Ortony, A., Clore, G. L., & Collins, A. (1988). What's basic about basic emotions? *Psychological Review, 97*, 315–331.

Panksepp, J. (2011). The basic emotional circuits of mammalian brains: Do animals have affective lives? *Neuroscience and Biobehavioral Reviews, 35*, 1791–1804.

Panksepp, J., & Biven, L. (2012). *The archeology of mind: Neuroevolutionary origins of human emotions*. New York: Norton.

Plato. [c. 385 BCE] (1989). *Symposium of Plato* [*Platonos Symposion*] (T. Griffith & P. Forester, Trans.). Berkeley, CA: University of California Press.

Plato. [380 BCE] (1965). *Plato II: Laches, protogoras, mene, euthydemes* (W. R. Lamb, Trans.). Cambridge, MA: Harvard University Press.

Plutchik, R. (1958). Outline of a new theory of emotion. *Transaction of the New York Academy of Science, 20*, 394–403.

Plutchik, R. (1980). *Emotion: A psychoevolutionary synthesis*. New York: Harper & Row.

Plutchik, R. [1962] (1991). *The emotions: Facts, theories, and a new model*, revised ed. Lanham, MD: University Press of America.

Plutchik, R. (1983). Universal problems of adaptation: Hierarchy, territoriality, identity, and temporality. In J. B. Calhoun (Ed.), *Environment and population: Problems of adaptation* (pp. 223–226). New York: Praeger.

Rohner, R. P. (1975). *They love me, they love me not: A worldwide study of the effects of parental acceptance and rejection*. New Haven, CT: HRAF Press.

Rohner, R. P., & Kaleque, A. (2005). *Handbook for the study of parental acceptance and rejection* (4th ed.). Storrs, CT: Rohner Research Publications.

Rousseau, J.-J. [1762] (1979). *Émile, or on education* (A. Bloom, Trans.). New York: Basic Books.

Sbarra, D. A. (2006). Predicting the onset of emotional recovery following nonmarital relationship dissolution: Survival analysis of sadness and anger. *Personality and Social Psychology Bulletin, 32*, 298–312.

Scherer, K. R., Schorr, A., & Johnstone, T. (2001). *Appraisal processes in emotion: Theory, methods, research*. Oxford, UK: Oxford University Press.

Shaver, P. R., & Hazen, C. (1988). A biased overview of the study of love. *Journal of Social and Personal Relations, 5*, 473–501.

Shaver, P. R., Morgan, H. J., & Wu, S. (1996). Is love a "basic" emotion. *Personal Relationships, 3*, 81–96.

Shewmon, D. A., Holmes, G. L., & Byrne, P. A. (1999). Consciousness in congenitally decorticated children: Developmental vegetative state as self-fulfilling prophecy. *Developmental Medicine & Child Neurology, 37*, 364–374.

Shneidman, E. S. (1993). *Suicide as psychache: A clinical approach to self-destructive behavior*. Northvale, NJ: J. Aronson.

Singer, I. (1984). *The nature of love, vol. 2, Courtly and romantic love*. Chicago, IL: University of Chicago Press.

Sroufe, L. A. (1997). *Emotional development: The organization of emotional life in the early years*. New York: Cambridge University Press.

Sullivan, S. (1999). *Falling in love: A history of torment and enchantment*. Basingstoke, UK: Macmillan.

TenHouten, W. D. (1996). Outline of a socioevolutionary theory of the emotions. *Journal of Sociology and Social Policy, 16*, 189–208.

TenHouten, W. D. (2007). *A general theory of emotions and social life*. London: Routledge.

TenHouten, W. D. (2013). *Emotion and reason: Mind, brain, and the social domains of work and love*. London: Routledge.

TenHouten, W. D. (2017a). *Alienation and affect*. New York: Routledge.

TenHouten, W. D. (2017b). From primary emotions to the spectrum of affect: An evolutionary neurosociology of the emotions. In A. Ibáñez, L. Sedeño, & A. M. Garcia (Eds.), *Neuroscience and social science: The missing link* (pp. 141–167). New York: Springer.

TenHouten, W. D. (2017c). Social dominance hierarchy and the pride–shame system. *Journal of Political Power, 10*, 94–114.

TenHouten, W. D. (2018). From *ressentiment* to resentment as a tertiary emotion. *Review of European Studies, 10*, 49–64.

TenHouten, W. D. (2019). Alienation and emotion: Hegel versus sentimentalism and romanticism. *Review of European Studies, 11*, 1–19.

Tiger, L. (1999). Hope springs internal. *Social Research, 66*, 611–623.

Tomkins, S. S. (1963). *Affect imagery consciousness, vol. II, The negative affects*. New York: Springer.

Valente, D., Theurel, A., & Gentaz, E. (2018). The role of visual experience in the production of emotional facial expressions in blind people: A review. *Psychonomic Bulletin & Review, 25*, 483–497.

Zweig, P. (1968). *The heresy of self-love: A study of subversive individualism*. New York: Harper & Row.

Warren D. TenHouten (Prof. Dr.) is a Research Professor at the Sociology Department at the University of California at Los Angeles. His research interests include neurosociology, affective neuroscience, the sociology of emotions, alexithymia, time-consciousness, reason and rationality, social exchange theory, and alienation theory. His books include Time and Society (SUNY 2005), A General Theory of Emotions and Social Life (Routledge), Emotion and Reason: Mind, Brain, and the Social Domains of Work and Love (Routledge 2007), and Alienation and Affect (Routledge 2016).

Chapter 7
Towards the Performance of Embodied Cultures of Love

Freddie Crous and Leigh Leo

Abstract In this chapter, love is approached from an embodiment perspective—an approach which makes it possible to develop and nurture cultures of wellbeing. Specific attention is given to psychological neoteny (extended youthfulness) as a personality structure within which love as a trait is incorporated. In sub-Saharan Africa, neoteny finds expression in a radical form of love known as *ubuntu*. Two performative instruments, namely the Positivity Projective and Enactment Technique, as well as the Rebirth symbol designed by the eminent artist, Michelangelo Pistoletto, can be used to develop, cultivate and expand cultures which are open and loving.

Keywords Love · Affability · Cultures of love · Embodiment · Neoteny · Performative instruments · Radical love · Ubuntu

7.1 Introduction

Approach to this chapter. Having analysed the major ideas in philosophy, the systematic philosopher, Stephen Pepper (1942), identified four so-called 'adequate' cognitive pathways for understanding the world. His use of 'adequate' is apt, because these world hypotheses as they are also known, adhere to the criteria of precision and scope. Each pathway has an underlying root metaphor: for formism it is form, for mechanism it is the machine, for organicism it is the living organism, and for contextualism it is the historical act in context. In this chapter, the organismic pathway is predominantly applied. A comprehensive discussion of Pepper's root metaphor theory falls outside the scope of this undertaking, but for a brief overview see Crous (2019b). Suffice to say that the nature of organicism is synthetic (rather than analytical) and integrative (as opposed to being dispersive). For this reason, its

---

F. Crous (✉) · L. Leo
Department of Industrial Psychology and People Management, University of Johannesburg, Johannesburg, South Africa
e-mail: fcrous@uj.ac.za

strength is its precision and its weakness, its relative inadequacy of scope. Organicism implies an embodied approach to understanding which, according to Schnall (2014), facilitates people's actions within both their physical and their social environments. Action, however, suggests contextualism. As such, with the introduction of performative instruments towards the end of the chapter, a contextual cognitive pathway is applied.

7.2 Orienting Love

The general belief is that the physiological feature that defines us as the human species—*Homo sapiens sapiens* (wise)—is our larger brains, but Maslin (2017) points out that this is not the case: in his view, the defining physiological feature of humankind is the fact that we walk upright. All other subsequent evolutionary developments, including psychological processes (in particular the cognitive) are contingent on the advent of humankind walking tall or vertically (UP), on two feet (i.e., becoming bipedal) (Kampourakis, 2018)—an event which first occurred on the African continent, according to Grayling (2019).

From an embodied perspective, bodily and psychological processes in general and cognitive processes in particular, are integrated (Shapiro & Stolz, 2019) to the extent that "states of the body modify states of the mind" (Wilson & Golonka, 2013, p. 58). If UP is therefore at the origin of humans' physical or bodily development as a species, then it also has to be fundamental for the development of the psyche/mind. For example, through our sensory-motor apparatus, we have evolved to internalise the experience of UP or verticality. The human mind has become spatially oriented to categorise and position everything that, in interaction with the physical and social environment, is experienced as positive or good (such as love) as UP, while everything that is experienced as negative or bad, such as aggression, is located as DOWN (Crous, 2019a; Lakoff & Johnson, 1980, 1999). Meier and Robinson (2004) provide empirical evidence for the tendency to represent good things as spatially UP and bad things as spatially DOWN: participants reacted faster to categorise positive words (such as 'love') as "good" when they appeared in the top segment of a computer screen, and negative words (such as danger) as "bad" when they appeared at the bottom of the screen. UP therefore provides a basic metaphoric structure or scaffold for conceptualising love (Schnall, 2014), in addition to offering a schema for wellbeing (Johnson, 1987). Given this embodied UP–DOWN orientation, people across all cultures are able to cognitively align their experiences of love, with wellbeing (see Lakoff & Johnson, 1980, 1999).

A major development in human evolution, namely neoteny has elevated love psychologically, so that it has assumed a trait-like nature. Neoteny (a precursor to walking upright), and in particular psychological neoteny, has not been adequately explored in the fields of the humanities or the social sciences, and as such needs to be explained.

7.3 Psychological Neoteny

Psychological neoteny—a term coined by Bruce Charlton (2006)—refers to the retention, into adulthood, of youthful attitudes and behaviours (or a personality characterised by prolonged youthfulness). While the term is relatively new to the field of psychology, the construct is deeply rooted in evolutionary theory. 'Neoteny', as defined in evolutionary biology, generally describes aspects of both physical and behavioural neotisation in the descendant of a species when compared to the ancestor; the latter of which (commonly referred to as behavioural neoteny) is comparable to the concept of psychological neoteny, as described by Charlton (2006). In *Growing young*, Montagu (1989) defines behavioural neoteny as a biologically based strategy that places a premium on learning and flexible adaption to the environment, and elevates the importance of youthful characteristics that enable such flexibility. Montagu states that we are prepared by evolution (provided that conditions are conducive) to learn and grow, to 'grow young' or employ youthful traits as we mature. Typical traits associated with behavioural neotisation in humans not only include curiosity, playfulness, the capacity to love, openmindedness, a sense of wonder, imagination, hope and trust, but also rebelliousness, irresponsibility, impulsivity and sensation seeking, among others.

Importantly, Montagu (1989) underlines the interconnected relationship between physiological and behavioural neotisation, explaining that they are inextricably intertwined, with physiological neotisation providing the structure for what is possible in human behaviour. Lorenz (1971), for instance, acknowledges the importance of fostering juvenile characteristics to maintain brain plasticity which, in turn, allows for ongoing learning and cognitive flexibility. This behavioural and cognitive malleability allows humans to rapidly adjust to changing environmental conditions, and provides a route for continued evolutionary change (Bateson, 1988). Despite the evident evolutionary and behavioural value of psychological neoteny in humans, theory pertaining to the construct has yet to coalesce around a firm core of ideas.

The lack of research and applied understanding of this construct can, perhaps, be attributed to established views on development. The idea that many of our childlike characteristics stay with us and continue to be important throughout our adult lives (Fletcher & Kenway, 2007) generally runs counter to established views on development. Traditionally, we rush into adulthood in order to acquire the restrictive lineaments of sophistication and 'maturity', quickly dismissing our childlike characteristics (Montagu, 1989). This is partly because of society's expectation of an orderly progression of development from infancy to adulthood (Hennig, 2010). Montagu (1989, p. 82) compares traditional perceptions of adulthood and childhood, stating: "In adulthood, we are serious, we produce, we focus, we fight, we protect and we have stable and strong beliefs; however, when we are young, we learn, we socialize, we play, we experiment, we are curious, we feel wonder, we feel joy, we change, we grow, we imagine, we hope."

Traditional views of adulthood and childhood are slowly changing, however, as the developmental cycle continues to shift, with traditional milestones in modern cultures (such as completing school, leaving home, becoming financially independent, getting married and having children) becoming delayed and stretching across a much longer lifespan than in the past (Arnett, 2000). As a result, some individuals in society may never achieve all five milestones, while others may reach them in a different order, for example, advancing professionally before committing to a relationship, having children young and marrying later, or leaving school to go to work and returning to school long after becoming financially secure (Charlton, 2006). Given the shift of traditional milestones in modern society, attaining what we would traditionally call 'adulthood' is happening later than ever (Hennig, 2010).

Charlton (2007) attributes the changing nature of adulthood in industrialised societies to the evolution of psychological neoteny. Presumably, based on the evolutionary origin of the construct, Charlton postulates that psychological neoteny has been achieved through the expedient postponing of psychological maturation. This he attributes to the prolonged average duration of formal education (people tend to delay having to assume important social roles, and their minds remain—in a significant sense—'unfinished'), leading to the postponement of a stable, integrated, adult personality being adopted. As a result, in any society people are likely to vary in respect of the level of psychological neoteny they display, due to differences in the roles they adopt in early adulthood (e.g., education, marriage, parenthood).

Psychological neoteny has been conceptualised as a unidimensional, multilevel personality trait, broadly characterised by neotenous traits that exemplify a collection of youthful qualities, including those that (a) promote exploration, discovery and learning (e.g., love of learning, curiosity, creativity, open-mindedness); (b) enable individuals to effectively adapt in the face of adversity (e.g., vitality, hope, resilience, optimism); (c) exemplify the impetuous qualities of youthfulness that can cause individuals to run counter to social conventions and behave in a free, candid, unrestrained or risky manner (e.g., rebelliousness, spontaneity, impulsivity, irresponsibility, playfulness and sensation seeking); and (d) aid in establishing and maintaining warm and friendly interpersonal relations (e.g., the capacity to love and be loved, sociability, cooperation, dependence, friendliness and trust) (Leo, 2019).

This initial description of the structure of psychological neoteny is further complimented when it is explained in the context of, and linked to, functional domains. Evolutionary developmental psychology provides the psychobiological framework from which a more complete (biological) understanding of psychological neoteny can be derived, providing an ultimate–proximate explanation for the construct. Ultimate explanations are generally concerned with the fitness consequences of a specific trait (or behaviour) and whether it is selected or rejected. By contrast, proximate explanations are generally concerned with the mechanism underpinning a trait or behaviour—that is, how it works (Scott-Phillips, Dickins & West, 2011). The ultimate explanation for the emergence of psychological neoteny, as derived from theory, positions the construct as an evolved psychological mechanism which enables greater flexibility and malleability in behaviour and cognition, thereby allowing humans to adapt to an increasingly complex and changing environment—in turn, that can lead to greater inclusive fitness. The proximate explanation for psychological neoteny includes (a) external triggers which prompt the retention of youthful traits into adulthood (continuous environmental pressures) and rapid cultural and social changes (which have modified the value of social roles in modern society); and also (b) internal mechanisms which are responsive to social and ecological variation, such as the epigenetic system, which enables the adaptation of physical, behavioural and psychological phenotypes, in the course of development, to different ecological conditions (Leo, 2019).

The inclination to take an interest in novelty, to actively assimilate, play and creatively apply our skills has, over the years, become a feature not only of childhood, but also of human nature, in that these traits ultimately affect our performance, persistence and wellbeing throughout the course of our lives (Ryan & LaGuardia, 1999). As a result, the emergence of psychological neoteny certainly has potential advantages and disadvantages for society, as well as different benefits and costs at the individual and personal levels (Charlton, 2007). Many researchers believe we are evolving towards greater psychological neoteny (Charlton, 2006, 2007; Fletcher & Kenway, 2007; Gould, 1977; Montagu, 1989), and promote the idea of cultivating youthful characteristics (Charlton, 2006, 2007; Lorenz, 1971; Montagu, 1989), thus making psychological neoteny a valuable concept in understanding emerging human behaviour. According to Montagu (1989), the potential benefits of an applied understanding of neoteny have not, as yet, been fully recognised. He states that such an understanding would encourage the celebration and nurturing of childlike traits, leading to significant adjustments in social institutions (e.g., our education systems and workplaces). Moreover, it would redefine society as a support system that contributes towards extending neotenous traits in all people.

One of the authors of this chapter (Crous, 2019a), informed by embodied cognition theory, also referred to as conceptual metaphor theory (CMT) and neoteny theory, developed a simple associative Positivity Projective and Enactment Technique (see Fig. 7.1). The design of this technique is represented by a logo-image consisting of an upright stick person (according to paleo-anthropologists, a slender or delicate build is associated with neoteny), superimposed onto a blobby typeface that resembles an amoeba-like word recognisable as UP. Moreover, the face resembles childlike/neotenic features retained into adulthood such as round-headedness, the absence of heavy brow ridges, a flat face, round eyes and a lack of hair. These

Fig. 7.1 The positivity projective and enactment technique

features provide the structure or scaffolding for neotenic-related behavioural/psychological characteristics such as affection, playfulness, optimism, trust, openness, joyfulness, humour, friendliness, lack of aggressiveness, among others (Charlton, 2006; Gould, 1977; Montagu, 1989). From Crous (2019a) it becomes clear how the technique, in conjunction with the positive action research method of Appreciative Inquiry, can be used to develop a nurturing culture in any system. Participants can be asked to have conversations to discover what is UP in their culture, what UP-image they have of their culture in a future manifestation, what social architecture should be designed to inculcate an UP culture, and how to make an UP culture part of their future.

Maturana and Verden-Zoller (2008) argue that love is the dominant quality of neoteny, because humans are love-dependent—without it, they are unable to survive. This view is in line with that of Fredrickson (2013), a scholar and researcher of positive emotions, who regards love as the supreme emotion, because love (or its absence) fundamentally changes the body's biochemicals, in turn altering key aspects of the body's cells that can affect not only physical health, but also psychological wellbeing. According to Fredrickson (2013), love is expansive in the sense that it unfolds and reverberates among people; it originates in the micro moments of authentic connections between them, and is perpetually renewable. Her observation supports Maturana and Verden-Zoller's (2008) suggestion that love expands the nature of *Homo sapiens sapiens* to include *Homo sapiens amans* (love). Following a comparative study with chimpanzees, Maturana and Verden-Zoller (2008) concluded that human life (embedded in neoteny) evolved to centre around cooperation rather than domination and submission, and that humans belong to an evolutionary history in which the basic emotion is love, not aggression and competition. In their view, humans are therefore a loving species that sometimes acts out aggressively, not an aggressive species that sometimes turns out to be loving (Maturana & Verden-Zoller, 2008). This state of being should, however, not be taken for granted but should be nurtured—a notion captured in a poem by the South African scholar and writer, Leon de Kock (2010, p. 55):

The Biology of Love

The Biology of Love
Says my new friend
Humberto Maturana
Is not a Question of Virtue
No, not a Moral Issue.
It is how we behave
To keep life close
Close to our hearts.
How we behave
To conserve
And serve
The Biology of Love.

This is our real intelligence
And if we nurture it
We open out

Like flowers
We become ourselves
Homo sapiens amans.
We recover our ground
The earth of our being.
Otherwise
We close down
We droop
We become ill
We shut others out
We 'develop'.
Homo sapiens aggressans.

It really is
As simple as that.
Any deviation
From this
Fundamentalism
Fundament of love
Of the Biology of Love
Is a heresy
A simple heresy
By which
We become
The cages
Of our selves.

Maturana and Verden-Zoller (2008, n.p.) emphasise that "love provides for those relational behaviours by which the other arises as a legitimate other in co-existence with oneself." On the African continent a very particular and radical form of love (Robinson-Morris, 2019) has developed, namely *ubuntu*, which grants love a social or community "personality" (Akinola & Uzodike, 2018).

7.4 Ubuntu

Fixed to the office door of one of the authors of this chapter (Crous), is a poster of Archbishop Desmond Tutu (see Fig. 7.2). What makes this poster exceptional, is Tutu's positive description of humanity, despite the atrocities he had to hear about as chair of the Truth and Reconciliation Commission hearings which followed the demise of apartheid in South Africa. Tutu's internalisation of the concept of *ubuntu* not only sustained him during his challenging tenure on the commission, but also empowered him to facilitate reconciliation amongst the different cultures in post-apartheid South Africa.

Tutu (2010, p.8) gave prominence to *ubuntu* with his belief that we are set in a delicate network of interdependence with our fellow human beings and with the rest of [nature]. In Africa recognition of our interdependence is called *Ubuntu*. It is the essence of being human. It speaks of the fact that my humanity is caught up and is

Fig. 7.2 Archbishop Desmond Tutu

inextricably bound up in yours. I am human because I belong to the whole, to the community, to the tribe, to the nation, to the earth, *Ubuntu* is about wholeness, about compassion for life.

Ubuntu is both a way of thinking and of being which is salient in Africa (Hoffmann & Metz, 2017)—an approach encapsulated by the defining phrase 'a person is a person through other persons'. As such, it takes on an ethical character (Grayling, 2019 p. 580), because it defines human moral existence in terms of mutuality, recognising "the essential and therefore constitutive, defining humanity-forming interconnectedness of persons to each other". *Ubuntu* can be positioned "between the over-ambitious 'love your neighbour' and the under-ambitious 'do no harm' as a realistically positive ethical principle" (Grayling, 2019, p. 581). But what does it mean to be a person through other persons? Metz (2015) indicates that sub-Saharan Africans regard a person (who exhibits *ubuntu*) as someone who lives an authentic life, displays ethical behaviour and shows human (moral) excellence (An UP person). In order to become a person 'through other persons', one has to enter into *community* with other people, wanting to live harmoniously with them (Metz, 2015). The first post-apartheid president of South Africa, Nelson Mandela, is widely recognised and heralded as a paragon of *ubuntu*, because he was able to internalise, enact and promote its values (Rodny-Gumede & Chasi, 2017) and lead South Africans to overcome their fear of cultural and racial differences. Mandela

Fig. 7.3 Michelangelo Pistoletto's rebirth symbol

believed love was an inherent part of *ubuntu* (see Akinola & Uzodike, 2018). The world took notice of Mandela's ability—as the embodiment of *ubuntu*—to break down the barriers that separated races and cultures. Recent local and international developments aimed at taking action (sometimes violently) against the idea of an open society and inclusivity, suggest that the time has come to restore *ubuntu* in South Africa and even to elevate it to a global level, thereby encouraging diverse cultures to establish a relational cosmopolitanism (see Graness, 2018). Since *ubuntu* suggests the joining of opposites (Meiring, 2015), a symbol of rebirth (see Fig. 7.3) which was developed by the eminent Italian artist, Michelangelo Pistoletto (2018), may be implemented as a performative instrument to facilitate and brand a culture of *ubuntu* in communities the world over.

The rebirth symbol is a reconfiguration of the mathematical symbol for infinity, which consists of an unbroken line intersecting itself to give form to two circles. For his rebirth symbol Pistoletto made the line cross itself twice, giving shape to three consecutive circles. The two outer circles represent all opposites. The process of connecting or joining them through the inner circle establishes the space for giving birth to a new (loving?) community or society. Through Cittadellarte (his foundation and eponymous centre), Pistoletto is already working collaboratively with communities around the globe to give expression to his symbol, taking hands by mapping meetings, establishing forums and hosting workshops, to realise the United Nations' Sustainable Development Goals, showing the way forward towards possibly establishing a flourishing, *ubuntu*-like culture of love.

7.5 Conclusion

As suggested here, from an embodiment perspective, in the first instance verticality as a schema allows love to be valued on a cognitive level. In the second, given the evolutionary development of psychological neoteny, which is embedded in physiological neoteny, love becomes trait-like within the affability domain of a larger neotenic personality structure.

Of particular interest here, are those neotenous traits that exemplify the positive interpersonal tendencies of youthfulness, namely the capacity to love and be loved, sociability, cooperation, dependence, friendliness and trust. These traits are collectively referred to as the affability domain, which is one of the four domains used to describe the concept of psychological neoteny. The highlighted traits describe a general tendency to value close relations with others; seek social interaction; strive for cooperation and social harmony; rely on others for guidance, support and approval; seek congenial relationships; and believe in the sincerity and good intentions of our fellow man.

With this embodied knowledge of love, one of the authors of the chapter (Crous) was able to design a simple associative technique to project and enact a flourishing culture in a group or community. In order to develop, nurture and expand on *ubuntu*, a radical form of love, the rebirth symbol created by the Italian artist Michelangelo Pistoletto, can be used as performative instrument for the creation of *ubuntu*-like cultures.

References

Akinola, A. O., & Uzodike, N. (2018). Ubuntu and the quest for conflict resolution in Africa. *Journal of Black Studies, 49*(2), 91–113. https://doi.org/10.1177/021934717736186

Arnett, J. J. (2000). Emerging adulthood: A theory of development from the late teens through the twenties. *American Psychologist, 55*, 469–480. https://doi.org/10.1037//0003-066X.55.5.469

Bateson, P. (1988). The active role of behaviour in evolution. In M. W. Ho & S. W. Fox (Eds.), *Evolutionary processes and metaphors* (pp. 191–207). New York, NY: Wiley.

Charlton, B. (2006). The rise of the boy-genius: Psychological neoteny, science and modern life. *Medical Hypotheses, 67*, 679–681. https://doi.org/10.1016/j.mehy.2006.05.003

Charlton, B. (2007). Psychological neoteny and higher education: Associations with delayed parenthood. *Medical Hypotheses, 69*, 237–240. https://doi.org/10.1016/j.mehy.2007.03.005

Crous, F. (2019a). The origin, development, validation and application of the positivity projective and enactment technique. In L. E. van Zyl & I. Rothman (Eds.), *Positive psychological interventions: Theories, methodologies and applications within multi-cultural contexts* (pp. 413–430). Cham: Springer.

Crous, F. (2019b). Indeterminateness in industrial and organisational psychological research: A root metaphor analysis. *SA Journal of Industrial Psychology, 45*, 5.

De Kock, L. (2010). *Bodyhood*. Johannesburg: Umuzi.

Fletcher, J., & Kenway, J. (2007, May). Consumer attitudes and behaviour: Marketing to the inner child. In *Paper presented at the ESOMAR consumer insights conference*. Milan, Netherlands: ESOMAR.

Fredrickson, B. (2013). *Love 2.0: How our supreme emotion affects everything we feel, think, do, and become*. London: Hudson Street Press.

Gould, S. J. (1977). *Ontogeny and phylogeny*. Cambridge, MA: Harvard University Press.

Graness, A. (2018). Ubuntu and the concept of cosmopolitism. *Human Affairs, 28*(4), 395–405.

Grayling, A. C. (2019). *The history of philosophy*. London: Viking.

Hennig, R. M. (2010). *What is it about 20-somethings?* [online magazine article]. Retrieved from https://www.nytimes.com/2010/08/22/magazine/22Adulthood-t.html

Hoffmann, M., & Metz, T. (2017). What can the capabilities approach learn from an Ubuntu ethic? A relational approach to development theory. *World Development, 97*, 153–164. https://doi.org/10.1016/j.worlddev.2017.04.010

Johnson, M. (1987). *The body in the mind: The bodily basis of meaning, imagination, and reason*. Chicago, IL: University of Chicago Press.

Kampourakis, K. (2018). *Turning points: How critical events have driven human evolution, life and development*. Cambridge: Cambridge University Press.

Lakoff, G., & Johnson, M. (1980). *Metaphors we live by*. Chicago, IL: University of Chicago Press.

Lakoff, G., & Johnson, M. (1999). *Philosophy in the flesh: The embodied mind and its challenge to Western thought*. New York, NY: Basic Books.

Leo, L. (2019). *Towards the development of the Neoteny personality questionnaire* (Unpublished doctoral thesis). University of Johannesburg, South Africa.

Lorenz, K. (1971). *Studies in animal and human behaviour*. Cambridge, MA: Harvard University Press.
Maslin, M. (2017). *The cradle of humanity*. Oxford: Oxford University Press.
Maturana, H., & Verden-Zoller, G. (2008). *The origin of humanness in the biology of love*. Exeter, UK: Imprint Academic.
Meier, B. P., & Robinson, M. D. (2004). Why the sunny side is up: Associations between affect and vertical position. *Psychological Science, 15*, 243–247. https://doi.org/10.1111/j.09567976.2004.00659.x
Meiring, J. J. S. (2015). Ubuntu and the body: A perspective from theological anthropology as embodied sensing. *Verbum et Ecclesia, 36*(2), 1–7. https://doi.org/10.4102/ve.v36i2.1423
Metz, T. (2015). African ethics and journalism ethics: News and opinion in light of Ubuntu. *Journal of Media Ethics, 30*, 74–90. https://doi.org/10.1080/23736992.2015.1020377
Montagu, A. (1989). *Growing young* (2nd ed.). Grandy, MA: Bergin & Garvey.
Pepper, S. C. (1942). *World hypotheses*. Los Angeles, CA: University of California Press.
Pistoletto, M. (2018). *The art of demopraxy*. Biella, Italy: Fondazione Pistoletto/Cittadellarte.
Robinson-Morris, D. W. (2019). Radical love, (r)evolutionary becoming: Creating an ethic of love in the realm of education through Buddhism and Ubuntu. *The Urban Review, 51*, 26–45. https://doi.org/10.1007/s11256-018-0479-4
Rodny-Gumede, Y., & Chasi, C. (2017). Ubuntu values individuals: An analysis of eulogies of Mandela. *Journal of Literary Studies, 33*(4), 106–123. https://doi.org/10.1080/02564718.2017.1403727
Ryan, R. M., & La Guardia, J. G. (1999). Achievement motivation within a pressured society: Intrinsic and extrinsic motivations to learn and the politics of school reform. In T. Urdan (Ed.), *Advances in motivation and achievement* (Vol. 11, pp. 45–85). Greenwich, CT: JAI Press.
Schnall, S. (2014). Are there basic metaphors? In M. J. Landau, M. D. Robinson, & B. P. Meier (Eds.), *The power of metaphor: Examining its influences on social life* (pp. 225–247). Washington, DC: American Psychological Association.
Scott-Phillips, T., Dickins, T., & West, S. (2011). Evolutionary theory and the ultimate–proximate distinction in the human behavioral sciences. *Perspectives on Psychological Science, 6*, 38–47. https://doi.org/10.1177/1745691610393528
Shapiro, L., & Stolz, S. A. (2019). Embodied cognition and its significance for education. *Theory and Research in Education, 17*(1), 19–39. https://doi.org/10.1177/1477878518822149
Tutu, D. (2010). Foreword. In D. Gluckstein (Ed.), *Dignity* (p. 8). New York: PowerHouse Books.
Wilson, A. D., & Golonka, S. (2013). Embodied cognition is not what you think it is. *Frontiers in Psychology, 4*, 458. https://doi.org/10.3389/fpsyg.2013.00458

Frederik (Freddie) Crous is Professor and head of the Department of Industrial Psychology and People Management in the College of Business and Economics at the University of Johannesburg. Freddie teaches, do research, and consults in the domain of positive industrial and organisational psychology. He prefers to approach life in general and work in particular from an appreciative stance.

Leigh Leo is a registered Industrial Psychologist with the Health Professions Council of South Africa (HPCSA). She recently completed her Doctoral Degree in Industrial Psychology at the University of Johannesburg, where her research focused on building a fundamental body of knowledge in the field of psychological neoteny through the development of a neoteny-based personality questionnaire. She has published in the domain of embodied cognition, consumer psychology, women in the workplace and assessment psychology. Her research interests are diverse, but generally lie in the field of positive industrial psychology. She currently works as a consulting psychologist with experience in areas of psychological assessment, talent management and process consultation.

Chapter 8
"A Friend? A Single Soul Dwelling in Two Bodies." Friendship—a Special Kind of Love

Elisabeth Vanderheiden

> *Friendship is essentially dependent on its duration—a two-week-old friendship doesn't exist.*
> (Hannah Arendt, 2002, translated by the author)

Abstract Scientific research shows that just thinking about a good friend can make people feel less stressed about their everyday problems. Other studies show that people with intact friendships are less stressed and have greater self-esteem. Other research indicates that friendships can even offset broken family relationships. This may also have something to do with the very nature of the friendship, because by its essence, friendships are the only human relationships that do without legal regulations, official founding rites, and mutual obligations. What a friendship looks like, why and how long it works, is negotiated only between the participants. At the same time, science is divided in terms of how exactly friendship should be defined. It is undisputed, however, that in classical Greek philosophy, friendship was clearly higher than love. Particularly in times of increasingly unstable couple and family relationships, increasing loneliness in old age—especially in Western cultures—and cultural and religious heterogeneity, friendship concepts are being examined more closely for their social value in the most diverse contexts. This chapter examines the question of what friendship is, to what extent it can be understood as a specific form of love relationship based on Aristotle, what its characteristics are, and to what extent it is universal or whether cultural differences can be described.

Keywords Love · Friendship · Cultural differences in the concepts and practice of friendship · Friendship and Well-being · Friendship in a digitalised world

---

E. Vanderheiden (✉)
Global Institute for Transcultural Research, Römerberg, Germany
e-mail: ev@keb-rheinland-pfalz.de

8.1 Introduction

Scientific research (such as that of Oberzaucher, 2019) shows that just thinking about a good friend can make people feel less stressed about their everyday problems. Other studies show that people with intact friendships are less stressed and have greater self-esteem (see Denissen, Penke, Schmitt & van Aken, 2008; Rubin & Bowker, 2018). Other research indicates that friendships can be a key factor in human happiness (Brumlik, 2008; Leibowitz, 2018). Friendship enhances positive developmental outcomes, including perspective-taking and social-cognitive skills (Rubin & Bowker, 2018). This may also have something to do with the very nature of the friendship, because by its essence, friendships are the only human relationships that do without legal regulations, official founding rites, and mutual obligations. What a friendship looks like, why and how long it works, is negotiated only between the participants. In the current scientific debate, interest in the topic of friendship seems to be increasing internationally, although understandings of the topic may differ, as will be shown below. Particularly in times of increasingly unstable couple and family relationships, increasing loneliness in old age, especially in Western cultures, and increasing cultural and religious heterogeneity, friendship concepts are continuously more examined for their social value in the most diverse contexts. This chapter examines the question of what friendship is, to what extent it can be understood as a specific form of love relationship based on Aristotle, what its characteristics are, and to what extent it is universal or whether cultural differences be described.

8.2 Approaching the Idea of Friendship

Science is divided as to how exactly friendship should be defined. Friendship seems to be an elusive term.

> The term 'friendship' is used very loosely and idiosyncratically, by both the general public and social scientists, to describe a diverse range of relationships. A 'friend' may be a casual companion with whom we play racquetball once a week, an intimate confidant with whom our most private thoughts and feelings are shared, someone we interact with every day, someone who lives across the country and we only exchange letters with several times a year, someone we just met a few days ago, or someone we've known all our lives. (Hay, 1988 as cited in Tang, 2012)

Already the sociologist and social theorist Niklas Luhman had characterised friendship in 1982 in contrast to love as "not delimitable" (Luhmann, 1982, p. 105). The German sociologist Schobin also comes to the conclusion that friendship is an amorphous term and that "friendship relations in modern societies are extremely diverse and fluid" (Schobin et al., 2016, p. 14). For him, friendship is therefore less a certain type of relationship with ascertainable characteristics than a network of social forms that is characterised less by a specific characteristic than by a bundle of characteristics (Schobin et al., 2016, pp. 15–16).

Many authors (see Baader 2008; Baader, Bilstein, & Wulf, 2008; Fröding & Peterson, 2012; Konstan, 2019; Leibowitz, 2018; Lu, 2009; McCoy, 2013; van der Meulen, 2016) still refer to Aristotle's definition in the derivation of their concept of friendship. That definition of friendship is briefly outlined here. In *Nichomachean Ethics*, Aristotle (2002) describes Philia, the love between friends, which is to be distinguished from Eros (physical love) and Agape (divine love) (see also chapters of Ryan, Chap. 11 and Mullen, Chap. 59 in this book). Characteristics of Philia are a common striving for a high goal and the feeling of a joyful connection in the search for virtue or wisdom. Friendship is described by Aristotle as a virtue. He distinguishes three kinds of Philia:

1. friendship based on mutual admiration
2. friendship based on mutual pleasure
3. friendship based on mutual advantage.

The first form of friendship is regarded as the purest and most perfect, because the friend is loved here only for his or her own sake, and the Philia applies to the whole person of the other. Philia's nature includes the joy of compassion for all that is beautiful and good, as well as compassion for the evil that befalls the friend.

As Konstan (2019) explains Philia is explicitly understood as a form of love:

> Here, then, Aristotle defines not philia but to philein. But before proceeding further, Aristotle pauses to offer a second definition (2.4, 1381a1-2): "A philos is one who loves [ho philôn: present participle] and is loved in return [antiphiloumenos]", and he adds: "Those who believe that they are so disposed toward one another believe that they are philoi [plural of philos]". Philoi, then, constitute a subset of those who love, namely, just those who both love and know or believe that their love is reciprocated. (Konstan, 2019, pp. 208–209)

But what really characterises friendship? This will be explored below.

8.2.1 Voluntariness, Closeness, Intimacy and Encounter at Eye Level as Constitutive Characteristics of Friendship

In the last decades, researchers such as Wright (1978) also distinguish friendship from other types of relationships by its voluntary character and by a personalistic focus in which individuals come to know and treat each other as whole persons, rather than simply as role occupants. Wright (1978, p. 1) stresses:

> Friendship involves investments of self in a relationship characterized by the partners' voluntary interdependence and personalized concern for one another.

Other researchers like van der Meulen (2016, p. 74) differentiate friendship from acquaintance, for instance, by the increased extent of closeness and intimacy, but also by the creation of symmetry, openness and sovereignty that distinguishes friendship from acquaintance.

The philosopher Foucault (1984) saw in friendship the possibility of meeting one another—at the same level and in freedom—together, freely and sovereignly assuming responsibility for the power that can result from this relationship, if necessary also as a place of resistance against certain social grievances. Within the framework of friendship, it is possible to freely negotiate rules and rituals with one another, and, according to Foucault's understanding, its specific sovereignty is nourished by the fact that it is wanted from within by those involved. Further characteristics include symmetry, since the participants meet each other at an equal level, as well as the ability to change, since it is at the discretion of those concerned how they develop themselves and their relationship.

Some researchers (see Fehr, 1996; Rubin, 1985) define friendship as a close relationship, which is voluntary, intimate, and non-romantic. Rubin and Bowker (2018, p. 2) agree:

> Friendships may be defined as voluntary, reciprocal, egalitarian relationships in which both partners acknowledge the relationship and treat each other as equals. Friendship is typically characterized by companionship, a shared history, and mutual affection....
>
> Also, throughout the life course, individuals typically choose, as their friends, those who are similar to themselves in such characteristics as gender, age, and behavioral styles. (Rubin & Bowker, 2018, p. 2)

8.2.2 Continuity Character, Changeability and Renunciation of Sexual Intimacy as Further Characteristics of Friendship

Many authors also emphasise the continuous character of friendship (Arendt, 2002; Michaelis-König & Schilling, 2019), assuming that there can be no "friendship at first sight" (Arendt, 2002), but only "a growing trust" arising in a lived practice of friendship, whether supported between two real friends or digitally (Michaelis-König & Schilling, 2019). Therefore, friendship is to be understood dynamically in the sense that it is changeable, as Brumlik (2008, p. 155) suggests, due to socialisation processes, for example.

> Friendship is explained ... as a relationship based on affection, cooperation and mutual adoption of perspective that plays a dynamic role in the development of interpersonal understanding of individuals. (Brumlik, 2008, p. 155, translated by Vanderheiden)

Another aspect that numerous authors (see Brumlik, 2008; Luhmann, 1982) underline as a constitutive feature of friendship is the renunciation of a sexual relationship within the framework of friendship. This is also proven by various studies. In a study on cross-sexual friendships (n = 40), the American communications researcher Reeder (2016) found that 28% of respondents find their close friends physically attractive and 14% wish to have a romantic relationship. A further 39%

also had romantic intentions at least earlier, but these intentions had declined over time (Reeder, 2016). However, friendship was a priority for most respondents and they did not want to change or jeopardise the relationship. This finding had already been confirmed in older studies such as one by the University of Athens, which concluded that although sexual attraction can potentially be a challenge, friendship is stronger in many cases (Halatsis & Christakis, 2009).

A notable exception here is the so-called "friends with benefits" relationships (see Vanderheiden's chapter (Chap. 9) on Friends With Benefits Relationships).

Now that the most important characteristics of friendship have been sketched out, the impacts friendships have or can have on the lives of those affected will be examined in more detail.

8.3 Impacts of Friendship

There are a number of studies investigating the positive implications of friendship on a physical and psychological level, with a variety of positive effects which can be demonstrated (see Blieszner & Ogletree, 2018; Holt-Lunstad, Smith, & Layton, 2010). These are comparable with, and sometimes even exceed, the positive effects of a romantic love relationship, as the following explanations illustrate.

8.3.1 Positive Impacts on Health

Positive impacts on health are essentially supported by two major meta-studies in a 2010 meta-analysis of 148 studies (Holt-Lunstad et al., 2010) that combined data on more than 308,000 people with 51% from the United States, 37% from Europe, 11% from Asia, and 1% from Australia. Across all studies, the average age of participants was 63.9 years, and participants were fairly evenly represented across gender (49% female, 51% male). Researchers found a strong connection between social relationships and lifespan. The size of this effect compares with better-known health-related effects of smoking and exercise, for example.

> The findings indicate that the influence of social relationships on the risk of death are comparable with well-established risk factors for mortality such as smoking and alcohol consumption and exceed the influence of other risk factors such as physical inactivity and obesity. (Holt-Lunstad et al., 2010, p. 2)

It has also been found that for family relationships, this effect cannot be demonstrated, and that friendships strengthen the immune system and reduce the risk of cardiovascular disease and depression.

In another 2015 analysis that compiled data on more than 3.4 million people across 70 studies between 1980 and 2014, Holt-Lunstadt and her colleagues (2015) provided quantitative data on mortality as affected by loneliness, social isolation, or living alone. They found that the absence of social connections carried the same health risk as smoking up to 15 cigarettes a day. Loneliness caused worse outcomes than obesity. They conclude:

> Overall, the influence of both objective and subjective social isolation on risk for mortality is comparable with well-established risk factors for mortality. (Holt-Lunstad et al., 2015, p. 1)

Essentially, studies by the behavioural biologist Elisabeth Oberzaucher (2019) also confirm this, showing that friendships between men, for example, lead to a reduction in the risk of suffering from cardiovascular diseases, and that such men also recover more easily from surgical interventions. According to her studies, the lack of friends among women is reflected, for example, in lower self-esteem (Oberzaucher, 2019).

Rubin and Bowker (2018) confirm similar effects—both for Western and non-Western societies—that friendships lead to apparently more positive feelings about oneself and the other and are associated with other positive effects on the physical level and for well-being, for instance in lower levels of anxiety and depression, higher levels of self-esteem.

A comparative cultural study by Denissen, Penke, Schmitt and van Aken (2008) noted similar effects, but found cultural differences, because their studies showed that in the United States or Greece, where people seem to have more frequent contact with their friends, the self-esteem of citizens appeared to be higher than in countries like Hungary or Japan, where people spend less time with their friends.

8.3.2 Positive Effects of Friendship on Finding Meaning

Friendship not only has positive effects on the physical level. A number of authors even argue that friendship is a component of happiness in life (see Brumlik, 2008; Leibowitz, 2018).

Huxhold, Miche, and Schüz (2013) were able to show in two national longitudinally representative studies with middle-aged adults (n = 2830) and older adults (n = 2032) that friendships made positive contributions especially among older adults (65 years and older). People not only looked more optimistically into the future, but friendships also had a beneficial effect on subjective well-being, for example by ensuring participation in social life and thus acting as a buffer against the negative effects of ageing.

Other research results also point to the special advantages of friendship as a social resource, such as the findings of James Fowler and Nicholas Christakis (2008), which indicate that friends who live nearby can significantly raise the overall level of happiness (Fowler & Christakis, 2008). The authors base their work on a network model through which friends are connected. In a study of family and partnership relationships and the sense of happiness of more than 12,000 inhabitants of an American town, these authors reconstructed the "social happiness network" of 1020 people. They found that happy and unhappy people do not spread evenly across the network, but rather occur in groups, and that unhappy people are rather at the edge of the social network which transmits happiness (Lenzen, 2010).

Ten Bruggencate, Luijkx and Sturm (2018) were also able to prove that friendship, in terms of its associated feeling of solidarity, has a positive effect on finding meaning.

8.3.3 Friendship as a Social Resource

Friendships represent an important social support structure (Blieszner, Ogletree, & Adams, 2019). Friends support each other, especially in old age (Selfhout, Burk, Branje, Denissen, van Aken & Meeus, 2010), with concrete help, from shopping to help in dealing with the authorities, but also in motivating each other to healthy activities, from walks to social activities such as taking part in rounds of games (Chang, Wray, & Lin, 2014). In this context, research that was carried out with older people, for example, or with lesbian, gay, bisexual and transgender (LGBT) relationships is of particular interest. Here, de Vries and Megathlin (2009) examined the significance of friendship in old age among older adults and came across concepts such as "families of choice" or "created families".

Almaatouq (2016) were able to demonstrate that the so-called "buddy effect" based on friendships can also have a positive effect on behaviour regardless of age. In their study, they were able to show that social pressure from groups of friends can lead to a spread of measurable behavioural changes, such as encouraging more physical activity or reduced consumption of calories, cigarettes and alcohol (Almaatouq 2016).

To what extent friendship may be regarded as universal and whether or to what extent cultural differences can be determined, is a question that will be explored in the next section.

8.4 Friendship Across and Between Cultures

Some researchers (such as Rubin & Bowker, 2018) regard friendship as universal and assume that most people

> of all ages, in Western (e.g., United States, the Netherlands) and non-Western (e.g., China, India) societies, have at least one person whom they consider a friend. (Rubin & Bowker, 2018, p. 2)

Some researchers understand friendship as a concept that constitutes a culture-free phenomenon in interpersonal relations (Argyle, Henderson, Bond, Iizuka & Cantarello, 1986; Argyle 1999), while others follow the idea that culture plays an essential role in how people define friendship (Triandis, Bontempo, Villareal, & Masaaki, 1988).

From a cultural studies perspective, Michaelis-König and Schilling (2019) assume that cultural rules apply to friendship and that friendship can be based either on equality of opinion or social equality.

Only few studies on friendship deal with cross-cultural or cross-cultural issues. Some selected studies will be presented here.

In 2015, Szarota, Cantarero and Matsumoto conducted a study with 100 respondents. The starting point was the question of whether central core values of Polish culture, such as sincerity and emotional openness, differed depending on whether a relationship was friendly, one of pure acquaintance or was with a stranger (Szarota, Cantarero, & Matsumoto, 2015). The results indicated that Polish participants find more expression in relationships with close friends than with acquaintances and strangers. The differences between these groups were quite large and resembled a pattern typical of collectivist cultures. On the other hand, the authors reported a high degree of total expressivity, which they describe as typical of individualism. Such high expressiveness was found for all the emotions studied, except for pride, which is consistent with earlier research on the importance of modesty in Polish culture. The ability to interact with strangers is seen as a primary characteristic of individualism (Oyserman, Coon & Kemmelmeier, 2002 as cited in Szarota et al., 2015); therefore the authors expected that in very individualistic cultures the differences between prescribed forms of interaction with strangers and acquaintances would be much smaller than in collectivist cultures. The aim of this research was to document the extent of emotional openness in the context of friendship. The researchers had assumed that Poles are not only more expressive in close friendships than with acquaintances or strangers, but that they also apply expressiveness to all the emotions studied, no matter how negative or socially disruptive they are. This was found to be true for all the emotions studied, except pride. It seems that pride is considered to be much less acceptable than other more negative emotions such as anger or sadness. Such an effect points to the qualities of Polish culture typical of collectivist cultures, where bragging about one's own achievements is typically avoided.

In a comparative study between two universities (Warsaw, Poland and Quito, Ecuador) 143 persons (68 females and 75 males aged from 18 to 27) took part. With the aim of examining the cultural conditions for emotional support in friendship, Zuzanna Wisniewska and her colleague Pawel Boski (n.d.), observed both similarities and differences between Polish and Ecuadorian cultures. Cultural differences occurred when personal problems revealed to the partner were confronted with "deficits" in terms of empathy, concern or care. The Polish participants were more sensitive to how the needs of the self-disclosing partner were met by their girlfriend, while the Ecuadorians placed more emphasis on the quality of interaction. The Poles were more interested in personal matters than were the Ecuadorians; the Poles rated intimate conversations more than trivial causal conversations, while the Ecuadorians showed the opposite tendency, because compared to intimate confessions, their preferences were in favour of mutual "small talk".

In a specific Indian context, Sarah Hilaly (2018) has examined friendship concepts, namely for the ethnic group of the Apatanis in the Ziro Valley in Arunachal Pradesh (Hilaly, 2018). The community is known for its seated agriculture among all-dry construction communities in this federal state. It is run without the use of traction and a local irrigation system. Located on a small remote plateau, its agriculture is the most efficient in terms of energy use. One of the traditional institutions of the Apatani is the workers' group Pataň. Its composition is largely based on a cross-gender village friendship, which is equally represented by the family unity. This aspect is reflected in a tradition during the Myoko Festival, where friends from different villages come to renew their relationships. The festival and the rituals associated with it also give friendship a special significance. The author describes as central to the functioning of this society a culture of friendship that permeates all spheres of life of the Apatani. Each of the practices through which friendship is structured aims to create networks of good will at different levels, ranging from family, clan and village to tribal level. This is linked to other socially sanctioned institutions that strengthen relationships that are very important for the maintenance of livelihoods, for a population concentrated in a small area, including friendly relationships between humans and non-humans, animals and spirits for example.

A recent representative study (SINUS Institute & YouGov, 2019), in which 2045 people participated, reported that, for Germany, 66% of the population have a best friend. On average, Germans have three to four close friends and count 11 people among their extended circle of friends. As a rule, these relationships are formed at work (45%), at secondary school or during training (22% each) and through sharing hobbies (21%).

According to the 2019 study open communication was rated as the most decisive factor: 71% consider honest interaction with one another to be valuable, 70% emphasise how important it is to be able to talk about everything, and 70% agree that good friendship is "what it takes to be there for each other when you need each other".

The relevance of shared values and beliefs seems to be declining and was only important for 41% of respondents. Many respondents say they have friends with different political views (60%) or are close friends with people of other religious beliefs (51%). Also, the importance of similarity does not seem to be so relevant for the emergence or persistence of friendship according to the study, in that 58% of respondents have friends with a lower level of education than their own, 46% are also friends with people of different origins and 38% have friends with a different sexual orientation.

Moreover, this study did not publish any difference in findings between East and West Germany in terms of friendships. This was not the case some years ago. Shortly after the fall of the wall between East and West Germany, educationalist Valtin (2008) conducted a study of the different concepts of friendship and identified significant differences. On the basis of an empirical study (n = 108) with 44 young people and 64 adults from West and East Berlin, Valtin (2008) came to the conclusion that East and West Berliners showed clear differences in friendship relations, which were bound to the structure of society (Valtin, 2008; Valtin & Fatke, 2017). In a highly structured society such as the German Democratic Republic (East), friendship relations were based on issues such as reliability, honesty, courtesy, solidarity and helpfulness, and friendship was seen more as help and support, especially in practical matters. In the more highly differentiated society of the Federal Republic of Germany (West), on the other hand, people showed a greater need for personalisation of their friendship relationships, which were characterised by high demands on emotionality and intimacy and were to be settled in the context of self-realisation and friends were understood as a "kind of new family" (Valtin, 2008, p. 282).

Some interesting studies are also less devoted to national or comparative cultural research, focusing instead on intercultural or cross-cultural issues.

A recent Australian study (Belford, 2017) examined how international students (Vietnam, Indonesia, South Korea, Mexico, Columbia, China, India and Italy) experience intercultural transitions after living and studying in Melbourne for a number of years, and in particular the participants' experiences of culture shock, social interaction and friendship development. Participants found that in some cases it was quite difficult to be part of a closed social circle of hosts or co-nationalities, but that friendship was crucial to support them in their process of adaptation.

A decisive factor for the success of an intercultural friendship was found to be the willingness of the members of a group to successfully negotiate their expectations and patterns of friendship.

At the same time, it is important to share similar values and beliefs in relationships and to understand each other's values and beliefs. A study of intercultural friendship (Krumrey-Fulks, 2001) pointed out that people in Chinese culture expect friends to show helpful behaviour, while American friends expect friends to be good listeners.

Sias and her colleagues (2008) examined intercultural friendship development through analysis of in-depth interviews with students. The sample was comprised of 30 individuals, including college students at a large Western university as well as residents from the surrounding community. They represented different countries and ethnic backgrounds including the United States, Armenia, Chile, China, Colombia, England, India, Japan, Korea, Poland, Philippines, Russia, Scotland, Spain, Taiwan, Uruguay, and Uzbekistan. Their analysis identified four factors that, according to respondents, influenced the development of their intercultural friendship. These were targeted socialising, cultural similarities, cultural differences, and prior intercultural experience. Results also indicated several ways in which communication both enables and hinders the development of intercultural friendships, providing evidence of the uniqueness and complexity of communication in these relationships. Sias et al. (2008, p. 2) define intercultural friendship as follows:

> Intercultural friendships are characterized by differences between individuals' cultures that bring unique rewards as well as challenges. Individuals must negotiate differences in cultural values and/or languages, and overcome enduring stereotypes. However, they also gain unique cultural knowledge, broaden their perspectives, and break stereotypes.

This study brought to light some very interesting results. It is well known that proximity is a decisive factor for the emergence of friendship. However, the cases of proximity reported in this study concerned all specific cultural events associated with the cultural networks of the participants (for instance a Chinese party) or the intercultural character of the student body at the university, which the authors interpret as meaning that cultural social functions contribute to creating the conditions for initiating and developing intercultural friendships.

The personal factors identified in this study also all focused on the cultures of the relationship partners in terms of cultural similarity, cultural differences and previous intercultural experience. Similar to intra-cultural friendships (see Sias & Cahill, 1998), perceived similarity was important for the development of intercultural friendships. The most significant similarity for the intercultural friendships studied, appeared to be the cultural similarity (such as being "Asian" or non-US American) and this made them culturally similar, in a way that promoted the initiation and development of their friendships. This led the authors (Sias et al., 2008) to the interesting conclusion that cultural differences reinforced rather than hindered the development of friendship. Cultural differences therefore encouraged the development of friendship, especially because the participants found these differences interesting and exciting. Language differences could both hinder and facilitate the development of these relationships. Those who have overcome the boundaries of language differences have been able to build rich and rewarding friendships. Sometimes language differences leads to the development of a unique language and vocabulary.

Globalisation not only affects who people can potentially make friends with, because today we are more mobile than ever before, both professionally and privately. The question also arises as to what influence digitalisation will have on our friendships: with whom we become friends and how we live and develop these special relationships. We will explore these questions in the next section.

8.5 Friendship in the Face of Digitalisation

The Internet and social media (messenger services, video chat and call programmes) make it easier today—in times of increased mobility and globalisation—to keep in touch with friends who are no longer as geographically close as they used to be. It is also possible to form new friendships between people who might never have met in a non-digitialised and less globalised world (Ben-Ze'ev, 2020).

Some researchers see this as a threat, fearing that it could lead to loneliness and greater isolation because people might prefer digital relationships to "analogue friendships" or neglect them because of excessive media consumption or Internet-based activities (f. e. Bedzow, 2020). Other authors (such as Fröding & Peterson, 2012) even doubt that digital friendships can exist. If, for example, Micha Brumlik (2008, p. 158) defines friendship as

> the form of life which takes place in the lived present, which is why living together in time and space is a necessary condition for its realization [,]

then the question arises what this could mean for a concept of friendship in the age of digitisation that might be redefined and renegotiated.

Currently, however, contrary and ambivalent tendencies can also be observed with regard to the concrete evaluation of friendship relationships in the digital environment. For example, the German Sinus Study (SINUS Institute & YouGov, 2019) found that 75% of respondents believe that real friendships can only be made in real life, but at the same time, 20% have Internet friends who do not know them personally. Another 52% fear that in the future, friendships through the Internet and the media may be less cultivated, but at the same time hope that around 70% will find friends through the Internet who they had lost sight of (SINUS Institute & YouGov, 2019).

This ambivalence is also reflected in the scientific discourse, while Fröding and Peterson (2012), for example, based on the Aristotelian definition of friendship, exclude virtual friendship from being considered real friendship. By "virtual friendship", the authors mean the kind of friendship that exists on the Internet and is rarely if ever combined with real-life interaction. A "traditional friendship", on the other hand, is the type of friendship that involves substantial interaction in real life, and the authors conclude that only this type of friendship can prove the quality of real friendship and thus qualify as morally valuable. In this sense, SINUS Institute and YouGov (2019) define virtual friendship as what Aristotle might have called a lower and less valuable form of social exchange.

On the other hand, Tang (2012, p. 417) asserts that

> [online friendship] reflects one additional way of relating. While online friendship may not provide as many types of social support as its offline counterpart, it adds to individuals' existing social network and provides additional resources.

Studies in connection with virtual support groups show, for example, that participants report a sense of mutual solidarity, as well as sympathy, acceptance and encouragement (see Tang, 2010, 2012). Positive feelings of closeness, acceptance, solidarity and support are experienced here just as they are felt in the "carbon world", because as Aaron Ben-Ze'ev rightly points out (Chap. 5 in this book), experiences in the virtual world are not "not real":

> online relationships are conducted between actual, flesh-and-blood people. Although this relationship involves many imaginative aspects, the relationship itself is not imaginary. Cyberspace is a part of reality; it is, then, incorrect to regard it as the direct opposite of real space. Cyberspace is part of real space, and online relationships are real relationships.

This is particularly logical since communication based on Luhmann could be assumed to be a central point of social relations (Luhmann, 1983).

Sabine Dahlheimer (2013) carried out a comprehensive online survey (n = 2179) and found that 95% of the respondents rated their trusted partner and also good friends, besides a good family life (78%), as being personally very important, and that friendship in general also had an independent value besides partnership and relationship. The results showed differences between the analogue and virtual worlds: the number of online friends correlated positively with the number of friends in the analogue world (Dahlheimer, 2013, p. 120). This research shows that there are differences in the choice of topics and depth of intimacy, depending on whether respondents are online or offline friends.

The question arises as to who is looking for friendships on the Internet and who is not. Research shows that women are more likely than men to make friends online. They also report more close friendships than men (Wolak, Mitchell, & Finkelhor, 2002). Obviously, women are also more willing to communicate about themselves online than men (Peter, Valkenburg, & Schouten, 2005).

Gender differences in friendships between men and women are discussed in more detail in the next section.

8.6 Friendships Between Women and Men

In 2012, a YouTube contributor known as Patvicious (2011a) put a video online in which he confronted a dozen of his fellow students from Utah State University on their way to the library with the question: "Can women and men be friends?" The women all answer this positively; the men doubt it or express themselves negatively, for example, "You are a man, you have your feelings, there is nothing you can do". On the way back, the filmmaker then asks the women once again how many of their male friends would secretly like to start a romantic or sexual relationship with them. The women suspect that all their male friends would like that. Since the upload, the video has been clicked almost 12 million times and discussed in over 30,000 comments, documenting the high interest in the topic. A second video a few months later (Patvicious, 2011b) on a variant of the theme was called up almost 700,000 times, concerning whether it was considered appropriate for people who live in a romantic relationship to have a friendship with someone who belongs to the opposite sex. Of course, this was not a study under scientific conditions, but scientific studies also show gender differences in the understanding and practice of friendship (see also Vanderheiden on Chap. 9 in this book), although the results are very disparate overall. Some selected studies will be presented below.

Valtin and Fatke (2017) examined gender differences in friendship relations in a study in West and East Berlin (n = 64) after German reunification, and found that women designate fewer persons as best/close friends, but significantly more women as their girlfriends, i.e. same-sex friends as closest friends, while men more frequently also count women among their friends. A friendship with several persons of both sexes is predominantly mentioned by men and by married persons or persons living in fixed relationships. Some of the men commented that their partners were responsible for establishing and maintaining the friendship relationship. The authors also emphasise:

> A close friendship between women and men, however, seems to be an exception, especially when it comes to single people. Our results show that friendships are obviously only possible if sexuality has been brought under some control. This can be the case, for example, if it is a matter of friendship with a couple or if it is a matter of "lost" love affairs. (Valtin, 1998, p. 3, translated by Vanderheiden)

According to Valtin, friendship is associated with three functions which, however, differ in their perception according to gender. The most frequently mentioned function was "sociability and exchange", which men understood as joint ventures, while women highlighted the importance of the role of conversations in friendship, from which they expected help in coping with problems as well as emotional support, comfort and sympathy. Moreover, for women, friendship was a protection against loneliness, and for them, the intimacy of the exchange of ideas was particularly important.

The second function of friendship in Valtin's study has been described as "support and assistance" and "help in emergency and crisis situations", whereby emotional support in friendship is more important for women than for men. On the other hand, the "culture of helpfulness" is obviously more developed among women. In this sense, the girlfriend is also used much more as a support structure in crisis situations, for example, in comparison with family members (Valtin, 1998, p. 6).

The third function of the study, "self-realisation", describes a function of friendship that creates an intimate sphere in which intimate feelings, thoughts and problems can be revealed without fear of social sanctions or loss of prestige. This was considered particularly important by West Berlin women in the study (Valtin, 2008).

Recent studies show quite comparable results. From a sociological point of view, Ann Cronin (2015) in a qualitative interview study ($n = 40$) in the United Kingdom has shown that intimacy is practised by participants in heterosexual friendship relationships as a zero-sum game and that their distribution is very limited. She argues that this distribution serves to create and strengthen boundaries of friendship and sexual couple relationships, and examines the implications of these results for the analysis of the relationship characteristics of friendship bonding. Among other things, Cronin (2015) discovered that heterosexual women use female friendships particularly as spaces to talk about partnership problems and to support their couple relationships, while life decisions (such as moving home or the job) are based on partnership obligations and not on other relationships such as friendships. Only the experience of being single for a longer period of time or having undergone a serious relationship crisis opens up a perspective for thinking about and realigning their deprioritising of friendships in the past or the significance of friendship. Here, too, Cronin (2015) found that it was women, above all, who were prepared to undertake such reflection and readjustment.

Other current studies also show clear gender differences Antony and Sheldon (2019) in a study on the role of forgiveness in maintaining friendship found gender differences ($n = 230$, 116 women and 114 men). There were not only differences between men and women with regard to the type and perceived severity of the described relationship transgressions in their friendships, but also in the strategies for mediating forgiveness. While male transgressions typically involve intervention in other intimate relationships and thefts, female transgressions are concerned with personal communication beyond the boundaries of friendship. Conflicts between male friends could escalate from verbal to physical aggression, while female friends were more concerned with other close relationships that threatened friendship. Men preferred to communicate forgiveness using the minimising strategy, while girlfriends generally opted for discussion and conditional forgiveness as the strategy.

Whereas Antony and Sheldon (2019) investigated the differences between women's and men's friendships, Reeder (2016) concentrated on heterosexual friendships that transcend gender and examined them in in-depth interviews (n = 40, 20 women and 20 men). She identified four types of attractions in cross-gender friendships, namely subjective physical/sexual attraction, objective physical/sexual attraction, romantic attraction and friend attraction. Friend attraction is subject to symmetry or asymmetry and may change over time. In a second study (n = 231, 128 women and 103 men) she used a questionnaire to evaluate the frequency of each type of attraction and the frequency with which the types of attraction change. The most common form of attraction was found to be friend attraction, and the least common was romantic attraction. In her studies, Reeder was able to show that the majority of the participants in this research did not experience any romantic or sexual attraction to their friends (Study II) Only 8.7% of participants said that their romantic appeal had grown over time, while 39% said that they once found this person romantically attractive but no longer did. Similarly, 20% of participants reported that their subjective physical/sexual attraction had increased, while nearly 40% reported that sexual attraction had decreased. Friendship attractiveness, on the other hand, showed the opposite trend, with 71% of respondents saying their friendship attractiveness had increased (Study I). Moreover, these studies show that the attractiveness is much more complicated than previous research suggests. Study I provided evidence that some cross-gender friends have experienced one or more types of attraction throughout their friendship. Others lack one or more types of attraction to their friend. In other cases, however, the participants experienced a certain form of attraction that changed later.

A relatively frequent change identified in Study I (Reeder, 2016) was the dissolution of romantic attraction, and Study II confirmed these results. Overall, research in Study II showed that romantic attraction and subjective physical/sexual attraction in cross-gender friendships decreases over time. Only 8.7% of the sample stated that their romantic attraction had increased over time, while 39% said that they once perceived this person as romantically attractive but no longer did so. Similarly, 20% of participants reported that their subjective physical/sexual attraction had increased, while nearly 40% reported that their subjective physical/sexual feelings had decreased. Friendship attractiveness showed the opposite trend: 71% of respondents said their friendship attractiveness had increased, while only 18% said it had decreased.

Possible reasons why the attraction to friendship is growing, while the romantic attraction and physical/sexual attraction is decreasing in most friendships, might be that friends who get to know each other over time begin to see faults in each other (either physically and/or in terms of personality) that make the other less attractive as a partner, or that these attractions may need to decrease in order to maintain friendships.

8.7 Conclusion

In this chapter friendship is presented as a special and specific form of the non-sexual and non-romantic form of love. It is universal, but shows different manifestations in different cultures. It has a strong positive impact on the immediate physical level, but also on the psychological level with possible far-reaching consequences for the creation of meaning as a relevant resource for happiness in life.

Friendships are becoming increasingly important as a relationship concept, on the one hand because traditional relationship models—especially in Western societies—are becoming relative as a result of the increasing number of divorces, childlessness of couples, and increased single households, and on the other hand because globalisation and digitalisation are creating completely new possibilities for initiating and shaping friendships.

8.8 Indications for Future Research Needs

Rubin and Bowker (2018) rightly criticise many friendship studies for referring exclusively or predominantly to Western societies. Future research projects should, to a greater extent, include other cultural contexts with their respective cultural norms and expectations.

Being more inclusive will also become massively important in view of the Fourth Industrial Revolution, as was explained in the previous chapter. Here research is still in its infancy and it could be worthwhile, for example, to pursue the following research questions:

- Will digitalisation and the Fourth Industrial Revolution fundamentally change the practices of making and maintaining friendships on the Internet, for example with regard to trans- or intercultural contexts, gender relations, generational relations?
- How might the Internet change the ideal of friendship?
- What role do the various cultural concepts of friendship play in this?
- Does digital media, automatisation, the increasing role of algorithms create new types and practices of friendship?
- What influence will digitalisation (which is part of the Third Industrial Revolution) and the increasing Fourth Industrial Revolution have on offline relationships?

This is the point at which research begins and global cross-cultural and interdisciplinary research projects are needed to investigate such questions.

A further important research question arises from the processes of change that are becoming more and more evident in Western societies, such as the growth in loneliness. In Germany, for example, a representative study on loneliness was conducted in both 2017 and 2019 (Splendid Research, 2017, 2019), (2017 n = 1039; 2019 n = 1009). According to this research, it became clear that people in Germany between the ages of 18 and 69 feel increasingly lonely and that the proportion of those affected has risen by 5–17% between the comparison years, with the proportion of women in particular rising (12% in 2017, to 19% in 2019) of women who feel frequently or constantly lonely. The same study (Splendid Research, 2019) concluded that apparently every fourth person in Germany struggles to find new friends, while a further 36% finds it sometimes difficult to do so. Here it could be rewarding to look into the question of which concepts and approaches—possibly using innovative socio-spatial or digital-based research techniques—could prove to be promising.

Acknowledgments This chapter is dedicated to my friends. A life without them could be conceivable, but for sure not worth living.

References

Almaatouq, A. (2016). Freundschaft: die gesündeste Beziehung. Tagesanzeiger. Retrieved 31 May 2020, from https://www.tagesanzeiger.ch/leben/gesellschaft/diegesuendeste-aller-beziehungen/story/31868506.

Antony, M., & Sheldon, P. (2019). "Is the friendship worth keeping:" Gender differences in communicating forgiveness in friendships. *Communication Quarterly, 67*(3), 291–311. https://doi.org/10.1080/01463373.2019.1573746

Arendt, H. (2002). *Denktagebuch, Dezember 1950*. München, Zürich: Piper.

Argyle, M. (1986). Rules for social relationships in four cultures. *Australian Journal of Psychology, 38*(3), 309–318. https://doi.org/10.1080/00049538608259017.

Argyle, M. (1999). Causes and correlates of happiness. In D. Kahneman, E. Diener, & N. Schwarz (Eds.), *Well-being: The foundations of hedonic psychology* (pp. 354–373). New York: Russell Sage Foundation.

Aristotle. (2002). *The Nicomachean ethics*. Oxford University Press: Oxford.

Baader, M. (2008). Freundschaft zwischen Ideal, Geschlecht und sozialer Aushandlung. In M. Baader, J. Bilstein, & C. Wulf (Eds.), *Die Kultur der Freundschaft: Praxen und Semantiken in anthropologisch-pädagogischer Perspektive* (pp. 47–59). Weinheim und Basel: Beltz.

Baader, M., Bilstein, J., & Wulf, C. (2008). *Die Kultur der Freundschaft*. Beltz: Weinheim.

Bedzow, I. (2020). *Friendship and social media*. Retrieved May 31, 2020, from https://www.academia.edu/11931351/Friendship_and_Social_Media

Belford, N. (2017). International students from Melbourne describing their cross-cultural transitions experiences: Culture shock, social interaction, and friendship development. *Journal of International Students, 7*(3), 499–521. Retrieved from http://jistudents.org

Ben-Ze'ev, A. (2020). Cyberspace: The alternative Romantice culture. In C. Mayer & E. Vanderheiden (Eds.), *International handbook of love*. Cham: Springer.

Blieszner, R., & Ogletree, A. M. (2018). Relationships in middle and late adulthood. In A. L. Vangelisti & D. Perlman (Eds.), *Cambridge handbook of personal relationships* (2nd ed., pp. 148–160). New York: Cambridge University Press.

Blieszner, R., Ogletree, A., & Adams, R. (2019). Friendship in later life: A research agenda. *Innovation in Aging, 3*(1), igz005. https://doi.org/10.1093/geroni/igz005

Brumlik, M. (2008). Freundschaft und Glück. In M. Baader, J. Bilstein, & C. Wulf (Eds.), *Die Kultur der Freundschaft: Praxen und Semantiken in anthropologisch-pädagogischer Perspektive* (pp. 152–161). Weinheim und Basel: Beltz.

Chang, P., Wray, L., & Lin, Y. (2014). Social relationships, leisure activity, and health in older adults. *Health Psychology, 33*(6), 516–523. https://doi.org/10.1037/hea0000051

Cronin, A. (2015). Gendering friendship: Couple culture, heteronormativity and the production of gender. *Sociology, 49*(6), 1167–1182. https://doi.org/10.1177/0038038514559321

Dahlheimer, S. (2013). *Freundschaft in Zeitalter virtueller Netzwerke. Eine explorative Studie zur Bedeutung von Freundschaften im Kontext spätmoderner Gesellschaften* (vol. 2, pp. 109–128). Neue Praxis.

Denissen, J., Penke, L., Schmitt, D., & van Aken, M. (2008). Self-esteem reactions to social interactions: Evidence for sociometer mechanisms across days, people, and nations. *Journal of Personality and Social Psychology, 95*(1), 181–196. https://doi.org/10.1037/0022-3514.95.1.181.

de Vries, B., & Megathlin, D. (2009). The meaning of friendship for gay men and lesbians in the second half of life. *Journal of GLBT Family Studies*, 5, 82–98. https://doi.org/10.1080/15504280802595394

Fehr, B. (1996). *Friendship processes*. Thousand Oaks, CA: Sage.

Foucault, M. (1984). *Von der Freundschaft als Lebensweise*. Berlin: Merve-Verlag.

Fowler, J., & Christakis, N. (2008). Dynamic spread of happiness in a large social network: longitudinal analysis over 20 years in the Framingham Heart Study. *BMJ, 337*(dec04 2), a2338. https://doi.org/10.1136/bmj.a2338

Fröding, B., & Peterson, M. (2012). Why virtual friendship is no genuine friendship. *Ethics and Information Technology, 14*(3), 201–207. https://doi.org/10.1007/s10676-011-9284-4

Halatsis, P., & Christakis, N. (2009). The challenge of sexual attraction within heterosexuals' cross-sex friendship. *Journal of Social and Personal Relationships, 26*(6–7), 919–937. https://doi.org/10.1177/0265407509345650

Hay, R. B. (1988). Friendship. In S. W. Duck (Ed.), *Handbook of personal relationships: Theory, research, and interventions* (pp. 391–408). New York, NY: Wiley.

Hilaly, S. (2018). Culture of friendship among the Apatanis of Arunachal Pradesh. *Space and Culture, India, 6*(1), 38–50. https://doi.org/10.20896/saci.v6i1.322

Holt-Lunstad, J., Smith, T., Baker, M., Harris, T., & Stephenson, D. (2015). Loneliness and social isolation as risk factors for mortality. *Perspectives on Psychological Science, 10*(2), 227–237. https://doi.org/10.1177/1745691614568352

Holt-Lunstad, J., Smith, T., & Layton, J. (2010). Social relationships and mortality risk: A meta-analytic review. *PLoS Medicine, 7*(7), e1000316. https://doi.org/10.1371/journal.pmed.1000316

Huxhold, O., Miche, M., & Schüz, B. (2013). Benefits of having friends in older ages: Differential effects of informal social activities on well-being in middle-aged and older adults. *The Journals of Gerontology Series B: Psychological Sciences and Social Sciences, 69*(3), 366–375. https://doi.org/10.1093/geronb/gbt029

Konstan, D. (2019). *Aristotle on love and friendship*. Retrieved 12 November 2019, from https://nsu.ru/classics/schole/2/2-2-konstan.pdf

Krumrey-Fulks, K. S. (2001). *At the margins of culture: Intercultural friendship between Americans and Chinese in an academic setting*. Unpublished doctoral dissertation, University of Kentucky, Lexington, KY

Leibowitz, U. (2018). What is friendship? *Disputatio, 10*(49), 97–117. https://doi.org/10.2478/disp-2018-0008

Lenzen, M. (2010). Nicholas A. Christakis u.a.: "*Connected!*": Um sechs Ecken herum kennen wir uns alle. Retrieved 10 November 2019, from https://www.faz.net/aktuell/feuilleton/buecher/rezensionen/sachbuch/nicholas-a-christakis-u-a-connected-um-sechs-ecken-herum-kennen-wir-uns-alle-1971788.html?printPagedArticle=true#pageIndex_2

Lu, C. (2009). Political friendship among peoples. *Journal of International Political Theory, 5*(1), 41–58. https://doi.org/10.3366/e1755088209000317

Luhmann, N. (1982). Liebe als Passion. In *Zur Codierung von Intimität*. Frankfurt am Main: Suhrkamp.

Luhmann, N. (1983). Soziale Systeme. In *Grunriss einer allgemeinen Theorie*. Frankfurt/Main: Suhrkamp.

McCoy, M. (2013). Friendship and moral failure in Aristotle's ethics. *Wounded Heroes*, 140–167. https://doi.org/10.1093/acprof:oso/9780199672783.003.0006

Michaelis-König, A., & Schilling, E. (2019). *Poetik und Praxis der Freundschaft (1800–1933)*. Heidelberg: Universitätsverlag Winter.

Oberzaucher, E. (2019). *Freundschaften wichtiger als Beziehungen* - oe3.ORF.at. Retrieved 3 November 2019, from https://oe3.orf.at/stories/2642539/

Patvicious. (2011a). *Why men and women can't be friends*. Retrieved 3 November 2019, from https://www.youtube.com/watch?v=T_lh5fR4DMA

Patvicious. (2011b). *In a relationship? Why men and women can't be friends* (part 2). Retrieved 3 November 2019, from https://www.youtube.com/watch?v=FYQmqxQgEBY

Peter, J., Valkenburg, P., & Schouten, A. P. (2005). Developing a model of adolescent friendship formation on the internet. *Cyberpsychology & Behavior, 8*(2), 423–430. https://doi.org/10.1089/cpb.2005.8.423

Reeder, H. (2016). "He's like a brother": The social construction of satisfying cross-sex friendship roles. *Sexuality & Culture, 21*(1), 142–162. https://doi.org/10.1007/s12119-016-9387-5

Rubin, L. B. (1985). *Just friends: The role of friendship in our lives*. New York: Harper & Row.

Rubin, K., & Bowker, J. (2018). Friendships. *The SAGE Encyclopedia of Lifespan Human Development*. https://doi.org/10.4135/9781506307633.n339

Schobin, J., Leuschner, V., Flick, S., Alleweldt, E., Heuser, E., & Brandt, A. (2016). *Freundschaft heute*. Bielefeld: Transcript Verlag.

Selfhout, M., Burk, W., Branje, S., Denissen, J., van Aken, M., & Meeus, W. (2010). Emerging late adolescent friendship networks and big five personality traits: A social network approach. *Journal of Personality, 78*(2), 509–538. https://doi.org/10.1111/j.1467-6494.2010.00625.x

Sias, P. M., Cahill, D. J., (1998). From coworkers to friends: The development of peer friendships in the workplace. *West. J. Commun. 62*, 273–300.

Sias, P., Drzewiecka, J., Meares, M., Bent, R., Konomi, Y., Ortega, M., et al. (2008). Intercultural friendship development. *Communication Reports, 21*(1), 1–13. https://doi.org/10.1080/08934210701643750

SINUS-Institut, & YouGov. (2019). *Studie zu Freundschaft*. Retrieved 3 November 2019, from https://yougov.de/news/2018/07/26/deutsche-haben-37-enge-freunde-offene-kommunikatio/

Splendid Research GmbH. (2017). Wie einsam fühlen sich die Deutschand. Eine repräsentative Umfrage unter 1.039 Deutschen zum Thema Einsamkeit. Hamburg.

Splendid Research GmbH. (2019). Wie einsam fühlen sich die Deutschand. Eine repräsentative Umfrage unter 1.006 Deutschen zum Thema Einsamkeit. Hamburg.

Szarota, P., Cantarero, K., & Matsumoto, D. (2015). Emotional frankness and friendship in polish culture. *Polish Psychological Bulletin, 46*(2), 181–185. https://doi.org/10.1515/ppb-2015-0024

Tang, L. (2010). Development of online friendship in different social spaces: A case study. *Information Communication and Society, 13*(4), 615–633. https://doi.org/10.1080/13691180902998639

Tang, L. (2012). Online friendship. *Encyclopedia of Cyber Behavior*, 412–421. https://doi.org/10.4018/978-1-4666-0315-8.ch035

ten Bruggencate, T., Luijkx, K. G., & Sturm, J. (2018). Social needs of older people: A systematic review. *Ageing & Society, 38*, 1745–1770. https://doi.org/10.1017/S0144686X17000150

Triandis, H. C., Bontempo, R., Villareal, M. J., & Masaaki, M. N. (1988). Individualism and collectivism: Cross-cultural perspectives on self–ingroup relationships. *Journal of Personality and Social Psychology, 54*, 236–250.

Valtin, R. (1998). Freundschaft - die zweitschönste Beziehung? Was Frauen und Männer darüber denken. Ergebnisse aus einer Interviewstudie. *Geschäftsstelle Des Zentrums Für Interdisziplinäre Frauenforschung Der Humboldt-Universität Zu Berlin, Bulletin Nr. 17/1998*, 43–53.

Valtin, R. (2008). Soziale Unterstützung contra Selbstverwirklichung. Freundschaftskonzepte von Jugendlichen und Erwachsenen im Ost-/West-Vergleich. In M. Baader, J. Bilstein, & C. Wulf

(Eds.), *Die Kultur der Freundschaft: Praxen und Semantiken in anthropologisch-pädagogischer Perspektive* (pp. 266–284). Weinheim und Basel: Beltz.

Valtin, R., & Fatke, R. (2017). *Freundschaft und Liebe. Persönliche Beziehungen im Ost/West- und im Geschlechtervergleich* (2nd ed.). Donauwörth: Auer.

van der Meulen, J. (2016). *Die Macht der Freundschaft*. Frankfurt am Main: Verlagsgemeinschaft Brüll & Heisterkamp KG.

Wisniewska, Z., & Boski, P. (n.d.). *Cultural conception of friendship: What do Ecuadorians and poles expect from a friend?* Retrieved 3 November 2019, from https://www.iaccp.org/wp-content/uploads/2019/06/35_Wisniewska.pdf

Wolak, J., Mitchell, K. J., & Finkelhor, D. (2002). Close online relationships in a national sample of adolescents. *Adolescence, 37*, 441–455.

Wright, P. H. (1978). Toward a theory of friendship based on a conception of self. *Human Communication Research, 4*(3), 196–207. https://doi.org/10.1111/j.1468-2958.1978.tb00609.x

Elisabeth Vanderheiden is a pedagogue, theologian, intercultural mediator, managing director of the Catholic Adult Education Rhineland-Palatinate, the President of the Catholic Adult Education of Germany and the CEO of the Global Institute for Transcultural Research. Her publishing focus is on the context of basic education for adults, in particular on trainings for teachers and trainers in adult education, as well as vocational, and civic education, edited books on intercultural opening processes and intercultural mediation. Her latest publications—together Claude-Hélène Mayer—focused on shame as resource as well as mistakes, errors and failure and their hidden potentials in the context of culture and positive psychology. She also works as an independent researcher. In a current project she is investigating life crises and their individual coping strategies from different cultural viewpoints. A topic that has also aroused her research interest is humour and how it appears in different cultural perspectives and from various scientific disciplines.

Chapter 9
"Have a Friend with Benefits, Whom off and on I See." Friends with Benefits Relationships

Elisabeth Vanderheiden

Abstract Friends with benefits relationships (FWBRs) can be defined as sexual relationships between two people who are friends. It is constitutive that there is no romantic love relationship between those involved, and sexual interactions happen more than once.

FWBRs were seen mainly as experimental relationships that are part of youth culture. Some researchers even argue that "FWB situations are common among young adults, not necessarily a replacement for romantic relationships but function as a romantic relationship. It's a different kind of engagement." Nevertheless, this phenomenon is not limited to adolescents since some research findings show that these are also meaningful relationships among older adults. Although the popularity of friendships (FBW) is increasing, there is still little research on the topic. In this chapter, relevant research results will be presented and discussed, in particular, with regard to possible significant factors such as gender and culture.

Keywords Love · Friends with beneftis (FWB) · Friends with benefits relationships (FWBR) · Gender · Well-being · Culture · Digitalisation

9.1 Introduction

As a relationship concept that is increasingly gaining importance also among adults, so-called "friends with benefits relationships" (FWBRs) are often practised as alternatives to love relationships, as a result of love relationships, or in preparation for love relationships. These no longer occur exclusively in the Western world, but with an increasing popularity. The purpose of this chapter is to provide a definition, to introduce what types of FWBR exist, and to explore the question of the extent to which these are or are not love relationships. The relationship between

---

E. Vanderheiden (✉)
Global Institute for Transcultural Research, Römerberg, Germany
e-mail: ev@keb-rheinland-pfalz.de

FWBR and well-being is described. The extent to which gender, age or cultural differences can be evaluated is also discussed and some case examples are presented.

> It's a physical act, like playing tennis. Two people should be able to have sex like they are playing tennis. No one wants to go away for a weekend after playing tennis. It's a game; you shake hands and keep going with your shit. . . .
> You swear that you don't want anything else? No relationship, no emotions, just sex—whatever happens we stay friends. ("Friends with Benefits (2011)—Just Sex Scene (5/10) | Movieclips", 2019)

The origin of the term "friends with benefits" is mostly traced back to the movie Friends with Benefits (2011), from which the above-mentioned dialogue between two friends, a young woman played by Mila Kunis and a young man played by Justin Timberlake, originates. A few researchers, such as the Canadian researcher Alex McKay (CBC News, 2019), however, attribute it to the hit song "Head over Feet" by Alanis Morissette (2019) from 1995:

> You're my best friend
> Best friend with benefits.

Friends with benefits (FWB) relationships (FWBRs) are defined as:

> a casual arrangement in which two people have both a friendship and sexual relationship at the same time. Though not romantic in nature, it is possible for romantic interest to precede the arrangement or develop as it unfolds. Friends with benefits have the potential to take various forms depending on the amount of emphasis placed on the friendship versus sexual component of the relationship as well as the motives, goals, and expectations that each partner brings. (Lehmiller, 2018)

There is a definitional ambiguity with regard to the consumption of alcohol or drugs (Lonardo, Manning, Giordano & Longmore, 2010; Manning, Longmore & Giordano, 2005). Some researchers, such as Wentland and Reissing (2014, p. 170), definitively exclude this:

> Sex between two people who have an existing friendship, these two may or may not engage in sexual activity when they hang out with each other, they are usually not under the influence of alcohol and/or drugs, these two engage in sex with each other regularly

while other studies show that this is quite common in certain cultural contexts (see Erlandsson, Jinghede Nordvall, Öhman, & Häggström-Nordin, 2012; Karlsen & Træen, 2012, p. 93).

The following elements are usually named as constitutive for FWBRs:

- access to sexual activity,
- emotional connection with a friend,
- avoiding the burdens of commitments which are commonly associated with romantic relationships (Mongeau, van Raalte, Generous, & Bednarchik, 2016, p. 2).

The FWBR can certainly be regarded as a hybrid form of relationship (García, Soriano, & Arriaza, 2014, p. 242; Mongeau et al., 2016; Hughes, Morrison & Asada,

2005), since it features elements of a romantic relationship, but also elements of friendship, neither of which are in a pure form, but are mixed (Jonason, Li & Cason, 2009; Jonason, Li & Richardson, 2011; Merriam-Pigg, 2012).

FWBRs were observed as a research topic around the turn of the millennium (see Afifi & Faulkner, 2000; Mongeau, Ramirez, & Vorrell, 2003; Bisson & Levine, 2009; Campbell, 2008; Eshbaugh & Gute, 2008; Fahs & Munger, 2015; Furman & Shaffer, 2011; Glenn & Marquardt, 2001; Grello, Welsh & Harper, 2006; Grello, Welsh, Harper & Dickson, 2003; Lewis, Granato, Blayney, Lostutter & Kilmer, 2012; Paul, McManus & Hayes, 2000; Puentes, Knox & Zusman, 2008). In contrast to other manifestations of casual sexual relationships such as hook-ups and one-night stands (relationships in which there is often no emotional or intimate component), most FWBRs are characterised by the fact that partners see themselves connected in true friendship, and most of those concerned do not consider the FWBR as a possible vehicle for romantic love (Lehmiller, VanderDrift, & Kelly, 2011). On the other hand, studies (see Lehmiller, Vanderdrift, & Kelly, 2012), which contrasted these to romantic love relationships, showed that FWBR partners were less likely to be sexually exclusive, had a lower frequency of sexual interaction, were less sexually satisfied, and generally communicated less about sex than romantic partners. However, compared to romantic partners, FWBR partners devoted relatively more time to sexual activity, practiced safer sex more frequently, communicated sexual experiences more frequently and reported a larger number of lifelong casual sex partners.

Most people who engage in FWBRs see this as a private matter and do not make it public in their social environment (Mongeau et al., 2016, p. 2; Karlsen & Træen, 2012, p. 90).

FWBRs are not a uniform construct, but differ greatly in terms of their origin, consequences and characteristics. Some arise in the aftermath of a former romantic relationship; others develop in the context of an initially platonically orientated friendship, when, for example, there is currently no partner available for a sexually orientated relationship. Others (though few) may arise as a preliminary stage to a later romantic relationship.

Based on analyses of participants' responses, researchers Mongeau (2016) and Mongeau, Knight, Williams, Eden, and Shaw (2013), identified seven types of FWBR in two studies with various students of different ethnic and age backgrounds. The (Fig. 9.1) and (Table 9.1) below show the distribution of the seven types of FWBRs and their specifics.

The table below gives an overview of the characteristics that define each type (Table 9.1).

The following case examples illustrate how some of these FWBRs manifest themselves in concrete terms.

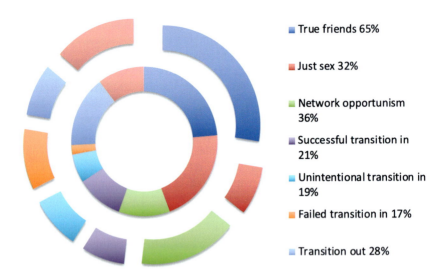

Fig. 9.1 Distribution of the seven types of FWBRs (Author based on Mongeau et al., 2013 and 2016)

Table 9.1 Types of FWBRs (Author based on Mongeau et al., 2013 and 2016)

Types of FWBRs	Definitions
True friends	Close friends who have sex on multiple occasions; partners express love, trust, and respect for an important friend who is considered a safe sexual partner; partners frequently interact in varied contexts. True friends appear similar to, but don't label themselves as, romantic partners
Just sex	Interact almost exclusively to arrange and carry out sexual interaction
Network opportunism	Sexual interaction between friends (though not particularly close) who share network connections; less breadth, depth, and frequency than true friends; shared networks enable partners to interact, typically including alcohol consumption. For these partners, sexual activities result if none of them has found another sexual partner for the night but is interested in sexual activities
Successful transition in	FWBRs may be related to romantic relationships, intentionally or not. Three forms of successful or unsuccessful transition to romantic relationships are distinguished. Type 1 describes the conscious and effective use of a FWBR to initiate a romantic relationship and transform a FWBR into a romantic relationship
Unintentional transition in	In the second type, a FWBR unintentionally results in a romantic relationship, although this was not the original intention of the respondent
Failed transition in	In type three, one or both partners unsuccessfully tried to create a romantic transition, but only friendship and sexual interactions remained
Transition out	FWBRs between partners from a terminated romantic relationship; partners no longer describe their relationship as romantic, but continue sexual interactions and a friendly relationship

9.2 Reseach Methodology

The case examples presented here were selected on the basis of random samples. Random sampling is a widely used method in social science research for selecting respondents and collecting data (see Acharya, Prakash, Saxena, & Nigam, 2013; Jansen, 2019). The two main components for the sample: randomness and known probabilities of selection, show personal experiences of those concerned with FWBR and willingness to provide information about the nature and design of the relationship. In each of the four case studies, the author had the opportunity to conduct a personal semi-structured interview with at least one partner in the FWBR (case examples 2, 3 and 4). In case example 1, a personal interview with L and a video interview with P were conducted. Motives for the FWBR, gender-specific and cultural differences as well as the nature and concrete design of the FWBR, were examined.

Case Example 1

L is 28 and lives in Germany, working as an IT-specialist in the game arena. Through a dating platform she met P from India 6 years ago, who is 32 and works as an data analyst. Their relationship began as, and continues to be, a cyber friendship. From the beginning P made clear that love is excluded: "Everything can happen between us, but love must not exist—not at all," he stressed. After several months of chat contact, he suggested a FWBR. At first L did not know exactly what it was about. P recommended she see the movie with the corresponding title Movieclips = ("Friends with Benefits (2011)—Just Sex Scene (5/10) | Movieclips", 2019). L, who had just separated and was still suffering from the separation, could not imagine at this time getting involved in a new commited love relationship, and therefore agreed to this relationship model. Over time, the relationship has become more intimate and—unintentionally—more binding. L, who has had other casual relationships at the beginning of the FWBR, is stopping them because her relationship with P has become increasingly important. After about a year, L declared that she felt deeper feelings for him, which led to a crisis, because for P as a Hindu believer, there was no question of marrying the woman whom his parents would choose for him, even if he himself felt different needs. There have been many discussions about needs, desires, agreements and understandings and the agreement to return to a friendship without intimate dimensions, as it was at the beginning of the relationship. They have lived this for several weeks; recently P has declared that he loves L. Since then, they feel like a couple, even though they never have met as persons in the non-digital world, and perhaps never will. There is now a high level of commitment for them in their relationship. The FWBR was the preliminary stage to this, so here, an FWBR is present as an unintentional transition. The extent to which it is a successful transition remains open.

Case Example 2

W is a construction worker and lives in Germany. He has, as he says, "somehow no luck in love". He is 45 and has had three longer relationships (1–2 years each), but they all ended with "finding his girlfriends in bed with someone else". He no longer believes in love and wants to "get involved with nothing". He is registered with all free online dating platforms known to him and finds many women there. Some he meets only for one-night stands; with two to three women he entertains longer-term FWBRs. One of these women could well imagine an intensification and stabilisation of the relationship, which he excludes, because he does not have such feelings for them. The other women share his need for sexual contact and limited emotional closeness and commitment. The FWBR has been his preferred relationship model for many years and still is now. Here, in particular, the FWBR serves the sexual satisfaction of the participants, who are not interested in more intensive emotional connections with each other. For the one woman who could well imagine more commitment and intensity from W, the FWBR could be regarded as a failed transition.

Case Example 3

K is a real estate agent in New York. She is 75 years old. She lived with C, who originally comes from Colombia, in a committed lesbian relationship for over two decades until C left her. However, when C is not in a committed relationship, she meets K and they occasionally have sex. Because they are also business partners and close friends, they define this for themselves as a FWBR and see themselves—now in a different form—as still connected in a more non-committal kind of love relationship. K does not want a relationship with high commitment anymore: "I'm too old for such nonsense", she says, "but sex still interests me of course". Here, the FWBR shows itself as a transition-out model after the end of the relationship.

Case Example 4

H is 50 and head physician of a large clinic. He has been married for 25 years and has two children. By chance 15 years ago, he met a married woman—also a doctor, but active in research—during an advanced training course. Through his sexual contact with her, he discovered his desire for sado-masochistic relationships in which he is the masochistic partner. Since then, they have met regularly about three to four times a year. In between, they talk on the phone and chat intensively. They define their relationship as a monogamous FWBR. For both, it is impossible for them to leave their spouses, especially for reasons of social acceptance and social obligation. But they also do not want to be without each other because they cannot satisfy these needs in their marriages and because they feel comfortable and connected with each other. In this case, the FWBR is an expression of network opportunism, but perhaps also of faithful friendship resulting from the same sexually interdependent orientation and the wish to keep it hidden.

These case studies give a first impression of the diversity and complex structure in which FWBRs manifest themselves. The examples also make it clear how, in different ways, they can become an expression of love relationships or how they can explicitly exclude this. They also demonstrate that people expect positive effects from this relationship model. The next sections will deal with these effects, preceded by a few remarks about the positive psychological and physical consequences of FWBRs.

9.3 Friends with Benefits Relationships and Well-Being

In the last 20 years there has been a paradigm shift in the scientific exploration of the relationship between sexual activities and well-being (see Bersamin et al., 2013; Eisenberg, Ackard, Resnick, & Neumark-Sztainer, 2009; García et al., 2014; Rosen & Bachmann, 2008; Levin, 2007). See also von Humboldt, Leal, & Low, Chap. 19 in this book. Whereas previous research into sexual health primarily focused on the possible negative consequences for health, such as sexually transmitted infections, HIV/AIDS, unwanted pregnancy, sexual coercion and sexual violence, the positive aspects have now moved more into the focus of researchers. Many studies show that sexual health, physical health, mental health and general well-being are positively associated with sexual gratification, sexual self-esteem and sexual pleasure (García et al., 2014). This is also the opinion of international professional organisations such as the Pan-American Health Organization, and the World Health Organization (Anderson, 2013, p. 242). Some studies have meanwhile examined in particular the health effects of FWBRs with regard to well-being. These are presented in the following paragraphs.

In 2014, Garcia and her colleagues (2014) conducted an online study on FWBRs and psychological well-being. They interviewed in an online survey 119 people (31 men, 88 women) who claimed to have a FWBR. (Cultural backgrounds or ethnic backgrounds were not surveyed.) The mean average age of participants was about 24 years. Almost 91% stated their sexual orientation as heterosexual, almost 2% said they were gay, 7% said they were bisexual, and almost 1% stated their orientation as pansexual. The majority of respondents gave positive feedback, with both men and women reporting that their emotional responses were more positive than negative.

> Men, as well as women, reported that their emotional reactions were more positive than negative. The most frequent was happy (47.1%), followed by desired (41.2%), satisfied (40.3%), excited and confused (both 26.9%), adventurer (26.1%), deceived (7.6%), used (5.9%); lastly, empty and clumsy (4.2%). It can be stated that, participants experienced the five positive categories more frequently, thus contributing to their psychological wellbeing. A higher percentage of women than men showed positive emotional reactions. As for negative emotional reactions, men showed a higher level than women, in all categories, except "confused" where women showed a higher percentage than men. (García et al., 2014, p. 244)

The study shows that male participants had more positive than negative emotions to express concerning FWBRs. The avoidance of engagement seems to be the central advantage for men, in addition to an increase in confidence and safety. Female participants also displayed more positive than negative emotions. They named the avoidance of engagement as the central benefit for themselves in a FWBR. They also listed winning confidence and safety. Those who expressed a negative emotional state chose to avoid commitments to gain confidence and safety. In summary, the authors come to the conclusion that, overall, positive emotions were selected significantly more frequently than negative ones, and women made up the majority of positive responses.

Eisenberg and her colleagues (2009) conducted a 2003–2004 survey of 1311 sexually active young adults (average age 20.5 years) in the form of a longitudinal study in Minnesota with the aim of measuring sexual behaviour and psychological well-being. According to the study, one fifth of participants reported that their youngest sexual partner was an occasional partner (i.e. an occasional partner or a close but non-exclusive partner). Occasional partnerships were more common among men than among women (29% vs. 14%), and the proportion of male and female respondents reporting a recent occasional partner varied according to ethnicity (men: from 16% of Asian-American background to 58% of men who indicated they were of "other" racial or ethnic background; women: 5% of Asian-American background to 36% of Native Americans). A variety of psychological sensitivities was generally consistent across all categories of sexual partners, and there were no significant differences between the different groups. The authors of the study conclude that young adults who engage in casual sexual encounters do not appear to be more vulnerable to harmful psychological consequences than sexually active young adults in more engaged relationships.

Owen, Fincham, and Manthos (2013) investigated the psychological and other implications of ending a FWBR. They interviewed 119 male and 189 female students with an average age of 19 years, the majority with a Caucasian background (63.6%).They all had been involved in FWBRs in the past 12 months that, at the time of the survey, no longer included a sexual component.

It became clear that the majority of FWBRs continued as friendships after sexual intimacy had ceased, and that about 50% of participants stated that they continued to feel close or closer to their FWBR partner. Those who did not remain friends reported that their FWBR was more sexual than friendly; they also reported a higher level of feeling of being deceived by their FWBR partner. At the same time, young adults who were no longer friends with their former FWBR partner reported greater feelings of loneliness and more depressive symptoms than young adults who remained friends. This can also be explained by the fact that those affected have lost not only a sexual partner, but also a friend. With regard to respondents who remained friends after the end of the sexual relationship, no significant differences were found in the level of mutual social attachment, loneliness or depressive symptoms (Owen et al., 2013).

Bersamin et al. (2013) collected data on identity, culture, psychological well-being and risky behaviour from 30 institutions in the United States in a multi-ethnic study of heterosexual adult students (n = 10,573 aged 18–25 years). The study did not explicitly refer only to FWBRs, but implied it as one of three casual sex forms (FWBRs, hookups and one-night stands). Special research interest lay on the psychological well-being and possible stress associated with casual sex. They found that a larger proportion of men (18.6%) compared to women (7.4%) reported having casual sex the month before the interview. Their results showed that for the interviewees, opportunity sex was negatively associated with well-being and positively associated with psychological stress. The gender difference proved not to be relevant here. Ethnic differences were apparently not investigated. They conclude that participation in casual sex can increase the risk of negative psychological outcomes (Bersamin et al., 2013).

The expectations associated with romantic relationships and the rules governing the shaping of sexual relationships are strongly determined by socio-cultural frameworks. Bersamin and colleagues (2013) also point this out:

> In the present study, we hypothesized and found that men were more likely than women to report a casual sexual encounter. But the current results suggest a different conclusion regarding the correlates of casual sex. As expected, latent variable modeling indicated a positive correlation between casual sex and psychological distress and diminished well-being—an association that, unexpectedly, appeared to be similar for men and for women. The results of the present study, therefore, argue that involvement in casual sex among college students is similarly associated with mental health outcomes for men and women. The lack of a gender interaction is surprising. Whereas a large meta-analysis found small gender differences in sexual attitudes and behaviors between 1993 and 2007, gender differences did emerge around attitudes toward casual sex, casual sex, and fear, anxiety and guilt toward sex. (Bersamin et al., 2013, p. 7)

The extent to which gender differences can actually be demonstrated in relation to FWBRs and what they consist of in detail will be examined in the next section.

9.4 Friends with Benefits Relationships and Gender Differences

Most studies on FWBRs have also investigated gender differences (see Epstein, Calzo, Smiler, & Ward, 2009; Gusarova, Fraser, & Alderson, 2012; Lehmiller et al., 2011; Owen & Fincham, 2011a). These results will be examined in more detail below.

A number of studies have shown that FWBRs are rated equally positively by women and men and that many are fundamentally open to such a form of relationship (see Lehmiller et al., 2011; Owen & Fincham, 2011a, b; Bell, 1981; Ben-Zeév, 2013; Taylor, 2013; Weaver, MacKeigan & MacDonald, 2011). Nevertheless, numerous gender-specific differences can be seen in detail. For example, Lehmiller et al. (2011) were able to prove in an online study (N = 411, 307 women, 104 men) that sexual desire was a more frequent motivation for men (72% men, 56% women) to start such relationships, while emotional interactions were a more frequent motivation for women (37% women, 25% men). Moreover, men were more likely to hope that the relationship would remain unchanged over time, while women were more likely to express a desire to transform the relationship into either a full-fledged romance or a fundamental friendship. However, it also turned out that both men and women were more committed to friendship than to the sexual aspect of the relationship. The authors suggest that traditional expectations of gender roles and sexual double standards in relation to the respective "scripts" can influence how men and women engage in FWBRs. This is related to the concept of the "sexual script" developed by Gagnon and Simon (2005). This approach describes the idea of an individual script for sexual action plans and for the specific processing of sexual stimuli linked to schemes of gender role behaviour and gender identity. They are associated with a certain role behaviour or specific schemes as cognitive representation of sexual experiences, models and attitudes in the sexual sphere. The sexual script includes, for example, the individual's ability and will to bind gender identity, sexual orientation or individual sexual reaction readiness, against the background of which sexual behaviour and activities manifest themselves. Cultural contexts and imprints are of decisive importance here:

> Sexuality and sexual behavior are "scripted" on three distinct levels: cultural scenarios which are instructions in collective meanings; interpersonal "scripts" which are applications of specific cultural scenarios by a specific individual in a specific social context; and intrapsychic "scripts" which are guidelines to the management of desires as experienced by the individual. (Gagnon & Simon, 2005)

Owen and Fincham (2011a) also refer to the concept of gender-related scripts and confirmed in their studies that men are obviously more willing to state at least one FWBR. Most men also appreciate that in the context of FWBRs a greater relational connection is possible than in other forms of casual sex (Epstein et al., 2009). This is confirmed by Gusarova et al. (2012) in a Canadian study. Here, too, both men and women rate FWBRs as predominantly positive to neutral, and women tend to associate entry into such a relationship model with the hope of dating.

Gusarova et al. (2012) come to the conclusion that, interestingly, in the context of FWBRs, traditional gender norms, both dissolve and seem to confirm.

In Figs. 9.2 and 9.3, for example, it can be seen that 42% of women clearly name true friends as an important type of FWBR more than men with 23%, while the

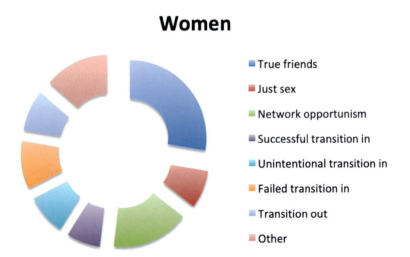

Fig. 9.2 Frequency of the seven types of FWBRs among women (Author based on Mongeau et al., 2013, p. 43). (True friends: 42%; Just sex: 12%; Network opportunism: 25%; Successful transition in: 11%, Unintended transition in: 13%; Failed transition in: 15%; Transition out: 13%; Other: 21%)

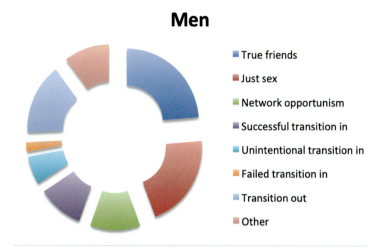

Fig. 9.3 Frequency of the seven types of FWBRs among men (Author based on Mongeau et al., 2013, p. 43). (True friends: 23%; Just sex: 20%; Network opportunism: 11%; Successful transition in: 10%, Unintended transition in: 6%; Failed transition in: 2%; Transition out: 15%; Other: 10%)

opposite phenomenon can be observed with regard to "just sex": 20% of men name it as a type of FWBR, while only 12% of women appoint it as a type. Also, almost all failed transition designations in FWBRs were mentioned by women (Women: 15, men: 2). Classic gender stereotypes therefore seem to be more likely to be confirmed here.

The case studies presented earlier in this chapter reflect these results. In three out of four examples, true friendship plays a decisive role in the relationship and distinguishes it in a certain way. In case example 1, the partners involved now understand their relationship as an exclusive love relationship, albeit possibly for a period of time until P enters into an arranged marriage. As a confirmation of a classical gender stereotype, it may be considered that it was L who initially spoke of having stronger feelings and wishing for a more intensive relationship with more commitment. However, these stereotypes and social scripts are in flux and are being renegotiated, so in case example 4 it was originally the woman who took the initiative for the relationship, which corresponds to her role as dominant partner. The statement of K in case example 3 to explicitly exclude a new committed relationship for herself but to demand the right to sexual satisfaction, also shows a new female self-confidence.

Nevertheless, there is still another—somewhat patriarchal—reality in which an FWBR is used by men primarily to satisfy their needs. Lehmiller et al. (2011, pp. 19–20) confirm this, at least in part. In their online survey of 411 persons (75% female), these researchers also found that men are often involved in several FWBRs at the same time and that they state a higher number of FWBRs than do women. In terms of motivation to start such a relationship, men clearly more often than women cited sexual desire as a motive, whereas women's need for emotional connection was much stronger than men's. Both sexes had the same level of commitment, but the commitment to friendship outweighed the commitment to sexual relations. There are clear differences in the future development: while most men hope to be able to continue the FWBR without fundamental changes, the majority of women hope that it can either be transformed into a romantic relationship or a deeper friendship.

For some researchers, this leads to a thoroughly critical evaluation of this form of relationship. García and Soriano (2017), for example, blame them for the emergence and cementing of emotional and sexual inequalities between women and men. They had interviewed 119 people in an online survey in Spain (31 men and 88 women) with the mean age of 23.69 years. The focus of their research was on the myths of romantic love of the people involved in FWBRs, and how far the myths of romantic love differ between men and women.

García and Soriano (2017) found that some gender stereotypes are still very lively and effective, for example, that men are still strongly orientated towards sexuality in the relationship, while women continue to desire the exclusivity of the relationship. In their study, significantly more women felt jealousy and the desire to feel special and unique. Interestingly, the study showed that both sexes are equally sceptical about believing in "true love" and love at first sight (García & Soriano, 2017, p. 207). On the other hand, the idea that love helps to overcome obstacles and difficulties was confirmed in the study in connection with an almighty vision of love. They conclude:

> The study results reinforce the belief that romantic love is an intrinsic part of the process of socialization and construction of gender relations, assigning attributes to men and women regarding their roles to take (Sanpedro (2004) as cited in García and Soriano, 2017, p. 207)

They points out that the romantic ideal culturally built offers the individual a model of loving behaviour organised around social and psychological factors.

It has been suggested several times that FWBRs are no longer limited to the Western context, although most studies still refer to Western contexts. The next section will examine whether and which possible cultural differences exist between and how they manifest themselves.

9.5 Friends with Benefits Relationships from Different Cultural Perspectives

Even though, as can be seen from the previous discussion, there are a respectable number of studies and scientific publications on FWBRs, it must be noted that there are very few studies that approach the topic from different cultural or cross-cultural perspectives. Most studies refer to the US. However, a few studies from recent years have placed cultural questions at the centre of their research.

Most studies, which have also looked at cultural issues, refer to a specific—mostly national—context. Kerstin Erlandsson and her colleagues (2012), for example, conducted a qualitative study with explorative and descriptive design in which she interviewed eight young people aged 16–18 years in Sweden to explore their thoughts, reflections and experiences regarding FWBRs. She conducted individual in-depth interviews with people who were engaged in FWBRs because they searched for physical and psychological intimacy without expectations and demands. The FWBRs were perceived as more advantageous when the partner was a close friend with whom the interviewee felt comfortable. There was ambivalence about the legitimacy of romantic feelings in a FWBR, although the ambivalence or romantic feelings was quite common. Sexual parallel relationships were, as their survey showed, common and often accepted. Sexual risk behaviour using alcohol and lack of contraception was considered common in FWBRs.

Monica Karlsen and Bente Træen (2012) conducted a study in Norway aimed at investigating the FWB phenomenon in young adults from a Norwegian heterosexual perspective. In particular, they orientated themselves on the theory of sexual scripts and conducted semi-structured interviews with 12 heterosexual women aged 21–28 years with experience in FWBRs as a research method. Various elements of the relationship were examined: Motives and functions, definition of a FWBR, emotions, intimacy and social influences. The results showed that the main function of the FWBR appears to be to meet physical needs in a safe context. In addition, the majority of respondents did not explicitly define the relationship or establish explicit rules for its regulation. Three types of FWBRs have been described: the good friends, the lovers and those who "hang on the hook" (those who suffered from unrequited love and accepted the FWBR to be close to the person for whom they had romantic feelings (Karlsen & Træen, 2012, p. 90)). The study showed that people in FWBRs "borrow" elements from friendship and love scripts and combine them into a FWBR script. It is interesting that in public space, the behaviour is controlled exclusively by this friendship script. Only in the private sphere is the friendship script and the love script available. Karlsen and Træen (2012, p. 90) stress that the results of their studies cannot be transferred to other subgroups of the population or to other societies and cultures:

> Through social processes sexuality is given the expression and that meaning which society imposes. This means that the expressions of sexuality are social constructions that the individual subordinates in interaction with his/her environment.

For the cultural space in which their studies are located, Karlsen and Træen (2012, p. 85) concretise this as follows:

> Sexuality in the Nordic cultures is traditionally regarded more or less as a gift to be handled with care. But sexuality is also subject to social sanctions and restrictions. Sexual behavior is accepted only when certain terms are fulfilled.

Most of the population legitimize sexual intercourse by love, and perceive of sexual conduct as an expression of love (Lewin, Fugl-Meyer, Helmius, Lalos, & Mansson, S. A., 2000; Træen & Hovland, 1998). The prevailing heterosexual script in the Norwegian context is therefore one that connects sexual activity to love, mutuality and responsibility (Helmius, 1990; Kvalem & Træen, 2000; Træen, 1993). This script is often referred to as the love script, and the majority of people follow this script (Træen & Gravningen, 2011; Træen & Hovland, 1998).

These implications may be an explanation for the fact that FWBRs Karlsen's and Træen's study follow the friendship script in public above all. In addition, this study revealed a certain carelessness or willingness to take risks with regard to sexual practice: some FWBRs had developed under the influence of alcohol after a party (Karlsen & Træen, 2012, p. 93) and were practised without the use of condoms (Karlsen & Træen, 2012, p. 94).

A survey from Sweden confirms this: Erlandsson and her colleagues (2012) interviewed eight young people aged 16–18 years in Sweden about their thoughts, reflections and experiences on FWBRs in a qualitative study with an explorative and descriptive design. In the in-depth interviews it became clear that sexual parallelism was common here and was often accepted. Sexual risk behaviour involving the use of alcohol and lack of contraception was considered by respondents to be common in FWBRs.

Saarenmaa (2013) initiated an intercultural study to improve the understanding of today's modern relationships by examining the nature of FWBRs. She sees FWBRs as an example of a current type of phenomenon in interpersonal relationships and a new field of research in interpersonal communication research. The FWBR was defined here as friendship in which the participants also have sex. She interviewed Finnish and American volunteers about their experiences in this area. Since earlier academic research on FWBRs had focused primarily on the study of American students and was mostly conducted as quantitative surveys, her study aimed to explore older adults outside the academic environment through research using qualitative methods.

For this purpose she used semi-structured thematic interviews as a method and collected a total of 21 interviews for this study. Ten interviews were conducted in Helsinki, Finland and 11 in San Francisco, US. The participants were heterosexual men and women aged between 24 and 54 years.

Saarenmaa found that the greatest differences were observed between different age groups and not between different cultures or sexes. Respondents agreed that the FWBR phenomenon is becoming more widely known and popular and should be discussed more openly. In regard to cultural differences between Finland and the US, she states:

> The biggest differences were how people acknowledged the FWB phenomenon when comparing Finland and the US. Also, the media showed more FWBRs in US culture. (Saarenmaa, 2013, pp. 60–61)

FWBRs were mainly seen as experimental relationships that are part of youthfulness. But they have also been observed as meaningful relationships between older adults. The experiences of the informants with FWBRs were predominantly positive. However, the participants did not want to have casual sex. Rather, they were looking for a deeper connection and the possibility of a romantic relationship.

Green and Morman (2008) examined a specific cultural context within the US. They interviewed approximately 200 students from a private Christian university in the southern states about their attitudes and activities regarding countersex friendships. In this study, only 20% of respondents stated that they had sex in their close, opposing friendships. Other studies on FWBRs reported far higher participation rates. McGinty, Knox, and Zusman (2007), for instance, reported a 57.3% participation rate for a FWBR; Afifi and Faulkner (2000) reported that 54% of their sample had sex with a friend at least once; and Mongeau et al. (2003) reported that 61.7% of study participants on one campus and 48.5% on another reported experiences with a FWBR. As possible explanations, the authors cite the sensitive issue and the location of data collection within the framework of a large private Catholic university and suggest that aspects of social desirability and religiosity may have benefited the final results of the current study.

Quiñones, Martínez-Taboas, Rodríguez-Gómez, and Pando (2017) studied the experiences of Puerto Rican college students with FWBRs (n = 156 students and the majority of them were women). Their particular research interest in this quantitative study was on how different levels of religiousness and sensationalism correlate among Puerto Rican university students reporting on FWBRs. Three instruments were distributed in Spanish to students from universities in the greater Puerto Rico area. While 61.8% of the students reported lifelong FWBRs, 17.9% mentioned current FWBRs. Forty per cent of those who had a FWBR reported more than one current FWBR. These rates varied considerably with regard to lifetime rates. Less than half (38.3%) of the total sample said they had never had a FWBR while 61.8% reported having one or more in their lifetime.

With regard to the socio-cultural context in Puerto Rico, Quiñones et al. (2017) note that most traditional denominations are in the Jewish–Christian tradition and most of these denominations consistently assume that sexual activity must be reserved for exclusive monogamous relationships.

But there was a clear difference in the group of people who were religiously strongly bound. Quiñones et al. (2017) found that participants with high levels of religiosity are less prone to be interested in FWBRs. This can be seen according to the values and beliefs fostered in the Jewish-Christian background, where partner exclusivity is encouraged (Quiñones et al., 2017, p. 24). It was also noted here that condoms were often not used. The higher the degree of intimacy in a FWBR, the more likely it was that condoms were dispensed with. This is not without problems, as 40% of respondents who stated that they had a FWBR also noted that they had more than one partner (Quiñones et al., 2017, p. 25).

Overall, it can be stated that too little attention is paid to the question of what possible differences the various cultural contexts of interviewed or affected persons might make, even if there is a corresponding culturally diverse group of participants, the data are usually only evaluated with regard to gender and age (for example, Wentland & Reissing, 2011, 2014).

In the present case examples, cultural differences were only explicitly and frequently addressed in the case of the first couple, although people from very different cultural backgrounds also come together in the constellation described in case example 3. However, the couple involved define this as a relevant influencing factor in their own right, since they had both been living in the US for a very long time or had come from the US. The situation is different for couple 1, who experience cultural requirements as a limiting factor for not being able to fully live their romantic relationship as an intimate relationship. Although P feels his commitment and desire for L he does not want to disappoint his parents. So he will one day agree to an arranged marriage to a woman whom his parents will choose for him on the basis of traditional religious and cultural guidelines. At the same time, it corresponds to his values that marriage is the appropriate context for a sexual relationship, or at least an exclusive monogamous two-person-relationship with high commitment to each other. On this, he and L agree. P works in an international corporation in transnational projects. L also works as a game developer in international teams. Both have much contact with people from different cultural backgrounds. A major difference between the two is that L regards cultural guidelines and limitations as clearly more negotiable than does P, who, through his professional contacts and also through what he experiences via media, social media, Youtube and the internet in general, gains extensive insights into other lifestyles and value systems and also toys with some options, but does not dare to take the "last step" and feels very strongly connected to his cultural environment and regards many framework conditions as non-negotiable.

9.6 Conclusion

FWBRs seem to be a form of relationship that is becoming increasingly attractive for people today, not only in adolescence. It is possible—and research on this is still pending—that it also relates to the way in which many relationships are currently established, namely by virtual means (see Ben-Zeév, Chap. 5 in this book). Access to potential partners is thereby significantly increased or potentially facilitated, but on the other hand the commitment seems to be reduced and the pressure increased by the fact that the number of potential partners is, at least theoretically, infinite. Under certain circumstances, relationship constructions that combine a secure emotional bond in the form of friendship with the fulfilment of sexual needs without demanding an alleged excess of commitment and determination forever, appear attractive. The FWBR appears to make it possible to "have your cake and eat it at the same time".

There are many reasons why such a form of friendship and/or love relationship could and can spread so strongly. It is therefore certainly worth considering this development through the lenses of the women's movement on the one hand and globalisation and digitalisation on the other. In the context of the women's movement, various effects are noteworthy that could, under certain circumstances, have an influence on a relationship construct such as the FWBR, for example a new self-image and the self-confidence of women (see also von Humboldt et al., Chap. 19 in this book and Vanderheiden on age-different relationships in Chap. 20), also with regard to the pluralisation of relationship concepts and, in particular, connected with gender-related sexual scripts. The option of contraception or the depathologisation of the menopause certainly also play a role. Despite all social changes, sexual relationships are still potentially more dangerous for women as a source of experiences of violence than vice versa, which is also why the interest of girls and women in this form of relationship can be explained, because they assume a higher level of safety for themselves than with other forms of casual sexual contact. At the same time, it is striking that both women and men generally do not live their FWBRs in public, but emphasise the friendship aspect there. Possibly this is an indication that for neither women nor men is too much sexual activity conducive to a good reputation in the social environment.

Globalisation and digitalisation not only lead to completely new travel behaviour and working conditions, but also to new communication and relationship models. Never before has it been so easy to get to know people, even over long distances, to keep in touch with them easily and free of charge, and to cultivate friendships and long-distance relationships. This is also interesting from a cultural perspective, because the question arises as to whether new transcultural models of friendship and love relationships could develop from this.

It is not known what effects these serious social upheavals will have on the concepts of love and lived practice. From a sociological point of view, Giddens (1992) had already assumed at the beginning of the 1990s that in Western societies romantic love would be replaced by confluent love. He combines his notion of confluent love or pure love with the assumption that individuals are looking to create meaningful relationships that are based on love and respect. Behind this lies the assumption that the individual seeks constant emotional satisfaction and "sets himself apart" from traditional concepts of romantic love in several respects: it presupposes emotional equality, it is not monogamous nor based on sexual exclusivity and therefore collides with the expressions, "forever" and "unique" which are typical of romantic love. In addition, it relies on the complacency of each individual person, beyond gender-specific inequalities, and focuses on being loved and loved so that the relationship remains stable as long as the individual feels satisfied (Giddens, 2000).

To what extent such concepts actually prevail over traditional ideas of romantic love is open and cannot yet be answered.

9.7 Further Research

Most of the research on FWBRs relates to the Northern America; valid studies from other cultural contexts are largely lacking or are only available in very isolated cases, such as for Scandinavia. But since it is clear that culture has a decisive influence on who people love, with whom they make friends, and with whom and how sexual relationships are lived, such studies would certainly be highly informative. The question posed above, regarding the influence digitalisation could have on FWBRs in connection with globalisation, would be a very exciting field of research. Most of the studies on FWBRs to date have questioned persons from a common cultural area, although some at least have taken different ethnic backgrounds into account. Researchers such as have been able to confirm in their studies that FWBRs are usually generated between people who have grown up in the same culture and with similar beliefs. It would certainly be an exciting project to examine more closely whether and, if so, what special features FWBRs have when people from significantly different cultural contexts live in relationships with one another.

References

Acharya, A., Prakash, A., Saxena, P., & Nigam, A. (2013). Sampling: Why and how of it?. *Indian Journal of Medical Specialities, 4*, (2). https://doi.org/10.7713/ijms.2013.0032

Afifi, W. A., & Faulkner, S. L. (2000). On being just friends': The frequency and impact of sexual activity incrossex friendships. *Journal of Social and Personal Relationships, 17*(2), 205–222.

Anderson, R. (2013). Positive sexuality and its impact on overall well-being. *Bundesgesundheitsblatt - Gesundheitsforschung - Gesundheitsschutz, 56*(2), 208–214. https://doi.org/10.1007/s00103-012-1607-z

Bell, R. R. (1981). Friendships of women and of men. *Psychology of Women Quarterly, 5*, 402–417.

Ben-Zeév, A. (2013). *Why are friends with benefits so happy?* Retrieved from https://www.psychologytoday.com/intl/blog/in-the-name-love/201304/why-are-friends-benefits-so-happy

Bersamin, M., Zamboanga, B., Schwartz, S., Donnellan, M., Hudson, M., Weisskirch, R., et al. (2013). Risky business: Is there an association between casual sex and mental health among emerging adults? *The Journal of Sex Research, 51*(1), 43–51. https://doi.org/10.1080/00224499.2013.772088

Bisson, M. A., & Levine, T. R. (2009). Negotiating a friends with benefits relationship. *Archives of Sexual Behavior, 38*(1), 66–73.

Campbell, A. (2008). The morning after the night before. *Human Nature, 19*(2), 157–173.

CBC News. (2019). We're happy with our sex lives, Canadian university students say | CBC News. Retrieved 19 July 2019, from https://www.cbc.ca/news/health/we-re-happy-with-our-sex-lives-canadian-university-students-say-1.1376119

Eisenberg, M., Ackard, D., Resnick, M., & Neumark-Sztainer, D. (2009). Casual sex and psychological health among young adults: Is having "friends with benefits" emotionally damaging? *Perspectives on Sexual and Reproductive Health, 41*(4), 231–237. https://doi.org/10.1363/4123109

Epstein, M., Calzo, J., Smiler, A., & Ward, L. (2009). "Anything from making out to having sex": Men's negotiations of hooking up and friends with benefits scripts. *Journal of Sex Research, 46*(5), 414–424. https://doi.org/10.1080/00224490902775801

Erlandsson, K., Jinghede Nordvall, C., Öhman, A., & Häggström-Nordin, E. (2012). Qualitative interviews with adolescents about "friends-with-benefits" relationships. *Public Health Nursing, 30*(1), 47–57. https://doi.org/10.1111/j.1525-1446.2012.01040.x

Eshbaugh, E. M., & Gute, G. (2008). Hookups and sexual regret among college women. *The Journal of Social Psychology, 148*(1), 77–90.

Fahs, B., & Munger, A. (2015). Friends with benefits? Gendered performances in women's casual sexual relationships. *Personal Relationships, 22*(2), 188–203. https://doi.org/10.1111/pere.12073

Friends with Benefits (2011) - Just Sex Scene (5/10) | Movieclips. (2019). Retrieved 18 July 2019, from https://www.youtube.com/watch?v=8Pd2fpoD0Xg

Furman, W., & Shaffer, L. (2011). Romantic partners, friends, friends with benefits, and casual acquaintances as sexual partners. *Journal of Sex Research, 48*(6), 554–564.

Gagnon, J. H., & Simon, W. (2005). *Sexual conduct: The social sources of human sexuality* (2nd ed.). New York, NY: Aldine Transaction.

García, H., Soriano, E., & Arriaza, G. (2014). Friends with benefits and psychological wellbeing. *Procedia - Social and Behavioral Sciences, 132*, 241–247. https://doi.org/10.1016/j.sbspro.2014.04.305

García, H., & Soriano, E. (2017). The romantic ideal of men and women involved in the relationship of friends with benefits. *Procedia - Social and Behavioral Sciences, 237*, 203–208. https://doi.org/10.1016/j.sbspro.2017.02.064

Giddens, A. (1992). *Sociología*. Madrid, España: Alianza Editorial.

Giddens, A. (2000). *Un mundo desbocado. Los efectos de la globalización en nuestras vidas*. Taurus: Barcelona.

Glenn, N., & Marquardt, E. (2001). *Hooking up, hanging out, and hoping for Mr. Right*. An institute for American values report to the independent women's forum. New York: Institute for American Values.

Green, K. J., & Morman, M. T. (2008). The perceived benefits of the friends with benefits relationship. *Human Communication. A Publication of the Pacific and Asian Communication Association., 14*(4), 327–346.

Grello, C. M., Welsh, D. P., & Harper, M. S. (2006). No strings attached: The nature of casual sex in college students. *Journal of Sex Research, 43*(3), 255–267.

Grello, C. M., Welsh, D. P., Harper, M. S., & Dickson, J. W. (2003). Dating and sexual relationship trajectories and adolescent functioning. *Adolescent and Family Health, 3*(3), 103–112.

Gusarova, I., Fraser, V., & Alderson, K. (2012). A quantitative study of "friends with benefits" relationships. *The Canadian Journal of Human Sexuality, 21*(1), 41–59.

Helmius, G. (1990). *Mogen För Sex?! Det Sexuellt Restriktiviserande Samhället Och Ungdomars Heterosexuella Glädje* (Mature enough for sex?! The sexually restricting society and adolescent heterosexual joy.) (Doctoral dissertation). Uppsala: University of Upsala.

Hughes, M., Morrison, K., & Asada, K. J. K. (2005). What's love got to do with it? Exploring the impact of maintenance rules, love attitudes, and network support on friends with benefits relationships. *Western Journal of Communication, 69*(1), 49–66.

Jansen, H. (2019). The logic of qualitative survey research and its position in the field of social research methods. Retrieved 28 October 2019, from https://doi.org/10.17169/fqs-11.2.1450

Jonason, P. K., Li, N. P., & Cason, M. J. (2009). The "booty call": A compromise between men's and women's ideal mating strategies. *Journal of Sex Research, 46*(5), 460–470.

Jonason, P. K., Li, N. P., & Richardson, J. (2011). Positioning the booty-call relationship on the spectrum of relationships: Sexual but more emotional than one-night stands. *Journal of Sex Research, 48*(5), 486–495.

Karlsen, M., & Træen, B. (2012). Identifying 'friends with benefits' scripts among young adults in the Norwegian cultural context. *Sexuality & Culture, 17*(1), 83–99. https://doi.org/10.1007/s12119-012-9140-7

Kvalem, I. L., & Træen, B. (2000). Self-efficacy, scripts of love and intention to use condoms among Norwegian adolescents. *Journal of Youth and Adolescence, 29*, 337–353.

Lehmiller, J. J. (2018). Friends with benefits. In T. Shackelford & V. Weekes-Shackelford (Eds.), *Encyclopedia of evolutionary psychological science*. Cham: Springer.

Lehmiller, J. J., VanderDrift, L. E., & Kelly, J. R. (2011). Sex differences in approaching friends with benefits relationships. *Journal of Sex Research, 48*(2–3), 275–284.

Lehmiller, J., VanderDrift, L., & Kelly, J. (2012). Sexual communication, satisfaction, and condom use behavior in friends with benefits and romantic partners. *The Journal of Sex Research, 51*(1), 74–85. https://doi.org/10.1080/00224499.2012.719167

Levin, R. J. (2007). Sexual activity, health and well-being - the beneficial roles of coitus and masturbation. *Sexual and Relationship Therapy, 22*(1), 135–148.

Lewin, B., Fugl-Meyer, K., Helmius, G., Lalos, A., & Mansson, S. A. (2000). *Sex in Sweden: On the Swedish sexual life*. Stockholm: National Institute of Public Health.

Lewis, M. A., Granato, H., Blayney, J. A., Lostutter, T. W., & Kilmer, J. R. (2012). Predictors of hooking up sexual behaviors and emotional reactions among US college students. *Archives of Sexual Behavior, 41*(5), 1219–1229.

Lonardo, R. A., Manning, W. D., Giordano, P. C., & Longmore, M. A. (2010). Offending, substance use, and cohabitationin young adulthood. *Sociological Forum, 25*(4), 787–803.

Manning, W. D., Longmore, M. A., & Giordano, P. C. (2005). Adolescents' involvement in non-romantic sexual activity. *Social Science Research, 34*(2), 384–407.

McGinty, K., Knox, D., & Zusman, M. E. (2007). Friends with benefits: Women want "friends", men want "benefits". *College Student Journal, 41*(4), 1128–1131.

Merriam-Pigg, L. (2012). *Lovers and friends. Understanding friends with benefits relationships and those involved*. San Jose, CA: San Jose State University.

Mongeau, P., Knight, K., Williams, J., Eden, J., & Shaw, C. (2013). Identifying and explicating variation among friends with benefits relationships. *Journal of Sex Research, 50*(1), 37–47. https://doi.org/10.1080/00224499.2011.623797

Mongeau, P. A., Ramirez, A., & Vorrell, M. (2003). *Friends with benefits: Initial explorations of sexual, non-romantic relationships*. Paper presented at the annual meeting of the Western States Communication Association, Salt Lake City, UT.

Mongeau, P., van Raalte, L., Generous, M., & Bednarchik, L. (2016). Friends with benefits. *Encyclopedia of Family Studies*, 1–4. https://doi.org/10.1002/9781119085621.wbefs500

Morissette, A. (2019). *Head over feet, Alanis Morissette's*. Retrieved 19 July 2019, from https://www.azlyrics.com/lyrics/alanismorissette/headoverfeet.html

Movieclips. (2019). *Friends with benefits* (2011) - *Just sex scene* (5/10). Movieclips.

Owen, J., & Fincham, F. D. (2011a). Effects of gender and psychosocial factors on "friends with benefits" relationships among young adults. *Archives of Sexual Behavior, 40*(2), 311–320.

Owen, J., & Fincham, F. D. (2011b). Young adults' emotional reactions after hooking up encounters. *Archives of Sexual Behavior, 40*(2), 321–330.

Owen, J., Fincham, F., & Manthos, M. (2013). Friendship after a friends with benefits relationship: Deception, psychological functioning, and social connectedness. *Archives of Sexual Behavior, 42*(8), 1443–1449. https://doi.org/10.1007/s10508-013-0160-7

Paul, E. L., McManus, B., & Hayes, A. (2000). "Hookups": Characteristics and correlates of college students' spontaneous and anonymous sexual experiences. *Journal of Sex Research, 37*(1), 76–88.

Puentes, J., Knox, D., & Zusman, M. E. (2008). Participants in "friends with benefits" relationships. *College Student Journal, 42*(1), 176–180.

Quiñones, R., Martínez-Taboas, A., Rodríguez-Gómez, J., & Pando, J. (2017). Friends with benefits in Puerto Rican college students. *Revista Interamericana De Psicologia/Interamerican Journal of Psychology (IJP), 51*(1), 19–28.

Rosen, R., & Bachmann, G. (2008). Sexual well-being, happiness, and satisfaction, in women: The case for a new conceptual paradigm. *Journal of Sex & Marital Therapy, 34*(4), 291–297. https://doi.org/10.1080/00926230802096234

Saarenmaa, E. (2013). *More than just friends?: A cross-cultural study on Finnish and American friends with benefits relationships*. Helsingin yliopisto: Helsinki.

Taylor, K. (2013). *Sex on the campus: She can play that game, too*. The New York Times. Retrieved from http://www.nytimes.com/2013/07/14/fashion/sex-on-campus-she-can-play-that-game-too.html?pagewanted=all

Træen, B. (1993). *Norwegian adolescents' sexuality in the era of AIDS: Empirical studies on heterosexual behaviour*. (Doctoral dissertation). University of Oslo, Norway.

Træen, B., & Gravningen, K. M. (2011). The use of protection for sexually transmitted infections (STIs) and unwanted pregnancy among Norwegian heterosexual young adults 2009. *Sexuality and Culture, 15*, 195–212.

Træen, B., & Hovland, A. (1998). Games people play: Sex, alcohol and condom use among urban Norwegians. *Contemporary Drug Problems, 25*, 3–48.

Weaver, A. D., MacKeigan, K. L., & MacDonald, H. A. (2011). Experiences and perceptions of young adults in friends with benefits relationships: A qualitative study. *The Canadian Journal of Human Sexuality, 20*(1), 41–53.

Wentland, J. J., & Reissing, E. D. (2011). Taking casual sex not too casually: Exploring definitions of casual sexual relationships. *Canadian Journal of Human Sexuality, 20*, 75–89.

Wentland, J., & Reissing, E. (2014). Casual sexual relationships: Identifying definitions for one night stands, booty calls, fuck buddies, and friends with benefits. *The Canadian Journal of Human Sexuality, 23*(3), 167–177. https://doi.org/10.3138/cjhs.2744

Elisabeth Vanderheiden is a pedagogue, theologian, intercultural mediator, managing director of the Catholic Adult Education Rhineland-Palatinate, the President of the Catholic Adult Education of Germany and the CEO of the Global Institute for Transcultural Research. Her publishing focus centres on in the context of basic education for adults, in particular on trainings for teachers and trainers in adult education, as well as vocational, and civic education, text collections on intercultural opening processes and intercultural mediation. Her latest publications focused on shame as resource as well as mistakes, errors and failure and their hidden potentials in the context of culture and positive psychology.

Chapter 10
Building a Culture of Revolutionary Love: The Politics of Love in Radical Social Transformation

Matt York

Abstract This chapter positions love as a key concept in political theory and philosophy and for performing a central (counter hegemonic) role in the revolutionary transformation of contemporary global capitalism—isolating a distinctive lineage of *revolutionary love* from the early twentieth century to the present day which has acted to animate a radical political culture aligned to the pursuit of freedom. Focusing through the works of anarchist/autonomist theorists Emma Goldman and Michael Hardt, it will explore how new love-based political subjectivities, practices, and group formations might present opportunities for a reimagining of the frame within which an *alter-globalisation* can occur—drawing on, and making links with contemporary ideas of love as a political concept for radical social transformation in the twenty-first century.

Keywords Love · Politics · Revolution · Transformation · Social change

10.1 Introduction: Love and Revolution in the Twentieth Century

Although often omitted by conventional political histories, there are many examples throughout the twentieth century of revolutionaries who have dared struggle to change the established order by revolutionising love to align with specific political and social ideals. It is here where the lines between the personal and the political blur, where we have seen glimpses of potentiality for love as a radically transformative force. It is here where we might discover that love has always performed an intimate catalytic role within revolutionary political cultures.

Perhaps not surprisingly, love played an important role for a number of feminist revolutionaries in the early twentieth century. Anarchist political activist and theorist Emma Goldman's concept of free love—as we shall explore in greater depth later in

---

M. York (✉)
Department of Government and Politics, University College Cork, Cork, Ireland
e-mail: matt.york@tuta.io

this chapter—called upon revolutionaries to 'ignite their inner desires' (Zittlow-Rogness & Foust, 2011, p. 148). Her conviction that revolution and love dare not be mutually exclusive led to her defence of causes such as sexual freedom, birth control and marriage reform for which even many of her fellow anarchists derided her, and that led to her eventual deportation from the USA to Soviet Russia in 1919 and subsequent exile from Russia in 1921 (Gornick, 2011). A contemporary of Goldman, Marxist revolutionary and Bolshevik Alexandra Kollantai also played a leading role in the revolutionary struggles of the time and was a key participant in the formation of the early Soviet state, becoming the first head of the new Department of Social Welfare (Ebert, 1999). Kollantai similarly found love to be a profoundly social and political emotion which was 'not in the least a private matter concerning only two loving persons' but possessed a uniting element 'valuable to the collective' (Kollontai, 1977, p. 108). Such positions argued the necessity of carrying out ideological struggle concerning the structure of gender and sexual relations simultaneously with social and economic struggles, and were highly contentious.

Love was also a recurring theme in the writings of Italian anarchist Errico Malatesta. Like Goldman he claimed that anarchists 'seek the triumph of freedom and of love' (Malatesta, 2015, p. 60). He argued for love as a central motivating force not only in anarchism but for all those possessing an anarchist spirit which aims at 'the good of all, freedom and justice for all, solidarity and love among the people' which he claimed was not an exclusive characteristic of self-declared anarchists, but a central inspiration for 'all people who have a generous heart and an open mind' (Malatesta, 2015, p. 110). Such a revolutionary love might offer potential insights for contemporary transnational struggles for radical social and political change through its transcendence of ideological differences which might otherwise hinder collaborative, coordinated struggle. Even Marx, claims Hardt (2011), proposed that love, in contrast to money, operates through proper exchanges:

> If we assume man to be man and his relation to the world to be a human one, then love can be exchanged only for love, trust for trust, and so on (Marx, 1975, p. 379).

Money on the other hand, claimed Marx, distorts such relations—exchanging 'every quality for every other quality and object, even if it is contradictory'—and thus undermines our ability to create relationships with each other and to form cohesive social bonds. Love then was positioned by Marx as providing a superior foundation for social organisation than money and current capitalist formations. There are however, as Hardt points out, limitations to Marx's considerations of love as simply a form of exchange, missing what might be the most important aspect of love as a political force—how it can transform us—as we will go on to discuss.

Decades later, like all modern revolutions, the Indian independence movement certainly suffered from internal flaws—not least its widespread acceptance of the caste system, with Gandhi himself accused of discrimination against the Dalit community (Roy, 2014). At its height however, the 'Gandhian revolutionary love' (Chabot, 2008, p. 816) which guided the Indian independence movement, undoubtedly did transform social consciousness, social relations and power relations in India. The independence movement's organisational structures were infused with this revolutionary love—allowing activists in the ashram communities to build alternative social structures and ways of life before the end of British rule, and to experiment with loving practices prior to engaging in non-violent direct action (Bondurant, 1971).

Twenty years on, Marxist revolutionary and guerrilla leader Ernesto Che Guevara (see Härkönen's chapter in this book) made a three month trip to Africa to offer his knowledge and experience as a guerrilla to the ongoing conflict in the Congo. During this time he urged his comrades to embrace a revolutionary love, claiming that 'the true revolutionary is guided by great feelings of love' (Guevara, 2003, p. 225). In reading a little deeper, however, we notice a parallel desire to escape the limitations of what Guevara referred to as 'the level where ordinary people put their love into practice'. The 'great feelings of love' he claims are necessary for the true revolutionary appear to be firmly situated in the public domain. He defers the 'love practices' involved in affective and caring labour to the 'ordinary people', one assumes mainly women, in order to unlock the mobility and freedom required for 'genuine' revolutionary activity. Such a theory and practice of love fails to acknowledge the different subject positions held within a group, movement or society itself, not to mention the transformative potential inherent in such ordinary love practices, and is therefore incomplete and deserves further interrogation.

In the 1960's and 1970's US civil rights movement, activists such as Martin Luther King Jr. and Ella Baker saw themselves as part of a 'beloved community'and aimed at a concept of social justice based in love and equality for all humans (Ferguson & Toye, 2017, p. 15). Martin Luther King Jr. asserted that a mistakenly bi-polar relationship between love and power had become accepted wisdom, which identified love with a 'resignation of power' and power with a 'denial of love'. He proceeded to remedy this misperception by arguing that power without love is 'reckless and abusive' and that love without power is 'sentimental and anaemic' (King, 1967). But the forces of revolutionary love which ignited multiple struggles across the twentieth century seemed to diminish by the late seventies, and hooks, (2000) notes that after the perceived failures of radical movements for social justice aimed at making the world a more democratic, peaceful place, people stopped talking about love. She describes a great feeling of despair as the leaders who had led struggles for peace, justice and love, one by one were assassinated, and that despair made 'capitulation to the existing social order' (hooks, 2000, p. 121) the only place of comfort.

10.2 Feminist Critiques of Love

By far the greatest constellation of theoretical work concerning love to date can be found within feminist scholarly literature. In the first and second wave feminism of the nineteenth and twentieth centuries, the literature tended to focus upon a critique of heterosexual romantic love relations within patriarchal societies (de Beauvoir, 1997; Firestone, 1971; Kollontai, 1977) and often in a fierce criticism of (state and church controlled) marriage as perpetuating gender inequality and masculine domination (Goldman, 2017a; Mitchell, 1974). As we shall explore further however, Goldman (2017b) also proposes such romantic modalities of love as a potential site for resistance to—and transformation of—patriarchal society. Moving beyond purely romantic relations of love, the *Combahee River Collective* (1983, p. 267) positioned their black feminist project as evolving from 'a healthy love for ourselves, our sisters, and our community which allows us to continue our struggle and work'. From the 1990's onwards, feminist theorising around love has fallen mainly into three core themes:

(i) the unequal and exploitative exchange of love within heterosexual love relations;
(ii) the exchanges of love (largely hidden and devalued within patriarchal society) which underpin parenting, caring, friendship and group solidarity; and
(iii) the potential of love as a political power in pursuit of women's liberation.

Jónasdóttir (1994, 2011, 2018) theorises such exploitative exchanges in (heterosexual) love relations through her concept of *love power* and describes how this power is appropriated by men in public and private life:

> If capital is accumulated alienated labor, male authority is accumulated alienated love (Jónasdóttir, 1994, p. 26).

She argues that the persistence of men's power over women in modern contemporary societies (which are formally, legally and socio-economically relatively gender equal) can be explained by the exploitation by men of women's love power. In this way love is positioned—alongside labour—as a 'fundamental causal human power' and 'agent of change' towards either liberation or domination according to its specific utilisation as a *creative/productive power* (Jónasdóttir, 2014, p. 14). Medina-Domenech, Estaban-Galarza, and Tavora-Rivero (2014) build upon Jónasdóttir's *love power* and theorise the concept of *love thought* which describes a specific cultural way of understanding and practicing love that tends to emphasise love above not only other emotions, but also other human dimensions (solidarity/ justice/ liberty) that emerge from modernity in western societies. They contend that this *love thought* is the root of a social order that is unequal in terms of gender, class, ethnicity and sexuality, and requires a heterosexual representation of parenting and family—concluding that a coherent theorisation of love in a rational and scientific sense is *not possible*. Whilst fully agreeing with many of the insights of Medina-Domenech et al. into the dangers of *how we love*, this author prefers to take their conclusion as a challenge to further explore how we might develop a theory of love that *does not* contribute to the consolidation of unequal gender, class and race relations, and that *does not* inadvertently reinforce heterosexuality as a norm and instrument of inequality—a project still in its embryonic stages, with much ground as yet uncovered.

There has also been a growing interest in what Ferguson (2014, 2018) calls the *affective economy*—the bodily and social exchange of energies and pleasures that overlaps with the biological reproduction of new human beings, in parallel to the reproduction of those who are involved in the material economy of the production of goods. In relation to the exchanges of love which underpin parenting, caring, friendship and group solidarity, Lynch, Baker, and Lyons (2009) claim that the activities which sustain such love should be recognised as a form of work, and use the term *love labour*—arguing that love labour is not simply a private matter but a public good which should be rewarded, funded and supported. Lynch (2014) builds upon Fraser's three dimensional theory of social justice (Fraser, 2005) based upon the principles of *redistribution, recognition* and *representation*, and adds a fourth dimension: *affective equality*—which she describes as 'the distribution of the nurturing provided through love, care and solidarity relationships' and as securing equality in *the doing of* emotional and other work involved in creating love, care and solidarity relations. The pursuit of affective equality concerns an understanding that the affective relations within which loving, caring and solidarity are grounded constitute discreet fields of social action. Taking account of affective relations and their role in framing human choices in this context becomes fundamental to reframing justice. Relations of love, care, and solidarity, Lynch argues, matter not only for what they can produce personally, but 'for what they might generate politically' in terms of encouraging 'alternative ways of relating beyond separateness and competition' (Lynch, 2014, p. 183). A recognition of the role of such affective relations would similarly recognise that human behaviour is not solely driven by competition and self-interest, encouraging a political discourse that would enable people to think *other-wise* rather than *self-wise*.

An increasing number of feminist theorists are now arguing that love, although historically a source of domination, is also a necessary condition for women's liberation. Lowe (2014) argues that love can indeed be revolutionised to conform to a political and social ideal—and a feminist ideal—rooted in the practice of freedom. A central theme of the work of *bell hooks* has been the construction of an activist approach to social transformation that recognises the intersections between gender, race and class—which imagines love as a powerful transformative political ethic. hooks, (2000) is primarily concerned with the ways in which the realisation of such a love ethic can happen *only as we relinquish our obsession with power and domination*, and makes the claim that 'domination cannot exist in any social situation where a love ethic prevails' (2000, p. 93). Adopting a similarly expansive vision, Sandoval's *methodology of the oppressed* (2000, p. 4) aims to reinvent love as a political technology: 'a body of knowledges, arts, practices and procedures for re-forming the self and the world'. Sandoval's postcolonial feminism positions love as central to a new decolonising theory and method for a new period of radical activism in pursuit of an 'internationalist, egalitarian, non-oppressive, socialist-feminist democracy' (Sandoval, 2000, p. 5). Ureña (2017) builds upon Sandoval's work to theorise *decolonial love* as an ongoing political and ethical act, and one which poses a direct challenge to systems of power that perpetuate coloniality. Colonial love, Ureña argues, is based on an imperialist, dualistic logic which fetishises the beloved object and participates in the oppression and subjugation of difference. Decolonial love by contrast is framed as *originating from below* and operates between those rendered *other* by hegemonic forces. She proposes that such a concept promotes love as an active, intersubjective process, and in so doing articulates an 'anti-hegemonic, anti-imperialist affect and attitude' that can guide the actions that work to dismantle oppressive regimes. Majewska (2014) notes that such work by feminists of colour is often depreciated for supposed lack of theoretical structure. This author fully concurs with Majewska that contrary to these opinions, the focus upon subjectivity as central within these theories has a great deal to offer the critics of neoliberalism inspired by Marx and the Frankfurt School.

10.3 Love as Freedom

In recent years a(n albeit small) number of anarchist political philosophers and social movement theorists have explored whether love can be utilised as a useful key concept for a new political theory of global revolution. This new body of work exploring love as a catalyst for the revolutionary transformation (*alter-globalisation*[1]) of contemporary global capitalism focuses on the long-term process of *transforming power* in our institutions and everyday lives, not primarily on *taking power* in the short term (Chabot, 2008). What is envisioned by these theorists is a radically different type of revolutionary movement not aiming at the seizure of political power through violent means, but with the 'liberation of imagination, desire and human creative potential' in our day to day lives, a revolutionary practice which is 'patient, constructive, organic and open ended' (Davis, 2011, p. 114). Simultaneously theorising love as political and as praxis challenges the boundaries between private and public, between personal and social, and draws connections between the emotional and the political in non-binary ways (Lanas & Zembylas, 2014).

Focusing through the works of influential anarchist/autonomist thinkers Emma Goldman[2] and Michael Hardt[3] and their theories and praxes of revolutionary love, this section will draw on, and make links with contemporary ideas of love as a political concept for radical social transformation in the twenty-first century. The convergence of Goldman and Hardt's ideas of love as a political concept can be traced to a wider alignment of political positions conforming to an anarchist

---

[1]The term *alter-globalisation* (from the French *alter-mondialisation*) is most closely associated with a specific movement wave spanning from the WTO protests in Seattle in 1999 into the first decade of the twenty-first century. This chapter reclaims and extends the meaning of the term *alter-globalisation* as a useful way of framing the ongoing series of movements whose proponents support global cooperation and interaction while opposing global capitalism—in general subscribing to anarchistic principles of freedom and the practice of a non-hierarchical democratic politics—and within which I would include movements such as the *Arab Spring*, Spain's *indignados*, radical environmental movements, and the global *Occupy* movement.

[2]Emma Goldman (1869–1940) was an anarchist political activist and theorist. She played a pivotal role in the development of anarchist political philosophy in North America and Europe in the first half of the twentieth century.

[3]Michael Hardt (born 1960) is an American political philosopher and literary theorist—best known for co-authoring the *Empire* trilogy with Antonio Negri.

revolutionary narrative which is anti-capitalist and that transcends party and state[4]. Goldman (2017a, p. 102) envisioned her revolutionary love as the 'creative, inspiring, elevating basis for a new race, a new world'. Throughout her revolutionary life, the numerous defeats at the hand of the State, imprisonment and eventual exile, Goldman consistently, patiently and with an unyielding zeal found the energy to resist, to rebel against domination, and this was perhaps her greatest act of (and victory in the name of) love. In a 1931 letter to Alexander Berkman she writes:

> as regards the masses, the inherent love of power to dominate others whoever wields that power, anarchists and syndicalists included, the still voice in me will not be silenced, the voice which wants to cry out against the wretchedness and injustice in the world (Goldman & Berkman, 1975, p. 50).

At the core of Goldman's anarchist politics was an unwavering belief that if the world was ever to give birth to a society free from class, gender or race based forms of systemic inequality, having moved beyond domination and oppression, that 'love will be the parent' (Goldman, 2017a, p. 102).

In alignment, Hardt's revolutionary love is the element that animates all other theoretical elements of his political theories, the *multitude* of the poor, the social productivity of *biopolitical labour*, and the *exodus* from capitalist command, into one coherent project (Hardt & Negri, 2011). Hardt (2012, p. 5) pursues a love which serves as the 'central, constitutive mode and motor of politics', an essential (and greatly undertheorised) concept for contemporary political thought. For him, this revolutionary love is the 'event that arrives from the outside and breaks time in two'—shattering the structures of this world and creating 'a new world' (Hardt, 2012, p. 4).

In relation to political struggle Hardt rejects a reason/emotion opposition, arguing that reason cannot be devoid from passions and affects (Özselçuk, 2016), and like Goldman and her anarchist contemporaries he positions solidarity, caring for others and cooperation as central human survival mechanisms. He contends that when we band together in social solidarity we form a 'social body' (Hardt & Negri, 2011, p. 180) that is more powerful than individual bodies, constructing 'a new and common subjectivity'. Hardt's revolutionary love produces affective networks, schemes of cooperation and social subjectivities. Rather than being spontaneous or passive as it is often presented, Hardt proposes love to be 'an action, a biopolitical event, planned and realised in common'. He takes a Spinozan perspective of love as an ontological event which marks a rupture with existing being to create new being, a production of the common that 'constantly aims upward', a creative expansion with ever more power, culminating in 'the love of nature as a whole, the common in

---

[4]While the work of Hardt is commonly positioned as post-anarchist, he personally rejects such labels. The autonomous Marxism associated with his co-author Antonio Negri more easily aligns with Hardt's own interest in reclaiming the 'common in communism'. In either case, whether libertarian socialist or social anarchist, the revolutionary love which ignites the politics of both Hardt and Goldman offers great potential in similarly igniting a politics of alter-globalisation no longer confined by party systems or nation states.

its most expansive figure'. Hardt's love remains beyond the control of capital, refuses to be privatised and is inherently open to all—clearly contradicting neoliberal values.

Similarly for Goldman, love is the revolutionary force she holds above all others in her pursuit of a free society:

> Love, the strongest and deepest element in all life, the harbinger of hope, of joy, of ecstasy; love, the defier of all laws, of all conventions; love, the most powerful moulder of human destiny' (Goldman, 2017a, p. 101).

She remarks on the notion of free love and questions if love could be anything other, claiming it can 'dwell in no other atmosphere'. Goldman understands that such a love is revolutionary because it remains elusive to capitalist and patriarchal control. Reflecting on the challenge presented to capitalism by such a love she remarks how 'all the millions in the world have failed to buy love' (Goldman, 2017a, p. 101) and how love is 'the element that would forego all the wealth of money and power and live in its own world of untrammelled human expression' (Goldman, 2017c, p. 18). She perceives a similar relationship between love and military oppression, noting how 'man has conquered whole nations, but all the power on earth has been unable to subdue love' (Goldman, 2017a, p. 101). She also provides a taste of the potentiality of love utilised as a dual power strategy, claiming that

> all the laws on the statutes, all the courts in the universe, cannot tear it from the soil, once love has taken root.

Just as Goldman had illuminated the inextricable interrelationality between the personal and the political in order to transform the political subjectivities and intersubjectivities of women and men, and in so doing created revolutionary subjects, Hardt similarly realises that love 'composes singularities' not in unity but as a 'network of social relations' (Hardt & Negri, 2011, p. 184). Bringing together these two faces of love—'the constitution of the common and the composition of singularities' argues Hardt, is the central challenge for understanding love as a political act. Using the example of the *Gezi encampment* at the centre of the 2013 wave of demonstrations and civil unrest in Turkey, Hardt describes how many of the activists involved had experienced this protest as love—as a transformative encounter (Özselçuk, 2016). Hardt claims that this transformative nature of love is central when considering love as a political concept. More than merely recognising solidarity and forming a coalition of *the same*, love transforms, love creates something new. In unity, through examining events such as the *Arab Spring*, *Occupy Movement* and *New Left*, Horvat (2016) suggests that we explore what connects these events in a deeper sense, which he proposes to be love:

> What connects them, more than anything, is something that can't be reduced to pure facts. What can't be reduced is this feeling of presence beyond classification or definitions; a presence of submergence; the feeling that you are completely alone but not abandoned, that you are more alone and unique than ever before, but more connected with a multitude than ever as well, in the very same moment. And this feeling can be described as love. Revolution is love if it wants to be worthy of its name. (Horvat, 2016, p. 6)

This apparent paradox concerning feelings of heightened individuality *and* solidarity during moments of revolutionary rupture animated by a spirit of love are further examined in the next section through the *entangled empathy* in which identity and agency are co-constituted by our social and material entanglements, with our individual subjectivities forming as an expression of entanglements across multiple interrelations.

Katsiaficas' work on developing the concept of the 'Eros effect' through a deep analysis of revolutionary events from the *Global Revolutions of 1968* through to the *Occupy Movement* and *Arab Spring* concludes that the 'activation' of such events are based more upon an *inherent* feeling of connection with others and an *instinctual* 'love for freedom' than with the specific economic or political conditions they oppose (Katsiaficas, 2017). When this 'Eros effect' is activated, their 'love for' and 'solidarity with' each other suddenly replace previously dominant values and norms—cooperation replaces competition, equality replaces hierarchy, and 'power gives way to truth'. But (as Katsiaficas enquires) can we make ourselves fall in love? Can we simply will ourselves to remain in love? Hardt pursues the same questions and concludes that such transformative events will not simply repeat themselves, suggesting that we can learn from such events, from the transformative power of love, and create habits which prolong or reproduce such encounters. New political constitutions of this kind will not be generated using conventional political logic. Neither 'we the people' (Hardt, 2012, p. 9) nor any singular identity can act as founder, for such a politics does not aim at unity. For Hardt, a political constitution *arising through* and *grounded in* a revolutionary love must generate encounters between different social multiplicities which produce new plural relationships, which in turn transform into smaller/larger multiplicities, requiring and generating new encounters. In reframing the conventional genesis of political constitution from unity to multiplicity, from fixed structure to dynamic process, Hardt's revolutionary love manages (theoretically at least) to prolong and extend the force of the revolutionary event to form and repeatedly transform social and political institutions, translating the 'force of the event' into a 'temporal process' (Hardt, 2012, p. 12).

Hardt's revolutionary love is not a unifying force aimed at some kind of *love monoculture*—a *love year zero*. Like Goldman he envisions free individuals living in cooperative social relations and in so doing constituting the common, the free society. In this way, love is not *anti-political* by ignoring the differences necessary for political contestation. Love could, claims Hardt, function as an 'antagonistic engagement of differences that form stable bonds' and which remain based on multiplicity (Özselçuk, 2016, p. 133). Of course, any political realist worth their salt would argue that such a society is as impossible now as it was in the time of Goldman. Through identifying the *corrupt* forms of love however, Hardt manages to displace *evil* as a primary element of human nature in favour of love, solidarity, caring for others and cooperation—human traits long held by anarchist theorists as the key mechanisms for human survival and prosperity. If evil, or as many Social Darwinists might describe it—*the individualistic competitive struggle for survival*—was truly the primary human drive then we would indeed need to yield to domination in order to restrain our fundamental human natures. Positioning love as primary suggests however that it holds the power to combat such corruptions, and therefore a revolutionary love has no need to 'accept the rule of a lesser evil' (Hardt & Negri, 2011, p. 198). Hardt cautions that we should not imagine that we can defeat evil once and for all, and clearly the corruptions of love will continue long into the future, but this does offer great optimism for political contestation and the struggle for an alter-globalisation. Like Goldman before him, Hardt is ultimately interested in *what human nature can become*. If evil, as he contends, is secondary to love, then 'the battle is ours to fight and win'.

10.4 Love beyond the Human: Entangled Empathy

The revolutionary love of both Goldman and Hardt succeeds in displacing the realist notion of sovereignty at the individual and social level, making clear the intimate relationality of social formation. This disorienting of conventional political schemas and the expansive trajectory of their political imaginary prealign Goldman and Hardt with some of the emerging theoretical work in posthuman theory in which a number of scholars are starting to extend their thinking about love to include non-humans, the environment, technology and even matter itself—challenging the anthropocentric bias of contemporary political thought. Hardt himself builds upon the concept of *multitude* by extending beyond the human singularities which compose the multitude to include non-human singularities, including machines. Young people now enter almost spontaneously into a digital world through which they find community, and while the kind of digital freedom promoted by corporate advertisers and marketing gurus is clearly far from free, Hardt views an opportunity to utilise what he terms the 'machinic subjectivities' and 'machinic assemblages' that are forming (Hardt & Negri, 2017, p. 120). Such assemblages are a dynamic composition of 'heterogeneous elements' that 'eschew identity' but nonetheless function together, subjectively, socially, and in cooperation (Hardt & Negri, 2017, p. 121).

Posthuman theory positions the (human) subject as fully immersed in and imminent to a network of non-human relations (Braidotti, 2013). This emerging field calls for a '*love of the world*' (Oliver, 2015, p. 104) leading to an ethics of 'political cohabitation' grounded in a respect for and responsibility towards our *more-than-human* plurality. Such a 'nontotalising, nonhomogenising earth ethics' (Oliver, 2015, p. 240) calls upon us to embrace our shared life on this planet with a multitude of *others*. The responsibility to engender response, or facilitate the ability to respond, in others and the environment, is the primary obligation of this *earth ethics*. The separation of epistemology from ontology assumes an inherent difference between human and non-human, subject and object, mind and body, matter and discourse. In remedy, Barad (2003, p. 829) proposes the use of an '*onto-epistemology*—the study of practices of knowing in being' as a better way to think through how we understand specific intra-actions to matter. The Anthropocene has coincided with an era of high technological mediation which challenges anthropocentrism from within (Braidotti, 2016). This decentring of *Anthropos* challenges the separation of *bios* (life) as the prerogative of humans, from *zoe* (the life of non-human entities). What has come to the fore instead is 'a nature-culture continuum' (Braidotti, 2016, p. 381) which reconceptualises the self as embodied, embedded, relational and extended. The frame of reference therefore becomes the world, in all its 'open-ended, interrelational, transnational, multisexed, and transspecies flows of becoming' (Braidotti, 2016, p. 388). As the author has argued elsewhere (York, 2018) the *more than human* inter-relationality being described by these theorists offers a frame within which a revolutionary love might work to build the critical consciousness required to animate the scale of activism necessary to avert an anthropogenic ecocide.

This emerging field usefully extends the work being undertaken through affect theory to explore how all bodies, human *and* non-human, come to matter through the world's 'intra-activity' (Barad, 2012, p. 69) and concludes that the very nature of materiality itself is an *entanglement*. From this perspective what we commonly take to be individual entities are not 'separate determinately bounded and propertied objects', but rather are (entangled parts of) phenomena that extend across time and space (Barad, 2011, p. 125). Ethics therefore shifts focus from finding the correct response to an externalised other to an obligation to be responsive to the other, who is not entirely separate from what we call the self. In pursuit of a revolutionary love, such an *entangled empathy* (Gruen, 2015, 2017) presents a robust relational ontology through which identity and agency are co-constituted by our social and material entanglements, with our individual subjectivities forming as an expression of entanglements in multiple relations across 'space, species, and substance' (Gruen, 2017, p. 458). We therefore care about others because they are *fundamentally* part of our own agency.

Of course the *newness* of this theoretical work might mask the fact that many indigenous peoples *have never forgotten* the entanglement of human and non-human, largely denied in western post-enlightenment thought. TallBear (2015, p. 234) explains how within many indigenous ontologies even objects and forces such as stones, thunder and stars are considered to be 'sentient and knowing persons' thus extending the frame of what is *living* (and what might be loved) far beyond the human. Such a radical solidarity can trace its lineage back through the many theorists and activists throughout history who have revolutionised love to align with their pursuit of freedom. The expansive, creative, disorienting, revolutionary love that is emerging through post human and entanglement theories is—we might argue—the very same force that animated Goldman's radical politics a century ago. In this neoliberal era, finally fulfilling the promise of a political theory and praxis grounded in a culture of revolutionary love constitutes a pressing political project for all those engaged in authentic contemporary struggles for an alter-globalisation, and one deserving significant further exploration.

10.5 Conclusion: Love as Liberation

Scholarly work from anarchist, feminist, affect theory and queer theory perspectives which explores love as a creative, productive and positive force, and the new posthuman theories which extend love to include non-humans and the environment offer exciting opportunities for new political cultures to emerge. Through examining aligning theoretical ideas throughout the twentieth century and emerging theory in the academy today we have been able to isolate a distinctive lineage of revolutionary love which acts to animate radical social and cultural transformation. Through exploring the inextricable interrelationality of the personal and political, this chapter has illuminated the processes through which love is perverted from its intrinsic course to manifest as domination within intimate asymmetrical power relations while also pursuing a theory and praxis of revolutionary love which aims at challenging and transforming such dominations and constituting the free society simultaneously.

It is clear from the experience of revolution in the twentieth century that authoritarian attempts at societal change towards alternative systems, however noble the intended outcomes, were conclusive failures. The literature suggests that if we are to successfully realise a more participatory, cooperative, non-exploitative, ecologically sustainable and peaceful world, the forms of organisation which lead the transition towards such a system (in order to avoid similar authoritarian results) require a pre-modelling of the quality of world envisioned, and could usefully adopt propositional activities grounded in revolutionary love. Such an approach might offer a clear, cohesive frame of reference within which the new system can be incubated, nurtured and sustained while simultaneously offering potential in constructing a counter-hegemony to subvert and supplant the failing neoliberal project.

The agency of a revolutionary love as explored in this chapter offers a direct (and directable) causal effect on the trajectory of our multiple loving-caring relations, and therefore to the extent to which they might lead to intimate or social relations of domination or liberation. Such a revolutionary love can be seen to materialise naturally in moments where our collective psycho-socio-material entanglement is realised, experienced and embodied. Conversely this revolutionary love can be invoked—activating a radical solidarity—a (more than human) psycho-socio-material commons. Operationalising this Agapeic Web might present us with both the means and the end when pursuing radical social and cultural transformation in the twenty-first century—facilitating the emergence of new love-based political subjectivities, practices, and group formations, and providing opportunities for a reimagining of the frame within which an alter-globalisation can occur.

References

Barad, K. (2003). Posthumanist performativity: Toward an understanding of how matter comes to matter. *Gender and Science, 28*(3), 801–831.
Barad, K. (2011). Nature's queer performativity. *Qui Parle, 19*(2), 121–158.
Barad, K. (2012). Matter feels, converses, suffers, desires, yearns and remembers. In R. Dolphijn & I. Van der Tuin (Eds.), *New materialism: Interviews and cartographies* (pp. 48–70). Ann Arbor, Michigan: Open Humanities Press.
Bondurant, J. V. (1971). *Conquest of violence: The Gandhian philosophy of conflict*. Berkeley: University of California Press.
Braidotti, R. (2013). *The posthuman*. Cambridge: Polity Press.
Braidotti, R. (2016). The critical posthumanities; or, is medianatures to naturecultures as zoe is to bios? *Cultural Politics, 12*(3), 380–390.
Chabot, S. (2008). Love and revolution. *Critical Sociology, 34*(6), 803–828.
Combahee River Collective. (1983). The Combahee River Collective statement. In B. Smith (Ed.), *Home girls: A black feminist anthology*. New York: Kitchen Table Press.
Davis, L. (2011). Love and revolution in Ursula Le Guin's four ways to forgiveness. In J. Heckert & R. Cleminson (Eds.), *Anarchism and sexuality: Ethics, relationships and power* (pp. 74–92). New York: Routledge.
De Beauvoir, S. (1997). *The second sex (translated by H. M. Parshley)*. London: Vintage.
Ebert, T. L. (1999). Alexandra Kollontai and red love. In *Solidarity US*. Retrieved from http://www.solidarity-us.org/site/node/1724
Ferguson, A. (2014). Feminist love politics: Romance, care, and solidarity. In A. G. Jónasdóttir & A. Ferguson (Eds.), *Love: A question for feminism in the twenty-first century* (pp. 250–264). London: Routledge.
Ferguson, A. (2018). Alienation in love: Is mutual love the solution? In A. García-Andrade, L. Gunnarsson, & A. G. Jónasdóttir (Eds.), *Feminism and the power of love: Interdisciplinary interventions* (pp. 36–54). New York: Routledge.
Ferguson, A., & Toye, M. (2017). Feminist love studies–editors introduction. *Hypatia, 32*(1), 5–18.
Firestone, S. (1971). *The dialectic of sex: The case for feminist revolution*. New York: Bantam Books.
Fraser, N. (2005). Reframing justice in a globalising world. *New Left Review, 36*, 69–88.
Goldman, E. (2017a). Marriage and love. In E. Goldman (Ed.), *Anarchism and other essays*. Los Angeles, CA: Enhanced Media.
Goldman, E. (2017b). Anarchy and the sex question. In T. Anderson (Ed.), *Publications by Emma Goldman*. Create Space: North Charleston, SC.
Goldman, E. (2017c). What I believe. In T. Anderson (Ed.), *Publications by Emma Goldman*. Create Space: North Charleston, SC.
Goldman, E., & Berkman, A. (1975). *Nowhere at home: Letters from exile of Emma Goldman and Alexander Berkman (edited by R. Drinnon & a.M. Drinnon)*. New York: Schocken Books.
Gornick, V. (2011). Love and anarchy: Emma Goldman's passion for free expression burns on. The Chronicle of Higher Education. Retrieved from https://www.chronicle.com/article/LoveAnarchy/129467
Gruen, L. (2015). *Entangled empathy: An alternative ethic for our relationships with animals*. New York: Lantern Books.
Gruen, L. (2017). Expressing entangled empathy: A reply. *Hypatia, 32*(2), 452–462.
Guevara, E. C. (2003). *Che Guevara reader: writings on politics and revolutions (edited by D. Deutschmann)*. Melbourne: Open Press.
Hardt, M. (2011). For love or money. *Cultural Anthropology, 26*(4), 676–682.
Hardt, M. (2012). *The procedures of love*. Ostfildern, Germany: Hatje Cantz Verlag.
Hardt, M., & Negri, A. (2011). *Commonwealth*. Cambridge: Harvard University Press.
Hardt, M., & Negri, A. (2017). *Assembly*. New York: Oxford University Press.
hooks, B. (2000). *All about love: New visions*. New York: Harper Collins.

Horvat, S. (2016). *The radicality of love*. Cambridge: Polity Press.
Jónasdóttir, A. G. (1994). *Why women are oppressed*. Philadelphia: Temple University Press.
Jónasdóttir, A. G. (2011). What kind of power is "love power"? In A. G. Jónasdóttir, V. Bryson, & K. B. Jones (Eds.), *Sexuality, gender and power: Intersectional and transnational perspectives* (pp. 45–59). New York: Routledge.
Jónasdóttir, A. G. (2014). Love studies: A (re) new (ed) field of knowledge interests. In A. G. Jónasdóttir & A. Ferguson (Eds.), *Love: A question for feminism in the twenty-first century* (pp. 11–31). London: Routledge.
Jónasdóttir, A. G. (2018). The difference that love (power) makes. In A. García-Andrade, L. Gunnarsson, & A. G. Jónasdóttir (Eds.), *Feminism and the power of love: Interdisciplinary interventions* (pp. 15–35). New York: Routledge.
Katsiaficas, G. (2017). From Marcuse's "political Eros" to the Eros effect. In J. Del Gandio & A. K. Thompson (Eds.), *Spontaneous combustion: The Eros effect and global revolution* (pp. 53–72). New York: SUNY Press.
Kollontai, A. (1977). *Selected writings of Alexandra Kollontai (edited & translated by a. Holt)*. New York: Horton.
King, Jr. M. L. (1967). Where do we go from here? Transcription from a speech given at 11th Annual SCLC Convention, Atlanta, Georgia. 16th August 1967. *King Encyclopedia*. Retrieved from http://kingencyclopedia.stanford.edu/encyclopedia/documentsentry/where_do_we_go_from_here_delivered_at_the_11th_annual_sclc_convention/
Lanas, M., & Zembylas, M. (2014). Towards a transformational political concept of love in critical education. *Studies in Philosophy and Education, 34*(1), 31–44.
Lowe, L. (2014). Revolutionary love: Feminism, love, and the transformative politics of freedom in the works of Wollstonecraft, Beauvoir, and Goldman. In A. G. Jónasdóttir & A. Ferguson (Eds.), *Love: A question for feminism in the twenty-first century* (pp. 193–205). London: Routledge.
Lynch, K., Baker, J., & Lyons, M. (2009). *Affective equality: Love, care and injustice*. London: Palgrave Macmillan.
Lynch, K. (2014). Why love, care, and solidarity are political matters: Affective equality and Fraser's model of social justice. In A. G. Jónasdóttir & A. Ferguson (Eds.), *Love: A question for feminism in the twenty-first century* (pp. 173–189). London: Routledge.
Majewska, E. (2014). Love in translation: Neoliberal availability or a solidarity practice? In A. G. Jonasdittir & A. Ferguson (Eds.), *Love: A question for feminism in the twenty-first century* (pp. 207–218). London: Routledge.
Malatesta, E. (2015). *Life and ideas: The anarchist writings of Errico Malatesta* (edited by V. Richards). Oakland, CA: PM Press.
Marx, C. (1975). *Early writings* (translated by R. Livingstone & G. Benton). London: Penguin.
Medina-Domenech, R. M., Estaban-Galarza, M. L., & Tavora-Rivero, A. (2014). Moved by love: How the research of love can change our deep rooted emotional understandings and affective consciousness. In A. G. Jónasdóttir & A. Ferguson (Eds.), *Love: A question for feminism in the twenty-first century* (pp. 158–170). London: Routledge.
Mitchell, J. (1974). *Psychoanalysis and feminism*. New York: Pantheon Books.
Oliver, K. (2015). *Earth and world*. New York: Columbia University Press.
Özselçuk, C. (2016). Fifteen years after the empire: An interview with Michael Hardt. *Rethinking Marxism, 28*(1), 124–138.
Roy, A. (2014, July). The mahatma Ayyankali lecture. In *Oral presentation given to the international seminar–re-imagining struggles at the margins: A history of the unconquered and the oppressed*. Thiruvananthapuram: University of Kerala.
Sandoval, C. (2000). *Methodology of the oppressed*. Minneapolis: University of Minnesota Press.
TallBear, K. (2015). An indigenous reflection on working beyond the human/not human. *GLQ: A Journal of Lesbian and Gay Studies, 21*(2–3), 230–235.
Ureña, C. (2017). Loving from below: Of (de)colonial love and other demons. *Hypatia, 32*(1), 86–102.
York, M. (2018). Revolutionary love and alter-globalisation: Towards a new development ethic. *Social Change, 48*(4), 601–615.

Zittlow-Rogness, K., & Foust, C. R. (2011). Beyond rights and virtues as Foundation for Women's agency: Emma Goldman's rhetoric of free love. *Western Journal of Communication, 75*(2), 148–167.

Matt York is a political theorist and activist. He holds a doctorate in government and politics, awarded by University College Cork, Ireland. His work on the politics of love can be found in a range of journals including *Social Change* and the *Radical Philosophy Review*.

Part III
Love in Religious and Belief Systems

Malaysian wedding (Photo: Aliff Hassan@Alex Hudson)

Chapter 11
Devotion: "Being Shore to the Ocean"

Thomas Ryan

Abstract Building on Robert Frost's phrase, this chapter examines devotion in terms of 'loyalty and love or care for someone or something' (Cambridge Dictionary). The first half explores foundational considerations about love as devotion through clarifying (a) language and (b) various understandings of love. Devotion is viewed, first, in the context of love as a universal phenomenon that finds expression across cultures, within committed relationships, families and between parents and children. Second, devotion is discussed in relation to agape, eros and philia. 'Robust concern' (carefully understood) is suggested as a possible description for devotion. On that basis, devotion can also function in social life as a deeply held loyalty to a cause or organization. It can also denote a bond between animals and humans. The chapter's second half illustrates devotion in daily life expressed in works of art using the framework of power-based relationships as in master-servant, kinship systems and social class. Such settings, found in selected modern films and literary texts (both ancient and contemporary), enable us to investigate the life-giving, ambiguous, and, finally, life-denying aspects of devotion. In the process, the various forms, benefits (and limits) of devotion emerge together with its necessary relationship to the guidance of moral wisdom.

Keywords Love · Agape · Care · Commitment · Concern · Loyalty

11.1 Introduction

The heart can think of no devotion Greater than being shore to the ocean-Holding the curve of one position, Counting an endless repetition. *Devotion* by Robert Frost (1928)

T. Ryan (✉)
Faculty of Theology and Philosophy, Australian Catholic University, NSW, Australia

Adjunct Associate Professor of the School of Philosophy and Theology University of Notre Dame, Fremantle, Australia
e-mail: tryansm@bigpond.net.au

In his poem 'Devotion', Robert Frost draws on the image of the seashore as the steady, reliable presence that borders, even, embraces, the ocean (Frost, 1928). Building on that insight, this chapter focusses on love as devotion. The abstract above serves as our guide in the two phases of the discussion. After clarifying language, we outline foundational considerations. Devotion (its forms and outcomes) is, then, seen 'at work' in everyday life through examining selected literary texts and modern films.

11.2 Love as Devotion: Foundational Considerations

In approaching this topic, we need, first, to clarify language and, second, explain relevant understandings of love in order to situate any discussion of 'devotion'.

11.2.1 Clarifying Language

'Devotion' has its roots in Latin 'devovere' = to dedicate by vow or solemn promise and is associated with loyalty, allegiance, fealty and setting apart.[1] Variants of 'devotion' such as the plural 'devotions' and 'devout' tend, in common usage, to be found in a religious context, namely, an habitual set of spiritual practices in a way of life or regular prayer directed to a higher being or an exemplar in some form, e.g., a saint. Words such as 'devotion', 'devoted' or 'devotee' have a connotation found in both a secular and a religious context and also towards persons or things. For the purposes of the discussion here, devotion can be defined as 'loyalty and love or care for someone or something' (Cambridge Dictionary, 2017).[2]

11.2.2 Clarifying Understandings of Love

Consider one word in the working definition just noted. 'Love' is a universal phenomenon (see Jankowiak and Nelson in this book, see Karandashev in this book). The descriptions and meanings of love vary across cultures and in relation to their underlying experiences and expressions. Concepts of love are subject to development in the context of cultural change. Western approaches to love can range from love as romantic, platonic, emotional and spiritual. There is a better

---

[1]Interestingly, 'devotion' is not amongst the contents of the *Stanford Encyclopedia of Philosophy* but 'loyalty' is listed as too, naturally, love.

[2]These usages seem to be reflected in a word search in libraries covering books and journals. While not comprehensive and definitive, it suffices for our purposes here.

appreciation of those understandings of love found in cultures that are non-Western. For all that, whatever the context or meaning, love is essentially an analogical term.

For our purposes, love seen as eros, philia or agape, offers a helpful point of departure while acknowledging that these forms of love are culturally embedded. Importantly, the modulations of love extend beyond private and intimate relationships. They find expression across cultures, within families and between parents and children. Again, love as benevolence is captured in the Nguni Bantu term 'ubuntu' which denotes 'humanity towards others' (see Crous' and Leo's in this book). This entails virtues that maintain harmony and a spirit of sharing with a group or society. It forms a parallel with notions of Benevolence (a character trait as in virtue ethics of David Hume) and Beneficence (actions and rules to benefit others as in John Stuart Mill).

Eros and philia presume an inter-personal relationship. Agape, however, includes such a setting but goes beyond it to embrace the social, communal and, even, transpersonal realms. Vacek suggests that the difference between these three 'traditional' forms of love is sharpened by asking the question 'for the sake of whom' we are loving. With eros, we love the beloved for our own sake, i.e., happiness through union with the beloved. Philia means that we love our beloved for the sake of the friendship we share with them. Agape entails love for the beloved for the sake of the beloved (Vacek, 1994, xv).

11.2.2.1 Devotion as Robust Concern

A variation of agape is love understood as 'robust concern' (Helm, 2017). Central to this view of love is not the creation of a 'we' as in union. It is a concern for the person for their own sake in so far as they are appreciated as a centre of value. Frankfurt considers that robust concern as a form of love is neither affective nor cognitive but, rather, volitional.

> That a person cares about or that he loves something has less to do with how things make him feel, or with his opinions about them, than with the more or less stable motivational structures that shape his preferences and that guide and limit his conduct (Frankfurt, 1999, 129).

This appears to be the language of character traits and of virtue.

Robust concern, understood thus, seems an apt description for devotion. Nevertheless, devotion can have its grounding in the relationship of union and of friends (eros or philia). Further, 'volitional' used in terms of the will is not confined to its capacity to choose. The will is an operation of consciousness whose object is the good or value. The will is drawn to what is valuable and good through desire (an affective movement). In that light, devotion's enduring foundation is, in fact, volitional (in that specific understanding of 'affective').

Desire, then, underlies and guides the will's intentionality and choice about 'caring', namely, wanting to nourish another's well-being or to promote a particular value or values. It will entail personal investment at a deeper affective level that persists in the face of passing feelings of impatience or anger in, for instance, caring for a disabled family member. To give in to such feelings and, even, to cease, even temporarily, in providing needed care can prompt a sense of guilt and shame—in failing the other person (and oneself).

The word 'robust' as applied to devotion seems, perhaps, to denote not so much intensity as, more typically, steady perseverance and the associated repeated choices that refine, deepen and strengthen concern. At times it involves courage, a determination not to be derailed from one's aims when things get difficult or, even, when one's efforts appear to futile. In other words, persistence, commitment and loyalty are part of the 'stable motivational structures' guiding one's behavior, noted earlier.

A word on 'loyalty' from the working definition of devotion used earlier. To consider loyalty as an option in life such that a person has no loyalties suggests a very deficient view of character and moral worth. Alternatively, loyalty can be attached to objects that are unworthy, e.g., a loyal Nazi or a sincere terrorist or rapist. Central, here, is the role of practical wisdom or *phronesis* as applied the virtues so that they 'would not be deficient, excessive or misplaced' (Kleinig, 2017). Loyalty (and devotion) are subject to the appraisal and guidance of practical wisdom.

11.2.2.2 Devotion's Many Faces

In the light of the discussion so far and the working definition (suggested above), devotion's scope can expand to include not only other persons but also 'things' (such as organizations, causes, clubs, faith communities).

Further, it can denote a bond between animals and humans. The aphorism of dogs as our 'best friends' is only too evident in television programs about the day to day life in veterinary practices. The mutual affection between the animals and its owners is perhaps part of the appeal for the viewers. It is found in novels such as *White Fang* by Jack London. The mutual bond and the loyalty of animals such as a dog can be viewed as an expression of affection if not a form of love. This reminds us that we must be careful in drawing a sharp line between human and animal behavior. Turner notes that 'there is some evidence that some animals use tools for purposes, intentionally.' In other words, they 'act for a reason.' Perhaps the boundary line between rational and nonrational animals is 'something more like a graded continuum of rationalities' (Turner, 2013, 272 n. 6). One can properly apply the term 'rational' to such purposeful or affectional behavior in animals even if it is only an incipient or partial mode of rationality.

There is a range of literature that explores the variations within devotion. For instance, we find studies on devotion in Christian religious practice (de Sales, 2002); on mindfulness and centering prayer (Frederick & White, 2015); on Vipassana meditation, love, devotion and surrender and their relation to illness and well-being (Parks, 2010); on devotion (bhakti) in Indian religions as a path to draw closer to the highest God, especially in meditation (Bronkhorst, 2011).

Alternatively, devotion can be found in misguided and, even, harmful forms. Loyalty to a belief system in the form of religious fanaticism can have profoundly destructive outcomes—as contemporary experience testifies. Distorted devotion in a Christian context, for instance, can take the form of the vice of religious hypocrisy, as in François Mauriac's *The Woman of the Pharisees*. This novel explores the impaired moral vision of a 'good' person of faith who is, nevertheless, a self-righteous zealot.

In a secular context, we find recent research on the impact of 'competing devotions to work and family' in academic scientists (Damaske, Ecklund, Lincoln, & White, 2014). In the market place, there are studies on the relationship between loyalty to certain 'brands' and 'consumer fanaticism' (Chung, Farrelly, & Beverland, 2017). Devotion expressed as an habitual and harmful attachment can take the form of an addiction, such as to pornography (Hilton & Watts, 2011).

It is beyond the scope of this discussion to investigate such a broad spectrum of academic research. Our focus from here is more practical. We have outlined some theoretical considerations about the nature of devotion and its characteristics and, then, indicated representative research. The most helpful step now may be to consider devotion 'at work' or 'in the flesh' through recourse to the arts, specifically, literature and films.

11.3 Devotion 'at Work'

Our discussion moves on to explore various 'faces' of devotion and how they are embodied in personal and inter-personal life. We will approach this with a limited focus, namely, within social, familial, class or cultural settings where there a form of master-servant relationship which, simultaneously, involves a mutual dependence. In so doing, we pick up the theme of love (as devotion) across cultures and as articulated in religious and secular forms.

Such a theme is explored in novels, plays and films. We will use four artistic 'case-studies' to illustrate the life-giving and life-denying aspects of devotion and how, at times, these are intertwined. In so doing, an effort to situate these artistic works within the categories of tragedy and comedy (and their respective 'modes') will be helpful.

For the positive side of devotion, we draw, first, on a biblical source, namely, *The Book of Ruth*, from the period of the monarchy in Israel c. 880 BCE [3] and, secondly, the 1989 film, *Driving Miss Daisy*. The twentieth century also offers two literary works where the interplay of the luminous and dark sides of devotion at are work. The first is the film version from 1983 of Ronald Harwood's play, *The Dresser*. The second is Kazuo Ishiguro's Booker Prize winning novel *The Remains of the Day* (1989).

---

[3]There is a film version *The Book of Ruth* released in 2004.

11.3.1 Devotion as Life-Giving

The Book of Ruth, the shortest 'book' in the Hebrew Scriptures, is an historical short story. Living in a foreign country (Moab), Ruth, Orpah (her sister) and Naomi (their mother-in-law) have all lost their husbands and are, now, all childless. In a shame/honor (and patriarchal) culture, without father, husband or sons, all three widows are powerless and economically vulnerable. Naomi encourages the two sisters to remain in their homeland (Moab). Initially, they both indicate their desire to accompany her to Bethlehem. Orpah finally accedes to Naomi's urgings and returns to her homeland (1:14). Naomi and Ruth travel to Bethlehem where they find protection with Boaz, a well-to-do 'kinsman' of Naomi's deceased husband Elimelech.

The axis of this devotion story is in Ruth's reply after Naomi urges the two sisters to stay with their own people. Ruth replies by assuring Naomi that she will accompany her wherever she goes, will live where she lives, will die where Naomi dies and, gentile 'outsider' though Ruth is, identifies herself with the Naomi's 'people' and their God (Ruth 1:16–17).

Ruth's gesture of human faithfulness triggers the rest of the story—one of redemption. This particular theme unfolds through human actions. The story traces the steps by which Ruth is led to finding a husband (Boaz) and Naomi to being healed of her emptiness and bitterness.

This story is illuminating for a number of reasons. First, Ruth's first gesture of loyalty (*hesed*) towards Naomi (noted above), which involves sacrifice and risk, is commended by Boaz (2:12). He later praises her for a second gesture of fidelity, namely, for 'seeking not a young husband' but rather 'an appropriate one' (Laffey, 557). Her action, in this instance, is out of respect for family claims and the social structure in which she lives. But it is also one in which she transcends the limits of her social role and cultural expectations as a woman. For this, Boaz invokes God's blessing on Ruth 'since this last act of kindness of yours is greater than the first' (3:10). The words 'kindness' and 'covenant fidelity' are other renditions of *hesed*. Faithfulness is associated with remembering; unfaithfulness with forgetting.

Ruth's state of mind and heart (*hesed*) are captured by the words noted above. Again, *hesed* can be viewed as 'devotion' described earlier: 'loyalty and love or care for someone or something' but also in in 'kindness' and thoughtfulness. Such words suggest an underlying affection going beyond duty. They point to a deeper aspect of the will's intentionality, namely, desire that animates and sustains the bond ('covenant') with another person.

Second, Ruth's original sense of caring responsibility for Naomi is centrifugal. It triggers Naomi's own concern for Ruth's own welfare and the various strategies her mother-in-law suggests concerning Boaz to achieve that. Later, Ruth's *hesed* prompts various shifts in Boaz: his concern for Ruth herself; his willingness to be her protector; his recognition ('honoring') of Ruth for her expressions of loyalty and care both towards Naomi and himself; his acknowledgement of Ruth by name (3:9–10), hence, as having an identity, a self, as a person (rather than, as culturally indicated, simply a possession, a part of his 'property').

Finally, as the story evolves, the 'devoted' Ruth, emerges as an instrument of healing for her 'empty' and 'bitter' mother-in-law (who, for that reason, had changed her name to Mara). In Naomi's eyes, God has not been faithful or loyal (devoted). In an act of forgetting, God has allowed Naomi to experience suffering and loss—without food, homeland, children or protector. All of these, indirectly (through Ruth), are restored to her.

Central in all this is the final scene. Ruth's mother-in-law receives new life and hope (is 'redeemed'), especially through the child of Ruth and Boaz who will be Naomi's 'comfort' 'life-restorer' and a 'prop of' her old age (4:15). These promises arise because the newborn son's mother is Ruth, the one who loves Naomi. Consistent with the story line, Ruth is now more like a daughter. She means more to Naomi than the ideal number of 'seven sons' (4:16). Ruth's loyal care and self-giving devotion have renewed, in Naomi, a sense of life, of love, of being blessed and of being honored—with an identity, a self.

Mention has been made above of Ruth (a foreigner and outsider) identifying herself with the God of Naomi (and of Israel). In what way, then, is the Book of Ruth religious? The plot is driven by the characters, in their actions and relationships with one another. This is a deliberate literary device suited to the author's overall religious purpose. Campbell notes that divine activity in the story is 'that of one in the shadows' yet God still remains 'the primary actor in the drama.' The story-teller's most 'characteristic way of 'making God manifest' is through 'working out a correspondence between the way God acts and the way the people in the story act.' This is particularly realized in the way 'people behave toward one another' through 'caring responsibility' (Campbell, 1981, 29).

God's action (and blessing), then, is mediated through human actions, namely, the determination to live a 'righteous and responsible life' as modelled in Ruth's acts of loyal devotion. Like the Good Samaritan (Luke 10: 30–37), Ruth is from an ethnic group 'despised and rejected by those who considered themselves to be the "people of God"' (Farmer, 1998, 892). She is representative of 'outsiders' and 'gentiles' who are receptive to God's call and included within the divine plan of salvation. Further, Ruth in her devotion is the instrument of the divine presence in the 'steady resolution' of Naomi's complaint and of her suffering. In this, Naomi is led gently to be 'the profound recipient' (Campbell, 1981, 30, 32). Naomi is enticed slowly to open herself to the gift of a renewed self, to again being honored—in the eyes of others, herself and of God.

What is presented in the *Book of Ruth* in the form of a somewhat human and secular story is a carefully crafted *novella* with a religious aim in mind, namely, God's saving desires and action working in unobtrusive mode. As commentator Kathleen Farmer points out 'reversal is the essence of redemption. Within the story world Naomi is the primary object of redemption. It is Naomi whose life is turned around, whose feelings of bitterness, emptiness, and hopelessness are reversed. Ruth's faithfulness is only the *instrument* God uses to accomplish Naomi's redemption.' We find here an encouragement to see 'not just that we ought to be like Ruth but that we are like Naomi' (Farmer, 1998, 892–3, italics in original).

The development of the plot in this novella clearly follows the comic curve in which the protagonist moves from low to high fortune, from unpleasant beginnings, through struggle, to a happy ending (Ghent, 1967, 66). This is true of both Ruth and Naomi. But it is also true of Boaz. Within his cultural context, to be childless (especially without a son) could be a source of profound shame for a man and a husband. It is through Ruth that Boaz's honour is preserved in being her kin-protector and, importantly, through the birth of a son.

We move on, now, to consider a second study in devotion as life-giving.

11.3.2 *Mutual Devotion as Dismantling Barriers*

Driving Miss Daisy is a film where the story and two main characters take 25 years to unfold.[4] One day in 1948, Daisy Werthan, a retired, wealthy, Southern Jewish widow (Miss Daisy) drives her car over the wall and finishes up in her neighbour's backyard. Her son (Boolie) insists her driving days are over. He employs an African-American chauffeur (Hoke Colburn). Miss Daisy keeps resisting the prospect of being driven. Hoke has to win her round. Hoke handles the proud and wilful Miss Daisy with endless patience, and a certain measure of quiet guile until she finally succumbs to being driven by the chauffeur.

This battle of wills, of two stubborn people, sets the scene for the next 25 years. Around 1963, when her housekeeper dies, we find the multi-skilled Hoke helping Miss Daisy with household tasks and looking after the garden. In turn, the retired teacher Miss Daisy, with tact and sensitivity, teaches her chauffeur to read. Over the years of mutual dependence and time together, the 'mistress' and 'servant' slowly get to know each other.

Driving Miss Daisy explores racism and anti-Semitism through this evolving devotion. The two characters are both outsiders: he, from the colour of his skin; she, from being Jewish in a society that is predominantly WASP. She may take pride in being Southern Jewish and liberal, but also has blind spots, for instance, about prejudice. She sees no parallel between an attack on her local synagogue and those of the Klu Klux Klan on African-American churches. Again, Hoke drives her to a dinner where there is speech by Martin Luther King. She has an extra ticket but does not consider directly asking him to accompany her. He is left outside, listening to the speech on the car radio.

Driving Miss Daisy's ends in 1973 with two converging 'movements': the widow's onset of dementia and the chauffeur's approaching retirement from failing eyesight. In the overlapping of the fading shadows of their lives they come to recognize a bond, if not a mutual devotion. It is a shared moment where racial (and class) boundaries dissolve; she recognizes Hoke as her 'best friend.'

---

[4]This 1989 film was based on the play of Alfred Uhry and starred Jessica Tandy and Morgan Freeman in the main roles.

Speaking of the film's director Bruce Beresford, one reviewer captures the beauty of this moment:

> He never steps wrong on his way to a luminous final scene in which we are invited to regard one of the most privileged mysteries of life, the moment when two people allow each other to see inside (Ebert, 1990).

In our wider discussion, this film illustrates not only the mutual form that devotion can take. It is a study in the slow emergence of a sense of personal safety between two people separated through race and class. Within this secure space, transparency and recognition come to characterise their relationship. While the film has an underlying element of social criticism, it is through the growing relationship of Miss Daisy and Hoke that there is a gradual dissolution of racial and class barriers. The key moment of insight at the end comes from a life-giving process rather than the pattern of tragic failure or flaw. The overall trajectory of this study of devotion, then, follows the same comic curve as that found in the story of Ruth—one that brings reassurance and hope.

We move on, now, to consider the life-denying and troublesome aspect of devotion.

11.3.3 Devotion: Its Distortions and Deceptions

We first consider a modern play.

11.3.3.1 Devotion as Love Unacknowledged

The Dresser is the story of the personal assistant (Norman) of an aging actor ('Sir') and the assistant's persevering efforts to maintain some sort of order in the 'master's' life (professionally and personally).[5] The assistant is constantly overlooked by 'Sir', despite his years of persistent and loyal efforts. His dedication in carrying out his task (and to 'Sir') has come at a personal cost; Norman equivalently has sacrificed any personal life that addressed his own individual needs and desires. One way he copes with 'Sir's' rants and whims is by taking the occasional nip of brandy from the small bottle kept in his back pocket.

After what will turn out to be his final performance, 'Sir' asks Norman to read from an autobiography he has just started. He reads aloud a list of 'thank you's—to audiences, other actors, stage hands. Nowhere does he acknowledge his dresser. Norman discovers 'Sir' has died while he was reading the list. The dresser, tipsy from the brandy, erupts with rage over the actor's dead body for the years of being overlooked, despite his persistent care for 'Sir.' This surge of emotion prompts a

---
[5]*The Dresser* (1983) is a film based on Ronald Harwood's play of the same name starring Albert Finney and Tom Courtenay.

moment of insight in Norman. He realizes his years of devotion are now over. But they are not lost. Even though never acknowledged by 'Sir', Norman now appreciates that the deceased 'master' is the only person he has ever loved.

Viewed in literary terms, this play is a tragicomedy in which devotion is portrayed in both its life-giving and distorted forms. The comic mode is present in that the elderly actor, by his own actions, is unmasked about his social and artistic pretentions. He is the recipient of his 'servant's' loyal concern but is oblivious to the dresser as a person, with his own life and his own needs. The actor, effectively, is exposed in his true nature and its impact on others.

It is in the dresser that the tragic curve of the play is realized. Norman arrives at a moment of self-discovery, about himself and, implicitly, a more realistic appraisal of his relationship with his 'master.' In this interweaving of the tragic and the comic, we find expressed, through dramatic chiaroscuro, the more ambivalent sides of devotion (Ghent, 1967, 67).

This brings us to the next phase of the chapter.

11.3.3.2 Devotion as Distorted Loyalty

The second study in devotion's darker side is the modern novel, *The Remains of the Day*.[6]

It is summer 1956. A man is driving through the west of England. His name is Stevens. He has been a butler at Darlington Hall for most of his life. He is travelling to see a former housekeeper, hoping she will return and resume that role. This outer journey is the context for Stevens' inner journey, namely, the meanderings of his memory and the evaluation of his life and of himself.

Our purpose here is not to engage in a full exegesis and interpretation of the novel. The aim here is very specific; to explore how the narrative illuminates our discussion of devotion. It needs to be noted that, in contrast with the film, the narrator in the novel is Stevens himself, hence, the action takes place predominantly in his mind. This gives the reader access to his efforts to rationalise and justify himself. Again, in contrast with the film's more sober and dignified Stevens, the butler in the novel tells lies, is foolish and impulsive. Cumulatively, then, this brings to his character an artless transparency that engages the reader's sympathy.

Steven's devotion is anchored in his family ties with Lord Darlington and the country residence. His father was the previous butler. Stevens is very good at what he does. He brings polish, thoughtfulness and discretion to the task. He is dedicated to his calling as a servant and to his master, Lord Darlington. He is part of a class system on which he depends (for his livelihood, his status and sense of worth) and which depends on him (for his loyalty and day to day functioning). The novel is a

---

[6]The 1993 film of the same name (starring Emma Thompson and Anthony Hopkins) was based on this novel.

social comedy; an unmasking of a social system around the English rural aristocracy and the various hierarchies—of the masters and of the servants.

Within this setting of a 'master-servant' relationship and his devotion in his task, there are repercussions for Stevens. When Lord Darlington is accused, and humiliated, as a Nazi sympathiser, his world collapses as also that of his butler (complicit by his silence). Stevens says, in tears, to a stranger in Weymouth near the end of the book that the Lord wasn't a 'bad man…he chose a path in life…it was a misguided one'.

But, significantly, he then says:

> As for myself, I cannot even claim that. You see, *I trusted*. In his lordship's wisdom.' Through his service of the Lord Darlington, Stevens 'trusted he was doing something worthwhile. I can't even say I made my own mistakes. Really—one has to ask oneself—what dignity is there in that? (Ishiguro, 1989, 243).

What is significant for our purposes is how this trust was to the detriment, even neglect, of Stevens' own personal emotional desires and his appreciation of the needs of others.

For example, when his father is dying after a stroke, Stevens gives priority to his public duty (a grand banquet). After the pleadings of Miss Kenton, he spares a moment and returns to his task.

Again, the most significant effect of his approach to devotion is found in his relationship with Miss Kenton during her time as housekeeper. She tells him of her feelings and senses he has similar feelings for her. This is a door to an ongoing relationship, even marriage. Stevens denies his feelings and puts priority on his job and his loyalty to Lord Darlington.

Again, Miss Kenton catches Stevens out reading a romantic novel (today's Mills and Boone?) which suggests the lurking of desire. Stevens resents the invasion of his privacy and says he was reading the book to improve his vocabulary.

Finally, Miss Kenton leaves to marry someone else. It is a letter from her that has prompted Steven's road trip and our share in his journey of memory into his life. But it is also an indicator that Stevens is hopeful of resuming the relationship with the former housekeeper. However, in the ensuing conversation between them, she (now Mrs. Benn) makes it clear that he had lost his opportunity many years ago. Further, married but separated, she has decided to return to her husband because of his need for her and to be near her pregnant daughter.

The book's final section is particularly illuminating about how devotion is at work in Stevens and how it is handled in the novel. He does know his place, is the perfect butler but, in so doing, he exercises a restraint of desire that, in many ways, has led him to have a wasted life. Nevertheless, as noted above, Stevens' tears while talking with the stranger on the pier at Weymouth bring a moment of insight and self-recognition. He acknowledges his self-deception but also what underlies it. His devotion was essentially a misplaced trust but also an abdication of any claim to being his own self. This entailed a blindness, if not a loss, with his own moral compass. His loyalty was not subject to the appraisal of practical wisdom. In arriving at this insight, the tragic side to Stevens is expressed.

Further, devotion in Stevens overrode his need for human warmth and intimacy. About that, there is a suggestion of the start of healing, even, of redemption. He has been encouraged by the stranger to look ahead and enjoy the remainder of his 'days.' Sitting on the bench, he observes the people shortly after the pier lights come on at twilight—a symbolic moment. He finds himself 'curious' about their behaviour. Stevens begins to 'look more enthusiastically' at how, through friendly banter and fun, strangers were able to, 'build such warmth among themselves so swiftly.' He even observes that 'in bantering lies the key to human warmth' (Ishiguro, 1989, 245).

It is difficult not to view this is a liminal moment for Stevens, even if a minimal one. The butler is far from his aristocratic cocoon, emotionally vulnerable, his 'blind dignity' exposed (Canby, 1993). It is now that he begins to actually see; he recognises and responds to the interactions of ordinary people. He starts to identify with common humanity. From this, he moves on to appreciate that such a gesture of human connection (banter) is a duty that is 'not unreasonable' in his professional role. He resolves to practice and develop his 'bantering skills' to pleasantly surprise his master (Ishiguro, 1989, 245). His defences are breaking down such that he is led to view his 'servant' role in a new light.

The novel's tragic thrust is realised in Stevens' acknowledgement of his distorted form of devotion but also in beginning to see people, and himself, differently. In so doing, he arrives at a regretful acceptance of loss, allied with a renewed (and healthier?) sense of purpose that is shaded, perhaps, with subdued contentment. The comic curve has found a level of resolution.

11.4 Conclusion

Our considerations of devotion have ranged from the theoretical through works of art illustrating its variations in daily life. We have spent time with people and texts that present the luminous, ambivalent but also the dark side of devotion (see Grosse on bad love). Devotion can be life-giving, can break down barriers, can override not being recognized, can be misguided and involve self-deception. In the process, certain qualities in devotion have emerged: desire, attachment, loyalty, perseverance and its momentum beyond the self. In devotion as robust concern, we find distilled love and care seasoned by thoughtfulness, strengthened by time, dependable through practice but always subject to the guidance of practical wisdom.

Devotion offers a contrary voice to consumerism and its throw-away mentality: where one 'falls in' and, therefore, 'out of' love; where life is a smorgasbord of choices making long-term commitment difficult; where we find the growing incidence of narcissism driven by 'I'm entitled'; where the surge of self-esteem literature prompts author Stephen Dovey to observe, 'you may be good but what are you good for?' (quoted in Dowrick, 1997, 78). (see Ungerer in this book).

By contrast, devotion appears as a steady, reliable beacon of light, a virtuous disposition with its own peculiar moral beauty both uplifting and inspiring. Or, to return to the metaphor of Robert Frost, devotion resembles the seashore in relation to the ocean in that it holds 'the curve of one position.'

Devotion or devoted people are part of all our lives—amongst families, friends, colleagues. Perhaps it is better to say that, far from trying to describe or analyze devotion, we should say 'I know it when I see it.' But what does devotion 'in full bloom' look like? Is there something about this form of care and love that naturally seeks the shadows, that does not seek to be noticed, a flower 'born to blush unseen'?

On that note, it is timely to mention a story that kept coming back to me while I was writing this chapter.

Without comment, I offer the story here by way of conclusion.

Some years ago, I was a chaplain at a residential care facility. There was one section set aside specifically for any residents who suffered from dementia (see Barrett et al. chapter in this book) and similar illnesses. There was a lady there (Mary) who was visited every day by her husband (Joe). He would come mid-morning, have a cup of tea, then take her out in her wheel-chair around the grounds, perhaps spending time in the sun. They would come back and have lunch together, perhaps a siesta in the easy chairs in the lounge. He might read to her, listen to music. Perhaps more time outside then afternoon tea and Joe would go home.

One day, one of the regular carers said to Joe 'Joe, you are wonderful with Mary. You are here nearly every day. You are so devoted. You know, if you ever wanted a break, there is always someone here to look after Mary. And it must be very difficult. Most of the time, Mary does not recognize you.'

Joe listened.

Then quietly, with an understanding smile (and without reproach), Joe replied: 'Yes—but I recognize her.'

References

Bronkhorst, J. (2011). *Karma*. Honolulu: University of Hawaii Press.
Cambridge Advanced Learner's Dictionary & Thesaurus. (2017). Cambridge University Press. Retrieved June 7, 2019, from https://dictionary.cambridge.org/dictionary/english/devotion
Campbell Jr., E. (1981). *Ruth: A new translation with introduction, notes, and commentary. The anchor bible* (Vol. 7). New York: Doubleday.
Canby, V. (1993, Nov. 5). Blind dignity–A Butler's story. *New York Times*.
Chung, E., Farrelly, F., & Beverland, M. B. (2017). Loyalty or liability: Resolving the consumer fanaticism paradox. *Marketing Theory, 18*(1), 3–30.
Damaske, S., Ecklund, E. H., Lincoln, A., & White, V. J. (2014). Male scientists' competing devotions to work and family: Changing norms in a male-dominated profession. *Work and Occupations, 41*(4), 477–507.

De Sales, F. (2002). *Introduction to the devout life*. New York: Vintage.
Dowrick, S. (1997). *Forgiveness and other acts of love*. Ringwood, Vic: Penguin Books.
Ebert, R. (1990). *Review of driving miss daisy*. Retrieved July 13, 1990, from https://www.rogerebert.com/reviews/driving-miss-daisy-1990
Farmer, K. A. R. (1998). *The book of Ruth: Introduction, commentary, and reflections, the new interpreter's Bible* (Vol. 2, pp. 891–946). Nashville: Abingdon Press.
Frankfurt, H. (1999). Autonomy, necessity, and love. In H. Frankfurt (Ed.), *Necessity, volition, and love* (pp. 129–141). Cambridge: Cambridge University Press.
Frederick, T., & White, K. M. (2015). Mindfulness, Christian devotion meditation, surrender, and worry. *Mental Health, Religion and Culture, 18*(10), 850–858.
Frost, R. (1928). *West running brook*. New York: Henry Holt and Co. Retrieved December 20, 2019, from https://www.goodreads.com/quotes/3939-the-heart-can-think-of-no-devotion-greater-than-being
Ghent, V. (1967). *The English novel: Form and function*. New York: Harper & Row.
Helm, B. (2017). *Love, the Stanford encyclopedia of philosophy* (Fall). Edward N. Zalta (Ed.), Retrieved June 06, 2019, from https://plato.stanford.edu/archives/fall2017/entries/love/
Hilton, D. L., & Watts, C. (2011). Pornography addiction: A neuroscience perspective. *Surgical Neurology International, 2*(1), 19–24.
Ishiguro, K. (1989). *The remains of the day*. London: Faber & Faber.
Kleinig, J. (2017). *Loyalty, the Stanford encyclopedia of philosophy* (Fall). Edward N. Zalta (Ed.), Retrieved July 13, 2019, from https://plato.stanford.edu/entries/loyalty/
Parks, T. (2010). *Teach us to sit still*. Emmaus, PA: Rodale Press.
Turner, D. (2013). *Thomas Aquinas: A portrait*. New Haven/London: Yale University Press.
Vacek, E. C. S. J. (1994). *Love: Human and divine*. Washington: Georgetown University Press.

Thomas Ryan (PhD) is a Marist priest based in Sydney, Australia. He has been an Honorary Fellow of the Faculty of Theology and Philosophy of the Australian Catholic University and is an Adjunct Associate Professor of the School of Philosophy and Theology of the University of Notre Dame Australia. Apart from chapters in books, he has published numerous articles in theological journals both nationally and internationally.

Chapter 12
Ashk: The Sufi Concept for Love

Çiğdem Buğdaycı

> *Someone asked, "What is loverhood?"*
> *I replied, "Don't ask me about these meanings –*
> *"When you become like me, you'll know;*
> *When it calls you, you'll tell its tale."*
> *Rumi*

Abstract *Eros*, *agapē*, and *philia* are distinct concepts of love, which the modern world has inherited from Plato. This paper discusses how the Islamic concept of love (Turkish *ashk*), while also rooted in Plato, has been omitted from the scholarship of love and philosophy. There are specialized studies of *ashk*; however, these deal only with the concept within the Islamic context, it has not been introduced into broader discussions of love. In Sufi cosmology, the world is created out of *ashk* and for the sake of *ashk*. *Ashk* is a concept, which transcends the division of sacred and profane. All beings are made of love and deserve care, compassion, and mercy. It is claimed here that the omission of *ashk* from general discussions of love has been ideological; the worldwide European cultural and economic expansion suppressed and ignored non-European elements. Likewise, the scope of the concept of romantic love has only recently been expanded from a Eurocentric to a world-embracing one, while the Eurocentric approach still abides in certain sectors of academia. This chapter proposes to position *ashk* next to *eros* and *agapē* as a missing link in the Platonic heritage. The particularity of Sufi *ashk*, and its parallels and disparities with *eros* are examined. This paper calls into question the historical neglect of *ashk* with regard to European colonialism as well as hostilities toward Sufism within the Islamic world.

Keywords Love · Ashk · Islam · Sufism · Platonic tradition - Eurocentricity

Ç. Buğdaycı (✉)
Amsterdam School for Cultural Analysis, University of Amsterdam, Amsterdam, The Netherlands
e-mail: bugdayci@yahoo.com

12.1 Introduction

In today's world, Islam and Sufism are terms, which can be understood variously. While Islam is most often regarded as a frightening religion that leads to terrorism, or to an apocalyptic clash between civilizations, or merely as a failed civilization (Ernst, 2003, p. xiii), Sufism is embraced by a variety of groups and organizations. These groups draw on eclectic forms of Sufism, sometimes called "New Age" Sufism, a type of self-help system both in Muslim and non-Muslim countries (Sedgwick, 2017). Islam is generally associated in popular media with jihadist figures whereas Sufism is taken out of its Islamic context and transformed by eclectic Sufi groups into a spiritual self-help discipline (El-Zein, 2000; Sedgwick, 2017).

If not formulated in opposition to Islam, Sufism is generally understood to be the mystical or esoteric side of Islam, developed subsequent to the Prophet Muhammad's mission. However, the great acclaimed Sufi mystics, in fact, never called themselves "Sufis"; nor did they call their teachings "Sufism". In the past, the word "Sufi" was not used as a generic term for spiritual teachers and their followers (Ernst, 1997). The present meaning of the word is primarily "a modern coinage laden with political baggage" (Chittick & Nasr, 2013, p. xvi).

Therefore, despite the widespread misunderstanding that Sufism is something distinct from Islam, it should be emphasized that this is a fabricated fact prevalent both in Muslim and non-Muslim countries. In general, Sufis use figurative and imaginative language often drawn from the Qur'an and Prophet Muhammad's *hadith*s[1]. When Islamic fundamentalists today make statements such as "Sufism has nothing to do with Islam", they are drawing upon the nineteenth-century work of Orientalists (Ernst, 1997, p. xv). Sufism continues to be disassociated from Islam in English translations of the thirteenth-century poet Rumi, who is currently a bestselling poet in the United States. The translations secularize his poetry by omitting Islamic expressions and Rumi's celebration of Prophet Muhammad (Furlanetto, 2013). In fact, the place of "Sufi love" in Islam is comparable to the centrality of agape in Christianity; however, there has been no detailed analysis of it.

What I have been referring to as Sufi love is termed $ashk^2$ in Turkish. *Ashk* is a commonly used word in the Muslim world, both in everyday life[3] and in the Sufi literature. Due to great Sufi authors and philosophers' discussion of it in varying and

---

[1]Hadiths are the sayings of Prophet Muhammad, which are one of the primary sources of knowledge in Islam.

[2]In modern Turkish written in the Latin alphabet, *ashk* is a loan word from Arabic. It is the common transliteration of the Arabic word عشق, *'išhq*, which is often taken to mean intense or passionate love. Due to lack of vowels in Arabic, it is read as "*ashk*" in Turkish while the Persians usually read it as "*eshq*". I use the word "ashk" for the Sufi love as it is used in Turkish.

[3]As in Turkish, *'Ashiq* (عاشق) in Arabic means "lover". The same word with the same meaning with a slightly different pronunciation appears in Urdu: *Aashiqui* (आशिक़ि), which is also frequently used by Hindi and Punjabi speakers. Bollywood produced a series of famous musical romance films with the title *Aashiqui* (1990) & *Aashiqui 2* (2013).

wide geography of Muslim countries, cultures, and languages, the word "ashk"—despite slight differences in its pronunciation—is a common property among the Muslims. Therefore, it needs closer scrutiny, especially in its relationship with the Platonic tradition of love.

This chapter aims primarily to examine the similarities between eros and ashk in order to display how ashk is a cognate of Platonic eros. Despite the prevalence of the "decline thesis", which holds that Muslim culture began to decline as early as the eleventh century, Islamic literature on ethics and proper behavior was extensive. It drew not only upon Islamic sources—Qur'an and hadith—but also illustrious examples from pre-Islamic societies, especially Greek philosophy (Ernst, 2003, pp. 119–124). The links between Greek philosophical thought and Sufism are, in fact, of the Islamic tradition itself.

Furthermore, the chapter aims to position Islam as a religion that has placed great emphasis on discussions of love, which have gone unremarked and even been subverted due to historical contingencies. Medieval Christian arguments about the insufficiencies of both Jewish and Muslim love have played a role in the development of Western thought and in the rise the history and philosophy of religion. Oft-repeated assumptions about Islam rooted in the early seventh century Christian views are that Islam is not a religion of love, but fear and violence; that when Muslims love, it is the flesh that they love, not the divine; and that even the vision of Paradise offered by their (false) prophet is one of merely carnal lusts writ large (Kaegi, 1969; Lamoreaux, 1996; Nirenberg, 2009; Tolan, 2002). The earliest translations of the Qur'an into Latin (like the one produced, with accompanying commentary, at the request of Peter the Venerable in 1140) were designed to demonstrate the depraved fleshiness of the prophet's passions and teachings (Burman, 2007; d'Alverny, 1947; Kritzeck, 1964; Nirenberg, 2009). Unlike the current perception of Islam as a puritanical and sex-phobic religion, the antique idea of Muslim lust aimed to articulate a sharper difference between an emerging "Christendom" and Islam (Nirenberg, 2009). Indeed, western commentators strongly criticized Islamic love poetry as indicative of Muslim lust to show their distance from Islam (Nirenberg & Capezzone, 2015, pp. 15–16).

The specific objective of this study is not to repeat the apologetics regarding the peacefulness of Islam but to discuss ashk's roots and significance by pointing at its context in the history of thought. This reassessment of Platonic eros and Sufi ashk has considerable importance in an age of ecumenical dialogue between religions while Islam is depicted as a fanaticism incapable of love, and, hence, dialogue (Nirenberg, 2008). It is especially important to remember that Sufism has become more marginalized within the Islamic community since the nineteenth-century rise of the Wahhabis, who considered Sufism contrary to Islamic teaching. In addition, the decontextualization of Sufism out of Islam, what Ernst has sarcastically called a "missionary phantasy" (Ernst, 1997, p. 15), has gained a new impetus in Muslim secular societies as well; this initially occurred as a result of the expansion of Western colonialism and the Orientalists' simultaneous fascination with Sufism and abhorrence of Islam.

12.2 Research Methodology

Three main concepts of love have come down to us from Greek philosophy in daily and academic usage: *philia*, *eros*, and *agape*. Philia is the general word for "love", which applies equally to family members, friends, and lovers, whereas eros refers to intense attachment and desire. Specifically, it concerns passionate love and desire, usually sexual, as well as the god who personified that state (Nehamas & Woodruff, 1989, p. xiii). While philia and eros can coexist in the Classical Greek literature, the noun agape is used most prominently in the New Testament. Anders Nygren claims in his *Agape and Eros* that agape is the authentic love proper to Christianity, while eros is an intruder (Osborne, 1994, p. 2). Challenging the traditional view that eros and agape are intimately connected, Nygren claims that they belong to two entirely separate spiritual worlds are incommensurable and (Nygren, 1953, p. 31).

In Sufism, theories of divine love have appeared since the tenth century, while its research does not have a long history. Despite the significant place of love in Sufism, few researchers addressed the issue through individual Sufi texts (Abrahamov, 2003; Bell, 1979; Chittick & Nasr, 2013). A major drawback of studying love is the difficulty of producing a comprehensive assessment of different attitudes towards love in Islamic literature. To overcome this, Joseph Normant Bell suggests that the historian of the idea of love should prepare monographs (Bell, 1979, p. 6). Although this approach is effective it does not allow for a broader discussion of the proximity between the Platonic idea of love and Sufi ashk.

Not much is truly known about how the Platonic idea of love is akin to Sufism. Plato was known quite well by the Muslim authors and poets; for instance, Ibn 'Arabi (1165–1240), known as the Great Shaykh, called Plato as *"Divine Plato [Aflāṭūn-i ilāhī],"*[4] (Addas & Kingsley, 1993, p. 105). Moreover, the writings of Sadr al-Din Qunawi, the student of Ibn 'Arabi, shows the intimate relationship between Ibn al-'Arabi's and Plato's philosophies (Chittick, Rustom, Khalil, & Murata, 2012, p. 114). Although direct quotations from translated texts are rare in their works, Plato, Aristotle, Hippocrates, Galen, and Empedocles were among the authorities most often cited on matters about love among the Sufis and Muslim philosophers (Bell, 1979, p. 4).

Even though it is commonly agreed that the exact relation is impossible to prove, some studies have accentuated the Platonic and Neoplatonic influences on Sufism or called for further research (Abrahamov, 2003; Holbrook, 2017; Murata, 2018; Bell, 1979; Morewedge, 1981). Some others have specified the intercultural aspects of

---

[4]Shahab Ahmet suggests that it is *meaningful* and *necessary* to characterize both Aristotle and Plato as *Islamic* in order to display how and to what extent they had been made part of the meaning-making process of Islam. By this he means that "It is not merely appropriate but is *meaningful and necessary to say Aristotle is Islamic* and *Plato is Islamic*—which means that Aristotle and Plato are made meaningful by and have particular meaning in the Muslim hermeneutical engagement with Revelation. It is equally necessary to speak of the "Islamic Aristotle" and "Islamic Plato" as meaning that there are elements of Plato or Aristotle that are *not* made meaningful by and in the Muslim hermeneutical engagement with Revelation" (Ahmed, 2017, p. 436).

Sufism (Izutsu, 1984; Murata, 1992). In her book *The Tao of Islam*, Sachiko Murata demonstrated a similarity between gender binaries in Islamic thought and the Chinese idea of yin/yang (Murata, 1992). On the other hand, Zaehner, a historian of religion who regarded Sufism to be a radical "distortion of the orthodox doctrine" (Zaehner, 1960, p. 2) thought that some great early Muslim mystics, such as Abu Yazid al-Bistami introduced Vedantian ideas into Sufism (Zaehner, 1960, p. 176).

In order to investigate the relationship between ashk and Platonic love, I adopt a comparative analysis. A comparison is a construction, which determines the elements or segments of social reality to be related to one another and along what dimensions. Therefore, it brings into fore a reality what appears as formless and chaotic in its totality (Azarian, 2011, p. 123). The axis of this chapter's comparative analysis bears a close resemblance to the method of motif-research, used by Nygren in his famous *Agape and Eros*. According to Nygren, a study of motifs can only be possible when we conceive the respective fundamental motifs of each tradition as "different general attitudes to life" that run side by side like parallel lines that never meet but constantly run into one another (Nygren, 1953, p. 34). He writes that

> (...) we must try to see what is the basic idea or the driving power of the religion concerned, or what it is that gives it its character as a whole and communicates to all its parts their special content and colour. It is the attempt to carry out such a structural analysis, whether in the sphere of religion or elsewhere, that we describe as motif-research (Nygren, 1953, p. 35).

Motif-research is, however, less concerned with the historical connections and origins of motifs than with their characteristic content and typical manifestations (Nygren, 1953, p. 35). According to him, a religion deprived of its fundamental motif would lose all coherence and meaning (Nygren, 1953, p. 37).

Inspired by Nygren's analysis of the differences and opposition between Christian agape and Platonic eros, this chapter analyzes ashk as the fundamental motif of Sufism. However, while Nygren opposes eros, in the Christian context affinities of ashk with Plato's eros are discussed in this chapter. Following eros, which is a motivating force for ascension to the Idea of Beauty, ashk strives to attain God's beauty. To establish links between Plato's eros and the Sufi ashk this chapter refers to seminal discussions of love in Plato's *Symposium* and *Phaedrus*. Also, Nygren's definition of agape is briefly mentioned to delineate the specificities of ashk. The principal benefit of using the motif-research is to further the specific types of love with regard to monotheistic religions and their relations with the Platonic concept of love.

We are aware that our research may have two major limitations. The first is that the Sufi literature spans almost a thousand years in a wide variety of Islamic cultures and various perspectives exist towards the conception of love (Abrahamov, 2003). The second is that it is not possible to prove whether there has been a direct influence of Plato's ideas on the formation of Sufi ashk. These limitations reveal the difficulty of establishing a comparison between eros and ashk within the scope of this article. Even though the Sufi authors have drawn on the Qur'an and Prophet's Muhammad's *hadith*s as their source, each of their work is unique which can only be assessed through textual analysis. It is a body of work, primarily, literary and religious, while many of them use parables and stories to teach the inherent meaning of the Qur'an, the sacred text. In spite of their differences in style and discussions, this chapter argues that the Sufi authors' focus on love reflects their general attitude to life and ashk has a central place as the fundamental motif of Sufism. This motif follows the path of the Platonic tradition, which involves a series of steps ascending from the material to the immaterial, and from sensory to the intelligible worlds.

12.3 Ashk

Philosopher Irving Singer, in his three-volume *Nature of Love*, notes that every discussion of love must *start* with Plato since courtly love, romantic love, and major emphases in religious love all take root in him. Indeed, Platonism is found throughout all Western theorizing about love (Singer, 1984, p. 47).

Prominent Sufi authors similarly expressed the centrality of love in Sufism as a relationship between human and divine and viewed the Qur'anic narrative as episodes in a love affair between God and humans. William Chittick, a distinguished scholar on Sufism, notes that if any single word can sum up the Islamic spirituality, that is the very heart of the Qur'anic message, it should surely be love (Chittick & Nasr, 2013, p. xi). Hence, Sufis and the Islamic philosophers described love as a divine energy that brings about the creation of the universe and drives every individual being to its own perfection (Chittick, 2014, p. 2). Likewise, Rumi's famous companion and teacher, Shams-i Tabrizi, called the Qur'an "the Book of Ashk" (*'ishq-nama*). Shams said if people do not understand that the Qur'an is a book about love, it is because they read the book with the eyes of jurisprudence, or theology, or philosophy (Chittick & Nasr, 2013, p. 41).

The word ashk means excessive love. It is generally considered to be the highest level in love as it is the origin of existence and the reason for creation. Nevertheless, it does not take place in the Qur'an, where another word for love, hubb, is used. The importance of *ashk* comes from the Sufi mystics' usage of it in their poetry and literature, specifically, popular romances and hymns. Chittick notes that ashk is used as a generic word in the early philosophical literature where most authors agree that it designates the intense and passionate love. This love can appear in a human relationship, which can even be a divine madness (*junūn ilāhī*), traceable to Plato's *Phaedrus* (Chittick & Nasr, 2013, pp. xxiv–xxv).

The "madman" for Plato, in *Phaedrus,* is the image of the philosopher. He is a "lover" because "the word 'lover' refers to a lover of beauty who has been possessed by this kind of madness". True beauty exists in the world of Ideas. Thus, Plato writes, "It is the highest kind of divine possession, it comes from the highest source, and it is the best, both for the one who has it and those who keep company with him" (*Phaedrus*, 249d–e). The similarity between ashk and eros concerning their divine nature is, in fact, more than that. According to Plato, the duality between the material world and the world of Ideas can only be overcome through the motivation of eros.

The main discussion of love takes place in Plato's *Symposium* where Socrates recounts the conversation he had with Diotima, a priestess from the city of

Mantineia, who was his teacher in "all matters of love". Diotima explains how love starts by loving "a beautiful body" and moves up to loving the Idea of "Beauty". Thus, the process of love is a move from the sensible world to the intelligible world with the goal to know the Idea of Beauty. In each stage of love, the lover/*philosophos* has an object of love—which changes from material to immaterial—and whose beauty strikes him/her (*Symposium*, 207b–212c). One of the most crucial ideas presented in the *Symposium* is "philosophy, the pursuit of wisdom, is motivated by love; it is, in fact, love's highest expression" (Nehamas & Woodruff, 1989, p. xix).

Similar to Platonic eros, Sufi ashk also describes the ascent of the human soul to the ultimate Beauty. The Sufi seeker has to purify his/her soul in order to attain perfection through love, as eros is an intermediary in Plato's account to reach the Idea of Beauty. Nevertheless, it should be noted that the contexts of eros and ashk are different from Plato's idea of eros in a significant way. Love for God is part of belief in Islam. When Prophet Muhammad was asked what belief is, he answers: part of "Belief means that God and His messenger are beloved by you more than anything else" (Abrahamov, 2003, p. 14). For this reason, different from the central idea of the *Symposium*, that eros is the motivating force to reach the Idea of Beauty and the Good; the Sufi sets on a quest toward the Beauty of God as part of his/her belief. While the conceptualization of beauty in both is crucial, a comparison of their respective object of love would be beyond the scope of this chapter.

Therefore, instead of what they pursue, the chapter discusses love in Sufism and Platonic eros through the emphasis they put on beauty in their quest. Two major hadiths that describe God's beauty plays a significant role especially in the general Sufi understanding of creation. Their importance for our discussion will be examined below.

12.4 Love and Beauty

For Muslim intellectuals and literary figures, together with love, beauty occupies a central place in the Universe and human life. They consider God to be beautiful in Himself, who created an inherently beautiful world. They also regard the pursuit of beauty at all levels, that is, material, ethical, spiritual, and divine, as part and parcel of the life of a good Muslim (Murata, 2018, pp. 2–3).

Beauty also plays a significant role in the Sufi understanding of creation. Love as the divine motivation of creating the universe finds its support in one of the most cited *hadith qudsis* (sacred hadith) of Prophet Muhammad, which goes as "I was a hidden treasure and I loved to be known; so I created the creatures and made Myself known to them; so they knew Me"[5] (Addas, 2002). The qudsi does not mean that

---

[5]Even though some scholars of hadith consider it a forgery, Ibn 'Arabi (1165–1240) states that it is authentic which he discovered through *kashf* (vision of the Prophet in dream) (Chittick, 1989, p. 391), also in (Addas, 2002).

God needs to be recognized but instead emphasizes that He *loved* to be recognized. God wanted to reveal His hidden treasure purely out of love. Thus, the cosmos is created as a result of His love, which is also the driving motif in His self-revelation. The hadith explains God's self-disclosure, first within Himself, then in creation, during which His beauty becomes manifest (Murata, 2018, p. 49). According to Aḥmad al-Ghazālī, since every existent thing is a self-disclosure (*tajallī*) of the Divine, everything is "a glance from loveliness (*kirishmeh-yi ḥusn*)" (Lumbard, 2016, p. 114). According to Ibn 'Arabi, Creation originates in divine love on a macrocosmic level and from an initiatic point of view, love and knowledge, the key-terms in this hadith, are distinct but inseparable and therefore there is no reason to contrast them (Addas, 2002).

Although not a Sufi, the Muslim philosopher Ibn-i Sina, well known in the West as Avicenna, a follower of Aristotle and commentator, reflects on the qudsi in a truly Platonic fashion and calls God as "the Absolute Good":

> If the Absolute Good did not disclose Itself, nothing would be received from It. If nothing were received from It, nothing would exist. . ., for Its self-disclosure (*tajalli*) is the cause of every existence. And since, by Its very existence, It loves the existence of everything caused by It, It loves the reception of Its self-disclosure (Chittick & Nasr, 2013, p. 286).

This ontological relationship between God and humans establishes that God's love comes before human love, in the Qur'an and this results from God's benevolence towards human beings. Therefore, the created beings must respond to God's creative love by loving Him in return (Chittick, 2014, p. 3).

It is here the path of ascent similar to Diotima's Staircase of Love appears. According to Lumbard, the path of ascent presents a soteriological relationship. This relationship is best expressed in the in the Qur'an verse "He loves them and they love Him (5:54)", which became the central verse for the discussion of love in the Sufi tradition. Lumbard notes that "As love is the true essence of all creation, the realization of love is neither an emotion nor a sentiment but the natural response of one's being to God, and its locus is the heart" (Lumbard, 2016, p. 115).

As stated in the above qudsi, love for God is not one-way: God appears as either lover or beloved in the Qur'anic verse 85:14: "And He is the All-forgiving and All-loving (*wadûd*)". Wadûd can either mean lover if we regard it as *nomen agentis* (*fâ'il*) or beloved if we regard it as *nomen patientis* (*maf'ûl*) (Abrahamov, 2003, p. 14). Therefore, "wadûd" means lover and beloved at the same time presenting the relationship between God and humans a reciprocal one. God is not only the beloved but also a lover of humans. This reciprocal relationship between God and human beings differs from Plato's notion of eros, which leads to Beauty in a nonreciprocal way.[6] Needless to say, Platonic Ideas do not have a love for human beings whereas

---

[6]However, in the famous Allegory of the Cave in the *Republic*, Plato explains the journey of the freed prisoner comprised of two ways. After the liberated prisoner sees the world of Ideas, he goes back to the cave to give the news to the captives.

God has. However, the concept of Sufi love differs from the Biblical notion, of agape, also understood as God's love. Nygren describes also agape as God's disinterested love for man. God's essence is identified with agape in the Gospel of John through the statement "God is love", which means that His love is eternal and exists even without an object (Nygren, 1953, p. 152). This contrasts with the hadith of the hidden treasure, which shows that God's love is not disinterested as God *loved* to have an object as a result of his overflowing love.

Together with the crucial creation narrative of the hidden treasure found in many Sufi texts, another key hadith refers to God's beauty: "God is beautiful and He loves beauty". Both hadiths have contributed to the idea that

> (...) creation was driven by God's desire to manifest His beauty so that it might be witnessed and known by others. Creation is then the self-disclosure (*tajallī*) of God's beauty as a result of His overflowing love for His own beauty. This process also brings about the duality of subject and object, knower and known, lover and beloved. Without God's creation, God's beauty could not have been known or loved by *anything else* (Murata, 2018, p. 19).

Thus, the general Muslim discourse on beauty has always been contemplated in the context of God's love. Since God is beautiful and created the cosmos out of love, Sufis stressed that the created beings must also love God (Chittick, 2014, p. 3). An early Sufi, Samani (d. 1067) comments on God's love:

> Although human beings should serve God, servanthood is the job description of the angels. Human beings were created for love, not service. They alone were created in God's image, manifesting the names of both majesty and beauty, severity and gentleness. They alone possessed readiness for love, for it demands separation and union, suffering and joy, trial and triumph (Chittick & Nasr, 2013, p. 47).

The Qur'an calls God the most beautiful creator in verse 23:14, which signifies two things: God is beautiful Himself, and what he creates is also beautiful (Murata, 2018, p. 75). Hence, human beings are created as the highest form of creation to be the mirror of God's beautiful names and endowed with the intellect to recognize God, which distinguishes them from all other creatures. This is also the meaning what the Sufis see in the Qur'anic verse 5:54, "He loves them, and they love Him" (Chittick, 2011, p. 67).

Since God granted intellect only to human beings, the Qur'an says in verse 38:72, "Then I breathed into him of My soul". Kazuyo Murata points out that the notion that the individual soul mirrors the beauty of higher-order has certain striking similarities with the Plotinian understanding whether there is direct or indirect influence (Murata, 2018, pp. 18–19). How one must beautify his/her soul following the significant example of Prophet Muhammad will be discussed later in the chapter.

Having discussed that not only cosmos was created out of God's love to disclose His beauty but also human beings were created out of love in a reciprocal relationship to God, the following section will explain the creation of humans and the first contract between God and human beings. This contract is called *Kalu bela,* which is referred to as "the Covenant of Love", and marks the nature of the relation between God and human beings.

12.5 Ascension to Beauty

In Sufism, God's beauty is not only the reason for the creation but also the cause for the beautification of the soul. Most Muslim thinkers and Sufis have understood that the search for beauty in various areas of human life is part of their religious path to human perfection since all beauty points to its origin, God (Murata, 2018, p. 26). The soul is described in need of ascending a stairway back to God in order to purify the lower self or soul (*nafs*) from its unrefined qualities. The term self, nafs, holds a significant role in Sufism as spiritual transformation comprises the nafs, traversing through seven stages, from impurity to purity. The self, almost always, begins the journey in the most unrefined level, what the Qur'an calls the commanding self (*al-nafs al-ammara*), or "the soul that incites to evil" (12:53). It is defined by self-centered and compulsive tendencies, such as selfishness, arrogance, oppression of others, lack of gratitude, greed, stinginess, envy, anger, cynicism, and laziness. Also, it loves the ephemeral attractions of the world. Similar to the Platonic notion of eros, the journey of the soul starts from the lower stages of beauty and rises up to higher stages, that is from the unrefined to the refined. The difficulty of transforming the nafs is reflected in the statement of Umm Talq, an early Sufi woman, who said, "The nafs is king if you indulge it, but is a slave if you torment it" (Shaikh 2012, p., 37).

Therefore, an example is necessary; the modal of beauty to be followed is Prophet Muhammad. In his *mi'raj*, the human being can go up the steps of the beautification of the soul, where each step is "an increase in proximity to divine beauty" (Murata, 2018, p. 22). God created Muhammad as the beautiful exemplar (33:21) for his community to follow. He made the last prophet actualize the fullness of human perfection by placing within him all the individual perfections of the previous prophets (Chittick & Nasr, 2013, pp. 150–152).

Nevertheless, this is not a one-way journey either since the Circle of Existence has two arcs, according to Sufism. Together with the ascension to God following the example of Prophet Muhammad in his *mi'raj*, the other arc represents a descent into the world (Chittick, 2000, p. 85). The journey of descent starts on what is commonly known as the Day of the Covenant, which is explained in the Qur'an 7:172: "And [mention] when your Lord took from the children of Adam—from their loins—their descendants and made them testify of themselves, [saying to them], 'Am I not your Lord?' They said, 'Yes, we have testified.' [This]—lest you should say on the Day of Resurrection, 'Indeed, we were of this unaware'".

Aḥmad al-Ghazālī and other Sufis understand it as a covenant made in and through love since God's question reflects His love for them and human beings' affirmation of their love for God. Therefore, only after God makes human beings beloved, they become lovers. All human love and love for God originates from God's pre-temporal love for human beings (Lumbard, 2016, p. 164). In the question, "Am I not your Lord?" God gives a clue to the question to which all the souls of eternity answer in an affirmation (Chittick & Nasr, 2013, pp. 46–47). All the souls say "yes" as they are stricken with the beauty of God's face and His voice. When they hear God's command, they descend level by level into the womb. However, on the earth, they are born in complete oblivion of the Day of the Covenant and the promise they made.[7] Therefore, the world and its attractions, influencing the nafs, remains to be all they know about. Only when they hear the ongoing despair in their soul, they start challenging their forgetfulness out of love. In Plato's *Phaedrus*, people see a beautiful object on the earth. They remember the divine beauty they experienced at the rim of the heavens. Thus, they start the reverse journey of descent, ascension toward God, as all things come from God (Chittick, 2000, p. 85). Human beings come to this world to display the attributes of God reflected within themselves, or, in other words, to "play his own part in revealing the Hidden Treasure". Simultaneously, whether they will remember their promise to love God on the Day of the Covenant is being tested. The question is whether they understand and acknowledge that they are "displaying God's Treasure", not their own (Jalal al-Din Rumi & Chittick, 1983, p. 69).

That God's Hidden Treasure manifests itself in creation, which is displayed in human beings, explains the course of love. The great philosopher and physician Ibn-i Sina (d. 1037), known in the West as Avicenna with his work translated into Latin, is famous for his synthesis of Greek and Islamic wisdom. He too expressed that all comes from God and goes to God as a result of His love and mercy in his *Ilahiyyat*: "He is the lover of His own Essence. As His Essence is an origin, It is the origin of all order and all good. Hence, the order of the good comes to be an object of His love accidentally". This was in the fashion of the Muslim scholar, Muhammad Ghazali (d. 1111), who wrote in his chapter exclusively on love in his *Ihya 'Ulum al-Din*, "When someone loves only himself, his acts, and his compositions, his love does not transgress his essence and the concomitants of his essence, since they are connected to his essence. Thus, God loves only Himself" (Chittick & Nasr, 2013, p. 115). According to this, love is a dynamic force because it moves the lover to God (Addas, 2002). The love of human beings ascends them to God when the human soul leaves behind the characteristics of his lower self and beautifies itself. Thus, the Sufi seeker's journey is both motivated and inspired by love. In this sense, ashk shows an affinity to eros in its motivation to pursue ultimate Beauty. However, it slightly differs from the Platonic eros since eros is an intermediary, that is "something in-between" in the *Symposium* (204b). Eros only leads to the Idea of Beauty, whereas ashk both comes from the Beauty of God and guides back to Him.

12.6 Conclusion

This chapter set out to establish a preliminary comparison between the understandings of love in the Islamic tradition and the Platonic tradition. The main goal of the current study is to position ashk within the Platonic tradition of love. The similarity

---

[7]Similarly, amnesia occurs to the psyche that drinks from the river of Lethe in the Myth of Er narrated in the *Republic*, 621b. In *Phaedrus*, the one who sees the beauty on earth remembers the true beauty (249d) and is called a "lover" (249e).

between ashk and eros is, in fact, one among many other attempts of comparison in philosophical and religious traditions.

Since Islam is a monotheistic religion while the accounts of Plato are rich with polytheistic stories of Greek gods and goddesses, their references, metaphors, and cultural context differ immensely. Despite such significant differences, the focus here has solely been on the links that can be drawn between two traditions considered to be distinct. While Plato's influence on Western civilization and philosophy is accepted to be a fact, it is entirely disregarded in the context of Islam even though Plato was known quite well by the Muslim authors and scholars. Therefore, the chapter has aimed to locate ashk as a motif that could question Eurocentrism in the field of love studies and philosophy by drawing attention to the Platonic influence on Islamic civilization.

It has been discussed that the path of love is described as ascension in both Platonic and Sufi traditions; while the philosopher tries to reach the ultimate Beauty, the Sufi lover tries to reach God. It has been shown that God is described as the ultimate Beauty whose love overflows and leads to creation in the Sufi perception. Ascension to God and His Beauty can only happen when human beings beautify their souls. The beautification of the soul is described in a Platonic way as it involves a move from the material to the spiritual, from the sensible to the intelligible world. Nevertheless, the reciprocal nature between God and human beings is not to be found in Plato's eros, described merely as an intermediary between the sensible and intelligible worlds. Ashk, on the other hand, emphasizes that God's love flows out of Him and goes back to Him through the account of creation expressed in the hadith of Hidden Treasure.

The proximity between Plato's eros and Sufi ashk requires more attention. This analysis suggests that the focus on beauty and ascension of the human soul through love are key axes of comparison between the two traditions. However, the major limitation of this study is that Sufi tradition is a broad literature composed over hundreds of years in different locales. Therefore, it has not been possible to address the historical specificities of ashk expressed by various authors and discuss it in more detail. This would be a fruitful area for further research.

There is, therefore, a definite need for discussion on cultural and historical usage of love as well as its meaning in different traditions. Paying attention to similarities and differences while articulating a common vocabulary could help solve a variety of conflicts that are beyond the scope of love. In consequence, this paper has contextualized ashk as discussed that a missing link in the Platonic tradition, whose importance has been disregarded as part of hostility towards Islam. Even though Christianity is considered to be the only monotheistic religion that focuses on love, the goal in this chapter has been to display its centrality in Islam as well. It is hoped that this analysis also clears the misconception of Islam as a religion of fear, propagated currently in popular media and politics and positions it instead as "the religion of ashk".

Acknowledgements I would like to express my profound gratitude to Dr. Victoria Rowe Holbrook for her support, availability, and comments on earlier versions of this chapter.

References

Abrahamov, B. (2003). *Divine love in Islamic mysticism: The teachings of al-Ghazâlî and al-Dabbâgh*. London: Routledge.

Addas, C. (2002). The experience and doctrine of love in Ibn 'Arabi (C. Twinch, trans.). *Journal of the Muhyiddin Ibn 'Arabi Society, 32*, 25–44.

Addas, C., & Kingsley, P. (1993). *Quest for red Sulphur: The life of Ibn 'Arabi*. Cambridge: Islamic Texts Society.

Ahmed, S. (2017). What is Islam?: The importance of being Islamic. In *Princeton*. Oxford: Princeton University Press.

Azarian, R. (2011). Potentials and limitations of comparative method in social science. *International Journal of Humanities and Social Science, 1*(4), 113–125.

Bell, J. N. (1979). *Love theory in later Hanbalite Islam*. Albany: State University of New York Press.

Burman, T. E. (2007). *Reading the Qur'an in Latin Christendom, 1140–1560*. Retrieved from https://doi.org/10.9783/9780812200225.

Chittick, W. C. (1989). *The Sufi path of knowledge: Ibn al-'Arabi's metaphysics of imagination*. Albany, NY: State University of New York Press.

Chittick, W. C. (2000). *Sufism: A short introduction*. Oxford: Oneworld Publications.

Chittick, W. C. (2011). The Koran as the lover's mirror. In *Universal dimensions of Islam: Studies in comparative religion*. Bloomington, IN: World Wisdom, Inc.

Chittick, W. (2014). Ibn Arabi. In E. N. Zalta (Ed.), *The Stanford encyclopedia of philosophy* (spring 2014). Stanford: Metaphysics Research Lab, Stanford University.

Chittick, W. C., & Nasr, S. H. (2013). *Divine love: Islamic literature and the path to god*. New Haven: Yale University Press.

Chittick, W. C., Rustom, M., Khalil, A., & Murata, K. (2012). *In search of the lost heart: Explorations in Islamic thought*. Albany, NY: State University of New York Press.

d'Alverny, M.-T. (1947). Deux Traductiones Latines Du Coran Au Moyen Age. *Archives d'histoire doctrinale et littéraire du Moyen Age, 16*, 69–131.

El-Zein, A. (2000). Spiritual consumption in the United States: The Rumi phenomenon. *Islam and Christian–Muslim Relations, 11*(1), 71–85. https://doi.org/10.1080/095964100111526

Ernst, C. W. (1997). *The Shambhala guide to Sufism*. Boston, MA: Shambhala.

Ernst, C. W. (2003). *Following Muhammad: Rethinking Islam in the contemporary world*. Chapel Hill: University of North Carolina.

Furlanetto, E. (2013). The 'Rumi phenomenon' between orientalism and cosmopolitanism: The-case of Elif Shafak's the forty rules of love. *European Journal of English Studies, 17*(2), 201–213.

Holbrook, V. (2017). Hüsn-ü Aşk'ın Arkeolojisi–I archeology of beauty and love- I. *ASOBİD: Amasya Üniversitesi Sosyal Bilimler Dergisi, 1*(1), 41–50.

Izutsu, T. (1984). *Sufism and Taoism: A comparative study of key philosophical concepts*. Berkeley: University of California Press.

Jalal al-Din Rumi, & Chittick, W. C. (1983). *The Sufi path of love: The spiritual teachings of Rumi*. Albany: State University of New York Press.

Kaegi, W. E. (1969). Initial byzantine reactions to the Arab conquest. *Church History, 38*(2), 139–149.

Kritzeck, J. (1964). *Peter the venerable and Islam*. Princeton, NJ: Princeton University Press.

Kumar, G., Bhatt, M. (Producers), & Bhatt, M. (Director). (1990). *Aashiqui* [Motion Picture]. India: Vishesh Films.

Kumar, B., Bhatt, M. (Producers), & Suri, M. (Director). (2013). *Aashiqui 2* [Motion Picture]. India: Vishesh Films.

Lamoreaux, J. C. (1996). Early Christian responses to Islam. In J. V. Tolan (Ed.), *Medieval Christian perceptions of Islam: A book of essays* (pp. 3–31). New York: Garland.

Lumbard, J. E. B. (2016). *Aḥmad al-Ghazālī, remembrance, and the metaphysics of love*. Albany: State University of New York Press.

Morewedge, P. (1981). Sufism, Neoplatonism, and Zachner's theistic theory of mysticism. In *Islamic philosophy and mysticism*. Delmar NY: Caravan Books.

Murata, S. (1992). *The Tao of Islam: A sourcebook on gender relationships in Islamic thought*. Albany: State University of New York Press.

Murata, K. (2018). *Beauty in Sufism*. Albany: State University of New York Press.

Nehamas, A., & Woodruff, P. (1989). *Symposium: Plato*. Indianapolis, IN: Hackett.

Nirenberg, D. (2008). Islam and the west: Two dialectical fantasies. *Journal of Religion in Europe, 1*(1), 3–33.

Nirenberg, D. (2009). Christendom and Islam. In *The Cambridge history of Christianity: Christianity in Western Europe c.1100–c.1500* (pp. 149–169). Cambridge: Cambridge University Press.

Nirenberg, D., & Capezzone, L. (2015). Religions of love: Judaism, Christianity, and Islam. In A. J. Silverstein & G. G. Stroumsa (Eds.), *The Oxford handbook of Abrahamic religions*. Oxford, UK; New York, NY: Oxford University Press.

Nygren, A. (1953). *Agape and Eros*. Philadelphia: Westminster Press.

Osborne, C. (1994). *Eros unveiled: Plato and the god of love*. Oxford; New York: Clarendon Press: Oxford University Press.

Plato, & Waterfield, R. (2002). *Phaedrus*. Oxford; New York: Oxford University Press.

Sedgwick, M. (2017). Eclectic Sufism in the contemporary Arab world. *Tidsskrift for Islamforskning, 11*(1), 65–82.

Shaikh, S. (2012). *Sufi Narratives of Intimacy Ibn 'Arabī, Gender, and Sexuality*. Chapel Hill, NC: University of North Carolina Press.

Singer, I. (1984). *The nature of love. 1: Plato to Luther*. Chicago; London: University of Chicago Press.

Tolan, J. V. (2002). *Saracens: Islam in the medieval European imagination*. New York, NY: Columbia University Press.

Zaehner, R. C. (1960). *Hindu and Muslim mysticism*. London: The Athlone Press.

Çiğdem Buğdaycı (Ms.), received her B.A. in Western Languages and Literatures at Boğaziçi University, and her M.A. in Cultural Studies at Istanbul Bilgi University. She is a Ph.D. candidate at ASCA (Amsterdam School for Cultural Analysis), the University of Amsterdam and writing her dissertation on the changing significations of the concept of Sufi love with regard to secularism and modernization of Turkey.

Chapter 13
Prema in kabIr's sAkhI: Indigenous Perspectives on Love

Dharm P. S. Bhawuk

Abstract In this paper, I analyze how the medieval mystic poet and saint *kabIr* (1398–1448) uses *prem* in his *sAkhI* or teachings by employing the collection of *kabIr sAhab*'s teachings published by the center in *dAmAkheDA, rAypur, chattisgaDha*, India. Eight themes emerged that provide a thick description of *prem* or love. Love is non-transient (or *aghaT prem piMjar base*). Love cannot be hidden (*prem chipAyA nA chipe*). Love is difficult (*kaThin galI hai prem kI or zISa kATa Age dhare*). Love is a drink (*kabIr pyAlA prem kA*). Love for God is superior to material love (*prem hai doya prakAra kA*). Love without understanding is useless (*prem akelA kyA kare*). Compassion causes humbleness, which in turn generates love (*jahAM dInatA tahAM prem*). Love, detachment and *sadguru* are interdependent ideas (*prem binA dhIraja nahIM*). The study contributes to global psychology by presenting an indigenous description, and the findings also help develop a more complex understanding of the construct of love.

Keywords Love · *kabIr* · *Prema* · *Bhakti* · *Priti* · Indigenous psychology

---

Harvard-Kyoto protocol for transliteration for *devanagarI* is used for all *saMskRit* and *hindI* words and names, and the first letters of names are not capitalized. All non-English words are italicized.
अ a आ A इ i ई I उ u ऊ U ए e ऐ ai ओ o औ au ऋ R ॠ RR ऌ lR ॡ lRR अं M अः H क ka ख kha ग ga घ kha ङ Ga च ca छ cha ज ja झ jha ञ Ja ट Ta ठ Tha ड Da ढ Dha ण Na त ta थ tha द da ध dha न na प pa फ pha ब ba भ bha म ma य ya र ra ल la व va श za ष Sa स sa ह ha क्ष kSa त्र tra ज्ञ jJa श्र zra

---

D. P. S. Bhawuk (✉)
Management and Culture and Community Psychology, University of Hawaii at Manoa, Honolulu, Hawaii, USA
e-mail: bhawuk@hawaii.edu

13.1 Introduction

Marsella (1998) presented the template of "global-community psychology." He entreated researchers to replace the Western cultural traditions by more encompassing multicultural traditions, and reiterated the need to emphasize the cultural determinants of human behavior, which has been discussed in the literature (Gergen, Gulerce, Lock, & Mishra, 1996; Pawlik, 1991). He recommended the systems orientation and noted that many indigenous psychologies are well equipped to deal with ascending dimensions of behavioral contexts, from individual to family to society to nature to spirituality. He further proposed that qualitative research including such methods as narrative accounts, discourse analysis, and ethnographic analysis should be encouraged. This paper enriches global-community psychology by presenting an indigenous construct, *prem*, which enriches our understanding of love, devotion, and spirituality.

Bhawuk (2003) analyzed how culture shapes creativity, and concluded that spirituality was a cultural value that has blossomed in India over thousands of years. He presented a table of saints, and *kabIr (kabIr sAhab* here after) appears prominently in the fifteenth century (1398–1448). *kabIr sAhab* was a disciple of *santa rAmAnanda*, who is considered the founder of *rAmAnandi saMpradAya*, the largest community of ascetic in India (Burghart, 1978; Kasturi, 2015). *santa rAmAnand* had many famous disciples, and most of them not *brahmans* like *pipA* (a *kSatriya*), *dhannA* (a *jAta* farmer), *narhari* (a goldsmith), *senA* (a barber), *sAdhana* (a butcher), and *raidAsa* (a cobbler). *kabIr sAhab* was in a vibrant historical period when love was being defined as the ultimate virtue, and definitely superior to knowledge. Therefore, analyzing love in the teachings of *kabIr sAhab* can be historically significant in understanding the meaning of love in the Indian context.

Inspired by Triandis (1994) and Marsella (1998), I have been working on indigenous psychology, especially focused on India, and over the years I have employed many different methods to identify and develop indigenous constructs like *manas, buddhi, ahaGkAra, Atman* (Bhawuk, 2011), *cit* or consciousness (Bhawuk, 2014), *adhyAtma* or spirituality (Bhawuk, 2019a, 2019b), *lajjA* (2017a, 2019c), *zraddhA* (Bhawuk, 2020), and *lokasaGgraha* (2008b, 2019e). I have also developed models of self (2005, 2008a, 2011), models of personal harmony (Bhawuk, 1999, 2011), and a spirituality-based theory of creativity (Bhawuk, 2003, 2019d). This effort has led to the employment of various methodology including historical analysis (Bhawuk, 2003), case analysis (Bhawuk, 2003; Bhawuk, Mrazek, & Munusamy, 2009), autoethnography (Bhawuk, 2009, 2017b, 2017c, 2019c), lexical analysis (Bhawuk, 2017a, 2019a, 2019b, 2019e), literary analysis (Bhawuk, 2017a), bridging life-world and scientific world (Bhawuk, 2019d), building models from scriptures (Bhawuk, 2005, 2008a, b, 2010a, 2010b, 2011, 2019d). In this paper, I add to the list of Indian constructs by deriving the meaning of the construct of *prem*, and contribute further to the literature by expanding the methodological scope by employing the literature in the tradition of *bhakti* or devotion, which is quite rich and voluminous. I employ the *sAkhI* of *kabIr sAhab* in this paper.

For indigenous research traditional sources should be utilized for two reasons. First, the material employed is cultural, since it is passed on from generation to generation. Second, it is likely to have been safeguarded from distortions of colonial rulers. Therefore, in this paper, the text, *zrI granth sAkhI: caurAsI aMga kI*, published by *zrI sadguru kabIr dharmadAsa sAhab vaMzAvalI, dAmAkheDA, rAyapur, chattisgaDha* (Paravatadas & Singh, 2013), which is one of the traditional *saMpradAya* or community of followers of *kabIr* in Northern India was employed. The text is organized into 84 cantos, and two of them pertain to the emotion of love; Canto 22, *aGga prem ko* has 38 verses, and Canto 60, *aGga priti ko,* has 23 verses.

In this paper, the collection of *kabIr sAhab*'s 38 verses pertaining to *prem* or love, were analyzed to develop a thick description of the construct of *prem*. The themes were found to be consistent with the 23 verses in aGga priti ko and the eight verses on *bhaktI* or love for God (Canto 17, *aGga bhakti ko*). The findings were further synthesized by doing a lexical analysis of the meaning of the word *prem* in *saMskRtam* and other Indian languages.

13.2 Methodology

All the 38 verses in the *aGga prem ko* or the section on love was analyzed individually. The question "What is love?" was utilized in the reflective analyses for each verse. Then the verses that are on the same sub-theme were analyzed together to recognize sub-themes. Following this, relevant verses from other *aGgas* of the *sAkhi* that pertain to *prem* or *prIti* were analyzed. Finally, all the sub-themes were synthesized, which provided a thick description of *prem* or love in the *bhakti* literature of *kabIr sAhab*. In the discussion section, the meaning of the word *prem* in *saMskRtam* and other Indian languages was employed to add to the generalizability of the findings.

13.3 *kabIr sAhab*'s *sAkhI* or Teaching

aGga prem ko, **verse 1:** *prem binA dhIraj nahiN, birah binA bairAg; satguru bin chUTe nahIM, man maMsA kA dAg.* If one does not have love, one does not have patience; and if one does not experience separation, one does not have a detachment. Without the blessings of *satguru*, the blemishes of manas are not removed. **What is love? Patience is born of love, or love is the antecedent of patience. We see this in how the mother, father, and teacher patiently nurture young ones. A farmer also patiently nurtures the plants.** *kabIr sAhab* **presents three ideas in this verse—love, detachment, and role of** *sadguru***. There are 65 verses pertaining to** *biraha* **or separation from the loved one, and one of them (verse 24) states that the day one is separated from the beloved one, love increases in the** *manas***. Thus, separation is related to both love and detachment; it is a love enhancer** and is also necessary for cultivating detachment. The role of the *sadguru* could be an indication that he or she is patient with us in helping us clean our attachments to the material world, which are not easy to remove.

aGga prem ko, **verse 2:** *prem prem sab koI kahai, prem na cinhai koya; ATha pahar bhInA rahe, prem kahave soya.* Everyone talks about love, but no one understands love. **What is love? It is that in which one is absorbed 24 hours** (*kabIr sAhab* uses eight *prahar* which is a measure of a full day and night).

aGga prem ko, **verse 3:** *chinahi caDhai chin Utarai, so to prem na hoya; aghaT prem pinJari basai, prem kahAvai soya.* Love does not happen this moment, and end that moment. Love that stays with the self without diminishing is called love. ***kabIr sAhab* defines love as non-transient. The choice of words are also interesting. Love is implicitly compared to a spirit that captures or possesses a person, and then described as not something a person this moment and leaves the next. Love possesses the person for good, and never diminishes. This is similar to the previous verse where love is said to be that which absorbs one all the time.**

aGga prem ko, **verse 4:** *hirdaya prem prakAziyA, Upar bhayA ujAs; mukh kasturI cAbate, bAhir phUTi bAs.* When one's inside is lit with love, the outside is also lit; just like when one chews something that is fragrant (*kabIr sAhab* refers to chewing *kasturi,* which is obtained from musk deer, zoological name Moschus Moschiferus), the fragrance pervades everything around the person. **What is love? It is something that cannot be hidden, and it is consistent; if there is love in the heart, then it is expressed in behavior.**

aGga prem ko, **verse 5:** *prem chipAyA nA chipe, jab tab pargaT hoya; jo kachu mukh se nA kahai, nain det hai roya.* Love cannot be hidden even if one tries to hide it, and it comes out unannounced. Even if one does not verbalize it, it is expressed by the eyes in tears. **What is love? Love is expressed by eyes with tears. In this verse, *kabIr sAhab* explicitly states what was implied in the previous verse.**

aGga prem ko, **verse 6:** *prem chipAyA nA chipe, jab tab hoya prakAza; dAbI dUbI nA rahe, kastUrI kI bAs.* Love cannot be hidden even if one tries to hide it, as it comes out occasionally, just like the fragrance of *kasturI* cannot be suppressed. **What is love? It is something that cannot be suppressed.**

aGga prem ko, **verse 7:** *prem pukAre bArane, aradh rain me pIva; prItm darzan dIjiye, tarsat merA jIva.* Love calls our from outside the door at midnight; and says, "My beloved, please give me *darzan;* my self is starving for a glimpse." **What is love? It is not bound by the propriety of time (and space) and the lover longs for a glimpse.**

aGga prem ko, **verse 8:** *jahAM dayA tahAM dInatA, jahAM dInatA tahAM prem; dayA prem nahIM dInatA, jahAM na JAve nem.* Where there is compassion, there is humbleness (or meekness); and where there is humbleness, there is love. One should not go where there is no compassion, love, and humbleness. **What is love? In this verse, *kabIr sAhab* gives us a causal network of three constructs, compassion leads to humbleness, and humbleness leads to love.**

aGga prem ko, **verse 9:** *kaThin galI hai prem kI, udmad cale na koya; udmad se DaratA cale, jA tan sudh na hoya.* The path of love is difficult, and not for those who are attached to the material world. Those who are afraid of the trappings of the material world, and can forget about their body can walk on this path. **What is love? In this verse, *kabIr sAhab* talks about spirituality and love, and notes that the path of spiritual love is not easy.**

aGga prem ko, **verse 10**: *ek pal bhagatI prem kI, koTa baras kA joga; jab lag pal pAve nahIM, tab lag jog vijog.* A moment of devotion of love is equivalent to ten million years of yoga practice. If one does not get that moment of love through the practice of yoga, then the practice of yoga is a waste. **What is love? kabIr sAhab emphasizes the importance of love in the practice of spirituality. This is consistent with the tradition (see *bhagavadgItA* 12.5 and 12.12).**

aGga prem ko, **verse 11**: *kabIr pyAsA prem kA, jal meM paiThA dhAya; gale zIza tak dUbiyA, piv bin pyAs na jAya.* A person who thirsts for love cannot quench it by going in water and submerging oneself up to the throat or head. As thirst does not go away without drinking water, without meeting the loved one the longing of a lover does not end. **What is love? *kabIr sAhab* compares love with thirst, and union of lovers with drinking of water.**

aGga prem ko, **verse 12**: *ye to pyAlA prem kA, tAkA paDA dukAl; kaheM kabIr kyoMkar pijIye, maMge zIza kalAl.* In this verse, *kabIr sAhab* uses the simile of drinking for love, and says that there is extreme shortage of servers or glasses to serve the wine of love. And the price asked for the drink of love is one's head or ego, meaning that one has to surrender completely to receive love. **What is love? It calls for erasing one's ego or requires total surrender.**

aGga prem ko, **verse 13**: *zISa kAT Age dhare, choDa kapaT kA bhAva; sAhab kabIr yoM kahe, aisA hoya to Ava.* One who can offer his head and quit cunningness, only those should come forward. **What is love? Here *kabIr sAhab* raises the standard for love, and the antecedents of love are said to be lack of cunningness or guile, and the ability to give up even one's life, what to talk about other material possessions.**

aGga prem ko, **verse 14**: *zISa kATa Age dharA, tA Upar paga dInha; kabIr saudA prem kA, sir kAte ham kinha.* *kabIr SAhab* calls love a market transaction (*saudA*) in which he traded his head for love. **What is love? The offering of one's head is repeated here, emphasizing the need for total surrender in love. Compared to the previous verse, in this verse *kabIr Sahiba* raises the bar by saying that it is not sufficient to offer one's head, but one should be able to stamp on it as if it is of no value or significance. This is often interpreted as total surrender, which is necessary in love.**

aGga prem ko, **verse 15**: *prem bikaMtA maiM sunA, mAthA sATe hAt, tanik vilamba na kIjiye, tat china dIje kATa.* I have heard that in the market love is sold in exchange for head. Do not waste any time; offer your head right away. This is the third verse where the head is being traded in the market place for love, and *kabIr sAhiba* says one should not waste any time, implying that it is still a bargain to buy love for one's head, or everything. **What is love? It is something that is traded in the market for life. It is so valuable that one should buy immediately by offering one's head, i.e., one's life.**

aGga prem ko, **verse 16**: *kabIr pyAlA prem kA, antar liyA lagAya, roma roma meM rami rahA, aur amal kyA khAya.* Here love is compared to intoxicants and said to be the most intoxicating. When one drinks from the goblet of love, and internalizes it, then love resides in every pore of the body. There is no use for any other intoxicant to such a person. **What is love? It is a goblet. It is an elixir filled goblet. It is something that can be internalized. When internalized, it can exude from every pore of our being. It is the ultimate addiction, upon tasting which all others pale by comparison.**

aGga prem ko, **verse 17:** *kabIr bhATI prek kI, sab koI baiThe Aya; premI hoya soI piye, aur se piyA na jAya. kabIr sAhab* uses lover (*premI*) for the first time in this verse. He says though all come and sit in the tavern of love, only a lover is able to drink; others are not able to drink. The simile of alcoholic drink is used again, and only a few, the lovers, are said to be able to drink. Just like in the previous verses love was said to be not easy, one had to offer one's head. Here again, love is said not to be easy for common people. **What is love? It is a tavern where all sit, but only lovers can drink. Others are not able to drink here. One could reject such a definition as tautological. But when an abstract concept is to be understood, sometimes it is helpful to know who personifies such a value or virtue. A lover is said to personify love (verse 17).**

aGga prem ko, **verse 18:** *rAtA mAtA maiM phiroM, rom rom [prem] ras pUra; chAMDi Asa zarIra kI, tab sAhab hAla hajUra.* I walk around intoxicated with my pores brimmed with love. When I gave up on the physical identity, only then was the Lord pleased. The love is said to be a rasa with which we can get filled. It is also said to be an elixir that is intoxicating. **By bringing the idea that only when we give up our physical identity do we get the grace of God,** *kabIr sAhiba* **alludes to the spiritual undermeaning of love. What is love? It is a rasa that can fill us up. It is an intoxicant (verse 18).**

aGga prem ko, **verse 19:** *prem bikaMte maiM sunA, sir sATe kA mol; koI jauharI le gayA jukti dhAr na tol. kabIr sAhiba* makes love the most expensive item sold in the market, which costs one life. He says that only a connoisseur buys love without doing any bargaining, and it is so valuable that he or she pays for it with life. **What is love? It is the most expensive item to be bought and sold in the market place. The price of love is life, and it is a bargain at that (verse 19).**

aGga prem ko, **verse 20:** *prem piyAlA jo piye so nahIM pIve nIra; bhAg baDA soI piye, bhar bhar deve kabIr.* One who drinks from the goblet of love does not need to drink water. Only the fortunate ones drink, and *kabIr* serves again again. **What is love?** *kabIr* **implies that it is something spiritual that so satisfies a person that the thirst for all physical and material entities are also quenched.**

aGga prem ko, **verse 21:** *sAheb kabIr ne yoM piyA bAkI rahI na chAka; pakkA kalaza kumhAra kA bahuri chaDhe na cAka.* Lord, *kabIr* so drank from the goblet of love that he has no desire to drink just like a baked pot does not need to be shaped on the potter's wheel. **What is love?** *kabIr* **uses his own experience in this** *sAkhI* **to emphasize that when one drinks from the goblet of love, one becomes completely contented. He further emphasizes the state of a person who is nourished by love by comparing the person to a baked pot that needs no shaping from the potter anymore. Only raw pots need to be shaped by the potter and are placed on the potter's wheel. Here it should be noted that** *kabIrA* was not shy proclaiming his experience. In another *sAkhI* he proclaims that he lived in the world so carefully that his life was not stained, and he left the world without being touched by the material world or touching the material world (*dAsa kabIr ne aisi oDhI, jyUM ki tyUM dhar dInhi cadariyA jhInI re jhInI*).

aGga prem ko, verse 22: *amRta ras kI moTarI, daI kabIr khola; Apa sarIkhA jo mile, tAhi pliAuM ghola.* Love is compared to nectar, and kabIr opens the package in which nectar is wrapped. He offers it to those who are like him. **What is love? It is the nectar that makes one immortal.** kabIr suggests that nectar is not readily available to everybody, since it is wrapped up. Only an able person can unpackage it. Then he says that he has unpackaged it, and is serving it to those who are like him. It is implied that love is not for common people. It is for those who care for nothing but love like *kabIr* did. It should be noted that *kabIr* proclaimed his nontraditional approach to life often in provocative terms like— *kabIrA khaDA bajAra meM, liye lukArI hAtha; jo ghar phUke Apana, cale hamAre Satha* (*kabIr* is standing with a torch in his hand in the market square; those who want to burn their homes should follow him.)

aGga prem ko, verse 23: *prem piyA tab jAniye, saba rasa bisare aur; prem jahAM nahIM nem hai, dujA jhUThI daur.* When one has drank from the goblet of love, all other desires are forgotten. Where there is love, there are no rules. Where there is no love, everything is false. **What is love? It is what makes one forget everything else. How do we know there is love? We know it because where there is love, there is no hindrance of rules. And where there is no love, everything is false; all the running around is for nothing.**

aGga prem ko, verse 24: *prem akelA kyA kare, samajha na hove hAta; dhanuSa bAna bina kheMciye, coTa akAratha jAta.* What can love alone do, when there is no wisdom. It is like stringing the bow and pulling the string without placing an arrow on the bow. The pulling of the string is wasted. **What is love? Love is the bow that requires an arrow of wisdom. Love needs to be applied properly, otherwise all effort is wasted. Here it is implied that love should be directed toward God, for all that is material is going to perish. It is also implied that one needs to live a life of service, because without it, love for God alone is not sufficient and is wasted effort.**

aGga prem ko, verse 25: *prem hai doya prakAra kA, so maiM dekhA joya; uttama sohi jAniye, jo sataguru se hoye.* I have seen that love is of two kinds. Know that the superior love is one that is for God. **What is love?** *kabIr sAhab* says that he has seen two kinds of love, one for material things and people of the world, and the other for God. He then proclaims that it is the love for God, not for other people and things, that is the superior one.

aGga prem ko, verse 26: *maiM matawAla prem kA, mada kA mAtA nAhi; mada ke mAte jo phire, te matawAle kAhi.* I am crazy for love, not for self indulgence. Those who are chasing self indulgence, they are not crazy for love. In this *sAkhI*, *kabIr sAhab* brings his personal experience and proclaims that he was crazy about love, love for God, not for self indulgence. **What is love? Love is not the passion for material world.**

aGga prem ko, **verse 27**: *rAtA mAtA nAma kA, pIyA prem aghAya; matawAlA dIdAra kA, mAMge mukti balAya.* One who is intoxicated with the name of the Lord, one who is satiated with love, such a person is crazy about seeing the Lord, and does not even care about *mokSa* or *nirvANa*. *kabIr sAhab* here presents the characteristics of an advanced spiritual person who constantly remembers the name of the Lord and is content with the love of the Lord; such a person does not even desire liberation, and seeks to be with the Lord all the time. **What is love? It is to be in a state where one does not care about even liberation, and only wants be in the presence of the Lord.** Earlier *kabIr sAhab* said one had to sacrifice one's physical self (or head) to buy love in the market place. Here he says that the epitome of love is not even to seek liberation.

aGga prem ko, **verse 28**: *bhukti mukti mAMgU nahIM, bhakti dAna de mohi; aura koI jacoM nahIM nizadin jAcoM tohin.* I do not seek pleasure and liberation. Give me *bhakti*. I do not have any other desire; I only seek you everyday. **What is love? Here love is used as a synonym of *bhakti* or devotion for the Lord, and *kabIr sAhab* seeks nothing but devotion of the Lord.**

aGga prem ko, **verse 29**: *Agi AMca sahanA sugama, sugama khaDag kI dhAra; neha nibahan prem rasa, mahAkaThina vyavahAra.* It is easy to bear the heat of fire; it is easy to walk on the edge of a sword; but it is extremely difficult to practice love. **What is love? It is the most difficult practice. Fire is symbolic of the ascetic practice of meditating with fire burning all around the person with the afternoon sun shining overhead called *paJca-agnI* or the fires in five directions. The path of spirituality is also compared to the razor's edge in *kaThopaniSad*. So, love is said to be even more difficult to translate in one's daily behavior than the ascetic practices.**

aGga prem ko, **verse 30**: *prem piyAlA jo piye, so saba taje vikAra; gatimukti sataloka ko, cale mAra paijAra.* One who drinks from the goblet of love gives up all material inflictions. Such a person proceeds to the spiritual world giving up all material desires. **What is love? It is the passport out of the material world to the spiritual world.**

aGga prem ko, **verse 31**: *yah to ghar hai prem kA, khAlA kA ghar nAhi; zIza utAre bhui dhare, tab paThe ghar mAhi.* This is the house of love, not of one's relative. One who wants to enter must surrender his or her head. **What is love? It is a pure place which can be accessed by surrendering ones physical self.**

aGga prem ko, **verse 32**: *prem na bAri Upaje, prem na hATa bikAya; rAjA prajA jehi ruchai, zIzA deya le jAya.* Love does not grow in the field. Love is not sold in the market. Whether kings or common people, those who want love should offer their head and take it. **What is love? It is something that does not discriminate between a king and a common person. Whoever wants love can have it by offering his or head; i.e. by totally surrendering oneself to the Lord.**

aGga prem ko, **verse 33**: *prem piyAlA so piye, zIsa dakSiNA deya; lobhI zIsa na de sake, nAma prem kA leya.* One who wants to drink from the goblet of love must give his or her head as the price. Those who are greedy only talk about love but are not able to offer their head. **What is love? It is the ability to sacrifice one's** physical identity and the material world. Those who are not able to do so only talk about love, but know nothing about it.

aGga prem ko, **verse 34:** *prem piyAlA bhari piyA, rAci rahyA guru jJAna; diyA nagArA zabda kA, lAla khaDA maidAna.* A person who drinks from the goblet of love and is submerged in the teachings of the spiritual *guru*, sees the Lord in the field when he beats the drum of *zabda*. *Zabda* refers to *akSara brahman* or the personification of the formless *brahman* in words. The sound *om*, which consists of three letters *a*, *u*, and *ma*, is said to be the representation of *brahman*. With extension, *zabda* has come to refer to all spiritual texts or the word of enlightened saints. *Zabad* also refers to all the verses in *guru grantha sahAba*, the *sikha* scripture, which includes verses written by Hindu and Muslim saints of India. There are 227 *pAdas in* 17 *rAgas and* 237 *slokas in zri guru grantha sahAba ji* that are attributed to *kabIr sAhab*. *zabda* is compared to the sound coming from beating the drum; just like the sound of drum jolts people, *zabda* jolts people on the spiritual path. Beating of the drum is also employed to gather people in a common place. Metaphorically, when the drum of zabda is beaten, the Lord comes in plain sight. **What is love? Love is what leads to the absorption of knowledge given by a spiritual teacher, and prepares one to beat the drum to bring God in plain sight.**

aGga prem ko, **verse 35:** *prem piyAre lAla soM, mana de kIje bhAva; sataguru ke partApa te, bhalA banA hia Dava.* One should love God with *manas* filled with *bhAva*. It is the grace of the spiritual *guru* that one is given the opportunity to love the Lord with emotion filled *manas*. **What is love? It is received with the grace of the spiritual teacher, which causes the mind to be imbued with deep longing for God.**

aGga prem ko, **verse 36:** *jA ghaTa prem na saMcare, so ghaTa jAnu masAna; jase khAla luhAr kI, swaMsa leta bina prAna.* The human body is compared to a pot. If the pot of human body is not filled with love, then know it to be a graveyard. Just like the blacksmith's bellow blows, and breathes lifelessly, so does a human being breathes but is without life if there is no love for God in that person's life. **What is love? It is what makes us different from the dead. In other words, we are dead without love for God.**

aGga prem ko, **verse 37:** *prem banij nahIM kari sakai, chaDhai na nAma ke gaila; mAnuSa kerI kholari, Odha phire jyoM bailaZ.* One who is not able to trade in the commodity of love, is not able to walk on the path of *nAma* or the spiritual path that leads to the Lord. Such a person is an ox in human form. **What is love? Love is what makes us different from animals. Our interactions need to be rich in love, else we are no different from animals**

aGga prem ko, **verse 38:** *prem bhAva ika cAhiye, bheSa aneka banAya; bhAve raho gRhahi meM, bhAve banameM jAya.* One can don anything, or be anybody—a householder or a monk, so long one has the emotion of love. **What is love? It is the prerequisite for being a human being in all phases of life. As noted earlier, without love one is an animal, or even worse, one is simply lifeless or dead.**

13.4 Results

In what follows, first the eight themes identified from the analyses of the 38 verses are presented.

Theme 1 (*aGga prem ko*, verses 2 & 3): *aghaT prem piMjar base* or love is non-transient. Love is not as simple as it seems. People talk about it but few understand what it is. A person in love is absorbed in love all the time, 24 hours a day. Love is that which does not diminish. Love is not waxing and waning. Love does not happen this moment, and end that moment. *kabIr sAhab*'s choice of words are also interesting. Love is implicitly compared to a spirit that captures or possesses a person, and then described as not something that possesses a person this moment and leaves the next. Love possesses the person for good, and never diminishes.

This theme is also supported in *aGga prIt ko* in verses 3, 5, 11, 15–20 and 22. In verse 3 the metaphor of flint is employed to state that love for a noble person does not change over eons, though it may remain dormant. In other verses, the true love is compared to that of a moth that gives its life in flame, a fish because it dies when it is separated from water, and the Hindu woman who sacrifices herself on the funeral pyre with her husband. The bee is said to have superficial love because it goes from one flower to another. Similarly, turtle, crocodile, frog, and gourd are said to have superficial love because they do not die like the fish when they are separated from water. The bucket wheel is also used as an example of superficial love as it approaches water when empty and turns away from it when filled. In verse 15, love is said to be unaffected by distance.

Theme 2 (*aGga prem ko*, verses 4–7): *prem chipAyA nA chipe* or love cannot be hidden. Love is compared to light, and if it is in the heart, there is light outside, meaning that the person in love can be identified clearly. A second example, that of *kasturI* or musk deer, which is often used in the Indian culture is also employed to highlight that love cannot be hidden. A third example is used to say that love cannot be hidden and is expressed in tears coming from the eyes. A fourth example of a devotee is used. The devotee cannot hide his or her love and knocks on the door of the teacher even at midnight. This theme is also supported in verses 2 and 21 of *aGga prIt ko*.

Theme 3 (*aGga prem ko*, verses 9–10, 12–15, 19, 29, 31–33): *kaThin galI hai prem kI* or *zISa kATa Age dhare* or love is difficult. *kabIr sAhab* compares love to a lane and says its a difficult path to follow. He states that only those who are carefully tread in the material world, who lose sense of their self, can walk in this lane. The difficult path is also rewarding. He states that even a moment of love is equivalent to millions of years of yoga practice, and in the absence of such a moment, eons of yoga practice is simply futile. This is consistent with the *bhagavadgItA* verse 12.5 where *kRSNa* also tells *arjuna* that the path of yoga is much harder than the path of devotion, for as *kabIr sAhab* says, all yoga and no love is futile.

Love is compared to thirst, continuing to make love difficult as thirst is unbearable. A thirsty person can submerge himself or herself in water but thirst will not be quenched until he or she drinks the water. Love is experiential. It has to be tasted. Tasting is union with God. Love is also compared to fire and force and *kablr sAhab* says that it is easier to bear fire burn or chopping by a sword, but extremely difficult to maintain a loving relationship.

He also compares love to a drink that has become hard to find. And when one finds it, one has to offer one's head for a goblet of love. Offering one's head reflects bravery, and so *kablr sAhab* is describing love in *vIra rasa*, to employ the Indian nine-part *rasa* theory or typology of emotion.[1] He uses many verses (12–15, 19, 31–33) where offering ones head is employed as a metaphor for the price of love. Thus, he adds much texture to how difficult love is. One interpretation of offering one's head is that one has to surrender completely to receive love of God. Another correlate of offering one's head is a complete lack of cunningness or guile. This is also shared with Rumi, who instructs—Sell your cunningness and buy bewilderment. Love and guile do not go together. He also uses the metaphor of the market place and says that the price of love is one's head, and that it is a bargain; one should immediately pay with one's head and buy love (see chapter on Sufism in this book).

This theme is also supported in *aGga prIt ko* in verses 1, 4, 9, 10, 12–14, and 20. In verse 1, the metaphor of riding a horse made of wax through fire is employed to emphasize how difficult it is to manage love. In verse 4, it is suggested that a lover should give up life simply with an exclamation of "Oh!" when separated from the loved one. In verse 9, *kablr sAhab* says that he could not find one person who knew how to love and who to love, pointing out the difficulty in understanding what love is. In verse 10, *kablr sAhab* says that if he knew love begets misery, he would have told the world about it. In the other verses, the difficulty of loves is expressed by showing how fish gives up its life or a Hindu woman burns on the funeral pyre.

Another facet of love is difficult emerges in Verse 30 of *aGga vizvAs ko*, which states *mAna mahAttama prem rasa, Adara bhAva saneha; ye paMco phIke paDe, jaba kahA kachU deha*. The moment one asks for a favor, one loses dignity, importance, love, respect, and affection. Love is an intangible quality like affection, dignity, importance, and respect. Like the other four, love is also lost the moment one asks for a favor. The non-transactional nature of love is illustrated with the example of other constructs. This also offers a guideline for social interaction—love is lessened if we expect favors.

Theme 4 (*aGga prem ko*, verses 11, 16–23, 30): *kablr pyAlA prem kA* or Love is a drink. It is a drink that quenches thirst, and in that love is like water that satisfies a thirsty person upon drinking (verse 11). One who drinks from the goblet of love, does not drink water anymore, for only love can quench one's thirst (verse 20). Then love is compared to an alcoholic drink, and said to be the most addictive. Sometimes

---

[1] *nAtyazAstra* of *bharat muni* presented an eight part theory rasa that included *zRGgAraH* (or romance), *hAsyam* (or laughter), *raudram* (or anger), *kAruNyam* (or compassion), *bIbhatsam* (or disgust), *bhay Anakam* (or horror), *vIram* (or heroism), and *adbhutam* (or amazement). Later, *zAntam* (or peace) was added as the ninth rasa, and now navarasa is accepted by all.

people use multiple substances to get a high. *kabIr sAhab* uses that situation and says that once one drinks from the goblet of love, the user has no need for other substance (verse 16). Following on the love is difficult theme, this drink is said to be not for ordinary people; only a few can drink it (verse 17). Similar to offering one's head, only when one relinquishes the self based in the body (this body is me!) is one able to drink from the goblet of love (verse 18). *kabIr sAhab* uses the metaphor of the making of a pot, and says that just like a baked pot does not go back on the potter's wheel, one who has love is content and has no desire left for any drink (verse 21). Love is compared to nectar, and only a select few like *kabIr sAhab* himself gets to drink it (verse 22). Finally, love is said to be the essence of essences, the *rasa* that makes one forget all others; and all rules are broken (verse 23). Drinking has social rules, but love is a drink that breaks all such social rules. One who drinks from the goblet of love proceeds to the satyaloka, the abode of truth and God. Thus, love is a drink that transports one to the spiritual world (verse 30).

Theme 5 (*aGga prem ko,* verse 25–28, 30, 34–38): *prem hai doya prakAra kA* or love for God is superior to material love. *kabIr sAhab* is is cognizant of people's love for material things and social relations. But he is also unequivocal about the superiority of spiritual *sAdhanA* or practice, love for God (verse 25). Love in that sense is a synonym of *bhakti* (verse 28). Love for God is such that one does not care about even liberation, and only wants be in the presence of the Lord. This idea raises the bar previously set where one had to sacrifice one's physical self (or head) to buy love in the market place. The epitome of love is not even to seek liberation (verse 27). In verses 6 and 7 of *aGga prIt ko*, how one should love a noble person and how two lovers become one is emphasized. In verse 8, the devotee calls out to God and wants not to be separated.

kabIr sAhab is an exemplar who is crazy about love for God, and inspires others with his example not to seek self indulgence (verse 26). It is important to reflect on the word *mada* in verse 26, which is translated as pride or arrogance. *Adi zaGkara* defines *mada* as being intoxicated with one's indulgence in the material world as the best course of action for oneself (commentary on *gItA* verse 18.35—"*viSayasevAm Atmano bahu manyamAno matta iva madam*"). *kabIr sAhab*'s use of *mada* clearly is in consonance with what *Adi zaGkara*'s interpretation. It should be also noted that *mada* is used along with *svapna* (dream), *bhaya* (fear), *zoka* (sorrow) and *visAda* (despair) as the characteristics of the *buddhi* associated with *tamogunNa*. Love is not the passion for material world.

zabda refers to *akSara brahman* or the personification of the formless *brahman* in words. The sound *om*, which consists of three letters *a*, *u*, and *ma*, is said to be the representation of *brahman*. With extension, *zabda* has come to refer to all spiritual texts or the word of enlightened saints. *Zabad* also refers to all the verses in *guru grantha sahAba*, the *sikha* scripture, which includes verses written by Hindu and Muslim saints of India. There are 227 *pAdas* in 17 *rAgas* and 237 *slokas* in *zri guru grantha sahAba ji* that are attributed to *kabIr sAhab. zabda* is compared to the sound coming from beating the drum; just like the sound of drum jolts people, *zabda* jolts people on the spiritual path. Beating of the drum is also employed to gather people in a common place. Metaphorically, when the drum of *zabda* is beaten, the Lord comes in plain sight. Love is what leads to the absorption of knowledge given by a spiritual teacher, and prepares one to beat the drum to bring God in plain sight (verse 34). It is received with the grace of the spiritual teacher, which causes the mind to be imbued with deep longing for God (verse 35). Love is what makes us different from the dead. In other words, we are dead without love for God (verse 36). Love is what makes us different from animals. Our interactions need to be rich in love, else we are no different from animals (verse 37). Love is the prerequisite for being a human being in all phases of life. As noted earlier, without love one is an animal, or even worse, one is simply lifeless or dead (verse 38).

Theme 6 (*aGga prem ko,* verse 24): *prem akelA kyA kare* or love without understanding is useless. This is a single verse but perhaps the most powerful one since *kabIr sAhab* makes love secondary to wisdom. The word *samajha* is a word used by people in everyday usage. It can mean *viveka* or the ability to discriminate between right and wrong; or, it can mean *buddhi*, the faculty that guides all thoughts and actions. Love for God has to be translated into love for all, and if that is missing, then love alone will not bear fruit. Love for one's teacher cannot be taken as rejection of the teachers of others, but it should lead to acceptance that for others their teachers are important as is one's teacher for himself or herself. Love for one's own spiritual path cannot be the reason to reject other people and the paths they are following. Thus, love should lead to love for all, and a non-hierarchical acceptance of all. One should always consider self as the servant of the servant. Thus, *kabIr sAhab* emphasizes the value of buddhi, viveka, or samajha to guide people in both their social and spiritual journeys.

In verses 12–16 of *aGga prIt ko*, highlighting the importance of understanding, the metaphors of fish and moth are presented to point out that one should only love if love is reciprocated, and one should not get into one-sided love. In verse 19, the example of a prostitute is used to caution that love to such people should be avoided. In verse 23, the example of welding is presented to point out how two pieces of iron can merge into one under proper conditions, emphasizing the need for understanding to look for such possibilities.

Theme 7 (*aGga prem ko,* verse 8): *jahAM dInatA tahAM prem* or compassion causes humbleness, which in turn causes love. Here *kabIr sAhab* gives us a causal model where the antecedent of humbleness or meekness is said to be compassion and love is its consequent. We could also interpret that humbleness is the proximal antecedent of love and compassion is a distal antecedent of love.

Theme 8 (*aGga prem ko,* verse 1): *prem binA dhIraja nahIM* or love, detachment and sadguru are interdependent ideas. What is love? Patience is born of love, or love is the antecedent of patience. We see this in how the mother and father patiently nurture young ones. A teacher nurtures students patiently. A mentor patiently nurtures a protege or mentee. A farmer also patiently nurtures the plants. In the workplace we can see that some managers are patient and nurture their subordinates, whereas some are only interested in the outcome. Sinha's (1980) nurturant-task leader intuitively taps this cultural milieu, and should be instructive to Indian managers, and managers in collectivist cultures in general. Misumi's

Performance-Maintenance model of leadership may also be tapping this aspect of the collectivist Japanese culture (Misumi & Peterson, 1985).

In the cultural context of India, we know that *vairAgya* is both an important characteristic of a spiritual person and a practice that is meticulously cultivated by spiritual aspirant. *kRSNa* proclaims in the *bhagavadgItA* that *abhyAsa* (mental practice of continuously dwelling on one word like *om*, or a *mantra*, or nothing; or simply gazing at the tip of the nose or between the eyebrows) and *vairAgya* (cultivating detachment by finding fault in all experienced and yet to be experienced pleasures) are the twin practices than help one calm the powerful and fickle *manas* (verse6.35). *vairAgya* become visible in the daily behavior of practitioners and in the life of saints, and hence it is a characteristic of spirituality.

Yet another cultural script is available to interpret the second idea, that separation leads to detachment. It is known that one has to strive for liberation with the desperation of a person who is drowning and gives his or her everything in trying to come out of water. Such a desperation is only possible when one feels the strong pangs (*viraha*) of separation from God. When such a strong emotion is felt, one gives all that one has got to get to God. Such desperation is needed for the cultivation of *vairAgya* is the second interpretation of the second idea presented in the verse.

kabIr sAhab relates love, *biraha*, and detachment in many verses in 65verse section on *biraha*, and lifts love from the mundane physical and social experience to the plane of spirituality. This is also supported in the third idea presented in the verse, that without a *sadguru* the blemishes of *manas* cannot be cleaned. It could be meant to challenge the idea that though one may cultivate *vairAgya* through one's effort, the grace of a guru is needed to purify or calm the *manas*. Also, the role of the *sadguru* could be an indication that *sadguru* is patient with us in helping us clean our attachments to the material world, which are not easy to remove. Sadguru is also love personified, and an exemplar of *vairAgya*, so the three ideas—love, detachment, and *sadguru* are interconnected.

13.5 Discussion

The two *saMskRtam* dictionaries by Monier-William and Apte show that from the root, *prI*, the verb form *prIyate* and its other forms are derived, which mean to please (or to be pleased or satisfied with), gladden, delight (delighted or delight in), enjoy, gratify, cheer, comfort, soothe, propitiate (or to wish to please), to like, love, be kind to, to refresh, and comfort. From the same root, *priya* is derived, which means beloved, dear to, liked, favorite, wanted, and own. With the root *kR*, it also gives the meaning to gain the affection of, win as a friend, to feel affection for, or love more and more. Other meanings of *priya* include dear, expensive, high in price, fond of attached or devoted to, pleasant, and agreeable, *priya* is also used for a friend, a lover, husband, a son-in-law, a kind of dear, and a certain type of medicinal plant. The feminine form, *priyA* is used to denote wife or even a mistress.

From *prI*, we also get *premin* (masculine or neuter gender) or *prem*, which means love, affection, kindness, tender regard, favour, predilection, and fondness. *Prem* is also compounded with many other words, which provide the scope of the meaning of the word. To name a few, *prempara* or intent on love, filled with affection, affectionate, loving, constant; *prempAtana* or tears of joy; *prempAtra* or an object of affection, a beloved person or thing; *prembandha* (or *prembandhana*) or the ties of love or affection; *prembhAva* or the state of affection; *premrAzIbhU* or to become one mass of affection; *premrddhi* or ardent love; *premlatikA* or creeping plant; *premvat* or full of love; *premvizvAsabhUmi* or an object of love and confidence; *premsAgara* or an ocean of love; *premAkara* or abundance of love; *premAmRta* or love-ambrosia; *premArdra* or overflowing with love; *premAzru* or tear of affection. Some famous *saMskRtam* texts that have appropriated *prem* in their title include, *premtattvanirUpaNa* (a Bengālī poem by *kRSNadAsa*), *prembhakticandrikA*, *prembhaktistotra*, *prempIyUSalatAkartarI*, *premrasAyana*, *premrasAyanAnurAga*, *premrAja*, *premendusAgara*, and *premoktyudaya*, to name a few. Most of these words are used in other languages derived from *saMskRtam* like *nepAlI*, *hindI*, *maraThI*, *gujaratI*, *bangAlI*, and others. Also, many book and film titles in these languages have appropriated the word *prem*. *Prem*, and all its other forms and words compounded with *prem*, indeed, are common words employed across India and Nepal in many languages of Indian origin. The following two dialogues between a spiritual aspirant and *nisargadatta mahArAja* presents insight on what is love, which is consistent with what has been deduced above from the verses of *kabIr sAhab*.

Dialogue 1

Q: I see so much evil in myself. Must I not change it?

NM: Evil is the shadow of inattention. In the light of self-awareness it will wither and fall off. All dependence on another is futile for what others can give, others can take away. Only what is your own at the start will remain your own in the end. **Accept no guidance but from within, ... keep quiet and look within; guidance is sure to come.** You are never left without knowing what your next step should be. The trouble is that you may shirk it. ... [**Emphasis added**.]

Q: You seem to advise me to be self-centered to the point of egoism. Must I not yield even to my interest in other people?

NM: Your interest in other is egoistic, self-concerned, self-oriented. You are not interested in others as persons, but only as far as they enrich or ennoble your own image of yourself. And the ultimate in selfishness is to care only for the protection, preservation and multiplication of one's own body. By body I mean all that is related to your name and shape—your family, tribe, country, race, and so on. To be attached to one's name and shape is selfishness. A man who knows that he is neither body nor mind cannot be selfish, for he has nothing to be selfish about. Or, you may say, he is equally "selfish" on behalf of everybody he meets; everybody's welfare is his own. **The feeling "I am the world, the world is myself" becomes quite natural; once it is established, there is just no way of being selfish. To be selfish means to covet, acquire, accumulate on behalf of the part against the whole.** [Emphasis added.]

Q: One may be rich with possessions, by inheritance, or marriage, or just good luck.
NM: If you do not hold on to, it will be taken away from you.
Q: In your present state can you love another person as a person?
NM: I am the other person, the other person is myself; in name and shape we are different, but there is not separation. At the root of our being we are one.
Q: Is it not so whenever there is love between two people?
NM: It is, but they are not conscious of it. They feel the attraction, but do not know the reason.
Q: Why is love selective?
NM: **Love is not selective, desire is selective. In love there are no strangers. When the center of selfishness is no longer, all desires for pleasure and fear of pain cease; one is no longer interested in being happy; beyond happiness there is pure intensity, inexhaustible energy, the ecstasy of giving from a perennial source.** [*I am That*, pp. 488–489. Emphasis added.]

Dialogue 2

Q: I have seen people supposed to have realized, laughing and crying. Does it not show that they are not free of desire and fear?
NM: They may laugh and cry according to circumstances, but inwardly they are cool and clear, watching detachedly their own spontaneous reactions. Appearances are misleading and more so in the case of a *jnAni*.
Q: I do not understand you.
NM: The mind cannot understand, for **the mind is trained for grasping and holding while the *jnAni* is not grasping and not holding.** [Emphasis added.]
Q: What am I holding on to, which you do not?
NM: **You are a creature of memories; at least you imagine yourself to be so. I am entirely unimagined. I am what I am, not identifiable with any physical or mental state.** [Emphasis added.]
Q: An accident would destroy your equanimity.
NM: The strange fact is that it does not. To my own surprise, I remain as I am—pure awareness, alert to all that happens.
Q: Even at the moment of death?
NM: What is it to me that the body dies?
Q: Don't you need it to contact the world?
NM: I do not need the world. Nor am I in one. The world you think of is in your mind. I can see it through your eyes and mind, but I am fully aware that it is a projection of memories; it is touched by the real only at the point of awareness, which can be only now.
Q: The only difference between us seems to be that while I keep on saying that I do not know my real self, you maintain that you know it well; is there any other difference between us?
NM: There is no difference between us; nor can I say that I know myself. **I know that I am not describable, nor definable. There is a vastness beyond the farthest reaches of the mind. That vastness is my home; that vastness is myself. And that vastness is also love.** [p. 506–507; Emphasis added.]

From the above two dialogues it is clear that when on an internal journey we are not grasping and holding or coveting and acquiring—"The *jnAni* is not grasping and holding." When one is on the internal journey his or her maturity is reflected in not being selfish—"Love is not selective, desire is selective. In love there are no strangers. When the center of selfishness is no longer, all desires for pleasure and fear of pain cease; one is no longer interested in being happy; beyond happiness there is pure intensity, inexhaustible energy, the ecstasy of giving from a perennial source." The advanced pursuant of spirituality naturally feels "I am the world, the world is myself," and lives in the "vastness beyond the farthest reaches of the mind" and becomes that vastness, which is love, himself or herself.

Let us examine what *jiddu kRSNAmurtiji* had to say about love to get a second perspective. He explains that ". . . most of us want the security of loving and being loved, but is there love when each one of us is seeking his own security, his own particular path? We are not loved because we don't know how to love. . . . I love my country, I love my king, I love some book, I love that mountain, I love pleasure, I love my wife, I love God. Is love an idea? . . . so to say, `I love God', is absolute nonsense. When you worship God you are worshipping yourself—and that is not love. . . . So what you are really saying is, `As long as you belong to me I love you but the moment you don't I begin to hate you. As long as I can rely on you to satisfy my demands, sexual and otherwise, I love you, but the moment you cease to supply what I want I don't like you.' So there is antagonism between you, there is separation, and when you feel separate from another there is no love. . . . **So when one loves there must be freedom, not only from the other person but from oneself."**

". . . fear is not love, dependence is not love, jealousy is not love, possessiveness and domination are not love, responsibility and duty are not love, self-pity is not love, the agony of not being loved is not love, love is not the opposite of hate any more than humility is the opposite of vanity. **So if you can eliminate all these, not by forcing them but by washing them away as the rain washes the dust of many days from a leaf, then perhaps you will come upon this strange flower which man always hungers after.** . . . By practising some method or system of loving you may become extraordinarily clever or more kindly or get into a state of non-violence, but that has nothing whatsoever to do with love. . . . If you don't know what to do, you do nothing, don't you? Absolutely nothing. **Then inwardly you are completely silent. . . . It means that you are not seeking, not wanting, not pursuing; there is no centre at all. Then there is love."**

"In what they call human love they see there is pleasure, competition, jealousy, the desire to possess, to hold, to control and to interfere with another's thinking, and knowing the complexity of all this they say there must be another kind of love, divine, beautiful, untouched, uncorrupted. . . . Really to care is to care as you would for a tree or a plant, watering it, studying its needs, the best soil for it, looking after it with gentleness and tenderness. . . . **And so love is not to do with pleasure and desire. When you totally abandon yourself to love there is not the other."**

". . . when there is love and beauty, whatever you do is right, whatever you do is in order. If you know how to love, then you can do what you like because it will solve all other problems. . . . It seems to me that one thing is absolutely necessary and that is passion without motive—passion that is not the result of some commitment or attachment, passion that is not lust. A man who does not know what passion is will never know love because **love can come into being only when there is total self-abandonment. . . . love is in which there is no thought and therefore no time. . . . to go beyond thought and time—which means going beyond sorrow—is to be aware that there is a different dimension called love.**"

Love is not about pleasure or desire, it is not about seeking, wanting, pursuing, and requires a total abandonment of self. Love is a different dimension, a vastness characterized by I am the world and the world is myself, and because it is different from the pursuance of material things, different from grasping and holding, without a center of selfishness, it is about spirituality. It is no surprise that in one of the famous verses of *kabIr sAhab* that is quoted in daily interactions by most people who speak *hindI states—pothI paDh paDh jag muA panDit bhayA na koi, DhAi Akhar prem kA paDhe so panDit hoye* (one does not become learned by studying scriptural texts but by understanding the two and one half letters that make the word *prem*). This paper presents many insights noted above to unravel the meanings of love in the Indian cultural context, and contributes to the literatures on both indigenous and global psychologies. It is hoped that other indigenous researchers would adopt the methodology employed in this research to present ideas on love for their cultures so that the global literature on love can be enriched beyond the limited Western view of the construct.

Texts are not random juxtapositions of clauses and that is why they have texture (Halliday & Hasan, 1976), which is a semantic property. A text is a semantic unit that has a unity of meaning (Lemke, 1991). When we study *sAkhIs* (or couplets) like the ones written by *kabIr sAhab*, the reader experiences the texture at multiple levels, in words, in feelings, and in some unnamable spiritual depth, all simultaneously or in an indeterminable sequence. As the examination of the *sAkhIs* on a theme progresses, as was does in this paper, the texture unexpectedly becomes a web of meaning, a thick description (Geertz, 1973; Ryle, 1949, 1971) of sorts. The analyses resulted in a discovery of the thick description of the meaning relations among the *sAkhIs* on ideas related to love—*prem* (love), *prItI* (love), and *bhakti* (devotion). The eight themes that emerged from the analyses of the 38 verses on *prem* or love (*aGga prem ko*) were found to also map the ideas captured in the 23 verses on *prItI* (*aGga prIti ko*). The eight themes present a thick description of what *prem* or love is in the Indian cultural context. Such a thick description has been missing in the literature on love, and so this paper contributes to both indigenous and global psychology by filling that lacuna.

Acknowledgements I would like to thank AcArya Satya Caitanya, Anand Chandrasekara Narayanan, and the editors for their constructive comments that helped improve the paper.

References

Bhawuk, D. P. S. (1999). Who attains peace: An Indian model of personal harmony. *Indian Psychological Review, 52*(2 & 3), 40–48.

Bhawuk, D. P. S. (2003). Culture's influence on creativity: The case of Indian spirituality. *International Journal of Intercultural Relations, 27*(1), 1–22.

Bhawuk, D. P. S. (2005). A model of self, work, and spirituality from the *Bhagavad-Gita*: Implications for self-efficacy, goal setting, and global psychology. In K. Ramakrishna Rao & S. B. Marwaha (Eds.), *Toward a spiritual psychology: Essays in Indian psychology* (pp. 41–71). Samvad Indian Foundation: New Delhi, India.

Bhawuk, D. P. S. (2008a). Anchoring cognition, emotion, and behavior in desire: A model from the *Bhagavad-Gita*. In K. R. Rao, A. C. Paranjpe, & A. K. Dalal (Eds.), *Handbook of Indian psychology* (pp. 390–413). New Delhi, India: Cambridge University Press.

Bhawuk, D. P. S. (2008b). Toward an Indian organizational psychology. In K. R. Rao, A. C. Paranjpe, & A. K. Dalal (Eds.), *Handbook of Indian psychology* (pp. 471–491). New Delhi, India: Cambridge University Press.

Bhawuk, D. P. S. (2009). Humiliation and human rights in diverse societies: Forgiveness & some other solutions from cross-cultural research. *Psychological Studies, 54*(2), 1–10.

Bhawuk, D. P. S. (2010a). Epistemology and ontology of Indian psychology: A synthesis of theory, method, and practice. *Psychology and Developing Societies, 22*(1), 157–190.

Bhawuk, D. P. S. (2010b). Methodology for building psychological models from scriptures: Contributions of Indian psychology to indigenous and global psychologies. *Psychology and Developing Societies, 22*(1), 49–93.

Bhawuk, D. P. S. (2011). *Spirituality and Indian psychology: Lessons from the Bhagavad-Gita*. New York: Springer. https://doi.org/10.1007/978-1-4419-8110-3

Bhawuk, D. P. S. (2014). citta or consciousness: Some perspectives from Indian psychology. *The Journal of Individual Psychology, 28*(1 & 2), 37–43.

Bhawuk, D. P. S. (2017a). lajjA in Indian psychology: Spiritual, social, and literary perspectives. In E. Vanderheiden & C.-H. Mayer (Eds.), *The value of shame–Exploring a health resource across cultures* (pp. 109–134). New York: Springer.

Bhawuk, D. P. S. (2017b). *Cultivating meditation for leading a peaceful life*. Spandan: Foundation for Human Values in Management and Society.

Bhawuk, D. P. S. (2017c). Developing theories and models to serve: A manifesto for indigenous psychologists. *Asian Journal of Social Psychology, 20*(2), 155–160.

Bhawuk, D. P. S. (2019a). adhyAtma or spirituality: Construct definition and elaboration using multiple methods. In S. K. Mishra & A. Varma (Eds.), *Spirituality in management: Insights from India* (pp. 19–41). Palgrave-Macmillan: London.

Bhawuk, D. P. S. (2019b). lajjA: Learning, unlearning, and relearning. In E. Vanderheiden & C.-H. Mayer (Eds.), *The bright side of shame: Transforming and growing through practical applications in cultural contexts* (pp. 35–49). New York: Springer.

Bhawuk, D. P. S. (2019c). Toward a spirituality-based theory of creativity: Indigenous perspectives from India. In K.-H. Yeh (Ed.), *Asian indigenous psychologies in the global context* (pp. 139–168). London, UK: Palgrave Macmillan.

Bhawuk, D. P. S. (2019d). adhyAtma or spirituality: Indian perspectives on management. In P. S. Budhwar, R. Kumar, & A. Varma (Eds.), *Indian business:Understanding a rapidly emerging economy* (pp. 256–266). London, UK: Routledge.

Bhawuk, D. P. S. (2019e). lokasaMgraha: An indigenous construct of leadership and its measure. In S. Dhiman & A. D. Amar (Eds.), *Managing by the Bhagavad Gita: Timeless lessons for Today's managers* (pp. 273–297). New York: NY.

Bhawuk, D. P. S. (2020). śraddhā: Construct definition from the Bhagavad-Gītā. *Psychology and Developing Societies, 32*(1), 1–16. https://doi.org/10.1177/0971333620906758

Bhawuk, D. P. S., Mrazek, S., & Munusamy, V. P. (2009). From social engineering to community transformation: Amul, Grameen Bank, and Mondragon as exemplar organizations. *Peace & Policy:Ethical Transformations for a Sustainable Future, 14*, 36–63.

Burghart, R. (1978). The founding of the Ramanandi sect. *Ethnohistory*, 121–139.

Geertz, C. (1973). *The interpretation of cultures: Selected essays*. New York: Basic Books.

Gergen, K., Gulerce, A., Lock, A., & Mishra, G. (1996). Psychological science in cultural context. *American Psychologist, 51*, 496–503.

Halliday, M. A. K., & Hasan, R. (1976). *Cohesion in English*. London: Longman.

Kasturi, M. (2015). *Sadhus, Sampradaya and Hindu Nationalism: The Dasnamis and the Shri Bharat Dharma Mahamandala in the early twentieth century* (NMML Occasional Paper, History and Society, New Series 79).

Lemke, J. L. (1991). Text production and dynamic text semantics. In E. Ventola (Ed.), *Functional and systemic linguistics: Approaches and uses* (Trends in Linguistics: Studies and Monographs 55, pp. 23–38). Berlin: Mouton/deGruyter.

Marsella, A. J. (1998). Toward a "global-community psychology": Meeting the needs of a changing world. *American Psychologist, 53*(12), 1282–1291.

Misumi, J., & Peterson, M. F. (1985). The performance-maintenance (PM) theory of leadership: Review of a Japanese research program. *Administrative Science Quarterly, 30*(2), 198–223.

Paravatadas, M., & Singh P. (2013). *zri grantha sAkhI: caurAsi aGga kI*. Chattisgadha, Raypur: *zrI sadguru kabIr dharmadAsa sAhab vaMzAvalI*.

Pawlik, K. (1991). The psychological dimension of global change [Whole Issue]. *International Journal of Psychology, 20*.

Ryle, G. (1949). *Concept of the mind*. London: Hutchinson and Company.

Ryle, G. (1971). Collected papers. In *Volume II collected essays, 1929–1968*. London: Hutchinson.

Sinha, J. B. P. (1980). *The Nurturant-task leader: A model of the effective executive*. New Delhi, India: Concept.

Triandis, H. C. (1994). *Culture and social behavior*. New York: McGraw-Hill.

Dharm P. S. Bhawuk (PhD, Prof.), is a professor of Management and Culture and Community Psychology at the University of Hawaii at Manoa. He brings with him the experience of living and growing in a developing economy, Nepal. He started his intercultural journey with a month at international children's camp in Artek, USSR, in 1972. His interdisciplinary training includes a Bachelor of Technology (B.Tech., Honors) from the Indian Institute of Technology, Kharagpur, in mechanical engineering, a Master of Business Administration (MBA) from the University of Hawaii at Manoa with a Fellowship from the East-West Center, where he did research with Prof. Richard W. Brislin in the area of intercultural training, and a Ph.D. in industrial relations with specialization in human resource management and cross-cultural psychology under the guidance of Prof. Harry C. Triandis at the University of Illinois at Urbana-Champaign.

Part IV
Love Within the Framework of Family and Intergenerational Relations

Sommer Romance (Photo: Carl Breisig)

Chapter 14
Videography of Love and Marriage Order

Elena Rozhdestvenskaya

Abstract The chapter is about staging a collective utopia of romantic love through a marriage ceremony. On the one hand, cultural rituals of love as a marriage ceremony meet national values, on the other hand, they are influenced by a wide range of modernization trends (from social demography to market influence and digitalization). Presented study is focused on the so-called outdoor wedding registration as a relatively new and expanding wedding trend in the Russian cultural context. As such a decoration, the author has chosen the Tsaritsyno Park (Tsaritsyno is a palace and park ensemble in the south of Moscow, founded by order of Empress Catherine II in 1776. It is an architectural and historical monument of the so-called "Russian Gothic". It was built by architects Vasily Bazhenov and Matvey Kazakov) located in Moscow, which sets its spatial and visual logic for the wedding narrative and its documentation with visual means. The theoretical focus of our research is on the dynamics and possible convergence of the pragmatic and romantic aspects of the modern phenomenon of love and marriage order which are embodied in media representations of changing, but preserving, traditional national moments of rituals. The empirical focus is actually on of the triad: the video media product, the opinion/ position of the professionals creating it, and the opinion/reaction of customers. The marriage ceremony as a counterpoint in the love story of the couple acquires in the process of production of a media product—a wedding video—not only a documentation of the most important life event. Thanks to the video, a love couple now identifies their wedding ceremony experiences and feelings with a commercial product. This media product delivers the narcissistic joy of reflection and recognition and thereby generates a modified reverse perspective on one's own lifeworld.

This chapter is an output of a research project implemented as part of the Basic Research Program at the HSE University, International Laboratory for Social Integration Studies.

E. Rozhdestvenskaya (✉)
Faculty of Social Sciences, International Laboratory for Social Integration Studies, HSE University, Moscow, Russia

Institute of Sociology Russian Academy of Sciences, Moscow, Russia
e-mail: erozhdestvenskaya@hse.ru

Keywords Love · Romantic love · Outdoor wedding registration · Wedding · Video · Videograph

14.1 Introduction: People Meet, People Fall in Love, They Get Married ...

Marriage statistics in Russia leave no doubt about how durable modern marriages are—with all the fluctuations, almost every second marriage ends in divorce.[1] Nevertheless, the choice in favor of the official ceremony of marriage with the sacramental "until death do us part...", already penetrating the Russian marriage tradition, is a manifestation of mutual faith in the long-term character, if not eternity of this event. VCIOM (Russian Public Opinion Research Center) recently decided to find out what drives the Russians upon marriage. It turned out that 30% of men (18% of women) get married of convenience (see Russian Newspaper, 2011). The majority—63% of people—get married out of a desire to officiate their being with the loved one. Women choose this reason more often—70% of cases, compared to 54% of cases for men. As for the image of an ideal family, the vast majority of Russians (81%) consider it as means of support and mutual respect for their spouses.

This data demonstrates a complex mixture of romance and pragmatism, the national recipe of which is likely to vary. In any case, the European cultural context has created an important distinction between love as passion (*amour passion*) and romantic love. According to Anthony Giddens (Giddens, 2004), passionate love has always been liberating, in the sense of breaking routine and everyday duties. This quality of passionate love placed it outside the existing institutions. On the contrary, the ideals of romantic love are loaded with normativity. Moreover, in his opinion, romantic love creates the illusion of control over the future, since it becomes predetermined, thanks to the expected scenarios of its implementation.

It is associated primarily with the growth of individualization, greater freedom in choosing a spouse, with the need to consolidate new forms of relations already within the marriage. Thus, special norms of communication have become in demand in society, which are implemented in the format of romantic love, but within a family, marriage, or partnership. And since it is love that presupposes the relations of individualized entities, it has become a condition, one of the important components in marriage, and vice versa, inability to love, lack of love has become a sufficient basis for refusal to marry or getting divorced. One of the consequences of this dramatic cultural shift has been the integration of sexuality into love and marriage. Thus, the scheme of romantic love combined sexuality and marriage.

In contemporary debates about the essence of love and its current formats, a number of works by Israeli sociologist Eva Illouz have become most important.

---

[1] The number of divorces per 1000 registered marriages was 655 in 2018, i.e. more than half of registered marriages end in divorce (Russian Demographic Barometer, 2019).

Given the wide European context, she wrote the book "Consuming the Romantic Utopia" about love in modern society, where she substantiates the coexistence of two models of love:

> I think in our culture there are two competing models of love. The romantic model is more about experience; it is spontaneous, sudden and overwhelming. We are blinded by the man in love. Another model is realistic; it is making us suspicious of this romance, telling us that it is fickle, just the product of Hollywood clichés. The meaning of another model is a joint victory over difficulties in everyday life, in supporting another person if he/she is sick. Both models coexist simultaneously (Illouz, 1997, p. 46).

The French sociologist Jean-Claude Kaufman is in solidarity with Illouz. In his book "The Morning After" (Kaufmann, 2002) he described the coexistence of the same two models of love, although he does not share Illouz's criticism of the pragmatism of the younger generation. If we talk about the relationship between romance and pragmatism, Illouz sees a serious roll in the dominance of a pragmatic model of love, which is facilitated by expanded opportunities for selecting potential partners, including online:

> The Internet has fundamentally changed the attitude of men and women regarding love because it opens up a huge pool of potential candidates. A search engine can provide up to 200 appointments per individual request. In the 19th century, a woman received maybe three offers in her life. She thought carefully over the second offer—whether she should reject it or not. Today we are extremely picky. And love arises as a rational search process, which is enhanced by the Internet. The choice is not based on physical presence or physical characteristics, but is made in accordance with preferences, level of education, status, age, etc. And only then does the filter of the first meeting come in.

By the way, the criteria formulated by Illouz were confirmed in the analysis of European dating forums conducted by the German sociologist Hans-Peter Blossfeld (Blossfeld, 2011).

So, despite the collective utopia of love as the last refuge of romance in the modern world of capitalism, there seems to be a successful convergence. In any case, they deeply condition each other. While the sphere of consumption seeks to produce romantic feelings, intimate relationships become more and more dependent on the staging and experience of consumption. The collective utopia of love, idealized as overcoming the market, becomes the preferred object of capitalist consumption and representation. At the same time, there are not so many socially oriented visual studies of commercial and amateur wedding videos. One might recall the works of C. Lewis (1998) on the professional shooting of the American middle-class wedding, J. Moran (1996) on the generation of consumers of home videos, a study by R. Adelmann (2002) on a commercial Indian wedding video, the work of J. Reichertz (2000) devoted to the analysis of media staging in the TV show "Dream Wedding" on RTL channel in Germany, a study by J. Raab (2002) called "The Most Beautiful Day of Life" on visual analysis and hermeneutics of wedding videos.

This performance of collective utopia of love is the main topic of this article. Its participants are not only a couple in love, but also relatives, friends, their social group, as well as involved mediators who organize and document the performance, as well as the cultural material context of the whole event. Through an analysis of the performance of the marriage ceremony and its video documentation, we want to show what new meanings and formats of feelings arise in the process of this performance. The article focuses on the so-called outdoor marriage registration as a relatively new and expanding wedding trend in the Russian cultural context. The author has chosen the Moscow Tsaritsyno Park as a place that hosts such outdoor ceremonies. The Tsaritsyno Park is not only a magnificent landscape and architectural background for the wedding, but also sets its spatial and visual logic for the wedding narrative and its documentation with visual means. The choice is based on the constant top position of the Tsaritsyno estate in the numerous ratings of places for outdoor marriage registration that are regularly made up by marriage agencies in Moscow.

14.2 Methodology

Empirically, our study is based on the principles of ethnographic research, partially implemented online and tightly describing a complex object—an outdoor wedding ceremony and its video documentation. But who is the subject of this process? The answer to this question is found by a whole group of those involved—the couple who are getting married, the wedding agency managers who organize the celebration, government officials for marriage registration and certification, and finally, photographers and videographers documenting the ceremony. Therefore, the methodological decision on the collection of empirical material consisted in choosing a qualitative approach through the collection of in-depth and contextualized observations. In this context, we turn to the concept of micro-ethnography. Thus, H. Knoblauch introduces the concept of focused ethnography (Knoblauch, 2005). Classical ethnographic research is necessarily associated with a long stay in the field and a description of the culture of a certain group, the meanings and structures operating in it. Microethnography focuses on the processes of communication, and not on social structures, on the process of production of meanings. In microethnography, the practice of attracting audio and video recordings is widespread, allowing us to capture the unfolding action and social situations in detail. The research plan consisted of the following steps:

1. The context of the outdoor ceremony—the park and the palaces of Tsaritsyno—was primarily subject to ethnographic observation.
2. We studied the proposals of online agencies offering a line of scenarios for an unforgettable Wedding Day, including an outdoor ceremony, its cost and organization.
3. An expert interview was conducted with a state employee from the territorial organization of Moscow (close to Tsaritsyno district), which has the right to register a marriage and issue certificates of marriage.

4. In addition, the immersive online ethnographic observation was conducted in special forums dedicated to visiting ceremonies of marriage (for 3 months). The forum discussions of brides were analyzed using a discourse analysis.
5. There were four offline interviews with professional video operators working on outdoor wedding registrations in order to make a definite impression of the normative structure of wedding video and photography, consumer requests, main style trends and the degree of influence of professionals on the final product—a wedding video report in Tsaritsyno.
6. The focus of micro-ethnography was implemented in detail in the analysis of the video clip about the wedding in Tsaritsyno, selected as the most typical among hundreds of such clips in the public domain on the YouTube online channel.

Organizing such a multidimensional research design, we pursued the goal of a dense description, in the words of K. Girtz. At the same time, it is necessary to mention the limitations of our study. Considering the wedding ceremony in the context of Tsaritsyno's imperial park, we are aware of the future need to triangulate this specific context with other formats of an outdoor wedding ceremonies. Perhaps then we will find other scenarios for rooting the myth of romantic love. In addition, the research plan did not include couples who limited themselves to amateur videos and photos without resorting to professional services. Perhaps these videos could reconstruct the emotional traces of love on Wedding Day, bypassing the market logic that feeds and at the same time commercializes the collective utopia of romantic love.

14.3 Outdoor Registration as a Format of Experience and Service on the Market

Attention to the current scenario of the wedding event is dictated by the assumption that the situation of experiencing emotion is an aspect of the emotion itself, which becomes a variable of the action played out (Barbalet, 2001). According to Arli Hochschild's (2003) theory of emotional management, emotional culture is the concept of the way people should feel in different contexts of action, served by different emotional ideologies. Hochschild identifies superficial and deep levels of emotional involvement of individuals in the processes of action. In a surface-flowing process of action, emotions are expressed in accordance with normative expectations. In the deep proceeding process of action, real work is done on the senses in order to really experience the expected emotions. In the implementation of emotional work, people are primarily motivated by maintaining the image of the *self* in accordance with the norms of a (national) emotional culture.

In the Russian cultural tradition, which seems to have sunk into oblivion, but shines through archetypal manifestations, the wedding is a single dramatic and ceremonial complex. The behavior of each its participants was strictly regulated and motivated both by the content of a certain ritual and by the behavioral canons of folk ethics, as the folklorist O. Balashova (2002) claims. Each stage of this often-multiday ceremony was accompanied by the corresponding magical actions, conspiracies, charms, songs, sentences, riddles, and was a collection of verbal and song texts subordinated for centuries to the worked-out laws of wedding action. The plot of the Russian wedding ceremony is dominated by the central motive of the struggle of family clans, which plays the role of a kind of "guide" of the main plot and combines the entire "speech" context of the wedding rite into a single whole. The main settings of the wedding rite are the continuation of the family clan, as well as the implementation of the rites of transition from one status to another (from being a girl to being married, from being a bachelor to being married). The process of development of the wedding story moves to the climax of the whole wedding—the "joining" and the official recognition of a new member of the clan. This socio-identification point is emphasized by another researcher. According to A. Bobrikhin (2009), the topic of a folk wedding is a sequence of actions aimed at overcoming borders and special obstacles, which symbolically leads to a change in the status of the main participants, while providing magical protection for the newlyweds at every stage.

Visual studies of the modern wedding photography reveal the continuity of ritual wedding activities that flow into the visual content of amateur photography. For example, O. Boytsova (2010) mentions in her study the bridegroom carrying the bride in her arms. The groom takes the bride across the thresholds of the registry office and the apartment, and across the bridge as the latter three are considered to be magically dangerous border zones. At the same time, a photograph of the groom with the bride in his arms visualizes the metaphor of newfound happiness—"being carried in one's arms" (meaning being treated like a queen). Other canonical wedding pictures are a visual image of kissing and hugging bride and groom, visualization of idioms "under the heel of the wife/whipped" and "marriage bond". O. Boytsova mentions a popular series of wedding photographs that depict one of the two main characters being smaller than the other one and "standing" in his arms. This is the ritual process of playing out of the plot of power and domination—'who is the boss in the house—which is deciphered by ritual actions such as breaking the loaf by the bride and groom. The joking code of the ritual game, however, refers to a very serious story about the upcoming family and gender roles of the newlyweds.

In addition to the canonization of the content of wedding photography, the concept of a "wedding photo session" holds a strong position in the modern wedding ritual. According to O. Tkach (2013), the schedule of the wedding walk, its route and the ritual actions that accompany it, are completely subordinated to the tasks of the photo shoot. That is, the modern "wedding city" is clearly "cropped" in accordance with the purposes of photographing.

Who takes control of the modern wedding rituals? Agencies that offer market services for weddings inspire the idea that a wedding day is the most unforgettable day in the life of any person, "which often happens only once" (a phrase taken from the website of one of such agencies). This motive encourages people to spare no money for organizing a wedding. But what should the wedding be like so that one does not mind spending a lot of money on it? Obviously, the efforts of various professional specialists, including a screenwriter, preferably with professional experience, experience in theatrical activities, knowledge of rituals and customs, and creative thinking; a host—not just an entertainer, but a presenter with the skills of a psychologist; a choreographer as a dance director of the wedding; a photographer with his/her own photo studio; a video operator; a limousine driver; a pyrotechnician responsible for the light show; a DJ and a designer; and finally, an administrator who will be able to quickly and efficiently negotiate with restaurant owners and future spouses regarding rentals. It is clear that it is incredibly difficult for the protagonists to be managers of this process, given the planned emotional work as described by A. Hochschild ("once in the lifetime"). Therefore, a number of logical research questions arise. What determines the choice of such a specific wedding format as outdoor registration of marriage in Tsaritsyno? What kind of emotions is this event charged with? What emotions does the product of its photo and video filming of a wedding in Tsaritsyno evoke?

The empirical interest in the outdoor registration of marriage in Tsaritsyno was preceded by an online analysis of the possibilities for organizing a wedding celebration. Only the Google search engine gives 60,400 links for the query "outdoor marriage registration". The wedding custom to visit city sights, as D.V. Gromov (2009) writes in his work, has been brought to its logical conclusion in this format of the wedding event. It started back in the 1970s with the generally accepted practice among newlyweds to visit various city sights after the official ceremony (Sosnina, 2009).

The dynamics of this service indicates an increase in its popularity among newlyweds. In fact, there are two types of outdoor registration of marriage. These are theatrical registration of marriage and the official state outdoor ceremony of registration of marriage, which are equally practiced in Tsaritsyno since it has its own registry office.

Below is an extract from an online advertising campaign:

> A wedding in the palace is what any bride dreams of in order to shine as the queen at the ball in a magnificent royal residence or in a family noble nest! We will offer you the most comfortable and beautiful palaces for weddings in Moscow and the Moscow region, we will develop a unique plot, we will think over a wedding banquet in the palace... And there's no need to say what [great] memories the wedding photo session held in the palaces leaves!
>
> In the Soviet era, our mothers, fathers and grandparents could enter the estate only as tourists. It never occurred to anyone that it was possible to combine two beautiful phenomena—the organization of a wedding and a palace. Today we have such an opportunity! Wedding estates of Moscow and the Moscow region hospitably open their doors to a fairy tale. Is it possible to refuse such an invitation?
>
> The most romantic event for those who love fairy tales about Cinderella and the Prince. Horseback riding, visiting old manors, classical music. There will be white horses and a picnic on the grass. The ceremony itself can take place in an open meadow decorated to your taste.

Outdoor registration of marriage—the wedding trend of recent years emerged as an alternative to marriage concluded in the registry office—has certain advantages over the traditional official procedure in the district registry office. They can be summarized as a negative reaction to an annoying cultural stereotype—the

Mendelssohn march, the common type of receptionist, administrative discourse that frightens the spouses with the use of the word "betrothed". But, of course, one negative reaction is not enough. A positive normative sample is also important and it is broadcast by the Western marriage fashion, visualized thanks to cinema, the Internet, glamorous magazines, thematic TV and reality shows. It is not surprising that the floral-arched design in the fresh air and against the backdrop of nature wins over the concrete box of the regional registry office and its conveyor of black and white characters. The last but not the least is the architecture—a fabulous castle which is called Tsaritsyno, as if offering to place the marrying couple into the story of the prince and princess...

But here a completely non-fabulous question arises—the price and access to the service. Many agencies prefer not to disclose the final price of an unforgettable day at all, indicating only ranges for certain positions (cafes, bride's bouquet, limousine rental, groom's suit, gifts for guests, video filming, etc.). Nevertheless, the lowest price announced is around 10,000 euros, and the highest level can be as high as the level of creativity and *vanity fair*. The normalized fee deduced by the agency for organizing a "turnkey" event is 10% of the wedding budget. This suggests that the couple is from the middle class, and their marriage mean less illusion but more work than before. Today, spouses in this social group are several years older on average than in the past.[2] They often earn more and can spend more on their family events. In addition, women work more often, they have less time, but they also have their own incomes. Thus, the organization of the main event is often delegated to professionals. They can also be instructed to organize a bachelorette party, flags for the "just married" car, even draft a marriage proposal.

Below is an extract from an interview with civil servant V. from the Tsaritsyno registry office:

> Usually, people that come to us are probably from the middle class, which can be seen if we look at the sums they are spending on a car, restaurant, and the dress of the bride. You know, there is probably even a scale—a wedding of economy class, middle class and business class. So Tsaritsyno hosts middle and business class weddings... Most of [the couples] are Russian, but 35-40 percent are weddings with an ethnical accent. In this case, we simply adapt the script of the ceremony, for example, remove such part as a kiss of the newlyweds that is usually accompanied by guests' cries "Gorko!" (similar to English "Kiss!").

In addition to economic preconditions and social taste, which is a characteristic of the class, Tsaritsyno (as, probably, other Moscow estates) has objectively limited opportunities for hosting those who want to conduct a wedding ceremony here. This leads to the problem of a queue—it is necessary to apply for an outdoor registration 2 months before the event.

The seasonal density of registration here is also variegated. It pulsates in tune with the general statistics of marriage registration in Russia. According to the

---

[2]There is a tendency towards the aging of the marriage and birth rate model with a shift in the age of the bride and groom all around Russia. The trend is as follows: the average age of the groom is increased by 2.7 years (28.7), the average age of the bride is increased by 1.9 years (26.1) (Zakharov, 2005).

statistics (Russian Demographic Barometer, 2012), the registration of marriages still retains a pronounced seasonal character—the least number of marriage registrations can be seen in May and the majority of marriage ceremonies are usually held in August. Commenting on these data, E. Shcherbakova notes that preferences for registering marriages in certain months are usually based on religious, cultural and financial reasons. For example, according to the church calendar, marriages are forbidden during fasting periods. Besides this, local customs, superstitions (for instance, that getting married in May means toiling for the rest of the life) and traditions related to the seasonal cycle of agricultural work stimulate autumn marriages in many cultures. It is hard to believe, but the long-eroded peasant habitat and conditional religiosity of the citizens less involved in church fuel the seasonality of such a phenomenon.

14.4 Online Wedding Forums as a Platform for Discussions Among Customers

By registering on several online platforms as a customer who plans to have an outdoor wedding ceremony in Tsaritsyno, the author of the article got the opportunity not only to get acquainted with the reflexed and evaluated experience of an outdoor wedding, but also to ask newlyweds—mostly females as the dominant contingent of such forums—relevant questions. It is significant that the questions that were asked were related to the general meaning and reasonable motivation for choosing the outdoor format of the wedding in Tsaritsyno. But it is precisely these things that future and accomplished brides do not discuss. The discourse of wedding forums is dominated by the practical issues of the upcoming event. With regard to outdoor registration, this is a problem of online recording or filing documents on the Internet, timing of registration procedures, and the cost of services, such as catering, photo and video shooting, the quality of equipment, design of gifts for guests, a wedding bouquet, weather conditions, the problem of access to vehicles on the territory of Tsaritsino park, etc. However, discussing these specific plots and going into the details of the upcoming celebration, the forum participants—of course, in an indirect form—mention important value preferences and motivations. Therefore, not only does the author anonymously quote female participants (not mentioning nicknames, emails and date when they made their entries), but also applies paraphrasing as a way of interpretation.

First of all, the author looks at the motive for abandoning the generally accepted places of outdoor registration and the roaming metaphor of the conveyor, which also affects them:

Re: Registry offices/Outdoor registration

But what if we don't want to do outdoor registration in any of these generally accepted places, because it's the same registry office, because in fact it is the same conveyor[3]... the same crowd of grooms and brides, a bunch of strangers, disposable glasses, long way to the entrance to the Kuskovo Palace where you meet 200 brides taking pictures under each bush and then another 50 couples who want to register in an Italian house... or, for example, Poklonnaya Gora. It is a place to worship the dead war heroes, and we will kiss there and drink champagne... none of these places inspires to hold a romantic wedding ceremony!

This post thematizes, firstly, the already familiar motive of running away from the wedding conveyor, which is blurring the uniqueness of the event, only changing the decorative background; secondly, the contextual inappropriateness of combining a wedding celebration with war cenotaphs, which has been reflected by new generations; and finally, the hidden disappointment caused by limited resources condemning to a low-budget level of provision of outdoor registration which is also obvious to others.

Re: Registry offices/Outdoor registration

We recently filed an application to the Tsaritsyno Museum-Reserve. Submission of the application takes place in the general queue and there is no way to do without it!!! I was in charge of forming the list and our couple was the first one on it, so for six months I kept lists so that we have a nice ceremony, and there were 45 more couples [on the list] (since there were everyone who submitted applications for 9 and 10 July for both registrations on the same day). They were on duty all night and drank champagne))), they all got to know each other and it was a lot of fun. We were very worried about the fact that half the list [successfully applied] and another half would fail. But in fact, the main thing on this day is not to get annoyed, but rather take a good mood with you))!!

Unlike the previous participant, this one has already made a decision, and the focus is shifted to the problems of rush demand during the peak season for registration. But incidentally, a high density of communication about the upcoming event can be seen (e.g. the practice of maintaining lists, a common night with champagne). This seems especially important in view of the exchange of not only practical information that helps in navigating about the thematic world of weddings, but also familiarization with the normative emotions that precede the event (fun and good mood).

Re: Registration in Tsaritsyno, organizational and other issues

We liked the registration, however, I myself love Tsaritsyno very much, and as soon as I found out that the registrations were taking place there, I wanted our marriage to be registered here)). But some of the relatives/friends, were puzzled finding out the price. They said it was meaningless. Among the real advantages there are the fact that weddings are clearly separated in time, and you do not intersect with anyone, a beautiful ceremony, and friendly staff. But whether it's worth the necessary effort and cost or not is up to you. We did not regret our decision. One of the disadvantages was that there was much less time than stated earlier, and we were politely asked to free the Opera House about 15 minutes earlier. As far as I understood, this is a common practice when there are a lot of couples. It is not very convenient that only one car is allowed into the territory (up to 6 m long), as a result, we

---

[3]Emphasized by the author hereinafter as semantic accents.

arrived by car, and the rest of the guests walked separately on foot (when the weather is bad, this matters). In the warm season, the problem is solved by the use of electric vehicles, but from October until spring they do not operate.

This is, perhaps, a rare case when a participant of the forum discussion had her own disposition in relation to Tsaritsyno. This is why the decision to put the most important event of her life in her favorite frame looks justified and motivated. This makes her romantic choice even more valuable, since it contradicts the pragmatics of high costs, which are not shared by relatives and friends. It is precisely this circumstance that can be considered as evidence of the individual values of the couple. It is the couple—and no one else—who pays for their shared emotions.

Re: Registration in Tsaritsyno, organizational and other issues

> I also liked the ceremony very much, and I do not regret at all that the wedding ceremony was held there. [T]he photos are amazing. [W]e wanted to have a wedding in a classic style, but make it as original, beautiful and modern as possible. [I]t's not a common registry office, there's an amazing hall. [I]f you want, I can email some photos. [T]here is original music. [T]here's an hour to register a couple, [and] nobody asked us to leave ahead of time. [T]here you can tune the bride's exit rather than make it just by the standard scenario as in the registry offices. [F]or example, it was my father took me to the groom. [T]here we danced first dance. [A]nd we also took advantage of the fact that we are in the park, did half the photo shoot there, and did not spend time traveling to some other place. [However] it's not very cool that they let one car out, but we ordered 1 electric car for 8-10 people, it cost 2,000 rubles both ways (1000 one way). [A]nd all the younger guests were walking for 12-15 minutes with no rush. [W]e entered [the park] in a regular car, because the newlyweds must arrive 15 minutes before the ceremony, sign the documents and have a rehearsal.

In this case, the familiar motive of fleeing from banality and stereotyping acquires an important positive expansion in addition to compaction. There arises a "new" procedural dramaturgy where the father takes the bride to the groom, the first dance is a demonstration of the couple to the guests, and the plot of the so-called mirroring is present. The registration process here is inseparable from its visualization with the help of a photoshoot. The purpose of the series of shots is to capture "stunning" shots, scenery, and characters.

Below is the answer to the question about the personal choice of registration in Tsaritsyno:

> It seems to me that everything here depends on personal perception: for me it was really something amazing, because Tsaritsyno is one of my favorite places in Moscow, and the whole format of our wedding was very suitable for this place. In my opinion, Tsaritsyno is a place for a classic wedding with a wedding-dress train, a veil and other attributes. Something original and modern will not fit to this place. Besides this, Tsaritsyno gives you an opportunity to be brought to the groom by your dad or another person that is close to you. [T]his is really something special in terms of the feelings you get.

In this sequent, partly close to the previous one, the priority of personal perception is being declared. The backstory of the habitual favorite place for walking in Moscow—the Tsaritsyno Park and Museum—proves again to be an important factor in deciding where to arrange outdoor registration. According to the forum participant, the romantic image of the Tsaritsyno architecture is also set by the wedding design—classic, with all the attributes—opening the space for experiencing emotions corresponding to the classic plot. And again, there is an archetypal motive of the father taking the bride to the groom. It is the father who wakes the bride's "special" emotions.

Re: Registration in Tsaritsyno

> The other day we had a wedding at the Tsaritsyno estate. The ceremony held in the Opera House was simply magnificent. Our wedding was somewhat unusual. All the guests, as well as the newlyweds, were dressed in clothes of the 19th century. All this looked very beautiful, spectacular. Random people walking around the park stopped by, congratulated the newlyweds, smiled and wished us all the best to the couple. It is worth mentioning that among the guests there were four children, also elegantly dressed. While the newlyweds took pictures in the palace, their guests walked and rested in the meadow. Mini-cars with police passed by, and the officer also told us we looked great and smiled))). What I am trying to say is when we were heading to the restaurant after walking for quite some time around the park, the clerk of the museum approached us with a security guard and demanded to leave the park, because, in her opinion, we were participants of a theatrical show. We answered that we had a wedding and generally we were not doing anything wrong. They told us that if we did not pay the fine, they would call the police. Yes... it would be interesting to see 15 people, including young children (the youngest of whom is 6 months old), put behind bars on a charge of refusing to pay a fine. This is it. Everything was just as usual.

This narrative, broadcasting negative experience, describes the costs of commercializing the Tsaritsyno brand. The "restored decoration" must be profitable, which explains why the park's employees and security guards were so vigilant and suspected the wedding group of not paying a fee or a hidden entertainment business. A probable hypothesis is that the administration of the park and museum may not be too loyal to self-entertaining groups that do not generate income. Although, the author believes that weddings groups walking around the park, especially costume groups, make their marketing contribution to increasing the tourist attractiveness of Tsaritsyno. People enjoy looking at them, they are photographed by visitors. When the author asked a passers-by in a similar situation:

> Do you like open weddings in Tsaritsyno?", the answer was: "Is looks as if the abandoned castle came alive and became inhabited by people.

Re: Did you like your wedding in Tsaritsyno?

> We were very pleased with the way OUR day went. There were no overlays; nobody let us down. Despite all my pre-wedding nightmares, the cars arrived [in time], the stylist and the photographer were on time, the bouquet was decorated even better than I expected. Besides this, after all the rainy days, it finally started snowing and the snow decorated the November gray. But I shuddered when I looked at the weather forecast foreshadowing snow and rain and the temperature of +/- 1 degrees. My only regret is that I was too nervous and the memories of my own wedding are more like a kaleidoscope of vivid pictures. Recently, my husband and I tried to remember what music accompanied the registration (we were offered several options to choose from)... and we realized that we don't even remember whether there was any music at all?!

This post documents an important aspect of the wedding as an event culminating and absorbing a lot of emotions, which results in the fact that certain circumstances are lost in memory, leaving just a chain of vivid images. Memory is not a reliable resource for memoires, without being supported by photos or a video. But what is the role of the photo document in provoking precisely those emotions that were experienced during the wedding? What place does Tsaritsyno's image take in designing these emotions?

14.5 Photo and Video Shooting of Outdoor Registration in Tsaritsyno

The author conducted several offline interviews with professional video operators working on outdoor registrations in order to make a definite impression about the normative structure of the video report on the wedding in Tsaritsyno and its features. It is important to say that in order to talk on this topic, the author needed to justify the absence of marketing intentions, since the respondents work in a highly competitive environment. Recruiting into a profession is not always associated with the education that directly serves it: a freelancer model is common, combining a screenwriter, a director, an operator, and a marketing manager. General characteristics of the product are associated with the brevity (30–40 min) of the final video compared to the volume of documentary that is many times bigger and often amounts up to 2–3 hours. In the "ideal case", the video is a narrative, the leitmotif of which is following the chronological structure of the events of the wedding day.

Vladimir, video operator:

> To make the final version of the video, you have to cut and assemble a lot, because it is necessary that the customer likes it, so that everyone looks beautiful, and no one picks their nose. You can't make a mistake, because video is not a photoshoot—you won't be able to reshoot it. But then a lot of material remains, sometimes something funny or awkward. However, some people think this is also important to them, so we give not only a final version of the video but all the documentary material. To my mind, this is exactly what is most valuable. I would now love to see my parents' wedding or show mine to my son. It seems to me that now there is more demand for it—for the present. What attracts people to Tsaritsyno? Outstanding views, a pond, the architecture is beautiful, it is much clearer there than in other places. Despite its pop reputation, Tsaritsyno has lots of spots away from palaces where you can make some videos.

Ruslan, video operator:

> Some people are fond of assembled inserts, swans, hearts, all kinds of animation. I try to avoid this, it's better to focus on the documentary part and add some good music so that it makes the video emotional. In general, the fashion for what a wedding video should be comes from the United States, not even from Europe. I look through the American relevant sites all the time, then we discuss this in our professional forums. There, in the West, emotions are more important, and for us, since we are wild people, it is important to demonstrate how much is invested, what kind of dress the bride has, the restaurant, the car. Therefore, we are the ones who formulate offer. Rarely does anyone formulate their wishes. [People] try to trust professionals. What attracts people to Tsaritsyno? I've already done 10 shoots there. It is possible to shoot a wide variety of romantic passages there. I already have my own professional practices guaranteeing successful panoramas. And customers, they often don't even know what Tsaritsyno is, and what the history of the Catherine's Palace is.

Alexander, video operator:

Of course, one can give their friends a video camera to shoot, but it is worth at least taking a look at their background in video shooting. Surely you will find a shot with a cropped head or just legs, too much sky, or vice versa, the floor. What should a wedding video have in it? I will describe to you step by step what should be there: video footage of the process of preparation and festive decoration at the bride's house, then panoramic views; then scenes captured outside and inside the registry office; then footage of registration, the couple signing the marriage license and exchanging rings, first kiss and congratulations; then, possibly, a trip to the church, its panoramic views, video footage of the scene of the church wedding and the newlyweds leaving the church, and congratulations from relatives and friends; then panoramic views before shooting in the restaurant, great toasts in the restaurant, the first waltz of the newlyweds, a table with gifts, the process of cutting the cake as well as people dancing, getting entertained and having fun. And each time the focus should be on a fabulous couple.

Georgiy, video operator:

What should a customer get? The format of the short artistic version of the wedding video includes the best moments, "cream", where there are no drawn moments, and the music and the connection of the episodes are carefully adjusted. In addition, a more detailed documentary version. Although the wedding video does not have strict standards. Who is our customer? Well, it's hard to say whether this is a middle-class couple. [N]ow it is blurry: a person might work at a factory but have a Volkswagen car. And the couple spend quite some money for the wedding. What attracts people to Tsaritsyno? A fabulous entourage, a well-groomed park, and restored buildings are the perfect backdrop for a classic wedding.

Summarizing the opinions of professionals, it is important to note the acute problems of documentary versus assembled inserts made during the editing process in the form of clichéd visual images that thematically serve the wedding plot. There is a steady demand for this embellishing design, but at the same time both the customer's request for reportage and the opinion of the professionals themselves about the boundaries of the supported taste are formulated.

This issue is raised repeatedly in forum discussions. This makes it more valuable to compare the impressions of female customers about the wedding video with the opinion of video operators.

Re: What should the wedding video be like?

It seems to me that it is individual for each person. We had a video operator who made a 2-hour-long video for us (and that is more than enough, otherwise guests are tortured to watch the video). He also made a 3- minute-long clip. He did everything lyrically enough, with his own zest of course. After all, all couples are different, as well as their behavior and the ability to pose for the camera. The clip is my favorite part. It contained the same song we danced to. The best moments he shot got to the video. Of course, the ransom part got there too but just about 20 minutes of it (there is no need in making this part longer). [The video operator] showed our way to the registry office accompanied by hilarious music. [The video also contained] several scenes shot at the registry office, including the ceremony. A walk without words, only the most delicate beautiful moments, a very beautiful music. [This part of the video] makes you have goosebumps, and the rest of the video is about the restaurant and all the best moments. But all these hearts, bunnies, cats, etc... I think is completely unnecessary. It distracts attention. Well, one can certainly make some kind of zest of their own, but no more than that. However, this is again individual for everyone.

While commenting on this sequence, it is necessary to focus on the recipe of "causing goosebumps," that is, on the condition of preserving and transmitting emotions through a video document, i.e. the same music acting as an associative key that renews that very experience in the memory, as well as the brevity of mise-en-scenes, which makes them closer to the format of the photo (and "and that is more than enough"). Furthermore, the expressiveness of the silent walk conveying sign language and body semantics in video format may channel more emotions in the shot than any spoken words might have done.

Re: What should the wedding video be like?

I would like the video to be shot only until we get to the restaurant, and that it mainly would the scenes of the walks. After all, the wedding video should be primarily informative! An ideal wedding video should last 20 minutes or 15 minutes. The operator should steer his own process, it is not necessary to making staged scenes. It would be obligatory for a photographer—required, for a video operator it is not. All these hearts, angels, page turning and from other cheap editing make me sick.

Re: What should the wedding video be like?

The video should be informative, that is true. It should include all the key scenes, but not the boring ones. [I]t would be good if all the guests get to the video at least once. In terms of timing, the perfect video would last like any feature film—from 1 h 20 minutes to 1 h 30 minutes. The video must be FULLY A REPORTAGE. One or two scenes with newly-weds walking by might be staged—but not more. Otherwise, you need to select a separate shooting day for a staged video, or even more than one. There should be no inserts in the video. Just simple editing featured with music.

Re: What should the wedding video be like?

All we got were just swans and rings. Ooooh. . . and I just hate it!!! But we took away all the video materials. . . I hope that one day I will make a good video)

Re: What should the wedding video be like?

Yesterday the whole family watched the video materials (2 clips and a video footage)!! I have some mixed feelings! At first it was really strange to look at ourselves from the side, especially on such a day. In general, I'm a critic, I sat and commented on every movement, while the rest of the family watched the video enthusiastically:)) At some point I caught myself watching [it] with my mouth open))) it was funny! Most of all I liked the way the walk (clip) and the abduction of myself in the restaurant were captured:)) (it was sooooo funny that the whole family laughed). There were also a few jokes from the groom during the ransom))) he was so cool, funny, and nervous:)))

Re: What should the wedding video be like?

The most important thing is that although everything is not that bad and you like at least some moments, the second time you watch [the video], it is even more interesting. That's for sure. . . You know, the video also distorts a lot [since] what we feel can never be transmitted by digital technologies. The main thing is that there is now a memory and your story is captured)))))))

A selection of statements made on the forum leaves no doubt that the visual documentation of the wedding ceremony is an important part of the general memorial process laying the semantic framework of the memory of the most important life event. People wait for a video or a clip impatiently and excitedly. They are inviting their relatives to share and relive this event. The traits of event recognition are not always predictable, but the degree of coincidence clearly depends on how much the video operator or director tended towards documenting. The importance of informativeness has been announced and repeatedly strengthened in the group discussion, but its content remains blurred. Do former brides mean the event density of the chronological flow or the high detail of investments ("I already said goodbye to my money and the video")? The majority of the forum participants reject or narrow down the possibility of "embellishment" of the video material due to animated inserts and symbols, but this raises the problem of a hidden mirror. As one of the forum participants admitted,

> a friend who taking pictures at my wedding has a lot of funny photos, but I want beauuuuuutiful ones. Therefore, I am waiting for professional photos. [A]t least I was silent during the staging for sure.

The narcissistic mirror requires a corrected and appropriate moment of reflection, which will not be embarrassing to present to your environment *("The dance was actually awful... It's a shame to show it")*.

However, perhaps the most important thing that the discussion of the wedding video makes clear is the expectation of a renewed experience. What looked pragmatic at the stage of preparation, analysis and weighting of justified or unjustified expenses, rational integration into event timing, and fully elaborated minute-by-minute wedding plan, is complemented by the renewal of emotions as if they had been hastily experienced in a situation of a wedding action. And from that moment, the memory of the event at the time of its experience on the wedding day will be constantly adjusted and possibly replaced by the image that is created in the commercial video product and carries traces of clichéd processing.

14.6 The "Wedding in Tsaritsyno" Video: Microanalysis

Hundreds of wedding videos uploaded to Tsaritsyno have been posted on YouTube (as of July 2018). There is practically no animation in them. They are built according to a similar scenario. It might slightly vary by making accents on a walk around the city in addition to the Tsaritsyno ceremony, some creative activities in the restaurant, a light or fire show, presence or absence of wedding transport, and the number of relatives represented. Various plots are united in the clips by a common musical theme and the leitmotif of a couple becoming one. For microanalysis, the author chose a maximally typical video, in which all the most frequently used scenes are presented in the sequence that is preferred by professional video operators.[4]

---

[4] The video clip can be freely accessed on YouTube (Wedding at the estate "Tsaritsyno", 2018)

Timer	Contents
0.00	Two wedding rings on a ribbon against the background of multi-colored balls.
0.06	Balloons on the chandelier. Panorama of the bride's apartment.
0.13	Close-up of pins, hairstyle, corset lacing, earrings, necklace, and the process of putting on a veil.
1.00	Panoramic walk of the bride and groom in Tsaritsyno park, over bridge; views of the pond.
1.17	Panoramas of the Catherine Palace. Couple in the palace.
1.35	Guests entering the Golden Hall while being accompanied by by the master of ceremonies. Concert of a costume orchestra.
1.48	Wedding rings close-up. The camera circles around a casket with rings.
1.51	Exchange of rings. First kiss.
2.05	The first dance of the newlyweds (guests applaud).
2.12	Newlyweds posing in static poses under portraits in the halls of the palace.
2.17	Kisses of a couple against the background of panoramic views of the Tsaritsyno reservoirs, inside the palace, on the bridge, on the stairs inside the palace, against the background of the Opera House, and in the rotunda.
2.50	A couple goes for a dance in the Golden Hall of the Catherine Palace, the video is shot from above.
2.55	Newlyweds dance in a restaurant in the evening with sparklers, under a red umbrella, with tinsel.
3.01	The couple dance in the Golden Hall of the Catherine Palace again.
3.11	Guests having fun and dancing in the restaurant in the evening, a newlywed bride dances with her father.
3.27	Kissing couple on the background of the palace buildings.
3.33	Close-up of a cake cut by the groom.
3.40	Kissing couple on the background of the Opera House.
3.46	Kissing couple on the steps of the palace.
3.47	Evening in the restaurant, people having fun and dancing with sparklers. Newlyweds dancing under a red umbrella.
3.49	A walk with a bouquet in Tsaritsyno park. Kisses under the veil. Close-up of rings.
3.59	Couple posing next to the palace, on the stair, against the background of golden balusters.
4.12	The couple dance in the Golden Hall again, in a circle of parquet, video shot from above.
4.16	A couple dance in a restaurant in the evening.
4.24–4.30	The couple dance in the Golden Hall again. Gradually, the video frame fades, becoming black and white.

If one traces second by second the change of plans and editing approach applied in a video, they can weigh the volume of meaningful scenes, and see their sequence in the visual narrative that is being created. What is a wedding story framed with? What visual and informative elements help telling a story about this event—a story that has a beginning, a climax and an end? The beginning was marked by a pair of rings hanging on ribbons shot against the background of multi-colored balloons creating a festive mood. This semantic key to the topic of the video shooting emerges a couple more times, i.e. at the culmination of the official registration and exchange of rings, and closer to the end, in the context of the couple's peaceful walk in the Tsaritsyno Park. Visual means designed to emphasize the meaning of history will be close-ups of hanging rings with visible engraving in honour of their owners, a luxurious box with rings, and rings on the newlyweds' hands as a *fait accompli*. The reportage itself develops from the scene in the bride's house, which has the character of a genre scene. The camera snatches a number of accessories that distinguish the bride from other elegant women who carefully bustle around her. This cramped private space is torn apart with a panoramic walk of the elegantly dressed couple along the Tsaritsyn boardwalks. The couple is separated from relatives, and the process of entering it into the palace and semi-palace spaces and premises begins. Such an important visual tool as editing plans and scenes is then used to densely fill the video with a variety of background designs that compress and open the space around the couple. The video operator plays with the chronology of scenes turning it into a prolonged period of time, since the repeated change of plans of the palace during the day and the restaurant in the evening as a background for the couple gives the impression of a disrupted day or that there were several days of walking celebrations. The things that would take the assigned hour for the couple to register and get congratulations in real time, grows into a construct of extended time period in the video. The spectacular completion of these manipulations is the visual method of fading, which smoothly translates the color scene of the presence of the couple at its main life event into the black-and-white mode of nostalgic memory of it.

Counting by the timer shows that the scenes of Tsaritsyno as an architectural and interior background amount to about 40% of the visual material, becoming an important part of the wedding action. A classic example of a figure in the background—"a wedding in Tsaritsyno"—develops into an organized, sequentially ordered visual form. The constants of the landscape, buildings, and interior captured by the camera, the image of the newlyweds holding hands, hugging and kissing, the background of the sky/grass/surface of the pond interrelate and give rise to a new quality. This indicates the integrity of the image perception of "wedding on the background of Tsaritsyno" and the specific order of such perception. The latter two arise due to the fact that the video operator applies the principles common to the gestalt logic (Arnheim, 1974), such as *affinity* (incentives placed side by side tend to be perceived together), *similarity* (incentives that are close in size, shape, color or form, tend to be perceived together), *integrity* (perception has a tendency to simplification and integrity), *closure* (which shows the tendency to complete the image in such a way that it takes on a full form), *adjacency* (proximity of stimuli in time and space), and *common region* (expectations and thoughts affect the interpretation of the perceived along with learning and past experience).

What does the newlyweds' image get close with? What is the way integrity is acquired? What are the plots or other collective images it is focused on?

First of all, the counterparty is "palace": boardwalks around the Catherine Palace, the Opera House, the Bread House, on the bridge, on the steps, in the rotunda, followed by walks inside the palace buildings, settling in the interiors (the newlyweds lean to the walls, sit down, whirl in dance, use usual everyday gestures, drinking a glass of champagne at a buffet table or putting their dresses in order).

The combination of these actions has the effect of saturation and settling in the palace with a fairytale couple that are more and more resembling a prince and a princess at home.

Another counterparty is a community of relatives and friends, minimally present in the video in Tsaritsyn's interiors, but dominating in another alternative space, that is a restaurant. This community becomes a must-have and inevitable backdrop for a couple that is dancing, drinking, and having fun. The effect of perception here is the 'integration' of those presented no longer separately, but rather as a couple of newlyweds, into a circle of friends and relatives. Having dinner and fun together creates a visual leitmotif that inscribes a couple of a prince and a princess who came off into the fairy Empyrean Heaven of the Tsaritsyno palace back into their social circle.

14.7 Conclusion

In this conclusion, the author is trying to summarize the diversified analysis of the video wedding staging in the context of the Tsaritsyno Park and Museum. The theoretical focus of this paper is on the dynamics and possible convergence of the pragmatic and romantic aspects of the modern phenomenon of love and marriage, which are embodied in media representations of changing rituals yet preserving traditional national features. The represented *topos* of the modern wedding is consistent with the folk one in terms of the sequence of actions aimed at overcoming borders and obstacles in the physical and imaginary social space, which symbolically marks a different status of the newlyweds, while ensuring legitimation from the significant environment. An important role in this staging of a collective utopia of romantic love is played by scenery in the broad sense of this word. The interiors and exteriors of Tsaritsyno Park and Museum make people play certain roles in the wedding scenario according to "the proposed circumstances". This results in a high degree of visualization with an imaginary figure of the inhabitants of these places, appropriating not only the subject space, but also social status. This is probably the case when a king or queen is not made by an retinue, but rather by a royal castle.

The empirical focus of this article is on the triad of the actual video product, the opinion/position of the professionals creating it and the opinion/reaction of consumer customers. It is absolutely clear that the management of the process of media sacralization of the utopia of romantic love is monopolized by professionals in this specific service market. Consumers actually delegate and alienate in their favor the right and power to interpret the most important events in their lives. According to J. Raab (2002), media sacralization through profane professionalization is achieved through a certain way of structuring visual material, manipulations with the flow of reportage shooting, accumulating the meaning of animated inserts or symbolic objects, and finally, musical accompaniment. Both professionals and customers note the emerging trend towards increased documentation of the wedding video, which is close to reportage shooting. The reflexive value of documenting an event, however, conflicts with the expectation of an embellishing mirror effect. In this sense, the projection of these expectations on the wedding video has a narcissistic character and indicates the inclusion of this media product in social exchange. This indicates the traces of the convergence of pragmatics and romance: analysis and weighting of justified or unjustified costs and rational integration into the timing of the wedding event are complemented by the renewal of experienced emotions when watching a video.

The video shooting of the wedding in Tsaritsyno is primarily intended for its customers, namely a couple of newlyweds, but thanks to their integration into certain social groups and social niches, it is addressed to a wider circle of individuals who get a copy of this video or are invited to share a joint viewing. This media product delivers the narcissistic joy of reflection and recognition and thereby generates a modified reverse perspective on one's own life. In this sense, an invariable document confirming romantic love is intended to strengthen the duration of the relationship, since its discursive accessibility involves endless reproduction and magical manipulations (scrolling in accelerated mode, slowing down, frame-by-frame stop) with a one-time and unique life event, and thereby the resumption of those very romantic feelings within the commemorative community. The target group of the proposed community is representatives of the predominantly Moscow "middle class" and social groups similar in lifestyle. The visual document reflects their taste as a social characteristic as well as their aesthetic preferences. The connection of the demonstrated taste with advertising samples is also unconditional. This is the way those social groups that are considered prestigious and worth being copied celebrate and visually design their weddings, choosing non-standard, not widely stereotyped formats of outdoor registrations in Moscow estates and palace complexes. Following the classical ritual, i.e. a bride dressed in white, luxurious palace apartments, a church, an orchestra, a limousine, pigeons in the air and a chic restaurant—is justified in the society that wants to appear stable and relatively in order.

References

Adelmann, R. (2002). Kommerzielle Hochzeitsvideos oder das 'Menschenrecht' gefilmt zu warden. In R. Adelmann, H. Hoffman, & R. F. Nohr (Eds.), *Video als mediales Phaenomen* (pp. 229–238). Weimar: VDG.

Arnheim, R. (1974). *Art and visual perception*. Moscow: Progreso.

Balashova, O. B. (2002). *Riddle and magic in the artistic system of a wedding. Abstract of dissertation for a PhD in philosophy*. Moscow: Moscow State University.

Barbalet, J. (2001). *Emotion, social theory, and social structure: A macrosociological approach*. Cambridge: Cambridge University Press.

Blossfeld, H.-P. (2011). Myths and facts about online mate choice. Contemporary beliefs and empirical findings (together with Andreas Schmitz, Susann Sachse-Thürer and Doreen Zillmann). *Zeitschrift für Familienforschung, 23*, 358–381.

Bobrikhin, A. A. (2009). Social pragmatics of ritual in folk culture. *Bulletin of the Chelyabinsk State University, 10*(30), 159–163.

Boytsova, O. Y. (2010). Amateur photography in the urban culture of Russia at the end of the 20th century. *Visual Anthropological Analysis.* Abstract of thesis for a PhD in History. St. Petersburg: University Press.

Giddens, A. (2004). *Transformation of intimacy.* St. Petersburg: Peter.

Gromov, D. V. (2009). "Wedding landmarks": Landscape and modern youth rites of passage. In F. Vlasova (Ed.), *Essays on Russian folk culture* (pp. 502–526). Moscow: Nauka.

Hochschild, A. R. (2003). *The commercialization of intimate life: Notes from home and work.* Berkley: University of California Press.

Illouz, E. (1997). *Consuming the romantic utopia: Love and the cultural contradictions of capitalism.* Berkeley: University of California Press.

Kaufmann, J.-C. (2002). *Premier matin.* Paris: Armand Colin.

Knoblauch, H. (2005). Focused ethnography. *Forum: Qualitative Sozialforschung/Forum: Qualitative Social Research, 6*(44). Retrieved November 04, 2019, from http://www.qualitative-research.net/index.php/fqs/article/view/20/43

Lewis, C. (1998). Working the ritual: Professional wedding photography and the American middle class. *Journal of Communication Inquiry, 22*(1), 72–92.

Moran, J. M. (1996). Wedding video and its generation. In M. Renov & E. Suderburg (Eds.), *Resolutions. Contemporary video practices* (pp. 695–702). Minneapolis: University of Minnesota Press.

Raab, J. (2002). 'Der schönste Tag des Lebens' und seine Überhöhung in einem eigenwilligen. Medium. Videoanalyse und sozialwissenschaftliche Hermeneutik am Beispiel eines professionellen Hochzeitsvideofilms. *Sozialer Sinn, 3,* 469–495.

Reichertz, J. (2000). *Die Frohe Botschaft des Fernsehens. Kultursoziologische Untersuchung medialer Diesseitsreligion.* Konstanz: Universitäts Verlag.

Russian Demographic Barometer. (2012). Retrieved November 6, 2019, from http://demoscope.ru/weekly/2012/0497/barom04.php

Russian Demographic Barometer. (2019). Retrieved November 4, 2019, from http://www.demoscope.ru/weekly/2019/0823/barom06.php

Russian Newspaper. (2011). № 5(5381). Retrieved November 4, 2019, from https://rg.ru/2011/01/14/brak.html

Sosnina, O. (2009). *Topography of happiness: Russian wedding. From the end of the 19th century to the beginning of the 21st century.* Moscow: Tzaritzino Museum.

Tkach, O. (2013). Wedding in the city: Going for a walk. In O. Brednikova & O. Zaporozhetz (Eds.), *Micro-urbanism. City in detail* (pp. 170–209). St. Petersburg: Aletheia.

Wedding at the estate "Tsaritsyno". (2018). Retrieved July 10, 2018, from http://www.youtube.com/watch?v=I3zpoyE3Ac0&feature=player_detailpage

Zakharov, S. (2005). Prospects for fertility in Russia: The second demographic transition. *Domestic Notes, 3*(24), 124–140.

Elena Rozhdestvenskaya is a Dr. of Sociology Hab. and a Professor at the Faculty of Social Sciences in National Research University Higher School of Economics (HSE), Leading Researcher in Institute of Sociology Russian Academy of Sciences, Co-Editor of the Journal "Interaction. Interview. Interpretation". Her major scientific interests lie on qualitative sociology, biographical method, memory studies, family sociology and visual sociology.

Chapter 15
Low-SES Parents' Love as Educational Involvement with Their Primary School Children: A Synthesis of Qualitative Research

Naomi Takashiro and Clifford H. Clarke

Abstract Parental love can be transmitted to children through parental involvement in education. Despite the abundant studies in the area, there are inadequate studies on low-socioeconomic status (SES) parental involvement from international perspectives. The purpose of our study was to examine how low-SES parents displayed their love through parental educational involvement with primary school children despite the odds. We employed a systematic qualitative research examining 19 existing Western and non-Western studies. Results showed that low-SES parents used different strategies to show their love. The identified four themes were: facilitated learning, using support from others, involved with school, and cultural influence. Although low-SES parents were disadvantaged, they emphasized the importance of education, provided good home environment, helped school assignment, cultivated learning experience, and established rapport with children. Support from family and outside of family members was also indispensable. Parents also attempted to resolve children's problems by establishing relationships with teachers. Some parents also showed unique cultural forms of love in motivation to compete, fulfilling traditional father's roles, and practicing religious beliefs. Our findings indicated that low-SES parents were dedicated to display love as their involvement with children's education despite the predicaments.

Keywords Low socioeconomic status · Synthesis of qualitative research · Parental educational involvement · Parental love

N. Takashiro (✉)
Department of Global Tourism, Kyoto University of Foreign Studies, Kyoto, Japan
e-mail: takashiron@mac.com

C. H. Clarke
School of Communications, University of Hawaii at Manoa, Honolulu, Hawaii
e-mail: chclarke@me.com

15.1 Introduction

Parental love is a form of affection towards children. Parents generally want their children to succeed in education. In order to achieve their goal, they can display their love through various forms of attitudes, behaviors, and thoughts, such as engagement, involvement, expectations, and support for educating children. In our chapter, we define parental love as parental involvement in their children's education. Reviewing the extant literature, Desforges and Abouchaar (2003) reported parental involvement took various forms of involvement at home and at school. Parental involvement included creating a stable home environment, facilitating learning, discussing with children, emphasizing the importance of educational and social values, aspirations for achievement, and creating good morals and social behavior. Parental involvement also included sharing information, taking part in activities and working at school, and school governance (Desforges & Abouchaar, 2003).

Given the evidence in the existing literature, parental involvement in children's education is related to many aspects of learning. For example, parental involvement positively influences children's academic performance, positive attitude toward school, self-esteem, classroom behavior, absenteeism, and motivation (Chen, 2018). This may suggest that parental involvement may have long-term effects on children's education. From the abundant research, researchers generally have acknowledged parents' involvement (e.g. Desforges & Abouchaar, 2003), especially in young children's education, such as that of primary school children. Parents' involvement reduces and changes the degrees of involvement when children grow older (Desforges & Abouchaar, 2003).

The degree of parental involvement is also associated with a number of parental factors. For example, parents' socioeconomic status (SES) and maternal educational level (Desforges & Abouchaar, 2003). That is, high-SES parents, educated mothers, tend to be more involved with children's education than their counterparts. It is understandable that disadvantaged parents are less likely to be involved with their children's education due to the language problems, unfamiliarity with the educational systems, and few home possessions. Low-SES parents are likely to be immigrants and minority. According to Lee and Bowen (2006), less educated parents may feel that their insufficient knowledge of the school system, educational jargon, low confidence level of communication with school staff, and their past negative school experiences may make them less involved with school.

Some low-SES parents despite being disadvantaged dedicate themselves to educate their children. Research indicated that low-SES parents showed higher levels of parental involvement in some dimensions (Wong & Hughes, 2006). Another study also indicated that low-SES parents were involved with children's education at home (Lee & Bowen, 2006). It seems that some low-SES parents do not use disadvantage as an excuse when it comes to their children.

Ethnicity is another factor to be considered for parental involvement (Desforges & Abouchaar, 2003). Researchers have suggested that the level of parental involvement varied depending on ethnicity (Desforges & Abouchaar, 2003). In addition, there is cultural variation regarding the definition of parental involvement. Results showed that parents from different cultures defined parental involvement differently and showed different degrees of involvement depending on contexts (Kim, An, Kim, & Kim, 2018; Wong & Hughes, 2006). Without considering cultural aspects of parental involvement, parents are often mislabeled as unloving and uncaring toward children.

Another issue is the research settings of parental involvement. Despite abundant studies that have been conducted in parental involvement in children's education, evidence from most studies is based on the U.S. or Western perspectives. Findings pertaining to the area from non-Western research are considerably inadequate (Yamamoto, Holloway, & Suzuki, 2016) and systematic research is mostly from the U.S. perspective (Desforges & Abouchaar, 2003). More research on parental involvement in the non-Western context is needed. For example, conducting more research on minority parental involvement is likely to contribute to diminishing the inequality in the education of minorities (Fleishmann & de Haas, 2016). The purpose of our study was to investigate how low-SES parents displayed their love through involvement in primary school children's education despite the odds.

15.2 Literature Review

Parental love can be transmitted through involvement in their children's education. In this section, we first review the definition of parental involvement in children's education and the previous studies in the field.

Many researchers have identified parents' involvement in the contexts of home and school (e.g. Desforges & Abouchaar, 2003). Others added community involvement in addition to family and school (Epstein et al., 1997). Examples of parental involvement in the previous studies are at home (e.g. parents encourage learning, secure places for study at home, visit educational places for intellectual stimulation, maintain regular routines, aspiration for personal achievement and good citizenship, and talk to children about schools), parental involvement in school (e.g. parents participate in volunteering, workshops, fundraising, school events, conferences, and activities) (Desforges & Abouchaar, 2003; Manz et al., 2004). Their parental involvement definitions also include low-SES elementary school students. This suggested that although there are significant cultural differences among ethnicities, the mainstream definition of parental involvement seem to be consistent throughout all ethnicities (Desforges & Abouchaar, 2003).

Desforges and Abouchaar (2003) provided an extensive literature overview of parental involvement, parental support, and family education in relation to student achievement and adjustment in school in Western countries and the U.S. These authors concluded that good home parenting was strongly related to children's achievement and adjustment. Parents' expectations and aspiration were most strongly associated with children's achievement. They also reported that the effect of ethnicity on achievement was small and that parental support and involvement differed among ethnicity. The authors mentioned that one of the limitations was that they might have omitted some of the articles, which are unpublished and unknown to the international scholars in the field.

Yamamoto and Holloway (2010) reviewed 35 studies on parental expectations and children's academic achievement relationships with different ethnic groups, which were published in U.S. settings between 1994 and 2007. They reviewed studies including children from kindergarten to 16 years old. The evidence showed that Asian American parents had higher parental expectations than other groups. Student prior academic performance was one of the successful predictors among European American parents, but not other minority parents.

Most of the minority or low-SES parental involvement studies in the U.S. focused on Mexican American and African American subjects. For example, Rojas-McWhinney and Bell (2017) conducted a study using interviews of 13 second-generation Mexican American parental involvements in the U.S. Some of the unique findings pertaining to Latino culture were speaking Spanish to maintain culture traditions and giving respect to others.

Another study (Jackson & Temillard, 2005) examined ten African American mothers' involvement in a low-SES neighborhood for primary school children's education in the U.S. The authors found that the parents emphasized the importance of education, monitored children's progress in school, assisted with homework, navigated a new approach for mathematics provided educational opportunities and materials, and created informal learning opportunities. Children being young, parents were able to assist with their homework.

Another qualitative research investigated six low-income parents' involvement in their primary school children in the U.S. (Smith, 2006). One of the findings was that the author presented broad definitions of parental involvement for low-income families. Their broad parental definitions included sending a child to school by getting up early, obtaining the available services and being present at school, and regular family activities at home. The author concluded that many low-income parents also were non-native speakers with limited English abilities, parental involvement was different from middle and high-SES parents. The inadequate home and school environmental factors may have influenced low-SES parents' perceptions of parental involvement. That is, low-SES parents may perceive parental involvement differently from their high-SES counterparts.

Watkins and Howard (2015) conducted a systematic review for low-SES parental factors for successful elementary school children in the U.S. They reviewed 30 qualitative and quantitative U.S. studies, which were published between 1999 and 2013. They found out that parental involvement with school, parental expectations, parenting styles, and home literacy environment were strongly related to children's academic success. Especially parental expectations showed most strongly to be associated with children's academic achievement.

Despite the scarcity of numbers of international studies compared to U.S. research, some research has been conducted in the area. Cabus and Ariës (2017) reported that immigrant and low-SES parents were involved in children's education as much as the average Dutch family in the Netherlands, however, their involvement was less effective in relation to children's academic achievement. In their study parental involvement was defined as their involvement in homework and parent-child communication on school matters. For low SES and immigrant parents having inadequate literacy competencies and time constraints, this type of parental involvement, such as helping in their children's advanced homework, may not be helpful for children's academic achievement.

Researchers studied how 77 Korean immigrant parents defined parental involvement and presented culturally unique findings on the definition (Kim et al., 2018). They reported that regardless of the level of parental educational attainments, supporting children at home was most important for the parents, and participating in school was least important. Among parental support at home, especially supporting nonacademic development and emotional/psychological development of children were more important than supporting children's academic success. Home-school connections, such as checking homework or communicating with teachers, were also identified by some of the parents. Korea being a Confucian society, the Korean immigrant parents perceived parental involvement as duty and obligation. Since parental involvement as duty appears to be rooted in Confucius culture (Kim et al., 2018), this parental definition seems to be influenced by the parents' culture wherein loving parents fulfill their obligations and duties. This is different from the perspective of mainstream western parental involvement.

Another cultural study done by Yamamoto et al. (2016) revealed that Japanese mothers compared to American counterparts were less likely to be involved with their primary school children's homework and cognitive engagement due to lower maternal responsibility, weaker parent-teacher interaction and other factors. The authors interpreted that the Japanese unique educational system of supplemental education outside of school may be one of the reasons for Japanese mothers' relatively lower engagement in school.

In summary, we reviewed the parental involvement literature up to the present. It appears that most researchers would agree with the mainstream definition of parental involvement, however, there was cultural variation. Due to the inadequate number of studies on low-SES, minority, and immigrants parents' educational involvement outside of the U.S. are especially needed. Exclusion of international research may create bias for various forms of parental love in children's education.

15.3 Method

15.3.1 Search Procedures

We conducted systematic qualitative research on low-SES parents' involvement with children's education by summarizing and synthesizing the existing data. According to Victor (2008),

> Systematic reviews are a method of identifying and synthesising all the available research evidence of sufficient quality concerning a specific subject (p. 1).

We used the electronic databases of Academic Search Complete via EBSCO host in order to locate relevant articles. We also used Internet searches and checked the Journal of Comparative Family Studies to reduce selection bias and not to overlook any relevant articles. The keywords we used were low socioeconomic status, low income, poor, poverty, parental involvement, parental engagement, parental participation, qualitative research or qualitative study.

15.3.2 Study Criteria

The indications of low socioeconomic status were selected based on the following criteria: (a) parents had high school or below high school educational attainments or (b) parents had low income in a working family or (c) parents lived in a low-income neighbourhood.

Since parent beliefs and concerns were likely to be different depending on children's ages (Rojas-McWhinney & Bell, 2017) and the level of parental involvement reduces with older children (Desforges & Abouchaar, 2003), we limited the literature to those studies focusing on primary school children.

According to our search results, articles on low-SES parental involvement outside of the U.S. did not appear much before the 2000s therefore articles published in English from 2000 to 2018 were included. We did not include non-peer reviewed articles due to the lack of rigorous reviews and possible lack of quality of evidence. Although some of the reviewed articles did not highlight low-SES parents' involvement in children's education, they were included as selected articles as long as they met our selection criteria. We included Western and U.S. studies as well as non-Western studies.

Research included in our study had two types of data as follows; (a) research consisting of participants' responses, such as interviews and focus groups and (b) data consisting of general conclusions based on parents' data. Selected articles included: parents' perspectives on parent educational involvement. This is because research indicated that others' perceptions, such as teachers' of parental educational involvement, were different from those of parents' (Wong & Hughes, 2006). Excluded articles included: (a) children's perspectives on their parents' academic engagement and (b) children with disabilities. As a result, we selected 19 articles for review.

15.3.3 Analysis

Our analysis was guided by the research question "How did low-SES parents display their love as involvement in children's education despite the odds?" The first author read each article several times to be familiar, entered the relevant data in Word, and wrote down notes. Then she compared those with other notes to identify similarities.

She grouped these similarities together and consulted with the second author about the grouping of the similarities. The first author then named the groups in order to answer the research question. The first author again shared her groupings and tentative themes with the second author to discuss. When we had disagreement during the process, we reviewed the discrepancies and discussed the issues until they were resolved.

15.4 Results

Before presenting the findings of our study, below is a succinct summary of the characteristics of the reviewed articles. Half of the reviewed studies focused on either Hispanic or African American or both from the U.S. The other 50 per cent came from outside of the U.S. About 50 per cent of the participants were mothers. Interviews and focus groups were common methods of data source. Please see the summary of the reviewed articles in the Appendix. Note that only relevant information pertaining to our study is listed.

Four themes were identified for parental love through their involvement in children's education: (a) facilitating learning (b) using support from others, (c) being involved with the school, and (d) living within cultural influences. The order of the themes is presented from the most frequent to the least frequent. Each theme with several subcategories is listed below.

15.4.1 Facilitating Learning

The first theme was facilitating children's learning. The parents used different strategies to facilitate children's learning. This theme consisted of four subthemes: (a) the importance of education, (b) providing a good home environment, (c) helping with school assignments, (d) cultivating children's learning experience, and (e) establishing rapport with children.

15.4.1.1 Advocating the Importance of Education

Parents expressed the importance of education in eight articles. A parent mentioned in one article, "I know how important education is..." (Gutman & McLoyd, 2000, p. 17). Although parents emphasized the importance of education, parental expectations ranged from just finishing high school to college. Most of the parents did not specify how far they wanted their children to go in terms of education. A few mentioned that they had lived hard lives and lacked resources. They did not want their children to repeat similar paths. For example, an Indonesian mother reported,

Yeah...our life adversity taught me that my son should be better than us, his education should be higher than us... (Yulianti et al., 2019, p. 263).

15.4.1.2 Providing a Good Home Environment

Some parents attempted to provide a good home environment for children by supplying educational materials, setting up rules, and providing a study area. This subtheme was identified in nine articles. Educational materials bought for children included new and used books, a tablet, Internet connection, CD-ROMs, and writing materials (Chin & Phillips, 2004; Milne & Plourde, 2006; Pan & Yi, 2011; Yulianti et al., 2019). Especially, books were the most common educational materials for children.

Several parents also regulated television viewing and allocated time for educational activities and other guidelines as parts of their rules and structures at home (Johnson et al., 2016; Milne & Plourde, 2006; Weiss et al., 2003; West-Olatunji et al., 2010). Supplying a good work area is also important for children to study. For example, Pan and Yi (2011) reported that a Taiwanese father provided a quiet study area for his children.

15.4.1.3 Cultivating Children's Learning Experience

Several parents cultivated children's learning experiences in seven articles. Most of the parents were engaged in specific activities together for children's learning experience, such as a field trip and library. Some of the examples reported by researchers were that a Japanese mother supported her son's interests in trains (Holloway, Yamamoto, Suzuki, & Mindnich, 2008) and that a Korean father had a family discussion every weekend (Kwon & Roy, 2007). Similarly, a parent took a daughter to a culture center to learn French as reported by researchers (Zellman, Perlman, & Karam, 2014).

One parent made a more aggressive approach to cultivate her daughter's music talent as reported by Pan and Yi (2011). A Taiwanese mother arranged music lessons for her daughter because she believed that her daughter should learn music although she did not know her interests in music.

15.4.1.4 Helping with School Assignment

Several parents were involved with children's homework in the following studies (Caissie, Gaudet, & Godin, 2017; Gutman & McLoyd, 2000; Johnson et al., 2016; Weiss et al., 2003; Pan & Yi, 2011). The homework assistance strategies involved both direct and indirect approaches. Some parents thought helping children's homework was manageable and others thought assisting homework was not possible. When parents were unable to assist homework, a Taiwanese parent just watched children doing homework as reported by Pan and Yi (2011) and Somali immigrant mothers praised children to complete homework although they were unable to check the accuracy of homework as reported by Yulianti et al. (2019). Just completing homework is inadequate for some parents. Yakhnich (2015) reported that one parent requested extra homework for her child. From our review, we identified that abilities for helping children's school assignment appears to be dependent on the level of parental educational attainment from no education to high school, self-confidence, language abilities, and children's grade school levels.

15.4.1.5 Establishing Rapport

Some parents in four articles established good rapport with children. Parents appeared to spend time with children to establish rapport. For example, some were engaged in non-specific activities to have conversations with children to encourage them, reported by scholars (Gutman & McLoyd, 2000; West-Olatunji et al., 2010). An African American parent reported, "They come talk to me and I listen" (West-Olatunji et al., 2010, p. 4). One father had a specific activity of taking a trip with a son (Chin & Phillips, 2004). Although taking a trip together would have increased father-child communication, it is unknown if the trip was involved with some educational activities.

15.4.2 Using Support from Others

The second theme was most frequently identified from the literature and it had two subcategories as follows: (a) support from family, and (b) support from school and community.

15.4.2.1 Support from Family

Besides themselves, families' own parents, relatives, and children's siblings provided support to children. Such support was found in seven journals. Various supports included providing transportation, providing a place to stay, giving educational opportunities, teaching English, and supervising children at school. For example, researchers quoted a Hispanic mother who had inadequate English language skills and was unable to help the child "So we have to ask her big sister what things mean" (Johnson et al., 2016, p. 449).

15.4.2.2 Support from School and Community

Support from school and community was identified in six journals. Parents had to rely on support from outside of family members: school teachers and community members' support. Community support included receiving and soliciting advice on homework, monitoring a child's behaviors, subsidizing educational costs, using an employer's computer, and modifying a parent's work schedule. School support consisted of tutoring and teacher's monetary contribution. Community help consisted of a neighbor, church members, employers, community leaders, and friends. For example, the mother's employer let her use the workplace computer for the child, and felt it was "really helping a lot" (Weiss et al., 2003, p. 17).

15.4.3 Involvement in School

The third theme was parental involvement in school. Several parents developed relationships with teachers for children in order to solve or proactively solve children's issues at school. This theme had two subcategories: (a) developing relationships with teachers and (b) guiding children's social behaviors and morals.

15.4.3.1 Developing Relationships with Teachers

This subtheme was identified in nine articles. Some parents perceived that developing relationships with teachers would solve and prevent children's future problems at school. For example, Gutman and McLoyd (2000) quoted a mother, who had said,

> I ask the teacher for a progress report in private to see how they are doing and just keeping in touch with the teacher, the counselor, and the principal on a monthly basis (p. 13).

A Japanese mother volunteered at her son's school to monitor the teacher, who was impatient with her son. They hoped that relationships with the son's teacher would be helpful for her son (Holloway et al., 2008).

15.4.3.2 Guiding Children's Social Behaviors and Morals

Some parents attempted to change children's unwanted social behaviors and to guide them to have good morals. Two articles had such indications. Researchers reported that a Hispanic immigrant mother guided her child on what was right and wrong (Johnson et al., 2016). Other scholars reported that a mother was eager to take action in disciplining her son's misbehaviors in school (Gutman & McLoyd, 2000). Parents told children how they should behave and gave advice.

15.4.4 Reflecting Cultural Influences

The fourth theme was identified as living within cultural influences. The three subthemes were: (a) motivation to compete, (b) the traditional role of fathers, and (c) religious beliefs. Each subcategory presented one quote respectively except the last one.

15.4.4.1 Motivating to Compete

A mother was convinced that studying in a rural school in Taiwan was not good for her daughters' future in their article (Pan & Yi, 2011). She was quoted as saying,

> When she was in the second grade, I decided I had to bring her to Taipei. I think [that studying in a rural school]... cannot compete with others, I like the competition. [The competition] makes progress... (p. 12).

The mother's strategy was to bring her daughter to a bigger city so that she was able to compete with high-achieving students. The mother perceived that her daughter would make academic progress by competing with other students.

15.4.4.2 Fulfilling Traditional Roles of Fathers

The roles of fathers are likely to be different across cultures. A Korean father perceived that he should be involved with children indirectly as the quote showed:

> Supporting is father's role—When I go home I don't talk much with the kids. Their mom takes care of them. I am always tired. But I have a conversation with them once a week...A father should always have dignity...In addition, a father has to support the kids economically (Kwon & Roy, 2007, p. 10).

The father mentioned that his busy work schedule prevented him for spending time with his children. He played a traditional father's role, which was to support children financially, but not children's cognitive development.

15.4.4.3 Practicing Religious Beliefs

Some African American parents used God in guiding children spiritually (Gutman & McLoyd, 2000; West-Olatunji et al., 2010). Their religious beliefs found in two articles were utilized to overcome academic difficulties and install morals in children. A mother's quote shows:

> I'm a faith-based household ... I feel that God placed the right people in my life at that time. In the beginning, matter of fact, I was told many detrimental things about her academic capabilities. (West-Olatunji et al., 2010, p. 5)

One parent experienced her daughter's academic capabilities, but she eventually resolved them by other's support, and she acknowledged God for such support.

15.5 Discussion

The purpose of our study was to identify how low-SES parents displayed their love by being involved with their children's education despite the odds. We conducted a qualitative systematic review of Western and non-Western studies. Although low-SES parents had limited resources and educational attainments, they expressed their desires and involved themselves in their children's education.

More specifically, we found that parents facilitated children's learning, used support from family and others, and were involved in the schools. We also identified some unique, culturally specific aspects of parental love. Some parents' love seems to be culture-universal and others seem to be culture-specific.

15.5.1 Facilitating Learning

15.5.1.1 Establishing Rapport

Similar to other findings, our results also showed that the parents listened, talked, did activities together, motivated, and gave advice to children (Desforges & Abouchaar, 2003). These daily activities are more likely to strengthen bonds between parents and children. This positive, supportive rapport with adults may help mitigate the negative effect of lower educated parents (McMillan & Reed, 1994). Clark (1990) suggested that daily interpersonal communication creates academic achievement. Some of the activities Clark (1990) suggested are also identified in our studies, such as listening, speaking, assisting homework and reading. Participating in various arrays of outside school activities create learning opportunities for children to extend their cognitive skills and be achievers. Clark (1990) also reported in a U.S. study that indicators of love were that parents and academically competent children tended to share personal problems and nurture each other. McMillan and Reed (1994) also suggested that good relationships with children and the attachment with children appear to be successful factors for children. Dedicated parents provide support, informal counselling, and assistance in guiding their children to succeed in school (McMillan & Reed, 1994) although they were lower educated parents and had few educational resources.

15.5.1.2 Advocating the Importance of Education

The parents were adamant about the importance of education for children. They did not want children to repeat the hardship of their lives, to have low educational attainment like them, and not to have any specific skills. Consistent with other findings, parents used their hardship from inadequate resources and lower educational attainment in order to emphasize the importance of education (Takashiro & Clarke, 2020).

Although some immigrant parents had inadequate language skills, they were willing to be involved in their children's education (Johnson et al., 2016). Immigrant parents told of the importance of education to children using emotional support through hard life stories to communicate their optimism, aspirations, and to motivate children to climb up the socioeconomic ladder via education despite their inadequate language skills and lack of knowledge in the educational systems. Parental support through emotional support is very important for educational success. Parents' strong commitment to education is likely to reduce the negative influence of lower educational attainment and limited resources (Rezai, Crul, Severiens, & Keskiner, 2015).

Our study also found that a few Somali immigrant parents used resilience to teach themselves the host language and became competent. In such cases, they became a role model and were able to help children. Parents' commitment to children's education can reduce the negative effects of low-SES (Pásztor, 2010).

15.5.1.3 Providing a Good Home Environment

Parents in our synthesis research provided a quiet study room, educational materials, and created rules at home. The results are consistent with others (Desforges & Abouchaar, 2003; Manz et al., 2004). Epstein et al. (1997) suggested six types of framework for developing programs for school and family programs. They indicated that parenting was one of the types of framework for the involvement of families. Parenting includes family establish home environment to support children's learning at home. Epstein et al. (1997) also indicated that providing a good home environment is not only helpful for children but also for parents. Some of the expected results for parents are that parents become aware of their own challenges in parenting, understand and be competent in parenting, in child development, and in changing home situations to improve opportunities for learning. Some of the expected outcomes for children are that they are able to complete homework, to gain skills, abilities, and to improve test scores associated with homework and classwork.

15.5.1.4 Helping with School Assignments

Researchers suggested that learning at home (e.g. helping with children's homework) is another one of the types of framework of family involvement (Epstein et al., 1997). Assisting children's homework is consistent with others (Cabus & Ariës, 2017; Jackson & Temillard, 2005; Kim et al., 2018; Manz et al., 2004). The parents in our synthesis study helped or monitored or even mimicked supervision of their children's homework. We identified that some less educated parents thought that helping homework with their primary school children was easy and others thought it was not. It appears that the level of parent's academic competence varies within low SES by the level of compulsory education completed. When parents realized that they were unable to directly assist with child's homework, they checked whether the child completed homework. Having inadequate language skills, some immigrant parents praised children for doing homework and doing well instead of directly helping children. For these parents, it may be more important that children complete homework rather than check the accuracy. Rezai et al. (2015) indicated that lacking abilities to assist their children's schoolwork and educational decisions, low-SES parents use emotional and financial support instead.

Congruent with research, parents made educational arrangements outside of school for children to cultivate their learning experiences (Jackson & Temillard, 2005; Manz et al., 2004; Watkins & Howard, 2015). These arrangements included library trips, culture center, music lessons, reading books, family discussion, and field trips. The informal learning activities may not be related to formal learning at school, but it seems to be helpful for children to learn. Jackson and Temillard (2005) indicated that low-SES parents supported their children's learning outside of school and their educational involvement with children occurred in daily activities. Parents supported, promoted and arranged such informal learning, but it was not associated with certain school activities. Parents also took initiative in providing additional informal learning that reflected their informal learning goals and assessment of these goals for children (Jackson & Temillard, 2005).

15.5.2 Using Support from Others

Our results showed that parents used support from family, extended family members, community members, and school staff. Low SES parents alone cannot educate children due to their lower educational backgrounds, limited language skills, inadequate material resources, and other reasons. In this case, they use family members and others' support in addition or to replace their roles. Support from family members is essential for young children to have academic success (Turner & Juntune, 2018). Consistent with a systematic qualitative study, various supports ranged from family, extended family members, teachers, community members, and employers (Takashiro & Clarke, 2020). Most successful at-risk children establish a close trusting relationship with any supportive and attentive family members (McMillan & Reed, 1994).

In addition to support from family members, we found that support from teachers, neighbors, church members, and tutors were also indispensable for children. The findings are congruent with others (Takashiro & Clarke, 2020). Tutoring from schools provided various opportunities for children to develop academic skills. Alvord and Grados (2005) suggested that support from caring teachers encourage resilience for children. McMillan and Reed (1994) indicated that participation in extracurricular activities at school provides opportunities for children to associate with peers and promote self-esteem. They continued that children's involvement in extra curricular activities at school and outside of school appear to promote self-esteem by relating to others and being recognized.

15.5.3 Involvement in School

15.5.3.1 Developing Relationships with Teachers

Congruent with others, our results also show that the parents developed relationships with teachers for their children (Manz et al., 2004). Some parents had regular contact with teachers to monitor children and others contacted teachers on an as needed basis. Although some parents contacted teachers about children's concerns, teachers were unable to help on certain issues. According to Manz et al. (2004), low-SES parents' involvement in home-school communication included contacting school through school conferences, phone, and notes. School-based involvement included volunteering, attending workshops, and fundraising. Another research indicated that parental involvement in school was associated with children's educational aspirations for less educated parents (Hill et al., 2004). That means, when low-SES parents were more involved in school, children tended to have higher educational aspirations. Involvement with school also may create network opportunities with other parents who have similar backgrounds. Lee and Bowen (2006) suggested that social networking with other parents or in parent-teacher conferences may help parents develop parenting skills, gain available resources, and gather information.

15.5.3.2 Guiding Children's Social Behavior and Morals

Parents can show their love to children through educating them in morals and appropriate social behavior. This was consistent with research indicating that when children acted up in school, some parents gave advice to children that they should obey the rules and respect teachers (Rojas-McWhinney & Bell, 2017). Parents also talked to teachers about children's behavior. Some parents believed that such guiding of children's behavior is important. For example, Rojas-McWhinney and Bell (2017) reported that showing respect, especially to older family members was one of the parental beliefs for Mexican American parents. In traditional Latino cultures, respect for others is one of the important cultural characteristics. We also found that educating children is not limited to just academic achievement but also to character-building. For Korean immigrant parents, support of nonacademic development and emotional/psychological development were more commonly identified as parental involvement than support of children's academic success. Nonacademic development included being a child's advisor, character education, and supporting caring peer relationships. Emotional/psychological development included, for example, love, encouragement, and self-esteem (Kim et al., 2018).

15.5.4 Reflecting Cultural Influences

We have discussed parental educational involvement for their children so far. These parents' perspectives tend to be universal and consistent throughout culture. Besides the mainstream parental involvement definitions, we found that some of the parental love as educational involvement seems to be influenced by culture. Our findings are consistent with others (Desforges & Abouchaar, 2003; Kim et al., 2018). Previous research indicated cultural influence of parents' involvement in children's education (Kim et al., 2018) and of the different degrees of parental involvement (Wong & Hughes, 2006). Ethnicity also influences parental involvement (Desforges & Abouchaar, 2003).

15.5.4.1 Motivating to Compete

In our reviewed study, we found a Taiwanese mother's unique form of love for her child to achieve academic success. Chinese parents tend to see children's academic failure as lack of tenacity, bad parenting or lack of parenting skills. Parents are likely to use punishment, shame, and criticism to correct children's undesirable behaviors. They also tend to override children's desires on behalf of what they think is best for children (Chua, 2011).

Parents are also likely to use competition for children in East Asia. Competition in education may not be perceived favorably in a western culture. However, comparing grades with other students is likely to accelerate and facilitate competition in order to gain academic excellence in East Asia. According to Cheng (2014), one should expect competition in East Asia such as Japan and Taiwan, because education is used for selecting elites. In East Asian countries, graduates from the most prestigious universities will be selected for good jobs in government and corporate sectors (Zorigt, 2019). Thus, educational competition is likely to facilitate and create such opportunities. Parents are likely to encourage educational competition in their children as a form of love in East Asian countries.

15.5.4.2 Fulfilling Traditional Roles of Fathers

The traditional roles of Asian fathers were identified in our reviewed study. A Korean father's role was to keep dignity and to be a family breadwinner. Seldom conversing with children and being tired, he expected his wife to take care of them. According to Hwangbo (2015), using the OCED data, Korean fathers spent about six minutes with children daily, which included reading books, assisting with homework, playing together, and supporting their physical needs. Consistent somewhat with the previous literature, the conventional view of Asian fathers' responsibilities was playing the role of a teacher and disciplinarian, assuring sufficient income, and supporting the mothers (McHale, Dinh, & Rao, 2014). That is, parental roles are also influenced by culture. Asian fathers tend to play the traditional roles of fatherhood as a sign of love for their children. It is also important to note; however, a recent trend for Asian fathers is to have more responsibilities and be involved with children's education and development, but this change is coming along slowly (McHale et al., 2014).

15.5.4.3 Practicing Religious Beliefs

Religious beliefs were seen among some African American parents. These parents relied on God's guidance and used it for their children's education. Consistent with other findings, some participants used their faith in God to cope with difficulties (Dass-Brailsford, 2005; Kumi-Yeboah, 2016). Researchers suggested that faith was related to high-achieving low-SES African students in South Africa (Dass-Brailsford, 2005) and that African Americans who actively practiced their religious faith achieved higher SES status than those who did not (Hill, 1993). Some parents use religious beliefs to show love to their children, which is unlikely to be seen in East Asian cultures.

15.6 Implications for Schools

As Kim et al. (2018) suggested, educators and schools should accept inclusive definitions of parental involvement in order to support low-SES parental education involvement. Although some culturally unique forms of parental educational involvement may not be familiar or seem strange to educators, educators should not label these parents as uncaring and unloving. Parents show their love through various types of educational involvement. Educators should understand this aspect when they deal with parents. Then educators and low-SES parents will be more likely to develop good rapport and work together for children's success.

15.7 Limitations

There are two limitations in this study. First, it was difficult to locate many international studies for our topic. As scholars have pointed out in the previous literature, parental involvement is mostly engaged from U.S. or Western perspectives. One half of the selected articles were from these regions. More international studies are needed in future research. The second limitation was that some articles had author s' interpretations of the results mostly with a few participants' quotations. We included these articles due to the difficulties in finding articles matching our criteria. Future studies should include more international studies to investigate different cultural forms of parental involvement.

15.8 Conclusion

We examined how low-SES parents showed their love as involvement in their children's education in a synthesis of qualitative research with Western and non-Western studies. In spite of low education backgrounds and limited material resources, low-SES parents displayed their love through educating their children. Parental involvement is not only limited to those who are advantaged. We identified that low-SES parents manifested love through facilitating children's learning, receiving support from others, and being involved in school. We also found culturally related parental love. That is, parental love is likely to be influenced if not determined by cultural context although there are some similarities across cultures as well. Despite our limitations, we extended the existing literature of parental involvement from the perspective of parental love with international studies. We hope that our chapter contributes to educators, researchers, school officials, and especially disadvantaged parents and children. Our desire is to inspire, encourage, and uplift those who are underprivileged but determined to be involved in their children's education despite their predicaments.

Acknowledgments We are grateful for our editors Claude-Hélène Mayer and Elisabeth Vanderheiden for their support, opportunities, and encouragement. We would not have completed this project without their help. We would also like to express our gratitude to those who were involved in this project. We are thankful for the ongoing support of our lovely feathered child, Pata-Pata, who is in heaven. We are immensely grateful to God for his sustaining guidance and support.

Appendix

Study characteristics

Author(s)/ year	Parents' ethnicity	Parental participants	Country/ setting	Children's age or grade	Data sources for parental participants
Caissie et al. (2017)	Unspecified	8 mothers	Canada	School age	Focus groups
Chin and Phillips (2004)	Latino, African American, and Asian American	Number of parents was unspecified	USA	Fifth grade	Observation, interviews, and surveys
Daniels (2017)	Somalia	4 mothers	South Africa	Primary school	Interviews
Dudley-Marling (2009)	African American and others	32 parents and grandparents	USA	Primary and middle school	Interviews
Gibbons, Pelchar, and Cochran (2012)	African American	1 mother	USA	10 years old	Interviews
Gutman and McLoyd (2000)	African American	34 parents and extended family	USA	Elementary and middle school	Interviews
Holloway et al. (2008)	Japanese	16 mothers	Japan	Preschool, first and second grade	Interviews
Jamal Al-deen and Windle (2017)	Muslim	25 mothers	Australia	Primary and/or secondary school	Interviews
Johnson et al. (2016)	Hispanic	92 mothers	USA	First grade	Interviews
Kwon and Roy (2007)	Korean	19 fathers	Korea	Under 12 years	Interviews
Milne and Plourde (2006)	Unspecified	Unspecified number of parents	USA	Second grade	Interviews
Parks (2017)	African American	8 mothers	USA	Prekindergardten to grade 1	Interviews and focus groups

(continued)

Author(s)/ year	Parents' ethnicity	Parental participants	Country/ setting	Children's age or grade	Data sources for parental participants
Pan and Yi (2011)	Taiwanese	5 Chinese	Taiwan	Adolescents recalled their past experience	Interviews
Weiss et al. (2003)	Not specified	20 mothers	USA	First and second grade	Interviews and observation
West-Olatunji et al. (2010)	African American	5 mothers and guardians	USA	Fifth grade	Focus groups and interviews
Yakhnich (2015)	Russian	17 parents	Israel	11–17 years	Interviews
Yoder and Lopez (2013)	Native American, Caucasian, Hispanic, and biracial	12 parents	USA	Preschool, elementary, middle, and high school	Interviews and focus groups
Yulianti et al. (2019)	Indonesian	16 parents	Indonesia	7–11 years	Interviews
Zellman et al. (2014)	Morroccan	16 parents	Morocco	Birth to 6 years	Focus groups

Note: Only those with information pertaining to our study is included

References

Alvord, M. K., & Grados, J. J. (2005). Enhancing resilience in children: A proactive approach. *Professional Psychology, 36*(3), 238–245.

Cabus, S. L., & Ariës, R. J. (2017). What do parents teach their children? The effects of parental involvement on student performance in Dutch compulsory education. *Education Review, 69*(3), 285–302.

Caissie, J., Gaudet, J. D., & Godin, J. (2017). Low-income, single-parent francophone mothers and the educational achievement of their children. *Canadian Journal of Education, 40*(4), 486–513.

Chen, G. (2018). *Parent involvement is key to student success*. Retrieved from https://www.publicschoolreview.com/blog/parental-involvement-is-key-to-student-success

Cheng, K. (2014). Does culture matter? Education reforms in East Asia. *Revue internationale d'éducation de Sèvres*. Retrieved from http://ries.revues.org/3804

Chin, T., & Phillips, M. (2004). Social reproduction and child-rearing practices: Social class, children's agency, and the summer activity gap. *Sociology of Education, 77*, 185–210.

Chua, A. (2011, January 8). Why Chinese mothers are superior. *The Wall Street Journal*. Retrieved from http://online.wsj.com/article/SB10001424052748704111504576059713528698754.html

Clark, R. M. (1990). Why disadvantaged students succeed: What happens outside school is critical. *Public Welfare, 48*(2), 17–23.

Daniels, D. (2017). Initiating a different story about immigrant Somali parents' support of their primary school children's education. *South African Journal of Childhood Education, 7*(1), 1–8.

Dass-Brailsford, P. (2005). Exploring resiliency: Academic achievement among disadvantaged black youth in South Africa. *South Africa Journal of Psychology, 35*(3), 574–591.

Desforges C., & Abouchaar, A. (2003). *The impact of parental involvement, parental support and family education on pupil achievement and adjustment: A literature review*. DfES Research Report 433.

Dudley-Marling, C. (2009). Home-school literacy connections. The perceptions of African American and immigrant ESL parents in two urban communities. *Teachers College Record, 111*(7), 1713–1752.

Epstein, J. L., Coates, L., Salinas, K., Clarke, K., Sanders, M. G., & Simon, B. S. (1997). *School, family, and community partnerships: Your handbook for action*. Thousand Oaks, CA: Corwin Press.

Fleishmann, F., & de Haas, A. (2016). Explaining parents' school involvement: The role of ethnicity and gender in the Netherlands. *The Journal of Educational Research, 109*(5), 554–565.

Gibbons, M. M., Pelchar, T. K., & Cochran, J. L. (2012). Gifted students from low-education backgrounds. *Roeper Review, 34*, 114–122.

Gutman, L. M., & McLoyd, V. C. (2000). Parents' management of their children's education within the home, at school, and in the community: An examination of African-American families living in poverty. *The Urban Review, 32*(1), 1–24.

Hill, R. B. (1993). Supporting African American families: Dispelling myths and building strengths. *The Roundtable, 7*, 2.

Hill, N. E., Castellino, D. R., Lansford, J. E., Nowlin, P., Dodge, K. A., Bates, J. E., et al. (2004). Parent academic involvement as related to school behavior, achievement, and aspirations: Demographic variations across adolescence. *Child Development, 75*(5), 1491–1509.

Holloway, S. D., Yamamoto, Y., Suzuki, S., & Mindnich, J. D. (2008). Determinants of parental involvement in early schooling: Evidence from Japan. *Early Childhood Research & Practice, 10*(1), 1–10.

Hwangbo, Y. (2015, October 20). *In South Korea, fathers are strangers*. Retrieved from http://english.hani.co.kr/arti/english_edition/e_national/713641.html

Jackson, K., & Temillard, J. T. (2005). Rethinking parent involvement: African American mothers construct their roles in the mathematics education of their children. *The School Community Journal, 15*(1), 51–73.

Jamal Al-deen, T., & Windle, J. (2017). 'I feel sometimes I am a bad mother': The affective dimension of immigrant mothers' involvement in their children's schooling. *Journal of Sociology, 53*(1), 110–126.

Johnson, S. B., Arevalo, J., Cates, C. B., Weisleder, A., Dreyer, B. P., & Mendelsohn, A. L. (2016). Perceptions about parental engagement among Hispanic immigrant mothers of first graders from low-income backgrounds. *Early Childhood Education J, 44*, 445–452.

Kim, Y. A., An, S., Kim, H. C. L., & Kim, J. (2018). Meaning of parental involvement among Korean immigrant parents: A mixed-methods approach. *The Journal of Educational Research, 111*(2), 127–138. https://doi.org/10.1080/00220671.2016.1220355

Kumi-Yeboah, A. (2016). Educational resilience and academic achievement of immigrant students from Ghana in an Urban School environment. *Urban Education, 10*, 1–30.

Kwon, Y. I., & Roy, K. M. (2007). Changing social expectations for work and family involvement among Korean fathers. *Journal of Comparative Family Studies, 38*(2), 285–305.

Lee, J., & Bowen, N. (2006). Parent involvement, cultural capital, and the achievement gap among elementary school children. *American Educational Research Journal, 43*(2), 193–218.

Manz, H. P., Fantuzzo, W. J., & Power, T. J. (2004). Multidimensional assessment of family involvement among urban elementary students. *Journal of School Psychology, 42*, 461–475.

McHale, J. P., Dinh, K. T., & Rao, N. (2014). Understanding coparenting and family systems among east and southeast Asian-heritage families. In H. Selin (Ed.), *Parenting across cultures: Childrearing, motherhood and fatherhood in non-Western cultures* (pp. 163–173). Springer: Cham, Switzerland.

McMillan, J. H., & Reed, D. F. (1994). At-risk students and resiliency: Factors contributing to academic success. *The Clearing House, 67*, 137–140.

Milne, A., & Plourde, L. A. (2006). Factors of a low-SES household: What aids academic achievement? *Journal of Instructional Psychology, 33*(3), 183–193.

Pan, L., & Yi, C. (2011). Constructing educational resilience: The developmental trajectory of vulnerable Taiwanese youth. *Journal of Comparative Family Studies, 42*(3), 369–383.

Parks, A. N. (2017). How do African American mothers in a rural community perceive resources for supporting family involvement in the early years? *Early Childhood Education Journal, 46*, 557–565.

Pásztor, A. (2010). Go, go on and go higher an higher. Second-generation Turks' understanding of the role of education and their struggle through the Dutch school system. *British Journal of Sociology of Education, 31*(1), 59–70.

Rezai, S., Crul, M., Severiens, S., & Keskiner, E. (2015). Passing the torch to a new generation: Educational support types and the second generation in the Netherlands. *Comparative Migration Studies, 3*(12), 1–17.

Rojas-McWhinney, J., & Bell, N. J. (2017). The negotiation of parenting beliefs by Mexican American mothers and fathers of young children. *Journal of Family Studies, 23*(1), 19–37.

Smith, J. G. (2006). Parental involvement in education among low-income families: A case study. *The School Community Journal, 16*(1), 43–56.

Takashiro, N., & Clarke, C. H. (2020). Low socioeconomic status students turn their academic failure to success: A synthesis of qualitative research. In C.-H. Mayer & E. Vanderheiden (Eds.), *Mistakes, errors and failures: Their hidden potential in cultural contexts*. Cham: Springer.

Turner, J. S., & Juntune, J. (2018). Perceptions of the home environments of graduate students raised in poverty. *Journal of Advanced Academics, 29*(2), 91–115.

Victor, L. (2008). Systematic reviewing. *Social research update, 54*, 1–4.

Watkins, C. S., & Howard, M. O. (2015). Educational success among elementary school children from low socioeconomic status families: A systematic review of research assessing parenting factors. *Journal of Children and Poverty, 21*(1), 17–46.

Weiss, H. B., Mayer, E. M., Kreider, H., Vaughan, M., Dearing, E., Hencke, R., et al. (2003). Making it work: Low-income working mothers' involvement in their children's education. *American Educational Research Journal, 40*(4), 879–901.

West-Olatunji, C., Sanders, T., Mehta, S., & Behar-Horenstein, L. (2010). Parenting practices among low-income parents/guardians of academically successful fifth grade African American children. *Multicultural Perspectives, 12*(3), 138–144.

Wong, W. S., & Hughes, J. N. (2006). Ethnicity and language contributions to dimensions of parent involvement. *School Psychology Review, 35*(4), 645–662.

Yakhnich, L. (2015). Immigrant parents in the educational system: The case of former Soviet Union immigrants in Israel. *Journal of Cross-Cultural Psychology, 46*(3), 387–405.

Yamamoto, Y., & Holloway, S. D. (2010). Parental expectations and children's academic performance in sociocultural context. *Educational Psychology Review, 22*, 189–214.

Yamamoto, Y., Holloway, S. D., & Suzuki, S. (2016). Parental engagement in children's education: Motivating factors in Japan and the U.S. *School Community Journal, 26*(1), 45–66.

Yoder, J. R., & Lopez, A. (2013). Parent's perceptions of involvement in children's education: Findings from a qualitative study of public housing residents. *Child and Adolescent Social Work Journal, 30*, 415–433.

Yulianti, K., Denessen, E., & Droop, M. (2019). Indonesian parents' involvement in their children's education: A study in elementary schools in urban and rural Java, Indonesia. *School Community Journal, 29*(1), 253–278.

Zellman, G. L., Perlman, M., & Karam, R. (2014). How Moroccan mothers and fathers view child development and their role in their children's education. *International Journal of Early Years Education, 22*(2), 197–209.

Zorigt, D. (2019). *Educational competition makes Asian countries more competitive*. Retrieved from https://www.austriancenter.com/educational-competition-asia/

Naomi Takashiro She received her Ph.D. in Educational Psychology and her M.A. in Communication with an emphasis on Intercultural Communication. She has been teaching English classes as adjunct faculty at the Kyoto University of Foreign Studies and its junior college in Kyoto, Japan. Her academic interests are socioeconomic status and inequality in education. She has been publishing articles in this area. She grew up in a low socioeconomic status family; her father was a high school dropout and mother is a middle school graduate. She has lived in Hawaii for twenty years and has worked in multicultural organizations before coming back to Kyoto six years ago. She has been looking for a full-time job at a university. In her spare time, she likes to cook, walk, swim, and read. She remains grateful for God's guidance in writing this book chapter.

Clifford H. Clarke He was raised in Japan by second-generation expatriate parents, whose own grand parents first moved to Japan in 1898 when the U.S. forced the Queen to abdicate her crown in the Kingdom of Hawai'i. Since arriving in Japan at the age of 7, his favorite pastime has been exploring cultural assumptions because at the age of 10 he was asked to become a bridge-between-cultures in Kyoto.

His higher education focused on the goal of becoming an effective "bridge person" by studying world religions and philosophies (B.A.), counseling across cultures (M.Div.), and interdisciplinary studies in the social sciences (ABD) at Stanford University's Graduate School of Education.

His four careers have evolved through 11 years of counseling foreign students at Cornell and Stanford universities, 8 years of teaching intercultural communication at Stanford and 5 years teaching at the University of Hawai'i at Manoa, 30 years of intercultural business management consulting in 13 countries in Asia, Europe, and North America, and 6 years of educational program design and evaluation in the State of Hawai'i public and charter schools.

Chapter 16
When a Mother's Love Is Not Enough: A Cross-Cultural Critical Review of Anxiety, Attachment, Maternal Ambivalence, Abandonment, and Infanticide

Sergio A. Silverio, Catherine Wilkinson, Victoria Fallon, Alessandra Bramante, and Aleksandra A. Staneva

Abstract Motherhood narratives pervade all cultures and are almost universally divided into the *'good and perfect'* or the *'bad and ugly'* mother discourses. A mother's love is commonly thought of as an emotional investment between those who mother, and those who are mother*ed,* and social expectations reinforce motherhood as being underpinned by an innate psychological bond. Historically comprising of nourishment, protection, and nurturing, in modernity a mother's love has evolved to encompass added meanings in view of the competing demands of personal, professional, and socio-political obligations. Consequently, with each new shape a mother's love assumes, its meaning becomes conceptually stretched and more fragile. Negotiating these demands, together with the intense societal scrutiny placed on modern mothers, renders the meaning of a mother's love ambiguous, and the traditional senses of motherhood increasingly difficult to achieve. Failure to bestow *'perfect'* motherhood can provoke a range of disordered constructions of love, and important consequences of the *'good mother'* discourse include

S. A. Silverio (✉)
Department of Women & Children's Health, King's College London, London, UK
e-mail: Sergio.Silverio@kcl.ac.uk; s.a.silverio@outlook.com

C. Wilkinson
School of Education, Liverpool John Moores University, Liverpool, UK
e-mail: C.Wilkinson@ljmu.ac.uk

V. Fallon
Department of Psychology, University of Liverpool, Liverpool, UK
e-mail: V.Fallon@liverpool.ac.uk

A. Bramante
Policentro Donna Ambulatory, Milan, Italy
e-mail: Alessandra.Bramante@gmail.com

A. A. Staneva
School of Psychology, The University of Queensland, St. Lucia, Australia
e-mail: Alessandra.Bramante@gmail.com

increased maternal anxiety. This can manifest as maternal ambivalence and mother-infant attachment issues which, in turn, may contribute to profound, lifelong implications for maternal and child mental health. In severe cases of strained mother-child bonds, a varied degree of presentations may occur, including maternal abandonment, or in the most troubling instances of rupture between mother and infant: Infanticide. Reflecting on such problematic issues, we suggest ways to navigate distress to avoid these detrimental outcomes and aim to hold society accountable, so mothers are not solely responsible for their sustained psychological health and are supported to provide their infants with the love they require.

Keywords Love · Motherhood · Anxiety · Attachment · Maternal ambivalence · Abandonment · Infanticide · Maternal mental health · Psychological health · The 'ideal feminine' · Women's health

16.1 Introduction

> *"The infant's life depends, to a very great extent, on the good will of others, but most especially, of course, that of the mother. Consequently, it has been the fate of mothers throughout history to appear in strange and distorted forms. They may appear as larger than life or as invisible; as all-powerful and destructive; or as helpless and angelic. Myths of the maternal instinct compete, historically, with myths of a universal infanticidal impulse."*
> ~**Nancy Scheper-Hughes** (1987)

The image of mother together with child is perhaps one of the most sacrosanct throughout history and across cultures. The relationship is one synonymous with adoration, cherishment, gentleness, kindness, nurture, warmth—one which is synonymous with *love*. However, the image of mother and infant has wider societal meaning. It is symbolic of the (re)productive potential of a people, and therefore can signify the guaranteed success of a nation state. Mother and infant together are both the aspiration and the reality of the (re)productive state and to ensure continued progeny, the mother-infant relationship must be harmonious; with the mother providing the environment in which a baby first develops from gametes to foetus and also safe delivery of the infant. Once born, the mother is the primary caregiver responsible for the continued protection of their infant within the world, and also the primary source of nourishment to ensure survival into a healthy adulthood, where they themselves can begin their own (re)productive lifecourse.

This view, though perhaps dated in presentation, remains true in the societal discourse today. Despite increased emancipatory policies, particularly in the Western World, a woman's lifecourse is marked by specific events, which act as rites of passage to womanhood and femininity (Silverio, 2019). These ideologies are created, distributed, and enforced *within*, and *by*, a hegemonic, heteronormative, and phallogocentric society—where men dictate and can quickly change what the new and current 'feminine ideal' is to be; forcing women to adapt, conform, or be outcast and ostracised for going against the new and everchanging norm (de Beauvoir, 1949/2011; Pickard, 2018). However, motherhood is one factor which has consistently been presented as key to the very fabric of the 'feminine ideal' (Nicolson, 2001), with even modern evidence suggesting *"underlying discourses that women are expected 'to marry', 'to carry', 'to bear', and 'to care'..."* (Silverio & Soulsby, 2020; p. 219).

The societal and socio-psychological implications associated with not being a mother are complex (Keizer, Dykstra, & Jansen, 2008; Shapiro, 2014), culturally mediated (Burkett, 2000; Silverio, 2018; Snitow, 1992; Tanturri & Mencarini, 2008), but usually negative (Park, 2002). To actively elect to not pursue motherhood has more severe implications for women in society (Letherby & Williams, 1999). It is often seen as taking a stand against womanhood and the 'feminine ideal', and therefore against the society (Morell, 1994). Often women who refuse to mother are seen to flout their societal (re)productive role and flagrantly disregard their duty to contribute to the next generation of their nation state (O'Brien, 1991), and therefore are often met with an *"organized response"* which in turn codifies childlessness as *"deviant"* (Blackstone & Stewart, 2012; p. 722). The normative lifecourse which includes motherhood has been so ingrained into societies across the globe that even our social story-telling perpetuates the myths of the childless woman, where non-mothers are seen as villainous, vain, and vengeful (Gandolfo, 2005; King, 2015; Mangum, 1999), and therefore any so-called deviation is immediately questioned, assessed in-line with the present societal norm for the 'feminine ideal' and—wherever possible—quashed (Silverio, 2016). These responses are often tacit, but can lead to social exclusion (Carey, Shelley, Graham, & Taket, 2009), stigmatisation (Park, 2002), and othering (Ramsay & Letherby, 2006), which further strain the already cracked identities of these women who *do not, will not,* or *cannot* conform to the normative lifecourse.

To mother, therefore, is to conform to society's desire for survival. To mother, therefore, is to show patriotism and adoration for one's country and people. However, to mother is burdened with the expectation that one must also be invested in the notion of a (re)productive society and is therefore intrinsically required to be invested in one's offspring. Though this statement may appear strong, it mirrors argumentation put forward by previous scholars of women's (re)productive freedoms such as Simone de Beauvoir (1949/2011). What is rarely explored in academic research, is what happens when this investment falters. Though we assume loving one's child is the most natural and innate response, especially as human babies are born so vulnerable; the act of unconditional love can sometimes become a difficult performance and ultimately can result in some very unfortunate outcomes.

This chapter draws upon international literature to frame arguments and provide context to the debates undertaken herein. Though based within Western(ized) countries, the authorship team have experience of cross-cultural issues in maternal (mental) health through the work they have, or are currently, conducting. This work, therefore, may appear embedded within a Western or high-income context, though this does not preclude the theories and argumentation being extrapolated to low- or middle-income (non-Western) settings. We urge readers, however, to err caution when doing so, without first engaging appropriate cultural, politico-social, and religious contextualisation.

This chapter proceeds as follows: First, we unpack conceptualisations of mothering, looking at the *'good and perfect'*, and the *'bad and ugly'*. We then proceed to review debates on anxiety, attachment, and maternal ambivalence, before moving on to consider what we deem are the more severely strained issues relating to mother-infant bonding—those of maternal abandonment and infanticide. In drawing the chapter to a close we suggest ways to negotiate these distressing ruptures between mother and infant, to avoid these unfavourable outcomes. We also question the role of society in propagating and proliferating such harmful discourses of what *'perfect'* versus *'ugly'* mothering is, in order to allow mothers to feel supported in sustaining good psychological health during difficult periods they may face with their infants, and ultimately to give them the resources to feel, and perform the unconditional love of a mother.

16.2 Constructing Motherhood

"One of the great things about being a new mother, especially of a first baby, is the amount of advice that pours in from all and sundry, people who have children themselves and others who have not. It starts in pregnancy and carries on at least until children are of school age. Perhaps this is why mothers tend to 'compare the products' and condition, the number of teeth, or whether it is sitting up or crawling yet, feeling that this kind of thing can show whether they are a good-enough mother." ~**Sheila Kitzinger** (1978)

Child-rearing guides of the past have often assumed mothers, living in heterosexual, nuclear families, will have primary responsibility for childcare, which entails raising healthy, disciplined, well-balanced children (Marshall, 1991). Over the past 40 years, a large body of work pertaining to mothering has been produced across several disciplines and theoretical fields. Recent feminist work in human and social sciences has explored the affective force and embodiment of motherhood (Clement & Waitt, 2017), intensive mothering ideologies (Hays, 1996; Parker & Morrow, 2017; Villalobos, 2014); and the notion of 'becoming' a mother (Holloway, Yamamoto, & Suzuki, 2016). Across the spectrum of mothering and motherhood, lies notions of the *'good mother'* (see Lane, 2014), the *'good-enough mother'* (see Pederson, 2016), the *'bad mother'* (see Kielty, 2008) and even, as we argue, the *'ugly mother'* (see also Haliburn's, 2017 discussion of mother-child incest for instance).

The traditional mother ideology, written about Western human, health, and social sciences, often define a *'good mother'* as full-time, at-home, white, middle-class, and entirely fulfilled through domestic aspiration (Boris, 1994; Hall & Hall, 1979; Johnston & Swanson, 2006; Kenny, 1978; Kinser, 2010). This no longer reflects contemporary understanding, but is more a reflection of the focus of academic research at the time. Further, it is argued that *'good'* mothers should facilitate the provision of a *'good'* childhood (Burman, 2008). Interwoven into debates on *'good'* mothering is the idea of *'intensive'* mothering. According to Hays (1996; p. 122), intensive mothering is a *"child-centred, expert-guided, emotionally absorbing, labour intensive, financially expensive"* ideology in which mothers are primarily responsible for the nurture and development of the child, and in which children's needs take precedence over the needs of their mothers. In other words, the mothering practices prioritise the needs of children through women's self-sacrifice (Baraitser, 2009; Choi, Henshaw, Baker, & Tree, 2005; Johnson, 2015; Kinser, 2010). Furthermore, research has found some women take a managerial approach to motherhood, through the hiring of tutors and scheduling in enrichment activities at great financial and time-resource cost, to ensure their children's future success (see Lareau, 2003). In some intensive mother-child relationships, mothers have further positioned children not only as substitute careers (Meeussen & van Laar, 2018), but also as substitute partners (see Villalobos, 2014). Whilst these forms of intensive mothering may provide ample opportunity to strain the mother-infant relationship, women who perform mothering of this kind, with a great deal of their own self-sacrifice, are deemed by society as positive role models in protecting and promoting their offspring to become the new generation of the (re)productive society.

On the contrary, mothers who do not, or are unable, to meet their children's needs are at risk of being labelled as *'deviant'* or *'bad'* mothers (Miller, 2007; Orton-Johnson, 2017). These are discourses which challenge what has been referred to as the unrealistic and unattainable constructions of how motherhood is portrayed in mainstream cultural narratives and societal discourse (Douglas & Michaels, 2005). In order to understand how the discourse of *'bad and ugly'* mothering is formulated, it is important to expose what constitutes and contributes to difficult mother-infant relationships, where more usually, literature has focused on what is required to be the *'good and perfect'* mother. In compiling this chapter, we address the psycho-social implications of maternal anxiety, attachment issues between mother and infant, maternal ambivalence, abandonment, and finally maternal infanticide. These issues, in isolation are enough to label mother's as *'not good-enough'* and even as *'bad and ugly'*. However we discuss how these factors are intrinsically linked and the very worst outcome between mother and infant—that of a mother abandoning or murdering their child—can be reached after seemingly quite rapid escalation and with very little resistance when performed in the context of a society which scrutinises every aspect of being a woman and individuals' performances of motherhood.

16.3 Anxiety

"Many mothers are excessively anxious about the health and safety of their children... There is some evidence that severe postpartum anxiety has adverse effects on the child, with a high proportion of insecure and disorganised attachments." **~Ian Brockington** (2004)

Maternal anxiety is receiving greater research attention, having been largely neglected previously. Historically obscured by a focus on maternal depression, there is now evidence to suggest anxiety occurs more frequently (Brockington, 2004; Kemp, Bongartz, & Rath, 2003; Muzik et al., 2000; Paul, Downs, Schaefer, Beiler, & Weisman, 2013; Wenzel, Haugen, Jackson, & Brendle, 2005) and independently of depression in the perinatal period (Matthey, Barnett, Howie, & Kavanagh, 2003; Wenzel et al., 2005). Anxiety is an emotion elicited from an impending non-specific threat cue (Cisler, Olatunji, Feldner, & Forsyth, 2010), and has well documented adverse effects for both mother and infant (Glasheen, Richardson, & Fabio, 2010). When experienced in the context of pregnancy and postpartum motherhood, the form and content of anxiety tends to be maternal and infant focused. It is often centred around fear of birth (Cowan & Frodsham, 2015; Sheen & Slade, 2018); bearing a physically handicapped child (Guardino & Schetter, 2014; van den Bergh, 1990); or parenting competence or infant safety and welfare in the postpartum (Fallon, Halford, Bennett, & Harrold, 2016). It is important to note here, the majority of sociological and psychological work concerning maternal anxiety has been conducted in Westernised contexts. Much of the literature, therefore, does not reflect socio-psychological implications *of,* and *for,* anxiety in the developing world, nor the global effects of anxiety on a mother's capacity to love.

Unlike other perinatal mood fluctuations, such as depression, which are largely maladaptive in nature (i.e. only producing negative effects on performance), anxiety can be adaptive (Matthey, 2016). According to the seminal psychological theory: The Yerkes-Dodson Law—performance increases with physiological or mental arousal (i.e. anxiety), but only up to a point (Teigen, 1994), whereby thereafter, or if repeated too frequently, it becomes ineffective or paralysing. In a childbearing context this obviously implicates performance or the ability to mother. Maternal anxiety at optimal levels therefore protects the mother and infant from threats to survival and sustained wellbeing (Matthey, 2016). To this end, anxiety can be seen as a necessary component of a mother's love, allowing mothers to remain vigilant to health in pregnancy, and respond to infant cues of distress in an appropriate, timely manner after birth. While researchers are still unable to predict which combinations of bio-psycho-social risk factors create the 'tipping point', perinatal anxiety is deemed problematic when it consumes a significant proportion of a woman's time, prevents her from fulfilling her mothering role, and interferes with self-care (Matthey, 2016). With increasing recognition of problematic anxiety both in research and societal discourse, it is important to consider how contemporary expectations of motherhood may exacerbate anxiety at an already vulnerable time in the woman's lifecourse.

A fundamental antecedent of anxiety is risk. Risk consciousness is a core feature of modern motherhood and *'good'* mothers are seen as having a moral and social responsibility to manage, minimise, and eliminate risks to their children (Knaak, 2010; Lee, Macvarish, & Bristow, 2010). Despite this, women are also seen as requiring expert guidance in order to effectively manage risk (Hays, 1996; Knaak, 2010). This begins in pregnancy where messages about risks to foetal health and development are increasingly articulated to prospective parents by policy makers and healthcare professionals (Lee et al., 2010). These messages concern modifiable health behaviours such as diet, physical activity, and alcohol use, yet they are often inconsistent (Hoddinott, Craig, Britten, & McInnes, 2012), and there is a lack of robust scientific evidence to support them (Lowe & Lee, 2010). Some researchers have argued this encourages hyper-cautious behaviour among women with regard to the relationship between behaviour in pregnancy and foetal development (Lee et al., 2010) and leads to disproportionate perceptions of risk (Fisher, Hauck, & Fenwick,

2006; Furedi, 2002). The most prominent example of this lies in childbirth itself. As birth in Western societies becomes increasingly medicalised, the knowledge and competency of women regarding childbirth has declined (Fisher et al., 2006). The construction of childbirth as threatening means women have become distrustful of birth and more accepting of medical interventions (Johanson, Newburn, & Macfarlane, 2002). However, medical management of birth further decreases the control experienced by the birthing woman, creates a power imbalance between the woman and healthcare professionals, and creates numerous conditions under which fear and anxiety are generated (Fisher et al., 2006; Johanson et al., 2002).

This climate of fear requiring hyper-vigilance and risk management thus becomes a key driver of anxiety which can push women to adopt a more intensive approach to motherhood in the postnatal period. After birth, women continue to be subject to public debate about how they feed their babies, talk to them, play with them, or discipline them (Kitzinger, 1978; Knaak, 2006; Lee, 2007; Zimmerman, Aberle, Krafchick, & Harvey, 2008). Furthermore, there is evidence women are disproportionately blamed for their children's actions, behaviours, health and well-being (Henderson, Harmon, & Newman, 2016). Thus, women are more prone to micromanage all aspects of motherhood in an effort to protect the child from any possible adverse experiences, whilst simultaneously constantly striving to optimise their child's health and development. According to Furedi (2002), this *'hyper-parenting'* leads to obsessive anxiety over the health and safety of children, and ever-increasing reliance on expertise and advice (see Hays, 1996; Johnson, 2015), which undermine the ability to mother and perpetuate insecurities from mother to child. Although some scholars have critiqued the ideologies of *'intensive'* motherhood for coming from a place of privilege (see Baca Zinn, 1990; Collins, 1994), researchers have identified the omnipresent state of these maternal expectations across most populations (Henderson et al., 2016). Crucially, this means even those women without the resources to parent intensively, still bear the emotional consequences of this pervasive school of thought.

The consequences of these ideologies are far reaching across the motherhood lifecourse. Anxiety in pregnancy has been linked to low birth weight, difficult temperament, and emotional problems in the infant (Zelkowitz & Papageorgiou, 2012), whilst fear of childbirth may prevent or interfere with the progression of labour, increase perceptions of pain, and contribute to the rising medical intervention rate (Fisher et al., 2006). After birth, maternal anxiety can force the well-intended and much desired reciprocal relationship with the infant to a point where it becomes just the opposite. Mothers with anxiety may have difficulty feeling closeness to their child, thus consistently implicating anxiety in the disruption of maternal sensitivity and bonding behaviours (Fallon, Silverio, Halford, Bennett, & Harrold, 2019; Mertesacker, Bade, Haverkock, & Pauli-Pott, 2004), and even more fundamental actions such as breastfeeding (Fallon, Halford, Bennett, & Harrold, 2018). It is clear each of these factors are key tenets of a mother's love, which women with high anxiety in the ante-, peri-, and post-natal periods may struggle to perform.

Perhaps most problematic, there is consistent evidence to support the intergenerational transmission of anxiety. Twin studies have demonstrated the transmission of anxiety from parent to child arises because of an environmental association between parents and their children, independent of genetics (Eley et al., 2015). This is in-line with developmental theories of anxiety which posit children may 'learn' anxiety from their parents through a variety of pathways such as modelling, negative information transmission, and parental behaviours such as over-protection (Stassart, Dardenne, & Etienne, 2017). Given the established effects of child anxiety on health and development (Swan et al., 2018), it seems the desire to minimise risk, achieve parenting perfection, and comply with societal ideals, paradoxically results in poorer performance of what Western society values as acts of maternal love, and has the potential to cause poorer outcomes for children.

16.4 Attachment

> *"...young children, who for any reason are deprived of the continuous care and attention of a mother or mother-substitute, are not only temporarily disturbed by such deprivation, but may in some cases suffer long-term effects which persist."* ~**John Bowlby & Colleagues** (1956)

Attachment theory was formulated to represent a universally applicable account of the bond between mothers and infants based on evolutionary and ethological considerations (Bowlby, 1969). Central to the theory is an infant's reflexive biological need to bond to their mothers in a critical period following birth and the importance of maternal sensitivity to enable secure attachments. Maternal deprivation and ambivalence during this period may lead to dysfunctional infant development across all domains, both emotional, mental, and physical. Some of the main components of maternal sensitivity represent undeniably important aspects of caregiving and the transmission of love from mother to infant. Availability and proximity are crucial to survival in that the infant is kept safe. Prompt responding is also conducive to infant wellbeing in that the infant will get fed when signalling hunger, protected when signalling fear, and cared for when signalling pain (Mesman, van Ijzendoorn, & Sagi-Schwartz, 2016). However, some researchers have argued traditional versions of attachment theory have shifted in emphasis to reflect contemporary ideologies of motherhood, chiming neatly with a social investment model (Thornton, 2011).

While Bowlby asserted a mother should be present and act responsively with her infant, the current emphasis is on a deliberated form of attachment parenting called *'intensive mothering'* (Gillies, Edwards, & Horsley, 2017). This parenting paradigm uses practices in line with tenets of attachment theory such as infant autonomy and security and includes on-demand and extended breastfeeding, infant-led weaning, and co-sleeping, which are all seen as evolutionarily and bio-culturally imperative (Faircloth, 2013). However, whilst on the surface it may appear to be a more loving form of parenting, thus highlighting these mothers as performing *'good'* motherhood, the intensity of the relationship can quickly become toxic as mothers stifle infants' innate drive for exploration and independence; use the bond as a coping mechanism for their own mental strife; or unnecessarily and inappropriately prolong physical aspects of attachment parenting—such as co-sleeping and breastfeeding—to satisfy their own deficit of intimacy. The role of *'good'* mother begins to lapse here whereupon—certainly in Western society—these extended physical encounters are interrogated on the grounds of possible incestuous inclinations (Korbman de Shein & de la Vega Morales, 2006; Schmied & Lupton, 2001; Williams & Finkelhor, 1995), and the psychic and emotional health of both mother and infant are brought under scrutiny (Cortesi, Giannotti, Sebastiani, Vagnoni, & Marioni, 2008; Rath Jr. & Okum, 1995). Furthermore, this form of attachment parenting *"both assumes and reinforces the traditional gender-based division of labour"* (Arendell, 2000; p. 1194), and idealises a parenting relationship in which mothers are *"totally responsive to an infant or child's emotional needs"* (Dear-Healey, 2011; p. 392). In Western culture, this form of attachment parenting is resource exhaustive and feeds into what Hamilton (2018; p. 33) calls yet another *"prescriptive doctrine"* women must follow to achieve *'good'* motherhood.

Attachment has, over the decades, been used as a key marker for assessing love and affection bestowed from a mother unto her infant. Although an inappropriate indicator, those mother-infant dyads with *'secure'* attachment are judged in society as the ultimate *'good'* mothers, whilst those who display *'avoidant'*, *'anxious'*, or *'fearful'* are seen to have failed the motherhood ideal. Modern thinking has shifted on attachment and attachment parenting and the concepts of attachment and love are slowly being disentangled for *"waiting a few minutes before intervening when crying or learning to fall asleep without parents tricking them by feeding or rocking allows for self-soothing"* (Wolke, 2019; p. 1023) does not mean any less love is felt for the infant, but rather this act is allowing the infant to develop their emotional regulation and independence; which they will require later in life, in more complex and, arguably, less safe and secure situations.

16.5 Maternal Ambivalence

> *"Motherhood is tough. Women's ambivalence towards their role and their babies is rarely acknowledged formally... There is little doubt and should be no surprises attached to the fact that this transition is likely to lead to mood and emotional lability."* ~**Paula Nicolson** (1999)

The link between anxiety, attachment issues and maternal ambivalence and split, or the co-existence of both maternal *love* and *hate*, is intricate, yet poignant. It is so, because the expectation for women is that should they have a baby, they will love them unconditionally and selflessly. However, those who are ambivalent to the role of motherhood or indeed, to their baby, are vilified (Murray & Finn, 2012). When levels of maternal distress rise as a result of the inner emotional stretch between polarities of *'perfection'* and idealization and their opposites of *'badness'* and denigration, mothers tend to collapse. Rozsika Parker (a British Psychoanalyst, writer, and a mother herself) explored the concept of maternal ambivalence in her seminal work *Torn in Two: The Experience of Maternal Ambivalence* (1995). In this text, she argues the seesaw of love and hate exists in so many women's feelings towards their children. She introduced the big *'unspeakables'* within the tightly constructed language of motherhood (Staneva & Wigginton, 2018), i.e. all those concepts we usually discursively *tip-toe* around, such as maternal *rage,* maternal *hate,* and maternal *disgust.* Not only is the relentless and unforgivable experience of the co-existence of both love *and* hate not readily accepted in society, it is hardly able to become accepted *within* and *by* the mother herself. Commenting in 2006 on her highly acclaimed, but (perceived as) controversial work, Parker shared the idea that she *"found it incredibly hard to weather being loved so much and blamed so intensely. As a mother of a small child you are endowed with the power to kiss everything better and then blamed bitterly when the pain is not cured".*

Raphael-Leff, another practicing psychotherapist and academic within the field of maternal health, explores the healthy maternal ambivalence and its necessary function. She suggests painful maternal experiences of resentment, persecution, and hatred remain under-explored, particularly within the psycho-therapeutic evidence (Raphael-Leff, 2010). In summary, it can be argued this exclusion or intellectual omission of discussing maternal ambivalence compels mothers to hide conflictual and shameful feelings from healthcare professionals—and from themselves—thus further hampering a mother's ability to perform the *'good and perfect'* mother role due to the manifesting inner psycho-emotional conflict.

Both Parker and Raphael-Leff offer an alternative and particularly useful interpretation of maternal ambivalence, namely as an *'unexpected gift'* of mothering, suggesting—as socially undesirable as it may well be—healthy maternal ambivalence is an inevitable feature of mothering, and a much needed one. Much psycho-sociological and feminist-informed work has focussed on unpacking the denigration of the maternal (O'Reilly, 2004, 2008, 2012; Rich, 1995). Along with Parker's psychoanalytic work, these efforts all form part of the same ongoing mission

> to enable mothers to own the malice, the hostility, the exasperation, the fury and dislike they feel—maybe only for a fleeting moment—towards their own children. If a mother experiences fear and shame in the face of her anger, a cycle can get going in which hatred really does end up outweighing love. The mother feels a bad, unnatural mother, her shame mounts and soon the child is perceived as nothing more than a guilt-inducing, hateful persecutor.

and hence, for her, the absolutely *"crucial difference between bearable and unbearable ambivalence".* (see Benn, 2006).

Only by acknowledging difficult feelings can a mother begin to perceive and experience—creatively—the real relationship she has with her child. Providing safe spaces, where sharing the *'unspeakables'* of *dislike* and *hate*, and hence converting them into mainstream *'speakables'* and valid characters in the maternal language, is a much-needed work for not only health professionals and academics, but also mainstream psychology, theory, and practice (see Nicolson, 1999, 2001). In doing so, it can be argued, these conversations can begin to change the pejorative societal discourses about *'failing'* mothers and *'not quite good-enough'* performances of motherhood, and thus change the perceptions of what the portrayals of motherhood may look like—from the *'good'* to the *'bad'*. When these portrayals become mainstream, we as a society can become more accepting of locating the cause of less desirable maternal actions to outside of the mother's direct control and realise it is down to society to help resolve the experience of maternal split, and not denigrate mothers for their experience of it.

16.6 Abandonment

> ...*it is part of a mother's relationship to her child to engage with that child's absolute corporeal uniqueness. It cannot be denied or avoided.* ~**Gillian Rose** (2003)

One of the key debates in the mothering and motherhood literature concerns abandonment. Literature on this topic is varied, including abortion (Abrams, 2015); surrogacy (Watson, 2016); denial of pregnancy and newborn abandonment (Lee, Li, Kwong, & So, 2006); and adoption at birth (Bonnet, 1993). The common thread amongst these types of abandonment, superficially, is that women who abandon their children are *'bad'*, even *'unnatural'*, going against Western culture's belief that women should love their children instinctively and selflessly. However, looking deeper into these different types of abandonment, the distinction between a *'good'* and *'bad'* mother becomes increasingly muddied.

To begin with abortion, which here we mean to be early in the gestation and elective, i.e. due to circumstances decided upon by and for the mother and not in relation to the foetus or foetal health. There has long been a stigma surrounding abortion, which to this day continues as it is seen as an abandonment of the motherhood role and thus the normative lifecourse of a woman. For some, the belief system surrounding abortion exists such that only a *'bad'* mother could reject their maternal role and abandon the life their child could have had (see Abrams, 2015). Aside from early elective abortion, the termination of a pregnancy due to foetal abnormality, has attracted some similar and some distinct social stigmatisation. Abrams (2015) notes how a pregnant woman choosing any form of termination of a pregnancy embodies the archetype of the *'bad'* mother by *'abandoning'* her unborn child. However, there are many reasons why women may terminate a pregnancy, and many do not relate to the apparently selfish desire a woman may have to live a childless life of untainted freedom. One such reason is medical, for instance if there is a genetic or structural anomaly, abnormality, or a non-viable foetus (Kersting et al., 2009). Here women are again viewed through two separate lenses—the first where they are constructed as *'good'* women who are only wanting to contribute healthy offspring to the (re)productive society, and secondly, as *'bad'* mothers who have abandoned their disabled offspring and failed to show the love of a mother to their foetus due to its propensity to be disabled. This second, more negative lens is often not felt as harshly by women as the narrative of a disabled foetus (and therefore future disabled offspring and disabled member of the (re) productive society) may work to recuperate a narrative of a *'good and moral'* mother for as McKinney (2019) reminds us; Western society often frames disabled lives as *unliveable, undesirable,* and potentially, *unlovable.*

Surrogacy is another area in which the *'good'* and the *'bad'* of motherhood discourses intertwine; for it can be questioned whether the *'good mother'* is the one who longs so much to have a child of her own, that she pays another woman to carry it or whether it is the *'bad mother'* who acts as the surrogate mother and who carries a child for nine months before abandoning it to a new mother who did not carry it. Considering surrogacy as *'womb rentals'* and *'baby-selling',* Watson (2016) questions whether the act undermines the human dignity and rights of both the surrogate mother and the child. Concerns also exist relating to how the surrogate mother, considering the assumption of maternal desire for all women, will love and wish to keep the baby as her own. This has been played out in social story telling across the Western world, with recent cases in the UK even granting a surrogate mother the right to keep the newborn (see Collins, 2011). The act of the surrogate mother keeping the baby arguably leads to involuntary abandonment of the prospect of motherhood for the infertile or non-carrying mother—whereby it is possible to accept both women showed unconditional love for the child with the prospective mother loving so much she asked for a surrogate to ensure the safe gestation of the infant, but the surrogate loving so much she could not abandon the infant after labour.

The topic of adoption is, too, a contested terrain in respect of notions of *'good'* or *'bad'* mothering (Lee et al., 2006). Whilst some discuss the *'victimisation'* of a newborn child through association of unwanted motherhood, others maintain the choice of adoption is a *"unique maternal act"* characterised by protection, opportunity, and love (Bonnet, 1993; p. 509). This perspective refutes use of the word *abandonment,* for this implies a denial of the positive motivations behind putting a child forward for adoption. Abbey (2013; p. XVIII) writing on the topic of 'unbecoming mothers' elucidates this point: *"...a mother without her children does not mean that the children are without their mother".* This notion maintains that, most often, a mother's actions to leave her child are informed by love, rather than personal pleasure. Here, the dichotomy of types of mother—those who are *'bad'* and give their baby up for adoption, and those who are *'good'* and adopt the *'abandoned'* child is blurred, as for many women, giving a child up for adoption is an agonising decision which leaves them *"bereft and traumatized"* throughout their lives (Greenway, 2016; p. 154).

Contrastingly, another form of perceived child abandonment is voluntary childlessness (see Bram, 1984; Shapiro, 2014). Voluntary childlessness is seen as flouting the social role a woman—certainly in Western society—should oblige, which is one of contributing to the (re)productive society. To not produce offspring is to abandon not only the role of 'mother', but to abandon the notion of being womanly, whilst simultaneously being a destructive citizen in the (re)productive cycle of the society. Though not as stigmatized as their counterparts who make an active choice to *'opt out'* of motherhood, women who do not have children due to circumstance are equally subjected to societal scrutiny for not fulfilling the 'feminine ideal' and thus abandoning motherhood (Silverio & Soulsby, 2020). Debates centre on the alien nature of childless women, believing they do not possess the innate desire to love a child. Instead, these *'non-mothers'* are characterised as longing freedom and liberation (Peterson, 2015). Research tells that women who declare themselves as voluntarily childless face disbelief, disregard, and even disgrace from others for their desires to be without children, all of which may have detrimental health and social outcomes to the ageing childless woman (Cwikel, Gramotnev, & Lee, 2006; Gillespie, 2000; Silverio & Soulsby, 2020). This is because women who choose voluntary childlessness are seen to go against the traditional construction of feminine identity which has long been synonymous with motherhood and mothering (Gillespie, 1999; Silverio, 2019). In more recent debates, Sappleton (2018) explores how women who are *'child-free by choice'* discuss the joys of *'otherhood'* as opposed to motherhood, whilst Smith (2018; p. 137) conceptualises these women as *"feisty and free"*.

In contrast to the other forms of so-called *'abandonment'*, less often framed in this way within the literature is the death of a mother; which carries the trademark emotional bearings of loss and grief. When a child is *'abandoned'* by their mother through no choice of her own—for instance a tragic accident or death from a terminal illness—the language surrounding the mother in social discourse and perpetuated by the media is often positively framed, for instance *"she loved her children unconditionally"* and *"she was a doting mother"*. Interestingly, just like other types of abandonment, the death of a mother is not free from stigma. Cain and LaFreniere (2015) discuss how children affected by parental bereavement have experienced taunting about their loss. This provides further evidence for the construct of motherhood love being intrinsically linked to the role of women in society, which in turn is embedded within the notion of a (re)productive state. To abandon the role of motherhood signals a twofold statement: First that the woman is incapable of loving their offspring; and second they have slighted the societal feminine role. Together these are viewed as active, destructive acts taken by the (childless) woman against the (re)productive society.

16.7 Infanticide

> *...the perpetrator of this act is often a victim too, and that recognition makes for a more paradoxical response. On the one hand is the image of a defenceless infant... On the other is the image of a mother, insane, isolated and imprisoned for a crime unthinkable to many.*
> ~**Margaret G. Spinelli** (2003)

Although rare, the most significant rupture in the mother-infant relationship is when the mother kills her child. This has been reported as an extreme version of maternal abandonment (Bloch, 1988), but what we would argue is better termed *'vexatious abandonment'* as the abandonment is achieved by murder. The rates of infanticide are said to fluctuate around approximately two girls and three boys (aged between birth and 17 years) per 100,000 of the population (Hatters Friedman & Resnick, 2007; Scott, 1973). For the purposes of this discussion, infanticide is being used as a blanket term to cover all infant murder caused by the parents, but can in fact be sub-categorized into neonaticide (where the infant is less than 24 hours old) and filicide (where the infant is between one and 17 years old). As a parental act, infanticide has been described for centuries across many different cultures and occurs in every socio-economic stratum around the world (McKee & Shea, 1998). Though complex, the law throughout the world is clear—infanticide is a crime, and one which can elicit emotions of sorrow, anger, and horror whilst arousing disappointment and a deep collective anguish from the (re)productive society in which the murder has taken place (Sieff, 2019; Spinelli, 2003). For this reason, when these acts occur, the societal view is often one positioning the mother as *'crazy', 'insane',* or at the very least, *'mentally disturbed'*. Even though this may be common opinion amongst society, considering these acts exclusively as expressions of madness, does not necessarily mean these behaviours have been influenced by underlying mental illness, disorders, or disease. In fact, there are circumstances in which the family environment and associated familial dynamics become pathological, leading to the occurrence of physical violence, mental or emotional torment, and/or sexual abuse—each of which, in the most severe cases, have the propensity to predispose murder.

This crime of infanticide *"is a subject both compelling and repulsive"* as the victim is innocent, but the perpetrator may also be a victim (Spinelli, 2003; p. XV). Infanticide committed soon after birth is psychologically comparable to *in vivo* late-term abortion. Neonaticides are often committed by poor, relatively young, single, sometimes drug and/or alcohol dependent women who attempt to prevent an emotional bond forming between the killer/mother and the killed/infant (Klier, Amon, Putkonen, Arias, and Weizmann-Henelius, 2019; Klier, Fisher, Chandra, and Spinelli, 2019). Denial of the pregnancy and of assuming the role of motherhood may have manifested early in gestation. These women often receive no antenatal or perinatal care, and by delivering the baby alone there is no-one available to prevent the killing of the neonate so soon after delivery. Frequently, this desire to prevent the formation of an emotional bond comes after a long period (through pregnancy) of the mother having feelings of alienation or hostility toward the as yet unborn child. These emotions manifest as the growing foetus is seen as an object feeding off a part of her body, a feeling which fails to be replaced by the development of a so-called *'maternal instinct'*. From a socio-psychological point of view, infanticide in the first year of life is different. In fact, the child in these instances is killed after the emotional bond and affective mother-infant relationship has developed. Usually, these cases are characterized by negative feelings towards the infant and/or struggles with this new life of co-existence.

Several investigators studying the reasons for infanticide have developed categories of the crime to aid in understanding the characteristics of this heterogeneous phenomenon. The first extensive reports of infanticidal parents were by Resnick (1969, 1970) who reviewed numerous filicide and neonaticide case reports from the international literature and introduced the idea of five categories of reasoning behind infanticidal acts by parents: Altruistic, psychotic, accidental, spousal revenge, and un-wanted child. More recent research (see Brockington, 2017; Spinelli, 2004;

Ussher, 2006) suggests the level of mothers and fathers committing infanticide is more equal today than previously, but that infanticidal women may also be driven by their clinical situation, or more iatrogenic sources of impulse to kill.

Often, parents who kill their children have diagnosed psychosis or major depression, with many reports of a high incidences of psychiatric symptomatology (Bourget & Bradford, 1990; Bourget, Grace, & Whitehurst, 2007; Resnick, 1969, 1970). In the late 1970s, d'Orbán studied women who were admitted for psychiatric observation in the hospital ward of a prison for acts of infanticide (d'Orbán, 1979). The findings suggested associations between maternal infanticide and the presence of certain stressors in the mother's life, such as being a survivor of domestic violence, early parental separation, and ongoing suicidality. In cases of neonaticide, d'Orbán confirmed an association with unmarried status and younger maternal age, though reported a lack of association with depression or psychosis.

Infanticidal mothers typically kill young children (of less than a year of age) and are as likely to kill boys as girls; most often using methods of beating or suffocation (Ussher, 2006). Hatters Friedman, Horwitz, and Resnick (2005); see also Hatters Friedman & Resnick, (2007) found maternal motives for filicide were predominantly altruistic (*'misguided love'*) or acutely psychotic (*'without rational motive'*), and that most mothers had experienced considerable developmental stressors, such as the death of their own mothers or incestuous abuse. Lack of social and marital support, economic difficulties, family stress, young maternal age, immaturity, and unrealistic expectations of motherhood have also been found to cause psychosocial stress. Studies from across the world (see Amon, Putkonen, Weizmann-Henelius, Arias, & Klier, 2019; Chandra, Venkatasubramanian, & Thomas, 2002; Klier, Amon, Putkonen, Arias, and Weizmann-Henelius, 2019; Klier, Fisher, Chandra, and Spinelli, 2019; Razali, Fisher, & Kirkman, 2019) of severely mentally ill postpartum women have found infanticidal ideation and infanticidal behaviours are common. Infanticidal behaviour was associated with female gender of the infant, adverse maternal reaction to separation from the infant, and psychotic ideas relating to the infant.

Most researchers agree mental illness is an important mediating factor in infanticide and filicide. Opinion, however, is divided on the presence of profound mental illness in women who commit neonaticide. Some believe such women have no discernible mental disorders (e.g. Bloch, 1988; Bourget & Bradford, 1990), while others report a significant proportion with remarkable symptoms of mental illness (e.g. Hatters Friedman et al., 2005; Hatters Friedman and Resnick, 2007; Resnick, 1969, 1970). Infanticidal women do not fit a homogenous profile, though they have in common the act of killing their own offspring. As discussed above, the rupture between mother and infant is not always due to a lack of love for their infant, but rather a complex inter-woven situation whereby the mother may be simply unable to love the child she once carried and bore.

16.8 Conclusions

> *"Many mothers and infants are mutually gratified through their relationship, and many mothers enjoy taking care of their infants. Still, when we say that the mother-infant relationship has been exclusive, mutual, and special, this means different things from the child's point of view than from the mother's".* ~**Nancy Chodorow** (1978)

Throughout this chapter we have spoken about what happens when a mother's love is not enough. By this we mean that the simple act of loving one's child no longer fulfils the societal expectation of what maternal love should entail. We have spoken in detail about how the *'good and perfect'* and the *'bad and ugly'* mother discourses are constructed and about the pressure these discourses place on new mothers to conform, irrespective of mental or physical capability. For women, motherhood has become an act of raising the next generation of the (re)productive society—it is no longer agentic nor autonomous—it is an expectation of the 'feminine ideal' (see Guttman, 1983; Silverio, 2019). Women are increasingly maligned for not embracing the role of motherhood as *overtly* displaying love for the infant is now a mandatory requirement of modern motherhood.

The discussion above has focused in detail on anxiety—something which has long been neglected in the maternal health literature and hence a sizeable space has been afforded to it here. This may have seemed in contrast to the following two sections on attachment and maternal ambivalence, though the reasons for each of these being smaller differ. Attachment has been written about extensively over the past few decades—the argumentation is less debated, and the position now somewhat lacks criticality due to the comprehensive empirical investigations and philosophical theorisations—hence here it is afforded some, but not central importance. On the contrary, little has been written about maternal ambivalence, and so what is documented above is a summarised *précis* of the available literature. The final two sections—on abandonment and infanticide—are trickier concepts to debate critically, when attempting to remain sensitive. These two important factors are demonstrable of the very worst which can happen when the act of love between mother and child fails, and we have documented the research and theory to support our critical perspectives on both outcomes. Perhaps most notable might be what is missing from this chapter, rather than what is present. Those with a keen eye and familiar to the field of maternal health will certainly have observed the omission of maternal depression or what Ussher (2006; p. 96) calls *"The curse of motherhood"*. Though depression in mothers has been noted as important for both maternal and infant health, it has often clouded other, distinct maternal health issues (e.g. anxiety; psychoses)—thus here it has been excluded from the debate.

A mother's love has the potential to provide the best possible foundation for an infant's emotional, physical, psychological, and social development. However, as documented here above, the conditions under which a woman is having to *perform* the act of loving their infant can strain the mother-infant relationship to points of rupture. The concept of a mother's love for an infant has changed over time and has been stretched to new and distorted—sometimes unrecognizable—shapes and forms. From once being about protection, nourishment, and nurturance, a mother's love is still required to provide all those factors, plus more. Furthermore, the responsibility for making an infant the best possible form to join the (re)productive society falls almost exclusively on the mother, who may not have wanted to take on the maternal role; or is ambivalent or resentful towards their child because of it. As Nicolson (2001; p. 180) states: *"The ultimate myth that motherhood is natural and desirable means that women take on its burden unconditionally."* and in doing so women accept the must live through the 'paradox of sacrifice' and accept motherhood as *"woman's greatest achievement and the means to fulfilling her femininity"* and *"also the potential source of her emotional destruction."* (Nicolson, 2001; p. 107).

Women can of course reject the 'maternal role' and deny the 'feminine ideal' (Bartlett, 1995), but the pressure to conform in our modern-day (re)productive society is often overwhelmingly strong (Silverio, 2019). Therefore, when women do go on to have (unwanted) children resentment can manifest as regret (Donath, 2015), but perhaps more sadly, can actively demonstrate a struggle to love one's infant in the context of performing *'perfect'* motherhood (see Røseth, Bongaardt, Lyberg, Sommerseth, & Dahl, 2018). Where these struggles become too great, we see anxiety build to a point of being maladaptive, attachment between mother and infant become disordered, and a disengagement from the infant by the mother due to her ambivalence towards it and her role. In the worst of these scenarios, infants are abandoned or killed by their mothers, leaving the mother both a *victim* and a *villain* within her society, though we would argue also a victim *of* her society.

What we hoped to have achieved by drawing upon and distilling literature on the *'dark side of motherhood'* from the past century is show how the act of loving one's infant can so easily be stretched and deformed by the changing societal narratives about how a woman, and more importantly, how a mother should look and act. If we can request for any change to come from this chapter, it would be to hold society accountable for perpetuating the demand for a (re)productive society, and begin to repair the fragile, fractured, and fragmented identities of women who become mothers. In doing so, we must re-negotiate the role of motherhood by reducing the expectation of being *'good and perfect'* all the time, and openly discuss how motherhood can be *'bad and ugly'*. Ultimately, women should be free to navigate womanhood and motherhood as they please, whilst being afforded the support of their society to ensure and sustain good mental health and psychological wellbeing, whether they choose to *become* 'Mother', or not.

References

Abbey, S. (2013). Foreword. In D. L. Gustafson (Ed.), *Unbecoming mothers: The social production of maternal absence* (pp. XVII–XVIII). New York: Routledge.

Abrams, P. (2015). The bad mother: Stigma, abortion and surrogacy. *The Journal of Law, Medicine and Ethics, 43*(2), 179–191.

Amon, S., Putkonen, H., Weizmann-Henelius, G., Arias, P. F., & Klier, C. M. (2019). Gender differences in legal outcomes of filicide in Austria and Finland. *Archives of Women's Mental Health, 22*(1), 165–172.

Arendell, T. (2000). Conceiving and investigating motherhood: The decade's scholarship. *Journal of Marriage and Family, 62*(4), 1192–1207.

Baca Zinn, M. (1990). Family, feminism, and race in America. *Gender & Society, 4*(1), 68–82.

Baraitser, L. (2009). *Maternal encounters: The ethics of interruption*. London: Routledge.

Bartlett, J. (1995). *Will you be mother? Women who choose to say no*. New York: New York University Press.

Benn, M. (2006, October 28). Deep maternal alienation. *The Guardian*. Retrieved from https://www.theguardian.com/uk

Blackstone, A., & Stewart, M. D. (2012). Choosing to be childfree: Research on the decision not to parent. *Sociology Compass, 6*(9), 718–727.

Bloch, H. (1988). Abandonment, infanticide, and filicide: An overview of inhumanity to children. *American Journal of Diseases of Children, 142*(10), 1058–1060.

Bonnet, C. (1993). Adoption at birth: Prevention against abandonment or neonaticide. *Child Abuse & Neglect, 17*(4), 501–513.

Boris, E. (1994). Mothers are not workers: Homework regulation and the construction of motherhood, 1948-1953. In E. N. Glenn, G. Chang, & L. Forcey (Eds.), *Mothering: Ideology, experience and agency* (pp. 161–180). New York: Routledge.

Bourget, D., & Bradford, J. M. (1990). Homicidal parents. *The Canadian Journal of Psychiatry, 35*(3), 233–238.

Bourget, D., Grace, J., & Whitehurst, L. (2007). A review of maternal and paternal filicide. *The Journal of the American Academy of Psychiatry and the Law, 35*(1), 74–82.

Bowlby, J. (1969). *Attachment and loss* (Vol. 1: Attachment). New York: Basic Books.

Bowlby, J., Ainsworth, M., Boston, M., & Rosenbluth, D. (1956). The effects of mother-child separation: A follow-up study. *British Journal of Medical Psychology, 29*(3–4), 211–247.

Bram, S. (1984). Voluntarily childless women: Traditional or nontraditional? *Sex Roles, 10*(3–4), 195–206.

Brockington, I. (2004). Postpartum psychiatric disorders. *The Lancet, 363*(9405), 303–310.

Brockington, I. (2017). Suicide and filicide in postpartum psychosis. *Archives of Women's Mental Health, 20*(1), 63–69.

Burkett, E. (2000). *The baby boon: How family-friendly America cheats the childless*. New York: Free Press.

Burman, E. (2008). Beyond 'women vs. children' or 'women and children': Engendering childhood and reformulating motherhood. *The International Journal of Children's Rights, 16*(2), 177–194.

Cain, A. C., & LaFreniere, L. S. (2015). The taunting of parentally bereaved children: An exploratory study. *Death Studies, 39*(4), 219–225.

Carey, G. E., Shelley, J. M., Graham, M. W., & Taket, A. (2009). Discourse, power and exclusion: The experiences of childless women. In A. Taket, B. R. Crisp, A. Neill, G. Lamaro, M. Graham, & S. Barter-Godfrey (Eds.), *Theorizing social exclusion* (pp. 127–133). New York: Routledge.

Chandra, P. S., Venkatasubramanian, G., & Thomas, T. (2002). Infanticidal ideas and infanticidal behavior in Indian women with severe postpartum psychiatric disorders. *The Journal of Nervous and Mental Disease, 190*(7), 457–461.

Chodorow, N. (1978). *The reproduction of mothering: Psychoanalysis and the sociology of gender*. Berkeley: University of California Press.

Choi, P., Henshaw, C., Baker, S., & Tree, J. (2005). Supermum, superwife, supereverything: Performing femininity in the transition to motherhood. *Journal of Reproductive and Infant Psychology, 23*(2), 167–180.

Cisler, J. M., Olatunji, B. O., Feldner, M. T., & Forsyth, J. P. (2010). Emotion regulation and the anxiety disorders. *Journal of Psychopathology and Behavioral Assessment, 32*(1), 68–82.

Clement, S., & Waitt, G. (2017). Walking, mothering and care: A sensory ethnography of journeying on-foot with children in Wollongong, Australia. *Gender, Place & Culture, 24*(8), 1185–1203.

Collins, P. H. (1994). Shifting the center: Race, class and feminist theorizing about motherhood. In E. Glenn, G. Chang, & L. Forcey (Eds.), *Mothering: Ideology, experience, and agency* (pp. 45–65). New York: Routledge.

Collins, N. (2011, January 22). Surrogate mother given right to keep baby. *The Telegraph*. Retrieved from https://www.telegraph.co.uk/

Cortesi, F., Giannotti, F., Sebastiani, T., Vagnoni, C., & Marioni, P. (2008). Cosleeping versus solitary sleeping in children with bedtime problems: Child emotional problems and parental distress. *Behavioral Sleep Medicine, 6*(2), 89–105.

Cowan, F., & Frodsham, L. (2015). Management of common disorders in psychosexual medicine. *The Obstetrician & Gynaecologist, 17*(1), 47–53.

Cwikel, J., Gramotnev, H., & Lee, C. (2006). Never-married childless women in Australia: Health and social circumstances in older age. *Social Science & Medicine, 62*(8), 1991–2001.

d'Orbán, P. T. (1979). Women who kill their children. *The British Journal of Psychiatry, 134*(6), 560–571.

de Beauvoir, S. (2011). *The second sex* (C. Borde & S. Malovany-Chevallier, trans.). London: Random House Company (Original work published 1949).

Dear-Healey, S. (2011). Attachment parenting international: Nurturing generations of mothers, children and families. In A. O'Reilly (Ed.), *The 21st century motherhood movement: Mothers speak out on why we need to change the world and how to do it* (pp. 383–393). Ontario, Canada: Demeter Press.

Donath, O. (2015). Regretting motherhood: A sociopolitical analysis. *Signs: Journal of Women in Culture and Society, 40*(2), 343–367.

Douglas, S., & Michaels, M. (2005). *The mommy myth: The idealization of motherhood and how it has undermined all women*. New York: Simon & Schuster.

Eley, T. C., McAdams, T. A., Rijsdijk, F. V., Lichtenstein, P., Narusyte, J., Reiss, D., et al. (2015). The intergenerational transmission of anxiety: A children-of-twins study. *The American Journal of Psychiatry, 172*(7), 630–637.

Faircloth, C. (2013). *Militant lactivism?: Attachment parenting and intensive motherhood in the UK and France*. New York: Berghahn Books.

Fallon, V., Halford, J. C. G., Bennett, K. M., & Harrold, J. A. (2016). The postpartum specific anxiety scale: Development and preliminary validation. *Archives of Women's Mental Health, 19*(6), 1079–1090.

Fallon, V., Halford, J. C. G., Bennett, K. M., & Harrold, J. A. (2018). Postpartum-specific anxiety as a predictor of infant-feeding outcomes and perceptions of infant-feeding behaviours: New evidence for childbearing specific measures of mood. *Archives of Women's Mental Health, 21*(2), 181–191.

Fallon, V., Silverio, S. A., Halford, J. C. G., Bennett, K., & Harrold, J. (2019). Postpartum-specific anxiety and maternal bonding: Further evidence to support the use of childbearing-specific tools. *Journal of Reproductive and Infant Psychology*.

Fisher, C., Hauck, Y., & Fenwick, J. (2006). How social context impacts on women's fears of childbirth: A Western Australian example. *Social Science & Medicine, 63*(1), 64–75.

Furedi, F. (2002). *Culture of fear: Risk taking and the morality of low expectation*. New York: Continuum International Publishing Group Ltd..

Gandolfo, E. (2005). A lesser woman? Fictional representations of the childless woman. In A. O'Reilly, M. Porter, & P. Short (Eds.), *Motherhood: Power & oppression* (pp. 111–123). Toronto, Canada: Women's Press.

Gillespie, R. (1999). Voluntary childlessness in the United Kingdom. *Reproductive Health Matters, 7*(13), 43–53.

Gillespie, R. (2000). When no means no: Disbelief, disregard and deviance as discourses of voluntary childlessness. *Women's Studies International Forum, 23*(2), 223–234.

Gillies, V., Edwards, R., & Horsley, N. (2017). *Challenging the politics of early intervention: Who's 'saving' children and why*. Bristol: Policy Press.

Glasheen, C., Richardson, G. A., & Fabio, A. (2010). A systematic review of the effects of postnatal maternal anxiety on children. *Archives of Women's Mental Health, 13*(1), 61–74.

Greenway, K. (2016). The hierarchy of motherhood in adoption: Literary narratives of kinship, maternal desire, and precarity. *Journal of the Motherhood Initiative for Research and Community Involvement, 7*(1), 147–162.

Guardino, C. M., & Schetter, C. D. (2014). Understanding pregnancy anxiety: Concepts, correlates and consequences. *Zero to Three, 34*(4), 12–21.

Guttman, H. A. (1983). Autonomy and motherhood. *Psychiatry, 46*(3), 230–235.

Haliburn, J. (2017). Mother-child incest, psychosis, and the dynamics of relatedness. *Journal of Trauma and Dissociation, 18*(3), 409–426.

Hall, F. S., & Hall, D. T. (1979). *The two-career couple*. Menlo Park: Addison-Wesley Publishing Company.

Hamilton, P. (2018). The 'good' attached mother: An analysis of postmaternal and postracial thinking in birth and breastfeeding policy in neoliberal Britain. In M. Fannin & M. Perrier (Eds.), *Refiguring the postmaternal: Feminist responses to the forgetting of motherhood* (pp. 28–49). Abingdon: Routledge.

Hatters Friedman, S., Horwitz, S. M., & Resnick, P. J. (2005). Child murder by mothers: A critical analysis of the current state of knowledge and a research agenda. *American Journal of Psychiatry, 162*(9), 1578–1587.

Hatters Friedman, S., & Resnick, P. J. (2007). Child murder by mothers: Patterns and prevention. *World Psychiatry, 6*(3), 137–141.

Hays, S. (1996). *The cultural contradictions of motherhood*. New Haven: Yale University Press.

Henderson, A., Harmon, S., & Newman, H. (2016). The price mothers pay, even when they are not buying it: Mental health consequences of idealized motherhood. *Sex Roles, 74*(11–12), 512–526.

Hoddinott, P., Craig, L. C. A., Britten, J., & McInnes, R. J. (2012). A serial qualitative interview study of infant feeding experiences: Idealism meets realism. *BMJ Open, 2*(504), 1–14.

Holloway, S. D., Yamamoto, Y., & Suzuki, S. (2016). What is a good mother? Historical shifts, divergent models in urban Japan. In T. Thelen & H. Haukanes (Eds.), *Parenting after the century of the child: Travelling ideals, institutional negotiations and individual responses* (pp. 35–56). Abingdon: Routledge.

Johanson, R., Newburn, M., & Macfarlane, A. (2002). Has the medicalisation of childbirth gone too far? *The BMJ, 324*(7342), 892–895.

Johnson, S. A. (2015). 'Intimate mothering publics': Comparing face-to-face support groups and internet use for women seeking information and advice in the transition to first-time motherhood. *Culture, Health and Sexuality, 17*(2), 237–251.

Johnston, D. D., & Swanson, D. H. (2006). Constructing the "good mother": The experience of mothering ideologies by work status. *Sex Roles, 54*(7–8), 509–519.

Keizer, R., Dykstra, P. A., & Jansen, M. D. (2008). Pathways into childlessness: Evidence of gendered life course dynamics. *Journal of Biosocial Science, 40*(6), 863–878.

Kemp, B., Bongartz, K., & Rath, W. (2003). Psychic disturbances in the postpartum period: An increasing problem? *Zeitschrift fur Geburtshilfe und Neonatologie, 207*(5), 159-165.

Kenny, M. (1978). *Woman x two: How to cope with a double life*. Feltham: The Hamlyn Publishing Group.

Kersting, A., Kroker, K., Steinhard, J., Hoernig-Franz, I., Wesselmann, U., Luedorff, K., et al. (2009). Psychological impact on women after second and third trimester termination of pregnancy due to fetal anomalies versus women after preterm birth – A 14-month follow up study. *Archives of Women's Mental Health, 12*(4), 193.

Kielty, S. (2008). Working hard to resist a "bad mother" label: Narratives of non-resident motherhood. *Qualitative Social Work, 7*(3), 363–379.

King, R. (2015). A regiment of monstrous women: Female horror archetypes and life history theory. *Evolutionary Behavioral Sciences, 9*(3), 170–185.

Kinser, A. E. (2010). *Motherhood and feminism*. Berkeley: Seal Press.

Kitzinger, S. (1978). *Women as mothers*. Glasgow: Fontana Books.

Klier, C. M., Amon, S., Putkonen, H., Arias, P. F., & Weizmann-Henelius, G. (2019). Repeated neonaticide: Differences and similarities to single neonaticide events. *Archives of Women's Mental Health, 22*(1), 159–164.

Klier, C. M., Fisher, J., Chandra, P. S., & Spinelli, M. (2019). Filicide research in the twenty-first century. *Archives of Women's Mental Health, 22*(1), 135–137.

Knaak, S. J. (2006). The problem with breastfeeding discourse. *Canadian Journal of Public Health, 97*(5), 412–414.

Knaak, S. J. (2010). Contextualising risk, constructing choice: Breastfeeding and good mothering in risk society. *Health, Risk & Society, 12*(4), 345–355.

Korbman de Shein, R., & de la Vega Morales, R. I. (2006). La curiosidad sexual infantil y el dormir con los padres. *Acta Pediátrica de México, 27*(5), 259–264.

Lane, R. (2014). Healthy discretion? Breastfeeding and the mutual maintenance of motherhood and public space. *Gender, Place & Culture, 21*(2), 195–210.

Lareau, A. (2003). *Unequal childhoods: Class, race, and family life*. Berkeley: University of California Press.

Lee, E. (2007). Health, morality, and infant feeding: British mothers' experiences of formula milk use in the early weeks. *Sociology of Health and Illness, 29*(7), 1075–1090.

Lee, A. C. W., Li, C. H., Kwong, N. S., & So, K. T. (2006). Neonaticide, newborn abandonment, and denial of pregnancy – Newborn victimisation associated with unwanted motherhood. Medical practice. *Hong Kong Medical Journal, 12*(1), 61–64.

Lee, E., Macvarish, J., & Bristow, J. (2010). Risk, health and parenting culture. *Health, Risk and Society, 12*(4), 293–300.

Letherby, G., & Williams, C. (1999). Non-motherhood: Ambivalent autobiographies. *Feminist Studies, 25*(3), 719–728.

Lowe, P. K., & Lee, E. J. (2010). Advocating alcohol abstinence to pregnant women: Some observations about British policy. *Health, Risk and Society, 12*(4), 301–311.

Mangum, T. (1999). Little women: The ageing female character in nineteenth-century British children's literature. In K. Woodward (Ed.), *Figuring age: Women, bodies, generations* (pp. 59–87). Indiana: Indiana University Press.

Marshall, H. (1991). The social construction of motherhood: An analysis of childcare and parenting manuals. In A. Phoenix, A. Woollett, & E. Lloyd (Eds.), *Motherhood: Meanings, practices and ideologies* (pp. 66–85). London: Sage.

Matthey, S. (2016). Anxiety and stress during pregnancy and the postpartum period. In A. Wenzel (Ed.), *The Oxford handbook of perinatal psychology* (pp. 132–149). Oxford: Oxford University Press.

Matthey, S., Barnett, B., Howie, P., & Kavanagh, D. J. (2003). Diagnosing postpartum depression in mothers and fathers: Whatever happened to anxiety? *Journal of Affective Disorders, 74*(2), 139–147.

McKee, G. R., & Shea, S. J. (1998). Maternal filicide: A cross-national comparison. *Journal of Clinical Psychology, 54*(5), 679–687.

McKinney, C. (2019). A good abortion is a tragic abortion: Fit motherhood and disability stigma. *Hypatia, 34*(2), 266–285.

Meeussen, L., & van Laar, C. (2018). Feeling pressure to be a perfect mother relates to parental burnout and career ambitions. *Frontiers in Psychology, 9*(2113), 1–13.

Mertesacker, B., Bade, U., Haverkock, A., & Pauli-Pott, U. (2004). Predicting maternal reactivity/sensitivity: The role of infant emotionality, maternal depressiveness/anxiety, and social support. *Infant Mental Health Journal, 25*(1), 47–61.

Mesman, J., van Ijzendoorn, M. H., & Sagi-Schwartz, A. (2016). Cross-cultural patterns of attachment: Universal and contextual dimensions. In J. Cassidy & P. R. Shaver (Eds.),

Handbook of attachment: Theory, research, and clinical applications (3rd ed., pp. 852–877). New York: The Guilford Press.

Miller, T. (2007). "Is this what motherhood is all about?": Weaving experiences and discourse through transition to first-time motherhood. *Gender and Society, 21*(3), 337–356.

Morell, C. M. (1994). *Unwomanly conduct: The challenges of intentional childlessness*. London: Routledge.

Murray, L., & Finn, M. (2012). Good mothers, bad thoughts: New mothers' thoughts of intentionally harming their newborns. *Feminism & Psychology, 22*(1), 41–59.

Muzik, M., Klier, C. M., Rosenblum, K. L., Holzinger, A., Umek, W., & Katschnig, H. (2000). Are commonly used self-report inventories suitable for screening postpartum depression and anxiety disorders? *Acta Psychiatrica Scandinavica, 102*(1), 71–73.

Nicolson, P. (1999). Loss, happiness and postpartum depression: The ultimate paradox. *Canadian Psychology/Psychologie Canadienne, 40*(2), 162–178.

Nicolson, P. (2001). *Postnatal depression: Facing the paradox of loss, happiness and motherhood*. Chichester: Wiley.

O'Reilly, A. (Ed.). (2008). *Feminist mothering*. Albany: State University of New York Press.

O'Reilly, A. (2012) (Ed.). *From motherhood to mothering: The legacy of Adrienne Rich's 'Of Woman Born'*. Albany, United States of America: State University of new York press.

O'Brien, M. (1991). Never married older women: The life experience. *Social Indicators Research, 24*(3), 301–315.

O'Reilly, A. (Ed.). (2004). *Mother matters: Motherhood as discourse and practice – Essays from the 'Journal of the Association for Research on Mothering'*. Toronto, Canada: Association for Research on Mothering.

Orton-Johnson, K. (2017). Mummy blogs and representations of motherhood: "Bad mummies" and their readers. *Social Media + Society, 3*(2), 1–10.

Park, K. (2002). Stigma management among the voluntarily childless. *Sociological Perspectives, 45*(1), 21–45.

Parker, R. (1995). *Torn in two: The experience of maternal ambivalence*. London: Virago Press.

Parker, B., & Morrow, O. (2017). Urban homesteading and intensive mothering: (Re)gendering care and environmental responsibility in Boston and Chicago. *Gender, Place & Culture, 24*(2), 247–259.

Paul, I. M., Downs, D. S., Schaefer, E. W., Beiler, J. S., & Weisman, C. S. (2013). Postpartum anxiety and maternal-infant health outcomes. *Pediatrics, 131*(4), e1218–e1224.

Pederson, S. (2016). The good, the bad and the 'good enough' mother on the UK parenting forum Mumsnet. *Women's Studies International Forum, 59*, 32–38.

Peterson, H. (2015). Fifty shades of freedom. Voluntary childlessness as women's ultimate liberation. *Women's Studies International Forum, 53*, 182–191.

Pickard, S. (2018). *Age, gender and sexuality through the life course: The girl in time*. Abingdon: Routledge.

Ramsay, K., & Letherby, G. (2006). The experience of academic non-mothers in the gendered university. *Gender, Work and Organization, 13*(1), 25–44.

Raphael-Leff, J. (2010). Healthy maternal ambivalence. *Studies in the Maternal, 2*(1), 1–15.

Rath Jr., F. H., & Okum, M. E. (1995). Parents and children sleeping together: Cosleeping prevalence and concerns. *American Journal of Orthopsychiatry, 65*(3), 411–418.

Razali, S., Fisher, J., & Kirkman, M. (2019). "Nobody came to help": Interviews with women convicted of filicide in Malaysia. *Archives of Women's Mental Health, 22*(1), 151–158.

Resnick, P. J. (1969). Child murder by parents: A psychiatric review of filicide. *American Journal of Psychiatry, 126*(3), 325–334.

Resnick, P. J. (1970). Murder of the newborn: A psychiatric review of neonaticide. *American Journal of Psychiatry, 126*(10), 1414–1420.

Rich, A. (1995). *Of woman born: Motherhood as experience and institution*. New York: WW Norton & Company.

Rose, G. (2003). Family photographs and domestic spacings: A case study. *Transactions of the Institute of British Geographers, 28*(1), 5–18.

Røseth, I., Bongaardt, R., Lyberg, A., Sommerseth, E., & Dahl, B. (2018). New mothers' struggles to love their child. An interpretative synthesis of qualitative studies. *International Journal of Qualitative Studies on Health and Well-Being, 13*(1), 1–10.

Sappleton, N. (Ed.). (2018). *Voluntary and involuntary childlessness: The joys of otherhood?* Bingley: Emerald Publishing.

Scheper-Hughes, N. (1987). The cultural politics of child survival. In N. Scheper-Hughes (Ed.), *Child survival: Anthropological perspectives on the treatment and maltreatment of children* (pp. 1–29). Dordrecht: D. Reidel Publishing.

Schmied, V., & Lupton, D. (2001). Blurring the boundaries: Breastfeeding and maternal subjectivity. *Sociology of Health & Illness, 23*(2), 234–250.

Scott, P. D. (1973). Parents who kill their children. *Medicine, Science and the Law, 13*(2), 120–126.

Shapiro, G. (2014). Voluntary childlessness: A critical review of the literature. *Studies in the Maternal, 6*(1), 1–15.

Sheen, K., & Slade, P. (2018). Examining the content and moderators of women's fears for giving birth: A meta-synthesis. *Journal of Clinical Nursing, 27*(13–14), 2523–2535.

Sieff, D. F. (2019). The death mother as nature's shadow: Infanticide, abandonment, and the collective unconscious. *Psychological Perspectives, 62*(1), 15–34.

Silverio, S.A. (2016). *Not a princess in a fairy-tale, but a female of society: A qualitative examination of gender identity in the never married older woman* (Unpublished master's thesis). Liverpool: University of Liverpool.

Silverio, S. A. (2018). From mothers to matriarchs: Modern constructions of ancient family values. *The Psychologist, 31*(11), OE1–OE5.

Silverio, S. A. (2019). Reconstructing gender to transcend shame: Embracing human functionality to enable agentic and desexualised bodies. In C.-H. Mayer & E. Vanderheiden (Eds.), *The bright side of shame: Transforming and growing through practical applications in cultural contexts* (pp. 149–165). Cham, Switzerland: Springer.

Silverio, S. A., & Soulsby, L. K. (2020). Turning that shawl into a cape: Older never married women in their own words – The "spinsters", the "singletons", and the "superheroes". *Critical Discourse Studies, 17*(2), 211-228.

Smith, H. (2018). Feisty and childfree: Voluntary childlessness as an alternative to mothering. In C. Nelson & R. Robertson (Eds.), *Dangerous ideas about mothers* (pp. 137–147). Perth: UWA Publishing.

Snitow, A. (1992). Feminism and motherhood: An American reading. *Feminist Review, 40*(32–51).

Spinelli, M. G. (2003). Introduction. In M. G. Spinelli (Ed.), *Infanticide: Psychosocial and legal perspectives on mothers who kill* (pp. XV–XXII). Washington: American Psychiatric Publishing.

Spinelli, M. G. (2004). Maternal infanticide associated with mental illness: Prevention and the promise of saved lives. *American Journal of Psychiatry, 161*(9), 1548–1557.

Staneva, A. A., & Wigginton, B. (2018). The happiness imperative: Exploring how women narrate depression and anxiety during pregnancy. *Feminism & Psychology, 28*(2), 173–193.

Stassart, C., Dardenne, B., & Etienne, A. M. (2017). The role of parental anxiety sensitivity and learning experiences in children's anxiety sensitivity. *British Journal of Developmental Psychology, 35*(3), 359–375.

Swan, A. J., Kendall, P. C., Olino, T., Ginsburg, G., Keeton, C., Compton, S., et al. (2018). Results from the child/adolescent anxiety multimodal longitudinal study (CAMELS): Functional outcomes. *Journal of Consulting and Clinical Psychology, 86*(9), 738–750.

Tanturri, M. L., & Mencarini, L. (2008). Childless or childfree? Paths to voluntary childlessness in Italy. *Population and Development Review, 34*(1), 51–77.

Teigen, K. H. (1994). Yerkes-Dodson: A law for all seasons. *Theory and Psychology, 4*(4), 525–547.

Thornton, D. J. (2011). Neuroscience, affect, and the entrepreneurialization of motherhood. *Communication and Critical/Cultural Studies, 8*(4), 399–424.

Ussher, J. M. (2006). *Managing the monstrous feminine: Regulating the reproductive body.* London: Routledge.

van den Bergh, B. (1990). The influence of maternal emotions during pregnancy on fetal and neonatal behaviour. *Journal of Prenatal and Perinatal Psychology and Health, 5*(2), 119–130.

Villalobos, A. (2014). Compensatory connection: Mothers' own stakes in an intensive mother-child relationship. *Journal of Family Issues, 36*(14), 1928–1956.

Watson, C. (2016). Womb rentals and baby-selling: Does surrogacy undermine the human dignity and rights of the surrogate mother and child? *The New Bioethics, 22*(3), 212–228.

Wenzel, A., Haugen, E. N., Jackson, L. C., & Brendle, J. R. (2005). Anxiety symptoms and disorders at eight weeks postpartum. *Journal of Anxiety Disorders, 19*(3), 295–311.

Williams, L. M., & Finkelhor, D. (1995). Paternal caregiving and incest: Test of a biosocial model. *American Journal of Orthopsychiatry, 65*(1), 101–113.

Wolke, D. (2019). Persistence of infant crying, sleeping and feeding problems: Need for prevention. *Archives of Disease in Childhood, 104*(11), 1022–1023.

Zelkowitz, P., & Papageorgiou, A. (2012). Easing maternal anxiety: An update. *Women's Health, 8*(2), 205–213.

Zimmerman, T. S., Aberle, J. T., Krafchick, J. L., & Harvey, A. M. (2008). Deconstructing the "mommy wars": The battle over the best mom. *Journal of Feminist Family Therapy, 20*(3), 203–219.

Sergio A. Silverio is an academic Psychologist who first trained in Psychological Sciences (Clinical & Health Psychology) at the University of Liverpool and later read for a Master's of Psychological and Psychiatric Anthropology at Brunel University London. He maintains a primary research interest in women's mental health over the lifecourse, in particular, assessing what contributes to poor mental health at key life transitions. Sergio has worked within various academic departments, notably as a Research Assistant in Qualitative Methods at the University College London's Elizabeth Garrett Anderson Institute for Women's Health where he is now an Honorary Research Fellow, and at the Department of Women & Children's Health at King's College London where he is now a Research Associate in Social Science of Women's Health. Most recently, he has been made an Honorary Fellow at the University of Liverpool's Department of Psychology, was elected as Fellow of the Royal Society for Public Health, and was nominated for Life Fellowship of the Royal Anthropological Institute. Sergio is also an Associate Fellow of The British Psychological Society, from whom he has won critical acclaim for his early work on ageing femininity and never married older women's social networks. His more recent work into antenatal anxiety was awarded the 40th Anniversary Thesis Prize by The Society for Reproductive and Infant Psychology. Having worked on various research projects on sensitive topics, Sergio has become an experienced interviewer and qualitative analyst, whilst also developing his theorisations on women's mental health and 'Female Psychology'. Sergio has an established track-record of successful publications, conference presentations, and invited talks; and maintains a strong network of international collaborators. With these colleagues and others, he continues to formalise a body of research with the aim of improving women's mental health.

Catherine Wilkinson is a Senior Lecturer in Education based at the School of Education at Liverpool John Moores University. Catherine has a creative interdisciplinary background with a BA (Hons) in Fashion Brand Management, an MSc in Marketing Management, and a PhD in Environmental Sciences. She has a recognised research achievement in researching 'with' children, young people and their families via creative and/or participatory approaches, including mixed methods, ethnographic and field-based qualitative research. Catherine completed her PhD in Environmental Sciences at University of Liverpool, funded by an ESRC CASE award. Undertaking 18 months of ethnographic research, Catherine adopted a participatory mixed-methods approach to explore the ways in which young people use community radio as a platform to find and realise their voices, build stocks of social capital, and create their own communities and senses of self. Catherine previously explored the portrayal of mothering a child with complex health care needs, considering the competing identities of mother, nurse, carer and advocate that these mothers fulfil as part of their daily regimes in 'being mum'. This paper was presented at the American Association of Geographers annual meeting, New Orleans, 2018, where Catherine was awarded funding from the AAG Enrichment Fund for her attendance as a 'distinguished non-geographer'. Though researching on diverse topics including youth voice, disfigurement, and eyebrows, Catherine's research is united under the theme of identity. Catherine is committed to culturally credible means of disseminating research, including the creation of audio artefacts, poetry, comic strips, and YouTube videos.

Victoria Fallon is a Lecturer in the Department of Psychology at the University of Liverpool. Her research interests concern perinatal mental health and early infant development, in particular, infant nutrition. Her PhD examined maternal anxiety and infant feeding from pregnancy to parenthood, from which she developed the Postpartum Specific Anxiety Scale [PSAS]—a validated, and reliable 51-item self-report tool designed to examine the frequency of anxieties specific to the postpartum period. Her research focus centres on maternal emotional distress and anxieties related to the women's newborn infants. This, along with her extensive use and teaching of research methods and statistics, in which she specialises in mixed methodologies and psychometrics, has seen Victoria publish in various international and impactful journals, and work together with colleagues in several countries. With these colleagues her most recent collaborative projects have been directed at formalising maternal mental health care and assessment across the Italian perinatal mental health sector, whilst co-founding the Families and Babies Laboratory at her home institution.

Alessandra Bramante is Psychologist, Cognitive Psychotherapist, and Clinical Criminologist. She has a PhD in Neuroscience, which focussed on the prevention of maternal neonaticide and filicide. With extensive research and clinical experience, she is a renowned expert in perinatal psychology and psychopathology. Alessandra currently works as a Consultant Psychologist at the Policentro Pediatrico, Milano [Paediatric Centre, Milan], routinely screening for postpartum depression and anxiety. Having worked clinically with mothers experiencing a wide range of mental illness including postpartum psychosis, obsessive compulsive disorder, and most anxiety, affective, attachment, and personality disorders, Alessandra was elected as the founding President of the Società Marcé Italiana per la Salute Mentale Perinatale [Italian Regional Group of The International Marcé Society for Perinatal Mental Health]. As part of Alessandra's ongoing and internationally reaching collaborations, she has authored numerous scientific publications on filicide, maternal suicide, and perinatal psychopathology.

Aleksandra A. Staneva has a PhD in maternal mental health. Through employing feminist, critical realist, and post-qualitative approaches, she is exploring experiences of depression and anxiety during pregnancy and early motherhood for women. Her research involves wellness, grassroots interventions, and the ethics of digital health. Aleksandra creates art, writes children's books, travels, and lives with her son and partner in beautiful Brisbane, Australia.

Chapter 17
A Semi-Peripheral Myth of the "Good Mother": The History of Motherly Love in Hungary from a Global Perspective

Gergely Csányi and Szabina Kerényi

Abstract Based on Foucault's theory of the soul, as well as the methodological insights of Fernand Braudel and world-systems analysis, this paper demonstrates how the myth of the good and the bad mother was created by certain actors during the various cycles of the capitalist world system, and how these myths have been embedded in the logic of capitalist accumulation. We show how on the one hand these myths contributed to securing the unpaid reproductive labour, care and love necessitated by accumulation, and how on the other hand they supported a new market segment from the nineteenth century onwards by manipulating maternal conscience. First we present an outline of the history of the myth of the good mother and motherly love in the core countries of the world system, then we summarise the socialist myth of the good mother. Finally, we use empirical examples to illustrate the ways the contemporary Hungarian myth of the good mother has been shaped by dependence on the core countries and on the socialist Soviet Union.

Keywords Love · Motherhood · Motherly love · Capitalist world system · Semi-periphery · Reproductive labour

17.1 Introduction

On 8 July 2018, the World Health Assembly (WHA) convened in Geneva with the partial aim of accepting a statement that breastfeeding and breast milk is the healthiest and most secure method of feeding infants, and that accordingly, member states of the UN needed to limit the (potentially) misleading marketing of companies producing infant formula. At one point, the US delegate interrupted the discussion by requesting that certain parts be removed from the statement, namely those in which the WHA would call on governments to protect and support breastfeeding and

G. Csányi (✉) · S. Kerényi
Centre for Social Sciences, Hungarian Academy of Sciences Centre of Excellence, Budapest, Hungary
e-mail: csanyiger@gmail.com; szabina.kerenyi@gmail.com

feeding breast milk to infants, and limit the popularisation of infant formula. When they were unsuccessful, the US representatives blackmailed the Ecuador delegation, who had intended to officially submit the statement, with the threat that unless they stepped back from this, the United States would instigate trade sanctions, as well as withdrawing their indispensable military assistance. As a result, besides Ecuador, representatives of a dozen South-American and African peripheral and semi-peripheral countries refused to submit the statement (Jacobs, 2018).

The strategy of the US delegation, which according to reports had astonished the assembly (Jacobs, 2018), is hardly surprising from a political economic perspective: it is in harmony with the economic policy of the Donald Trump government, which aims to deal with the new-old crisis of US hegemony through protectionist measures (for example protecting US companies from the limiting measures of international bodies) and a rhetoric of economic nationalism (Parnreiter, 2018). The infant formula industry is an approximately 70-billion-dollar industry, and is dominated by a small number of European and US companies with significant interest in sales in peripheral countries (Jacobs, 2018).

A similar story was the Nestlé boycott in in 1977. The boycott initiated by anti-poverty organisations, and preceded, among others, by the exploratory work of journalist Mike Muller (1974), which went by the unrestrained title *The Baby Killer*. These demonstrated that the aggressive marketing policy of infant formula production is directly responsible for the death of thousands of newborns in peripheral countries, where due to unhygienic circumstances, including the lack of clean water, feeding through formula entails significantly more risk than breastfeeding, to the decreasing of which it has contributed.

The above stories are highly instructive. The above not only shows that the "private sphere" is not the least bit independent from the "public sphere," but also that transnational relations permeate even the most intimate of human (love) relations. For instance, how breastfeeding, an act of motherly love, is perceived by the mother is—at least in part—decided within the field of the power of interests related to transnational commodity production.

In this chapter, we accept as our starting point that the defining of "motherhood" and the right way to love as a mother—the creation of the myth of the "good mother"—takes places according to the interests of various actors. For this, we partly rely on Foucault's philosophical anthropology, according to which "[t]he soul is the effect and the instrument of a political anatomy; the soul is the prison of the body" (Foucault, 1995, p. 30). Based on Foucault, we look at how certain actors construct the "motherly soul," and how they are able to manipulate the mother's conscience according to their interests. On the other hand, we rely on the methodology of Fernand Braudel and world-systems analysis, according to which history can be grasped in the dialectic of "great" historical events and "everyday life" (Braudel, 1977); and the relations between people can be understood within the context of those greater relations that they are part of (Wallerstein, 2004). On the basis of this, we look at the ways in which motherly praxes of love and care considered to be appropriate at a particular point in time are embedded into socio-economic structural dynamics. Thus the objects of this study are the ways in which the motherly "soul" as a construct is determined, and how practices such as child-rearing, that are considered particularly intimate, are related to great historical events—or how the mother–child relationship is embedded into broader human relations, that is, the dominant commodity production and market relations.

17.2 Who Is a Good Mother?

Who Is a Mother? The mother is a woman who has a child. This statement, while seemingly banal, is the foundation of any historical enquiry regarding motherhood. After all, we may state that being a mother always entails being the mother of somebody. Being a mother is therefore not a quality or substance, but a relative position. It is a position that can only be interpreted in relation to the child or children. Inversely, the word "child" refers to two things in contemporary society. Firstly, it refers practically to everyone, since everyone is the child of somebody independently of their age. Secondly, it refers to people before the age of puberty, independently of who their mother is. In the first sense, "child" is also a relative position, the opposite relative position of "mother," and they use this relation to position each other. In the second sense, being a "child" is a quality, that is, an absolute position. In contemporary societies, the emphasis is on the second sense, which also means that the child is an absolute position that designates a relative position, that of the mother.

While we were working on this research project, a colleague of ours shared a personal experience with us. On three consecutive occasions, her 5-year-old daughter was taken to the doctor by the father. On the last occasion, when the (male) paediatrician saw the father with the daughter, he asked, "Does this daughter have no mother?!" Our colleague, who had learnt about this from the father, was in tears when she shared the story with us.

What Is Motherhood? The case above can be interpreted in a way that based on the age (the absolute position) of the girl, the paediatrician was expecting a praxis positioned by him relative to the girl's age, that is, the mother's praxis—of bringing her daughter to the doctor. Motherhood as a human relation is therefore manifest in contemporary societies as everyday practices of reproductive tasks—care and love—that are necessary for the child to survive and live in welfare and well-being according to heterogenous social norms.

Who Is a Good Mother? A good mother is a mother who is not bad. Behind this second seemingly banal statement lies an important theoretical and methodological insight. We can state that the good mother is defined negatively, that is, a good mother is somebody who does not fail to perform the tasks belonging to the praxis of motherhood, and performs them "correctly"—which in effect means loving her child "correctly." In other words, the myth of the good mother is always constructed together with the myth of the bad mother. The question "Does this daughter have no mother?!" suggests that a mother not present in caring tasks (taking the child to the doctor) is a mother neglecting her praxis, and therefore is a bad mother. The expression of this expectation elicits an emotional response for this reason—this is the way the motherly soul, in a Foucauldian sense, works: it constructs a motherly conscience and reacts to the accusation of being a bad mother with internalised shame and guilt. The motherly soul is the prison of the motherly body.

17.3 An Outline of the History of the Myth of the Good Mother in the Core Countries

The Myth of the Good Mother Is a Capitalist Myth Although narratives about motherhood existed in the Middle Ages, most importantly the cult of the Virgin Mary, but in the Middle Ages, the ideal of the "good mother" was not clearly normalised or standardised (Thurer, 1995). According to Philippe Ariés,

> [n]obody thought, as we ordinarily think today, that every child already contained a man's [sic] personality [...] This indifference was a direct and inevitable consequence of the demography of the period (1965, 39).

According to the social historian Edward Shorter, who draws on Ariès, among others, there is also a reverse connection: mothers looked at the development of their children below the age of two with disinterest, which in turn contributed to high infant mortality (Shorter, 1975). According to Lloyd deMause's description of life in the Middle Ages (1974), neither the nuclear family, nor private life in the bourgeois sense existed, and infanticide was a regular feature of family planning. Cohabitation was first and foremost a community of labour, not love.

But as Ariès (1965, p. 39) himself asks, if social constructions of the child and the mother (or the lack of these) were determined by demographic relations, why did the modern myths of the child and motherly love begin to appear almost 300 years before the demographic transition?

The First Bad Mother: The Myth of the Witch Firstly, between 1315 and 1322, the Great Famine and plague epidemic that followed resulted in the death of 30–40% of the European population, and the "Black Death" mostly hit peasants, day-labourers, vagabonds and craftsmen. Secondly, in the society of the Middle Ages, due to limited access to land and the protectionist limitation of craft guild membership, it was neither desirable nor possible for peasants or craftspeople to have large numbers of children. Moreover, communities of peasants and craftspeople regularly made efforts to control the birthrate in Europe. Various methods of both contraception and also pregnancy termination existed, but infanticide was also regular. These two combined factors led to a demographic crisis by the sixteenth and seventeenth centuries, peaking between 1620 and 1630 (Federici, 2004).

But the first seeds of the newly emerging capitalist world-system necessitated a constantly available labour force—for which the states and church had to interfere with reproduction patterns (Federici, 2004). Thus the answer to the question asked by Ariès of why the social construction of the mother–child relationship was radically transformed in the fifteenth century—several hundred years before the first phase of the demographic transition—is that this was due to a well-organised campaign on the part of European states and church aimed at managing the demographic crisis. It took place through the interference with reproductive patterns in order to secure the labour force basis of the capitalist mode of production. One of the most didactic examples of this is from sixteenth-century Germany, where a mother could face punishment if it was considered that she had not made enough physical effort during labour, or if she had not shown enough love for her baby after giving birth (Rublack, 1996, p. 92).

At the same time, European states and churches began to wage a war on non-reproductive sex, birth regulation, abortion and infanticide through the use and bureaucratisation of witch-hunts. Witch-hunts were a manifestation of the newly emerging world-system, with the extension of bureaucracy and the state apparatus imposing its logic onto human relationships (Wallerstein, 1974)—in this particular case onto love and sex relationships. This "war" claimed the lives of hundreds of thousands of women: prostitutes, unmarried mothers, midwives, women who had, or were said to have committed adultery, or women who were unable to produce their living infant to authorities after giving birth. Primarily, members of the lower classes (Federici, 2004). The witch myth of the sixteenth century became the first myth of the bad mother. It was no coincidence that a central element in witch trials was that witches were presumed to sacrifice children to the devil (Federici, 2004). The neglecting of loving and caring for children came to be considered a terrible crime, while the myth of the good mother also appeared alongside that of the bad mother.

The Myth of the Angelic Bourgeois Mother By the end of the seventeenth century, in most parts of Europe, the family and the education system—which had been established by that time—removed children from adult society, and this was accompanied with an expectation towards their parents from society to treat them with special care.

In addition, after 200 years of terror, first with the rise of the Dutch and then the British hegemony, with the bourgeoisie along with it, constructions of femininity also changed radically. The bourgeois woman—according to the expectations of the period—was without passion, asexual, pure, and was attached to her husband through tender friendship and faithfulness rather than sexual love. For the bourgeoisie, the family home had become completely isolated from the outside world; it became the sphere of the woman supported by her husband, while work and politics remained the sphere of the bread-earning husband (Federici, 2004; Foucault, 1990; Laqueur, 1992; Somlai, 1984). All this formed an organic part of the class identity of the bourgeoisie and its symbolic separation from other classes. The bourgeois man–woman relationship was materially and symbolically determined by the ways in which the bourgeoisie was embedded into the system of social relations of the period.

Elisabeth Badinter, in her search for motherly love, points to the fact that out of 21,000 babies born in Paris in 1780, approximately (or less than) 1000 were nursed by their mothers at home, and another 1000 by live-in wet-nurses. The remaining 19,000 were sent away to wet-nurses (Badinter, 1981, p. 43). However, "[a]fter 1760 publications abounded advising mothers to take care of their children personally and 'ordering' them to breast-feed" (Badinter, 1981, p. 117). By this time it had become an accepted view among the Western-European bourgeoisie that children deserved pleasure with the mother. From this period onwards, even though the practice of wet-nursing had been prevalent among the upper classes for centuries, it was the woman not nursing her child—for whatever reason—that received scorn on account of not loving her child.

According to the slowly spreading bourgeois myth of motherhood, the mother was an angelic creature without desire, ready to sacrifice anything for the warmth of the home and her children. The image of the child had also radically transformed—it had come to assume primarily emotional value rather than economic, and thus in a certain sense it had become priceless. By the second half of the eighteenth century, the strict punishment-centred pedagogy of the seventeenth century had disappeared (Thurer, 1995). Child-rearing advice had been institutionalised, but this meant that any behavioural or welfare discrepancy of the child became the sole responsibility of the mother. In sum, the accusation of being a bad mother constantly hovered over the bourgeois mother, and accordingly, she was haunted by the conscience of the bad mother.

From the nineteenth century, Darwinism began to permeate the ideology of the bourgeoisie. Motherhood received an evolutionary tinge. The successful woman became the one who was "good" at reproducing. Since no "decent" woman was permitted to have sexual desires, birth defects were interpreted as evidence of the indecent thoughts of the mother. Thus the myth of the bad mother was scientifised (Thurer, 1995).

As a result of the industrial revolution, the British hegemony that was built on it, and the economic prosperity that sprang from the world-system, new markets emerged (Silver & Arrighi, 2003). One consequence of this was the expansion of products made particularly for children, creating a market based on parental love. For instance, one of the best-known children's toys, the Teddy Bear, was created in the first years of the twentieth century. The mother who failed to love her children enough or sacrifice enough for them, which from the nineteenth century had come to include purchasing the appropriate products, committed an unforgivable sin—she was a bad mother.

By the beginning of the twentieth century, the bourgeois family model and the bourgeois myth of the good mother had come to serve as a standard in all social classes (Thurer, 1995). From the perspective of the ideology of the ruling class, the working-class mother was no less deviant (Badinter, 1981; Somlai, 1984; Thurer, 1995). The mother working in the labour market became the perfect example of the myth of the bad mother, namely the neglectful mother, and it did not count as a mitigating factor that it was necessary for her to work. Mothers in working-class families typically had to work, and as a result they frequently had to leave their children alone for an entire day. Opium and swaddling were popular methods for keeping children safe during this time (Thurer, 1995). All this resulted in working-class mothers being perceived as bad mothers not only by others, but also by themselves.

The Fordist Myth of the Good Mother During the time of the two wars women had integrated into the formal labour market to an unprecedented extent. The Fordist mode of production and the lack of male workforce helped construct a new and special case of the myth of the good mother, which was clearly different from the myth of the bourgeois woman ready to sacrifice everything for her child. The breastfeeding and infant-care principles of the time, which propagated routine breastfeeding and feeding at set intervals, can be tied to this myth. Benjamin Spock's *The Common Sense Book of Baby and Child Care* was published in 1946 in the United States, which, in accordance with the defining child psychology theory of the time, recommended separation as soon as possible, and a withholding of love from the child. And even though he discusses at length the advantages of breastfeeding, he in fact suggests a breastfeeding practice that would be very difficult to maintain it in the long term (feeding at four-hour intervals, the introduction of additional food from the age of 3 months, regulating the duration of breastfeeding). In addition, he dedicates a separate chapter to the topic of "spoiling" the child, arguing that infants that are picked up and carried around for 3 months became somewhat spoilt. The approach represented by Dr. Spock not only mirrored the position of the child, but also the value of labour and production in a society where the biorhythm of infants needed to adapt to the dynamics of production. In sum, too much motherly love suddenly became undesirable.

The Modern Myth of the Good Mother During the period of upturn for the US hegemony, by the 1960s the expansion of education, technological development, economic prosperity and the development of mass media turned motherhood into a battlefield, with various actors constantly attempting to redefine it according to their own interests. Capital was continuously looking for new forms of investment, while the household began to operate as a constantly growing market, based to a great extent on parental love.

As psychology became heterogenised, commercialised and embedded into pop culture (Rose, 1999), psychological and psychologising labels regarding bad mothers also spread widely. The myth of the bad mother was further scientifised and psychologised: the "overprotective mother" emerged, along with the "neglectful mother," the "over-solicitous mother," the "rejecting," "dominating," and "smothering mother" (Thurer, 1995, pp. 225–286). With the fragmentation of the myth of the bad mother, the myth once again became practically impossible to live up to.

Consumption habits and advertisements became closely aligned with habitus and identity. Commercials frequently re-romanticised pregnancy and the household, while propagating a "scientific" household management. Moreover, motherhood and the household as a market gained renewed momentum after the overproduction crisis of the 1970s. From the 1980s, doctors were able to determine the sex of unborn children with high probability, so expecting parents were able to purchase baby items particularly designed for girls or boys. The individualisation of products in turn created new supply and demand, thus further expanding the market. This is, for instance, when pink became the "colour for girls" (Paoletti, 2012). From this period, market relations making use of the "goodness" of motherhood became increasingly influential with regard to the social and cultural construction of the myth of the "good mother." Buying goods became the ultimate scale of motherly love.

17.4 The Socialist Myth of the Good Mother in Hungary

By the 1930s in the Soviet Union, s, in relation to initial reform plans, the Soviet efforts of industrialisation had institutionalised the subordinated and informal forms of female reproductive labour, similarly to the forms of capitalist modernisation (Csányi, Gagyi, & Kerékgyártó, 2018). On the other hand, similarly to almost all European countries, the Soviet leadership began pronatalist propaganda, in the period between the two world wars. In 1936, all contraceptive methods were removed from the market (Hoffmann, 2003). Subsequently, the Pravda published an editorial about socialist morals and the importance of family and child-rearing, as well as an article that depicted the loving relationship between Stalin and his elderly mother (Somlai, 1990). Mothers with seven or more children were promised monetary compensation regardless of their family background—even in cases where their husbands had been convicted of engaging in counter-revolutionary activity. The propaganda emphasised that a child was a natural and necessary part of a woman's life, a pleasure rather than a burden (Hoffmann, 2003, p. 102).

The first period of Hungarian state socialism was characterised by the female labour force being channelled into the transformation of the mode of production. Full-time motherhood, where a woman would use her labour for her own family and not for the whole of socialist society, was unacceptable for the contemporary propaganda. Contrary to the bourgeois myth of motherhood, the "good mother" could not be "a mother only." Officially, motherhood was portrayed as not challenging, so that a woman could easily perform—even outperform men—in factories and agriculture besides being a mother. As such, motherhood as praxis and love was not part of official propaganda. Bringing up children to become self-confident workers and socialists was at the forefront, but was not the means to this end.

From 1952, however, the regulation of motherhood became a clear direction for the party. It was ordered that "the public prosecutor give the greatest possible support to the police force" in order that people contributing to abortions could be identified and convicted (Schadt, 2003, pp. 135–137). These criminal cases were treated as serious and involved imprisonment and a restriction from participation in public affairs as well as medical praxis (ibid.). This tightening matched the concept of motherhood as an openly social function:

> [i]t has to be clear that abortion is not a private matter, but a matter concerning the entirety of the people, it is a serious criminal offence committed against our working people and future" (Schadt, 2003, pp. 136–137; our translation).

Abortion measures were complemented by a tax liability of those without children, which—also based on a Soviet example—required people above 24 years of age but not yet retired and without children to contribute 4% of their income (Schadt, 2003, pp. 136–137).

In its latent content, the myth of the good socialist mother in many ways resembled the Fordist myth of motherhood, which emerged in the core position of the world system. This resemblance is not coincidental, as they were constructed by similar dynamics, and built around a similar idea of maternal care. In both, breastfeeding was adapted to the cyclical monotony of industrial production. A proposal submitted to the Council of Ministers in 1953 outlined a practice similar to what Spock had recommended on a psychological basis:

> If the working woman breastfeeds her child in an on-site crèche or one that is close to her workplace, or her home that is close, during the first six months, she is entitled to two nursing breaks of 30 minutes, then, until the ninth month, one break of 30 minutes, which is included in working time and remunerated with the average wage. If the mother breastfeeds her child in her home or in a crèche that is distant from the workplace, upon her request, the two 30-minute breaks can be taken as one hour-long break. (KSH, 1953, 92; our translation)

It was the so-called "Ratkó generation" (named after Anna Ratkó, Minister of Welfare, later Health, between 1949 and 1953) that was most directly hit by all of this, since as a result of the ban on abortions, the number of births had escalated, while at the same time mothers only received 6 weeks of maternal leave. Afterwards they had to return to work, and infant care was entirely organised around the pace of their work. We can learn the following from the memories of a nurse working at a factory crèche at the time:

> The shoe factory began at quarter to six, but the children had to be brought there at around quarter or half past six so that their mothers could get to occupy their places by the so-called assembly lines by the time the factory whistled at quarter to six. [...] The children would come in the winter darkness, crying, the streets would echo with their crying [...] On many occasions, you had to forcefully remove the naked children from around the necks of their mothers, so that they could run to work. (Szülők Kézikönyve [Handbook of Parents], 2015)

Although the abortion ban was replaced by a relatively liberal abortion regulation practice in 1956, and the childless tax was also abolished in 1957, the socialist myth of the good mother only began to erode in Hungary during the late 1960s. Besides the narrative of Stalinist industrialisation, the country had already taken out western loans in 1952, and was on the brink of bankruptcy. Due to the changing structure of the world system that came with the beginning of the period of global financialisation, Hungary, which had primarily exported food and raw materials, ended up in a worse trade position. Parallel to these processes, maternity benefit (GYES) was introduced in 1967, and extended to 3 years in '69. The introduction of GYES was narrated as a pronatalist measure on the one hand, and as a measure of child wellbeing on the other on the basis that a continuous experience of motherly love is crucial for the child in the first few years. In reality, however, it was an economic policy decision driven by the exhausted socialist economy and the total failure of full employment: it made it possible to remove a large proportion of (female) workforce from production without creating unemployment. The three-year benefit, which could be extended to a longer period with more children, reinforced a bourgeois image of the mother that had never entirely gone away—that of the full-time mother.

With the combination of the socialist myth of the good mother, the bourgeois myth of the good mother—which had been reinvigorated by the introduction of the maternal benefit—, and western constructions of femininity, which had increasingly begun to filter in, mothers found themselves facing expectations that they would not have been able to fulfil, even under much better material circumstances.

As Susan Zimmermann observes,

> a reporter described with abhorrence the young mothers they met at the tiny landing of a high block of flats, they were killing time there in tracksuits or swimsuits, surrounded by four screaming, crawling toddlers and three sleeping babies lying around like 'potato sacks' on a couch (Zimmermann, 2012, 109; our translation).

The "GYES mother" (benefit mother) appeared in the contemporary discourse as a woman locked into an environment lacking in stimuli, half-mad with boredom and abandoned—which, in some cases, may not have been very far from the truth. "The phrase 'GYES depression' or 'GYES illness' was being used as a cliché in public discussions" (ibid.). In contrast, during the same period, the expression "latchkey child" ("kulcsos gyerek") also appeared, which referred to children who had no one waiting for them at home after school or during a school holiday, and so were able to freely move between school, public libraries and home with their house keys hung around their necks. The expression itself emphasised the lack of adult—primarily motherly—care, and the bourgeois family model with a full time stay-at-home mother. The heterogeneity and ambivalence of social expectations regarding motherhood, along with the crisis of the socialist myth of the good mother, expressed the ambivalence and crisis of the socialist system on the level of discourse and interactions.

17.5 The Contemporary Myth of the Good Mother in Hungary

The mounting debt of Hungary and the rest of the socialist bloc and their economic dependency on western core countries, along with Western-European countries no longer being able to sell their investment commodities on their own domestic markets, contributed to a formal reintegration of the region into the world system. By signing the Maastricht Treaty, joining NATO and later the EU, Hungary was completely integrated into the formal circulation of the world system (Éber et al., 2014). This integration meant both a source of cheap labour, and a new market for the core countries. Along these two aspects, the core countries colonialised motherly love and constructed the contemporary myth of the "good mother" in a semi-peripheral country.

One of the primary means of making labour cheap is increasing the share of informal reproductive patterns in relation to the share of wages and welfare institutions in the costs of subsistence. Although the post-transition governments consistently cut back on the social security system of the former state socialist regime, due to the constant demographic drop, none of these governments radically changed the exceptional, although not entirely unique, lengthy maternity benefit. Nevertheless, while between 1967 and 1985, child-rearing ensured women had an active role in society due to the benefit being equal to a normal wage, after the regime change the provided amount was only a fraction of an average wage, which intensified the role of women as carers, and destabilized their position in the labour market.

Moreover, demographic indicators did not improve regardless of the possibility of lengthy maternity leave. And since Hungary entered the competition for cheap labour within the region, problems of demography came to the foreground - Accordingly, one of the first parliamentary debates after the regime change was centred around the tightening of the abortion law. The phrase "full-time mother" was reborn in the rhetoric of right-wing parties, establishing a role model of a properly caring mother, who devotes her life to her family. In addition, from the regime change onwards, but especially after the 2008 crisis which had irreversibly eroded the promise of catching up with the West, the right-wing rhetoric started to place emphasis on a woman's duty to give birth. In connection with this, as another effect of reintegrating into the world-system, from the 1980s an increasing number of western, particularly American, films entering the Hungarian market had communicated the superiority of the lifestyle of the core countries, especially the life of American suburbia (Taylor, 1996). In Hungary, the film Home Alone (1990), broadcast every single Christmas from the mid-'90s, regularly implanted the sentimentalism of motherly love into viewers. These kinds of films do not thematise the material basis of households, only the importance of the warmth of the (American suburban) home and motherly love framed within wealth and consumption. All of this has resonated very well up until today with both the bourgeois myth of the mother, invoked in Hungary from the 1960s, reinvigorated after the regime change and again with renewed strength after the 2008 crisis, and the neoliberal narrative.

Along with this, a pronatalist campaign video—masked as a celebratory video for Mother's Day—of the so-called Young Families Club (Fiatal Családosok Klubja) from 2017 employs the aesthetic of the US hegemony to present an idealised picture that is radically different from the everyday reality of the majority of the Hungarian households. The short film depicts the everyday lives of two well-off families, and uses every possible motif already familiar to us from the upper-middle-class lives of the aforementioned family films. The campaign video ends with the motto "Motherhood involves less sacrifice and more happiness than you would think"—which perfectly summarizes how the pronatalist redefinition of the myth of the good mother takes place in similar ways, in similar cycles, in different regions of the global commodity production system. This sentence is not essentially different from the rhetoric of the Soviet pronatalist campaign of the Pravda in the 1930s or 1940s, only this time it was made in accordance with the aesthetic of the US film industry.

In addition, as we observed above, from the end of the nineteenth century, but especially from the last third of the twentieth century, the household have functioned as a segment of the market based on motherly love and conscience. Thus, Hungarian households and mothers have also functioned as a market for the industries of the core countries. Although commercials of domestic products aimed particularly at children were already present in Hungary in the 1970s—for instance, commercials of baby food—, these did not yet operate with the myth of the good mother. TV commercials appearing from the 1980s onwards—as well as advertisements that later appeared on the internet—which primarily popularised products from the western core countries, were characterised by the negativistic definition of the bourgeois myth of the good mother. One of the first non-Hungarian and non-Eastern European TV commercials directly aimed at mothers with young children was a nappy advert of a Swedish company. In the commercial, the babies are happy because they are wearing the nappies of the given brand, which keeps their bottoms dry. According to the logic of the commercial, if somebody fails to buy the given brand, she fails to do everything in order to prevent her child from harm, and therefore lacks in motherly love—she is, in the bourgeois sense of the word, a bad mother. To give a different example, the slogan of a German baby formula from the late '90s went, using a catchy tune: "what is good for the baby, is a pleasure for mummy," suggesting that a good mother loves her child so much that it is a pleasure for her to purchase that particular formula. This successfully linked the pressure to consume—unfamiliar in (early) state socialist regimes—with the quality of motherhood.

Furthermore, with the broadening of the supply of mass media, the internet, social media and books, the third phase of the scientification of the myth of the good mother has been imported into Eastern Europe. Official or self-appointed experts and celebrities have constantly redefined what being a good mother means and how a child should be loved. Adapting to this, commercials frequently present the operating mechanism of the product with the help of an experiment or animation that looks scientific, and is adapted to the requirements of scientific household management—since the good mother is also a good manager of the household.

Thirdly, commercials affect the shaping of the habitus and the identity, and operate with the reinforcing of personal competencies. It is quite typical for a baby "using" a particular brand of nappies to be given this brand name as a nickname adjective. Commercials beginning with "mothers know that . . ." are also cliché, which often refer to competencies that are otherwise hardly connected to motherhood. In other words, they suggest that a good mother needs to excel not only at motherhood, but also in other areas of family life and the household, and consequently put the burden of parental care on mothers exclusively.

According to the latest marketing trends, formula producers operate with the respect of the private sphere by emphasising competences associated with motherhood and the freedom of choice. In one formula advertisement, for instance, mothers feeding their babies with formula and with mother's milk—the two identity groups—make peace by the end of the commercial and accept each other's maternal praxis. The name of the product is only visible for two seconds at the end of the video, encouraging unsuspecting mothers to enthusiastically share this message of freedom and acceptance through the channels of social media, often not even aware that they are partaking in the viral marketing campaign of a formula company that builds on the idea that formula feeding is identity-shaping, and as an identity is beyond criticism. This is a good example of how the myth of the good mother has come to be tied to the myth of choice as a liberal value and the implication that choice is given for everyone: the good mother is somebody that keeps herself informed and educated in all areas, and chooses the best for her child in every situation—preferably on a scientific basis—, and this choice is typically connected to practices of consumption.

In all, the good mother is somebody who is striving to give the best to her children and entire family in every situation and on every level all by herself, by making conscious choices: she cares and entertains at the same time, binds the family together, and places her needs, if she has them, behind those of the family. The constant redefining of the myth of the good mother continuously increases general frustration in mothers as it is impossible to fulfil the variety of abstract expectations. Moreover, in addition to expectations, through the positioning of the mother in this way, all responsibility of decisions regarding children and the family are attributed to the mother.

Finally, it is important to mention the problem of motherhood in public discourse, and also its place within the Hungarian feminist discourse. With the reintegration of the Eastern European region, Western European and US discourses have also filtered in. And while both during and directly after state socialism, women's movements primarily addressed the world of work (an example is the debate surrounding the extension of the retirement age in 1992), within civil society as a whole, including feminism, issues around the question of liberty soon gained priority (Fábián, 2009). The latter is especially interesting since the question of abortion was at the forefront of reproduction discourses of the regime change, and there was little difference in policy between governments on the left and on the right. Moreover, the problematising of motherhood and family planning remained almost entirely in the conservative discourse, while on the left, it appeared in a somewhat reactionary approach, primarily as the denial of the intrinsic value of population growth, and through the emphasising of the right to have power over one's own body. The movement Másállapotot a szülészetben! ("Respectful Maternal Care"), which emerged in 2016 and was also novel as a political movement in more than one way, partly broke through this rigid framework and presented the question of motherhood in a new light. The movement, partly growing out of the home birth movement, problematised pregnancy and birth as general questions affecting all social classes. At the same time, moving away from short-term political goals, it embedded the questions of giving birth and having children in a general context of female autonomy as a systemic critique of the patriarchal regime—as a result of which, the leftist, feminist direction employing systemic critique appeared simultaneously with the conservative family-centric direction in the movement.

17.6 Summary

Relying on Marxist feminist (c.f. Seccombe, 1974) and world-systems perspective (c.f. Dunaway, 2012) literature, in sum, we can state that within the household, an "accumulation of human capital" takes place, since it is there that the future labour supply is produced (Dunaway, 2012, pp. 102–103; Terleckyj, 1975, pp. 230–231). Firstly, this necessitates parents' labour of care, love, consumption, socialisation, and in a certain sense, ideology (Seccombe, 1974, pp. 15–16). Secondly, the costs of "human capital accumulation" are also relegated to households. In this sense, by being the primary locations of socialisation, they are also the place where the cost of capital return is made cheap. Thirdly, the household can be considered a market, since households with a higher income are encouraged to consume well above subsistence by the advertising industry and mass media.

Moreover, we can state that the myth of the good and the bad mother and the correct ways of motherly love and care comprise a segment of the dominant ideology that ensures the status quo of the given global system of accumulation: on the one hand, it makes certain that the majority of the labour necessary for the "accumulation of human capital" is assigned to women, and on the other, that households, and in particular their female members (using their own earnings), secure the costs necessary for "human capital accumulation," and even those beyond what is necessary.

Furthermore, we can state that the constructions—myths—of motherhood function in a way that if the woman in the relative position of motherhood fails to perform the motherly praxes of love, care, and consumption, she will appear as a bad mother to herself and her environment. Since motherhood is narrated as defined by humanity, a sacral order, or evolution, being an unloving mother counts as a sin against humanity, God, or nature, and thus it is a sin especially grave and shameful. After all, in the myth of the good and the bad mother, it is those acts of the woman that contradict the logic of capital accumulation that are interpreted as grave sins, thus causing pain for the motherly soul crafted through centuries of capitalism.

At the same time, in those periods and regions of the capitalist commodity production system where mothers' labour is needed on the formal labour market, the myth of the good mother is adapted in a way that it facilitates the channelling of motherly labour into formal productive labour. In these periods and regions, being a good mother is typically defined in a way that the praxis of motherhood does not make the praxis of wage labour impossible.

The contemporary myth of the good mother in Hungary is romantic, sentimental, scientific, and based on self-sacrifice and consumption. It can be viewed as a present end point of a constant redefinition of several centuries' worth of transnational structural dynamics embedded into semi-peripheral positions. In it the expectations of cheap labour, reproduction of semi-peripheral development combine with narratives of the modern transnational market. The good Hungarian mother performs all reproductive labour for her child in a selfless manner, sacrificing herself within the household, and acquires all products from the market that contribute towards her child's well-being as a sign of unlimited love. The good Hungarian mother is conscious and informed, she is aware of the work of the experts of motherhood, and leads the household in a scientific manner. She primarily self-identifies as a mother, and expresses this identification through her conscious consumption practices. If the good Hungarian mother does not succeed in performing these praxes for any reason, she experiences guilt and shame, as this is how the motherly soul functions.

Acknowledgements Funded by the project titled "EFOP-3.6.3-VEKOP-16-2017-00007- Young researchers from talented students—Fostering scientific careers in higher education" which is co-financed by the European Union (European Social Fund) within the framework of Programme Széchenyi 2020.

References

Aries, P. (1965). *Centuries of childhood: A social history of family life*. New York: Vintage.
Badinter, E. (1981). *Mother love: Myth and reality: Motherhood in modern history*. New York: Macmillan.
Braudel, P. F. (1977). *Afterthoughts on material civilization and capitalism* (P. P. Ranum, Trans.). Baltimore: The Johns Hopkins University Press.
Csányi, G., Gagyi, Á., & Kerékgyártó, Á. (2018). Társadalmi reprodukció. Az élet újratermelése a kapitalizmusban. *Fordulat, 24*, 5–29.
DeMause, L. (1974). *The history of childhood*. New York: The Psychohistory Press.
Dunaway, W. A. (2012). The semiproletarian household over the longue durée of the modern world-system. In R. E. Lee (Ed.), *The longue durée and world-systems analysis* (pp. 97–136). Albany, NY: SUNY Press.
Éber, M. Á., Gagyi, Á., Gerőcs, T., Jelinek, Cs., & Pinkasz, A. (2014). 1989: Szempontok a rendszerváltás globális politikai gazdaságtanához, *Fordulat, 21*, 10–63.
Fábián, K. (2009). *Contemporary women's movements in Hungary: Globalization, democracy and gender equality*. Washington, DC: The Woodrow Wilson Center Press.
Federici, S. (2004). *Caliban and the witch*. New York: Autonomedia.
Foucault, M. (1990). *The history of sexuality, Vol. 1: An introduction*. New York: Vintage.
Foucault, M. (1995). *Discipline & Punish: The birth of the prison* (A. Sheridan, Trans.). New York: Vintage Books.
Hoffmann, D. L. (2003). *Stalinist values. The cultural norms of Soviet modernity [1917–1941]*. Ithaca, NY: Cornell University Press.
Jacobs, A. (2018). Opposition to breast-feeding resolution by U.S. Stuns World Health Officials. *The New York Times*. Retrieved August 8, 2019, from https://www.nytimes.com/2018/07/08/health/world-health-breastfeeding-ecuador-trump.html
KSH. (1953). Az 1952–53. *Évi népesedéspolitikai program Magyarországon*. Retrieved August 8, 2019, from http://demografia.hu/kiadvanyokonline/index.php/tajekoztatofuzetek/article/view/2225
Laqueur, T. (1992). *Making sex: Body and gender from the Greeks to Freud* (Reprint edition). Cambridge, MA: Harvard University Press.
Muller, M. (1974). *The baby killer. War or want*. Retrieved August 8, 2019, from http://archive.babymilkaction.org/pdfs/babykiller.pdf
Paoletti, J. B. (2012). *Pink and blue: Telling the boys from the girls in America*. Bloomington: Indiana University Press.
Parnreiter, C. (2018). America first! Donald Trump, the demise of the U.S. hegemony and chaos in the capitalist world-system. *Zeitschrift für Wirtschaftsgeographie, 62*(1), 1–13.
Rose, N. (1999). *Governing the soul*. London: Free Association Books.

Rublack, U. (1996). Pregnancy, childbirth and the female body in early modern Germany. *Past & Present, 150*, 84–110.
Schadt, M. (2003). *"Feltörekvő dolgozó nő". Nők az ötvenes években*. Pécs: Pannónia Könyvek.
Seccombe, W. (1974). The housewife and her labour under capitalism. *New Left Review, I, 83*.
Shorter, E. (1975). *The making of the modern family*. New York: Basic Books.
Silver, B. J., & Arrighi, G. (2003). Polanyi's "double movement": The Belle Époques of British and U.S. hegemony compared. *Politics and Society, 31*(2), 325–355.
Somlai, P. (1984). A "hagyományos háztartások" és a "polgári intimitás": Két típus a családi kapcsolatok társadalomtörténetéből. *Szociológia: A Magyar Tudományos Akadémia Szociológiai Bizottságának Folyóirata, 1*(2), 1–23.
Somlai, P. (1990). A szabad szerelemtől az ellenőrzött magánéletig. Családpolitika a Szovjetunióban 1917 után. *Társadalmi Szemle, 1990*(6), 25–40.
Szülők, K. (2015). *SZKK interjú, Koch Alajosné, nyugalmazott gondozónő*. Retrieved August 8, 2019, from https://www.youtube.com/watch?v=ABHt2iZRvgc&t=470s
Taylor, P. J. (1996). What's modern about the modern world-system? Introducing ordinary modernity through world hegemony. *Review of International Political Economy, 3*(2), 260–286.
Terleckyj, N. (1975). *Household production and consumption*. National Bureau of Economic Research.
Thurer, S. (1995). *Myths of motherhood: How culture reinvents the good mother* (Reprint edition). New York: Penguin Books.
Wallerstein, I. (1974). *The modern World-System I. Capitalist agriculture and the origins of the European World-Economy in the sixteenth century*. New York, San Francisco & London: Academic.
Wallerstein, I. (2004). *World-systems analysis: An introduction*. Durham: Duke University Press.
Zimmermann, S. (2012). A társadalmi-nemi (gender) rezsim és küzdelem a magyar államszocializmusban. *Eszmélet, 24*(96), 103–131.

Gergely Csányi is a sociologist. His research field is the social-economic embeddedness and historical change of psychic structures, intimacy, body conceptions and gender. He is a PhD student of the University of Pécs. Csányi is member of the Working Group for Public Sociology "Helyzet".

Szabina Kerényi is a social anthropologist. Her research field is post-socialist spaces and movements, and discourses of reproduction. She is based at the Centre for Social Sciences, Hungarian Academy of Sciences. Kerényi is member of the Working Group for Public Sociology "Helyzet".

Chapter 18
Loving Like I Was Loved: Mother-Child Relationship from the Malay Muslims' Perspective

Dini Farhana Baharudin, Melati Sumari, Suhailiza Md Hamdani, and Hazlina Abdullah

Abstract As a woman takes on the role of mothering, her identity grows and develops. A mother's role has long been influenced by dynamic changes owing to social, political, and economic factors. However, becoming a mother is often described as a satisfying and empowering experience. Love in the mother-child relationship is worth examined given the challenges of parenting in contemporary Malaysia nowadays due to technological advances and globalisation. This paper examines how Malay Muslim mothers learn about the act of giving and receiving love through observations and examples they experienced in the cycle of life. Terminologies related to love, the concept of love between mother-child, and the value and strength of mother-child love in Malay Muslim culture are explained. A qualitative approach was used for this study. Interviews were conducted with 12 participants who are mothers and daughters. The responses from participants on love in the mother-child relationship which include the present bond with their child as well as the messages communicated about love from their mothers, and the influences of their culture were also included. This paper supports previous studies that show links between love and affection in childhood and positive well-being and happiness in the future. Meaningful positive relationships between mother and child also serves as the foundation to a stronger connection with Allah (*hablum min Allah*) and other human beings (*hablum min annas*).

Keywords Love · Mother-child · Parenting · Muslim · Malaysia

D. F. Baharudin (✉) · S. M. Hamdani
Faculty of Leadership and Management, Universiti Sains Islam Malaysia, Nilai, Malaysia
e-mail: dini@usim.edu.my; suhailiza@usim.edu.my

M. Sumari
University of Malaya, Kuala Lumpur, Malaysia
e-mail: melati2112@gmail.com

H. Abdullah
Faculty of Major Language Studies, Universiti Sains Islam Malaysia, Nilai, Malaysia
e-mail: hazlina@usim.edu.my

© Springer Nature Switzerland AG 2021
C.-H. Mayer, E. Vanderheiden (eds.), *International Handbook of Love*,
https://doi.org/10.1007/978-3-030-45996-3_18

18.1 Introduction to Love in the Described Context

Malaysia is a country with the total population of 32.4 million situated in the Southeast Asia which comprises people from multicultural background that adhere to collectivistic values (Department of Statistics Malaysia, 2018). Out of this number, the female population is 15.7 million (48.4%) and the male population 16.7 million (51.6%). Malaysia has made significant changes from an agricultural society to a modern one. At present, not only men play a role in ensuring socioeconomic growth, but women are also increasingly seen as equally important in the development of the country. Equipped with certain educational background, women nowadays are given the opportunity of going out to work to help support the family finances in addition to continue doing their duties as mothers. Due to this dynamic change in the society, a mother's role has also experienced changes. Becoming a mother is often described as a satisfying and empowering experience and as a woman takes on the role of mothering, her identity grows and develops. Given the challenges of parenting in the present contemporary Malaysia due to technological advances and globalization, love in the mother-child relationship is worth examined.

As mothers and also daughters, we reflected on these matters and this led us to conduct a study on how love was experienced in the mother-child relationship in today's setting as compared to experiences of being loved in the past. Therefore, we share in this chapter some of the findings. In this chapter, we describe the responses of 12 mothers who are also daughters themselves to questions relating to their experiences of love in their present relationship with their children and legacy of their own mothers' love. Hence, to better understand the descriptions, we first situate this chapter in some of the current scholarship relating to love, the family, mother-child relationship, as well as noting other theoretical influences on our interpretation of the data gathered.

18.2 Love as Part of Human Nature

Hatfield, Rapson, and Martel (2007) posit that love is an important human feature from birth to death. Ever since the mid-twentieth century, there is a growing interest in understanding love, but much remains to be uncovered (Neto & Wilks, 2017; Peterson & Seligman, 2004). Recently, research on love is now looking into the capacity to love and be loved which is seen as an innate human tendency that has powerful effects on life from infancy through old age.

Love is usually defined as an intense feeling of deep affection. This has been evidenced by the various classifications of love proposed by scholars. For example, six styles of love ranging from intense and possessive manic lover to patient and selfless agape lover (Hendrick & Hendrick, 1989); Lee's Six Love Attitudes which includes eros, ludus, storge, pragma, mania, and agape (1973), Sternberg's (1986) Theory of Triangular Love (see the chapter of Nel and Govender) comprising intimacy, passion, and commitment and Hatfield and Rapson's (1993) passionate and companionate love. All of which points to the fact that love is not only what one feels but also enacts. In many circumstances, love between human beings is relational that is when you love someone you will show it. For that reason, what we feel is very much reflected in what we do.

In the field of positive psychology, love is categorised as a positive emotion. Love has been found to be a prominent predictor of subjective well-being (Diener & Lucas, 2000) and altruistic love is related to happiness (Smith, 2009). Under the broaden-and-build theory of positive emotions, people's daily experiences of positive emotions compound over time to discover and build a variety of consequential personal resources, for example, the ability to give and receive emotional support, or maintain a sense of mastery over environmental challenges (Fredrickson, 1998, 2001). In other words, by having these personal resources people have more potential to meet life challenges effectively, become more successful, healthier and happier, and as a whole increase their life satisfaction (Lyubomirsky, King, & Diener, 2005; Tomasulo, 2010; Waugh & Fredrickson, 2006). At the interpersonal level, induced positive emotions increase people's sense of 'oneness' with close others and their trust in acquaintances (Dunn & Schweitzer, 2005). People who experience or express positive emotions more than others also show increases in optimism and tranquility over time (Fredrickson, Tugade, Waugh & Larkin, 2003), and also enhance the quality of their close relationships (Gable, Gonzaga, & Strachman, 2006; Waugh & Fredrickson, 2006).

Peterson and Seligman (2004, p. 29) identified love and the capacity to love as one of the strengths and virtues in human beings. It is defined as "valuing close relations with others, in particular those in which sharing and caring are reciprocated".

According to Al-Ghazali (1967), the many forms of love include love for God and the Prophet, love for fellow beings, love for other creatures, love for knowledge, and love for goodness. Peterson and Seligman (2004) mentioned that there are three prototypical forms of love:

1. child's love for a parent,
2. parent's love for a child, and.
3. romantic love.

Hence, relationships can involve different types of love at different point of time. For example, people may gradually shift from a child-parent to parent-child form of love as they grow up and their parents get older.

18.3 Love: Cultural and Religion Perspectives

As culture affects how people define love and the importance they place on love (Fehr, 1993; Hatfield & Rapson, 1996), a further understanding of Malay Muslim mothers in terms of their cultural and religious values, relevant characteristics, and challenges is needed.

From the total population of 32.4 million, the Malays count as the majority in Malaysia followed by the Chinese (20.8%), Indians (6.2%), and others (0.9%) (Department of Statistics Malaysia, 2018). Article 160(2) of the Malaysian Constitution defines 'Malay' as a person who professes the Muslim religion, habitually speaks the Malay language, and conforms to Malay customs (Hafriza, 2006). Islam plays an important role in almost every aspect in the life of the Malays; and is central to the Malay identity. As Muslims, the Malays by Islam; thus, upholding Islam as their religion and at the same time maintaining their cultural values (Ahmad Munawar, Zakaria, Mohd. Yusof, & Mashitoh, 2012; Hafriza, 2006). Prophet Muhammad once asked his companions of "the firmest handhold of faith", and the Prophet declared that "the firmest handhold of faith is to love for the sake of God and to hate for the sake of God, to befriend God's friends and to renounce His enemies" (Al-Kulayni, 1397, p. 126). This signifies that Islam truly recommends Muslims to love people and optimise kind and sincere relationships.

Similar to other collectivistic culture, extended family ties and strong kinship networks are emphasised. The socio-cultural system of the Malays is basically hierarchical and relationship-oriented. Even in the phase of rapid industrialisation and technological changes, class-based social structure continues in the way Malays express respect for elders and fulfil mutual obligations which is rooted from their value of *budi bahasa* (courtesy). For the Malays, *budi bahasa* is considered as the key ingredient for harmonious living in a collectivistic society as it serves as a guide to the way they relate with others with appropriate conduct, politeness and good manners in their everyday life (Dini Farhana, Zuria, & Salleh, 2013, 2015; Hashim, Normahdiah, Rozita, & Siti Sarah, 2012; Ismail & Muhammad Azaham, 2000; Mardiana, Halimatun Halaliah, & Asnarulkhadi, 2011; Wan Norhasniah, 2012; Zawawi & NoorShah, 2012). This can be observed by the way Malays obey their elders' instructions and depend on them to offer guidance, the way Malay extended families take care and look after their elderly folks, and specific ways of communicating values in verbal or non-verbal communications such as the use of honorifics for elders, and appropriate body postures when walking or sitting in front of them as a sign of respect (Abdullah & Pedersen, 2003; Mardiana et al., 2011).

The family is the core of the Malay culture. Relationship between husband and wife is seen as complementary with the man taking the leading role and the wife following him in order to preserve harmony. Being patient, humble, and having a caring posture of concern and support for others will ensure that there is peaceful coexistence among family members and community at large. The Malays also acknowledge the patriarchal nature of the society in which males are regarded as the head of the house, while women are expected to attend to their household duties in nurturing their children despite being career women. The values of respect for elders and other family-based values are taught by parents and internalised by the young early in life. The extended family concept plays a key role in providing emotional bonds and support for aging relatives. This form of living arrangement encourages family members to maintain warm, close-knit and intense relationships of interdependence and mutual help. Most Malay parents therefore expect their children to obey their instructions. Work, duties and responsibilities are distributed accordingly [in the family structure]. Malays think highly of those who are loyal, moderate in their ways, discipline and obedient. In the Malay Muslim culture, harmonious relationships will be maintained if children show these values and do not challenge their parents. All of these values are in line with Islamic teachings.

In Islam, love is viewed from a broader and more comprehensive perspective. Al-Ghazali (1967) classifies love into seven dimensions namely the love of Allah at the highest level, the love of the Prophet Muhammad, followed by self-love, the love of parents, love of creatures, love of knowledge, and love for goodness (Abu Zahrin, Ismail, & Idris, 2014). Love includes a sacred vertical relationship with the Creator, Allah (divine love) and horizontal relationship with human beings and other creatures (Al-Ghazali, 1967; Nor Asiah, 2001). A total submission to Allah is required, and Muslims do this by performing certain compulsory practices contained in the Pillars of Islam and Pillars of Iman, alongside other religious practices such as reading the Quran, saying their prayers and executing other religious practices such as fasting in the month of Ramadhan, performing Hajj and executing other works of charity, which are all aimed at becoming closer to Allah (Ali & Aboul-Fotouh, 2012; Padela, Killawi, Forman, Demonner, & Heisler, 2012; Utz, 2012). Not only the relationship with Allah, but also establishing good relationships with fellow human beings is also demanded by Islam.

In the realm of family and marriage, three concepts that relate to love can be found in the Holy Quran, specifically in verse 21 of Chap. 30 (al-Rum). The concepts are *sakeenah* (tranquility), *mawaddah* (love), and *rahmah* (mercy). Islam highlights that the purpose of marriage is to form a united *sakeenah* family based on *mawaddah* and *rahmah*. Sakeenah is the purpose of marriage which means to achieve peace, tranquility, and calmness after a physical or spiritual turmoil. This is because after marriage, a man will naturally feel at ease with the presence of his wife. Likewise, a woman will feel comfortable in the presence of her husband. The physical and spiritual state of fear that is associated with sin when not yet married can be changed into a calm and peaceful feeling after marriage. From the point of view of family, *sakeenah* is the result that family members achieve after adapting to transition in the family life cycle. *Sakeenah* is a dynamic concept because family life will not always be a bed of roses, but it takes courage, patience, and faith (*taqwa*) to overcome problems or challenges based on a strong desire for peace and tranquility of the soul and the pleasure of God. In other words, *sakeenah* can also be interpreted as family well-being. Second is the concept of '*mawaddah*'. *Mawaddah* can be defined by looking at three perspectives:

1. with reference to the Quran, Chapter 30 (Surah al Rum), verse 21, *mawaddah* refers to the feelings that exist between a man and a woman who are husband and wife, as passionate love or an intense emotion that is characterised as a state of longing for union with one another. Some scholars also interpret this as sexual intercourse between the husband and wife;
2. reference to Surah asy-Syura, Chapter 42, verse 23—*mawaddah* refers to maintaining kinship, while
3. reference to Surah al-Baqarah, Chapter 2, verse 96 means to desire.

Finally, *rahmah* which derives from the word '*rahim*' which means to have mercy on another, to be tender, or to have compassion upon another. Linguistically, it is also known as the womb, where the child is cared for and nourished. Love is the gift of Allah that enables one to do good and even the best for others, not only the spouse but also the children resulting from the marriage, which is proven by sincere sacrifice. A person who sacrifices and endures pain, for example, a mother giving birth, will naturally kiss her baby even though she was in a state of extreme stress and pain during labour, which portrays the kind of love that ultimately centers on the good of others. In a family context, parents show *rahmah* by responding to children's distress with sympathy and supportive behaviours, and through child focused efforts to foster children's positive development. This can be seen from the hadith of Bukhari and Muslim, "Whoever does not love, will not be loved".

18.4 Love in Mother-Child Relationship

The Malay Muslim mothers interviewed in this study shared their experiences of love in the mother-child relationship at present as compared to experiences of being loved in the past by their own mothers. Although there are some differences in the experiences from the present and the past, the understanding of what love is was maintained across the different generations. Love is part of mothers' nature to commit through the care they provide for their children to whom they are dedicated to protect, nurture, and train with the goal of helping them to become good individuals. Being career women, they still try to balance their professional commitment with family life. All the mothers selected in this study have children of both genders, all of whom are of different ages ranging from baby to young adult.

Description of the Study
The study employed a qualitative research approach with the use of two sessions of focus group discussion with 12 working mothers to obtain extensive sharing of experience. The participants were selected through purposive sampling in order to provide as much insights as possible into the phenomenon under examination i.e. the experiences of mothers regarding their experiences of love received from their mothers, and also love towards their children. All the mothers are married. The mothers are between 40 and 50 years of age with varied educational backgrounds. Six of them hold master degrees while the other six possess doctorate degrees. The age group of their children is quite diverse—those between 3 and 24 years.

The first session of the focus group discussion comprises six mothers (labeled as P1–P6) which lasted for about two and a half hours, while the second session consists of another six mothers (labeled as P7–P12) that took about 3 hours. The participants were asked semi-structured questions such as what is love to you as a mother?, how do you express love?, how did your mother show love?, what are the challenges in expressing love to your children?, which were based on an interview protocol prepared by the authors. All interviews were recorded and transcribed for data analysis. To maintain the confidentiality of the participants, each participant was given a label P1 to P12.

Researchers also did do follow up interview with participants until data is saturated.

Data Analysis

Data gathered from the Focus Group Interview were transcribed verbatim and analysed. Thematic analysis was used in identifying, analysing and interpreting of patterns or themes within qualitative data. Based on this analysis, the study identified two main themes. The themes are present and past love in mother-child relationship and messages conveyed through love in different era.

Unraveling Mothers' Love: Present and Past

In this section, we describe findings from the study which we divide into two parts based on the emerging themes. The first part involves narratives that articulate the mothers' experiences of love in the present bonding with their child, which encompass the physical, emotional and spiritual signs of love. The second part conveys the messages communicated about love from their mothers that represents the notion of love from a different epoch. All the narratives demonstrate intergenerational and cultural influences in the experience of love in mother-child relationship.

18.4.1 Present Love in Mother-Child Relationship

18.4.1.1 Physical Experience of Love

The physical experience of love was shown through touch, material rewards, and routine responsibilities. All of these were experienced by the participants in this study during their role as a mother to their children; and as a daughter to their mother.

Mothers' physical touch was experienced through hugs and kisses. Participants in this study build their relationship with their children through kissing and hugging throughout their lifetime, especially during their childhood. Some also shared that they received the same act of kissing and hugging from their children. This can be seen from the statements below

> I show that I love them by hugging and kissing them. (P3)
>
> Although they have all grown up, I would still kiss them. As a matter of fact, I kiss them [my sons] even in public. That is my way of showing my love for them. (P12)
>
> If we say we love them, we have to hug them regularly... we should also not feel ashamed to train our boys to hug and hold us in front of public. I am in the process of training my children to do that, especially the boys so that they are not shy to kiss and hug me till they grow up. (P5)
>
> With the kids, I will surely show my love, because during my childhood we never hugged our parents. The most we did was to shake and kiss their hands to show respect. Parents nowadays are different because of the surrounding and the reading culture... so, if you love someone demonstrate it. (P4)

The participants acknowledged the power of physical expression of love, and they agreed that love must be demonstrated explicitly to their children. Nevertheless, one of the challenges shared by some of the participants is that when the children grew up into adolescents, the children stopped the act of kissing and hugging in showing affection because they felt ashamed. However, when they grew older, they took the initiative to kiss and hug again probably due to the fact that maturity has made them realize and appreciate the value of family love. This can be seen in the following excerpts;

> But when they grow into teenagers they were embarrassed [if in front of friends]... now after he has become a young adult, he started to kiss and hug me. And I hug and kiss back. It was really a nice surprise. (P3)
>
> When I am with the children, if I want to hug and hold them, like my eldest 12 years old, he seems to avoid... shy. But at times, he will come to me [to hug] and I am okay with that. (P1)
>
> I feel that at a certain stage, boys... even though they were very attached to us before entering school, but once they enter school, there will be a stage when they become shy. But when they live in the hostel, they become attached again. It's like they appreciate us more. (P3)

Then again, some of the participants shared that they did not experience hugs and kisses when they were with their own mother. For example:

> My mom rarely shows her love [by kissing or hugging]. At times when we get together watching TV, that is the time we chat about school, friends, and she will listen even though she is busy... she's a career woman. Another thing, tea-time is so precious and important—we eat toasts together, eating, and drinking. (P2)
>
> It's difficult to interpret [love] because my mother is not the type that shows affection. It's just... I could see my mother hugs my younger brothers and sisters... not that I'm jealous. There was this one time when I have to bring glue (starch) to school but my mom just kept quiet. But the next morning the glue was ready. (P1)
>
> I learnt about love and affection from the family of my mother-in-law. My husband up till now, he still can kiss and hug my mother-in-law. So, I try to practice that in my family [because it was not done by my own mother]. (P6)

Even though there were minimal signs of hugs and kisses from their own mothers, the participants still express their love by hugging and kissing their own mothers when they were old. This may due to them being more open, and possibly because of the changes in culture and acceptance to express love. This is so because they have better education that has led them to understand the need of physical affections in strengthening family love.

> I also noticed that I did the same with my own mother—show love by hugging and kissing her when I grow older. (P2)
>
> I feel like a mother is the role model for children. Whenever I go back to kampung to see my mother, I would first shake her hand and then I would hug and kiss her. Perhaps my children saw this and that's why they feel that hugging and kissing their mother is okay. (P12)

Physical touch in the form of hugs and kisses is also promoted in Islam. Parents should kiss and hug their children when they are young as a symbol of love and affection, as exemplified by Prophet Muhammad. When a companion of the Prophet admitted that he never kissed his children, the Prophet said that the love was torn from the heart. In this sense, the Prophet's view is different from the traditional Malay parents who seem reluctant to show affection to their children fearing that it would make them lose respect towards the parents. However, participants in this study do not only extend their love to their children through touch but also materials in the form of gifts or rewards from the mothers to their children and vice versa.

> My mom after resigning she used her savings to help my father and buy us school supplies and other things that we needed. I do the same with my children. I don't mind using up all my salary for them. (P5)
>
> Mother would also entertain my siblings and I each month after receiving her salary. She would also take us to town and have lunch as a reward for our excellent achievement in school. It encourages us to excel in our studies. I also do the same [to my children]. (P9)
>
> "I saw her sacrifice. We know there are things luxurious and hard to get such as going for trips [because of our parents' salary]. My mother and father would still try their best to give it to us." (P2)

Participants also reminisced how their mother would pamper them with gifts or rewards. They enjoy this moment and perceive it as luxury. Despite earning minimal income during those days, mothers tried their best to meet the request of their children and developed love in the family. They perceived this as their mothers' sacrifices. Additionally, most of them appear to apply the same gesture to their own children.

Gifts or rewards are visible, tangible evidence of love. The very nature of a gift is not something that the children deserve but given because the parents yearn to share unconditional love with their children. Nevertheless, some parents fail to realize this; they think by just giving gifts to their children without the presence of 'inner', 'deeper' feeling is an ample act of love when in reality, they are simply paying them for a service rendered, or because they wanted to hide their 'guilt' for being too busy or being absent. When this happens, they are not really conveying love to their child.

The mothers also considered routine responsibilities such as cooking, doing housework, and providing education as their way of showing love to their children. They also shared how their own mothers did the same sacrifice.

> This is something that I still struggled with [to do with my children] but I try as best as I could... My mom was an accountant. She would only be free on weekends. But I remember no matter how busy she was, she would always cook and prepare food for us and would wake up at 4 a.m. Mon would prepare everything before going to work. When we came back, lunch would be ready. I guess that was mom's way of showing love. (P6)
>
> Mother cooked, she observed what we like to eat... although she is a teacher and had a maid, but she still cooked. It was as if we could taste the love and tenderness through her meals. My mother is my role-model so, I do the same. I want my children to feel the same. (P2)
>
> I followed my mother's example in educating the children especially on religious education. In the past, mother always have this routine—before maghrib prayers, we must bath and eat dinner, between the evening prayers, we must recite the Quran or other religious activities, then only do homework or any other activities. This is related to responsibilities of parent to child. Because we love them, we must teach and emphasize on religion. (P3)

Performing acts of service even though they are sometimes considered as daily routine is part of the experience of showing and receiving love. Malay Muslim mothers often feel that carrying out routine chores for the family comes naturally for them and is already a form of expression of love. This may be the reason why traditional Malay parents rarely say or show their love openly. For them, parenting is a responsibility that they take seriously as a service-oriented vocation that has already represented love. For them, in this case, actions definitely speak louder than words.

In addition, the participants also mentioned about the importance of spending time with their children as an expression of love. Once again, as career women who realise that time is important in juggling between work and family, the participants confessed that quality time is indeed an essence to indicate love.

> Love is to spend time together, especially for my children whom reside in the boarding-school. When they come home, we entertain and provide them with more attention. (P4)
>
> During weekends, we go out window-shopping. That will give us quality time—the time in the car where I will talk to my children. My own mother did not do this when growing up because she's too busy with her business. (P7)
>
> I often dedicate about 30-minutes of my time to have one-on-one special time with my child without interruptions of phones, siblings, housework, and work commitments. Sometimes, we have a snack at his favourite place, sometimes, we go to see the movie, or other times we play. (P10)

A further significance of spending time as a way to demonstrate love is shown through another participant who mentioned that with the advent of smartphones and other technological advances, in addition to the need for women to work, it is easy to get distracted and have a disinterested lifestyle towards loved ones. Thus, she kept reminding herself that she needs to make time for her children.

> Love means—we must make time for them. (P5)
>
> I make sure that I will put down any electronic devices when I talk to him. I try to make eye contact with him so that he would understand that I care and that he has got all my focus on him. (P12)

Likewise, another mother shared how she needs to be creative in coming up with ways to share quality time with her children. Despite being busy, she feels the need to connect with her children as she herself did not experience the same with her mother.

Expressing love through providing quality time for the children is giving undivided attention to them. Children must feel that they are the center of attention which allows more opportunity for meaningful conversations.

18.4.1.2 Emotional Experience of Love

Besides physically displaying their love, in order to create a positive and healthy relationship, it is also important to have empathy in mother-child relationship. Empathy refers to appreciating other people's feelings and thoughts especially when related to negative experiences (Gonzalezmena, 2006). Without empathy it is difficult to have positive relationship between parents and their children. Mothers who provide love to their children with their gentle, caring, and sympathetic approach are closer to their children, and help develop positive growth and success in them (Sidek, 2010). The confessions below signal how the participants believe that children need emotional support;

> As teachers we can see students who are pressured by their parents. As a teacher and mother, I don't expect too much [from my children]. Just support what they are good at. If they are weak, we assist but don't put too much pressure. We must be realistic. (P2)
>
> Children have different talents. Some love sports or painting. In academic we send to extra classes. Other than that, we leave it to Allah because we have tried our best. We give support and do not compare them [children]. (P1)

At times, mothers give advice and encouragement to their young ones on various matters and for older children, they may be the ones asking for advice from the mothers. Besides support, mothers also possess special instinct that can sense if something is wrong or otherwise. Furthermore, children would still require advice and attention from their mothers in every phase of their lives as they face different challenges at different stages of their life. This shows the close relationship that enriches the love between a mother and the child.

> Mothers have instinct. If we call, even just by listening to ours voice, they know that we have problem... I always share my problems with my mother. But now after being married, I don't want to worry her. Once, she couldn't sleep because I shared my sad story! (P3)
>
> I give advice to my daughters. That as a female, they should be able to do housework... I told them that women have to be able to cook. I was telling them the realities of being a woman. (P7)
>
> With my teenage son, I have to talk to him to know what he feels. Encourage him when he feels down. And I am also thinking about how to be closer to him and know his feelings." (P3)

18.4.1.3 Spiritual Expression of Love

Apart from the physical and emotional aspects, the participants also show their love by not failing to pray and supplicate for their children to achieve excellence in the world and the hereafter. They believe that their parents' prayer is one of the major factors contributing to their success—which also reflects the Islamic view—hence they correspondingly pray for the success and wellbeing of their own children.

> Indeed, teenagers are a challenge. There will be a phase where they will 'run' away from us. There's a barrier. We must handle them, either they are close to us or they will find other people for attention. We have to pray to avoid this and to read on how to curb the problem. My son, the turning point was when he was in Secondary 4. When he went to boarding school, and saw other unfortunate people, that time he became more appreciative, and started to demonstrate love to us. But we prayed a lot [for him to change for the better]. We have to constantly pray. (P3)
>
> Another thing, when my mother scolds me, she will use positive words because she said, 'The sky will open up when I say something' [in Islam, a mother's prayers will always be fulfilled by Allah]. So, mother will always say positive things [even when angry]. (P4)

In relation to that, the mothers believe that prayers should come together with efforts and then, leave everything in the hands of Allah (tawakkal). Indeed, Islam stresses that in everything we do, prayers must be accompanied by great effort and the rest will be determined by Allah.

> Every time my children are about to take any examination or test, regardless if they are married or not, they would never miss to call for the mother and seek her blessing. And I would always pray for their success [regardless of whether they requested or not]. (P11)

A loving mother would always pray for the welfare of her children even though they are hurt by the children's attitude and action. The Malay Muslim mothers believe that a prayer is an ultimate symbol of love from parents to their children. Prayers would result in children feeling the genuine, natural intimacy and love showered by the parents. In addition to prayers, mothers also show the importance of having good values as part of love. Some examples of good values include obedience and patience as evident in the excerpts below.

> My son when he's angry, whether for a moment or so, will always message or call me to apologize. And I praised him for this. If his little sister did something wrong, he would tell her that 'syurga di tapak kaki ibu' [a saying that heaven is under the mother's foot to indicate a symbol of the high position of the mother; hence, need to be obeyed and respected]. (P3)
>
> I remembered we were so afraid of hurting her [our mother's] feelings. In the end, we did not go to the river because she did not approve. We believe it might be risky because 'kalau masin mulut ibu' [means the wisdom of a mother's advice indicates the importance of having children to listen to and obey what their elders want them to do] we might get into trouble. (P12]
>
> I rarely get angry. I will talk and advise. If I'm so angry, I might shout at them. But I rarely get angry... usually I'm patient. And my mom is very patient." (P8)

18.4.2 Messages Conveyed Through Love Across Different Era

Among the point of comparison that the participants drew between their role as mothers and that of their own mothers was that they were, in addition to being mothers, also working longer hours because they partake various types of jobs and handle higher expectations compared to their mothers. Additionally, there are also challenges in terms of technology (gadgets) and higher cost of living in the present setting that differ in the past. All of these add to the challenges of parenting as they are expected to be able to cope with their work, home, family, and other life responsibilities in a balanced manner. However, it can be concluded that despite the differences observed, the meaning and experience of love have not gone through major changes.

Mothers in this study have defined love as emotions, attitudes, and actions related to selfless concern and giving of oneself for the well-being of their children. Examples can be seen from the participants' responses.

> To me, the meaning of true love is when we are open to giving and receiving. There are sincerity and sacrifices involved. (P1)
>
> Love is so abstract if translated into action, it means there should be sacrifices. (P2)

> Love is giving sincerely and sacrifices. In my marriage of fifteen years, I realize how important sacrifices is in order to see my children's success. (P3)

The mothers show that their love contains feelings, conditions, and behaviors that are focused on caring, and orientation toward supporting, helping, and extending beneficence to another. They make voluntary choices to give oneself for the good of their children which includes efforts to promote prosperity and decency. The mothers also associate love to rights and responsibilities as a mother where their love is unconditional but conditional (because of the responsibilities).

> Either we are willing or not, we have to sacrifice for the family. (P2)
> As mothers, our love is unconditional. (P3)
> Being responsible is a form of love towards the children. Islam shows that children are born as clean slate. We are the ones shaping them." (P5)

The mothers also mentioned about the challenges that they faced in providing 'equal' love to their children. Here, the concept of equality in Islam is apparently adopted where mothers perceived that being fair in giving love is to position things at its proper place. In the case of attending to children, being equal and just is imperative, taking into consideration factors such as age, gender, [dis]ability, and needs of the child. This was exemplified by the mothers' responses in this study;

> We don't compare our children with others. We accept them the way they are and sometimes we see our children lacking in some aspect but great in other aspect. My parents also never compare we with others. (P2)
> Children have different talents. Some love sports or painting. In academic we send to extra classes. Other than that, we leave it to Allah because we have tried our best. We give support and do not compare them [children]. My parents in the past also did not compare me with others. (P1)

Despite the hope of parents to provide equal love to their children, in reality, children are different not only in terms of their gender but also age levels, and specific needs. Therefore, love must all be harmonized with the physiological, emotional, intellectual, spiritual, and social changes that are taking place inside the child. They value and respect their children regardless of imperfections.

According to the participants, love is also a life-long, continuous cyclical process. The participants gradually shift from a daughter receiving love from their mother to becoming a mother giving love to their children as they grow up and their parents get older.

> We thought only little children need attention... but once [my son] graduated [from college], other issues appear... so it's forever. After this my son is getting married and so there are issues still. (P2)
> My parents' love for the youngest was so obvious. The age difference between us is 20 years. I got married when he was 5. Imagine how spoiled he is when with us. But he is the one who spends more time with my mother. Now he is the one taking care and living with her. We really appreciate this. (P3)

Overall, the themes identified in this study have shown the influence of culture and religion with specific reference to Islam, on the experience of love obtained by the participants from their mothers. There is a clear sign of the existence of the element of blessing (*rahmah*), which is a prominent aspect in Islam in the understanding and practice of love in the Malay Muslim mother-daughter relationship. It is also interesting to note the importance of the concept of justice in the experience of love which is also interpreted in an Islamic perspective by the participants in this study.

18.5 Conclusion

From the narratives of all 12 mothers who participated in this study, the mother-child love is influenced by multiple persons and factors that come at it from multiple directions, and thus shape and reshape the way one love. Even though love is a part of mothers' nature (*fitrah*) to love their children, the expressions and manifestations of love might differ from one person to another. Among the challenges that mothers face would be in balancing and providing equality when having many children of different age and gender so that every child will feel loved. In spite of that, the mothers continue to go through life transformative process in the ways that they love, care, and nurture their children.

In summary, a mother's love and compassion are the most pertinent ingredients for the family's well-being and success. Since in the womb until adulthood, with the mercy of God, loving mothers shower their children with love and kindness. They nurture their children with love without expecting any rewards. As a Muslim, the most powerful motivation for human action is to get Allah's blessings. Mothers in this study demonstrate their love and affection to their children in many ways. They would kiss and hug their children, provide material and emotional support, and pray for the success of each of the children. They continuously give physical, socio-emotional, and spiritual experiences of love to the children. As a consequence, the sincerity of love fosters the children's self-esteem, motivation, success, and well-being and tranquility of family life.

All the narratives demonstrate intergenerational and cultural influences in the experience of love in mother-child relationship. This chapter supports previous studies that show links between love and affection in childhood and positive well-being and happiness in the future. Meaningful positive relationships between mother and child also serve as the foundation to a stronger connection with Allah (*hablum min Allah*) and other human beings (*hablum min annas*). Professionals working with Malay Muslm community need to be more culturally aware and sensitive about the cultural belief regarding love between mother and child. The culture of Muslim in general need to be applied with caution on this community because Malay Muslim culture is embedded between the Malay cultural tradition and Islamic values.

Further studies ought to be carried out to understand family relationships of the Malay Muslims, not only love between parent and child but also married couples. It is hoped that the narratives of mothers shared in this chapter have provided valuable information that can be used by mental health practitioners in a practical form. One limitation is the small number of samples that limits the generalization of the findings. Research in other areas that are related to love such as attachment in the

Malay Muslim community could also be addressed as it would also help to explore this issue and beyond.

References

Abdullah, A., & Pedersen, P. B. (2003). *Understanding multicultural Malaysia: Delights, puzzles, & irritations*. Petaling Jaya: Pearson Prentice Hall.

Abu Zahrin, S. N., Ismail, R., & Idris, F. (2014). Concept of love in Islam and its relationship with rational thinking. *Jurnal Psikologi Malaysia, 28*(2), 102–119.

Ahmad Munawar, I., Zakaria, S., Mohd. Yusof, O., & Mashitoh, Y. (2012) Islam dalam Pendidikan dan hubungannya dengan pembentukan jati diri bangsa Melayu di Malaysia. *Jurnal Hadhari, Special Ed.*, 37–50.

Al-Ghazali, al-Imam A'bi Hamid Muhammad bin Muhammad. (1967). *Ihya' cUlum al-Din, al-Juzu' al-Thalith*. Qaherah: Muassasah al-Halabi wa syarakahu li nasyri wa al-Tauzi`.

Ali, O., & Aboul-Fotouh, F. (2012). Traditional mental health coping and help-seeking. In S. Ahmed & M. Amer (Eds.), *Counseling muslims: Handbook of mental health issues and interventions* (pp. 33–55). New York, NY: Routledge Press.

Al-Kulayni. (1397). AA.H., Kitab al-Iman wal-Kufr. *Bab al-Hubb fi Allah wal-Bughd fi Allah, 6*, 126.

Department of Statistics Malaysia. (2018). *Population & demography*. Retrieved August 15, 2019, from https://www.dosm.gov.my/v1/index.php?r=column/ctwoByCat&parent_id=115&menu_id=L0pheU43NWJwRWVSZklWdzQ4TlhUUT09

Diener, E., & Lucas, R. E. (2000). Explaining differences in societal levels of happiness: Relative standards, need fulfillment, culture, and evaluation theory. *Journal of Happiness Studies, 1*, 41–78.

Dini Farhana Baharudin, Zuria Mahmud, & Salleh Amat. (2013). *Pandangan golongan Melayu dewasa tentang kesejahteraan: Satu penerokaan awal*. Paper presented at the PERKAMA Counseling Convention 2013. Persatuan Kaunseling Malaysia. Kuala Lumpur, June 9-11.

Dini Farhana Baharudin, Zuria Mahmud, & Salleh Amat. (2015). Wellness from the perspective of Malay Muslim Adults in Malaysia. *Al-Abqari Journal of Islamic Social Sciences and Humanities, 6*(2015), 79–100.

Dunn, J. R., & Schweitzer, M. E. (2005). Feeling and believing: The influence of emotion on trust. *Journal of Personality and Social Psychology, 88*, 736–748.

Fehr, B. (1993). How do I love thee? Let me consult my prototype. In S. Duck (Ed.), *Understanding relationship processes series, Vol. 1. Individuals in relationships*. London: Sage Publications https://doi.org/10.4135/9781483326283.n4

Fredrickson, B. L. (1998). What good are positive emotion? *Review of General Psychology, 2*, 300–319.

Fredrickson, B. L. (2001). The role of positive emotions in positive psychology: The broaden-and-build theory of positive emotions. *American Psychologist, 56*, 218–226.

Fredrickson, B. L., Tugade, M. M., Waugh, C. E., & Larkin, G. (2003). What good are positive emotions in crises? A prospective study of resilience and emotions following the terrorist attacks on the United States on September 11th, 2001. *Journal of Personality and Social Psychology., 84*, 365–376.

Gable, S. L., Gonzaga, G. C., & Strachman, A. (2006). Will you be there for me when things go right? Supportive responses to positive event disclosures. *Journal of Personality and Social Psychology, 91*, 904–917.

Gonzalezmena, J. (2006). *Child, family, and community: Family-centered early care and education* (5th ed.). Pearson.

Hafriza Burhanudeen. (2006). *Language & social behaviour. Voices from the Malay World*. Bangi: Penerbit Universiti Kebangsaan Malaysia.

Hashim Musa, Normahdiah Sheik Said, Rozita Che Rodi & Siti Sarah Ab. Karim. (2012). Hati budi Melayu: Kajian keperibadian sosial Melayu ke arah penjanaan Melayu gemilang. *GEMA Online Journal of Language Studies, 12*(1), 163–182.

Hatfield, E., & Rapson, R. L. (1993). *Love, sex, and intimacy: Their psychology, biology, and history.* New York: Harper Collins.

Hatfield, E., & Rapson, R. L. (1996). Stress and passionate love. In C. D. Spielberger & I. G. Sarason (Eds.), *Stress and emotion: Anxiety, anger, and curiosity.* New York: Routledge.

Hatfield, E., Rapson, R. L., & Martel, L. D. (2007). Passionate love and sexual desire. In S. Kitayama & D. Cohen (Eds.). *Handbook of cultural psychology.* New York: Guilford Press.

Hendrick, C., & Hendrick, S. S. (1989). Research on love: Does it measure up? *Journal of Personality and Social Psychology, 56*, 784–794.

Ismail Noor & Muhammad Azham. (2000). *The Malays par excellence... warts and all. An Introspection.* Subang Jaya: Pelanduk Publications.

Lee, J. A. (1973). *The colors of love: An exploration of the ways of loving.* Don Mills, ON: New Press.

Lyubomirsky, S., King, L., & Diener, E. (2005). The benefits of frequent positive affect: Does happiness lead to success? *Psychological Bulletin, 131*, 803–855.

Mardiana Mohamad, Halimatun Halaliah Mokhtar, & Asnarulkhadi Abu Samah. (2011). Person-centered counseling with Malay clients: Spirituality as an indicator of personal growth. *Procedia Social and Behavioral Sciences, 30*, 2117–2123.

Neto, F., & Wilks, D. C. (2017). Compassionate love for a romantic partner across the adult lifespan. *European Journal of Psychology, 13*(4), 606–617.

Nor Asiah Jusoh. (2001). *The psychology of love: Comparative study of al-Ghazali and Maslow.* Unpublished directed research report. International Islamic University Malaysia.

Padela, A., Killawi, A., Forman, J., Demonner, S., & Heisler, M. (2012). American Muslim perceptions of healing: Key agents in healing and their roles. *Qualitative Health Research, 22*, 847–858.

Peterson, C., & Seligman, M. E. P. (2004). *Character strengths and virtues: A handbook and classification.* New York: Oxford University Press.

Sidek, B. (2010). Keluarga sakinah. Shah Alam: Alaf 21.

Smith, T. W. (2009). Loving and caring in the United States: Trends and correlates of empathy, altruism, and related constructs. In B. Fehr, S. Sprecher & L. Underwood (Eds.). *The science of compassionate love: Theory, research, and applications.* Malden, MA, USA: Blackwell.

Sternberg, R. J. (1986). A triangular theory of love. *Psychological Review, 93*, 119–135.

Tomasulo, D. (2010). *Love 2.0 book review.* Retrieved August 15, 2019 smith 2009 from https://psychcentralreviews.com/2016/love-2-0/

Utz, A. (2012). Conceptualizations of mental health, illness, and healing. In S. Ahmed & M. Amer (Eds.), *Counseling muslims: Handbook of mental health issues and interventions* (pp. 15–32). New York, NY: Routledge Press.

Wan Norhasniah Wan Husin. (2012). *Peradaban dan Perkauman di Malaysia.* Kuala Lumpur: Penerbit Universiti Malaya.

Waugh, C. E., & Fredrickson, B. L. (2006). Nice to know you: Positive emotions, self-other overlap, and complex understanding in the formation of new relationships. *Journal of Positive Psychology, 1*, 93–106.

Zawawi, I., & NoorShah, M. S. (2012). Indigenising knowledge and social science discources in the periphery: Decolonising Malayness and Malay underdevelopment. In Z. Ibrahim (Ed.), *Social science and knowledge in a globalising world* (pp. 1–35). Kajang: Persatuan Sains Sosial Malaysia.

Dini Farhana Baharudin (PhD) is a lecturer at the Faculty of Leadership and Management, Universiti Sains Islam Malaysia, Nilai, Malaysia. She holds a degree in Law, Master degrees in Community Counseling (MA) and in Education (MEd), and a PhD in Counseling. She is also a Registered and Licensed Counselor in Malaysia. Besides teaching, she is actively involved in research and publications on multiculturalism and diversity in counseling, marriage and family counseling, addiction counseling, and holistic wellness.

Melati Sumari (PhD) is a Senior Lecturer at the University of Malaya, Kuala Lumpur, Malaysia. She has been working at the university since 1997. She obtained a Bachelor and Master degrees in Education (Counseling), both from the University of Malaya, and a doctoral degree in Counselor Education and Supervision from Western Michigan University, USA. She has published two academic books in counseling, more than ten book chapters and journal articles in counseling. She has also been awarded a number of research grants. Her research and writing focus mainly on marriage, family, and addiction counseling in cultural context. She also presented in local and international conferences.

Suhailiza Md Hamdani (PhD) is lecturer at the Faculty of Leadership and Management, Universiti Sains Islam Malaysia, Nilai, Malaysia. She has a Bachelor degree in Usuluddin from the University of Malaya, Malaysia, a Master degree in 'Aqeedah from the University of al Al Bayt, Jordan. She currently finishes her PhD in 'Aqeedah from the Islamic International University of Malaysia. Her interests are in da'wah, psycho-spiritual therapy, and 'aqeedah.

Hazlina Abdullah (PhD) obtained her PhD from the International Islamic University Malaysia (IIUM), M.Ed TESL from Universiti Pendidikan Sultan Idris (UPSI), and her B.Ed TESOL degree from the University of Warwick. She has gained vast teaching experience through her teaching career at secondary and tertiary levels. She is currently attached to Universiti Sains Islam Malaysia (USIM).

Chapter 19
Sexuality, Love and Sexual Well-Being in Old Age

Sofia von Humboldt, Isabel Leal, and Gail Low

Abstract Age significantly influences older adults' perspectives of love and sexuality. The frame of proof concerning sexual well-being (SWB) of older adults is starting to increase. Older adults experience love, sexual desire and engage in sexual activities, although, our understanding of their SWB is still insufficient and often not consensual. Additionally, up to date, cultural aspects lack in the literature.

SWB correspond to an emotional and cognitive evaluation of an individual's sexual life, and is positively related with physical and mental health, well-being, psychological growth, and successful aging. Current literature focuses on sexual dysfunctions and difficulties; however SWB include sexual satisfaction, sexual functioning, sexual interest, self-esteem, intimate satisfaction, and psychosexual variables.

Different factors may influence SWB and contribute to sexual unwellness (SU), such as physical and mental health, psychological variables, culture, daily stress, relationship quality and duration, intercourse difficulties, general sexual dysfunctions, and sexual communication.

Policy and intervention programs, which comprise love and SWB dimensions, concerns and cultural aspects, may contribute to the health and well-being of older individuals and to understanding the needs of older dyads.

The present chapter discusses SWB within the context of love and intimacy in old age, including an empirical exploration of SWB, comprising pertinent research, policy programs and interventions. Given that love and SWB may contribute to successful aging, and that older adults may try to explore relationship

---

S. von Humboldt (✉)
William James Center for Research, ISPA – Instituto Universitário, Lisboa, Portugal
e-mail: sofia.humboldt@gmail.com

I. Leal
William James Center for Research, ISPA – Instituto Universitário, Lisboa, Portugal
e-mail: ileal@ispa.pt

G. Low
Faculty of Nursing, Edmonton Clinical Health Academy (ECHA), University of Alberta, Edmonton, AB, Canada
e-mail: gail.low@ualberta.ca

© Springer Nature Switzerland AG 2021
C.-H. Mayer, E. Vanderheiden (eds.), *International Handbook of Love*,
https://doi.org/10.1007/978-3-030-45996-3_19

issues and sexual problems, but not obtain adequate attention, it is pertinent to improve our knowledge and to analyze love and SWB in old age in depth in order to elaborate future tailored policies and interventions with older populations. Moreover, since old people in different cultures show diverse meanings for their love relationships and sexual experiences, specific knowledge about love and SWB is essential for planning culture-adapted interventions in old age. The chapter will conclude with a discussion of the limitations and future perspectives for research and interventions.

Keywords Love · Aging · Older adults · Sexuality · Sexual unwellness · Sexual well-being

19.1 Introduction

The number of older adults is increasing exponentially worldwide (2.6% per year) and at a much faster rate than the remaining population, with great impact upon society, including increasing costs with social support and health care, and cross-cultural challenges about aging well (World Health Organization [WHO], 2012). Indeed, the group of people over age 65, will more than double by the year 2030 (Hillman, 2008; von Humboldt, Leal, & Monteiro, 2016). Consequently, knowledge about love relationships and sexual well-being (SWB) of the older population is going to be of major significance in the next years as we witness the growth of the population (von Humboldt et al., 2016).

19.2 Love and Sexuality Among Older Adults in Different Cultures

Age significantly influences individual concepts of love and sexuality in old age (Neto, 2012). A number of studies highlighted older participants who verbalized not only of the desire to have sex, but also of the need for physical love and affection (Davis, 2015; Hillier & Barrow, 2010). Furthermore, Neto (2012) indicated that older women believe that love comes before sex, and that older men consider that love is essential in relationships. In the same study, both men and women were similar in the conviction that sex is a demonstration of love (Davis, 2015).

Aging is a complex and unique process that involves cultural, ethnic and gender differences. Indeed, attributes such as love, sexual intimacy and sexuality significantly contribute to older adults' life expectancy, well-being, health and quality of life (von Humboldt, 2016; Langer, 2009).

Love is a concept shaped by culture and time, and has changed throughout history and individual lives, in a surprising way (Barusch, 2008). Experiences associated with love can be explained by human biochemistry and physiology, however the way we interpret and shape them is determined by the culture and time, in which we live (Barusch, 2008) (see also Chaps. 2, 4, and 29).

In a different perspective, some religions such as Sufism (see Chap. 12) and Mahayana Buddhism, and other spiritual and contemplative traditions highlight that love and compassion may be a path to wisdom. Additionally, in some Western cultures, research highlights the difficulty in achieving more elevated, productive and mature forms of love and therefore, wisdom (Barusch, 2008; Fromm, 1956). In relation to this, in a previous cross-cultural study, with older participants from Western and Asian countries, participants completed a survey with measures assessing cultural indicators of quality of love, self-transcendence, and wisdom. Outcomes indicated that a cultural syndrome and individualism were positively associated with immature love, and negatively related to self-transcendence (Le & Levenson, 2005). A different study indicated significant worldwide cross-cultural results (Buss, 1989, 2016). Love partners who offered good economic resources, as well as the capacity of long-term resource acquisition, such as ambition, hard work and social status, were much desired, in particular by older women. Older men prioritized physical attractiveness and relativized youth. Cultures also differed dramatically in what concerns the desire for virginity in a potential spouse. Swedes, for example, did not value virginity, while Chinese indicated virginity practically indispensable (Buss, 1989, 2016).

Universal preferences for love partners in old age include the desire for kind, understanding, intelligent, reliable, emotionally stable, and healthy love partners. Interestingly, old people around worldwide feel happier with partners with whom they are in love and in turn are in love with them, overturning some conventional beliefs indicating that love is an Western creation and not universal in all cultures. Indeed, the feeling of love is found throughout the world, serves as a form of psychological commitment, and appears in long-term relationships throughout old age (Buss, 1988, 2016; Frank, 1988). In this context, successful partner retention tactics incorporate love, attention, kindness, affection, resource flow, and sexual access (Buss, 2016) and sexuality, is present in every existential trajectory and overpasses sexual activity because it includes love (Frugoli & Júnior, 2011).

19.3 Are Older Adults Sexually Active?

Sexual activity in later life is multi-established, with substantial variation between older and younger groups (Bell, Reissing, Henry, & Van Zuylen, 2017) (see Chap. 20). Research indicates that older people engage in sexual activity less often when compared to younger groups (Fileborn et al., 2015). In a previous study, the old age cohort (age 65–74) reported lower frequency of recent sexual activity with partners, e.g., vaginal, oral, anal, other genital contact (Mercer et al., 2013).

Some previous studies have ingrained ageist convictions about asexuality in old age, resulting in a lack of understanding about the sexuality of older adults (Gott & Hinchliff, 2003). However, existing research reiterates that sexuality is perceived by older adults as having substantial value in later life (Gott & Hinchliff, 2003; von Humboldt et al., 2016).

A previous study indicated that sexual desire is the stage of sexual behaviour least affected by senescence. Interestingly, older adults are more physically capable of having sex than they are willing to participate in sexual activity (Sharpe, 2004). Therefore, the myth of asexuality in old age is incompatible with this expression of sexuality (Sharpe, 2004). Indeed, there is substantial proof that many older people are sexually active and see sex as both agreeable and rewarding (Ferris et al., 2008; Fileborn et al., 2015; Lee, Nazroo, O'Connor, Blake, & Pendleton, 2016; Lee, Vanhoutte, Nazroo, & Pendleton, 2016; Waite, Laumann, Das, & Schumm, 2009).

In a study by Hillman (2008), 25% of participants aged 70 to 80 had sexual activities during the previous year, and reported a frequency of sexual activity greater than once a week. In a different study, 73% of older people were engaging in sexual relationships, and 65% of these indicated regular sexual activity with a partner (Lindau et al., 2007). In another study, two-thirds of older people reported having sexual activity (Syme, Klonoff, Macera, & Brodine, 2013).

In an institutionalized setting for older people with caregivers, 50% of caregivers reported that older people were interested in sexuality, 33.3% had a need to express sexuality and 16.6% considered that older people should have more sexual experiences, indicating positive opinions concerning sexuality in later life (Monteiro, von Humboldt, & Leal, 2017).

Moreover, the conclusions of the representative Australian Longitudinal Study of Health and Relationships indicated a high percentage of heterosexual women and men reporting an active sex life as relevant to their well-being (78%: women; 91%: men) and underlined that their sexual relationship was 'very' emotionally satisfying (72%: women; 86%: men) (Ferris et al., 2008). Conclusions from ELSA-Wave 6 indicated a positive relation between sexual activity and SWB. Subsequently, the positive influence of sexual activity in health and well-being in old age has been progressively highlighted in health materials and campaigns (Tetley, Lee, Nazroo, & Hinchliff, 2016).

Ussher, Perz, Gilbert, Wong, and Hobbs (2013) indicated that heterosexual and gay older adults renegotiated sexual activity after cancer treatment and experienced sexual satisfaction from sexual activities not involving an erect penis (e.g. masturbation, mutual genital touching).

In a study with older married couples, only 2 out of 28 participants said sex was not relevant (Hinchliff & Gott, 2011). The last National Study of Sexual Attitudes and Lifestyles (Natsal-3) (Mitchell et al., 2013) defined levels of sexual function for sexually active older adults compared to younger groups: a combination of sexual response, sexual function within a relationship, and self-appraisal of sexual life. Results indicated that sexually active participants reported having at least one same-sex or distinct-sex sexual partner in the previous year (Mitchell et al., 2013). Another study with heterosexual old couples highlighted the importance and role of sexuality in later life (Gott & Hinchliff, 2003).

19.4 Older Adults' Sexuality in a Cultural Context

There is a lack of data regarding cultural aspects related to SWB. From a cultural view point, sexual activity in old age is commonly considered seen as pathological or exceptional (Bieńko, 2014) (see Chap. 20). Moreover, perspectives about sexuality in old age may be accompanied by surprise and disbelief (Bieńko, 2014). Popular culture models prefer a youthful appearance rather than looking 'old' as more sexually attractive. Conversely, old age is usually associated with dependence, passivity, disease and unattractiveness (Bieńko, 2014). For example, sexual activity has been seen in some cultures as an energy-demanding activity, one not of necessary to preserving health and longevity (Bieńko, 2014).

Cultural bias tends to stereotype older individuals as asexual, lacking emotions and feelings. Moreover, culturally, older women and men do not perceive their sexuality in the same way. Women's sexuality is often associated with the ability to reproduce and raise children. Women may feel that beyond the age of 40 to 45 years, when they begin to feel bodily changes, mainly due to menopause, sexual activity should be ruled out. Men's sexuality is not expected to change throughout life. Additionally, cultural differences seem to exist in different areas of the globe. For instance, African older women are not expected to discuss their sexuality, although in a recent study they very openly shared their sexual experiences (Okiria, 2014). However, this is not consensual. Research also highlights the emergence of another cultural stereotype, based on the perception of health, vitality, love and pleasure, while engaging in sexual activities in old age. Additionally, in some cases medical intervention for increasing sexual performance is expected (Gott, 2005).

19.5 Sexual Well-Being

SWB has been defined as the emotional and cognitive evaluation of an individual's sexual life, and may be evaluated in terms of pleasure judgments across various areas, such as physical and emotional aspects of relationships, sexual activity, and other aspects of comparative significance of an individual's sexuality (Rosen & Bachmann, 2008). Although SWB is often omitted and misunderstood in old age (Kalra, Subramanyam, & Pinto, 2011), it is an important component of general well-being in old age (Hooghe, 2012).

SWB is positively linked to health and well-being, and physical activity (Laumann et al., 2006). Additionally, some aspects of SWB, such as sexual interest, functioning and satisfaction have been related to physical health, relaxation, cardiovascular benefits and reduced pain sensitivity (Brody, 2010; Chen, Zhang, & Tan, 2009; Jannini, Fischer, Bitzer, & McMahon, 2009), and with psychological benefits, such as reduced levels of depression, greater quality of life, internal growth, well-being, and self-esteem (Trudel, Trugeon, & Piché, 2010).

Although leading directly and indirectly to successful aging, SWB has been a consistently avoided construct (Mona et al., 2011). Definitions of SWB differ considerably across studies and frequently focus on sexual dysfunctions and difficulties (Mona et al., 2011). However, this important concept contains important components, such as sexual satisfaction, functioning and interest, self-esteem, healthy intimate relationships, and psychosexual variables (Mona et al., 2011; Rosen & Bachmann, 2008).

Some authors suggest that SWB denotes the perceived quality of a person's sexuality, including sexual function, relationships and pleasure, body image, and one's sex life in geneal (Laumann et al., 2006). Across cultures, Laumman and colleagues (2006) proposed that men showed consistently higher levels of SWB than women with respect to emotional satisfaction, physical satisfaction, satisfaction with sexual function, and the relevance of sex. In the same study, pleasure with sexual activity was associated with physical and emotional satisfaction. In addition, physical and emotional satisfaction were the variables most positively correlated with SWB (Laumann et al., 2006). In another cross-national study with older people, care and affection, and physical and sexual health were the strongest indicators of SWB, while sexual touching and contact, and a sexual desire for others were least relevant to SWB (von Humboldt et al., 2016; von Humboldt et al., 2020a,b). Despite the rising interest in SWB, most studies have focused on sexual difficulties, sexual function and sexual activity, and less on the emotional and relational variables related to SWB (Laumann et al., 2006).

Currently, what is SWB from the perspective of older adults? In a previous study, 86% of participants were involved in sex-affective activities, such as kissing, cuddling, caressing, sexual contact, sexual touching, self-stimulation, expressing affection, and oral sex (American Association for Retired Persons (AARP), 2005). Indeed, relationships allow for proximity between individuals, interpersonal engagement, and shared interests, which determine partnership, care, eroticism and intimacy (AARP, 2005; Stroebe, Stroebe, Abakoumkin, & Schut, 1996). Moreover, research has given less attention to the impact of significant others upon SWB, although social relationships show a significant influence on health of older adults. Currently, there is still no connection between research on SWB and affective relationships (Hinchliff & Gott, 2011), although relationship status seems to have a significant impact on SWB (Hinchliff & Gott, 2011).

In a study by Gott and Hinchliff (2003), 44 participants aged 50 to 92 were asked to estimate the relevance of sex to their quality of life, based on the World Health Organization Quality of Life (WHOQOL) scale. Their replies were fairly equally divided between three types: very important, moderately important, and not important. The majority of the participants who mentioned sex was not important ascribed the reason to health problems. Those who replied that sex was very important explained it was an expression of love, a giving and receiving satisfaction. For this cohort, SWB did not necessarily comprise sexual intercourse; sex could include only tenderness and care. Lastly, for the 'very important' group, the preeminent aspect of sex was showing and sharing affection (Gott & Hinchliff, 2003).

Indeed, literature indicates old people perceive sexual activity in broader terms than younger adults (Bouman, 2013; Hinchliff & Gott, 2004b; Waite et al., 2009), i.e. as encompassing physical intimacy and not solely penetrative sexual contact. Moreover, physical intimacy and sexual activity as part of intercourse have been found to play a part in the quality of sex life in later life (Hinchliff & Gott, 2004b; Tetley et al., 2016).

19.5.1 Dimensions of Sexual Well-Being

There has been a relevant change in some domains of public health whereby SWB in later life is viewed as pertinent for successful aging (Marshall, 2010). This tendency dovetails with a more western societal change from considering older adults as asexual to a sexually-driven agent (von Humboldt et al., 2016).

The physiological condition of older adults is improving as well. For example, more individuals are living to be older and show better health due to developments in health care, which permit older people to be more physically and physiologically capable of maintaining a satisfactory sex life (WHO, 2015).

In this context, the current literature points out different dimensions of SWB among older people, such as care and affection, sexual touching, intimacy with a partner, sexual expression and openness, sensuality and eroticism, physical health, sexual health, feeling attractive, sexual desire for others, sexual contact, mental health and emotional well-being (von Humboldt et al., 2016).

Additionally, the importance of care and affection (e.g., hugging, cuddling and kissing) for SWB, and the relevance of sexual touching and sharing intimacy (e.g., caressing, touching with the lips, massaging, rubbing, and fingertips) with a partner (von Humboldt et al., 2016) has been reiterated in the literature.

19.5.2 Factors Affecting Sexual Well-Being and Sexual Unwellness

Sexual unwellness (SU) has been defined as encompassing an absence of sexual pleasure and an incapability to maintain sexual relationships due different factors such as mental and physical health issues (Syme, Cordes, Cameron, & Mona, 2015). Although, older adults declare their sexual life as significant for their successful aging and well-being, a number of elements can negatively influence their SWB, including chronic health issues, losing one's partner, reduced libido, menopause, problems of erectile functioning, problems of body image, and general sexual dysfunctions (e.g., orgasmic disorder, vaginal dryness and penetration with pain) (Syme et al., 2015; von Humboldt, Silva, & Leal, 2017).

Rosen and Bachmann (2008) established that emotional well-being was positively linked to sexual activity and pleasure, although a casual relation could not be determined. Furthermore, older adult well-being was positively related with a satisfying sexual activity (Laumann, Paik, & Rosen, 1999).

Cultural differences may affect old adult SWB. Cultures show different views of sexual activity in old age (Syme & Cohn, 2016). For instance, western society frequently shows greater openness to manifestations of sexuality in younger adults than in older age (Syme & Cohn, 2016; von Humboldt et al., 2016). Furthermore, factors such as the increase in age at first marriage, separation, sexual revolution, cohabitation, and out-of-wedlock births, declines in fertility, and modifications in the family structure and sexual partnering have changed cultural perspectives, and consequently older adult SWB (Syme & Cohn, 2016).

As individuals age, sexual expression may change, with less focus on orgasm or vaginal contact and more on sexual touching (Galinsky, 2012). In addition, age is associated with decreases in sexual function and with a partner's decreasing health and the absence of a partner, which in turn, affect sexual activity in old age (American Association for Retired Persons, 2005). When obstacles to sexual activity are seen as part of the normal aging process, there is a decrease in reports of distress regarding sexual dysfunction (Gott & Hinchliff, 2003). This is mainly visible with erectile dysfunction conditions.

Younger adults with identical or lower degrees of erectile dysfunction were much more distressed then older adults, who perceived it as a natural consequence of aging (Hinchliff & Gott, 2004a). Women going through menopause experienced this change as distressing, because they associate their loss of reproductive ability with a significant loss of sexual attraction (Hinchliff & Gott, 2004b). Alternatively, women in general who considered menopause as a natural, inevitable consequence of aging were found to enjoy sex more, because they had no worries about getting pregnant (Hinchliff & Gott, 2011).

As they become older, adults maintain their intimacy and relationships with a dynamic, satisfying sex life. However, during aging, a number of challenges may also generate sexual issues (Aldwin, Jeong, Igarashi, Choun, & Spiro, 2014). Although older adults report their sexual life as pertinent for their successful aging and well-being, several elements may affect their SWB: chronic health conditions, losing a partner, reduced libido, menopause, body image issues, and general sexual dysfunctions (e.g., erectile dysfunction, orgasmic disorder, vaginal dryness and penetration with pain) (Syme et al., 2015). Significant life circumstances, in particular changes in health, may also affect the sex life of older adults (Fileborn et al., 2015).

Older adult health and physical condition (e.g., diabetes and hypertension, medication intake, urinary incontinence, pelvic organ prolapse, and malignant prostate cancer) may have an important effect on their capacity for sexual intercourse (Lindau et al., 2007; von Humboldt et al., 2016). Sexual activity is also influenced by some long-term situations that are more frequent in people in their 60s and older. Indeed, mental and physical health conditions may have negative effects upon SWB, by decreasing sexual desire, making it more difficult to maintain a sexual position, or increasing anxiety (e.g. that sexual activity might trigger a heart attack) (Bouman, 2013). Specific chronic conditions, such as hypertension and diabetes, are related with decreases in sexual activity (Lindau et al., 2007). Health issues in old age may also compromise other sexual activities, such as sexual contact and touching (Karraker, DeLamater, & Schwartz, 2011).

The impact of physical health upon sexual activity may influence how age is related to reduced sexual activity in couples (Call, Sprecher, & Schwartz, 1995; Galinsky & Waite, 2014). In addition, a given health condition may have a different impact on sexual activity for older women and men. For instance, hypertension can limit the mechanics of intercourse for older men because of erectile dysfunction, but a similar condition in older women may not restrict their capacity for vaginal intercourse (Dennerstein, Alexander, & Kotz, 2003).

Physical health conditions are also positively related to sexual health and sexual relationships (Lindau et al., 2007). Physical health influences the ability of older adults and their partners to engage in sexual relations, and mortality affects the availability of sexual partners (Karraker et al., 2011). Moreover, the lack of access to sexual education and services, the absence of protection from discrimination, and the insufficient confidentiality and privacy within health and social care services may have a negative effect on SWB and sexual health (World Health Organization, 2015). Sexual health and sexual function may be influenced by physical function and medication (e.g., hypertension, diabetes) (DeLamater & Sill, 2005). Additionally, specific drugs used for chronic diseases may negatively influence sexual activity (Syme et al., 2015). Indeed, medication may have sexual side effects, e.g. hypertensive drugs, prescribed for many people aged 60 and older, may produce erectile issues (Bouman, 2013). Bouman (2013) refers that control of drug-related sexual issues is higher in older adults, given their susceptibility to the side effects of medication.

Older adults may experience daily stress, which may add to concerns about aging, diseases, retirement, surgeries, disability and lifestyle transformations, all of which may cause sexual difficulties (Aldwin et al., 2014).

Research indicates that lack of physical or emotional pleasure with sex appears to be more connected to the presence of a partner than to individual health (Syme et al., 2015). In a different study, participants indicated loss of their partner, loss of interest, and their own health or that of their partner as reasons for sexual inactivity (Ekström et al., 2018).

To date, the literature appears to undervalue the potential of older people to deal with their concerns about sexual activity within dyads (Hinchliff & Gott, 2011), although sexual desire in later life appears to be more linked to relational or social sharing of care and affection than to physiological variables (DeLamater & Sill, 2005). Indeed, intimate relationships with a partner may ease dealing with poor sexual activity, and thus protect older adult psychological well-being from sexual concerns (Hinchliff & Gott, 2011).

Psychological elements may also influence the expression of sexuality between older adults (Lindau et al., 2007). Beliefs and attitudes appear to affect sexual expression, which can in turn involve a feeling of discomfort and shame, and ultimately abstinence and sexual restraint (Syme et al., 2015). Older adults' perspectives can influence their views about sexual activities (Lindau et al., 2007). Negative self-perceptions may stimulate negative views about their own attitudes, feelings and behaviours towards sexuality (Lindau et al., 2007). Moreover, poor mental health (e.g. depression) may negatively influence sexual behaviour and well-being in older age (Carpenter, Nathanson, & Kim, 2009).

SWB may be influenced by the quality and duration of intercourse (Lindau et al., 2007). A decrease in sexual frequency may be due to long-term relationship predictability (Lindau et al., 2007).

For older people, in particular older women, physical attractiveness influences their self-esteem (Lindau et al., 2007). Furthermore, direct communication with significant others helps older adults balance their sexual expectations and expression of affection, eroticism and sensuality (Hinchliff & Gott, 2011). Both partner emotional and psychological well-being may affect partnered sexual expression and sexual function (Laumann, Das, & Waite, 2008). Additionally, how older people express their sexual activity may predict their mental and emotional well-being (Hinchliff & Gott, 2011). Inversely, declines in mental health and cognitive function related to aging may as well influence sexual expression (Cole & Dendukuri, 2003). For example, depression is related to reductions in sexual activity and well-being comparable to those experienced by an older individual with chronic health conditions (Wells & Burman, 1991). Additionally, antidepressant drugs are associated with decreases in sexual desire (DeLamater & Sill, 2005). Although older people don't often spontaneously verbalize their sexual issues, these are widespread among older adults (Hirayama & Walker, 2011).

Late life sexuality has been frequently considered a specialized medical subject (Gott & Hinchliff, 2003), but other health interventions—such as nursing services, medication intake, nutritional and fluid intake, personal hygiene, physiotherapy interventions—and other daily routines are prioritized over sexuality issues (Bauer, Chenco, Rhonda, & McAuliffe, 2013). In addition, treatment for normative sexual situations in late life—such as prevention of sexually transmitted illness and risky sexual behaviour—is the area most addressed regarding older adult SWB (Kenny, 2013). The literature has reiterated that older adults do not frequently search help for their sexual problems (Hinchliff & Gott, 2011). Additionally, health professionals do not regularly ask older patients about their SWB, regarding topics such as safety, discomfort and decrease of sensitivity (Gleser, 2015; Mellor et al., 2013; Wei & Mayouf, 2009).

19.5.3 Policies and Interventions

Older patients frequently tarry to feel comfortable and secure when searching help from their GP (e.g. due to embarrassment) (Wei & Mayouf, 2009). In previous research, older adults who sought assistance from their health professional reported that such help was not useful and ageist (Wei & Mayouf, 2009). Other studies recognized similar obstacles when older adults enquired health professionals about love relationships and SWB, namely discomfort, lack of safety, supposition of asexuality and less responsiveness (Mellor et al., 2013), and embarrassment due to the patient's age (Wei & Mayouf, 2009).

Policy programs and community interventions—which contain dimensions of love and SWB, such as physical health and sexual health, affection and care—contribute to older adult health and well-being (von Humboldt et al., 2016). Additionally, interventions that encompass older dyads may also contribute to a combined understanding of love and sexual needs in old age (von Humboldt et al., 2016).

19.6 Concluding Remarks and Future Perspectives

The older population is increasing rapidly and consequently researchers and health professionals have progressively approached concerns about well-being and health in old age. Older adults regularly recognize love and sexuality as essential to general health and aging well (Sandberg, 2015). Moreover, love and SWB is relevant for older adults and it is culturally self-perceived in different ways (von Humboldt et al., 2016).

Contrary to the stereotypical image of an asexual older age, an increasing body of literature has reiterated that older adults develop love relationships and are sexually active (Sandberg, 2015). Sexual stereotypes concerning older adults are founded on societal assumptions regarding the aging process that are out of date. These persist however in part because views rooted in the culture take time to modify (Sandberg et al., 2015; von Humboldt et al., 2016). Indeed, the stereotype of an asexual old age is disproven by plentiful evidence that older people maintain love relationships and are sexually active (Sandberg, 2015).

Culture may influence love and sexuality in older populations, however studies are lacking (Rao, Ismail, Darshan, & Tandon, 2015), and the literature is not consensual. The quality of love and sexual self-perception in older age differs significantly across cultures and by biological sex. Indeed, older women have especially difficulty recognizing and expressing their sexuality (Carpenter, Nathanson, & Kim, 2006). Moreover, recent cultural perceptions of 'old' age point out that older adults may show pleasure, vitality and health while performing sexual activities (Rao et al., 2015).

SWB is an frequently neglected concept that may lead (via physical, emotional, psychological, and social variables) to aging well, health, physical activity, relaxation, cardiovascular benefits and reduced pain sensitivity (Brody, 2010; Laumann et al., 2006), reduced levels of depression, and increased quality of life, well-being and self-esteem (Trudel et al., 2010).

Definitions of SWB show great variability and frequently contemplate only sexual dysfunctions, e.g., inability to perform sexual activities, problems with the sexual response cycle, among others (von Humboldt et al., 2016). However, SWB is the multi-dimensional, including domains such as intimate relationships, sexual satisfaction, sexual attractiveness and desire, affection, sexual interest and functioning, sexual openness, eroticism, and psychosexual variables (von Humboldt et al., 2016). Moreover, SWB in later life has been proposed to be more associated with relational than physiological variable, with less emphasis on sexual relations and more on sexual touching (von Humboldt et al., 2016).

While little is known about how older adults address love and SWB, sexual concerns are predominant in old age, and older people do not frequently report them (von Humboldt et al., 2017). Although the literature frequently focuses on the medical aspects of older adult sexual functioning, they continue to enjoy and be involved in sexual activities. However, health problems (e.g., fatigue, sexual pain, diabetes, depression, and poor self-rated health) can interfere with their SWB (von Humboldt et al., 2017). In fact, not all older adults are, would like to or intend to be sexually active. Motives encompass different factors, such as lack of well-being, cultural differences, unavailability of a sexual partner, mental and physical health problems, side effects of medication (e.g. those used in the management of long-term chronic conditions), intercourse difficulties, living environment (e.g. lack of privacy) and other sexual difficulties, such as sexual intercourse and sexual communication (Bouman, 2013). Moreover, older people face everyday challenges, which add to the normative and non-normative concerns of the aging process, incapacity, retirement, illness, surgery, and lifestyle changes, all of which may affect their availability for sharing love and SWB (von Humboldt et al., 2017).

Although there is an increasing focus on older individuals' aging well, elements connected with love and sexuality have been less examined in the literature (Hooghe, 2012). The lack of research on this topic, together with the rapid aging of the population, underline the need for more research relating sexual unwellness and older adults' well-being (Lee, Nazroo, O'Connor, Blake, & Pendleton, 2014). Although research in this area is less abundant than for younger adults, knowledge is rapidly increasing. Quantitative research has determined the frequency and type of sexual activity of older adults, whereas qualitative study has provided a deeper understanding of their love relationships and sex life (e.g. Lee, Nazroo, et al., 2016). However, the few studies addressing SWB in old age show no consensus (Lee, Vanhoutte, et al., 2016). Criticisms of the present literature include incomplete definitions of love, SWB, cross-sectional nature of research, emphasis on sexual unwellness, and absence of cultural evaluations and inclusion of a complete set of bio-psychosocial elements (von Humboldt et al., 2016). Additionally, and to our knowledge, so far no research has considered the impact of a longitudinal community-based intervention for increasing older adults' love in relationships and SWB.

Omitting these issues negatively influences a comprehensive care service. Governments and organizations must recognise the sexual health needs of older adults, and the importance of future research and results leading to proof-based recommendations for application.

Several studies have recognized recurrent obstacles when older adults enquire health professionals about love relationships and SWB, namely concerning absence of partners, discomfort, absence of safety, suppositions of asexuality and less responsiveness (Mellor et al., 2013), and embarrassment due to the age of the patient (Wei & Mayouf, 2009).

Policy and intervention programs, which encompass dimensions of love and SWB—such as physical health and sexual health, affection and care—may contribute to the health and well-being of older individuals and towards understanding the needs of older dyads (von Humboldt et al., 2016).

The observed significance of love and sex towards healthy aging and well-being in old age implies that sexual functioning is encouraged presently as part of an aging well agenda, which heightens concerns about SWB. Indeed, the WHO (2015) indicated that sexual health is a life-long concern. This focus on SWB is a transformation, taking place progressively and visibly, especially in high-income countries. The sexual health needs of older adults are probably receiving greater attention partly due to societal changes driven by feminist and lesbian, gay, bisexual and transgender activism, and resulting changes in attitudes towards sex, relationships and being older.

More studies into the conceptual framework of love and SWB in older age are necessary. For example, considering an extensive set of bio-psycho-social risk elements is recommended. Further interventions with older adults can increase their efficiency by comprising love and SWB variables. Moreover, there is a continued necessity for professionals to be open to talk about love, sexuality and evaluate the love and SWB concerns of older people (von Humboldt et al., 2017). A future SWB model should include more knowledge on how older adults from various cultures describe their SWB (von Humboldt et al., 2016).

Cultural elements may be essential factors in older adult love, sexual behaviour and sexual activity (Winn & Newton, 1982). Considering that love and SWB in old age is self-perceived and that people in various cultures manifest varying experiences, combined research and adjusted interventions permit a deeper knowledge of the different experiences and perspectives of older people (e.g. Karraker et al., 2011; Schwartz, Diefendorf, & McGlynn-Wright, 2014). Consequently, studies on the multi-cultural and multi-dimensional context of love and SWB is relevant for increasing our capacity to deepen SWB and relevant components, for predicting risk of health and SU and, ultimately, for developing cost-effective love and SWB interventions in late adulthood (von Humboldt et al., 2016).

Community intervention and policy programs, which comprise specific indicators of love and SWB, may contribute to older adult well-being. Currently, our knowledge of love relationships and SWB among older populations is still restricted. Future interventions with older people can increase efficacy by including relevant love and SWB variables. Thus, there is a continued need for professionals to be open to talk about love, sexuality and evaluate SWB issues in old age.

Future intervention and educational programs should take into account recent findings, in order to increase the discussion of these issues and to stimulate intimate love and SWB (Monteiro et al., 2017).

In sum, this chapter discussed the multidimensional nature of love and SWB in old age. Consequently, we believe that love and SWB is an essential aspect for older adults, and that studies and health care professionals may use these user-driven outcomes in future health care planning and cross-cultural community interventions with older adults.

References

Aldwin, C. M., Jeong, Y. J., Igarashi, H., Choun, S., & Spiro, A. (2014). Do hassles mediate between life events and mortality in older men? Longitudinal findings from the VA Normative Aging Study. *Experimental Gerontology, 59*, 74–80. https://doi.org/10.1016/j.exger.2014.06.019

American Association for Retired Persons (AARP). (2005). *Sexuality at midlife and beyond: 2004 update of attitudes and behaviors*. Washington, DC: Author.

Barusch, A. (2008). *Love stories of later life: A narrative approach to understanding romance*. New York: Oxford University Press.

Bauer, M., Chenco, C., Rhonda, N., & McAuliffe, L. (2013). Sexuality in older adults: Effect of an education intervention on attitudes and beliefs of residential aged care staff. *Educational Gerontology, 39*(2), 82–91. https://doi.org/10.1080/03601277.2012.682953

Bell, S., Reissing, E. D., Henry, L. A., & Van Zuylen, H. (2017). Sexual activity after 60: A systematic review of associated factors. *Sexual Medicine Reviews, 5*(1), 52–80. https://doi.org/10.1016/j.sxmr.2016.03.001

Bieńko, M. (2014). *The sexual aspects of intimacy in old age, in the public and private spheres*. Institute of Applied Social Sciences University of Warsaw.

Bouman, W. P. (2013). Sexuality in later life. In T. Dening & A. (Eds.), *The Oxford textbook of old age psychiatry* (pp. 703–723). Oxford: Oxford University Press.

Brody, S. (2010). The relative health benefits of different sexual activities. *Journal of Sexual Medicine, 7*, 1336–1361. https://doi.org/10.1111/j.1743-6109.2009.01677.x

Buss, D. M. (1988). Love acts: The evolutionary biology of love. In R. J. Sternberg & M. L. Barnes (Eds.), *The psychology of love*. New Haven: Yale University Press.

Buss, D. M. (1989). Sex differences in human mate preferences: Evolutionary hypotheses tested in 37 cultures. *Behavioral and Brain Sciences, 12*, 1–14.

Buss, D. M. (2016). *The evolution of desire* (pp. 1–5). Springer International Publishing.

Call, V., Sprecher, S., & Schwartz, P. (1995). The incidence and frequency of marital sex in a national sample. *Journal of Marriage and the Family, 57*, 639–652. https://doi.org/10.2307/353919

Carpenter, L. M., Nathanson, C. A., & Kim, Y. J. (2006). Sex after 40?: Gender, ageism, and sexual partnering in midlife. *Journal of Aging Studies, 20*(2), 93–106.

Carpenter, L. M., Nathanson, C. A., & Kim, Y. J. (2009). Physical women, emotional men: Gender and sexual satisfaction in midlife. *Archives of Sexual Behavior, 38*, 87–107. https://doi.org/10.1007/s10508-007-9215-y

Chen, X., Zhang, Q., & Tan, X. (2009). Cardiovascular effects of sexual activity. *Indian Journal of Medical Research, 130*, 681–688.

Cole, M. G., & Dendukuri, N. (2003). Risk factors for depression among elderly community subjects: A systematic review and meta-analysis. *American Journal of Psychiatry, 160*(6), 1147–1156. https://doi.org/10.1176/appi.ajp.160.6.1147

Davis, M. C. (2015). *Exploring how sex and love are defined in adulthood: Conversations with women about romantic relationships*. Western Carolina University.

DeLamater, J., & Sill, M. (2005). Sexual desire in later life. *Journal of Sex Research, 42*(2), 138–149. https://doi.org/10.1080/00224490509552267

Dennerstein, L., Alexander, J. L., & Kotz, K. (2003). The menopause and sexual functioning: A review of the population-based studies. *Annual Review of Sex Research, 14*, 64–82.

Ekström, M., Johnson, M. J., Taylor, B., Luszcz, M., Wohland, P., Ferreira, D. H., et al. (2018). Breathlessness and sexual activity in older adults: The Australian Longitudinal Study of Ageing. *NPJ Primary Care Respiratory Medicine, 28*(1), 20. https://doi.org/10.1038/s41533-018-0090-x

Ferris, J. A., Smith, A. M., Pitts, M. K., Richters, J., Shelley, J. M., & Simpson, J. (2008). Selfreported sexual activity in Australian sexagenarians. *British Medical Journal, 337*, a1250. https://doi.org/10.1136/bmj.a1250

Fileborn, B., Thorpe, R., Hawkes, G., Minichiello, V., Pitts, M., & Dune, T. (2015). Sex, desire and pleasure: Considering the experiences of older Australian women. *Sexual and Relationship Therapy, 30*(1), 117–130. https://doi.org/10.1080/14681994.2014.936722

Frank, R. H. (1988). *Passions within reason: The strategic role of the emotions*. New York: WW Norton.

Fromm, E. (1956). *The art of loving: [An enquiry into the nature of love]*. Harper.

Frugoli, A., & Júnior, C. A. D. O. M. (2011). A sexualidade na terceira idade na percepção de um grupo de idosas e indicações para a educação sexual. *Arquivos de Ciências da Saúde da UNIPAR, 15*(1).

Galinsky, A. M. (2012). Sexual touching and difficulties with sexual arousal and orgasm among U.S. older adults. *Archives of Sexual Behavior, 41*, 875–890. https://doi.org/10.1007/s10508-011-9873-7

Galinsky, A. M., & Waite, L. J. (2014). Sexual activity and psychological health as mediators of the relationship between physical health and marital quality. *The Journals of Gerontology Series B: Psychological Sciences and Social Sciences, 69*(3), 482–493. https://doi.org/10.1093/geronb/gbt165

Gleser, H. (2015). Sex, women and the menopause: Are specialist trainee doctors up for it? A survey of views and attitudes of specialist trainee doctors in Community Sexual and Reproductive Health and Obstetrics & Gynaecology around sexuality and sexual healthcare in the (peri) menopause. *Post-reproductive Health: The Journal of the British Menopause Society, 21*(1), 26–33. https://doi.org/10.1177/2053369115574448

Gott, M. (2005). *Sexuality, sexual health and ageing*. New York: Open University Press, McGraw International.

Gott, M., & Hinchliff, S. (2003). How important is sex in later life? The views of older people. *Social Science and Medicine, 56*, 1617–1628. https://doi.org/10.1016/S0277-9536(02)00180-6

Hillier, S. M., & Barrow, G. M. (2010). *Aging, the individual, and society* (9th ed.). Belmont, CA: Wadsworth Publishing.

Hillman, J. (2008). Sexual issues and aging within the context of work. *Professional Psychology: Research and Practice, 39*(3), 290–297. https://doi.org/10.1037/0735-7028.39.3.290

Hinchliff, S., & Gott, M. (2004a). Perceptions of well-being in sexual ill health: What role does age play? *Journal of Health Psychology, 9*(5), 649–660. https://doi.org/10.1177/1359105304045361

Hinchliff, S., & Gott, M. (2004b). Intimacy, commitment, and adaptation: Sexual relationships within long-term marriages. *Journal of Social and Personal Relationships, 21*(5), 595–609. https://doi.org/10.1177/0265407504045889

Hinchliff, S., & Gott, M. (2011). Seeking medical help for sexual concerns in mid and later life: A review of the literature. *Annual Review of Sex Research, 48*(2), 106–111. https://doi.org/10.1080/00224499.2010.548610

Hirayama, R., & Walker, A. J. (2011). Who helps older adults with sexual problems? Confidants versus physicians. *Journals of Gerontology Series B: Psychological Sciences and Social Sciences, 66B*(1), 109–118. doi: https://doi.org/10.1093/geronb/gbq021.

Hooghe, M. (2012). Is sexual well-being part of subjective well-being? An empirical analysis of Belgian (Flemish) survey data using an extended well-being scale. *Journal of Sex Research, 49*(2–3), 264–273. https://doi.org/10.1080/00224499.2010.551791

Jannini, E. A., Fischer, W. A., Bitzer, J., & McMahon, C. G. (2009). Is sex just fun? How sexual activity improves health. *Journal of Sexual Medicine, 6*, 2640–2648. https://doi.org/10.1111/j.1743-6109.2009.01477.x

Kalra, G., Subramanyam, A., & Pinto, C. (2011). Sexuality: Desire, activity and intimacy in the elderly. *Indian Journal Psychiatry, 53*(4), 300–306. https://doi.org/10.4103/0019-5545.91902

Karraker, A., DeLamater, J., & Schwartz, C. R. (2011). Sexual frequency decline from midlife to later life. *The Journals of Gerontology Series B: Psychological Sciences and Social Sciences, 66*, 502–512. https://doi.org/10.1093/geronb/gbr058

Kenny, R. T. (2013). A review of the literature on sexual development of older adults in relation to the asexual stereotype of older adults. *Canadian Journal of Family and Youth, 5*(1), 91–106. https://ejournals.library.ualberta.ca/index.php/cjfy

Langer, N. (2009). Late life love and intimacy. *Educational Gerontology, 35*(8), 752–764. https://doi.org/10.1080/03601270802708459

Laumann, E. O., Das, A., & Waite, L. J. (2008). Sexual dysfunction among older adults: Prevalence and risk factors from a nationally-representative U. S. probability sample of men and women 57-85 years of age. *Journal of Sexual Medicine, 5*, 2300–2311. https://doi.org/10.1111/j.1743-6109.2008.00974.x

Laumann, E. O., Paik, A., Glasser, D. B., Kang, J., Wang, T., Levinson, B., et al. (2006). A cross-national study of subjective sexual well-being among older women and men: Findings from the global study of sexual attitudes and behaviors. *Archive of Sexual Behavior, 35*(2), 145–161. https://doi.org/10.1007/s10508-005-9005-3

Laumann, E. O., Paik, A., & Rosen, R. C. (1999). Sexual dysfunction in the United States. *Journal of the American Medical Association, 281*, 537–544. https://doi.org/10.1001/jama.281.6.537

Le, T. N., & Levenson, M. R. (2005). Wisdom as self-transcendence: What's love (& individualism) got to do with it? *Journal of Research in Personality, 39*(4), 443–457.

Lee, D. M., Nazroo, J., O'Connor, D. B., Blake, M., & Pendleton, N. (2014). Sexual health and well-being among older men and women in England: Findings from the English Longitudinal Study of Ageing. *Archives of Sexual Behavior, 45*(1), 133–144. https://doi.org/10.1007/s10508-014-0465-1

Lee, D. M., Nazroo, J., O'Connor, D. B., Blake, M., & Pendleton, N. (2016). Sexual health and well-being among older men and women in England: Findings from the English Longitudinal Study of Ageing. *Archives of Sexual Behavior, 45*(1), 133–144. https://doi.org/10.1007/s10508-014-0465-1

Lee, D. M., Vanhoutte, B., Nazroo, J., & Pendleton, N. (2016). Sexual health and positive subjective well-being in partnered older men and women. *Journals of Gerontology. Series B: Psychological Sciences and Social Sciences, 71*(4), 698–710. https://doi.org/10.1093/geronb/gbw018

Lindau, S. T., Schumm, L. P., Laumann, E. O., Levinson, W., O'Muircheartaigh, C. A., & Waite, L. J. (2007). A study of sexuality and health among older adults in the United States. *New England Journal of Medicine, 357*, 762–774. https://doi.org/10.1056/NEJMoa067423

Marshall, B. L. (2010). Science, medicine and virility surveillance: 'Sexy seniors' in the pharmaceutical imagination. *Sociology of Health and Illness, 32*(2), 211–224. https://doi.org/10.1111/j.1467-9566.2009.01211.x

Mellor, R. M., Greenfield, S. M., Dowswell, G., Sheppard, J. P., Quinn, T., & McManus, R. J. (2013). Health care professionals' views on discussing sexual wellbeing with patients who have had a stroke: A qualitative study. *PLoS One, 8*(10), e78802. https://doi.org/10.1371/journal.pone.0078802

Mercer, C. H., Tanton, C., Prah, P., Erens, B., Sonnenberg, P., Clifton, S., et al. (2013). Changes in sexual attitudes and lifestyles in Britain through the life course and over time: Findings from the National Surveys of Sexual Attitudes and Lifestyles (Natsal). *The Lancet, 382*(9907), 1781–1794. https://doi.org/10.1016/S0140-6736(13)62035-8

Mitchell, K. R., Mercer, C. H., Ploubidis, G. B., Jones, K. G., Datta, J., Field, N., et al. (2013). Sexual function in Britain: Findings from the third national survey of sexual attitudes and lifestyles (Natsal-3). *The Lancet, 382*(9907), 1817–1829. https://doi.org/10.1016/S0140-6736(13)62366-1

Mona, L. R., Syme, M. L., Goldwaser, G., Cameron, R. P., Chen, S., Clemency, C., et al. (2011). Sexual health in older adults: Conceptualization and treatment. In K. Sorocco & S. Lauderdale (Eds.), *Cognitive behaviour therapy with older adults: Innovations across care settings* (pp. 261–285). New York: Springer.

Monteiro, A., von Humboldt, S., & Leal, I. P. (2017). How do formal caregivers experience the sexuality of older adults? Beliefs and attitudes towards older adults' sexuality. *Psychology, Community and Health, 6*(1), 77–92.

Neto, F. (2012). Perceptions of love and sex across the adult life span. *Journal of Social and Personal Relationships, 29*(6), 760–775.

Okiria, E. M. (2014). Perspectives of sexuality and aging in the African culture: Eastern Uganda. *International Journal of Sociology and Anthropology, 6*(4), 126–129.

Rao, T. S., Ismail, S., Darshan, M. S., & Tandon, A. (2015). Sexual disorders among elderly: An epidemiological study in south Indian rural population. *Indian Journal of Psychiatry, 57*(3), 236.

Rosen, R. C., & Bachmann, G. A. (2008). Sexual well-being, happiness, and satisfaction, in women: The case for a new conceptual paradigm. *Journal of Sex and Marital Therapy, 34*, 291–297. https://doi.org/10.1080/00926230802096234

Sandberg, L. (2015). Sex, sexuality and later life. In J. Twigg & W. Martin (Eds.), *Routledge handbook of cultural gerontology*. London: Routledge. https://www.book2look.com/embed/9781136221026

Schwartz, P., Diefendorf, S., & McGlynn-Wright, A. (2014). Sexuality in Aging. In D. L. Tolman & L. M. Diamond (Eds.), *APA handbook of sexuality and psychology* (Person-based approaches) (Vol. 1, pp. 523–551). Washington: American Psychological Association. https://doi.org/10.1037/14193-017

Sharpe, T. (2004). Introduction to sexuality in late life. *The Family Journal, 12*, 199–205. https://doi.org/10.1177/002216780426410

Stroebe, W., Stroebe, M., Abakoumkin, G., & Schut, H. (1996). The role of loneliness and social support in adjustment to loss: A test of attachment versus stress theory. *Journal of Personality and Social Psychology, 70*, 1241–1249. https://doi.org/10.1093/geronb/gbr058

Syme, M. L., & Cohn, T. J. (2016). Examining aging sexual stigma attitudes among adults by gender, age, and generational status. *Aging Mental Health, 20*, 36–45. https://doi.org/10.1080/13607863.2015.1012044

Syme, M. L., Cordes, C. C., Cameron, R. P., & Mona, L. R. (2015). Sexual health and well-being in the context of aging. In P. A. Lichtenberg & B. Carpenter (Eds.), *APA handbook of clinical geropsychology*. Washington, DC: American Psychological Association. https://doi.org/10.1037/14459-015

Syme, M. L., Klonoff, E. A., Macera, C. A., & Brodine, S. K. (2013). Predicting sexual decline and dissatisfaction among older adults: The role of partnered and individual physical and mental health factors. *Journals of Gerontology Series B: Psychological Sciences and Social Sciences, 68*(3), 323–332. https://doi.org/10.1093/geronb/gbs087

Tetley, J., Lee, D., Nazroo, J., & Hinchliff, S. (2016). Let's talk about sex: What do older men and women say about their sexual relations and sexual activities? A qualitative analysis of ELSA wave 6 data. *Ageing and Society, 38*(3), 497–521. https://doi.org/10.1017/S0144686X16001203

Trudel, G., Trugeon, L., & Piché, L. (2010). Marital and sexual aspects of old age. *Sexual and Relationship Therapy, 25*(3), 316–341. https://doi.org/10.1080/14681991003750467

Ussher, J. M., Perz, J., Gilbert, E., Wong, W. T., & Hobbs, K. (2013). Renegotiating sex and intimacy after cancer: Resisting the coital imperative. *Cancer Nursing, 36*(6), 454–462. https://doi.org/10.1097/NCC.0b013e3182759e21

von Humboldt, S. (2016). Conceptual and methodological issues on the adjustment to aging: Perspectives on aging well. New York, NY: Springer. https://doi.org/10.1007/978-94-017-7576-2

von Humboldt, S., Leal, I., & Monteiro, A. (2016). Are older adults well sexually? Sexual well-being among a cross-national sample of older adults. *Review of European Studies, 8*(1), 134–144. https://doi.org/10.5539/res.v8n1p134

von Humboldt, S., Low, L., & Leal, I. (2020a). Are older adults satisfied with their sexuality? Outcomes from a cross-cultural study. *Educational Gerontology, 46*, 284–293. https://doi.org/10.1080/03601277.2020.1744805

von Humboldt, S., Ribeiro-Gonçalves, J. A., Costa, A., Low, G., & Leal, I. (2020b). Sexual expression in old age: How older adults from different cultures express sexually? *Sexuality Research and Social Policy*, 1–15. https://doi.org/10.1007/s13178-020-00453-x

von Humboldt, S., Silva, S., & Leal, I. (2017). A study on sexual unwellness in old age: Assessing a cross-national sample of older adults. *Review of European Studies, 9*(3), 207–216. https://doi.org/10.5539/res.v9n3p207

Waite, L. J., Laumann, E. O., Das, A., & Schumm, L. P. (2009). Sexuality: Measures of partnerships, practices, attitudes, and problems in the National Social Life, Health, and Aging Study. *The Journals of Gerontology Series B: Psychological Sciences and Social Sciences, 64*(B), 56–66. doi:https://doi.org/10.1093/geronb/gbp038

Wei, L., & Mayouf, M. A. (2009). The effects of the social status of the elderly in Libya on the way they institutionally interact and communicate with younger physicians. *Journal of Pragmatics, 41*, 136–146. https://doi.org/10.1016/j.pragma.2008.09.001

Wells, K. B., & Burman, M. A. (1991). Caring for depression in America: Lessons learned from early findings of the medical outcomes study. *Psychiatric Medicine, 9*, 503–519. https://doi.org/10.1016/0163-8343(91)90056-3

Winn, R. L., & Newton, N. (1982). Sexuality in aging: A study of 106 cultures. *Archives Sexual Behavior, 11*(4), 283–298. https://doi.org/10.1007/BF01541590

World Health Organization [WHO]. (2012). *Good health adds life to years – Global brief for World Health Day 2012*. Geneva: The Author.

World Health Organization [WHO]. (2015). *Sexual health, human rights and the law*. Geneva: The Author.

Sofia von Humboldt (Dr.) is a clinical and health psychologist with a long-standing experience with older adults. Her current research interests include sexual well-being, adjustment to aging, well-being, mental health, and cross-cultural studies with older populations. Dr. von Humboldt is Associate Professor and Principal Investigator in William James Center for Research at ISPA- Instituto Universitário. Deeply committed to working with older adults, she has written papers, chapters and books on the multidimensional and cross-cultural approach to sexual well-being and health and mental in old age.

Isabel Leal is PhD in Psychology (1991) from the Catholic University of Louvain (Belgium). She is full professor of ISPA- Instituto Universitário (Lisbon, Portugal) where is Head of the Department of Clinical and Health Psychology and researcher of the William James Center for Research, I&D).

Her research interests focus on the interface of Health and Psychology, in particular on sexual and reproductive health and on the issues of adaptation in lifecycle among them the aging and the disease.

She has published 250 articles in specialized journals and is the author, co-author and editor of 50 books. ORCID: http://orcid.org/0000-0002-1672-7912

Dr. Gail Low has a practice background in acute care, surgical, respiratory, and home care nursing. Dr. Low has worked as a Clinical Nurse Specialist in transitional and extended care settings. She joined the Faculty of Nursing at the University of Alberta in 2005. Dr. Low currently teaches undergraduate Nursing students about research methods and statistics.

Dr. Low's research focuses on factors that affect the psychological well-being of adults at midlife and in later life. She is currently exploring how older people psychological adapt to their own process of aging and how psychological beliefs about aging affect psychological well-being.

Chapter 20
"A Matter of Age?" Love Relationships Between Older Women and Younger Men: The So-called "Cougar" Phenomenon

Elisabeth Vanderheiden

Dispositioned Hearts
It has been some time, tonight on the Ninth -
Well it has to be because I'll try to break through
To hear the sweet eternal voice I have missed,
The other week I was so close, but I just can't...
Hold the tongue, the one once soul-kissed,
Between bitten, adored and older lips

The remaining desires of our carcass
It always must come, close-down to it,
Because those numbers reign in mind
Try to reason and again reach,
The understanding of the truth
But for how long again, will you sustain?

In eyes of my favourite shades,
Irises that mirror and drape mine
Blind and dilate coyly with flavour
Afterwards you whispered the ageless question,
"Do you still love me?", the four lettered
Word that is seldom pure,
This night let it be, let us speak
With dispositioned hearts

Daniel J. Thorssøn

Abstract While love relationships between older men and younger (adult) women have been well-researched, the equivalent relationship of elder women with younger men has led a shadowy existence in research so far. At the same time, public interest in such relationships is growing, evidenced by interest in celebrity relationships such as those of Demi Moore, the *90 Day Fiancé* reality TV star Jenny Slatten and her Indian partner Sumit, or the French President Macron and his wife Brigitte Macron,

E. Vanderheiden (✉)
Global Institute for Transcultural Research, Römerberg, Germany
e-mail: ev@keb-rheinland-pfalz.de

© Springer Nature Switzerland AG 2021
C.-H. Mayer, E. Vanderheiden (eds.), *International Handbook of Love*,
https://doi.org/10.1007/978-3-030-45996-3_20

with a corresponding mainstream media. In public discussion, the older women in such relationships are often labelled as "cougars". The slang term "cougar" is often used to label older females who seek a relationship (or relationships) with younger males (The Oxford British and World English Dictionary, 2012). and the younger men as "toyboys" or "cubs".

This chapter focuses on the impact that age difference has on relationships, the issues that arise for the partners, and which opinions and prejudices they have to face. In this chapter, relevant current research results are presented and discussed. In particular, possible significant factors such as gender and culture are considered in detail.

Keywords Love · Love relationships between older women and younger men · Gender · Age · Culture · So-called "Cougar" Phenomenon

20.1 Introduction

The purpose of this chapter is have a closer look at love relationships between older women and younger men. This type of relationship is not only becoming increasingly popular in the media owing to certain celebrities who live this relationship model, but it is also gaining increasing importance as a research object (see Casterline, Williams, & McDonald (1986), Banks & Arnold (2001), Leahy (2002), Proulx, Caron, & Logue (2006), Pyke & Adams (2010), Drefahl (2010), Skopek, Schmitz, & Blossfeld (2011), Collard (2012), Conway, Noe, Stulp, & Pollet (2015), Gustafson & Fransson (2015), Montemurro & Siefken (2014), McKenzie (2013), see also Chap. 43). This chapter will present the relevant current state of research on this specific form of love relationship, showing to what extent traditional social scripts reflect or contradict these relationships in terms of age and gender. It will be shown how far such relationships are realised, what self-images the affected persons have of themselves and their partners, what specific problems they are confronted with, and how they define their relationships. Some case examples are presented.

Love is a highly complex topic and includes "a variety of emotions and experiences" (Karandashev, 2020). From a psychological perspective, Sternberg (1988) understands love in the context of triadic theory as part of intimacy, passion and commitment.

From an evolutionary psychological perspective, Helen Fisher and her colleagues take a counter position and classify love primarily as a "drive", like hunger and thirst, rather than as emotion, and assume that love, like the universal expressions of sex, attachment and intimacy, is provoked by the human neuronal and hormonal system, and is therefore to be understood as a generic term for the articulation of sex, attachment and intimacy (Fisher, 1992, 1995, 2004; Fisher, Aron, Mashek, Li, & Brown, 2002).

In 1992 Jankowiak and Fischer (Jankowiak & Fischer, 1992, p. 153; Jankowiak & Paladino, 2008, p. 7) (see Chaps. 2 and 3) published from a cultural anthropological perspective a cross-cultural study of romantic love in which they examined

166 societies, concluding that romantic love is a cultural universal, or almost universal, phenomenon (Jankowiak & Fischer, 1992, p. 153).

This conclusion modifies that of Lindholm (2001)—also from an anthropological point of view—when he says that

> romantic love as we know it is a modern phenomenon that arises from the intersection of human needs and historical-cultural context.

This is also reflected in the fact that love relationships are still closely interwoven with social norms and are defined by corresponding scripts, especially with regard to gender and age (Eckert & McConnell-Ginet, 2019, p. 2). These scripts (Buddeberg & Maake, 2005, pp. 30–33) play an important role in individual concepts of relationship, the understanding of love relationships and the shaping of sexuality (see Chap. 9). These scripts are not only individually biographical, but also culturally founded (Buddeberg & Maake, 2005, pp. 30–33). The concept of scripts goes back to Simon and Gagnon (1989) and can also be understood as a synonym for sexual identity. Those scripts contain ideas about what a person wants to do or is allowed to do sexually, where, and with whom. In each individual, socially and personally shaped sexual scripts overlap. These are learned and expanded in the course of a lifetime (Kasif & Band-Winterstein, 2017, p. 7; Montemurro & Siefken, 2014).

Alternatively, the term "lovemaps" (Money, 1986) is often used. A lovemap is, so to speak, a person's internal blueprint for their ideal erotic situations. Also lovemaps are conceived as a culture-related and lifelong modifiable concept. These lovemaps are shaped from an early age by experiences in the non-sexual realm. For example, through relationships with others, through how a person perceives herself or himself and her/his own body, through the way in which s/he deals with the family, and much more. Precisely because they are culture-related, these scripts and lovemaps present themselves very differently for women and men. Researchers in this field speak of "social scripting" (see Sanchez, Fetterolf, & Rudman, 2012; Wiederman, 2005). According to the assumptions of social scripting, social scripts assign certain rules to the members of a society regarding appropriate behaviour and interpretation associated with certain behaviours. In most cultures, therefore, gender-specific rules apply to who may love whom, and who may have intimate relations with whom (Kreager & Staff, 2009; Montemurro & Siefken, 2014).

> Social scripting theory rests on the assumption that people follow internalized scripts when constructing meaning out of behavior, responses, and emotions. With regard to potentially sexual situations, scripts provide meaning and direction for responding to sexual cues and for behaving sexually. As men and women exhibit certain differences in sexuality, we might say that the two sexes follow separate but overlapping (and often complementary) scripts. (Wiederman, 2005, p. 496)

In addition to gender, age and socioeconomic status are also important factors, which can lead to stigmatising double standards (Gazso & Bischoping, 2018; Kreager & Staff, 2009; McKenzie, 2013; Sontag, 1972). These double standards lead to disadvantages, especially for women. Susan Sontag sums up what the social relationship script for men and women ideally looks like, at least in the Western context:

The double standard about aging shows up most brutally in the conventions of sexual feeling, which presuppose a disparity between men and women that operates permanently to women's disadvantage. In the accepted course of events a woman anywhere from her late teens through her middle twenties can expect to attract a man more or less her own age. (Ideally, he should be at least slightly older.) They marry and raise a family. But if her husband starts an affair after some years of marriage, he customarily does so with a woman much younger than his wife. Suppose, when both husband and wife are already in their late forties or early fifties, they divorce. The husband has an excellent chance of getting married again, probably to a younger woman. His ex-wife finds it difficult to remarry. Attracting a second husband younger than herself is improbable; even to find someone her own age she has to be lucky, and she will probably have to settle for a man considerably older than herself, in his sixties or seventies. Women become sexually ineligible much earlier than men do. A man, even an ugly man, can remain eligible well into old age. He is an acceptable mate for a young, attractive woman. Women, even good-looking women, become ineligible (except as partners of very old men) at a much younger age. Thus, for most women, aging means a humiliating process of gradual sexual disqualification. Since women are considered maximally eligible in early youth, after which their sexual value drops steadily, even young women feel themselves in a desperate race against the calendar. They are old as soon as they are no longer very young.[1]

Sanchez and her colleagues (2012) have researched the consequences and predictors of the traditional gender roles of female submission and male dominance in sexual relationships and found that the sexual roles of men and women become more equal over time. Nevertheless, empirical evidence suggests that traditional sexual roles continue to dominate heterosexual relationships (see Chap. 19). This has negative effects on the sexual satisfaction of women in particular. Therefore, they conclude that traditional sexual scripts are harmful to both women and men. They also emphasise that although sexual scripts and needs can be expressed more equally than in the past, there is still evidence of sexual inequalities to the disadvantage of women. At the same time, however, they were able to demonstrate that relationships that reject the traditional sexual script lead to greater sexual satisfaction and better relationship outcomes (Sanchez et al., 2012). This in turn can also have an effect on love relationships.

Against the background of social scripting and lovemaps, age-differentiated love relationships between older men and younger women are still judged socially by the majority quite differently from love relationships between older women and younger men (McKenzie, 2013; Montemurro & Siefken, 2014; Proulx et al., 2006). Older women (women over the age of 40, according to Montemurro, 2019) and old women are generally still depicted as de-sexualised in society, in the media or the public. For example, they are not or are only rarely perceived as people who are sexually attractive or have sexual needs themselves or are sexually active (Montemurro, 2019). There are three types of sexual scripts:

1. cultural scenarios: models for behavior that allows individuals to imagine a desired response and expected course of action

---

[1] Sontag, 1972, "The double standard of aging", *Saturday Review,* vol. 23, pp. 29–38.

2. interpersonal scripts: govern interaction between individuals in sexualized situations
3. intrapsychic scripts: how individuals process or cognitively interpret cultural scenarios (Montemurro, 2019; Alarie, 2019a, 2019b, 2019c).

Women who have relationships with younger men, whether purely sexual or love affairs, are often referred to in the media (Kaklamanidou, 2012) and public discourse as "cougars". (Cougar is actually the name of the mountain lion or puma native to the Americas.) It is assumed that the slang term cougar was coined in the 1980s by the Canadian ice hockey team, The Vancouver Canucks. The team used the term to describe older, single women who went to the team's games because they had a sexual interest in the players (Lawton & Callister, 2010). The term first appeared in the print media in 2001, when the Canadian newspaper *The Toronto Sun* published a news story about cougars. This story was triggered by the launch of "Cougardate.com", a Canadian dating site that sought to bring older women together with younger men. The author of the story, *Toronto Sun* columnist Valerie Gibson, subsequently published *Cougar: A Guide for Older Women Going Out with Younger Men* in 2002.

"Cougar" is an interesting term, in that it evokes associations of a predator hunting in search of a helpless and innocent victim to be beaten and devoured. Love and sexual relationships of women are thus clearly animalised and sexualised here. Consistent with this approach is the fact that not only is there generally very little research on love relationships between older women and younger men (much less than on older men and their relationships with younger women), but what does exist usually arises in sexual-scientific contexts and is rarely located in psychological or sociological contexts. This could suggest that this form of relationship is primarily seen as a sexual arrangement rather than a love relationship.

There are therefore many women who find the term "cougar" inappropriate, incompatible with their self-image and discriminatory (see Alarie, 2019a, 2019b, 2019c; McKenzie, 2013). Others such as Montemurro (2019) however, understand the cougar concept as evidence of changing sexual scripts and a new, more self-determined sexual script for older women. Montemurro (2019) sees it as an encouragement to older women to demonstrate their sexuality and to pursue self-determined corresponding needs. In this context, the author differentiates dominant from alternative sexual scripts, and classifies "cougar" as an alternative sexual script for women that moves them from a passive, heteronomous role into an active one, allowing them control over their own sexuality, and additional options for positioning and acting (Montemurro, 2019).

20.2 Statistical Facts on (Love) Relationships Between Older Women and Young Men

> The outside world confronts us with a barrage of abstractions: statistics, figures, formulas, all indicating how imperilled we are, and almost all of them elude our comprehension. Loving is a kind of rebellion, a way of getting in touch with forces to counteract the intangible and unintelligible existence we find ourselves in.
> (Beck & Beck-Gernsheim, 1995, p. 178)

Owing to the limited research in this area, there is little reliable data on how many women and men live in such a type of relationship. In some cases, however, national statistics on marriages of people of different ages are available, and some are presented here as examples. The selection is random and arbitrary to the extent that corresponding valid data were available at all.

For **Germany** in 2017 for example, it can be stated that in almost three quarters of the partnerships (73%), the man was older than his partner; in 17% the woman was older. In relation to the total population, relationships with a large age difference were rather rare, as only 6% lived with a partner who was more than 10 years older (Statistisches Bundesamt, 2019).

For **Switzerland**, it can be observed, during 2013, that in three out of ten couples, both partners were approximately the same age (± 1 year), while the majority of men were at least 2 years older than women. Couples in which the woman was older were much rarer (14%). For most couples, the age differences were relatively small. In 22% of couples the man was at least 6 years older than the woman and only in 4% of couples the woman was 6 or more years older than the man. Only one tenth of couples had an age difference of 10 years or more (9% were men at least 10 years older; 1% were women at least 10 years older). The average age difference between partners was 4.8 years in couples where the man was older, and 2.9 years in couples where the woman was older (Bundesamt für Statistik, 2016).

It is interesting to note that the age differences between partners are greater when the partnership has only begun at a later stage in the life of both or at least one partner.

In **France**, the situation, at least for 2012, was that for heterosexual couples, both spouses had an age difference of only 1 year in three out of ten cases. In six out of ten couples, the man was older than the woman. In only one in ten couples, the man was younger. This constellation of relationships is gaining in importance: the proportion of couples who met in the 2000s was 10% of those in the 1960s, and 16% of those in the 1960s. The more qualified the men were, the more often they had a partner their age, and the less frequently they had a spouse younger than they were. At the same time, it becomes clear that the more educated the women were, the more often they had a partner of their age and the less often they had an older spouse. In couples with at least one immigrant partner, the man was more often the eldest. This was the case for 71% of couples where both spouses were immigrants (Daguet, 2016).

In the **US**, also (US Bureau, 2013), it can be seen that a great many more men were married to younger women than vice versa and that there were greater age differences than among older women with younger partners.

The National Family and Health Survey (International Institute for Population Sciences, 2016) found in a survey of nearly 64,000 couples in **India** in 2015 and 2016 that only just over 2% of married men had a wife who was older. Three quarters of men, on the other hand, were at least 2 years older than their wives. Overall, however, the age difference in the age cohorts is decreasing, e.g. it was still 6.9% for those aged 50 to 54, and only 2.4% for those aged 20 to 24. Regarding the different religious groups, the Hindus, Muslims and Christians showed the strongest age difference between husband and wife (an average of a little over 5 years), the lowest was shown among Sikhs (just 3.6 years).

A study by the Chinese Academy of Social Sciences (as quoted in the South China Morning Post, 2019 and the Global Times, 2019) found that only 13% of marriages registered in the 1990s in **China** involved a younger groom. This figure rose from 14.37% in 2000 to 40.13% in 2010, while the traditional combination of an older man and a younger woman dropped to 43.13%, from 68.09% in the same period. The causes cited in this study were better educational and employment opportunities for women and a serious gender imbalance, which contributed to the decline of a centuries-old tradition that states that Chinese husbands must be older than their wives. This is above all a metropolitan phenomenon.

Lawton and Callister (2010) published a study in 2010 based on census data (1986 and 2006) that analysed the relationships of older women aged 40, 50 and 60 with younger men in **New Zealand**. Among 40-year-old women in 2006, almost 1% had a partner who was 30 or younger, i.e. 10 or more years younger than themselves. This is a small change from 1986, but the proportion of partners who were 5 or more years younger has shifted more. In 1986, 3.8% of 40-year-old women had a partner who was 35 years or younger. Until 2006 it was 5.8%. Among 50-year-old women, 1.4% had a partner who was 10 or more years younger in 1986, rising to 1.8% in 2006. For women who were 60, 1.0% had a partner who was 10 or more years younger in 1986; this figure rose to 1.7% in 2006. For women aged 60 with a partner five or more years younger, the figures were 4.0% in 1986 and 5.4% in 2006. Lawton and Callister (2010) conclude that these relationship constructions are rare, but are increasing as a proportion of all couples. Not considered in the census data, were comparable informal relationships in which couples do not live in the same house. For various reasons, researchers suspect that there are higher rates of short-term relationships in which the woman is older than the man, but which do not appear in official statistics.

Thus, there seems to be evidence in various cultural and national contexts that the proportion of women living in legalised relationships with younger men is still much smaller than the proportion of men living in such relationships with younger women, and that age differences are smaller. This is confirmed by a study from a psychological perspective (Dunn as cited in Addison, 2010) which, in the context of online dating, collected age references of 22,000 men and women using online dating sites across 14 countries and two religious groups. Participants were people from

Australia, Brazil, Britain, Canada, China, Greece, Germany, Indonesia, Japan, Kenya, Mexico, Russia, South Africa, and Ukraine. The majority of younger men, aged 20–25, chose either women in their age group or slightly younger. Older men expressed a clear preference for significantly younger women. This pattern seems to be cross-culturally consistent.

The fact that women—especially when the difference in age is only a few years—enter into (love) relationships with older men, meets with far greater skepticism and resistance than vice versa. This is essentially attributed to compliance with the relevant social scripts or lovemaps (Alarie, 2019a, 2019b, 2019c; Montemurro & Siefken, 2014; Sanchez et al., 2012).

In certain other national and cultural contexts, however, there has been a slight increase in (love) relationships between older women and men, for example in China, France and New Zealand. The reasons proposed for this are seen in particular as being the higher level of education of women and the better socio-economic conditions associated with education, but also in an increased self-confidence (see Alarie, 2019a, 2019b, 2019c; Lawton & Callister, 2010; McKenzie, 2013). Other researchers assume that when partners of an appropriate age are not available, people compensate by "crossing traditional age limits to choose a partner" (Berardo et al., 1993, p. 102; Blumstein & Schwartz, 1983, p. 32). This could potentially be the case, for example in India and China, but further long-term studies are yet to prove this.

The main issues discussed in this section have been the extent—at least statistically—of partnerships and marriages between older women and younger men, the extent of age differences and comparisons of relationships between older men and younger women. The next section will focus on the assumptions made about these relationships and the qualitative research findings which examine these specific relationships.

20.3 Case Examples: Research Methodology

The following case studies have been collected as random samples (Kromrey, Strübing, & Roose, 2016; Müller-Böling & Klandt, 1996). The cases that could provide the most comprehensive information were selected (Misoch, 2015, p. 186). The decisive criterion was that the interviewee lived in a relationship with an age gap at the time, and that the female partner was older. The couples were identified through a snowball system (Przyborski & Wohlrab-Sahr, 2008) in the author's closer and wider circle of acquaintances.

Case Example 1[2]

Greta is 82, was a teacher, and has German and Polish roots; Richard now 70, was an engineer, and both live in Germany. They have been married for 50 years and

---

[2] In the interest of better clarity and unambiguity, the case studies and corresponding comments as well as quotes from respondents in this chapter are set in italics.

have one child and grandchildren. Both are Catholic and got to know each other through religious education at school. Richard, at the age 16, fell in love with Greta, but Greta gave him no chance; she was his teacher and initially regarded this situation and also the age difference as big obstacles. Richard then began to get involved in her parish outside school, to spend more time with her. It was only after several years, when he was no longer her student, that Greta began to consider him as a potential partner: "It was crucial to me how seriously and consistently he courted me. Whether someone in his circle of friends laughed at him or his family put him under pressure because of the age difference, he did not let himself be distracted in his courtship of me. He simply did not give up. And when I 'gave in', everything happened very quickly: I fell in love with him, we got married when he started studying after his military service and became parents. I have never regretted that."

For Richard it was not and is not about relationships with older women in general: "I'm not interested in older women in general. I felt and still feel attracted to Greta: her attitude, her humour, her looks, the peace she radiates, the way we can talk to each other. The happiness I feel when we are together. For me, she is the greatest woman in the world."

Case Example 2
Nathalie is 73 and was a judge in the US; now she is retired. Tom is 30 and a teacher of children with special needs. They are a couple and have been living together for 3 years. They got to know each other through a dating platform. Tom was actively looking for an older woman after he separated from his high school girlfriend at the end of his studies. He had some (more sexually orientated) affairs with older women before his relationship with Nathalie. Nathalie is divorced. She and her ex-husband were of the same age. Nathalie and Tom love each other and neither wants to have a life without the other. But for some time now there has been no sexual contact. Nathalie was not ready for an interview. Tom: "Nathalie says she has lost the desire for sex. She is a 'seldom' lady. In the beginning I tried to be patient. But I am young and I want and need sex. We negotiated a deal that I can have sex with other women. But this has nothing to do with Nathalie, even though I know that it is hard for her sometimes. I love her; I don't want to imagine a life without her". Tom actively searches for older women on dating platforms, pretending to be 60 years old and presenting himself with a photo that is very blurry, shows him at a distance and makes him appear much older. Only when he comes into closer contact with potentially interested women does he reveal his true age, but not his relationship status. So he has frequent and irregular sexual contacts with different older women.

Tom enjoys these sexual encounters: "I have great fun having sex, but sometimes I feel guilty about Nathalie because she knows where I am and what I am doing. But I try not to let that happen because we have that deal. And she wants my love and I give it to her only."

Case Example 3
Helen is 60, a medical doctor who is divorced and lives in UK, Ram is 30, an engineer and lives in India. They know each other through a dating platform and have lived an intense virtual love relationship for 5 years. In the non-virtual world

they have not yet met each other, but dream about it and often talk about it. Ram feels rooted in the traditional values of Hindu society. Above all, it is important to him to live in accordance with those values and to be a valuable member of society, to do the right thing. Therefore, it is out of the question for him one day to get involved in an arranged marriage and marry the woman who his parents choose for him. He has succeeded in delaying this day so far. He deliberately sought an older woman outside India through an international dating platform. Ram: "I've always felt attracted to older women, but I can't live that here. Helen and I are a perfect match. I appreciate her character, her looks so much, her big heart. I admire how hard she works and how successful she is. I find her attractive and very sexy. She is the perfect woman for me. Everything fits." He finds the connection between them to be very intense: "I can't imagine that our relationship could ever be over, even if it probably could one day happen. Sometimes, when I think about something, I have a problem or have to make a decision, I hear her voice in me like a voice mail, or feel her energy. There is a very close connection between us."

Helen is basically open in her relationships. She has had relationships with men and women, but has not consciously searched for a relationship with a young man. Of her relationship with Ram she says: "For me, his age doesn't really matter. Often I have to consciously remind myself how old he is. For example, he likes ten- or twenty-year-old music titles or films much better than I do, I often draw his attention to new releases, not the other way round. That's what we amuse ourselves about. He has an old soul, I often think. Actually, he forgets a lot more than I do, sometimes I jokingly call him 'old man' because of that. Between us, age is less an issue than the limitations that arise for him from cultural demands. Because I could just jump on a plane and fly to India and we could meet in the carbon world, but that would force him to lie to family and friends. That's why we don't want to and can't do that—at least at the moment. Sometimes it's okay, sometimes it's hard to stand. Sometimes we just imagine that we are married." In Ram's environment nobody knows about the connection; in Helen's environment friends and some colleagues know about it. Helen says: "The difference in age doesn't really interest anyone, but rather some people find that it feels like a purely virtual love affair, as if it were something unreal. For us this is very real. But if we were experienced together in the carbon world, there would certainly be many here in England who would take offence at our great age difference." Helen also feels this intensive connection: "Sometimes I can feel almost physically when he misses me particularly strongly, there is then a special and strong energy. That's usually very nice, but sometimes it makes me sad because I don't know if we'll ever meet in the analogue world."

20.4 Current State of Research on Age-Differential Relationships Between Older Women and Younger Men

Even though the issue of age-different couples of older women and younger men receives a lot of media attention, as already mentioned there are still only a few studies that deal with it scientifically. The main progress results are presented below.

Gender researcher Alarie (2019a, 2019b, 2019c) published a qualitative study in Canada in which she conducted 55 interviews with women aged 30 to 60 who had one or more intimate partners younger than themselves. The women were asked, among other things, how they imagine the "cougar" and why they accept or reject this label. At the same time, the research examined how these women talk about their own intimate relationships in relation to age. One of the main objectives of the study was to understand the expectations of these women, of their intimate relationships and what might influence their desire to seriously engage (or not) with a younger partner. Any relationship qualified by the participant as sexual, amorous and/or romantic was taken into account. The sample of 55 women consisted of 21 women in their 30s, 19 in their 40s, and 15 in their 50s. The vast majority of participants identified themselves as "white"; only two participants indicated that they belonged to a different group. For the majority of the women interviewed, the term "cougar" had a negative connotation and the majority of those affected rejected it for themselves. The vast majority of the participants associated the term "cougar" primarily with sexuality, especially sexual appetite and seduction orientation. In fact, most of them perceived this label as an insinuation that middle-aged women interested in younger men have abnormal or even unhealthy sexuality. Many of the women in the age cohort over 50 found this inappropriate; they reported that younger men often actively sought a relationship with them and not vice versa (Alarie, 2019b, 2019c). The younger women also rejected the term because they felt too young to be labelled as such (cougar is associated with being silver-haired).

One result of the study was that women in such relationship constructions seem to find it easier to deal with certain aspects of these scripts in a more playful, free or challenging way (Alarie, 2019c, p. 1) and in return receive positive feedback from younger men (Alarie, 2019c, p. 4). Thus, many respondents described their relationships as contexts in which they feel encouraged as women to present themselves as highly desirable and self-confident, and in which they can easily ensure that their needs are taken into account. At the same time, the researcher found that in contrast to the usual cultural reception of "cougars", very few women perceive themselves as seducers who pursued younger men, while younger men passively waited to be courted. The tendency to present oneself in a more passive role in the relationship process was more pronounced among participants over 40 than among 30-year-olds and was then attributed to something beyond their control, such as the attractiveness of the man. However, women over 40, and over 50 years of age in particular, described the relationship-building process as initiated by the younger men (Alarie, 2019b, p. 473). Alarie attributes this finding to the fact that women find it difficult to renegotiate the gender-specific relationship-building script because it is constrained by common cultural discourse that indicates that a woman's value decreases with age, and by the cultural discomfort with the sexuality of older women. It could be critically noted that, in addition to this interpretation, there is actually the possibility that the male partners were more actively engaged in initiating relationships. Because this corresponded to their idea of gender-equitable behaviour, it is possible that they had an explicit interest in the relationship with an older woman.

Here it is interesting to note that in the three case studies presented, the initiative was also taken exclusively by the male partner. None of the women had previously had a (sexual) relationship with a younger man or explicitly felt the need to do so. On the contrary, at the beginning of the relationship, all three women had initially hesitated to enter into a corresponding relationship, mainly because of the large age difference, partly also because of additional framework conditions (namely the teacher–pupil relationship and the long-distance relationship).

In another study, based on data from the National Survey of Family Growth in Canada, Alarie and Carmichael (2015) examined the characteristics of middle-aged women who reported sexual relations with younger men in the last 12 months (age gap ≥ 5 years, n = 201; age gap ≥ 10 years, n = 67). They found that about 13% of sexually active women between the ages of 35 and 44 had slept with a man who was at least 5 years younger. Contrary to conventional assumptions, the results show that, in the context of this study, it is mainly low-income women and those who identify themselves as "other races" (not white or black) who opt for an age-hypogamous sexual relationship. Women are most likely to opt for such a relationship with a younger partner if they have previously been married. Finally, the results also suggest that age-hypogamous relationships are not simple sexual affairs. The researchers were able to identify a total of 240 age-hypogamous sexual relationships in which women were at least 5 years older than their partner (note that some women had more than one younger male partner in the last 12 months). Of these relationships, about 54% lasted at least 2 years. In addition, 87 of the 201 (43%) women in age-hypogamous sexual relationships (using the 5-year age difference definition) were actually married to or living with their younger partner. These results are a clear indication of the longevity of women's sexual relationships with younger men, clearly showing that about half of these relationships are long-term and that many of them involve marriage or cohabitation.

These results are also reflected in the case studies. In case examples 2 and 3, the older women are both divorced. All three relationships have already lasted several years, with the first case example having lasted for several decades.

There are no significant educational differences between the couples; all have at least one university degree, only Nathalie and Tom have a slight educational gap because she has a Master's degree and he has a Bachelor's degree.

As far as the economic gap is concerned, the case of couple 1 is even contrary to conventional assumptions, because Greta gave up her job and stayed at home after the birth of her child, as was usual in the Catholic milieu in Germany at that time, in order to take care of the upbringing of the common child.

With Nathalie and Tom, there are considerable financial differences due to the age difference and the associated professional careers, from which Tom certainly profits when Nathalie invites him to travel, for example. Tom is, however concerned about the balance in the relationship, and for him it is an expression of his manhood and the seriousness of his feelings to regularly invite Nathalie for dinners or events and give her presents.

Helen and Ram also have a large economic difference, owing to their different places of residence (the UK and India) and the remuneration systems in their home countries, but both consider this to be irrelevant because there is no transfer of money or gifts between them.

It is interesting to note that from both studies (Alarie, 2019c; Alarie & Carmichael, 2015) the clear self-confidence of the women speaks in favour of their relationship with a younger man, even if the women perceive negative feedback and criticism for this form of relationship as burdensome, especially the women over 40 years of age.

The stigmatisation of this form of relationship can be traced back to a long tradition as an object of research: In 1996 for example, Warren conducted a sociological study of interviews with married, cohabiting and divorced older women (n = 7) and younger men (n = 8), which examined the effects of this type of age difference on relationships and on oneself, but above all drew attention to the stigmatisation aspect. Both women and men were aware of the stigmatising potential of their relationships, especially that the woman could be confused with the man's mother. Although the couples' fear of audience reaction diminished over time, the stigma aspect played an important role in their self-esteem. For the women, their body image, particularly the aging process of body and face, was the most problematic. For the men, the major problems were the lack of a common history with their wife, the distance from peers and the preliminary decision for other age-related roles, such as being a grandfather at a young age. Both the women and the men reported in the interviews that the difference in age was initially irrelevant with regard to mutual attraction, getting to know each other and the initiation of the relationship. Then they formulated a relevance of the age-related qualities for the continuation of the love relationship. The younger men named as special qualities of the older women their depth, care, sexuality, maturity, responsibility, "three-dimensionality" and financial security. The women compared their relationships with the younger partners especially with previous partnerships and emphasised the intensity of the current relationship.

In the decade before the 1996 study, statements about such relationship constructions were even more stereotypical:

> The women in the December–May group apparently had unavailable, narcissistically involved mothers and highly competitive fathers who were high achievers and with whom the women tended to identify. The men in these relationships had powerful mothers and passive-aggressive fathers, some high achievers. (Singer-Magdoff, 1988, p. 144 as cited in Warren, 1996, p. 80).

Here too, the related language images are a good reflection of the time and cultural context of typical scripts: the older woman associates with December, the month in which nature appears cold, dead and lifeless, before the year draws to a close. The man, in this description is connected with the association of the awakening, budding nature after the long dead winter, full of irrepressible energy and vitality and sensual joie de vivre. The derivation of the causal connections for the relationship decision of a couple from the presumed psychological profile of the parents can be regarded as fatal.

The use of these linguistic images is by no means part of the past (Collisson & De Leon, 2018). In a recent study (Collisson & De Leon, 2018), Collison and his colleague investigated which negative stereotypes and prejudices are associated with age-differentiated couples. They found that age gaps were more unpopular and perceived as less appropriate compared to age-appropriate couples. In exploratory analyses, the age-differentiated relationships have repeatedly led to significantly more prejudice than other types of couples. Collison and colleagues conducted an online investigation in Arizona and interviewed 62 men, 35 women and two participants who had not reported gender. Participants were identified as Caucasian (50%), Asian (37%), African American (7%) and Hispanic (4%). Participants were aged 19 to 63 years and the survey was conducted on age-dissimilar couples. In general, couples with a greater age difference were less popular than couples of similar age. There was an explicitly greater acceptance of the relationship between women and older men (81.95%) than of women in relationships with younger men (55.45%) (Collisson & De Leon, 2018, p. 4). The study showed that the interviewees' own age and gender did not positively influence their prejudices against couples with age gaps. However, the exploratory analyses showed differences in the level of prejudice caused by different types of couples (e.g. couples differing in race, weight or finances). Interestingly, people rated age-gap pairs as less appropriate than interracial, mixed-weight, or mixed socioeconomic status pairs. The older relationship partner was given a particularly negative rating because he/she was assumed to derive the greater benefit from this relationship. The more strongly this assumption was formulated, the more prejudices were expressed against this kind of relationship.

Advantages over such relationship constellations do not only seem to persist in Western contexts. One of the few studies dealing with relationships between older women and younger men in the non-Western context comes from South Africa (Phaswana-Mafuya et al., 2014). In this study, Phaswana-Mafuya and her colleagues investigated relationships between "sugar mommies" and their younger partners in terms of their appearance, their acceptance and the perceived reasons why older women and younger men enter into these relationships. An explorative qualitative study with 135 participants from 11 different focus groups on age, gender (women = 27%) from the nine South African provinces was conducted. Focus group interviews collected data on the participants' views, opinions and experiences with "sugar mommy" practice. The study found that the sugar mommy model was widespread in South Africa.

The prejudices with which the older women were confronted were:

domination, reduction of stress, physical attraction, procreation, lack of self-control, youthful feeling, migrancy, difficulty in finding partners of compatible age, and young men seen as not demanding (Phaswana-Mafuya et al., 2014, p. 259).

The following motives were attributed to the young men:

reduction of stress, being enticed, rejection by women of compatible age, peer influence, and the belief that older women are purer (Phaswana-Mafuya et al., 2014, p. 259).

Some of the interviewees (number not named) were unprejudiced about this form of relationship and named entirely different non-functionalising reasons for the relationship, such as "love knows no age" or because "here is nothing wrong with it" (Phaswana-Mafuya et al., 2014, pp. 259–260).

20.5 Experiences, Insights and Motives of Couples in Relationships Between Older Women and Younger Men

Proulx and colleagues (Proulx et al., 2006) conducted one of the basic qualitative studies in 2006 with eight couples living in an age-different relationship where the woman was 10 or more years older than her husband. The interviews were carried out with each participant separately and focused on three main areas: The impact of the age difference on the relationship, the problems that arose for the couple, and any differences in the experience of husbands and wives. The men were aged from 24 to 51 years, and the women from 34 to 61 years. Age differences between men and women ranged from 10 years to 17 years. All but one of the participants identified themselves as white, except one man of Asian descent. Most couples belonged to the middle class with at least one university degree.

The age of women at the time of marriage was between 34 and 53 years, with 75% of women in their late 30s and early 40s (6:8). For men, their age at marriage was 23 to 43 years, with 75% of men in their early to mid-twenties (6:8) at the time of marriage. The couples were married between 7 months and 15 years and had files ranging from less than 1 year to 5 years before marriage. Many of the women (6:8) had been married at least once before, while most men (6:8) had never been married before.

From the point of view of the couples, age differences were associated with various advantages that women and men rated differently, as shown in Fig. 20.1. Men described the greater life experience and maturity of the partner predominantly as a main benefit (6:8 compared to 1:8 women) and also stated more frequently than their partner's career/finances being more secure was also seen as an advantage (4:8 compared to 2:8 women).

These findings are also confirmed in the case examples presented. This is explicitly formulated by Richard and Ram, who describe life experience/maturity as very attractive in relation to Greta and Helen respectively. For Ram, it also acts

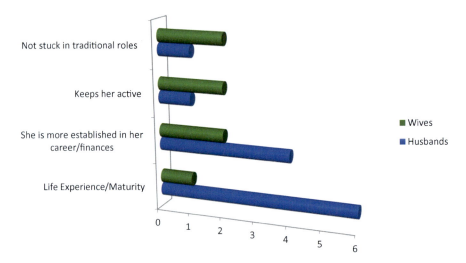

Fig. 20.1 Benefits of the age difference (8 husbands, 8 wives). Vanderheiden based on Proulx et al. (2006)

as an attractor that Helen is so professionally established and successful. Tom makes no specific statement about this; he seems to be attracted mainly physically to older women, but he does not give up on Nathalie, although he is denied sexuality here.

Another current study supports the relevance of maturity. From an anthropological–sociological point of view, Lara McKenzie conducted a study in Australia in 2013 (McKenzie, 2013) with age-different couples who had a romantic relationship, focusing on three aspects

1. Characteristics of romantic love, especially in contemporary Western contexts
2. Age-related relationships as a social phenomenon
3. Interplay between autonomy and connectedness through the lens of Romantic love in age-related relationships.

She conducted interviews with 24 people in Perth who lived in relationships with age differences. The smallest age difference was 7 years, the largest 30 years. The interviewees were between 22 and 76 years old and the duration of the relationship was between 2.5 months and 29 years. Eleven men and 13 women were interviewed: 9 persons lived in a relationship in which the woman was older than the man (average age difference 11.9 years; average relationship duration 7.2 years) and 15 persons lived in a relationship in which the man was older (average age difference 17.1 years; average relationship duration 9.7 years). For all respondents, a minimum and appropriate level of maturity seemed crucial for starting and maintaining a love relationship (McKenzie, 2013, p. 118).

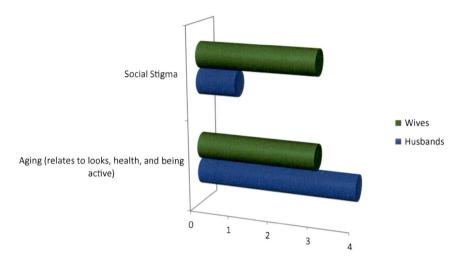

Fig. 20.2 Drawbacks due to the age difference (8 husbands, 8 wives). Vanderheiden based on Proulx et al. (2006)

Asked about the potential drawbacks with regard to their relationship, two aspects were mentioned: aging—related to looks, health, and being active—and the aspect of social stigma (see Fig. 20.2). For women, more often than for men, the social stigma seems to be a disadvantage of this type of relationship (citing 3:8 women and 1:8 men).

This is also reflected in the case examples presented. Greta is worried about the age difference, but not so much about attractiveness: "I know that Richard wouldn't leave me because I'm getting older or less attractive. I'm worried that, of course, as I grow older, I won't have as much time with him as I'd like. And that I will probably be the one who has to go first and leave him behind. That worries me in terms of age." For Helen, it is different: "Sometimes I already feel like time flies and I get older and older and then I ask myself what it will feel like when Ram one day won't find any arguments to prevent an arranged marriage and I'll be single again and find myself on the search for a new partner in my mid-sixties or so. That won't be easy."

She does not perceive the age difference as a social stigma, however, Ram experiences it differently. "Often, when I go home to my parents and I'm on a train or bus at night, I imagine telling them about Helen, how wonderful she is and how happy we make each other. But of course that's out of the question".

Greta and Richard faced very negative experiences regarding their age difference at the beginning of their relationship. Greta remembers: "It was a scandal, and at that time very unusual. Everyone made stupid remarks, he would leave me when I get old and unattractive, such a relationship would be sick and abnormal".

With regard to the question whether the age difference attracted the partners to each other, 6 of the 16 participants in Proulx study stated that the age difference had played a role in the initial attraction to their spouse, and 3 of the 6 stated that they had always felt attracted to the age difference.

This, too, is fully confirmed by the statements of the couples presented in the case examples.

In McKenzie's (2013) study most respondents shared the understanding that relationships are based on similarity or compatibility. They stated that they sought and maintained relationships with certain types of partners and that similarity in social class, culture, religion, education, gender and even age strongly influenced their choice of partner. While most interviewees stated that race, class and culture would not influence whom they loved, many believed that the similar interests of partners, as well as similar intellectual abilities and educational qualifications, were highly desirable in a relationship (McKenzie, 2013, p. 150). This was associated with a concept of love that sees love as "blind" to social traits such as age, culture and ethnicity and considers them irrelevant to the development of love. Love continued to be understood by most as a largely autonomous force that brought couples together and controlled with whom a relationship arose (McKenzie, 2013, pp. 156–157). All respondents believed that romantic love should be the basis of a marriage or couple relationship (McKenzie, 2013, p. 162) and also that partners should choose each other freely, unburdened by demands and expectations from family, friends or society.

This also applies to the interviewees in case examples 1 and 3, but there are no reliable statements from case 2. Ram and Helen see themselves as lovers, feel closely connected, sometimes struggle with the limitations that prevent them from living together. But they perceive these limitations as culturally conditioned and not as caused by their age difference. Ram: "We couldn't get married if Helen was thirty years old." Greta and Richard (case example 1) have long since overcome social prejudices and family reservations and shown that their love is lasting and sustainable.

20.6 Conclusion and Future Research Needs

Most studies on age-different couples are quantitative and rather descriptive in character, often based on national statistics or micro-census, and nearly all come from the Western cultural context.

The few qualitative studies in existence concentrate primarily on the problems that arise (or could arise) from age inequality, while very few concentrate on questions such as how older women and younger men want to understand and shape their relationships, what makes their relationship special and different from others, what relationship concept they want to live, what assumptions they make about themselves and their partner, what aspirations they have and what values they share. With this in mind, it appears that love as a theme in this context is explicitly addressed only by McKenzie (2013).

Perhaps this inflexible focus on sexuality and problems, which is expressed in most studies, reflects how pointed many social scripts still seem to be today, unbroken and unquestioned, and obviously preventing these couple relationships from being viewed also as love relationships. In the spirit of Beck and Beck-Gernsheim (1995, p. 191): "Lovers are free and active agents, personally accountable, taking decisions which are intentional and their own".

With a view to future research needs, it would be desirable to take a closer look at the love and relationship concepts of people who live their relationship as couples of older women and younger men. The researchers have also focused on the attitudes and self-awareness of those affected to date, in order to examine the lived practice of these relationships, which may also be worthwhile.

Most studies refer to the Western context; it might be fruitful to include other cultural perspectives in the research, both in different cultural contexts and in relation to relationships between people with different cultural backgrounds.

It could also be exciting to investigate the influence of digitisation on the emergence of this relationship construction and its maintenance or practice, for instance, in establishing to what extent such relationships emerge via dating platforms or are practised in the context of globalisation as inter-cultural or transcultural cyber love relationships.

It is hoped that more intensive and sophisticated research on love relationships between older women and younger men will prove Lawton and Callister (2010, p. 20) to be correct when they conclude:

> With women increasingly better educated than males, there will, inevitably, be far more couples where the woman is better educated and, sometimes, better paid than her partner. It will take time to see if there also continues to be growth in couples where the woman is significantly older than her partner. If there is further major growth, it is likely the somewhat negative predatory term cougar will disappear or at least change its current connotations.

Acknowledgement I would like to thank Daniel J. Thorssøn, a poet and artist from the Manawatu, New Zealand, for his generous permission to cite his poem here (Thorssøn, 2016).

References

Addison, S. (2010). *"Cougar" trend of women chasing younger men a myth*. Retrieved July 26, 2019, from https://www.reuters.com/article/us-britain-cougars/cougar-trend-of-women-chasing-younger-men-a-myth-idUSTRE67H61Q20100819

Alarie, M. (2019a). «Je ne suis pas une cougar! » - Quand l'âgisme et le sexisme compliquent l'expression du désir sexuel féminin. *Recherches Féministes, 32(1), 49–70.* 49-70.

Alarie, M. (2019b). "They're the ones chasing the cougar": Relationship formation in the context of age-hypogamous intimate relationships. *Gender and Society, 33*(3), 463–485. https://doi.org/10.1177/0891243219839670

Alarie, M. (2019c). Sleeping with younger men: Women's accounts of sexual interplay in age-hypogamous intimate relationships. *The Journal of Sex Research*, 1–13. https://doi.org/10.1080/00224499.2019.1574704

Alarie, M., & Carmichael, J. (2015). The "cougar" phenomenon: An examination of the factors that influence age-hypogamous sexual relationships among middle-aged women. *Journal of Marriage and Family, 77*(5), 1250–1265. https://doi.org/10.1111/jomf.12213

Banks, C., & Arnold, P. (2001). Opinions towards sexual partners with a large age difference. *Marriage and Family Review, 33*(4), 5–18. https://doi.org/10.1300/j002v33n04_02

Beck, U., & Beck-Gernsheim, E. (1995). *The normal chaos of love*. Cambridge: Polity Press.

Berardo, F., Appel, J., & Berardo, D. (1993). Age dissimilar marriages: Review and assessment. *Journal of Aging Studies, 7*(1), 93–106.

Blumstein, P., & Schwartz, P. (1983). *American couples: Money, work, sex*. New York: Morrow.

Buddeberg, C., & Maake, C. (2005). *Sexualberatung*. Stuttgart: Enke.

Bundesamt für Statistik. (2016). *Paarbeziehungen Erhebung zu Familien und Generationen 2013. Erhebung zu Familien und Generationen*. Retrieved July 24, 2019, from https://www.bfs.admin.ch/bfs/de/home/statistiken/bevoelkerung/erhebungen/efg.html

Casterline, J., Williams, L., & McDonald, P. (1986). The age difference between spouses: Variations among developing countries. *Population Studies, 40*(3), 353–374. https://doi.org/10.1080/0032472031000142296

Collard, R. (2012). Cougar figures, gender, and the performances of predation. *Gender, Place and Culture, 19*(4), 518–540. https://doi.org/10.1080/0966369x.2011.610179

Collisson, B., & De Leon, L. (2018). Perceived inequity predicts prejudice towards age-gap relationships. *Current Psychology*. https://doi.org/10.1007/s12144-018-9895-6

Conway, J., Noë, N., Stulp, G., & Pollet, T. (2015). Finding your soulmate: Homosexual and heterosexual age preferences in online dating. *Personal Relationships, 22*(4), 666–678. https://doi.org/10.1111/pere.12102

Daguet, F. (2016). *An increasing number of couples where the man is younger than the woman - Insee Première - 1613*. Retrieved July 24, 2019, from https://www.insee.fr/en/statistiques/2534182

Drefahl, S. (2010). How does the age gap between partners affect their survival? *Demography, 47*(2), 313–326. https://doi.org/10.1353/dem.0.0106

Eckert, P., & McConnell-Ginet, S. (2019). *Language and gender*. 2nd edition. Retrieved July 24, 2019, from https://web.stanford.edu/~eckert/PDF/Chap1.pdf

Fisher, H. (1992). *Anatomy of love*. New York, NY: Fawcett Columbine.

Fisher, H. (1995). The nature and evolution of romantic love. In W. Jankowiak (Ed.), *Passionate love* (pp. 57–71). New York, NY: Columbia University Press.

Fisher, H. (2004). *Why we love: The nature and chemistry of romantic love*. New York, NY: Henry Holt.

Fisher, H. E., Aron, A., Mashek, D., Li, H., & Brown, L. L. (2002). Defining the brain systems of lust, romantic attraction, and attachment. *Archives of Sexual Behavior, 31*, 413–419.

Gazso, A., & Bischoping, K. (2018). Feminist reflections on the relation of emotions to ethics: A case study of two awkward interviewing moments [35 paragraphs]. *Forum Qualitative Sozialforschung/Forum: Qualitative Social Research, 19*(3), Art. 7. https://doi.org/10.17169/fqs-19.3.3118

Global Times. (2019). *An increase of older women snagging younger men in China has caught the public's attention - Global Times*. Retrieved July 27, 2019, from http://www.globaltimes.cn/content/1075597.shtml

Gustafson, P., & Fransson, U. (2015). Age differences between spouses: Sociodemographic variation and selection. *Marriage and Family Review, 51*(7), 610–632. https://doi.org/10.1080/01494929.2015.1060289

Jankowiak, W., & Fischer, T. (1992). A cross-cultural perspective on romantic love. *Ethnology, 31*, 149–155.

Jankowiak, W., & Paladino, T. (2008). Desiring sex, longing for love: A tripartite conundrum. In W. Jankowiak (Ed.), *Intimacies: Love and sex across cultures* (pp. 1–36). New York, NY: Columbia University Press.

Kaklamanidou, B. (2012). Pride and prejudice: Celebrity versus fictional cougars. *Celebrity Studies, 3*(1), 78–89. https://doi.org/10.1080/19392397.2012.644722

Karandashev, V. (2020). Cultural diversity of romantic love experience. In C. Mayer & E. Vanderheiden (Eds.), *International handbook of love*. Cham: Springer International.

Kasif, T., & Band-Winterstein, T. (2017). Older widows' perspectives on sexuality: A life course perspective. *Journal of Aging Studies, 41*, 1–9. https://doi.org/10.1016/j.jaging.2017.01.002

Kreager, D., & Staff, J. (2009). The sexual double standard and adolescent peer acceptance. *Social Psychology Quarterly, 72*(2), 143–164. https://doi.org/10.1177/019027250907200205

Kromrey, H., Strübing, J., & Roose, J. (2016). *Empirische sozialforschung*. Konstanz: UTB.

Lawton, Z., & Callister, P. (2010). *Older women–younger men relationships: The social phenomenon of "cougars." A research note*. Retrieved from http://ips.ac.nz/publications/files/be0acfcb7d0.pdf

Leahy, T. (2002). *Negotiating stigma: Approaches to intergenerational sex*. Victoria Park, WA: Books Reborn.

Lindholm, C. (2001). *Culture and identity: The history, theory, and practice of psychological anthropology*. Boston: McGraw Hill.

McKenzie, L. (2013). *Ageless love? Shared understandings of age-dissimilar, romantic relationships in Perth, Western*. Dissertation. University of Western Australia, Perth.

Misoch, S. (2015). *Qualitative interviews*. Berlin: De Gruyter.

Money, J. (1986). *Lovemaps*. New York: Irvington.

Montemurro, B. (2019). *Cougars: New sexual scripts for older women*. Retrieved 25 July 2019, from https://www.youtube.com/watch?v=H4alBxLGAxc

Montemurro, B., & Siefken, J. (2014). Cougars on the prowl? New perceptions of older women's sexuality. *Journal of Aging Studies, 28*, 35–43. https://doi.org/10.1016/j.jaging.2013.11.004

Müller-Böling, D., & Klandt, H. (1996). *Methoden empirischer Wirtschafts- und Sozialforschung. Methoden empirischer Wirtschafts- und Sozialforschung: eine Einführung mit wirtschaftswissenschaftlichem Schwerpunkt*. Köln: FGF c/o Univ. Dortmund.

Phaswana-Mafuya, N., Shisana, O., Davids, A., Tabane, C., Mbelle, M., Matseke, G., et al. (2014). Perceptions of sugar mommy practices in South Africa. *Journal of Psychology in Africa, 24*(3), 257–263. https://doi.org/10.1080/14330237.2014.906086

Proulx, N., Caron, S., & Logue, M. (2006). Older women/younger men. *Journal of Couple and Relationship Therapy, 5*(4), 43–64. https://doi.org/10.1300/j398v05n04_03

Przyborski, A., & Wohlrab-Sahr, M. (2008). *Qualitative Sozialforschung*. München: Oldenbourg Verlag.

Pyke, K., & Adams, M. (2010). What's age got to do with it? A case study analysis of power and gender in husband-older marriages. *Journal of Family Issues, 31*(6), 748–777. https://doi.org/10.1177/0192513x09357897

Sanchez, D., Fetterolf, J., & Rudman, L. (2012). Eroticizing inequality in the United States: The consequences and determinants of traditional gender role adherence in intimate relationships. *Journal of Sex Research, 49*(2–3), 168–183. https://doi.org/10.1080/00224499.2011.653699

Simon, W., & Gagnon, J. H. (1989). Sexual scripts: Permanence and change. *Archives of Sexual Behavior, 15*, 97–120.

Skopek, J., Schmitz, A., & Blossfeld, H. (2011). The gendered dynamics of age preferences – Empirical evidence from online dating. Zeitschrift Für Familienforschung, Heft 3(23. Jahrg.), 266–290. Retrieved from https://www.budrich-journals.de/index.php/zff/article/viewFile/5733/4860

Sontag, S. (1972). The double standard of aging. *Saturday Review, 23*, 29–38.

South China Morning Post. (2019). *Educated Chinese women with good jobs are opting for younger husbands*. Retrieved July 27, 2019, from https://www.scmp.com/news/china/society/article/2113990/no-country-older-men-chinas-better-educated-well-paid-women-are

Statistisches Bundesamt. (2019). *Ab welchem Altersunterschied es kritisch wird*. Retrieved July 24, 2019, from https://www.t-online.de/leben/liebe/id_73316790/altersunterschied-ab-diesem-abstand-wird-es-problematisch.html

Sternberg, R. J. (1988). *The triangle of love*. New York, NY: Basic Books.
Thorssøn, D. (2016). *Dispositioned hearts by a perfect circle*. Retrieved October 28, 2019, from https://allpoetry.com/poem/12614013-Dispositioned-Hearts-by-A-Perfect-Circle
US Bureau. (2013). *Current population survey (CPS)*. Retrieved July 24, 2019, from https://www.census.gov/programs-surveys/cps.html
Warren, C. (1996). Older women, younger men: Self and stigma in age-discrepant relationships. *Clinical Sociology Review, 14*(1), Article 7. Retrieved July 25, 2019, from http://digitalcommons.wayne.edu/csr/vol14/iss1/7
Wiederman, M. (2005). The gendered nature of sexual scripts. *The Family Journal, 13*(4), 496–502. https://doi.org/10.1177/1066480705278729

Elisabeth Vanderheiden (Second state examination) is a pedagogue, theologian, intercultural mediator, managing director of the Catholic Adult Education Rhineland-Palatinate, the President of the Catholic Adult Education of Germany and the CEO of the Global Institute for Transcultural Research. Her publishing focus centres on in the context of basic education for adults, in particular on trainings for teachers and trainers in adult education, as well as vocational, and civic education, text collections on intercultural opening processes and intercultural mediation. Her latest publications focused on shame as resource as well as mistakes, errors and failure and their hidden potentials in the context of culture and positive psychology.

Chapter 21
A Table for One: The Homosexual Single and the Absence of Romantic Love

Aliraza Javaid

Abstract The expression 'A Table for One' is borrowed from Lahad (*A table for one: A critical reading of singlehood, gender and time*. Manchester University Press, Manchester, 2017) to metaphorically signify the sheer loneliness, solitude and invisibility that some single homosexuals embody in the midst of individualism and secularization. This book chapter, then, critically details the ways in which gay love is often constructed as taboo, deviant and made stigmatized during social relations. Drawing on the works of Goffman, I attempt to understand how homosexual singles are subjected to hostility, social disapproval and stigma, often resulting in the absence of same-sex love. Love is usually out of reach for many gay men because of the rise of fleeting sexual and fluid intimacy. Therefore, I argue herein that the exposure to such intimacy can reproduce a homosexual single identity that becomes stigmatized during social relations, in which their singlehood ascribes a 'spoiled identity' (Goffman, 1963a). That is, the single stigmatized homosexual identity, with whom no one to go out with, is interactional and socially accomplished. The homosexual single, although he can be seen, is *unnoticed* and fades into the background for he has nothing to converse about regarding coupldom at family gatherings, Birthday parties, and at other social events occupied by heterosexuals and non-heterosexuals, singles and non-singles. Gay singles are like 'non-persons' since they are "treated in social interactions as if they are not there" (Goffman, E., *The Presentation of Self in Everyday Life* (p. 152). Anchor Books, New York, 1959). The 'double stigma' emanating from embodying both a homosexual and a single identity can draw in social exclusion and alienation during everyday encounters with strangers and non-strangers. Their *singlehood career* (Lahad, *A table for one: A critical reading of singlehood, gender and time*. Manchester University Press, Manchester, 2017) evokes the absence of romantic love, leaving the homosexual single eating alone at a table for one.

Keywords Love · Gay love · Single identity · Gay singlehood · Gay love as taboo

A. Javaid (✉)
University of East London, University Square, London, UK
e-mail: ali_2p9@hotmail.co.uk

21.1 Introduction

Each year, as a homosexual single, I sit at a table for one, I eat alone, I drink alone, I go to nights out alone, and it seems that wherever I go, I am invariably alone. My singlehood is reinforced when other gay and bisexual men often reject the possibility of having a romantic date with me. It becomes further reinforced through my doing of fleeting and fluid intimacy, having multiple sexual partners to remind me of my singlehood identity and loneliness. Whilst I fall hopelessly into entrapments of such fleeting sexual encounters with multiple men, I do so voluntarily in the hope that my singlehood identity becomes vanquished. Rather, it becomes reemphasized. Being a homosexual single in the midst of their being an absence of love, I attempt to make sense of this single, often stigmatizing, identity that is socially and interactionally accomplished. I argued previously that, "at times, certain identities, such as singlehood, being single, being alone, were imposed on me so I was imprisoned and entrapped in singlehood" (Javaid, 2018a: 95). I use the metaphor, 'A Table for One' borrowed from Lahad (2017), to metaphorically signify the sheer loneliness, solitude and invisibility that some single homosexuals, like myself, embody in the midst of individualism and secularization. It refers to the position that singles either take up or do not take up and matters regarding their legitimacy and (in)visibility in public life. We have entered a social world that is occupied by digital apps that make the arrangement of casual sexual encounters so much more easier and fluid; the formulation of these 'digital worlds' seemingly leave romantic love for gay singles unproblematic and unquestionable. In this book chapter, I attempt to offer some critical engagement of the homosexual single, situated in a confused world where 'offline/online' becomes blurred and unnecessarily questioned.

Whilst casual gay encounters become normalized for some single gay and bisexual men, but made deviant by many, Ken Plummer (1975) suggests that the homosexual single is socially constructed and is unlikely to echo one form of homosexuality but rather represent many versions. He discusses the homosexual single as embodying a "homosexual way of life" or a "career type" of sexuality. The majority of heterosexuals, as he argues, construct this homosexual culture as deviant and abnormal and so restricting their everyday movement. The deviance of homosexuality needs to be understood in a cultural and historical context (Plummer, 1975). Homophobia or heterosexism can and does limit homosexual singles' movement in public life, resulting in many remaining in the closet and so remaining closed off from the possibility of falling in love with another man (Javaid, 2018a). The confession of same-sex love can put one at the center stage and he may become a target of homophobic violence and abuse. He may retreat by way of disdaining romantic love.

This book chapter, then, critically examines singlehood and the ways in which gay love is often constructed as taboo, deviant and made stigmatized during social relations. Drawing on the works of Goffman, I attempt to understand how homosexual singles are subjected to hostility, social disapproval and stigma, often resulting in the absence of same-sex love. Love is usually out of reach for many gay men because of the rise of fleeting sexual and fluid intimacy. Therefore, I argue herein that the exposure to such intimacy can reproduce a homosexual single identity that becomes stigmatized during social relations, in which their singlehood ascribes a 'spoiled identity' (Goffman, 1963a). That is, the single stigmatized homosexual identity, with whom no one to go out with, is interactional and socially accomplished. The homosexual single, although he can be seen, is unnoticed and fades into the background for he has nothing to converse about regarding coupldom at family gatherings, Birthday parties, and at other social events occupied by heterosexuals and non-heterosexuals, singles and non-singles. Gay singles are like 'non-persons' since they are "treated in social interactions as if they are not there" (Goffman, 1959: 152). They do not 'belong'. The 'double stigma' emanating from embodying both a homosexual and a single identity can draw in social exclusion and alienation during everyday encounters with strangers and non-strangers. Their singlehood career (Lahad, 2017) evokes the absence of romantic love, leaving the homosexual single eating alone at a table for one. In this book chapter, I consider the question whether or not a homosexual single can legitimately occupy a respectable designated position absent from the nuclear family. By considering this dilemma, questions around respectability emerge that a homosexual single may defy in everyday social life. Can a homosexual single occupy the position of singlehood without stigma? The non-homosexual and the nuclear family are traditionally marked as legitimate and respected, so does this mean that the homosexual single is accountable for this deviation?

21.2 Homosexuality and Singlehood: Storying the Unloved, the Deviant and the Abnormal

I argue that same sex love is often restrained in the midst of heteronormativity, resulting in many gay singles being unable to find and sustain love. I define heteronormativity as the normalization of heterosexuality in all segments of everyday life; it is institutionalized across social institutions, such as the family, the education system, and everyday public life and discourses. It places heterosexuality as culturally 'normal' and valued, placing non-heterosexualities at the borders of significance, such as homosexuality. Gay social conduct or the embodiment of gay lacks cultural and symbolic value (Javaid, 2018c). Homosexuality is culturally stigmatized through social relations (Plummer, 1995). Because of heteronormativity, homosexuality is positioned as the 'abnormal' or the 'other'. Stevi Jackson (2018: 138) argues that, 'even in the most liberal places much of everyday life still proceeds on the assumption that everyone is heterosexual unless known to be otherwise. Heteronormativity is mobilised and reproduced in everyday life through routine activities in which gender, sexuality, and heterosexuality interconnect'. James Messerschmidt (2018: 14) writes that:

> [T]he relationship between hegemonic masculinity and emphasized femininity underpins what has become known as *heteronormativity*, or the legal, cultural, organizational, and interpersonal practices that derive from and reinforce the discursive structure that there are two and only two naturally opposite and complementary sexes (male and female), that gender is a natural manifestation of sex (masculinity and femininity), and that it is natural for the two opposite and complementary sexes to be sexually attracted to each other (heterosexuality) ... the notion that men's and women's bodies are naturally compatible and thus "made for each other" (emphasis in original).

Consequently, if a gay single 'embodied practices are read as effeminate this can lead to imputations of homosexuality and undermine his claims to masculinity' (Jackson, 2018: 138). He becomes not only stigmatized, for he is socially excluded, but also the finding and maintaining of same sex love becomes problematic. First, this is because the homosexual single may perform femininity or campiness, which is likely to be distasteful to some other gay men who may embody notions of heteronormativity, such as the performance of 'straight-acting' masculinity. Second, many gay or bisexual men remain in the closet and so this concealment of their sexual identity makes it difficult to pursue a romantic and loving gay relationship with another. Instead, many of these men carry out clandestine sexual activities with multiple men because of the threat of heteronormativity that breeds homophobia, trapping many gay and bisexual men in the closet. Gay and bisexual men are coerced to mirror heterosexual lifestyles and cultures, normalized into gay culture. We see many heterosexuals at the gay scene to remind gay and bisexual men of their presence, emphasizing that even heterosexuals 'own' gay spaces (Javaid, 2018b). Heterosexuals occupy all spaces given that non-heterosexuals' bodies are deemed

> as non-conforming and as non-heteronormative, failing to embody heteronormative notions of gender and/or sexuality (Javaid, 2018d: 751).

Jackson (2006) argues that the construction of heterosexuality is formed in a way that is characterised as the normal way of life, a normal way of being, and everyone is assumed to be heterosexual until shown otherwise. Thus, when one confesses their non-heterosexuality, they are vulnerable to homophobia. A hierarchy of sexuality emerges, in which heterosexuality remains at the top as the leading form of sexuality, the most honored and glorified. I have stated that,

> though this sexual hierarchy is dynamic and changing, it nonetheless compartmentalises homosexuality near the bottom tier as a deviation to heterosexual standards, expectations, and norms. The normalisation of heterosexuality underpins all social action (Javaid, 2018c: 46).

As "heteronormativity regulates the lives of heterosexual as well as non-heterosexual identified people" (Richardson, 2018: 16), gay singles are regulated in the midst of heterosexual spaces. There is a dichotomy between heterosexuality and homosexuality, whereby the public/private division is a spatial marker within the control of sexualities regarding who has access to particular spaces and rights; as a form of zoned tolerance, gays are pushed to the private sphere (Javaid, 2018b; Richardson, 2018; Richardson and May, 1999). As a consequence, the public confession of same sex love is almost forbidden, made into a taboo, and so any men disclosing their love for another man can expect their to be some sort of antagonism in the public space of heterosexuality. Same sex love is relegated to the bedroom, out of public sight, so that heteronormativity can be perpetuated and reinforced.

However, despite my critical take on this dichotomy and of gay men's inability to confess same sex love in heterosexual spaces at certain contexts, times and places, we are seeing some constructions of the 'normal' gay whereby the confession of same sex love can be accepted and less negatively regulated and sanctioned. For example, Steven Seidman (2002) states that the normal gay is:

> associated with specific social behaviours. For example, the normal gay is expected to be gender conventional, link sex to love and a marriage-like relationship, defend family values, personify economic individualism, and display national pride (p. 133).

One could argue, then, that some may accept the normal gay if he mirrors a heteronormative life style. This includes same-sex marriage or a civil partnership, perpetuating dominant intimate norms, by showing their devotion to a loving, stable, marital-style couple relationship. I argue that there is a hierarchy of homosexuality, just as there is a hierarchy of heterosexuality (Seidman, 2002). In this hierarchy, gay men who engage in social practices underpinned by heteronormativity, such as marriage or a heterosexual-like relationship, are more likely to be able to confess their love for another man publically. In contrast, those gays who drastically deviate from heteronormativity, such as those whom engage in sexual promiscuity or do not marry, are more likely to be constructed as 'deviant', making it problematic to confess their same sex love. I do not claim that this hierarchy is static and unmoving, however, but rather negotiated through social and power relations.

I argue that the homosexual single is 'doubly stigmatized' in and through social interaction. Stigma is defined in and enacted through social interaction as intended by the original formulation of the theory (see Goffman, 1963a). The 'double stigma' is socially accomplished, firstly, because of his homosexual identity, and, secondly, because of his singlehood identity, both of which are discreditable stigmas for they are initially unknown and can be concealable until they manifest through confession to others or through telling sexual stories to others (Plummer, 1995). The emergence of stigma through social relations lies in the "rules" that guide social conduct at certain contexts, times and places through the definition of what is allowable, acceptable, or 'normal'. Ken Plummer (1975) formulates the notion of 'sexual stigma' to distinguish the link between homosexual identity and stigma, arguing that homosexuality is unproblematically linked to deviance. Plummer demonstrates that sexuality is only sexual via the meanings people attach to certain forms of social conduct. In other words, nothing is sexual until it has been given sexual meaning. To understanding the homosexual single as 'doubly stigmatized and deviant', the interaction and encounter are significant. As Plummer highlights (1975), though, we are reliant on societal reactions in order for one to be constructed as a homosexual. The social audience reinforces one's homosexual single identity, grounded in social relations and encounters. During such encounters and social relations, we tell sexual stories (Plummer, 1995) or stories about our singlehood as a homosexual. By doing so, we confess our and affiliate with a homosexual single identity. Plummer (1995) writes that the:

> [T]he telling of a story has no simple, unitary or fixed character. For setting it out like this deconstructs, decentres and destabilises the story. Stories depend upon a constant flow of joint actions circulating between tellers, coaxers, texts, readers and the contexts in which the stories are told: tellers can only select, coaxers can only sift, texts can only sieve and readers can only interpret. Each of these processes compounds the others till the link between reality and the story become very fragile ... Texts are connected to lives, actions, contexts and society (p. 95).

Grounded in social practices and organization, then, the practice of story telling about one's own single and homosexual identities are not a uniform and straightforward exercise. Rather, the meanings we attach to our homosexual singlehood career (Lahad, 2017) cannot be determined nor assumed, but actively moving and changing. The process of storytelling gives us hope and despair for we are fought with new challenges and opportunities associated with our gay singlehood career. Goffman (1963a) establishes that degradation may result in a 'spoiled identity' if one's embodied self presentation, story and practice are conceptualised by others as 'failed'. The appearance of the homosexual single is likely to be degraded and constructed as 'failed' for deviating from the status quo of heteronormativity, whereby the heterosexual couple is categorized as 'normal' and competent. Given that robust participation within everyday life rests on the successful presentation of self, the homosexual single is likely to be 'read' as transgressing the gender and sexual order.

21.3 Drinking Alone?

Gay solo drinkers are familiar with the 'just one glass?' question so often asked by bar staff when a bottle of wine is ordered, as they peer behind one, expecting to see late-arriving companions. In this section, I want to think about the particular ways that gay men might position themselves or be positioned in public settings as alone at particular times, such as during a night out, and how their position in this context is either liberating and constraining. Gay men drinking alone are never truly alone. They are surrounded by people, including the bar staff, the bouncers at the door, and other people who are drinking, but are drinking with others. Goffman (1963b: 22) writes about co-presence, being in the presence of others, writing that it "renders persons uniquely accessible, available, and subject to one another". The homosexual single is sat drinking alone, making his presence visible and known to others who are not drinking alone. He can be seen, but unnoticed; he is, at the same time, susceptible to others. In other words, he makes himself available for others, should they enter his 'single space'. The quest of finding love on a night out may be persistent for the homosexual single, who is alone to find love. Drawing on Goffman's (1972[1971]) theoretical work on participation units, which are interactional units of public life that help persons cope with co-presence, the homosexual single disrupts the status quo of drinking with others for he poses the question as to whether he 'fits in' within the public space of gay bars and clubs. Is he afforded public protection from others during his drinking in the evening at a gay bar/club? Others may see him alone, but do not go over to drink with him; without any obligation to invite the homosexual single, others may inadvertently single him out and socially exclude him from the informalities of the nightlight and celebrations. In turn, arguably, stigma is likely to be enforced onto the single because he is constructed as 'coming alone' and is positioned as 'out of place' (Javaid, 2018b), and because, for Goffman, "evening activities... provide unfavorable information about unaccompanied participants, especially damaging in the case of [single gay] participants" (Goffman, 1963b: 103–104). Gay singles, therefore, are "a potential target of uncivil attention ... [they are] aware of being out of place in the evening as opposed to the daytime" (Lahad and May, 2017: 1.4) and are "nakedly expose[d] ... to invasions of privacy" (Goffman, 1963a: 16). Others may stare at the gay single, with repeated sneaked stares, coupled with pitiful stares from bar staff and bouncers, forcing the gay single to be self-aware and "to be self-conscious and calculating about the impression he is making" (Goffman, 1963a: 14). He may suffer "the pain of being stared at" (Goffman, 1963b: 88).

Homosexual singles drinking alone momentarily break interaction order. Their sense of belonging is questioned and potentially disapproved of by others because they have no safety net, that is, others to safeguard them from public scrutiny. May (2013) argues that belonging equates to sustaining some level of comfort or ease in a person's environment. It also indicates the recognition of others, identifying their cultures (May, 2013). The homosexual single may be recognizable by others as the one who is alone, the one without any friends or a romantic boyfriend. This becomes his identification at a particular context, time and place. Drinking alone at gay bars and clubs is a process of what May (2011) calls 'territorialising space'. In other words, the homosexual single makes this space his own, navigating through the bars/clubs not only as alone, but also as someone who attaches symbolic meanings to these spaces. They are significant to him for they represent something close to him; they mean something to him, whether it represents a new chapter in his life, a new moment in which he had met someone who he thought would be the love of his life, or he had met his potential husband at these bars/clubs, and so on. These symbolic meanings attached to these geographical spaces can be his only avenues to gaining a sense of belonging. They offer him hope.

His out of place position during his drinking alone activity at the evening time, thereby, evokes stigma for he is socially excluded, drinking and partying alone. Lahad and May (2017) suggest that, when one is alone, he is seen to be lonely and perceived as lacking social value and social standing, incurring suspicion and being frowned upon; in turn, he becomes stigmatized as a social outcast. I argue that this stigma is consequential of gay single's 'participation unit' (Goffman, 1972[1971]). Thus, as they are solo drinkers on a night out, they occupy the single position, deviating from any sense of togetherness:

A single is a party of one, a person who has come alone, a person by 'himself', even though there may be other individuals near him ... A with is a party of more than one whose members are perceived to be 'together' (Goffman, 1972[1971]: 41).

Goffman (1972[1971]: 49) states that "the fundamental arrangement in public life is that singles and withs are to be treated as though sealed off from their setting" given that the gay single out alone in public during the evening poses risks to 'withs', which includes a more than one individual. A single participation unit will be recognized by 'withs' as those who are single. As Lahad and May (2017: 3.4) write, such singles "constitute a 'single' participation unit and when appearing in public they lack the required togetherness of the 'with' that is usually expected" on a night out. Gay bars and clubs are geographically created for 'withs'. For example, the tables are often large to accommodate large groups of drinkers, the seating areas are multiple with several chairs and tables close to each other, and the smoking terrace is also large with several chairs and tables aligned to each other to suggest that these are spaces for 'withs'. Where does the single situate? He contravenes social conventions and the architecture of gay bars/clubs given their design as spaces conducive to sharing and togetherness. Consequently, gay solo drinkers can feel uncomfortable in, and in some cases are excluded from, shared public spaces. Their isolation stems from the visible reminder that he is alone amongst people who form a group that he stands outside of. This social isolation of the single because of the design of gay bars/clubs reflects a bounded and restrained invitation to public space, symbolically suggesting that the gay single drinker's right to claim a territory of the self is questionable. 'Territory' means an individual's capability to temporarily claim possession of public space (Goffman, 1972[1971]). In this case, their claim possession of a personal space within a busy gay bar or club; their claim is contextual and situational. The deviant gay single has nowhere to hide; symbolically and metaphorically, he may not even have a place at the table. The gay single's sense of belonging in the public space of the gay bar/club is diminishing (see May, 2011). I argue, then, that gay singles can feel unable to claim entitlement to shared public spaces, such as gay bars and clubs.

However, the gay singles can negotiate their stigma or their 'spoiled identity' (Goffman, 1963a) during social relations by finding a potential dating partner on a night out. He may be successful and 'clicks' with someone whom he met, even if brief, and they passionately share a kiss together. As a consequence, the gay single momentarily saves 'face' (a positive social value; see Goffman, 1955) by actively becoming a part of a 'with' participation unit but contextually bound. He is situationally no longer alone but now occupies a 'with' identity. Stigma momentarily becomes diluted since he is no longer socially excluded or isolated from the main 'event' (I refer here to the drinking and partying that is happening as a collective activity with more than one people). In this fleeting context for the gay single, who briefly encounters a romantic lover with whom to momentarily drink with, social displacement and the deviation of social norms become unimportant for he is now safeguarded by another who helps him to save 'face' (Goffman, 1955) to form a presentation of self (Goffman, 1959) that is situationaly 'normal'. After all, the gay single who drinks alone "is being told that [he] is encroaching upon public space (and time) that has certain conventions that delineate who is entitled to belong, where to (and when)" (Lahad and May, 2017: 5.4). When a gay single briefly engages with another guy, dancing and kissing with him, locking eyes together and thinking he could be 'the one', civil inattention could be momentarily secured as both are 'behaving properly'. A strong social gaze of the gay single may be, for a short time, warded off. His 'knight in shining armour' has arrived, but for how long?

21.4 The Homosexual Single Mourner: Ghostly Invaders

I previously argued that, "The functioning of mourning ... is symbolically and metaphorically painful, most times even literal. It is symbolically and culturally violent. Mourning is a social process" (Javaid, 2018a: 129). Mourning requires a social audience to reaffirm its existence. The process of mourning begins when a significant other leaves us, either through breaking up with us or through death, which reaffirms our gay single identity. Ostler (2002) eloquently describes this social process of mourning for the single as the following: "if it's the termination of a relationship you're still feeling a little bruised over, it can feel like a death. That's because you're mourning the death of your hopes and dreams and perhaps even—gulp—your wedding plans" (p. 50). When a significant other leaves a homosexual single, he mourns not only of him, but also of the hopes and dreams that came along with this no-longer-present romantic other. He takes with him his heart and dreams. This 'romantic theft', as Falk (2007) argues, induces fear in the single whereby once the single believed that romantic love will rescue him only to find that being alone is the real fear. That fear of loneliness underpins mourning, knowing that those we love are irreplaceable (Milligan, 2014). For when we mourn, we keep that significant other 'alive' or 'with us' in a spiritual and romantic sense, rather than in a literal and physical sense. Although they are not physically here 'with us', they are in our memories that we cling on to in order to keep them 'alive'. They are ghosts that haunt us in our dreams, on the train, at work, and anywhere during which we think we are alone.

In 'Mourning and Melancholia', Freud (1917) writes about mourning and the process of grieving, which has some relevance for the gay single mourner. From a psychoanalytic framework, Freud contests the taken-for-granted view that grieving over a loss loved one fades with time; in other words, time heals. Freud, instead, argues that mourning is a profound psychic crisis, not a more or less prolonged phase of suffering. For him, grieving fades via—created by the loss of a loved one—a psychical working out of the pain. Melancholia is on a spectrum of possible responses. The gay single becomes disinterested in the social world, he is unable to select a new love object, and chooses not to pursue romantic relationships within melancholia and mourning. Not able to detach itself from the love object, the gay single simply identifies so completely with it—so much so that he lives in constant pain or, what I call, endures symbolic violence (Javaid, 2018a). Although unacknowledged and unconsciously done, the love object lives with the gay single. He, then, may no longer construct himself as completely 'single' for he may consider himself as never truly alone, clinging onto the love object. For instance, as Inglis (2013: 100) writes, "Mourning practices are a method of gradually loosening the ties that bound the lovers together. Mourners will often put up photographs or carry mementos." The gay single mourner holds onto the loved object through items, such as photographs or carrying mementos because, by doing so, the loved object is tightly held on to so as to reduce stigma of the gay single whilst making this mourning process visible and seen by others, making the loss of a loved one public. This is because the public sharing of grief is deemed to lighten the loss, and reducing stigma for the bereaved (Inglis, 2013). Although the physical ties are broken, to which Inglis refers, the gay single mourner can still hold onto the loved object through memorialized and symbolic items. Grieving over a loved one is cultural. For example, "Grieving is the process of coming to terms with loss. The loss of a loved one can be so overwhelming that the lover never fully recovers. People can die of a broken heart ... the way people deal with grief ... is profoundly cultural" (Inglis, 2013: 98).

The private face of stigma often involves feelings of grief. In extreme cases, the gay single mourner is reduced in our minds from "a whole and usual person to a tainted, discounted one" (Goffman, 1963a: 12) during the social process of mourning over a lost loved one. Non-singles can watch the gay single mourner. This observation ensures that their non-single identity is reinforced in relation to the discredited 'Other'—a process known as Othering—and that stigmatization essentially works to protect a sense of normality; that is, the normality of couplsom. Drawing on Goffman (1961), one could argue that the gay single mourner becomes stigmatized by their differentiation, and their subsequent dehumanizing treatment of pity by others, particularly by non-singles, as well as the gay single's efforts to re-establish himself as human by their telling of a 'sad tale' to explain their predicament: "he died in an accident" or "he left me brokenhearted". Scott (2005: 95) refers to what she calls 'the Competent Other' to indicate that, during social interactions, there "is a generalized image of one's fellow actors as being relatively well equipped for interaction, coupled with the fear of one's own perceived incompetence being revealed through an inadequate front-stage performance". Non-singles could be construed as 'the Competent Others' since they are able to present a performance of togetherness, without the public demonstration of mourning. They are able to rely upon each other through trials and tribulations; the gay single does not have a romantic other with whom to rely on. The gay single actor who mourns will be concerned about how others view his public confession of loss, which interlinks with loneliness, laying oneself exposed to scrutiny about how one ought to manage their mourning. At some point, they may be expected to 'get over it'.

To avoid such pity or stigma, the gay single mourner might grieve at the 'backstage', keeping it as a private matter. With reference to Goffman's (1959) theory of performativity, the gay single can actively select which parts of their biography or identity to reveal to others during public social interaction, reliant upon 'impression management'. Gay single mourners are storytellers; they choose which parts of their story to tell to others at certain times, places and contexts. Goffman (1963a) makes a distinction between individuals who are discredited, that is, whose stigma is publically known or noticeable, and individuals who are discreditable, that is, whose stigma is not known and can be hidden from sight. If, for example, a single ethnic minority gay mourner loses a loved one through either divorce or a breakup, they are 'doubly stigmatized': (1) they are subjected to discredited stigma through their visible racial/ethnic identity, known to others during social interactions, certainly to non-singles; (2) they are exposed to discreditable stigma through their confession of being gay, divorced or being broken up with by a loved one and so are publically mourning over their loss loved one. This 'double stigmatization' can result in the single embodying what Goffman (1963a) calls internalized stigma, which refers to, "The stigmatized individual tends to hold the same beliefs about the identity that we do. [This may cause him] to agree that he does indeed fall short of what he really ought to be. Shame becomes a central possibility" (p. 7). Through mourning, the gay single may think that he will be single forever due to his multiple stigmas.

When a stigmatized gay single interacts with non-singles ('normal') during the process of mourning, social interactions "can become tense, uncertain, and ambiguous for all participants, especially the stigmatized one" (Goffman, 1963a: 41). The gay single may encounter statements from non-singles like, "I'm so sorry to hear about your loss", "you will find someone else", "there are many more men out there", to remind the gay single of his situational loss of a 'normal' status as a non-single. The gay single is now expected to find someone else to dilute the stigma that they momentarily possess; otherwise, they are subjected to social exclusion. For instance, the gay single mourner may not be invited to attend social gatherings, hosted by non-singles; he may not want to go out in order to privately mourn since mourning is often a private matter (Inglis, 2013); or he may be so 'doubly stigmatized' that it metaphorically and symbolically transposes itself onto potential future dating partners, a process Goffman (1963a) calls 'stigma by association'. A gay single mourner, then, reinforces his own single identity and stigma through social isolation and, sometimes, social exclusion.

21.5 Concluding Thoughts

This book chapter attempted to grapple with the social and cultural construction of the homosexual single, whose identity is 'made' during social and power relations. He may not always become single from his own choosing, but is often positioned in singlehood by others. Their singlehood career (Lahad, 2017), coupled with their homosexual identity, are transgressions to social and interactional orders like tripping while walking on the street or having your zipper open resulting in situational stigma manifesting. However, stigma for gay singles is much more pronounced, I argue, because it becomes their 'master status' or their 'deviant career'. They are known as the homosexual single with no one to go out with, to eat with, or to drink with. He is marked not only as suspicious but also as 'doubly stigmatized' for embodying both a single and homosexual identity. I have attempted to demonstrate that homosexual singles are subjected to hostility, social disapproval and stigma, often resulting in the absence of same-sex love. Love is usually out of reach for many gay men because of the rise of fleeting sexual and fluid intimacy. This increase of fluid intimacy or fleeting sexual and romantic encounters or what Bauman (2003) calls 'liquid love' is in part down to individualism, secularization and consumerism. For Bauman (2003), many relationships today are 'connections' rather than romantic relationships. Because many such encounters are contextual and brief, they can reinforce a homosexual single identity for the single insofar that they can induce a 'spoiled identity' (Goffman, 1963a). The gay single is reminded of his singlehood identity; he gains nothing other than fleeting, sexual encounters that lack substance and meaning. They dilute any possibility for a romantic relationship, one that is meaningful. His 'spoiled identity' is further reinforced when he has nothing to converse about regarding (heterosexual) coupledom at family gatherings, Birthday parties, and at other social events occupied by others. Subsequently, though he can be seen, he is unnoticed and fades into the background. This, I argue, is especially the case given that homosexuality is positioned as the 'abnormal' or the 'other' because of heteronormativity that places the homosexual single at a table for one.

References

Bauman, Z. (2003). *Liquid love: On the frailty of human bonds*. London: Polity Press.
Falk, F. (2007). *On my own: The art of being a woman alone*. New York, NY: Harmony Books.
Freud, S. (1917). Mourning and melancholia. *Standard Edition, 14*, 243–258.
Goffman, E. (1955). On face-work. *Psychiatry, 18*(3), 213–231.
Goffman, E. (1959). *The presentation of self in everyday life*. New York: Anchor Books.
Goffman, E. (1961). *Asylums: Essays on the social situation of mental patients and other inmates*. New York: Anchor Books.
Goffman, E. (1963a). *Stigma: Notes on the management of spoiled identity*. Harmondsworth: Penguin.
Goffman, E. (1963b). *Behavior in public places: Notes on the social organization of gatherings*. New York: Free Press.
Goffman, E. (1972[1971]) *Relations in public: Microstudies of the public order*. Harmondsworth: Penguin Books.
Inglis, T. (2013). *Love*. London: Routledge.
Jackson, S. (2006). Gender, sexuality and heterosexuality: The complexity (and limits) of heteronormativity. *Feminist Theory, 7*(1), 105–121.
Jackson, S. (2018). Why "heteronormativity" is not enough: A feminist sociological perspective on heterosexuality. In J. W. Messerschmidt, P. Y. Martin, M. A. Messner, & R. Connell (Eds.), *Gender reckonings: New social theory and research* (pp. 134–155). New York: New York University Press.
Javaid, A. (2018a). *Masculinities, sexualities and love*. Abingdon: Routledge.
Javaid, A. (2018b). Out of place: Sexualities, sexual violence, and heteronormativity. *Aggression and Violent Behavior, 39*, 83–89.
Javaid, A. (2018c). *Male rape, masculinities, and sexualities: Understanding, policing, and overcoming male sexual victimisation*. Hampshire: Palgrave.

Javaid, A. (2018d). 'Poison ivy': Queer masculinities, sexualities, homophobia and sexual violence. *European Journal of Criminology, 15*(6), 748–766.

Lahad, K. (2017). *A table for one: A critical reading of singlehood, gender and time*. Manchester: Manchester University Press.

Lahad, L., & May, V. (2017). Just one? Solo dining, gender and temporal belonging in public spaces. *Sociological Research Online, 22*(2), 12.

May, V. (2011). Self, belonging and social change. *Sociology, 45*(3), 363–378.

May, V. (2013). *Connecting self to society: Belonging in a changing world*. Basingstoke: Palgrave Macmillan.

Messerschmidt, J. (2018). *Masculinities and crime* (25th Anniversary Edition). London: Rowman and Littlefield.

Milligan, T. (2014). *Love*. London: Routledge.

Ostler, S. (2002). *Get on with it! How to be sassy, successful and single*. Crows Nest: Allen & Unwin.

Plummer, K. (1975). *Sexual stigma: An interactionist account*. London: Routledge.

Plummer, K. (1995). *Telling sexual stories: Power, change and social worlds*. London: Routledge.

Richardson, D. (2018). *Sexuality and citizenship*. London: Polity.

Richardson, D., & May, H. (1999). Deserving victims?: Sexual status and the social construction of violence. *Sociological Review, 47*(2), 308–331.

Scott, S. (2005). The red, shaking fool: Dramaturgical dilemmas in shyness. *Symbolic Interaction, 28*(1), 91–110.

Seidman, S. (2002). *Beyond the closet: The transformation of gay and lesbian life*. New York: Routledge.

Aliraza Javaid is a senior lecturer in criminology at the University of East London. Dr Aliraza Javaid has a BSc (Hons) Criminology, an MSc Clinical Criminology, an MRes Social Sciences, and a PhD in Sociology and Social Policy. His research interests are gender, sexualities, masculinities, police and policing, sexual violence, the sociology of 'evil', and the sociology of 'love'. His first sole-authored book, which is entitled Male Rape, Masculinities, and Sexualities: Understanding, Policing, and Overcoming Male Sexual Victimisation, has been published by Palgrave (2018). His second sole-authored book, entitled Masculinities, Sexualities, and Love, is published by Routledge (2018). His third book, entitled Violence in Everyday Life: Power, Gender, and Sexuality, is published by Zed Books (2020). His other publications around his research interests can be found at https://alirazajavaid.wordpress.com/publications-2/

Chapter 22
On Homosexual Love and Right to Same-Sex Marriage: Questioning the Paradox of #LoveWins Discourse

Tinnaphop Sinsomboonthong

> *This study is a part of a research report, "The #LoveWins as a Discourse: Researching Homosexual Love and Right to Same-Sex Marriage in Thai Social Media". It focuses on the ways in which the hashtag, #LoveWins, is used by Thai social media users on Twitter to explore the changing definitional boundary of online ethnographic research.*

Abstract As the decriminalization of homosexuality becomes a global trend, support for the legalization of same-sex marriage in many countries can be found on social media. Since the hashtag, #LoveWins, first erupted on social media—when the US Supreme Court affirmed the constitutional rights of same-sex marriage in June 2015—it has become one of the most cited hashtags for celebrating the decriminalization of homosexuality and the legalization of same-sex marriage across the globe. Amidst the ongoing confrontation between advocates of the junta-backed legislation related to same-sex marriage laws, known as 'Thailand's Civil Partnership Draft Bills,' and its detractors, the hashtag has widely been employed by active Thai social media users for creating an LGBT-friendly atmosphere while attempting to neutralize the bi-polarized politics of the law. Again, during the national elections of 2019, it was widely used for rebranding parties' gay-friendly image. The use of #LoveWins, and any hashtags quoting 'love' and 'wins', is a discursive tool and an expression of the Western-centric normativity of homosexual love, which itself is associated with Eurocentric modernity and heteronormativity. This chapter, as a Netnographical study, focuses on how #LoveWins is used by analyzing its discursive implications in the hypertexts of the hashtag as articulated by Thailand's social media users on Twitter during the Drafted-Bills period and the national election in late 2018 to mid-2019. Specifically, it considers how this dynamic seeks to decolonize the discourse of the universality of love and advocate for a more inclusive non-heteronormative meaning of love, a so-called 'queer love', in a non-imperialist manner.

T. Sinsomboonthong (✉)
Faculty of Sociology and Anthropology, Thammasat University, Bangkok, Thailand
e-mail: tinnaphopsinsomb@gmail.com

Keywords Love · LGBT rights · *#LoveWins* · Queer · Same-sex marriage · Social movement · Thailand

22.1 Introduction

It took almost 50 years to recognize LGBT rights on the global stage, from the time of the founding of the UN in 1945 to the 4th World Conference on Women in 1995, that was held in Beijing, China. This is where sexual orientation was first raised as a potentially relevant aspect of women's rights despite later being discarded. Again, however, it was not sufficient to propel LGBT rights onto any UN platforms as a global issue.

Despite this, the situation started to change when the Yogyakarta Principles emerged from a meeting in Yogyakarta, Indonesia, during November 6–9, 2006. These Principles were launched as a global charter on March 26, 2007 at the United Nations Human Rights Council (UNHRC) in Geneva and later became formally known as 'Additional Principles and State Obligation on the Application of International Human Rights Law in Relation to Sexual Orientation, Gender Expression and Sex Characteristics to Complement the Yogyakarta Principles' (the so-called 'Yogyakarta Principles +10'). This was the first time that LGBT rights were recognized and respected on the global stage.

As the decriminalization of homosexuality has become a global trend after a long history where homosexuality had been forbidden,[1] support for the legalization of same-sex marriage in many countries can be found on social media. Since the hashtag, #LoveWins, first erupted on social media following the US Supreme Court affirming the constitutional rights of same-sex marriage in June 2015, it has become one of the most cited hashtags for celebrating the decriminalization of homosexuality and legalization of same-sex marriage in many countries. This hashtag has been used in various posts and Tweets on Facebook, Twitter and other applications to express users' support of global LGBT rights. This is also the case for social media users in Thailand.

Although this hashtag has at times circulated on social media in Thailand, it was particularly visible in many posts on Twitter during two main periods of time- the politics of same-sex partners' legal status since late 2018 and the first national election after 5 years under the military junta led by Prayut Chan-o-cha, which was held in the early 2019.

---

[1]The first country in the world that started to decriminalize homosexual acts was eighteenth century France (1791), while Monaco, Luxembourg and Belgium decriminalized homosexuality in 1793, 1794 and 1795 respectively. Step by step, more countries across the globe pursued this path from the nineteenth to twenty-first centuries. The United States, in particular, recently decriminalized homosexuality in 2003, while Thailand, the focus country of this chapter, decriminalized homosexuality in 1956 (Sanders 2013).

First and foremost, amidst the ongoing confrontation between celebrators of the junta-backed legislation concerning same-sex marriage laws, known as 'Thailand's Civil Partnership Draft Bills,' and its detractors, the hashtag was widely used among active Thai social media users for creating an LGBT-friendly atmosphere and attempting to neutralize the bi-polarized politics of the law. While the Drafted Bills' supporters frequently flooded a number of Facebook posts and Tweets to celebrate the advancement of their agenda, the opposition claimed that the government had a hidden agenda when it enacted this law. In their view, the government only became enthusiastic about the law when it could generate popular support before the national election (Fullerton, 2018; Yodhong, 2018). Another period of high #LoveWins hashtag usage among social media users was during the national election in 2019. This time, however, a number of politicians from significant political parties (particularly the Future Forward Party and the Democrat Party) became more enthusiastic than other parties to use the hashtag because it constituted a useful tool for rebranding their parties as gay-friendly.

While the utilization of #LoveWins and any hashtags associated with 'love' and 'wins' by Thai social media users are generally associated with the political confrontation between the Bill supporters and the Bill opposers, the use of the hashtag, and indeed the hashtag itself, emphasized the discourse of modernity related to the notion of 'right to (homosexual) love' and 'right to same-sex marriage'. That is to say, the hashtag was no longer merely a decoration on a post or a way to link one post to another across a virtual world via a search engine; rather, it was a discursive tool and a method of highlighting the Western-centric normativity of homosexual love, which is associated with Eurocentric modernity and heteronormativity. Thai social media users employed this hashtag to promote equality and prioritize a particular type of homosexual love while various non-normative sexual and gender identities were still subordinated and othered as shown on Thailand's popular social media platforms, particularly on Twitter.

Hence, this chapter focuses on how #LoveWins is generally utilized among Thai social media users. The research focus includes:

1. the discursive relationship between the hashtag, together with any relevant hashtags, and the text where it is included on Twitter posts;
2. the core subtext of those selected Twitter posts; and
3. the functional hypertext of the hashtag.

This analysis is effected through an online-research ethnography (a 'Netnography' (Kozinets, 2009); a virtual ethnography (Hine, 2000); digital ethnography (Murthy, 2008); etc.) in order to analyze the discourse of development-modernity in #LoveWins as expressed among Thailand's social media users. The period of examination shall cover, but is not limited to, the Drafted-Bills politics in late 2018, the national election in early 2019 and the time when the new government of Thailand was installed.

22.2 Love, Heteronormativity, Homonormativity

It is said that love is vital, being an integral part of the human condition (see Buss, 2006; Gottschall, 2008; Jankowiak, 1995 and other chapters in the same book; Jankowiak & Fischer, 1992; Lenon, 2011; Shaver, Morgan, & Wu, 1996). The loving culture is one of the most prominent human cultures as Illouz (2011, 195–196) notes, the culture of (romantic) love is a life-long personal project aiming to maintain *"long-lasting and yet exciting feelings"* while extending *"the experience of love throughout one's life."* As argued by Illouz (2011), all men and women in human society tend to be generally regulated by love. She points out,

> The emotion of romantic love cannot be separated from social rules pertaining to the control of women's and men's sexuality, the regulation of marriage, and the ways in which property is transmitted. (Illouz, 2011, 194).

According to her, the institutionalized nexus of love, heterosexuality and marriage is socially united to sustain the social order. Then, so-called 'romantic love' is institutionally constructed through that combination and presents itself as the supreme ideology behind every marriage.

This study does not focus on all types of love but solely on romantic love or what Lewis (1960) termed 'Eros'. The concept of romantic love has been investigated by scholars to understand how it is expressed in literature and society (see also Dion & Dion, 1996; Kephart, 1967; Rubin, 1970). Heterosexuality is a central component and it plays a crucial role in emphasizing the binary ideals of masculinity and femininity (Illouz, 2011, 197). Essentially, both are constructed on the basis of heterosexual imaginary, which

> prevents us seeing how institutionalized heterosexuality actually works to organize gender while preserving racial, class, and sexual hierarchies. (Ingraham, 2011, 304)

Institutionalized heterosexuality—so-called heteronormativity—constitutes *"the standard of legitimate and expected social and sexual relations,"* (Ingraham, 2011, 305) leading to the determination and limitation of imaginary boundaries, paradigms, perceptions, conceptions and narratives of heterosexual love.

According to Sternberg (1986), the totality of love is the conjunction of intimacy (psychological feelings), passion (physical-sensual response), and commitment (social relationships). The component of decision/commitment is defined as the decision to love someone in the short term and the maintenance of love in the long term (Sternberg, 1986, 119) and is assigned as one of the most crucial components of love leading to marriage in empty love (an arranged marriage without intimacy nor passion), fatuous love (a swift marriage without intimacy), companionate love (a long-termed committed friendship in a marital relationship), and consummate love (the ideal relationship that includes all these three components) (Sternberg, 1986, 123–124). In order to transform love (an emotion) into a marriage (a social institution), commitment becomes an integral part of this.

According to Johnson (1991), commitment refers to a linkage between the future and the motivation to continue a relationship. Marital commitment, in particular, refers to a way in which a person forms and maintains a marriage to a particular partner or simply *"the partners' estimates of the likelihood that they will marry their partners . . ."* (Surra & Hughes, 1997, 6). This type of commitment necessitates a marriage as the telos of all committed relationships throughout the modern European history while constituting a wedding ceremony in a church as its righteous beginning of a marriage to earn God's approval in Christianity. Hence, a wedding is not simply a short-lived ceremony, it forms a crucial part of Western culture.

The culture of a wedding in the West is made possible and framed by heteronormativity. This wedding culture refers to a form of sociological-ideological regulation. It socially privileges and appropriates human coupling through a wedding ceremony while having the idea of romantic love at its heart (Ingraham, 2011, 306). As a wedding is required, marriage, as a social institution, is maintained by the power of romantic love and the wedding culture.

Romantic love is widely discussed from different perspectives (see also Berlant, 2001; Firestone, 1970; Friedman, 2003; Illouz, 2012; Johnson, 2005 and Langford, 1999). The claim on the universality of love is one of them. The phrase, 'romantic love', is often thought to be something all human beings long for, irrespective of one's geographic location. Love and sexual psychology are, then, claimed to be naturally created, essential to humanity (Johnson 2005, 24; see also Buss, 1988; Perper, 1985; Tennov, 1984). Therefore, such love is assumed to be universal.

Critically engaging with the universalists' claim about (romantic) love are authors such as Aries (1962), who argues that romantic love is unique to Anglo-American and European societies. Likewise, Stone (1988, 16) maintains that romantic love originated from Europe and contends that if romantic love existed outside of Europe,

> it only arose among the nonwestern nation-states' elite who had the time to cultivate an aesthetic appreciation for subjective experiences.

However, according to Giddens (1992), love is not a universal social phenomenon but rather is unstable and changeable in accordance with the social structures and discourses of the time. Romantic love, in his view, is neither universally determined as a basic human instinct nor an elite-only asset. Love has the potential to affect everyone but in a variety of ways as it is differently shaped by its particular socio-cultural, economic, historical and political context.

Not only does the universality of romantic love in different cultures need to be reviewed but also that of heterosexuality as its main component in order to understand a more inclusive and contemporary meaning of love. As the world embraces greater sexual and gender diversity, as witnessed through the case of Yogyakarta Principles, most countries are influenced by this global transformation of rights and this recognition is expressed in legal actions associated with same-sex marriage and the decriminalization of homosexuality. Consequently, the basis of romantic love has shifted from the heterosexual binary ideals to the more inclusive heterosexual-homosexual binary ideals.

Homonormativity is what Duggan (2003) defines as a way in which homosexuals transform conservative values and the mainstream (sexist) characteristics of social institutions into their homosexual values, norms and institutions. Consequently, it is built on the same basis of heteronormativity, which Brandzel (2005, 196) argues to consistently include whiteness, the middle-class, childrearing and materiality. Homonormativity frames the way that romantic love plays a crucial role in the homosexual world, makes (romantic) homosexual love possible, and it generates the logic of homosexual right to marriage from (heterosexual) social institutions.

Therefore, under homonormativity, homosexual love is closely associated with heteronormativity, which allows heterosexual couples the right to marriage and being socio-legally recognized and accepted. Logically then, homosexual love is warranted the same rewards. However, while homosexual love is closer to gaining equal acceptance as that of heterosexual love, it seems that access to legally-recognized marriage between homosexuals and heterosexuals are still discrepant. LGBT movements in all countries, together with their supporters, must call for the state to sanction homosexual love and same-sex marriage. Homosexual love and same-sex marriage are closely intertwined and represent one of the most critical claims in the politics of identity in this post-Marxist era (Brown, 1993; Gitlin, 1993). This is clearly shown in the way that social media users in developing countries (e.g., Thailand) try to advocate for homosexual love and the right to same-sex marriage by using the hashtag, #LoveWins, on social media platforms (see Gibson (2018) for the relationship between same-sex marriage and social media; see also Barlik (2017) for the use of social media for promoting same-sex marriage in Poland; and Khatua, Cambria, Ghosh, Chaki, and Khatua (2019) for the use of social media for promoting same-sex marriage in India).

22.3 Researching the Hashtag

This chapter is an online ethnographic study focusing on the use of a particular hashtag and its so-called 'hypertextuality,' which, in this case, refers to a network of electronic informatic tools that connect blocks of texts (Landow, 2006) in an automatic and instantaneous manner (Rost, 2002, 3) without a univocal sense or principle of domination (Bolder, 1990, 25). Formulated by literary scholars, the concept of hypertextuality may simply refer to a type of text that is co-constituted by authors who produced a number of other related texts based on that text and presented as a coherent textual entity (Jackson, 2007; see also Blaszka, Burch, Frederick, Clavio, & Walsh, 2012; Grubišić, 2017; and Brunner, Hemsley, Dann, Togher, & Palmer, 2018). As noted by Albu & Etter (2016, 13), a hashtag is a hypertext as it connects all linked texts within existing power relations. Accordingly, the hypertextuality of the hashtag, #LoveWins, is discussed in the same way in order to understand what lies behind the linkage of those blocks of texts.

The use of the hashtag, #LoveWins, and the hashtag itself are both discursively investigated in this chapter within a context of the hashtag being utilized as part of a discourse of development and modernity. The hashtag is no longer just a decoration in a post or a linkage to other posts. Instead, it is considered to be a discursive practice by which cultural meanings of the hashtag are produced and understood among Thai Twitter users.

This study concentrates on two significant political periods in LGBT politics in Thailand when the hashtag was widely used in Thai social media. Specifically, it considers

1. Thailand's Civil Partnership Draft Bills since late 2018 and
2. the national election period around mid-2019.

The data collection process of this study was not real-time but was conducted later from February–August 2019.

22.3.1 Data Collection

During this time of data collection, Twitter advanced search engines were regularly used to observe if there would have been more relevant posts/Tweets to collect (particularly those that were endlessly generated during the national election from March to July 2019). This study only focuses on Twitter as it is the most popular among Thai social media users. After crude surveys concerning the use of #LoveWins, it was found that this hashtag appeared most frequently on Twitter, Facebook, and Instagram. Although Facebook and Instagram could be considered to be popular platforms for the hashtag, a number of initial surveys for this study showed that, in fact, Thai social media users tended to generally use the hashtag on Facebook and Instagram without a descriptive content. The hyperlink of the hashtag alone on both applications could not lead to its hypertextuality, which is the main focus of this study. Therefore, only Twitter, where the hashtag accompanies descriptive content, is relevant to the scope of this analysis., Other applications (e.g. Facebook, YouTube, Instagram, etc.) and popular blogs in Thailand (e.g. Pantip.com, Palm-Plaza, etc.) will not be included in this study.

A number of preliminary surveys were conducted in December 2018 and, more intensely, in January 2019. The data survey on Twitter was officially conducted twice during February and April 2019 while the data collection was done during May–June 2019. Any public posts on Twitter in which the hashtag, #LoveWins, featured, were collected, organized and curated as screen shots. Particularly during the 2019 national election, only two (Future Forward Party and Democrat Party) of all the parties focused on promoting right to same-sex marriage and included other LGBT rights issues in their campaigns. The hashtag was once again widely used among these two parties' supporters across social media in Thailand. Therefore, Future Forward Party and Democrat Party politicians' posts and tweets were primarily considered in terms of how the hashtag was utilized by people and politicians during this important political time in March 2019. The data collection not only covered politicians' posts and Tweets, but also extended to their supporters' reactions on social media (e.g. re-Tweets and shared posts) as this illuminate how people employed the hashtag as a response to the changing political climate.

22.3.2 Ethical Considerations

Before the data were all collected and then presented in this chapter, ethical considerations are observed to ensure that there are no violation of rights or invasion of privacy. There are three ethical considerations and four research limitations to be considered. The first issue concerns privacy and publicity of data. All data used in this study are public posts on Twitter. Content creators (which refers to those owners of Twitter posts that are used in this study) post their contents and include the hashtag, #LoveWins, without concealment or concern for privacy. However, according to Kozinets (2009), public posts on social media like Facebook and Twitter ethically require the owner's permission regarding use of their specific content in order to prevent a possible threat to their privacy as their real account names and their messages can be easily found on Google or on the advanced search engine on Facebook, Twitter and Instagram. Ethical considerations should not be neglected even though their data are publicly available. However, Thelwall (2010) argues that, as content creators can decide the extent to which individual content is exposed, it can be assumed that public posts permit usage for academic purposes. In order to avoid identifying content creators and sharers based on their descriptive contents, and prevent the violation of online privacy and copyright, this study only analyzes public posts that can be found by the Twitter advanced search function. Also, the focused content is not socio-politically sensitive. Lastly, this chapter is intentionally presented in English for ethical reasons so any descriptive content can be protected from a literal search on Google or in the advanced search engine of each application. Moreover, all data is not presented as direct quotes but rather in a translated-and-paraphrased form in English.

The second ethical concern relates to the invisibility of the researcher. According to Bengtsson (2014), this issue is increasingly serious among Netnographers as the nature of online platforms does not allow a researcher to have face-to-face interactions with content creators and sharers. There are a number of perspectives on this issue: one side claims that Netnographers may cover their identities throughout the research process, known as the 'cyberstealth' (Ebo, 1998, 3 in Pananakhonsab, 2017, 66), or they can reveal themselves at the very end of the data collection process (see also Gatson & Zweerink, 2004). However, Kozinets (2009) advocates for another viewpoint, claiming that researchers should always reveal themselves before collecting data in order to avoid causing problems with/for content creators and sharers.

A further ethical matter concerns the authenticity of content creators and sharers. In other words, in some cases, the identity of each content creator cannot be confirmed as they are avatar accounts. However, although the presented name of each account may be anonymized by content creators, according to Bruckman (2002, 221 in Kozinets, 2009, 145), the revelation of avatar accounts' names could still put them at risk as they might sometimes disclose information about their true identity. So, pseudonyms are used for all accounts' names in this study to doubly protect data sources and owners.

22.3.3 Research Limitations

Last but not least, the changing nature of a field site (from 'a location' to 'a space') and the changing definition of ethnography, as noted by Kozinets (2009), stands as the first research limitation. As many online ethnographers have experienced, there is no physical boundary in a focused online community. The systematic approach of a real-life ethnography can no longer be applied to one in the virtual world. Although it may seem that the collective use of a particular hashtag does not guarantee a social relationship or a sense of belonging between hashtag users, this does not mean that there is no determinable boundary to identify a particular community through the study of a hashtag. A community may still exist. As the hashtag is widely used among content creators and sharers on social media, particularly on Twitter, all descriptive contents are hyperlinked to each other by this hashtag. A new version of the community is thus created by the hashtag. As a result of the changing nature of a field site, as discussed above, the outdated definition of ethnography must also be reconsidered. Hence, the research space and the data collection are creatively designed and carefully determined.

According to Kozinets (2009, 63–65 cited in Pananakhonsab, 2017, 64), an online ethnography, or 'Netnography', can be differentiated into two types:

1. 'online communities' that refer to studies of a particular online space with a clear-cut boundary (e.g. Facebook page, Facebook group, chatroom, etc.); and
2. 'communities online' that refer to interactions of online accounts on the same topic or linkages between people online (e.g. hashtag, video-content sharing, etc.).

The designation of the research space in this study is based on the latter, as the use of #LoveWins demonstrates the way in which individuals indirectly interact via this hashtag. So, the relationship between Twitter accounts is somewhat loose as most of these accounts do not directly reply nor re-Tweet from each other, except in some cases where the hashtag features in a chain of replies and re-Tweets.

This study, however, cannot answer why Thai social media users unconsciously employ the hashtag nor how the hashtag is collectively perceived by said users as in-depth interviews were not implemented in this study. There were two reasons for this,

1. the disclosure of avatar account users' identification would risk their privacy, and
2. this study does not focus on personal viewpoints or the personal background of each content creator but instead aims to present the data on its own terms.

Also, compared to other research on the use of hashtags, this analysis does not tally the repetition of the use of the hashtag over a particular duration and/or in a specific space. This study only focuses on applying a qualitative research method, an online ethnography, throughout its data collection process. Therefore, this study might not deliver a total count regarding the hashtag usage or any other quantitative results, but it does examine a set of findings generated through an online ethnographical approach over a particular timeframe, within a set period of research and in a specific country, one that is filtered by the Twitter advanced search function.

The searching process itself is limited by the use of #LoveWins: in some cases, content-related posts and Tweets might be simply excluded as those posts and Tweets do not contain the hashtag. Sometimes, the hashtag, #LoveWins, is adjusted, supplemented or even translated in Thai. The data collection might eventually risk overlooking a number of relevant sources of data (see Lorentzen & Nolin, 2015). Accordingly, the data collection does not only focus on the hashtag, #LoveWins, but also any hashtags with 'love' and 'wins' both in English and Thai languages.

22.3.4 Data Analysis

Embedded in this hashtag is a close association with modernity and development, which are tightly interlinked with a long history and are often used interchangeably by modernization theorists. This is shown in their descriptive contents hoping that Thailand would be more 'developed and modernized' like Western countries and Taiwan, seen as the LGBT capital in Asia. Thus, calls for the 'right to homosexual love' and the 'right to same-sex marriage' in Thailand are shaped and formulated within the discourse of modernity, development and love. Hence, postcolonial theory is the principle lens employed in the research analysis process. Specifically, discourse analysis is primarily applied in order to reveal the presence and nature of Eurocentric modernity within the hashtag. At the same time, this approach attempts to decolonize the minds of those who embrace the hashtag, #LoveWins, without any awareness of the innate colonial character of this call to rights. With this knowledge, people can gain the ability to

> read and write otherwise, to rethink our understanding of the order of things, [and it] contributes to the possibility of change, McLeod (2000, 23),

so that a more inclusive, non-heteronormative meaning of love, a so-called 'queer love' in a non-imperialist manner, can be possible.

22.4 Research Findings: Development, Modernity and #LoveWins

Although all data from Twitter are systematically collected, there are fewer linkages between each post as all of this data do not derive from a particular bounded community, rather, it represents all public posts that are found via Twitter advanced search function. Another consideration is that, apart from being used on many personal posts about a couple's relationship, the hashtag, #LoveWins, is also used on Twitter in irrelevant posts, for example, criminal news, entertainment news, and product marketing, etc. Therefore, it is necessary to categorize all data in order to differentiate the degree of relationship between the text and the core subtext shared by all texts that are hyperlinked with the hashtag.

The use of #LoveWins can be categorized into 3 levels, including

1. banal decoration,
2. homosexual love celebration, and
3. colonial discourse on homosexual love.

22.4.1 Findings: Three Categories of the Use of #LoveWins

The first category refers to the way in which the hashtag is used in entertainment news (e.g., a celebrity breaks up with her boyfriend, kissing scenes on TV), criminal news (e.g., suicides, murder cases, etc.), and advertisements (e.g., sneakers, skincare products, condominiums, etc.). The hashtag use in these cases are decorative as, since Pride Month of June 2019, any LGBT-related hashtags (e.g., #LoveWins, #Pride, #LGBT, #GayPride, #LoveIsLove, etc.) have been in rainbow colors on social media platforms. The discursive political linkages between the hashtag and posts are too unclear to conclude that its usage is to deliver a political message or call for socio-political change in terms of the LGBT politics of rights. As most posts in this category contain no descriptive content, the analysis of data in this category is unachievable.

The second level refers to any posts with the hashtag used to celebrate personal-to-social homosexual love. Some posts in this category contain no descriptive content, while the rest contain cheerful descriptive content of love presented in a short-to-long messages (e.g., a post describing the content creators' intimate relationship, wedding ceremony in foreign countries, and posts celebrating the legalization of same-sex marriage in Taiwan in May 2019, etc.). However, this category could only be counted as crude evidence of LGBT-rights support on social media as the posts themselves articulate no political message or demand for socio-political change. In other words, they are only celebratory rather than seeking change. Therefore, this type of data is also excluded from this study.

The third level concerns the manner in which content creators and sharers use the hashtag to deliver a political message and advocate for socio-political change in terms of the LGBT politics of rights. These posts are always presented as extended messages. Some are contained solely to their own content, while others continue to elaborate in the replies. Also, in most cases, original posts generate even more conversations as other Twitter users reply and re-tweet from each original post. The focal point of this category is that many posts reflect the discourse of development and modernity, presenting LGBT-rights in terms of a Western representation of development, modernity and civilization.

Several posts suggested that Thailand should use the legalization of same-sex marriage to represent itself as another LGBT paradise in Asia. A few other posts claimed that Thailand could maximize the opportunity to connect more to global tourism and generate greater income from it if it becomes another Asian country where same-sex marriage and registration of marriage are both legal. Interestingly, a number of posts celebrated LGBT rights in Taiwan while simultaneously satirizing Thailand's LGBT rights. Moreover, a number of posts criticize both Thailand's LGBT rights and the (un-)reliability of the Junta-endorsed 'Civil Partnership Draft Bill' at the same time. These posts, in particular, communicate the view that Thailand is not yet 'modern' enough as it has stalled halfway to (Western) modernity as represented by its unfinished project regarding the Drafted Bills. Even more damning in these posts is that Thailand's underdevelopment is visible from the content within the Drafted Bills that remains rather superficial in terms of the whole spectrum of LGBT rights, being confined to the issue of same-sex marriage. The Bills lack a profound understanding of LGBT-rights apart from granting permission for homosexual weddings and the legalization of the same-sex marriage. Other LGBT-related rights and protection are silenced in these discussions. The ongoing political project of LGBT rights in Thailand, consequently, represents a worthless exploit in the push towards development and modernity.

From September 2018 to August 2019, the total number of posts in Thai on Twitter with the hashtag, #LoveWins, which were found as a result of the Twitter advanced search function, were 377. Within this number, each post carried a variable number of replies and re-Tweets. Out of 377 posts, 87% of posts can be categorized as belonging within the first and second categories, while only 13% are in the third category, which is the main focus in this study. However, although the number of posts in the third category represent only a few compared to both former categories, most of them comprise a number of replies and re-Tweets. This indicates the way that the hashtag can lead to the re-production of the core subtext, derived from all relevant texts (hyperlinked with the hashtag) as well as their replies and re-Tweets, which in turn are related to the discourse of development and modernity.

22.4.2 Analyzing the Discourse of Development/Modernity

Focusing mainly on the data in the third category, as a result of findings on Twitter, it seems that the use of #LoveWins on social media platforms is not only influenced by homonormativity but also by the discourse of development and modernity. Homonormativity works together with the discourse of development and modernity to demarcate and determine the way in which people frame their perceptions. Their political desires, values and prospects are located within the Western homonormative frame, which also limits the hashtag users' definitional understanding of development to the discourse of modernity, analogous to what Rostow (1991) and other modernization theorists described. In other words, development as a process is only defined as modernization as long as development is a result/a state/reflective of Western modernity. According to Quijano (2007), modernity is intertwined with development and the drive for the accumulation of power and wealth. Through post-WWII history, the interchangeability of modernity and development has been internationally accepted for decades as a universal and rational state for all countries. Therefore, the criteria for Thailand to become a developed country rests on it replicating the way that Western developed countries have recognized homosexual love and legalized their right to same-sex marriage.

The reason why this study focuses on the third category of data is that it is the only category containing sufficient descriptive content. In the data analysis process, the linkage between all of the data is focused on establishing the core subtext within the discourse of development and modernity. As a result, the discourse behind the hashtag and its use needs to be problematized. As evident in all posts' hypertexts and their core subtext, the hashtag has never been used to celebrate other types of relationships or even the state of being single. The hashtag solely focuses on a same-sex couple who endorse Western monogamous values and commit to a life-long relationship certified by marriage. The discourse of #LoveWins does not offer a space for people who prefer a non-committed relationship or people who prefer celibacy. The hashtag, #LoveWins, thus excludes other types of relationships. As celibacy indicates a non-marital status, it is situated outside the normative realm in LGBT community, therefore, the hashtag also excludes this status. Ruti and Cocking (2015) advocate for being single against heteronormativity and homonormativity as this position challenges the expectation of both normativities. In this sense, being single can be considered a queer political practice against normativities. Similarly, Cobb (2012) advocates for being single against normativities and supports the idea of adding the letter 'S' to the LGBT acronym, in addition to 'Q' (refers to questioning), 'I' (refers to intersex), and 'A' (asexual).

The use of #LoveWins as a way to celebrate the LGBT movement for equality and freedom may well reflect the reality that the movement's calls for change do not encompass all but are only reserved for a particular group. As the movement's aspiration is selective, some people might be left behind. Due to these reasons, the use of #LoveWins can be understood as a de-queering love, or the ways in which a more inclusive love for all is contained and limited. The movement's stance on gender identity, sexual orientation and relationships are no more inclusive. Only particular types of gender identity, sexual orientation and relationships that reflect heterosexual institutions are acceptable and advocated. Moreover, the hashtag normalizes heterosexual institutions from the West. Like knowledge, as we learn from Mignolo (2009), Western love is banally portrayed as universal. However, its universality is based on the pre-determined 'colonial difference' that constructed the illusionary dichotomic objectivity between the Self (the West) and Other (the Rest) through coloniality. Additionally, the hashtag users' perceptions, behaviors, expectations, imaginary and prospects are shaped by the discourse of development and modernity framed within the homonormative regime of truth. Therefore, the use of the hashtag emphasizes the legitimacy of Western civilization as the global aesthetic and ethical standard of civilization.

22.5 Conclusion

The use of a hashtag might not be just a careless, inexplicable and irrational action, instead it is used among Thai social media users in a systematic and rational manner. Hashtags, particularly #LoveWins, are generally used at a particular moment for a specific number of reasons. It is therefore essential that any online researchers understand the virtual politics of LGBT rights in Thailand, particularly at important political moments in history when the legislation of same-sex marriage bi-polarizes Thai online society.

However, this study does not aim to argue that right to same-sex marriage are naturally problematic or socially undesirable. In fact, it seeks to raise a question among those who cherish right to same-sex marriage and other LGBTQ rights in Thailand and who also use this hashtag. When the hashtag claims that love always wins, the question remains "over what exactly does it win?" So, instead of rejecting homosexual love and right to same-sex marriage in Thailand, this study intends to suggest that homosexual love should be more inclusive and less standardized. Therefore, it is preferable that queer loves are redefined into the definitional realm of 'acceptable loves' rather than confined to a mere essentialist-traditionalist homosexual love. Also, right to same-sex marriage should be queered to expand its realm of rights and revolutionized, from same-sex to no-sex, in order that many other gender identities and sexual orientations are more socially accepted. Finally, homonormativity must be deconstructed, and love must no longer be reserved for only one particular type of relationship that is standardized from/by the West. It must become more inclusive.

Although homosexual love might seemingly be framed by homonormativity, it does not always manifest this way everywhere. According to Lenon (2011)'s work, which claims that a racial norm of whiteness plays a crucial role in the Canadian politics of LGBT rights, homosexuals could earn respectability and lead ordinary and unremarkable lives—referring to the shift from same-sex to no-sex—through the language of romantic love. Sexual difference as the basis of rights in the legal realm is desexualized and ethically bleached by the language of romantic love in the same way. In this case, love is used as a primary condition equating to one's humanity and it is presented as an ethical value that cannot be denied and disavowed (Lenon, 2011, 367). So, instead of arguing that homosexual love is universally framed by the same homonormativity, the same process and the same result, this study argues that homosexual love might not always operate in the same manner in online and offline spaces across the globe. Instead, cultural diversity and differing social structures significantly determine and shape these dynamics.

In closing, as Thai social media users employ the hashtag, #LoveWins, to express their perceptions and political desires—that are themselves framed within Western-derived homonormativity—there is still insufficient evidence to generalize from this case in terms of its application to other countries. More studies are required to understand how homosexual love relates to homonormativity and the discourse of development and modernity. Therefore, this chapter wishes to call attention to the need for further research on the use of #LoveWins in different platforms, cultures and methods. As the decriminalization of homosexuality and the legalization of same-sex marriage in many countries are more and more promoted, the hashtag has been continuously used among social media users in different cultures to celebrate the widespread of the Western development-modernity via the use of #LoveWins. Eventually, when the global use of #LoveWins and its discourse of development and modernity are differently studied and understood, the universality of love and the unification of development-modernity can be contested, subverted and decolonized.

Acknowledgments I would like to acknowledge the invaluable kindness of Assistant Professor Dr. Wilasinee Pananakhonsab for her fruitful advice throughout the research process. Also, I would like to sincerely thank Mr. Chanatip Tatiyakaroonwong for his invaluable help as a research assistant in the data collection process.

References

Albu, O. B., & Etter, M. (2016). Hypertextuality and social media: A study of the constitutive and paradoxical implications of organizational Twitter use. *Management Communication Quarterly, 30*(1), 5–31.
Aries, P. (1962). *Centuries of childhood: A social history of family life*. New York: Vintage.
Barlik, J. (2017). Twitter w kampaniach informacyjnych o związkach osób tej samej płci w Polsce i w USA [Twitter in awareness campaigns on same-sex unions in Poland and in the USA]. *Studia Medioznawcze [Media Studies], 4*(71), 61–76.
Bengtsson, S. (2014). Faraway, so close! Proximity and distance in ethnography online. *Media, Culture and Society, 36*(6), 862–877.
Berlant, L. (2001). Love (a queer feeling). In T. Dean & C. Lane (Eds.), *Homosexuality and psychoanalysis* (pp. 432–451). Chicago: University of Chicago Press.
Blaszka, M., Burch, L., Frederick, E., Clavio, G., & Walsh, P. (2012). #WorldSeries: An empirical examination of a Twitter hashtag during a major sporting event. *International Journal of Sport Communication, 5*, 435–453.
Bolder, J. D. (1990). *Writing space: The computer in the history of literacy*. Hillsdale: Lawrence Erlbaum.
Brandzel, A. L. (2005). Queering citizenship? Same-sex marriage and the state. *GLQ: A Journal of Lesbian and Gay Studies, 11*(2), 171–204.
Brown, W. (1993). Wounded attachments. *Political Theory, 21*(3), 390–410.
Bruckman, A. (2002). Studying the amateur artist: A perspective on disguising data collected in human subjects research on the internet. *Ethics and Information Technology, 4*, 217–231.
Brunner, M., Hemsley, B., Dann, S., Togher, L., & Palmer, S. (2018). Hashtag #TBI: A content and network data analysis of tweets about traumatic brain injury. *Brain Injury, 32*(1), 49–63.
Buss, D. M. (1988). Love acts: The evolutionary biology of love. In R. J. Sternberg & M. L. Barnes (Eds.), *The psychology of love* (pp. 100–118). New Haven: Yale University Press.
Buss, D. M. (2006). Evolution of love. In R. J. Sternberg & K. Weis (Eds.), *The new psychology of love* (pp. 65–86). New Haven: Yale University Press.
Cobb, M. (2012). *Single: Arguments for the uncoupled*. New York: New York University Press.
Dion, K. K., & Dion, K. L. (1996). Cultural perspectives on romantic love. *Personal Relationships, 3*, 5–17.
Duggan, L. (2003). *The twilight of equality: Neoliberalism, cultural politics, and the attack on democracy*. Boston, MA: Beacon Press.

Ebo, B. (1998). Internet or outernet? In B. Ebo (Ed.), *Cyberghetto or cybertopia?: Race, class, and gender on the Internet* (pp. 1–12). Westport, CT: Preager.

Firestone, C. (1970). *The dialectic of sex: The case for feminist revolution*. New York: William Morrow.

Friedman, M. (2003). *Autonomy, gender, politics*. Oxford: Oxford University Press.

Fullerton, J. (2018, December 27). Thai government backs same-sex civil partnership bill. Resource webpage. *The Guardian*. Accessed August 16, 2019, from https://www.theguardian.com/world/2018/dec/27/thai-government-backs-same-sex-civil-partnership-bill

Gatson, S. N., & Zweerink, A. (2004). Ethnography online: 'Natives' practicing and inscribing community. *Qualitative Research, 4*(2), 179–200.

Gibson, R. (2018). *Same-sex marriage and social media: How online networks accelerated the marriage equality movement*. London: Routledge.

Giddens, A. (1992). *The transformation of intimacy: Sexuality, love and eroticism in modern societies*. Cambridge: Polity Press.

Gitlin, T. (1993). The rise of 'identity politics'. *Dissent, 40*(2), 172–177.

Gottschall, J. (2008). *Literature, science, and a new humanities*. New York: Palgrave Macmillan.

Grubišić, M. (2017). Addressing the notions of convention and context in social media research. *Jezikoslovlje, 18*(3), 473–497.

Hine, C. (2000). *Virtual ethnography*. London: Sage.

Illouz, E. (2011). Romantic love. In S. Seidman, N. Fischer, & C. Meeks (Eds.), *Introducing the new sexuality studies* (pp. 193–200). New York: Routledge.

Illouz, E. (2012). *Why love hurts: A sociological explanation*. Cambridge: Polity Press.

Ingraham, C. (2011). One is not born a bride: How weddings regulate heterosexuality. In S. Seidman, N. Fischer, & C. Meeks (Eds.), *Introducing the new sexuality studies* (pp. 303–307). New York: Routledge.

Jackson, M. H. (2007). Fluidity, promiscuity, and mash-ups: New concepts for the study of mobility and communication. *Communication Monographs, 74*, 408–413.

Jankowiak, W. R. (1995). *Romantic passion: A universal experience?* New York: Columbia University Press.

Jankowiak, W. R., & Fischer, E. F. (1992). A cross-cultural perspective on romantic love. *Ethnology, 31*(2), 149–155.

Johnson, M. P. (1991). Commitment to personal relationships. In W. H. Jones & D. Perlman (Eds.), *Advances in personal relationships* (pp. 117–143). London: Jessica Kingsley.

Johnson, P. (2005). *Love, heterosexuality and society*. Basingstoke: Routledge.

Kephart, W. M. (1967). Some correlates of romantic love. *Journal of Marriage and the Family, 29*, 470–474.

Khatua, A., Cambria, E., Ghosh, K., Chaki, N., & Khatua, A. (2019). Tweeting in support of LGBT? A deep learning approach. *CoDS-COMAD '19 Proceedings of the ACM India joint international conference on data science and management of data* (pp. 342–345). Kolkata: ACM.

Kozinets, R. V. (2009). *Netnography: Doing ethnographic research online*. London: Sage.

Landow, G. P. (2006). *Hypertext 3.0: Critical theory and new media in an era of globalization*. Baltimore, MD: The Johns Hopkins University Press.

Langford, W. (1999). *Revolutions of the heart: Gender, power, and the delusions of love*. London: Routledge.

Lenon, S. (2011). 'Why is our love an issue?': Same-sex marriage and the racial politics of the ordinary. *Social Identities, 17*(3), 351–372.

Lewis, C. S. (1960). *The four loves*. New York: Harcourt, Brace & World.

Lorentzen, D. G., & Nolin, J. (2015). Approaching completeness: Capturing a hashtagged Twitter conversation and its follow-on conversation. *Social Science Computer Review, 35*(2), 277–286.

McLeod, J. (2000). *Beginning postcolonialism*. Manchester: Manchester University Press.

Mignolo, W. D. (2009). Epistemic disobedience, independent thought and decolonial freedom. *Theory, Culture and Society, 26*(7–8), 159–181.

Murthy, D. (2008). Digital ethnography: An examination of the use of new technologies for social research. *Sociology, 42*(5), 837–855.
Pananakhonsab, W. (2017). Withīkān wijai choēng chāttiphan wannanā nai chumchon online [Ethnographic methods in online communities]. *Thammasat Journal, 36*(2), 58–76.
Perper, T. (1985). *Sex signals: The biology of love*. Philadelphia: ISI Press.
Quijano, A. (2007). Coloniality and modernity/rationality. *Cultural Studies, 21*(2–3), 168–178.
Rost, A. (2002). The concept of hypertext in digital journalism. *23 Conference and General Assembly*, IAMCR/AIECS/AIERI International Association for Media and Communication Research. Barcelona.
Rostow, W. W. (1991). *The stages of economic growth: A non-communist manifesto* (3rd ed.). Cambridge: Cambridge University Press.
Rubin, R. (1970). Measurement of romantic love. *Journal of Personality and Social Psychology, 6*, 265–273.
Ruti, M., & Cocking, A. (2015). When love is not all we want: Queers, singles and the therapeutic cult of relationality. In D. Loewenthal (Ed.), *Critical psychotherapy, psychoanalysis and counselling* (pp. 108–124). London: Palgrave Macmillan.
Sanders, D. (2013). Recognizing same-sex relationships in Thailand. *CMU Journal of Law and Social Sciences, 6*(1), 27–55.
Shaver, P. R., Morgan, H. J., & Wu, S. (1996). Is love a 'basic' emotion? *Personal Relationships, 3*(1), 81–96.
Sternberg, R. J. (1986). A triangular theory of love. *Psychological Review, 93*(2), 119–135.
Stone, L. (1988). Passionate attachments in the West in historical perspective. In W. Gaylin & E. Person (Eds.), *Passionate attachments* (pp. 15–26). New York: Free Press.
Surra, C. A., & Hughes, D. K. (1997). Commitment processes in accounts of the development of premarital relationships. *Journal of Marriage and Family, 59*(1), 5–21.
Tennov, D. (1984). *Love and limerance*. New York: Norton.
Thelwall, M. (2010, July 12). *Researching the public web*. Resource webpage. eHumanities. Accessed August 29, 2019, from https://www.ehumanities.nl/researching-the-public-web
Yodhong, C. (2018, February 13). *Leūoen leūaktang mai penrai, tāe tǫng dāi jotthabīen khūchīwit: Kān kao mai thūk thī khan khǫng klum LGBTQ [Never mind postponing the election, the marriage certificate matters: When an LGBTQ group chases its tail]*. Resource document. The Matter. Accessed August 12, 2019, from https://thematter.co/thinkers/sex-ray/democracy-and-lgbtq/45578

Tinnaphop Sinsomboonthong is a lecturer at the Faculty of Sociology and Anthropology, Thammasat University, Thailand. He received his master's degree in Development Studies at London School of Economics (LSE), UK, where his research focused on the transnationality of gender mainstreaming and rights discourses in a Thailand's borderland. He has researched and published on a range of topics including queer culture and sexuality; gender and international development; politics race and ethnicity; and decolonization of rights. His current research examines how the Third World discourse and Eurocentric modernity in the mainstream global development impact the social life of queer movements in Asia.

Chapter 23
Love and Conflicts Between Identity-Forming Values

Michael Kühler

Abstract What we deeply value or care about at least partially constitutes our identity. If so, we cannot ignore our identity-forming values without abandoning who we are. Naturally, we also care deeply about the persons we love. Thus, we cannot simply ignore what they value. However, what if our own identity-forming values come into conflict with the identity-forming values of the persons we love? In a pluralistic society, in which people's identities are shaped by different cultural backgrounds, such conflicts arise all too often and not only pose a severe practical challenge for lovers but also a theoretical challenge for theories of love and identity. How exactly can and should such conflicts be analyzed, and is there a theoretical as well as practical chance of resolving them? This chapter addresses these questions and discusses them against the background of three influential philosophical theories of love and their relation to the lovers' identities, whereas the focus lies on romantic love: (1) individualist accounts, (2) interpersonal accounts, and (3) union accounts. While all three theories are able to analyze conflicts between identity-forming values plausibly, albeit differently, it is argued that attempts at resolving them ultimately hinge on an understanding of both love and identity as something we can actively shape, thus rejecting the prominent idea of romantic love as something that happens to us as well as the analogous essentialist idea of our identity as something we can merely discover but not actively change.

Keywords Love · Identity · Essentialism · Freedom · Value conflicts

23.1 Introduction

Some things and some people are especially important to us. So much so that any answer to the question who we are—assuming that the question does not simply aim at finding out our name—would have to be considered incomplete if it did not

M. Kühler (✉)
Academy for Responsible Research, Teaching, and Innovation (ARRTI), Karlsruhe Institute of Technology (KIT), Karlsruhe, Germany

Münster University, Münster, Germany
e-mail: michael.kuehler@uni-muenster.de

include references to these things and people. For example, imagine you answered this question without referring to the hobby you value most, or imagine Romeo answering this question without any reference to his love of Juliet. Consequently, if answers to the question who we are may be considered describing our *identity*, the things or persons we value most or love may be considered *identity-forming values*. They make us, at least in part, who we are. Hence, we cannot ignore them in our lives without abandoning who we are.

Furthermore, loving a person arguably includes caring about the beloved's well-being, whereas their well-being appears to be directly influenced by how well their identity-forming values fare in their lives, just like our identity-forming values in ours. If so, it looks like loving a person includes caring about her identity-forming values. At the very least, it appears that, as lovers, we cannot simply neglect what the persons we love care about the most. Imagine parents who completely fail even to recognize what their children value most in their lives. Surely, this would imply a lack of parental love.

However, what if our own identity-forming values come into conflict with the identity-forming values of the persons we love? Imagine someone loving the opera in this identity-forming sense while the person's lover hates it, or imagine a couple with one person being deeply religious while the other person considers herself an atheist. In a pluralistic society, in which people's identity-forming values are shaped by different cultural backgrounds, such conflicts may arise all too often and for a vast number of reasons. This not only poses a severe practical challenge for the lovers in question but also poses a theoretical challenge for theories of love and of personal identity. How exactly can and should such conflicts be analyzed, and is there a theoretical as well as practical chance of resolving them?

This chapter addresses these questions and discusses them against the background of influential philosophical theories of love and their relation to the lovers' identities, whereas the focus lies on romantic or erotic love, i.e. the kind of love between adults that is said to be *more* than *just* friendship. What exactly this surplus or difference consists in and how this kind of love may be analyzed in more detail is, of course, a matter of debate (see Helm 2017a, 2017b, and the chapters in the first section in this handbook). For the purpose of this chapter and its central question about possible conflicts between identity-forming values, it is helpful to distinguish between three broad types of theoretical approaches to romantic love:

1. individualist accounts, according to which romantic love is a purely individual stance which takes the beloved merely as its object,
2. interpersonal accounts, according to which love is to be analyzed in terms of a dialogical relation between the lovers who are both considered subjects of their loving relationship, and
3. union accounts, according to which the lovers abandon their individual identities and together form a new *we*-identity.

While all three approaches are able to analyze conflicts between identity-forming values plausibly, albeit differently, attempts at resolving them ultimately hinge on an understanding of both love and identity as something we can actively shape, thus rejecting the prominent idea of romantic love as something that happens to us as well as the analogous essentialist idea of our identity as something we can merely discover but not actively change.

The chapter proceeds as follows. Firstly, the theoretical background is spelled out in more detail, comprising brief explanations of the concepts of identity and identity-forming values as well as of the three mentioned theoretical approaches to romantic love, including their bearing on the lovers' identities and identity-forming values. Secondly, possible conflicts of identity-forming values among lovers are discussed, including, thirdly, the question whether they allow for being resolved.

23.2 Theoretical Background

23.2.1 Identity and Identity-Forming Values

It is a matter of debate how to define a person's identity in the above sense, i.e. how to give a plausible answer to the question who a person is. Subjectivist accounts refer to a person's individual characteristics, e.g. her character traits, personal values, or what she cares about. Arguably, these personal characteristics and values may be influenced by the person's cultural background, since they need to be articulated, which, in turn, relies on social conditions, such as language and available definitions (Taylor, 1977a, 1977b). Social-relational accounts, on the other hand, highlight the person's social relations and especially the social roles the person occupies, e.g. being a teacher or a parent. At this point, a person's cultural background obviously has a tremendous impact on how exactly social roles are defined or interpreted. Finally, narrative accounts claim that the answer has to be given in the form of the person's life story, whereas a person's cultural background comes into play once again due to socially accepted or appraised forms of narratives (for an overview of these approaches, see Kühler and Jelinek, 2013). However, arguably, all of these approaches would have to include what or who the person *loves* or else miss a crucial aspect of the person's identity. This may be spelled out in terms of love as a subjective characteristic, including its object, or as a specific social relation to another person, or as a specific love story within the person's overall life story.

For the purpose of this chapter, subjective accounts provide a helpful point of reference. In recent decades, Harry G. Frankfurt has spelled out an exemplary and influential subjective philosophical account of a person's identity, which directly emphasizes the importance of what we care about and love (Frankfurt 1971, 1987, 1994, 1999, 2004, 2006). He advocates a *volitional* approach, according to which who we are ultimately comes down to the multi-level structure of our will. On a first level, we may desire any number of things in the world, e.g. ice-cream. Yet, on a second level, we may have desires which have first-order desires as their objects, e.g. a so-called second-order desire *not* to have the first-order desire for ice-cream. Furthermore, on this second level we may want specific first-order desires to be action-guiding, which Frankfurt calls second-order *volitions*, e.g. the second-order volition that our first-order desire for ice-cream may, indeed, be action-guiding (Frankfurt, 1971; for an exemplary critical discussion of Frankfurt's position, see Buss and Overton, 2002).

While being capable of having volitions constitutes personhood, as Frankfurt initially argued, he has later shifted his attention to questions of personal autonomy, for which a person's identity turns out to be an essential prerequisite. Still, Frankfurt keeps his volitional approach and argues that what constitutes our identity is "what we care about" in comparison to things we merely desire (Frankfurt, 1999). Accordingly, he describes "caring" as a multi-level structure of our will with which we also wholeheartedly identify (Frankfurt, 1987). Yet, with what we identify is not a matter of active choice. We can merely discover what we care about, or what our "volitional necessities" are, of which love is a special kind. Hence, according to Frankfurt, our identity is ultimately defined by what we love (Frankfurt, 1994, 2004). He gives the example of a woman who initially wants to give up her child for adoption and has taken all necessary steps to do so. Yet, on the day she has to give her child away she discovers that she simply cannot bring herself to do so. She encounters what Frankfurt describes as a person's volitional limits, which, in turn, may be considered marking the contours of the person's identity (Frankfurt, 1993, p. 111). Hence, when we discover what we love or what our volitional limits are, we have learned something about who we are. A person's identity is, therefore, constituted by what the person loves or, put differently, by her identity-forming values, which the person cannot, or even wants to, go against.

23.2.2 *Individualist Accounts of Love*

Individualist accounts of romantic love come in different flavors. They might analyze love in terms of a specific emotion, volition, or a more general stance. They might argue that love is rational in that there are reasons *for* love, or they might argue that, on the contrary, love is arational and is, conversely, the source of reasons, namely reasons *of* love (for an overview, see Helm, 2017a; Kroeker and Schaubroeck, 2016). However, what all of these flavors have in common, and what is important for the purpose at hand, is that individualist accounts take love to be something attributable exclusively to the lover, with the beloved merely being the *object* of this love.

Since Frankfurt already draws a close connection between identity and love, as explained in the previous section, and because Frankfurt's account of love, despite not primarily aiming at romantic love, is clearly an individualist account, his position provides an apt example for the discussion here. As touched upon before, for Frankfurt love is a special kind of volitional necessity, i.e. what a person cares about. If the object of love is a person, this means that individualist love consists in the lover caring about the beloved's well-being and wanting him or her to flourish. As Frankfurt puts it, the lover is "disinterestedly devoted to" the beloved's interests and ends, which obviously includes what the beloved, in turn, cares about and loves (Frankfurt, 1994, p. 135). Consequently, loving someone in this sense means that the lover cannot simply ignore the beloved's identity-forming values because these are particularly important for the beloved's well-being. If, for instance, a person cares about a career in music and identifies with being a musician, loving this person means, among other things, taking this seriously and wanting the person to flourish in this regard—although it should be noted that taking it seriously does not exclude the possibility of being critical about it. Yet, ignoring such an identity-forming value altogether would mean that there is no love.

If so, how exactly do the beloved's identity-forming values become important to the lover? Following Frankfurt's line of thought—although he has not addressed the question himself—the lover only cares about the beloved's identity-forming values insofar as they present themselves as suitable means to promote the beloved's well-being. This means that the lover does not care about these values him- or herself but that they are important to the lover only *indirectly* and *instrumentally*. Consequently, these values do not necessarily play any role within the lover's own identity, as it is at least in part constituted by his or her own identity-forming values. For instance, if the beloved identifies him- or herself as a jazz musician, the lover does not necessarily also have to care directly about jazz. Jazz would become important for the lover only indirectly as a means to promote the beloved's well-being, for example by noticing interesting jazz concerts nearby and informing the beloved about them or inviting him or her to them, all the while not caring directly about jazz him- or herself at all.

Still, it should be noted that the lover may indeed come to care about the beloved's identity-forming values directly. However, this would not happen because of his or her love but only incidentally due to encountering something which the lover comes to find valuable on its own terms, just like when we in general encounter things in our life we come to value. The crucial point is, therefore, that, according to individualist accounts of love, like Frankfurt's, the beloved's identity-forming values do not necessarily have an impact on the lover's own identity. The lover's identity in principle stays the same, which will be the decisive starting point for analyzing possible conflicts between identity-forming values among lovers later on.

23.2.3 *Interpersonal Accounts of Love*

While individualist accounts of love are easily capable of including cases of unrequited love, mutual love can only be understood in terms of two individual stances of love, which are completely independent of each other and just so happen to have the respective other person as object. Interpersonal accounts of love, on the other hand, take mutual love as their starting point and emphasize this *shared* relationship. Recently, Angelika Krebs has formulated and defended such an account in great detail (Krebs, 2014, 2015). According to her, love is *dialogical* in nature in that mutual lovers, who are both taken as subjects of their shared love, each have an intrinsic interest in sharing their lives. "Partners share what is important in their emotional and practical lives. [...] [L]ove is the intertwining of two lives" (Krebs 2014, p. 22). This includes having joint feelings and sharing activities, neither of which can be reduced to two people merely feeling or doing the same in parallel.

Based on the philosophical debate on joint agency (for an overview, see Roth, 2017), the crucial difference between individual and shared agency may be described simply by considering two people going for a walk individually and in parallel in comparison to two people going for a walk together. In the latter case of shared action, the two people at the very least need to coordinate their individual actions and see them as intentional contributions to the shared action of going for a walk together. The same holds for the idea of interpersonal love, whereas this encompasses the lovers sharing what is important in their lives. Moreover, the lovers are intrinsically interested in doing so and in having a dialogical form of intimacy for its own sake, including being open to what is of identity-forming value to the beloved (Rorty, 1987). Pursuing such a dialogical relationship and sharing one's lives is precisely what interpersonal love is about.

Interpersonal accounts of love, then, substantially change the way how the identity-forming values of one of the lovers become important for the other lover, too. First of all, lovers, once again, cannot simply ignore or not care at all about each other's identity-forming values. Moreover, the idea of sharing their lives *for its own sake* and being open to each other's identity-forming values is incompatible with merely acknowledging them as a suitable means to promote the beloved's (individual) well-being. Consider the case of the jazz lover again. Sharing this identity-forming value means taking an intrinsic interest in it *together out of love*. At the very least, the other person now has to be intentionally open for the possibility to become a jazz lover herself. Hence, when loving in the interpersonal sense, each lover's individual identity will unavoidably—and willingly—be affected by their dialogical love. "In sharing emotions and actions, the partners engage in a mutual building of selves. How they view and respond to each other shapes their characters." (Krebs, 2014, p. 22)

However, while lovers need to be open to changes to their respective individual identities based on their shared lives and respective identity-forming values, this still does not necessarily lead to adopting the other person's identity-forming values *directly*. As shared values, they still become important only *indirectly*. Yet, since the values are *shared*, this happens *out of love* and *for its own sake*. Consider again the case of the jazz lover. Although the person's partner needs to be open to jazz and engage in shared jazz-related activities, it is perfectly conceivable that she does so only out of love and not because she values jazz directly herself. Accordingly, assuming that the loving relationship would end, so would the person's intrinsic interest in jazz as a shared value—at least if the person did not come to value jazz directly at some point independently of her love. However, if jazz as a shared value will necessarily become indirectly important to the person's partner out of love and for its own sake, and if the partner also has to be open to the possibility of valuing jazz directly, this marks a substantial change in comparison to individualist accounts when it comes to how the identity-forming values of one's beloved become important for oneself and to discussing possible conflicts between identity-forming values later on.

23.2.4 Love as Union

The idea of love as a union between the lovers has been of tremendous influence on our understanding of romantic love at least since Plato's *Symposium*. According to the myth Aristophanes tells (Sheffield and Howatson, 2008, pp. 189c–193d), we were all once "double-creatures" with four legs, four arms, and two heads. Because of our strength and hubris, we even posed a threat to the gods themselves, so Zeus split us in two halves, i.e. in our current appearance. Each of these halves then desperately looked for its other half and yearned for being reunited once again. Thus, love is nothing but the desire for unity and, if fulfilled, the union itself—whereas the proper relationship between the *desire* for unity and the union *itself* is a matter of substantial dispute in the analysis of union accounts of love.

While the union metaphor is, of course, not to be taken literally, the central idea of recent union accounts basically takes the direction of interpersonal accounts one step further, namely by claiming that the lovers not only share their lives but have a *shared identity*, a *we-identity* (Fisher, 1990, pp. 26–35; Nozick, 1990, p. 82; Solomon, 1994, p. 193). Unsurprisingly, it is a matter of contention what exactly this means (see, e.g., Merino 2004). Yet, the general idea is that lovers see themselves no longer as independent individuals but as fundamentally belonging together. Even friends or bystanders would no longer primarily refer to them as individuals but first and foremost as a couple. For instance, when trying to answer the question, who Romeo is, any plausible answer would have to describe him primarily in terms of his loving relationship with Juliet, and vice versa. Following union accounts, both Romeo and Juliet would belong together in a way that makes it virtually impossible to define their identities independently, and neither of them would be inclined to do so anyway. It is always Romeo *and* Juliet, as Solomon remarks (Solomon, 1994, p. 192f.).

Still, it is helpful to add a rough distinction between weak and strong versions of union accounts at this point. Weak versions claim that this new we-identity is merely a supplement to or partial modification of the lovers' respective individual identities. Strong versions, on the other hand, claim that the new we-identity completely redefines and, thus, replaces the lovers' prior respective individual identities. The difference between weak and strong versions, therefore, essentially marks a difference in how important or encompassing the we-identity is for each lover, i.e. whether the lovers may still have their own individual identities and perspectives, which are only considered to be less important than the shared we-identity, or whether they lose their individuality altogether, being only able to take up the shared we-perspective from there on. Accordingly, weak versions would still allow for each lover, for instance, to have individual preferences about how to design their shared apartment. Yet, these would always be considered to be less important than the lovers' shared we-preferences about it. Strong versions, on the other hand, would imply that the lovers (willingly) abandon their prior individual identities completely, which would mean that neither of them even has any individual preferences anymore. Instead, such lovers would always and solely understand themselves in terms of their shared we-identity. Following the above example, the practical question for them would be: how would *we* like to design *our* apartment?

In any case, both versions comprise the idea of the lovers' prior individual identities merging into a shared we-identity, which implies a merging of the lovers' prior individual identity-forming values. Consequently, these shared identity-forming values now become constitutive of the shared we-identity, although both how this is exactly to be analyzed and the degree to which each lover's individual identity-forming values may be featured in the shared we-identity remain a matter of debate (Friedman, 1998; Merino, 2004). An important critical question is, for instance, whether the merger of identities may be considered fair to each lover instead of one lover's identity-forming values dominating the shared we-identity. However, the crucial point for the purpose at hand is that union accounts of love imply that the shared identity-forming values become *directly* important for both lovers in terms of their shared we-identity. Consequently, possible conflicts between identity-forming values will directly affect the lovers' very we-identity, which marks a substantial difference in comparison to individualist and interpersonal accounts of love.

23.3 Conflicts Between Identity-Forming Values Among Lovers

23.3.1 Analyzing Conflicts Between Identity-Forming Values Among Lovers

The theoretical background has provided the following picture of how the beloved's identity-forming values become important for the lover: According to individualist accounts of love, these values merely become *indirectly* and *instrumentally* important to the lover, i.e. as a suitable means to promote the beloved's well-being. The lover's own identity remains unaffected. Interpersonal accounts of love take their starting point in mutual love and analyze it in terms of a dialogical relationship, which consists in the lovers sharing what is important to each of them individually. This includes each lover being intentionally open for their own identity to change based on the beloved's identity-forming values. However, while the lovers share their respective identity-forming values in their life together *for its own sake*, this still only means that one person's values become *indirectly* important to the other, namely *out of love*. The lovers' individual identities are still not necessarily affected. Finally, union accounts of love comprise the claim that due to the merging of the lovers' prior individual identity-forming values, these values now become *directly* important to both lovers in terms of their shared we-identity. Following this theoretical landscape, what are the implications for the analysis of possible conflicts between identity-forming values among lovers, and do these conflicts allow for being resolved without the loving relationship unavoidably coming to an end?

Consider again the case of the jazz lover and imagine that the person's partner *hates* jazz. Or imagine a loving relationship between a deeply religious person and an atheist to whom any religious faith is irrational superstition. First of all, it is important to emphasize once again that, for the topic at hand, such conflicts are to be considered conflicts between *identity-forming values* and not merely conflicts between rather unimportant preferences or likings. Hence, when facing such conflicts, the lovers' respective individual identities or their shared we-identity are at stake. Addressing such conflicts, therefore, has a direct impact on who the lovers (individually) will be from there on. For instance, it looks like the jazz lover's partner could no longer be a person who hates jazz in the same identity-forming sense if their loving relationship is supposed to last, and vice versa.

Secondly, pluralistic societies, in which people's identities are at least partially shaped by different cultural backgrounds, introduce an additional layer of complexity for such conflicts. For, conflicts might then not only occur between different conflicting identity-forming values, like in the case of the religious person and the atheist, or due to different stances toward the same value, like in the case of the jazz lover and hater, but they might stem from different cultural definitions or interpretations of values. Consequently, even if lovers apparently share the same identity-forming value, they might interpret it differently due to their different cultural backgrounds, thereby leading to a further type of conflict between identity-forming values. For example, imagine that both lovers value *being nice and polite* to others in the identity-forming sense mentioned. Yet, what *being nice and polite* exactly means and entails crucially hinges on cultural interpretations. Consequently, lovers might end up in a conflict over the very meaning of the value with which they both identify themselves as well as how exactly to pursue it.

Assuming that these types of conflict are not far-fetched but rather occur quite often, one way how to handle them in real life might simply consist in ignoring them. The reasoning would be that such conflicts could never be fully avoided anyway, that life is not perfect, and that we just have to accept that loving relationships are complex and often enough full of conflict. Therefore, the point would be to accept and live with them instead of trying to resolve them.

While this strategy indeed seems to be employed quite often and looks like a realistic depiction of social life, it is equally plausible to be critical about it and argue that, although it may help for a while, eventually the conflict will erupt and pose a serious threat to the loving relationship that can no longer be ignored, precisely because the lovers' identity-forming values and, thus, their very identities are at stake. Hence, simply sweeping conflicts between identity-forming values under the rug—best not to talk about them—may be considered neither a lasting way how to deal with them nor a real solution in the first place.

The three accounts of love described above, then, lead to different analyses of such conflicts. Firstly, one might think that at least within individualist accounts of love the lover's identity remains unaffected by such conflicts because the beloved's identity-forming values merely become indirectly and instrumentally important to begin with. As explicitly pointed out above, the lover's identity remains the same. However, things are not that simple. In order for a conflict between identity-forming values to arise in general, realizing or promoting at least one of the beloved's identity-forming values would go directly against realizing or promoting at least one of the lover's identity-forming values, and vice versa. Now, according to individualist accounts of love, the beloved him- or herself is one of the lover's identity-forming values, including the intention of promoting the beloved's well-being, which is why the beloved's identity-forming values become indirectly and instrumentally important to the lover. Hence, even if the lover only promotes the beloved's identity-forming values out of instrumental reasons, this means that his or her own conflicting identity-forming value gets diminished by it. For instance, the jazz lover's partner could not realize his or her goal of avoiding jazz altogether—because of his or her hatred of it—when accompanying the beloved to jazz concerts, even if doing so only for instrumental reasons. Or consider the atheist. How could the atheist promote the beloved's religious faith and practices, again even if only for instrumental reasons, if this meant, according to the atheist's own identity-forming values, promoting an irrational practice of superstition? How could the atheist promote and at the same time reject or even fight against the beloved's religious faith without experiencing a conflict within his own identity? Hence, conflicts between identity-forming values among the lovers will create a conflict within the lover's identity even against the background of individualist accounts of love.

Interpersonal accounts of love only up the ante when it comes to such conflicts because they would obviously take place at the heart of dialogical love, i.e. within the account's central idea of lovers *sharing* their life and identity-forming values *for its own sake* and *out of love* as well as *being open* to changes in their own respective individual identities in light of the beloved's identity-forming values. Consider a dialogical love between the jazz lover and his or her partner who hates jazz. How could these lovers share both of these directly contradicting identity-forming values for its own sake, even if the other's identity-forming value became important only indirectly out of love? Furthermore, how could the lovers be open to each other's identity-forming values if this implied adopting the exact opposite identity-forming value to one's original identity-forming value, e.g. in case of the atheist who would have to be open to becoming a religious person and, thus, to rejecting his identity-forming atheist conviction, and vice versa?

Following union accounts, such conflicts would even threaten the successful constitution of the lovers' shared we-identity. Assuming a merger of the lovers' original individual identity-forming values, the shared we-identity would have to include directly contradicting identity-forming values, e.g. loving *and* hating jazz at the same time. Analogously, Frankfurt originally argued that cases of unresolved conflicts between second-order desires, i.e. cases in which one is unable to develop a second-order volition, even pose a danger to one's personhood (Frankfurt, 1971,

p. 21). Even if Frankfurt's conclusion may be considered going too far, an analogously conflicted we-identity would at the very least make it impossible to give a coherent answer to the question who the lovers are, i.e. to give a consistent description of the lovers' we-identity. This holds for the lovers as well. The lovers themselves would not know who they are in terms of their shared we-identity: do we love jazz or do we hate it? Are we religious or are we atheistic? For, obviously, *we* cannot be both at the same time.

In sum, all three accounts of romantic love lead to the conclusion that conflicts between identity-forming values among lovers pose a threat to the coherency of the lovers' respective (original) individual identities or their shared we-identity. Moreover, given that the lovers' (original) individual identities are at least partially shaped by their respective cultural background, conflicts between identity-forming values also pose a threat to the lovers' respective cultural ties. If so, could the lovers do something about it? Is there a chance of resolving such conflicts based on either of these three accounts of love? Or do such conflicts inevitably lead to love coming to an end—or to failing to develop fully in terms of constituting a consistent shared we-identity to begin with? Following the three accounts described above, love would have to be considered coming to an end if the original individual identity-forming values simply remain stronger than the beloved's identity-forming values, leading either to disregarding the latter as a means to promote the beloved's well-being, or to not being open to changes in ones' identity and being unable to share conflicting identity-forming values out of love, or to resisting the constitution of a shared we-identity. However, assuming that the lovers at the same want their love to last, is there something they can do to resolve such conflicts?

23.3.2 Can Conflicts Between Identity-Forming Values Among Lovers Be Resolved?

First, it should be noted that conflicts between identity-forming values may not only be resolved in terms of one conflicting value being rejected or disappearing completely. A conflict may already be considered resolved if the initially conflicting values are revised in such a way as to make them compatible. For example, the conflict between the deeply religious person and the atheist may be considered resolved if the atheism and religious belief involved no longer include each other's explicit rejection. Imagine the atheist retaining his or her atheist conviction but only in terms of a personal stance, so that it no longer includes the rejection of religious beliefs as irrational superstition. Instead, the atheist would accept religious beliefs as viable personal options for other people. Conversely, the religious person would hold on to his or her religious belief likewise only in terms of a personal conviction and would refrain from seeing atheists as misguided people who cannot be trusted. This way, the two revised identity-forming values may be considered compatible and the original conflict resolved.

Still, this holds only as long as the lovers retain an individual identity, i.e. only against the background of individualist and—in part—interpersonal accounts of love. In case of union accounts and the idea of a shared we-identity, mere compatibility will not suffice because the lovers would still be torn between identifying themselves as either a religious or an atheistic *we*, i.e. how their shared we-identity may be defined in this regard. Likewise, following interpersonal accounts, it may very well be possible to share each other's, now compatible, identity-forming values. However, lovers cannot be open to adopting each other's identity-forming values in this regard, since this would still mean having to reject their own conflicting identity-forming value, including any cultural ties that come with it.

In any case, the crucial question at this point is whether lovers, assuming they want to hold on to their love, can actively take steps to revise or change their identity-forming values in order to resolve a conflict between these values, be it in terms of reaching compatibility or in terms of a more substantial change in one's identity. In this regard, it is helpful to distinguish between *contingent conflicts* and *inherent conflicts*. Contingent conflicts derive from contingent social or cultural circumstances when it comes to the pursuit of different values or the definition or interpretation of a value. For instance, it might be considered impossible to love both jazz and heavy metal, or to be a catholic and love a protestant, or to be nice and polite to others if this were interpreted differently in different cultures. However, in all three cases the conflict would arguably depend only on contingent historical, social, or cultural circumstances. Inherent conflicts, on the other hand, stem from directly opposing stances toward the same value, e.g. loving vs. hating jazz, or being a deeply religious person vs. being an outspoken atheist, which are both opposing stances toward religious beliefs.

While resolving contingent conflicts may all too often be hard to do, given that it involves changing the social or cultural circumstances which led to the conflict between the values in question in the first place, from a theoretical point of view it is easily conceivable that the lovers can actively take steps to achieve this goal and, thus, resolve the conflict. For example, over time people's actions have led to social and cultural change and to resolving the conflict between being a catholic and loving a protestant, and vice versa. More trivial examples, like the conflict between jazz and heavy metal, might even be easier and quicker resolvable by way of critically reflecting on the reasons of this (apparent) conflict and coming to the conclusion that neither of the two values comprise any convincing reason as to why one should not be able to love both styles of music. In either case, the identity-forming values would then be compatible.

However, inherent conflicts pose a more serious challenge, for they are only resolvable if one of the conflicting stances toward the value in question is given up. Consider again the above-mentioned changes in atheism and religious belief necessary for reaching compatibility. In this regard, it should be noted that giving up one's own conflicting stance does not necessarily mean adopting the opposite stance. For instance, the person who hates jazz does not have to become a jazz lover but only needs to lose his or her hate for it and become neutral toward it. Still, the three accounts of love again have different implications at this point. For, only individualist accounts allow for complete neutrality. Interpersonal accounts would not only require giving up one's hate for jazz but comprise one's openness to becoming a jazz lover when revising one's stance toward it. Union accounts would even require adopting a shared stance toward jazz in order to constitute a consistent we-identity, i.e. one of the conflicting stances would, indeed, have to be given up completely.

Furthermore, inherent conflicts raise the bar in terms of whether lovers can do something to resolve such a conflict because it would involve actively changing or even giving up some of one's identity-forming values, including any underlying cultural ties. Following once more Frankfurt's account on identity, according to which a person's identity is constituted by the person's volitional *necessities*, this would be impossible. According to Frankfurt's *essentialist* account of identity, we are merely able to discover who we are and what we love (Frankfurt, 1994, p. 136ff.). This also fits well the popular idea of romantic love as something over which we have no say. Love is something that *happens* to us. We *fall* in love. If so, inherent conflicts prove to be unavoidably unresolvable by the lovers. Lovers could merely hope that they undergo changes over time in their identity-forming values that happen to resolve the conflict.

Consequently, if one wants to defend the idea that lovers can do something to resolve even inherent conflicts, both the essentialist account of identity and the popular idea of romantic love being something that happens to us have to be rejected (Kühler, 2014). Ultimately, this leads one to adopt an *existentialist* account on identity and love. According to existentialism, we not only can but have to choose who we are or want to be, since our human mode of existence is one of existential freedom (Sartre, 1943, part 4, Chap. 1; Crowell, 2017); hence Sartre's slogan "existence precedes essence" (Sartre, 1946, p. 20), i.e., existential freedom precedes and creates one's identity. With regard to love, Erich Fromm has famously claimed that "[t]o love somebody is not just a strong feeling—it is a decision, it is a judgment, it is a promise" (Fromm, 1956, p. 52)—although Fromm admits that including both aspects amounts to a paradox, which he merely acknowledges.

The question whether essentialism or existentialism proves to be more convincing can be left open for the purpose at hand. The crucial point is simply to draw out the theoretical implications of the idea that lovers can or cannot actively do something to resolve inherent conflicts between their respective identity-forming values. Moreover, assuming that identity-forming values comprise a cultural dimension, the challenge posed by conflicts between identity-forming values among lovers also includes the question whether lovers can actively shed their respective cultural ties.

In any case, both essentialism and existentialism are in principle compatible with all three accounts of love. Following individualist accounts, a lover may either be able only to discover what he or she loves and who he or she is or be able to choose freely what and who to love and, thereby, who to be. Following interpersonal accounts, lovers would likewise either only be able to discover their own identity-forming values and whether they are open to changes based on the beloved's identity-forming values or be able to choose such openness and change freely and engage in the sharing of each other's lives accordingly. Finally, following union accounts, lovers would either only be able to discover whether the constitution of a consistent shared we-identity is possible to begin with or be able to choose freely how they want to shape their shared we-identity in terms of merged identity-forming values. Hence, inherent conflicts between identity-forming values amongst the lovers would either amount to unavoidable tragedy and to love coming to an end—or failing to constitute a shared we-identity in the first place—or pose a practical challenge for the lovers in terms of facing the question who they want to be from now on in light of the conflict and their love.

23.4 Conclusion

Starting from the idea that a beloved's identity-forming values necessarily become important to the lover, the above discussion has shown that the way they do so depends on the presupposed account of love. According to individualist accounts, the beloved's identity-forming values merely become indirectly and instrumentally important to the lover as a means to promote the beloved's well-being. Following interpersonal accounts, lovers share their respective identity-forming values for its own sake and out of love. Moreover, lovers are intentionally open to changes to their own identity based on the beloved's identity-forming values. Finally, union accounts argue that the lovers' individual identity-forming values merge and constitute a shared we-identity.

Conflicts between identity-forming values among lovers then have proven to pose a substantial challenge to the lovers' individual identities—or their shared we-identity. While contingent conflicts may be considered actively resolvable in that they stem from historical, social, or cultural circumstances that are in principle open to change, thus eliminating the contingent conflict between the values in question, inherent conflicts are not that easily resolvable. Resolving inherent conflicts requires substantial changes in the lovers' individual stances toward the same value. However, actively changing such a stance means changing who one is and what one loves, including one's cultural ties. Theoretically allowing for such freedom ultimately presupposes an existentialist account of identity and love, which also means rejecting both an essentialist account of identity, according to which we can merely discover who we are, and the popular idea of romantic love being something that just happens to us.

References

Buss, S., & Overton, L. (Eds.). (2002). *The contours of agency. Essays on themes from Harry Frankfurt*. Cambridge: The MIT Press.
Crowell, S. (2017). Existentialism. In E. N. Zalta (Ed.), *The Stanford encyclopedia of philosophy* (Winter 2017). https://plato.stanford.edu/archives/win2017/entries/existentialism/

Fisher, M. (1990). *Personal love*. London: Duckworth.
Frankfurt, H. G. (1971). Freedom of the will and the concept of a person. In *The importance of what we care about* (pp. 11–25). Cambridge: Cambridge University Press, 1988a.
Frankfurt, H. G. (1987). Identification and wholeheartedness. In *The importance of what we care about* (pp. 159–176). Cambridge: Cambridge University Press, 1988b.
Frankfurt, H. G. (1993). On the necessity of ideals. In *Necessity, volition, and love* (pp. 108–116). Cambridge: Cambridge University Press, 1999a.
Frankfurt, H. G. (1994). Autonomy, necessity, and love. In *Necessity, volition, and love* (pp. 129–141). Cambridge: Cambridge University Press, 1999b.
Frankfurt, H. G. (1999). On caring. In *Necessity, volition, and love* (pp. 155–180). Cambridge: Cambridge University Press.
Frankfurt, H. G. (2004). *The reasons of love*. Princeton: Princeton University Press.
Frankfurt, H. G. (2006). *Taking ourselves seriously and getting it right*. Stanford: Stanford University Press.
Friedman, M. (1998). Romantic love and personal autonomy. *Midwest Studies in Philosophy, 22*, 162–181. https://doi.org/10.1111/j.1475-4975.1998.tb00336.x
Fromm, E. (1956). *The art of loving* (p. 2006). New York: Harper Perennial.
Helm, B. W. (2017a). Love. In E. N. Zalta (Ed.), *The Stanford encyclopedia of philosophy* (Fall 2017). https://plato.stanford.edu/archives/fall2017/entries/love/
Helm, B. W. (2017b). Friendship. In E. N. Zalta (Ed.), *The Stanford encyclopedia of philosophy* (Fall 2017). https://plato.stanford.edu/archives/fall2017/entries/friendship/
Krebs, A. (2014). Between I and thou – On the dialogical nature of love. In C. Maurer, T. Milligan, & K. Pacovská (Eds.), *Love and its objects. What can we care for?* (pp. 7–24). Basingstoke: Palgrave Macmillan.
Krebs, A. (2015). *Zwischen Ich und Du: Eine dialogische Philosophie der Liebe*. Berlin: Suhrkamp.
Kroeker, E. E., & Schaubroeck, K. (Eds.). (2016). *Love, reason and morality*. New York: Routledge.
Kühler, M. (2014). Loving persons. Activity and passivity in romantic love. In C. Maurer, T. Milligan, & K. Pacovská (Eds.), *Love and its objects. What can we care for?* (pp. 41–55). Basingstoke: Palgrave Macmillan.
Kühler, M., & Jelinek, N. (2013). Introduction. In M. Kühler & N. Jelinek (Eds.), *Autonomy and the self* (pp. ix–xxxvi). Dordrecht: Springer.
Merino, N. (2004). The problem with "we": Rethinking joint identity in romantic love. *Journal of Social Philosophy, 35*, 123–132.
Nozick, R. (1990). Love's bond. In *The examined life. Philosophical meditations* (pp. 68–86). New York: Simon & Schuster.
Rorty, A. O. (1987). The historicity of psychological attitudes: Love is not love which alters not when it alteration finds. *Midwest Studies in Philosophy, 10*(1), 399–412.
Roth, A. S. (2017). Shared agency. In E. N. Zalta (Ed.), *The Stanford encyclopedia of philosophy* (Summer 2017). https://plato.stanford.edu/archives/sum2017/entries/shared-agency/
Sartre, J.-P. (1943). *Being and nothingness. A phenomenological essay on ontology*. Translated and with an introduction by Hazel E. Barnes, New York: Washington Square Press, 1992.
Sartre, J.-P. (1946). *Existentialism is a humanism*. New Haven: Yale University Press.
Sheffield, F. C. C., & Howatson, M. C. (Eds.). (2008). *Plato: The symposium*. Cambridge: Cambridge University Press.
Solomon, R. C. (1994). *About love. Reinventing romance for our times*. Indianapolis: Hackett Publishing, Reprint 2006.
Taylor, C. (1977a). What is human agency? In *Philosophical papers 1. Human agency and language* (pp. 15–44). Cambridge: Cambridge University Press, 1985a.
Taylor, C. (1977b). Self-interpreting animals. In *Philosophical papers 1. Human agency and language* (pp. 45–76). Cambridge: Cambridge University Press, 1985b.

PD Dr. Michael Kühler is Assistant Professor ("wissenschaftlicher Mitarbeiter") at the Academy for Responsible Research, Teaching, and Innovation (ARRTI) at Karlsruhe Institute of Technology (KIT), Germany, and "Privatdozent" at Münster University, Germany. His areas of expertise include ethics, metaethics, political philosophy, and the philosophy of love. His publications include: "Liebe, Identität und die Freiheit zu gehen," in: Dietz, Simone/Wiertz, Svenja/Foth, Hannes (eds.): Die Freiheit zu gehen, Dordrecht: Springer, 2019, 195–222; "What if I Cannot Do What I Have to Do? Notions of Personal Practical Necessity and the Principle 'Ought Implies Can'," in: Bauer, Katharina/Mieth, Corinna/Varga, Somogy (eds.): Dimensions of Practical Necessity. "Here I Stand. I Can Do No Other," Houndmills: Palgrave Macmillan, 2017, 87–107; and "Loving Persons. Activity and Passivity in Romantic Love," in: Maurer, Christian/Milligan, Tony/Pacovská, Kamila (eds.): Love and Its Objects. What Can We Care For?, Basingstoke: Palgrave Macmillan, 2014, 41–55.

Chapter 24
The Importance of Family Members in Love Letters

Paul C. Rosenblatt

Abstract In an analysis of the love letters of 10 couples living in the nineteenth or twentieth centuries in the United States or Europe, close family members were typically mentioned early and often in the letters. Letter writers told lovers about family members and family members about lovers and reported on the process of the family acceptance of the lover. Letter writers expressed concern and caring for members of the lover's family and were told of expressions of caring for them from members of their lover's family. Family members would reach out to a lover and a lover would reach out to members of the other's family. These findings suggest the possibility that in an escalating couple relationship in some cultural contexts the couple is not an isolated dyad. They may be connected to their families of origin and communicating that to their lover and perhaps quite possibly looking forward to a committed couple relationship in which family members of one or both of them will have a significant place. Culture intersects these matters in a number of ways, including the etiquette of what is said about one's own and the other's family in letter writing, cultural expectations for where married couples will live, cultural ideas about the role of male family authorities in the lives of unmarried women, and cultural expectations regarding in-law relationships and exchanges of help between married couples and their families of origin.

Keywords Love · Couples · Culture · Family · Love letters · Written communication

P. C. Rosenblatt (✉)
Department of Family Social Science, University of Minnesota, St. Paul, MN, USA
e-mail: prosenbl@umn.edu

24.1 Introduction

Years ago I read some unpublished courtship letters written in the early 1800s between a young clergyman living in Minnesota and a young woman living hundreds of miles away in Illinois. The letters were intriguing because they provided over many months every bit of communication between the two. It is very rare for those of us interested in the development of couple relationships to have such rich data on what precisely two potential partners communicate to each other. One ongoing tension in the couple's correspondence concerned where the woman's mother would live after the couple married and settled in Minnesota, where the clergyman was leading a church. The woman wanted her mother to live with them; the man did not, and offered, over a number of letters, an array of reasons why the woman's mother should not live with them. That collection of letters had me thinking about the place of parents and other relatives in love letters and led me to want to do a more systematic study of how much and for what reasons families of origin are mentioned in love letters. This chapter is a report of that study.

24.1.1 Possibilities

There is tension in psychology and the social sciences between generalizing broadly and sensitivity to cultural diversity. I think cultural diversity is extremely important and have written about the costs of overgeneralization based on data and perspectives from one particular culture (e.g., Rosenblatt, 2017, 2020). So I am aware that even if 10 love letters collections, with their rich over-time data, might be useful for stimulating our thinking about couple relationships, they do not justify broad generalizations about couples. At best, they suggest possibilities. So in the end I address the question, "Do these 10 letter collections written in the nineteenth and twentieth centuries offer potentially useful possibilities in thinking about some couple relationships?" The letters analyzed for this chapter were written long ago, in various geographic locations, and in several different languages, and handwritten love communications nowadays are probably not common in more technologically advanced countries, though they still occur in some countries (e.g., Nepal—Ahearn, 2003, Uganda—Parikh, 2015). It is certainly possible that love letters written in the past are not of value for understanding couples in technologically advanced countries. So this chapter's analysis of love letters only raises the possibility that a couple in an escalating relationship in their own particular cultural and historical context builds their relationship with reference to and connection with members of their families or origin. Thus, it is possible that in a sense some people marry a family or at least some members of the other's family and also a sense in which some people who marry do not turn away from key members of their family or origin. Can we still use the term "love" when we talk about one person and her or his family coming together with another person and her or his family? The answer depends on how one defines love, but I think it is clear that in almost all of the 10 letter collections the correspondents expressed something they thought of as love for one another.

24.1.2 What Are Love Letters?

Love letters available to scholars are generally considered love letters because they were labeled "love letters" by archivists who first had access to the letters and by the editors of books in which published couple letters appear. But even if both partners in a couple exchanging letters say "I love you," we cannot assume that what they mean by love is the same as another couple exchanging letters in a different cultural or historical location. Moreover, what is called "love" by a couple or by an archivist or editor may be very different from what might be called "love" in recent social psychological writings. Furthermore, in what might be called "love letters," expressions of love might be fueled by and represent much that is not love, for example, interest in escaping the parental household, sexuality, economic insecurity, or the desire to meet community expectations for young adults. Because I sampled letter collections only of people who eventually married and because in some eras and cultural locations in which those letters were written the correspondence of unmarried heterosexual unrelated individuals was expected to lead to marriage, I think many of the love letters I worked with were as much heading-toward-marriage letters as they were love letters.

24.2 Theoretical Background and Context

Given that seven of the 10 cases used in this chapter are from the United States, I turn for theoretical background and context to relatively recent sociological literature from the United States. That literature offers ideas and starting places for thinking about the letters, but of course it is about more recent times than the seven love letter cases. Also, to the extent that the United States has been and is culturally diverse, the sociological literature I cite may be of limited relevance to some of the love letters from the United States.

Although in some data from the United States marriage significantly reduces the contact of adults with their families of origin (Sarkisian & Gerstel, 2008), it remains common for young married couples to live with or very near the family of at least one of the partners (Merrill, 2011). Thus, issues of possible or anticipated contact in early marriage with family members of at least one of the partners might need to be addressed in the course of exchanging love letters. More generally, adult children and their parents in the United States, whether they live near each other or not, often remain in substantial communicative contact (e.g., Huo, Napolitano, Furstenberg, & Fingerman, 2020; Logan & Spitze, 1996; Rossi & Rossi, 1990; Zarit & Eggebeen, 2002). That suggests that relatively few U.S. couples, as they communicated about a future together, would have been anticipating a marital future that is out of contact with their families of origin.

There are also issues of family influence in that in some, perhaps many, cultures and historical eras someone considering a particular person as a possible marital partner would be dealing with family member attempts to influence their choice and might value such influence. Thus, there would be the expectation and understanding that family members will have and should have a say in the life choices the young person makes (Thornton, 2009), which suggests that love letter exchanges might well touch on the opinions of family members as a couple moves toward possibly marrying. This might be especially true if it seems at all likely that parents or other family members of one or both lovers might at some point provide material assistance to the couple (Fingerman, Miller, Birditt, & Zarit, 2009).

Because family members might try to influence their choices or be influential in their choices, letter writers might correspond about the attempted or actual influence. Then, too, in anticipation of marrying, lovers might want to write about how close to family members they would like to live after marrying, what their future relationships with and obligations to the families of one or both partners might involve, and how to maintain appropriate relationships with their families. Thus, letter writers might write about their families of origin and even use their couple correspondence to build connections with one another's families. Related to that, letter writers may want their relatives to accept their future spouse and may want to be accepted by the relatives of their future spouse, and that too may lead to writing in love letters about family. In addition, in some cases, a new spouse may step immediately into demanding roles in the spouse's family, for example, as caregiver for the motherless children of a spouse who is a widower, and that too is a reason to write about family. I would further argue that in instances where family considerations are important, family members may be written about even in the first letters a couple exchanges.

24.3 Research Methodology

I analyzed 10 published love letter collections. Working with published letters makes it easier for others to check on what is claimed in this chapter about the letters. Also, published letters are easier to read than hand written letters, and the layout and informational clarity of a printed set of letters makes it easier to sample from the set. Issues of copyright are clear with published letter collections, and problems of determining the dates of letters and letter authenticity are resolved, to the extent they can be, by the editor of a letter collection. So I turned to published collections of love letters.

In this research I consider letter collections to be love letter collections if the editor of a published collection labeled it as a love letter collection. I searched my university's online catalog for books of love letters (using the search term "love letters") exchanged by heterosexual couples who at the beginning of their correspondence were not married and who eventually married. I looked for collections in which there were at least 30 premarital letters, in which letters were written in or had been translated into English, and in which there were letters from both parties. This report is based on the first 10 love letter collections I found in the library's holdings that fit the criteria. The 10 love letter collections are listed in the first of the two reference sections at the end of this chapter.

Fourteen of the 20 letter writers were from the United States, two from Russia, and one each from Great Britain, Germany, the Austro-Hungarian Empire, and Australia. The letters were written as early as the 1820s and as recently as the 1940s.

Some letter collections were brief (not much more than 30 letters) and others were extensive (over 1000 letters). I did not want to weigh the large letter collections more than the small ones in data analysis, nor did I want to research rare events in love letters but to research what was common, which made sampling from the letter collections appropriate. Since I wanted to sample across the trajectory of the couple relationship, the sampling strategy was to use the first 10 (in chronological order), middle 10, and last 10 letters before each couple married. I considered the middle 10 letters to be those written half way between the date of the first love letter in the collection and that of the last love letter before marriage. With the Sandburg-Steichen letters (Sandburg, 1987) I respected the editor's assertion that the first published Sandburg and Steichen letters were not love letters, and chose as the first love letter the one the editor said was the one that marked the beginning of the love relationship.

Focusing on the first, middle and final 10 letters before marriage in each letter series I used thematic analysis (Patton, 2002, pp. 452–471) to identify love letter references to family members. Coding began with noting love letter passages referring to family members. Sometimes, a bit of research was needed to determine whether a person named was a relative or not. Next I carried out an inductive categorization of the types of references to family members. Categories were created that were descriptive, not inferential, and were linked closely to the words letter writers used. The findings section of this paper offers illustrations of each theme, which enables readers to check the fit between the data and the themes generated in my analysis.

24.4 Findings

24.4.1 Frequency of Love Letter Content About Family Members

In every letter collection, family members were referred to. Across the 10 letter collections 47% of the letters sampled referred to one or more family members of the letter writer or the letter recipient. The range in letters mentioning family members was from 90% of the letters of Dickinson and Norcross to 17% of the letters of Freeman and Palmer. Even for Freeman and Palmer, who were older than most letter writers in this study and who were not living with family members, her parents received meaningful attention in the couple correspondence.

Another important finding is that family members were referred to early (in at least one of the first 10 letters) in every letter collection. In fact family was referred to in four of the first letters in the 10 letter collections and in the first four letters in nine of the 10 letter collections.

24.4.2 Building Links Between Lover and Family

24.4.2.1 Telling Family Members About the Lover

Early in some letter collections it is clear that one or both partners had acted to build relationships between key members of their family and their lover by telling the family members about the lover and the couple relationship. That led to family conversations they wrote about to their lover. Consider the following from the first love letter from Mileva Marić to Albert Einstein, October 10, 1897.

> Papa gave me some tobacco that I'm to give you personally. He's eager to whet your appetite for our little land of outlaws. I told him about you—you absolutely must come back with me sometime—the two of you would really have a lot to talk about. But I'll have to play the role of interpreter. I can't send the tobacco, however, because should you have to pay duty on it, you would curse me *and* my present (Einstein & Marić, 1992, pp. 3–4).

With these lines Marić informed Einstein that she had told her father about him and her father was reaching out to Einstein. That suggests that for Marić and her father Einstein's relationship should be not only with her but also with her father.

Here is another illustration, from the fourth love letter exchanged by Zelda Sayre and F. Scott Fitzgerald, February, 1919. Sayre wrote:

> I s'pose you knew your Mother's anxiously anticipated epistle at last arrived—I am so glad she wrote—Just a nice little note—untranslatable, but she called me 'Zelda' (Bryer & Barks, 2002, p. 12).

We learn from this passage that Scott had told his mother about Zelda, had given his mother Zelda's address, and his mother had written to Zelda. That is another example of the couple relationship, early on, being not just a dyadic one but involving a parent of one of the lovers.

Telling key family members about the couple relationship can be a step toward receiving family approval for the relationship and toward creating a space in the family for the outsider. Here is an illustration from the letters of Woodrow Wilson to Edith Bolling Galt. Wilson, a widower with three adult children, wrote the following to Galt on August 3, 1915, in the first of the middle 10 letters sampled, a bit more than 3 months after the first love letter between them.

I took [my daughter] Nell in the music room ... and told her of the great happiness that had come to us, my precious One, and I know you would have been touched and delighted if you could have seen and heard how she took it—with unaffected joy that I should have found escape from my loneliness and comfort and support now and in the days to come, and even the little she had seen of you had given her an impression of you that made her glad that it was *you* she was to welcome. Isn't it wonderful how ... all three [of my daughters] understand and how their sweet love for me interprets the whole thing to them perfectly? (Link, Hirst, Little, & Gordon, 1980a, p. 73).

In a case that shows the value of telling family members relatively early about a developing romance, John Miller's mother made great difficulty for him when he was close to marrying Sally McDowell, because his mother felt that she had not been given enough time to get used to the two having a relationship and moving toward marriage. The following is from the next-to-last letter written before the couple married, Miller to McDowell October 29, 1856:

Mother, whose health is feeble, came into my room & told me yesterday that after deliberation she was opposed to the suddenness of my movements & could not approve it: & then to my utter horror & surprise went on to make me understand that she could not repeat her invitation [to you to visit her] (Buckley, 2000, p. 870).

Some couples already knew one or a few members of the other's family before the love letter exchange began. A prior relationship could be a valuable link between the two lovers and could make the couple relationship more durable. Consider the following from the second love letter between Olga Knipper and Anton Chekhov. Knipper wrote on June 22 or 23, 1899:

Marya Pavlovna, your sister, is she sketching or just being idle? Give her my best love and tell her I will write ... My brother, Karl, and his wife, Elena, are very nice people. You would be happy here. Think about it. Not long ago we made an excursion to Aleksandropol by the new railway ... It was beautiful ... Last evening we walked about eight miles, we explored an interesting little valley. There was no road and we had to walk on pebbles ... We spent an eternity on the road to the Caucasus. Travel is never easy there ... Give my compliments to your mother, your sister (Benedetti, 1996, pp. 7–8).

In this passage Knipper may have been using her connection with Chekhov's sister to bolster her claim to a relationship with him. She also seems to have been pushing Chekhov to vacation with her and to meet her brother and his wife. She concluded by giving her "compliments" to Chekhov's mother and sister. Although giving those compliments may have conformed to Russian social conventions at that time (Janning, 2018) and it may have been a courteous thing to do in a wide range of letter-writing relationships, her giving her compliments might also have meant that she acknowledged their importance to Chekhov and showed him that she respected them and either already had a relationship with them or aspired to have a relationship with them.

24.4.2.2 Telling the Lover About One's Family

Some love letter material about members of the writer's family seems to have been only a report of news (including bad news) about important people in the writer's life. For example, Alice Freeman wrote George Herbert Palmer about her concerns about the health of her parents. Marian Smith wrote Eugene Petersen repeatedly about her concerns about her brother, who was missing in action in World War II. But for some letter writers it seems that references to family members were in part a way to help the other to know their family and to know who they were for the letter writer. Consider the following from the fourth love letter exchanged by Lilian Steichen and Carl Sandburg, April 6, 1908:

> I had just seen [W, a family friend]. Mother & I had stepped in to explain that we would not stay overnight at his house ... Edward [my brother] used always to compare him with Christ. When Edward was about twenty W used to wear a beard so that he really resembled the old-master pictures of Christ—and Edward's greatest aspiration was to paint a Christ with W as model (Sandburg, 1987, p. 53).

With her references to her mother and brother, Steichen was telling Sandburg that she and her mother travel together and visit others and that her brother is an ambitious and imaginative artist whose creative ideas she finds interesting. Perhaps Sandburg already knew those things, but even if he did, her including those things in an early love letter was a way of reinforcing the importance of that knowledge.

Then there is this in the third love letter from Edward Dickinson to Emily Norcross, April 10, 1826: "I feel anxious about my brother at your Academy—and fear he will not conduct himself properly" (Pollak, 1988, p. 9). With this statement Edward might have been saying that his brother was important to him, that he had higher standards than his brother, and that if his brother did something inappropriate or shameful at the academy in the town where Emily lived Edward should not be judged by what his brother did.

24.4.2.3 Progress Report on Family Acceptance of the Other

For a while some letter writers withheld information about their romantic partner from parents and other family members. For example, in the second love letter exchanged between Agnes Miller and Olaf Stapledon, on April 4, 1913, Miller wrote: "I shall tell Mother all about it sometime, and if you like you can talk to her afterwards" (Crossley, 1987, p. 9). But with family being so important to many of the letter writers, with the other's family anticipated to have an important role in the marital future of many letter writers, and with family approval being strongly desired or even necessary for the couple relationship to go forward, many correspondents provided progress reports on family acceptance of the other. For example, in the fifth love letter exchanged between Lillian Steichen and Carl Sandburg, April

6, 1908, there is a long account of her mother acknowledging to a family friend the marital future of Lillian and Carl and then having a long discussion with that family friend and others about what form marriage should take.

> B cornered mother ... and asked ... about you ... When he heard how long you had been with us—he guessed the rest and practically got mother's confirmation of his guess—mother can't keep anything in ... I really felt grateful to mother for having talked too much ... B thereupon announced that he would go out to dinner with us ... And what a dinner it was! ... The subject was" The Sex-question in general—our 'possible' marriage in particular! ... Mother represented a modified form of the accepted conventional Church-view of marriage ... Life-long mating by *contract, promise* before state or church authorities (Sandburg, 1987, pp. 56–57).

In some letter exchanges the progress reports were mixed. The family of one correspondent might be more positive about the couple relationship than the family of the other. In letter 9 of the first 10 letters between F. Scott Fitzgerald and Zelda Sayre, Scott wrote that he was sending Zelda his mother's engagement ring, which meant that his mother knew about Zelda and accepted her. Zelda, by contrast was concerned about her parents accepting Scott. As Zelda wrote Scott March, 1919, "I'm not exactly scared of 'em, but they could be so unpleasant about [my marrying you]" (Bryer & Barks, 2002, p. 15). In other letters to Scott she mentioned her mother fearing that Scott could not earn a decent living as an author and that Scott was an alcoholic.

24.4.3 Expressions of Connection Between Lover and Family

24.4.3.1 Writing Caring Things About the Lover's Family

Some lovers communicated to the other that they were interested in the other's family or cared about them. One can take that as an expression of caring about the other. That is, since the other cares about her or his family, showing that one is interested in the other's family or cares about them is a way of saying to the other that "I care about you." But also, expressing interest in the other's family and care for them is a way of acknowledging that marrying the other means that one will be part of that family.

Some letter writers asked questions about their lover's family. For example, Edward Dickinson often asked Emily Norcross about the whereabouts and health of members of her family. The following is from the ninth love letter exchanged by them, June 18, 1826: "How is your brother, who has been ill—& how is [your brother] William—when do you expect him home?" (Pollak, 1988, p. 23).

Another form of expressing care about the other's family was to include greetings to them or regards for them in a love letter. Doing so could be a way of acknowledging the possibility or likelihood that the other's family members will become one's relatives and of showing that one approves of the other's family. It is also a way of acknowledging the importance of the other's family for the other. Even if expressing regards for another's family is a courteous way of writing letters to anyone one knows rather well or whose family one knows, in a love letter such expressions may have additional gravitas. Such greetings were expressed by six of the 20 letter writers. For example, Edith Bolling Galt wrote the following to Woodrow Wilson in the second of the last 10 letters before the couple married, November 2, 1915: "My tender love to that sweet [daughter of yours] Margaret, and I do hope her cold is much better" (Link, Hirst, Little, & Gordon, 1980b, p. 161).

24.4.3.2 Family Members and Lovers Reach Out to Each Other

In the sampled letters, 10 of the 20 letter writers mentioned reaching out to family members of the other or being reached out to by family members of the other. For example, some letters mentioned a gift sent between one lover and a family member of the other, a letter sent to or from one lover and a family member of the other, or a visit to one lover of a family member of the other. Thus, as mentioned above, in the first love letter in the Einstein-Marić exchange, Marić wrote to Einstein that "Papa gave me some tobacco that I'm to give you personally." Then there was the reference above to Zelda Sayre receiving a letter from F. Scott Fitzgerald's mother. Albert Einstein mentioned receiving letters from Marić's sister:

> Your dear sister, whom I already know from her cheerful letters, will certainly enjoy being with us—I don't need to tell you that she's welcome—such a carefree, ornery little thing (Einstein & Marić, 1992, pp. 33–34).

And Edward Dickinson wrote to Emily Norcross about receiving a letter from her father concerning the stove that was going to be installed in the house Emily and Edward would occupy after marrying.

Sometimes the reaching out was engineered by the other. For example, Marian Elizabeth Smith wrote to Eugene T. Petersen February 9, 1945:

> I've asked Mother to send you *Flight to Arras* so you'll probably get it in a month or so. I'll be anxious to know how you like it (Petersen, 1998, p. 47).

By asking her mother to send the book to Petersen, Smith engineered a reaching out from her mother to Petersen.

Sometimes reaching out seemed a matter of etiquette and not of caring or affection for the family members. For example, in an era and location where it was considered inappropriate for an unrelated woman and man to be alone together, a simple invitation might have to encompass members of the other's family. Thus, John Miller wrote in the first letter between him and Sally McDowell, August 5, 1854:

> Mr. Miller's compliments to Mrs. McDowell & begs, if she or either of her sisters or either of her brothers will ride with him in a little uncomfortable no-top buggy to-day or to-morrow (Buckley, 2000, p. 1).

Miller's invitation was of necessity not just for her but also for one of her siblings. Similarly, where a couple's relationship could not escalate toward marriage without the consent of the woman's father and without his input on such issues as the date of the wedding, the man courting her would have to reach out to her father. Thus Edward Dickinson wrote Emily Norcross March 7, 1827, in the fifth of the middle 10 letters of their correspondence:

> I should certainly desire that our union might take place whenever it should be thought safe by you and your [family], to entrust your person and preservation & promotion of your happiness to my care. I intend, if agreeable to you, to converse with your father on the subject (Pollak, 1988, p. 97).

24.4.3.3 Meeting the Lover's Relatives

Some letters included a lover's words about anticipating meeting one or more members of the other's family for the first time. For example, Einstein wrote the following to Marić September 19, 1900, in anticipation of Marić's sister staying with them.

> Thanks for your sweet letter and ... the plan to bring your fat little sister along and introduce her to our 'European culture.' To impress her with it even more and to give her a high opinion of us as well, I've already bought two little coffee spoons for our household ... Your dear sister, whom I already know from her cheerful letters, will certainly enjoy being with us—I don't need to tell you that she's welcome—such a carefree, ornery little thing (second of middle 10 letters, Einstein & Marić, 1992, pp. 33–34).

24.5 Discussion

24.5.1 Importance of Family in Love Letters

Family members were referred to in every one of the 10 letter collections and in nearly half of all the letters. That seems to indicate that family was important to the letter writers and important in their growing relationship with each other. In fact, family members were referred to early in all 10 of the letter collections. That suggests that family members were so important to the correspondents and in their conceivable future that they had to be mentioned early in a correspondence that could lead to marriage. Reflecting that importance, the most common family references in the letters included accounts of having told family members about the other, helping the other to know more about one's family, reports on progress on family acceptance of the other, and expressions of connection between one letter writer's family and the other (for example, writing caring things about the other's family or reaching out to the other's family).

The findings from the 10 letter collections suggest that it could be a mistake to depict a couple with an escalating relationship as though they were simply a dyad. Depending on culture and context, they may be embedded in and connected to their families, and family members and family issues will be entangled in the relationship escalation and anticipated future. At the very least, for anyone in an escalating couple relationship who is living with family members it is conceivable that coresident family members would not be easily ignored while communicating to the other about what is going on in their life. And quite possibly for some couples in escalating relationships, loyalty, love, and caring for family members would guarantee that they would want the other to know about their family members and to accept a future in which those family members are important.

24.5.2 Limitations

The 10 letter collections providing data in this chapter are not a random sample of a well-defined universe of letter collections. They are simply 10 letter collections that were available in print and in English. The 10 collections are from diverse times, but none more recently than the 1940s. They are also only from the culture or cultures they are from.

24.5.3 Culture

There may be shared cultural elements across the 120 years of letters examined for this chapter, across the countries in which the letter writers lived, and across the three languages in which the letters were originally written. But scholars who write about love letters alert us to the potential for cultural differences (Janning, 2018; Lyons, 1999, 2013; Paldam, 2018), and I have tried to be alert to possible cultural differences among the 20 letter writers represented in this chapter. Even if the cultural differences of which I am aware do not seem to make a difference regarding the general patterns of writing about family in the letters, underlying the patterns and in the details of reference to family there are clearly cultural differences. For example, there was often a sense for nineteenth century women letter writers that they were not in a position to marry without the approval of their father or father surrogate.

There were also cultural factors limiting correspondence. In some cultural settings letter writers could not assume that their letters were private—for example the letters of soldiers in World War I (Stapledon) and World War II (Petersen) were reviewed by military censors. Some couples concealed from family and community members that they were corresponding, and the concealment said something about the cultural forces, particularly on women (Eustace, 2001), against seeming to have or actually having a romantic involvement. Thus, in some cultural settings it harmed a woman's reputation to be seen to have a romance (Norcross, Freeman) and it could harm a widower's reputation to be interested in another woman soon after his wife's death (Wilson).

This chapter could be taken as a comment on contemporary popular culture in the United States and Europe, in which films, fiction, drama, and popular music often offer an image of an isolated couple falling in love and becoming committed to each other (Amato, 2009). It is a popular culture that often seems to idealize the isolated couple falling in love or newly in love with stories that omit or say very little about parents and other relatives of the lovers. In the past and arguably in the present in many cultures in the world it has been and is rare for two individuals to come together unconnected to family and without intentions to be connected to family in the future (Thornton, 2009).

In a time of increased digitalization, the cultural meaning and significance of love letters written on paper may be changing (Janning, 2018). Electronic media confronts some emerging adults with the challenge of having and perhaps being able to maintain several escalating relationships (Konstam, 2019), and electronic media may drive changes in what and when lovers communicate and what they deal with in their exchanges (Paldam, 2018). But that does not mean that family no longer is important in the exchanges of lovers. Some people may value aspects of digital romantic communication (Janning, 2018), and digital romance may be flirtatious in ways that are far different from what was common in paper communication (Wyss, 2009), but there may still be family content in the electronic exchanges of some couples. It remains to be seen, from research using electronic love communications, how and how much family members are referred to.

24.6 Conclusion

The research reported in this chapter indicates that romantic correspondence is not necessarily about two people standing alone but may be about two people in families, planning to stay in families, supported by and supporting family members, perhaps seeing things in part through the eyes of family members, and with a degree of enduring obligation to family members.

24.7 Recommendations in Theory and Practice

24.7.1 Theory

The research reported here suggests that theorizing about escalating couple relationships as though family is irrelevant to their current or anticipated future relationships may be a mistake. The two who are coming together may remain players in their families, and their developing relationship may in part be about who each will be in relationship to the family of the other, and how the couple will in the future interact with their families.

24.7.2 Practice

A key implication for practice from the research reported in this chapter is that in helping couples or prospective couples, practitioners may make a mistake to assume that the two partners are the only players in their relationship. It is important to be alert to the possible significance of their family relationships, and to recognize that interventions may have to take into account and possibly involve members of their families.

The Love Letter Collections

Benedetti, J. (1996). *Dear writer, dear actress: The love letters of Anton Chekhov and Olga Knipper*. Hopewell, NJ: Ecco Press.

Bryer, J. R., & Barks, C. W. (2002). *Dear Scott, dearest Zelda: The love letters of F. Scott and Zelda Fitzgerald*. New York: St. Martin's Press.

Buckley, T. E. (Ed.). (2000). *"If you love that lady don't marry her": The courtship letters of Sally McDowell and John Miller 1854–1856*. Columbia: University of Missouri Press.

Crossley, R. (1987). *Talking across the world: The love letters of Olaf Stapledon and Agnes Miller, 1913–1919*. Hanover, NH: University Press of New England.

Einstein, A., & Marić, M. (1992). Albert Einstein & Mileva Marić: *The love letters*. J. Renn & R. Schulmann (Eds.), S. Smith (translator). Princeton, NJ: Princeton University Press.

Link, A. S., Hirst, D. W., Little, J. E., & Gordon, D. (1980a). *The papers of Woodrow Wilson, vol. 34, July 21 – September 30, 1915*. Princeton, NJ: Princeton University Press.

Link, A. S., Hirst, D. W., Little, J. E., & Gordon, D. (1980b). *The papers of Woodrow Wilson, vol. 35, October, 1915 – January 27, 1916*. Princeton, NJ: Princeton University Press.

Palmer, A. F., & Palmer, G. H. (1940). *An academic courtship: Letters of Alice Freeman and George Herbert Palmer, 1886–1887*. Cambridge, MA: Harvard University Press.

Petersen, E. T. (1998). *Chance for love: The World War II letters of Marian Elizabeth Smith and Lt. Eugene T. Petersen, USMCR*. East Lansing: Michigan State University Press.

Pollak, V. R. (1988). *A poet's parents: The courtship letters of Emily Norcross and Edward Dickinson*. Chapel Hill: University of North Carolina Press.

Sandburg, M. (1987). *The poet and the dream girl: The love letters of Lilian Steichen and Carl Sandburg*. Urbana: University of Illinois Press.

Tribble, E. (1981). *A president in love: The courtship letters of Woodrow Wilson and Edith Bolling Galt*. Boston: Houghton Mifflin.

References

Ahearn, L. M. (2003). Writing desire in Nepali love letters. *Language and Communication, 23*, 107–122.

Amato, P. R. (2009). Institutional, companionate, and individualistic marriage: A social psychological perspective on marital change. In H. E. Peters & C. M. Kamp Dush (Eds.), *Marriage and family: Perspectives and complexities* (pp. 75–90). New York: Columbia University Press.

Eustace, N. (2001). "The cornerstone of a copious work": Love and power in eighteenth-century courtship. *Journal of Social History, 34*, 517–546.

Fingerman, K., Miller, L., Birditt, K., & Zarit, S. (2009). Giving to the good and the needy: Parental support of grown children. *Journal of Marriage and Family, 71*, 1220–1233.

Huo, M., Napolitano, L., Furstenberg, F. F., & Fingerman, K. L. (2020). Who initiates the help older parents give to midlife children. *The Journals of Gerontology, Series B, 75*(4), 907–918.

Janning, M. (2018). *Love letters: Saving romance in the digital age.* New York: Routledge.

Konstam, V. (2019). *The romantic lives of emerging adults: Getting from I to we.* New York: Oxford University Press.

Logan, J. R., & Spitze, G. D. (1996). *Family ties: Enduring relations between parents and their grown children.* Philadelphia, PA: Temple University Press.

Lyons, M. (1999). Love letters and writing practices: On *écritures intimes* in the nineteenth century. *Journal of Family History, 24*, 232–239.

Lyons, M. (2013). *The writing culture of ordinary people in Europe, c. 1860-1920.* Cambridge: Cambridge University Press.

Merrill, D. M. (2011). *When your children marry: How marriage changes relationships with sons and daughters.* Lanham, MD: Rowman & Littlefield.

Paldam, C. S. (2018). Overcoming absence: From love letters to skype. In A. Malinowska & M. Gratzke (Eds.), *The materiality of love: Essays on affection and cultural practice* (pp. 68–84). New York: Routledge.

Parikh, S. (2015). *Regulating romance: Youth love letters, moral anxiety, and intervention in Uganda's time of AIDS.* Nashville, TN: Vanderbilt University Press.

Patton, M. Q. (2002). *Qualitative research and evaluation methods* (3rd ed.). Thousand Oaks, CA: Sage.

Rosenblatt, P. C. (2017). Researching grief: Cultural, relational, and individual possibilities. *Journal of Loss and Trauma, 22*, 617–630.

Rosenblatt, P. C. (2020). Diversity in human grieving: Historical and cross-cultural perspectives. In M. H. Jacobsen & A. Petersen (Eds.). *Exploring grief: Towards a sociology of sorrow* (pp. 37–51). New York: Routledge.

Rossi, A. S., & Rossi, P. H. (1990). *Of human bonding: Parent-child relations across the life course.* New York: Aldine de Gruyter.

Sarkisian, N., & Gerstel, N. (2008). Till marriage do us part: Adult children's relationships with their parents. *Journal of Marriage and Family, 70*, 360–376.

Thornton, A. (2009). Historical and cross-cultural perspectives on marriage. In H. E. Peters & C. M. Kamp Dush (Eds.), *Marriage and family: Perspectives and complexities* (pp. 3–55). New York: Columbia University Press.

Wyss, E. L. (2009). From the bridal letter to online flirting: Changes in text type from the 19th century to the internet era. In C. Rowe & E. L. Wyss (Eds.), *Language and new media: Linguistic, cultural, and technological evolutions* (pp. 99–128). Cresskill, NJ: Hampton Press.

Zarit, S. H., & Eggebeen, D. J. (2002). Parent-child relationships in adulthood and later years. In M. H. Bornstein (Ed.), *Handbook of parenting* (Children and parenting) (Vol. 1, pp. 135–161). Mahwah, NJ: Lawrence Erlbaum Associates.

Paul C. Rosenblatt (PhD) has a Ph.d. in Psychology and is Professor Emeritus of Family Social Science at the University of Minnesota. He has published 14 books and roughly 200 journal articles and chapters in edited books. Much of his work has focused on the social psychology, anthropology, and sociology of people's closest relationships and what the personal and relationship impacts are of the ending of a close relationship. His research has included studies of ethnic cultures within the United States, ethnographic work in Mexico and Indonesia, and collaborative writings focused on Korean culture, Zulu culture, and Chinese culture. Rosenblatt carried out pioneering research in the 1960s and 1970s on love in cross-cultural perspective and has written extensively about couples in which the partners differ in cultural background and about family relationships and relationship losses across cultures. His chapter for The Handbook of Love in Cultural and Transcultural Contexts is based on analysis of personal documents (love letters). His previous research includes a number of studies using personal documents such as autobiographies, memoirs, and diaries.

Part V
Love in the Context of Counselling, Psychotherapy and Psychiatry

Self Love (Photo: Claude-Hélène Mayer)

Chapter 25
Love at the Psychiatric Ward

Dominic Harion, Sarah Francesca Löw, Sascha Settegast, and Dominik Zink

Abstract If (love) relationships in clinical, hospitalized settings are understood as specific forms of a more comprehensive concept of "love", the question arises how possible theoretical approaches to and therapeutic implications of such forms of *exiled love* can be conceptualized, since the efforts to classify and evaluate these relationships are manifold and are modelled differently from the perspectives of various disciplines. Against this backdrop, the present article focuses on the salutogenic potentials of love at psychiatric wards and in rehabilitation milieus. Starting with an overview of the legal and ethical aspects, which have been increasingly discussed especially since the 1980s, both the effects of love relationships in clinical settings that interfere therapy and those that benefit therapy are addressed. The cultural-historical framework for this approach is based on the differentiation of love into *eros, philia* and *agape*, which are reflected in regard to their therapeutic and ethical-normative potentials and lead to an understanding of love as an "ontological rootedness", which can provide the basis for resource-oriented therapeutic work.

Keywords Love · Eros · Philia · Agape · Ontological rootedness · Compassion · Empathy · Psychiatry · Resource-oriented psychotherapy · Therapeutic milieu · Salutogenesis · Cultural sciences

---

D. Harion
Luxembourg Centre for Educational Testing (LUCET), University of Luxembourg, Esch-sur-Alzette, Luxembourg
e-mail: dominic.harion@uni.lu

S. F. Löw (✉)
Trier, Germany
e-mail: sarah.loew@web.de

S. Settegast
Department of Philosophy, Trier University, Trier, Germany
e-mail: settegast@uni-trier.de

D. Zink
Department of German Studies, Trier University, Trier, Germany
e-mail: zinkdo@uni-trier.de

© Springer Nature Switzerland AG 2021
C.-H. Mayer, E. Vanderheiden (eds.), *International Handbook of Love*,
https://doi.org/10.1007/978-3-030-45996-3_25

25.1 Introduction

Love relationships between patients at psychiatric clinics present themselves as a both multi-layered and auspicious topic for research, given that illness "is always also an expression of unsettled relationships, either to oneself, to other people, or to the meaning-conferring power." (Krolzik, 2000: 145. Translated by authors.) Particularly if approached from the perspective of cultural studies, which considers both the clinic as an institution and 'love' in its various forms as products of cultural formation processes, a focus on the phenomenon of love relationships at the clinic promises to illuminate both, given that the regime of hospitalization and the various types of love challenge, and thus shape, each other in multifaceted ways.

A phenomenon definitely observable in everyday clinical interactions, such relationships are frequently defined in the literature as "sexual and emotional involvement" (Buckley & Wiechers, 1999: 533). On this, Dein and Williams (2008) remark:

> New relationships are, in our experience, viewed with more concern than previously existing ones (284).

Kastner (2013) reports prevalence rates in-between 1.5% and 8% in psychiatric acute care facilities for adult patients. According to Steinberg, Rittner, Dormann, and Sprengler-Katerndahl (2012), the likelihood of sexual contact increases with the length of retention time at an institution; assisted living facilities, however, will be excluded from this article as they represent an altogether separate topic. While fewer than 3% of patients interviewed by Kastner (2013) at a rehabilitation clinic reported relationships or '*Kurschatten*', none of them reported sexual contacts. Kastner attributes these inconsistent prevalence rates to a lack of precise terminology: "for example, there are no adequate translations for '*Kurschatten*' into other, non-German languages" (105. Translated by authors). In what follows, we will use 'clinic' to denote any type of hospital aimed at the stationary care of patients with psychological disorders. Such care may represent a coercive context, which Großmaß (2010) understands as comprised of all the influences leading up to institutionalization that do not emanate from clients themselves. Großmann counts amongst these influences subjectively experienced push and pull factors (i.e., pressures and incentives) exerted by clients' formal and informal networks, as well as legal provisions, which are sometimes also understood as coercive contexts in a more narrow sense. Our contribution will focus on love in a clinical context between co-patients, not between patients and clinical staff since

> from a scientific, clinical, and psychotherapeutic point of view, any sexual contact during psychotherapeutic treatment represents without a doubt an abuse of the psychotherapist's position of power (Schleu, Tibone, Gutmann, & Thorwart, 2018: 11. Translated by authors)

and thus constitutes a separate, albeit rarely investigated topic for research. In this area, research particularly into child abuse within institutions has only recently been re-emphasized as a genuine desideratum (Andresen et al., 2019).

Since intimate relations among lovers

within clinics are never independent of the institutional context, even though individuals may hope for or fantasize this (Wellendorf, 2000: 58. Translated by authors),

we will begin with a survey of legal and ethical aspects, which have been subject to continually increasing study on the part of clinical researchers since the 1980s. We will complement this overview with an exposition of further objections to love at the clinic as raised by researchers from the perspective of psychodynamics.

Subsequently, we will describe love as a factor which is conducive to therapy. To this end, we will first indicate the importance of social support and emphasize the role of meaningfulness as a further crucial component. We will then explicate the concepts of *eros*, *philia*, and *agape*, as these represent diverging forms of love that need to be differentiated in terms of their therapeutic and ethical-normative potential. We will explore this potential in connection with the notion of 'ontological rootedness' in group-therapy settings, which recognizes in the concept of love something akin to a secular soteriology. Finally, we will broach some of the practical implications of our approach and specifically discuss how clinical staff might respond to cases of love at the clinic.

Both the institution of the clinic and the three concepts of love, which we will describe in greater detail later in this contribution, represent cultural constructs. We understand the term 'culture' to signify a context that, although in principle variable and changing, remains relatively stable over a given period of time and provides a frame of reference that renders particular utterances and actions intelligible as such. Thus, we presuppose a constructivist, non-essentialist conception of culture as a *signifying system* (Mecklenburg, 2009: 15). In Western culture since the advent of modernity, i.e. roughly from the late eighteenth century onwards, the leading concepts of love as much as the various kinds of hospital have been marked by their relation to the specifically modern form of subjectivity (cf. Foucault, 1973 for the case of the clinic and Foucault, 1978 for the case of love and desire). In relation to love relationships at psychiatric clinics, the tension between autonomy and heteronomy that is so decisive for the Western conception of subjectivity represents a neuralgic point. While implicitly presupposed for the most part, we will conjoin this discourse analytical point of departure with salutogenic approaches focusing on the connection between love and health (Mayer, 2012, 2018).

If, as Mayer (2018: 37) describes, love plays a crucial role in facilitating Antonovsky's sense of coherence and thus acts as a key factor in his salutogenic conception of health, then investigating the relationship between love and clinic is nothing short of essential, since the clinic is *expressis verbis* the institution devoted to the aim of restoring health. Within this triangulation of love, health, and clinic, situations in which the different types of love come into conflict with the regime of hospitalization will prove of particular interest, as they promise to produce new insights into all three objects of investigation.

25.2 Love at the Clinic: In-Between Self-Determination and Protection

The development of bourgeois society, particularly through the rise of the nuclear family, precipitated the emergence of a specifically bourgeois notion of love (Luhmann, 1994). A central constituent of this distinctively modern conception is the conviction, first articulated in Early German Romanticism, that one's choice of partner should be free and independent of social pressures and institutional constraints, i.e. subject to no authority beyond the feelings and emotions of the individuals involved. As much as this ideology and its aspirations diverged from lived reality during the late eighteenth and nineteenth centuries, it seems true enough that, since the 1960s, Western societies typically know "no directive institutions that would prescribe how to proceed, what to do and what not to do" (Bausinger, 2002: 4. Translated by authors) in choosing one's partner. On the contrary, there now appears to be "great freedom, free choice" (Ibid., 5. Translated by authors). Naturally, this should not be mistaken for a total absence of constraints relating to love and desire, but rather implies the internalization of such rules as currently govern intimate relationships. "[A]ny young person has to confront the fact of internalized control" (Ibd. Translated by authors). Accordingly, some have described this seemingly authentic and 'free' submission to personal feelings as a privileged access point for the operation of social power and social normalization tendencies (Foucault, 1978).

Sexuality represents a quintessential expression of this bourgeois notion of romantic love. Yet, both in ethical and legal respects, sexuality is also a special matter of patient care and supervision within the context of the psychiatric clinic. Given that sexual self-determination forms an incontestable constituent of modern subjectivity, it confronts the institution of the clinic with problems so grave that these tend to dominate any discussion of the topic 'love at the clinic'. For that reason, we will begin with a survey of current clinical practice in regard to sexual relations among patients.

Legally speaking, there is no doubt that sexual self-determination is a key constituent of individual liberty:

> The *Grundgesetz* (GG) of the Federal Republic of Germany enumerates sexuality [...] indirectly and implicitly among the personal liberties in Article 2 (Steinberg et al., 2012: 377. Translated by authors).

> In the field of action, the right to sexual self-determination secures a person's freedom to live out their sexuality according to their wishes and beliefs, be it alone or in consent with a partner, as well as their freedom from sexual exploitation or harassment. The individual's right to sexual self-determination ends where its exercise would come at the expense of another's protected sphere of self-determination (Zinsmeister, 2013: 48. Translated by authors).

This right is equally recognized in the US:

> Legally, consensual sexual relationships between adults are a right in our society (Dobal & Torkelson, 2004: 68).

Hence, it follows that

> the patient should have the right to privacy and also have the right to make the decision about engaging in a sexual relationship (Binder, 1985: 124).

At the same time, Steinberg et al. (2012) emphasize the responsibility of attending staff concerning sexual relations among patients, since staff is subject to guarantor liability in the context of child and adolescent psychiatry as well as in case of disorders and disabilities among adult patients, which limit or offset their capacity for free and informed decision-making. In such cases,

> [t]he disorder must [...] exclude free choice. In addition to the patient's capacity for comprehension, the voluntariness of their decision is of crucial import. It depends on whether a free examination of all relevant considerations is possible. Conversely, it is not possible to speak of free decision-making where the person concerned is subject to external influences on their will or their decision-making is determined by uncontrollable drives and thoughts (BayOlG NJW, 1992: 2100. Translated by authors),

which requires ascertainment by an authorized expert in a court of law. Provided no other legal guardian has yet been appointed, a mental health court will then determine a custodian. Disorders that may require such custodianship are, for example, primary dementias, intellectual disabilities, alcohol dependence and drug abuse in cases where the addiction has effected severe cerebral modifications, as well as cases of acute mania and of acute or severe chronic schizophrenia, although the latter have to be evaluated individually.

Where free decision-making is impossible, it is in custodians' responsibility to protect patients from the consequences of their actions, since we must assume that they would act differently if their present state of illness did not impair their capacity for responsible choice (Crefeld, 2011). If such patients undergo stationary treatment at an institution, they are in custody of the clinic, which may be held liable for possible consequences:

> One of the legal implications of sex between patients is that a female patient may press legal charges against the hospital or the assailant, claiming rape as a result of her hospital stay (Binder, 1985: 123).

While Dein and Williams (2008) specifically point out the "vulnerability of women to sexual abuse and exploitation" (285), men are also affected, although precise numbers are difficult to determine since an unspecifiable number of cases may remain unreported due to social stigma. Holbrook (1989) describes the climate of fear, particularly prevalent in the US, which surrounds potential lawsuits targeting staff and hospitals in cases of sexual contact between patients where these are not immediately reported to police, as well as the resultant over-reporting. Further problems are posed by the occurrence of pregnancies due to lack of contraceptives, by the transmission of sexually transmittable diseases (Buckley & Wiechers, 1999; Ford et al., 2003), and by patients "exchanging sex for money and goods" (Buckley & Wiechers, 1999: 532). As the authors of one study report, of 56 clinical experts asked to put their concerns in regards to patient sexuality in a hierarchy, the largest percentage placed sexual assault as the primary concern (46.4%) (Buckley & Wiechers, 1999: 532).

Hence, as is often the case in psychiatry, clinical staff is confronted with an ethical tension between the two poles of patient self-determination and patient protection. Given that

> [t]he patient has the right to be protected from exploitation during the course of a hospitalization (Binder, 1985: 124),

patients' liberty to engage in sexual acts must be restricted to competent adults, who are capable of free and informed decision-making. Any actual determination that a person's decision-making is not free, in the form of a judicial assessment and the appointment of a legal guardian, will usually represent the endpoint of a lengthy process. In the course of this process, therapeutic staff may alternatively arrive at the conclusion that, even though free decision-making remains possible to a patient overall, a dependent personality structure or relevant prior experiences with the patient nonetheless cast the patient's ability to consent into serious doubt. Holbrook (1989) discusses this complicating factor for patient protection under the heading of the "incompetent patient" (76).

In this respect, while in-between 25% (Buckley & Wiechers, 1999) and 87% (Buckley & Robben, 2000) of clinics polled in the US reported on having instituted hospital policies, "there is currently no standard for a sexual behavior policy for psychiatric inpatients" (Ford, Rosenberg, Holsten, & Boudreaux, 2003: 346). This has prompted several groups of researchers (Ford et al., 2003; Steinberg et al., 2012) to develop proposals concerning the regulation of sexuality at psychiatric hospitals, including possible measures for responding to violations of sexual self-determination. Patients, however, often actively undermine such hospital policies, in ways comparable to other policies such as smoking bans, as these may be read to stand in symbolically for the social reality principle from which they suffer in everyday life (Haubl, 2012). In such cases, patients may attempt to conceal their relationship from clinical staff. Thus, Warner et al. (2004) report that roughly a third of respondents engaged in sexual activities despite a 'no sex' policy. In contrast, some patients also deliberately arrange discovery of their relationship, which can then be factored into therapy (Bernhard & Lamprecht, 1991). Kastner and Linden (2011) characterize the ambience surrounding this hide-and-seek game as "holiday camp atmosphere" (18. Translation by authors).

A further aspect is that the prohibition itself can provoke a transference of aggression onto third parties, in that patients may come to perceive staff, insofar as it enacts the prohibition, as the source of their problems. On the patient side, this can represent a strategy for evading the issues that occasioned institutionalization in the first place. As to why love relationships are sought out *within* the context of the clinic, given that day release policies and weekend leaves of absence would usually allow for outside contacts, one may presume that the allure precisely lies in the interplay of prohibition and concealment. Patients thus come to use the hospital ward as a space for restaging real life areas of conflict—a circumstance that staff should not meet with censure or disdain but with an attitude of sympathy and understanding (Schauenburg, 2007).

It may seem as though these fields of conflict arise purely from the special circumstances of hospitalization, and specifically from the restrictions placed on lived sexuality at the clinic. More accurately, however, the context of the clinic merely foregrounds dynamics that are already comprised within the bourgeois notion of love itself, albeit in a mostly latent form. These dynamics can be summed up in the concept of yearning or longing, which represents a crucial constituent of romantic love. Yet, at the same time, longing is also a somewhat paradoxical element of love, for it does not merely consist in desiring an object that is unavailable. In its specifically romantic form, longing consists in an *infinite* movement toward the beloved, which is predicated on their ultimate unavailability, and as such acts both as the very source of one's lust for them and as the defining attribute of romantic love. Only where our longing for the other can never be satisfied, where our desire for them is infinite, are we faced with romantic love in its most genuine and paradigmatic form.

In its concrete manifestations, the dynamic of longing can take varied forms. In Friedrich Schlegel's novel *Lucinde* (1797), one of the first genuinely modern attempts at depicting a successful romantic love relationship, romance is framed as an infinite romantic game; a playful back and forth resembling a work of art. More common, and more akin to the clinical setting, however, are narratives of tragic romance, as these reveal how external obstacles can function as markers of authenticity for one's love. This aspect is perhaps most clearly articulated in what is arguably the greatest proto-narrative of romantic love ever written: Shakespeare's *Romeo and Juliet*. Although it is rare for love to be held onto even at the price of death, it is true that the bourgeois narrative of romantic love and longing contains as an essential feature an element of resistance and rebellion. Against this background, contexts of hospitalization appear predestined for the development of love relationships because the lovers may experience the kind of opposition these contexts enable as both an authentic revolt against subjectively illegitimate restrictions on their love as well as a confirmation that their feelings are genuine. Thus, it is precisely the perceived restriction of individual liberty which produces a desire that deems itself an authentic form of resistance (as described, e.g., in Foucault, 1978).

This illustrates very clearly how the concept of romantic love can come to conflict with the institution of the clinic in salutogenic respects. On the one hand, romantic love can contribute to a sense of coherence by creating meaningfulness and comprehensibility, for to love romantically is to comprehend one's relationship as meaningful. In this context, the longing inherent to romantic love is not perceived as an obstacle to manageability, but rather the reverse is true, for it acts as a guarantee for the infiniteness of one's love. On the other hand, however, the hospitalization regime regarding patient sexuality is at odds with this dimension of manageability, as the clinic needs to limit patients' sexual autonomy and, in consequence, will be experienced as an obstacle to manageability by them. Given the character of bourgeois romantic love, this basic conflict may be exacerbated through a self-reinforcing feedback loop: one's love may be experienced as particularly genuine and authentic precisely because the hospitalization regime is perceived as an obstacle to it. This dynamic may represent an underrated risk of love at psychiatric clinics.

25.3 Further Objections to Love at the Clinic

Even apart from the problems highlighted in the previous section, the literature abounds with objections to love relationship at the clinic. Frequently, the relationship is considered a potential threat to therapeutic success and interpreted, not as progress, but as resistance (Bernhard & Lamprecht, 1991) or as a way for patients to evade their problems (Kobbé, 1999).

One way for love to be counterproductive to therapy is secondary morbid gain, as when patients receive special care and attention precisely because they are ill, which tends to promote the perpetuation of their illness (Lackinger, 2013). Thus, patients might misattribute the attention they receive as part of the love relationship to their illness, and consequently hamper their recovery. A further, potentially problematic factor is the idealization of the other, which occurs as a pathological feature, e.g., in narcissistic personality disorder (Ermann, 2017), but also represents a commonplace precondition for falling and staying in love more generally (Kernberg, 1998). Stendhal (1944) famously called this 'crystallization', by which he meant the ongoing discovery of ever-new merits ('positive facets') in the beloved person. In extreme cases, the overestimation of the other's qualities can effect a dissolution of the boundaries of the self, when the "beloved and desired object of transference takes the place of the I" (Bernhard & Lamprecht, 1991: 106). This may at the same time function as a strategy for positive self-presentation.

> By loving someone who represents an ideal, I can partake in their brilliance (Mitscherlich, 2014: 163. Translated by authors),

which facilitates warding off or attenuating feelings of inferiority (Ibid.); a phenomenon Cialdini et al. (1976) refer to, in the case of identification with sports idols, as 'basking in reflected glory'. This reattribution of their situation, which is consequent on their idealization of the other, may then lead patients to an assessment of their own problems as less grave and their situation as less in need of change, since 'now that I am with my new partner, everything will be fine'. In ways comparable to vacation settings, patients' knowledge of the spatiotemporal limitations of their stay in stationary therapy, particularly of its finite character, fosters their relationship curiosity and motivation by the pleasure principle (Bernhard & Lamprecht, 1991: 105). This, in turn, facilitates denial of uncongenial characteristics and thus helps in sustaining the idealization; a pattern also observable in the case of 'vacation flings'.

Binder (1985) describes the spectrum of possible negative consequences when relationships between patients fail:

> The range of psychological response of patients to sexual contact includes observations that the experience was harmful and caused ego disintegration and psychotic regression, led to an emotional symbiosis that caused a decreased impetus towards independence, separation, and

growth, retarded recovery, and resulted in sexual promiscuity, acute decompensation or suicide when the patient experienced rejection at the end of the relationship (122).

Kastner (2013) adds emotional dependence and separation or divorce from a previous partner to this list. Hammelstein and Roth (2006) cite disinhibition as a facet of sensation seeking and describe it as a tendency to socially and sexually unconstrained patterns of behavior, impulsivity, and arousal seeking, as in high-risk sexual practices. Patient relationships exhibiting these factors can take on the character of deliberate risk-taking behavior and self-harm. A paradigm disorder displaying such tendencies is mania in its acute stages (Keitner & Grof, 1981), although patients do not exhibit sexually disinhibited behavior while in stable condition. According to Keitner, Baldwin, and McKendall (1986), certain diagnoses increase the probability of patients' engaging in relationships:

> Patients with a diagnosis of personality disorder, eating disorder, and bipolar disorder were more likely to be involved in relationships than patients with other diagnoses (169).

Kernberg (1998) differentiates various motivations for promiscuous behavior according to disorder, which range from feelings of guilt to feelings of arousal evoked by another person's withholding of their body.

In summary, the literature on love at the clinic contains significant objections to love relationships among patients. Nonetheless, and even before considering potential positive salutogenic effects that love relationships might exhibit in therapeutic contexts, it is necessary to acknowledge the inevitability and indispensability of patient relationships in the context of the therapeutic community. Against this background, we argue that lived sexuality, understood as a privative mode of romantic love, represents too narrow a notion of love to chart patient relationships in clinical contexts accurately, as is apparent when considering the difficulties that attach to drawing distinct boundaries between permitted and prohibited expressions of sexuality at the clinic. Which forms of sexual interaction are included in the prohibition? Should it also comprise kissing? If so, what about the erotic dimensions of intimate embrace? To avoid such ambiguities and come to a more differentiated assessment of patient relationships, we propose an expansive notion of love on which positive relationships of any type, such as acquaintances and friendships, exhibit at least one of love's different forms.

To this end, we will consider differing perspectives on and interpretations of 'love' as these are conditioned by their historicity and cultural anthropological background, for the various shapes that love at the clinic may take cannot be derived from any one concept of 'love' considered in isolation. Even our common practice of talking about love, in ordinary language and everyday contexts, and our emotional ability to recognize love phenomenally draw on a cultural and historical manifold of handed-down and intertwined concepts. In a nutshell, we are faced with an originally Hebrew and, more precisely, Old Testament inheritance, which has been enriched in the course of Western intellectual history with influences from the New Testament and from the philosophies of Plato and Aristotle:

> If love in the Western world has a founding text, that text is Hebrew. Before Plato and Aristotle—the other dominant sources of Western concepts of love—and well before Jesus, Hebrew Scripture provides [...] ideas that have guided the course of love ever since (May, 2011: 14).

In what follows, we will try to further differentiate these strands of conceptual development, within the limits of the present contribution, in order to present a richer picture of love's place at the clinic and its cultural framing. To that end, we will discuss patient relationships within the psychosomatic rehabilitation milieu and situate them in relation to the aforementioned Biblical, Platonic, and Aristotelian concepts. Naturally, these very concepts will also structure and predetermine the character and results of any such investigation from the very outset, given the constructivist conception of culture presupposed here.

25.4 Love as a Therapy-Conducive Factor

From a systemic point of view, it is important to note that remembered, imagined, lost, and longed for relationships fundamentally co-determine the experience of self and world, and that even patients eschewing the community and seeking to avoid or withdraw from relationships thereby exhibit a particular type of relation (that of rejection) to their therapeutic environment. At the clinic, there is no being 'outside' the web of relationships. On the contrary, and this separates love in clinical contexts from other types of 'exiled love', these relationships usually form an explicit subject for discussion—and often they are pathologically and diagnostically relevant, for example in the guise of the "Agony of Eros" described by Byung-Chul Han (2012). Consequently, patient relationships at the clinic, including love relationships, should not be considered as something that is merely to be tolerated or ideally even to be avoided. Rather, they should be recognized as harboring a therapeutic potential that can be seized on and developed in therapy-conducive ways. How then does love at the clinic need to be framed theoretically in order to enable a resource-oriented view of it?

Two cultural conditions for such a framing have emerged from our discussion so far, one relating to the genesis of our concept of 'therapeutic milieu', the other to our understanding of what we call 'love'. In the beginning, we claimed that there is a tension between both, which is at core defined by a conflict between autonomy and heteronomy. This point may be further substantiated in recourse to a discourse-analytical approach to the culture of the 'clinic', which highlights the 'therapeutic milieu' as one that is both hospitalized and hospitalizing. It embodies the operations of law and legal practice in a salutogenic context, which express themselves, in this constellation, as a type of "caring coercion" (Brink, 2010: 480. Translation by authors): Within the clinic, both the care of the patient and the self-care of the institutionalized system require coercive safeguards against love. Yet, phenomenally, the breaking out of 'love' tends to elude such restrictions, as it generally tends to elude any planning of surrounding conditions at the clinic. Ultimately, love operates according to its own laws: It just happens, often despite all efforts to contain it, and sometimes precisely because of them.

As discussed before, the phenomenon of 'love' blends together a number of culturally and historically grown concepts, whose difference and, at times, disparity may become particularly salient under restrictive coercion within the clinical context. For this reason, we will begin in what follows with a brief survey of current findings on (love) relationships within therapeutic milieus, in order to connect these with their own cultural-historical conditions. To that end, we will carve out the different roots of our concept of 'love' and, finally, consider their potential salutogenic characteristics.

Social support is an important therapy-conducive factor. It is one result of Kastner's (2013) survey that only one patient reported that their contact to other patients was worsening their therapy results. The majority of patients interviewed (159 patients), however, estimated that these contacts were improving their therapy results. On average, patients felt supported by their co-patients, either through receiving tangible practical help, comfort, or encouragement when asking for it. Moreover, they did not feel particularly burdened in emotional or practical terms by their co-patients (Kastner, 2013):

> In relation to therapy results, it needs to be emphasized that patients who classified their co-patients as friends exhibited better therapy results than those without friendly contacts to their co-patients (Kastner, 2013: 105).

Consequently, non-romantic relationships to co-patients are helpful and desirable from a therapeutic point of view, since bonding with others represents a central human need from early childhood on. It is already manifest in infancy that stable bonds to attachment figures are a crucial precondition for trust (Erikson, Erikson, & Kivnick, 1986). Hence, the experience of social support can function as an important resource for individuals. According to Bengel and Lyssenko (2012),

> perceived support—that is, the stable expectation to receive the desired and hoped for type of support in case of need (91. Translated by authors)—

has a protective effect.

Yet, as Mayer (2018) argues, not only functional social support but also love can have such a health-conducive effect. She emphasizes that love, health, and culture are closely interconnected. Binder (1985) similarly highlights the positive aspects:

> [r]eports suggest that emotional and sexual relationships may in fact have positive aspects because patients feel helpful to each other or patients may learn how to handle relationships or the patient may become more cheerful, energetic, and engaged in treatment (122).

Intimate relationships offer the opportunity to avoid feelings of loneliness and experience meaningfulness. Indeed, dyadic relationships have come to play a central role in the search for meaning since traditional horizons of meaningfulness, as provided by intact families, religious orientations, or commonly recognized social values, have become increasingly problematic and less important (Bausinger, 2002). Following Antonovsky (1979), meaningfulness, next to comprehensibility and manageability, is a key aspect of salutogenesis. Accordingly, Mayer (2018) emphasizes that,

> in order to promote health in a culture-specific and intercultural way, love has to be perceived as comprehensible, manageable, and meaningful (38. Translated by authors).

A striking literary illustration of an encouragement of romantic-emotional relationships among patients as a therapeutic strategy is provided by Paul Coelho (2000).

On the other hand, Kastner (2013) criticizes that

> it remains an open question whether confounding variables might explain the correlations, i.e. through which further factors patients might feel supported or burdened by their co-patients (35. Translated by authors).

She calls for a closer investigation into the efficient factors and side effects of patient relationships. In the context of our contribution, we intend to pursue this aim not empirically but by outlining a theoretical framework for such investigations. Correspondingly, in what follows we will describe love relationships in clinical contexts primarily, not from a legal, but from a salutogenic perspective in order to examine their therapeutic and ethical-normative potential. We have emphasized that, since sexuality represents one of its core components, the bourgeois notion of romantic love poses both ethical and legal challenges for the institution of the clinic and may, in salutogenic respects, also impede patient convalescence. For that reason, we will now attempt to untangle the various conceptual strands that, culturally and historically, have gone into framing our current understanding of love, in order to come to a more differentiated assessment. We emphasize the ethical-normative aspect because love within the conditions of a specific institutional framework takes on the form of a particular shaping of

> benevolence, in one person for this or that person. So conceived, love generates and shapes a certain relationship between them, and often these relationships involve roles. These role-relationships differ from one another in several ways, including the form of love for which they call [...], the level of good will they demand, and how important the distinctive type of good will is within the relationship. This variance generates a relativity that is crucially internal to morality (Garcia, 2019: 326).

The salutogenic and therapeutic potential of love relationships is connected to this perception of action-guiding roles, and thus to the individual motives and goals that condition and shape these relationships in the clinical contexts.

In order to provide some terminological clarification and capture the various types of love relationships in practically applicable concepts, it is helpful to consider the classic differentiation of love into *eros*, *philia*, and *agape*, which has been the subject of ample study from a cultural historical point of view by various disciplines. In this context, we will give particular emphasis to *agape* and its significance for salutogenesis. On the one hand, *agape* initially represents an elusive phenomenon from a contemporary point of view and thus requires careful re-articulation. On the other hand, as a form of love, it proves particularly congenial to current practical research on empathy and to the ethics of compassion; it thus exhibits great normative and psycho-educative potential.

25.5 Love as Eros, Philia, Agape

All three types of love have important historical roots. Both *eros* and *philia* derive from the Greek and particularly from the Platonic-Aristotelian tradition (Plato: Symposium, Phaedrus; Aristotle: Nicomachean Ethics VIII, IX), where *eros* is understood as passionate (but by no means only or predominantly sexual) love and *philia* designates the love in friendship. *Agape*, on the other hand, originally derives as a concept from the New Testament, where it signifies the love of God in its broadest sense, although later interpretations identify it with a 'boundless love' in the sense of charity (usually understood as *caritas*).

Eros is a form of love that promises no enduring happiness since passionate love is marked by *desire*, and desire particularly for what we do not have but seem to find in our partner. Only as human beings characterized by lack are we capable of loving erotically; and this is a love we experience both in romantic infatuation and in sexual desire, which often complement each other but may also occur separately. *Philia*, on the other hand, we experience in happily succeeding relationships, particularly in all types of friendship, of which exclusive relationships between two people represent a marginal case. For while *eros* and sexuality may equally belong to such relationships, they are not the only key features defining them. Thus, both forms of love can be connected, and in the development of our relationships, we may at times experience an oscillation between them. Classic interpretations often consider the appealing, *attractive* power of *eros* to reside in its ability to move us toward other, 'higher' forms of love: from a particular and insular love with its egoistic components to love's more universal forms. (For a more extensive explication of these concepts than can be given here, cf. the transdisciplinary studies of Comte-Sponville (2014) and Wischmeyer (2015), which also offer valuable and detailed surveys of the literature to date.)

While *eros* and *philia* thus remain congenial to modern ways of life and modern understandings of love, *agape* initially presents itself as much less accessible due to its original dependence on a specific sociohistorical context. The Greek term '*agape*' originally designates an early Christian form of communal life, while its Latin equivalent '*caritas*' accentuates, on current interpretations that take its early Christian background into account, an active and practical love of others (cf. Wischmeyer, 2015: 248 and Benedikt XVI, 2016). Thus,

> [w]ithin the postmodern discourse on love, neither a simple adoption of nor even a qualified recourse to this early Christian concept are possible: The basic religious and social-institutional conditions for the concept are no longer in place, neither in Western societies overall nor within the Christian churches specifically. This not only applies to the concept of *agape* in general, but also to that of charity (Wischmeyer, 2015: 255. Translated by authors. Also cf. Guanzini, 2016).

What is meant here, however, is the original notion of charity as developed in the first century CE. As such, *agape* is not obsolete but rather transformed, in the context of current discourses on love, into an ideal vanishing point that requires re-articulation apart from its Christian roots:

> Charity is, if it exists at all, a love liberated from the ego: a love without egoism, without possessiveness, an impartial and boundless love. Hence, charity seeks the universal, even though it does so within the singularity of a particular encounter (Comte-Sponville, 2014: 47. Translated by authors. Also cf. Wischmeyer, 2015: 255–265).

Of course, these three forms of love are only distinct from one another in theoretical reflection, and it would be senseless to accord (even normative) primacy to one of them. They represent culture-specific concepts handed down in tradition, which characterize various ways in which love relationships can take shape. They interfere with and permeate one another, and may condition and transition into each other: "We might more profitably use words like 'eros', 'agape' and 'philia' to name not distinctive types of love, but rather three modes of love's mature attentiveness" (May, 2012: 248). As such, these ways of loving are easily recognizable as aspects of our humanity on a purely phenomenal level.

25.6 Transitions: Agape and Caritas, Compassion and Empathy

Against the background of this triadic concept of love, Arthur Schopenhauer offers an important and, for the purposes of our contribution, helpful differentiation and interpretation of love in one of his more well-known dictums:

> [A]ll true and pure love is compassion *[Mitleid]*, and all love that is not compassion is selfishness. Selfishness is ερως; compassion is αγαπη. Both often occur in mixed form (Schopenhauer, 1844: § 69. Translated by authors).

Schopenhauer's view is particularly relevant for an understanding of love in clinical contexts because it has been deeply influential on current (neuro-) psychological, therapeutic (cf. Birnbacher, 2005; Lukits, 2016; Yalom, 2005), and ethical discourses and plays a role in contemporary research into empathy. Within the latter, it is known mostly as the 'ethics of compassion' *(Mitleidsethik)*, as encapsulated in the imperative:

> Harm no-one; rather, help anyone as much as you can (Schopenhauer, 1986. Translated by authors).

Unfortunately, Schopenhauer's notions of true love and compassion are often summarized under the heading of 'empathy', which represents a somewhat misleading constriction of his views, even though his writings are sometimes suggestive of it.

> Whatever kindness, love and generosity do for others, it is always only alleviation of suffering, and thus what can move them toward good deeds and works of love is only the

cognition of another's suffering, which is immediately intelligible from our own and equal to it. From this, it follows that pure love (αγαπη; caritas) is by its nature compassion; no matter whether the suffering it alleviates is big or small, as in any ungratified wish (Schopenhauer, 1844: §69. Emphasis and translation by authors).

It may thus seem obvious to identify Schopenhauer's 'compassion' with 'empathy'. On the one hand, however, such an interpretation neglects Schopenhauer's metaphysics of the will, which represents the basic framework that shapes his understanding of compassion. On the other hand, it proves anachronistic, as Titchener introduces 'empathy' in 1909 as the English translation of the German '*Einfühlung*' (Titchener 1909, 21f.).

Thus understood as a capacity, empathy represents a general human disposition that is capable both of neuropsychological description and of pedagogical and psycho-educative conceptualization (cf. e.g. Howe, 2013). Hence, empathy and whether it can be taught or learned receive particular attention in developmental psychology, where it is discussed in relation to the internalization of norms, the formation of conscience, and the development of social competence (Hopf, 2005; Hopf & Nunner-Winkler, 2007). Similarly, recent publications on therapeutic settings adapt empathy and 'compassion training' to therapeutic settings, especially for the shaping of therapist-patient-interactions (cf. Howe, 2013; Staemmler, 2009). In these contexts, empathy is typically differentiated into an emotional and a cognitive component, with the latter being prior to any experience of compassion as such. Compassion, or 'suffering with someone', is only possible where we are, in principle, capable of 'feeling with someone', and it is crucial to misunderstand this neither as an un-distanced 'emotional contagion' nor as 'sympathy'. Compassion does not consist in being overwhelmed by another's feelings. Rather,

in any moment, we remain clear about and alive to the fact that *he* is the one who suffers, not *we*: and that we feel this suffering *in his person*, not in ours. [...] We suffer *with* him, that is, *in* him; we feel his pain as *his* and are not under the illusion that it is ours (Schopenhauer, 1986: 743. Translated by authors).

Given this element of non-identification,

[e]mpathy cannot [...] simply be counted as either 'positive' or 'negative'. It appears more neutral, more directed toward comprehension of the other's state, more distanced in its integration of emotional and cognitive elements. From a certain distance, empathy holds the intermediate ground between self and other—a space, where the *pathos* or being affected, which results from the encounter, is linked with one's own interested activity of wanting to understand (Breyer, 2013: 13. Translated by authors).

In traversing this space, empathy is capable of several gradations:

In *cognitive* empathy we recognize what another person is feeling. In *emotional* empathy we actually feel what that person is feeling, and in *compassionate* empathy we want to help the other person to deal with his situation and his emotions (Ekman, 2003: 180).

Given these differentiations, empathy in itself cannot be equated with love, neither with *eros*, nor *philia*, nor *agape*, and love itself "is not reducible to empathy or social commitment" (Wischmeyer, 2015: 17. Translated by authors). Nonetheless, empathy represents a precondition for entering into resonance with other people, for reflecting feelings cognitively and emotionally, and thus for *cultivating* any form of love.

Schopenhauer's conception of love as compassion and its consequent identification with *agape* and *caritas* thus very much fit into current debates concerned with re-articulating the value and demands of charity. This is particularly true of the ethical impetus of Schopenhauer's view, which finds its counterpart in some more recent contributions to this debate.

> Even if charity does not exist, even if it is only an ideal, it still points us in a direction we can take: by loving ourselves a little less or a little better, by loving the other a little more for his sake and thus perhaps a little less for our own sake (Comte-Sponville, 2014: 148).

Yet, in asserting the ethical-normative character of compassion, Schopenhauer does not overlook the real life combinations of *eros* and *agape*, their mixings and tensions in any actual relationship.

> Even true friendship is always a mixture of selfishness and compassion: the former lies in our enjoyment of the friend's presence, whose individuality conforms to ours, and it almost always comprises the largest part; compassion expresses itself in our sincere sympathy with his weal and woe and the unselfish sacrifices we make for it (Schopenhauer, 1844: §67. Translated by authors).

In the discourse on exiled love in clinical contexts, empathy, love as compassion and *agape* form the conceptual framework for an understanding and practice of love as *ontological rootedness*.

25.7 Ontological Rootedness in Group Therapy Settings

In Simon May's history of love, 'ontological rootedness' designates a secular concept derived from a diagnosis of contemporary culture not unlike the one found in Han's *Agony of Eros*.

> Simon May assumes that the Christian concept of love has deeply influenced Western notions of value, and that this influence has even increased with the general weakening of the Christian religion within Western culture. While the foundational framework of the Christian religion wanes, the enormous demands directed at love remain in place (Wischmeyer, 2015: 251. Translated by authors).

May (2012) thus detects a vacuum, a kind of vacancy in the place we want to experience as love. This vacancy finds expression in a longing for *ontological rootedness*, which determines our understanding of what love is:

> Love is the rapture we feel for people who (or things that) inspire in us the experience or hope of ontological rootedness—a rapture that triggers and sustains the long search for a vital relationship between our being and theirs. We experience their mere presence as grounding—or as a promise of grounding—because it seems to be receptive to, to recognize, to echo, to provide a powerful berth to what we regard as most essential about us. Which very much includes our origins, and the strengths, vulnerabilities, sensibility and fate with which they endow us. And which, far from being purely private, is deeply influenced by models that we absorb from our parents, society and peers (240).

The strength of the clinical setting consists in the possibility of experiencing ontological rootedness within the protected space of the therapeutic community, i.e. apart from therapist-patient-interactions, which precisely do not allow for a love relationship as a horizon for making experiences, and in the possibility of integrating these experiences into the therapeutic process. It may appear doubtful whether this longing for ontological rootedness is ultimately capable of fulfillment, just as it appears doubtful whether charity as an ideal can actually be attained. Within the clinical setting, however, what is important is not their actual realization but the process of emotional and cognitive reflection on this longing and its potential fulfillment in (love) relationships, and on our role within such relationships. Depending on indication and therapy concept, the therapeutic setting and the community of co-patients may provide a suitable context for such reflection as well as suitable techniques. In various clinical group settings, particularly in emotion-focused psychotherapeutic rehabilitation centers, therapeutic communities are already being carefully introduced to the principles and techniques of non-violent communication and transaction analysis, and not merely with the aim of furthering a healthy climate within the group. Rather, by means of resource-oriented communication methods, co-patients are becoming co-therapists, who accompany each other in their individual processes of recovery. While this does not exclude conflicts among co-patients as part of the unfolding group dynamic, the importance of such conflicts for personal development is explicitly recognized and utilized within therapy.

Apart from such communication training, providing a suitable context for reflection on relationships and on the techniques of self-care and care for others may also be achieved by means of emotion- and empathy-focused psycho-education, which develops both the cognitive and emotional components of empathy and allows patients to derive individual options for action from it. The ideal of charity, as marked by the triad of *eros*, *philia*, and *agape*, can function both as the background for this education and as the goal of the group dynamical processes. It seems then that clinical settings are particularly suitable for corrective emotional experiences and cognitive reappraisals (Strauß, Kirchmann, Schwark, & Thomas, 2010) of satisfying community or successful separation, both of which are existentially human phenomena. As Hales, Romilly, Davison, and Talor (2006) remark:

> People who have been in abusive relationships perhaps need to be able to test more healthy ones, in safety, as part of rehabilitation (262).

Similarly, Johnson, Burlingame, Olsen, Davies, and Gleave (2005) count among "key group therapeutic relationship constructs—group climate, cohesion, alliance, and empathy" (310). These have a positive influence on therapeutic processes (Bormann & Strauß, 2012).

Even where relationships are only short-lived and merely represent 'pleasant momentary distractions' akin to 'vacation flings', empathetic persons are capable of exploring the reasons for separation and integrate them into a coherent narrative, without being broken by the experience. Where relationships are successful, they represent an opportunity for experiencing resonance, if the love directed at an intimate partner [...] becomes, in the sense of Martin Buber, the central place for the relationship between I and You in a world dominated by impersonal relationships, and the central space in which the things that *touch*, *grip* and *move* us manifest themselves (Rosa, 2016: 364f. Translated by authors).

25.8 Therapeutic Implications

Summarizing the current situation, there is a number of studies on the negative consequences of love relationships at the clinic while the opportunities offered by relationships between co-patients are seldom utilized for therapy:

> Where hospital policies exist, there is an understandable tendency to focus on the potential for coercion and dangerous sexual activity, but few seek to facilitate healthy relationships (Hales et al., 2006: 261).

If empathy represents an important precondition for healthy love relationships within the clinical setting—a hypothesis that would require further empirical study—it is equally required from therapeutic staff. Yet, according to Binder (1985), staff tends to react negatively to relationships between patients:

> Staff may feel angry [...] because they perceive the sexual behavior as a challenge of their authority (124),

which is already apparent in the choice of terminology to describe such relationships between patients. In English, these relationships are sometimes referred to as 'pairings', a term that designates "originally the mating behavior of rats (sic!)" (Kobbé, 1999: 12. Translated by authors). In regard to staff response, Keitner and Grof (1981) report that "23% separated the involved patients" (189), again a choice of words reminiscent of handling animals or quarreling children. In this connection, Dein and Williams (2008) explicitly warn not "to infantilise patients" (285). The feelings of shame that may be occasioned by this constellation find a particularly drastic but not fully unrealistic depiction in the movie *One Flew Over the Cuckoo's Nest*, in which the head nurse's negative reaction to discovering a patient's sexual activity ultimately drives him into suicide.

Perlin (1994) subsumes the prejudices against mentally ill persons and their sexuality under the heading of "sanist myths of the mentally ill" (537), which he summarizes as follows:

> Mentally ill individuals are 'different,' and, perhaps, less than human. They are erratic, deviant, morally weak, sexually uncontrollable, emotionally unstable, lazy, superstitious, ignorant, and demonstrate primitive morality. They lack the capacity to show love or affection (Perlin, 1994: 537).

As Wan-Yuk Harley, Boardman, and Craig (2012) report, patients and staff tend to come, to some extent, to differing assessments of patient relationships:

> The researcher was up to three times more likely to report a problem than the participant (1297).

It is therefore necessary for staff to reflect on their own therapeutic stance and possible prejudices, and to muster empathy for any kind of relationship between patients, irrespective of staff's own evaluation of its functionality. Yet, such empathy should not come to take on the form described by Binder (1985):

> Staff may also feel that a relationship is helpful to a patient and may give tacit silent approval by not reporting the event (125).

At the same time, every relationship needs to be evaluated on its own individual terms, and this renders the enforcement of universal rules, which need to apply equally to all, more difficult.

Institutionalization is often necessary for patients with severe personality disorders (Schauenburg, 2007), whose ego weakness often entails a far-reaching attachment disorder that expresses itself in an insecure, fearful-ambivalent or disorganized attachment style (Strauß, 2012).

> Persons with an insecure attachment style often are less capable of empathy, and have greater difficulty perceiving and communicate their emotions (Bengel & Lyssenko, 2012: 87. Translated by authors).

Nonetheless, as described above, empathy can be fostered and facilitated in a clinical setting, for example by means of perspective-taking, another central technique of psychotherapy that is equally useful both for patients and therapists in assessing clinical relationships.

A notable limitation of our approach consists in the fact that we have mostly considered research from Central Europe and Northern America, which we take to be representative of a 'Western approach' to love at the clinic and which does not allow conclusions regarding other cultural contexts. Hofstede (2001), in an attempt at differentiating cultures at the macro-level, devises the categories of 'individualism' and 'collectivism' and states that, e.g.,

> Chinese culture countries score considerably lower on individualism than those of the Western world (210);

a difference that would surely also impact respective framings of love. Within the confines of the present contribution, we can only indicate such differences in culturally shaped interpretations of love; a closer investigation might be a promising direction for future research. Moreover, research into whether there are gender-differences in the way relationships at the clinic are experienced represents another important desideratum (Wan-Yuk Harley et al., 2012).

In conclusion, as the history of the *Kurschatten* demonstrates (Bleymehl-Eiler, 2007), attitudes to love at the clinic are zeitgeist dependent. Regarding the developmental trajectory of research, it is noticeable that research on the issue has moved since its beginnings in the 1980s from polling hospital staff (e.g. Keitner et al., 1986) to polling the patients concerned (e.g. Kastner, 2013); a tendency that may be interpreted as a turn toward the subject and away from a mere objectification of patients. Similarly, there has been a decrease of paternalistic and moralizing assessments over time:

It was felt that this particular relationship was destructive for both patients for a number of reasons. It was inappropriate for Mrs. A. because she was married, because she was older than Mr. G. [...] (Keitner & Grof, 1981: 190).

It remains to hope then that patient relationships at the clinic will be regarded in a more resource-oriented manner in the future, and that ontological rootedness will play a larger role in future research into love at the clinic.

References

Andresen, S., Briken, P., Bergmann, C., Keupp, H., Kavemann, B. Katsch, M., et al. (2019). *Geschichten die Zählen. Bilanzbericht 2019 der unabhängigen Kommission zur Aufarbeitung sexuellen Kindesmissbrauchs, Band I.* Verfügbar unter https://www.aufarbeitungskommission.de/wp-content/.../Bilanzbericht-2019_Band-I.pdf [20.5.2019].

Antonovsky, A. (1979). *Health, stress, and coping. New perspectives on mental and physical well-being.* San Francisco: Jossey-Bass.

Bausinger, H. (2002). *Anbandeln, Anbaggern, Anmachen. Zur Kulturgeschichte der Annäherungsstrategien. Vortrag, gehalten am 6.7.02 in Tübingen zum 25.* Jubiläum der pro familia Tübingen/Reutlingen.

BayOLG (Bayerisches Oberstes Landesgericht). (1992). *Neue Juristische Wochenschrift, 2100*.

Benedikt, XVI. (2016). Gott ist die Liebe: Die Enzyklika "Deus caritas est". Vollständige Ausgabe. Ökumenisch kommentiert von Bischof Wolfgang Huber, Metropolit Augoustinos Labardakis, Karl Kardinal Lehmann. Freiburg i. Br.: Herder

Bengel, J., & Lyssenko, L. (2012). Resilienz und psychologische Schutzfaktoren im Erwachsenenalter – Stand der Forschung zu psychologischen Schutzfaktoren von Gesundheit im Erwachsenenalter. Bundeszentrale für gesundheitliche Aufklärung (Hrsg.). *Forschung und Praxis der Gesundheitsförderung, 43*, 1–147.

Bernhard, P., & Lamprecht, F. (1991). Die verheimlichte Beziehung – der "Kurschatten". *Praxis der Psychotherapie und Psychosomatik, 36*, 104–112.

Binder, R. L. (1985). Sex between psychiatric inpatients. *Psychiatric Quarterly, 57*(2), 121–126.

Birnbacher, D. (2005). Schopenhauer und die moderne Neurophilosophie. *Schopenhauer-Jahrbuch, 86*, 133–148.

Bleymehl-Eiler, M. (2007). *Der Kurschatten: Ein Tabu bei Licht betrachtet. Eine Ausstellung der Stiftung Kur-, Stadt-, Apothekenmuseum Bad Schwalbach* [August 2006 bis Februar 2007].

Bormann, B. & Strauß, B. (2012). Therapeutische Beziehungen in Gruppen. In B. Strauß & D. Mattke (Hrsg.), Gruppenpsychotherapie: Lehrbuch für die Praxis (S. 69–84). Berlin: Springer.

Breyer, T. (2013). *Grenzen der Empathie. Philosophische, psychologische und anthropologische Perspektiven.* Paderborn: Fink.

Brink, C. (2010). *Grenzen der Anstalt. Psychiatrie und Gesellschaft in Deutschland 1860–1980.* Göttingen: Wallstein.

Buckley, P. F., & Robben, T. (2000). A content analysis of state hospital policies on sex between inpatients. *Psychiatric Services, 51*(2), 243–245.

Buckley, P. F., & Wiechers, I. R. (1999). Sexual behavior of psychiatric inpatients: Hospital responses and policy formulation. *Community Mental Health Journal, 35*(6), 531–536.

Cialdini, R. B., Borden, R. J., Thorne, A., Walker, M. R., Freeman, S., & Sloan, L. R. (1976). Basking in reflected glory: Three (football) field studies. *Journal of Personality and Social Psychology, 34*(3), 366–375.

Coelho, P. (2000). *Veronika beschließt zu sterben.* Zürich: Diogenes.

Comte-Sponville, A. (2014). *Liebe. Eine kleine Philosophie.* Zürich: Diogenes.

Crefeld, W. (2011). *Beurteilung der Fähigkeit zur freien Willensbildung. Thesenpapier zur Einführung in das Thema der Arbeitsgruppe 9 des 2.* Bayerischen Betreuungsgerichtstags 20.07.2011.
Dein, K., & Williams, P. S. (2008). Relationships between residents in secure psychiatric units: Are safety and sensitivity really incompatible? *Psychiatric Bulletin, 32*, 284–287.
Dobal, M. T., & Torkelson, D. (2004). Making decisions about sexual rights in psychiatric facilities. *Archives of Psychiatric Nursing, 18*(2), 68–74.
Ekman, P. (2003). *Emotions revealed: Recognizing faces and feelings to improve communication and emotional life.* New York: Times Books.
Erikson, E. H., Erikson, J. M., & Kivnick, H. Q. (1986). *Vital involvement in old age.* New York: Norton.
Ermann, M. (2017). *Psychoanalyse heute: Entwicklungen seit 1975 und aktuelle Bilanz* (3. Aufl.). Stuttgart: Kohlhammer.
Ford, E., Rosenberg, M., Holsten, M., & Boudreaux, T. (2003). Managing sexual behavior on adult acute care inpatient psychiatric units. *Psychiatric Services, 54*(3), 346–350.
Foucault, M. (1973). *The birth of the clinic.* New York: Pantheon Books.
Foucault, M. (1978). *The history of sexuality.* New York: Pantheon Books.
Garcia, J. L. A. (2019). Love and moral structures: How love can reshape ethical theory. In A. M. Martin (Hrsg.), *The Routledge handbook of love in philosophy* (S. 325–332). London: Routledge.
Großmaß, R. (2010). Hard to reach – Beratung in Zwangskontexten. In C. Labonté-Roset, H.-W. Hoefert & H. Cornel (Hrsg.), *Hard to reach. Schwer erreichbare Klienten in der Sozialen Arbeit* (S. 173–185). Berlin: Schibri.
Guanzini, I. (2016). Agape – (Post)Modern? Žižek, Badiou, Taylor: (Post-)Säkulare Rezeptionen einer biblischen Kategorie. *Aisthema, 3*(2), 39–64.
Hales, H., Romilly, C., Davison, S., & Talor, P. J. (2006). Sexual attitudes, experience and relationship amongst patients in a high security hospital. *Criminal Behaviour and Mental Health, 16*, 254–263.
Hammelstein, P. & Roth, M. (2006). Das Bedürfnis nach stimulation: "sensation seeking". In B. Renneberg & P. Hammelstein (Hrsg.), *Gesundheitspsychologie* (S. 67–72). Heidelberg: Springer.
Han, B.-C. (2012). *Agonie des Eros.* Berlin: Matthes & Seitz.
Haubl, R. (2012). Der institutionelle und organisatorische Kontext von Gruppen am Beispiel stationärer Gruppenpsychotherapie. In B. Strauß & D. Mattke (Hrsg.), *Gruppenpsychotherapie. Lehrbuch für die Praxis* (S. 99–107). Berlin: Springer.
Hofstede, G. (2001). *Culture's consequences* (2nd ed.). Thousand Oaks, CA: Sage.
Holbrook, T. (1989). Policing sexuality in a modern state hospital. *Hospital and Community Psychiatry, 40*(1), 75–79.
Hopf, C. (2005). *Frühe Bindungen und moralische Entwicklung. Aktuelle Befunde zu psychischen und sozialen Bedingungen moralischer Eigenständigkeit.* Weinheim: Juventa.
Hopf, C., & Nunner-Winkler, G. (2007). *Frühe Bindungen und moralische Entwicklung. Aktuelle Befunde zu psychischen und sozialen Bedingungen moralischer Eigenständigkeit.* Weinheim: Juventa.
Howe, D. (2013). *Empathy. What it is and why it matters.* Oxford: Random House.
Johnson, J., Burlingame, G. M., Olsen, J., Davies, D. R., & Gleave, R. L. (2005). Group climate, cohesion, alliance, and empathy in group psychotherapy: Multilevel structural equation models. *Journal of Counseling Psychology, 52*, 310–321.
Kastner, S. (2013). *Beziehungen und soziale Unterstützung zwischen Patienten in psychosomatischer Rehabilitation.* (Elektronisch publizierte Dissertation, FU Berlin). Verfügbar unter https://refubium.fu-berlin.de/handle/fub188/13682?show=full&locale-attribute=en [21.05.2019].
Kastner, S. & Linden, M. (2011). Beziehungen im sozialen Netz und im therapeutischen Milieu. In M. Linden (Hrsg.), *Therapeutisches Milieu. Healing Environment in medizinischer*

Rehabilitation und stationärer Behandlung (S. 15–28). Berlin: Medizinisch Wissenschaftliche Verlagsgesellschaft.

Keitner, G. I., Baldwin, L. M., & McKendall, M. J. (1986). Copatient relationships on a short-term psychiatric unit. *Hospital and Community Psychiatry, 37*(2), 166–170.

Keitner, G. I., & Grof, P. (1981). Sexual and emotional intimacy between psychiatric inpatients: Formulating a policy. *Hospital and Community Psychiatry, 32*(3), 188–193.

Kernberg, O. F. (1998). *Liebesbeziehungen: Normalität und Pathologie*. Stuttgart: Klett-Cotta.

Kobbé, U. (1999). Vom Begehren des anderen . . . Paarbildungen in der stationären Suchttherapie: Fortschritt oder Widerstand? In H. Westendarp & M. Zumhagen (Hrsg.), *Sexualität in der stationären Suchttherapie. Beiträge zur Differenzierung der Suchttherapie* (S. 8–26). Klinik Brilon-Wald.

Krolzik, U. (2000). Heilsame Dialoge in Begegnungen. In W. Ruff (Hrsg.), *Heilsame Begegnungen: Netzwerke in der stationären Psychotherapie* (S. 149–156). Göttingen: Vandenhoeck & Ruprecht.

Lackinger, F. (2013). Primärer und sekundärer Krankheitsgewinn bei delinquenten Patienten. *Persönlichkeitsstörungen– Theorie und Therapie, 13*(1), 33–42.

Luhmann, N. (1994). *Liebe als Passion. Zur Codierung von Intimität*. Suhrkamp: Frankfurt/M.

Lukits, G. (2016). Empathie und Empirie: Rogers' Verstehenszugänge und ihre Voraussetzungen in der Erkenntnistheorie Schopenhauer. Ein philosophischer Anstoß. *Personnel, 20*(1), 63–71.

May, S. (2012). *Love. A history*. New Haven: Yale University Press.

Mayer, C.-H. (2012). Der Einfluss von Kultur und Spiritualität auf die Gesundheit. *Der Mensch, 44*(1), 15–21.

Mayer, C.-H. (2018). Die Liebe – Interkulturelle Perspektiven auf ein universelles Konzept zur Gestaltung von Gesundheitskulturen. *Der Mensch, 56*(1), 34–29.

Mecklenburg, N. (2009). *Das Mädchen aus der Fremde. Germanistik als interkulturelle Literaturwissenschaft*. München: Iudicum.

Mitscherlich, M. (2014). *Eine Liebe zu sich selbst, die glücklich macht*. Frankfurt/M: Fischer.

Perlin, M. L. (1994). Hospitalized patients and the right to sexual interaction: Beyond the last frontier. *New York University Review of Law and Social Change, 20*(3), 517–548.

Rosa, H. (2016). *Resonanz – Eine Soziologie der Weltbeziehung*. Berlin: Suhrkamp.

Schauenburg, H. (2007). Stationäre psychodynamisch–psychoanalytische Psychotherapie. *Psychotherapie im Dialog, 8*(1), 16–20.

Schleu, A., Tibone, G., Gutmann, T., & Thorwart, J. (2018). Sexueller Missbrauch in der Psychotherapie. Notwendige Diskussion der Perspektiven von Psychotherapeuten und Juristen. *Psychotherapeutenjournal, 17*, 11–19.

Schopenhauer, A. (1844). *Die Welt als Wille und Vorstellung* (Vol. Bd. I). Leipzig: Suhrkamp.

Schopenhauer, A. (1986). *Preisschrift über die Grundlage der Moral*. In Ders.: Sämtliche Werke. Textkritisch bearbeitet u. hrsg. v. Wolfgang Frhr. von Löhneysen. Frankfurt/M. Bd. 3, S. 743f.

Staemmler, F. M. (2009). *Das Geheimnis des Anderen – Empathie in der Psychotherapie. Wie Therapeuten und Klienten einander verstehen*. Stuttgart: Klett-Cotta.

Steinberg, R., Rittner, C., Dormann, S., & Sprengler-Katerndahl, D. (2012). Verantwortlicher Umgang mit Sexualität – Empfehlungen in einer klinischen Einrichtung. *Der Nervenarzt, 83*, 377–383.

Stendhal. (1944). *Über die Liebe*. München: Zinnen.

Strauß, B. (2012). Die Gruppe als sichere Basis: Bindungstheoretische Überlegungen zur Gruppenpsychotherapie. In B. Strauß & D. Mattke (Hrsg.), *Gruppenpsychotherapie: Lehrbuch für die Praxis* (S. 86–96). Berlin: Springer.

Strauß, B., Kirchmann, H., Schwark, B., & Thomas, A. (2010). *Bindung, Sexualität und Persönlichkeitsentwicklung*. Stuttgart: Kohlhammer.

Titchener, E. B. (1909). *Lectures on the experimental psychology of the thought processes*. New York: The Macmillan Company.

Wan-Yuk Harley, E., Boardman, J., & Craig, T. (2012). Friendship in people with schizophrenia: A survey. *Social Psychiatry and Psychiatric Epidemiology, 47*(8), 1291–1299.

Warner, J., Pitts, N., Crawford, M. J., Serfaty, M., Prabhakaran, P., & Amin, R. (2004). Sexual activity among patients in psychiatric hospital wards. *Journal of the Royal Society of Medicine, 97*, 477–479.

Wellendorf, F. (2000). Die Institution Klinik als Netzwerk von Begegnungen. In W. Ruff (Hrsg.), *Heilsame Begegnungen: Netzwerke in der stationären Psychotherapie* (S. 57–68). Göttingen: Vandenhoeck & Ruprecht.

Wischmeyer, O. (2015). *Liebe als Agape. Das frühchristliche Konzept und der moderne Diskurs.* Tübingen: Mohr Siebeck.

Yalom, I. (2005). *The Schopenhauer cure.* New York: Harper.

Zinsmeister, J. (2013). Rechtsfragen der Sexualität, Partnerschaft und Familienplanung. In J. Clausen & F. Herrath (Hrsg.), *Sexualität leben ohne Behinderung* (S. 47–72). Stuttgart: Kohlhammer.

Dominic Harion M.A. is a research and development specialist for educational sciences and didactics at the Luxembourg Centre for Educational Testing (LUCET) at the University of Luxembourg. He studied German language and literature, philosophy, and educational sciences at the University of Trier, where he was a research fellow with the German department from 2011 till 2015 and recently finished his PhD. He is a certified behavioral trainer and university instructor in German studies, educational sciences, and the didactics of ethics.

Dr. Sarah Francesca Löw M.Sc. received her Ph.D. from the Europa-Universität Viadrina Frankfurt (Oder) in 2017 for a dissertation on resilience and resources. Since 2017 she is being apprenticed as a psychological psychotherapist (Depth Psychology) at the Rhein-Eifel Institute Andernach. From 2015 till 2018, she worked as research fellow at the university hospital in Regensburg, and from 2018 till 2019 as resident psychologist at a psychiatric acute care facility in Trier. From 2008 till 2014, she studied psychology, sociology, philosophy, and ethnology at the Universities of Trier and Santiago de Compostela (ES).

Sascha Settegast M.A. is research fellow in philosophy at the University of Trier, where he is currently working on a doctoral dissertation on the concepts of nature and human nature in contemporary neo-Aristotelian virtue ethics. He studied philosophy and history at the University of Trier and at Jesus College Oxford. Prior to his appointment in Trier, he held a position at the University of Oslo and also did research at the University of St Andrews and the University of Arizona. He specializes and has published in normative and applied ethics.

Dr. Dominik Zink is research fellow at the University of Trier, where he is currently writing a book on literary conceptions of truth around the year 1800 as part of his habilitation. He studied German language and literature studies and philosophy at the Universities of Würzburg and Trier and received his PhD in 2016 from the Europa-Universität Flensburg for a dissertation titled "Interkulturelles Gedächtnis. Ost-westliche Transfers bei Saša Stanišić, Nino Haratischwili, Julya Rabinowich, Richard Wagner, Aglaja Veteranyi und Herta Müller". Apart from intercultural German studies, theories of cultural memory, and poetology, he also works on German-Jewish literature, culinary arts, and on Early German Romanticism both in its literary and philosophical guises.

Chapter 26
Love from a Psychotherapeutic Perspective Including Case Studies: The Need for Effective Altruism

Hans-Jörg Lütgerhorst, Sabine Diekmeier, and Jörg Fengler

Abstract A distinction has to be made between erotic love and love for one's neighbor in the sense of charity. While the former implies a serious rupture in the therapeutic alliance requiring immediate supervision and termination of psychotherapy in most cases, the latter in everyday language in various cultures is used as a synonym for extended sympathy presupposing empathy, affection, compassion, care, reliability and effort taking. However, the perception of a good therapeutic alliance and culture by the client also complies with an ascription of competence to the therapist and an early improvement of clients' complaints. Therefore the term "effective altruism" is outlined.

In general, effective psychotherapy requires basic emotional-social intelligence, knowledge about disturbances and disorders, about intervention methods and techniques, self-care and treatment competence including intercultural and group-therapy treatment experiences. It should draw upon different value systems and concepts of meaningfulness, gender, religion, level of education and linguistic patterns, especially in intercultural scenarios in order to promote effective altruism. Furthermore, the knowledge of a critical window for success within the early sessions ought to be modified in terms of an extended number of sessions for intercultural settings. A "culture of analyzing ruptures" is suggested to deal with stagnation or even failures in psychotherapy. Six case vignettes are presented to illustrate how "love" can be realized by active charity/effective altruism (The terms are used synonymously) in intercultural psychotherapeutic settings and how transference and countertransference are involved.

H.-J. Lütgerhorst (✉)
Akademie für Verhaltenstherapie, Köln, Germany
e-mail: Hans-Joerg@Luetgerhorst.de

S. Diekmeier
Justus-Liebig-University, Gießen, Germany
e-mail: sabine.diekmeier@psychol.uni-giessen.de

J. Fengler
Fengler-Institut für Angewandte Psychologie, Köln, Germany
e-mail: info@fengler-institut.de

© Springer Nature Switzerland AG 2021
C.-H. Mayer, E. Vanderheiden (eds.), *International Handbook of Love*,
https://doi.org/10.1007/978-3-030-45996-3_26

Keywords Love · Psychotherapy · Erotic love · Active charity · Empathy · Treatment competence · Intercultural experiences · Analyzing ruptures · Effective altruism · Group therapy

"Love thy neighbour as thou lovest thyself" (Matthew 22:39, NT-KJ) and corresponding commandments in the Koran and in other religions outlined in chapters in this book.

Our view is restricted to psychotherapy as carried out by clinical psychologists, psychiatrists, counselors and other psychosocial professionals.[1] We include all of these when using the term "psychotherapist" or in short "therapist".[2] We favor a multi-method, transdiagnostic and eclectic orientation based upon behavior therapy, psychodynamic and systemic elements.

26.1 Love Within the Therapeutic Alliance, Transference and Countertransference

Using the broad term of love within the psychotherapeutic context can elicit a diversity of reactions, depending on the cultural frame of reference, the linguistic meaning of the word love and the therapeutic background. Clients developing loving feelings towards their therapist form a common risk in all these professions, partly accounted for by the intimacy of the therapeutic setting and relationship. Spending a considerable amount of time in a one-to-one setting, sharing biographical and emotional experiences in a safe and appreciative setting can elicit warm feelings towards the therapist showing attention, closeness and empathy. Vice versa, being on the giving side of this interaction can easily satisfy the therapist's own needs for admiration, power, feeling needed etc. The differentiation between helpful and harmful needs, motives and behaviors within such an intense interpersonal yet professional relationship, lays therefore a basis for working effectively within the healthcare profession. It is however seldom a concrete part of the training for becoming a psychosocial professional. This lacking can be attributed to the resistance against and tabooing of talking about a subject that might involve breaking the code of medical and psychotherapeutic ethics as elaborated in country specific codes of conduct or respective literature (Pope & Vasquez, 2016).

Concerning the therapeutic relationship, a lot of literature has been written, as the quality of the therapeutic bond between the therapist and the client is one influential factor for the success of therapy (Clarkson, 2003; Gelso & Hayes, 1998; Lambert &

---

[1] Hereunder, we are referring to male, female and diverse when using the masculine form.

[2] Likewise, the terms "psychotherapy" or "therapy" refer to all of these professions and we also include "counseling", for in various countries there is no distinct differentiation made between the two.

Barley, 2001; Norcross & Lambert, 2019). We refer to the concept presented by Gelso & Hayes (1998), who differentiate between three elements of the therapeutic relationship: the real relationship, the working alliance and the transference-countertransference configuration.

In their understanding the real relationship describes the personal contact, characterized by the genuineness and authenticity the two parties show each other and the realism between therapist and client ("do I perceive my counterpart in ways that match the other"). A strong real relationship would be characterized by fundamentally positive feelings toward the other, in a setting which allows one's own authenticity and the realistic perception of the other. The fundament of positive valence does not exclude the arising of negative emotions during the process of therapy, nor does it exclude loving or erotic feelings occurring at some stages. As groundwork on the therapist's side, there should be an unconditional positive regard towards the client. In optimum, you would find feelings of compassion and altruistic charity towards the client.

The working alliance can be conceptualized as the joining of a client's reasonable side with a therapist's working or analyzing side (Gelso & Hayes, 1998): Do client and therapist act in concert? In a good working alliance, there's a mutual understanding: therapist and client agree on the goals the client wants to achieve, the tasks that need to be fulfilled to reach set goals, and share a strong bond formed by the trust that set tasks will lead to set goals (Bordin, 1979). During the therapeutic process the working alliance is dynamic, as it is an ongoing negotiation between the therapist and the client, between the interventions the therapist offers and the client's willingness to engage with them. The working alliance contains the ongoing processes of agreeing, pursuing and negotiating the goals and aims to get there in relationship to the values of the client, e.g. are the goals the client expects us to reach realizable? Is the client motivated to implement what he is learning within the therapy sessions etc.? In this part, feelings of love are not expected to occur.

The transference-countertransference is explained below. It has historically been of special interest within psychoanalysis, where the concept originated. While there are several definitions of these concepts, we will refer to Gelso & Hayes' working definition: Transference as the process during which the client's rather unconscious psychological structure, his experiences and derived expectations influence his perception and behavior towards the therapist—though the contribution of the therapist's person and behavior to transference shouldn't be neglected. Different therapists can elicit different transferences, according to their own characteristics. Transference represents a displacement of earlier relationships toward the current one, so to say the role of a former attachment figure, assigned by the client to the therapist. Countertransference on the other hand describes the therapist's rather unconscious internal and external reactions to the client, derived from his own unresolved conflicts and vulnerabilities (Gelso & Hayes, 1998), as well as his attachment experiences and present attachment style (Peter & Böbel, 2020). It can also depend on the role assigned to the therapist and the perceived transference, and the therapist's unfulfilled needs, be it only the one for romantic love, as two of the authors being supervisors can confirm.

A client with desire for close and intensive relationships, who's feeling helpless without them may in transference make the therapist seem to be the good Samaritan, the savior. The client might perceive the therapist as the person capable of fulfilling the desire for a strong counterpart that soothes, supports, and solves the patient's problems. This might be accompanied by romantic feelings and idealization towards the therapist. In countertransference, the therapist might experience concern, responsibility, but also the fear of being engrossed by the client's neediness. If the therapist accepts the role of the savior and acts upon it, this might be counterproductive as it might fortify the client's dependency on a strong counterpart keeping him in a passive state, and harbors the risk of the development of dysfunctional dynamics.

In cognitive behavioral therapies (see Chap. 59), the occurrence of loving feelings on the client's side is widely acknowledged, though falling short of the theoretical implications and options for therapeutic intervention that the psychodynamic theories offer. In cognitive behavioral therapies it is rather handled as a possible critical situation which should be addressed empathetically but clearly, while psychodynamic therapies can use interpretations to aim at increasing the client's insights on his transference and subjacent patterns of perception, experiencing and interpretation.

If a therapist notices romantic feelings towards a client these are often supposed to be understood in the light of countertransference processes and preferably not to be disclosed to the client (Gelso, Pérez Rojas, & Marmarosh, 2014). It is clearly communicated as a reason to seek supervision and not to be acted out, as this would mean a severe disruption of the therapeutic relationship with harmful consequences on the client as well as the therapist.

26.2 Judicial Aspects

Judicially, sexual activity with a client within a counseling, treatment or care relationship—even with consent—is considered a felony and can be penalized with up to 5 years imprisonment (in Germany). It is therefore clear that love or—more accurately—erotic love within a therapeutic alliance has a very destructive impact. In the Anglo-American area, an anonymous survey revealed 7.1% of the male psychiatrists having had sexual encounters with clients, while 3.1% of female psychiatrists admitted having done so (Gartrell, Herman, Olarte, Feldstein, & Localio, 1986). When asking therapists how many clients reported sexual contact to a former therapist or health-worker (not differentiating between nurses, psychiatrists, psychotherapists), the numbers rose to 22.7% (Halter, Brown, & Stone, 2007). Due to feelings of guilt and shame, the number of cases reported by clients may only represent a fraction of a larger dark figure, though professional sexual misconduct can lead to sexual traumatization, massive ambivalence or despair on the clients side (Trabert 2014). In the context of sexual "love", it is remarkable to note that according to the well-known psychoanalyst Kernberg (1999) it often is the female client who seduces the therapist and the therapist thus is less responsible for sexual abuse. As we oppose this conviction, we strongly suggest that the therapist seeks help in supervision or peer consulting as soon as empathy and care turn into an experienced erotic desire in order prevent a sliding transition into what might end in a disaster.

26.3 Respectful Physical Touch and Humaneness in Therapy

It is a thin line to walk, distinguishing between contact that can be kind and human, and erotic or even sexual nuances during therapy. While physical touching used to be a complete no-go in psychoanalysis, neo-analysts and psychodynamic therapists are less strict (Adler, 1931; Ferenczi, 1988; Yalom, 1980) if applied with respect to the integrity of the client. Adler and also Ferenczy ("No healing without sympathy") strongly opposed the Freudian concept of complete abstinence and favored aspects of humaneness including love in the sense of charity which might include embracing (Smith, Clance, & Imes, 2001). Moreover, in behavior therapy, integrative psychotherapy (Geib, 1998) and in hypnotherapy (Levitan, 1986) *respectful physical touch* has become a useful tool for anchoring resourceful and coping experiences. Turning away from deficit orientation even in psychodynamics (Wöller, 2017), the theory and practice of positive and philosophical psychology (Dalai Lama, Tutu, & Abrams, 2016; Seligman, 2002) in the early 2000s discovered the value of virtues like humaneness explicitly to favor well-being, change and salutogenesis. Frankl (1985), in his existentialistic approach, had already drawn upon humaneness in a broader sense of love within the context of spirituality and the personal experience of sense of life as a virtue.

26.4 Fromm's Categories of Love

Some of the many forms of love were already differentiated by Fromm (1956), who presented a differentiation within the broader term "love" into the categories of erotic love, parental love, self-love, love for God and altruistic love.

Erotic love being driven by the desire for complete unification with another person, therefore being exclusive and contrasting the other categories, which claim to be more universal forms of love. He considered erotic love to be inappropriate for the therapeutic alliance especially from the therapist's side, as the client's side can barely be controlled. The remarks above should have endorsed the reasoning behind it. Concerning parental love, Fromm distinguished between motherly and fatherly love, describing motherly love as unconditional love and affirmation of the children's existence, desires, and needs: a love that is given—or not—but cannot be generated or controlled by the child as the recipient. The love that is experienced passively in that kind of relationship that is characterized by inequality by the division into a giving and a receiving part. However, in the therapeutic setting motherly love might be experienced as supportive by the client, but is not necessarily productive, if accommodating a client's passivity. In contrast, the fatherly figure is described as one of authority leading the way into society and the world and teaching how to deal with the world's problems that await the child. The fatherly love in contrast to the motherly love is described as a love that is bound to conditions, that can therefore be influenced and controlled by fulfilling expectancies. The client can find a similar guidance and authority figure in his therapist, but experiencing only the therapist's approval—in accordance with demands and expectations attributed to the therapist—would be obstructive to the growth of the client finding his own expression of his self. Self-love must be distinguished from egomania, as these are opposites according to Fromm. Self-love is considered as an expression of being able to grant positive affirmation, regard and care to oneself and to grant love to others equally. Fromm (1956) describes love of God as a religious desire to overcome the feeling of separation and to reach union, while altruistic love ("love for one's neighbor") for him is the most fundamental and underlying all other forms of love. It contains a striving for responsibility, care, regard and insight towards all living beings and the intention to foster such a kind of life. His concept and recommendation is the therapeutic relationship as one of utmost realism and participation.

26.5 Basics of Effective Altruism

We try to take a closer look at the productive forms of this altruistic love within a therapeutic setting and focus on effective altruism of the therapist including empathy, humaneness, care, effort, reliability, temporary postponing of own needs and resilience facing difficult situations requiring treatment competence and effectiveness. The effectiveness of natural healers, magicians, wizards and sangomas in non-European cultures (cf. other articles in this book) should in our opinion however not only be attributed to the experience of their disposal of such characteristics, but also to their being culture-bound referring to the power of ancestors and to the ascription of spiritual power to mediate between clients and their ancestors.

As this book deals with cultural and intercultural perspectives of love and our contribution deals with the psychotherapeutic perspective, it should not remain unmentioned that Asian views on healing by facilitating attachment and promoting energy flow by Tantra-massages or by a Kundalini-exercises must be considered as detrimental to the client. Tantra is very intimate and can include sexual stimulation. Kundalini within the seven chakras explicitly refers to a sexual chakra in order to experience life energy. It does not mean taking a European point of view to strictly recommend refraining from such approaches even if allegedly embedded in a western psychotherapeutic encounter.

The social and philosophical movement of "effective altruism" of the early 2010s aims at determining the most effective ways to benefit others, identifying and acting according to one's values, looking for the biggest possible positive impact for others (Gabriel, 2017).

In psychosocial aid and psychotherapy, we therefore add "effective" to the term altruism and conceive of effective charity or effective altruism as an attitudinal concept involving emotional, cognitive, conative and behavioral characteristics, in which the perceived quality of the therapeutic alliance is one decisive factor defined by agreeableness, empathy, warmth, reliability, genuineness, affection and a caring attitude. However, by "effective" we are also driving at concrete intervention methods and techniques illustrated further below.

It almost goes without saying that psychosocial professionals need basic social-emotional intelligence including an altruistic attitude like "agape", a profound knowledge of mental and behavioral disturbances and disorders as well as of intervention methods and techniques and a supervised experience leading to treatment competence. It may seem bizarre, but just imagine a therapist resembling a "forest gump", smoking with an overflowing ashtray in an untidy room smelling oddly and his fingernails being dirty. Therefore, also some situational features might prevent the client from feeling comfortable in spite of all those above mentioned positive characteristics being present. And last but not least, complete unselfishness of psychosocial professionals lacking self-care presumably leads to detrimental exhaustion and also forms a bad and dysfunctional role-model.

Taking a closer look at the bottom 10% of therapists who perform worse than average reveals that their clients have a higher chance not to change at all or even to deteriorate (Baldwin & Imel, 2013). Presumably, these therapists do not possess the ability to form an empathetic therapeutic alliance, they also lack self-care, suffer from disruptions in their own private life, see too many clients per day, or suffer from compassion fatigue; whereas those who perform better than average and possess good interactive emotional and verbal skills, self-esteem, self-care, a supportive social network and are perceived as reliable and conscientious. Skill-training is highly recommended for novice therapists (Hill & Knox, 2013) and in our view should be supplemented by a training in intercultural knowledge and skills.

In this context it goes without saying that self-experience, supervision and peer consulting of therapists should be made use of.

26.6 Intercultural Case Vignettes

In order to illustrate love in the sense of active charity/effective altruism, but also transference and countertransference in intercultural therapy settings, six case vignettes are presented, two of them obtained in South Africa, three in psychosocial aid for refugees in Germany and one in supervision of a case of intercultural misunderstanding.

Case Vignette 1

A supervisory meeting referring to intercultural issues between a German therapist in training and his client with migration background (contribution by Jörg Fengler).

Supervisory meetings are a common method for quality assurance of a therapist's work. During these supervisory meetings, a specially trained and experienced psychotherapist (supervisor) is reviewing an ongoing therapy with the treating therapist. This can contain problems, interventions, recapitulation etc. and aims to minimize the influence of individual "blind spots" the treating therapist might have and optimize aspects of the therapeutic relationship and intervention.

A therapist is reviewing a group therapy session, in which he had a peculiar experience after finishing the last session with that group. The group therapy consisted of clients with different sex and disturbances in a psychosomatic hospital. The last session serves the purpose of reflecting on the process of the therapy. Especially emotional experiences and perspectives towards the future were reviewed. There was feedback for every patient, as well as for the therapist. In supervision, the therapist recalled giving a female patient feedback.

He recalled having said: "I was especially impressed, how individually and empathically your feedback in the group has been and how you took a constructive influence in the group's course by stating your position. I appreciated this a lot and it has been helpful to other patients in this group".

Two days later, this patient asked for an urgent conversation before her departure. The client was a 40-year old, well-groomed and educated woman, who worked as an engineer in a major enterprise and was born in a southern European country. She opened with the sentence: "You are well aware of proposing marriage to me officially during the last group therapy. Now we need to talk to my parents and I need to divorce my current husband".

Supervisor: "So? How did you reply to this?"

Therapist: "I answered rigid, formal and fiercely 'What do you mean? I am married as well, happily married and I have three children, and you are married as well'. But I am unsatisfied with this intervention. How else could I have reacted?"

Supervisor: "Maybe you should consider the option of recognizing the patient's affection, but not as love or impending marriage, but as appreciation of your empathy during the therapy sessions. Maybe then you can proceed to a friendly, but clear boundary".

Therapist: "This sounds good. But now it is too late, as the group is terminated and the client returned home."

Supervisor: "I agree. Establishing new contact with her might induce misunderstandings and breach the dictate of abstinence (from personal contacts to patients) and secrecy. But what did you learn from this situation for developing your own therapeutic competence?"

Therapist (slightly afflicted): "Well, now I feel invited to pay even more attention to possible cultural differences in the perception of courtship and to dose friendliness more carefully, even when I consider it right at this moment".

Conclusion: The implicit meaning of openly shown sympathy can vary drastically between cultures.

Case Vignettes 2–4

Encountering refugees between Sept 2015 until Jan 2018 as a German clinical psychologist at voluntary work (first author).

Preface: Because of the extremely over-demanding political situation with huge numbers of refugees, the psychosocial care was limited to only a few contacts and the need for short-time interventions in an intercultural context.

Case Vignette 2

23 year old Syrian man, Muslim. Epileptic seizures in the accommodation for refugees in terms of falling on the floor with head-banging, spatial disorientation for a few minutes were neurologically assessed as psychoreactive. Imprisoned during army service in Syria because his intention to join the "Free Syrian Army" had become known. Tortured in various brutal ways, traces visible on his back. Imprisoned in a room with a large number of others with little space. During flight traumatic experiences in an over-occupied rubber boat.

Sequentially preceding such seizures were crowds and loud noise in the accommodation, a feeling of help- and powerlessness, then headaches und flashbacks referring to the Syrian prison and sea-crossing from Turkey to Greece, then seizures. He was short of money, but refused to accept offered cash from the clinical psychologist.

Diagnosis: Untypical PTSD involving psychoreactive seizures.

In countertransference he evoked empathy, compassion and the altruistic caring need to effectively mitigate his complaints thereby implying intercultural love. No intercultural barrier seemed to interfere with the therapeutic alliance and confidence seemed to be mutual. Under the given limited conditions of care, he was then administered a rapidly acting benzodiazepine (Tavor Expidet, 2.5 mg) and told to take one as soon as headaches were sensed, and moreover to avoid noise and crowds during meals within the tent and inside the building and to go outside, or if unavoidable to put cotton wool into his ears.

He was seen three times thereafter, reported only one instance for taking the medication, but no further seizures. Further follow-up was by telephone, because he had been transferred to another city. He then reported a steady state compared to his initial complaints thus satisfying the need to grant effective altruistic care.

Conclusion: Even in intercultural encounters, it sometimes needs direct and concrete interventions to display effective altruism full of affection. In such cases it is not sufficient to listen empathically.

Case Vignette 3

51 year old man from Afghanistan, Muslim, but unreligious, belonging to the Hasara ethnic minority, fled because of the war, not afflicted by directly experienced traumata, discriminated and disadvantaged by authorities, no regular job, poor living circumstances in terms of temporary work for a farmer. Borrowed a large sum to pay the people smugglers. In the accommodation for refugees together with his wife and

two children. Reason for appointment: complaints of the personnel that he had been seen threatening other refugees with a knife during loud arguing with Iraqis.

During the interview he complained about "racial discrimination" by these. After unsuccessful attempts together with his wife to solve the issue with them, he had become resentful and furious and had shown them his knife with which he had pointed in their direction not really intending to stab anyone of them.

Diagnosis: Acute stress reaction.

In countertransference he evoked at first a state of increased alertness and worry, then partial understanding for his emotions, then affectionate intercultural compassion and pity because of the present situation he was in, then confidence in his ability to act according to his insight, but also a feeling of responsibility for the surrounding refugees. He apparently also responded with confidence which was confirmed by the translator. He was then requested to fetch and deliver the knife, which turned out to be a small kitchen knife from his service in the kitchen. His knife was collected and he was asked to promise by referring to Allah not to repeat such threatening. He appeared to be confident in the therapist, trustworthy and reliable. Consecutively, the need to protect others in his direct surroundings and society in a more general sense was fulfilled. Iraqis who had been involved were instructed that such prejudiced behavior would be detrimental to applying for asylum. Follow-ups proved no re-occurrence. Thus, the intervention seemed to comply with effective altruism.

Conclusion: In this case the therapeutic alliance involved mutual affection in the sense of intercultural love and active charity/effective altruism. Respect for and reference to the client's religious belief ensured sufficient insight to prevent bringing himself and others into danger.

Case Vignette 4

45 year old woman, black African Muslima from Northern Nigeria wearing a head cloth, she had fled together with her 27 year old daughter because of the killing of civilians committed by the Boko Haram rebels involving her husband recently and of her parents-in-law previously. Atrocious experiences during the flight on transporting pick-ups and trucks through the Sahara Desert and in Libya in terms of robbery, hunger, thirst, being beaten, endless seeming trips day and night with a lot of stops and changing vehicles.

Medical investigation showed no physical illness except scars on her legs due to transport conditions whereas she complained about pain allover her body, headache, partial anesthesia in her right arm, and a conviction that she had been bewitched or was haunted by ancestors as the cause of suffering from all these complaints. Her English was sufficient, however she spoke softly and seemed to be very shy so that gender matching had to be considered by having a female nurse attend. After repeated questioning, she complained about sometimes feeling frozen or numb, sometimes easily irritated, nightmares, flashbacks at daytime hours referring to experiences at home and during the flight. But all this was due to the ancestors as she underlined.

Obtained case history concerning youth and early adulthood further revealed that years ago when it was still possible to travel south, she had once traveled to Lagos/

Nigeria to see a "doctor for mental problems". At that time, she had felt sadness esp. in the morning, slept badly, suffered from lack of energy and vitality. He had prescribed a fluctine medication which had helped her after two weeks of taking it. She could afford to go on paying for these pills, because her husband had had a job. During the flight, she had run out of these pills.

Diagnosis: PTSD, severe recurrent depressive episode (presently manifested as masked depression).

In countertransference, she evoked at first a feeling of bewilderment and helplessness because she refused a handshake, which changed into a professional and effective altruism mindset in order to enable a differentiation between indications for interventions matching with the diagnosis. Affection on the background of intercultural knowledge and the motivation for effective care led to consider convictions about the influence of ancestors as culture-bound and thus not as paranoid had they been stated by a European woman. Obvious cultural and value differences therefore were perceived without impeding interventions and thus did not overshadow the empathy in the therapeutic alliance. An SSRI-antidepressant was administered for the severe masked depressive episode. Additionally, general physical activation exercises were supported by staff members including small talk about former resources and those granting a minimum of well-being under the given circumstances. PTSD-symptoms were initially treated by meditative and relaxing breathing exercises before the transfer to another city took place. These exercises involved a training in skills to counteract preceding signs of flashbacks by pressing a rubber ball and by mindful and verbally expressed counting of visual, audible, olfactory and gustatory features in the presently perceived environment. Haptically perceived sensations were omitted in order to prevent her focusing on somatic symptoms. While it took about two weeks to find an improvement of depression including lessening of masked symptoms, a slight recovery from PTSD-symptoms could be found after one week though only referring to a decrease in frequency and amplitude of nightmares and daytime flashbacks.

On the day of her transfer, the black Muslim woman with a head cloth wanted to embrace the therapist in order to express her trust and gratitude. That gesture increased a feeling of sympathy and being deeply touched and was responded by appreciation of her embrace.

Conclusion: Practical interventions in terms of effective altruism were very much facilitated on the basis of empathetic acceptance of her Nigerian cultural background and her traumatic experiences.

Case Vignettes 5–6

Encountering AIDS-clients as a German volunteer clinical psychologist (first author) in an AIDS-clinic run by an NGO in a South African township between Jan 2011 and Sept 2014.

Preface: Clients were seen several times during periods of ten to 21 days. Most of them were in medical and nursing care because of AIDS-infection and under ARV-medication. Transcultural challenges were obvious.

Case Vignette 5

18 year old South-Sotho juvenile living in a township in the Free State province together with his mother, grandmother and siblings, attending school irregularly because teachers could not handle his panic attacks, therefore no prospect of passing exams. Father had left the family 16 years ago and was living 150 kilometers away, seldom contact. Fair knowledge of English to enable communication, at times a nurse supported by translating. No HIV-AIDS-infection, appointment in the clinic with complaints about recurrent "sudden anxiety feelings" while no appropriate care was granted in the township. Several preceding hospital admissions in a unit for internal medicine. No cardiac illness was found. Allergic asthma successfully treated by Aerosol on demand. Epilepsy without seizures for two years under medication. He appeared physically slim but without nutritional deficiency. Exploration revealed panic disorder mainly out of the blue but presently mostly triggered by grandmother asking to fetch her alcohol, though anger was not experienced consciously. First panic symptoms at age 10. What was striking in his reporting was a feeling of constantly being underestimated by peers and school teachers according to his real talent and abilities, whereas he believed himself to be bright and intelligent because a deceased uncle had said so to him and that he would become famous as an adult and a leader.

He had frequently contacted the clinic with recurrent somatic complaints centered around his heart. His panic symptoms included palpitations, fear of a heart attack and of fainting, pain in both lower legs, strong perspiration and lasted for 15–30 minutes each. He had developed a generalized avoidance behavior except for seeking refuge in the clinic. Suspicion of secondary gain by getting attention for cardiac complaints. An attempt to have his intelligence tested by a Sotho-language or a non-verbal test by a black African colleague had failed because he defaulted appointments. He also complained about lack of money and not being sufficiently fed by his mother. Direct contact with his mother revealed that the latter was untrue.

Diagnosis: Panic disorder with hypochondriac features on the basis of a juvenile self-esteem conflict.

In countertransference, he evoked at first a fatherly feeling of affection and love for granting orientation and support, then affection and compassion were contrasted by uncertainty as to the strong difference of black culture from that of the therapist. This uncertainty was then outbalanced because of the therapist's knowledge of life within a township including a visit at his home seeing his mother. The remaining uncertainty referred to the patient's belief in the impact of his deceased uncle as an ancestor who had made idealizing (but unrealistic) predictions to him. The clinical impression during the interventions gave rise to the assumption of a normally intelligent juvenile. His resources were drawing, listening to classical music, Christian religiousness and an interest in nature.

Interventions aiming at concrete help and thus at effective altruism were at first overshadowed when the patient spent money donated by the interviewer for sweets instead of paying the donated money for fees for enrolling in a program for school defaulters or drop-outs. Because of the widely spread shortage of money of township inhabitants, in contrast to European ethical standards there were no remorses of the interviewer to donate money. Annoyance about lack of reliability was then expressed leading to a more compliant attitude of the patient; also money was then only granted after he had accomplished gardening on the clinic premises as agreed upon before in order to establish contingencies and self-responsibility. The panic syndrome was treated by breathing and relaxation exercises and by physical exercises like push-ups granting a perception of the variability of heart beats caused intentionally. Then techniques of ego state psychotherapy were applied involving the contrasting ego states, which had been caused by his uncle's previous prediction and the present experience of being overlooked and underestimated—speak and negotiate with each other to attain a compromise. The compromise was then made the topic of a hypnotherapeutic intervention interspersing the mentioned resources and aiming at self-acceptance as a person with slightly above average intelligence whose uncle would be glad to see him make his way by finishing his schooling and then trying to lead a normal life. Resources were supplemented by calming and joyful amplified experiences of nature at a river and then drifting in a boat downstream anchoring these imaginations by touching one hand and shifting to these whenever negative feelings like anger disappointment about being underestimated would come up induced by suggestions anchored before at the other hand. He was trained to apply such shifts himself at stressful instances indicated and signaled by an imagined yellow traffic light.

Furthermore, the role of ancestors in black African culture was embedded and made use of by ascribing a helpful role to his uncle instead of discarding or refuting his unrealistic prediction as would be suggested in European value systems.

Follow-ups showed a decrease in frequency of panic symptoms after four weeks with weekly appointments. At a follow-up one year after intake, he reported complete lack of symptoms, attendance and progress at the school program and confidence in attaining a grade necessary for later professional schooling.

Conclusion: The therapist's knowledge of the black-African township culture served to gradually establish a therapeutic alliance including a fatherly-loving and empathetic relationship with the client and this laid the ground for effective altruistic interventions.

Case Vignette 6
28 year old black South-Sotho woman with HIV under ARV-medication which she had collected previously. Child two years old and still breast-fed. At the last appointment she was poorly dressed and smelled badly. As she seemed very strange to the nurse on duty at the AIDS-clinic, she was seen by a clinical psychologist with the translating nurse present. She appeared to be in an almost catatonic state with thought blocking, mute for a while and staring at the ceiling. She had previously been admitted in the local general hospital for a few days without any improvement. When asked whether she was hearing or seeing something others could not necessarily perceive, she mentioned with a very soft voice "Tokoloshi" who commanded her to go into the nearby Vaal river and drown the little boy and herself. "Tokoloshi" was explained by the nurse to be a powerful bad spirit in black African culture. An immediate decision was made not to understand this in terms of a deviant culture, but to diagnose a paranoid-hallucinatory schizophrenic illness and to refer her to a

psychiatric hospital about 90 kilometers away without telling her about that indication and decision. In accordance with the diagnosis, there were no detectable affective reactions on her part nor was there any facial expression. The clinical psychologist then left the room where she was attended by the nurse. Fifteen minutes later she had to be given fast acting benzodiazepine suppository on a stretcher because of a state of catatonic excitation. Within these fifteen minutes, a number of black counselors and home-based caregivers had executed exorcism on her which had obviously caused the aggravation. She then calmed down under medication. The counselors and home-based caregivers were strictly requested not to do this again and they agreed without credible consent. A quick home visit in the company of two female caregivers, not involved in the exorcism, was secured to have the baby taken care of by neighbors. Her living circumstances were found to be far below township standards with almost no furniture or food and dirty. The little furniture had been destroyed by her. Her mother reported that she had been in a very altered mentally and behaviorally aggressive state for a few days, seemingly shouting at someone not present. Sandwiches were fetched to grant immediate support.

Diagnosis: Paranoid-hallucinatory schizophrenia.

In countertransference, she evoked at first a strong feeling of empathy, loving compassion and pity, but also a conviction to act professionally. After the attempted exorcism a feeling of responsibility came up to protect her against black counselors and caregivers who had been involved and to organize effective support concerning the acute state she was in. The therapist's loving compassion and pity also referred to her miserable living conditions.

Transport to the hospital was then organized by having her sit in the middle of the back seat with the two before mentioned female caregivers next to her in order to prevent suicide by her jumping out of the car upon presumed commands by "Tokoloshi". She was admitted to the psychiatric hospital and stayed there for three weeks treated with antipsychotic medication and continuation of ARV-medication. After discharge and readmission to out-patient treatment in the AIDS-clinic, the antipsychotic medication was continued by the medical doctor in charge and familiar with psychopharmacology. At a home visit he found a cleaned house with mother and another lady taking care of her. Money was left to secure buying of food. However, she had taken the double dosage of antipsychotic medication for one week and suffered from considerable side-effects. Therefore, two black care-givers whom she knew from the transport supported her every second day and surveilled adherence. No further clinical psychological intervention took place.

Upon follow-up by the medical doctor five months later, she was found compliant, had come to scheduled appointments twice a week, reported a general state of well-being and was going to marry. More money was given to her mother for buying food. The side-effect of slightly increased weight was considered to be advantageous according to male black African preferences. In spite of the initial referral from the care-giving AIDS-clinic to a psychiatric hospital, the way of dealing with the disturbances was considered to comply with effective altruism and thus the black South African concept of "Ubuntu".

Conclusion: In spite of the ancestor related culture of the client it was helpful to abstain from further relating to it and rather intervene directly and realize empathy by effective altruism to prevent an extended suicide.

26.7 Recommendations for Effective Therapeutic Practice and Conclusions

Taking it for granted that the earlier-mentioned positive prerequisites apply (Lütgerhorst, 2017), we leave it up to the reader to take the following recommendations into consideration, illustrating how **active charity/effective altruism** can be implemented in counseling and psychotherapy and **within intercultural settings**. We thus conceive of charity not only as an attitude, but as concrete interactional behavior and we make these suggestions on the basis of a multi-method, transdiagnostic and eclectic orientation (Hessler & Fiedler, 2019) as an attempt to increase treatment competence:

Remember: *There is no perfect solution for any human problem. No therapist is perfect all of the time.*

- As the quality of the therapeutic alliance has a high predictive value for outcome, it is empathetic understanding, warmth and care that are decisive. Competence in different aspects of empathy should therefore be on hand: cognitive, emotional and somatic empathy. The latter implies that even physical sensations are reflected if not mirrored in the therapist. Thus, empathy is not restricted to emotions.
- Favorably, the focus in process orientation should be on all modalities of experiencing of the client (Lütgerhorst, 2014) and also include imaginations, impulses and cravings. If lacking, self-experience and supervision might be beneficial to increase these competencies.
- Not being paralyzed by compassion or even pity with a view towards what is required both for the client and the therapist's self-care. Again, using self-experience and supervision might be beneficial for setting healthy boundaries when necessary.
- General knowledge and readiness to tailor interventions beyond conventional psychotherapy and approaches like (cognitive) behavior therapy, psychodynamic therapy, psychoanalysis, hypnotherapy, systemic therapy etc. according to the client's needs. If suitable, the combination of approaches and use of add-ons like mindfulness exercises, music, singing, sports etc. is advised. Within the process of scientific verification of therapy manuals, the complexity of disturbances is reduced, and such manuals have been mainly developed with monosyndromal samples rarely to be found in naturalistic, especially not in intercultural settings. Moreover, manuals do not take the compliance of therapeutic goals with the fulfillment of the below mentioned basic needs sufficiently into regard, therefore we encourage to expand the therapist's view.

- The ongoing clarification of problems, obstacles, goals, motives, concerns, attractors of avoidance and of striving for change, basic needs, sense of life, and of assignments and tasks presented to the therapist in order to consolidate a stable working alliance.
- A general resource- instead of deficit orientation as the activation of resources is a predictive factor in therapy success (Grawe, 1998; Grawe et al., 1995). This may include a client's skills, abilities, capabilities, talents, positive experiences in nature, gratitude as a general attitude, but also for single experiences, as gratitude is one of several character strenghts facilitating recovery from mental problems (Niemiec, 2018).
- The linking of interventions to the fulfillment of basic needs is a therapeutic focus which can be used across psychological disturbances and disorders. This involves the need for attachment/fear of loss of it, need for control/fear of loss of it, need for augmenting self-esteem/fear of loss of it, need for gaining pleasure/avoidance of displeasure, need for new experiences vs. avoiding them (Grawe et al., 1995).
- Presupposing a bio-psycho-social understanding of psychological illness, it is crucial to take stressful context conditions into account such as housing, working conditions or unemployment, relationships etc. These aspects are common beyond cultural and intercultural issues and ignoring them might counteract therapeutic efforts.
- Balancing between empathetic listening and pacing, structuring and flexibility with regard to change from symptom-orientation to person- or background-orientation, and vice versa (Gall-Peters & Zarbock, 2012); likewise, a view for the implicit, unconscious or preconscious mode of functioning bearing more meaning than what is explicitly stated (Gendlin, 1982); in this context it is important to notice experiential avoidance present when emotional or somatic experiences are suppressed, because of an immediate evaluation of a subject as negative, strong and uncontrollable even before it becomes conscious (LeDoux, 1996). Thus, flexibility with a view for such subtle process characteristics is called for in contrast to strict adherence to methods.
- Taking somatic deficits and need for psychopharmacological support into account. E.g. severe and ongoing sleeping disturbances impede concentration necessary for therapy and might temporarily require medication, if the promotion of basic functions of concentration and of focusing attention cannot be attained otherwise, e.g. by mindfulness or slowing-down exercises.
- If possible, required, and with the client's consent, a multi-professional exchange of information in the sense of networking is advised.
- Matching also according to rather formal aspects at intake interviews before starting therapy sessions, concerning severity of the disturbance and professional competence, to sex, age, level of education and treatment expectancies of the client.
- Within an ongoing therapy, the conversation should not be indoctrination and tuition, but a dialogue, though the in-between use of a flip-chart can be useful e.g. to clarify short-term and long-term advantages and disadvantages of maintaining vs. changing attitudes and behaviors.

- If the client previously has made dreadful attachment experiences or dreadful experiences in general, it is especially important to enable corrective experiences in a climate of empathy, for change is difficult if early primed bad experiences prevail.
- Pay attention to specific rules that apply with suicidal clients; and also with PTSD-clients affording stabilization before addressing the trauma and secure permanent distance from the assaulter in cases of a man-made trauma.
- Preparing the client for "zones of discomfort" to be tolerated during change processes, for obstacles and for delayed relief and success, as this is crucial for managing expectations, de-pathologization and implementing transparency.
- Dosed interpretation close to consciousness and supported by further exploration especially if clients tend to restrict themselves to enumerating external events and avoid the experience of evaluations (as precursors of emotions), emotions and physical sensations.
- Dosed confrontation with dissonant or contradictory elements of experiencing and needs as well as with unrealistic goals.
- Furthermore, the degree of indispensable self-responsibility and cooperativeness is usually much higher than in somatic medicine, which clients should be informed about at the beginning as a passive treatment expectancy is frequent.
- If the therapist is confronted with clients' divergent values or unwillingness to adapt to societal norms of the given environment, dosed self-disclosure might be helpful. Another option would be to view and evaluate the interaction from higher ground, i.e. from a meta-perspective as if a supervisor were present as a mediator.
- Using supervision might also be helpful to get feedback about non-verbal aspects of an interaction like mimics and gestures. Moreover, supervision might serve to get feedback about the tone and hue of voice, and about formal aspects like length of verbal contributions of both therapist and client and their balance.
- Meaningful and summarizing take-away messages and feasible homework-assignments, while keeping in mind that complete compliance in fulfilling these is different from concordance covering not negotiated steps towards a meaningful goal which had not yet been focused upon.
- Intensifying resource and coping experiences in a state of deep relaxation which can merge into trance if hypnotherapy is applied.
- Use of mottos like the following in order to facilitate change processes and solution orientation once problems and goals have been specified and outdated mottos need to be rescripted:
    > **"It is better to light a candle than to complain about the dark"**
    > "You cannot plough a field, if you turn it over in your mind"
    > "You cannot sail the ocean, unless you dare to lose sight of the shore"
    > "While one man waits for change to come, the next one turn to things undone"
    > "God gives you nuts, but he does not crack them"
- Use of myths, stories and narrations etc. can be an effective therapeutic tool.

- Psychoeducation and information about psychotherapy and counseling should not be limited to the pre-therapy phase but rather be interspersed in order to bring about enlightenment and de-pathologization.
- General openness for analyzing ruptures, crises and mistakes in order to find more appropriate pathways whenever stagnation or failure is occurring. This kind of an open attitude is recommended, for in 5–10% of all treatment cases in RCT-research there is no change or deterioration (Lambert, 2013). This also occurs in single cases with therapists who in general perform well, for no therapist is flawless. Moreover, multimorbid disorders, which are more frequent in naturalistic settings than in RCT, yield even more non-responders. Here, a general motivation of the therapist for constructive learning by mistakes is preferable to over-demanding perfectionism including rigid maintenance of failing methods and techniques which might in turn result in diminishing the therapist's self-esteem. Therapists who encounter their mistakes constructively (Yalom, 2002), suffer less from guilt feelings and shame—A certain restriction in assuming "resistance" of the client is recommendable, as change processes imply natural anxiety or caution when leaving old patterns behind in favor of new pathways (Sullivan, 2012).
- Special competence in dealing with restraint, distrust, hostility and negativism which are the most frequent reasons for ruptures.
- It might be useful to change the therapist in cases when ruptures cannot be negotiated in that particular therapeutic alliance even though a climate free of fear to criticize had been provided.
- Additional settings and options should be taken into account, like integration into self-help groups or the usage of bibliotherapy and cinematherapy. Internet-based treatments can offer a low-threshold access and be beneficial in cases of regional lack of care.
- Interviewing relevant relations and other stakeholders with the client's consent, for these can be supportive or form obstacles and thus facilitate or hinder progress in therapy.
- Special emphasis on spirituality, transcendence and experienced meaning or sense of life as regard for these dimensions are helpful for coping with disturbances and for recovery into a state of well-being.
- Preparedness that the empirical finding of success predictability within the "critical window" in early sessions, often does not apply with clients of different cultural background, which demands patience and persistence.
- Direct intercultural experiences. In order to get acquainted with other cultures, it is often not sufficient to know about different kinds of Weltanschauung, to spend holidays abroad, read books, learn from the media or attend seminars. We therefore recommend intercultural experiences first hand whenever possible.
- Intercultural treatment experiences under supervision with special regard to divergent values and habits, uprooting and culture shock experiences of migrants.
- Attention for discordance of words with gestures and mimics. Peer-consulting with colleagues who themselves have a different cultural background can be fruitful.

- Advanced proficiency in the pertaining foreign language, if no interpreter is available, as language, concept formation and culture are closely linked (Chomsky, 2006); also some knowledge of vernaculars, dialects and regiolects within one culture is helpful.

26.8 Special Recommendations Applying to Group Settings

Many therapists avoid group settings because of fear of criticism and negative evaluation and of being overwhelmed by the amount of information difficult to synthesize (cf. Yalom & Lesczc, 2005, for helpful suggestions for coping). However, groups offer the chance for positive interpersonal and vicarious learning. We therefore present additional information for clients to get acquainted with and for therapists to attend to, hereby enlarging the suggestions of Fengler (2008):

- The group therapist should explicitly accept his role as an active leader, moderator and mediator and counteract the development of clients feeling excluded or outsiders.
- An increased group-related ability to balance between structuring and flexibility.
- Focus on complaints as well as on resources and solution orientation.
- Engendering and facilitating group coherence which replaces the predictive factors of quality of the therapeutic alliance in single settings. Experiencing sharing and solidarity was found to be important for group settings (cf. the approach of Yalom & Lesczc, 2005) as it increases motivation which is one important predictor for change.
- Experience in group dynamics beyond mastering psychotherapeutic methods.
- Present group rules like confidentiality, authentic openness and self-disclosure with regard to weaknesses, guilt and shame, but also to resources; demanding respect for abstention from hostility and insults.
- Preparedness for different cultural and intercultural values and habits of the attendants.
- Competence for divided attention, i.e. while focusing on one group member perceiving reactions of others at the same time.
- An emphasis on feedback of group members while temporarily withholding own impulses.
- Invitation to support each other and form networks.
- Appreciation of expressed emotions including those for group members, for attempts to (re)gain confidence and for making corrective interpersonal experiences.
- Limitation of statements about traumatization as this might put an over-demand on other group-members.
- Presenting life topics like unavoidable uncertainties, discomforts and crises, loneliness, illnesses, separation and death.

References

Adler, A. (1931). The meaning of life. *The Lancet, 65*(5), 226–228.
Baldwin, S. A., & Imel, Z. E. (2013). Therapist effects. Findings and methods. In M. J. Lambert (Ed.), *Bergin & Garfield's handbook of psychotherapy and behavior change* (Vol. 6, pp. 169–218). Hoboken, NJ: Wiley.
Bordin, E. S. (1979). The generalizability of the psychoanalytic concept of the working alliance. *Psychotherapy: Theory, Research and Practice, 16*(3), 253–260.
Chomsky, N. (2006). *Language and mind*. Cambridge: Cambridge University Press.
Clarkson, P. (2003). *The therapeutic relationship* (2nd ed.). Philadelphia, PA: Whurr.
Dalai Lama, Tutu, D., & Abrams, D. C. (2016). *The book of joy: Lasting happiness in a changing world*. New York: Avery-Penguin.
Fengler, J. (2008). Gruppentherapie. In M. Hermer & B. Röhrle (Eds.), *Handbuch der therapeutischen Beziehung* (pp. 1413–1433). Bd 2. Tübingen: dgvt-Verlag.
Ferenczi, S. (1988). *Ohne Sympathie keine Heilung: das klinische Tagebuch von 1932*. Frankfurt a. M.: Fischer.
Frankl, V. E. (1985). *Man's search for meaning*. New York: Simon & Schuster.
Fromm, E. (1956). *The art of loving*. New York: Harper and Row.
Gabriel, I. (2017). Effective altruism and its critics. *Journal of Applied Philosophy, 34*(4), 457–473.
Gall-Peters, A., & Zarbock, G. (2012). *Praxisleitfaden Verhaltenstherapie/Störungsspezifische Strategien, Therapieindividualisierung, Patienteninformationen*. Leipzig: Pabst Science.
Gartrell, N., Herman, J., Olarte, S., Feldstein, M., & Localio, R. (1986). Psychiatrist-patient sexual contact: Results of a national survey, I: Prevalence. *American Journal of Psychiatry, 143*(9), 1126–1131.
Geib, P. (1998). The experience of nonerotic physical contact in traditional psychotherapy. In E. W. L. Smith, P. R. Clance, & S. Imes (Eds.), *Touch in psychotherapy: Theory, research, and practice* (pp. 109–126). New York: Guilford Press.
Gelso, C. J., & Hayes, J. A. (1998). *The psychotherapy relationship: Theory, research, and practice*. Hoboken, NJ: Wiley.
Gelso, C. J., Pérez Rojas, A. E., & Marmarosh, C. (2014). Love and sexuality in the therapeutic relationship. *Journal of Clinical Psychology, 70*(2), 123–134.
Gendlin, E. T. (1982). *Focusing*. New York: Bantam.
Grawe, K. (1998). *Psychologische Therapie*. Göttingen: Hogrefe.
Grawe, K., Donati, R., & Bernauer, F. (1995). *Psychotherapie im Wandel: von der Konfession zur Profession* (4th ed.). Göttingen: Hogrefe.
Halter, M., Brown, H., & Stone, J. (2007). *Sexual boundary violations by health professionals–an overview of the published empirical literature*. London: Council for Healthcare Regulatory Excellence.
Hessler, J. B., & Fiedler, P. (2019). *Transdiagnostische Interventionen in der Psychotherapie*. Stuttgart: Klett-Cotta.
Hill, C. E., & Knox, S. (2013). Training and supervision in psychotherapy. In M. J. Lambert (Ed.), *Bergin & Garfield's handbook of psychotherapy and behavior change* (Vol. 6, pp. 775–811). Hoboken, NJ: Wiley.
Kernberg, O. F. (1999). Persönlichkeitsentwicklung und Trauma. *Persönlichkeitsstörungen – Theorie und Therapie (PTT), 3*(1), 5–15.
Lambert, M. J. (2013). The efficacy and effectiveness of psychotherapy. In M. J. Lambert (Ed.), *Bergin & Garfield's handbook of psychotherapy and behavior change* (pp. 169–218). Hoboken, NJ: John Wiley & Sons.
Lambert, M. J., & Barley, D. E. (2001). Research summary on the therapeutic relationship and psychotherapy outcome. *Psychotherapy: Theory, Research, Practice, Training, 38*(4), 357–361.

Levitan, A. A. (1986). The role of touch in healing and hypnotherapy. *American Journal of Clinical Hypnosis, 28*(4), 218–223.

Lütgerhorst, H.-J. (2014). Der "englische Patient". PTBS-Exploration, multimodale Exposition, methodischer Brückenschlag. In S. Trautmann-Voigt & B. Voigt (Eds.), *Brückenschläge zwischen Systemischer Therapie und Verhaltenstherapie* (pp. 77–99). Claus Richter: Köln.

Lütgerhorst, H.-J. (2017). Gütemerkmale der therapeutischen Allianz und Therapieerfolg. In S. Trautmann-Voigt & B. Voigt (Eds.), *Psychodynamische Psychotherapie und Verhaltenstherapie – Ein integratives Praxisbuch* (pp. 115–133). Stuttgart: Schattauer.

Niemiec, R. M. (2018). *Character strengths interventions/a field guide for practitioners*. Boston: Hogrefe.

Norcross, J. C., & Lambert, M. J. (2019). *Psychotherapy relationships that work: Vol. 1: Evidence-based therapist contributions*. Oxford: University Press.

Peter, B., & Böbel, E. (2020). Significant differences in personality styles of securely and insecurely attached psychotherapists: Data, reflections and implications. *Frontiers in Psychology, 11*, 1–12.

Pope, K. S., & Vasquez, M. J. T. (2016). *Ethics in psychotherapy and counseling: A practical guide* (5th ed.). Hoboken, NJ: Wiley.

Seligman, M. E. P. (2002). Positive psychology, positive prevention, and positive therapy. In C. R. Snyder & S. J. Lopez (Eds.), *Handbook of positive psychology* (pp. 3–9). New York: Oxford University Press.

Smith, E. W. L., Clance, P. R., & Imes, S. (2001). *Touch in psychotherapy: Theory, research, and practice*. New York: Guilford Press.

Sullivan, H. S. (2012). Conceptions of modern psychiatry. The first William Alanson White memorial lectures. *Psychiatry, 75*(1), 3–17.

Trabert, W. (2014). Wenn der Therapeut zum Täter wird: Sexuelle Traumatisierung in Psychiatrie und Psychotherapie. *Psychotherapie im Dialog, 15*(1), 50–53.

Wöller, W. (2017). Tiefenpsychologisch fundierte Psychotherapie als ressourcenbasiertes integratives Verfahren. In S. Trautmann-Vogt & B. Vogt (Eds.), *Psychodynamische Therapie und Verhaltenstherapie/Ein integratives Praxishandbuch* (pp. 134–145). Stuttgart: Schattauer.

Yalom, I. D. (1980). *Existential psychotherapy*. New York: Basic Books.

Yalom, I. D. (2002). *The gift of therapy*. New York: Harper-Collins.

Yalom, I. D., & Lesczc, M. (2005). *Theory and practice of group psychotherapy*. New York: Basic Books.

Hans-Jörg Lütgerhorst (Dr. of Medical Science) worked for 35 years full-time as a clinical psychologist/psychotherapist in state hospitals for psychiatry, psychotherapy and psychosomatics; since 2010 in an ambulatory practice (www.praxis-am-richterbusch.de). Lecturer, supervisor, self-experience coach and examiner of the provincial boards of examiners for Medicine, Pharmaceutics and Psychotherapy of two federal states. Lectures and workshops at national and international congresses. Concluded training and further training in behavior therapy and CBT, client-centered psychotherapy, focusing therapy and hypnotherapy. Further training in ego state therapy not yet concluded. Voluntary work with AIDS-patients in South Africa and with refugees in Germany.

Sabine Diekmeier (M.Sc. Psychology) is a therapist-in-training in Cognitive Behavioral Therapy in Gießen, currently working as a psychologist in a hospital for rehabilitation. Previous experiences include working as research assistant in the teaching hospital of Gießen in the Department of Psychosomatic Medicine and Psychotherapy, internships in psychiatric hospitals as well as voluntary work with HIV/AIDS patients at the Aids Federation Gießen.

Jörg Fengler Professor em., Psychological Psychotherapist, Supervisor (DGSV), Senior Coach (DBVC), 35 years professor at the University of Cologne, specialization: Clinical and Educational Psychology. Lectures in Luxemburg, Belgium, Switzerland, Austria, Kenia, Korea, Russia. Twelve scientific books about group dynamics, burnout prevention, drug prevention, feedback, deaf people, psychology of handicapped persons. Director of Institute of Applied Psychology in Cologne, Germany.

Chapter 27
Coming Home to Self: Finding Self-Compassion and Self-Love in Psychotherapy

Aakriti Malik

Abstract Love as an emotion is a deeply rooted one. Being felt in differential ways, it withholds a great potential to unravel deep-seated trauma and a gamut of emotions in the context of psychopathology in psychotherapy. Clients often seek therapy as a means to treat their symptoms or manage their mental and emotional health. However, the process of psychotherapy opens up layers of past history around being loved that determine a client's present belief systems around love, being loved or loving someone. What often gets lost is the question of self-love. While client may come with presenting complaints of lack of confidence, feeling inferior to others, it takes great skill as a therapist to acknowledge the lack of self-love the client has for him/herself. Research suggests that as children we internalise our parents' conversations which later become our internal self-talk in our mind. The criticality or kindness offered in these scripts, in addition to the lack or the presence of love received greatly determine an individuals' love for themselves. Self-compassion as a psychotherapeutic approach has been found to heighten people's physical and mental well-being with an emphasis on an unconditional acceptance of oneself as they are. The current chapter aims at understanding love through different theoretical perspectives, its link with psychopathology and how it presents itself with other emotions. Selected case examples have been utilised to emphasize on the healing properties of compassion-based therapy with clients from an Indian background and its role in alleviation of symptoms.

Keywords Love · Self-love · Self-compassion · Psychotherapy · Culture · India

A. Malik (✉)
Middlemore Hospital, Auckland, New Zealand
e-mail: aakritimalik26@gmail.com

27.1 Introduction

Love has been a universal human emotion that has permeated through many aspects of life. It has been defined as a strong emotional attachment toward another person or thing that can produce feelings of euphoria and joy—or sadness and despair (Thaik, 2014). Love can be considered both as positive and negative. As a virtue, it encompasses human emotions of kindness, compassion and affection towards others. As a vice, it has the potential to be considered akin to vanity, selfishness, egotism, potentially leading people to a type of obsessiveness or co-dependency (Merriam Webster, 2012). The ancient Greek philosophers identified five types of love; they were: familial love (*Storge*), platonic love (*Philia*), romantic love (*Eros*), guest love (*Xenia*) and divine love (*Agape*). It is only recently that modern researchers have started focusing on self-love as one of the many types.

Self-love refers to the act of valuing one's own happiness and well-being. It involves an unconditional sense of support, caring and a core of compassion for the self. Essential to the aspect of self-love is a consideration and a willingness to meet personal needs, allow non-judgmental thinking, and view the self as essentially worthy, good, valuable, and deserving of happiness. Khoshaba (as cited in Wood, 2016) defines self-love as a state of appreciation for oneself that grows from actions that support one's physical, psychological, and spiritual growth.

One of the significant components of self-love is self-compassion (see Chap. 31). One of the ways to embrace one's love for the self is through offering it with self-compassion. Kristin Neff (2003b), a pioneer in the field defines self-compassion as

> being touched by and open to one's own suffering, not avoiding or disconnecting from it, generating the desire to alleviate one's suffering and to heal oneself with kindness. Self-compassion also involves offering non-judgemental understanding to one's pain, inadequacies and failures, so that one's experience is seen as part of the larger human experience.

Thus, it consists of three main components: self-kindness, common humanity and mindfulness. According to her, self-compassion allows people to maintain an equanimity in the face of unpleasant circumstances, opening up to life in the present moment rather than running away from one's problems or shortcomings.

27.2 The Flip Side: What Is Not Self-Love

Interestingly, an addition of the word 'self' before love and the Merriam Webster (2012) dictionary states it as "love of self" and "conceit" and "regard for one's own happiness or advantage" as the definition of self-love. It comes as no surprise then that for the longest of times the word 'self-love' has often been considered synonymous to either being selfish or narcissistic.

While much has been debated over the etymology of the word 'narcissus', the Greek mythology speaks of a beautiful young man who pined for love of his own reflection only to die and become a flower. In linguistics, the word narcissism refers to someone who is ego-centric, self-absorbed and self-centred. This is much in contrast to the meaning of self-love which refers to loving oneself without the need to downgrade others, taking pride in one's accomplishments and offering oneself the much-needed compassion when life gets difficult.

In the traditional psychoanalytical parlance, Freud (as cited in Fromm, 1956) assumed love to be a manifestation of libido. It could either be turned towards others or oneself. Self-love then meant the turning of libido towards oneself (which was the same as narcissism). Thus, love and self-love as concepts were mutually exclusive in the sense that more of one led to less of another. Eric Fromm (1956), in the book Art of Loving, disagrees about love and self-love being inherently exclusive. On the contrary, he writes

> The affirmation of one's own life, happiness, growth, freedom is rooted in one's capacity to love, i.e., in care, respect, responsibility, and knowledge.

If an individual is able to love productively, he loves himself too; if he can love *only* others, he cannot love at all.

Fromm (1956) distinguishes clearly between selfishness and self-love and calls them as opposite entities. According to him, an individual who is selfish thinks only of his own interests and pleasure with total disregard for others' needs, interests, respect for their dignity and integrity. With this respect, a selfish person lacks the ability to love others. Further, a selfish individual instead of loving himself too much only loves himself too little. His lack of fondness for himself leaves him empty and frustrated only to block the satisfactions of life from himself which he wishes to achieve. Thus, Fromm (ibid) concludes by saying

> it is true that selfish persons are incapable of loving others, but they are not capable of loving themselves either.

Much like self-love, self-compassion has also been confused with narcissism although research indicates no link between self-compassion and narcissism (Neff, 2003a; Neff & Vonk, 2009). As studied by Neff, Hseih, and Dejitthirat (2005) and Neff and McGeehee (2010):

> Narcissism is a reactive attempt to bolster our self-image when we fail ("I'm smart—it was just a stupid test!"), whereas self-compassion implies openness to failure, the ability to comfort ourselves, to assess the situation, and to work to improve it.

Thus, unlike narcissism which aims at berating and downsizing external factors so as to elevate one's own status, self-compassion is a healthy inner response to misfortune that makes us feel better (Neff & Vonk, 2009).

27.3 Conceptual Framework: Understanding Self-Love Through Theories

Research in the area of developmental psychology has highlighted the effects of early attachment with the caregiver and parenting styles on numerous aspects of later adult life such as cognition, romantic relationships, mental and physical health among many others. Bowlby's attachment theory (1969) explained that early life experiences with primary caregivers played a significant role in the formation of internal working models. These included self-perceptions of one's own value and worthiness of care and perceptions of others' ability to provide such care in times of need.

Inherent in Bowlby's theory (1973) is the assertion that individuals often treat themselves and others as they were treated throughout childhood by their primary caregivers. Kohut (1971, 1977) argued that an individual's ability to be self-reassuring and soothing in times of personal failure or to act out one's narcissistic rage towards the self could be internalised based on early experiences with the caregivers.

Fromm (1956) writes:

> At any rate, the sense of falling in love develops usually only with regard to such human commodities as are within reach of one's own possibilities for exchange.

Thus, the language parents use with their children, especially in instances involving failure and disappointments later comes to form the child's inner voice or their self-talk. One of the essential aspects of the self-talk is the criticism towards one's self. According to Gilbert, Clarke, Hempel, Miles, and Irons (2004) there is clinical evidence that a dominant–subordinate self-to-self relationship can be acted out internally (e.g. with one part of the self-issuing threats and shaming put-downs while another part of the self submits and feels beaten down). Mongrain, Vettese, Shuster, and Kendal (1998) and Enns, Cox, and Inayatulla (2003) found self-criticism to be associated with feelings of being inferior, having poor affiliative relationships, leading to rejection from others.

Gilbert et al. (Ibid, 2004) speak primarily of two main components of self-criticism. One, where the self is critical when it dwells on the mistakes and the inadequacies and the second, when the self wishes to hurt itself resulting from feelings of self-hate and self-disgust. In the former, a parent's threats or punishments towards a child worded as "You're not trying hard enough" or "If you don't accomplish X, then nobody will like you or you won't get on in the world" can make a lasting impression. People who internalise this form of self-regulation justify their self-attacking voice to be aimed at correcting their behaviour. With respect to psychopathology, people diagnosed with anxiety issues (social anxiety, generalised anxiety, OCD) and mood disorders are often found to have this pattern.

The self-criticality which is aimed at hurting oneself often emanates from past experiences wherein as children, they have had their significant others calling them names, abuses, or accusing them of things they were not responsible for. For instance "You're stupid, you'll never be good" or "You're always pathetic and annoying" or "It's because of you we don't have enough". Such expressions give children a sense of being bad from within, something they cannot fix. Often such instances occur in invalidating environments where children find it difficult to comprehend their and other's emotions, live in unpredictable situations or have parents who are emotionally dysfunctional. One of the most common examples of such self-criticality occurs in clients who present with borderline personality disorder.

Thus, no matter which theoretical perspective one takes, an essential component that weaves them all together is that of receiving and giving of love. A baby can inculcate the capacity to offer only that love which s/he has received from their significant other. Whether one calls this introjection in the psychoanalytical language or learnt behaviour makes no difference. It is the way s/he has been loved that also translates to their way of expressing their needs with regards to love. The kindness or the criticality, the closeness or the distance, the acceptance or the rejection, the acknowledgement or the ignorance, all act as sediments that lay the foundation of the bed-rock of love. In a similar way how a person treats one's self with love is intrinsically related with their true experience of how they came to be loved.

27.4 Self: Criticism or Compassion: Relationship with Psychopathology

Once thought to be only related with depression, self-criticism has been considered as a trans diagnostic risk factor for different kinds of psychopathology (Kannan & Levitt, 2013; Shahar, Doron, & Szepsenwol, 2015). Individuals who are self-critical experience feelings of unworthiness, inferiority, failure and guilt. They are constantly engaging in harsh self scrunity and evaluation and fear being disapproved, criticized and losing the approval and acceptance of others (Blatt & Zuroff, 1992). Several researchers have found self-criticism to have a negative impact on interpersonal relationships throughout the life (Besser & Priel, 2003; Wiseman, Raz, & Sharabany, 2007). Studies have shown self-criticism to be high for people suffering from depression (Ehret, Joormann, & Berking, 2015; Fazaa & Page, 2003), PTSD (McCranie & Hyer, 1995; Sharhabani-Arzy, Amir, & Swisa, 2005), eating disorders (Dunkley, Masheb, & Grilo, 2010; Kelly, Carter, Zuroff, & Borairi, 2013) and anxiety disorders (see Chap. 59).

In a study by Brewin and Firth-Cozens (1997) self-criticism in fourth-year medical students predicted depression 2 years later, and—in males—10 years later in their medical careers better than a history of depression. Another research with 5877 respondents in the National Comorbidity Survey (NCS) found self-criticism to be robustly associated with social phobia after controlling for factors such as current emotional distress, neuroticism, and lifetime history of mood, anxiety, and substance use disorders (Cox, Fleet, & Stein, 2004).

In contrast recent literature has found that the greater the self-compassion, the lesser the psychopathology (Barnard & Curry, 2011). This has also been supplemented by a study that found large effect sizes when examining the link between self-compassion and depression, anxiety and stress (MacBeth & Gumley, 2012). The presence of self-compassion has also been found to be associated with less body dissatisfaction, body preoccupation, and weight worries, greater body appreciation and less disordered eating (Ferreira, Pinto-Gouveia, & Duarte. 2013;

Kelly et al., 2013). With respect to PTSD, Beaumont, Galpin, and Jenkins (2012) found self-compassion to be a protective factor for posttraumatic stress. Additionally, according to Dahm (2013) combat veterans with higher levels of self-compassion show lower levels of psychopathology, better functioning in daily life, and fewer symptoms of posttraumatic stress.

Studies in the field of neuroscience have found that engaging in self-criticism, on an fMRI, activates the brain regions of lateral prefrontal cortex and dorsal anterior cingulate cortex which are responsible for processing error detection and correction. In contrast, engaging in self-reassurance has been found to activate the left temporal pole and insula areas, previously found to be activated in compassion and empathy. Thus, people who are self-critical tend to show an activated dorsolateral prefrontal activity, while those who engage in self-assurance show an activated ventrolateral prefrontal cortex (Longe et al., 2010).

27.5 Self-Criticism Versus Self-Compassion: A Cultural Perspective

Culture has been defined as a "group's shared set of distinct basic assumptions, values, practices, and artifacts that are formed and retained over a long period of time" (Taras, Rowney, & Steel, 2009). Cultural psychology is of the view that the self is born of the interaction between the person and a set of culturally derived beliefs, values, institutions, customs, and practices (Fiske, Kitayama, Markus, & Nisbett, 1997; Nisbett, Peng, Choi, & Norenzayan, 2001). The self and attendant psychological structures and processes are thus supported by a web of cultural meanings, and likewise, the interaction of individual selves creates and sustains the cultural environment. Thus, in this way, culture and self are significantly intertwined with each other (Shweder, 1990). Research in cultural psychology maintains that culture is implicated in psychological processes at a far more fundamental level (e.g., Markus & Kitayama, 1991).

Cross-cultural investigations of self-compassion and self-criticism are sparse. Of the existing few, it was found that while both self-enhancing and self-critical capacities exist among people from eastern and western culture, Easterners are more self-critical than Westerners (Heine & Hamamura, 2007; Lo, Helwig, Chen, Ohashi, & Cheng, 2011). A study by Neff, Pisitsungkagarn, and Hsieh (2008) found that self-compassion levels are governed by cultural practices that are more nuanced than a simple East-West dichotomy.

Traditionally, India as a country sees high interdependence, with a prevailing importance given to the family (Mishra, 1994; Saraswathi & Pai, 1997). Strong kinship networks and extended families have existed, although in urban compared to rural areas there has been an increase in the nuclear families (Roopnarine & Hossain, 1992). Though social and economic changes have impacted the socialization practices, traditional cultural beliefs have continued to influence child-rearing (Mishra, Mayer, Trommsdorff, Albert, & Schwarz, 2005; Saraswathi & Ganapathy, 2002).

Given the Indian cultural background and the expectations imposed on growing children and adolescents (mostly from lower and middle-class families) with regards to academic achievement, the prevalent parenting styles in India are either authoritarian or authoritative.

Even in the twenty-first century, India continues to fight with stereotypes concerning careers and academics with respect to gender. All the above factors while highlighting excellence mostly miss out on the aspect of self-love and self-compassion. To match with the level of stress and pressure are the rising statistics of mental illnesses of depression, anxiety disorders and most disturbingly, youth suicide. A 2012 Lancet report found India to have the world's highest rate of suicide for youth aged 15–29 years old (Saha, 2017). In a scenario such as this, the aspect of self-compassion becomes highly significant and need of the hour.

27.6 Self-Compassion and the Psychotherapeutic Process

> You yourself, as much as anybody in the entire universe, deserve your love and affection—
> Buddha

Compassion focused therapy (CFT), according to Gilbert (2010), is a multimodal therapy which builds on a range of traditional cognitive behavioural therapies and other interventions. It emphasises on attention, reasoning, rumination, behaviour, emotions, motives and imagery. Self-compassion helps in deactivating the threat system (linked with feelings of insecure attachment, defensiveness and autonomic arousal) and activates the caregiving system. This is associated with feelings of security, safety, attachment and oxytocin-opiate system (Gilbert & Procter, 2006).

Compassion focused therapy caters to the need of the clients who come from harsh backgrounds, thus making it difficult for them to access their soothing emotion regulation systems. In other words, such clients can understand the logic of CBT but continue to not feel any different after using alternative thoughts. CFT enables them to utilise affect systems that allow them to experience feelings of reassurance and safety. According to Desmond (2016) when clients develop more compassion for themselves, they can more easily move through difficult material, forgive themselves and others, and become more productive and happy human beings. In an uncontrolled pilot study by Rose, McIntyre, and Rimes (2018) twenty-three university students with significantly high levels of self-criticism underwent six individual weekly treatment sessions with an emphasis on methods from compassion focused therapy. Findings revealed statistically significant improvements between pre- and post-intervention for self-criticism, functional impairment, mood, self-esteem and maladaptive perfectionism with medium to large effect sizes at both post-intervention and follow-up. Gains were maintained or increased between post-treatment and 2-month follow-up.

In a research carried out in Norway on 170 patients at a university clinic meeting, who met for the criterion of anxiety and depression related disorders, the relationship between self-image and outcome in psychotherapy was measured. Self-image was measured with the Structural Analysis of Social Behavior (SASB-I) introject pre and post-treatment. Findings revealed that an increase in self-love and decrease in self-blame (pre to post) predicted reduced symptoms at post-treatment, whereas decrease in self-attack and self-control, as well as increase in self-affirm, predicted reduced interpersonal problems. Thus, the study suggested an improvement in a client's self-image to be related to a positive psychotherapy outcome (Ryum, Vogel, Walderhaug, & Stiles, 2015).

Tim Desmond, in his book Self-Compassion in Psychotherapy (2016) describes the five ways he likes to inject self-compassion into the healing therapeutic process:

1. Unlocking the client's natural well of compassion by focusing first on a person, pet, or object that they care deeply for, then helping them expand it.
2. Using compassion to help the client transform their suffering in the present by accepting their current struggle, validating feelings associated with it and offering themselves kindness, love, and understanding in the present moment.
3. Using compassion to transform the client's past suffering, by reflecting on the past, picturing themselves as a child, and offering love and compassion.
4. Helping clients understand why they engage in self-criticism (related to anxiety/depression or their inner critic) and showing ways to overcome it, for example a dialogue with the inner critic and the kind self.
5. Therapist's own practice of self-compassion which helps them relate with clients and assist them in the journey of becoming a kinder and a compassionate person to their own self.

Hence, more often than not, underlying the many clinical symptoms which clients bring to psychotherapy are core issues rooted in the sense of an inadequate self thus leading them to feel small, incapable and incompetent. Thus, when a therapeutic stance which is grounded in core mindfulness concepts of acceptance and self-compassion is adopted, it gives the client an opportunity to sit with their difficult emotions rather fight or flee from them. This further strengthens their capacity for distress tolerance and emotion regulation, skills frequently taught in various presentations of clinical symptoms and mental illnesses.

27.7 Methodology

The current chapter cites a case study with a client which involved psychotherapeutic work for over 16 sessions spread over a time span of a year. The gap between the sessions was caused due to factors such as family gatherings, festival celebrations, holidays and exam schedules at the client's end.

27.7.1 The Journey With-in

> Love and compassion are necessities, not luxuries. Without them humanity cannot survive.—Dalai Lama

Riya, a 22-year-old girl who was pursuing her Masters in Psychology wanted to seek psychotherapy sessions for some of her concerns and also to understand what it felt like to be a client. She came with concerns of poor self-esteem, low confidence and issues related to her body-image. She would spend hours rehearsing her conversations with people and refrained expressing her views in class discussions out of fear of being evaluated and mocked at by others. It was also observed that she carried many "shoulds" and "oughts" in her mind. Riya was governed by a sense of not being "good enough" thus constantly feeling small and inadequate in different areas of her life (which included academics, family, romantic life, body-image and self-perception).

27.7.2 The In-Adequate Me

One of the underlying themes that came across in many sessions, as presented by Riya, was that of "feeling inadequate" and "not good enough". In one of the early sessions while exploring her anxiety to speak in social situations, Riya shared that she felt there was a shadow within her which watched how she talked and spoke to others. We addressed one of her thoughts and a downward arrow technique was utilised to understand the roots of it.

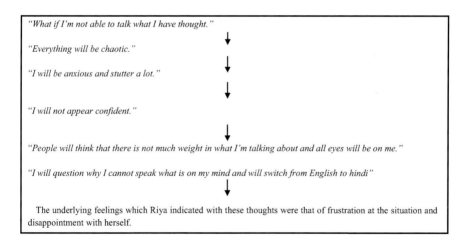

On exploration it was found that that her social awkwardness began when she entered college. Seeing others perform better than her fanned her insecurities.

As she spoke, I offered her an image that was forming in my mind and asked if she connected with it "I see a 6-year-old Riya extremely overwhelmed by people's talents, to see that they are "better than" me. When asked what she felt in her body she described her chest feeling heavy with the colour dark grey.

The therapist reflected back to her the entire process of the triggers that would overwhelm her and how the child in her was still alive and would mentally shutdown at the pretext of talking and expressing her opinion in front of others. Riya responded by saying "*I cannot be lesser than them*". This further led to an exploration of how she considered being the elder child (the first-born child) of parents to be a responsible task. Her parents expected her to do well.

Her inner critic smirked at her, expressing its' disappointment, for her not being able to do what she wanted to.

The idea of surpassing herself, being seen as falling short of anything, would often lead to rehearsing a conversation she would use at a later point in time. The therapist reflected back to Riya of how akin her experience was to Adler's concept of compensating for the underline felt inferiorities, thus, leading her continuously to strive for superiority. Riya's face lit up as if she had stumbled upon a bright lamp on a dark alley. She nodded her head vigorously and smiled, affirming the reflection that she was offered.

27.7.3 *The Parent and the Inner Critic*

Riya was found to share a fairly secure attachment bond with her parents. They had offered her, like many middle-class Indian homes, an authoritative style of parenting which came with freedom and healthy limits. Inquiry into her inner critic led us to understand the voice to be judgemental and often laden with disappointment, shame and an internal expectation of perfectionism.

Interestingly, it was found that Riya's internalised parental voice was harsher than her parents' opinions or voices in the present-day context. In one of the earlier sessions she was suggested to read Neff's book on Self-Compassion (2011) and Daring Greatly by Brene Brown (2012) as part of bibliotherapy. The following session Riya came back with an insight which was suggestive of a clear blue sky that had seen months of heavy rains. She shared having an inner dialogue with her critic. She shared a victory of expressing herself in her class for the very first time. Riya shared "*Being critical doesn't really help*" and quoted "*Like Brene Brown says that the credit belongs to the man in the arena*".

Natterson (2015) in his book, Psychotherapy as a mutual loving process, writes:

> Most patients bring developed but inhibited loving capabilities to therapy. These inhibitions originate from strictures imposed by loving but neurotic parents. Therapy logically becomes a process of removing these inhibitions and releasing the loving self. From this it follows that love and self are inseparable and mutually reinforcing, and that the authentic self is the loving self.

The therapy process with Riya was focused on helping her gather her own inner resources of compassion which she already possessed. Behind the veil of her presenting complaints was a self which was in genuine need of love, safety and self-compassion. The therapist's compassionate and humanistic stance and the ability to channel her inner critic to these resources provided Riya with sufficient practice to utilise them outside therapy sessions as well.

27.7.4 Inviting the Loving Self

Along with the many concerns Riya brought to therapy, one of them was how she viewed her own body. She had always been a chubby kid but her perception towards her body weight, appearance and height affected her self-worth. According to her height, Riya was overweight. She expressed that she tried to make-up for her looks by drowning herself in studies but that didn't come to her aid. In one of the earlier sessions she said

> I'll never be that whole package...I have always had this thought, that only if I lose weight, I'll be perceived as great in every way. There's a dark curtain on this idea that there is more to me than my weight.

Through the sessions, we worked together on her image of her body, what it meant to her and what she could do attain her goals of a healthier self.

In a later session in therapy, Riya shared her wish to lose weight as a cousin's marriage was approaching. She shared how her earlier attempts at losing weight had failed. I reflected back at her

> ... it appears that you are saying that because I've failed earlier, I'll fail again". To this she responded by saying "That's true. Time is running out. I'll be devastated if it doesn't work this time.

The therapist adopted an approach wherein words such as "fat", "calories", "thin" were intentionally refrained and the focus was on encouraging Riya to make realistic goals, eating healthy and connecting with her body that sustained her. Every time Riya mentioned of her efforts, she was encouraged and appreciated. The sessions also focused on keeping a non-judgemental and an observational stance towards her inner critic.

As the therapy sessions came to a close, Riya, in one of the last sessions shared that she had lost 6 kilograms of weight. She was congratulated and praised for her efforts. When asked what helped her, she spoke of continuing with her usual consumption of three home-cooked meals combined with running and exercises inspired from youtube videos. To this she added

> one of the biggest changes for me was the change in the perception of how I'm not good enough because I'm fat and that I'm stupid.

Riya credited her work on being compassionate to herself as one of the tools that aided her in the process. She shared experiencing the fine-tunement of her capacity to step-out from the inner critic's voice. "*Self-compassion is like a good sign on a bumper sticker. We read it but don't do and act upon it until using it becomes our only choice*" she remarked. In sync with Riya's experience are words written by Natterson (2015). He says:

> When the loving self emerges from hiding, the patient's loving capabilities are always enhanced. Self and love are inseparable partners, wrapped around each other like a double helix. Love moves from the longing to be loved, to the belief that one is worthy of being loved, to the confident certainty that one has or will have love. Parallel to this, the self unfolds, moving from self-doubt to self-trust, self-respect.

27.7.5 Utilising the Insights for Days to Come

> The process of learning an art can be divided conveniently into two parts: one, the mastery of the theory; the other, the mastery of the practice.

As the client connects with the knowledge, grief and learnings of how their past lessons on love add to their current perception and treatment of oneself, the seed of a new kind of love begins to grow in their soil of self. The therapist like a gardener encourages her client to slowly rely on their newly developed resources of self-compassion. Through continuous practice and watering the client gradually begins to see the seed blossoming into a love that's there to protect them and be with them no matter what the circumstances. In my sessions with Riya it is the repeated and gentle reminders to utilise self-compassion and practice non-judgmental acceptance of the current emotional state that enabled her to tap into her inner resources.

Her efforts to soften the critical voice that was anxiety provoking allowed her to express her opinions which she would earlier shy away from. Self-compassion, for her, created new spaces to explore and do things which couldn't be thought of. She recognised a change in her perception towards her body which allowed her to embrace it than fight with it. This led her to work for it than against it, which she reported in her victory of losing weight. Understanding her inner critic, it's unreasonable expectations from herself and softening its' voice, with a gentle stance of the therapist, encouraged Riya to connect with her ever-loving presence of herself. She found the courage to speak her mind, challenge her negative thoughts and test them only to find them baseless and untrue. Additionally, one of the significant learnings that touched Riya was her ability to give space to emotions than resist them. She wrote (in one of the mails she had sent to the therapist):

> I realised that suppressing my emotions was only making me hollower from inside. Truly feeling what I was feeling and what I wanted to feel made me such a lighter being. Now I embrace my emotions and try to understand where they are coming from.

Being compassionate to herself through practicing within and outside (by journal writing) allowed Riya to ease and let go of the many expectations she had created in striving to be that "perfect" friend, daughter, sister, student and a girlfriend. The many inadequacies Riya had presented with in the beginning of the sessions were taken care of in the sessions. The insights and her victories saw her becoming that ideal self that she had dreamed of, only to find it in her present self. Natterson (2015) writes:

> Therapy's basic process is not to fill vacancies, but to liberate what has been kept hidden, which is, first and foremost, the loving self. Therapists sometimes see cases in which a patient's fluent loving capability emerges and prevails within a relatively short period of time. Such events suggest that the loving self had survived intact from early childhood, but had been inhibited and stifled.

To see Riya grow and blossom through the sessions was deeply satisfying. Her growth was nothing short of phenomenal. In one of the last sessions, she expressed:

> You (the therapist) helped me to understand each part of myself one by one where some layers I unravelled myself with the help of the strength I had built. Today, I think it's safe to say, that I have come a long way. It always brings tears to my eyes when I think about the journey I have had with myself and I am only filled with gratitude.

27.8 Conclusion

Thich Nhat Hanh says "When someone says to us, *Darling, I care about your suffering, a deep healing begins*". Regardless of what symptoms a client presents to us, one thing that stays true to each one of them is their deep need for unconditional love. As psychotherapists and psychologists, utilising compassion focused therapeutic approach allows clients to heal with great kindness, non-judgmental-ness and acceptance offered to none other than the loving self. The self which had endured years of bruises, scars, rashes, pains of the inner critical voice melts and weeps the moment it is touched by the love of self-compassion. It is in moments such as these that healing begins to take place. The client's heart which was earlier shut and withdrawn towards life slowly begins to feel a release. It's nothing short of a new lease of life. What makes self-compassion and compassion focused therapy an excellent tool to use is the fact that it makes our clients self-reliant and accepting of their current and future struggles. It is in this act of open-ness that a new world blossoms at their door-step, with a self that finds its own companion for life, that which is loving, caring and kind.

Acknowledgements I'd like to extend my sincere gratitude to Ms. Manpreet Kaur and Ms. Nisha C, trained Clinical Psychologists from NIMHANS, Bangalore, India, for their reading of the earlier version of this chapter and offering insightful suggestions at a very short notice.

References

Barnard, L. K., & Curry, J. F. (2011). Self-compassion: Conceptualizations, correlates, & interventions. *Review of General Psychology, 15*(4), 289–303.

Beaumont, E., Galpin, A., & Jenkins, P. (2012). 'Being kinder to myself': A prospective comparative study, exploring post-trauma therapy outcome measures, for two groups of clients, receiving either cognitive behaviour therapy or cognitive behaviour therapy and compassionate mind training. *Counselling Psychology Review, 27*(1), 31–43.

Besser, A., & Priel, B. (2003). A multisource approach to self-critical vulnerability to depression: The moderating role of attachment: Depression in married couples. *Journal of Personality, 71*(4), 515–555. https://doi.org/10.1111/1467-6494.7104002

Blatt, S. J., & Zuroff, D. C. (1992). Interpersonal relatedness and self-definition: Two prototypes for depression. *Clinical Psychology Review, 12*(5), 527–562. https://doi.org/10.1016/0272-7358(92)90070-O

Bowlby, J. (1969). *Attachment and loss: Vol. 1. Attachment*. New York: Basic Books.

Bowlby, J. (1973). *Attachment and loss: Vol. 2. Separation: Anxiety and anger*. New York: Basic Books.

Brewin, C. B., & Firth-Cozens, J. (1997). Dependency and self-criticism as predictors of depression in young doctors. *Journal of Occupational Health Psychology, 2*(3), 242–246. https://doi.org/10.1037/1076-8998.2.3.242

Brown, B. (2012). *Daring greatly how the courage to be vulnerable transforms the way we live, love, parent and lead*. New York: Penguin Group.

Cox, B. J., Fleet, C., & Stein, M. B. (2004). Self-criticism and social phobia in the US national comorbidity survey. *Journal of Affective Disorders, 82*(2), 227–234. https://doi.org/10.1016/j.jad.2003.12.012

Dahm, K. A. (2013). *Mindfulness and self-compassion as predictors of functional outcomes and psychopathology in OEF/OIF veterans exposed to trauma*. Retrieved from https://repositories.lib.utexas.edu/handle/2152/21635

Desmond, T. (2016). *Self-compassion in psychotherapy*. New York: W. W. Norton.

Dunkley, D. M., Masheb, R. M., & Grilo, C. M. (2010). Childhood maltreatment, depressive symptoms, and body dissatisfaction in patients with binge eating disorder: The mediating role of self-criticism. *International Journal of Eating Disorder, 43*(3), 274–281.

Ehret, A. M., Joormann, J., & Berking, M. (2015). Examining risk and resilience factors for depression: The role of self-criticism and self-compassion. *Cognition and Emotion, 29*(8), 1496–1504. https://doi.org/10.1080/02699931.2014.992394

Enns, M. W., Cox, B. J., & Inayatulla, M. (2003). Personality predictors of outcome for adolescents hospitalized for suicidal ideation. *Journal of the American Academy of Child and Adolescent Psychiatry, 42*, 720–727.

Fazaa, N., & Page, S. (2003). Dependency and self-criticism as predictors of suicidal behavior. *Suicide and Life-threatening Behavior, 33*(2), 172–185. https://doi.org/10.1521/suli.33.2.172.22777

Ferreira, C., Pinto-Gouveia, J., & Duarte, C. (2013). Self-compassion in the face of shame and body image dissatisfaction: Implications for eating disorders. *Eating Behaviors, 14*(2), 207–210. https://doi.org/10.1016/j.eatbeh.2013.01.005

Fiske, A. P., Kitayama, S., Markus, H. R., & Nisbett, R. E. (1997). The cultural matrix of social psychology. In D. T. Gilbert, S. Fiske, & G. Lindzey (Eds.), *Handbook of social psychology* (4th ed., pp. 915–974). New York: McGraw-Hill.

Fromm, E. (1956). *The art of loving*. New York: Harper and Row.

Gilbert, P. (2010). *Compassion focused therapy: The CBT distinctive features series*. London; New York: Routledge; Taylor & Francis Group.

Gilbert, P., Clarke, M., Hempel, S., Miles, J. N. V., & Irons, C. (2004). Criticizing and reassuring oneself: An exploration of forms, styles and reasons in female students. *British Journal of Clinical Psychology, 43*(1), 31–50. https://doi.org/10.1348/014466504772812959

Gilbert, P., & Procter, S. (2006). Compassionate mind training for people with high shame and self-criticism: Overview and pilot study of a group therapy approach. *Clinical Psychology & Psychotherapy, 13*, 353–379.

Heine, S. J., & Hamamura, T. (2007). In search of east Asian self-enhancement. *Personality and Social Psychology Review, 11*(1), 4–27. https://doi.org/10.1177/1088868306294587

Kannan, D., & Levitt, H. M. (2013). A review of client self-criticism in psychotherapy. *Journal of Psychotherapy Integration, 23*(2), 166–178. https://doi.org/10.1037/a0032355

Kelly, A. C., Carter, J. C., Zuroff, D. C., & Borairi, S. (2013). Self-compassion and fear of self-compassion interact to predict response to eating disorders treatment: A preliminary investigation. *Psychotherapy Research, 23*(3), 252–264. https://doi.org/10.1080/10503307.2012.717310

Kohut, H. (1971). *The analysis of the self*. New York: International Universities Press.

Kohut, H. (1977). *The restoration of the self*. New York: International Universities Press.

Lo, C., Helwig, C. C., Chen, S. X., Ohashi, M. M., & Cheng, C. M. (2011). The psychology of strengths and weaknesses: Assessing self-enhancing and self-critical tendencies in eastern and western cultures. *Self and Identity, 10*(2), 203–212. https://doi.org/10.1080/15298861003751272

Longe, O., Maratos, F. A., Gilbert, P., Evans, G., Volker, F., Rockliff, H., et al. (2010). Having a word with yourself: Neural correlates of self-criticism and self-reassurance. *NeuroImage, 49*(2), 1849–1856. https://doi.org/10.1016/j.neuroimage.2009.09.019

MacBeth, A., & Gumley, A. (2012). Exploring compassion: A meta-analysis of the association between self-compassion and psychopathology. *Clinical Psychology Review, 32*, 545–552.

Markus, H. R., & Kitayama, S. (1991). Culture and the self: Implications for cognition, emotion, and motivation. *Psychological Review, 98*(2), 224–253.

McCranie, E. W., & Hyer, L. A. (1995). Self-critical depressive experience in posttraumatic stress disorder. *Psychological Reports, 77*(3), 880–882. https://doi.org/10.2466/pr0.1995.77.3.880

Merriam Webster. (2012). *Love – Definition of love by Merriam-Webster*. merriam-webster.com. Archived from the original on 12 January 2012. Retrieved December 14, 2011.

Mishra, R. C. (1994). Individualist and collectivist orientations across generations. In U. Kim & H. C. Triandis (Eds.), *Individualism and collectivism: Theory, method, and applications* (pp. 225–238). Thousand Oaks, CA: Sage.

Mishra, R., Mayer, B., Trommsdorff, G., Albert, I., & Schwarz, B. (2005). The value of children in urban and rural India: Cultural background and empirical results. In G. Trommsdorff & B. Nauck (Eds.), *The value of children in cross-cultural perspective. Case studies from eight societies* (pp. 143–170). Lengerich: Pabst Science.

Mongrain, M., Vettese, L. C., Shuster, B., & Kendal, N. (1998). Perceptual biases, affect, and behavior in relationship of dependents and self-critics. *Journal of Personality and Social Psychology, 75*, 230–241.

Natterson, J. (2015). *Psychotherapy as a mutual loving process*. Chevy Chase, MD: International Psychotherapy Institute.

Neff, K. (2003a). Development and validation of a scale to measure self-compassion. *Self and Identity, 2*, 223–250.

Neff, K. (2003b). Self-compassion: An alternative conceptualization of a healthy attitude toward oneself. *Self and Identity, 2*(2), 85–101. https://doi.org/10.1080/15298860309032

Neff, K. (2011). *Self-compassion: The proven power of being kind to yourself*. New York: Harper Collins Publishers.

Neff, K. D., Hseih, Y., & Dejitthirat, K. (2005). Self-compassion, achievement goals, and coping with academic failure. *Self and Identity, 4*, 263–287.

Neff, K., & McGeehee, P. (2010). Self-compassion and psychological resilience among adolescents and young adults. *Self and Identity, 9*, 225–240.

Neff, K. D., & Vonk, R. (2009). Self-compassion versus global self-esteem: Two different ways of relating to oneself. *Journal of Personality, 77*, 23–50. https://doi.org/10.1111/j.1467-6494.2008.00537.x

Neff, K. D., Pisitsungkagarn, K., & Hsieh, Y.-P. (2008). Self-compassion and self-construal in the United States, Thailand, and Taiwan. *Journal of Cross-Cultural Psychology, 39*(3), 267–285. https://doi.org/10.1177/0022022108314544

Nisbett, R. E., Peng, K., Choi, I., & Norenzayan, A. (2001). Culture and systems of thought: Holistic versus analytic cognition. *Psychological Review, 108*(2), 291–310. https://doi.org/10.1037/0033-295X.108.2.291

Roopnarine, J. L., & Hossain, Z. (1992). *Parent-child socialization in diverse cultures*. Norwood, NJ: Ablex.

Rose, A., McIntyre, R., & Rimes, K. A. (2018). Compassion-focused intervention for highly self-critical individuals: Pilot study. *Behavioural and Cognitive Psychotherapy, 46*(5), 583–600. https://doi.org/10.1017/S135246581800036X

Ryum, T., Vogel, P. A., Walderhaug, E. P., & Stiles, T. C. (2015). The role of self-image as a predictor of psychotherapy outcome. *Scandinavian Journal of Psychology, 56*(1), 62–68. https://doi.org/10.1111/sjop.12167

Saha, D. (2017). Every hour one student commits suicide in India. *Hindustan Times*. Retrieved from https://www.hindustantimes.com/health-and-fitness/every-hour-one-student-commits-suicide-in-india/story-7UFFhSs6h1HNgrNO60FZ2O.html

Saraswathi, T. S., & Ganapathy, H. (2002). Indian parents' ethnotheories as reflections of the Hindu scheme of child and human development. In H. Keller & Y. H. Poortinga (Eds.), *Between culture and biology: Perspectives on ontogenetic development* (pp. 79–88). New York: Cambridge University Press.

Saraswathi, T. S., & Pai, S. (1997). Socialization in the Indian context. In H. S. R. Kao & D. Sinha (Eds.), *Asian perspectives on psychology* (pp. 74–92). Thousand Oaks, CA: Sage.

Shahar, B., Doron, G., & Szepsenwol, O. (2015). Childhood maltreatment, shame-proneness and self-criticism in social anxiety disorder: A sequential mediational model: Shame and self-criticism in social anxiety. *Clinical Psychology & Psychotherapy, 22*(6), 570–579. https://doi.org/10.1002/cpp.1918

Sharhabani-Arzy, R., Amir, M., & Swisa, A. (2005). Self-criticism, dependency and posttraumatic stress disorder among a female group of help-seeking victims of domestic violence in Israel. *Personality and Individual Differences, 38*(5), 1231–1240. https://doi.org/10.1016/j.paid.2004.08.006

Shweder, R. A. (1990). Cultural psychology: What is it? In J. W. Stigler, R. A. Shweder, & G. Herdt (Eds.), *Cultural psychology: Essays on comparative human development* (pp. 1–46). Cambridge, England: Cambridge University Press.

Taras, V., Rowney, J., & Steel, P. (2009). Half a century of measuring culture: Review of approaches, challenges and limitations based on the analysis of 121 instruments for quantifying culture. *Journal of International Management, 15*(4), 357–373. https://doi.org/10.1016/j.intman.2008.08.005

Thaik, C. M. (2014). The kind of love that does your heart good. *Psychology Today*. Archived from https://www.psychologytoday.com/hk/blog/the-heart/201403/the-kind-love-does-your-heart-good

Wiseman, H., Raz, A., & Sharabany, R. (2007). Depressive personality styles and interpersonal problems in young adults with difficulties in establishing long-term romantic relationships. *Israel Journal of Psychiatry Related Sciences, 44*(4), 280–291.

Wood, H. (2016). A Christian understanding of the significance of love of oneself in loving god and neighbour: Towards an integrated self-love reading. *HTS Theological Studies, 72*(3), 1–10.

Aakriti Malik is a Clinical Psychologist currently working at Middlemore Hospital in Auckland, New Zealand. An Indian by origin, she is registered with the New Zealand Psychologists Board and the Rehabilitation Council of India. Her recent migration to New Zealand has given her the capacity to personally recognize and empathise with the struggles of migration and its effect on individual's social, psychological and emotional lives. Having worked with people from diverse cultural backgrounds for the past eight years, in India and through tele-mental health platforms, Aakriti considers her profession a privilege. It allows her to connect to the deeper realities of people and encourage them to reach their true potential. Additionally, her fondness for writing and teaching has seen her greatly contribute in the area of research. She has worked as a lecturer teaching undergraduate students from various courses in both government and private institutions in India and Malaysia. Her publications include articles and book chapters in Indian and international journals. Further, she has to her credit multiple workshops and seminars conducted for mental health professionals, students, teaching and the parent community. Aakriti has also been an expert columnist in renowned newsletters such as the New Indian Express and Times of India.

Chapter 28
How to Research Performances of Love with Timelines

Sharon Rose Brehm

Abstract This chapter provides a methodological addition to ethnographic approaches to study love. It tackles the question, how we can investigate performances of love. Love itself is a concept that is fluid and develops meaning not only through words but also bodies. To explore love as a researcher therefore means to consider the diverse materiality of love. The narrations of love are just as important as bodily reactions.

This research on migration experiences of German-Russian couples is based on a combination of ethnographical and systemic psychotherapeutic methods. Intensive 2-year long research provided the basis to use a sculpture work. This method is called "timeline" and ropes are used to symbolize the lives of interview partners. The couples formed with ropes their lives on the floor. Thereby they could literally walk the interviewers through their migrations experiences as marriage migrants. The qualitative, actorfocusing method was conducted with five German-Russian couples in Germany.

This method gives the possibility to include the different perspectives and experiences of love even within one relationship. Especially in order to understand binational or transcultural relationships it is important to avoid reductions. Additionally, this method is a potent research practice to collect narrative, emotional and non-verbal aspects of love at the same time. How intimacy is created as well as what love means for binational couples concerning life choices is presented. This article sets out a research design to study the complex performance of love and proposes further inclusion of systemic methods in qualitative research designs.

Keywords Love · Migration · Russia · Binational couples · Applied ethnography

---

S. R. Brehm (✉)
Munich, Germany
e-mail: Sharonrose.brehm@gmail.com

28.1 Introduction

> What we know, wish to know, struggle to know, must try to know about love or rejection, being alone or together and dying together or alone—can all be streamlined, put in order, match the standards of consistency, cohesiveness and completeness set for the lesser matters? Perhaps it can—in the infinity of time that is. (Bauman, 2013, p. 2)

Love is a complex subject as several articles in this book already laid out. The complexity stems from the hardship to deal with emotions and the stigmatization of vulnerability we experience in our societies as well as in academia. Love is experienced through the fluidity of moments and challenges us to put something in words we also experience with our bodies. This chapter provides a methodological addition to ethnographic approaches to study love and thereby addressing these issues. Semi-structured interviews revealed how limited classical interview situations can be analyzed and interpreted in regard to concepts and performances of love. Due to that the methodic canon of cultural anthropology was expanded and opened to a method from systemic therapy. The timeline uses ropes to symbolize biographies of interview partners.

Intensive 2-year long research provided the basis to use the timeline for qualitative research. Ropes symbolize the lives of interview partners. The couples were given ropes to form their lives on the floor. Thereby they could literally walk researchers through their migration experiences. Hence, fieldwork became an exploration of not only told but incorporated stories.

Integrating a timeline shifted the focus on interactivity and momentums of love of German-Russian couples. This whole study shows the interdependencies between the legal process and private relationships of migrating couples, concentrating on the actors' perspectives (Brehm, 2020). Through the timeline method, two components of love became more detailed. First, the timeline made different shades of closeness and intimacy more apparent. Second, love also got the meaning of a permission to be changed by one's partner.

28.2 Aim of the Chapter

This chapter sets out a research design to study the complexity of love, its physical and corporeal symbols, and proposes further inclusion of systemic methods in cultural anthropological studies.

The objective of this chapter is adding variety and sensory depth to qualitative research methods, which is essential when we study multifaceted concepts like love. Language and words offer essential insights, and yet nonverbal communication is just as full of meaning. Thereby social scientists need to adapt, strengthen and extend their methodic repertoire. This chapter presents a methodological approach to study love and migration experiences of German-Russian couples and concentrates on the different displays of love. The timeline was used to gather corporeal, physical and symbolic findings about love.

This study about German-Russian couples lies in a complex context. German-Russian couples find themselves in a unique situation, which the research literature also revisits. One branch of literature analysis the bureaucratical site. Governmentality, vigilance and the role of the state play essential functions. Other research literature dwells on more intimate details, like communication, exchange of values and family relationship between two people with different upbringings and backgrounds. These academic contributions also include the effect of history and traditions for the used discourses.

Thereupon *Grounded Theory* (Glaser & Strauss, 1967) defines the research paradigm. Not only does *Grounded Theory* support the post-structural idea that we continually construct and deconstruct meaning. It also establishes a fruitful exchange between researcher and interviewees. It initiates a circle of gathering data, analysis, of going back and meeting again with interview partners—and thereby creates the grounds to understand love's complexity.

Next to *Grounded Theory,* Sara Pink's *Sensory Ethnography* (2015) offers a methodological framework and orientation. She highlights the materiality of knowledge. She proposes how to integrate sensory and sensuality data.

The timeline resulted out of these theoretic considerations and aimed to gather data about love. As the timeline originates from systemic therapy, it is important to describe why its values fit into the conducted ethnographic fieldwork. The description of the couples and data provide the methodic grounds for the research methodology. The timeline as a methodical addition developed out of the process and the adaption to the individual research situation. Semi-structured interviews, a more classical approach, led to the use of systemic methods.

The second phase commenced with intense preparation and allowed the execution to be open, focusing on the actors and allowed sensitivity towards more than words. This chapter answers practical questions in regard to research love, from how to start the method, what to say, how to explain it to interview partners and on what to focus.

28.3 Context and Literature Review

A duality frames the migration experiences of German-Russian couples who want to live together in Germany. The research literature mirrors the complicated situation, as well. Therefore, the literature overview shows the two intervening spheres and links them to the context. Thereafter, the sample clarification follows.

28.3.1 Love Migration: Bureaucratical Framework and Governmentality

On the one hand, bureaucratical processes, the sphere of the state and control influence the practices of German-Russian couples: From collecting documents to preparing themselves to be tested if their marriage is a scam. Their relationship, privacy and intimacy are the foundation for their migration experience. Interview partners didn't migrate for a job or a limited amount of time. They moved to Germany in the belief of living together with their spouses.

The constitution of Germany includes the right for family and marriage in §6. For that reason, the visa for family reunification offers a unique legal situation for spouses of German citizens. For example, migrating spouses get the same rights as their German citizens, and they can apply earlier for German citizenship.

As it is challenging to define marriage and as certain marriage constellations are associated with marriage scam and fraud, the migration process is managed by German officials. Until now, the term "mail-order marriage" stigmatizes German-Russian couples (Constable, 2003; Luehrmann, 2004). Beneath this stereotype lies the fear that migrants use marriages as a tool to obtain access to the German welfare system and to use people only as a visa sponsor. A specific set of regulatory practices is brought into life to secure the German border against marriages of convenience and security holes (Williams, 2010). Besides German language tests, marriage migrants might face the need to justify their relationship in interviews.

Scientists such as Anna-Maria D'Aoust (2010), Sabine Hess (2009) and Miriam Gutekunst (2013, 2018) address this situation. They focus on vigilance and governmentality in spousal and marriage migration processes.

The Canadian political scientist Anna-Marie D'Aoust (2010) examines the tension between love and regulation on a discursive and medial level. Hess and the Transit Migration-Group initiated the concept of border regime analysis. This ethnographic approach brings together institutions and individual lives. They analyze borders as a space of observation and control (Hess, 2009; Hess & Tsianos, 2010). Miriam Gutekunst also applies this methodological approach in her studies about German-Moroccan and German-Northern African couples. She examines the question of immobilization through the border regime (Gutekunst, 2013, 2018).

28.3.2 Questions of Intercultural Communication About Binational Relationships

Locating political and power-immanent aspects in the phenomenon of marriage migration is a relatively new field of research that has been developing since 2010. Previously, ethnographic studies about family reunification of binational couples focused on questions of intercultural communication, individual narratives and the contextualization of subjects.

Communication techniques, experiences of difference and instrumentalizations of differences within a couple's relationship are at the forefront of this research perspective (Beer, 1996; Glowsky, 2011; Johnson, 2007; Kreckel, 2013; Lauser, 2004; Waldis, 1998; Wießmeier, 1993). Andrea Menz (2008) describes that discourses in Germany view binational couples still as encounters of cultures on a small scale.

Indeed, questions regarding everyday life are equally important to the couples: How to overcome physical distance? How to establish intimacy? What does it mean to be close? What role do family and cultural background play for the expectations about a partnership?

28.4 Description of the Research Field

The political-legal framework limited the research field. The legal situation changed considerably in 2005 with the introduction of the Immigration Act—the change from the "Zuwanderungsgesetz" to the "Aufenthaltsgesetz"—and in 2007 with further constitutional amendments. Because of this timeframe, this study is about migration experiences that emerged after 2007. As a legal frame was used, the terms "Russian" and "German" relate to the citizenship of a person.

Since 2007 basic German language skills are a necessity to migrate. For this reason, the Goethe-Institute—a center to learn more about German language and culture—functioned as a gateway to find most of the interview partners. The people who learn German at the Goethe-Institute are not limited to a specific age, milieu or educational level.

Five couples of the sample were open to this systemic method. The five couples are structurally similar: They are all between their mid-20s and mid-30s, they all have an academic degree. It is always the women, a Russian citizen, who moves to her German husband.

The comparison with statistic data about marriage migrants reveals that interview partners are consistent with average. Official statistics suggest that 80% of spousal migrants to Germany are between the age of 18 and 34, and 55% do either have a final degree or professional qualification (Büttner & Stichs, 2014).

> Earlier research [...] has shown that people who 'marry out' tend to be either highly educated, professional middle class or working class, to marry later than the average age of their particular group and to come from families with previous cross-cultural marriages. They also tend to marry those of similar status to themselves (Khatib-Chahidi, Hill, & Paton, 1998, p. 50).

A closer look at the couples reveals the abundance and complexity of the entire field. Manuel was doing his doctorate in humanities and met Dunja in Germany through friends. She studied business administration and worked as a manager in Russia. They are about 30 years old. Dunja grew up in a big city, Manuel in a suburb. They married in Russia.

Kunduz and Thomas also married in Russia. They met during a training in America, but they only became a couple back in their home countries. Both are lawyers and over 30 years old at the time of the wedding.

Ekaterina and Iwan got to know each other in Germany, while Ekaterina worked as an au pair in Germany. Before that, she studied German as a teacher in Russia and was in Germany for several language courses before her au pair time. Iwan works in the IT department of a medium-sized company. Iwan and Ekaterina are in their mid-20s and live in a rural area in Germany.

Gregor and Elen are as well in their mid-20s. Elen lived her whole life in a big city in Russia and is a doctor by profession. Gregor previously worked in the family's business and is now a manager in a medium-sized company. The two got to know each other via the internet.

Anna and Bastian met during a festival in Russia. Bastian is studying engineering in a small town in Germany. His parents are Russian Germans, so he speaks Russian, but has German citizenship. Anna worked in an agency for tourism. Anna and Bastian are about 30 years old, and they married in Germany.

28.5 Theoretical Considerations on Research About Love

28.5.1 *Grounded Theory: To Approach Love Step by Step*

Cultural ethnographers discover a research field via words, pictures, with their senses and by participating. Even if researchers do not want to be visible, the production of knowledge never takes place from an objective position. Hence, as social scientists, it is crucial to get hold of these construction processes, to witness the variety of meaning. By creating a research process in which not only we as researchers hold the power of interpretation but our interview partners stay the experts for their lives, we establish a power balance.

One way to ensure this balance is *Grounded Theory*. Anselm Strauss and Juliet Corbin initially developed *Grounded Theory* the 1960s. Besides the definition of concrete research steps, *Grounded Theory* is famous for developing new models and theories out of the data. The approach works bottom-up instead of top-down (Glaser & Strauss, 1967).

Data collection, analysis, and interpretation became interdependent research steps and the collected categories and codes were repeatedly shared and discussed with interview partners. Through this circle, researchers ensure to stay open to new hypothesis and to create knowledge based on empirical data. The fluidity and complexity of love can thereby be approached step by step. Grounded Theory allowed the integration of the timeline as a result of semi-structured interviews in the first phase of this research. Thereby more senses and new perspectives got into the focus. Structuring the study via *Grounded Theory* offered the opportunity to get closer to performances of love.

28.5.2 Sensory Ethnography: To Approach Love's Physical and Corporeal Dimensions

> Reality (being) and knowing are co-constitutive. We can perceive and know only that for which our sensitivities have prepared us, and these sensitivities depend on aspects of our being. (Anderson & Braud, 1998, p. 22)

Our researches are already full with nonverbal sign and symbols. It is not that research needs to create interview situations in which gestures, movements, displays of emotions are allowed, but rather a question of focus and providing space for senses, emotions, gestures—and this is important for a concept such like love.

The way we talk about love in our everyday life shows a rich sensuality: butterflies in our stomach, heartbroken, being head over heels for somebody. And there is still room to integrate love's materiality to research. Sara Pink's approach doing *Sensory Ethnography* is a way to "go beyond language and take into account all the sensory, often unspoken phenomena that are part of lived experience." (Pink & Leder Mackley, 2014, p. 96).

Pink lists "perception, place, knowing, memory and imagination" (Pink, 2015) as the principles for *Sensory Ethnography*, and they apply to the timeline as well. Using timelines interview partners create a space and sculpture to bring memories and imaginations to the front stage. In this creation and imagining, also sensations they felt during their migration process become present again as a way of memorizing.

28.6 Integration of Systemic Methods into Ethnographical Research to Study Love

Systemic therapy originated from the work with families, so the timeline was a way to get back to its roots: understanding relationships and concepts of love.

Family therapy and systemic therapy still claim to be more than just another form of treatment. Systemic therapy techniques arise from the question of how people in social systems create their reality jointly, which premises underlie their thinking and experience, and which possibilities exist to question and "disturb" these premises (Schlippe & Schweitzer, 2007, p. 17). It was only in the middle of the twentieth century, that therapists acknowledged the importance of family systems for the healing of their patients. Nowadays, systemic practitioners see families as one system out of many others like our workplace, academia, partnerships, friendships. People live in systems. People are systems.

Because of analogous values in the work with the research subjects or clients, the methodical transfer from therapy to empirical cultural science suggested itself. First, the shared belief that truths that are always perspective. Secondly, a de-hierarchized relationship between researcher/therapist and field/client. Thirdly, the way of working is equally characterised by creativity and respect. Fourthly, it is about the analysis of connections and networks of relationships, and fifthly about the significance of language as an interactive practice in an active system.

28.7 Research Methodology

The research methodology stands out due to the used broad approach, typical for multi-sited ethnography. Not only did the research took place in Germany and Russia, but also the language signalizes variety. During the interviews, we spoke German, Russian and English.

In the beginning, the focus laid on semi-structured interviews with couples, which were complemented with group discussions and interviews with experts. The idea to integrate methods from systemic therapy into qualitative research arose out of challenges during the beginning and the aim of this study:

The first interviews were accompanied with a slight hesitation from interviewees to talk about their relationship after having a conversation about documents and bureaucracy. This division is already known to other researchers as well. Stefanie Sommer writes about her research with Russian elites migrating to Germany, that she was forced to acknowledge and accept the historically grown dividing line between the private and public spheres. A boundary that is already associated with other Eastern and Southeastern European countries. To her, the former appeared family-like, intimate and friendly, while the latter seemed to be unfriendly, dangerous and sometimes even hostile (Sommer, 2015, p. 67).

Some interviewees mentioned that it is more difficult to talk about aspects related to their relationship because of the shadows of migration management procedures. It seemed like the interview structure, considering both personal relationships and paperwork, imported some of the fear and worries which couples might face during their contacts with the embassy and other officials. My interview partner Jekaterina, for example, reflected that it is hard to find other interview partners, because of their peripheral and insecure legal status. The standard procedure is to renew the visa year after years. She stated that any "misbehaviour" could be a risk to their legal status.

Conducting a formal interview reminded some of the interview partners moreover of the need to prove that their relationship and love is real. Besides, we know from less intimate research fields, that not everybody feels confident being in the spotlight of attention and laying out their romantic story in front of a stranger.

In addition to these challenges, the goal of the research is a reason to not only conduct interviews. The centre of this study are the perspectives of German-Russian couples who migrated to Germany. Changing the conventional setup of interviews, from the atmosphere to questionnaire, offered interview partners more control and presence over their migration stories.

The timeline addresses both the aim and challenges of this research. This systemic method offers a more corporeal and visual approach for remembering, and therefore includes not only narratives and verbal expressions but also feelings, pictures or body movements into the research process. Furthermore, the timeline also captures the migration process as a process.

28.7.1 Second Phase

This section focuses on the execution of the method and resembles a how-to-guide for timelines. It dwells on what is essential to consider, how to start the process, what to say, how to explain it to interview partners and on what to focus.

The first thing is preparation. As this method originates from a therapeutic context, it is important to ensure that it isn't a therapy surrogate.

A method like the timeline can simply capture the interviewees' experiences and be used to look back in a person's history. It gives enough space for differentiation and individual interpretation, as it is a view from above and includes bodies.

After deciding which method to import, the timeline was tested, discussed with ethnographers and systemic counsellors, and its specifications of executions were planned.

Two ropes in different colours with the same length are necessary. The strings should be several meters long. Moderation cards saying "now" and "first meeting" were used. However, I also included other moments of particular interest to my research like "wedding" or "migration act" for example.

Permission to conduct this method was granted by the interview partners before the meeting, explaining the aim of this systemic method extensively.

The revenue for this method should offer enough space and privacy. In this study the interviewees decided where to meet and where they would feel most comfortable. All interview partners chose to meet in their private homes for this reason.

The session started with follow-up questions from earlier interviews. After some minutes, I as the interviewer switched to the timeline-method, explained it a second time and gave the basic instruction, that these ropes shall symbolize their lives, and they can thereby show their migration experience as a part of their biography.

Then, the couples chose their ropes and agreed on the direction of the timeline. They defined where to start, their current situation and their future is.

As the rope functions as a metaphor for life, it is essential to pay attention to the following details: First, the point of today should be at the middle of the rope or even closer to birth. By doing this, interviewers ensure that people have still the perception of enough life to experience. It has a negative psychological effect on the interviewees if it seems that not enough time remains.

Second, if possible, the future should offer a view out of the window instead of facing a wall. It constitutes a different atmosphere if people have vision or run against something. If you need to choose between view and future space, I'd prioritize to have enough rope for the future.

People have different interpretation of the courses of the ropes. Interview partners might add symbols, crossovers or wavy lines and give their pathways thereby significant meanings. There is no limit to the creativity and scope of interpretation.

During this forming much time, silence and patience is necessary. This process can take several minutes. Some couples discussed their biography and the outline of their ropes first. Others put them down immediately and changed it several times, repeatedly checking from different perspectives if the strings fit. This process is already fruitful as it gives first impressions of their biography and the meaning attached to specific steps in their life. It also shifts the atmosphere from a classical interview top-down-situation to a focus on their relationship.

The interview partners in this study didn't agree to be video-taped, so it was necessary to describe actions, gestures and nonverbal communications with words. It is important to note why interview partners frowned, smiled, moved in a certain way, hugged each other, got stiffer at specific questions. This instant reflection offered an immediate discussion of the movement directly with interview partners instead of rescheduling a follow-up or interpret their action during analysis. It was a change from challenge to chance.

As soon as interview partners finished their sculpture work, the first question was, what comes to their mind seeing their migration process like this—with a view from above. They also took the possibility to explain why they formed their rope. During this part, interview partners were able to share their reflection from a meta-perspective.

Next, they were asked to stand on the first time they met which they marked with a moderation card and literally walk me through their migration experiences. Every time the couples took a step forward is a moment of particular interest. Researchers should pay attention to bodily reactions. If interviewees changed their body language, researchers can ask why they did what they did and to share what comes to their mind, what is unique to this situation, or what they are thinking at this moment in their lives. The pictures in their mind led my interview partners to tell meaningful stories and offered more insight into their relationship. If there were any prominent emotions, I encouraged them to talk more about their joy, fear, excitement, confusion, longing.

In this way, the timelines continue through crucial milestones, like the moment they became a couple or their wedding, the moment they decided to move together to Germany and the actual migration.

When the couples arrived in the present, they were asked to look back and reflect how it all felt. How it was going all these steps.

Some last remarks: As the ropes symbolize the lives of interview partners, researchers shouldn't change them on their behalf as they would symbolically just change the life of another person. The timeline offered depth to findings which were not so prominent in the interviews and even new perspectives. Each method has a different impact on the results and findings about love.

28.8 Findings in Respect to Love

When we allow ourselves as researchers to be open and vulnerable, our interview partners experience this openness also and share with us the depths and colours of their lives. In this study, love was present from the beginning in the interviews and group discussions. It was hard to grab nonetheless, because the interviews reproduced the discourse about love being a feeling.

Interview partners said that they migrated mainly for their relationships. If it weren't for their partners, they wouldn't have chosen Germany or moved at all. Most of them had no connection to Germany before their relationship. When inquired how they define love, interview partners and participants in group discussions would answer: "You know it when you feel it.", "I just felt I could trust him." or "Do German women not know what love is?" Love as a feeling turned out to be such a solid concept that on the one side, its branches over the world. On the other, it's difficult to narrow it down with only words. Love stayed in a cloud of abstract words.

To get closer to the core, interview partners were asked to share instances and moments in which they consciously felt love. The interviewed women talked about signs of caring, safety and connection: They knew it was love when he prepared tea when she was sick; when he calls every day; when he takes his vacation to be with her; when he sends books and wants her to visit him in Germany. They named everyday life situations. The timeline then created a bigger picture. It integrated the theme behind the instances in the overall experience of closeness and growth. The timeline in the second phase offered more profundity and information to these first impressions.

28.9 Love: Different Shades of Closeness

The timeline presented a new view on being close. The couples used the ropes to symbolize getting closer, meeting or being separate for different reasons and thereby established closeness as a symbol for love. In other contexts, closer ropes could also express arguments or individual life courses with ups and downs.

The couples' proximity had different qualities: emotional, physical and concerning life choices. It always turned out that the couples experienced the closeness with their significant other as something unique.

Physical closeness is a topic that is often discussed within and about a long-distance relationship. The geographic distance reduces the quantity of physical touch. The physical connection is not only about the absence of physical presence. The timeline showed that moments of physical contact are extremely important to the long-distance relationships the Russian-German couples experience.

Elen, for example, experienced an intense physical longing, and pictures felt like an insufficient substitute. To not be able to touch during times of separation was frustrating, and so the couple decided to skype without video. Also, as the visa situation is difficult, the couples needed to be creative with finding places where they could physically meet. They looked for destinations for vacations which do not need a visa. Anna joined Bastian during his semester abroad in South America so that they have time together, for example. But it is not only a question, how to deal with physical absence, but moments of touch became milestones.

Situations like the first kiss got a significant meaning and succeeded in a different quality of their relationships. Their first kiss often marked the transformation from friends to lovers and put the question of having a long-distance-relationship on the table. Moments of becoming a couple were then reproduced during the interview by sharing a kiss, hugging, and smiling faces—all demonstrations of the sensuality of love, its small and big gestures.

Due to this tangible way of remembering, the atmosphere and vibration of the interview changed. These expressions of affection contrast with other interview situations in which—if that—they merely expressed affection verbally. The timeline made crystal-clear: Love is a performance.

Besides the physical closeness, emotional closeness was also a common theme. Thomas, for instances, mentions a closeness he never experienced with other female friends. Elen describes nightlong talks and that they even continued writing during their breakup. She didn't talk about this aspect in former interviews. However, during the timeline, their break became a vital point and proof of their commitment. All couples experienced and established through permanent communication this emotional closeness. New technologies like Skype, Whatsapp or Facebook play therefore an essential role in long-distance relationships.

Besides the physical and emotional closeness, some couples also highlight nearness concerning life choices via the timelines. Dunja and Manuel used the forming of the rope to show that they somehow were always close through their whole life, but never touched before their first meeting: "The relationship was somehow always meeting and meeting again, and yet never touched until this moment." The couples refer to exchange programs, to internships and study abroad, to language courses, to vacations where they were living in the same street and yet didn't meet.

Dancing brought Anna and Bastian together, and their shared interest carried them through their distance, as Anna puts it. Kunduz and Thomas met because of their job. Thomas highlights that their shared professional background helped them in the creation of their life in Germany. It is a mutual understanding which delivers patience and admiration.

All interview partners agreed that family plays a vital role in their lives. When asked what helped them to go through difficult times like separation, longing and migration management, Elen noted that it is the knowledge that family is just as crucial to her husband. This mutual priority made it doable. It wasn't difficult anymore but a necessity to create the life and relationship they imagined together.

Having similar perspectives on life—same interests, similar academic background, professions, or priorities created closeness—and is both the foundation and effect of their love. All couples showed that their biographies were not a straight line and yet they had the commitment to stay together, because of what draws them together.

Love for the interviewed binational couples got the meaning of getting as close as possible, living the original meaning of intimacy. Intimacy means, the closest to the inner, and shows one important facet of love in transcultural matters.

28.10 Love as the Permission to Be Changed

The timeline provided the grounds for a second finding about love. Love also equals growth and the acceptance of change. Even before the method, it was apparent, that the interviewed German-Russian couples crossed boundaries. It was a way to transform. Yet the interview data suggested it to be related more to the migration act than to love, to be more applicable to the women than to the men:

Before the timeline the interviewed women highlighted the necessity of migration and that, if you migrate to live with your love, it is doable. They felt no hesitation to move to Germany and had no problems with authorities. As the timeline breaks out of conventional narration patterns and works on a more emotional level, the interview partners committed that migrating was difficult and full of adversities.

Jekaterina, like most interviewed Russian women, said that she didn't experience any major problems or difficulties. Yet, when asked to look back on her migration path during the timeline, she threw herself on the ground and moved next to the ropes like she was in a military training: "Migration was hard work."

The couples crossed boundaries of nation-states as they applied for visas and physically migrated, as well as language barriers. Most of my interview partners learnt a new language. As the timeline revealed, migration felt like a break of their old life. The whole life path of my Russian interview partners changed. Their jobs and careers did not proceed. No matter if the women were lawyers or doctors, they didn't continue at the same level, or even the same job, as they did in Russia. They had to learn to overcome a new distance to their family and friends. This remoteness became visible, especially in everyday life situations. They felt separated from German society as simple tasks like going to a doctor or shopping, working, bureaucratical matters or meeting with friends as they first had to find new ones, were things they couldn't do as easily as before. The timeline showed the difficulty of migration in a new light.

That migration changed the life of the migrating women was clear, but the timeline showed that also the German partner evaluated their boundaries and transformed throughout the process.

The moment that was vital for that understanding happened during the timeline with Kunduz and Thomas, when asked why they committed to each other despite the distance. Out of this question emerged this short conversation.

Kunduz: Here is our wedding, and that is "now".
Researcher: Closer?
Thomas: You need to add more squiggles.

Fig. 28.1 Ropes of Thomas and Kunduz (Sharon Brehm)

This scene shows the limitation of words. Not the words, but the actions are illuminating. Kunduz kneeled and put the ropes closer together. However, she didn't move her string, but the one of Thomas. She literally meshed with Thomas' biography and her gesture showed, she changed his course of life too. Moreover, he let her change his life. He even encouraged her with words, his smile, the tone of his voice, eye contact. The timeline shed light on the perspective of the not-migrating men: their lives were also changing. For the interviewed men it was the start of another phase in their life: becoming a husband. Taking the financial, emotional, social responsibility for someone else. They also invested time and resources to build and maintain their relationship, by flying to Russia, applying for visas, opening their social circles, learning Russian themselves, looking as well for job opportunities for their girlfriends and wives (Fig. 28.1).

The timeline showed that love is allowing another person to change oneself, our life path, our vision. It encourages to cross boundaries, borders and thereby let us grow, thereby expanding our comfort zone. Love in this transcultural matter assembles the power to bridge the 'trans'.

The findings promote a linkage between method and outcome by presenting the empirical findings that were only possible through the timeline.

Finally, the discussion reflects on the advantages and pitfalls of the method. Researchers need to weigh out effort and outcome. As the method is not yet established, she needs more resources like time, discussions and mental flexibility.

28.11 Discussion

The timeline as a more corporeal and physical method was used to contribute findings about love. It is crucial to reflect upon disadvantages and advantages on how to research love and to discuss findings in respect to the presented literature about binational couples.

28.11.1 Disadvantages

One disadvantage is the intensive preparation and additional qualification. Using a rope in an interview setting doesn't happen intuitively for both researchers and interview partners. From the initiation before the method to the guiding during the meeting it differs from the skills and procedures learned during most academic trainings.

Compared to semi-structured interviews, timelines offer and need more mental flexibility. When we as social scientists have a questionnaire, we can cling to our thought of structure and have a safe container. Ropes on the contrary reassemble individual lives with their ups and downs, symbols and patterns. The safety of known structure is disrupted. Therefore, this method needs intense preparation.

One recommendation therefore is to have regular interviews before applying the timeline, so to get a stable relationship and then having more capacities during the timeline to pay attention to new details, structure and outcomes.

The second disadvantage is the openness of interview data. It is more difficult to compare timeline situations as biographies are often very diverse. On the plus side, this creates new perspectives and helps to avoid blind spots. For that reason, focus on a limited number of interviews. *Grounded Theory* worked well as a tool for analysis and allows to adapt the methodological procedure steadily.

The third disadvantage is a question of privacy. The interviewees in this study didn't want to be filmed due to personal considerations. Using innovative methods doesn't stop at the preparation or the execution but needs also to be open to other ways of gathering and analysing data. Sharing and describing actions immediately during the timelines captured meaningful movements and respected the need for privacy at the same time.

28.11.2 Advantages

Despite its difficulties the timeline provides multiple benefits while researching love: Most important, it allowed to collect different kind of data about love. The interview partners made more use of nonverbal communication and created new symbols. The timeline opened analytical lenses to capture gestures and movements.

Second, the timeline made it possible to gather different perspectives about love. Not only did the women for example changed their life but also the men. Both partners allowed the other one to be transformed in the course of love. At the same time, the different acts and perspectives were not messed up but can be distinguished. When it comes to couples it is important to not merge them into one person, but to understand the different perspectives. Even within one relationship, partners do not necessarily share the same interpretation. Especially in order to understand binational or transcultural relationships it is important to avoid reductions and create space for difference. Moments like the beginning of a timeline, when partners create a sculpture with their ropes together already show the construction of different perspectives.

Third, the timeline ensured a research-sideways situation. Due to the atmosphere and openness, the interview partners had the space to show how their migration experience and relationship looked like the way they pictured it. Individual spatialization of structures, processes, networks in order to achieve deeper associations, images and stories.

Forth, the timeline itself functions as a golden threat. In case interviewees drifted apart with their stories, researchers always have a visual reminder on what to focus or how to get back to the bigger picture.

28.11.3 Binational Couples: More than a Question of Communication

Research literature on binational couples either focuses on governmentality—private relationships as being monitored and regulated by the state—or how to communicate when primary identity categories are different.

The findings about love, gathered by timelines, emphasize how couples construct, produce and experience love as closeness. Instead of highlighting what separates binational couples—from communication to bureaucracy—and how to bridge the gap, it analyses the act of coming together and to create relationships.

Love is conceptualized around heightened emotionality and relationships. Yet, traditional interviews talk about emotions. The timeline—from shaping the sculpture to gestures through the process of walking through someone's life—shows how love shapes interactions and decisions. The performance of love can only be talked about to a certain degree. From hugs, kisses, eye contact, speaking patterns and letting someone change the course of your own life. These kind of data is not yet fully analyzed in social sciences.

28.12 Conclusion

This chapter offered a more physical and symbolic methodological framework for qualitative research. The study focused on German-Russian couples who migrate to Germany. This methodological approach concentrated on the perspective of the actors and on how to overcome research intrinsic challenges. As the timeline originates from systemic therapy, the values behind its origin provide a solid basis for collaboration.

The question then is how to integrate methods from another field of expertise into academia on a practical level. The foundation was built on curiosity and openness, provided by *Grounded Theory*. Despite the requirements, this visualisation technique cannot be replaced by simpler ones. The method in a way mirrors and meets the complexity of love.

Findings in respect to love presented different perspectives on known love themes like intimacy and growing together. These aspects of love became more tangible through verbal and non-verbal communication. They shed light on symbols and practices that weren't so clear or prominent before. Allowing another person to change the course of one's life is a new perspective on love.

28.13 Recommendations in Theory and Practice

Our methodological approach influences the data we are gathering. If our aim is to get a hold of new perspectives or to broaden our horizon, evaluating our research methods is a commendable strategy. Especially fluid, multifaceted concepts like love which are not only thoughts, but also bodily reactions, emotions or personal goals need to be met. What doesn't this study cover about love and German-Russian couples?

First, the methodical repertoire from systemic therapy is yet to be discovered as a toolbox to research love and other feelings. A modification of the "inner team", another method from systemic therapy, would have been a second option to understand the multitude of love: Different aspects of love like caring and nurturing, excitement and adventure, and so on, could have been visualised in order to understand why different, even paradoxical needs are attached to love. Using visual techniques provides clarity. A picture can tell more than a thousand words.

Two aspects of love are only touched in this study, although they promise to be fruitful research topics. The performance of love outside of stereotypical behaviour is a field of study that could demystify and differentiates it from falling in love.

Second, that love brings people together leads to two perspectives. The first often researched is looking into the past and see what obstacles, variances and distanced binational conquered. The second is to investigate the being and present of a couple, and see how intimacy and closeness are experienced.

References

Anderson, R., & Braud, W. (1998). Conventional and expanded views of research. In R. Anderson & W. Braud (Eds.), *Transpersonal research methods for the social sciences: Honoring human experience* (pp. 1–26). Thousand Oaks: Sage.

Bauman, Z. (2013). *Liquid love: On the frailty of human bonds*. Cambridge: Polity Press.

Beer, B. (1996). *Deutsch-philippinische Ehen: Interethnische Heiraten und Migration von Frauen*. Berlin: Reimer.

Brehm, S. (2020). *Die Liebe und das Ferne? Migrationserfahrungen deutsch-russischer Ehepaare*. München: Universitätsbibliothek der Ludwig-Maximilians-Universität München.

Büttner, T., & Stichs, A. (2014). *Die Integration von zugewanderten Ehegattinnen und Ehegatten in Deutschland*. BAMF-Heiratsmigrationsstudie 2013. Nürnberg.

Constable, N. (2003). *Romance on a global stage: Pen pals, virtual ethnography, and "mail-order"-marriages*. Berkeley: University of California Press.

D'aoust, A.-M. (2010). Circulation of desire: The security governance of the international "mail-order brides" industry. In M. de Larrinaga & M. G. Doucet (Eds.), *Security and global government. Globalization, governance and the state* (pp. 113–132). New York: Routledge.

Glaser, B., & Strauss, A. (1967). *The discovery of grounded theory: Strategies for qualitative research*. New York: de Gruyter.

Glowsky, D. (2011). *Globale Partnerwahl: Soziale Ungleichheit als Motor transnationaler Heiratsentscheidungen*. Wiesbaden: VS Verlag für Sozialwissenschaften.

Gutekunst, M. (2013). *Liebe ohne Grenzen?!: Binationale Paare und ihr Umgang mit Immobilisierung durch Grenzregimes*. München: Herbert Utz Verlag.

Gutekunst, M. (2018). *Grenzüberschreitungen – Migration, Heirat und staatliche Regulierung im Europäischen Grenzregime: Eine Ethnographie*. Bielefeld: transcript.

Hess, S. (2009). Man schickt doch auch nicht eine Ersatzbraut zum Altar: Zur Konfliktualität der neuen Formen des Regierens in und von Europa. In G. Welz & E. Baga (Eds.), *Projekte der Europäisierung: Kulturanthropologische Forschungsperspektiven* (pp. 181–196). Frankfurt am Main: Inst. für Kulturanthropologie und Europ. Ethnologie.

Hess, S., & Tsianos, V. (2010). Ethnographische Grenzregimeanalyse. In S. Hess & L.-M. Heimeshoff (Eds.), *Grenzregime: Diskurse, Praktiken, Institutionen in Europa* (pp. 243–264). Berlin: Assoziation A.

Johnson, E. (2007). *Dreaming of a mail-order husband: Russian-American internet romance.* Durham: Duke University Press.

Khatib-Chahidi, J., Hill, R., & Paton, R. (1998). Chance, choice and circumstance: A study of women on cross-cultural marriages. In R. Breger & R. Hill (Eds.), *Cross-cultural marriage: Identity and choice* (pp. 49–66). Oxford: Berg.

Kreckel, J. (2013). *Heiratsmigration: Geschlecht und Ethnizität.* Marburg: Tectum Verlag.

Lauser, A. (2004). *Ein guter Mann ist harte Arbeit: Eine ethnographische Studie zu philippinischen Heiratsmigrantinnen.* Bielefeld: transcript.

Luehrmann, S. (2004). Mediated marriage. Internet matchmaking in provincial Russia. *Europe-Asia Studies, 56*(6), 857–875.

Menz, M. (2008). Biographische Wechselwirkungen: Genderkonstruktionen und "kulturelle Differenz" in den Lebensentwürfen binationaler Paare. Bielefeld: transcript.

Pink, S. (2015). *Doing sensory ethnography.* Los Angeles: Sage.

Pink, S., & Leder Mackley, K. (2014). Framing and educating attention. In L. M. Arantes & E. Rieger (Eds.), *Ethnographien der Sinne: Wahrnehmung und Methode in empirisch-kulturwissenschaftlichen Forschungen* (pp. 93–110). Bielefeld: transcript Verlag.

Schlippe, A. V., & Schweitzer, J. (2007). *Lehrbuch der systemischen Therapie und Beratung.* Göttingen: Vandenhoeck & Ruprecht.

Sommer, S. (2015). *Postsozialistische Biografien und globalisierte Lebensentwürfe: Mobile Bildungseliten aus Sibirien.* Bielefeld: transcript.

Waldis, B. (1998). *Trotz der Differenz: Interkulturelle Kommunikation bei maghrebinisch-europäischen Paarbeziehungen in der Schweiz und in Tunesien.* Berlin: Universitätsverlag Freiburg Schweiz und Waxmann Münster.

Wießmeier, B. (1993). *Das "Fremde" als Lebensidee: Eine empirische Untersuchung bikultureller Ehen in Berlin.* Berlin: LIT.

Williams, L. (2010). *Global marriage. Cross-border marriage and marriage migration in context.* Basingstoke: Palgrave Macmillan.

Sharon Rose Brehm (PhD) is a cultural anthropologist and wrote her PhD on German-Russian couples. She graduated from the interdisciplinary Elite Graduate Program for East European Studies from Ludwig-Maximilians-University and University of Regensburg. Her focus lied on cultural anthropology, intercultural communications and economics. She works as a systemic counselor for couples and as a trainer for intercultural communication in Munich, Germany.

Part VI
Love in the Context of Globalisation

Newari Marriage Ceremony—Nhyākaḥmū (Photo: Rupak Shrestha)

Chapter 29
Correlates of Love Across Relationship Types and Cultural Regions

Charles T. Hill and Collaborators

Abstract A cross-cultural study of intimate relationships explored correlates of love around the world. Structural Equation Modeling found similar factors associated with love across nine cultural regions, as well as across eight relationship types defined by men and women, married or unmarried, in opposite-sex or same-sex relationships. The correlates are similar in spite of any variations in mean levels of the factors. The correlates occur in the following categories: motivation, partner suitability, intimacy dimensions, exchange processes, conflict resolution, and well-being. The findings have implications for future research, self-reflection, and couples counseling.

Keywords Love · Intimate relationships · Cross-cultural · Relationship types · Couples counseling

29.1 Introduction

Our comprehensive cross-cultural study of intimate relationships, which is described in the book (Hill, 2019), provides a unique opportunity to conduct new analyses to compare correlates of love across many cultures. This chapter describes the comprehensive nature of the study, its measure of love, how the correlates are tested, the sets of factors that are correlated with love, the categories of the correlates of love, conclusions and limitations, and the implications of the study for future research, self-reflection, and couples counseling.

C. T. Hill (✉)
Department of Psychological Sciences, Whittier College, Whittier, CA, USA
e-mail: chill@whittier.edu

29.2 How Is the Study Comprehensive?

The study is comprehensive in several ways. It investigates a wide range of factors found relevant to intimate relationships in previous research, instead of focusing on just a few factors. It includes participants from all over the world, instead of just a few countries. The participants are in a variety of types of romantic or sexual relationships, instead of just one or two types. And it develops models that include many factors in conceptually meaningful categories that make similar predictions across the cultural regions and the relationship types.

Participants answered a many-factor survey of intimate relationships that is online in multiple languages at https://cf2.whittier.edu/chill/ir. Students and non-students were recruited from nine cultural regions: (1) North America, (2) Latin America, (3) Western Europe, (4) Eastern Europe, (5) Central, West, and South Asia, (6) East Asia, (7) Southeast Asia, (8) Africa, and (9) Oceania. Hill (2019) lists the numbers of participants from the more than 70 countries in which they reside.

The study compares those with or without a current romantic or sexual partner. Among those with a partner, the study compares eight relationship types, defined by men or women, in opposite-sex or same-sex relationships, who are unmarried or married.

The study includes participants recruited by obtaining marriage license records and mailing letters to opposite-sex and same-sex newlyweds, plus others who saw recommendations of the study on two LGBTQ+ websites posted by participants in the study. They also include couples in parent choice (arranged) marriages and own choice (love) marriages, who completed a printed questionnaire in Urdu in Pakistan. And they include some former participants in the Boston Couples Study (Hill, Rubin, & Peplau, 1976), who were each mailed a letter with a unique code to enter online to create a 38-year follow-up of their previous responses.

The study develops a comprehensive model of factors that predict having a current partner, and a comprehensive model of the predictors of commitment through relationship satisfaction as well as factors that predict commitment whether relationship satisfaction is high or low (Hill, 2019). The models are comprehensive, by including many categories of factors, which make similar predictions across the nine cultural regions and across the eight relationship types.

This chapter extends the study by conducting new analyses of the correlates of love across cultural regions and relationship types.

29.3 How Is Love Conceptualized and Measured?

Love is an emotion, while relationship satisfaction is a cognitive evaluation. This is similar to the distinction in well-being between happiness as an emotion and life satisfaction as a cognitive evaluation (Diener, Oishi, & Lucas, 2002). But it is difficult to measure love as an emotion, since physiological measures of emotions are not unique. For example, heart rate increases with anger, fear, and excitement, but decreases with sadness. Blood rushes to the face with anger, but flees the face with fear. So Rubin (1970) measured love as an attitude, asking subjects to agree or disagree with statements representing components of love.

Rubin (1970) conceptualized love as having three components: caring, attachment, and intimacy. Berscheid and Walster (1969, 1978) made a distinction between passionate love and companionate love. Sternberg (1986) conceptualized love in terms of intimacy, passion, and commitment. And Lee (1973) conceptualized love in terms of six love styles.

In our study, Confirmatory Factor Analysis using Structural Equation Modeling revealed that a Four Component Love Scale had consistent loadings on a single factor across nine cultural regions and eight relationship types (Hill, 2019).

The four components, and the items that measure them, are the following, in which CP means Current Partner:

CARING: One of my primary concerns is CP's welfare. (Rubin, 1970)
ATTACHMENT: It would be hard for me to get along without CP. (Rubin, 1970)
INTIMACY: I have a relationship of mutual understanding with CP. (Sternberg, 1986)
I give considerable emotional support to CP. (Sternberg, 1986)
PASSION: My relationship with CP is very romantic. (Sternberg, 1986)

Commitment is conceptualized as separate from love in the study, and is measured in a different scale as described in Hill (2019). Lee's love styles do not load on the Four Component Love Scale. The new data analyses in this chapter are based on the 5352 participants who completed the Four Component Love Scale concerning a current partner.

29.4 How Are the Correlates Tested?

Pearson correlations are used to determine which factors are correlated with the Four Component Love Scale, for all participants. Correlations with r < 0.10 are called Trivial Correlations in the study (Hill, 2019), because r-squared is <0.01 which means that less than 1% of the variation in one variable is associated with variation in the other variable.

Statistically significant correlations are marked with ∗ for $p < 0.05$, ∗∗ for $p < 0.01$, and ∗∗∗ for $p < 0.001$. Due to the large number of participants, even trivial correlations are statistically significant although they are not very meaningful. Non-trivial correlations are emphasized in the findings.

All scales used in the study are based on Confirmatory Factor Analysis using Structural Equation Modeling (SEM) that reveals consistency in factor loadings across the nine cultural regions and eight relationship types, with goodness of fit measures CFI > 0.950, RMSEA < 0.05. That means that the factor loadings do not differ statistically significantly from each other across the nine cultural regions and across the eight relationship types. Hence the scales can be meaningfully used to make comparisons across the cultural regions and relationship types.

Scales are identified in this chapter by the number of items in them, such as Sexual Satisfaction (3) for the 3-item Sexual Satisfaction Scale. The wordings of the items in each scale, and of the factors not in scales, are described in Hill (2019), which cites the sources of the theoretical concepts measured by the scales and other factors. Most items have responses from 0 = NOT AT ALL to 8 = COMPLETELY.

To test for consistency of correlates across cultural regions and relationship types, SEM Structural Models are used with sets of factors that are correlated with the Four Component Love Scale. The results reported in this chapter have goodness of fit measures CFI > 0.950, RMSEA < 0.05. That means that the regression coefficients do not differ statistically significantly from each other across the nine cultural regions and across the eight relationship types. Hence the associations of the factors with love are similar, although not necessarily identical, across the cultural regions and relationship types.

Note that correlations ignore the mean level of the measures in their calculation, as illustrated in Fig. 1.7 of Hill (2019). This is also true for regression coefficients in SEM analyses. Hence correlations, and regression coefficients in SEM, can be similar in spite of any variations in mean levels of the factors. For example, the association between love and relationship commitment is similar across married and unmarried persons, even though both love and commitment are generally higher among married persons than among unmarried persons (Hill, 2019).

As in Multiple Regression, when the factors in a set are correlated with each other, the factors with the highest regression coefficients may capture the effects that they have in common, leaving low regression coefficients for the other factors.

In this study the factors that capture the effects of other factors, or have effects beyond the effects of other factors, are called Central Factors (Hill, 2019), if they have non-trivial regression coefficients. Trivial coefficients are those that are less than 0.10, which add little to the explained variance.

However, when a set of factors is correlated with each other, it is called multicollinearity and is considered a problem, because the correlations among the factors may vary in other studies. Thus the factors that capture the effects of other factors may vary, and the factors considered Central Factors or Trivial Factors may vary. Hence the category of a set of factors that are correlated with each other is more important than the specific factors in the predictive models. These categories will be discussed in Sect. 29.25.

29.5 How Is Love Correlated with Relationship Reasons?

Participants are asked the question and items shown in Table 29.1. Correlations between the Four Component Love Scale and relationship reasons are shown in the first column of Table 29.1. Items are ordered from highest to lowest correlations.

Table 29.1 Reasons for being in a committed relationship

How important to you are each of the following as reasons for being in a marriage or other committed relationship?		
	Corr.	Regr.
Commitment to stay together	0.22***	0.20
Emotional closeness	0.21***	0.21
Exclusivity (monogamy)	0.09***	0.00
Sexual activities	0.07***	−0.00
Someone to cook and clean	−0.07***	−0.05
Having a child	0.05***	0.00
Financial security	−0.02	−0.04

The reasons for being in a committed relationship that are most closely associated with loving the partner are a desire for commitment and a desire for emotional closeness. The other reasons have trivial correlations with love.

Regression coefficients from SEM analyses are shown in the second column, which are similar across cultural regions (CFI = 0.988, RMSEA = 0.015) and relationship types (CFI = 0.992, RMSEA = 0.010). They reveal that desire for commitment and desire for emotional closeness are both Central Factors in loving the partner, across nine cultural regions and eight relationship types.

29.6 How Is Love Correlated with Life Goals?

Participants are asked the question and items in Table 29.2. Correlations between the Four Component Love Scale and life goals are shown in the first column of Table 29.2. Items are ordered from highest to lowest correlations.

The life goals that are most closely associated with loving the partner, are having a committed relationship, having a romantic or sexual partner, taking care of a home, spending time with family, and helping others. These goals are correlated ($p < 0.001$) with the Higher-Order Value of Self-Transcendence (Schwartz, 2012) discussed in the next section.

Regression coefficients from SEM analyses are shown in the second column, which are similar across cultural regions (CFI = 0.998, RMSEA = 0.010) and relationship types (CFI = 0.996, RMSEA = 0.013). They reveal that having a committed relationship is a Central Factor in loving the partner. It accounts for the effects that it has in common with the other factors correlated with loving the partner, across nine cultural regions and eight relationship types.

Table 29.2 Life goals correlated with love

How important to you is each of the following as a goal in your life?		
	Corr.	Regr.
Having a committed relationship	0.32***	0.34
Having a romantic or sexual partner	0.19***	0.04
Taking care of a home	0.17***	0.08
Spending time with family	0.15***	0.08
Helping others	0.12***	0.04
Supporting a family	0.09***	0.01
Having time for leisure activities	0.08***	0.02
Participating in cultural events	0.07***	0.00
Being financially self-supporting	0.06***	0.09
Raising children	0.05***	−0.04
Spending time with friends	0.05***	−0.06
Having my own biological child	0.04**	−0.05
Having a career	0.02	−0.09
Making as much money as possible	−0.01	−0.07

29.7 How Is Love Correlated with Values?

Scales measuring the four High-Order Values identified by Schwartz (2012) are described in Hill (2019). These represent groupings of values that are related to each other. Correlations between the Four Component Love Scale and these High-Order Values are shown in the first column of Table 29.3. Items are ordered from highest to lowest correlations.

The High-Order Values most closely associated with loving the partner are the Self-Transcendence Scale, which includes items measuring the values of universalism and benevolence, and the Conservation Scale, which includes items measuring the values of security, tradition, and conformity. Openness to change and Self-enhancement are not correlated with loving the partner.

Regression coefficients from SEM analyses are shown in the second column, which are similar across cultural regions (CFI = 0.991, RMSEA = 0.011) and relationship types (CFI = 0.984, RMSEA = 0.020). They reveal that Self-Transcendence, treating others equally and valuing others, is a Central Factor in loving the partner. It is more important than Conservation values, across nine cultural regions and eight relationship types.

Table 29.3 High-order values correlated with love

	Corr.	Regr.
Self-transcendence (4)	0.15***	0.20
Conservation (3)	0.11***	0.09
Openness to change (3)	0.02	−0.04
Self-enhancement (4)	−0.00	−0.04

29.8 How Is Love Correlated with Relationship Attitudes?

Participants are asked the question and items shown in Table 29.4. Correlations between the Four Component Love Scale and attitudes about relationships are shown in the first column of Table 29.4. Items are ordered from highest to lowest correlations.

The relationship attitudes most closely associated with loving the partner are the romantic beliefs "To be truly in love is to be in love forever" and "As long as they at least love each other, spouses or partners should have no trouble getting along together," plus the Secure Attachment statement "It is easy for me to become emotionally close to others" (Hazan & Shaver, 1987). Negatively associated with loving the current partner are being interested in finding a partner and having had difficulty finding a partner. The other relationship attitudes have trivial correlations.

Regression coefficients from SEM analyses are shown in the second column, which are similar across cultural regions (CFI = 0.990, RMSEA = 0.013) and relationship types (CFI = 0.992, RMSEA = 0.011). They reveal that the romantic belief "To be truly in love is to be in love forever" is a Central Factor in loving the partner. It accounts for the effects in common with other factors that are correlated with loving the partner, across nine cultural regions and eight relationship types.

29.9 How Is Love Correlated with Stereotypic Gender Traits?

Participants are asked the question and items shown in Table 29.5. Correlations between the Four Component Love Scale and stereotypic gender traits are shown in the first column of Table 29.5. Items are ordered from highest to lowest correlations.

Table 29.4 Relationship attitudes correlated with love

To what extent does each of the following statements describe your feelings about relationships?		
	Corr.	Regr.
To be truly in love is to be in love forever	0.19***	0.12
If in love have no trouble getting along	0.13***	0.06
Secure attachment	0.11***	0.09
Interested in finding a partner	−0.14***	0.01
Difficulty finding a partner	−0.13***	−0.03
Avoidance attachment	−0.09***	−0.02
Anxious attachment	−0.08***	−0.06
Concerned about losing friendship	−0.08***	−0.04
Concerned about rejection	−0.07***	−0.07
Not marry against advice of parents	−0.05**	−0.05

Table 29.5 Stereotypic gender traits correlated with love

For each of the following characteristics, select the number which best reflects your personal opinion about yourself

	Corr.	Regr.
Emotionally expressive	0.17***	0.10
Nurturing	0.17***	0.11
Sensitive	0.13***	0.05
Assertive	0.07***	0.02
Independent	0.04	0.01
Competitive	0.01	−0.04

The stereotypic gender traits most closely associated with loving the partner are the stereotypic feminine traits of being emotionally expressive, nurturing, and sensitive. The stereotypic masculine traits have trivial correlations. This is not surprising, since the stereotypical feminine traits involve emotional empathy, while the stereotypical masculine traits do not. Emotional attachments and nurturing behaviors are strongly associated with love in research on the effects of oxytocin (Carter & Porges, 2013).

Regression coefficients from SEM analyses are shown in the second column, which are similar across cultural regions (CFI = 0.996, RMSEA = 0.009) and relationship types (CFI = 0.988, RMSEA = 0.015). They reveal that being emotionally expressive and nurturing are Central Factors in loving the partner. They account for effects in common with being sensitive, across nine cultural regions and eight relationship types.

29.10 How Is Love Correlated with Mate Selection Factors?

Participants are asked the question in Table 29.6, with items that combined into the scales shown in Table 29.6. Correlations between the Four Component Love Scale and the mate selection scales are shown in the first column of Table 29.6. Items are ordered from highest to lowest correlations.

The mate selection factor most closely associated with loving the partner is the Personality Important Scale, which includes the items personality, attitudes and values, and sense of humor. Note the trivial negative correlation for the Attractiveness Important Scale, which includes the items physical attractiveness, height, and weight. Although some research has found effects of physical attractiveness on marital satisfaction (Meltzer, McNulty, Jackson, & Karney, 2014), the present study has found personality to be more important than physical attractiveness for both love and relationship satisfaction (Hill, 2019), across nine cultural regions and eight relationship types, including married and unmarried men and women in opposite-sex and in same-sex relationships. In the Boston Couples Study, physical

Table 29.6 Mate selection factors correlated with love

How important to you is each of the following characteristics in selecting a partner for marriage or other committed relationship?		
	Corr.	Regr.
Personality important (3)	0.14***	0.29
Social status important (3)	−0.08***	−0.09
Attractiveness important (3)	−0.06***	−0.06
Ethnicity important (3)	−0.02	0.03

attractiveness did not predict couples staying together, getting married, or staying married (Hill & Peplau, 1998).

Regression coefficients from SEM analyses are shown in the second column, which are similar across cultural regions (CFI = 0.995, RMSEA = 0.010) and relationship types (CFI = 0.990, RMSEA = 0.015). They reveal that Personality Important is a Central Factor in loving the partner. It is more important than social status, attractiveness, and ethnicity, across nine cultural regions and eight relationship types. To understand this, it is helpful to reflect on the following:

> Think about the people you love. They come in all shapes and sizes. Do you love them because they look like models in the media, or because of their personality and how they treat you?

29.11 How Is Love Correlated with Partner Similarity?

Participants are asked the question in Table 29.7, with items that combine into the scales shown in Table 29.7. CP means Current Partner. Correlations between the Four Component Love Scale and partner similarity factors are shown in the first column of Table 29.7. Items are ordered from highest to lowest correlations.

Loving the partner is associated with similarity scales on all four of the mate selection factors, plus similarity on intelligence and similarity on willingness to have children, which do not load on the other factors. Note that similarity on personality has the highest correlation, while similarity on ethnicity has the lowest correlation. Our findings support the well-known similarity hypothesis of attraction (Byrne, 1971).

Regression coefficients from SEM analyses are shown in the second column, which are similar across cultural regions (CFI = 0.988, RMSEA = 0.012) and relationship types (CFI = 0.978, RMSEA = 0.022). They reveal that the Personality Similarity Scale is the strongest Central Factor in loving the partner, and that similarity in willingness to have children and similarity in intelligence are also Central Factors. When those are taken into account, similarity in social status, attractiveness, and ethnicity are much less important in loving the partner, across nine cultural regions and eight relationship types.

Table 29.7 Partner similarity factors correlated with love

To what extent are you and CP similar on each of the following characteristics?		
	Corr.	Regr.
Personality similarity (3)	0.39***	0.35
Similarity in willingness to have children	0.33***	0.16
Similarity in intelligence	0.29***	0.16
Social status similarity (3)	0.22***	0.03
Attractiveness similarity (3)	0.16***	−0.04
Ethnicity similarity (3)	0.10***	0.01

29.12 How Is Love Correlated with Ratings of Partner and Self?

Participants are asked the two questions in Table 29.8, with items shown in Table 29.8 for each question. Correlations between the Four Component Love Scale and ratings of partner and self are shown in the first column of Table 29.8. Items are ordered from highest to lowest correlations.

Loving the partner is associated with rating the partner desirable as a partner in a committed relationship, rating the partner intelligent, and rating the partner attractive. It is also associated with rating the self desirable as a partner in a committed relationship, and rating the self intelligent and attractive. High self-ratings indicate self-confidence in finding a desirable partner and establishing a loving relationship. They may be either a cause of success or an effect of success in having a current partner.

Regression coefficients from SEM analyses are shown in the second column, which are similar across cultural regions (CFI = 0.989, RMSEA = 0.017) and relationship types (CFI = 0.995, RMSEA = 0.014). They reveal that rating the partner desirable as a partner, rating the partner intelligent, and rating the self desirable as a partner are all Central Factors. This means that they each have effects beyond what they have in common. Rating the partner attractive is captured by rating the partner desirable as a partner, and rating the self as intelligent and attractive are captured by rating the self as desirable as a partner, across nine cultural regions and eight relationship types.

29.13 How Is Love Correlated with Lee's Love Styles?

Participants are asked the question in Table 29.9, with the items shown in parentheses that are from Hendrick and Hendrick (1986), to measure Lee's (1973) Love Styles that are listed in Table 29.9. Although they do not have consistent factor loadings with the Four Component Love Scale, some of the items do have

Table 29.8 Ratings of partner and self correlated with love

For each of the following characteristics, click on the number which best reflects your personal opinion about yourself		
For each of the following characteristics, circle the number which best reflects your personal opinion about CP		
	Corr.	Regr.
Rate partner: desirable as a partner	0.56***	0.43
Rate partner: intelligent	0.37***	0.18
Rate partner: attractive	0.31***	0.09
Rate self: desirable as a partner	0.22***	0.11
Rate self: intelligent	0.17***	0.02
Rate self: attractive	0.10***	−0.08

Table 29.9 Correlations with items measuring Lee's love styles

For each of the following statements indicate how true that statement is of your feelings toward CP		
	Corr.	Regr.
Eros (We were meant for each other)	0.70***	0.38
Agape (I sacrifice my own wishes)	0.45***	0.13
Storge (Our friendship merged into love)	0.30***	0.05
Mania (I am miserable when CP ignores me)	0.28***	0.04
Ludus (I kept other lovers secret)	−0.08***	−0.03
Pragma (CP would help my career)	0.02	−0.05

correlations with that scale. These correlations are shown in Table 29.9. Items are ordered from highest to lowest correlations.

The Four Component Love Scale is non-trivially correlated with the items representing Eros, Agape, Storge, and Mania, but not Ludus or Pragma.

Regression coefficients from SEM analyses are shown in the second column, which are similar across cultural regions (CFI = 0.983, RMSEA = 0.018) and relationship types (CFI = 0.992, RMSEA = 0.016). They reveal that Eros (we were meant for each other), and Agape (I sacrifice my own wishes to let my partner achieve my partner's wishes), are Central Factors in loving the partner. They account for the effects of Storge and Mania on loving the partner, across nine cultural regions and eight relationship types.

29.14 How Is Love Correlated with Emotional Intimacy?

Correlations of the Four Component Love Scale with other measures of emotional intimacy are shown in Table 29.10. Items are ordered from highest to lowest correlations.

Table 29.10 Correlations with other measures of emotional intimacy

	Corr.	Regr.
I and my partner are in love	0.77***	0.32
Emotional closeness	0.71***	0.22
I express affection to partner (3)	0.65***	0.20
Partner expresses affection (3)	0.58***	0.05

The love scale is correlated with agreement with "I and my partner are in love," "How emotionally close would you say your relationship with CP is right now," expressing affection to the partner (verbally and nonverbally), and partner expressing affection (verbally and nonverbally). The correlation is not 1.00 because both being in love may not be to the same degree as one partner being in love.

Regression coefficients from SEM analyses are shown in the second column, which are similar across cultural regions (CFI = 0.997, RMSEA = 0.013) and relationship types (CFI = 0.998, RMSEA = 0.013). They reveal that saying "I and my partner are in love," emotional closeness, and expressing affection to partner are all Central Factors in loving the partner. They each have effects beyond what they have in common, and they account for effects of partner expresses affection, across nine cultural regions and eight relationship types.

29.15 How Is Love Correlated with Communication?

Correlations of the Four Component Love Scale with measures of communication are shown in the first column of Table 29.11. Items are ordered from highest to lowest correlations.

Loving the partner is associated with self-disclosure to the partner, the partner knowing you, knowing the partner, partner self-disclosure, trusting the partner not to lie, how often you communicate with the partner, never lying to the partner, and how often you see the partner. Byers (2005) found communication to be important for relationship satisfaction and sexual satisfaction.

Regression coefficients from SEM analyses are shown in the second column, which are similar across cultural regions (CFI = 0.993, RMSEA = 0.017) and relationship types (CFI = 0.997, RMSEA = 0.015). They reveal that all but the last two are Central Factors, which means that they each have effects beyond what they have in common. The effects of the last two are captured by the other factors, for example, how often communicate with partner captures effects of how often see partner, across nine cultural regions and eight relationship types.

Table 29.11 Correlations with measures of communication

	Corr.	Regr.
Self-disclosure to partner (4)	0.61***	0.24
How well partner knows me	0.60***	0.18
How well I know partner	0.59***	0.13
Partner self-disclosure (4)	0.58***	0.12
I trust partner not to lie to me	0.53***	0.15
How often communicate with partner	0.45***	0.36
I never lie to partner	0.43***	0.09
How often see partner	0.29***	0.07

29.16 How Is Love Correlated with Sexual Intimacy?

Correlations of the Four Component Love Scale with various aspects of sexual intimacy are shown in Table 29.12. Items are ordered from highest to lowest correlations.

Loving the partner is associated with sexual satisfaction (overall, with frequency of sex, and with types of sexual activities), frequency of sexual activities, and ideal frequency of sexual activities. While being pressured to have sex when you don't want to might decrease love, being willing to engage in sex when you don't want to might reflect loving the partner, hence its overall correlation with love is trivial. Muise and Impett (2015) found that people who are motivated to meet a partner's sexual needs have partners who are more satisfied and committed to their relationships.

Regression coefficients from SEM analyses are shown in the second column, which are similar across cultural regions (CFI = 0.965, RMSEA = 0.019) and relationship types (CFI = 0.975, RMSEA = 0.023). They reveal that Sexual Satisfaction and ideal frequency of sexual activities with the partner are Central Factors, which account for the effects of the other sexual intimacy factors, across nine cultural regions and eight relationship types.

29.17 How Is Love Correlated with Sex outside the Relationship?

Correlations of the Four Component Love Scale with measures of sexual activities with others outside the relationship are shown in the first column of Table 29.13. Items are ordered from highest to lowest correlations.

Approving partner having sex outside the relationship, having had sex outside the relationship, partner approving your sex outside the relationship, and believing the partner had outside sex are all negatively associated with loving the partner. Walters and Burger (2013) explored reasons for cheating and consequences of disclosing cheating.

Table 29.12 Correlations with aspects of sexual intimacy

	Corr.	Regr.
Sexual satisfaction (3)	0.33***	0.33
Frequency of sexual activities	0.18***	0.02
Ideal frequency of sexual activities	0.18***	0.12
Equal interest in having sex	0.07***	−0.09
Engaged in sex when didn't want to	−0.05***	−0.01

Table 29.13 Correlations with measures of sex outside the relationship

	Corr.	Regr.
I approve of partner's outside sex	−0.23***	−0.10
I have had outside sex	−0.20***	−0.08
Partner approves of my outside sex	−0.17***	−0.03
Partner has had outside sex	−0.11*	−0.13

Regression coefficients from SEM analyses are shown in the second column, which are similar across cultural regions (CFI = 0.969, RMSEA = 0.023) and relationship types (CFI = 0.953, RMSEA = 0.035). They reveal that approving partner having outside sex, and believing the partner had outside sex, are Central Factors. They capture the effects of all of the other factors, across nine cultural regions and eight relationship types.

29.18 How Is Love Correlated with Social Exchange Measures?

Correlations of the Four Component Love Scale with measures of social exchange (Blau, 1964) are shown in the first column of Table 29.14. Items are ordered from highest to lowest correlations.

Feeling that you have gained benefits from the relationship, being equally involved in the relationship, feeling invested in the relationship, having equal disclosure and equal power, and having made sacrifices, are all associated with greater love for the partner. Research on equity in intimate relationships is reviewed by Hatfield, Rapson, and Aumer-Ryan (2008).

Regression coefficients from SEM analyses are shown in the second column, which are similar across cultural regions (CFI = 0.965, RMSEA = 0.022) and relationship types (CFI = 0.967, RMSEA = 0.027). They reveal that all of the factors except the last are Central Factors. That means that each has effects beyond the effects they have in common. Making sacrifices is captured by investing in the relationship. These effects are consistent across nine cultural regions and eight relationship types.

Note that the highest SEM regression coefficient is for being equally involved in the relationship. In the Boston Couples Study, being equally involved was one of the

Table 29.14 Correlations with measures of social exchange

	Corr.	Regr.
Gained benefits from relationship	0.49***	0.31
Equally involved in relationship	0.34***	0.51
Feel invested in relationship	0.33***	0.16
Equal disclosure in relationship	0.18***	0.12
Equal power in relationship	0.16***	0.14
Made sacrifices in relationship	0.10***	0.02

best predictors of staying together (Hill, Rubin, & Peplau, 1976), and eventually marrying one's college dating partner (Hill & Peplau, 1998).

29.19 How Is Love Correlated with Conflict Measures?

Correlations of the Four Component Love Scale with measures of conflict are shown in Table 29.15. Items are ordered from highest to lowest correlations.

Loving the partner is associated with using positive responses to conflict (trying to find a mutual solution, trying to find out what is stressing partner, partner trying to find out what is stressing you; cf. Gottman, 1999). Conflict over expectations, uncertainties, and high conflict items (time management, poor communication, our personalities, leisure activities) are negatively associated with loving the partner. Using negative responses (imposing your way, criticizing, and being criticized) is not associated with loving the partner.

Regression coefficients from SEM analyses are shown in the second column, which are similar across cultural regions (CFI = 0.986, RMSEA = 0.018) and relationship types (CFI = 0.979, RMSEA = 0.029). They reveal that Positive Responses to conflict is a Central Factor in loving the partner. It captures the effects of the various kinds of conflict on loving the partner. How you deal with conflict is much more important than the amount of conflict. These effects are consistent across nine cultural regions and eight relationship types.

29.20 How Is Love Correlated with Responses to Dissatisfaction?

Correlations of the Four Component Love Scale with responses to dissatisfaction (Rusbult, Zembrodt, & Gunn, 1982) are shown in Table 29.16. Items are ordered from highest to lowest correlations.

Loving the partner is positively associated with Voice (discuss to fix things up), and negatively associated with Exit (leave the relationship) and neglect (get angry and not talk). The correlation for loyalty (wait hoping it gets better) is trivial.

Table 29.15 Correlations with measures of conflict

	Corr.	Regr.
Positive responses to conflict (3)	0.51***	0.50
Conflict over expectations (4)	−0.19***	−0.08
Conflict over uncertainties (4)	−0.19***	−0.09
Conflict over high conflict items (4)	−0.17***	−0.03
Negative responses to conflict (3)	−0.01	0.07

Table 29.16 Correlations with responses to dissatisfaction

	Corr.	Regr.
Voice (discuss to fix things up)	0.44***	0.34
Exit (leave the relationship)	−0.33***	−0.18
Neglect (get angry and not talk)	−0.10***	0.04
Loyalty (wait hoping it gets better)	−0.07***	−0.01

Schumann found that an apology is more likely to be perceived as sincere and lead to forgiveness in a loving relationship (Schumann, 2012).

Regression coefficients from SEM analyses are shown in the second column, which are similar across cultural regions (CFI = 0.985, RMSEA = 0.017) and relationship types (CFI = 0.980, RMSEA = 0.015). They reveal that Voice (discus to fix things up) is a positive Central Factor, and Exit (leave the relationship) is a negative Central Factor in loving the partner. They account for the effects of Neglect (get angry and not talk), across nine cultural regions and eight relationship types.

29.21 How Is Love Correlated with Intimate Partner Violence?

Correlations of the Four Component Love Scale with jealousy and intimate partner violence are shown in the first column of Table 29.17. Items are ordered from highest to lowest correlations.

All except two of the correlations of loving the partner with intimate partner violence are trivial. This is likely due to very low reported incidence of intimate partner violence in this study. However, expressing jealousy is positively associated with loving the partner, while partner breaking up and coming back is negatively associated with loving the partner.

Regression coefficients from SEM analyses are shown in the second column, which are similar across cultural regions (CFI = 0.995, RMSEA = 0.014) and relationship types (CFI = 0.995, RMSEA = 0.018). They reveal that expressing jealousy is a Central Factor. All other factors have trivial coefficients, across nine cultural regions and eight relationship types. While results were similar for men and women in the eight relationship types in this study, Aylor and Dainton (2001) found gender differences in feelings and expressions of jealousy.

Table 29.17 Correlations with intimate partner violence

	Corr.	Regr.
I expressed jealousy	0.16***	0.14
P broke up for a period of time	−.10***	−0.09
I broke up for a period of time	−0.08***	−0.04
Partner shoved	−0.08***	−0.06
Partner hit	−0.07***	−0.01
Partner expressed jealousy	0.05**	−0.02
I used verbal violence (3)	0.04**	0.05
I shoved partner	−0.03*	−0.03
I hit partner	−0.02	0.01
Partner used verbal violence (3)	−0.01	−0.03

29.22 How Is Love Correlated with External Factors?

Correlations of the Four Component Love Scale with factors outside the relationship are shown in the first column of Table 29.18. Items are ordered from highest to lowest correlations.

Parents and others (closest friends, and co-workers or classmates) approving of the partner, and parents, closest friends, and co-workers or classmates knowing the partner, are correlated with loving the partner. Life domains (your job or career, your friendships, your activities by yourself) impacting the relationship, or the relationship impacting these life domains, are negatively associated with loving the partner. But coping with stress (feeling in control of events in your life, feeling able to cope with stress, and having social support from others) is positively correlated with loving the partner.

Regression coefficients from SEM analyses are shown in the second column, which are similar across cultural regions (CFI = 0.991, RMSEA = 0.014) and relationship types (CFI = 0.981, RMSEA = 0.026). They reveal that parents, friends, and others approving of the partner is the strongest Central Factor, and parents and closest friends knowing the partner are also Central Factors. The other factors have trivial coefficients when these are taken into account. These effects are consistent across nine cultural regions and eight relationship types.

Bell and Hastings (2015) found that parental approval of interracial couples helped buffer negative outside experiences. Apostolou (2016) explored parental reactions to same-sex attractions. And van Zantvliet, Kalmijn, and Verbakel (2015) explored parental influences on dating between immigrants and natives.

Racial-ethnic identities, and religious identities were measured, but all have trivial correlations with loving the partner. They are not presented in tables in order to simplify the data presentation. Other factors matter more.

Table 29.18 Correlations with external factors

	Corr.	Regr.
Parents and others approve of partner (3)	0.48***	0.28
Parents know partner	0.38***	0.10
Closest friends know partner	0.36***	0.11
Co-workers or classmates know P	0.23***	0.00
Life domains impact relationship (3)	−0.16***	−0.09
Relationship impacts life domains (3)	−0.14***	0.02
Coping with stress (3)	0.14***	0.03

29.23 How Is Love Correlated with Emotional Well-Being?

Psychologists view happiness as an emotional response, and life satisfaction as a cognitive evaluation (Diener et al., 2002). Correlations of the Four Component Love Scale with measures of emotional well-being are shown in Table 29.19. Items are ordered from highest to lowest correlations.

Loving the partner is positively associated with happiness, and negatively associated with depression and anxiety. It is likely that the causal direction goes both ways—loving a partner increases emotional well-being, and emotional well-being increases loving the partner.

Regression coefficients from SEM analyses are shown in the second column, which are similar across cultural regions (CFI = 0.993, RMSEA = 0.015) and relationship types (CFI = 0.989, RMSEA = 0.020). They reveal that Happiness is a Central Factor in loving the partner. It accounts for effects of depression and anxiety, across nine cultural regions and eight relationship types.

29.24 How Is Love Correlated with Evaluative Well-Being?

Correlations of the Four Component Love Scale with cognitive evaluation measures of well-being are shown in the first column of Table 29.20. Items are ordered from highest to lowest correlations.

Loving the partner is associated with considering life to be fulfilling and meaningful, general life satisfaction, self-esteem, job satisfaction, and appearance satisfaction. Satisfaction with number of children, which does not load on the other satisfaction scales, is trivially correlated with loving the partner.

Regression coefficients from SEM analyses are shown in the second column, which are similar across cultural regions (CFI = 0.993, RMSEA = 0.015) and relationship types (CFI = 0.989, RMSEA = 0.020). They reveal that considering life fulfilling and meaningful, and general life satisfaction, are Central Factors in loving the partner. They account for effects of self-esteem, job satisfaction and appearance satisfaction. These effects are consistent across nine cultural regions and eight relationship types.

Table 29.19 Correlations with emotional well-being

	Corr.	Regr.
Happiness	0.39***	0.45
Depression	−0.22***	−0.03
Anxiety	−0.13***	0.05

Table 29.20 Correlations with cognitive evaluation measures of well-being

	Corr.	Regr.
Life is fulfilling and meaningful (4)	0.22***	0.22
General life satisfaction (5)	0.21***	0.12
Self-esteem	0.16***	0.02
Job satisfaction (3)	0.11***	−0.01
Appearance satisfaction (3)	0.11***	0.00
Satisfaction with number of children	0.03*	0.00

To promote well-being in association with intimate relationships, Singles Counseling has been developed to help single clients prepare for a happy marriage or single life (Aydın, 2017, 2018). It explores gender roles in relation to the basic human needs of autonomy and relatedness (Kağıtçıbaşı, 1996), and is applicable in both individualistic and collectivistic cultures.

29.25 What Are the Categories of the Correlates of Love?

This chapter reveals that loving the partner is associated with many kinds of factors that have consistent effects across nine cultural regions and eight relationship types. The kinds of factors can be classified in terms of the following categories, which list the Central Factors and their regression coefficients in this study:

Motivation

- Relationship reasons: commitment 0.20, emotional closeness 0.21
- Life goals: having a committed relationship 0.34
- Values: Self-transcendence (universality and benevolence) 0.20
- Traits: emotionally expressive 0.10, nurturing 0.11

Partner Suitability

- Mate selection: personality important 0.29
- Partner similarity: personality 0.35, willingness to have children 0.16, intelligence 0.16
- Rate partner: desirable as a partner 0.43, intelligent 0.18
- External factors: parents and others approve of partner 0.28, parents know partner 0.10, closest friends know partner 0.11

Intimacy Dimensions

- Love styles: Eros (meant for each other) 0.38, agape (sacrifice own wishes) 0.13
- Emotional intimacy: both in love 0.32, emotional closeness 0.22, express affection 0.20
- Communication: self-disclosure to partner 0.24, how well partners knows me 0.18, how well I know partner 0.13, partner self-disclosure 0.12, trust partner not to lie 0.15, how often communicate 0.36
- Sexual intimacy: sexual satisfaction 0.33, approve of partner's outside sex −0.10

Exchange Processes

- Exchange measures: gained benefits 0.31, equally involved 0.51, feel invested 0.16, equal disclosure 0.12, equal power 0.14

Conflict Resolution

- Conflict measures: positive responses to conflict 0.50
- Responses to dissatisfaction: voice (discuss) 0.34, exit (leave) −0.18
- Intimate partner violence: express jealousy 0.14

Well-Being

- Emotional: happiness 0.45
- Evaluative: life fulfilling and meaningful 0.22, general life satisfaction 0.12

The first category (Motivation) is the same as the first category in the Comprehensive Partner Model that predicts who has a current partner (Hill, 2019). This is not surprising, since wanting a partner involves wanting someone to love. The other categories in the Comprehensive Partner Model are Confidence, Readiness, and Opportunity, which are involved in finding a partner to love but are not correlates of love.

The middle four categories (Partner Suitability, Intimacy Dimensions, Exchange Processes, and Conflict Resolution) are the same as the categories of the Comprehensive Commitment Model (Hill, 2019). The categories of factors associated with loving the partner are similar to the categories of factors that predict relationship satisfaction and commitment, since the emotion of love for the partner is strongly correlated with the cognitive evaluation of relationship satisfaction ($r = .72$) and relationship commitment ($r = .77$) in this study.

The last category (Well-being) is also strongly associated with relationship satisfaction and commitment in this study (Hill, 2019). The emotion of loving someone, and the cognitive evaluation of having a satisfying and committed relationship, capture important emotional and cognitive contributors to well-being.

29.26 Conclusions and Limitations

The many factors that are correlated with love are not surprising, in light of previous research on intimate relationships. What is surprising is that the factors associated with love are similar across nine cultural regions and eight relationship types. This is true even though the mean levels of the factors may vary across cultures and relationship types. How the factors vary is reported in Chap. 11 of Hill (2019).

Since the study is online (except in Pakistan), participants are limited to those who have access to the internet, and to those willing to answer an online questionnaire, as noted in Hill (2019). They are likely to be younger, and better educated than the general public.

As noted in the discussion of Structural Equation Modeling in Sect. 29.3, the correlations may vary in other studies, and so the factors considered Central Factors or Trivial Factors may vary. But the categories of the factors are very likely to be similar, since they capture a wide range of factors found important in intimate relationships in previous research (Hill, 2019).

29.27 Implications of the Study

For Future Research, this study reveals the usefulness of conducting comprehensive research that explores many factors, not just a few, and compares many cultures and many relationship types. It also demonstrates the usefulness of identifying Central Factors and Trivial Factors, while recognizing that categories of the factors may be similar even if the Central Factors and Trivial Factors vary across studies.

For Self-Reflection, it is useful to ask oneself questions about the categories of the correlates of love, such as the following (cf. Hill, 2019):

Motivation: What are my reasons for wanting an intimate relationship? What are my life goals, my values, and my personality traits?
Partner Suitability: How similar is the partner in personality, intelligence, and desirability as a partner in a committed relationship? To what extent do my parents and friends know and approve of the partner?
Intimacy Dimensions: Are we both in love? How well do we know each other? How often do we communicate? How satisfying is our sexual intimacy?
Exchange Processes: To what extent have I gained benefits from the relationship? Are we equally involved in the relationship?
Conflict Resolution: How do we respond to conflict? Do we discuss things and come to a mutual understanding? Do I try to understand what is stressing the partner?
Well-Being: Does the partner make me happy? Does the relationship contribute to making my life fulfilling and meaningful? How does it affect my life satisfaction?

For Couples Counseling, therapists should help individuals and couples explore the questions for Self-Reflection.

Collaborators The following collaborators translated the questionnaire, recruited participants, or did both, which were crucial in conducting the study on which this chapter is based. Collaborators also made comments on chapter drafts.

Kâmile Bahar Aydın, Ankara Yıldırım Beyazıt University, Turkey; Maria Rivas Barros, Universidad del Magdalena, Colombia; Diana Boer, University of Koblenz-Landau, Germany; Claudia C. Brumbaugh, Queens College, City University of New York, United States; José Enrique Canto y Rodriguez, Universidad Autónoma de Yucatán, Mexico; Rodrigo J. Carcedo, Universidad de Salamanca, Spain; Elena Chebotareva, Moscow State University of Psychology and Education, National Research University Higher School of Economics, Russia; Sylvia Xiaohua Chen, and Algae K. Y. Au, The Hong Kong Polytechnic University, Hong Kong SAR, China; Artemis Z. Giotsa, University of Ioannina, Greece; Victoria V. Ilchenko North Ossetian State University, Vladikavkaz, Russia; Valery L. Sitnikov, Herzen State Pedagogical University, St. Petersburg, Russia; Elena Sinelnikova, Emperor Alexander I St. Petersburg State Transport University, Russia; Loredana Ivan, National University of Political Studies and Public Administration (SNSPA), Bucharest, Romania; Ilona Kajokiene, Mykolas Romeris University, Vilnius, Lithuania; Rukhsana Kausar, Vice Chancellor, Government College Women University, Sialkot, Pakistan; and Shehnaz Bano, University of the Punjab, Pakistan; Mie Kito, Meiji Gakuin University, Japan; Karolina Kuryś-Szyncel and Barbara Jankowiak, Adam Mickiewicz University, Poznań, Poland; Zsuzsa F. Lassú, Eötvös Loránd University, Hungary; Olufemi A. Lawal, Lagos State University, Nigeria; Xiaomin Li, University of Arizona, United States; Guillermo Macbeth and Eugenia Razumiejczyk, National Scientific and Technical Research Council of Argentina (CONICET) and Pontific Catholic University of Argentina (UCA); Silvia Mari, Università di Milano-Bicocca, Italy; Takafumi Sawaumi, Ryutsu Keizai University, Japan; and Tsutomu Inagaki (Fujii), Kagoshima University, Japan; Jenny Lukito Setiawan, Universitas Ciputra Surabaya, Indonesia; and Immanuel Yosua, Atma Jaya Catholic University of Indonesia; Vered Shenaar-Golan and Ofra Walter, Tel Hai Academic College, Israel; Suhas Shetgovekar, Indira Gandhi National Open University, India; Mein-Woei Suen, Asia University/Chung Shan Medical University, Taiwan; Cláudio V. Torres, University of Brasília, Brazil.

References

Apostolou, M. (2016). The evolution of same-sex attractions: Parental and intimate partners' reactions to deviations from exclusive heterosexual orientation. *Personality and Individual Differences, 101*, 380–389.

Aydın, K. B. (2017). *Bekar Danışmanlığı ve Özerk-İlişkisel Bekar Danışmanlığı Modeli: Türkiye'de Yeni Bir Kavram, Araştırma, Uzmanlık ve Çalışma Alanı* [Single Counseling (SC) an Autonomous-Relational Single Counseling Model (ARSCM): A New concept, research, specialization and work field in Turkey]. *TURAN-SAM, 36*(9), 707–715.

Aydın, K. B. (2018). *Model of autonomous-relational singles counseling (MARSC) in collectivist cultures: The Turkey model*. Poster presented at the 24th congress of the International Association for Cross-Cultural Psychology, Guelph, Canada.

Aylor, B., & Dainton, M. (2001). Antecedents in romantic jealousy experience, expression, and goals. *Western Journal of Communication (includes Communication Reports), 65*(4), 370–391.

Bell, G. C., & Hastings, S. O. (2015). Exploring parental approval and disapproval for black and white interracial couples. *Journal of Social Issues, 71*(4), 755–771.

Berscheid, E., & Walster, E. H. (1969). *Interpersonal attraction*. Boston: Addison Wesley.

Berscheid, E., & Walster, E. H. (1978). *Interpersonal attraction* (2nd ed.). Reading, MA: Addison Wesley.
Blau, P. M. (1964). *Exchange and power in social life*. New York: Wiley.
Byers, E. S. (2005). Relationship satisfaction and sexual satisfaction: A longitudinal study of individuals in long-term relationships. *Journal of Sex Research, 42*(2), 113–118.
Byrne, D. (1971). *The attraction paradigm* (Vol. 11). New York: Academic.
Carter, C. S., & Porges, S. W. (2013). The biochemistry of love: An oxytocin hypothesis. *EMBO Reports, 14*(1), 12–16.
Diener, E., Oishi, S., & Lucas, R. E. (2002). Subjective well-being: The science of happiness and life satisfaction. In C. R. Snyder & S. J. Lopez (Eds.), *Handbook of positive psychology*. Oxford: Oxford University Press.
Gottman, J. M. (1999). *The marriage clinic: A scientifically based marital therapy*. New York: Norton.
Hatfield, E., Rapson, R. L., & Aumer-Ryan, K. (2008). Social justice in love relationships: Recent developments. *Social Justice Research, 21*(4), 413–431.
Hazan, C., & Shaver, P. R. (1987). Romantic love conceptualized as an attachment process. *Journal of Personality and Social Psychology, 52*, 511–524.
Hendrick, C., & Hendrick, S. (1986). A theory and method of love. *Journal of Personality and Social Psychology, 50*, 392–402.
Hill, C. T. (2019). *Intimate relationships across cultures: A comparative study*. New York: Cambridge University Press.
Hill, C. T., & Peplau, L. A. (1998). Premarital predictors of relationship outcomes: A 15-year follow-up of the Boston couples study. In T. N. Bradbury (Ed.), *The developmental course of marital dysfunction* (pp. 237–278). New York: Cambridge University Press.
Hill, C. T., Rubin, Z., & Peplau, L. A. (1976). Breakups before marriage: The end of 103 affairs. *Journal of Social Issues, 32*(1), 147–168.
Kağıtçıbaşı, Ç. (1996). The autonomous-relational self: A new synthesis. *European Psychologist, 1*(3), 180–186.
Lee, J. A. (1973). *The colors of love*. Englewood Cliffs, NJ: Prentice Hall.
Meltzer, A. L., McNulty, J. K., Jackson, G. L., & Karney, B. R. (2014). Sex differences in the implications of partner physical attractiveness for the trajectory of marital satisfaction. *Journal of Personality and Social Psychology, 106*(3), 418–428.
Muise, A., & Impett, E. A. (2015). Good, giving, and game: The relationship benefits of communal sexual motivation. *Social Psychological and Personality Science, 6*(2), 164–172.
Rubin, Z. (1970). Measurement of romantic love. *Journal of Personality and Social Psychology, 16*(2), 265–273.
Rusbult, C. E., Zembrodt, I. M., & Gunn, L. K. (1982). Exit, voice, loyalty, and neglect: Responses to dissatisfaction in romantic involvements. *Journal of Personality and Social Psychology, 43*(6), 1230–1242.
Schumann, K. (2012). Does love mean never having to say you're sorry? Associations between relationship satisfaction, perceived apology sincerity, and forgiveness. *Journal of Social and Personal Relationships, 29*(7), 997–1010.
Schwartz, S. H. (2012). An overview of the Schwartz theory of basic values. *Online Readings in Psychology and Culture, 2*(1).
Sternberg, R. (1986). A triangular theory of love. *Psychological Review, 93*(2), 119–135.
van Zantvliet, P. I., Kalmijn, M., & Verbakel, E. (2015). Early partner choices of immigrants: The effect of preferences, opportunities and parents on dating a native. *Journal of Ethnic and Migration Studies, 41*(5), 772–794.
Walters, A. S., & Burger, B. D. (2013). "I love you, and I cheated": Investigating disclosures of infidelity to primary romantic partners. *Sexuality & Culture, 17*(1), 20–49.

Charles T. Hill is Professor of Psychology at Whittier College, California, where he won the Nerhood Teaching Excellence Award. He has a PhD in Social Psychology from Harvard University, an MA in Sociology and an MS in Physics from the University of Washington, and a BA in physics from the Honors College of the University of Oregon. He is a member of Phi Beta Kappa, the American Psychological Association, the American Sociological Association, and other professional organizations. He is on the editorial board of Online Readings in Psychology and Culture, published by the International Association for Cross-Cultural Psychology. He is the author of *Intimate Relationships Across Cultures: A Comparative Study*, conducted with collaborators he met at international conferences around the world.

Chapter 30
Love in a Time of Globalization: Intimacy Re-imagined Across Cultural Flows

Bahira Trask

Abstract This chapter examines how love and intimate relationships are changing in a time of globalization. As it becomes exponentially simpler to connect with others around interest areas and inclinations, new conceptualizations of intimate relationships are becoming common place in near and far places in the world. As Naomi Quinn pointed out in 1992, love is socially constructed and interconnected with other domains of social life such as gender relations, family, and work life. While love is often presented as "natural" and immutable, it is however intimately tied to cultural systems of meaning. This presents the question of what is meant by love and intimate relationships in varying cultural and socio-economic contexts, contexts that are rapidly transforming due to social, political, economic and technological transformations.

Globalization has been primarily analyzed through the prism of economics and politics with little attention on how more intimate processes and concepts are being simultaneously reshaped. And yet we know that globalization is introducing new concepts of romance, love, and intimate relationships which are transformed in local contexts. Technology facilitates these flows and encourages the ensuing hybridity that characterizes our time. In this paper I will examine how experiences of love and intimacy are transforming in various contexts in response to globalization. There will be a specific emphasis on differences in these concepts based on class, race, nationality, sexualities, and geographic location.

Keywords Love · Globalization · Gender · Culture · Global transformations · Hybridization

---

B. Trask (✉)
Department of Human Development and Family Sciences, University of Delaware, Newark, DE, USA
e-mail: bstrask@udel.edu

© Springer Nature Switzerland AG 2021
C.-H. Mayer, E. Vanderheiden (eds.), *International Handbook of Love*,
https://doi.org/10.1007/978-3-030-45996-3_30

30.1 Introduction

This chapter examines how love and intimate relationships are changing in a time of globalization. As it becomes exponentially simpler to connect with others around interest areas and inclinations, new conceptualizations of intimate relationships are becoming common place in near and far places in the world. As Strauss and Quinn pointed out several decades ago, love is socially constructed and interconnected with other domains of social life such as gender relations, family, and work life (Strauss & Quinn, 1992). While love is often presented as "natural" and immutable, it is however intimately tied to cultural systems of meaning. This presents the question of what is meant by love and intimacy in varying cultural and socio-economic contexts, contexts that are rapidly transforming due to social, political, economic and technological transformations. Specifically, as individuals are increasingly interconnected, values and beliefs are changing rapidly in ways that are not always obvious or clear-cut. We know a great deal about love, relationship formation, and marriage in the West, and specifically amongst the white middle-class in the United States (see for example, Cherlin, 2004, 2009). However, when we look to various sub-groups in the United States or at other regions in the world, despite the proliferation of communication technologies, it is less clear the extent to which more relaxed Western values around sexuality, partnerships before marriage and norms around intimacy have been adopted and by whom (Hull, Meier, & Ortyl, 2010; Plummer, 2001). We know even less about partnerships between individuals of different backgrounds (nationalities, religions, ethnicities, and gender identities) and how they negotiate and decide on their short-term and longer-term relationships. Nevertheless, a growing literature depicts a global, albeit uneven, trend towards models of intimate relationships and families that are based on chosen love rather than founded on social obligation and the reproduction of kinship systems (Padilla, Hirsch, Munoz-Laboy, Sember, & Parker, 2007).

The concept of intimacy is predicated on relationships and attachments between individuals that are close psychologically and/or geographically speaking. But intimacy connotes much more than this. Intimacy refers to a certain type of relationship: one that is unique and involves emotions between those involved. Ara Wilson defines the concept as capturing

> deeply felt orientations and entrenched practices that make up what people consider to be their "personal" and "private" lives and their interior selves, and includes positively valued feelings like affection but also problematic feelings like fear and disgust (Wilson, 2012, p. 32).

Intimacy from this perspective is deeply tied to our sense of who we are and how we relate with others.

In contemporary analysis, however, intimacy has come to be primarily associated with the sexual realm (Sehlikoglu & Zengin, 2015). This primarily Western perspective ignores and discounts a wide variety of other types of intimacies that exist between individuals and within groups. As Roseneil and Budgeon (2004) pointed out, a focus on sexuality limits our understandings of emotions and what it truly means to be intimate with someone. Thus, a Western discourse of love (again with a focus on romantic and sexual love) and "choice" increasingly structures the meaning and practices of intimate relationships and families, as well as the research on these topics. Concurrently, particularly in other parts of the world besides the United States and western Europe, love, and specifically romantic, sexual love, is now understood to be synonymous with being "modern" (Donner, 2012). One result of this phenomenon has been the global growth of commercialized experiences of "love" and intimacy. Valentine's day (a uniquely Western celebration of intimacy and love) has spread to other parts of the world, with the accompanying practice of greeting cards, restaurant dinners and elaborate gifts. However, this practice has not been universally embraced, and has instead also led to a backlash in certain places. For instance, in recent times there have been multiple attacks on couples celebrating these types of holidays as they are perceived as a "Western infringement" on traditional cultural beliefs (Kreil, 2016).

We increasingly find ourselves in a situation where a specific definition and practice of love and intimacy exists in contrast, and at times in conflict, with the realities of nationhood, social class, gender, regionality, race and ethnicity (Svasek & Skrbis, 2007). Globalization is playing a critical role in this process. On the one hand, globalization promotes certain aspects of love and intimacy such as spreading the concept of personal inclination, romance, and choice. On the other, as will be seen in this paper, globalization also undermines the very values and practices that it promotes by being at the heart of economic and political processes. The mechanisms behind what is happening are complex and multi-varied, necessitating a nuanced discussion of the interrelationship between intimacy, love and globalization. We are only now beginning to explore and understand how individuals are more interconnected to the economic and political processes encouraged and supported by globalization, and how this in turn, affects social life, values and practices. The spread and hybridization of values and belief systems are a key component of this discussion.

In this chapter I explore the relationship between globalization and changing norms around love and intimacy, These complicated issues involve questions of value and belief systems, religion, public order, gender relations and individual preferences. My goal with this paper is to initiate and further the discussion with the understanding that there is much work yet to done in this particular area.

30.2 What Is Globalization?

Even though globalization is a hotly contested phenomenon, there is some agreement that globalization entails a new form of bridging geographic and cultural distances, and that these developments are the product of constantly evolving transportation, communication and information technologies. From the mid-1990s onwards, there has been an increased emphasis on the part of social scientists on the effects of globalization. Specifically, the movement of capital, the changing role of the nation-state, the increased transnational migration of individuals, and the growth and expansion of multinational corporations and transnational organizations have been the focus of study. More recently, globalization has been understood to be particularly important as it influences cultural change as well (Pieterse, 2019). Despite this more nuanced perspective on globalization, an understanding of the relationship between this phenomenon and social concerns such as love, intimacy, and close relationships is still in its infancy. This oversight has occurred, despite the fact that the meaning of the very categories which are a part of globalization have been altered through a process of hybridization: the nation-state, economies, communities, social class, gender, race, ethnicity, and intimacy and love are now understood to be in a state of perpetual change. Thus approaches to globalization that focus exclusively on economic and political dimensions, do not capture the dynamism or the human consequences that are an inherent feature of this phenomenon.

A small but vocal minority of scholars, represented most prominently by Anthony Giddens have argued that globalization has moved us past modernity into an age of postmodernity (Giddens, 1990). Giddens has argued that modernity is inherently globalizing, and that the consequences of this process have taken us into a new world that we currently do not understand very well. He stated,

> In the modern era, the level of time-space distanciation is much higher than in any previous period, and the relations between local and distant social forms and events become correspondingly 'stretched.' Globalization refers essentially to that stretching process, as the modes of connection between different social contexts or regions become networked across the earth's surfaces as a whole (p. 64).

As Giddens (1990) pointed out, we are in a fundamentally different world where the trajectory for transformation is accelerating at unimagined speeds and across wide distances. This form of globalization can also be termed as a form of global connectivity (Kelly, 2001).

While change is an inherent aspect of the human experience, the rapidity and spread of a wide-ranging set of values and norms makes contemporary analyses of social life very complicated and at times, even inaccurate. In a context with multiple interacting belief systems, norms, and values, it is increasingly difficult to identify which aspects of a society's ideology individuals draw from. However, throughout this discussion about globalization, love, and intimacy, it is important to recognize that individuals are active agents who are neither the victims of dominant ideologies, nor autonomous representatives of self (Valentine, 2006). They have the potential to resist or re-imagine conflicting representations that may result in alternative constructions to previously existing, dominant discourses.

As stated above, until relatively recently, globalization has been primarily discussed from an economic and political perspective. However, new scholarship repeatedly highlights that most aspects of social, economic and political life are closely interrelated are constantly being reshaped. Globalization is introducing and affecting concepts of romance, love, and intimate relationships which are subsequently transformed in local contexts (Pieterse, 2019; Swidler, 2001). Technology facilitates these flows and encourages and stimulates a hybridity that is a critical part of this process. In order to begin to understand the role that globalization plays in the transformation of love, intimacy and relationships, it is necessary to begin with some perspectives on the detraditionalization of intimate relationship formation.

30.3 The Detraditionalization of Relationship Formation: How Did We Get Here?

The transformation of global perspectives on intimacy, love and marriage cannot be simply explained through the spread of media images, as is so common in mainstream discourses (Valentine, 2006). Instead, transformations in the intimate sphere are in all likelihood a response to a confluence of factors including wide spread changes in gender roles, the spread of new ideologies and values pertaining to intimate relationships, and economic forces that have elicited new behaviors.

Over the last 50 years the path to forming intimate relationships and marriage has changed dramatically in the United States and many European countries. Age of first marriage has increased, more and more couples are living in neolocal households, and fertility is declining. Interestingly, however, values around forming intimate relationships, specifically "being a family" have not markedly changed (Esping-Anderson & Billari, 2015).[1] Large scale surveys (see for instance, Pew, 2015) indicate that in the United States for example, most individuals still want to find a long-term partner and a relatively high number of individuals want to become parents. What has changed noticeably, specifically in many Western countries, are attitudes around sexuality, gender, and love. In the United States and most European countries we have more open, commodified sexual cultures, and there exist more choices for most individuals around gender construction and identities. Trends in other parts of the world are not quite as obvious but ethnographic research indicates that open dialogues about sexuality and personal fulfillment though love relationships are becoming more common in areas as diverse as Mexico (see for example, Hirsch, 2003), Egypt (see, Inhorn, 2003), China (see, Ji, 2015), and India (see, Sandhya, 2009). This raises the question about why have attitudes about the need for forming intimate relationships remained relatively stable, but values associated with sexuality and gender changed? And how are these changes linked to the beliefs and practices associated with love.

Until relatively recently, marriage, children, and relatively traditional gendered, expectations around family life were the norm for most individuals in societies around the world. The division of labor based on sex was relatively unquestioned, and divorce despite being available was stigmatized (Coontz, 1992; Gross, 2005; Smith, 1993). While in the United States and Europe, there were exceptions to this

---

[1]It is important to note that the term "family" is used to connote a variety of living arrangements including single parents, divorced couples, same-sex relationships and so on.

norm, most individuals adhered to a pretty formulaic path to family formation and once married, to relatively stable gender roles. It is against this backdrop of an entrenched model of "acceptable" partnership formation and family life, that major changes have taken place.

Contemporary theorists have pointed out that the transformations in intimate relationships and their accompanying expectations, have undergone a process of detraditionalization (Gross, 2005). Social and cultural beliefs and traditions around intimate life have been reconfigured and at times even abandoned. In order to understand these changes, contemporary primarily ethnographic studies have specifically focused on new values and mechanisms around pairing up and mating amongst the anonymity of urban life (Padilla et al., 2007; Patico, 2009; Zelizer, 2005).

In most societies, couples who married as shortly as two generations ago, spoke about their relationships as bonds of obligation and the mutual fulfillment of responsibilities. Hirsch (2007) in an ethnographic study of a small town in Mexico depicted how for most couples, until recently, marriage was not about passionate, romantic love but about gendered responsibilities. However, this gendered division of labor that has characterized so much of human history in so many societies, has given way to a wide variety of arrangements. For instance, in the United States, over 40% of women are now the primary or main breadwinner and gender convergence, the sharing of roles between men and women, is increasingly the norm (Pew Research, 2015). In addition, in many Western countries, a relatively high percentage of children are born into unions that are not necessarily cemented through a marriage contract. In fact, what we have witnessed is a pluralization of accepted practices around couple formation and intimate relationships. These transformations and accompanying multiplicity of choices have also led to an increase in anxiety in some individuals: the very notion of intimacy has changed, how we find and maintain love relationships has been altered, and the blueprint for what is considered acceptable is constantly being reworked (Sehlikoglu & Zengin, 2015).

Globally, a specific Westernized notion of romantic, sexualized love is replacing the traditional model of reciprocal duty and responsibility that is foundational to intimacy in much of the world. In the new model, a strong relationship and/or marriage is characterized by shared decision-making, shared time together, and shared duties. In other words, a companionate, egalitarian partnership is increasingly the ideal for younger couples around the world (Padilla et al., 2007). That said, I wish to emphasize again however, that the ideal of forming a family, be it through marriage or living together and with or without children, remains prevalent throughout the world (Esping-Anderson & Billari, 2015).

Various social theorists have struggled to explain the detraditionalization of the contemporary relationship formation. Manuel Castells, a major social theorist, posited in *The Power of Identity* (1997) that a confluence of factors came together to lead to our contemporary phenomena. In particular, he pointed to the second-wave of feminism with its emphasis on creating and opening up educational and occupational opportunities for women as a main driver of ideological change. Castells suggested that the feminist foci of that time, on denaturalizing the here-to-for taken for granted assumption of "natural" sex differences, set the foundation not just for a reconceptualization of the capabilities and potentials of women but also allowed for the emergence of the acceptance of same-sex relationships. This larger ideological movement has led to the diversification of intimate relationships and a decline to traditional forms of patriarchy. With the demise of traditional models of power relations within intimate relationships, new forms of love, intimacy and coupling were able to gain a foothold—at least in many Western countries.

From a somewhat different perspective, the social theorist Anthony Giddens, suggested that it is specifically through globalization that intimacy and concepts such as love and marriage have been detraditionalized. He claimed that as financial and communication systems have gained strength, traditional institutions such as the breadwinner/homemaker family have weakened. The locus of authority has shifted to communication and financial systems, which transcend state boundaries and according to Gidden's, have gained enormous social power (1992). He also suggested that intimacy has been freed from traditional restraints specifically by the influence of mental health systems. The increased emphasis on individual self-fulfillment and development have become, at least in the West, the main standard by which intimate relationships are evaluated (Gross & Simmons, 2002). Instead of the emphasis being on lifelong relationships and procreation, for an increasing number of individuals around the world, intimacy is defined virtually exclusively by sexual fulfillment and personal growth. These ideas are spread through ever faster, ubiquitous communication technologies and social media that promote norms and behaviors that are at times very removed from the customs and locales to which they spread. In some locales, especially in the non-Western part of the world, these messages have not resonated with public custom. In response, counter responses are developing that emphasize traditional roles, especially for women. In these places, a return to "traditional" gender roles is being emphasized, at least in the public sphere. Some recent studies illustrate that for example in countries in North Africa, the Middle East and South East Asia, a return to women's veiling is, in part, a response to negotiating these varied discourses on gender roles (Macleod, 1993; Secor, 2002). When women veil and work outside the home, they send a symbolic message that they are "traditional" and "modern" simultaneously. Their veiling sends the message that while they have taken on the new norms of working for pay that have been brought on by globalization, they are still retaining their local traditions around piety and religiosity. In fact, some studies (Secor, 2002) describe how men will specifically look for veiled women as their future wives, as this move also suggests to the outer world their own adherence to their faith. Thus, what we find is that intimacy and gender roles are being constantly re-negotiated in the face of globalizing processes.

Rebhun (1999) suggested a different impetus for the de-traditionalization of intimate partner relationships. Instead she takes a historical perspective and argues that when social relations shifted from small, kinship-based villages to those in wage-labor-based cities, the definition and expression of intimacy and attachment became less instrumental and more romantic. As young people are increasingly living and working in urban environments, the home-work distinction has increased.

This is in contrast to the lives of their parents who were living in more rural settings and in smaller, more bounded environments. While there are more economic opportunities for women, there are fewer for men, creating economic tensions between individuals in relationships. Simultaneously, couples are exposed to Western notions that focus on emotional intimacy as the primary driver for relationship formation. Thus, Rebhun (1999) argues, the traditional supports (extended family, the expectation of land inheritance, and norms and values) are not in place to support these relationships that are built on fragile bonds. The result are couples with short-term relationships and few supports for maintaining their relationships when things go awry.

A critical aspect of this discussion are also the changes that have accompanied new belief systems around sexuality. The ability to control fertility through contemporary contraceptive measures is an important aspect of the transformation around behaviors and values. New improved contraceptive technologies have allowed women to be freed from the fear of unwanted pregnancies. This has allowed women to also embrace the ideal of sexual fulfillment and made it a condition for staying in relationships. Gross and Simmons (2002) argued that the severing of sexuality from reproduction has also allowed for a move away from heterosexuality being the normative standard by which all other relationships are judged. This move has allowed for the emergence of a perspective that does not rely on "natural" gender complementarities anymore and has opened up the discourse to gender identity, same sex relationships and the like.

30.4 Intimacy, Love and Economics

The relationship between economics and intimacy is critical, complex, and foundational to understanding changing social values including those around the construction of love. At the root of most relationships is an exchange of some sort. In our contemporary environment, the discourse around love and intimacy assumes what is sometimes referred to as a "pure" relationship (Giddens, 1992). Two individuals come together to form an intimate partnership based on an emotional connection. However, the historical record, and even a large body of contemporary ethnographic research suggest a different story. Intimate and other types of relationships are based on transactional exchanges—and many of those transactions are economic in nature. Thus, money and resources are often exchanged for intimate and sexual services and tend to have a gendered underpinning.

Some anthropologists suggest that the sexual exchange of girls and women has been historically and cross-culturally an integral social aspect of many societies and cultures. They argue that this gendered exchange is embedded in the belief and practices of a multitude of family and kinships systems. From this perspective, historically, groups traded their women as peace offerings and as a "gift" with which they created social relationships and achieved important alliances (Long, 2004; Mauss, 1990). This has created, in many places, a cultural template that deems transactions involving women as "normal" and embedded in various cultural systems. At the extreme end of this type of transaction is sexual trafficking where girls and women (and at times boys and men) are used against their will for "intimacy" services. But there are also others who argue that even "traditional" marriage is a form of economic and sexual transaction. For instance, Constable (2009) wrote,

> More recent scholarly research on sex work, sex tourism, prostitution, and comfort women points to the fluidity between paid sexual labor and marital relations and to interconnections between paid forms of intimacy and those that are assumed to be 'free'.

Today we understand that individuals weave together complex notions about "appropriate" behaviors with the opportunities or lack of opportunities that they are faced with. Capitalist, global processes offer new opportunities for love and intimacy but they are not necessarily defined by them. Instead, individuals draw on these ideas as is expedient for them under various circumstances.

A key component of exchanges is if they are equal or not. "Pure" relationships are built on the concept of equal exchange. However, inequality characterizes much of contemporary social life. A major consequence of globalization has been the growing inequality between and within societies. We have witnessed a growing gap between expectations and opportunities, especially for young people. Traditional media such as films and shows, as well as social media have spread images about how some wealthy people live, to places and individuals that may never access anything even remotely close to these types of lifestyles (Constable, 2009). Moreover, the display of wealth through luxury goods in stores, expensive cars, and mansion type houses, now co-exist in many places right alongside with malnutrition, poor sanitation, and sub-standard housing. This juxta-position of extreme wealth with extreme poverty has altered expectations for life styles and consumption choices. Concurrently, particularly in low-income countries, the ability to earn an income has actually declined (Hirsch, 2003). Structural adjustment policies set by the International Monetary Fund (IMF) have led to unintended consequences such as economic stagnation, inflation and rising unemployment. Coupled with a lack of affordable housing, these economic conditions have had serious implications for young people looking to form families. They are unable to embark onto long-term partnerships as the economic risks of forming a family are too high.

In an ethnographic study of love and marriage in Senegal, Hannaford and Foley (2015) illustrate that while spousal compatibility, intimacy and love have traditionally been an important aspect of marriage there, these days economic challenges are de-emphasizing those same characteristics in unions. Instead, individuals pursue relationships with the desire to secure immediate financial gains, with much less interest in emotional closeness and intimacy.

> The goal of marriage as a long-term project has given way to strategies in which heterosexual unions are seen as a means to extract immediate financial benefit from male partners (Hannaford & Foley, 2015).

Thus, the consumer lifestyle promoted through globalization has impacted the relationship and intimacy choices of young people in particular.

While we have seen a global emphasis on "love," concurrently we are witnessing an outsourcing of "caring" at least in high-income countries. Love as "pleasure" and for the purpose of self-satisfaction has replaced a more multi-dimensional notion of love as mutual dependency and commitment (Hirsch, 2007). This more limited notion of love becomes particularly problematic in more collectivized contexts where the emphasis on responsibility for the larger extended family remains central—such as in societies in the Middle East, Southeast Asia, and South Asia. Our discourses emphasize romantic love and an idealized egalitarian relationship between partners, that which Giddens (1992) termed a "pure relationship." Giddens describes this relationship as one in which "a social relation is entered into for its own sake, for what can be derived by each person from a sustained association with another; and which is continued only insofar as it is thought by both parties to deliver enough satisfactions for each individual to stay within it" (58). This type of a relationship has a strong element of personal development contained within.

In reality, however, even in Western societies a large literature indicates that many if not most relationships, despite egalitarian foundations, do not necessarily result in long-term equal partnerships. Thus, a notion of intimacy and partnership is spreading around the world that in actuality is not truly viable for most individuals—including for those who are involved in intimate relationships within cultural systems that promote idealized notions of love and intimacy as uniquely satisfying.

30.5 Technology and Intimacy

A significant aspect of globalization is the proliferation of communication technologies. Early discussions of specifically the Internet viewed this type of communication as disembodied from individuals and thus as dangerous. Communicating through this medium was perceived as facilitating deceitful behaviors and a lack of accountability (Valentine, 2006). More contemporary scholarship has disputed these early fears. In fact, some research indicates that Internet interactions encourage greater self-disclosure and communication. New communication technologies have allowed individuals from varied regions and backgrounds to interact in a 24/7 manner that was unheard of in previous eras. However, in reality intimate relationships across boundaries are not new. Historically, it was not unusual for marriages to be arranged by correspondence between interested parties or through the third-party intervention of parents. In today's environment, new technologies offer unique mechanisms for creating transnational intimacies and for sharing and promoting new beliefs and practices around intimate relationships.

The Internet and social media provide a wide variety of offerings of intimate relationships ranging from access to a multitude of interest groups for potential mates and friends to the commodification of any imaginable sexual service. Moreover, online intimacies between potential partners are much more easily established and maintained (Constable, 2007). In particular, the Internet and social media provide new spaces for those individuals who until recently were excluded from public interactions. For instance, individuals who are gay and lesbian have been at the forefront of using these technologies to initiate intimate relationships (Valentine, 2006). The Internet has also provided a place where individuals can find information about lifestyles, behaviors and practices that until recently were hidden from view or not particularly prevalent. Moreover, it has allowed for the formation of support groups for those who people seeking those types of relationships.

Recent scholarship indicates that for heterosexual and homosexual individuals, courtship, dating, marriage and other forms of sexual partnerships have expanded exponentially through new communication technologies. Simultaneously, there has been an enormous proliferation of for profit-oriented matchmaking services that utilize digital services (Constable, 2003). In other words, the "marriage market" and the availability of sexual services of any sort have been greatly commodified. For instance, in contrast to the past, individual sex workers now can advertise themselves over the Internet and also communicate with their clients using communication technologies. Sexuality does not necessarily need to be brokered through a third-party agency, and negotiations now take place over the privacy of the Internet. Thus, the Internet has allowed for a proliferation of intimacy and sexual services some of which are clearly commodified. Interestingly, Bernstein has also pointed out that the language used to describe sexual workers over the Internet is increasingly market-based: special "sales," markdowns and guarantees, treat individuals as marketable goods (2007).

But is it really true that globalization and the processes it facilitates have commodified intimate relationships more than in the past? Older social science perspectives advocated for ideal types that juxta-posed market and domestic spheres (Zelizer, 2000). From this view, the domestic sphere was a "haven" from the rough, impersonal arena of market capitalism. Intimate relationships were assigned to the domestic sphere and thus were shielded from capitalistic intervention. However, today we realize that this is not necessarily the case. The trade in sexuality is as old as human civilization and transactions around intimate relationships and money are exceedingly complex. In fact, as was highlighted above, some scholars even argue that "traditional" marriage with the breadwinner/homemaker family at its base is an economic transaction. From this perspective, globalization has not so much changed the basic bargain as much as providing new and faster mechanisms for accessing the "transaction" which in this case are intimate relationships.

From a somewhat different perspective, Bernstein (2007) argued that "traditional," "procreative," and "companionate" models of sexuality are these days being replaced by a "recreational sexual ethic." This perspective emphasizes that an increasing number of individuals only seek physical sensations and a false, acquired sense of relationships. She uses the example of the "girlfriend experience" offered by some contemporary sexual workers, as indicative of this new type of commodification of intimate relationships. And Constable (2009) cites the work of Allison (1994) amongst Japanese salary men who spend time in hostess clubs where they engage with women and receive their "care" without the necessity of an ongoing relationship with them. However, these are not necessarily examples of "new" types of intimate relationships. Instead, they provide evidence for the fact that economic transactions between individuals in exchange for "love" and intimacy have always been a part of social life. What is different today is not so much the transaction of economics for intimacy but (1) The mechanism for accessing the transactions; (2) The privacy that surrounds the transactions, and (3) The ease with which individuals can access a wide array of these types of relationships. These examples allow us to gain insight into how gender relations and social norms are changing and how globalization provides new mechanisms for accessing and conducting intimate relationships. Moreover, we can better see that intimacy is often related to commercial practices and material exchanges (Constable, 2009). In the most extreme example, globalization is helping to promote the growth of a sex tourist industry dominated by countries such as Thailand, which are able to play off erotic stereotypes contrasting active Western masculinity with submissive Asian femininity (Altman, 2001).

30.6 Discussion

What we learn from an examination of the complex interrelationship between globalization, love and intimacy, is that human emotion and connectivity remain at the root of the human experience (Esping-Anderson & Billari, 2015; Jankowiak & Fischer, 1992). Love provides the foundation for human connections and it is the glue that holds people together. The discourse and terminology may change, however, humans seek out others for close intimate relationships. Confusion and uncertainty about changing life trajectories increasingly characterize our time, but the foundation of what we seek from others in the intimate sphere remains the same. That said, we are not witnessing a globalization or homogenization of love per se. While the spread of common ideas about love (for instance, greater individual choice in choosing partners and private negotiations about the types or relationships someone may want) is becoming more prevalent, there are other forces at work as well (Gross & Simmons, 2002). Despite global changes that have opened up opportunities for women, traditional gendered conceptualizations of roles in mating and marriage remain, and at times have actually strengthened. Even in the United States which is considered an extremely "modern" country, in practice men and women remain ambivalent about the breadwinner-homemaker model that dominated in former times (Cherlin, 2004). And in some places like China, a return to traditional gender roles has actually increased, resulting in the phenomenon of "leftover women"—women who have chosen to continue working instead of marrying at the culturally appropriate time (Ji, 2015).

Importantly, the global always becomes hybridized with the local, i.e. local meanings are created by local actors at specific historical moments. As Ahmed and Donnan wrote in 1994, "Even though the same cultural 'message' may be received in different places, it is domesticated by being interpreted and incorporated according to local values" (p. 3). Thus, the significance of regionality and locality in discussions about love and intimacy cannot be discounted. We are not witnessing a Westernization of the world. Instead, we are undergoing a complex process of disseminating practices and beliefs that are simultaneously being re-worked and re-interpreted in local fashions. Love and intimacy are part of this processes. In the words of Constable (2009),

> Globalization does not simply result in greater commodification of intimate sexual, marital, and reproductive relationships; it also offers opportunities for defining new sorts of relationships and for redefining spaces, meanings, and expressions of intimacy that can transform and transgress conventional gendered spaces and norms (p. 58).

Through the spread of ideas, globalization provides a new environment for individuals to rethink what they may want with respect to their intimacy needs and how to put into practice their beliefs, values and personal inclinations. But it is important to remember that individuals do not operate in isolation: they are part of larger contexts and these environments provide other opportunities and constraints. Economic prospects, or the lack thereof, an increase in consumer culture, greater exposure to lifestyles through mass media, and traditional beliefs, customs, and practices all coexist in the same space. Moreover, love and intimacy take place in physical spaces and are affected by laws and national boundaries, not just by beliefs and values. For instance, Sehlikoglu and Zengin (2015) pointed out that states are playing an increasingly important role in evaluating bi-national marriages (marriages between citizens of two different countries). Civil servants have been tasked with having to decide if there is truly "love" or "intimacy" between two individuals and where the boundaries are between acceptable and unacceptable forms of relationships. The preservation of national identity and borders are an important aspect of this process. It is through the determination about who "belongs" and is allowed to stay, and those who are deemed as not intimate enough and needs to leave, that concepts about legal identity are enforced. We see from this example that states can be closely involved with defining intimacy, and thus, enforcing certain normative models of love that are specific to cultural contexts.

30.7 Conclusion and Recommendations

Globalization influences how we perceive notions of love and intimacy: socio-historical contexts, economic and political factors, and technology all play an important role in altering and at times solidifying local concepts. And as the discussion above has indicated, due to globalizing influences we are witnessing a hybridization of values and behaviors around the world. Thus, it is extremely difficult to disentangle how various factors interact with one another and it is questionable, if we can really draw generalities or conclusions from what are primarily small-scale ethnographic studies on love and intimacy. There is currently no large-scale analysis that takes a more holistic, cross-cultural approach to this issue. In addition, virtually all cross-cultural studies of intimate relationships are based on heteronormative models. And yet, there is an overarching need to rework assumptions about how individuals define love and intimacy and how these ideas factor into mate selection, long-term partnerships, marriage and domesticity. Berlant (1998) suggested that "intimacy's norms, forms and crimes," need to be catalogued and then proceeded to ask "how public institutions use issues of intimate life to normalize particular forms of knowledge and practice and to create compliant subjects (p. 188). Constable (2009) built on this concept and pointed out that for instance men are specifically portrayed as highly sexual but their nurturing and caretaking sides rarely explored nor do we currently have any real understanding of various gendered experiences of love and intimacy.

In order to understand changing notions of love and intimacy we need a wide variety of studies conducted by interdisciplinary teams (for instance, psychologists, anthropologists and economists) with strong cross-cultural awareness and perspectives. For instance, social scientific studies are needed that examine the role that various types of social media play on dating and mating behaviors in different cultural settings and amongst individuals of different ages. We also need more studies that take into account the role of economics, and their relationship to partnership formation and maintenance. As an increasing number of women around the world have joined the paid labor force, we need to understand how their notions of a "suitable" partner are evolving—and the same is true of men's, trans-gendered, and same-sex individual's perspectives. Are relationships becoming more commodified? Less commodified? How is intimacy being defined in collectivistic settings where extended families still play a primary role in individual's lives? Intimacy and love also need to examined from other analytic perspectives. For instance, studies on language usage provide insight into how the actual words "love" and "intimacy" are linguistically malleable and change over time. As one example, Garais and Wilkins explore how the concept "zu lieben" and "zu hassen" (to love and to hate in German) have different connotations today than they did in the past. Those changes have come about through globalization as a specifically American way of using the words to love have influenced German culture (2011). These kinds of issues and questions can provide insight into how globalization is altering notions of love and intimacy.

Contemporary movies, television series, and media have created a unique perception of love and intimacy that stresses the romantic, eros nature of relationships. However, great literature and the arts in general have left us a historical record that depicts human love and intimacy as more complex with elements of caregiving, nurturance and long-term attachment as also foundational. What we can understand from this discussion is that close, intimate relationships the world over are characterized by their flexibility, adaptability and multiplicity. We need to better capture this diversity and the underlying processes in order to understand the dynamism and strengths of intimate relationships and love which are foundational to the reproduction, survival, and happiness of humans.

References

Ahmed, A. S., & Donnan, H. (1994). Islam in the age of postmodernity. In A. S. Ahmed & H. Donnan (Eds.), *Islam, globalization and postmodernity* (pp. 1–20). London: Routledge.

Allison, A. (1994). *Nightwork: Sexuality, pleasure, and corporate masculinity in a Tokyo Hostess Club*. Chicago, IL: Univ. Chicago Press.

Altman, D. (2001). *Global sex*. Chicago, IL: University of Chicago Press.
Berlant, L. (1998). Intimacy: A special issue. *Critical Inquiry., 6*, 181–188.
Bernstein, E. (2007). *Temporarily yours: Intimacy, authenticity, and the commerce of sex*. Chicago, IL: University of Chicago Press.
Castells, M. (1997). *The power of identity*. New York: Wiley-Blackwell.
Cherlin, A. (2004). The deinstitutionalization of American marriage. *Journal of Marriage and Family, 66*, 848–861.
Cherlin, A. (2009). *The marriage go-round: The state of marriage and the family in America today*. New York: A Knopf. (Connell, R.W. (2005). Change among the gatekeepers: Men, masculinities, and gender equality in the global arena. *Signs, 30*, 1801–1825.)
Constable, N. (2003). *Romance on a global stage: Pen Pals, virtual ethnography, and "mail-order" marriages*. Berkeley: University of California Press.
Constable, N. (2007). Love *at* first sight? Visual images and virtual encounters with bodies. In M. Padilla, J. S. Hirsch, M. Munoz-Laboy, R. E. Sember, & R. G. Parker (Eds.), *Love and globalization: Transformations of intimacy in the contemporary world* (pp. 252–269). Nashville, TN: Vanderbilt University Press.
Constable, N. (2009). The commodification of intimacy: Marriage, sex, and reproductive labor. *Annual Review of Anthropology, 38*, 49–64.
Coontz, S. (1992). *The way we never were: American families and the nostalgia trap*. New York: Basic Books.
Donner, H. (2012). Love and marriage globally. In *Anthropology of this century* (Vol. 4).
Esping-Anderson, G., & Billari, F. (2015). Re-theorizing family demographics. *Population and Development Review, 41, 1–31*.
Gareis, E., & Wilkins, R. (2011). Love expression in the United States and Germany. *International Journal of Intercultural Relations, 35*, 307–319.
Giddens, A. (1990). *The consequences of modernity*. Stanford: Stanford University Press.
Giddens, A. (1992). *The transformation of intimacy: Sexuality, love and eroticism in modern societies*. Cambridge: Polity.
Gross, N. (2005). The detraditionalization of intimacy reconsidered. *Sociological Theory, 23*(3), 286–311.
Gross, N., & Simmons, S. (2002). Intimacy as a double-edged phenomenon? An empirical test of Giddens. *Social Forces, 81*, 531–555.
Hannaford, D., & Foley, E. (2015). Negotiating love and marriage in contemporary Senegal: A good man is hard to find. *African Studies Review, 58*, 205–225.
Hirsch, J. (2003). *A courtship after marriage: Sexuality and love in Mexican transnational families*. Berkeley: University of California Press.
Hirsch, J. S. (2007). 'Love makes a family': Globalization, companionate marriage, and the modernization of gender inequality. In M. Padilla, J. S. Hirsch, M. Munoz-Laboy, R. E. Sember, & R. G. Parker (Eds.), *Love and globalization: Transformations of intimacy in the contemporary world* (pp. 93–106). Nashville, TN: Vanderbilt Univ. Press.
Hull, K., Meier, A., & Ortyl, T. (2010). The changing landscape of love and marriage. *Contexts, 9*, 32–37.
Inhorn, M. (2003). Global infertility and the globalization of new reproductive technologies: Illustrations from Egypt. *Social Science and Medicine, 56*, 1837–1851.
Jankowiak, W., & Fischer, E. (1992). A cross-cultural perspective on romantic love. *Ethnology, 31*(2), 149–155.
Ji, Y. (2015). Between tradition and modernity: "Leftover" women in Shanghai. *Journal of Marriage and Family, 77*, 1057–1073.
Kelly, R. M. (2001). *Gender, globalization and democratization*. Lanham, MD: Rowman & Littlefield Publishers.
Kreil, A. (2016). The price of love: Valentine's day in Egypt and its enemies. *Arab Studies Journal, 24*, 128–146.

Long, L. D. (2004). Anthropological perspectives on the trafficking of women for sexual exploitation. *International Migration, 42*, 5–31.

Macleod, A. (1993). *Accommodating protest: Working women, the new veiling and change in Cairo*. New York: Columbia University Press.

Mauss, M. (1923/1990). The gift. New York: W.D. Halls.

Padilla, M., Hirsch, J. S., Munoz-Laboy, M., Sember, R., & Parker, R. G. (Eds.). (2007). *Love and globalization: Transformations of intimacy in the contemporary world*. Nashville, TN: Vanderbilt University Press.

Patico, J. (2009). For love, money, or normalcy: Meanings of strategy and sentiment in the Russian-American matchmaking industry. *Ethnos, 74*, 307–330.

Pew Research Center. (2015). Retrieved September 15, 2019, from https://www.pewsocialtrends.org/2015/12/17/1-the-american-family-today/

Pieterse, J. N. (2019). *Globalization and culture: Global Melange*. New York: Rowman & Littlefield.

Plummer, K. (2001). The square of intimate citizenship: Some preliminary proposals. *Citizenship Studies, 5*, 2.

Rebhun, L. A. (1999). *The heart is unknown country: Love in the changing economy of Northeast Brazil*. Stanford: Stanford University Press.

Roseneil, S., & Budgeon, S. (2004). Cultures of intimacy and care beyond 'the family': Personal life and social change in the early 21st century. *Current Sociology, 52*(2), 135–159.

Sandhya, S. (2009). The social context of marital happiness in urban Indian couples: Interplay of intimacy and conflict. *Journal of Marial and Family Therapy, 35*(1), 74–96.

Secor, A. J. (2002). The veil and urban space in Istanbul: Women's dress, mobility, and Islamic knowledge. *Gender, Place and Culture: A Journal of Feminist Geography, 9*, 5–22.

Sehlikoglu, S., & Zengin, A. (2015). Introduction: Why revisit intimacy? *The Cambridge Journal of Anthropology, 33*(2), 20–25.

Smith, D. E. (1993). The standard North American family: SNAF as an ideological code. *Journal of Family Issues, 14*, 50–65.

Strauss, C., & Quinn, N. (1992). Preliminaries to a theory of culture acquisition. In H. L. Pick Jr., P. W. van den Broek, & D. C. Knill (Eds.), *Cognition: Conceptual and methodological issues* (pp. 267–294). Washington, DC: American Psychological Association.

Svasek, M., & Skrbis, Z. (2007). Passions and powers: Emotions and globalisation. *Identities, 14*(4), 367–383.

Swidler, A. (2001). *Talk of love: How culture matters*. Chicago, IL: University of Chicago Press.

Valentine, G. (2006). Globalizing intimacy: The role of information and communication in maintaining and creating relationships. *Women's Studies Quarterly, 34*, 365–393.

Wilson, A. (2012). Intimacy: A useful category of transnational analysis. In G. Pratt & V. Rosner (Eds.), *The global and the intimate: Feminism in our time* (pp. 31–56). New York: Columbia University Press.

Zelizer, V. (2000). The purchase of intimacy. *Law and Social Inquiry, 25*, 817–848.

Zelizer, V. (2005). *The purchase of intimacy*. Princeton, NJ: Princeton University Press.

Bahira Trask is Professor and Chair of Human Development and Family Sciences at the University of Delaware. She holds a B.A. in Political Science with a concentration in International Relations from Yale University and a Ph.D. in Cultural Anthropology from the University of Pennsylvania. Her research focuses on globalization, women's employment and family change in Western and non-Western countries, and she presents regularly on these topics at international forums. Dr. Trask has authored and edited a number of books including *Women, Work, and Globalization: Challenges and Opportunities* (Routledge, 2014), *Globalization and Families: Accelerated*.

Chapter 31
The Expression of Compassionate Love in the South African Cultural Diversity Context

Rudolf M. Oosthuizen

Abstract Compassionate love is a form of altruistic, caring love that emphasises concern for the other's wellbeing (Kim, Wang, & Hill, *Journal of Positive Psychology and Wellbeing, 2*(1), 23–44, 2018; Miller, Kahle, Lopez, & Hastings, *Developing Psychology, 51*(1), 36–43, 2015). Recently, there has been an increase in prejudice toward some culturally diverse outgroups. In response, the South African government and citizens have called for compassion. In four studies, Sinclair, Fehr, Wang, and Regehr (*Social Psychological and Personality Science, 7* (2), 176–183, 2016) found that people who are high in compassionate love tend to express less prejudice than those who are low. Furthermore, they found that people high in compassionate love had more positive attitudes toward culturally diverse outgroups, including foreigners. Building personal relationships with culturally diverse outgroup members is an important catalyst for positive cultural intergroup attitudes. The objective of the chapter was to present a critical review of the way in which compassionate love holds promise as a positive pathway to prejudice reduction. A compassionate love scale can be used, in alternative forms, to assess compassionate or altruistic love for different targets (e.g. culturally diverse outgroups and all of humankind). Compassionate love was found to be associated positively with prosocial behaviour, as directed both to close others and to all of humanity. Evidence was found that compassionate love is distinct from empathy (Collins et al., *Journal of Social and Personal Relationships*, 1–29, 2014; Sprecher & Fehr, *Journal of Social and Personal Relationships, 22*(5), 629–651, 2005).

Keywords Love · Compassionate love · Cultural diversity · Prejudice · Outgroups compassionate love scale · Intergroup

---

R. M. Oosthuizen (✉)
Department of Industrial and Organisational Psychology, University of South Africa, Pretoria, South Africa
e-mail: oosthrm@unisa.ac.za

31.1 Introduction

With talk of cultural diversity reform in South Africa, there has been vigorous discussion of the value of showing compassion toward outgroups. Despite this call, relatively little is known about compassion or how it shapes judgements and actions. This chapter focuses on the concept of compassionate love and its promise as a positive pathway toward prejudice reduction. This chapter specifically seeks to demonstrate that compassionate love for culturally diverse outgroups and other stigmatised groups is associated with reduced prejudice and discrimination (Sinclair, Fehr, Wang, & Regehr, 2016).

Compassionate love may be characterised as a collection of states of mind, cognitions, feelings and activities related to caring concern and giving of oneself for the prosperity of others (Underwood, 2009). This concept is related to but is not synonymous with compassion, which is characterised as an emotional reaction to the suffering of another that fosters making a difference and a desire to reduce that suffering (Goetz, Keltner, & Simon-Thomas, 2010). Instead of alluding to a particular affective state or being restricted to the suffering of others, compassionate love also incorporates endeavours to advance others' human prospering and development. Key highlights of compassionate love include making choices unreservedly to make oneself available for the good of the other; a degree of understanding of oneself (for example, as possessing propensities and confinements), the other individual (for example, their needs and sentiments) and the circumstances (for example, what might offer assistance to advance the other's wellbeing); valuing and considering another individual notwithstanding their imperfections, and heartfelt, positive, emotional engagement (Underwood, 2009). Compassionate love has been described as being similar to unconditional love and at its core is ultimately about giving of the self for the good of the other (Miller, Kahle, Lopez, & Hastings, 2015).

The objective of this chapter is to present a critical review of the promise compassionate love holds for a positive pathway to prejudice reduction.

31.2 Theoretical Background

31.2.1 Compassion

Compassion is characterised as having sentiments of concern and care for those who are suffering, and carrying out benevolent acts to assist in lightening their burdens and fulfilling their needs (Holt-Lunstad & Smith, 2012) (see Chap. 27). Compassionate love shapes a maintained mien toward caring and making a difference for the other and produces benefits comparable to compassion (Sprecher & Fehr, 2005). Compassionate love has been shown to be more beneficial than kindness because of its persevering focus on benevolence, care and concern for the wellbeing of the other. Compassionate love does not anticipate reciprocity, but is given unreservedly and includes being moved by another's suffering or need. The four characteristics of compassionate love include concern for the wellbeing of others, openness to their experience, regard and deference, and understanding and acknowledgment (Reis, Maniaci, & Rogge, 2014). Although compassionate love is related to empathy, it is more closely associated with a prosocial orientation that is longer lasting than empathy alone (Batson, 2009). Moreover, compassionate love involves a disposition to perform self-sacrificial acts (Fehr & Sprecher, 2009). Compassionate love can be directed toward humanity as a whole, strangers, close others and specific individuals (Sprecher & Fehr, 2005). Compassionate love directed toward humanity/strangers in particular has been found to increase individual wellbeing, as it involves contributing to one's environment and the happiness of others (Fingerman, 2004). Similarly, compassionate love for humanity/strangers is also related to the increased enactment of prosocial acts, such as volunteerism, compared to compassionate love for close others. Additionally, higher compassionate love is correlated with greater spiritual experiences (Underwood, 2002) and higher religious service attendance (Kim, Wang, & Hill, 2018; Sprecher & Fehr, 2005).

Research on intimate relationships illustrates that more noteworthy sanctioning of compassion between accomplices is related to increments in relationship fulfilment for both beneficiaries and members (Reis et al., 2014), whereas a nonattendance to compassion inside the relationship is related with diminished relationship fulfilment (Clark, Lemay, Graham, Pataki, & Finkel, 2010). This may be because people who are higher in compassionate love are more adjusted to the troubles of their partners, experience more sincere sympathy for their partners, and give more tender and caring messages to back them (Collins et al., 2014). Additionally, people who both give and receive more significant compassionate love experience increased wellbeing, far better mental wellbeing, and lower mortality rates (Holt-Lunstad & Smith, 2012; Kim et al., 2018).

31.2.2 Empathy and Compassion

At first glance, it may be difficult to distinguish compassion, including compassionate love, from empathy. Indeed, compassion is similar to empathy, as it is derived from empathy. When researchers studied the effects of adversity and hardship on empathy and compassion, they found that increased adversity was correlated with greater empathy, which ultimately led to more compassion (Lim & Desteno, 2016). However, although these two constructs are related, they are distinct in important ways and produce different effects (Lim & DeSteno, 2016; Steffen & Masters, 2005). Like empathy, compassion includes having a profound emotional and cognitive understanding of another's torment but their forms are separate, as compassionate sentiments infer expansive charitable behaviours that fulfil the requirements of others, whereas empathy does not (Batson, Chang, Orr, & Rowland, 2002; Lim &

DeSteno, 2016; Steffen & Masters, 2005). Besides, research on empathy indicates that sharing feelings of torment with those who are suffering can lead to empathic trouble, which can deliver solid needs to cope by pulling back from the suffering person, which in turn decreases the likelihood of engaging in helping behaviours (Kim et al., 2018; Singer & Klimecki, 2014).

Compassion, on the other hand, is not necessarily characterised by sharing the same feelings as the sufferer. Instead, it involves feeling concern and love for the individual, which then produces a strong motivation to alleviate pain and improve the other's wellbeing (Singer & Klimecki, 2014). Batson (2009) discovered that individuals with high empathy that led to compassion engaged in more helping behaviours than those who only experienced empathy that led to empathic distress. Compassion is also distinguished from empathy through the ways it can help overcome empathic distress. Vachon (2016) found that compassion training can be used as a coping strategy to reverse the negative effects of empathic distress. Similarly, in a study conducted by Klimecki, Leiberg, Ricard, and Singer (2014), researchers discovered that after increasing negative affect through empathy training that produced empathic distress, compassion training could reverse these effects by lowering negative affect to baseline and increasing positive affect (Kim et al., 2018).

Neuroimaging studies have moreover supported the two constructs on both a neural and an experiential level. When people have empathic reactions to others' torment, the front midcingulate cortex and front insula are activated, ranges related to negative influence. They moreover detail an increment in negative influence on an experiential level (Klimecki et al., 2014). Brain systems included in compassion contrasted with those included in empathy; compassion was related to activation in the average orbitofrontal cortex, insula and ventral striatum, which are zones related to reward and positive influence, such as adoration and fondness (Beauregard, Courtemanche, Paquette, & St-Pierre, 2009; Kim et al., 2018; Singer & Klimecki, 2014).

The concept of empathy has a long history in the prejudice literature. As might be expected, studies have found that empathy is negatively correlated with prejudice (Batson et al., 2002; Finlay & Stephan, 2000; Oswald, 1996). However, it has also been suggested that empathy alone may not be sufficient to reduce prejudice. According to Stephan and Finlay (1999), empathising with outgroup individuals who are suffering may create uneasiness which, in turn, may lead to indeed more prominent preference. In a later audit of Stephan and Finlay's (1999) work, Cikara, Bruneau, and Saxe (2011) concluded that it is essentially the suffering of in-group individuals that inspires empathy. In reality, individuals may indeed take delight in the suffering of outgroup individuals instead of empathising with them. However, given the affiliation between empathy and prejudice that has been found in past research, it is imperative to illustrate that compassionate love is not basically an intermediary for empathy (Sinclair et al., 2016).

31.3 Literature Review

31.3.1 Compassionate Love

Scholars have long recognised that the word "love" is far too ambiguous to represent the many kinds of feelings and experiences for which people use this word. Plato, as an early example, distinguished love as sexuality, as the search for a soul mate, or as a means of contemplating the divine in another person (Aron & Davies, 2009). Over the millennia, philosophers, poets, lay writers and scientists have proposed various typologies of love, a list that includes, in the past half century, several typologies developed by relationship researchers. In a recent review, Berscheid (2010) argued that a fourfold distinction was most theoretically coherent: companionate love, romantic love, adult attachment love, and compassionate love (Mikulincer & Shaver, 2007). Compassionate love is a relative newcomer to the relationship-science literature and has received scant attention (Reis et al., 2014).

31.3.1.1 What Is Compassionate Love?

Compassionate love is "an attitude toward other(s), either close others or strangers or all of humanity; containing feelings, cognitions, and behaviours that are focused on caring concern, tenderness, and an orientation toward supporting, helping, and understanding the other(s), particularly when the other(s) is (are) perceived to be suffering or in need" (Monin, Schulz, & Feeney, 2015; Sprecher & Fehr, 2005, p. 630). It has been contended that compassionate love may be the kind of love that promotes the most prominent social good (Fehr & Sprecher, 2009). This kind of love has been characterised in different ways. In any case, most definitions emphasise caring for, valuing and concern for the beneficiary. For illustration, Sprecher and Fehr (2005) characterise compassionate love as sentiments, cognitions and behaviours that are centred on caring, concern and tenderness, and an introduction to supporting, making a difference and understanding another individual or people. This kind of love is habitually activated by the discernment that another individual is in trouble. Accordingly, Berscheid (2010) maintains it is this predecessor that separates compassionate love from other sorts of love (e.g. passionate/romantic and companionate). Compassionate love is additionally characterised by a feeling centred on advancing the welfare of another (Berscheid, 2006). In spite of the fact that it is comparable to empathy (Batson, 2009), it is considered to be a longer lasting, prosocial emotion/orientation that can be experienced in both a social setting and with outsiders (Collins et al., 2014; Fehr & Sprecher, 2009; Sprecher & Fehr, 2005).

Research has indicated that with regard to targets, compassionate love is linked to a number of prosocial introductions. Of most prominent significance to the investigation of display, compassionate love for strangers/humanity is related to compassion, helpfulness and volunteerism (Fehr, 2010, 2013; Fehr & Sprecher, 2009,

2013). Recently, researchers have made conceptual distinctions between prosocial constructs such as compassionate love, compassion and empathy. Those who distinguish between compassionate love/compassion and empathy contend that the critical contrast is that empathy includes feeling what another individual is feeling, while compassionate love/compassion incorporates the motivation to provide assistance (Fehr & Sprecher, 2013; Goetz et al., 2010; Hein & Singer, 2010). Sprecher and Fehr (2005) maintain that compassionate love includes feeling empathy but is a broader concept that includes actions taken to alleviate distress or promote the wellbeing of the other. Consistent with these views, in empirical studies, measures of compassionate love and empathy tend to be moderately to strongly correlated (Fehr & Sprecher, 2013; Sinclair et al., 2016).

31.3.2 The Compassionate Love Scale

Sprecher and Fehr (2005) created a Compassionate Love Scale that can be utilised, in totally different adaptations, to assess compassionate love for humanity/strangers, close others (family and companions), and a particular close other. They found that individuals experience compassionate love to a more prominent degree for close others than for humanity/strangers, the scores of which on the Compassionate Love Scale are emphatically related to prosocial behaviour with close connections and in society. For example, compassionate love experienced for close others and for a specific partner is associated with the provision of social support to loved ones (as measured by self-report), and compassionate love for humanity is associated with engaging in volunteer behaviour and other forms of helping (Sprecher & Fehr, 2005). Individuals high in compassionate love are more likely to anticipate enhanced positive mood when they imagine helping others (Sprecher, Fehr, & Zimmerman, 2007). They are also more likely to choose compassionate strategies for ending their relationships, strategies that would reduce the negative impact of the breakup and protect the partner from further harm (Sprecher, Zimmerman, & Abrahams, 2010).

31.3.2.1 Descriptive Information on the Compassionate Love Scale

The psychometric properties of the Compassionate Love Scale, both for the close others version and for the humanity–strangers version, indicated that the item-to-total correlations were high, ranging from 0.46 to 0.81. Cronbach's alpha was found to be 0.95 for each version of the scale. The mean total score was 5.96 (SD = 0.70) for the close others version and 4.32 (SD = 1.07) for the humanity version. This difference was significant (paired $t(351) = 34.34$, $p < 0.001$). In addition, scores on the two forms of the Compassionate Love Scale were positively correlated, $r = 0.56$, $p < 0.001$. A gender comparison indicated that women scored significantly higher than men on the Compassionate Love Scale, both for close others (M = 6.10, SD = 0.62 vs. 5.68, SD = 0.75; $t = 5.58$, $p < 0.001$) and for strangers

($M = 4.56$, $SD = 0.98$ vs. 3.88, $SD = 1.08$; $t = 5.99$, $p < 0.001$) (Sprecher & Fehr, 2005).

31.3.2.2 Factor Structure of the Compassionate Love Scale

Sprecher and Fehr (2005) conducted an exploratory analysis of the factor structure of each version of the Compassionate Love Scale, using principal component analysis with varimax rotation. A scree test in each analysis indicated one primary factor that explained 45.79% and 51.45% of the variance and that had eigenvalues of 9.59 and 10.81, respectively. Two other factors with eigenvalues slightly above 1.0 and explaining 5–8% of the variance were also extracted in each analysis. If a three-factor model was adapted, the factors, based on the items loading (>0.45) on each, are defined as tenderness and caring, acceptance and understanding, and helping and sacrifice. However, for two reasons, they present the scale as measuring a single underlying factor. Firstly, and as already noted, the scree test demonstrated a distinct break between the first factor and all the others. Secondly, the items loading on the second and third factors correlate with other variables (e.g. empathy, helpfulness) similar to items in the first factor.

31.3.2.3 Reliable and Validity of the Compassionate Love Scale

The Compassionate Love Scale is internally reliable, further confirming the findings of the pilot samples based on a preliminary version of the scale. Compassionate love was moderately, but not highly, correlated with empathy, thereby providing convergent validity for the Compassionate Love Scale, and indicating that empathy and compassionate love are distinct concepts. Furthermore, compassionate love was associated positively with self-reports of helping behaviour directed toward others (neighbours, the handicapped, the elderly), also providing validation for the scale and consistent with predictions that compassionate love may serve as an important motivator of prosocial behaviour (Sprecher & Fehr, 2005).

31.4 Research Methodology

31.4.1 Study Design

A critical review of the research literature entailed a broad systematic review of contemporary research on the themes of compassion, empathy, compassionate love, cultural diversity, prejudice, outgroups, and the Compassionate Love Scale. This approach allowed the author to evaluate documented research on compassionate love as a positive pathway to prejudice reduction.

31.4.2 Study Eligibility Criteria

The boundary of the systematic review was demarcated to include only documented contemporary research in the field of positive psychology published from 2015 to 2019. A search was done by means of an online information technology service, including search engines such as EBSCOhost/Academic Search Premier, and Google Scholar academic databases. The terms "compassion", "empathy", "compassionate love", "cultural diversity", "prejudice", "outgroups", and the "Compassionate Love Scale" were used in the search. The full texts of publications were downloaded from the databases in order to ascertain which articles to include or exclude from the systematic review. The inclusion criteria for articles reviewed for the purpose of this chapter were studies exploring compassionate love as a positive pathway to prejudice reduction. The research articles were treated as the sources of data.

31.4.3 Data Analysis

A qualitative approach was followed in exploring compassionate love in the South African cultural diversity context. In the first stage, the author read the studies carefully to form an understanding of the phenomenon of compassionate love under exploration. In the second stage, the author synthesised a portrait of the phenomenon of compassionate love that accounts for the relations and linkages within its aspects. Stage 3 consisted of theorising about how and why these compassionate love relations appear as they do, and Stage 4 consisted of re-contextualising the new knowledge about the compassionate love phenomenon and relations back into the context of how other authors have articulated the evolving knowledge. Seventeen studies were identified in a systematic search for relevant research published between January 2015 and August 2019 in the following electronic databases: EBSCOhost/Academic Search Premier and Google Scholar Academic database. Publications were evaluated for quality and eight studies were identified as the primary sources for exploration.

31.4.4 Strategies Used to Ensure Data Quality

Systematic, rigorous and auditable analytical processes are among the most significant factors distinguishing good from poor quality research. The researcher therefore articulated the findings in such a manner that the logical processes by which they were developed are accessible to a critical reader, the relationship between the actual data and the conclusions about data is explicit, and the claims made in relation to the data set are rendered credible. Considerations were also made in terms of potential publication bias (e.g. the assumption that not all research on the topic may have been published), trustworthiness or credibility, true value and quality, appropriateness and reflection on the research endeavour in its entirety, as well as best practice. Value and quality were assured by reviewing each article with regard to scientific and methodological rigour in exploring smart technology, artificial intelligence, robotics and algorithms, and employees' perceptions and wellbeing in future workplaces. All data were retained for possible future scrutiny.

31.5 Discussion and Practical Implications

31.5.1 Compassionate Love and Prejudice in the South African Cultural Diversity Context

Competition between culturally diverse groups and dividing the world into culturally diverse ingroups and outgroups are important factors in understanding compassionate love and prejudice in the South African cultural diversity context. Xenophobia in South Africa is also a reality that need to be contended with.

31.5.1.1 Competition Between Culturally Diverse Groups

One of the most used and easiest clarification of prejudice is that competition between culturally diverse groups can fuel ill will. In the event that two culturally diverse groups compete for scarce assets, such as occupations and reasonable lodging, one group's gain is the other's misfortune. The reasonable group strife hypothesis attests that intergroup antagonistic vibes and prejudice are characteristic consequences of intense competition between groups. A classic study at Robbers' Cave State Park in Oklahoma provided support for this hypothesis. The members were 11-year-old boys going to a 3-week summer camp. They did not know that the camp guides were really researchers (their guardians did know). The boys were randomly assigned to one of two groups. During the primary week, the boys got to know the other individuals in their groups through ordinary camp activities. Along these lines they created group identities, calling themselves the Rattlers and the Falcons. In the second week, the two groups competed in a football game, a treasure hunt and a tug of war, with trophies and other prizes at stake. As predicted by realistic group conflict theory, hostile feelings quickly erupted between the two groups. Food fights broke out in the dining hall, cabins were ransacked and group flags were burnt (Weiten, 2018).

31.5.1.2 Dividing the World into Culturally Diverse Ingroups and Outgroups

When people join together in groups, they often divide the social world into "us versus them", or ingroups versus outgroups. People tend to evaluate culturally diverse outgroup members less favourably than ingroup members. People also tend to think simplistically about culturally diverse outgroups—tending to see diversity among the members of their own group but to overestimate the homogeneity of culturally diverse outgroups (Boldry, Gaertner, & Quinn, 2007; Weiten, 2018).

31.5.1.3 Prejudice Toward Culturally Diverse Outgroup Members

Prejudice has been a defining feature of life in South Africa. As a social problem, it harms victims' self-conception, suppresses their potential, creates enormous stress in their lives and promotes tension and strife between groups (Inzlicht & Kang, 2010; Ong, Fuller-Rowell, & Burrow, 2009). Prejudice and discrimination are closely related concepts that have been used conversely in popular use. Be that as it may, social researchers tend to characterise their terms accurately. Partiality could be a negative opinion held towards individuals in a group. Like many other attitudes, prejudice can include three components: beliefs (for example. 'Coloureds in South Africa are alcoholics and drug users'), emotions (for example. 'I am afraid of people with HIV') and behavioural dispositions (for example. 'I wouldn't invite a lesbian to my house'). Indeed, in spite of the fact that South Africa's national history is linked transcendently with racial prejudice, these cases show that prejudice is not constrained to ethnic groups. Women, gay men, lesbians, transgendered individuals, older adults, individuals with inabilities and individuals analysed with physical or mental disorders are also targets of broad prejudice. Prejudice may lead to discrimination, which includes carrying on in an unexpected way, ordinarily unjustifiably, towards the individuals of a group. Homophobia, ageism, sexism and ableism are all instances where individuals of a specific groups suffer unjustifiable treatment. As a demeanour, prejudice may result from forms of individual discernment, with one such process being stereotyping. Homophobia is based on negative states of mind but discrimination is extended to all non-heterosexual outgroups and, for this reason, 'sexual prejudice' could be a more encompassing social phenomenon (Weiten, 2018).

The reduction of prejudice has been a long-standing goal of social psychology (for example, Allport, 1954). The aim of much of the research that has been conducted over the decades has been to decrease negativity (for example, conflict and tensions) between members of different social groups. Recently, there has been a call to move beyond the goal of "mere tolerance" of outgroups and, instead, strive to promote positive relations between groups (Tropp & Mallett, 2011). The work of Crocker and Garcia (2009) on the role of ego-system (self-focused) versus ecosystem (other-focused) motivation in intergroup relations is an example of this more positive approach (Migacheva, Tropp, & Crocker, 2011).

Sinclair et al. (2016) found that compassionate love was associated with lower levels of prejudice toward a variety of culturally diverse outgroups, including foreigners. Further, it was found that the relationship between compassionate love and prejudice toward foreigners was mediated by the inclusion of outgroup members in the self. Thus, individuals who were high in compassionate love were more likely than those who were low to incorporate foreigners within the self, which, in turn, led to more positive states of mind toward this culturally diverse outgroup. In spite of the fact that consistent support was found for the mediator targeted in these studies, there are other candidates who ought to be put to the experimental test (for example, dehumanisation and ethical shock). It is equally important to rule out factors that do not mediate the affiliation between compassionate love and prejudice. Sinclair et al. (2016) found that empathy and positive affect do not explain why people who are high in compassionate love express more positive attitudes and behavioural intentions toward foreigners.

However, these variables still need to be ruled out when examining prejudice toward other stigmatised culturally diverse groups. People who brought to mind a personal experience of compassionate love reported less prejudice toward foreigners than those who brought to mind an experience of empathy, positive mood or, in the control condition, a neutral experience. Thus, asking people to report on a time when they put themselves in someone else's shoes does not appear sufficient to reduce prejudice toward a stigmatised culturally diverse outgroup. Nor is it the case that a simple "feel good" manipulation is an effective prejudice reduction strategy. Rather, findings suggest that prejudice is lessened when people focus on an experience of giving of themselves for the good of another (Sinclair et al., 2016).

Sinclair et al. (2016) state that there are, of course, other possible causal pathways. For example, it could be the case that people who are high in compassionate love show less prejudice, which, in turn, could result in the inclusion of stigmatised culturally diverse groups in the self. A recalculation of mediation analyses to test this possibility indicated that prejudice did emerge as a mediator of the relation between compassionate love and inclusion. However, these findings must be treated with caution given that in all of the studies, prejudice was measured after inclusion of others. It could be that there are different causal pathways. In terms of application, these discoveries recommend that basic apprises of regular encounters with compassionate love guarantee the diminishment of prejudice. Whatever the case, the development of intercessions for expanding compassionate love past the momentary effects are encouraged and were investigated within the research organisation. For example, close cross-group companionships may be a vehicle for creating compassionate love for individuals of other groups (Brody, Wright, Aron, & McLaughlin-Volpe, 2009). Intercessions along these lines may be very useful for changing attitudes to suffering.

Participants who were high in compassionate love were less inclined to slash funding from a foreign student group. They also reported greater willingness to assist foreign students (for example, sharing their notes) and support for a mentorship programme for foreign students. Thus, the more positive attitudes toward foreigners expressed by those who were high in compassionate love also translated into more positive behavioural intentions. Finally, the findings might be explained in terms of a construct that has a long history in the prejudice literature, namely empathy. Certainly, there is evidence in the literature that empathy is negatively associated with prejudice. Moreover, measures of empathy and compassionate love tend to be moderately correlated, raising the possibility that the construct of compassionate love is merely old wine in a new bottle. The non-significant findings for empathy might best be interpreted in light of Cikara et al.'s (2011) finding that it is primarily the suffering of ingroup members that elicits empathy. In fact, they suggest that rather than empathising with outgroup members, people may take pleasure in their suffering. In short, a case can be made that compassionate love brings something new to the prejudice table (Sinclair et al., 2016).

31.5.1.4 Xenophobia in South Africa

Xenophobia refers to a fear of foreigners. Rydgren (2004) ascribes the development of xenophobic beliefs to faulty cognitive processes that emerge from false conclusions about individuals, based on what the person knows about the social group or category to which another individual belongs (stereotyping). The South African Constitution promotes tolerance, inclusiveness and human rights, yet at least 67 people perished in incidents considered to be xenophobic attacks between the years 2000 and 2008. In the South African context, immigrants from other African countries are known by the derogatory term magweregwere. McDonald (1998) identifies and challenges some xenophobic stereotypes about migrants from Africa. According to Weiten (2018), the belief that a great deal of 'illegal aliens' enter South Africa (by any means possible) to obtain work and utilise health and other social services, bringing with them disease and crime is unfounded.

31.6 Chapter Conclusion

31.6.1 Relationship Between Compassionate Love and Prejudice Toward Culturally Diverse Outgroup Members

Compassionate love entails feelings of concern and tenderness, understanding the needs of others, along with a desire to help alleviate suffering and promote wellbeing (Underwood, 2002, 2009). Thus, people who experience this kind of love would be inclined to incorporate foreigners into their sense of self, which, in turn, would lead to less prejudice. Aron, Lewandowski, Mashek, and Aron (2013) define the inclusion of the other in the self as treating another person's identity, perspectives and resources as if they were one's own. In short, the other becomes a part of one's self.

Sinclair et al. (2016) state that people who are high in compassionate love, that is, people who feel tenderness and caring for others and are motivated to alleviate others' distress and would be inclined to include foreigners in the self. However, there is substantial evidence that when people include outgroup members in the self, they show more positive attitudes toward that group (Brody et al., 2009; Dys-Steenbergen, Wright, & Aron, 2015).

Sinclair et al. (2016) found that as compassionate love increased, prejudice toward various outgroups, including foreigners, decreased. Empathy scores were also negatively associated with ratings of various outgroups. However, the correlations were not as strong as those found for compassionate love. As in other research (Sprecher & Fehr, 2005; Underwood, 2002), compassionate love was correlated with empathy. Compassionate love predicted prejudice for all of the groups, whereas empathy was generally non-significant when compassionate love was in the equation. Gender differences were not found in any of the analyses.

References

Allport, G. W. (1954). *The nature of prejudice*. Reading, MA: Addison-Wesley.
Aron, A., & Davies, K. M. (2009). Aristotle and Plato on relationships. In H. T. Reis & S. Sprecher (Eds.), *Encyclopedia of human relationships* (Vol. 1, pp. 108–110). Thousand Oaks, CA: Sage.
Aron, A., Lewandowski, G. W., Mashek, D., & Aron, E. (2013). The self-expansion model of motivation and cognition in close relationships. In J. A. Simpson & L. Campbell (Eds.), *The Oxford handbook of close relationships* (pp. 90–115). New York: Oxford University Press.
Batson, C. D. (2009). These things called empathy. In J. Decety & W. Ickes (Eds.), *The social neuroscience of empathy* (pp. 3–15). Cambridge, MA: MIT Press.
Batson, C. D., Chang, J., Orr, R., & Rowland, J. (2002). Empathy, attitudes, and action: Can feeling for a member of a stigmatized group motivate one to help the group? *Personality and Social Psychology Bulletin, 28*, 1656–1666.
Beauregard, M., Courtemanche, J., Paquette, V., & St-Pierre, E. L. (2009). The neural basis of unconditional love. *Psychiatry Research, 172*, 93–98.
Berscheid, E. (2006). Searching for the meaning of "love". In R. J. Sternberg & K. Weis (Eds.), *The new psychology of love* (pp. 171–183). New Haven, CT: Yale University Press.
Berscheid, E. (2010). Love in the fourth dimension. *Annual Review of Psychology, 61*, 1–25.
Boldry, J. G., Gaertner, L., & Quinn, J. (2007). Measuring the measures: A meta-analytic investigation of the measures of outgroup homogeneity. *Group Processes & Intergroup Relations, 10*(2), 157–178.
Brody, S., Wright, S. C., Aron, A., & McLaughlin-Volpe, T. (2009). Compassionate love for individuals in other social groups. In B. Fehr, S. Sprecher, & L. G. Underwood (Eds.), *The science of compassionate love: Theory, research, and applications* (pp. 283–308). West Sussex: Wiley-Blackwell.
Cikara, M., Bruneau, E., & Saxe, R. (2011). Us and them: Intergroup failures of empathy. *Current Directions in Psychological Science, 20*, 149–153.
Clark, M. S., Lemay, E. P., Graham, S. M., Pataki, S. P., & Finkel, E. J. (2010). Ways of giving benefits in marriage norm use, relationship satisfaction, and attachment-related variability. *Psychological Science, 21*, 944–951. https://doi.org/10.1177/0956797610373882
Collins, N. L., Kane, H. S., Metz, M. A., Cleveland, C., Khan, C., Winczewski, L., et al. (2014). Psychological, physiological, and behavioural responses to a partner in need: The role of

compassionate love. *Journal of Social and Personal Relationships, 31*, 1–29. https://doi.org/10.1177/0265407514529069

Crocker, J., & Garcia, J. (2009). Downward and upward spirals in intergroup interactions: The role of egosystem and ecosystem goals. In T. D. Nelson (Ed.), *Handbook of prejudice, stereotyping, and discrimination* (pp. 229–245). New York: Psychology Press.

Dys-Steenbergen, O., Wright, S. C., & Aron, A. (2015). Self expansion motivation improves cross-group interactions and enhances self-growth. *Group Processes and Intergroup Relations, 19*, 60–71. https://doi.org/10.1177/1368430215583517

Fehr, B. (2010). Compassionate love as a prosocial emotion. In M. Mikulincer & P. R. Shaver (Eds.), *Prosocial motives, emotions, and behaviour: The better angels of our nature* (pp. 245–265). Washington, DC: APA Press.

Fehr, B. (2013). The social psychology of love. In J. A. Simpson & L. Campbell (Eds.), *The Oxford handbook of close relationships* (pp. 201–233). New York: Oxford University Press.

Fehr, B., & Sprecher, S. (2009). Compassionate love: Conceptual, measurement, and relational issues. In B. Fehr, S. Sprecher, & L. G. Underwoods (Eds.), *The science of compassionate love: Theory, research, and applications* (pp. 27–52). Malden, MA: Wiley/Blackwell.

Fehr, B., & Sprecher, S. (2013). Compassionate love: What we know so far. In M. Hojjat & D. Cramer (Eds.), *Positive psychology of love* (pp. 106–120). New York: Oxford University Press.

Fingerman, K. L. (2004). The consequential stranger: Peripheral relationships across the life span. In F. Lang & K. L. Fingerman (Eds.), *Growing together: Personal relationships across the life span* (pp. 183–209). New York, NY: Cambridge University Press.

Finlay, K., & Stephan, W. (2000). Improving intergroup relations: The effects of empathy on racial attitudes. *Journal of Applied Social Psychology, 30*, 1720–1737.

Goetz, J. L., Keltner, D., & Simon-Thomas, E. (2010). Compassion: An evolutionary analysis and empirical review. *Psychological Bulletin, 136*, 351–374. https://doi.org/10.1037/a0018807

Hein, G., & Singer, T. (2010). Neuroscience meets social psychology: An integrative approach to human empathy and prosocial behaviour. In G. Hein & T. Singer (Eds.), *Prosocial motives, emotions, and behaviour: The better angels of our nature* (pp. 109–125). Washington, DC: American Psychological Association.

Holt-Lunstad, J., & Smith, T. B. (2012). Social relationships and mortality: Social and personality. *Psychology Compass, 6*, 41–53. https://doi.org/10.1111/j.1751-9004.2011.00406.x

Inzlicht, M., & Kang, S. K. (2010). Stereotype threat spillover: How coping with threats to social identity affects aggression, eating, decision making, and attention. *Journal of Personality and Social Psychology, 99*(3), 467–481.

Kim, G. Y., Wang, D. C., & Hill, P. C. (2018). An investigation into the multifaceted relationship between gratitude, empathy and compassion. *Journal of Positive Psychology and Wellbeing, 2*(1), 23–44.

Klimecki, O. M., Leiberg, S., Ricard, M., & Singer, T. (2014). Differential pattern of functional brain plasticity after compassion and empathy training. *Social Cognitive and Affective Neuroscience, 9*, 873–879. https://doi.org/10.1093/scan/nst060

Lim, D., & DeSteno, D. (2016). Suffering and compassion: The links among adverse life experiences, empathy, compassion, and prosocial behaviour. *Emotion, 16*, 175–182. https://doi.org/10.1037/emo0000144

McDonald, D. A. (1998). *Challenging xenophobia: Myths & realities about cross border migration in Southern Africa*.

Migacheva, K., Tropp, L., & Crocker, J. (2011). Focusing beyond the self: Goal orientations and intergroup relations. In L. R. Tropp & R. K. Mallett (Eds.), *Moving beyond prejudice reduction: Positive pathways to intergroup relations* (pp. 99–115). Washington, DC: APA Press.

Mikulincer, M., & Shaver, P. (2007). *Attachment patterns in adulthood: Structure, dynamics, and change*. New York, NY: Guilford Press.

Miller, J. G., Kahle, S., Lopez, M., & Hastings, P. D. (2015). Compassionate love buffers stress-reactive mothers from fight-or-flight parenting. *Developing Psychology, 51*(1), 36–43. https://doi.org/10.1037/a0038236

Monin, J. K., Schulz, R., & Feeney, B. C. (2015). Compassionate love in individuals with Alzheimer's disease and their spousal caregivers: Associations with caregivers' psychological health. *Gerontologist, 55*(6), 981–989. https://doi.org/10.1093/geront/gnu001

Ong, A. D., Fuller-Rowell, T., & Burrow, A. L. (2009). Racial discrimination and the stress process. *Journal of Personality and Social Psychology, 96*(6), 1259–1271.

Oswald, P. (1996). The effects of cognitive and affective perspective taking on empathic concern and altruistic helping. *Journal of Social Psychology, 136*, 613–623.

Reis, H. T., Maniaci, M. R., & Rogge, R. D. (2014). The expression of compassionate love in everyday compassionate acts. *Journal of Social and Personal Relationships, 31*, 651–676. https://doi.org/10.1177/0265407513507214

Rydgren, J. (2004). Mechanisms of exclusion: Ethnic discrimination in the Swedish labour market. *Journal of Ethnic and Migration Studies, 30*(4), 697–716.

Sinclair, L., Fehr, B., Wang, W., & Regehr, E. (2016). The relation between compassionate love and prejudice: The mediating role of inclusion of out-group members in the self. *Social Psychological and Personality Science, 7*(2), 176–183. https://doi.org/10.1177/1948550615609736

Singer, T., & Klimecki, O. M. (2014). Empathy and compassion. *Current Biology, 24*, 875–878. https://doi.org/10.1016/j.cub.2014.06.054

Sprecher, S., & Fehr, B. (2005). Compassionate love for close others and humanity. *Journal of Social and Personal Relationships, 22*(5), 629–651. https://doi.org/10.1177/0265407505056439

Sprecher, S., Fehr, B., & Zimmerman, C. (2007). Expectation for mood enhancement as a result of helping: The effects of gender and compassionate love. *Sex Roles, 56*, 543–549.

Sprecher, S., Zimmerman, C., & Abrahams, E. M. (2010). Choosing compassionate strategies to end a relationship: Effects of compassionate love for partner and the reason for the breakup. *Social Psychology, 41*, 66–75.

Steffen, P. R., & Masters, K. S. (2005). Does compassion mediate the intrinsic religion–health relationship? *Annals of Behavioural Medicine, 30*, 217–224. https://doi.org/10.1207/s15324796abm3003_6

Stephan, W. G., & Finlay, K. (1999). The role of empathy in improving intergroup relations. *Journal of Social Issues, 55*, 729–743.

Tropp, L. R., & Mallett, R. K. (2011). *Moving beyond prejudice reduction: Positive pathways to intergroup relations*. Washington, DC: APA Press.

Underwood, L. G. (2002). The human experience of compassionate love. In S. G. Post, L. G. Underwood, J. Schloss, & W. B. Hurlbut (Eds.), *Altruism and altruistic love* (pp. 72–88). Oxford: Oxford University Press.

Underwood, L. G. (2009). Compassionate love: A framework for research. In B. Fehr, S. Sprecher, & L. G. Underwood (Eds.), *The science of compassionate love: Theory research, and applications* (pp. 3–25). Malden, MA: Blackwell Press.

University of Oklahoma, Institute of Group Relations, & Sherif, M. (1961). *Intergroup conflict and cooperation: The Robbers Cave experiment* (Vol. 10, pp. 150–198). Norman, OK: University Book Exchange.

Vachon, M. L. (2016). Targeted intervention for family and professional caregivers: Attachment, empathy, and compassion. *Palliative Medicine, 30*, 101–103. https://doi.org/10.1177/0269216315624279

Weiten, H. (2018). *Psychology themes and variations* (3rd SA ed.). Andover: Cengage Learning EMEA. ISBN: 9781473748583.

Rudolf M. Oosthuizen (DLitt et Phil) received a BA degree (Cum Laude) from the University of Pretoria in 1992 and obtained a BA (Honours) in Psychology at the same university in 1993. In 1999, he received an MA degree in Industrial and Personnel Psychology from the Potchefstroom University for Christian Higher Education. In 1999, he registered as Industrial Psychologist with the Health Professions Council of South Africa. In 2005, he completed a DLitt et Phil in Industrial and Organisational Psychology at the University of South Africa (Unisa). Currently Rudolf is an associate professor in the Department of Industrial and Organisational Psychology at the University of South Africa.Rudolf is the manager for the MComIOP programme, and he is responsible for the lecturing of honours subjects and the supervision of master's and doctoral students. He has presented conference papers at national and international conferences, and published articles in accredited scientific journals. Rudolf's fields of interests are (1) career psychology, career development and management from an individual, group and organisational perspective in the twenty-first century world of work; (2) positive psychology, with the focus on salutogenesis and well-being, sense of coherence, locus of control, self-efficacy, the hardy personality and learned resourcefulness; (3) employment relations and the improvement of the quality of employment relations in organisations and in society in general; and (4) the fourth Industrial Revolution (Smart Technology, Artificial Intelligence, Robotics, and Algorithms).

Chapter 32
Love in the Context of Transnational Academic Exchanges: Promoting Mental Health and Wellbeing

Rashmi Singla and Ulrike de Ponte

Abstract Educational and cultural dimensions of transnational academic exchange such as student exchanges, double degree programmes, internships have been researched but the romantic dimensions are almost overlooked, especially qualitatively, while Green (*EU's Erasmus study abroad programme is 'responsible for 1m babies'*, 2014) documents that one quarter students on Erasmus exchange scheme met their long-term partner while studying abroad.

The chapter explores love, with focus on formation of intimate relations in academic exchanges in the European settings. The method is case-studies drawn from two projects based in Denmark, the first about ethnically intermarried couples (Singla, *Intermarriage and mixed parenting: Promoting mental health & wellbeing, crossover love*. Palgrave Macmillan, 2015) and the second, an ongoing project about LAT (Living Apart Together) transnational couples (Singla & Varma, *LAT (Living Apart Together) transnational couples: Promoting mental health and wellbeing*, 2018), moving beyond 'methodological nationalism and- conjugalism'.

The theoretical framework is Cultural Psychology and foreground is a combination of Narrative Psychology, intersectionality, digital emotional reflexivity and transnationalism. Moreover, aspects related to figuring out criteria of the exchange situation abroad, which can underpin explaining the high rate of long-term relationships while studying abroad, are included. Those aspects are based on a framework, in which intercultural and developmental psychological findings are linked.

The 3–4 case studies are drawn from empirical research with eight couples in the first study and 20 couples in the second. The narratives are thematically analysed, whereas two themes regarding participants' motivation for establishing relationship despite differences and long-term sustaining of the relationship are described in the chapter.

R. Singla (✉)
Department of People and Technology, Roskilde University, Denmark
e-mail: rashmi@ruc.dk

U. de Ponte
Department of Natural Sciences and Cultural Studies, Applied University of Regensburg (OTH Regensburg), Regensburg, Germany
e-mail: ulrike.de_ponte@oth-regensburg.de

© Springer Nature Switzerland AG 2021
C.-H. Mayer, E. Vanderheiden (eds.), *International Handbook of Love*,
https://doi.org/10.1007/978-3-030-45996-3_32

Preliminary findings nuance the phenomenon of love in academic exchanges, invoking concepts such as educational homogamy, balancing independence and togetherness, diversities of connectivities intersecting social media and intimacies. Furthermore, the significant others' support and opposition of these couples' love dynamics are covered, along with considerations linked to the concept of the emotional availability (Saunders, Kraus, Barone & Biringen, Frontiers in Psychology, 2015) based on Bowlby's attachment theory and the shared third (Benjamin, *Psychoanalytic Quarterly, 73*(1), 5–46, 2004).

Lastly, 'good practices' for promoting the mental health and wellbeing of such academic exchange couples are delineated along with suggestions for relevant services for those experiencing psychosocial problems.

Keywords Love · Academic exchange · Intimate relationship · Narrative psychology · Educational homogamy · Diversities of connectivities · Emotional availability

32.1 Introduction

This is an exploration of love and intimate relationships made while one or both partners were students abroad. It draws on both academic literature and qualitative research with couples whose relationships began as students away from home, in a transnational context.

Learning that 27% of Erasmus[1] alumni met their life partner while abroad (Green, 2014), inspired us to explore the themes presented in this chapter. We decided to probe further into the dynamics of the phenomenon of love in the context of academic exchange across national borders which leads to long-term relation. For us, the movement of students across nations mirrors processes of globalisation, understood as the increased global movement of persons, ideas and goods as well as increased developmental tasks for those people.

32.1.1 Background

Family relationships, especially transnational intimate couple of relations, along with the promotion of mental health and wellbeing and psychosocial intervention have been primary research areas for the first author (Singla & Varma, 2018, Singla,

---

[1]Erasmus programme begun in 1987 and have helped more than three million students study overseas until 2014. Named after the well-travelled Dutch philosopher Desiderius Erasmus of Rotterdam, it covers the 28 European Union (EU) countries as well as Iceland, Liechtenstein, Norway, Switzerland and Turkey (Green, 2014).

2004, 2006a, 2006b, 2008, 2015). The second author has been conducting research in the field of the international youth exchange (de Ponte, 2017, 2019; de Ponte & Jäger, 2015) and on re-entry issues for Bachelor-level students after 1-year mandatory time abroad—one semester for study and one semester for internship.

The invitation to contribute to this "Handbook of Love in Cultural and Transcultural Contexts", a primary reference exploring transcultural perspectives on love, motivated us to combine our two areas of scientific research. Our focus is on intimacy related to movement across national borders (Singla & Varma, 2018) for study and internships. We are also interested in the development of intercultural competence (Jensen, 2007) through this increasing form of migration. We consider how love develops and leads to long-term relationships. Movement for education and professional development has increased remarkably in the past three decades as described in the next section.

32.1.2 Increased Academic Exchanges

In exploring the field of academic exchange, it is important to note that globalisation is intricately linked to migration and entails international migration for some students and their partners. Bauman (1998) argues that freedom of mobility is at the centre of present day polarisations with some on the top, some on the bottom of the hierarchy, with the bulk of population—the new middle class, oscillating between the two extremes, being local in a globalised world can be seen as a sign of social deprivation. Already in 2007, Koser predicted a growing trend towards increased movement of students across national borders, linking it to the fact that in most countries foreign students pay higher fees than nationals so recruiting them represents a good investment for universities. It is also clear that today's foreign students are the skilled migrants of tomorrow. An illustrative case at European Union level is the aforementioned Erasmus programme, in which 3244 students participated in its first year 1987 and which has gone on to support 3.3 million students in the programme's first three decades. Over 797,000 students participated in 2017 (Erasmus, 2019) under Erasmus+ in the fields of youth education, training, and sport for 2014–2020.

The Erasmus Impact study (EIS, 2014) documents that students' mobility strongly influences their careers as well as their social life. Top motivations to study or train abroad are the opportunity to live abroad and meet new people, improve foreign language proficiency and develop transnational skills. On average, Erasmus students have better employability after a stay abroad. Erasmus students have a more international life as 80% stated that they have improved their intercultural awareness. 33% of Erasmus alumni have a life partner with a different nationality compared to 13% of non-mobile alumni. 27% of Erasmus alumni state that they met their current life partner during their stay abroad (EIS, 2014, p. 14). These statistics from a particular case of academic exchange explicitly show how transnational exchanges may lead to changes in an array of life domains including the formation of intimate couple of relationships as this chapter argues.

Using a developmental-psychological perspective, mobility represents a new educational task during the postmodern student-life-cycle. What sounds inspiring has a flipside however, and students in Germany, for example, have described that they experience going abroad as a necessity to stay competitive in the job market. Even worse, going "only to England" is hardly appreciated anymore, the same with "only" traveling to Austria, Switzerland or the Netherlands. It has to be further away. We note that along with an increased "outside" freedom of mobility, there is an emerging apperception of an "inner" compulsion of mobility. Furthermore, de Ponte's doctoral thesis suggests that there is a need to add—according to Havighurst's developmental tasks (see also de Ponte, 2017, 2019)—a new developmental task which adolescents and young adults have to face nowadays, which can be defined as "mental safety in insecurity"; it can be operationalised by ambiguity tolerance, emotional agility and the ability of mentalising (de Ponte, in progress). To eleborate more on de Ponte's findings, we focus on how romantic love features in these settings in the next section.

32.1.3 Romantic Love

The complex issue of existential insecurity understood as a consequence of globalisation entails a close connection between human experiences, trust and a search for intimacy, and is seen as a transformation of intimacy during past decades (Giddens, 1992). Romantic love as a part of couple relationships has become paramount in contemporary societies, invoking the concept of the 'pure relationship' which relates love to a continuum with individualism and self-satisfaction at one end and collectivism and self-abandonment or personal non-existence at the other, shaping 'our black-and-white-view' of the world. According to Giddens

> Romantic love seems to be a normal part of human existence, rather than a distinctive feature of modern culture. [...] The emphasis on personal satisfaction in marriage has raised expectations which cannot be met, and this is one factor involved in increasing rates of divorce (1992, p. 398).

Romantic love is thus an aspect of being human and explains both intimate relationship formation and dissolution. Giles (2006) emphasises that romantic love is closely related to sexual desire, which is perceived as a response to human conditions and is determined by neither biology nor culture, though constrained by both. Moreover, in agreement with Giles (2008), we are critical of romantic love being considered as just a Western phenomenon and accept its universal nature with local variations.

Karandashev (2015) (Chap. 4) formulates similar views of cultural perspectives on romantic love and emphasises romance as a fanciful, expressive and pleasurable feeling based on emotional attraction towards another person. In accounts of love and sex from couples living apart together (LAT) in the British context, Carter, Duncan, Stoilova, and Phillips (2016) contend that commitment is inseparable from love and emphasise elements of love, time and investment in commitment. Romantic love can also be seen as linked to the oath "for better and for worse" in many contexts. Benjamin, however, does not use the term "romantic love", but establishes the intersubjective concept of co-created experience with mutual recognition (2004, 18), called the 'shared third', in which

> we [...] come to the felt experience of the other as a separate yet connected being with whom we are acting reciprocally (p. 6).

We elaborate the important concept of the shared third later in this chapter.

32.1.4 Rationale for the Chapter

A quick look at relevant publications describing psychological studies of international youth exchange indicates, among other things, the added value of coping with the classical developmental tasks, such as developing a partnership between boyfriend or girlfriend (Havighurst, 1972), avoiding heteronormativity, we also add same gender relationship for some. Issues such as the development of multicultural identity (Thomas, 2017a, 2017b), enhancement of openness towards people from other cultures (Abt & Stumpf, 2017) have been researched but the role of 'love' in young people's lives is barely covered.

According to Green (2014), Umberto Eco, Italian novelist and professor of semiotics, described the international student exchange programme Erasmus as a "sexual revolution" sweeping Europe. He also highlighted this programme's creation of "the first generation of young Europeans," stating:

> I call it a sexual revolution: a young Catalan man meets a Flemish girl—they fall in love, they get married and they become European, as do their children. The Erasmus idea should be compulsory—not just for students, but also for taxi drivers, plumbers, and other workers. By this, I mean they need to spend time in other countries within the European Union; they should integrate. (Ibid, 2014, p. 2)

Despite the celebratory tone of this assessment of student exchange promoting a sexual revolution in Europe, there is not much emphasis on love relationships in academic exchange, which this chapter aims to investigate theoretically and empirically through case studies invoking first person voices. In this chapter, we have already provided some background on the significance of exchange at personal and conceptual level. In the following we provide a theoretical framework and then present our methodology along with two case studies and the major findings. Finally, we present a discussion and recommendations for theory.

32.2 Theoretical Framework: An Integrative Framework

For an academic exploration of love in academic exchange situations and its long-term continuity, a single perspective did not seem adequate, thus we developed an integrative theoretical framework combining the following diverse perspectives:

32.2.1 Cultural Psychological Concepts and Intersectionality

This theoretical framework is based on a socio-cultural psychological approach described by Valsiner and Rosa (2007), in which human beings are perceived as social as well as uniquely personal—subjective, affective, and individually goal-oriented, creating meaning. This approach emphasises the various levels and the dynamic nature of human relationships.

> The symbolic ambiguity of human meaning fields is corroborated in the landscape of human relationships. Human beings strive towards belonging to one or another social unit, [a couple], group, community, nation, or even humankind (e.g. feeling of being the "citizens of the world")—and consequently, they are in the process of moving away from the past relationships, (...) continuing family traditions of the past, the family unit prepares itself for future life (Valsiner, 2007, p. 171).

Complimenting this approach, recognition of intersectionality provides an ontological framework in understanding social relationships; establishing that social existence is never singular, and that everybody belongs simultaneously to multiple categories that mutually constitute each other (Phoenix, 2011). These categories are historically and geographically located, comprising power relations that shift over time. The three major categories ethnicity, gender and class or socio-economic position, are the "Big Three", frequently invoked in social analyses. It is important however, to move beyond these three categories to include categories such as age, nationality, and locality (Moodley, 2011; Phoenix, 2011). Love and intimacy in transnational contexts is not free from the economic and structural inequalities of an unequal world. Shared households, shared financial and social aspects of relationships are defined as 'materialized testimonies of genuine feelings' by Pananakhonsab (2019) which confirm the socio-material aspects of love relationships.

32.2.2 Transnationalism and Digital Communication

The concepts of transnationalism and diaspora imply interconnections across national borders (Karla et al., 2005; Singla, Shajahan, & Sriram, 2020) and include spatial aspects related to global marriages (Williams, 2010). These concepts are included in our framework, especially to aid understanding of the continuity of intimate relationships across countries and time.

Similarly, theories related to communication through distance (Holmes, 2014) and technology (Turkle, 2011) are also important. This particular aspect of long-distance relationships entails balancing autonomy and togetherness as in most intimate relationships. This makes emotional reflexivity, perceived as the capacity to interpret one's own and others' feelings along with acting on them, very significant (Holmes, 2014). While Turkle (2011) argues that technology has become the architect of our intimacies and that, paradoxically, relentless connection leads to a new solitude. Based on an exploration of our lives in the digital terrain, she critically analyses the experience of feeling overwhelmed and depleted by lives which technology has made possible. Thus, in exploring the phenomenon of love forged in an academic context, a critical perspective on emotional reflexivity, technological connection across distance and time is part of the theoretical framework.

32.2.3 The Distinctiveness of the Situation of Staying Abroad and the Intercultural Encounter

The high percentage, 27%, of Erasmus alumni who met their current life partner during their stay abroad (EIS, 2014, p. 14) evoked our curiosity to scientifically study the situation abroad and we identify four aspects that can explain this phenomenon. As Layes (2000) pointed out, 'situation' is a term that cannot stand-alone as an action always implies a situation in which it is performed. He states:

> In this sense, a situation represents a necessary structural prerequisite for the execution of actions, but it is not identical with the actions carried out in it (Layes, 2000, p. 24).

Therefore, the first aspect of how the situation abroad (two cultures) makes a difference to the situation at home (monoculture) is a structural prerequisite: we give a different meaning and sense to misunderstandings. In a "monocultural" setting, one faces the danger of conflict when there is a misunderstanding. People living abroad, expect the strange and therefore unknown. Though we are aware that the situation at home as is not necessarily monoculture—members of the at-home-culture are often not aware about the fact that they bring culture into a situation themselves, only think the others do. As Thomas (2010) explains, being abroad is a

> ... learning, experiencing and acting field.

So more concrete, what happens is "The Strange", which one simply does not know until being abroad, but one can learn about it from the other who is interested in sharing with oneself. The second aspect can be found in the especially intense state one gets into, the moment we dawn on "the strange"[2] and something passes off unexpectedly, inducing a feeling of losing orientation inside us. These situations are labelled as "intercultural critical incident" by Thomas (2017a, p. 34).

This state is very energy demanding, so we need to solve the misunderstanding with the other. The feeling of the need of the other who can explain and ease our uncertainty, can be named from an intersubjective view as an urge to share. This might be seen as a third aspect. A fourth aspect linked to our third, is that we experience ourselves and the other, who might be undergoing the same process, as highly emotional available (Saunders, Kraus, Barone, & Biringen, 2015), described as "... the ability of two people to share a healthy emotional connection" (ibid., p. 2). After returning home, students often report their experience with people from abroad as more intense than at home.

These four aspects represent basic pointers to understanding the special features of the situation of living abroad. Summing up, the other becomes significant when the interaction is felt as a "co-created" experience (Benjamin, 2004, p. 6). At the same time there is a mutual interest in reflecting together on behaviour of both persons in an emotional intense setting. Summarising the special feature of the situation abroad, we conclude that the intercultural encounter bears the characteristics of the shared third.

32.2.4 Emotional Availability and the Shared Third

To understand the creation of the shared third, we highlight some considerations of the role of emotional availability in the process (for additional discussion, see de Ponte, in progress). Being emotionally available is crucial to the emergence of romantic love, yet it is hard to find research with this psychodynamic focus.[3]

Biringen, Derscheid, Vliegen, Closson, and Easterbrooks (2014) define emotional availability (EA) as a construct which refers to the capacity of a dyad to share an emotionally healthy relationship. The term was first used by Mahler, Pine, and Bergman (1975; cited in ibid.) to describe

> ... a mother's supportive attitude and presence in the context of infant/toddler explorations away from her. They noted that healthy mother-child relationships allow for exploration and autonomy, at the same time recognizing the importance of physical contact and emotional 'refueling'. [This includes] not merely (...) physical presence, but also emotional signaling and awareness of such signaling from others (Biringen et al., 2014, p. 115).

---

[2] About when a difference turns to be experienced as strange (see Utler, 2014). Utler wrote her thesis about when the strange can be experienced as strange.
[3] Research is found in the context of parent-child-contact; e.g. the chapter "Can the Parent Look Good Without the Child?" (Saunders et al., 2015, p. 4).

What can be seen as important is that this affective attunement includes negative as well as positive emotions. EA is operationalised by six components, four relating to the caregiver and two relating to the care-receiver, in this case a child:

> The four caregiver components are sensitivity, structuring, non-intrusiveness, and non-hostility. The two child components are the child's responsiveness to the caregiver and the child's involvement of the caregiver (2014, p. 114).

In order to translate this insight into our situation with two adult partners, we double these six components reciprocally: Both partners behave sensitive, structuring, non-intrusive and non-hostile to each other, and to experience the other as responsive and involved. This makes clear that if both partners experience the other mutually as an emotionally available partner, there will be good conditions for a partnership.

What then is the speciality of the shared third referred above? Benjamin (1988, 2004) conceptualised the shared third through her intersubjective perspective of the quality of interactions in the two directions: "the doer" (pull-you or the one in third) and "the done-to" (push-the third in one or me). The shared third emerges the moment each partner acts "like an agent helping to shape a co-created reality" (Benjamin, 2004, p. 9) and recognises the other as "an equivalent center of being" (Benjamin, 1995, p. 6).

To summarise, we draw the conclusion that the shared third depends on the extent to which both partners are able and willing to co-create. Regarding the situation abroad, the six components listed above show differentiations in respect to culture. When someone is experienced as approachable, when someone responds or shows involvement can differ across culture, and stronger spatial invasion can be interpretated as interest or intrusiveness. The moment both partners exchange and share their "inner world", acknowledge and witness each other's view, a psychological space outside the dyad is created: the shared third. However, at the same time the materiality of love also needs to be learned and recognized by the partners and the authorities involved (Pananakhonsab, 2019; Patcharin, 2019).

32.3 Methodology

32.3.1 *Empirical Studies and Ethical Considerations*

The two case studies discussed below represent two different situations of academic exchange and were selected from the studies published in Singla (2015), which discusses the life histories of eight couples, and an ongoing research project, Singla and Varma (2019) which features the experiences of 20 couples. The two couples met in an academic exchange context and have continued their relationship 5–8 years later. Intermarriage and mixed parenting were the focus of the first study, while the second one deals with living apart together transnational (LATT) couples. Both studies include couples who are ethnically as well as nationally mixed.

In both studies, the participants were recruited through key people in their networks who functioned as gatekeepers and researchers' own contacts. They were contacted by using phone and e-mails, in-depth interviews were conducted primarily in Danish and English. The research was conducted in line with ethical standards delineated for the Nordic psychologists by the relevant Psychological Associations (Ethical Principles, 2019). Ethical considerations included assuring confidentiality with pseudonyms, full, informed consent, adherence to non-maleficence or 'no-harm' research principles and addressing issues of researcher positionality.

In the first study, the interviews were face to face, while in the second there was a combination of face to face and skype/telephone interviews, primarily because the participants are living in different parts of the world. A Swedish member of research team, herself in a mixed marriage (Swedish–Danish) conducted the interviews in 2010 (Dunger, 2010), while, in the second study, the first author conducted the interviews during 2017–2018 along with a research associate (Singla & Varma, 2019). The interviews were recorded and transcribed. The data was subjected to thematic analyses based on close reading, meaning condensation and interpretive strategies. Only two themes are covered here, the other four themes are analysed elsewhere (Singla, 2015).

32.3.2 The Case Studies

32.3.2.1 Danish Katja and Indian Rajiv: Master Level Internship in Mumbai

This couple met in Mumbai, India during Katja's internship as a part of master's level studies affiliated to Copenhagen University, Denmark. They have been married for 3 years.

Katja, 32, who introduced herself as "Danish, with Danish parents", originates from Fynen, and her parents are divorced and remarried, having mid-level jobs. She has a number of siblings from the same parents and 'bonus' ones from her parents' subsequent relationships. She has lived in a middle-class Copenhagen neighbourhood for the past 3 years. She has a master's degree and works full time in a dynamic international organisation.

Rajiv 35, introduced himself thus: "I am from India. Indian". He grew up in a metropolis with a well-placed father and stay-at-home mother, one older sister and "a million cousins", implying a large extended family. He has a master's degree and has worked in the advertising sector. He was previously married to an Indian woman for a short period and then divorced. Currently he is part-time self-employed in the health sector. They have 1-year-old daughter. Their ethnic and job identities were prominent as they met each other in a metropol in India.

32.3.2.2 Danish Lena and Spanish/Peruvian Pedro: Erasmus Study Exchange in Madrid

Danish Lena, 31, and Spanish Pedro, 39, met during Lena's Erasmus study exchange in Spain at Masters level (International Marketing and Spanish) and have been a LATT (living apart together transnational) couple for almost 8 years. Currently Lena works in Denmark and Pedro in Spain.

Lena introduced herself as "Danish, from a Suburb near Copenhagen". She is the daughter of a divorced mother and has two siblings.

Lena informed that Redro is from Peru but lives in Spain, while his family remain in Peru. He has been in Spain for the last 10 years. He studied and works with electronics and recently obtained Spanish citizenship.

32.4 Major Findings

Our main question in this chapter is 'How do young people from different national settings and ethnic backgrounds 'come together'?' The answers we have found show a commonality of coming together through the process of "falling in love" and the creation of a shared third (Benjamin, 2004) combined with pragmatic aspects despite contextual variations. These narratives reflect globally dominant discourses of love and intimacy.

32.4.1 Motivation for Establishing Relationships Despite Differences

Katja met Rajiv in Mumbai, India, which was foreign for her during 1-year internship. She was introduced to Rajiv through a common friend and she states her falling in love happened within a period of just 2 months.

32.4.1.1 Then We Started Hanging Out as Friends and Eh Yeah a Couple of Months Later 'Love'

Rajiv answered in the interview that the reason he came to Denmark was Katja, whom he met through a musician friend in Mumbai. The narrative below documents their reciprocal attraction based on shared interests and values, despite their differences. Their first contact lead to awareness of mutual positive feelings and the mutual experience of being emotional available, though Katja was disoriented and found the Indian setting 'strange' due to her focus on 'exotic' aspects in the beginning. Katja was initially hesitant in articulating her feelings because of the ongoing process of the dissolution of Rajiv's first marriage. He explains:

> ... We ended up meeting and we really liked each other. It was so nice. Then she was travelling around, and then she came back to Mumbai. ... we were already together in the first trip and we spend the last 12 days together and then she left and we were always in touch and then when I came back from Africa, that was when she said, like ok. That was when I really felt that there would be a future with her and that I felt something for her. But she had felt so all the time, but she did not really want to talk about it about it because she felt that I was still married like. Married yeah [in the process of a consensual divorce from his Indian wife, after two years of marriage].

For Lena, during an Erasmus Exchange in Madrid, the specific situation of being in Spain was motivation for developing an intimate relationship with Pedro from Peru. She also pointed to the high level (90%) of fellow students participating in academic exchange abroad.

> I was an Erasmus exchange student in Madrid. I studied in (name of the Danish university). I did International Marketing and Spanish. I chose to learn Spanish out of interest. I finished in 2016. I was an exchange student in Madrid in 2009. From my class I would say about 90% [were on exchange] they encourage people in university to travel abroad and make it easy. ...However, we all studied Spanish, so it was very common to travel to Spain to practice language skills.

When further questioned about the intimate relationship, Lena's reply foregrounded her openness, the chance factor of meeting and positive emotional dynamics—'chemistry'—implying a basis for emotional availability and later a shared third.

> No, he [Pedro] was just working. When I first travelled to Madrid, I had to find an apartment to stay. One of the advertisements I saw online was in his apartment. I went to see his apartment and we got to know each other. But we did not live together. I did not choose that room because I did not like it that much. But that is how I got to know him. We only speak in Spanish, because I already knew the language. He only speaks Spanish. He is learning English now...

> We had a very good chemistry. The same night we met each other, we went out, together with his best friend. I found an apartment very close to his, about 15 minutes. Walking distance. He is a bit older than I am. So only eight years older.

32.4.1.2 The Responses of Significant Others

When asked about the reaction of those close to them to their relationship, Katja described the mostly positive reactions of the people around her. The exceptions being, one of her close colleague's mother who reacted negatively by displaying shock at seeing Rajiv's picture focusing on his hierarchically negative phenotype as "black":

> ...just one of my closest colleagues, her mother, ..., but she is Dansk Folkeparti [member of the Danish national far right party] ... she knew that I had an Indian husband and it was totally fine, but then my colleague show her a picture of us at some point and she was like 'oh

my God he is black' and then she told me and I was like 'okay that's really weird' what does she expect, he is from India so yes he is black, so that's the only thing that I really noticed.

Furthermore, she described her grandmother's negative stereotype of India as "a terrible country, bringing up a baby there is totally insane". Katja rejects this as just 'grandmother talk' and points to positive acceptance of Rajiv:

> It has nothing to do with him, she loves him, but she is happy that we chose Denmark and not India.

On the other hand, Rajiv emphasises his positive experiences with Katja's large family with stepparents and a large number of stepsiblings, as well as her friends.

> …her parents live there, and that was the only thing, I think that I have blended nicely, it was so kind, they were so kind, all her friends and they welcomed me, and that was cool.

In summing up, Katja and Rajiv' intimate relationship came through a pathway of being romantically bonded in the Indian context, where Katja's openness towards the other, their mutual attraction and indication of being emotional available, socio-material aspects such as Rajiv's privilege and power as a successful professional were pivotal. The ethnic differences and family reactions were in the background.

For Lena, there was a period of not revealing the relationship to close family members as she expected family reactions to be rejecting. When revealed later, they were not positive as there was shock about a 'stranger' as a future family member.

> We met each other in 2009 August, and I told my parents about the relationship after Christmas 2009. They were a bit shocked because they did not know anything about him. They were a bit nervous, if he was going to treat me well. If he wanted to be with me to be able to go to Denmark.

Lena expressed her family's negative reactions in the beginning which turned to being neutral and then to tolerance through emphasising the stigmatisation and negativity of outsiders.

> They were not surprised about the distance relationship. They were more nervous about the cultural differences, the religious views. I got neither support not hindrance from my family. They said, "It is your decision. We don't mind."—Neutral. My friends and family were the same.

> People from outside were really negative though.… Most part I ignore the comments and I think, "You don't know better", and that it is not going to change my relationship.

32.4.1.3 Major Strategies for Managing in the First Phase of the Relationship

The main strategies exhibited in our case studies for managing the first phase of meeting their future partner in the context of academic exchange were being open to differences but also open to similarities—interest in music, concentrating on the relationship, exploring the emotional dynamics, which together built up a shared third (Benjamin, 2004). This served to calibrate expectations, overcome differences in meanings and interpretations of behaviour and helped to find ways of staying close to each other against the negative responses of others. The significant others of our couples were either positive or neutral and in the case of stigmatisation from an elderly family member, the response was to ignore the negative evaluation of partner. With no plans to dissolve the relationship this even strengthened the relationship.

In the next section, attention is directed towards sustaining the love relationship across the borders of nations, time and ethnicity.

32.5 Long-Term Sustaining of the Relationship

The dynamics of sustaining love and the relationship through separation is foregrounded here. Katja and Rajiv had to endure a period of 1 year apart and Lena and Pedro are separated for a period of almost 8 years. According to Schaeffer-Gabriel, ideals of flexibility and mobility are way to idealise intermarriage (2006, p. 4) and which open up the possibility of cosmopolitan citizenship of the world. This is a general discourse of drawing upon cosmopolitan identity as emphasised by Katja and Lena in the 'strange' settings of Mumbai and Madrid.

32.5.1 Managing Everyday Life

At the time of the interview, Katja and Rajiv's everyday life was structured around family and work, as they have a 1-year-old daughter. Rajiv is working part-time and Katja works many hours per week. The gender roles are different as well, as Katja declares: 'I am the one in-charge' and they negotiate couple equality in their own manner. While Lena and Pedro still live in Denmark and Spain respectively, 8 years after falling in love during the academic exchange, they visit each other every 3–4 months and are together for periods varying from 3 days to a month. Despite the sadness of parting, Lena explains the positive aspect of autonomy and free choice of activities in being a LATT couple. Recognising the other as separated yet connected and reciprocally acting promotes the idea of the shared third. Lena is aware of the autonomy existing within the intimacy yet aiming at cohabitation with Pedro in the near future will be their own decision, dependent on the reunification situation, in contrast to the conclusion in other studies about LAT couples in Europe, that the social pressure exerted by family and friends to live together is a major factor (Ayuso, 2019).

> The positive things are that I am freer. . . . I do not have to stay with my boyfriend every day. It may seem a bit strange to a lot of people, but I can do whatever I want. If I want to go to the gym, swimming pool and train every day, I can do it. . . .When we meet . . .In summer is it Spain and in winter it is Denmark, especially for Christmas.

At the same time, keeping up the intimate contact through digital media is also invoked along with the plans of living together in Denmark in near future.

32.5.2 Digital Communication, Emotional Availability and the Shared Third

As Katja and Rajiv have been married and living together, the 1-year, pre-marriage period marked by contact through digital media and visits was now a memory. On the other hand, for Lena and Pedro, digital communication plays a vital role in sustaining their love relationship.

Sharing and mutual understanding implies a high level of emotional reflexivity and emotional availability as interpreted in the narrative of Lena and Pedro. She stated how an empathetic listening by her partner is related to the feeling of his being almost present. This expresses an experience of being separated yet connected as described by the notion of the shared third (Benjamin, 2004).

> When I am in a bad mood, he asks me the details, because he knows it makes me feel better to talk about it, it helps. It is almost as if he is there.

About the form of digital communication, Lena explains:

> In the beginning, we used the telephone .... Afterwards, we used Skype, both on the phone as well as on the computer. Now we use WhatsApp to communicate—messaging, calling and video calling. It costs about a dollar a year after the first year, which is almost free service.

In the beginning of Lena and Pedro's relationship, the telephone had a high economic cost. Through the use of digital communication such as Skype, there is now almost no economic cost and both are emotional available for each other. In sustaining relationships over distance, one has to learn to write and communicate supportively which means being more explicit in sharing emotions and overtly contributing to the nurturing of the relationship. Successful encounters on a virtual level imply learning how to build a shared third. Abilities that can be seen to promote connection are: expressing feelings with words, making empathy explicit through caring words, and through making the other feel "seen". Together these actions promote acknowledgment and witnessing which are themselves linked to the establishment of the shared third and valued as "transcendental" (Benjamin, 2019, p. 25). This capacity to maintain the shared third, interpert and act on emotions are conceptualised as emotional reflexivity (Holmes, 2014) entailing emotional availability (Biringen et al., 2014) which has contributed to the sustaining of their relationship through a period of almost 8 years. At the same time, it can be interpreted that Lena and Pedro, while living apart, have a relationship, which demonstrates love, time and investment as delineated by Carter et al. (2016). At the same time the relationship is also seen as a contingent commitment reflecting their job situation and restrictions on their reunification. However, these accounts lack mention of the negative aspects of these free digital communications, such as Skype, WhatsApp, Facebook, by which the consumer themselves are the product (Hendriks, 2018).

32.5.3 Future Perspectives

Despite or maybe because of the specific setting of being in a relatively new, strange setting of academic exchange, both Katja and Lena showed a cosmopolitan stance, openness and acceptance the differences between their Danish homes and the setting in Mumbai and Madrid respectively. Both cases show the creation of a shared third, conceptualised by Benjamin (2004) as 'The felt experience of the other as a separate yet connected being with whom they are acting reciprocally'(p. 6). Both were able to establish emotional closeness related to sexual attraction (Giles, 2006) and their cosmopolitan outlook supported relationships with their partners from across national and ethnic borders.

Regarding the future, Katja and Rajiv have established a family in Denmark and aspire to stay together. Lena has waited for Pedro's Spanish citizenship for the past years due to the highly restrictive family reunification legal rules in Denmark. At the time of interview, Pedro planned to move to Denmark as he had recently obtained Spanish citizenship. Lena sums up the positive aspects of their living in Denmark with reference to socio-material conditions—that is the relatively easier labour market and preferential conditions for raising children.

32.6 Personal Developmental Aspects: Identifying Criteria for Promoting Health and Well-Being

Our two case studies underline the psychological and socio-material aspects involved in the development of intimate relationship in the context of academic exchange. Both the personal and contextual levels and the interplay between them are significant. Openness to differences implying ambiguity tolerance, management of perspectives, mental safety in insecurity and a cosmopolitan stance are vital at the personal level. For both Katja and Lena, openness and being involved with and receptive to the potential partner were important along with the positive or at least neutral attitudes of the significant others in their family and life situations. In addition, developing an explicit style in the use of digital media and in being each emotionally available and caring implying emotional reflexivity. These personal and interpersonal aspects should be identified and enhanced in order to promote students' positive mental health and wellbeing and their implications for theory and practice are taken up further in the final section.

32.7 Discussion

Studies such as EIS (2014) demonstrate that every fourth Erasmus exchange student in Europe meets their intimate life partners during the exchange. These numbers are important, but they do not tell us about the emotions and aspirations of the people behind these numbers. To try to understand these deeper motivations we have analysed the lived experiences of two young couples to explore these loving, transnational relationships in the academic context.

The narratives, along with the theoretical conceptualisations, demonstrate that the feeling of being 'citizens of the world' or cosmopolitans (Valsiner, 2007) leads to the development of a multicultural identity (Thomas, 2017a, 2017b) and openness towards the other (Abt & Stumpf, 2017). The developmental task of couple formation (de Ponte, 2017) and the special nature of being away from home, forms a background for falling in love with a person abroad; someone who is perceived as the other, 'separated yet connected' (Benjamin, 2004) This combines with acting reciprocally and being emotionally available during the exchange. In line with Phoenix's work (2006) considering simultaneously the diverse attributes and sense of belonging of young people, going beyond just their gender and socio-economic belonging/class and ethnicity but also their nationality and locality, has been constructive. In the academic exchange settings, the differences in belongings such as ethnicity, nationality and locality are backgrounded and socio-material aspects such as the social-economic similarity, especially the commonality of social values and personal interests such as music are foregrounded.

32.8 Recommendations for Theory and Practice

This analysis and discussion has a range of implications for both theory and practice in the area of love and academic exchange. It also has implications for promoting mental health and wellbeing. There is a need to develop theoretical concepts which address newer complexities such as the coexistence of love and commitment in LAT relationships (Carter et al., 2016) and the development of intimacy despite visible differences (Green, 2014). Moreover, we should develop and refine concepts which include complex on-going transformations brought about by transnational marriages both at the local and global level (Williams, 2010) and relationships without the conventional bonds of co-residency (Ayuso, 2019; Holmes, 2014) and beyond.

A supportive, positive context gains significance for enhancing relationships across different frames of belonging and has implications for both the sending and receiving institutions as well as societies at both personal, group and structural level. The psycho-social preparation of students promoting openness and receptivity towards difference, developing ambiguity tolerance, encouraging self-perception as 'citizens of the world' and dealing with emotional intensity (Saunders et al., 2015) are among aspects that could promote and enhance positive mental health and wellbeing.

Both preparation before leaving home as well as re-entry debriefing (see discussion of re-entry courses working on emotions, de Ponte, 2019, and her lecture course at the Applied University of Regensburg) are vital for developing good practice related to the phenomenon of love in the academic exchange context. Experiences of encounter with the other can be both negative and positive and, for some, may need sharing and working through with staff, peers and/or professionals, to understand emotions that might still be activated. This can be done in an academic way by working on 'critical incidents' (Flanagan, 1954), and should, include encounters both unexpectedly positive or experienced negatively with a special focus on emotions (de Ponte, in progress). Prototypes of this work have been evaluated by students, who evaluate it as supportive and empowering. Furthermore, the creation of approachable, welcoming circumstances in receiving institutions and society are also significant. It was an introduction by a common friend that led Katja to contact Rajiv, while a chance factor and openness on the part of Pedro in the Spanish context brought Lena in contact with Pedro. Through experiences of discrimination, involvement with "the strange", there emerges a conscious process reflecting one's own cultural attitudes and "what we know" (see Lena's comment: "you don't know better"), overcoming norms and leading to find one's own style and way to deal with new forms of relationships. This leads to 'mental safety in insecurity' (de Ponte, 2020). Further research should show if and in what sense it can permeate throughout extended families too and challenge xenophobia and ethnic discriminatory practices in the society which affect people and couples as also entailed in Singla & Ganapathy-Coleman, 2020). Lastly, there should be provision of counselling and psychotherapy services (de Ponte & van Eck, 2017; Singla, 2017) for also those who form 'mixed' love relationships across national, ethnic, religious borders and who experience psychosocial challenges which are difficult to manage without professional help.

We can take the recommendations a step further, as these lessons are very applicable to young people arriving in the European countries as refugees. Now they get no or very little support in developing healthy relationships and there have been many problems involving issues of consent. Some of these insights and suggestions for training etc. would be very valuable. Looking into healthy intimate relationships between refugees and citizens would be though another research project!

32.9 Concluding Comments

This chapter started with the finding that "27% of Erasmus alumni meet their life partner while abroad" (EIS, 2014) and we conclude from our own academic work that falling in love or being 'stuck' in some negative feeling evoked by an encounter abroad, involves both complex emotions and socio-material consequences. These issues are often seen as "too personal" to be suitable for academic analysis, so are rarely included in exchange students' academic world. It is our view that these themes should be taken into account and addressed in preparation and return courses following academic exchanges. Understanding more about how love relationships are experienced would be supportive and promote positive mental health and wellbeing.

We hope that our modest scientific analysis can contribute to improving the situation of people who happen to fall in love with the other during their transnational academic exchange. We feel there is much to learn about building the shared third, commitment and how to sustain intimate relationships through time and distance, despite difference in nationality and other forms of identity and belonging. Hopefully this chapter contributes to increased transnational academic exchange including positive and sustainable love relationships, promoting the cosmopolitan stance and recognition of our shared humanity across borders.

References

Abt, H., & Stumpf, S. (2017). Effects of international youth exchanges on openness & mobility in professional careers. In Thomas (Ed.), *Cultural and ethnic diversity: How European psychologists can meet the challenges* (pp. 193–202). Gottingen: Hogrefe.

Ayuso, L. (2019). What future awaits couples living apart together (LAT)? *The Sociological Review, 67*(1), 226–244.

Bauman, Z. (1998). *Globalization: The human consequences*. Cambridge: Polity Press.

Benjamin, J. (1988). *The bonds of love: Psychoanalysis, feminism, and the problem of domination*. New York: Pantheon.

Benjamin, J. (1995). Recognition and destruction: An outline of intersubjectivity. In *Like subjects, love objects*. New Haven, CT: Yale University Press.

Benjamin, J. (2004). Beyond doer and done to: An intersubjective view of tiredness. Psychoanalytic Quarterly, 73 (1): 5–46.

Benjamin, J. (2019). *Anerkennung, Zeugenschaft und Moral [Acknowledgement, Witnessing and Moral]*. Gießen: Psychosozial.

Biringen, Z., Derscheid, D., Vliegen, N., Closson, L., & Easterbrooks, M. A. (2014). Emotional availability (EA): Theoretical background, empirical research using the EA scales, and clinical applications. Elsevier. *Developmental Review, 34*, 114–167. Online: https://www.sciencedirect.com/science/article/pii/S0273229714000033

Carter, J., Duncan, S., Stoilova, M., & Phillips, M. (2016). Sex, love and security: Accounts of distance and commitment in living apart together relationships. *Sociology, 50*(3), 576–596.

de Ponte, U. (2017). Developmental-psychological contributions to international youth exchanges. In A. Thomas (Ed.), *Cultural and ethnic diversity: How European psychologists can meet the challenges* (Chap. 20, pp. 187–192). Göttingen: Hogrefe.

de Ponte, U. (2019). The use of transformative learning in the prevention of radicalisation. *Intellectual Out*, 1. Theoretical Framework, ERASMUS+-project (PR)IDE; project leader KulturLife gGmbH, Kiel. https://kultur-life.de/fileadmin/kundendaten/pdf/Erasmus-plus-PRIDE-IO1-Research-Contribution.pdf

de Ponte, U. (2020). *Resilienz-Entwicklung als Teilaspekt der interkulturellen Kompetenz-Entwicklung bei in Deutschland sozialisierten jungen Erwachsenen* [Arbeitstitel; working title: Developing resilience as a partial aspect of developing intercultural competence among young adults socialised in Germany]. Dissertationsvorhaben an der Ruhr-Universität Bochum, Prof. Dr. J. Straub.

de Ponte, U. & Jäger, J. (2015). Interkulturelle Begegnungserfahrung von Jugendlichen als Mehrwert der Besonderen Förderung. In IJAB – *Fachstelle für Internationale Jugendarbeit der Bundesrepublik Deutschland* (S. 124–132) e. V. (Hrsg.): Forum Jugendarbeit International 2013-2015 (Kinder- und Jugendhilfe transnational gestalten), Bonn.

de Ponte, U. & van Eck, H. (2017). Aspects of transcultural counselling and psychotherapy. In A. Thomas (Ed.), *Cultural and ethnic diversity: How European psychologists can meet the challenges* (Chap. 20, pp. 153–141). Göttingen: Hogrefe.

Dunger, F. (2010). *Making sense of intermarried identities*. Unpublished project report International Development Studies, Roskilde University.

EIS. (2014). *The Erasmus impact study*. Retrieved August 15, 2019, from https://ec.europa.eu/programmes/erasmus-plus/sites/erasmusplus2/files/erasmus-impact_en.pdf

Erasmus. (2019). Retrieved September 14, 2019, from https://ec.europa.eu/programmes/erasmus-plus/about/statistics_en

Ethical Principles for Nordic Psychologists. (2019). Retrieved August 2, 2019, from https://www.dp.dk/wp-content/uploads/etiske-principper-for-nordiske-psykologer-1.pdf

Flanagan, J. C. (1954, July). The critical incident technique. *Psychological Bulletin, 51*(4), 327–358.

Giddens, G. (1992). The transformation of intimacy: Sexuality, love and eroticism. In *Modern societies*. Oxford: Polity Press.

Giles, J. (2006). Social constructionism and sexual desire. *Journal for the Theory of Social Behaviour, 36*(3), 225–238.

Giles, J. (2008). *The nature of sexual desire*. Lanham: University Press of America.

Green, C. (2014). *EU's Erasmus study abroad programme is 'responsible for 1m babies'*. Accessed December 16, 2018, from https://www.independent.co.uk/student/news/eus-erasmus-study-abroad-programme-Responsible-for-1m-babies-9751749.html

Havighurst, R. J. (1972). *Developmental tasks and education*. New York: McCay.

Hendriks, V. (2018). *Reality lost: Markets of attention, manipulation and misinformation* [with Mads Vestergaard]. New York: Springer Nature.

Holmes, M. (2014). *Distance relationships: Intimacy and emotions amongst academics and their partners in dual-locations*. Basingstoke: Palgrave Macmillan.

Jensen, I. (2007). *Introduction to: Cultural understanding*. Roskilde: Roskilde University Press.

Karla, V., Kaur, R., & Hutnyk, J. (2005). *Diaspora & hybridity*. New Delhi: Sage.

Karandashev, V. (2015). A cultural perspective on romantic love. *Online Readings in Psychology and Culture, 5*(4). https://doi.org/10.9707/2307-0919.1135

Koser, K. (2007). *International migration: A very short introduction*. Oxford: Oxford University Press.

Layes, G. (2000). *Grundformen des Fremderlebens: Eine Analyse von Handlungsorientierungen in der interkulturellen Interaktion* [Basic forms of experiencing otherness: An analysis of action orientations during an intercultural interaction] (Internationale Hochschulschriften). New York: Waxmann Verlag.

Mahler, M., Pine, F., & Bergma, A. (1975). *The psychological birth of the human infant: Symbiosis and individuation*. New York: Basic Books.

Moodley, R. (2011). *Outside the sentence: Readings in critical multicultural counselling and psychotherapy*. Toronto: CDCP.

Pananakhonsab, W. (2019). Migration for love? Love and intimacy in marriage migration processes. *Emotion, Space and Society, 31*, 86–92.

Patcharin, L. (2019). *Love, money and obligations: Transnational marriage in a Northeastern Thai Village*. Singapore: NUS.

Phoenix, A. (2011). Psychosocial intersections: Contextualizing the accounts of adults who grew up in visibly ethnically different households. In Lutz, Vivar, & Supik (Eds.), *Framing intersectionality: Debates on a multi-faceted concept in gender studies* (pp. 137–152). Surrey: Ashgate.

Saunders, H., Kraus, A., Barone, & Biringen, Z. (2015). Emotional availability: Theory, research, and intervention. *Frontiers in Psychology* [published: 28 July 2015]. https://doi.org/10.3389/fpsyg.2015.01069. Retrieved from https://www.researchgate.net/publication/280520657

Singla, R. (2004). *Youth relationships, ethnicity and psychosocial intervention*. New Delhi: Books Plus.

Singla, R. (2006a). Changing patterns of intimate partnership formation and intergenerational relationships among ethic minority youth in Denmark. In G. J. Øverland (Ed.), *Sociology at the frontiers of psychology* (pp. 149–171). New Castle: Cambridge Scholars Press.

Singla, R. (2006b). *Den eneste ene – hvordan etniske minoritetsunge i Danmark Danner par, Konflikt og intervention* [The one and only – How ethnic minority youth in Denmark form intimate partnerships]. Retrieved from www.akademia.dk

Singla, R. (2008). *Now and then – life trajectories, family relationships and diasporic identities: A follow-up study of young adults* (Vol. 46). Copenhagen Studies in Bilingualism University of Copenhagen.

Singla, R. (2015). *Intermarriage and mixed parenting: Promoting mental health & wellbeing, crossover love*. Basingstoke: Palgrave Macmillan.

Singla, R., Shajahan, P., & Sriram, S. (2020). Indian diasporic communities in a people-centered perspective: Exploring belonging, marginality and transnationalism. In Banerjee, Carney, & Hulgård (Eds.), *People – Centred social innovation: Global perspectives on an emerging paradigm* (pp. 156–178). New York: Routledge.

Singla, R. (2017). Intermarried couples negotiating mixedness in everyday life in Denmark: Lessons for psychologists. In A. Thomas (Ed.), *Culture and ethnic diversity in how European psychologists can meet the challenges* (pp. 159–167). Hogrefe Publishing GmbH: Hogrefe & Huber Publishers.

Singla, R., & Varma, A. (2018). *LAT (Living Apart Together) transnational couples: Promoting mental health and wellbeing*. Keynote abstract Fourth ICCP Conference, Bengaluru, 3rd–6th January 2019. Retrieved from https://www.iccp2019.com/

Singla, R., & Varma, A. (2019). Changing demographics and intimate relation patterns among Indian diaspora in Denmark. In S. I. Rajan (Ed.), *India migration report; Diaspora in Europe* (pp. 249–272). London: Routledge.

Singla, R., & Ganapathy-Coleman, H. (2020). Intermarried couples: Transnationalism, and racial dynamics in Denmark & Canada. In S. Safdar, C. Kwantes, & W. Friedlmeier (Eds.), *Wiser world with multiculturalism: Proceedings from the 24th Congress of the International Association for Cross-Cultural Psychology*. https://scholarworks.gvsu.edu/iaccp_papers/276

Thomas, A. (2010). Internationaler Jugendaustausch – ein Erfahrungs- und Handlungsfeld für Eliten? In IJAB – Fachstelle für Internationale Jugendarbeit der Bundesrepublik Deutschland e.V. (Hrsg.), *Forum Jugendarbeit International* (S. 18–27). Bonn.

Thomas, A. (2017a). Orientation in cultural and ethnic diversity. The concept of cultural standards. In Thomas (Ed.), *Cultural and ethnic diversity: How European psychologists can meet the challenges* (pp. 36–48). Göttingen: Hogrefe.

Thomas, A. (2017b). Development of multicultural identity in international youth exchanges. In Thomas (Ed.), *Cultural and ethnic diversity: How European psychologists can meet the challenges* (pp. 211–220). Göttingen: Hogrefe.

Turkle, S. (2011). *Alone together: Why we expect more from technology and less from each other*. New York: Basic Books.

Utler, A. (2014). *"Aber der Tongchun is echt komisch"– Differenzerfahrungen im Migrationskontext* [But Tongchun is really strange – Experiences of difference in the context of migration]. Bochum: Westdeutscher Universitätsverlag.

Valsiner, J. (2007) *Culture in minds and societies: Foundation of Cultural Psychology*. New Delhi: Sage Publication.

Valsiner, J., & Rosa, A. (2007). *The Cambridge handbook of sociocultural psychology*. Cambridge: Cambridge University Press.

Williams, L. (2010). *Global marriage: Cross-border marriage migration in global context*. Basingstoke: Palgrave Macmillan.

Rashmi Singla PhD, Psychology Masters (Copenhagen University), MSc (Delhi University), Associate Professor, Department of Psychology and Educational Research, Roskilde University, Denmark since 2000. Affiliated to NGO-Transcultural Therapeutic Team for Ethnic Minority Youth and Families since 1991. Participation in international projects about health, family, globalization, contested childhoods. Member of Nordic Migration Research (NMR) board for 2018–2022. Migrated from India to Denmark in 1980 and has academic interest in movements across borders (transnationalism and diaspora), family life, couple and peer relations, ethnicity, inclusion/exclusion processes and psychosocial intervention. Interplay between Eastern and Western Psychology such as meditation, yoga, organizational diversity management are also areas of interest. Published extensively, see—www.ruc.dk/rashmi, last book: intimate Intermarriage and Mixed Parenting: Promoting Mental Health and Wellbeing (2015) Palgrave Macmillan.

Ulrike de Ponte (Dipl.-Psych., PhD. scholar in Social Psychology & Sociology at Ruhr University Bochum, Germany), since 2011 managing director of the Additional Study Programme "Intercultural Competence" at the Applied University Regensburg and Head of the programme for the part psychology. Before she worked 10 years as a trainer and researcher close to Alexander Thomas, full professor of intercultural psychology, and his Institute of Cooperation Management. She did research and published several articles in miscellanies as well as a monography in the field of international youth exchange. Recently she participated in a Erasmus+-project about preventing radicalisation through developing identity as knowledge partner and is convenor of the Board on Cultural and Ethnic Diversity of the European Federation of Psychologists' Association (EFPA) since 2015. She is a member of Hermeneutic Research Group with Psychodynamic Approach founded by Professor Hans-Dieter König, Johann Wolfgang Goethe University of Frankfurt a. Main.

Chapter 33
Living with Love in Today's World: Philosophical Reflections on Some of Its Complexities

Ondřej Beran and Camilla Kronqvist

Abstract In contrast to many philosophical accounts of love, which analyse it as a special kind of valuation of the beloved, or a special concern for her well-being, we elaborate on the minority observation characterising love as making a difference to one's whole life (endowing it with meaning). Our aim is not to suggest that this is an external, one-dimensional relationship. We consider not just the difference love makes to (our perception of) life, but inquire into how certain features of our life may make a difference for how we come to conceive of love. We first discuss the importance of the compartmentalisation of our lives and the interplay between our lives of love and those parts of our lives that are based elsewhere. Then we focus on such tonalities and modalities of love as the sense of responsibility and perseverance. These analyses relate to the phenomenon of environmental despair (first section) and high-functioning burnout (second section), relying equally on real-life and fictional examples. We indicate possible consequences that follow from these discussions for the *philosophy* of love. One of these is that philosophy's insights can be sharpened if it remains conscious of the relations between its own conceptual analyses and the approaches and findings of cultural critique and the social sciences.

Keywords Love · Language of love · Environmental grief · Burnout · The understanding of life · Examples

O. Beran (✉)
Department of Philosophy, Centre for Ethics as Study in Human Value, University of Pardubice, Pardubice, Czech Republic
e-mail: Ondrej.Beran@upce.cz

C. Kronqvist
Department of Philosophy, Åbo Akademi, Turku, Finland
e-mail: camilla.kronqvist@abo.fi

33.1 Introduction

Our lives are not unitary enterprises, but typically unfold in several loosely rather than tightly interconnected domains. One of these segments of life can markedly outweigh the others, becoming thus what Fingarette (1988, 100) calls one's "central activity". Although the "list" of these domains would vary across different cultures, some of the items will exhibit a considerable transcultural constancy. One of such nearly ubiquitous items is the domain of personal (family) life. And at least in the contemporary developed Western societies, the typical picture of life will combine this domain of the private with a few significant others—with those of professional occupation, leisure activities, civic or political engagements, or religion. This list is not supposed to be exhaustive, but to outline a picture in which most readers with this kind of cultural background can find themselves.

In this chapter we consider the interconnections between these domains in the light of the revival of interest that Western philosophy saw in the phenomenon of love around the middle of the twentieth century.[1] Most of the central discussions in this revival stem from the analytical tradition, or, to put it more broadly, they reflect the register of concepts, arguments, and framings characteristic of the Anglophone philosophy (or philosophy of the kind most typically cultivated in English today). Though this philosophical upbringing necessarily mirrors a particular cultural spectre of examples and concerns, most thinkers engaged in the debate genuinely intend their observations and analyses to capture something about (the concept of) love "as such". This chapter shares this background, but with the intention of distinguishing itself in a certain direction. Our key opening point is that of discerning a divide between those philosophers who locate love only in one of the life domains outlined above (by default, that of personal life) and those who see it as a more pervasive phenomenon.

Among the first, we find philosophers who analyse love mostly as a particular kind of emotion centring on the beloved person. Some authors suggest that love consists of the appreciation, or appraisal, of a particular value (Velleman, 1999); some prefer to see love as bestowing this value onto the other (Singer, 2009). The appreciation itself of the value then involves a special concern for the beloved's well-being, trumping preferentially any *impersonal* consequentialist-like or Kantian-like considerations (Williams, 1981a; Frankfurt, 1999). Other theorists stress the essence of love as the emergence and existence of a particular bond, or union (Nozick, 1991). Yet another philosophical tradition reads love as a particular kind of vision of the beloved (or a transformation thereof) (Jollimore, 2011; see also Murdoch, 1970, although her focus is not on erotic or partner love). Love sees the

---

[1] The motivation for this revival of interest in love as a subject for moral and philosophical psychology, largely derived from renewed readings of Plato or Aristotle, who devoted much attention to erotic love, friendship, or the citizen's love for their country. It also went along with a broader interest in philosophical theories of emotions that, in contrast to the study of passions, inquired into the cognitive and motivational structures and aspects of emotions.

other as fully real and independent (Murdoch, 1997a, 1997b), as infinitely precious (Gaita, 2002), or involves one in the practical acknowledgment of the other's independence (Weil, 2009). The cognitivist turn in thinking about emotions (Solomon, 1973; Nussbaum 2004) also opened space for asking the question about the *reasons* for (or against) loving a person (Frankfurt, 2004).

Partly in criticism of the focus on the reasons for love of a particular person, some philosophers have observed that an exhaustive description of love (for a particular person) should not stop at those aspects of love that *directly thematise* the beloved person. Harry Frankfurt (2004) suggested that rather than looking for reasons for love, it is instructive to consider love itself as "a source of reasons." Similarly, Robert Solomon (1990) suggested that love is no mere emotional attitude the lover takes to the beloved, but rather that love involves both lovers in a "loveworld" where the relationship sets the stage for a renewed sense of shared self. While he is rooted in the continental tradition, Agamben (2009, 25) offers a complementary observation that the beloved stands so "excessively close" to the lover that the lover cannot focus on *her* and incorporates her instead into the frame of *how* she sees everything that she sees.

Here, however, we will approach the question of how love pervades our conception of life from an alternative viewpoint, and consider the sense in which love shapes the meaning we see in life, through Rush Rhees's (1997, 42) remark that

> religion makes a difference to a man's life, and obviously being in love does too. (...) the person in love is different; life is different for him, or the whole world is different for him.

It is common to express sentiments of this kind in everyday language, also in negative terms, such as when it is claimed that love makes one "see everything through rose-coloured glasses". It is, however, important to Rhees that the difference that love makes cannot be reduced to a set of experiences causing us to see things differently. The difference centrally involves, and is internal to, the "language of love". As one of us (Kronqvist, 2017) put it in an elaboration of Rhees's sketchy remark, unravelling what sense can be made of love as "a passion for life," love (pure love, at least) involves a feeling that everything "falls into place" (36). This, however, is not a vague feeling, but rather a way of characterising the fact that love brings about an awareness of "the significance a life with another person has to us, in the sense we make of life" (37).

These observations contribute to a "phenomenology" of life in which love has a (central) place. One's own life, life as such, appears to oneself in a certain light. Of course, the lover cares about the well-being of the beloved, but she also gains a new *vision,* or *understanding,* of her whole life and its events. By "vision" we mean the complex of judgments, emotional responses, practical attitudes, etc., as characterised by Murdoch (1997b, 80). For example: as I am in love, I find something touchingly humane in my colleagues (who previously struck me as annoying, hardly bearable), Or, my love for my children helps me find meaning in my struggle of the political campaign against a local factory contaminating the air—I now (spontaneously) sense a point in this (otherwise, "objectively," exhausting and demoralising) endeavour. And so forth.

In these examples, as in Kronqvist's earlier account, the dialectic between how one conceives of one's life and one's love, is mainly explored through a consideration of the significance love has for the sense one makes of (sees in) one's life, including those parts of it that do not feature love explicitly or overtly. Here, our aim is to work against the temptation to interpret the relation between love and life as an external, one-dimensional relationship. We supplement the view of this phenomenology with aspects of love, and life, which diversify the picture of what may be entailed in the experience that things fall into place. We consider not just the difference love makes to (our perception of) life, but also inquire into how features of our life make a difference for how we come to conceive of love.

In the first section, we discuss the interplay between our lives of love and those parts of our lives that are based elsewhere. The second section focuses on tonalities of love beyond passion (for one's life), in particular the sense of responsibility and perseverance that may become the characteristic feature of love. In the first section, we attend to a real-life example, whereas the second concerns a fictional one. Both these examples are taken from a rather particular cultural setting, and as such they allow us a glimpse into what living with love—living which is always necessarily somewhere—is like.

In the concluding section, we indicate possible implications of discussing these examples for the *philosophy* of love, namely, that it can sharpen its insights if it remains conscious of the relations between its conceptual analyses and the approaches and findings of cultural critique and the social sciences. One notable point: despite the heterogeneous conceptual landscape accessible only through joint forces of these disciplines, which any single example always reflects unevenly (being more "at home" somewhere than somewhere else), the language that the example speaks still makes what it has to say a talk of love. (There is an important difference between this talk and a talk of "what the people of the culture/society/community X think is love"; a difference in relied-upon notions and assumed elaborations.)

33.2 Love Under a Shadow

Insofar as love makes a difference to one's life *beyond* home (which it unmistakably does), it becomes important to make sense of the nature of this impingement. We have referred to a possible account of this impingement: proceeding in terms of the light in which we *see* and understand things that happen in our lives, now that love is present in them.

Our interests now lie with influences flowing in the, as it were, "opposite" direction: what difference the changed light in which we see and understand the events of our lives makes for how we can, or cannot anymore, understand our love. Here, we would like to consider a tragic event that took place in New York in 2018. David Buckel, a renowned lawyer, committed for many years to environmental and LGBT issues and causes, immolated himself as a protest against a politics that is blind towards climate change. Though his friends and family later reported his increasing depression, nobody knew that its intensity was such that it would lead to suicide.

His memorandum sent to the media shows, however, that his feelings of guilt and helplessness may have been deep and overwhelming, but for what he considered good reasons rather than a pathology. He says:

> Pollution ravages our planet, oozing inhabitability via air, soil, water and weather. Most humans on the planet now breathe air made unhealthy by fossil fuels, and many die early deaths as a result—my early death by fossil fuel reflects what we are doing to ourselves[,]

adding that

> [m]any who drive their own lives to help others often realize that they do not change what causes the need for their help.

The opening of his note bears the mark of a man who has considered the consequences of his actions:

> My name is David Buckel and I just killed myself by fire as a protest suicide. I apologize to you for the mess.

(About Buckel's life and farewell note, see Mays, 2018.)

Buckel's death can be read as a case of environmental grief or despair (as described e.g. by Cunsolo & Ellis, 2018). The general "symptoms" of this "diagnosis" are such that facing the progressive, probably irreversible, deterioration of the environment, many people sink into depression, lose interest in their day-to-day lives, and exhibit suicidal tendencies. We speak of "symptoms" and "diagnosis" in scare quotes, for rather than being a mental-health issue, environmental grief seems to be one possible reaction of an attentive mind to the changed shape of our lives. It is changed to an extent that we suggest is "grammatically disruptive": it interferes with what we used to be able to meaningfully think and say.

The notion of environmental despair points us to cases in which any sense of balance in one's life is abolished. Unlike, say, clinical depression, which tends to directly disrupt the attitudes and relationships of love in various ways (Fiske & Peterson, 1991), environmental despair seems a more lucid condition. In an eerie way, it coexists with one's love. One does not become a different personality (no longer invested in the relationship), yet environmental despair overshadows the love that previously illuminated the whole of one's life. Severing the links of vision that pervaded the continuity of one's life, environmental despair does not need to eradicate love for loved ones. Nevertheless, love no longer makes a crucial difference to one's life as a whole. It may even be the *only* area of life that makes sense. David Buckel lived in a happy family, he and his partner had a daughter, and their relationship was by no means in a crisis or fading. And yet, it is not meaningless to think that though he really loved his family, his love could not cure his environmental despair. Being the person he was, he could not help feeling that "the world has just gone off the rails," and that love could do nothing to diminish the burden of this realisation.

This case has some noteworthy implications:

1. There is an intriguing kind of cognitive dissonance here. That things are falling into place is not something one simply sees happening. Rather, one implicitly assumes that, when in love, everything *should* fall into place. Yet, sometimes it simply does not. The disaster of the climate crisis is of almost absurdly awful size: we cannot retreat to a domain that we can reasonably try to influence by our own powers. When we despair about our situation, or the whole world, a part of what makes it still bearable is the sense that we are not powerless in trying to prevent at least something we value from falling apart. But environmental despair creeps into the everyday components of the fabric of even the most personal and intimate domains of our lives. It brings about, among other things, a heightened awareness of the harrowing modes that concern the one I love—she is being poisoned by air and water, or is complicit in the destruction in subtle ways ("Privilege is derived from the suffering of others," reads Buckel's note), or both. Once these pathways of thinking about one's own life have been entered—again, we do not need to see them as delusional—it seems difficult to recover the viewpoint of "everything falling into place." Should one overlook climate change? Should one reinterpret it so that it does not matter to love? Would the one who loves then live with her eyes intentionally half-closed?

2. Love serves no real consolation; if anything, it rather exacerbates the situation. As horrid as the climate crisis is for one's own sake, it is even more so for the sake of one's *children*. Love for one's children, if suffused by a sense of responsibility and worry about them, only makes it worse. One does not worry about what might happen to one's nearest and dearest; one simply knows that it *will* happen. Again, one experiences a cognitive dissonance here: this is not something love *should* bring into our lives—the certainty that one is committing a sin against one's own children by being complicit in bequeathing an uninhabitable future to them.

3. The general sense that there is no future left, which accompanies environmental despair, plays a significant structural role in itself. Sentiments such as, "So long as we have each other, I know I don't have to be afraid of anything. We will endure" are characteristic of love. Now, love no longer offers a refuge from the world around us. We do not understand environmental degradation as a cyclical calamity (like war or economic crisis), but rather as an irreversible degradation of the once familiar richness and variety of our form of life. Face to face with this kind of understanding of the world, love may no longer offer the sense of reassurance that there is a private sphere in which, or through which, one can resist or hide from the public sphere. Analogously, terminally ill adolescent patients often fail to see a real purpose in learning in school—what for should they? (Cf. Davis, 1989, 239.) In these extreme cases, appeals to instrumental rationality make little sense. And though it may be argued that the point of loving someone or educating oneself does not fall within the sphere of instrumental rationality, a *pinch* of it is still embedded in the motivational structures behind our understanding of why loving someone or educating oneself makes sense.

Against this background, environmental despair raises the demand for a concept of love purified of grammatical structures of worldly temporality. Statements to the effect that "When I grow up, I want to be alive"[2]—do of course have their literal meaning. But the environmental crisis is also, as we put it clumsily, grammatically disruptive: once we realise its urgency, it becomes drastically more difficult for us to *understand* our lives as having a future. This understanding necessarily goes hand in hand with what we do with our lives right now, and how we do it in relation to love.

The strong interconnection between the lost sense of balance in one's understanding of the world and of one's love—as, for example, in Buckel's story—cannot therefore mean that we are simply living in *too* hard times. As a philosophical observation, the statement that our relationships of love crumble and fail under the burden of life's adversities feels trivial.[3] Our concern is rather with showing the difference that our changed understanding of the world (its future) will make to the way we understand, experience and analyse our very concept of love.

It is hard to imagine how love could not involve a heightened attention to those aspects of the "here and now" that shape one's understanding of the beloved's person and of what one owes to her. This means to take into account the potentialities of the course of one's life. This life is *in* the world, and some of the life potentialities (of people one cares about) *will* be drastically curbed by aspects of a world in which everything does not fall into place. Loving one's children is not disconnected from the wish, however vague or implicit, for them to have a full life. Such a desire can be manifest in thinking, "When my little girl grows up, she can go study at a university, whatever subject, because she is super-smart." To someone who perceives the impact of the climate change crisis, however, a *natural* expression of love can rather be that it is "not fair," or "not right" that the future of one's children is being taken from them (consider an analogous case: if one's child is terminally ill). Similarly, the realisation that the climate change crisis is not a transitory or reversible hardship can be expressed in the decision to remain childless. A growing number of people have made such a decision, thinking that they have no future to offer to their children (Astor, 2018).

What we allude to here is that a historically and culturally conditioned shift may be looming in our conceptions of love. The idea of the full life that one can "reasonably" wish for one's children (such as the university wish above) is a reflection of a relatively stable life in stable, relatively rich societies with public social welfare systems. Such contents are slowly being elided from the lived notions

---

[2]The title of a documentary film about the movement Fridays for Future, which is based on a direct quotation from one of the striking students.

[3]It seems preposterous to expect philosophy to outline a minimal set of life's (material) conditions that would guarantee a reasonably probable viability of love. Nevertheless, some philosophers engage in considerations of this kind (cf. Ben-Ze'ev 2019; see Chap. 5). A part of the temptation derive from a vaguely Aristotelian idea of the good life, one that has to do with the fulfilment of a "reasonable man's" expectations from his life. (Which is divorced from the "extremist" Platonic intuitions of the principal significance of the sense I make of my life whatever its conditions "materially" are; the significance of our moral aspirations and aspirations to understanding.)

of love even in these societies, and with that, there are changes in the ways we relate to our lives, and to what we can do with them in terms of love life or family life.

33.3 Love Exhausted

In the first section, we discussed the impact of the changed stage for the way we experience the characteristic aspects of love, such as the emotions of care or joy, or the attitude of valuation, centring round the person of the loved one. Here, we discuss the aspects of love that, though not excluded are not usually given a central position in typical characterisations of love: the senses of responsibility and perseverance (see Chap. 58). To highlight them we make use of a fictional example.

Michael Haneke's 2012 film *Amour* tells the story of an elderly couple trapped in the deadlock of exhausting care. When Anne suffers a paralysing stroke, her husband, Georges, starts taking care of her, with the partial help of hired nurses. This duty is exacting for him (being an elderly man in frail health), and as the story unfolds towards its seemingly inevitable ending, we can see his love for Anne manifested in the repeated daily tasks performed under increasing strain and exhaustion.

The progress and prospects of his relationship with his wife are not sources of perceived meaning in Georges's life. They do not charge him with energy or enthusiasm. Thus, his love for Anne cannot really be characterised as something that "keeps him going" in the sense of providing him with a support against other kinds of hardship in life. This does not mean that his love for Anne is imperfect, but the tonality of their relationship changes significantly. Love still "keeps him going," for he knows he must stand by Anne as long as he can, but this "must" is not of the kind of "moral necessity" explored by Williams (1981b), with alternatives viscerally perceived as "unthinkable." Here we witness a phenomenon of a more Kantian sort.

As in the previous section, the phenomenology of this case has noteworthy implications:

1. Love may not (always) be exhaustively characterised by the experience (*Erlebnis*) that one "gets" from it, or simply as anything that one gets. It also requires one to give. This *giving* is often gratuitous, and in the best cases the thought about what one is giving may not occur for all that one receives in return. Yet, speaking about giving does not only have a "metaphorical" sense—giving one's love, giving of oneself. In the most concrete of ways, love often asks one to give something to the other that in another case could have been "spent" on oneself. And sometimes what one is asked to give is something that one lacks, be it money, time, energy, or attention. This doesn't mean that if a parent dedicates most of her free time to her children, thereby having no time left for her own long-standing, oft-postponed dreams (to finish the half-written detective novel, say), making this decision will make her unhappy. On the contrary. But what makes her happy is *not* that she has no time for her detective novel. She may never stop regretting that.

The case of Georges and Anne is a version of this dedication, albeit an extreme one. Georges is not an adult in his prime, and Anne is not a beautifully growing, increasingly independent child. The "resources" (time, care, energy) that Georges needs to put into the relationship are scarcer than they used to be and not renewable. This huge giving out is not a matter of enjoyment in itself; rather, Georges acts out of the sense that he simply "owes" this to Anne. This is what their love means for him. This sense may not, in the moment of giving what he "owes" (natural as it is), feel elevating or joyful. If one's beloved is seriously or terminally ill, then the only available expression of love may be to stay, out of love, with the loved one until the end. Yet, this stage of life is often painful and draining, and the beloved's death can be perceived as a relief. Not only a final relief for the ill person, from the pain and suffering, but also a relief from the burden carried by his or her companion.

In a situation like that of Georges, one may draw strength from various sources. One may go back, in one's thoughts, to what one experienced as good and beautiful and not simply as draining. Still being able to do this adds one more thing to be grateful for, apart from the shared time. Yet, these kinds of resources may also *not* be available (anymore) for the carer; she may only be supported by such understanding that revolves round the ideas of duty, responsibility, or loyalty. Only death may allow her to think once more about what was good and beautiful.

The carer may also be so afflicted by the situation that she no longer sees (or even cares about seeing, or tries to see) any answer to the question, "How did I end up here?" (or, as she may phrase it for herself, "Why do I have to be here?"). Empirical psychology may be interested in the causal factors leading a person into these various mind-sets; for a philosopher, these scenarios are interesting as varieties of understanding, as contributions to how one can make sense of one's life and one's love.

2. Related to the above phenomenon: caring for a seriously ill spouse, partner, or child sometimes leads to burnout similar to that which is an endemic threat in caring professions (nurses, physicians, etc.). Various studies have stressed that the onset of burnout should be studied not as an episodic phenomenon, but rather as developing over a long period during years that appear practically stable (Schaufeli et al., 2011; Bakker & Costa, 2014). Reaching the acute burnout episode (a collapse) takes some time, and one can (or may have to) *live with one's burnout* for a long time, which gives it the nature of a *chronic* condition.

If the loving carer is burning out, this is manifest in her slowly failing and faltering endeavour. There is a difference in phenomenological tonality between being driven (unstoppably) and persevering out of a sense of "must". Yet,. there is no sharp boundary between going on, with a sense of responsibility, and going on "somehow", with buzzing head, blunted senses, and ever-shrinking capacity for, and interest in, having any sense of why it is worthwhile to keep going—proceeding towards an episode of acute burnout. On a scale between a clear sense of responsibility and a breakdown, the various stages of a "high-functioning burnout" emerge.

In her memorable story, Anne Helen Petersen (2019) describes millennials as the "burnout generation"—an entire generation for whom life has (irreparably assumed) the shape of a meaningless tangled web of plodding and toiling. Yet, they know no other life, and so they have to live this one, without much joy and with the undercurrent of fatigue in all their undertakings. This vision of life is related to the changed structure of the job market, social security systems, and so on. Again, it seems to be life under the burden of a cognitive dissonance: the notion that life should not be like this (perhaps when compared to what one's parents considered "realistic" life aspirations) and yet so often and overwhelmingly is. It is as if hard work, and the self-denial that hard work sometimes involves, has lost the capacity of being of genuine value, a source of healthy satisfaction for the worker. Only the toil is left.

The gradually vanishing sense of value in the toil seems to be a characteristic shared by forms of chronic burnout, of both precarised millennials up to their eyes in debt and the loving carer. The carer perseveres as long as it is possible—for the sake of the loved one—but the sense of her love as the source of the meaning and value inherent in the toil may shrink over time, while toil may gain centrality as the defining feature of how her life shows itself to her.

3. These shifts in our understanding of love respond to features (that change over time) of our lives in particular societies. Much as the story in *Amour* seems universal, what makes it sound familiar is its connection to characteristics of life in contemporary developed Western countries. Longevity and life expectancy is growing. Families tend towards a certain geographical, social, and economic atomisation into nuclear families that are, on average, better off than their ancestors a century ago, but that also more often need to face the twists of their lives "on their own." The availability, quality, and "offer" of social services and state-run social welfare systems is a major factor that simply is considered, in life situations of this kind, as a default, to an extent without parallel previously or elsewhere. (And how these services work also serves characteristics of the cultures of various countries not unrelated to, but not directly dependent on, their economic development; compare the Scandinavian countries with the U.S.)

The observation that love can be exhausting and exhausted would not be a great discovery, though its uncompromising artistic elaborations, like *Amour*, can strike us as revelatory. This observation tells us little if meant as a side-note to the contents of a universal and timeless concept ("'love' is ... and apart from that, it can also be ..."). There is no such universal and timeless concept; our familiarity with love is built from the ground up. Georges's story would not have looked like it did without its particular setting, and without appreciating these particulars it would be very difficult to understand his story as the story of love that it is.

On the other hand, though a particular cultural background might help one appreciate finer nuances of the narrative, this is by no means a requisite of understanding the story as a story of *love* (rather than a story about "what wealthy cultured French pensioners think is love"). Even a recipient from a distant culture can watch it and feel the emotional pressure. This *trans*cultural openness is not possible *despite* the story's not being *a*-cultural. If the story did not take place somewhere and did not take turns characteristic of this setting, there would be nothing to tell, and therefore nothing to translate and transfer either.

33.4 Lessons to Be Learned?

The focus issue of the first section was taken from real life. The same goes for the second section, but we borrowed our example from fiction. This may appear unjustified if one thinks that philosophy should have the ambition to write about real lives and the real world. Yet, the "data" on which philosophy relies differ from the empirical data collected through the methods of the natural or social sciences. Philosophy's investigations are *conceptual*, and we learn about our concepts from various sources. By reading Austen's, Tolstoy's, or Coetzee's novels one is not "mining" empirical data about historical locations of human shallowness, poverty, war, or cruelty. Their works show what it *means* to live in poverty or war, or to be afflicted by cruelty, what form a life may take in such circumstances, what characterises the life of a shallow person. These examples, as well as our thinking through them, imagining ways of re-describing them (cf. Hertzberg, 2006; Moi, 2015), are philosophy's "data."[4]

The aim of the above explorations of the concept of love, as it appears in the light of these settings, was to show the complexity of the working of love—phenomenologically relevant and often neglected—that "keeps one going." In exploring its details, two points deserve special focus:

1. The image of love as that in which one can "enclose oneself from the world." While drawing thus on one's happy and harmonious personal life is psychologically natural, interpreting it as an integrative experience of the meaningfulness of life may falsify the phenomenon. Relying on strong experiences of love as a safeguard against life's vicissitudes may prove foolhardy and wrongheaded. Such attitudes, however, should not be conflated with putting one's faith in love, or in one's beloved, finding occasions for wonder and gratitude in one's life despite the recognition that one's love won't change the world, in some of the most relevant senses. One's love will neither prevent climate change nor burnout. It may not even prevent one from losing faith in love when faced with dire circumstances. Faith in one's love (in its meaning) is *not* the same as a prediction of its own persistent continuity. This faith rather sheds the light in which one perceives one's here and now. (Compare Kronqvist's [2011] analysis of the important difference between an analogous pair of relationships towards love's future—prediction and promise.)

---

[4] We owe this observation to Sophie-Grace Chappell's comments made during a lecture on the topic of love.

These considerations bear interesting similarities to different reactions we may have to the fact that we are dying. Although the death in question is not specifically one's own, climate depression can be seen as a form of death anxiety. Rather than despairing, however, another possible reaction to the climate crisis is acting-out of the idea that the only thing one can do in the face of death is to persevere in one's love, as Georges does. This "love despite" may nurture no hope that it will be better, but express a kind of a disillusioned clear insight into why what one is doing is good, perhaps even the impossibility of living with oneself (with who one would become), if one chose to be somewhere else than by the loved one. Here the distinction between escapism and optimism becomes vital. David Buckel did not lose the capacity to "enclose himself from the world;" he was never (we suppose) a self-indulgent escapist, he rather lost his optimism. His self-immolation was pre-meditated, but it was not so as a "consequence drawn" from the prediction of imminent death (the lack of perspective of his love). He did not *choose to be elsewhere* because there was no perspective for him *here*; he lost faith. His expressed intention to *do something* about the attitude towards climate change through his death, however, can also be read as a hope of affecting the world so that faith in love and life, as he seemed to understand it, would be an intelligible option again.

2. The image of love as something that fills us (with various emotions). Of course, love does this, but it doesn't consist in this subjective experience, for we can learn much about it from cases and situations where it *empties* rather than fills us. A burnout carer gives a lot of her life away; what is at play are not her emotions, but rather her life. "This is my life to give away." "What happened to my life, where did it disappear?" To describe such words as a failure to "feel the same as before" (when everything was rosy) misses what the situation is about (unlike the inability to "go on like that," and being full of regret and guilt on that account). Whether love is blooming, or crumbling, it may be useful to resist the temptation to locate these happenings in one's *feelings*.

Wittgenstein (1981, § 504) points out:

Love is not a feeling. Love is put to the test, pain not. One does not say: "That was not true pain, or it would not have gone off so quickly."

Love, in the sense of something that, if true, is unlikely to "go off quickly," is connected with what actions one perceives as thinkable and unthinkable. (Failing, for one reason or another, to do what one once perceived as unthinkable not to do does not amount to closing one's eyes to what one sees in the light of such a love.) Whatever Georges's love for Anne is like—it may have gone far from what he used to feel towards her decades ago—and however difficult it appears for him to carry on, wondering about which fleeting emotions come and go is to misunderstand in what sense Amour is a story of love. We may argue about how well he stands his test, but what is (metaphorically speaking) put to the test are not his feelings.

Love, in the sense of persevering, or doing what is good, may be the only way left to Georges to make sense of his life, perceived as a whole. This shows that love is not only accidentally exposed to life's hardships. The example helps us see how all aspects of life, in some ways, involve us in love, more specifically, in *labours of love*.

A joint lesson from these two points would be: don't underestimate the complexity of the relationship between our lives and loves. Love pervades the whole of our lives, acting (powerfully) *in* and *upon* many areas or dimensions, though in ways responding also to the changing circumstances of our lives, as we understand them. Our circumstances may demand changes in our conception of love, yet how we come to conceive of our (transformed) circumstances may as well borrow much from previous conceptions of love. The despair with which environmental crisis may fill us—which, nevertheless, allows us to see its urgency more clearly—owes something to dreams we may once have cherished, such as those about the rosy future of our university-bound children.

This dialectic between the difference that love makes for us and the way in which we see the world—what we find in it, in response to what the world puts forward to us—deserves attention and exploration. Love is *not* our whole life (cf. Rorty's 2016, 347) observations about the *difficulties* of love). If it were, "moving on" would not be *one* of the *legitimate* ways of dealing with grief and bereavement.

We need to take the situated *variability* of this dialectic into account. Things develop in our lives, and we develop along with them. The array of responses that love for a child requires from a parent differs strongly when the child is one year old and when she is 16. There is something desecrating about the idea of being angry with a toddler, but it may be a natural form of respect paid to one's teenage child, because anger may be a sign that you see that person as your equal. (Depending, of course, on what it is you are angry about.) The array of what one is capable of "investing" in the relationship also changes with time (the time spent in the relationship as well as the time of one's life). There is the slow shift from the enthusiasm of youthful gestures (tearing up a train ticket in order to be able to spend a few more hours with the other) to the more sedate perseverance of the fifty-something sharing the household chores and remembering to buy the other's (unintelligibly) favourite brand of beer.

Our love changes as we change in it (cf. Rorty's, 1987) analysis of the historicity of love). But there are several patterns of the development of human life, and they do not exhibit a timeless, a-cultural character. The options of disposing of one's life in relation to those whom one loves have been changing strikingly. The two case studies discussed above show the shifts in our forms of life—shifts in what slowly becomes intelligible—that disrupt some ingrained "grammatical" structures of "the language of love." Other, new ways of talking about love may be taking root, though, allowing us to do differently the things that Rhees mentioned as capacities inherent to the familiarity with this particular language, such as recognising love in others, or feigning love.

Love, in this view, is not simply an adaptation to the changing world. The sense in which we can think of life as a continuous whole, rather shows that this world itself, as we inhabit it, offers profound motivations for considering love as something that mustn't cling to its realisation within this world. There is a risk of corruption inherent in becoming too attached to certain aspects of our life, and the darker turns of our lives serve as reminders of the necessity to emancipate ourselves from such attachments. The claims that love for one's children places on the parent may be considered absolute, unconditional, and timeless, yet a lot depends on how such ideas are unpacked in practice. There are important differences between wishing for a better future for our children, striving for it and expecting it, as well as being disappointed if it does not happen (for example, with whom is one disappointed?). How we deal with a future that is less splendid than what "reasonable" people feel assured to wish for, thus offers a kind of test to which a parent's love is put. The latter responses especially might highlight that certain understandings of what is involved in a better future (its material, secular sense—a university career, and so on) may have involved, from the very beginning, the potential to become rotten.

There is nothing rotten *per se* with a working-class single parent hoping for a better (perhaps university-related) future for her children and doing all she can to make it happen. One thing is notable, however: the hope of upward social mobility as an expression of one's love for one's children, including the ways in which it can rot, was not always an available and intelligible form of parental love. During the Early Middle Ages in Europe, these conceptions of love might have been considered accidental or unintelligible. Later societal and cultural shifts brought them to life, or at least to the forefront. When philosophers think about love (the concept of love), they thus cannot safely ignore bits and pieces of the history of ideas, which they can find pretty much everywhere, though, including in works of fiction. As Peter Winch (1990, 23) puts it,

> [a] man's social relations with his fellows are permeated with his ideas about reality. Indeed, "permeated" is hardly a strong enough word: social relations are expressions of ideas about reality.

And there is a note worth adding: we need to be aware of the incessant, if slow, movement of the complex of these ideas.

A number of observations can be made in this endeavour. One is that our lives have turned out to be, to an unprecedented extent, lives without a sustainable future. The mostly secularised notion of what one owes to one's children, in terms of their future, underscores the bitterness of this awareness.

Another observation: on the one hand, our lives unfold in response to massive rearrangements of a globalised society that suffers from inequality and exploitation and expects us to rely primarily on ourselves to organise our lives efficiently. On the other hand, there are ideas in the air about the injustice of these pressures.

Yet another observation: love has become the subject of massive attention from the expert and self-help genres. We have to accommodate in our lives, in one way or another, the expertise about the kinds of expressions of love that are most conducive to the well-being of our loved ones, such as the idea that the best kind of love for one's children manifests itself in spending time with them. What options does this imperative leave open for a single mother working 12-h shifts in a supermarket to cover the commercial rent for her flat? For one thing, it provides a source for an intelligible concern of hers that she does not know them anymore, not having enough time to keep track of what is important for them at their respective ages.

We mentioned at the beginning that we would like to follow a "phenomenology" of love, as suggested by some minority voices of philosophy. We hope that it transpires clearly now that we do not have in mind anything like Husserl's (1970, 226) "invariant set of essential types" that "furnishes us in advance" with the "lifeworld itself." The idea of phenomenology employed here needs to take into account the variant, the contingent, and the particular. If you think of love's interaction with environmental grief, or with burnout, you are engaging with stories about what our lives are to us that could not have been told in the same way 100 or 200 years ago. We would not want to call the contemporary historicity of the experiences that David Buckel, or Georges, must have gone through "essential" for love. (There seems to be no essence of love in the sense of the essence in which Husserl apparently was interested.) But we need to keep track of these changes, otherwise the language of love we are speaking will feel flat. We will also be unable to capture the full meaning of those stories of love that are set in the real world now.

Our present stories of love could not have been told in the past for various reasons. There is the material course of history—there was no point in coming to terms with environmental grief in the pre-industrial world in which Jane Austen's novels *about love* are set. There was poverty and exhaustion and misery back then, too. There was no burnout, though, because "burnout" is also an *idea* that developed to make sense of some forms of this exhaustion, and that helped, in turn, to shape the ways in which we think about and try to deal with these forms in our lives.

No historical and cultural shift, however, needs to make the older stories about love uninteresting or uninspiring. Just as it was *Pride and Prejudice* 200 years ago, today it is, *Amour* or, who knows, *Normal People* that teaches us about love—thanks as much to what remains the same (or similar) as to what has changed substantially. The philosophy of love that wants to do justice to this insight is not replaced by the history of ideas, or by cultural critique, or by social science, but it has good reasons to be interested in communicating with these disciplines.

References

Agamben, G. (2009). *What is an apparatus?* (D. Kishik & S. Pedatella, Trans.) Stanford, CA: Stanford University Press.
Astor, M. (2018, February 5). No children because of climate change? Some people are considering it. *New York Times*. Retrieved 8 September 2019, from https://www.nytimes.com/2018/02/05/climate/climate-change-children.html
Bakker, A. B., & Costa, P. L. (2014). Chronic job burnout and daily functioning: A theoretical analysis. *Burnout Research, 1*(3), 112–119.
Ben-Ze'ev, A. (2019). *The arc of love*. Chicago, IL: The University of Chicago Press.
Cunsolo, A., & Ellis, N. R. (2018). Ecological grief as a mental health response to climate change-related loss. *Nature Climate Change, 8*(4), 275–281.
Davis, K. G. (1989). Educational needs of the terminally ill student. *Issues in Comprehensive Pediatric Nursing, 12*(2–3), 235–245.
Fingarette, H. (1988). *Heavy drinking*. Berkeley, CA: University of California Press.

Fiske, V., & Peterson, C. (1991). Love and depression: The nature of depressive romantic relationships. *Journal of Social and Clinical Psychology, 10*(1), 75–90.
Frankfurt, H. (1999). *Necessity, volition and love*. Cambridge: Cambridge University Press.
Frankfurt, H. (2004). *Reasons of love*. Princeton, NJ: Princeton University Press.
Gaita, R. (2002). *A common humanity*. London: Routledge.
Hertzberg, L. (2006). Trying to keep philosophy honest. In A. Pichler & S. Säätelä (Eds.), *Wittgenstein: The philosopher and his works* (pp. 82–97). Frankfurt a. M.: Ontos Verlag.
Husserl, E. (1970), *The crisis of European sciences and transcendental phenomenology* (D. Carr, Trans.). Evanston, IL: Northwestern University Press.
Jollimore, T. (2011). *Love's vision*. Princeton, NJ: Princeton University Press.
Kronqvist, C. (2011). The promise that love will last. *Inquiry: An Interdisciplinary Journal of Philosophy, 54*(6), 650–668.
Kronqvist, C. (2017). A passion for life: Love and meaning. *Nordic Wittgenstein Review, 6*(1), 31–51.
Mays, J.C. (2018, April 14). Prominent lawyer in fight for gay rights dies after setting himself on fire in prospect park. *New York Times*. Retrieved September 8, 2019, from https://www.nytimes.com/2018/04/14/nyregion/david-buckel-dead-fire.html
Moi, T. (2015). Thinking through examples: What ordinary language philosophy can do for feminist theory. *New Literary History, 46*(2), 191–216.
Murdoch, I. (1970). *The sovereignty of good*. London: Routledge.
Murdoch, I. (1997a). The sublime and the good. In I. Murdoch (Ed.), *Existentialists and mystics* (pp. 205–220). London: Chatto and Windus.
Murdoch, I. (1997b). Vision and choice in morality. In I. Murdoch (Ed.), *Existentialists and mystics* (pp. 76–98). London: Chatto and Windus.
Nozick, R. (1991). Love's bond. In R. C. Solomon & K. M. Higgins (Eds.), *The philosophy of (erotic) love* (pp. 417–432). Lawrence, KS: University Press of Kansas.
Nussbaum, M. (2004). Emotions as judgments of value and importance. In R. C. Solomon (Ed.), *Thinking about feeling: Contemporary philosophers on emotions* (pp. 183–199). New York: Oxford University Press.
Petersen, A.H. (2019, January 5). How Millennials became the burnout generation. *BuzzFeed News*. Retrieved September 8, 2019, from https://www.buzzfeednews.com/article/annehelenpetersen/millennials-burnout-generation-debt-work.
Rhees, R. (1997). Religion and language. In D. Z. Phillips (Ed.), *Rush Rhees on religion and philosophy* (pp. 39–49). Cambridge: Cambridge University Press.
Rorty, A. O. (1987). The historicity of psychological attitudes. *Midwest Studies in Philosophy, 10*(1), 399–412.
Rorty, A. O. (2016). The burdens of love. *The Journal of Ethics, 20*(4), 341–354.
Schaufeli, W. B., Maassen, G. H., Bakker, A. B., & Sixma, H. J. (2011). Stability and change in burnout: A 10-year follow-up study among primary care physicians. *Journal of Occupational and Organizational Psychology, 84*(2), 248–267.
Singer, I. (2009). *The nature of love: Plato to Luther*. Cambridge, MA: The MIT Press.
Solomon, R. C. (1973). Emotions and choice. *The Review of Metaphysics, 27*(1), 20–41.
Solomon, R. C. (1990). *Love: Emotion, myth and metaphor*. New York: Prometheus Books.
Velleman, J. D. (1999). Love as a moral emotion. *Ethics, 109*(2), 338–374.
Weil, S. (2009). Forms of the implicit love of God. In S. Weil (Ed.), *Waiting for God* (E. Craufurd, Trans., pp. 79–142). London: Routledge.
Williams, B. A. O. (1981a). Persons, character, and morality. In B. A. O. Williams (Ed.), *Moral luck: Philosophical papers 1973–1980* (pp. 1–19). Cambridge: Cambridge University Press.
Williams, B. A. O. (1981b). Practical necessity. In B. A. O. Williams (Ed.), *Moral luck: Philosophical papers 1973–1980* (pp. 124–131). Cambridge: Cambridge University Press.
Winch, P. (1990). *The idea of a social science and its relation to philosophy* (2nd ed.). London: Routledge.
Wittgenstein, L. (1981). *Zettel* (G. E. M. Anscombe, Trans.). Oxford: Basil Blackwell.

Ondřej Beran is a researcher, based at Centre for Ethics as Study in Human Value (University of Pardubice). He works mainly in the philosophy of language and ethics, with occasional outreaches to other areas. He is the author of *Examples and Their Role in Our Thinking* (Routledge 2021) and *Living with Rules* (Peter Lang 2018) and co-editor of *From Rules to Meanings* (Routledge 2018, with Vojtěch Kolman and Ladislav Koreň).

Camilla Kronqvist is a researcher, and currently also teacher, in philosophy at Åbo Akademi University, in Turku, Finland. Her doctoral dissertation (2009) dealt with the different kinds of conversation we may have about love, and what may be learnt by considering them in the discussions of philosophy. She has worked on questions concerning emotions and ethics, and their interconnections, moral relativism, and the philosophy of education. Her articles appeared in *Inquiry*, *Philosophical Investigations*, and *Philosophia*. She co-edited several books, most recently *Evolution, Human Behaviour and Morality* (Routledge 2016).

Part VII
The Dark Side of Love

Trump (Photo: Pete Linforth)

Chapter 34
Love in Unhappy Couples

Paul C. Rosenblatt

Abstract Defining love as attachment to and caring for the other, I argue that some unhappy couples feel love for one another, a love they may not speak about to one another and that they may not even recognize they feel. To focus the discussion of what might be love in unhappy couples, the chapter offers a fictional short story about a married couple with a long history of difficult marital interaction and who, despite their history, cannot exist apart from each other. The idea that love may be unspoken or not in awareness of partners in unhappy couples contrasts with the view that is common in social psychology and in English language dictionary definitions of "love," that love must be verbalized and in a person's awareness in order to be counted as existing. It also contrasts with the view that love cannot coexist with an enduring pattern of strongly negative feelings and prolonged conflict. Although unhappy couples may remain together for reasons other than love (for example, economic dependency, thinking there is no better alternative, a belief that divorce is wrong), I argue that some unhappy couples remain together because of love, even possibly a love that is unspoken and out of their awareness. The chapter offers a number of conceptual paths to understanding how strong negativity may be linked to love, including that in some cultural contexts negativity may be a form of expressing love and not even be perceived as negativity.

Keywords Love · Culture · Marital conflict · Unconscious · Unhappy couples

34.1 Introduction

In this chapter I focus on the kind of love that involves attachment to and caring for one's partner. With this definition in mind, I argue for the possibility that some unhappy couples love one another, and the love may be unspoken and perhaps not

P. C. Rosenblatt (✉)
Department of Family Social Science, University of Minnesota, St. Paul, MN, USA
e-mail: prosenbl@umn.edu

even in the awareness of the partners. This argument contrasts with common dictionary definitions of "love" and common understandings in social psychology of love. In English language dictionary definitions of "love" and in my reading of the social psychology literature on love, I think a basic assumption is that love cannot be considered present if a person does not make or endorse statements of love and does not act in ways that are defined in the culture as loving. In psychology, this is consistent with the long tradition of studying behaviors and not what psychoanalytic scholars would call the "unconscious." The social psychology literature has produced insightful analyses of love, but I argue in this chapter that love can be present and in some ways detected or inferred even if it is unvoiced and even if it seems out of the awareness of the person who in some sense is loving.

34.2 Theoretical Background and Context

It may be difficult for some to accept that unhappy couples may love one another. In English language dictionary definitions of "love" and in the social psychological literature love is contrasted with negative feelings and actions such as hate, disrespect, disdain, conflict, dislike, and contempt, as though love and the negative dispositions cannot coexist. But negative feelings and actions do not preclude love and in fact there is considerable evidence that love of another and negative feelings and actions directed at that other often coexist. People may, for example, ambivalently feel strong love and strong negatives toward a partner (Benedek, 1977; Usher, 2008). In addition, most couple relationships are likely to include times of feeling emotionally hurt, hurting the partner emotionally, conflict, disapproval, and disappointment (e.g., Feeney, 2009; Frost, 2013; Gottman & Gottman, 2017; Illouz, 2012; L'Abate, 2016; Usher, 2008). The commonality of alternating times of love and of strongly negative feelings may represent something important about long term couple relationships. Walsh (2016, p. 25), for example, asserted that many thinkers have seen a linkage between love and relational conflict and aggression. He cited the ethologist Konrad Lorenz as saying that the linkage is necessary for relationships to be maintained peacefully and for coordinated efforts toward common ends in a species like humans with so much capacity for aggression. In fact, building on Gottman's (1993) assertion that conflict and the airing of differences may be foundational to a couple staying together, one might surmise that conflict is foundational for love in couple relationships. This suggests that an unhappy couple may stay together despite their evident unhappiness because they love each other (Perez-Testor, Davins, Aramburu, Aznar-Martinez, & Salamero, 2013) in the sense of feeling attachment to and caring for one another.

To contextualize this discussion further in terms of the social psychological literature on love, that literature has evolved to give a sense of there being a multiplicity of loves (e.g., Berscheid, 2006, 2010; Fehr, 2013), one of which is romantic or passionate love. In social psychology, the overwhelming focus of research has been on romantic or passionate love (Fehr, 2013). That focus should not be taken to imply that the attachment and caring love that I think is present in some unhappy couples is trivial. Rather, I would argue that in many couples, including some unhappy ones, attachment to and caring love is central and may be built on a foundation of familiarity, proximity, similarity, perhaps fear of being alone (Perkel, 2007), and a history of doing things for one another. Attachment and caring love may also be rooted in problematic attachment needs developed early in life and fueled by or entangled in difficult marital dynamics (Usher, 2008; Vincent, 2007). The view of attachment offered in this chapter is linked to the very substantial social psychological literature on attachment (e.g., Shaver & Mikulincer, 2006), but focuses particularly on unverbalized and possibly unconscious attachment processes in some unhappy couples (and I have not found writings about that sense of attachment in the social psychological attachment literature).

34.3 Methodology: Case Study of a Fictional Unhappy Couple

To ground this chapter's exploration of the possibilities for love in unhappy couples, I offer a fictional case study in the form of a short story about a couple who despite a long history of unhappiness with one another find that they cannot exist apart from each other. I offer this story as a route into thinking about the unspoken and possibly unconscious attachment and caring love that I think exists in some unhappy couples.

34.3.1 Arnie and Clarice

Arnie and Clarice had been married for 43 years, and for 43 years they had criticized and insulted each other. On most days Clarice felt contempt for Arnie, a contempt based on years of profound disappointment in him. On most days Arnie hated Clarice. They lived together in a toxic atmosphere of anger, disappointment, hurt feelings, disgust, and dissatisfaction. Relatives, neighbors, and acquaintances were so put off by the couple's warfare that they sooner or later decided to avoid Arnie and Clarice. So as the years passed Arnie and Clarice were ever more alone with each other.

Things between them were not always grim. At first they were drawn to each other. She had a nice smile, beautiful hazel eyes, and a quick wit. He liked that about her the evening they met at a singles event. Also, she had smooth, flawless skin, which Arnie found very attractive, but perhaps he was most drawn to her precise pronunciation and quick intelligence. She liked it that he had a good income as a roofing salesman, striking blue eyes, and an attractive smile, she also liked that he appreciated her intelligence, knew a lot about current events, and shared her politics.

At the time they met, they were both past the age that most people married. She had always been choosy, and her penetrating sarcasm had driven all her previous suitors away. He had always been good at drawing women to him. He was, after all, a salesman and was good at selling himself. But he never had been good at keeping women interested in him. Some caught on quickly that he always wanted things his way. Women who got to know him better learned that he hoarded many things (including newspapers, magazines, junk mail, and roofing scraps). They also learned that he kept detailed records of his bowel movements. To top things off, he was quite rigid in his ways. And so women who at first found him interesting came to think that married life with him would be a nightmare.

Theirs was a small wedding at city hall. Her sister, who is now dead, was there. Two salesmen Arnie didn't know very well who worked where he worked were there. And that's all.

Clarice had wanted children. Arnie couldn't stand children and thought Clarice would be a horrible mother. They argued for years about whether to have children, and in the end they had one daughter, Betty. In her childhood Betty would at times keep the peace between her parents, partly because Clarice focused so much of her critical energy on Betty and partly because Betty learned to charm them out of bad moods. Betty also learned at an early age to distract her parents so they would briefly stop their warfare. But now Betty was an adult and in a marriage of her own. One thing she liked about the man she married was that his job required him to live hundreds of miles from Arnie and Clarice. Betty wanted great distance from the Arnie and Clarice battle zone. But there were the obligatory family visits, and this was the time for Arnie and Clarice's annual December visit to Betty and her husband.

Arnie and Clarice left early in the morning on their long drive. But it was later than they had talked about leaving, and so the trip began with Clarice scolding Arnie for taking so long to finish packing and to have a bowel movement. Arnie was at first silent, bearing the weight of Clarice's disgusted criticism. But after 10 minutes he fired back at her, not only about her not understanding that the time they agreed to leave was just an estimate, like the departure time of an airline flight, but also that had they left at the time they talked about leaving they would have been caught in stop-and-go rush hour traffic.

It was a windy, bitingly cold, but sunny day. Arnie was driving, and Clarice was telling him what was wrong with his driving. She was always irritated by his driving, and at the moment she was anxious about how fast he was going. He was angry with her, feeling defensive, and once again wondering why he had married her.

"Stay in the middle of your lane," Clarice said in her precise, chiding way of criticizing Arnie. "And you are too old to be driving this fast."

Arnie was watching the road ahead and also a giant semi-trailer truck coming up on their left. He scowled at what Clarice had just said and replied in a tight, disgusted, defensive voice, "This is the speed I have to go. I'm just two miles an hour over the speed limit and keeping up in my lane, the 'slow' lane."

The truck pulled even with them and slowed down, staying beside them. Then it started creeping over the dashed white line into Arnie and Clarice's lane. Arnie honked his horn, but the truck kept on coming. It was a foot into their lane, then two feet, and then it looked like they were going to be hit by the truck's enormous right front wheel. Arnie yanked the steering wheel to the right to get onto the shoulder. But the turn was more than their Dodge could handle at that speed. In an instant the car was rolling into the roadside ditch and up the embankment. It rolled and rolled, with the sound of glass shattering and metal bending and tearing until it hit a scrubby pine tree at the top of the highway embankment. And then there was silence.

Twenty minutes later Arnie and Clarice stood side by side at the top of the embankment, stunned and sad, watching a tow truck backing up to their car, watching a highway patrol officer directing traffic out of the right hand lane, and watching the ambulance attendants wheeling their lifeless bodies into the ambulance.

Clarice scowled at Arnie and said in an accusing, mocking voice that made clear that she knew more than he, "If you had been a careful driver, we would still be alive. If you had been ready to leave the house on time we would still be alive." Arnie seemed not to hear her. Perhaps he didn't hear her, or perhaps it was his passive aggressive way of getting back at her.

They continued to stand there, not bothered by or even feeling the icy wind, but dreadfully bothered to be together. Each was furious and full of contempt for the other. It had never taken long for them to get to the boiling point with each other, but this time was different. For both of them the fatal accident was the last straw.

Clarice walked away from Arnie a few steps, turned to him, and said, "I was an idiot to marry you. You were a loser, and I knew it. I no longer want to be with you."

Arnie's arms were crossed in front of him almost as though they were holding his body together. He turned angrily to Clarice and snarled, "You are so nasty, and you have no 'off switch.' All you've got to offer is nastiness, hatred, and criticism. I thought when I died that I would finally be free of you. But I was wrong. I'm dead and you're still with me, still criticizing me. Well, I've had it. I'm leaving." He turned and started walking in the direction of an abandoned farmhouse a hundred yards away.

As he turned, Clarice said with a tone of moral indignation in her voice, "Don't *you* leave *me*. I'm leaving you, you worthless old man. I may be dead, but there's still a life for me to live, and it's going to be infinitely better without you." She walked down the embankment toward the tow truck, thinking she would ride in it to someplace far from Arnie.

But oddly, as Arnie headed toward the abandoned farmhouse and Clarice headed for the tow truck and as the distance between them increased, something happened to both of them. Arnie felt himself starting to fall apart, disintegrate, and become less whole. He stopped, confused and scared. Since it was his first hour of being a spirit he wondered if this was just part of being a spirit, or if it had to do with the wind. He glanced toward Clarice, and he could see that she had stopped too. Clarice looked worried and confused. Something was happening to her. Her solidity was disappearing and she was becoming almost a mist without solid boundaries. She touched her belly with her hands, and neither the hands nor the belly felt solid. She glanced at Arnie and could see he was struggling too.

Each started walking back toward the other. As they came closer, they each started feeling more solid, more real, more substantial. When they were just a few feet apart, the sense of disintegrating, dissolving, becoming a mist, losing their outlines, and becoming less whole was gone. Close together they felt whole. Close together they felt that they were real and could last a long time.

"Damn," muttered Arnie.

"Unbelievable, simply unbelievable," said Clarice to herself.

Each understood what had happened to the other and what the other had felt. Each could see how wholeness had been restored for the other when they were again close.

Arnie felt trapped. He had hoped desperately to be free from Clarice, happily free from her criticism, anger, sarcasm, and nastiness, happily free from the tension of knowing that her verbal assaults would happen again and again. But he wanted to continue to exist, not to disappear into nothingness. He wanted to have a continuing consciousness and reality. He steeled himself, swallowed, calmed himself, and stared at the abandoned farmhouse. Then he shrugged his shoulders and said to Clarice in a tight, quiet voice, "I'm sorry. It's not going to work out for me to be away from you." He hated saying that. He felt defeated, not just for the moment but possibly forever.

Clarice nodded, and with a look of wonderment on her face said in an uncharacteristically gentle voice, "I am sorry too. I thought I had enough of you. But now it seems the only way I can go on is to be with you." And then she added, with a critical edge to her voice, "Try not to make a mess of this."

With a sour look on his face Arnie fired back, "Try not to make a mess of this? Can't you see we both have to make this work?"

He turned and started walking as fast as he could toward the farmhouse. Clarice stood staring at him. As he walked farther from Clarice his boundaries began to break up and he felt like he could not continue to be himself, that he was about to disappear. He realized that he had once again gone too far from her. He stopped and turned toward Clarice.

Clarice, what was left of her as she was breaking up, stared at him in worry about herself. He could tell that she was in trouble with him having walked away from her. They both were in trouble. He took a hesitant step toward her, and she started drifting toward him. She said, in a voice that sounded resigned and almost loving, "Yes, Arnie, we both have to make this work. It seems we are actually one, not two. We cannot seem to exist apart. That means all our inadequacies and mistakes are ours, both of ours. I can criticize you or I can criticize me, but either way we two are one and have to be one to exist."

Arnie waited for her to reach him, then turned and started walking slowly toward the abandoned farmhouse with her by his side. He was aware that Clarice was saying something too softly for him to hear, and he thought that it was probably critical of him. He sighed and thought, "It's going to be a hell of an after-life." And then, almost as if she could read his mind, she said in an affectionate and playful voice, "I was saying, 'Let's see if we can make it to the farmhouse without getting ourselves killed.'"

34.4 Possibilities for Love in the Story of "Arnie and Clarice"

We each can read a story in our own way. From the perspective of the literature on reader responses to texts (Tompkins, 1981), my having written "Arnie and Clarice" does not give me more claim to make sense of the couple's relationship than anyone else has. That said, I think something positive exists between Arnie and Clarice, and that something is so powerful that they begin to disappear if they move too far from each other. Despite their history of mutual nastiness they become less themselves and may disappear completely if they separate.

Can love be present in unhappy couples like Arnie and Clarice? Unhappy couples may stay together not because of love but because of economic dependency, because they do not believe in divorce, or for the sake of their children or parents. Perez-Testor et al. (2013) add to the list of reasons other than love for unhappy couples to stay together mutual control, ambivalent provocation, and inseparable dependence. Despite these and other possible factors pushing unhappy couples to stay together without loving one another, it is possible for unhappy couples like Arnie and Clarice to stay together because of love. A case can be made that love is some, much, or all of what holds some unhappy couples together and makes them whole and themselves. How can they love each other when the negatives are so strong? If they never use the word "love" when talking to each other and never seem aware of loving each other, can we legitimately say they love each other? Can people love each other when there is great negativity between them?

34.5 The Ups and Downs of Marital Relationships

Times of negativity in a couple's relationship do not preclude times of love. Many couples have their downs as well as their ups, their times of unhappiness with each other as well as their times of loving each other. For decades, professionals who provide therapy to couples have asserted that many couples struggle at times, perhaps even most or all the time, with personal differences, misunderstandings, communicative challenges, family of origin burdens, encounters in which harsh things are said, disappointments, frustrations, unmet needs, personal dispositions that can annoy one another, and difficulties that arise from being too close or too distant emotionally (e.g., Charny, 1969; Cuber & Harroff, 1965; Frost, 2013; Gottman & Gottman, 2017; Illouz, 2012, p. 220; Perez-Testor et al., 2013; Perkel, 2007; Thompson & Tuch, 2014; Usher, 2008). Normal couple relationships have their ups and downs (e.g., L'Abate, 2016; Thompson & Tuch, 2014; Vangelisti & Alexander, 2002). Thus, with most couples there may be times of feeling love and times where the feelings about the partner that are at the surface and in awareness may be anger, resentment, disgust, disappointment, and the like. Consequently, two partners may at times feel loving and act loving and at other times may not be aware of feeling love for one another and may not act loving. Conversely, couples in relationships that are at times quite negative may at other times feel and be aware of love for one another.

The story of Arnie and Clarice, however, makes it seem that for years they did not have times of expressing love for each other. Perhaps they could be understood as like long-term, apparently stable couples that Cuber and Haroff (1965) called "conflict habituated," which means they experience considerable ongoing tension, conflict, quarreling, nagging, and harshness with each other. One could marvel that a couple stays in a relationship like that, but Cuber and Haroff (1965, pp. 44–46) argued that many conflict habituated couples put some limits on their conflict so that it does not become physical or extremely brutal psychologically. Furthermore, Cuber and Haroff argued that the deep need to do psychological battle actually holds many conflict habituated couples together and is a basis for something that could be labeled affection and caring for one another. Thus, from a Cuber and Haroff perspective, if Arnie and Clarice can be seen as "conflict habituated" there would be affection and caring between them (even if such times were not included in the story about them).

34.6 Unhappy Relationships in the Perspective of the Language of Love

The literature on the language of love (e.g., Thompson & Tuch, 2014, pp. 262–266) makes clear that there are a number of different languages a love. So someone may experience feeling love, giving love, or receiving love in ways that an observer might not understand as love. Thus in the relationship of Arnie and Clarice, Clarice's critical comments may be a loving language. That Arnie did not seem to experience those comments in that way does not mean Clarice did not love him, but only that for him some other language of love was what mattered. In that regard, for them being together could be a shared language of love, and the ultimate in loving for them might be that neither abandons the other.

34.7 Unhappy Couples and Love of the Conflict

The love of some unhappy couples, and conceivably of Arnie and Clarice, may be fueled by their conflict. Their love may even flourish because of their ongoing battle and struggle together. It may be where they find life meaning and feel energized. It may be where they feel the most intimacy in terms of revealing feelings and thoughts, knowing the other's feelings and thoughts, and engaging with one another. It may be a struggle they miss when they are not together. And if one partner were to lose the other through separation, divorce, or death, the conflict may be sorely missed by the other in part because the conflict was a vehicle for loving the other and being loved by the other.

34.8 Ego Defenses that Mask Love

For Arnie and Clarice, saying, or even thinking, "I love you" may make them feel intolerably and frighteningly vulnerable to being hurt in a burst of negativity from the other. They may even feel safer in their negativity with each other than they would feel with the uncertainties and vulnerabilities of a fully and openly loving relationship (Pickering, 2008, pp. 115–116). One can see such vulnerability and the ego defensive silence about love that accompany it as coming at least in part out of irrational unconscious individual processes, quite possibly linked to childhood experiences. But they may be rational in the sense of reflecting a realistic assessment of the situation one is in and one's vulnerabilities. The interplay of ego defenses can be understood as relational in the sense that, as the psychoanalyst Carl Jung saw marriage, it is a problematic bilateral unconscious psychological container (Meyerowitz-Katz, 2018; Pickering, 2008, p. 89). In any case, mutual love may be present but hidden behind an ego-defensive wall.

34.9 Ambivalence

From a psychoanalytic perspective (e.g., Benedek, 1977; Usher, 2008), people may feel toward a partner an ambivalent mixture of love and such negative reactions as fear, insecurity, and hate. The energy that drives passion, attraction, love, and other strong feelings in the relationship may be fueled by the internal conflicts linked to the ambivalence. Related to this, love feelings might only be achieved as a result of considerable effort to achieve those feelings through a process of adapting to and overcoming the polarities that are inevitable with ambivalence and with partner differences (Benedek, 1977). How could the fictional Arnie and Clarice remain together despite so many negatives? They both might feel love for the other as a way to control the centripetal force of the negatives they feel. And the achievement of that love might be based on considerable effort to control or otherwise deal with the forces that push the partners apart. From this perspective, one can read the negative things the partners say to each other as not simply criticism but as signs of the struggle to overcome the negatives and continue to love the other.

34.10 Dialectics

One can say that there are dialectics to relationships (Migerode & Hooghe, 2012) such that negative and positive feelings fit together or are always in play, so that even when we see only positives or only negatives, only loving or only angry couple interactions, negative and positive feelings are in play together. In fact, both poles may be necessary for the relationship to continue. Each partner cannot simply feel and say loving things to the other, but must blend or balance the love with the negatives. For example, one cannot say "I love you" without there being somewhere inside of one and perhaps pushing one to say "I love you," a sense that the other in some way offends, frightens, disappoints, annoys, frustrates, or is in other ways not purely positive for one. Indeed, the dialectic polarities can be said to energize the relationship. That is, in a dialectic framework neither would fight the other so intensely if there were not so much love; neither would love the other so intensely if there were not strong negatives in play.

34.11 Negativity Does Not Mean Love Is Absent; Indifference Would

Some would suggest that having strong negative feelings about a spouse or partner means that there is still caring present, still hope for a good relationship, still a hunger to love and be loved. This line of thinking comes from the perspective that the opposite of love may not be intense negative feelings but indifference (Abbasi & Alghamdi, 2017; Pickering, 2008, p. 31; Thompson & Tuch, 2014, p. 166). That Arnie and Clarice are so intensely engaged with each other in negative ways may mean that they have deeply loving, caring feelings for each other or at least still have hope of such feelings in their relationship.

34.12 Cultural Contexts for Unvoiced and Out-of-Awareness Feelings of Love

Imagine that Arnie and Clarice come from a culture in which couples do not voice feelings of love and in which feelings of love are often out of a person's awareness, but under the surface there may be love. The cultural possibilities are diverse, since the concept of love has quite a range of lexical and more or less untranslatable meanings cross culturally (Lomas, 2018), but for purposes of illustration, here are two examples that I think make plausible that in some cultures a couple with as much negativity in their relationship as Arnie and Clarice might love each other:

1. In the culture of my childhood, one of Eastern European Jews who had immigrated to the United States, there were quite a few couples who seemed to me to be more or less like Arnie and Clarice, seemingly emotionally distant from each other and often more or less at war. Those couples puzzled me and still do, which is one reason I wrote the Arnie and Clarice story. I think a piece of what was going on with some couples was that what seemed to me to be warfare was to them rather playful and affectionate, that the couples were not as emotionally distant or as hostile to each other as I thought. Another piece of what was going on was that many of the elders in my life would avoid saying loving things to those they loved because of fear that saying a loving thing would bring death to the loved one. The death might come because the loving thing made someone, a passer-by for example, jealous and lead the person to put the evil eye (a conscious or unconscious and possibly fatal curse) on the loved one. Or the death might come from the loving statement attracting the attention of the angel of death who would then take the life of the loved one. So in my growing up years when my grandmother wanted to use a term of endearment with me she would call me (in Yiddish) "you bastard." The insult was said in a loving way and by expressing love in this way she was, in her thinking, protecting me from the danger of having something unambiguously loving said to me. I believe that such beliefs drove avoidance of public affection by married couples and made some couples seem less loving in public than they were in private.
2. A powerful lesson for me about culture and love was when I carried out a pilot research project on Chinese television soap operas with a Chinese doctoral student, Xiaohui (Sophie) Li. In married couples in the soap operas a common pattern was for the woman to nag and criticize her husband. I naively assumed that the nagging and criticism were not loving, but Xiaohui Li assured me that in the Chinese cultural context (see Chap. 50) nagging and criticism aimed at pushing a husband to better himself were expressions of real love by a wife for her husband. In Chinese married couples the language of loving and caring was often, at least when wives talked to husbands, one of criticism and of nagging the partner to do better.

These two cultural examples suggest that love can be present in a couple relationship that on the surface seems unloving. Indeed there is potentially a cultural challenge in any enduring couple relationship in which what seems to go on is quite negative, that the couple may experience their relationship as loving and not negative, but some observers may have an ethnocentric or culturally limited view of what constitutes a loving relationship. That suggests that rather than the social science observer defining what is love in a couple relationship it makes sense for what a couple does in an ongoing relationship to be seen as defining love (Migerode & Hooghe, 2012).

34.13 Discussion

This chapter uses a fictional short story as a vehicle to make the case that some chronically unhappy couples love each other, although they may not speak of love and might not be aware of their love feelings. The conceptual routes to recognizing the possibilities of love being present in unhappy couples have included framing the unhappiness in the literatures on the ups and downs of ordinary couple relationships, on conflict-habituated couples, and on the language of love. The conceptual routes to recognizing the possibilities for love in unhappy couples also included considerations about the positives for couples in their mutual conflict, about the possibilities that ego defenses mask love, about the inevitability and dynamics of ambivalence in couple relationships, and about dialectic processes in couples. Further, the chapter explores the idea that strongly negative feelings may (in contrast to indifference) mean that there are also positive feelings in play. In addition, the chapter makes the case that there are cultures in which what seems quite negative in couple relationships may, in those cultures, be understood as loving and positive.

This chapter is a thought experiment, not a report of research. That means that this chapter succeeds to the extent that it legitimates the possibility that a couple who seems to be quite unhappy may love one another. To accept that perspective, one may have to be open to the possibilities that there are unconscious processes at work, that love may be hidden from observers, that there are diverse languages of love, and that cultures may differ radically in what is considered loving in couple relationships.

The major implications of this chapter are that unhappy couples may also be loving, which helps to understand why some unhappy couples stay together, the potential for some unhappy couples to persist in a demanding course of couple counseling to get to a more openly loving place, and what the losses might be for a person in an unhappy marriage whose spouse dies. The chapter implies that there are real limits to understanding couple relationships if we overlook the possibilities for love in relationships with considerable negativity, in relationships in which love is not voiced, and in relationships in which partners seem not to be aware that they feel love for one another. Furthermore, the chapter implies that using a social psychological approach rooted in behavioral assessment and Euro-American culture to understand and assess love may misunderstand or overlook strong expressions of love in a number of cultures. A related implication is that there is much to be learned about love by studying the variability of expressions, forms, and meanings of love in diverse cultures.

This chapter suggests several next steps in researching love. One would be to develop methods for assessing unvoiced and unconscious love, perhaps drawing on psychoanalytic approaches for getting at what people cannot or will not say and that they seem not to be conscious of. Another next step is to study love in diverse cultures, starting in each culture not with frameworks or methods built in Euro-American social psychological research, but learning from people in each culture how they might meaningfully understand and evaluate what love is. A thought piece based on a short story with elements counter to what may be consensual reality is only a heuristic for thinking about love in unhappy couples, and that suggests that another line of research that might be worthwhile pursuing is to develop case studies of unhappy couples, drawing on what the partners in those couples have to say and on what can be observed. Of course, if there are elements of love they cannot voice or are not conscious of, the case studies will have their limits, but we may be surprised at what we learn from what people can put to words.

34.14 Conclusion and Recommendations in Theory and Practice

This essay suggests that there can be love in terms of attachment and caring in some unhappy couples.

We who study love are inevitably embedded in academic cultures and larger cultures (in the anthropological sense) that give us vocabularies, standards for evidence, literatures and academic theories to draw on, intellectual goals, and matters to focus on as we try to make sense of the world. Our cultures are limiting in the sense that they make it challenging to appreciate the ways that other academic and anthropological cultures make sense of what falls at least to some extent in the domain we call love. Although we live in multicultural societies and although scholars in many different academic cultures address love, I fear that the realities of how we live in our own cultures and the realities of how academic cultures operate mean that much of the work done on love is monocultural. Thus knowledge is advanced in ways that ignore the realities of other cultures (academic and anthropological) that could illuminate our own cultural realities in possibly intriguing and insightful ways. I have my cultural limitations, but I have tried with this chapter to bring some of the psychoanalytic culture realities about love (the possibilities for unconscious and unvoiced love) into relationship with the social psychological realities. I have also tried to bring the realities of Chinese culture and the Jewish culture of my childhood into confrontation with social psychological realities, with the idea that negative interactions, such as those in the fictional unhappy couple, may not mean that two partners do not love each other. In fact, there may be considerable love underlying, fed by, or represented by their negativity. Unhappy couples may have much to teach us about researching love and about carrying out clinical work with couples if we can find cultural standpoints that allow us to be open to and understanding of the love that may be present.

References

Abbasi, I. S., & Alghamdi, N. G. (2017). Polarized couples in therapy: Recognizing indifference as the opposite of love. *Journal of Sex and Marital Therapy, 43*, 40–48.

Benedek, T. (1977). Ambivalence, passion, and love. *Journal of the American Psychoanalytic Association, 25*(1), 53–79.
Berscheid, E. (2006). Searching for the meaning of "love". In R. J. Sternberg & K. Weis (Eds.), *The new psychology of love* (pp. 171–183). New Haven, CT: Yale University Press.
Berscheid, E. (2010). Love in the fourth dimension. *Annual Review of Psychology, 61*, 1–5.
Charny, I. W. (1969). Marital love and hate. *Family Process, 8*, 1–24.
Cuber, J., & Harroff, P. B. (1965). *The significant Americans*. New York: Appleton-Century.
Feeney, J. A. (2009). When love hurts: Understanding hurtful events in couple relationships. In A. L. Vangelisti (Ed.), *Feeling hurt in close relationships* (pp. 313–335). New York: Cambridge University Press.
Fehr, B. (2013). The social psychology of love. In J. Simpson & L. Campbell (Eds.), *The Oxford handbook of close relationships* (pp. 201–233). New York: Oxford University Press.
Frost, V. K. (2013). Tensions of marriage: Love, cooperation, capitulation, annihilation. *Clinical Social Work Journal, 41*, 100–111.
Gottman, J. M. (1993). The roles of conflict engagement, escalation, and avoidance in marital interaction: A longitudinal view of five types of couples. *Journal of Consulting and Clinical Psychology, 61*, 6–15.
Gottman, J., & Gottman, J. (2017). The natural principle of love. *Journal of Family Theory & Review, 9*, 7–26.
Illouz, E. (2012). *Why love hurts: A sociological explanation*. Cambridge: Polity.
L'Abate, L. (2016). Intimacy and sharing hurts. In G. Weeks, S. T. Fife, & C. M. Peterson (Eds.), *Techniques for the couple therapist: Essential intervention from the experts* (pp. 151–154). New York: Routledge.
Lomas, T. (2018). The flavours of love: A cross-cultural lexical analysis. *Journal for the Theory of Social Behaviour, 48*, 134–152.
Meyerowitz-Katz, J. (2018). Gathering fragments: Steps in the evolution of a creative coupling. In P. Jools, J. Berg, & N. Byrne (Eds.), *Working with developmental anxieties in couple and family psychotherapy: The family within* (pp. 112–129). New York: Routledge.
Migerode, L., & Hooghe, A. (2012). 'I love you'. How to understand love in couple therapy? Exploring love in context. *Journal of Family Therapy, 34*, 371–386.
Perez-Testor, C., Davins, M., Aramburu, I., Aznar-Martinez, B., & Salamero, M. (2013). Hatred in couples: Neither with you nor without you [French]. *Le Divan Familial, 31*, 153–163.
Perkel, A. (2007). Fusion, diffusion, de-fusion, confusion: Exploring the anatomy of the couple psyche. In M. Ludlam & V. Nyberg (Eds.), *Couple attachments: Theoretical and clinical studies* (pp. 43–62). London: Karnac.
Pickering, J. (2008). *Being in love: Therapeutic pathways through psychological obstacles to love*. New York: Routledge.
Shaver, P. R., & Mikulincer, M. (2006). Attachment theory, individual psychodynamics, and relationship functioning. In A. L. Vangelisti & D. Perlman (Eds.), *The Cambridge handbook of personal relationships* (pp. 251–271). New York: Cambridge University Press.
Thompson, J. M., & Tuch, R. (2014). *The stories we tell ourselves: Mentalizing tales of dating and marriage*. New York: Routledge.
Tompkins, J. P. (1981). *Reader-response criticism: From formalism to post-structuralism*. Baltimore, MD: Johns Hopkins University Press.
Usher, S. F. (2008). *What is this thing called love? A guide to psychoanalytic psychotherapy with couples*. New York: Routledge.
Vangelisti, A. L., & Alexander, A. L. (2002). Coping with disappointment in marriage: When partners' standards are unmet. In P. Noller & J. A. Feeney (Eds.), *Understanding marriage: Developments in the study of couple interaction* (pp. 201–227). New York: Cambridge University Press.
Vincent, C. (2007). Touching the void: The impact of psychiatric illness on the couple. In M. Ludlam & V. Nyberg (Eds.), *Couple attachments: Theoretical and clinical studies* (pp. 133–144). London: Karnac.
Walsh, A. (2016). *Love: The biology behind the heart*. New Brunswick, NJ: Transaction.

Paul C. Rosenblatt (PhD) has a Ph.d. in Psychology and is Professor Emeritus of Family Social Science at the University of Minnesota. He has published 14 books and roughly 200 journal articles and chapters in edited books. Much of his work has focused on the social psychology, anthropology, and sociology of people's closest relationships and what the personal and relationship impacts are of the ending of a close relationship. His research has included studies of ethnic cultures within the United States, ethnographic work in Mexico and Indonesia, and collaborative writings focused on Korean culture, Zulu culture, and Chinese culture. Rosenblatt carried out pioneering research in the 1960s and 1970s on love in cross-cultural perspective and has written extensively about couples in which the partners differ in cultural background and about family relationships and relationship losses across cultures.

Chapter 35
"A Silver Duck in the Dish Washing Water" or Love and Crime in the Context of Positive Victimology

Claude-Hélène Mayer

> *All journeys have secret destinations Of which the traveller is unaware.*
> Martin Buber

Abstract Crime in the context of love has always drawn attention in public and has recently become a growing area of research. This chapter aims at providing an insight on the complex topic of love and crime research, focusing particularly on hate and love crimes, love, relationship crime in gendered and cultural contexts, and love and the desistance from crime.

In this chapter it is argued that a positive criminology and positive victimology perspective in the context of love and crime can help to overcome criminal acts from the point of view of the offender, as well as that of the victim. Positive criminology and victimology perspectives can support a positive, loving and thereby health-related (salutogenic) view of the criminal act. Particularly positive victimology can support the victim through specific interventions to overcome trauma and re-establish self-esteem and self-assurance beyond the experienced crime.

The chapter provides insights into 12-step and 16-step programmes as a potential positive psychology and positive victimology intervention tool for crime victims. It presents a case example of a female victim of criminal acts within the context of a divorce and her process of rehabilitation and de-traumatisation through the 16-step programme. The case example is based on the victim's private diary notes, talks, interviews and messages. Conclusions and recommendations are provided.

C.-H. Mayer (✉)
Department of Industrial Psychology and People Management, University of Johannesburg, Johannesburg, South Africa

Institut für therapeutische Kommunikation und Sprachgebrauch, Europa Universität Viadrina, Frankfurt (Oder), Germany
e-mail: claudemayer@gmx.net

Keywords Love · Crime · Positive criminology · Positive victimization · Hate and love crime · Offending - Relationship crime · Love and desistance · 16-step process

35.1 Introduction: Love and Crime in Positive Criminology and Victimology

The topic of love and crime fills huge quantities of literature, short stories, film material, as well as documentaries, news and musicals. The musical "Chicago", for example, tells the story of several female offenders from different socio-economic, societal, cultural and relationship backgrounds who committed a crime in the context of love. In the musical, these female offenders who have been arrested for their criminal acts, are fighting to escape their sentence and the prison by showing their innocence or creating a situation which will absolve them of the crime.

Crime in the context of love—also termed "crime d'amour" (Courneau, 2010)—and the interrelationship of these two concepts has been researched scientifically from different cultural and disciplinary perspectives, with varying aims, methodologies and theories (see Gardell, 2015; Levy & Levy, 2017; McCarthy & Casey, 2008; Naffine, 2019; Rayburn & Wright, 2018; Walsh & Beyer, 1987). Varese (2017) emphasised that love is an important aspect of organised crime structures, and that love relationships often contribute to crime in mafia organisations, besides being recognised in hate and love crime contexts (Balboni & McDevitt, 2001; Fairfax, 2002; Levy & Levy, 2017) or relationship crime (Jones, 2008; Walsh & Beyer, 1987). Love clearly plays an important role in various crime contexts and criminal acts.

Criminal acts are related to automatic information processing in cognitive theory (Beck, 1995). This means that criminal acts take place founded in cognitive schemata which lead to habitual behaviour which is scarcely reflected on or critically (re-)evaluated. Based on this assumption, the cognitive schemata relate to positive and negative thinking patterns and might lead, according to Beck (1995), to thinking errors, irrational thinking and categorisations without nuances. Habitual negative interpretations can promote misinterpretations of situations, negative feelings, and destructive behaviour which might lead to criminality and criminal acts, and even mental illness (Beck, 1995).

Developing a value system that contradicts criminal acts and which is incompatible with criminal behaviour is important in rehabilitation of offenders (Bergström, 2012). Rehabilitation is also strongly connected to salutogenic social support (Chen, 2006). This means that healthy relationships and social contacts can contribute to decreased criminal acts and desistance from crime. At the same time, positive mental health and healthy relationships are created during daily life activities, such as work, play, learning and love (WHO, 1986). Bauer et al. (2019) have called for new research paradigms for salutogenic research, moving beyond the traditional contexts of health research. In this train of thought, Bergström (2012) argues that it is not enough to logically process criminality and criminal acts, but that it is also of importance that the change towards healthy and salutogenic behaviour is connected to salutogenic rituals, symbols, and new forms of actions, as well as to the ability to share the new experiences. At the same time, negative emotions can be transformed into positive emotions (Bergström, 2012).

By using this kind of positive criminality perspective (Ronel & Elisha, 2011; Ronel & Segev, 2015), individuals can develop personally and socially and transform their self-image, as well as their emotions towards the positive (Johnson, 2003), thereby creating change.

Positive criminology, as a new conceptual perspective of criminology, integrates several theoretical models and approaches and focuses on the positive aspects in life which help to distance individuals and groups from deviance and crime. The focus on the positive can be reached through formal or informal interventions and therapeutic programmes, but also through auto-didactical learning and self-help interventions (Ronel & Elisha, 2011). In the context of crime and crime intervention, Ronel & Elisha, (2011) propose that these positive aspects can be exposure to goodness, social acceptance, reintegrative shaming, or even positive personal traits or concepts, such as coherence or resilience.

Positive criminology usually focuses on the positive aspects of offenders and perpetrators. It is argued here that the positive criminology perspective should also be applied to crime victims, and used for victims to debrief from crime experiences or trauma treatment. Very little research has been conducted with regard to victims' treatment in police investigations, trial cross-examinations and even the challenges of dealing with victimisation within criminal justice systems (Jaishankar & Ronel, 2013; Moore, 2013). However, a new term has developed in this context: "positive victimology" (Dancig-Rosenberg & Pugach, 2015; Ronel & Toren, 2012), which uses the concepts of positive criminology, focusing on the positive aspects and strengths of the victims, their surroundings and their capabilities to minimise the impact of the damage experienced during criminal acts. Further, positive victimology is about empowering victims themselves and encourages social growth by transforming the negative experiences.

It is argued here that love, as a deep-rooted emotion which creates connection and longing between self and others (Mayer, 2018b), can support positive victimology by taking on a positive, loving perspective on self and others. By doing so, individuals contribute to creating health and well-being (Mayer, 2018a), even in a challenging situation. Karandashev (2015) (see Chap. 4 in this book) describes love as a connection of the soul. Love can be viewed as a strong resource in meaning-making, a spiritual act or connection (Grün, Hüther & Hosang, 2017) and a form of self-transcendent and self-loving emotion (Neff & Knox, 2017). Love is further viewed as not being of natural origin, but rather resulting from commitment and practice, constant renewal and also creativity (Pozsar, Dumitrescu, Piticas, & Constantinescu, 2018).

This is not only important and true for offenders, but also for victims of crime and criminal acts (Hill, 2009). Hill (2009) has pointed out that victims of crime often face enduring challenges which they have to cope with. Coping of crime victims can be supported through "loving" relationships (Hill, 2009). Fredrickson, Tugade, Waugh, and Larkin (2003) support this idea by emphasising that positive emotions, such as love, gratitude or interest can help people to cope with difficult life situations.

This chapter purposefully focuses on crime and criminal acts in the context of love—thereby taking selected perspectives into account—as well as love in the context of coping with crime and victimisation. A case study provides insights into working through a 16-step programme with a victim who experienced criminal acts during a divorce process.

35.2 Hate Crime and Love Crime

Balboni and McDevitt (2001) asked almost 20 years ago about the interconnectedness of hate crime and love crime. The questions seem to be even more relevant today, although it is probable that many hate crimes are not reported and even fewer are punished (Lantz, Gladfelter & Ruback, 2019).

Hate crime, according to the FBI (2019), is: "a traditional offense like murder, arson, or vandalism with an added element of bias". It is further a "criminal offense against a person or property motivated in whole or in part by an offender's bias against a race, religion, disability, sexual orientation, ethnicity, gender, or gender identity." Hate crime is therefore by definition interlinked with a discriminative and prejudiced bias (Lantz et al., 2019). Research on hate crime has different foci, such as politically motivated crime in the context of ultra-nationalist crime and violence (see for example, Gardell, 2015), but also crime against lesbian, gay, transsexual and bisexual individuals (LGTB) (Levy & Levy, 2017). In a study on hate crime, Levy & Levy (2017) point out that public policies on gay and lesbian rights affect the incidence of hate crimes based on sexual orientation. They further argue that legal inequalities influence and even increase hate crimes through their bias in discrimination and violence. Walters and Hoyle (2017) highlight the fact that hate crime usually causes great harm to members of minority groups and threatens multicultural societies. The punishments for hate crime offenders have accordingly been strengthened in the past. However, dealing with hate crime is not a simple matter, in that it is described as arising from feelings of hating "the other", but also from feelings of loving "the own" group (Gerstenfeld, 2017). Schweppe and Walters (2017) affirm that hate crime has become a globalised and internationalised issue which needs to be addressed on a global and international level in terms of legislation, different governmental and state actions, protective measures and policing. Further, responses to hate crime at the level of individuals, minority–majority groups, communities and nations, as well as in the digitalised worlds need to be newly recognised and addressed. In his article on "What's love got to do with it?" Gardell (2015) addresses the discussed interrelationship of hate and love with regard to ultra-nationalist crime and violence. The author points out that perpetrators of hate crime are often viewed as angry white men. This group of individuals declare that they "act out of love and not out of crime" (Gardell, 2015). Gerstenfeld (2017) states that hate crime perpetrators often claim not to hate individuals of other groups, but instead to love their own group, therefore committing the crime on those grounds. Hate crime is often reinforced by struggles of intra- and interpersonal hate and love, and by feelings of displacement with specifically defined identity borders, which need to be taken into consideration when aiming to understand a crime.

35.3 Love, Relationship and Crime in Gendered and Cultural Contexts

Violence and crime need always to be observed, understood and addressed by including the influences of the context, such as the social structures, the socio-economic circumstances, the cultural values and norms, the history, as well as the gender roles and relationship components. Several authors already highlighted in the 1970s that crime and violence against women is anchored in socio-economic structures, gendered power relations, and the roles ascribed with interpretations of inferiority (see for example, Walker, 2017).

Perspectives on love and crime are strongly gendered and women in the context of love are often misrepresented as sexual objects, victims, or holders of inferior feminine positions (Lemish, 2004; Nuytiens & Christiaens, 2015). In the crime context, toxic forms of love, which usually refer to manipulation, power struggles, relationship problems and abusive relationships are at play when love and crime or criminal acts are observed (Jenkins, 2017). In this case, toxic (love) relationships might lead to "crimes of passion" (Jenkins, 2017), criminal exploitation, love addiction and dependency in relationships—which might be used in criminalisation or criminal acts. Often, the question which arises with regard to crimes of passion, is whether the offender is "bad or mad" (Colquhoun, 2014). It has been observed previously that often women are judged as "mad" while male offenders are judged as "bad" (Colquhoun, 2014). Jones (2008) comments that the relationship between male and female offenders plays an important role, highlighting that most of the female offenders in their study were manipulated and physically abused to ensure their compliance with criminal activities. In their research titled "From 'Crime of Passion' to 'Love does not kill'", Herbst-Debby and Gez (2012) explore the murder of 122 women in the 1990s in Israel, when the Israeli public debate increased the critical feminist discourse on violence against women publicly. Several of those murdered were women wanting to leave their partners, and women who had left partners or were in a divorce process (Herbst-Debby & Gez, 2012) to escape from toxic love and/or abusive and manipulative relationships.

Richie (2018) describes the gender entrapment of battered black women who—in comparison to white women—enter their intimate relationships with lower self-esteem and fewer expectations. African American women in particular, were increasingly vulnerable to violence from intimate partners and this impacted strongly on their behaviour patterns which were dominated by their own experience of abuse

(Richie, 2018). Through the gender and relationship entrapment, African American women join illegal activities and commit crime or criminal acts. Richie (2018) describes different paths into crime taken by these women: death of one of their children, violent crimes to men other than the batterer, arrest for crimes in the context of illegal sex work, property damage and assault of their batterers during abusive episodes.

Martsolf et al. (2012) focus in their article on patterns of dating violence across adolescence and have identified several different types of dating violence in romantic love relationships. McCarthy and Casey (2008) highlight research findings that adolescent dating often correlates with depression, interpersonal violence, conflict with parents, school failure, as well as association with delinquents, substance use and offending behaviour. However, the two researchers also find that romantic love relationships in adolescents may encourage young adults to refrain from crime and criminal activities, while adolescent sexual activity may increase the frequency of offending. When sex is interlinked with a romantic love relationship, it is less stressful and less consequential for crime (McCarthy & Casey, 2008).

Naffine (2019) shows how "erotic love" as a concept in Western societies is reflected in the English common law and has been reflected in the English and Australian rape law. Here, love between a heterosexual couple is defined by gender roles which are reflected in the law, mirroring the importance of man's autonomy and potency and women's entanglement in love and commitment (Naffine, 2019). This shows that not only concepts of crime and love are gendered, but also the reactions of the law towards crime in the context of love.

A relatively new field of crime is love and cybercrime (Rege, 2009; Whitty, 2018). Research has shown that internationally, love fraud and love scams are on the rise (Whitty, 2018). Here, individuals (often middle-aged women), become victims of scams in which potential partners whom they meet through online dating platforms promise love, romantic relationships and the end of loneliness (Rege, 2009). The potential partner then requests financial assistance to relocate to the person, receive the money and disappear (Rege, 2009). This kind of romance or "sweetheart scam" has become a serious threat when focusing on the number of victims worldwide (Whitty, 2015) and is based on the concept of faked online profiles through which the scammers create love relationships with their victims, fake their love by "grooming" their victims and thereby "creating a hyperpersonal relationship" until they request financial aid from the victim and consequently end the relationship, taking the money (Whitty, 2018).

Love and relationship crimes have many facets and are in the process of being researched further.

35.4 Love and Its Impact on Desistance from Crime

Different studies deal with the question of what makes people desist from crime (McCarthy & Casey, 2008; Rayburn & Wright, 2018; Walsh & Beyer, 1987; Wyse, Harding & Morenoff, 2014). Focusing on crime, Walsh and Beyer (1987) have found that love deprivation is prevalent in adolescent delinquents, and assume that both love and deprivation of love impacts strongly on delinquency. Rayburn and Wright (2018) present findings concerning desistance from substance use and homelessness which show that stable, successful romantic relationships incline formerly homeless substance abusers to desist from crime, homelessness and substance abuse. Their study shows that successful romantic love relationships are an important motivator for desistance (Rayburn & Wright, 2018). McCarthy and Casey (2008) also highlight that adolescent romantic relationships may fill the void of weakening parental guidance and bonds in adolescence and the onset of adult attachments. They further suggest that positive romantic relationships may discourage involvement in crime, while sexual activity without the frame of a romantic relationship might lead to an increase in offending from experienced relationship-related stress (McCarthy & Casey, 2008). Wyse, Harding and Morenoff (2014) study the influence of fluid romantic relationships on desistance processes and observe that even romantic relationships (and not only marriage) can hinder or foster criminality and desistance. The authors state that for male offenders and substance users, marriage and romantic relationships can impact positively on crime desistance, particularly when they are in processes of informal social control. The role of romantic relationships in female desistance is less researched: romantic relationships can increase criminal acts in women ex-offenders, decrease it or have no impact at all.

Leverentz (2006) has pointed out that for female ex-offenders, romantic relationships can become a source of support or hindrance. Often, female ex-offenders get into romantic relationships with drug users and/or ex-offenders and these relationships can be constructive or destructive for female ex-offenders depending on the context.

From their research in various cities in Greece, Russia and Ukraine, authors Antonaccio, Tittle, Botchkovar and Kranidiotis (2010) conclude that criminal and deviant behaviour correlates with age and deviant peer association. Their study does not support research highlighting that gender and marital status correlate with criminal and deviant behaviour in specific cultural contexts nor does it emphasise that the research on crime, love relationships and deviances needs to become far more culture-sensitive. Their research shows that religiosity and crime and crime deviance correlate, meaning that a high degree of religiosity is associated with a low risk of crime. However, this statement also needs to be reflected sensitively with regard to culture and context of research according to Antonaccio et al. (2010).

Love can play a role in desisting from crime with impact on the offender, as well as the victim. In the following, a positive victimology perspective is taken into account to transform criminal act experiences into experiences of growth and love.

35.5 Positive Victimology in the Context of Love Crime

Victims of crime have often been neglected in crime-related studies and research; however, during the past years the literature on victimology has been growing (Freeman & Turvey, 2012). Instead of focusing on victimology in the course of investigation, or in the victim's history or victim-related interpretation of crime, this chapter explores a salutogenetic (health-related) and love-based approach to dealing with the experience of crime from a positive victimology perspective. For that reason, the 12-step and 16-step programmes of transformation are briefly introduced. The 16-step programme, as an expansion of the 12-step programme of transformation, is used in a case study of a female crime victim who transforms and regains strengths through a reconnection with spirituality and love, to overcome traumatisation and victimhood.

35.6 The 12-Step Process of Transformation

According to Glaser (2008), the 12-step programme is well anchored in the Jewish tradition; however, because it is a group therapy process, it is difficult to evaluate. It has been criticised since it has not undergone clinical testing, is seldom used in single therapy settings and is embedded in a specifically religious frame (Glaser, 2008) and is seen as most appropriate for white male Americans; however, Hillhouse and Fiorentine (2001) have shown the 12-step-process to be equally as effective for women and ethnic minorities. Lee, Pagano, Johnson, & Post (2016) describe the 12-step process in terms of two concepts: love and service as spiritual base, and virtues which might help certain perpetrators of crime to change for the better. Spirituality is viewed as a force that supports mental health and well-being, openness to (divine) love and service to others and results in character development which is not compatible with criminality and delinquency (Lee, Veta, Johnson, & Pagano, 2014). Love enhances the impact of service and affects leadership, but it is most effective when spirituality and altruism (service to others) are combined (Lee et al., 2016).

Research has shown that the 12-step-programme, originally introduced by Bill Wilson, a co-founder of Alcoholics Anonymous, impacts positively on sense of coherence and positive affect, and reduces criminal thinking (Lindblom, Eriksson, & Hiltunen, 2017). The belief in a higher power and meaning in life can contribute to coping with difficult life situations, suffering and the experience of crime and violence (Chen, 2010). The 12-step programme has previously been developed and used in the context of crime science and rehabilitation, for example, in the work with offenders and victims of suffering of drug abuse (Chen, 2010; Chen & Gueta, 2015). It is argued here that this 12-step programme could also support offenders and victims of crime in the context of love. The 12-step programme is a spiritually-based programme which focuses on meaning-making and the recreation of meaning in the context of transformation and self-transcendence on physical, emotional and spiritual levels (Chen & Gueta, 2015). It has been previously highlighted (see Mayer, 2020) that meaning is created through the experience of love and the experience of loving relationships which, at the same time, are viewed as spiritual experiences. Having said that, this article supports the idea that attributing positive meaning to negative experiences and emotions initiates self-transcendence (Frankl, 1965, 1988). Additionally, spirituality has long been overlooked in criminology and should be seen as a source of social response, crime desistence, rehabilitation and prevention (Ronel & Yair, 2017) and provides access to positive emotions and meaning in life (Chen & Gueta, 2015), such as love, and through love, to transformation and self-transcendence. The programme could therefore also be viewed as a valuable contribution for offenders and victims who are moving towards positive meaning-making in the context of love and crime. Summarising, the programme relates to self-change at three levels of integration (Chen & Gueta, 2015), namely decrease in negative feelings towards the self and increase in sense of coherence, social acceptance and inclusion, and spiritual-increase in meaning of life and decrease in self-centredness. The 12 steps are as follows (Chen, 2010):

1. Spiritual principles of honesty, acceptance, surrender and humility and admission of addiction and sense of helplessness
2. Spiritual principles of openness and hope towards a higher power (religious or belief system based on higher power)
3. Conscious decision to choose either spiritual recovery or a descent into disease
4. Examining moral inventory including seeing the damage caused by addiction
5. Sharing insights gained on the wrong-doings (towards the self, others and higher power)
6./7. Advice on further spiritual growth, also recognising stumbling blocks to spiritual progress (often relates to higher power)
8./9. Restitution steps involving willingness to name and make amends to those harmed previously
10./11. Maintenance steps: focus on present, emphasise on continuous spiritual practice, connection to higher power and continued self-development and transcendence through prayer and/or meditation
12. Spiritual awakening after implementing the previous steps and sharing the message with others

This 12-step process has been expanded by Kasl into a 16-step process which is particularly used for female offenders (Kasl, 1992, 2012). Both processes are originated in the US. It is proposed in this chapter that the process can also be useful for victims of crime, to support a salutogenic and positive process of self-recovery and debriefing from crime. The 16-step programme also involves a more transcultural and trans-religious approach to transformation than the 12-step programme, as explained below.

35.7 Kasl's Extended Programme: 16-Step Process for Female Offenders

Kasl (1992, in an interview with White, 2013, p. 4) points out that particularly (battered) women who have been in abusive relationships and need to learn to trust themselves again, are in focus in the 16-step process. One of the steps Kasl (1992) has added to the 12-step programme: "I know my reality. I know what I see. I know what I feel. I know what I know." Thereby these women often have to overcome co-dependency. Kasl calls co-dependency an "internalised oppression syndrome" (1992, in White, 2013, p. 8). The author offers the following two options for Step 1 from the 12-step-programme (Kasl, 2012; White, 2013: 1a) "We affirm we have the power to take charge of our lives and stop being dependent on substances or other people for our self-esteem and security", or alternatively 1b) "I am an addict and I am powerless over the addiction".

It is argued here that this programme can be used not only to work with offenders, but also with victims. This assumption is empowered by Kasl's 16-step-programme for discovery and empowerment, especially of women in co-dependency and under internalised oppression. Kasl (in an interview with White, 2013), points out that women and minority groups might need to use a different approach in her programme. First, she criticises regarding the 12-step process that particularly women seem to struggle with surrendering to a new "male power", such as the image of "God" as used in the 12-step process. Further, Kasl specifies that those working through the programme need not only to acknowledge who they have harmed, but also who they have been harmed by. The author has provided another step which says: "We release guilt and shame and anything that keeps us from loving ourselves or others" in order to neutralise the sense of shame, blame and guilt which oppressed people tend to assume quite easily (Kasl, in an interview with White, 2013). Kasl (1990) also highlights the importance of clearing out negative energy by making amends and sharing grievances in a respectful way.

The 16-step-programme is based on love, empowerment, humanness—placing it into "a social context of hierarchy, patriarchy, and understanding internalized oppression" (White, 2013, p. 7), distinguishing it from other programmes and expanding the 12-step programme, by connecting to power and joy instead of pain. The progress of the 16-step process is "action-oriented, encourag[ing] people to explore their thinking patterns, learn self-care, take control of their lives, set goals, expand their creativity and develop supportive relationships" (White, 2013, p. 5). From her earlier writings, Kasl (1999) draws on her teachings of love and spirituality, viewing these as a basis for becoming more fully human, empowered and prepared for intimate relationships without co-dependence, and anchored in loving kindness.

35.8 A Case Study: The 16-Step Programme of a Female Victim in the Context of Love and Crime

This case example shows how a female victim of the abusive and criminal acts of her husband transformed the experience of suffering, destructive behaviour, and pain during a process of separation and divorce through meaning-making, spirituality and love guided by the 16-step programme.

35.8.1 The Context

M, a German middle-aged woman, was married for 16 years when she decided to separate from her husband and divorce him. The process of separating, together with her three children (aged 16, 14 and 8 at the time), took several years. Before the separation she had tried to move out twice, always returning to her husband, hoping to revive the relationship.

The couple had moved to the US shortly after their marriage, where they both worked as expatriates in a German multinational company. When she fell pregnant for the first time, she quit her professional career and became a housewife. He focused on his career, changed jobs after a few years and became a major role-player in a new industry sector which had been unfamiliar to him. With the new professional pressure, he became a depressive, started drinking and in turn became violent and aggressive at home.

After several years of conflict within her marriage, M moved out during a night of violence, fleeing with the children to her best friend, where she stayed with the children for the first weeks of separation. The husband threatened her and the children with buying a gun and shooting them if they did not return. He started to denounce her with the relevant authorities, to have the children removed from her, and contacted friends and family to manipulate them, announcing she was mentally ill. He also did not respect her boundaries and invaded their new home and property, after she had moved out with the children. He contacted the paediatrician to get examination reports which he aimed to hold against her, refused to pay maintenance and started legal action against her at different levels. To destroy her new life, he gave false signatures in relevant official documents and gave wrong information to the authorities, thereby conducting criminal acts. She got into debt to fight his legal proceedings and was trapped in her feelings of victimisation and abuse.

When M decided to start the 16-step process, she had been through two and a half years of physical and verbal attacks from the husband, including legal proceedings, court cases against his claims, and criminal offences towards her and her children. She felt exhausted and decided that she needed a new focus in her life. Since her aim was to return to the state of inner peace and well-being she had known long before, she decided to join a self-help and empowerment group of (battered) women who worked through Kasl's 16-step process.

The following paragraphs are based on personal interviews with M, together with excerpts from M's notes taken while working through the 16-step-programme. Findings provide insights into working through victimisation in the context of love and crime.

35.8.2 Transforming Through Kasl's 16-Step Programme

In this section, each step in the process is presented and then individually discussed in terms of M's experience.

1. **(a) We affirm we have the power to take charge of our lives and stop being dependent on substances or other people for our self-esteem and security [or] (b) We admit we were out of control with / powerless over _____ yet have the power to take charge of our lives and stop being dependent on substances or other people for our self-esteem and security.**

   In the beginning, M chose option 1a, emphasising that she has the power to take charge of her life and stop being dependent on her husband. Ever since she had stopped working and had her first child, she had felt dependent on him. In this process, she realised that not only had she felt financially dependent, but that she had also felt a dependence which related to her fears. These fears were of not being able to make it on her own, not being good enough, or not being able to manage things in the new country they lived in, not being able to manage both family and work, or not being as capable as he was on the job. Her husband implicitly told her that she had a low self-esteem and a high need for security, although people in her social environment usually mirrored to her that she seemed to be highly independent and risk-taking, curious, and open to new experiences. Her self-image clashed with the way others viewed her, and she became aware that her self-talk of being dependent was not contributing to her process of separation and divorce, feeding into her fears of failing in court and with processes of legitimation, perhaps even having to return to him again.

2. **We come to believe that [choose what fits] God / The Goddess / Universe / Great Spirit / Higher Power awakens the healing wisdom within us when we open ourselves to that power.**

   M remembered that, at one time, she had felt a very strong connection to God, which had then become the belief in a higher power. She realised that she had lost her belief entirely during the past years of struggle, focusing only on her safety and that of the children, staying aware of the alcoholism of her husband and keeping it in control, looking after the financial security of her children and herself. She remembered about the higher power's strength in her life before her marriage, but could not reconnect with it. However, occasionally, she began to remember the power that had given her power.

3. **We make a decision to find our authentic selves and trust in the healing power of the truth.**

M made a conscious decision to find her authentic self and to trust herself again. In this process, she realised that she had lost trust in herself while only believing in her husband, in his truth and his (professional) abilities, his knowledge and wisdom, and anything he had said. She realised that she had unconsciously stopped listening to her inner voice and could not believe that she was now dealing with her husband's criminal acts in court. For her, it was still surreal that it was he who was doing this to her. After 3 months of working with the 16-step process, she made the decision to trust herself and her abilities again, but it took some more months until she felt herself strong enough to apply for new jobs again.

Sometimes within the 16-step process, when she had to have contact with her husband and his legal claims, she believed that she was actually wrong and that she had done something wrong (not being the right wife for him, not being clever enough, or even being the cause of his heavy drinking) and these were exactly the times when she realised she needed her empowerment group to strengthen her trust and belief in herself.

4. **We examine our beliefs, addictions, and dependent behaviour in the context of living in a hierarchal, patriarchal culture.**

M realised that the more her husband drank, the less she had enjoyed drinking, and she became conscious of her internalised co-dependency. She also saw that her entire married life had been built around supporting his career, while she fitted herself into traditional role behaviour which was very foreign to the way she had grown up. In spite of coming from a highly educated family—her father a professor, her mother a high school teacher—and with a focus on gender equality, M had lost herself in a traditional family setting which was dominated by her husband's career and she representing him as the wife of the successful manager.

5. **We share with another person and the Universe all the things inside of us for which we feel shame and guilt.**

At first, M did not know what to share about shame and guilt within the group. However, after she had listened to other women's experiences in her group, she became aware of feeling guilty for having neglected her own professional career, and ashamed of having become so dependent on her husband. This new awareness helped her to make the decision to apply for new jobs to return to a life on her own.

6. **We affirm and enjoy our strengths, talents, and creativity. We do not hide these attributes from ourselves and others.**

When it came to the step of affirming and enjoying her strengths, M was uncertain what to do. First, she looked at strengths in her professional career, but she had lost many years of professional experience and felt unable to catch up with the speed of the times. Then she started focusing on sports which she had loved before she got married, and re-joined a sports group (running) which made her feel more active and alive. The new focus on something positive and enjoyable helped her to defocus from the court cases, threats, protection orders and her financial problems. She even started to go out with new acquaintances from her sports club and managed to have a glass of wine with them, claiming her independence from the husband's co-dependency.

7. **We become willing to let go of guilt, shame and any behaviour that keeps us from loving ourselves and others.**

For many months, M felt angry with herself and guilty that she had stayed in this relationship for such a long time. At the same time, she was ashamed that she had let go of her career and had led herself into the domestic violence, the legal cases and her social and financial co-dependency. Theoretically, she was prepared to let go the guilt, shame and destructive mindset and move on, but in practice she struggled to apply it for quite some time.

8. **We make a list of people we have harmed and people who have harmed us, and take steps to clear out negative feelings by making amends and sharing our grievances in a respectful way.**

M thought that by staying in the abusive relationship and becoming a victim, she had done harm to her children, herself, and to her parents (particularly since the parents had always warned her against marrying this man). She felt deep guilt about this fact. She felt harmed by her husband on different levels: the physical, violent level, the abusive verbal and non-verbal levels, the professional level and also on financial levels. In the group, she highlighted that, for her, the hardest realisation was that she had become a victim and stayed in this victimisation for so many years. She believed that she could—by joining this group process—only make a beginning to clear out negative feelings towards herself and her husband, and that it would probably take more time to clear these feelings, beyond the group process.

9. **We express love and gratitude to others, and increasingly appreciate the wonder of life and the blessings we do have.**

M expressed love and gratitude to her children, also to her parents and herself. However, she could not express gratitude to her husband although she knew it was the right thing to do for all the good things he had done for her apart from the negative aspects. She also knew that only by feeling gratitude to him could she move forward in her spiritual and loving development and her healing process. However, she was so angry with him that the anger overwhelmed her when she attempted to express gratitude.

10. **We continue to trust our reality and daily affirm that we see what we see, we know what we know and we feel what we feel.**

Since M had not trusted herself for many years, this step was a major, ongoing process and often when she opened letters from the lawyers or talked to her husband, she became confused about her own reality, but at last she began to realise when this was the case. She then started to put coping mechanisms in place, such as talking to her friends, calling them to discuss her views, writing down her views and his views, meditating and reflecting on the situation.

11. **We promptly acknowledge mistakes and make amends when appropriate, but we do not say we are sorry for things we have not done and we do not cover up, analyse or take responsibility for the shortcomings of others.**

M had learned in her family of origin that it is polite and kind to say "sorry", even when one had done nothing wrong. She had learned to take on the responsibility for things that went wrong (as the eldest child in her own family). Therefore it was particularly challenging, and she worked very hard not to assume the blame for other people's mistakes. Sometimes she even felt sorry for having to "fight back" her husband. The most difficult part for her was to work with the idea that she caused her husband's drinking problem, his violence and his depression (as he had claimed). She felt constantly responsible for the shortcomings of her husband and tried to cover up for him where she could, for instance financially, and by providing education and entertainment for the children. Until the end of the 16-step group process, she could not entirely give up feeling responsible for his shortcomings.

12. **We seek out situations, jobs, and people who affirm our intelligence, perceptions, and self-worth and avoid situations or people who are hurtful, harmful, or demeaning to us.**

M continued applying for jobs. Eventually she took on work that was below her educational and financial level in terms of the needed income, because she believed that she could not secure a position she actually deserved in terms of her professional background and experience. However, as soon as she became aware that she was spending time with people who would do her no good, or that she attracted people who were similar to her husband, she started to withdraw from these relationships.

13. **We take steps to heal our physical bodies, organise our lives, reduce stress, and have fun.**

M decided to take steps to heal by taking a vacation with the children, visiting the grandparents, attending a course to reduce stress in her life, and doing sports activities. She decided to make the best out of the weekends, going on trips with her children, visiting friends and having fun in family camps.

14. **We seek to find our inward calling, and develop the will and wisdom to follow it.**

Since M had been unable to grasp her inward calling, but had longed to know it for many years, she started meditating. During one of these sessions while meditating about her future, an image appeared before her inner eye. It was a silver duck in a dish washing water. The duck had slanted eyes and peered over the rim of a white sink. The dish washing water was dirty and grey, with little bubbles of washing liquid.

This unusual image struck her with surprise; she could not stop thinking about it.

When M returned to the group meeting, she told the group about the image. At first, she did not have any interpretations of the "silver duck", but when she reflected further, she realised that ducks can swim anywhere, no matter how warm or cold the temperature, and they do not mind how the water looks. She associated ducks with togetherness, never living alone, being either with a partner or in a group. The duck also reminded her of time spent with her grandmother, feeding ducks in a pond near their home. She had always been fascinated by ducks and how they adjusted so easily to their surroundings. They could swim, walk or fly—adapting themselves to whatever was needed in the environment, being able to float on water, no matter if it was clear, dirty, rough or quiet.

After the group meeting, M wrote that she felt like a silver, precious and shiny duck which was swimming in dirty water. M loves silver and associates it with shine, strength, value, and its ability to be polished if it becomes old or dirty. She saw the silver duck as an image of herself: a duck trapped in the dirty washing-up water in the kitchen sink, without even realising it could fly to escape. The duck's slanted eyes were, for her, a sign that the duck was prepared to fight and take on external attacks. Maybe those eyes were even expressing her own anger.

A few days later, M realised when she stood one morning in her kitchen, that her coffee plunger reminds her of the duck. This coffee plunger was a very important part of her life, because she believed she could not live without coffee, and the plunger was one of the few pieces she had retained from her marriage.

From the image, she developed her calling to make the best out of the situation, to shine, no matter how dirty the water, and to stay afloat. Several excerpts in her notebook referred to this image and the struggle to always see herself as the silver duck and not to focus on the dish washing water.

15. **We accept the ups and downs of life as natural events that can be used as lessons for our growth.**

M's inward calling fitted well with her transformation efforts and with her aim to grow during the very stressful time of divorce and law cases, not only for her personal growth and benefit, but also in becoming a female role model for her children. However, M highlighted that the ups and downs were not easy for her, and to stay positive was a major effort.

16. **We grow in awareness that we are interrelated with all living things, and we contribute to restoring peace and balance on the planet.**

At the end of the 16-step programme, M knew that she had worked through many issues, but that she still needed time to fully overcome her sense of victimisation, lingering feelings of fear and doubt of her self-worth. However, she also felt less traumatised and knew what to do when she recognised her old behaviour and thought patterns. Although all of her decisions had somehow made sense to her in the past, it was now time to change direction, standing up for herself and her children. She also decided to no longer apply for positions that were underpaid or below her qualifications, and opted for positions which—instead of being anchored in the web design industry—were in her area of expertise and interest (business) and where she could contribute to the greater good of the society.

35.9 Discussion and Conclusions

An argument has been presented in this chapter that positive victimology can contribute positively to the way in which victims of violence and criminal acts manage these experiences. Based on a positive victimology perspective which takes salutogenic (health-related) and loving attitudes into consideration, victims may be able to overcome and de-traumatise from their experiences in a sustainable way. The 16-step programme was established originally as a process to support female criminal offenders, in particular, to overcome their criminal backgrounds. This chapter demonstrates, with a case example, that the 16-step process might also support female victims with overcoming their trauma, and strengthen them in their efforts to reconnect with themselves. Because the 16-step programme does not refer to a specific religion, but instead focuses on spirituality as a broader concept in a non-paternalistic belief system, this process might be used across cultures and could even be adjusted in culture-specific terms for different contexts and concepts. The process can be used to transform negative experiences of both offenders and victims, thereby leading to personal growth and freedom beyond the criminal acts and experiences.

Love, as a deep-rooted, emotional concept across cultures (Mayer, 2018b), can provide a strong base for positive victimology in general and specifically within the 16-step process which is anchored in spirituality (thereby the opinion that everything is connected) and the belief that a positive focus is the core to healing and de-traumatisation. By connecting and reconnecting to the soul with a loving attitude (Karandashev, 2015), and through a reactivation of spirituality in life with the social support of the 16-step process (Kasl, 2012), victimisation can be overcome.

In this case example, the author does not look at hate or love crime; however, as Gardell (2015) points out, hate crime and love crime seem to be interconnected. Therefore, it can be assumed that in the case presented, the husband's love (which already appears to include abusive and toxic aspects of love) turns into feelings of hate after the victim's separation. For this case, this assumption is true on an individualised family conflict level, not for a group bias or group level and membership context.

The case study further illustrates how the violence against the female victim, as well as against the children, is anchored in socio-economic structures, gendered power relations, and the roles ascribed with interpretations of inferiority (Walker, 1979). The perspectives are gendered, in that the female victim occupies an inferior feminine position (Lemish, 2004; Nuytiens & Christiaens, 2015), not in the beginning of the marriage, but towards the end where manipulation, toxic love concepts, power struggles, relationship problems and abusive relationship patterns (Jenkins, 2017) are clearly manifested. As described by Jones (2008) with regard to criminal activities, the female victim in the case example complies for many years with manipulative acts, toxic love concepts and abusive relationship patterns before re-establishing her own identity and belief system through a long process of self-development (shown, in part, in the 16-step process). As Herbst-Debby and Gez (2012) describe in their study of murdered Israeli women, these women were in the process of marital separation when their husbands murdered them. In the case presented in this chapter, the husband does not murder the victim, but he abuses and attacks her (physically, verbally, non-verbally), threatening her with "buying a gun" and turning extremely violent with the aim of destroying her life.

As highlighted in the 12-step programme (Chen & Gueta, 2015), the case example shows how new meaning is created for the female victim throughout the 16-step programme, drawing on spirituality and a loving attitude towards self and others. In this example, M feels trapped in an abusive relationship, particularly towards the end. When she separates, she finally recognises the strength of the suppression and toxic love relationship she has been in. By working through the 16-steps and sharing her experiences with other women who are caught up in similar relationship patterns with abuse and co-dependency, either as female crime offenders or as victims, she feels and experiences support in the process of healing.

For M, the broadened 16-step process of Kasl (2012) works particularly well, because she has never been very religious or believed in a male God, but rather in God as a higher power. Steps 8 and 9 are also effective for M, in that she believes she has not harmed others primarily, but rather has been harmed in the first instance. Only with hindsight, does she realise that by allowing herself to be harmed and suppressed, she has also harmed her children. Shame and guilt are key concepts in this process (Kasl, 1990). M feels guilty about her husband becoming someone who now harasses her and turns to criminal acts to destroy her. She also experiences shame and blame by her social environment, and feels greatly relieved on learning that other women in her group feel the same, but need to transform the feelings of shame and guilt into a loving kindness towards themselves. Through the process, M increases her awareness of suppression through hierarchies, male suppression, patriarchy and internalised oppression (White, 2013) and learns that she can reconnect to her own power, her (self-)love and courage, instead of to her pain and anxieties. In the end of the process, M realises that she will not only have to deal with the criminal acts and attacks of her husband, but also with her own goals, the meaning in her life, her own power and empowerment struggles, self-care, self-control and personal transformation. She also notes that before entering any new relationship, she needs to develop further, to avoid making the same mistakes.

In conclusion, the 16-step programme has supported M, as a female victim of criminal acts in the context of love (and hate): it has greatly contributed to her salutogenic development and the transformation of anger, fear and pain into loving kindness, spiritual development and connection and love in the context of humanness.

Future research should take the impact of positive psychology, positive criminology and positive victimisation into account and study the interconnectedness of crime and love, relationship and spirituality further. Interventions such as the 12- and the 16-step programme, need to be researched in mixed method studies, empirically underpinning their success in specific contexts. However, these intervention programmes should also be researched across cultures, with regard to their impact on gender, offenders and victims, particularly in love and crime contexts.

Theories of concepts such as salutogenesis, spirituality, meaningfulness, love and loving kindness should be taken into consideration to build a theoretical and empirical base for the intervention programmes. On a practical level, such programmes should be implemented in different cultural and contextual settings and be adjusted to the socio-cultural surroundings and gender aspects, taking the diversity and intersectionalities of participants and their abilities to work with the programme into account.

Acknowledgements I would kindly like to thank Ruth Coetzee and Elisabeth Vanderheiden for their support to developing this chapter.

References

Antonaccio, O., Tittle, C. R., Botchkovar, E., & Kranidiotis, M. (2010). The correlates of crime and deviance: Additional evidence. *Journal of Research in Crime and Delinquency, 47*(3), 297–328.

Balboni, J. M., & McDevitt, J. (2001). Hate crime reporting: Understanding police officer perceptions, departmental protocol, and the role of the victim is there such a thing as a "love" crime? *Justice Research and Policy, 3*(1), 1–27.

Bauer, G.F., Roy, M., Bakibinga, P., Contu, P., Downe, S., Eriksson, M., et al. (2019). Future directions for the concept of salutogenesis: A position article. *Health Promotion International,* Jun 20. pii: daz057. https://doi.org/10.1093/heapro/daz057. (Epub ahead of print).

Beck, J. S. (1995). *Cognitive therapy: Basic and beyond.* New York: Guilford Press.

Bergström, G. (2012). *Kriminalitet som livsstil 5: Erev. Upplagan.* Lund: Studentlitteratur.

Chen, G. (2006). Social support, spiritual program, and addiction recovery. *International Journal of Offender Therapy and Comparative Criminology, 50,* 306–323.

Chen, G. (2010). The meaning of suffering in drug addiction and recovery from the perspective of existentialism, Buddhism and the 12-step program. *Journal of Pychoactive Drugs, 40*(3), 363–375.

Chen, G. & Gueta, K. (2015). Application of positive criminology in the 12-Step-program. Chapter 15. In N. Ronel & D. Segev (Eds.), *Positive criminology* (pp. 208–220). London: Routledge Taylor & Francis

Colquhoun, K. (2014, April 6). Trials of passion: Crimes in the name of love and madness review—Convincing, enlightening. *The Observer.* https://www.theguardian.com/books/2014/apr/06/trials-passion-crimes-name-love-review

Courneau, A. (2010). *Crime d'Amour.* SBS Films.

Dancig-Rosenberg, H., & Pugach, D. (2015). Between secondary victimization and positive victimology. In N. Ronel, & D. Segev (Eds.), *Positive criminology* (pp. 292–306). London: Routledge Taylor & Francis.

Fairfax, L. M. (2002). The thin line between love and hate: Why affinity-based securities and investment fraud constitutes a hate crime. *U.C. Davis L. Rev., 36,* 1073.

FBI. (2019). Hate crimes. https://www.fbi.gov/investigate/civil-rights/hate-crimes

Frankl, V. E. (1965). *Man's search for meaning.* New York: Washington Square Press.

Frankl, V. E. (1988). *The will to meaning: Foundations and applications of logotherapy* (Expanded ed.). New York: Penguin.

Freeman, J., & Turvey, B. E. (Eds.). (2012). *Interpreting motive. Criminal profiling: An introduction to behavioural evidence* (4th ed.). San Diego: Elsevier Science.

Fredrickson, B. L., Tugade, M. M., Waugh, C. E., & Larkin, G. R. (2003). What good are positive emotions in crises? A prospective study of resilience and emotions following the terrorist attacks on the United States on September 11th 2001. *Journal of Personality and Social Psychology, 84*(2), 365–376.

Gardell, M. (2015). What's love got to do with it? Ultranationalism, islamophobia, and hate crime in Sweden. *Journal of Religion and Violence, 3*(1), 91–116.

Gerstenfeld, P.B. (2017). Hate crime. The Wiley handbook of violence and aggression. Hoboken, NJ: Wiley.

Glaser, E. R. (2008, July 5). Judaism and the 12-step program. Tammuz, Torah Portion. https://www.aish.com/sp/pg/48937302.html

Grün, A., Hüther, G., & Hosang, M. (2017). *Liebe ist die einzige Revolution. Drei Impulse für Ko-Kreativität und Potenzialentfaltung*. Herder: Breisgau.

Herbst-Debby, A., & Gez, Y. (2012). From "crime of passion" to "love does not kill": The murder of Einav Rogel and the role of Na'amat Women's Organization in the construction of violence against women in Israel. *Israel Studies, 17*(2), 129–155.

Hill, J. K. (2009). Victimization, resilience and meaning-making: Moving forward in strength. Victims of Crime Research Digest, 2. https://www.justice.gc.ca/eng/rp-pr/cj-jp/victim/rd09_2-rr09_2/p1.html

Hillhouse, M. P., & Fiorentine, R. (2001). 12-Step program participation and effectiveness: Do gender and ethnic differences exist? *Journal of Drug Issues, 31*(3), 767–780.

Jaishankar, K., & Ronel, N. (Eds.). (2013). *Global criminology. Crime and victimization in a global era*. Boca Raton, FL: CRC Press Taylor & Francis.

Jenkins, C. S. (2017). 'Addicted'? to 'love'? *Philosophy, Psychiatry, & Psychology, 24*(1), 93–96.

Johnson, M. (2003). *Självkänsla och anpassning*. Lund: Studentlitteratur. Häftad, Svenska.

Jones, S. (2008). Partners in crime: A study of the relationship between female offenders and their co-defendants. *Criminology & Criminal Justice, 8*(2), 147–164.

Karandashev, V. (2015). A cultural perspective on romantic love. *Online Readings in Psychology and Culture, 5*(4). https://doi.org/10.9707/2307-0919.1135

Kasl, C. S. (1990). *Women, sex, and addiction: A search for love and power*. New York: Harper & Row Perennial Library.

Kasl, C.S. (1992). *Many roads, one journey. Moving beyond the 12 steps*. New York: Harper Perennial.

Kasl, C. S. (1999). *If the Buddha dated. A handbook for finding love on a spiritual path*. Penguin Random House.

Kasl, C. S. (2012, August 10). *Sixteen annotated steeps for discovery and empowerment.* https://charlottekasl.com/category/articles/

Lantz, B., Gladfelter, A. S., & Ruback, R. B. (2019). Stereotypical hate crimes and criminal justice processing: A multi-dataset comparison of bias crime arrest patterns by offender and victim race. *Justice Quarterly, 36*(2), 193–224.

Lee, M. T., Pagano, M. E., Johnson, B. R., & Post, S. G. (2016). Love and service in adolescent addiction recovery. *Alcoholism Treatment Quarterly, 34*(2), 197–222.

Lee, M. T., Veta, P. S., Johnson, B. R., & Pagano, M. E. (2014). Daily spiritual experiences and adolescent treatment response. *Alcoholism Treatment Quarterly, 32*(2), 271–298.

Lemish, D. (2004). Exclusion or marginality: Portrayals of women in Israeli media. In K. Ross & C. M. Byerly (Eds.), *Women and media: International perspectives* (pp. 39–59). Malden, MA: Wiley Blackwell.

Leverentz, A. M. (2006). The love of a good man? Romantic relationships as a source of support or hindrance for female ex-offenders. *Journal of Research in Crime and Delinquency, 43*(4), 459–488.

Levy, B. L., & Levy, D.L. (2017). When love meets hate: The relationship between state policies on gay and lesbian rights and hate crime incidence. *Social Science Research, 61*, 142–159.

Lindblom, S., Eriksson, L., & Hiltunen, A. J. (2017). Criminality, thinking patterns and treatment effects – evaluation of the Swedish cognitive intervention programme 'new challenges' targeting adult men with a criminal lifestyle. *Journal of Scandinavian Studies in Criminology and Crime Prevention, 19*(2), 204–224.

Martsolf, D. S., Draucker, C. B., Stephenson, P. L., Cook, C. B., & Heckman, T. A. (2012). Patterns of dating violence across adolescence. *Qualitative Health Research, 22*(9), 1271–1283.

Mayer, C.-H. (2018a). Die Liebe. Interkulturelle Perspektiven auf ein universelles Konzept zur Gestaltung von Gesundheitskulturen. *Der Mensch, 56*(1), 34–39.

Mayer, C.-H. (2018b). Liebe aus kulturellen Perspektiven: Ansätze zur Gestaltung interkultureller Gesundheitskulturen? *Impulse, 98*, 3–4.

Mayer, C.-H. (2020). Stories of love in cultural perspectives: Meaning-making through expressions, rituals and symbols. In C.-H. Mayer & E. Vanderheiden (Eds.), *International handbook of love: Transcultural and transdisciplinary perspectives*. Cham: Springer.

McCarthy, B., & Casey, T. (2008). Love, sex, and crime: Adolescent romantic relationships and offending. *American Sociological Review, 73*(6), 944–969.

Moore, C. (2013). Beguiling eve and her innocent counterpart: Victim-offender identities in the criminal justice process. In K. Jaishankar & N. Ronel (Eds.), *Global criminology. Crime and victimization in a global era* (pp. 289–314). Boca Raton, FL: CRC Press Taylor & Francis.

Naffine, N. (2019). *Criminal law and the man problem*. New York: Hart Publishing.

Neff, K. D., & Knox, M. C. (2017). Self-compassion. In: V. Zeigler-Hill & T. K. Shackelford (Eds.). *Encyclopedia of personality and individual differences* (pp. 1–8). Cham: Springer. https://doi.org/10.1007/978-3-319-28099-8_1159-1

Nuytiens, A., & Christiaens, J. (2015). Female pathways to crime and prison: Challenging the (US) gendered pathways perspective. *European Journal of Criminology*. https://doi.org/10.1177/1477370815608879

Pozsar, M. H., Dumitrescu, A. I., Piticas, D., & Constantinescu, S. (2018). Dating Apps in the life of young Romanian women. A preliminary study. *Analize, Journal of Gender and Feminist Studies, 11*, 216–238.

Rayburn, R. L., & Wright, J. D. (2018). "I stopped shooting up when i got married": Desistance, crime, and love. *Deviant Behavior, 39*(10), 1294–1304.

Rege, A. (2009). What's love got to do with it? Exploring online dating scams and identity fraud. *International Journal of Cyber Criminology, 3*(2), 494–512.

Richie, B. (2018). *Compelled to crime. The gender entrapment of battered, black women*. London: Routledge. E-book.

Ronel, N., & Elisha, E. (2011). A different perspective: Introducing positive criminology. *International Journal of Offender Therapy and Comparative Criminology, 55*(2), 305–325.

Ronel, N., & Segev, D. (2015). *Positive criminology*. London: Routledge Taylor & Francis.

Ronel, N., & Toren, Y. (2012). Positive victimology—An innovation or "more of the same?". *Temida, 15*(2), 171–180.

Ronel, N., & Yair, B. (2017). Spiritual criminology: The case of Jewish criminology. *International Journal of Offender Therapy and Comparative Criminology, 62*(7), 2081–2102.

Schweppe, J., & Walters, M. A. (2017). *The globalisation of hate. Internationalising hate crime*. Oxford: Oxford University Press.

Varese, F. (2017). *Mafia life: Love, death and money at the heart of organized crime*. London: Profile Books.

Walker, L. E. (1979). The battered woman. New York: Harper & Row.

Walker, L. E. (2017). *The battered women syndrome* (Fourth ed.). New York: Springer.

Walsh, A., & Beyer, J. A. (1987). Violent crime, sociopathy and love deprivation among adolescent delinquents. *Adolescence, XXII*(87), 705.

Walters, M., & Hoyle, C. (2017). Healing harms and engendering tolerance: The promise of restorative justice for hate crime. In: N. Chakraborti (Ed.), *Hate crime. Concepts, policy, future directions* (pp. 228–248). London: Willian.

White, W. L. (2013). Sixteen-step groups for discovery and empowerment: An interview with Dr. Charlotte Kasl. www.williamwhitepapers.com

Whitty, M. T. (2015). Mass-marketing fraud: A growing concern. *IEEE Security and Privacy, 13*, 84–87.

Whitty, M. T. (2018). Do you love me? Psychological characteristics of romance scam victims. *Cyberpsychology, Behavior and Social Networking, 21*(2), 105–109.

World Health Organization (WHO). (1986). *Ottawa charter for health promotion*. Geneva: World Health Organization.

Wyse, J. J. B., Harding, D. J., & Morenoff, J. D. (2014). Romantic relationships and criminal desistance: Pathways and processes. *Social Forum, 29*(2), 365–385.

Claude-Hélène Mayer is a Full Professor in Industrial and Organisational Psychology at the Department of Industrial Psychology and People Management at the University of Johannesburg, an Adjunct Professor at the European University Viadrina in Frankfurt (Oder), Germany and a Senior Research Associate at Rhodes University, Grahamstown, South Africa. She holds a Ph.D. in Psychology (University of Pretoria, South Africa), a Ph.D. in Management (Rhodes University, South Africa), a Doctorate (Georg-August University, Germany) in Political Sciences (socio-cultural anthropology and intercultural didactics) and Master degrees in Ethnology, Intercultural Didactics and Socio-economics (Georg-August University, Germany) as well as in Crime Science, Investigation and Intelligence (University of Portsmouth, UK). Her Venia Legendi is in Psychology with focus on work, organizational, and cultural psychology (Europa Universität Viadrina, Germany). She has published numerous monographs, text collections, accredited journal articles, and special issues on transcultural mental health and well-being, salutogenesis, transforming shame, transcultural conflict management and mediation, women in leadership in culturally diverse work contexts, coaching, culture and crime and psychobiography.

Chapter 36
Free to Love: Experiences with Love for Women in Prison

Estibaliz de Miguel-Calvo

Abstract This chapter describes the relational dynamics of romantic relationships of incarcerated women, in the context of the reflection on the agency of criminalized women. Women's experiences with love in prison are means of redefinition of one's identity and one's decisions in the realm of emotions. Imprisoned women try to maintain their integrity and reverse the negative effects of their deteriorated identity constructed by the different disciplinary agents, where love is a fundamental pillar of resistance, even if it means inserting oneself into a framework of normative gender relations, at least in the first instance. Experiences involving love also constitute a way for the participants to articulate the meaning of prison life and redefine the self. Being in love in contemporary Western society is sociologically understood as a means of self-validation and experiencing freedom, which has a particular symbolic value for incarcerated women, who lack freedom and tend to carry social a stigma derived from penal punishment. Partner relationships thus become a source of positive identity and a way to succeed under conditions of social stratification.

Keywords Love · Sociology of love · Gender · Prison · Women in prison · Agency

36.1 Introduction

There is a growing academic interest in analyzing the situation of incarcerated women and their relationships in different geographic contexts (i.e. Estevez-Grillo, 2018 and Bouças do Lago, 2014 in Brazil; Ojeda, 2013 in Argentina; Kolb & Palys, 2018 in the U.S. Padovani, 2016, and De Miguel-Calvo, 2015b in Catalonia and the Basque Country in Spain; Joël-Lauf, 2012 in France). Recently, research on social ties, as well as couple relationships, heterosexual and homosexual (Einat & Chen, 2012; Forsyth, Evans, & Foster, 2002; Herrero-Riesgo, 2015; Joël-Lauf, 2013;

E. de Miguel-Calvo (✉)
Department of Sociology and Social Work, University of the Basque Country, Leioa, Spain
e-mail: estibaliz.demiguel@ehu.eus

Pardue, Arrigo, & Murphy, 2011), are being conducted from different disciplines such as socio-legal studies, sociology or psychology, and it is usually done from a gender perspective.

Prisons, as total institutions, constitute a world of relations (Goffman, 2001 [1961]). Incarceration does not only result in the rupture of relationships and separation from loved ones but it also operates remaking personal bonds (Haney, 2013), moreover, producing a new set of relationships inside. As an example, Padovani (2016) describes how Brazilian women in Catalonian prisons reframe their family and love ties while they are incarcerated, in the quest for improving their living conditions. Kolb and Palys (2018) explore how incarcerated women tend to create personal relationships in prison in the form of 'pseudo-families' or couples, based on heteronormative patterns. In addition, the space of confinement generates the conditions for non-normative sexual practices, such as homosexuality. Incarcerated women and their relationships, however, have been generally framed in the field of family life. Much scholarly attention has been given to women who are mothers behind bars, especially in relation to the impact of imprisonment on children, associating women with motherhood (Barberet, 2014b) and largely ignoring other aspects of the experiences of incarcerated women such as love, sexuality, and personal life (May & Nordqvist, 2019; Smart, 2007) in a broader sense.

Here, I describe the relational dynamics of romantic relationships of incarcerated women inside prison walls, while I reflect on the agency of incarcerated women through their emotional experiences. The analysis is grounded in the recent body of literature on the affective experiences during incarceration based on different parts of the world, including research I carried out in the Basque Country (Spain), with 49 in-depth interviews and 15 months of participant observation. I also mention 'Dyke Jails', a documentary-research on lesbian experiences of women in prison in Spain. Hence, research on the topic places a part in the dialogue in this chapter, as some themes resonate with each other.

The theoretical basis for the analysis of the romantic relationships of imprisoned women is the sociology of love, as well as feminist theories about love. With this stand, I reflect on the possibilities of incarcerated women to be agents under the prison regime. Experiences with love may be interpreted as forms of resistance to the pains of imprisonment and their consequences in the shaping of a damaged identity as 'bad women'. Thus, the concept of agency is discussed here. Love may function as a strategy for surviving in the context of prison, also as an invaluable resource to reshape their damaged identity by being included in the collective utopia of love in Western societies. Prisons thus are specific contexts for the research on love, intimacy, and sexuality taking into consideration the multiplicity of relationships and interactions from inside of prison to the outside, as well as interactions that have to do with emotional and sexual content behind walls. In this context, I contend that incarcerated women are agents as they act as subjects in the realm of affectionate relationships, challenging in some ways the gendered prison regimes of punishment and discipline.

In what follows, I analyze the couple relationships of women in confinement understood as forms of resistance to the pains of imprisonment and the stigma derived from imprisonment (Añaños-Bedriñana & Jiménez-Bautista, 2016; Ariza & Iturralde, 2017; García, Boira, Gómez-Quintero, Marcuello, & Eito, 2015; Mageehon, 2008; Moran, 2012; Schlosser, 2008). I begin with the main characteristics of the issues of women in prison, framed in the discussion on the disciplinary regimes for incarcerated women, as gendered punishment this being oriented to the re-feminization of criminal women considered deviant women of the gender norms. Then, I briefly trace the possibilities of agency in the emotional realm based on sociological and feminist understandings on love. This is followed by a description of results on the couple relationships of women in prison derived from research in various contexts, putting special attention to investigations in Spain in which I participated. The chapter concludes with some ideas on the limits and possibilities of 'emotional agency' in prison for incarcerated women as well as some proposals to focus further research on love relationships in prison.

36.2 Women in Prison. Gendered Disciplinary Regimes

714,000 women and girls are held prisoners in penal institutions worldwide, according to the World Female Imprisonment List (Walmsley, 2018). More than 200,000 are held in the United States of America, constituting the highest female population rate in the world (65.7 per 100,000 of the total population in the country) in the context of 'mass incarceration' in the territory. The next countries with the largest population of women in prisons are China (107,000 women inmates), Russian Federation (almost 49,000) and Brazil (about 44,700). These four countries altogether hold more than half of the world's female prison population. Besides this, the number of women and girls in prison has increased during the last decades, 53% since the year 2000 according to the report of the Institute of Criminal Research (Walmsley, 2018). An increase which does not correspond to the rise in the global population figures. Still, these figures of incarcerated women are expected to continue rising even faster than their male counterparts. Much of the incarceration of women is due to the punitive policies against drugs, resulting in a high criminalization of women, who usually play a role in the lowest links of drug trafficking organizations (Almeda, Di Nella, & Navarro, 2012; GCDP-Global Comission on Drug Policy, 2014; Giacomello, 2013; Ribas, Almeda, & Bodelón, 2005; Sudbury, 2002).

Incarcerated women worldwide are a minimal proportion with respect to men in the prison system. Women prisoners tend to be between 2 and 9% of the total, so usually, they do not constitute more than one in ten prisoners. This weak numerical position, together with an androcentric vision of incarceration, has led to overshadow the situation of women behind bars, both for criminal system operators and for criminological researchers (Barberet, 2014a). Consequently, issues of women in prison have been largely ignored until the emergence of feminist criminology in the 1970s. Feminist perspectives of the criminological discipline expand the object of study (Smart, 1990) putting in the forefront women in criminological studies and offering an alternative to the persistence of blind perspectives to gender in the discipline (Gelsthorpe & Morris, 1990; Smart, 1977). Research shows that the judicial and the criminal system tend to contribute to the creation of a normal woman (Chesney-Lynd, 1986; Larrauri, 1994; Smart, 1977; Worrall, 1990), as opposed to the abnormal and deviant criminal on the basis of discourses of femininity clustered around notions of domesticity, sexuality, and pathology (Carlen & Worrall, 1987). Crime is associated with hegemonic masculinity (Juliano, 2011; Messerschmidt, 1993) as action, initiative and transgression. In this sense, criminal women are conceived as monstrous since their behavior do not correspond to the normative definition of women—passive, caretakers and conforming the norms, showing that there are different modes of control that women experience compared to men (Carlen, 1983, 1988; Chesney-Lind, 2006; Larrauri, 1994). Not only patriarchy but also capitalism and racism are understood as the basic structures of oppression being articulated in our contemporary societies. Critical criminology highlights the criminalization of poor and racialized women (Davis, 2003; Rice, 1990; Richie, 1996).

In short, identity is a central element in women's prison discipline, the stigmatization of women is a form of power exercised by criminal and penitentiary institutions. As Butler notes in reference to Foucault's theorization, the prison acts on the prisoner's body, but it does so by forcing the prisoner to approximate an ideal, a norm of behavior, a model of obedience (Butler, 1997). The normative ideal that is instilled in the prisoner is a form of psychic identity. In this way, research on criminalized women is relevant for two main reasons.

On the one hand, it puts at the forefront their experiences in the criminal justice systems and their life paths as marginalized women, where issues of gender, class, race with personal and structural violence intersect (Carlen, 1988; Rice, 1990; Richie, 1996). In general, incarcerated women have experienced multiple forms of social exclusion prior to their imprisonment. Literature on the topic has highlighted the tendency to the criminalization of poverty (Carlen, 1988), together with the criminalization of foreign and migrant women (Martín-Palomo, Miranda, & Vega, 2005; Padovani, 2016; Ribas-Mateos & Martinez, 2003; Ribas et al., 2005), ethnic minorities (Equipo Barañi, 2001; Imaz & Martin-Palomo, 2007; Jewkes, 2011; Richie, 1996) and drug users (De Miguel-Calvo, 2015a, 2016; Malloch, 2000). Hence, there is an overrepresentation of these groups also in prison.

On the other hand, the analysis of the forms of social control exercised on incarcerated women "gives light on the various prisons in which all women live" (Lagarde, 2005, 642). In this regard, Angela Davis states:

> Scholars and activists who are involved in feminist projects should not consider the structure of state punishment as marginal to their work" as "the gendered character of punishment both reflects and further entrenches the gender structure of the larger society " (Davis, 2003, 61).

Hence, the prison is a total institution (Goffman, 1993) and a privileged place to analyze the ways of exercising power in our society (Foucault, 1995) and, in this case, the forms of social control towards women.

General problems in the prison systems are overcrowding, a lack of effective programs for rehabilitation and reintegration, an emphasis on security, and insufficient or ineffective application of alternative measures to imprisonment (Maiello, Carter, Companies, & Min, 2019). The literature on the topic foregrounds the disadvantaged position of women (and other non-hegemonic groups) among the problems identified in the penal institutions worldwide (see for example, Almeda, 2005; Barberet, 2014a; Dobash & Dobash, 1986; Penal Reform International, 2008). Women suffer from the inadequacy of the institutions designed for men and specific regimes of formal control under prison institutions. They suffer special repression 'because of their quantity' (Falcón, 1977). The Global Prison Trends report states:

> Designed, built and managed for men, our criminal justice systems continue to be mostly ill-equipped to respond to the needs of specific populations, such as children, women, older people, and lesbian, gay, bisexual, transgender and intersex prisoners (Maiello et al., 2019, 3).

Within the global literature on the issues of women in prison, it has been underscored the androcentric and clearly discriminatory perspective of the prison system in relation to women, punished with a marked gender character. Incarceration for women is characterized by discourses or "femininity regimes" that seek to regulate their behavior through three control mechanisms: monitoring their appearance, work and regulating their behavior (Bosworth & Carrabine, 2001). These features remain still today in new forms of punishment, as Ballesteros-Pena (2018) describes for the Respect Modules in Spain, in which (gendered) discipline and obedience underlie the idea of responsibilization.

However, feminist critical criminology has been criticized for its structuralist vision, which puts an excessive focus on the disciplinary power to impose itself and on the gendered regimes of the prison institution. They have been accused of moving into a binary conception of domination/resistance, leaving issues related to the agency of women prisoners in a more than a second level and presenting them as "ideal victims," which is not always a safe or successful feminist option. (Fili, 2013, 4). I propose that epistemological and theoretical feminist proposals of a post-structuralist stance, which have been developed in recent times since they offer insight to appreciate the capacity of action of imprisoned women articulated with institutional power relations.

36.3 Resisters Behind Bars

Recent work has underscored the agency of women in prison (Bosworth, 1999; Bosworth & Carrabine, 2001; De-Miguel Calvo, 2017; Fili, 2013), noting that incarcerated women do not remain passive in relation to the exercises of power. In this regard, Fili states:

> Prisons are sites of human interaction where prisoners are in a constant dialogue with the institution, and during the dialogue, all participants negotiate and constitute the definition of the situation in which they find themselves (2013, 18).

Feminist studies of a post-structuralist orientation offer a theoretical basis to develop the reflection on the agency of imprisoned women, based on the grounds of the reflection of Butler (1997) on power and resistance. Judit Butler describes the Foucaultian understanding of power, not as opposed to resistance, as both are inseparable but rather as a result of power. Understanding power not as monolithic or fixed, but rather formative or productive, malleable, multiple, proliferative, and conflictual, which therefore is constantly recreated. This perspective allows us to escape the blindness (and fascination) that power tends to produce in the researcher Medina-Doménech (2013). Beyond the dichotomy between passive victims and active resistances, it is possible to grasp the multiple levels that are operating in social relations within the prison and how they are negotiated (Fili, 2013). Hence, it is possible to grasp criminalized women's capacity for action, while they navigate multiple structural constraints (Bernard, 2012), even in the most limiting circumstances such as the space of confinement.

Tracking the agency of imprisoned women requires theoretical tools that allow us to go beyond the understanding that has been held so far about resistance in prison, which have primarily had a strong political, collective character and have had an explicit ideological approach (Rosón & Medina Doménech, 2017). As Bosworth and Carrabine suggest,

> we need to advance a way of thinking that recognizes that resistance should not be simply equated with rudimentary forms of political action and transformation (2001, 506).

In this sense, Dolores Juliano (1998) states that the problem lies in the epistemological perspective in the approach to the object of study, since it is often assumed that women of popular sectors are passive recipients of a culture that assigns them a subordinate role, setting aside how they continuously develop subversion strategies and avoidance of system impositions. Bosworth and Carrabine (2001) expand on the notion of resistance through three notes. First, resistance is not always visible to an audience, that is, it can refer to issues of authority framed personally or intimately. Second, it cannot be taken for granted that people who do not seem to question authority are accepting the legitimacy of the institution. Finally, they propose to move away from conceptions of resistance that are closely associated with the use of violence and explicit protest.

I draw on the notion of an agency described by Bosworth (1999) which includes the possibility of resistance. The author uses the term agent to express two attributes of imprisoned women: on the one hand, their role as subjects and, on the other, their ability to act and, specifically, to act negotiating power and resisting. According to Bosworth, resistance is one of the forms adopted by the agency, which, in turn, illuminates the attempts of the protagonists to distort power relations on the microscale but taking into account, at the same time, the status quo. Thus, the notion of agency is not merely individual or psychological but rather takes into account social conditions (Pollack, 2000).

Tattoos (Ribeiro & Mendoza, 2013), music and clothing (Estevez Grillo, 2018), as well as sports (Martinez-Merino, 2018; Martinez-Merino, Martos-Garcia, Lozano-Sufrategui, Martín-González, & Usabiaga, 2018) have been interpreted as ways of resistance in prison. Ribeiro and Mendoza (2013) analyze the tattooed body of a prisoner as a discursive space, as a communication resource in which they can write and differentiate their bodies from each other, as well as express protests. In this way, through the tattoo, the prisoners carry out an exercise of reconfiguration and redefinition of themselves and their relationship with others, which allows them to affirm their existence as social beings and establish social bonds. Estevez-Grillo (2018) describes three main sources of resistance in incarcerated girls in the Fundação CASA: affections, musicality and what the author calls 'materialities'— in relation to the material aspects during incarceration. The author mentions the use of objects and clothes for embellishing themselves, as well as for altering their appearance. These are interpreted as strategies for resisting standardization, and as a way of preserving individuality. Music has relational connotations, as incarcerated women choose certain songs for sending messages. On the other hand, Mageehon (2008), in his description of the ways in which incarcerated women negotiate power, recognizes the fragility of their position regarding criminal power and that of prison staff, but appreciates that they act by adopting forms of conformity and passive resistance, which resonates in the tactics that (Scott, 1990) calls 'infrapolitics of the dominated'.

Bosworth (1999) includes the negotiation of the notion of femininity as a resistance strategy, where womanhood can function as a means of oppression, but also as a form of resistance. For the author, women in prison co-opt a definition of allegedly universal and homogeneous femininity, to appropriate it and extend its margins until they can join their own experiences. They take control over the definition of femininity itself by making an alternative proposal, acting through the role of mother and other identities of femininity, such as wives, girlfriends, and lovers. Worrall (1990) also highlights the importance of femininity as a battlefield, since for the author criminalized women exploit the contradictions of the 'gender contract' as a feminization process based on certain parameters of domesticity, sexuality, and pathology. As Worrall (1990) states, women's resistance

> has the important effect of undermining the authority of official discourses and keeping open the possibilities of the creation of new knowledge about them -both as women and as law-breakers (Worrall, 1990,163).

Fili (2013) aligns with this idea when she analyses the agency of women in Greek prisons, as she finds that incarcerated women develop strategies to alleviate discomfort caused by prison. These strategies are framed in formulas for the preservation of identity, which are aimed at resisting the essentialization of women. Identity and femininity are therefore two fundamental axis of the resistance of criminalized women. Femininity is a key element in the construction of identity, and for the resistance against the gendered prison regimes.

The redefinition of identity, and more precisely femininity, is articulated with the emotional field, which I intend to develop through underlying the implications of the couple's love experience. This idea will be developed in the next section when I describe the contributions of feminist theories with regard to the role of (heterosexual) love in the formation of gender subjectivities, understanding love relationships as a metaphorical form of 'liberation' (De Miguel-Calvo, 2015b). This focus can be useful to understand how romantic relationships behind bars are saturated with dense metaphorical connotations in that context. Nari et al. (2000) find that women try to survive to confinement through formulas where affectivity plays an important role. The emotional field is a key area to articulate strategies. This proposal implies understanding feelings, not as something fixed, but conceiving that they have a plasticity that social actors shuffle more or less consciously (Esteban, 2010). The efforts for creating a loving environment can be understood as strategies that allow transcending situations of material and emotional scarcity:

> In the day to day, in the urgent need to rebuild a daily life, perhaps the strongest strategy within the prison is to love. Loving a couple, loving a daughter, loving a mother, loving a father, loving a sister. It does not matter that they are not, it does not matter that the bond lasts for the duration of the confinement (Nari et al., 2000, 17).

Love in prison might be interpreted as a form of 'emotional resistance', a term coined by Rosón and Medina-Doménech (2017, 420) to refer to

> delicate procedures elaborated by people which, provided with affectivity, potentially challenge the different forms of power and the emotional regimes that sustain those powers.

36.4 Sociological and Feminist Understandings on Love

Love and emotions have not been traditionally subject to inquiry within the social sciences, which is assumed to be the domain of psychology (Smart, 2007), reinforcing the idea that these are individual rather than social phenomena. However, the social sciences, and specifically the discipline of sociology, are paying more attention to the different aspects involved in the shared experiences with emotions and love, stressing the idea that they are socially constructed (Jackson, 1993)

The analytical proposal presented here takes contributions from two bodies of ideas on love. On the one hand, sociological approaches devoted to the study of the role of love in the processes of individualization and subjectivation generated in Western countries. On the other, feminist ideas analyzing the role of love in the generation and perpetuation of gender inequalities (Esteban, Medina, & Távora, 2005). In both cases, it is underlined the importance of romantic love experience in the configuration of subjectivity, with the difference that the social sciences have not accentuated so clearly on the generation of gendered subjectivities as in the case of feminist theories.

As for the first line, there is currently a growing interest in love relationships within the discipline of sociology, as they are increasingly appreciated as a central component for social and personal life (Jackson, 1993, 2014; Smart, 2007). In this sense, love plays a role in shaping the subjectivity of the modern individual, and in configuring social practices (Esteban, 2011a; Esteban, Távora, & Medina, 2007).

Various sociologists have focused on the relationship between late modernity processes and love relationships (Bauman, 2003; Evans, 2003; Giddens, 2008; Gómez, 2004) highlighting the role of intimacy and love life for individuals, to the point that Beck and Beck-Gernsheim (1998) have come to regard love as 'the new secular religion of our time.' Based on the thesis of the de-traditionalization, these authors suggest that Western societies are in a historical moment of increasing individualization and secularization, where the traditional ties of pre-modern societies have practically disappeared whereas love has taken a central position for people's lives. The source for 'enchantment' is no longer the institutionalized religion but the intimate relationships in the sphere of intimacy:

> The more referents are lost for stability, the more we direct the relationship we feel to give meaning and roots to the relationship with the couple to our life (1998, 93).

Langford (1999) emphasizes the meaning of couple love as 'salvation', the meaning of life, happiness or way of transporting out of the daily routine to a special place. In this context, there is room for a new role of social actors and human agency. Personal choice is a key element, emphasizing freedom as an essential value of our society that is recreated in human relationships (Giddens, 2008; Illouz, 2012).

In this line of analysis of the relationship of love with the processes and characteristics of today's society, Eva Illouz (2009) states that the couple's relationship is related to the new consumption styles of advanced capitalism, where a collective imaginary of romance is constructed in which differences of social class and gender are blurred. Participating in what we could call 'consumption of love' is a form of social inclusion, that is, a way of participation in the collective utopia of romantic love. However, access to these romanticized assets as well as to the commercialization of romantic love is not available to everybody. Socioeconomic differences in the field of love only blur in the imaginary, but not in the field of social practices. At this point, the author expresses that

> the social organization of love is not only structured in terms of patriarchy but also, and in equal or greater measure, in terms of socioeconomic class (Illouz, 2009, 42).

Beyond socioeconomic conditions, Illouz (2012) also points out that love contributes to a sense of personal worth as if the couple disappears; the basic personal psychological support disappears. This is one of the keys to understand the inclination of imprisoned women towards relationships, especially considering that their sense of personal worth is deeply undermined, as women and as criminals.

As for the second line of analysis, from a more multidisciplinary nature, feminist theories describe the crucial role of love in the configuration of gender subjectivities (differentiated, opposed, complementary and hierarchical), through discourses and practices in different orders of life (Medina Doménech, 2013). In this line, Lupton (1998) analyses the differentiation in the construction of a discourse on emotions about men and women in the western world, represented in the models of 'emotional woman' and 'man without emotions'. In the creation of these stereotypes, interactions in everyday life and mass media contribute to the idea that women have a greater capacity to feel emotions and express them, understanding that it is they who are most familiar with the world of emotions. Hochschild (1979), meanwhile, describes the 'emotional norms', which are constructed differently for men and women, in a sexual division of emotional labor.

In this way, the realm of the couple appears as central in the feminine existence (Bosch & Ferrer, 2013; Esteban & Távora, 2008; Lagarde, 2000, 2008).

> [Women are] beings for love, beings of love, says Lagarde (2000, 347).

Their experience with love is defining their gender identity, so being in a relationship tends to be associated with being socially valuable and, on the other hand, being single is related to having some type of failure (Langford, 1999). Thus, love is "what makes us men and women" (Esteban, 2009, 2010, 2011b; Esteban et al., 2005), the scenario par excellence where femininities and masculinities are performed, as well as where gender inequalities are perpetuated through the 'emotional specialization' of women in the field of love (Coria, 2001; Eichenbaum & Orbach, 2007; Hite, 1988; Lagarde, 2000). Gendered and hierarchical identities create the conditions of possibility for the 'exploitation of the power of love' of women by men, the main way of perpetuating gender inequalities (Jónasdóttir, 1988, 1998; Jónasdóttir & Ferguson, 2014). This is also at the root of gender violence within the couple (Amurrio & Larrinaga, 2010; Amurrio, Larrinaga, Usategi, & De Valle, 2010; Bosch, 2011; Bosch & Ferrer, 2013).

In sum, despite some remarkable exceptions (such as Hooks, 2001 and Lorde, 2003) feminist theorizations on love have been at the forefront of what Carol Smart (2007) has called the 'disdainful approach', assuming that love functions as a kind of 'false consciousness' in which women are trapped. However, feminist criticisms of love as oppressive and legitimizing inequalities can lead us to a dead-end:

> Once the oppressive nature of love for women is exposed, trying to do explorations beyond seemed at best banal and at worst, ideologically unsound (Jackson, 1993, 204).

It is necessary to open paths beyond oppression, overcoming the idea that women who have negotiated the senses of love, eroticism, and romantic illusion are 'cultural fools', 'wrong', 'degrading' or complicit with sexist violence and patriarchy (Felitti & Elizalde, 2015).

Carol Smart offers a way of overcoming the cul-de-sac, suggesting to focus on the 'doings of love' rather than on the discursive representations, which means to inquire into the doings and meanings in everyday lives. Similarly, Medina-Doménech (2013) suggests differentiating between the discourses on love and the practices of love of women under the dictatorship in Spain, therefore, differentiating between what she calls the science of love (discourses of the power) and the knowledge of love in women's everyday lives. With the aim to conflate the realm of hegemonic powers in relation to romantic love and the everyday experiences of incarcerated women, love relationships in prison have been explained as a form of metaphorical 'liberation' (De Miguel-Calvo, 2015b). Drawing on the concept of 'captivity' of anthropologist Marcela Lagarde, I contrast the metaphorical and objective 'captivities' of incarcerated women, both as women in the patriarchal system and as incarcerated women, held in prison. In this sense, love may be understood as a way to hold captive criminalized women in the realm of patriarchal love, but also as a metaphorical way of setting free behind bars. More recently, research on love have developed insights on the ways hegemonic understandings on love are challenged on a day-to-day basis by feminist women (García-Fernández, 2017) and by practitioners of non-monogamy and polyamory (Enciso-Dominguez, 2018; Enciso-Domínguez, Pujol, Motzkau, & Popper, 2017; Klesse, 2018). Homosexual encounters also challenge the hegemonic heterosexual scripts on love, experiences occurring also behind bars, as it will described further on the next section where love experiences of women in prison are portrayed.

36.5 Love, Affection, and Sexuality Behind Bars

The literature on relationships in prison emphasizes the tendency of incarcerated women to be in relationships. This has been generally interpreted as a form of agency, considering that networks of affection produce thwarts to the powers of the institution (De Miguel-Calvo, 2017; Estevez-Grillo, 2018; Ojeda, 2013; Padovani, 2016). Friends, acquaintances, family, and couple relationships form a means to survive the deprivations of imprisonment (Comfort, 2008), a coping mechanism (Severance, 2005) or a way of getting security (Ojeda, 2013). Moreover, Kilty and Dej (2012) find that close relationships are important for criminalized women who use drugs because, through these connections, women develop a sense of self-worth.

A recent body of research in Brazil has emphasized the affective and relational dimensions of criminalized women and girls during incarceration (Bouças do Lago, 2014; Estevez-Grillo, 2018; Padovani, 2016). Estevez-Grillo (2018) researched on the living conditions of the girls held at the CASA Foundation in Sao Paolo, a resource for educational detention measures. The author finds that, while boys make affections clandestine, in girls the demonstration of affectivity in a dehumanized space such as jail is a resistance strategy.

Bouças do Lago (2017) pays attention to the female partner figure of the prisoner as part of the relations of affection that occur inside/outside the prison. In her analysis of the visits that the couple of the male prisoners make to the prison, he describes the interactions that occur between the female wives of the prisoners. These interactions are filled with tensions and hierarchies. Protagonists create categories in order to differentiate between them in a way to express that one has a more valid relationship than the others do. Comfort (2008) a leading voice in the theme of 'secondary prisonization'—the consequences of the prison for the families, focuses on the ambivalence of the incarceration of the partner for women. In her work Doing Time Together, the author notes that the dynamics of love and intimacy are altered in the carceral space, where the prison functions as "a peculiar refuge in which couples can enact idealized versions of romance and cohabitation" (2008, 17). This shows that incarceration can reinforce romantic attachment and, more importantly, heightens the status of women, leading men to the feminine realm of love.

However, not all the visions have been so positive. Greer (2000) depicts an environment of mistrust towards sexual relationships among inmates, as they are seen as based on manipulation primarily where money plays a significant role. Certainly, material interests are not out of the equation in romantic relationships (Padovani, 2016). In addition, jealousy and conflict derive from the relationships behind bars (Ojeda, 2013).

Pardue, Arrigo, and Murphy note that women prisoners "may view sex as an expression of freedom, especially as sexual intimacy is one of the few aspects of their lives they can control" (2011: 291). Certainly, aspects related to the body are the ones that can ensure the exertion of freedom, in the stretched limits of the prison. Moreover, the specific context of the prison favors homosexual transactions. Thus, lesbian relationships are a significant component of the subculture of women's prisons (Forsyth, Evans, & Foster, 2002). According to the literature, homosexuality is experienced more or less openly in jail, without any restrictions by the prison staff, together with relative acceptance by other women prisoners (De Miguel-Calvo, 2015b; Joël-Lauf, 2012; Nari et al., 2000). 'Dyke Jails' ('Cárceles Bolleras'), the documentary directed by Cecilia Montagut, is the visual result of the research in which Raquel Osborne sociologist and myself participated. The documentary, precisely, contends the idea that prisons are favorable environments for the transformation of desire, and that lesbian desire is a means of resistance to the powers of prison. Katia, one of the participants in the documentary, spoke about her desire as a form of affirmation of herself against the institution. She contended that she presented herself as a woman who feels desire and that to speak about that openly with other confined women. This resonates with Lorde's power of the erotic. Herrero-Riesgo (2015) show similar findings, understanding prison as sites for the transformation of desire, but stressing that this transformation moves in two directions, towards others and towards oneself, in the sense of knowledge of oneself. This possibility of enhancing self-consciousness and knowledge about oneself resonates with the idea of Jaggar (1989) to show emotions as via for knowledge.

There is also evidence that some women have their first lesbian experience in prison. Some authors have reflected around these relationships differentiating between 'true' and 'false' lesbians (Pardue et al., 2011). However, recent research has challenged this differentiation—those who were lesbian before entering prison and the others who engage sexually with other women only while they are in prison. Challenging this idea, Andrea, another participant in the documentary 'Dyke Jails' recalled that there was a woman in prison who coined the term 'jail lesbian' to express the contingency of her practices. It also shows her agency in the very act of defining herself.

Certainly, there is a constant suspicion about the validity and veracity of any experience that occurs within the prison. As with lesbian practices that occur behind bars, any relationship that begins within the prison is considered suspicious of not having continuity. 'Prison love, passenger love' ('Amor taleguero, amor pasajero') as expressed in the phrase that I often heard from the participants of my research (De Miguel-Calvo, forthcoming). Relationships that have been established in prison are considered a kind of parenthesis in the 'real' life, something that one passes through. In a way, that is not 'true', implying that love outside prisons is authentic.

Finally, it is interesting to note the contrast between the experience of heterosexual relationships and lesbian practices. Joël-Lauf (2013) examines the benefits of homosexual relationships in women's prisons, contending that women prisoners find pleasure in lavishing and receiving affection, as well as in being desired. In this sense, compared to experiences with men, often violent, the interviewees emphasize that, among women, they have the opportunity to be treated with tenderness and respect. However, these relationships are not only about affection and care. In this vein, some informants for 'Dyke Jails' research project reported abusive conducts of some women towards their partners. Some other research have also noted exploitative components of same sex relations in prison among women (Einat & Chen, 2012; Greer, 2000; Joël-Lauf, 2013). Economic interests, jealousy, conflict and violence are not absent in lesbian relationships in prison.

36.6 Conclusion

In this chapter, I have aimed at showing how prison is a specific field of study of love and that the couple relationships of imprisoned women are fundamental in their experience of imprisonment. At the same time, my goal has been to develop the idea that the love environment in prison works for women prisoners, not always as a reproducer of gender inequalities, but that can also be an axis of resistance. This resistance is not political and collective, but rather in the field of identity and in terms of interactions at the micro level. Still, these resistances put into question the exercises of power over women. Taking into account that the main axis of punishment is articulated on the idea that criminalized women are inadequate women and that the penitentiary response must be aimed at feminization. At this point, the analysis of the disciplinary power over women and their resistances is especially interesting for debates about the social control of women, as well as for the heating debates that are currently taking place about the political subject 'Woman'.

Recent literature on women in prison has acknowledged the agency of women and their capacity for resisting the punishment of prison through a wide range of strategies. Different behaviors and practices behind bars have been understood as ways of affirming their existence as social beings, seeking establishing social bonds. Moreover, incarcerated women try to resist standarization and preserve individuality. Here, the negotiation of the notion of femininity appears at the core of the agency. Co-opting the definition of femininity, they create new knowledge about themselves. This applies also for the realm of emotions and relationships. Here I gather literature on imprisoned women that has revealed the importance of the emotional world behind bars as a way to resist the pains of imprisonment, as well as a way to achieve security and even economic benefits. In this sense, those meanings and those identities (either with their positive connotations or with their negative connotations of stigma), are aspects that are being negotiated regularly.

Women resist taking the available emotional resources that allow them to reformulate the meanings and disrupt the logics of confinement. However, few studies consider in any depth the debates on love in sociological and feminist studies. I propose to connect reflections on love in prison with the debates that currently are taking place in the sociological discipline as well as within feminism related to collective experiences with love.

Based on the sociological reflections on love, it can be affirmed that women prisoners are inserted in the social meanings of love, which are highly valued. Thus, by having a partner, confined women affirm their existence as social beings with significant links. Love counteracts, in this way, the social stigma of being a woman prisoner, given that love provides a sense of self-worth in current Western understandings of romantic relationships. Moreover, the love of a couple plays an important role, since it allows to be inserted in a frame of a socially shared sense, where the invisibility to the participation in a social utopia is left behind. Nowadays, love means freedom, abundance, salvation and escape from reality. These values gain special connotations in the context of prison, characterized by a lack of freedom, material and emotional scarcity for those who have been juridically and morally 'condemned'. Besides, love conforms a collective utopia of enchantment, affirmation of individuality and freedom from social constraints. These ideas are highly valuable in the context of imprisonment, especially for women.

Feminist reflections of love have revolved around the role of (heterosexual) couple relationships in the perpetuation of gender inequalities, assuming that love works as a sort of 'false consciousness' trapping women into exploitative relationships with men. These gender inequalities can only occur based on subjectivities that are constructed as differentiated between women and men. Love, thus, is the realm in which gender identities are performed, defining women as 'emotional beings'/'beings for love'. In this sense, when incarcerated women insert themselves to the realm of love, they are expanding normative understandings on womanhood, as they claim to be also 'beings for love', who worth being loved.

It is possible to grasp these meanings of love for incarcerated women, if we expand the reflection on love beyond oppressions. An excessive attention to power might be blinding. A differentiation between discourses and practices allows us to grasp the individuals' capacity to resist.

However, behaviors that seek to undermine authority can also be self-destructive; therefore, they are not exempt from ambiguity. Certainly, agency is a problematic object of study and I understand that there has not been enough debate when it comes to clarifying the different layers of the notion of resistance and its limits. Tensions between structuralist and post-structuralist views of the role of emotional experiences in contexts of deprivation remain here, as general conditions of incarceration are not put into question by these forms of agency. Further debate is needed in order to maintain a critical view about structural constraints while, at the same time, deepen into a more nuanced notion of agency.

References

Almeda, E. (2005). Women's imprisonment in Spain. *Punishment & Society, 7*(2), 183–199. https://doi.org/10.1177/1462474505050442

Almeda, E., Di Nella, D., & Navarro, C. (2012). Mujeres, cárceles y drogas: datos y reflexiones. *Oñati Socio-Legal Series, 2*(6), 122–145.

Amurrio, M., & Larrinaga, A. (2010). Love and violence in learning about relationships. In M. L. Esteban & M. Amurrio (Eds.), *Feminist challenges in social sciences. Gender studies in the Basque Country* (pp. 158–173). Reno, NV: University of Nevada.

Amurrio, M., Larrinaga, A., Usategi, E., & De Valle, A. I. (2010). Violencia de género en las relaciones de pareja de adolescentes y jóvenes en Bilbao. *Zerbitzuan, 47*, 121–134.

Añaños-Bedriñana, F., & Jiménez-Bautista, F. (2016). Población y contextos sociales vulnerables: la prisión y el género al descubierto. *Papeles de Población, 22*(87), 63–101.

Ariza, L., & Iturralde, M. (2017). Mujer, crimen y castigo penitenciario. *Política Criminal, 12*(24), 731–753.

Ballesteros-Pena, A. (2018). Responsibilisation and female imprisonment in contemporary penal policy: 'Respect Modules' ('Módulos de Respeto') in Spain. *Punishment & Society, 20*(4), 458–476. https://doi.org/10.1177/1462474517710241

Barberet, R. (2014a). *Women, crime and criminal justice*. London: Routledge.

Barberet, R. (2014b). Women and incarceration. In *Women, crime and criminal justice* (pp. 159–188). London: Routledge.

Bauman, S. (2003). *Amor líquido. Acerca de la fragilidad de los vínculos humanos*. Madrid: Fondo de Cultura Económica.

Beck, U., & Beck-Gernsheim, E. (1998). *El normal caos del amor*. Barcelona: El Roure.

Bernard, A. (2012). The intersectional alternative: Explaining female criminality. *Feminist Criminology, 8*(1), 3–19. https://doi.org/10.1177/1557085112445304

Bosch, E. (2011). *Del mito del amor romántico a la violencia contra las mujeres en la pareja*. Madrid: Instituto de la Mujer.

Bosch, E., & Ferrer, V. (2013). *La violencia contra las mujeres. El amor como coartada*. Madrid: Anthropos.

Bosworth, M. (1999). *Engendering resistance: Agency and power in women's prisons*. Aldershot: Ashgate.

Bosworth, M., & Carrabine, E. (2001). Reassessing resistance: Race, gender and sexuality in prison. *Punishment and Society, 3*(4), 501–515. https://doi.org/10.1177/14624740122228393

Bouças do Lago, N. (2014). *Mulheres na prisão: Entre famílias, batalhas e a vida normal*. Universidad de Sao Paulo.

Bouças do Lago, N. (2017). Mulher de preso nunca está sozinha: gênero e violência nas visitas à prisão. *ARACÊ – Direitos Humanos Em Revista, 4*(5), 35–53.

Butler, J. (1997). *The psychic life of power. Theories in subjection*. Stanford, CA: Stanford University Press.

Carlen, P. (1983). *Women's imprisonment: A study in social control*. London: Routledge and Kegan Paul.

Carlen, P. (1988). *Women, crime and poverty*. Milton Keynes: Open University Press.

Carlen, P., & Worrall, A. (1987). *Gender, crime and justice*. Milton Keynes: Open University Press.

Chesney-Lynd, M. (1986). Women and crime: The female offender. *Signs: Journal of Women and Culture in Society, 2*(1), 78–96.

Chesney-Lind, M. (2006). Patriarchy, crime, and justice: Feminist criminology in an era of Backlash. *Feminist Criminology, 1*(1), 6–26. https://doi.org/10.1177/1557085105282893

Comfort, M. (2008). *Doing time together. Love and family in the shadow of the prison*. Chicago: University of Chicago Press.

Coria, C. (2001). *El amor no es como nos lo contaron...ni como lo inventamos*. Buenos Aires: Paidós.

Davis, A. (2003). *Are prisons obsolete?* New York: Seven Stories Press.

De Miguel-Calvo, E. (2015a). Mujeres usuarias de drogas en prisión. *Praxis Sociológica, 19*, 141–159.

De Miguel-Calvo, E. (2015b). *Relaciones amorosas de las mujeres encarceladas*. Bilbao: UPV/EHU Servicio Editorial.

De Miguel-Calvo, E. (2016). Mujeres, consumo de drogas y encarcelamiento. Una aproximación interseccional. *Política y Sociedad, 53*(2), 529–549. https://doi.org/10.5209/rev_POSO.2016.v53.n2.47421

De Miguel-Calvo, E. (2017). Explorando la agencia de las mujeres encarceladas a través de sus experiencias amorosas. *Papers. Revista de Sociología, 102*(2), 311–335.

De Miguel-Calvo, E. (forthcoming). Amor taleguero, amor pasajero. Relaciones sexo-afectivas de mujeres dentro de la cárcel. In B. S. Stock & R. Dotta (Eds.), *Género y Prisiones*. Sevilla: Athenaica.

Dobash, R. P., & Dobash, R. E. (1986). Imprisonment of women. (S. Gutteridge, Ed.). New York: Basil Blackwell Inc.

Eichenbaum, L., & Orbach, S. (2007). *¿Qué quieren las mujeres? (7a)*. Madrid: Talasa.

Einat, T., & Chen, G. (2012). What's love got to do with it? Sex in a female maximum-security prison. *Prison Journal, 92*(4), 484–505. https://doi.org/10.1177/0032885512457550

Enciso-Dominguez, G. (2018). Rethinking the monogamy script: Contributions from Poliamory oractices: Gender, jealousy and quotidianity. In *National problems through psychological view* (pp. 232–259). Mexico: Universidad Autónoma de México.

Enciso-Domínguez, G. E., Pujol, J., Motzkau, J. F., & Popper, M. (2017). Suspended transitions and affective orderings: From troubled monogamy to liminal polyamory. *Theory and Psychology, 27*(2), 183–197. https://doi.org/10.1177/0959354317700289

Equipo Barañi. (2001). *Mujeres gitanas y sistema penal*. Madrid: Metyel.

Esteban, M. L. (2009). Identidades de género, feminismo, sexualidad y amor: los cuerpos como agentes. *Politica y Sociedad, 46*(1y2), 27–41.

Esteban, M. L. (2010). Algunas ideas para una antropología del amor. In *Emociones y sentimientos* (pp. 229–246). Cuenca: Universidad de Castilla-La Mancha.

Esteban, M. L. (2011a). *Crítica del pensamiento amoroso: temas contemporáneos*. Barcelona: Bellaterra.

Esteban, M. L. (2011b). *Critica del pensamiento amoroso*. Barcelona: Bellaterra.

Esteban, M. L., Medina, R., & Távora, A. (2005). ¿Por qué analizar el amor? Nuevas posibilidades para el estudio de las desigualdades de género. In X Congreso de Antropología de la FAAEE C1—Sevilla. Retrieved from http://cdd.emakumeak.org/ficheros/0000/0599/Sevilla-05122.pdf

Esteban, M. L., & Távora, A. (2008). El amor romántico y la subordinación social de las mujeres: revisiones y propuestas. *Anuario de Psicología, 39*(1), 59–73.

Esteban, M. L., Távora, A., & Medina, R. (2007). El amor romántico dentro y fuera de Occidente. In L. Suárez, E. Martín, & R. A. Hernández (Eds.), *Feminismos en la antropología: Nuevas propuestas críticas*. XI Congreso de Antropología de la FAAEE (pp. 157–172). Ankulegi: Donostia. Retrieved from http://www.ankulegi.org/wp-content/uploads/2012/03/0609Esteban.pdf

Estevez-Grillo, N. (2018). Força pra subir, coragem na descinda: um estudo sobre as resistências das meninas na Fundação CASA. Pontificia Universidade Católica de Sao Paulo.

Evans, M. (2003). *Love: an unromantic discussion*. Oxford: Blackwell.

Falcón, L. (1977). *En el infierno. Ser mujer en las cárceles de España*. Barcelona: De Feminismo.

Felitti, K., & Elizalde, S. (2015). "Vení a Sacar a La Perra Que Hay En Vos": Pedagogías de la seducción, mercado y nuevos retos para los feminismos. *Revista Interdisciplinaria de Estudios de Género, 2*(julio-diciembre), 3–32.

Fili, A. (2013). Women in prison: Victims or resisters? Representations of agency in women's prisons in Greece. *Signs: Journal of Women in Culture and Society, 29*(1), 1–26. https://doi.org/10.1017/CBO9781107415324.004

Forsyth, C. J., Evans, R. D., & Foster, D. B. (2002). An analysis of inmate explanations for lesbian relationships in prison. *International Journal of Sociology of the Family, 30*(1), 66–77.

Foucault, M. (1995). *Discipline and punish. The birth of prison*. New York: Second Vintage Books.
García, J., Boira, S., Gómez-Quintero, J. D., Marcuello, C., & Eito, A. (2015). Imprisoned women and professional intervention in Spain. *International Journal of Law, Crime and Justice, 43*(4), 439–455. https://doi.org/10.1016/J.IJLCJ.2014.11.004
García-Fernández, N. (2017). Love and its contradictions: Feminist women's resistance strategies in their love narratives. *Journal of Popular Romance Studies, 2017*. Retrieved from http://www.jprstudies.org
GCDP-Global Comission on Drug Policy. (2014). Asumiendo el control: Caminos hacia políticas de drogas eficaces. Retrieved from www.globalcommissionondrugs.org/reports
Gelsthorpe, L., & Morris, A. (1990). *Feminist perspectives in criminology*. Buckingham: Open University Press.
Giacomello, C. (2013). *Mujeres, delitos de drogas y sistemas penitenciarios en América Latina*. London: IDPC. Retrieved from http://idpc.net/es/publications/2013/11/mujeres-delitos-de-drogas-y-sistemas-penitenciarios-en-america-latina
Giddens, A. (2008). *La transformación de la intimidad. Sexualidad, amor y erotismo en las sociedades modernas*. Madrid: Cátedra.
Goffman, E. (1993). *Asylums. Essays on the social situation of mental patients and other inmates*. Penguin Random House: London.
Goffman, E. (2001). *Internados. Ensayos sobre la situación social de los enfermos mentales (1st in Spanish)*. Buenos Aires: Amorrortu.
Gómez, J. (2004). *El amor en la sociedad del riesgo*. Barcelona: El Roure.
Greer, K. R. (2000). The changing nature of interpersonal relationships in a women's prison. *The Prison Journal, 80*(4), 442–468.
Haney, L. (2013). Motherhood as punishment: The case of parenting in prison. *Signs. Journal of Women and Culture in Society, 39*(1), 105–130.
Herrero Riesgo, I. (2015). Deseo(s) y resistencia(s) en las cárceles: algunas experiencias de mujeres ex-presas. UPV/EHU.
Hite, S. (1988). *Mujeres y amor. Nuevo informe Hite*. Barcelona: Plaza y Janés.
Hochschild, A. (1979). Emotion work, feeling rules and social structure. *American Journal of Sociology, 85*(3), 551–575.
Hooks, B. (2001). *All about love*. New York: Harper Perennial.
Illouz, E. (2009). *El consumo de la utopía romántica. El amor y las contradicciones culturales del capitalismo*. Madrid: Katz.
Illouz, E. (2012). *¿Por qué duele el amor? Una explicación sociológica*. Madrid: Katz.
Imaz, E., & Martin-Palomo, T. (2007). Las otras otras: extranjeras y gitanas en las cárceles españolas. In B. Biglia & C. San Martín (Eds.), *Estado de Wonderbra: Entretejiendo narraciones feministas sobre las violencias de género* (pp. 217–227). Madrid: Virus.
Jackson, S. (1993). Even sociologists fall in love: An exploration in the sociology of emotions. *Sociology, 27*(2), 201–220.
Jackson, S. (2014). Love, social change, and everyday heterosexuality. In A. Jonasdóttir & A. Ferguson (Eds.), *Love. A question for feminism in the twenty-first century* (pp. 33–47). New York: Routledge.
Jaggar, A. M. (1989). Love and knowledge: Emotion in feminist epistemology. *Inquiry, 32*(2), 151–176. https://doi.org/10.1080/00201748908602185
Jewkes, Y. (2011). Autoethnography and emotion as intellectual resources: Doing prison research differently. *Qualitative Inquiry, 1*(18), 63–75.
Joël-Lauf, M. (2012). *La Sexualite en Prison De Femmes*. Université Paris.
Joël-Lauf, M. (2013). Coûts et bénéfices de l'homosexualité dans les prisons de femmes. *Ethnologie Francaise, 43*(3), 469–476. https://doi.org/10.3917/ethn.133.0469
Jonasdóttir, A. (1988). Sex/gender, power and politics: Towards a theory of the foundations of male authority in formal equal society. *Acta Sociologica, 31*(2), 157–174.
Jónasdóttir, A. (1998). *Why women are oppressed?* Philadelphia, PA: Temple University Press.
Juliano, D. (1998). *Las que saben. Subculturas de mujeres*. Madrid: Horas y Horas.

Juliano, D. (2011). *Presunción de inocencia: riesgo, delito y pecado en femenino*. Donostia: Gakoa.
Kilty, J. M., & Dej, E. (2012). Anchoring amongst the waves: discursive constructions of motherhood and addiction. *Qualitative Sociology Review, VIII*(3), 6–23.
Klesse, C. (2018). Theorizing multi-partner relationships and sexualities – Recent work on non-monogamy and polyamory. *Sexualities, 21*(7), 1109–1124. https://doi.org/10.1177/1363460717701691
Kolb, A., & Palys, T. (2018). Playing the part: Pseudo-families, wives, and the politics of relationships in women's prisons in California. *The Prison Journal, 98*(6), 678–699. https://doi.org/10.1177/0032885518811809
Lagarde, M. (2000). Claves feministas para las negociaciones en el amor. In M. Lagarde (Ed.), *Para mis socias de la vida. Claves feministas para el poderío y la autoestima de las mujeres, los liderazgos entrañables y las negociaciones en el amor* (pp. 383–485). Madrid: Horas y Horas.
Lagarde, M. (2005). *Los cautiverios de las mujeres: madresposas, monjas, putas, presas y locas*. México: UNAM.
Lagarde, M. (2008). Amor y sexualidad. Una mirada feminista. In Curso de verano: Sexualidades en movimiento, derechos a debate. Santander: UIMP—Universidad Internacional Menéndez Pelayo. Retrieved from https://www.academia.edu/8006688/Amor_y_sexualidad_Marcela_Lagarde
Langford, W. (1999). *Revolutions of the heart. Gender, power and the delusions of love*. London: Routledge.
Larrauri, E. (1994). *Mujeres, derecho penal y criminología*. Madrid: Siglo XXI.
Lorde, A. (2003). *La hermana, la extranjera*. Madrid: Horas y Horas.
Lupton, D. (1998). *The emotional self*. London: Sage.
Mageehon, A. (2008). Caught up in the system. How women who have been incarcerated negotiate power. *The Prison Journal, 88*(4), 473–492.
Maiello, L., Carter, S., Companies, C. G. L., & Min, B. (2019). *Global prison trends*. London.
Malloch, M. S. (2000). *Women, drugs and custody*. Winchester: Waterside Press.
Martinez-Merino, N. (2018). *Understanding the meaning of sport and physical activity in prison: revealing incarcerated women's voices*. Universidad del País Vasco y Universitat de València.
Martinez-Merino, N., Martos-Garcia, D., Lozano-Sufrategui, L., Martín-González, N., & Usabiaga, O. (2018). Frictions, cracks and micro-resistances: physical activity and sport as strategies to dignify imprisoned women. *Qualitative Research in Sport, Exercise and Health, 11*(2), 217–230. https://doi.org/10.1080/2159676X.2018.1493526
Martín-Palomo, M. T., Miranda, M. J., & Vega, C. (Eds.) (2005). *Delitos y fronteras: Mujeres extranjeras en prisión*. Madrid: Instituto de Investigaciones Feministas.
May, V., & Nordqvist, P. (2019). *Sociology of personal life*. London: Macmillan and Red Globe Press.
Medina-Doménech, R. M. (2013). 'Who were the experts?' The science of love vs women's knowledge of love during the Spanish dictatorship. *Science as Culture, 23*(2), 177–200. https://doi.org/10.1080/09505431.2013.809412
Messerschmidt, J. W. (1993). *Masculinities and crime: Critique and reconceptualization of theory*. Lantham M.D.: Rowman and Littlefield.
Moran, D. (2012). Prisoner reintegration and the stigma of prison time inscribed on the body. *Punishment and Society, 14*(5), 564–583. https://doi.org/10.1177/1462474512464008
Nari, M., Fabre, A., Hauser, S., Calandra, N., Fraguas, N., & Friedman, J. (2000). Me queda la palabra. Estrategias de resistencia de las mujeres encarceladas. In M. Nari & A. Fabre (Eds.), *Voces de mujeres encarceladas* (pp. 19–64). Buenos Aires: Catálogos.
Ojeda, N. S. (2013). Cárcel de mujeres. Una mirada etnográfica sobre las relaciones afectivas en un establecimiento carcelario de mediana seguridad en Argentina. *Sociedad y Economía, 25*, 237–254.
Padovani, N. (2016). Plotting prisons, flows and affections: Brazilian female prisoners between the transnational drug trade and sex markets in Barcelona. *Criminology and Criminal Justice, 16*(3), 366–385. https://doi.org/10.1177/1748895816646611

Pardue, A., Arrigo, B. A., & Murphy, D. S. (2011). Sex and sexuality in women's prisons: A preliminary tipologycal investigation. *The Prison Journal, 3*(91), 279–304.
Penal Reform International. (2008). Women in prison: incarcerated in a man's world. *Penal Reform Briefing, 1*. Retrieved from http://www.penalreform.org/wp-content/uploads/2013/06/brf-03-2008-women-in-prison-en.pdf
Pollack, S. (2000). Reconceptualizing women's agency and empowerment. *Women & Criminal Justice, 12*(1), 75–89. https://doi.org/10.1300/J012v12n01_05
Ribas, N., Almeda, E., & Bodelón, E. (2005). *Rastreando lo invisible. Mujeres extranjeras en las cárceles*. Barcelona: Anthropos.
Ribas-Mateos, N., & Martinez, A. (2003). Mujeres extranjeras en las cárceles españolas. *Revista Sociedad y Economía, 5*, 65–80.
Ribeiro, R., & Mendoza, N. O. (2013). El cuerpo preso tatuado: un espacio discursivo. *Andamios. Revista de Investigación Social, 10*(23), 283–303.
Rice, M. (1990). Challenging orthodoxies in feminist theory: a black feminist critique. In L. Gelsthorpe & A. Morris (Eds.), *Feminist perspectives in criminology* (pp. 57–69). Milton Keynes-Philadelphia: Open University Press.
Richie, B. (1996). *Compelled to crime: the gender entrapment of battered black women*. New York: Routledge.
Rosón, M., & Medina Doménech, R. (2017). Resistencias emocionales. Espacios y presencias de lo íntimo en el archivo histórico. *Arenal. Revista de Historia de Las Mujeres, 24*(2), 407–439.
Schlosser, J. A. (2008). Issues in interviewing inmates. Navigating the methodological landmines of prison research. *Qualitative Inquiry, 14*(8), 1500–1525.
Scott, J. C. (1990). *Domination and the arts of resistance*. New Haven, CT: Yale University Press.
Severance, T. A. (2005). "You know who you can go to": Cooperation and exchange between incarcerated women. *The Prison Journal, 85*, 343–365.
Smart, C. (1977). *Women, crime and criminology: A feminist critique*. London: Routledge and Kegan Paul.
Smart, C. (1990). Feminist approaches to criminology or postmodern woman meets atavistic man. In L. Gelsthorpe & A. Morris (Eds.), *Feminist perspectives in criminology* (pp. 70–84). Buckingham: Open University Press.
Smart, C. (2007). *Personal life*. London: Polity.
Sudbury, J. (2002). Celling black bodies: Black women in the global prison industrial complex. *Feminist Review, 70*(1), 57–74. https://doi.org/10.1057/palgrave.fr.9400006
Walmsley, R. (2018). World Female Imprisonment List fourth edition Women and girls in penal institutions, including pre-trial detainees/remand prisoners. Retrieved from www.prisonstudies.org.
Worrall, A. (1990). *Offending women: Female lawbreakers and the criminal justice system*. Londres y Nueva York: Routledge.

Estibaliz de Miguel Calvo (PhD) in Sociology. Awarded 'Micaela Portilla' Prize for the best PhD in feminist/gender studies at the University of the Basque Country (2012). Visiting fellow at the Morgan Centre for the Study of Relationships and Personal Life in the Department of Sociology at the University of Manchester (2010 and 2011). Selected for the PhD workshop at the European Sociological Association (ESA) Conference in Geneva, 2011. Member of the EMOCRITICAS-Research Network on Emotions and Feelings from a gender/feminist perspective. Research interests: women in prison, social exclusion, love and emotions.

Chapter 37
Hatred, Life Without Love, and the Descent into Hell

Warren TenHouten

> [H]ate is the unmet wish to be loved, the inability actively To love anyone (self or other), and the consequent abject dependency on others to magically fill with love a bottomless pit, an inferno—the self—that is utterly empty of love.
> James Gilligan (1997, p. 54)

Abstract Love and hatred are often seen as opposites. From a standpoint of emotion classification, love can be defined as a mixture of joy and acceptance, the joyful acceptance of and by another. The opposites of joy and acceptance are sadness and disgust, respectively. From this it has been inferred (in the previous chapter) that the opposite of love is not hatred but rather loneliness–forlornness. Hatred and loneliness share the primary emotion disgust, as the object of hatred is rejected and even seen as morally disgusting. But hatred does not involve sadness; hatred rather involves a dynamic of anger and fear. More specifically, three primary or basic emotions—anger, fear, and disgust, are the hypothesized elements of hatred. These three emotions combine in pairs to form three secondary emotions: frozenness/tonic-immobility (anger & fear), revulsion (fear & disgust), and contempt (anger & disgust). This chapter identifies an absence of love as a causative factor in the mentality and behavior of hate-infused violent criminals, their hatred of life, and their hellish experience of life as the living death. A comparison is made of the present hierarchical-classification theory's model of hatred and Sternberg's triangulation theory of hate.

Keywords Love · Hatred · Emotion · Anger · Fear · Disgust · Contempt · Repugnance · Frozenness/Tonic-immobility · Violence · Hell

W. TenHouten (✉)
Department of Sociology, University of California at Los Angeles, Los Angeles, CA, USA
e-mail: wtenhout@g.ucla.edu

37.1 Introduction

The powerful emotion hatred has been described as the most destructive affective phenomenon in human history (Royzman, McCauley & Rozin, 2005). Hatred finds manifestation in many ways, including a reaction to a romantic love unraveling, in the mentality and destructive behavior of the adult who was unloved and abused as a child, and in the potentially violent behavior of the theologically-driven ideologue. Hatred has long been of interest in psychiatry, criminology, social work, psychology, political science, and sociology (Fischer, Halperin, Canetti, & Jasini, 2018). Hatred has been described in various ways: as a kind of generalized anger (Bernier & Dozier, 2002), a generalized evaluation (Ben-Ze'ev, 2000) (see his chapter in this book), a motive to devalue others (Rempel & Burris, 2005), a single emotion (Elster, 1999), and a family of emotions, including at least anger, disgust, and contempt (e.g., Fischer et al., 2018). While hatred has gained interest when considered in the forms of hate crime and hate speech (Levin & McDevitt, 2002), there is little theorizing and limited empirical research on this emotion. This is not surprising given that it is neither feasible nor ethical to experimentally induce hatred in a laboratory setting. Individuals are additionally apt to deny that they have ever felt hatred, in part because it is not considered an admirable emotion and is given a negative moral evaluation (Aumer, Bahn & Harris, 2015; Halperin, 2008).

The primary objective of this chapter is to model the structure of hatred in a context of emotion theory. This theoretical aim is realized by using an emotions-classification system which defines hatred as a complex emotion comprised of more basic emotions. Hatred was considered a fundamental, basic, elementary, or primary emotion by many medieval and early modern thinkers, including St. Thomas Aquinas (1265–1274), Descartes (1649), and Locke (1689). No longer oriented to theological considerations, contemporary emotion theorists and researchers have seldom included hatred it in inventories of emotions (Fischer et al., 2018; but cf. Fitness & Fletcher, 1993, Halperin, 2008). Yet, hatred would appear to be a culturally universal and socially important emotion, arguably an intrinsic capability of human nature, with deep evolutionary roots (Eibl-Eibesfeldt, 1972).

Hatred is closely associated with anger–rage, which has been shown to involve the "rage system," a brain infrastructure shared by humans and many other animal species (Panksepp, 1998, ch.10; Panksepp & Biven, 2012, ch. 4). In complex emotions comprising mixtures of primary emotions, one constituent emotion can play a key role. For example, in resentment, anger is the central emotion, and researchers often refer to an "angry resentment" stimulated by feelings of unfairness or of relative deprivation (Smith et al., 2012, 217–218; see also Folger, 1987, TenHouten, 2018b). Similarly, intense anger–rage is described as "the emotional core of hatred," and as "a sustained emotion of rage that occupies an individual through much of his life, allowing him to feel delight in observing or inflicting suffering on the hated one" (Gaylin, 2003, p. 33).[1]

Having described hatred as a kind of rage, Gaylin (2003, p. 33) opines that

> regardless of how advanced modern biological psychology may become, we are unlikely to find a way to objectively define, calibrate, or titrate an emotion.

But emotions most certainly can be classified. If hatred is not a primary emotion, and not just an expression of anger–rage, it can be asked: What kind of emotion is it? If all emotions are socially or psychologically constructed, as many sociologists of the emotions and affective neuroscientists believe, then hatred, like all other emotions, would exist *sui generis*. Some researchers hold this view in part because emotions such as love and hate are complicated, interrelated, and come about amidst a veritable tangle of strong feelings, sentiments, wishes, intentions, drives, desires, and stresses. Further, verbal expressions of emotions can gloss the inner experience of very different emotions and reasons (Gay, 1993, pp. 69, 91–92, 198). However, if hatred is not entirely socially or psychologically constructed, and if is not a primary emotion, then it might well be a complex emotion, comprised of two, or even three, primary emotions. It is possible to become enraged with another person over some event or utterance without feelings of hatred, and we can hate in a way that inhibits expression of anger. This suggests other emotions are interior to hatred.

This necessarily leads to the problem of emotion classification. Among emotions researchers, there is no consensus regarding which emotions, if any, are primary (for an inventory of primary-emotion classifications, see TenHouten, 2013, pp. 14–15). However, a classificatory definition of hatred is possible. As argued elsewhere (and summarized in the Chap. 6 of this volume), this author holds that Robert Plutchik (1958, 1962, 1980) has gotten the primary emotions exactly right (TenHouten 1996, 2007, p. 15; 2013, p. 15; 2017a, 2017b). Plutchik identified eight primary emotions as the prototypical adaptive reactions to four fundamental problems of life: acceptance/disgust address the problem of social identity; joy/sadness, temporality; anger/fear, hierarchy; and anticipation/surprise, territoriality.

Beyond identifying the primary emotions, Plutchik ([1962] 1991, pp. 117–118) interpreted all but five of the 28 pairings of the eight primary emotions as secondary-level emotions. Plutchik, however, never pursued this important step he had taken in contributing to the classification of emotions, leaving his definitional system as a rough approximation which has undergone considerable revision (TenHouten 2007, p. 111; 2013, pp. 18–19; 2017b). Plutchik ([1962] 1991, p. 118, emphasis added) defined the emotions resentment and hate in two ways, claiming that:

1. Anger + surprise = outrage, *resentment, hate*;
2. Disgust + anger = scorn, loathing, indignation, contempt, *hate, resentment*, hostility.

---

[1]Delight, however, is not interior to hatred. Elsewhere, delight is defined as a mixture of joy and surprise (TenHouten 2007, pp. 77–78), and the enjoyment, pleasure, and delight taken in inflicting harm on others is defined as *maliciousness* = *anger & delight* (TenHouten 2018a, 241).

In definition 1, it is entirely reasonable to define *outrage* = *anger & surprise* (TenHouten 2007, pp. 100–101): One feels outraged upon perceiving surprising, harmful behavior adjudged to be *out*side of, or in violation of, normative boundaries, which can induce intense feelings of anger, of *rage*. Resentment has been defined elsewhere as a tertiary-level emotion, as *resentment* = *anger & surprise & disgust* (TenHouten 2018b). Resentment thus includes outrage, but is a more complex emotion, as it also contains disgust and, therefore, two other secondary emotions, *contempt* = *anger & disgust* and *shock* = *surprise & disgust* (TenHouten 2007, pp. 82–84, 88–90). Plutchik's inclusion of "hate," however, appears problematic, for while hatred includes anger, it does not involve surprise.

In definition 2, scorn and loathing might be behavioral expressions of hatred. Indignation is synonymous with anger, but can also imply outrage. Contempt is defined above as a mixture of anger and disgust. Hostility is a personality trait, and a form of behavior, rather than an emotion. Hate and resentment share contempt, and differ only in that resentment includes surprise but hate includes fear. Thus, Plutchik's first definition of hate is incorrect in including surprise, and his second definition is incomplete, it is proposed here, in not including fear. To his credit, however, Plutchik has justifiably linked hatred to three primary emotions, which enables defining hatred as a tertiary emotion:

Hatred$_1$ = *anger & disgust & fear*;

There are three secondary emotions latent in this definition: *contempt* = *anger & disgust*, *frozenness/tonic-immobility* = *anger & fear*; and *repugnance* = *disgust & fear* (TenHouten 2007, ch. 14). The resulting classificatory model of hatred is shown in Fig. 37.1.

Hatred, like all tertiary-level emotions, can take eight forms: the three primary emotions, three mixtures of one primary and one secondary emotions, three secondary–secondary mixture, and the three secondary emotions. What is required is that all three primary emotional components be present, either explicitly or implicitly, embedded in a secondary-level emotion. The three primary emotions are next briefly described, and the hypothesized forms of hatred are then considered.

37.2 The Three Primary Emotions of Hatred

37.2.1 Anger–Rage

In humans, anger is culturally universal and unlearned. Anger finds early expression, as the approach-oriented nature of anger is visible in infancy (He et al., 2010). Even a ten-week-old will respond differently to an angry face than to a sad face (Haviland & Lelwica, 1987). The origin of aggression (anger & anticipation) emerges in the earliest forms of infantile body movements, which allows the infant to discover his or her limitations, and to discover the difference between the 'me' and the 'not-me', essential for the later establishment of 'object relations' (Winnicott, 1971).

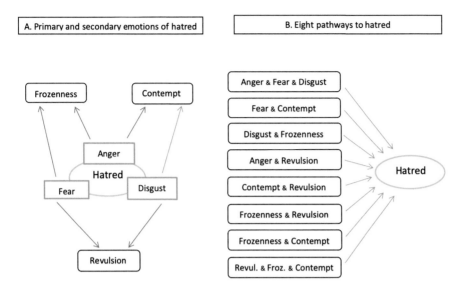

Fig. 37.1 The emotional components of hatred: (a) Primary and secondary emotions of hatred; (b) Eight pathways to hatred

Anger–rage is an essential component of hatred, but there is a distinction between these two emotions. Like anger, hatred is ordinarily directed to a particular person but it can also be directed to groups or categories of people: strangers; women; men; members of despised or invidiously stereotyped racial, ethnic, or religious minorities; members of privileged, abusive, and exploitative ruling elites. But whereas anger arises in response to some specific act of another person, hatred is not limited to specific circumstances but extends to general traits. Elster (1999, pp. 64-65) observes that in anger we believe that "because they do bad things, they are bad," but in hatred we believe that "because they are bad, they do bad things." While anger is suddenly evoked and can also leave quickly, as in irritation and bristling at an unkind remark, hatred is a long-term emotion, typically not triggered by a personal offense; over time, it evolves into a stable sentiment. Individuals can become angry with a close other, and even hate the one they love (Ben-Ze'ev, 2008; Schoenewolf, 1996). Feelings of hatred, often unacknowledged, can also develop for an individual, group, or category of persons that are more distant, which typically involves depersonalization together with prejudicial feelings. The object of hatred, whether close or distant, is thus more general than that of anger.

37.2.2 Fear

Hatred also involves fear. The potential harm to oneself that is perceived by the one who hates is believed to stem from fundamental traits of the other person or group, and hated groups are often seen as potentially powerful and able to inflict great harm to one's welfare and way of life. For this reason, fear, the primary emotional reaction of self-protection, is interior to hatred. Ben-Ze'ev (2000, p. 381) argues that

> the negative character of the other person and the danger inherent in the other's continued power is...central to hate.

The putatively negative character that we fear in others, are in some cases projections of shadowy and unacknowledged aspects of the self.

The hatefulness manifested by individuals toward others, and toward the self, can suggest a self that is psychologically damaged. Hatred can be an effort to adapt to a deeply shamed self, which fears being laughed at, stared at, held in contempt, made a fool of, or treated as an object of disgust. Out of self-protection, the self-hating, deeply shamed individual will aggressively react to the slightest perceived act of denigration. It is this fear that can generate hatred toward others, and can stimulate anger, aggressiveness, and violence. Such deep shame involves both fear and sadness, but the fearfulness typically goes unacknowledged, so that only the sadness is recognized (Lewis, 1992, pp. 143–144).

37.2.3 Disgust

In hatred, there is typically little prospect for altering the undesirable, despised, even disgusting characteristics of the other, so there is a natural inclination to stay as far away as possible from the hated other, or to endeavor to make the noxious other disappear from one's life-space. Disgust is reactive to the negative experience of social identity, and more generally of social inequality. Indeed, hate can be conceptualized as a "measure of inequality between subject and object" (Holbrook, 1972, p. 42). Moreover, hatred involves a pathology of incorporation, of ingesting (the function of the primary emotion, acceptance), which is the most primal meaning of disgust. The interiority of disgust to hatred can be seen in the phenomenon of loathing. If the disgust component of hatred is intense, the other is perceived as unpleasant to the senses, and there develops an urgent feeling to have the object relocated or removed, or if that is not possible, to relocate oneself, as the disgusting qualities of the other become sickening and enervating (Miller, 1997, p. 35).

37.3 The Three Primary–Secondary Expressions of Hatred

37.3.1 Contempt and Fear

Contempt is a negative sociomoral evaluation, either of another person's or group's nature or behavior, or of its perceived negative characteristics. Contempt is close in meaning to disgust, and includes disgust, but there is an important difference. In disgust, the other is merely displeasing but not necessarily inferior; in contempt, the object might be socially inferior or superior in social-dominance position, but holds some features held to be inferior, and is seen as potentially negatively impacting the welfare and well-being of the one feeling contempt. Thus, contempt expresses the subject's feeling of superiority over the object of contempt, or at least over their problematic features.

Social-dominance hierarchy is thus involved in contempt, and this introduces anger as the adaptive reaction of asserting or defending one's own social status (Ben-Ze'ev, 2000, p. 391; Miller, 1997, pp. 220–222; Plutchik, [1962] 1991, pp. 78–84). We might feel anger over a specific action of another, but contempt focuses on perceived undesirable characteristics of the other, such as uncouth behavior, greediness, and ruthlessness. The kind of anger we feel in contempt involves a sense of indignant disapproval of such unpleasant, even disgusting characteristics.

Given that contempt is composed of anger and disgust, and hatred of anger, disgust, and also fear, it follows that the difference between contempt and hatred is spanned by fear. Contempt and hatred are both negative evaluations of some other: In contempt, we see something inferior about this other, something to look down upon; but in hatred, we also fear that this contemptable other, while inferior in some way(s), is nonetheless potentially dangerous. By substituting 'contempt' for 'anger & disgust' in $Hatred_1$, a second definition of hatred is derived:

$Hatred_2 = contempt\ \&\ fear$.

To hold an individual or category of individuals in contempt attributes moral inferiority to them. Contempt is "the feeling or actions of a person toward someone or something considered low, worthless, or beneath notice" who is "scorned, considered worthless, and despicable" (*Webster's*, 1988, p. 300). These feelings or actions of contempt are directed toward what is despised or disdained, suggesting anger and its associated behavior of moving toward its object; this object is simultaneously rejected and avoided as if contaminated and eliciting disgust. As these opposed behavioral tendencies of anger and sociomoral disgust interact, they create a second-order emotion, contempt, that is characterized by an inner tension.

Numerous scholars have seen a close relationship between contempt and hate (Fischer et al., 2018; Fitness & Fletcher, 1993; Halperin, 2008; Sternberg, 2005). Ben-Ze'ev (2000, p. 392) observes that,

> in contempt the emphasis is on the inferiority of the object, whereas hate stresses the object's dangerous nature.

Ben-Ze'ev considers as an example the difference between the Nazis' attitude toward the Jews, and whites toward blacks during the period of American slavery. The Nazis were hateful, the whites contemptuous. The Nazi ideology saw Jews as powerful, dangerous, and irredeemably evil, so that their survival could not be risked. During the Holocaust, "the only good Jew was a dead Jew," whereas during American slavery, "the good black was a properly subservient black" (Ben-Ze'ev, 2000, p. 392). Ben-Ze'ev further explains, and emphasizes, that hatred implies a reaction to a perceived threat, to something which is to be feared. The Nazis had no pity for the Jews, for they lived in fear of their power, influence, even of their gaze (*Judenblink*).

37.3.2 Disgust and Frozenness/Tonic-Immobility

By substituting 'frozenness/tonic-immobility' for 'anger & fear' in Hatred$_1$, a third pathway to hatred is derived:

Hatred$_3$ = disgust & frozenness/tonic-immobility.

Individuals experiencing hatred of another will typically regard the object of their hatred as morally nauseating or evil, that is, as profane and disgusting (Fischer et al., 2018, p. 310). Disgust, by itself, inhibits attacking or aggressing upon the object of hatred, because disgust is an emotion functioning to keep us away from contamination and what is seen as unpleasant or toxic.

Because anger and fear, when experienced together, require opposing behaviors, one of advance and the other of withdrawal, one state of anger is disgust, arising when those who are hated are permitted to go about their daily lives, while being unable or afraid to act against them. Faced with a sociomorally disgusting other, and being immobilized, unable to socially exclude or attack the other, the interaction between these two emotions, disgust and tonic-immobility, can contribute to the generation of feelings of hatred toward this other.

Tonic immobility is an unstable balance between anger and fear, an emotional state that can result either in close encounter or in distancing, as anger or fear becomes the stronger feeling. If fear comes to outweigh anger as a determinant of hateful behavior, one will become motivated to keep as far away as possible from the other. But when bouts of anger temporarily suppress and outweigh fear, the result can be an emotional tension filled with verbal aggression, with potential to boil over into physical violence.

37.3.3 Anger and Repugnance

A fourth way to define hatred is as a combination of repugnance and anger. Here, the object of hatred is abhorred and elicits great antipathy. Given that *fear & disgust = repugnance*, it follows from substitution in the formula for Hatred$_1$ that

Hatred$_4$ = anger & repugnance.[2]

---

[2] This definition contrasts sharply with Plutchik's ([1962] 1991, p. 118) proposal that "fear + disgust = shame, prudishness." Prudishness is not an emotion but a personality trait, and shame can be better defined as a secondary emotional mixture of fear and sadness (TenHouten 2017c).

The meaning of repugnance conveys the meaning of an extreme dislike or distaste (a form of rejection and disgust) but also means aversion (the behavioral aspect of fear), such that "repugnance applies to that...from which [a person] instinctively draws away" (Fernald, [1914] 1947, p. 52). A synonym of repugnance, *abhorrence*, implies a shuddering. especially sociomoral, recoil. We abhor that which makes us shudder (a source of disgust) and recoil (move away from, a reaction of fear).

The difference between anger and hatred is spanned by repugnance. In anger, there is a cognitive appraisal that the behavior of the other can be influenced or changed (TenHouten, 2019). But in hatred, the other is seen as repugnant, a perceived realization of the others' malicious intent, malevolent nature, and repulsive characteristics and behavioral patterns that cannot be changed. In appraisal of a hated other, the negative evaluation is of the object itself, not any particular behavior of the object. The hated object is appraised with a focus on its repugnant "innate nature, motives, and characteristics," such that "a momentary change of certain behavioral patterns will not...diminish levels of hatred" (Fischer et al., 2018, p. 310; see also Ortony, Clore & Collins, 1988; Royzman, McCauley, & Rozin, 2005).

37.4 Mixtures of Secondary Emotions

There are additional pathways to hatred, for all three pairings of the secondary emotions of hatred—contempt, frozenness/tonic-immobility, and repugnance—can occur together (as shown in Fig. 37.1).

Contempt–Revulsion An individual could feel a deep sense of contempt for some other person, group, or category of persons, while simultaneously experiencing revulsion. There is an inner tension in this affective experience, for contempt (with its anger component) can lead to fantasizing about attacking and harming the other: but to actually do so would mean exposure to the repulsive, repugnant other, so that the constituent feelings of fear and disgust (in both of these secondary emotions) urge not attack but withdrawal.

Frozenness–Revulsion The acting out of anger is inhibited by fear, as attack behavior must respect the social power, even social dominance, of the angering other. The resultant antithetical emotional experience is of being frozen, or 'trapped' in one's social place, and stuck with the presence of another that one has come to see as an object of revulsion but can neither eliminate or escape. This kind of hatred can, as Sternberg (2005, p. 400) suggests, boil over and possibly lead to violence.

Frozenness–Contempt In this pathway to hatred, the individual feels frozen in place, trapped in the sense of being unable either to destroy or avoid the presence of an unwanted other or group. The individual is apt to obsessively focus on this other's contemptible nature, appearance, and behavior, and thereby cultivate a deep, passionate, even seething, sense of hatred of this other, who comes to be reviled.

Frozenness–Revulsion–Contempt It is also possible that all three of these secondary-level pairings can occur together, and in empirical data analysis, factor together—as a three-way interaction, with the other forms of hatred.

37.5 Affect-Spectrum Theory vs. the Triangulation Theory of Hate

The present theoretical model of the emotions—Affect Spectrum Theory (AST)—includes a three-level classification system. In this theory, hatred includes 3 of the 8 primary emotions, 3 of 28 secondary emotions, and 1 of 56 tertiary emotions. AST bears similarities and differences to Robert Sternberg's (2005, pp. 38–41; see also Sternberg & Sternberg 2008, chs. 3–4) "triangular theory of the structure of hate" (TTH). Sternberg identifies three aspects of hate:

(i) The "negation of intimacy (distancing) in hate; repulsion and disgust";
(ii) "Passion in hate: anger—fear"; and
(iii) Decision–commitment in hate: devaluation–diminution through contempt.

The most notable continuity of the two theories is that both AST and TTH view disgust, anger, and fear as essential ingredients of hate; Both theories also involve contempt. These four concepts, however, are seen quite differently.

Sternberg (2005, p. 39, emphasis added) defines "passion" as "anger *or* fear in response to a threat," citing Galdston (1987, p. 371, emphasis added), who, in referring to the "passion component" of hatred, asserts that,

> hatred allows for the super-imposition of a psychosomatic process upon the sensorimotor reflex of fight or flight in response to the stimuli of perceived danger.

Thus, for Sternberg, passion as anger–fear involves either anger/fight *or* fear/flight. While anger can be seen, at least metaphorically, as a passion, fear is not describable as a passion. AST focuses on the combination of anger *and* fear as a secondary emotion, frozenness/tonic-immobility. This secondary emotion, which has not previously been linked to hatred, is most certainly not a passion, but is rather inhibitory, making of hatred a frustrating and aggravating sense of impotence and powerlessness.

Both Sternberg and present theory see disgust as an emotion interior to hatred. Sternberg (2005, p. 39) refers to "repulsion and disgust" as "the first potential component of hate," and as "the negation of intimacy," which seeks distance from an object seen as noxious, "arousing repulsion and disgust in the person who experiences hatred." The hated individual, or category of persons—either from personal experience or from propaganda and ideology, are seen as subhuman, inhuman, and incapable of closeness or warmth (Leyens et al., 2000, cited in Sternberg, 2005, p. 39).

Sternberg's (2005, p. 39, emphasis added) third component of hate, decision–commitment, is characterized by "*cognitions* of devaluation and diminution through contempt for the target group" or individual. On the group level, hatred for a targeted other can be cultivated through propaganda and 'educational' programs that can, and have, gone as far as to include 'brainwashing'. While the role of contempt is well explained by Sternberg, the present classification holds that *contempt = anger & disgust*, so that contempt includes anger, an emotion of approach, anger, together with disgust, an emotions of distancing. Contempt is an ingredient of hatred, because it mixes tendencies of approach and withdrawal, but in TTH it is involved in "cognitions" and "decision–commitment" processes. In AST, contempt involves complex sociocognitive appraisal processes, but, as a mixture of disgust and anger, is essentially an emotion,

Sternberg (2005, p. 40) implicitly defines the mixture of disgust and anger as an emotion, as he defines "boiling hate" as "revulsion (disgust of negation of intimacy + anger)." Here there is a real difference in the two conceptualizations. In present classification, the equation *revulsion = fear & disgust* joins disgust to fear, not to anger. When we perceive another as repulsive or revolting, our immediate reaction is not to boil over with anger and engage in attack behavior, but rather to avoid contact and quickly withdraw from the sight, sound, and smell of the fear-inducing and potentially contaminating other. Both fear and disgust are triggers of withdrawal-related or escape behaviors.

Both theories identify three elements of hate, three pairings of these elements, and one manifestation of all three elements. AST sees contempt as an emotion, defined as *contempt = anger & disgust*, whereas Sternberg defines contempt as a cognitive element, a "cognition of devaluation and diminution." Of course, contempt, like all emotions, involves a cognitive-appraisal process, so either characterization is justified. The difference is that AST sees contempt as a secondary-level combination of elements of hatred, while TTH rather sees contempt as an irreducible component of hate.

AST defines repugnance as a secondary component of hatred, as *repugnance = fear & disgust*. Sternberg, in contrast, sees repugnance as an irreducible "component" of hatred.

In triangulation theory, the taxonomic differences in kinds of hate are described as quantitative differences in intensity. Using the metaphor of temperature, hatred can be cold (contempt), cool (disgust), hot (anger–fear), simmering (disgust, contempt), boiling (disgust, anger–fear), seething (anger–fear, contempt), and burning (disgust, anger–fear, contempt). While Sternberg claims that his three elements of hatred—contempt, disgust, and anger–fear, alone or in pairs are tantamount to hatred heated to varying temperatures. In AST, all eight varieties of hatred must include (either directly or embedded in secondary emotions) all three hypothesized primary elements of hatred—anger, fear, and disgust. In AST the different kinds of hatred are thus only qualitatively different, but for Sternberg, the differences, it is claimed, are also quantitative, ordered by intensity/temperature. Having analyzed the affective infrastructure of hatred, we next consider its development in the self, and consider the extremes of hatred that can develop in the absence of love.

37.6 Hatred and Social Identity

> When we hate someone, what we hate is something in him that is part of ourselves.
> Hermann Hesse ([1919] 2013, p. 91)

Descartes found himself thinking and inferred, "*Cogito, ergo sum.*" But he did not ask an obvious next question, "*What* am I?" Guntrip (1968, p. 267) endeavored to show that the answer to this question contains the secret of hatred. The origins of hate must be found in the foundations of identity, in Being. This means that an understanding of hatred requires examination of what experiences, in the earliest stages of life, promote the foundations of the attainment of a normal and healthy human identity. We are born with a primary urge to survive, physically and psychically, and to grow and develop into full human beings. The foundation of identity, Winnicott (1965a) held, is in the development of a sense of self. At birth, the infant does not know that he or she is a whole person separate from the not-me. A stable and attentive mother with the capacity to 'be' an adequate source of security enables the normal development of object-relations, first with the mother, then with others caregivers and beyond. The child develops a not-me world and participates as a 'subject' in a world of 'objects', all the while developing intellectual abilities and undergoing symbolic elaboration and the acquisition of language, culture, and a social identity, a self. Winnicott (1965b, p. 368) saw transition objects, cuddly blankets and teddy bears, as the first cultural artifacts, the first use of symbols (of the union of the baby and mother and his or her internalization of the mother) that makes it possible to be alone, separate, as a human being.

Hatred is incubated in early experiences which inhibit the development of a self, and prohibit the self's possession of *ruth*, the ability to empathize with others. Hate does not emerge from any primary animal aggression or from a Freudian Thanatos but rather "from frustrated love and the inevitable imperfections of our formative environment" (Holbrook, 1972, p. 35). Hatred is just as ambiguous as love or aggression: it is a manifestation of a need to survive, and can thus be both a life-seeking and an anti-human force (Holbrook, 1972, p. 35). A concern for other people, ruth, is a positive achievement of humanity and the moral sense on which civilization can be constructed. When the earliest experiences are abusive and pathological, the result can be weakness and failure to develop ego-strength, and failure to develop empathy for others. When the young child experiences excessive unpleasure, an inner feeling of hatred can emerge and become a stable and enduring feeling of hostile destructiveness. Abuse and the resulting unpleasure leads to an emotionally shamed and over-sensitive self that can easily be hurt, "and [this] can then be felt as a weakness to be resisted, resented, and hidden behind a tough exterior" (Winnicott, 1965b, p. 368). When this inner hatred further develops, the individual comes to hate being itself, as a manifestation of the emotionally over-sensitive and fearful self (Holbrook, 1972, p. 20). As this fearfulness turns into its own opposite, anger, a hidden resentment can develop of the mother and others responsible for caregiving, who have failed to *be* for the child at a time when he or she was totally dependent. Not accepted by the mother and responsible others, acceptance can turn into its opposite, into an internalized sense of self-rejection and self-disgust. Such an individual—who has experienced rejection will be prone to provoke rejection by others, fearing exposure of the shadowy, unacceptable and destructive aspects of their own self.

Descartes ([1649] 1988, p. 62) contrasted love and hate as passions, seeing love as an excitation of the soul, caused by the motion of the spirits, which incites us to join itself in volition to the objects that appear to be suitable to it.

Hatred, for Descartes, was conceptualized as, "the will to be separated from the objects that are presented to it." In love, we imagine a whole in which we are an integral part, but in hatred we see ourselves alone as a whole, entirely separated from an object of aversion. Indeed, hate can arise from frustrated love and the inevitable imperfections of our early environment: when we are rejected in love, this shattering experience can leave an individual feeling painfully alone in an empty wholeness, existing only as a self in-itself.

When we hate, we show a lack of concern for others, a lack of ruth, and we cannot, or choose not to, live up to the moral sense upon which civilization ultimately depends (Holbrook, 1972, p. 35). Ruth has its cost, in anxiety, guilt, and pain, but without it we are not fully human. To be ruthless is to have a divided self, and to be in a less-than-human state of normless anomie (TenHouten 2016, 2017a, pp. 79–80, 85).

Love and hate are often linked, even considered opposites, with one latent in the other.

This suggest there are continuities between the two emotions, and indeed they are, as outlined by Gaylin (2003, pp. 13–29). (1) While both love and hatred have cognitive content, and are manifested only following some multi-stage cognitive appraisal process, both are essentially powerful emotions that require an object, and this object can be an individual, a group, a category of people, a community. We cannot really love ice cream and hate spinach,[3] but we can love our family members and hate members of a category of people. (2) The emotions of love and hate are experienced with intensity, as passions. (3) Love and hate, as passions, must be sustained over a considerable period of time: a weekend tryst, with a fleeting passion, is not yet love; an unpleasant encounter with the other stimulated sense of prejudice, but this is not tantamount to hatred. (4) Both love and hate involve misperception, bias, and distorted perception. The individual in love with another sees the other with 'rose tinted' glasses, idealizes, feels he or she has always known this other (true, insofar as perception is projection). And (5), others become objects of love or hate only if they become preoccupations, so that the person in love cannot stop thinking about the other, and a bigot only becomes a hater through obsessive rumination and worry about the despised other. Given these continuities, it is not difficult to understand that these two oppositely-valenced emotions might be linked and seen as opposites.

---

[3]In everyday talk, the terms 'love' and 'hate' are used very broadly. For example, Locke ([1689] 1995, p. 161) definition of love ranged from loving grapes to finding continuous delight in one's family members; hate, from hating spinach to feeling pain over the presence or absence of an object or being.

While love and hate are not opposites, they are opposed. As love begins to erode, to slip away, the acceptance component of love begins to wane, and the opposite of acceptance, rejection, informs one's view of the love object. In present classification, *acceptance & rejection–disgust = ambivalence'*, and ambivalence gradually can turn into rejection of the now devalued other. Rejection of the other also requires breaking a bond, and doing so involves an act of social power. This involves both anger and fear, the adaptive reactions to the existential problem of hierarchical-ranking. The joy that had been experienced in a love relationship can also turn into its opposite, a sadness of losing shared enjoyment with the loved other. The emergence of sadness can trigger a variety of emotions, which have been called the emotions of 'troubled intimacy'. But hatred is not among these emotions, for hatred does not involve either joy or sadness.[4] Hatred rather involves social power, and while we would like to express our anger, we fear the consequences of doing so, and are thereby frozen in place, faced with an individual, group, or social-identity category we abhor, and find disgusting, but cannot eradicate.

Hatred can emerge for various reasons, and love gone wrong is only one possible pathway. While the loss of love always involves sadness, the human capability to hate follows from human nature, as the human is, at least potentially, "one of the world's most aggressive beasts who fundamentally enjoys torturing and killing other animals, including his fellow man" (*Time* 1969, Jan 17, p. 34, cited by Eibl-Eibesfeldt, 1972, p. 1). This Hobbesian beast has, historically, been partially tamed through a civilizing process (Elias, 1939). Such a dark view of humankind is an exaggeration, no doubt, but the fact is that 'civilized' humanity has long perpetuated warfare, conquest, and violence, and this will continue as long as it is perceived of as adaptive behavior, and as long as territory and resources can be acquired and retained by force.

37.7 Absence of Love, Hatred, and the Descent into Hell

The loss of love can be devastating, often referred to in literature as an experience of hell. Even more devastating is the experience of never having been loved, for the result can be an inner feeling of deadness. Dante Alighieri was profoundly on the mark when he described the lowest circle of hell not as an inferno of flames but of ice, of absolute coldness, of the total absence of warmth. The relationship between a lack of love in childhood and the emergence of hatred, described above in terms of object-relations theory, can be seen empirically by examining individuals who were,

---

[4]Descartes ([1649] 1988, pp. 94, 96) argued that hatred "is never without Sadness." However, whereas hatred is a motivation for destructive action (inhibited primarily by fear), sadness is characterized by inaction. Descartes implicitly acknowledges this, as he described sadness as "bestowing caution and apprehension, disposes one in a way toward Prudence." the opposite of sadness, Descartes saw as more problematic than sadness insofar as it predisposes individual to "abandon themselves to it unthinking and rash" actions.

as children, abused, raped, prostituted, tortured, set on fire, scalded, and beaten. Such violence is "the ultimate means of communicating the absence of love by the person inflicting the violence" (Gilligan, 1997, p. 47; see also Cartright, 2002; Hadreas, 2007). To be abused and humiliated destroys the capacity for experiencing joy, acceptance, and love. Gilligan (1997, p. 273n3) observes that,

> Where there is love, there is joy; and where there is joy, there is love. Conversely, where there is no love, there is no joy (this is the condition called hell, in theological language).

The other aspect of being unloved is rejection, being treated as an unwanted object of disgust. Gilligan (1997, p. 47) puts this starkly: To be beaten deliberately is to be rejected and unloved." To be treated with violence can kill the soul, so those who later kill have been 'murdered' themselves, or feel they were, or are about to be, destroyed, so they kill in acts they perceive as self-defense.

One consequence of lacking the experiences of joy and acceptance is that one is rendered unable to love either the self or others. It is not possible to combine emotions one does not possess. Being an abused and unloved child creates a sense of shame at the level of a deep humiliation, but even the experience of shame gives way to an emotional deadness. The individual who cannot love eventually becomes unable to experience *any* feelings, including primary emotions such as joy and sadness, and even "primordial emotions" such as pain and pleasure (Denton, 2006). These levels of emotion are interdependent, because only individuals who are capable of risking pain can experience joy. This absence of feeling is tantamount to a feeling of deadness, and the resulting "joyless life is a synonym for hell," as it is "the most intolerable of...torments" (Gilligan, 1997, p. 52).

Gilligan (1997, p. 53) describes the psychological and social condition of violent men, hardened criminals, incarcerate in maximum-security U. S. prisons. He found that without either the experiences of, and capacity, for love, and especially for self-love, "the self collapses, the soul dies, [and] the psyche goes to hell." These men strive to protect themselves from the reality of having being deprived of love by emptying their souls of love for others, and a soul empty of love fills with hatred. The murderers and rapists Gilligan interviewed were engulfed by hate, and saw the world itself as hateful. These prisons house and contain the living dead, including those who mutilate themselves hoping they are capable of experiencing pain, a 'something' preferable to a 'nothing'. These men, the living dead, who feel neither pain nor love, have acted upon the urge to harm and kill others because for them the it is intolerable to see that others are still alive. Feeling emotionally dead, in what is perceived of as a hateful world, many of these violent men prefer physical death, and choose suicide (in the U.S.A. and beyond, at a rate hundreds of times greater than for the general population). Without love, and filled with a hatred of being itself, the dichotomy between life and death breaks down, so that while the body lives, there is a spiritual and emotional death. Without love, these individuals come to hate life, to experience life as a living death, and see themselves as zombies, vampires, robots, demons, or monsters, for whom the feeling of physical pain is preferable to feeling nothing at all, so that self-mutilation becomes a futile gesture of bringing themselves back to life.

37.8 Discussion

On the level of behavior, anger is a painfully negative experience for all involved, but it is also positively-valenced, goal-directed, approach-oriented emotion (Carver & Harmon-Jones, 2009; Plutchik, [1962] 1991, pp. 75–84). The other two primary emotional components of hatred—fear and disgust, are negative-valenced, withdrawal-oriented emotions. The combination of these three component emotions, insofar as they combine in form hatred of other social beings, is overall a negative sentiment. The valence of mixed emotions obeys no algebraic rule, and hatred is no exception, for even hatred, a destructive emotion, can have a creative and positive aspect, as in the case where there is hatred of an oppressive and sadistic political elite, in which social justice and social rights can be restored only through the destruction of a corrupt and evil system of rule. A second example might be an anti-war movement in opposition to an unjust or unwise military adventure, in which the participants feel both anger and disgust fused in a hatred of what is be being done in their name, such as bombing residential areas and torturing prisoners. And hatred can lead to concentration-camp incarceration or genocidal extermination of people treated as subhuman and deserving of no consideration or pity. In anger, there is always the hope that its expression will lead the targeted individual or group to behave in a more considerate manner in the future, so that the circumstances that trigger anger can be altered. But in hatred, there is little prospect for altering the undesirable, despised, disgusting characteristics of the other.

This chapter has endeavored to conceptually break hatred down into its elementary emotional components. The result of this effort is not a theory of hatred, but rather an exploration of hatred within a general classificatory theory of the emotions. Hatred is conceptualized as being comprised of 3 of 8 primary emotions, which combine in pairs to form 3 of 28 secondary emotions. In this hierarchical classification, hatred emerges as 1 of the 56 tertiary-level emotion combinations. If we regard the eight expressions of tertiary emotions as a group of complex emotion, then the total number of emotions jumps by 392, to 484. This does not at all shrink the significance of hatred, but rather points to the amazingly broad spectrum of the emotions enabled by the central and peripheral systems' brain and heart.

The present classificatory effort suggests there is an intrinsic inner tension embedded in the tertiary-level emotions of hatred. The anger component of hatred instills an urge to approach and attack the object of hatred, but the fear and disgust components rather motivate an opposite reaction of withdrawal and distancing. This tension involves a sense of frozenness, an unpleasant feeling of being torn between the opposed impulses of other-destruction and self-protection. The tension of tonic immobility is reinforced by the secondary emotion, contempt, wherein anger is approach-motivating but disgust motivates withdrawal and distancing.

The development of hatefulness has been causally linked to life without love, especially in the early years of life. This lack of love is never simply an absence of a positively-valenced emotion, for it finds its early roots in negative experiences, especially childhood abuse and neglect. However pathological and destructive hatred can be, like all emotions it is intended as an adaptive reaction to problems of life, particularly to social relationships that involve the dimension of social hierarchy and social identity.

References

Aquinas, T. [1265–1274] (1947–1948). *The summa theologica.* New York: Benziger.
Aumer, K., Bahn, A. C. K., & Harris, S. (2015). Through the looking glass, darkly: Perceptions of hate in interpersonal relationships. *Journal of Relationships Research, 6*, e3.
Ben-Ze'ev, A. (2000). *The subtlety of emotion.* Cambridge, MA: Harvard University Press.
Ben-Ze'ev, A. (2008). Hating the one you love. *Philosophia, 36*, 277–283.
Bernier, A., & Dozier, M. (2002). Assessing adult attachment: Empirical sophistication and empirical bases. *Attachment & Human Development, 4*, 171–179.
Cartright, D. (2002). *Psychoanalysis, violence and rage-type murder: Murdering minds.* Hove, East Sussex, UK: Brunner-Routledge.
Carver, C. S., & Harmon-Jones, E. (2009). Anger is an approach-related affect: Evidence and implications. *Psychological Bulletin, 135*, 183–204.
Denton, D. (2006). *The primordial emotions: The dawn of consciousness.* London: Oxford University Press.
Descartes, R. [1649] (1988). *The passions of the soul*, trans S. Voss. Indianapolis, IN: Hackett.
Eibl-Eibesfeldt, I. (1972). *Love and hate: The natural history of behavioral patterns*, trans. G. Strachan. New York: Holt, Rinehart and Winston.
Elias, N. [1939] (1994). *The civilizing process*, Vol. I, *The development of manners*, trans E. Jepcott. New York: Urizen Books.
Elster, J. (1999). *Alchemies of the mind: Rationality and the emotions.* Cambridge, UK: Cambridge University Press.
Fernald, J. C. [1914] (1947). *Standard handbook of synonyms, antonyms, and prepositions*, rev. edn. New York: Funk and Wagnalls.
Fischer, A., Halperin, E., Canetti, D., & Jasini, A. (2018). Why we hate. *Emotion Review, 10*, 309–320.
Fitness, J., & Fletcher, G. J. (1993). Love, hate, anger and jealousy in close relationships: A prototype and cognitive appraisal analysis. *Journal of Personality and Social Psychology, 65*, 942–958.
Folger, R. (1987). Reformulating the conditions of resentment: A referent cognition model. In J. C. Masters & W. P. Smith (Eds.), *Social comparison, social justice, and relative deprivation* (pp. 183–215). Hillsdale, NJ: Lawrence Erlbaum.
Galdston, R. (1987). The longest pleasure: A psychoanalytic study of hatred. *International Journal of Psycho-Analysis, 68*, 371–378.
Gay, P. (1993). *The cultivation of hatred* (vol. III, The bourgeois experience: Victoria to Freud). New York: W. W. Norton.
Gaylin, W. (2003). *Hatred: The psychological descent into violence.* New York: PublicAffairs.
Gilligan, J. (1997). *Violence: Reflections on a national epidemic.* New York: Vintage Books.
Guntrip, H. (1968). *Schizoid phenomena, object relations, and the self.* New York: International Universities Press.
Hadreas, P. (2007). *A phenomenology of love and hate.* London: Routledge.
Halperin, E. (2008). Group-based hatred in intractable conflict in Israel. *Journal of Conflict Resolution, 52*, 713–736.
Haviland, J. M., & Lelwica, M. (1987). The induced affective response: 10-week-old infants' response to three emotion expressions. *Developmental Psychology, 23*, 97–104.

He, J., Amey, K., McDermott, J. M., Henderson, H. A., Hane, A. A., Xu, Q., et al. (2010). Anger and approach motivation in infancy: Relation to early childhood inhibitory control and behavior problems. *Infancy, 15*, 246–259.

Hesse, H. [1919] (2013). *Demian: The story of Emil Sinclair's youth*. New York: Penguin Books.

Holbrook, D. (1972). *The masks of hate: The problem of false solutions in the culture of an acquisitive society*. New York: Pergamon Press.

Levin, J., & McDevitt, J. (2002). *Hate crimes revisited: America's war on those who are different*. Cambridge, MA: Westview Press.

Lewis, M. (1992). *Shame: The exposed self*. New York: The Free Press.

Leyens, J.-P., Paladino, P. M., Rodrigues-Torres, R., Vaes, J., Demoulin, S., Rodriguez-Peres, A., et al. (2000). The emotional side of prejudice: The attribution of secondary emotions to ingroups and outgroups. *Personality and Social Psychology Review, 4*, 186–197.

Locke, J. [1689] (1995). *An essay concerning human understanding*. Amherst, NY: Prometheus Books.

Miller, W. I. (1997). *The anatomy of disgust*. Cambridge, MA: Harvard University Press.

Neufeldt, V., & Guralnik, D. B. (Eds.) (1988). *Webster's new world dictionary of American English*. New York: Webster's New World,

Ortony, A., Clore, G. L., & Collins, A. (1988). *The cognitive structure of emotions*. Cambridge, UK: Cambridge University Press.

Panksepp, J. (1998). *Affective neuroscience: The foundations of animal and human emotions*. New York: Oxford University Press.

Panksepp, J., & Biven, L. (2012). *The archeology of mind: Neuroevolutionary origins of human emotions*. New York: W.W. Norton.

Plutchik, R. (1958). Outline of a new theory of emotion. *Transaction of the New York Academy of Sciences, 20*, 394–403.

Plutchik, R. [1962] (1991). *The emotions: Facts, theories, and a new model* (revised edn.). Lanham, MD: University Press of America.

Plutchik, R. (1980). *Emotion: A psychoevolutionary synthesis*. New York: Harper & Row.

Rempel, J. K., & Burris, C. T. (2005). Let me count the ways: An integrative theory of love hate. *Personal Relationships, 12*, 297–313.

Royzman, E. B., McCauley, C., & Rozin, P. (2005). From Plato to Putnam: Four ways to think about hate. In R. J. Sternberg (Ed.), *The psychology of hate* (pp. 3–35). Washington, DC: American Psychological Association.

Schoenewolf, E. (1996). The couple who fell in hate: Eclectic psychodynamic therapy with an angry couple. *Journal of Contemporary Psychotherapy, 26*, 65–71.

Smith, H. J., Pettigrew, T. F., Pippin, G. M., & Bialosiewicz, S (2012). Relative deprivation: A theoretical and meta-analytic review. *Personality and Social Psychology Review*, 16, 203–232.

Sternberg, R. J. (2005). Understanding and combatting hate. In R. J. Sternberg (Ed.), *The psychology of hate* (pp. 37–49). Washington, DC: American Psychological Association.

Sternberg, R. J., & Sternberg, K. (2008). *The nature of hate*. New York: Columbia University Press.

TenHouten, W. D. (1996). Outline of a socioevolutionary theory of the emotions. *Journal of Sociology and Social Policy, 16*, 189–208.

TenHouten, W. D. (2007). *A general theory of emotions and social life*. London: Routledge.

TenHouten, W. D. (2013). *Emotion and reason: Mind, brain, and the social domains of work and love*. London: Routledge.

TenHouten, W. D. (2016). Normlessness, anomie, and the emotions. *Sociological Forum, 31*, 465–486.

TenHouten, W. D. (2017a). *Alienation and affect*. London: Routledge.

TenHouten, W. D. (2017b). From primary emotions to the spectrum of affect: An evolutionary neurosociology of the emotions. In A. Ibáñez, L. Sedeño, & A. M. Garcia (Eds.), *Neuroscience and social science: The missing link* (pp. 141–167). New York: Springer.

TenHouten, W. D. (2017c). Social dominance hierarchy and the pride–shame system. *Journal of Political Power, 10*, 94–114.

TenHouten, W. D. (2018a). Anger and contested place in the social world. *Sociology Mind, 8*, 226–248.
TenHouten, W. D. (2018b). From *ressentiment* to resentment as a tertiary emotion. *Review of European Studies, 10*, 49–64.
TenHouten, W. D. (2019). Anger, social power, and cognitive appraisal: Application of octonionic sociocognitive emotions theory. *Journal of Political Power, 22*, 40–65.
Winnicott, D. W. (1965a). *The family and individual development*. New York: Basic Books.
Winnicott, D. W. (1965b). *The maturation process and the facilitating environment: Studies in the theory of emotional development*. New York: International Universities Press.
Winnicott, D. W. (1971). *Playing and reality*. New York: Basic Books.

Warren D. TenHouten (Prof. Dr.) is a Research Professor at the Sociology Department at the University of California at Los Angeles. His research interests include neurosociology, affective neuroscience, the sociology of emotions, alexithymia, time-consciousness, reason and rationality, social exchange theory, and alienation theory. His books include *Time and Society* (SUNY 2005), *A General Theory of Emotions and Social Life* (Routledge 2007), *Emotion and Reason: Mind, Brain, and the Social Domains of Work and Love* (Routledge 2013), *Alienation and Affect* (Routledge 2016), and *Anger: From Primordial Rage to the Politics of Hared and Resentment* (Nova 2020).

Chapter 38
When the Love Is Bad

Patricia L. Grosse

Abstract Modern popular theories of emotion distinguish between loves: there is true love and puppy love, parental love and child love, friendly, Platonic love, the love for and of our pets, the love for and of non-human others. What is often considered a different category all together are states like obsession, lust, the desire for domination, the laser focus of an abuser on their victim. These series of emotional states are set over and against love: they are false loves, they masquerade as the real thing but deep down have their origin in violence and hatred, misogyny and rage. These states provoke a common response in champions of love: they are not real love. But what if these vicious states are kinds of love? What if they come from the same place from whence the purest of loves springs? What if they are, in fact, forms of Bad Love? This chapter provides a selective philosophical history and analysis of "bad love" in several of its myriad forms. The methodology used for this analysis is gleaned from feminist theory, the history of emotions, and the moral psychology of Augustine of Hippo. There are two major sections of this essay: "When Love Was Bad," provides a brief background on the philosophical history of "bad love." Beginning with Platonic "bad love," this section swiftly turns to Augustine's analysis of love and emotion. The second major section, "Bad Love, Revisited," synthesizes Augustine's account of emotion with Susan Brison's feminist philosophical account of the effect of trauma on the psyche. The chapter concludes with a reexamination of Platonic negging and Augustinian emotion, thus reaffirming the slipperiness of Bad Love. This essay contributes to the philosophical literature on the history of the emotions as well as philosophy of love.

Keywords Love · Concupiscence · Abuse · Augustine · Emotion · Moral psychology

---

P. L. Grosse (✉)
Laurium, MI, Hancock, USA
e-mail: patricia.grosse@gmail.com

38.1 Introduction: You'd be Prettier if you Smiled More

This essay seeks to provide a limited historical and theoretical framework of the nature of the kind of love that has in the past (and presently) been considered "Bad Love."[1] While this essay is centered on the Western canon of philosophical thought, it is indeed transcultural—this chapter examines the transformation of loves in the Ancient Greek philosophical thought of Plato to the Late Antique Christian Philosophy of the North African Roman theologian St. Augustine of Hippo. In a way this essay is also transcultural in that it seeks to draw a line between modern practices and understandings of Bad Love to those of the Ancient and Late Antique world. This Introduction will provide a short overview of the philosophical methodology of the essay, the concept of Bad Love in modern culture today, and finally, the structure of this essay.

This essay is a contribution to the Philosophy of Love, which is an umbrella term for the field of philosophy which seeks to understand the nature of love.[2] Discipline of philosophy that is concerned with the history, ethics, and nature of love in its many forms. This category of philosophy attracts scholars with diverse methodological backgrounds. The methodology of this essay is grounded in feminist theory, the history of emotions, and moral psychology.[3] The essay focuses in on certain themes in the works of Plato and Augustine regarding Bad Love and explores them as such: this kind of focused analysis can be found in the works of philosophers and theologians such as Miles (for example, 2005 and 2006), Webb (2013), and Aumiller (2019).

Defining the true nature and definition of love actually is outside of the purview of this essay. Instead, this essay seeks to explore but one facet in the nature of love (Bad Love), its history and its present. Modern popular theories of emotion distinguish between loves: there is true love and puppy love, parental love and child love, friendly, Platonic love, the love for and of our pets, the love for and of non-human others. What is often considered a different category all together are states like obsession, lust, the desire for domination, the laser focus of an abuser on their victim.

This last series of emotional states are set over and against love: they are false loves, they masquerade as the real thing but deep down have their origin in violence and hatred, misogyny and rage. These states provoke a common response in champions of love: they are not real love. But what if these vicious states are

---

[1] While there are many scholars who discuss the term "bad love" (such as Reid, 2019), the usage of this term comes from the author's analysis of Augustine's *City of God* (Augustine, 2003; Grosse, 2017a, 2017b) and will be discussed in Sects. 38.2 and 38.3.

[2] For an extensive overview of the philosophy of love, see Helm's (2017) excellent entry, "Love" in the *Stanford of Encyclopedia of Philosophy*.

[3] The References section of this essay provides a limited bibliography of various essays, collections, and monographs, that are helpful for those wishing to explore further readings in feminist epistemology, the history of emotions, and, especially, the history of St. Augustine's thoughts on emotion.

kinds of love? What if they come from the same place from whence the purest of loves springs? What if they are, in fact, forms of Bad Love?

Bad Love abounds in modern romances. An example of this can be found in the modern practice of negging, in which a man insults a woman in a particular way in order to lower her self-esteem enough for him to trick her into sex. There are many popular dating-advice articles (for example, Helm, 2017; Howard, 2017; Pugachevsky, 2019; Woolf, 2012) that define and decry this act. Pugachevsky (2019), a writer for *Cosmopolitan Magazine*, defines negging as

> ... when a person who is objectively less of a catch than you finds ways to manipulate you into feeling bad about yourself so that you'll want to impress them (i.e., sleep with them).

What may come as not much of a surprise is that this modern practice of negging is not new. In Plato's dialogue on love, *Phaedrus* (1997), the titular character shares a speech given to him by Lysias, a rhetorician who sought to persuade the young Phaedrus into to having sex with older men who did not love him. The *Phaedrus* itself explores the nature of love, the soul, and rhetoric, but what is most relevant to this essay is the shrewdness of Socrates, who immediately cuts through the false narrative Lysias has provided the handsome Phaedrus: of course Lysias desired Phaedrus, he was merely *lying* in order to achieve his goals. Phaedrus was being tricked into sex through the act of negging—Lysias lies Phaedrus about his actual love for him at the same time that he gives back-handed complements on Phaedrus' intellect.

Socrates is intimately familiar with the technique of negging for good reason: he practices it himself. In Plato's *Lysis* (1997), a dialogue ostensibly about the nature of *philia*, friendship-love, Socrates explains how important it is not to sing the praises of potential lovers but to knock them down a peg or two in conversation, thus keeping young would-be-beloveds in their place as lesser intellectuals in order to leave them gasping for the wisdom within their older pedagogue.

Thus, two Platonic dialogues on love and friendship have a worm within their hearts: insult masquerading as friendship, lies masquerading as truths, bad lovers masquerading as friends. In the intervening 2500 years much has been written on the nature of desire and the nature of love, this chapter explores this sinister side of love.

There are two major sections of this essay: 2. "When Love Was Bad" and 3. "Bad Love, Revisited." "When Love Was Bad," provides a brief background on the philosophical history of "bad love." Beginning with Reid's (2019) conception of Platonic "bad love," this section swiftly turns to Augustine's analysis of love and emotion in Book 14 of *The City of God* (2003). Augustine, whose own definitions of love tend to be slippery, wrote in a time that love as a whole was considered to be "bad." Augustine's defense of love as fundamental for human emotion provides the groundwork for an understanding of Augustinian Bad Love.

The second major section, "Bad Love, Revisited," synthesizes Augustine's account of emotion with Susan Brison's feminist philosophical account of trauma. Brison's (2003) account of the splintering effect of trauma on the psyche provides a framework for better understanding the effect of Bad Love on human moral structures. This essay concludes with a reexamination of Platonic negging and

Augustinian emotion, thus reaffirming the slipperiness of Bad Love, which defies categorization at the same time it invites an epistemological account of its nature. Ultimately, Augustine's account of love as the foundation for all emotion is valuable for reimagining the nature of love in general and Bad Love in particular.

38.2 When Love Was Bad

As discussed above, the definition love is a difficult one to pin down—it is impossible to provide a detailed account of every aspect of love in the world or that which is found in the fourth century B.C.E. philosopher Plato or the fifth century CE philosopher theologian Augustine. Christian children hear that God is love, and that there should be a kind of "neighborly love" for friends. Most people love their families and friends. Readers with children may love them, too. The author of this essay has cats (and loves them, too).

What is love? Is it an emotion? A feeling? An affect (if we wish to separate these terms)? If love is an emotion is it a basic or a complex emotion? These questions and more are explored in the field of Philosophy of Love. The scope of this essay is more narrow.

In his chapter "Plato on Love and Sex," Jeremy Reid (2019) provides an account of the representation of love given in Plato's *Laws* as fundamental for understanding Plato's overall account of love. He emphasizes the duality that is loving for Plato: there is "bad love" and "good love." As Reid shows in his interesting essay, the good kind of love is one-sided and calm, not dark and stormy. He writes,

> The bad kind of love involves a desire primarily directed at the beloved's body, and (though explained with ancient reticence) aims at gaining sexual pleasure from him.

He claims that this bad kind of love involves the love of a particular beloved's and is focused on sexual gratification. Thus, on Reid's view, for Plato bad love is bodily, earthly, and aims only at what one can gain from the object. Reid (and Plato) contrast this bad love with good love, which is,

> directed at the beloved's soul... the lover is happy merely to look upon the beloved (Reid, 2019, 106).

This account of disinterested love focused on the goodness and essence (i.e. soul) of the beloved maps onto modern perceptions of "true love" as a state of disinterestedness. The bad lover, however, only wants things from their beloved, such as sexual or personal gratification.

The Bad Love that is the focus of this chapter is not the bad love Reid attributes to Plato. There was a time long ago that all loves were considered bad by certain groups. It is this during this time that Augustine of Hippo (354–430 CE) discussed the nature of human love in his hugely important theological text, *The City of God*. In Augustine's time there was a desire to not only to distinguish between good love and bad love, but between love itself (as bad) and other, calmer mental states.

The confusion caused by the nature of something so fundamental to human life as love is, of course, not lost on Augustine. The difficulty of pinning down the nature of love is seen in Augustine's terminology for love in its many forms *amor/amare, caritas/dilectio/diligere, libido, appetitus, concupiscentia, cupiditas/cupere*, etc. Augustine does not maintain a strict vocabulary in discussing things like love and God and body and soul—his language evolves over time and, as a rhetorician, he is always utilizing words that are the best for his audience.

In *"Cupiditas and Caritas: The Early Augustine on Love and Fulfillment,"* William Babcock (1993) distinguishes between two kinds of love in Augustine: "true object" and "false object" loves—this dichotomy, as we have seen, is present in other philosophical engagements with love. The two categories Babcock (1993) delineates are, ultimately, *caritas* and *cupiditas*, between "true love" and desire. It is tempting to place *amore* and *caritas* over and against *libido, appetitus, concupiscentia,* and *cupiditas*. However, this dualism implies that *caritas* and *cupiditas* are something other than love (*amore*).

This duality is certainly at play in the subject of this chapter: obsessive states are often described as not-love. The desire to control, to dominate is said to be the motivating factor of abusers. Reid's Platonic "good love" and "bad love" seem to map onto what Augustine's account of love is—the true form of love and its negation.

Augustine's accounting of love is much more complex than a simple dichotomy, however. The next two subsections—"The Love that is Emotion" and "When the Love is Bad: The Love that is Concupiscent Desire"—both examine Augustine's understanding of the relationship between (bad) love and emotion. These sections will explore Augustine's texts directly in order to provide an account of the Bad Love that this essay seeks to qualify.

38.2.1 The Love that Is Emotion

Many theories within the philosophy of love claim that love is a kind of emotion. However, the concept of love precedes that of emotion. In her essay "Emotion in Augustine of Hippo and Thomas Aquinas: A Way Forward for the Im/passibility Debate?", Anastasia Scrutton (2005) writes,

> In fact, the concept of the emotions is exclusive to the modern era. The term did not crop up in English until the mid-sixteenth century, when it was used to denote a public disturbance, and was not given its current meaning until the early nineteenth century.

> Furthermore, no exact translation or equivalent is found in Latin or any of the ancient languages. In contrast to the preference of the modern world for a single overarching category, the ancients and mediaeval worlds had a diversity of descriptions of human experiences. *Passiones, motus, motus animae, passions animae, affectus, affectiones, libidines, perturbations* and *libido* are all Latin terms now generally translated 'emotions' or 'feelings'—translations which can negate the original implications of each term. (Scrutton, 2005, 170)

Emotions and feelings, on Scrutton's account, are represented by a plethora of words in Latin, none of which convey what modern accounts of emotion seek to convey. However, Augustine's account of the nature of feelings (what can generally be described as emotions), is important for moving forward in the philosophy of love and emotions.[4] Love, for Augustine, is not an emotion at all, and neither is it a proto-emotion.

In Book 14, Chap. 7 of *City of God*, Augustine is speaking against stoics and skeptics who deny the validity of love, emotion, and feeling.[5] He seeks to defend his claims about what is and is not love in terms of Christian identity with Scripture.

In Augustine's interpretation of John 21, 15–19,[6] he emphasizes that Christ actually asks *"Diligis me?"* twice and *"Amas me?"* once. Augustine writes,

> The reason why I thought I should mention this is that quite a number of people imagine that fondness (*dilectionem*) and charity (*caritatem*) are something different from love (*amorem*). They say, in fact, that 'fondness' is to be taken in a good sense, 'love' in a bad sense. [...] My task, however, was to make the point that the Scriptures of our religion, whose authority we rank above all other writings, do not distinguish between 'love' and 'fondness' or 'charity.' *For I have shown that 'love' is also used in a good sense.* (Augustine, 2003, XIV.7, 557, emphasis mine)

Here the difficulties of understanding love in Augustine become clear. Augustine is working towards proving the importance of many forms of love by founding love, *amore*, in Scripture. That is, in this Scripture he finds more than merely fondness (*diletionem*) or charity (*caritas*). He folds together many forms of love as interchangeable states that are both distinct and the same.

The "good sense" and "bad sense" dichotomy in the passage above comes up again in terms of the object of love and the objects of desire in relationship to the emotions later in this chapter and in the overall text. Augustine immediately follows the above discussion of the presence of love in the Scriptures by defining the relationship between the human will and the objects of its love:

---

[4] Jennifer Greenwood (2015) writes of a parallel between current debates in the field of emotion theory and that of philosophy of mind in her book *Becoming Human: The Ontogenesis, Metaphysics, and Expression of Human Emotionality*: "Theorists in emotion theory argue that emotions are either predominantly inborn, biological, or 'natural' devices or predominantly learned, cultural, or 'nurtured' devices. Intracranialist theorists in philosophy of mind argue that cognition takes place entirely in the head, and transcranialists argue that it can and frequently does take place in cognitive systems that extend into the natural, technological, and sociocultural world" (Greenwood, 2015, xi).

[5] Augustine claims that the emotions we experience are of *this* world, and that the way we live the "agitations of the mind" today is "not the life we hope for in the future" (Augustine, 2003, 14.9, 564), i.e. in heaven. So on the one hand he fights for the "goodness" of love and on the other he denies emotions. Augustine is certainly a philosopher of many contradictions.

[6] An interesting aspect of this exchange is that Simon Peter is "hurt" by the questioning of Christ. The entire passage Augustine is referring to is here in full: "*When they had finished eating, Jesus said to Simon Peter, 'Simon son of John, do you love me more than these?'* 'Yes, Lord,' he said, 'you know that I love you.' Jesus said, 'Feed my lambs.' *Again Jesus said, 'Simon son of John, do you love me?'* He answered, 'Yes, Lord, you know that I love you.' Jesus said, 'Take care of my sheep.' *The third time he said to him, 'Simon son of John, do you love me?' Peter was hurt because Jesus asked him the third time, 'Do you love me?'*" (John 21, 15–19, emphasis mine)

And so a rightly directed will (recta uoluntas) is love in a good sense (bonus amor) and a perverted will (uoluntas peruersa) is love in a bad sense (malus amor). Therefore a love which strains after the possession of the loved object is desire (cupiditas); and the love which possesses and enjoys that object is joy (laetitia). The love that shuns what opposes it is fear, while the love that feels that opposition when it happens is grief. Consequently, these feelings are bad, if the love is bad, and good if the love is good. (Augustine, 2003, XIV.7, 557)

In this passage we are given Augustine's account of human emotion: all emotions are kinds of love (*amor*) that are either good (*bonus*) or bad (*malus*). The goodness or badness of any given emotion has to do with the will with which one loves—*recta* or *peruersa*.

In this list it would seem that Augustine offers contrasts, rightly directed will vs. perverted will, good love vs. bad love, and desire verses joy. However, this reading of Augustine's use of parallelism neglects the final sentence: "these feelings are bad, if the love is bad, and good if the love is good." Desire, joy, fear, and grief are all good "feelings" when the love that grounds them is good.

One can see this in action through an example: grieving over the ending of a romantic relationship for a short time can be good. Caused by a love that wants what it can no longer have, grief gives comfort to the scorned. However, that grief ought to be rightly willed—a grief over a future that will not occur and a past that is no longer grounded in the present. If the grief is grounded in a perverted will, it hurts the individual feeling that feeling: the scorned party, unable to move forward, breaks the windows of her lover's truck, goes to his work to confront him in public, etc.

This bad love is not related to the object of that love, but in the will of the person possessing that love. It is necessary to determine what, exactly, love is doing here in the equation. Thus, the next section, "When the Love is Bad: The Love that is Concupiscent Desire," explores the nature of sexual desire and its relationship to both the emotions and bodily loves.

38.2.2 When the Love Is Bad: The Love that Is Concupiscent Desire

As shown above, a distinctive facet of Augustine's conception of emotion as love is the fact that all emotions involve a love that is oriented towards an object. Desire (*cupiditas*) has at its heart the inability to possesses its object—when we possess and object we no longer desire it, when we have it we now are in a state of joy. Both states, whether possessing or not-possessing their objects, are forms of love. This section examines the nature of *concupiscentia* and whether it is a candidate for an understanding of the account of Bad Love that was promised in the beginning of this essay.

Concupiscentia is a word with cupid at its heart, it is considered to be the kind of desire that uncontrolled lust. It is a bad love, some say, and Augustine himself uses the term often interchangeably with *cupiditas*. *Concupiscentia* is a love that is not to be desired as it is unrestrained desire.

Many scholars of Augustine on love read *concupiscentia* as directly related to sexual desire. This is understandable, considering how Augustine discusses "dread lust" in Chaps. 16 and 18 of the fourteenth book of *City of God*. In these chapters Augustine takes a break in his discussion of the Edenic Fall to discuss sexual desire:

> We see then that there are lusts (*libidines*) for many things, and yet when lust is mentioned without the specification of its object the only thing that normally occurs to the mind is the lust that excites the indecent parts of the body (*obscenae partes corporis excitantur*). This lust assumes power not only over the whole body, and not only from the outside, but also internally; it disturbs the whole man, when the mental emotion combines and mingles with the physical craving, resulting in a pleasure surpassing all physical delights. So intense is the pleasure that when it reaches its climax there is almost total extinction of mental alertness; the intellectual sentries, as it were, are overwhelmed. [...] Sometimes the [sexual] impulse is an unwanted intruder, sometimes it abandons the eager lover, and desire (*concupiscentia*) cools off in the body while it is at boiling heat in the mind. Thus strangely does lust refuse to be a servant not only to the will to beget but even to the lust for lascivious indulgence; and although on the whole it is totally opposed to the mind's control, it is quite often divided against itself. It arouses the mind, but does not follow its own lead by arousing the body." (Augustine, 2003, XIV.16, 577)

Here it seems clear that, for Augustine, lust and concupiscence are neither emotions nor bodily—they are related to the will but are not equal to it.

In general, lust excites the "indecent parts of the body" at some moments and at others, while ravaging the mind, refuses to move those same indecent parts. This passage brings to mind the Porter scene in Act II Scene III of Macbeth:

> *Porter (to MacDuff)*: Marry, sir, nose-painting, sleep and urine. Lechery, sir, it provokes, and unprovokes; it provokes the desire, but it takes away the performance; therefore, much drink may be said to be an equivocator with lechery: it makes him, and it mars him; it sets him on, and it takes him off; it persuades him, and disheartens him; makes him stand to, and not stand to; in conclusion, equivocates him in a sleep, and, giving him the lie, leaves him. (Shakespeare, 1998, II.iii.5–8, pp. 131–132)

Lust takes over resonates in both flesh and mind in ways that do not necessarily lead to the sex that is desired. These passages, however, concern themselves with sexuality after the Fall—that is, they concern themselves with punishment for the Fall. For Augustine, it is not possible to love rightly when one is overwhelmed with a lust that seeks to control others, a lust that cannot even be trusted to arise when one wishes.

According to Augustine, we human beings associate desire with the body because that is the most universally present reminder of what little control we have over our own desires and our own selves. Thus this kind of love is a candidate for the Bad Love at the heart of the viciousness we humans can do to each other. However, we know from other texts of Augustine that concupiscentia is also associated with any kind of desire whose object one does not yet possess. Concupiscentia thus moves beyond mere love of sexual gratification to the kind of love one has have for things like cats, lovers, friends, blood-sport, and even the kind of love parents have for their children, children for their parents, etc. In this way, concupiscentia becomes the primary mode that human beings experience and express amor.

The "bad love" Augustine claims to be the origin for bad emotions is not concupiscentia—the desire for an object outside of oneself is not bad in itself. All love pulls itself out of the inner space of the heart/soul and stretches outwards into the world. Caritas also stretches out and within that inner cubiculum of the heart.[7] The previous section (with its two parts) focused on the account of emotion and concupiscent desire given in Augustine's text. It has been shown that emotion, for Augustine, is a kind of love, and whether the emotion is good or bad depends on the object of that love. Moreover, the category of desire (as concupiscentia) has been shown to be more expansive that of just desire for sexual pleasure. The next section explores the nature of concupiscent love in relationship with the kinds of trauma it can lead to.

38.3 Bad Love, Revisited

One's experience of the world as it is not one that can be radically intrapersonal, though the effect of the world on one's ability to experience the world is very real and important. In *Aftermath: Violence and the Remaking of a Self*, Susan Brison (2003) recounts in harrowing detail the effects of the brutal, life-halting rape she suffered. She writes,

> At the time I did not yet know how trauma not only haunts the conscious and unconscious mind, but also remains in the body, in each of the senses, ready to resurface whenever something triggers a reliving of the traumatic event. I didn't know that the worst—the unimaginably painful aftermath of violence—was yet to come. (Brison, 2003, x)

In the aftermath of experiences of great trauma there are scars on the psyche that present themselves physically. Brison's trauma caused her to reknit herself, to make herself again, not the same but reborn.

After a traumatic experience the victim is often left with the pain of others waiting for them to "get better"—to become themselves again. Under extreme trauma, according to Brison, there is no going back. One's feelings and emotions, too, are splintered and left to re-heal. This splintered affect can be seen in Augustine's writings of the human Fall (after Adam and Eve taste of the forbidden fruit and are both made to see the difference between good and evil as well as to leave paradise) as well as his discussions of what it is to be human—I wonder how many sins can be attributed to Bad Love—the kind of love, perhaps, that seeks control rather than union.

---

[7] My thanks to Erika Kidd for this understanding of "cubiculum of the heart," which she discussed in her delightful talk "Praying in the Bedchambers of the Heart: Augustine on Prayer and Intimacy" at the 2017 North American Patristics Society Meeting.

For Augustine, *concupiscentia* is natural to the human person; it existed in the Garden of Eden through to today, and is resurrected in the world that is to come. Whenever Augustine discusses the deep mythology of the Christian faith he is not speaking in absolutes—he is seeking to expand upon what he takes to be a central component of human life—love is embodied and extends to fill everything up from within, spilling out into the world.[8] But love is not necessarily stable and often troublesome—we often love things we shouldn't, and even occasionally identify with those who hurt us rather than ourselves. Love complicates things, much more so when love as a concept is bracketed and shuffled off as not something to be discussed right now.

Love permeates human life, and its presence and lack has a great impact on not just one's mood but one's way of processing the world. *Concupiscentia* is a bodily kind of love—it is the love for worldly things and people; it is a love that is associated with physical feeling, with quivering movements and yearning leaning toward despair. But *caritas* too has these moments. Augustine's account of *caritas*— the human love of God—abounds with libidinal imagery. *Caritas* is bodily as it is extended, as is *concupiscentia*. There is perhaps no human love that is not bodied. And yet there are aspects of love that are necessarily outward reaching and seemingly unembodied: love is a pulling and striving toward another outside of oneself.

For Augustine, the Fall of Adam and Eve led to a splintered affect in all humans, a *concupiscentia* that has come unstuck from its place in the hierarchy in the human soul and abandoned to the whims and caprices of the world. Any child of Adam is necessarily born with such a splintered affect, and with each new trauma comes another cascade of shards, moving into many different kinds of directions. And yet, for all its weakness, the human body is needed for sensing beatitude, but also for being beautiful in its right.

Returning to Chap. 7 of Book 14, Augustine unpacks his account of love and emotion in terms of scripture in a way that provides a deeper understanding of what it means to will and to love:

> The Apostle 'desires (*Concupiscit*) to depart and to be with Christ" (Phil 1, 23); and, 'My soul has desired (*Concupiuit*) to long (*desiderare*) for your judgments' (Ps. 119, 20), or (to put it more appropriately), 'My soul has longed to desire your judgments'; and, 'The desire (*concupiscentia*) for wisdom leads to sovereignty' (Wisd. 6, 20). All the same, it is the established usage that when we use 'desire' (*cupiditas* or *concupiscentia)* without specifying its object it can only be understood in a bad sense. (Augustine, 2003, XIV.7, 558)[9]

---

[8] I explored the relationship between Augustine's account of *caritas* and *concupiscentia* in relation with Extended Mind theory elsewhere in my doctoral dissertation, *Embodied Love and Extended Desire* (2017). I am influenced by Jan Slaby's (2014) account of "extended emotion," which is a response to the bracketing of emotions in the work of Andy Clark (2010) and others.

[9] In the Latin this passage is replete with concupiscence itself (emphasis mine): *Quod dicimus, de scripturis probemus.* Concupiscit *apostolus dissolui et esse cum Christo; et:* Concupiuit *anima mea desiderare iudicia tua, uel si accommodatius dicitur: Desiderauit anoma mea* cuncupiscere *iudicia tua; et:* Concupiscentia *sapientiae perducit ad regnum. Hoc tamen loquendi obtinuit consuetudo, ut, si cupiditas uel concupiscentia dicatur nec addatur cuius rei sit, non nisi in malo possit intellegi.*

Scripture is replete with right-willed *concupiscentia*-desire. Augustine clarifies again that it is the object of the desire (what is willed for) that makes the desire either good or bad. "In a bad sense" is repeated several times in Book 14, Chap. 7 of *The City of God* (I have included several of the uses of the phrase in this essay). For Augustine, it is only when there is not a clear object of concupiscent desire is the term meant "in a bad sense" in Scripture. It is object-less desire-love that leads to Bad Love: it is the kind of love which overreaches its object.

In this chapter, Augustine gives humanity three bodies: one mythic and natural, one temporal and wild, and one spiritual. He goes to great lengths to insist that the first body—that of Adam and Eve—naturally had emotions, desire, and the capacity for sexuality. He then claims that the mode by which emotions are expressed in both this world and the next to be loving, as we saw earlier in Chap. 7, love is the extension by which one wills into the world and is affected by the world. And yet Augustine seems to claim in Chap. 9 that emotions (apart from joy) do not belong in the ecstatic state of things (Augustine, 2003, XIV.9, 564). And so what can be thought of this seeming contradiction?

In the Chap. 14, Book 9 of the *City of God*, after having discussed the nature of love, the naturalness of love, the relationship between love, will, and emotions, Augustine turns to apatheia, the state of being so longed for by stoics and other philosophers. *Apatheia* is to be unmoved by *pathos* (passio), to be unmoved by the world or by one's own emotions and, indeed, to kill one's emotions and replace them with passionless, isolated reason.

Apatheia is the parent of the motherless nous that has guided Western Philosophy's desire for reason. Augustine is not a fan of *apatheia*:

> Moreover, if *apatheia* is the name of the state in which the mind cannot be touched by any emotion (*affectus*) whatsoever, who would not judge this insensitivity (*stuporem*) to be the worst of all moral defects? There is therefore nothing absurd in the assertion that the final complete happiness will be exempt from the spasms of fear and from any kind of grief; but only a man utterly cut off from truth would say that love (*amorem*) and gladness (*gaudiumque*) will have no place there. (Augustine, 2003, XIV.9.565)

Henry Bettenson, the English translator of this text, charitably translates "*stuporem*" as "insensitivity"—the word connotes in Latin what it sounds like in English—stupidity, stupefaction, numbness. Those who think that the desirable state of being to be emotionless (both internally and externally) are themselves in a stupor, on Augustine's view. In this way Augustine provides a kind of philosophical background to Susan Bordo's (1987, 2004) (among many other feminist thinkers) insights into the falseness of "objectivity" in philosophy and science.[10]

---

[10]This is not to say that love does not also lead one into stupidity, a fact that musician Kacey Musgraves (2013) eloquently discusses in her song, "Stupid": "Stupid love is stupid/Don't know why we always do it/Finally find it just to lose it/Always wind up looking stupid/Stupid." In another way, through reading Augustine as a feminist concerned with the falseness of objectivity in accounts of reason and emotion, Augustine becomes an ally against those whose views he would categorize with the word *stuporem*.

Given my reading of Book 14 of the *City of God*, Augustine does not seek a beatitude (that is, heaven) that is unbodied or unloving or emotionless. Because there is joy in the next world, there could, too, be some kind of heavenly *concupiscentia*; this heavenly *concupiscentia* is necessary for there to be relation with other humans in beatitude. Again, Augustine does not make clear that *cupiditas/concupiscentia* involves a bad love. The feelings associated with it are bad only when the love is bad, and the love is bad only when its object is unfixed.

To return to the "negging" example given in the Introduction: the seducer lies to his victim in order to have sex with her (or, perhaps, to punish all women), but the seducer does not want sex with *her*, or, indeed, any specific woman at all. The seducer wants to seduce *any woman*. Thus the seducer's desire is necessarily one that overreaches any one object.

This section has expanded on Augustine's account of *concupiscentia* in order to arrive at an understanding of what, for him, is Bad Love. For Augustine being human is a murky business—pulled by a desire/love that is constantly shattered and rejoined the goal for some may be the cessation of all desire/love. But for Augustine all love is rooted in desire, and all desire is rooted in love. These are facets of the same stone, and can in theory be viewed separable but are in fact inseparable.

38.4 Conclusion: But, Babe, I Love You

This chapter must conclude with an affirmation of the elusiveness of the category "Bad Love." The kinds of bad love that are delineated in the introduction of this chapter do not map onto Augustine's account of *concupiscentia* at all. This is due to the fact that the nature of love is murky itself, and it is only when the love is bad that the feeling is bad, and, by extension, it is when the will that is doing the loving is perverse that the love that results is manipulative, controlling, hurtful.

Denying that those that use love as a weapon actually, truly love covers over one epistemological problem with another: love becomes more and more narrowed when its bad persona is denied. Augustine's account of love on the one hand is closer to a common-place understanding of what love is: love is less and emotion than it is a reframing of one's existence towards an unstable other (and we are all unstable objects of love). On the other hand, it opens an epistemological space for an understanding of the category of Bad Love as Love in the Bad Sense.

I opened this chapter with a reference to the negging found in the Speech of Lysias in Plato's *Phaedrus*. Augustine has choice words to say about Plato's conception of the human person, and spends some time in Book 14 mocking the *Phaedrus* for its absurdity. On Augustine's view, the Platonic theory of body/soul makes flesh responsible for moral failings in a way that is illogical (Augustine, 2003, XIV.5, 554). He describes Plato's horses and their status as the cause for the re-embodiment of souls: the horse representing dread lust throws the triune soul out of joint with itself: unable to maintain its life in the ideal realm, the soul falls back into any body that happens to be ready. Thus lust, on Plato's account, is already in the soul and not in the body. Augustine writes,

> Thus on their own confession, it is not only from the influence of the flesh that the soul experiences desire and fear, joy and distress; it can also be disturbed by those emotions from a source within itself (Augustine, 2003, XIV.5, 555).

The severance of passionless reason from reasonless emotion is made circumspect in Plato's *Phaedrus*. In the *Phaedrus*, Socrates and his friend and student Phaedrus discuss a written speech of the orator Lysias. In this speech, Lysias argues that it is better for the young man to have sex with an older man who does not really love him than with one who does. Socrates makes many objections to this speech, not least of which is that Lysias is lying. Socrates alleges that there is eros secretly hidden in the motivation of the speaker: Lysias actually desires the boy he claims to not desire. The claim of Lysias, that it is preferable to sleep with a man who does not love you rather than one who does, is the claimed avowal of a certain kind of reason over passion, *logos* over *eros*.

This division is necessarily a false one: we are never really separate from our emotions when we reason. The *Phaedrus* offers an interpretation of reason that is not without love and puts to the test the myth of passionless logic. It is a lie people tell themselves when they claim to be making rational choices when in fact they are choosing what kind of desire to live with.

Augustine's exploration into the relationship between love, desire, and emotion is one that has been greatly influential to Western thought on love. Augustine's actual account of the emotions as kinds of loving, and Bad Love as objectless loving is one that is worth revisiting in modern scholarship on the philosophy of love as well as the psychology of those whose love seeks to dominate, such as emotional abusers.

Acknowledgments I would like the editors of this volume as well as the anonymous reviewer for feedback on this chapter. This chapter has benefitted from feedback from several conferences and trusted colleagues, especially Sarah Vitale, Rachel Aumiller, and James Wetzel.

References

Augustine. (2003). *City of God* (H. Bettenson, Trans.). London: Penguin.
Aumiller, R. (2019). Fantasies of forgetting our mother tongue. *Journal of Speculative Philosophy, 33*(3), 368–380.
Babcock, W. S. (1993). *Cupiditas* and *Caritas*: The early Augustine on love and human fulfillment. In R. J. Neuhaus (Ed.), *Augustine today* (Encounter series 16) (pp. 1–34). Grand Rapids, MI: Eerdmans.
Bordo, S. (1987). *The flight to objectivity: Essays on Cartesianism and culture*. Albany, NY: State University of New York Press.
Bordo, S. (2004). *The unbearable weight: Feminism, Western culture, and the body* (Tenth Anniversary Ed.). Berkeley, CA: University of California Press.
Brison, S. J. (2003). *Aftermath: Violence and the remaking of a self*. Princeton, NJ: Princeton University Press.

Clark, A. (2010). *Memento*'s revenge: The extended mind extended. In R. Menary (Ed.), *The extended mind* (pp. 43–66). Cambridge, MA: MIT Press.

Greenwood, J. (2015). Becoming human: The ontogenesis, metaphysics, and expression of human emotionality. In *Life and mind: Philosophical issues in biology and psychology*. Cambridge: The MIT Press.

Grosse, P. (2017a). *Embodied love and extended desire*. PhD Diss. Villanova University, Villanova, PA.

Grosse, P. (2017b). Love and the patriarch: Augustine and (pregnant) women. *Hypatia: A Journal of Feminist Philosophy. Special Issue: Feminist Love Studies in the 21st Century, 32*(1), 119–134.

Helm, B. (2017). Love. *Stanford encyclopedia of philosophy*. Accessed October 30, 2019, from https://plato.stanford.edu/entries/love/.

Howard, L. (2017). What is negging? *7 Signs someone is doing it to you*. Bustle. Accessed October 30, 2019, from https://www.bustle.com/p/what-is-negging-7-signs-someone-is-doing-it-to-you-72174.

Miles, M. R. (2005). Sex and the city (of God): Is sex forfeited or fulfilled in Augustine's resurrection of body? *Journal of the American Academy of Religion, 73*(2), 307–327.

Miles, M. R. (2006). *Desire and delight: A new reading of Augustine's confessions*. Eugene: Wipf & Stock Publishers.

Musgraves, K. (2013). Stupid. In *Same trailer different park*. Nashville: Mercury, Compact Disc.

Plato. (1997). In J. M. Cooper (Ed.), *Plato: Complete works*. Indianapolis: Hackett.

Pugachevsky, J. (2019). Here's how to tell if your date is full-on Negging you. *Cosmopolitan*. Accessed October 30, 2019, from https://www.cosmopolitan.com/sex-love/a28507230/negging-dating-meaning/.

Reid, J. (2019). Plato on love and sex. In A. M. Martin (Ed.), *The Routledge handbook of love in philosophy* (pp. 105–115). New York: Roudledge.

Scrutton, A. (2005). Emotion in Augustine of hippo and Thomas Aquinas: A way forward for the Im/passibility debate? *International Journal of Systematic Theology, 7*(2), 169–177.

Shakespeare, W. (1998). In N. Brooke (Ed.), *Macbeth*. Oxford: Oxford University Press.

Slaby, J. (2014). Emotions and the extended mind. In M. Salmela & C. von Scheve (Eds.), *Collective emotions: Perspectives from psychology, philosophy, and sociology* (pp. 32–46). Oxford: Oxford University Press.

Webb, M. (2013). On Lucretia who slew herself: Rape and consolation in Augustine's *De ciuitate dei*. *Augustinian Studies, 44*(1), 37–58.

Woolf, N. (2012). "Negging": The anatomy of a dating trend. *New Statesman*. Accessed October 30, 2019, from https://www.newstatesman.com/blogs/voices/2012/05/negging-latest-dating-trend.

Patricia L. Grosse is Assistant Professor of philosophy at Finlandia University in the Upper Peninsula of Michigan in the United States. Her research and teaching interests include feminist readings of religious thought, embodied and extended emotion theory, the thought of Augustine of Hippo, and the philosophy of pop culture. Her current research project, *Moving St. Monnica's 527 Bones*, explores the philosophical life and afterlife of St. Monnica, the mother of Augustine.

Part VIII
Love in Literature

Reading Girl (Photo: Anuja Mary Tilj)

Chapter 39
Cosmopolitan Love: The Actuality of Goethe's Passions

Rainer Matthias Holm-Hadulla and Alexander Nicolai Wendt

> *Heavenly jubilating, deadly despaired; happy is only the soul who loves.*
> *Goethe, Egmont (Translation by the authors)*
>
> *This chapter is dedicated to Professor Otto Dörr Zegers on the occasion of the award of the "Premio Nacional de Medicina" de Chile*

Abstract Love can appear in manifold ways: in the motherly affection and in the ecstasy of nature, in sacred prayers as well as in the intimate unification of lovers. That is to say, love constitutes the meaning of many, if not all regions of life. Yet, only in the most vivid biographies, the entire spectrum of love's manifestations can be found. As it were, the phenomenology of love benefits from the diligent and faithful investigation of truly exceptional lives. One example is the biography of Johann Wolfgang von Goethe who augmented his experience of love with his poetic abilities but also enabled his poetry by experiencing love. This chapter depicts the life of Goethe in order to highlight the different aspects in which love expresses itself. Throughout personal tragedies and greatest beatitude, Goethe was able to see love as the fabric that "holds the world together in its innermost core" (Faust I). The biographical experiences ultimately amount to a mutual meaning of the diverse aspects: *cosmopolitan love*. The notion is discussed in the context of Schelerian phenomenology of love.

Keywords Cosmopolitan love · Goethe · Scheler · Storge · Eros · Philia · Agape

---

R. M. Holm-Hadulla · A. N. Wendt (✉)
Heidelberg University, Germany
e-mail: rainer@holm-hadulla.com; alexander.wendt@psychologie.uni-heidelberg.de

39.1 Introduction

Since antiquity, philosophical just as poetic minds have been exploring the manifold aspects that compose the experience of love. Five traditional Greek notions of love highlight its many-sided nature, namely στοργή (*storge*) as the affectionate side of love, φιλία (*philia*) as friendship, φιλαυτία (*philautia*) as self-love, ἔρως (*eros*) as romantic love, and ἀγάπη (*agape*) as charity and spiritual love.

A popular contemporary account about love, however, cannot represent the entire depth to the more than two-millennial inquiry into the nature, meaning, and even function of love as it has been conducted in, for example, theology, philosophy, but also psychology. Moreover, the danger that lies in the taxonomic separation of different aspects of love is to alienate the reflection from life itself. In the end, the true source for any acquaintance with love can only be the loving encounter. Thus, it is the most vivid life, the life that bears the greatest depth and meaning where any attempt to accomplish an encompassing reflection about the essence of love ought to begin.

This approach to the investigation of love is genuinely phenomenological. It was Max Scheler who said that "love and hate as ultimate essences of acts can only be intuited, not defined" (1923, 176). Intuition, in other words, means an unmediated confrontation with the phenomenon itself, to witness love without conceptualization. Only when faithful contemplating the presence of love in all its purity, its actual meaning can come to the fore. Therefore, the memory of eventful and diverse lives is one of the most valuable treasures of occidental cultural heritage—a vigorous pioneer of life can be the prototype for an entirely new lifestyle for generations to come.

One of the prime examples of German history is the life of Johann Wolfgang von Goethe who not only experienced a manifold of adventures but passed them on to posterity in the most prolific of all forms: art. Goethe lived through the ups and downs of love during his 82-years-long life. He was not only one of the world's most influential poets, but also a politician and scientist who produced novel insights on love. Furthermore, his innovative contribution was transcultural since he integrated classical European concepts of love-philosophy, Greek mythology and Hebrew, Christian, Muslim religion as well as Persian, Indian and Chinese thought. Hence, his life is an ideal occasion for a thorough and encompassing contemplation on love. The following pages will track his biographical development in order to shed light on the meaning of love for his life. Thereafter, general considerations about the different aspects of *cosmopolitan love* become possible.

39.2 The Manifold Presence of Love in Goethe's Life and Work

Throughout his long life, Goethe suffered bitter disappointments and was affected by severe mood swings. Despite being a gifted child, a well-loved poet, and an influential politician, he devoted his entire life to an errant search for love; nonetheless, he had the exceptional ability to overcome emotional pain and to commute it into his creative activity. The way in which he harnessed his passions is an important aspect of his poetic heritage. Even 200 years later, cultural experience is influenced by Goethe's unique life-long struggle for love in its divergent forms. A more detailed psycho-biographical account of his amorous acquaintances can be found in "Goethe's Path to Creativity" (Holm-Hadulla, 2019).

Most importantly, Goethe's life is a story of great resilience against various emotional crises. Family relationships and friendships, political, scientific and poetic work, as well as passionate love were indispensable for him to overcome emotional turmoil and melancholia. Even the quasi-mythical experience of birth plays an important role in Goethe's autobiographical reflections and can be seen as one of the origins for his family-love (*storge*) and self-related (*philautia*) love. He returned to the topics of birth and personal growth on the one hand and the threat of death on the other at all stages of his life. He conceived of his own striving for love and creativity as a continuous process of "dying and becoming". When interpreting his poetry, these fundamental reflections should be considered, for example in the verses that he included in a letter to Auguste zu Stolberg, in which he states that he had been given everything entirely, "all joys, the infinite ones, /all pains, the infinite ones, entirely" (HA 1, 1981, p. 142). For Goethe, joy and despair were often conjoined: at the time he wrote these lines, his living situation would have been the envy of many, but he had also just received news of his beloved sister's death.

Besides the loving family relationships Goethe playfully explored his life-world. He developed profound *philia* for nature and culture. However, his poetic work was dedicated to erotic love. After being rejected by a young lady as a student, he found himself in an emotional crisis that could not be overcome for more than a year. Yet, he found words for his sufferings and wrote his first significant poems which he dedicated to a friend (*Odes to Behrisch*). His later poetic breakthrough was evoked by another unfortunate love 2 years later when he was 22. The resulting misery led to the seminal novel "*The Sufferings of Young Werther*".

Goethe's erotic relationships can be characterised as despairing and even chaotic since their very beginning. The encounter between 13-year-old Goethe and 16-year-old Gretchen, can be seen as the end of his childhood. She was the pubescent poet's first love, and he never let go of the memory, even in old age:

> This girl's image never left me from that moment; it was the first durable impression made upon me by any woman (*Poetry and Truth*, vol. 1, p. 146).

Gretchen, however, did not take him seriously. When she left Goethe's circle of friends, he spent his days and nights shifting between agitation and exhaustion. His family was even afraid that he might harm himself. Therefore, they hired a young man as his daily companion. Ultimately, Goethe became not only mentally but physically affected and began to

> torment myself by weaving the wildest romance of sorrowful events, all leading to an inevitable and tragic catastrophe (Poetry and Truth, vol. 1, p. 190).

These tendencies indicate a feature of Goethe's intimate romantic attachment that anticipates the nature of his later relationships: Goethe dedicated his entire being to the loving relationship, dissolving all boundaries, only to turn away from his partner just as rigorously in the end; any defeat would then provide inspiration for his poetry. He drew creative energy from disappointment and rejection, which he then conveyed to his writing. The women he loved—including Gretchen, but later also Käthchen Schönkopf, Friederike Brion, Charlotte Buff, Frau von Stein, Marianne Willemer, and Ulrike von Levetzow—were the source of his feelings and ideas.

During the years of his departure from home, Goethe's mood grew more sombre and he admitted to his sister that he often felt depressed. At the beginning of Easter Week in 1766, he wrote to his sister,

> I frequently become melancholic. I do not know from whence it comes. Then I stare fixedly at those around me like an owl ... And then a darkness overwhelms my soul, a darkness as impenetrable as October fog (FA 28, 1985–1999, p. 603).

However, the *agape*-love with his sister didn't stabilize him enough since he still bemoaned his "melancholy" and the "fog of doubt". In times like these, he wrote that he was unable to build up any self-esteem.

Instead, it was *erotic* love that could help him when coping with his self-tormenting ruminations. A short time later, though, his letters would begin to sound more optimistic again:

> I am often in a good mood, sister. In a very good mood! Then I visit the pretty women and the pretty girls ... I am hard-working, I am cheerful, and I am happy. Farewell" (FA 28, 1985–1999, p. 604).

He also drew on his friendship with Behrisch who could give him a feeling of security. Endorsed by this *philia*-love, Goethe could delve into his active and self-assuring creative love for poetry. He became able to transform his desires into text.

It is easy to disregard Goethe's enthusiasm as juvenile extravagance, but it cannot be denied that his relationships allowed him to work his internal tensions. Goethe's creativity required an amorous counterpart in order to experience his wishes and longings, even his personality, as coherent. His affection helped to promote his self-esteem and to find his place in his *cosmos*. Only love could provide this support: Visiting his family (*storge*), making friends like Behrisch (*philia*), stabilizing his self-respect by intellectual work (*philautia*), engaging in romance (in this time by poetry), and reaching a higher sense of creativity (*agape*).

Goethe arrived in Strasbourg in 1770. He resumed his legal studies and attended university lectures in other fields. In the social circles of university, he established an important *philia*-relationship with the slightly older Gottfried Herder, who at this time, was already a recognized author. Furthermore, Goethe was inspired by *erotic* love. He flirted with the daughters of his dancing instructor and fell in love with the 18-year-old Friederike Brion. Unlike his first love, Friederike returned his affection, and, thus, they spent many happy months together. He began his *Songs of Sesenheim,* e. g., the famous *"May Song".* Goethe's bliss, however, did not last very long. His passionate relationship with Friederike began to trouble him, and the other parts of his life in Strasbourg started to change. His dissertation was rejected, and he cozld not achieve the degree in law which he had planned to achieve. In his letters, he spoke of "deep unease", without being able to give a reason for it.

Thus, Goethe repelled from Friederike despite being able to tell why he did so. He mentioned odd mood swings and a strange loss of interest. After leaving her, Friederike was profoundly disappointed. When they separated, she could not articulate her feelings and fell ill soon afterwards. In a retrospective letter to Charlotte von Stein, Goethe confessed, "I had to leave her at a moment that almost cost her life …".

On his return from Strasbourg into his parent's house he was still in a state of instability, because

> there was still something over-strained about him, which did not point to perfect health of mind (Poetry and Truth, vol. 2, p. 51).

Since Goethe disliked the legal work at the court in Frankfurt, he continued to read and to dedicate himself to his poetic vocation. This helped him to deal with feelings of guilt over his treatment of Friederike. Urged by his sister and his important friend Johann Heinrich Merck, Goethe completed the historical drama *Goetz von Berlichingen* in less than 2 months, although it did not appear in public until 1773 in an extensively revised version. The play was greatly acclaimed and made his breakthrough possible. Once more the biographical importance of love in the life of Goethe reflects in his creative genius, connecting the romantic tragedy between Friederike and him, but also his friendship, with the development of the play.

The encounter with Charlotte Buff, who was engaged with another man, made Goethe fall into unrequited love yet another time. The following period of disappointment and desolation turned out to be the most productive time in his life. Goethe exposed himself to subjects that would come to characterize his entire literary oeuvre, such as the material for his tragedy *Faust.* Creative love or love for creation (*agape*) enabled him to transform despair and suicidality. His creation became his preferential method of maintaining connections with his loved ones.

After a long incubation period, Goethe finally wrote *The Sufferings of Young Werther* in February of 1774. In these days, Goethe received many invitations from Frankfurt society and was celebrated as a young genius. In one of these occasions, he was introduced to Lili Schönemann, the 16-year-old daughter of a banker. He could not deny "a sweet and gentle attraction" (*Poetry and Truth*, vol. 2, p. 213). However, despite falling in love with Lili, Goethe became acquainted with Countess Auguste zu Stolberg, too. The countess, who lived in a convent, had received *Werther* with great admiration and wrote to the poet in order to share her enthusiasm. Goethe was so pleased with her letter that he immediately replied,

> My dear ——, I will give you no name, for what are the names Friend, Sister, Beloved, Bride, Wife, or a word which comprises a complex of all those names, beside the direct feelings — to the —— I cannot write further, your letter has caught me at a wonderful time. Adieu, though at the first moment! —— Yet I return —— I feel you can endure it, this disjointed stammering expression, when the image of the Eternal stirs in us. And what is that but Love? —— If He was forced to make man after His own image, a race that should be like Himself, what must we feel when we find brothers, our likeness, ourselves doubled? (Bell, 1884, p. 222)

Messages like these established a subtle and poetic relation with Auguste zu Stolberg. Goethe took this complete stranger and turned her into his most important confidant, assigning her a variety of roles—friend, sister, beloved, bride, wife—and trusting her with all of his lively emotions and feelings. Curiously, this self-therapy-by-letter began even though his relationship with Lili Schönemann had started to become more serious. "*New Love, New Life*", a poem that was composed during this period, reveals his ambiguous expectations and contradictory feelings.

In this troubled state, it was Auguste zu Stolberg who could comfort Goethe and reassure him in his projects. Goethe assumed that the erotic love with Lili was a serious threat to his creativity since he felt confused and unproductive. A few days after attending Carnival ball with Lili, he confessed to Auguste:

> God knows I am a poor youth ... I wish I could rest on your hand, repose in your eyes ... In vain, my head is overstrained ... Oh, if I did not write dramas now, I should perish! (Bell, 1884, pp. 228–229)

Shortly after his engagement, Goethe began to avoid Lili and fled to Switzerland. Nevertheless, the poet couldn't rest properly since the trip was cut short and he had to return to Frankfurt without seeing Italy. In these days, his troubled mind was pushing him even further into a new crisis, and once again, he thought about suicide. He said that the suffering of Werther was nothing but the babbling of children when compared to his current state. In July 1775, he resumed his self-therapeutic correspondence with Auguste zu Stolberg:

> If I become too miserable, I will turn north, where she will be 200 miles behind me, dear sister [Auguste] ... I must be blown about even more, and then a moment against your heart! — That has always been my dream, my prospect as a result of a great deal of suffering ... Do not cease to be on my side as well. (FA 28, 1985–1999, pp. 460f.)

This emotional letter is a testimony to Goethe's struggle with his sorrowful sentiments. In Auguste, he had found a reliable, actively reassuring and creative *philia*-love which helped him to order his inner chaos. One year later, the Duke of Saxony-Weimar, 18-year-old Carl August, requested an encounter due to the curiosity of his mother, Anna Amalia. Anna Amalia was highly educated, composed music, and Goethe had come to her attention thanks to her passion for literature. The poet's work had even inspired her own creativity since she composed music that was meant to accompany Goethe's ballads. They became lovers in the sense of *storge*, *philia*, *philautia*, and *agape*. Perhaps erotic vibrations were present as well. This holds true for Goethe's love with duke Carl August and Charlotte von Stein, too. Especially the latter served Goethe to condense *storge*, *philia*, *philautia*, sublimated *erotic* and *agape* love. Charlotte von Stein had a certain resemblance with Cornelia, Goethe's sister, but she had also suffered a fate similar to that of Catharina Elisabeth, Goethe's mother, which may have contributed to his exalted love for her. When poetizing that, "in ages long past", she would have been his "sister or his wife", Goethe seems to be including her to the constellation of relationships that connected him to his mother, to his sister, to Auguste zu Stolberg, and to other women.

Being occupied with the new acquaintances, Goethe lost interest in older contacts, for example Auguste zu Stolberg,. He allowed himself to become entirely captivated by Charlotte von Stein. Not only did he make her his platonic ideal of a beloved, he also revitalized his emotional and creative conflicts with her. Some of the time, this relationship resembled the therapeutic relationship found in psychoanalysis, much like his earlier relationship with Auguste zu Stolberg. In April 1776, he described their mysterious and spiritual affinity:

> I cannot explain the significance, the power, that this woman has over me in any other way than by the transmigration of souls. Yes, we once were man and wife! Now we know each other -- but veiled, in an ethereal aura. I have no name for us -- the past -- the future -- the universe. (Boerner, 2005, p. 44)

The letter lucidly illustrates that Goethe's infatuation expresses the concentration of various types of loving relationships. On the one side, the relationship incarnates the erotic longing for human completeness achieved by the union of man and woman. On the other side, his advances toward Charlotte fulfilled his wish for secure bonding (*storge*), friendly understanding (*philia*), self-actualization (*philautia*), and love for universal values (*agape*). In the poem *"To Charlotte von Stein"*, he strives to enunciate the nature of this complex intimacy:

> Why did you give us the deep insight/enabling us to see hints of our future,/so that we can no longer, in a blissful delusion,/trust our love, our earthly happiness?/Why, fate, did you give us feelings/enabling us to read each other's hearts/in order to spy out our true situation/ amid all the strange turmoils? (Appelbaum, 1999, pp. 45–46)

In these verses, the poetical self bestows order upon the emotional chaos by mirroring itself in the beloved. Thus, Goethe transforms *storge*, *philia*, *philautia* and *erotic love* into a cosmopolitan *agape*. Beyond poetry, Goethe cared devotedly for Charlotte's son Fritz. His motivation for educating the boy, on a deep, unconscious level, may have been the resurrection of his dead siblings. Apparently he was dedicating himself to life in order to combat his own fear of death. This concentration of hopes and fears, however, meant that their relationship had to remain unfulfilled in respect to erotic love. Likewise, his creative processes can be understood as a dialectic interplay of inclinations and renunciation (Holm-Hadulla & Wendt, 2020).

During his first few months in Weimar, Goethe developed an important friendship with Duke Carl August, that should last for over 50 years. They shared many adventures, but more importantly, they could trust one another. Goethe was very successful in inspiring Carl August's personal interests, which the court at Weimar observed with appreciation. The Duchess Anna Amalia was especially pleased with his cultivating effect on her son, while Goethe himself found emotional stability in the company of Carl August.

Another impressive condensation of the different forms of love can be found Goethe's Italian Journey from 1786 to 1788. He characterized it as a "true new birth". In Weimar, the restless wanderer had become a sedate minister and respected teacher. Not only had he achieved great prestige in the society of Weimar (active/ *philia*) but his friendship with Duke Carl August comforted him (relational/*storge*) just as his poetic fulfilment (self-love/*philautia*). He had become a recognized man who could occupy himself with politics, economy and science (creative love/*agape*). But his erotic longings remained unfulfilled and, thus, some of his poetic aspirations. In a letter to Carl August in January 1788, he explained the motive for his trip:

> The chief reason for my journey was: to heal myself from the physical-moral illness from which I suffered in Germany and which made me useless; and, as well, so that I might still the burning thirst I had for true art. In the first point, I was somewhat successful, and in the latter, quite so. (Richards, 2003, p. 137; HA Letters 2, 1981, p. 78)

Secure bondings (*storge*) and respectful friendships and interests (*philia*), self-esteem (*philautia*) and engagement in politics, economy and science (*agape*) needed to be complemented by lived sexuality and living poetry (*eros*). In his notes for his *Italian Journey*, he wrote that the journey was "changing [him] within and without" and "continues to work" (Works 12, 1985–1999, pp. 249, 251). His erotic striving and poetical work once again made it possible for him to validate himself and to process the events that were assailing him. The "true new birth" was as well poetic as erotic. In one of his letters to Carl August from Italy, he expressed himself thusly:

> I may well say: in this one-and-a-half years of solitude I have found myself again; but as what?—As an artist! What I am beyond that, you will judge and make use of ... Take me in as a guest, allow me to complete the full measure of my existence by your side and take pleasure in life. (HA Letters 2, 1985–1999, p. 85)

After his return, Goethe, revivified by his recent experiences, continued to debauch in *eros*-love. He had become more open while in Italy and now, beyond the restraint of courtly etiquette, was enchanted by Christiane Vulpius. Christiane, a 23-year-old seamstress from a poor family, tried to improve her brother's meagre situation as a writer by approaching Goethe on his behalf. Apparently, she immediately won Goethe's sympathy who reciprocated her erotic affinity. For the first time, he could enjoy the erotic love without the burden that had come with his previous relationships. *The Erotica Romana*, which were later renamed the *Roman Elegies*, were written during this period.

Since he could rely on familial security (*storge*), friendships and interests (*philia*), self-esteem and self-actualization (*philautia*) as well as a deep love for creativity in nature and culture (*agape*), he could now engage in a deep and lasting romantic relationship:

> We lovers are pious, we quietly revere all demons, /wishing every god and every goddess to be favorably inclined toward us. (Appelbaum, 1999, p. 93)

Creation finds a perfection in *eros*-love that includes *storge*, *philia*, *philautia* and *agape*:

> Yes, we gladly confess it to you all: our prayers,/our daily service, is always consecrated to one goddess in particular./Roguishly, briskly, and earnestly we celebrate secret feasts,/and silence befits all initiates perfectly. (Appelbaum, 1999, p. 93)

Considering her profound emotional significance for Goethe, it is easy to understand that he was deeply affected by Christiane's death in June of 1816. She died of kidney failure and suffered such immense pain before her death that she bit through her own tongue. The women caring for her had to leave her room since they could no longer bear to hear her screams of pain. Goethe himself was confined to his bed with high fever, and so she was alone during her final hours. He was also kept from her bedside by his dread of illness and death. Goethe recorded in his journal that he felt "emptiness and deathly stillness in and around me". On the day of her death, he wrote the following verses for her epitaph:

> In vain you try, o sun,/To shine through the dark clouds!/The whole value of my life/Is to weep for her loss. (HA 1, 1981, S. 345)

After the tragedy, Goethe sought refuge in his administrative, scientific, and artistic work. Additionally, he was seeking the company of his friends Boiserée, Zelter, and Wilhelm von Humboldt. Hence, during times of sorrow, Goethe was supported by his work and his friends, but he was also assisted by his disciplined lifestyle. His routine included to wake up early, a regular diet, and exercise in nature. Consequently, he built up resilience that facilitated his administrative and scientific work, but it cut him off from the "pathological wellspring" of his poetry, hence his lack of productivity in writing poetry during this period.

However, even in his eighth decade, Goethe experienced yet another unexpected change in his life. The world-renowned statesman, scientist, and poet had actually achieved everything he wanted to and could now calmly look on both his life and his death with the wisdom of age. Thanks to his poetry was able to judge that the narrow boundaries of one's own person are dissolved in favor of being taken up in a greater love for the cosmic whole (*agape*). Inspired by ideas from the Far East, this dissolution is experienced not as a threat, but as bliss: "Self-surrender is a pleasure". As in Taoism, this does not mean cessation, but rather activity in a higher sense, where the creative being is not dispersed, but rather remains completely present while outside of himself. The "eternal", which is found in activity, is one of Goethe's central themes in his later poem "*Legacy*", where he expresses "no being can crumble into nothingness"—while in "*The One and the All*", the dialectical antithesis is declared: "everything [must] crumble into nothingness". Fading into the stream of life is a prerequisite for the eternal, "if it [insists] on remaining in its momentary state" (see Holm-Hadulla, 2019).

Suddenly and unexpectedly, Goethe experienced a romantic disappointment in 1823 which descended on him as a deep crisis. While staying in Marienbad, he fell in love with the 19-year-old Ulrike von Levetzow. The 74-year-old Goethe even considered to marry the maiden. Amalie von Levetzow, Ulrike's mother, initially thought of the proposition as a joke, but once she realized that Goethe was serious, she and her daughter escaped from Marienbad. Regardless of the circumstances, Goethe followed the two, but his proposal was rejected yet again; deeply disappointed and in despair, he composed the famous "*Marienbad Elegy*" during the pitiful journey home to Weimar. Along the poems "*To Werther*" and "*Reconciliation*", the *Elegy* composes the *Trilogy of Passion*. Remembering the emotional anguish he had depicted almost 50 years earlier in *The Sufferings of Young Werther*, he titled the first poem "*To Werther*". It is remarkable that Goethe was still so deeply connected to feelings he had experienced 50 years before. Werther's "much-lamented shade" was still imminently near to him. The world of emotions in Werther, which mirrored Goethe's life-world during the years 1772–1774, was still very present to the 74-year-old, as if he had never stopped to experience *The Sufferings of Young Werther*. Werther preceded him in death, "and didn't lose much". Goethe, on the other hand, continued to live, "for weal or woe"; he was plagued by his passions and "embroiled in repeated amorous plights". In the end, even the poetical self must face the inevitable: "separation is death!" But then the poet lifts up his voice to avoid death. He is "entangled in such torments" and calls out to a god, "to express what he endures".

Goethe's creative culture of work and of remembrance saved him again and again from suicide and made it possible for him to produce timeless creations. In the *Trilogy of Passion*, he expresses his gratitude for his ability to transform his misery by means of creativity.

During this erotic crisis, he reinvigorated himself in the company of his friends and indulged himself in his interests (*storge*, *philia*, *philautia*), but he also dedicated his time to his grandchildren (generative *agape*) and the latest works (transcendental *agape*): "Self-surrender is a pleasure".

In February of 1829, he commented to Eckermann,

> Man should believe in immortality; he has a right to this belief; it corresponds with the wants of his nature" (Oxenford, 1850, vol. 2, p. 122).

The unshakable will to live that reflects itself in this belief also came to the fore in Goethe's last creative projects. He dedicated his final years to completing *Wilhelm Meister's Travels* and *Faust II*, in which he worked through two elementary conflicts: Wilhelm Meister recognizes his own boundaries but renounces them, while Faust strives to overcome his own earthly limitations. Nine month before his death on March 22, 1832, the entry in his diary stated that he had completed Faust, and hence "the main business achieved". He considered Faust his legacy; with it, he gave lasting and universal expression to his mortal struggle with relational love, activity, self-actualization, *erotic* and creative love—*storge*, *philia*, *philautia*, *eros* and *agape*—cosmos and chaos.

39.3 Cosmopolitan Love as the Uniting Principle in Goethe's Life

Goethe's exceptional biography inspired his contemporaries as well as generations to come, ultimately making him the German national poet by the end of the nineteenth century. Many referred to his work with greatest reverence and his words permeated even the colloquial German tongue. Similarly, Goethe and his worldview became subject to several philosophical reflections—among them also reflections about the subject of love, such as the seminal contribution to the phenomenology of love, Max Scheler's 1913 "the nature of sympathy" (second edition from 1923). In the inquiry, Scheler critically investigates the meaning of empathy, the possibility of intersubjectivity, but most importantly, the essence of love. Curiously, by adapting the Husserlian phenomenology, he reaches a philosophical understanding of love that converges with Goethe's manifold biographical encounters. Hence, it is a promising enterprise to re-examine Goethe's love-imbued life from a Schelerian standpoint.

Scheler's premise is that there have been two primary conceptions of love in history. The first one can be found, for example, in Indian and Chinese philosophy as well as spiritualism but also in Plato. It entails the tendency to dissolve personality through a primordial union with the entire *cosmos*, ultimately withdrawing from all worldly matters, such as the individual pain or suffering. He calls this form of love "*cosmistic* identification" (Scheler, 1923, XI), meaning an identification with the κόσμος (cosmos, the entire being, universe). A typical example for such an understanding of love is the Platonic idea of complete unity between lovers. In his *Symposium*, Plato had envisaged the loving relation between man and woman by virtue of the legend of the spherical people: Since the original men—creatures with two heads and four arms as well as four legs—had been too powerful, the gods decided to split them in halves. Thus, love can be understood as the reunion with one's complementary half. Scheler does not believe that this conception of love is veritable since it entails a possible end for the search for love, a point of completion. Furthermore, the *cosmistic* love neglects the importance of the autonomous person, favouring the unification with the other—and ultimately with the entire *cosmos*.

The traditional alternative is called "*a-cosmistic*" (ibid., 116) love. Quite unlike the idea of unification, it centres on the nature of God as an absolute person. Consequently, it entails the idea of a hermetic communion with God as it can be found in the eremitic lifestyle of Christian monasteries but also in classical Greek spirituality. Scheler concludes that this form of retreat from the world might almost always lead to worldy isolation:

> A love for God like the Greek love for God, that leads men beyond the community of mankind but not to deeper or more inclusive collective relations with their brethren, may consequently only end on a mountain where the lonely anchorite rejects all human connections (Scheler, 1913, 153f).

Both forms of love can be found in Goethe's biography. The poet has been searching reclusion in *agape* or *philautia* with a definite *a-cosmistic* tendency, but he also relished in the intensity of *cosmistic* interaction with fellow humans or nature, be it *eros*, *philia*, or *storge*. However, neither of the two extremes of love could ever satisfy him. His creative search led him to an encompassing sense of love that did neither sacrifice community for exaltation nor personality for exhilaration. Rather, as he expressed in the West-Eastern Divan,

> The slave, the lord of victories,/The crowd, whene'er you ask, confess/In sense of personal being lies/A child of earth's chief happiness (Dowden, 1914, 114).

This declaration of the importance of the autonomous personality as the centre of human nature embraces both, the *cosmistic* and the *a-cosmistic* aspect of love. This mutual fulfilment of the different forms of love can also be found in Schelerian thought. In his article on "Eros and Agape in Scheler", Guido Cusinato highlights the reciprocal dependence of the different forms of love. He says:

> Eros and Agape work together but they have different natures: Agape is a divine endowment whilst Eros is primarily the striving of a human who seeks self-assertion. They belong to different levels. Eros is a function and Agape an act. For Scheler, functions—even the highest—only reach the psychic self and not the person. Moreover, Eros is not just any type of function. One could even say that it is the true task of Eros to connect itself with the Agapeic act in order to give Agape room to move (Cusinato, 2003, 95).

The holistic meaning of love, thus, is substantiated in the interplay of its different aspects. It cannot be reduced to some apparent function that reaches for a goal-state like the *cosmistic* self-dissolution or the *a-cosmistic* revelation of the absolute. On the contrary, love is the liveliest of all experiences and therefore the ideal inspiration for poetic creativity—or rather, it manifests itself in poetry as its expression. In this sense, Scheler reads Goethe as a pioneer of sentimentalism who made the "universal field of expressions of the world as a single organism" (Scheler, 1923, 96) accessible. In other words, the poetic transformation of perception by virtue of love facilitates the experience of an "universal grammar of expression, a cosmic mimic art and mime" (ibid.).

For Scheler, these considerations about the nature of love lead to solidarism as a moral attitude that promotes solidarity with the manifold forms of life that exist because it requires cooperation to disclose the "universal field of expression". He says: "Only the diachronic and contemporary cosmopolitan cooperation and complementation of irrepresentable parts of humanity may empower the complete power of knowledge that resides in humanity" (ibid., 34). Cosmopolitan love, thus, does not merely dissolve the beloved person in ecstatic unity or withdraw from other persons on the quest for divine redemption. Cosmopolitan love engages with the diversity and depth of all kinds of experience in the natural process of growth that characterises life. This aspect has been elaborated most profoundly by the Chilenian psychiatrist and cosmopolitan Otto Dörr (e.g. 2007). Overarching the versatile aspects of love, cosmopolitan love takes responsibility for the other as an autonomous person in the πόλις (polis) as a community because their irreplaceable personal complexity is a realm of independent and valuable meaning.

However, following Goethe, it must be pointed out that love is fundamentally shaped by chaos and it is common sense that love can produce blissful feelings as well as the deepest despair. Goethe, especially during his first twenty years, lived through several crises which were related to *erotic* love, as well as his friendships—in the sense of *philia* and well-being—in his later life. His self-love—*philautia*—was often challenged. His intense caring for nature and culture and a higher sense of cosmopolitan values, such as *agape*, allowed him to survive his passionate love affairs. Indeed, these were not affairs only, but rather an expression of enduring longing for family-bonding, friendships and interests (*philia*), self-respect (*philautia*), romantic love (*eros*) and love for the divine, political, and scientific creation and cultural creativity (*agape*). Ultimately, these experiences led him to the discovery of cosmopolitan love as an all-encompassing foundation of life which expresses itself in its diverse aspects.

39.4 Conclusion

Johann Wolfgang von Goethe lived an exceptional life. Its surviving records are a prolific source for the acquisition of new knowledge, be it philosophical or psychological. Reading Goethe's life as a history of love, it can be shown that no particular concept can suffice to condense the poet's manifold experiences. Instead, it is imperative to factor in all aspects of love that compose Goethe's biography, especially *philia, philautia, eros, storge*, and *agape*. Yet, beyond these particular viewpoints, the creative unity among them reveals an overarching layer. This encompassing sphere of love might be called *cosmopolitan* love. It conveys the particularities of the different forms of love, but also reflects their dynamics with reference to the social integration of the life-world.

In dialogue with philosophy, Goethe's biography offers a vivid source for the inquiry concerning the nature of love. Schelerian phenomenology bears great resemblance with Goethe's own path towards *cosmopolitan* love. Therefore, the meaning of Goethe's life can be discussed in a more reflective fashion. Drawing on Scheler's interpretation of Goethe, the poet's experience of love allowed him to comprehend the manifold expressions of life. Complementary, love made Goethe's poetry visionary. A possible field of research in this direction is the investigation of expressions, such as the different aspects of love. Cosmopolitan expressions of love require a *cosmo-vital* relation to the world.

References

Boerner, P. (2005). *Goethe*. London: Haus Publishing.
Cusinato, G. (2003). Eros und Agape bei Scheler. In C. Bermes, W. Heckmann, & H. Leonardy (Eds.), *Vernunft und Gefühl. Schelers Phänomenologie des emotionalen Lebens* (pp. 83–108). Königshausen & Neumann: Würzburg.
Dörr, O. (2007). *La Palabra y la Musica*. Santiago de Chile: Editorial Universidad Diego Portales.

Holm-Hadulla, R. M. (2019). *Goethe's path to creativity: A psycho-biography of the eminent politician, statesman and poet.* London, New York: Routledge, Taylos an Francis Group.
Holm-Hadulla, R. M., & Wendt, A. N. (2020). Dialectical thinking: Further implications for creativity. In M. Runco & S. Pritzker (Eds.), *Encyclopedia of creativity* (3rd ed.). Amsterdam, Boston: Academic Press/Elsevier.
Scheler, M. (1913). Liebe und Erkenntnis. In M. Scheler (Ed.), *Schriften zur Soziologie und Weltanschauungslehre* (pp. 161–195). Leipzig: Der Neue Geist-Verlag.
Scheler, M. (1923). *Wesen und Formen der Sympathie.* Bonn: Cohen.

Goethe's Works

FA: Johann Wolfgang Goethe. (1985–1999). In D. Borchmeyer, et al. *Sämtliche Werke. Briefe. Tagebücher und Gespräche. Frankfurter Ausgabe* (Vol. 40). Frankfurt: Deutscher Klassiker Verlag.
HA: Goethes Werke. (1981). In E. Trunz (Ed.), *Hamburger Ausgabe* (10th ed., revised.) Munich: C. H. Beck'sche Verlagsbuchhandlung.

Translations

Appelbaum, S. (1999). *103 great poems: A dual-language book = 103 Meistergedichte/Johann Wolfgang von Goethe.* Mineola, NY: Dover Publications.
Bell, E. (1884). *Early and miscellaneous letters of JW Goethe, including letters to his mother.* London: George Bell & Sons.
Dowden, E. (1914). *West-Eastern Divan.* London, Toronto: Dent & Sons.
Oxenford, J. (1850). *Conversations of Goethe with Eckermann and Soret* (Vol. 2). London: Smith, Elder, and Co.
Richards, R. J. (2003). The erotic authority of nature: Science, art, and the female during Goethe's Italian journey. In L. Daston & F. Vidal (Eds.), *The moral authority of nature* (pp. 127–154). Chicago: University of Chicago Press.

Rainer Matthias Holm-Hadulla is a professor for psychiatry, psychosomatic medicine, and psychotherapy at Heidelberg University, Germany. He is a training analyst (IPA) and teaches at universities in Buenos Aires and Santiago de Chile and at the Pop-Academy, Mannheim. Professor Holm-Hadulla is the author of over 100 scientific papers, as well as six books on creativity, counselling, and psychotherapy, including The Art of Counselling and Psychotherapy (Karnac, 2004) and The Recovered Voice: Tales of Practical Psychotherapy (Karnac, 2017). His Psycho-Biography of Johann Wolfgang von Goethe (Routledge, 2019) has been published in German, Spanish, Italian, and Persian language.

Alexander Nicolai Wendt is a research associate at the chair for Experimental and Theoretical Psychology at Heidelberg University, Germany. He is currently conducting a research project at the University of Verona, Italy, on concrete psychology in Schelerian phenomenology.

Chapter 40
On the Discoursive Construction of the Spanish Hero in Intercultural Romances

María-Isabel González-Cruz

Abstract This chapter explores the different strategies employed for the construction of the Spanish identity of male protagonists in a sample of romances published between 1955 and 2003 by Harlequin/Mills & Boon. Set in a Spanish-speaking area, the Canary Islands, many of these novels narrate the love stories of mixed couples, invariably a hero of Spanish origin and an English-speaking heroine. After a brief review of the romantic idea of love in popular culture and the concepts of identity and national character, the perceptions of Spaniards and the image of Spain throughout history are examined. Then the chapter focuses on the multiple facets of the hero's Spanishness, including references to his physical features, personality and behaviour. His characterization also draws from a number of literary and historical figures, which apparently work as inspirational sources. The role of language is also highlighted, since the texts tend to be interspersed with Spanish terms and expressions. All together, these elements seem to effectively contribute to the discoursive construction of the romantic Spanish hero.

Keywords Discourse on Spain and Spanishness · Spanish identity and stereotypes · Concepts of identity and national character · Love in popular culture · Romance fiction

40.1 Introduction

Reputed as a reactionary genre, popular romance fiction has proved to be one of the most successful publishing phenomena and a significant cultural artefact, despite its double stigma as popular and feminine (Sánchez-Palencia Carazo, 1997, p. 153). In the last decades, challenging the denigrated view so prominent in the Academia, a number of scholars have approached the study of romance novels in a more positive

M.-I. González-Cruz (✉)
Department of Modern Languages, University of Las Palmas de Gran Canaria, Las Palmas, Spain
e-mail: isabel.gonzalezcruz@ulpgc.es

way, with critical rigour and avoiding the condescending treatment of previous analyses (Dixon, 1999; Kamblé, 2014; Regis, 2003; Vivanco, 2011). Today, romances tend to be viewed as historical documents which "must be read in the context of the time and manner of their production" (Auchmuty, 1999, p. x). As cultural barometers, these works portray patterns of gender roles and relationships (sex, love, marriage, motherhood), representing sociocultural differences through stereotyping but also by deploying binary oppositions (feminity/masculinity; identity/alterity). These oppositions are "crucial for all classification, because one must establish a clear difference between things in order to classify them" (Hall, 1997, p. 236). In fact, quite often romances include protagonists who have very different backgrounds, either from each other, the intended reader, or both: they may come from different countries and cultures, speak different languages, belong to very different social strata or are, in some other way, an "Other" to the rest of the characters. This justifies my aim to explore the discursive strategies employed in a sample of Harlequin/Mills & Boon romances[1] to construct the Spanish identity of the male protagonists. Before studying the characterization of the Spanish heroes and the representation of Spanishness in this type of texts, a brief revision of the concepts of romantic love, identity and national character is required. The chapter will then focus on the analysis of those factors that contribute to the literary depiction of the Spaniard. By examining the way Spanishness is projected in these novels, I also corroborate Lindsay's claim that "perceptions of identity can never be value-neutral" (2015, p. 134).

The selected romances are totally or partially set in the Canaries, a well-known Spanish all-year-round tourist resort off the African coast. They narrate the love stories of mixed couples: a hero of Spanish origins[2] and an English-speaking heroine who, for various reasons, settles temporarily on the islands, stereotypically described as an exotic paradise with very different sociocultural traditions. Thus, although devoted par excellence to telling love stories, these romances of intercultural merging also tend to bring to the fore several cross-cutting issues. This confirms Pérez-Gil's idea that beneath their apparently simple and predictable plots these novels often pose "questions of gender, class, race and ethnicity that merit deeper analysis" (2019, p. 169). Interestingly, with their "distinctive status as the despised and rejected 'other' of modern literary writing" (Selinger & Frantz, 2012, p. 3), the texts provide insight[3] for the analysis of identity and otherness, alongside gender, sociocultural and national identity and stereotypes. By portraying the characterization of Spanish heroes, this chapter contributes to a multidisciplinary view of

---

[1]The sample of 15 romances belongs to the wider corpus compiled for Research Project FFI2014–53962-P, funded by the Spanish government. This grant is hereby gratefully acknowledged.

[2]Airlie (1958) is the only exception: the hero is a Briton relatively Spanishized after being long established in the Canaries, where he has close social bonds. Hispanicisms and interesting comments on Spanish character abound, which justifies its inclusion as a primary source.

[3]They are also useful to explore topics such as paradise discourse, language contact, environmental awareness and political attitudes (González-Cruz, 2015, 2017a, forthcoming; Vivanco, 2016).

romance studies, evidencing these novels' "complicity with discourses of national identity" as they stereotype difference and reveal "the ethnocentric views that the English may have of the Spaniards" (Pérez-Gil, 2018, p. 952).

40.2 Some Theoretical Background

This section will approach two key aspects the study relies on; namely, the idea of love that predominates in popular culture, particularly in romance fiction, and the connection between the concepts of identity and national character.

40.2.1 *Love in Popular Culture*

Despite the variety of values that different societies and cultures have attached to love throughout history, it remains a complex and difficult concept to define. Research on love and romance proves that this universally known term has been experienced, expressed, represented and studied from very different perspectives. Yet, scholars in Critical Love Studies, such as Gratzke, are still sceptical "regarding our ability fully to understand the object of our studies," claiming not only that "we cannot grasp its full potentiality" but also that "love is relational", both to an object, "as fleeting as that may be," and to a set of rules which define the validity of love in a given socio-historic context" (2017, pp. 2–4). During the Romantic period, previous religious views of God as "the sole source and guarantor of love" were replaced by the idea of "love as a religion. Love hence became an end in itself" (Gratzke, 2017, p. 5). In turn, following the physical law of Negative Entropy and the rule of order in the universe, biologist Griffith (2011, pp. 33–34) claims that "here on Earth love is the underlying theme of existence," as long as all types of matter become ordered into larger wholes, from atoms into multicellular organisms. Therefore, for this scientist, love can be described as "unconditional selflessness," and it seems to be "the glue that holds the world together."

From the several senses given to the word 'love' in the *Oxford English Dictionary*, the one typically portrayed in popular narratives such as romance fiction has to do specifically with "[a]n intense feeling of romantic attachment based on an attraction felt by one person for another; intense liking and concern for another person, typically combined with sexual passion." Interestingly, Dixon mentions Cawelti's classic description of "the moral fantasy of romance" as "a simple case of love overcoming all problems and obstacles" (1999, p. 166), while Harders notes how "romance persists in idealizing the institution of marriage" (2012, p. 149). In fact, as Regis explains, love and the happy ending, which includes marriage, are precisely "the elements most associated with the popular romance novel" (2003, p. 21). This type of fictional writing shares certain features with other forms of social media such as "film, television, magazine, music, advertising and self-help books," as Weisser proves in part VII of her reader. Thus, in addition to their preoccupation with romance, their audience is mostly formed by women; and most importantly, with their focus on romantic love, they play a crucial role in constructing masculinity and femininity while "representing the ideal of romance" (2001, p. 299).

40.2.2 Identity and National Character

Conceived as the "cultural, literary, and popular representations of collective peculiarities and behaviour," the idea of national characters is said to be "stereotypical in nature" and consists of "attributions and prejudices established intertextually" (Hoonselaars & Leerssen, 2009, p. 251). This seems to contradict one of the most commonplace facts, "that each of us is a unique human being with our own thoughts and personal identities" (Clark, 2013, p. 7). We must bear in mind, though, that the concept of identity is complex and multilayered, including not only the internal psychological one but also cultural and social facets. Hence, factors such as language, religion, ethnicity or nationality (Joseph, 2004) play an important part in the creation of an individual's identity. These elements are often very closely intertwined, as is the case with nationality and language, the latter being one of the most defining attributes of the individual, "an important part of our sense of who we are—of our identity," (Edwards, 2009). Besides, as many sociolinguists have proved, in the creation of nations, the adoption of a specific language or "linguistic variety that belongs to that 'nation'" has always played a crucial role, "marking one nation from another" (Clark, 2013, pp. 39/41). This explains why Spanish vocabulary and expressions are constantly interspersed in the English discourse of the novels.

The concept of a nation as a mental construct emerged during the Enlightenment, quickly unfolding all its "emotional appeal and social binding force" (Wodak, de Cillia, Reisigl, & Liebhart, 2009, p. 186). Now it is understood more as a cultural artifact, as proposed by Anderson (1991), who defined nations as *imagined communities* that are limited and sovereign. On the one hand, they are imagined because, obviously, nobody is expected to ever be able to get to know all his/her compatriots "yet, in the image of each lives the image of their communion" (1991, p. 4). On the other hand, they form a *community*, because "whatever its inequalities and divisions, its members are bound by a deep horizontal comradeship" (Clark, 2013, p. 39), a sense of groupness which contributes to the belief that "nationality is associated to one's belonging." In sum, each nation is said to have a number of identifiable characteristics, this leading to "the assumption that every nationality has an ascertainable national character," as Altenbernd (1979, p. 9) put it.

This apparently innocent idea, which has gone unchallenged for centuries, "is the product of discourse" (Wodak et al., 2009, p. 22) and seems to be deeply entrenched in the popular culture and the imaginary of all human societies. Most people tend to unconsciously believe that "the citizens of a nation share widely a set of relatively stable traits of physique and personality, patterns of behaviour, and attitudes"

(Altenbernd, 1979, p. 9). Examples abound but, to mention just one, I will quote a few statements translated from a long political joke in Spanish, titled "And God created the Spaniard," which is circulating these days via WhatsApp. The joke typically encodes culturally specific assumptions and argues that "when God created the world, he decided to grant men different virtues for them to prosper. Thus, the Swiss were tidy and compliant with the law; the Englishmen, persistent and bookish; the Japanese, hardworking and patient; Italians, cheerful and romantic, and the French, cultured and refined."

These are only a few popular stereotypes but the reader is bound to be familiar with many others which tend to associate an individual's specific geographical origin (even at smaller, more local levels) with certain personal defects or qualities. Obviously, the representation of national characters "cannot be empirically measured against an objectively existing *signifié*. They are rather discursive objects: narrative tropes and rhetorical formulae" as Leerssen (2016, p. 16) notices. Actually, it is through popular culture and popular literature, including travelogues, that all these stereotypical ideas are usually reproduced and diffused, "highlight[ing] or even caricature[ing] some real or supposed trait" (Edwards, 2009, p. 21). In Pérez-Gil's words, "[a]dvertently or inadvertently, literary works may feed creatively on prevalent national stereotypes that mirror the beliefs of the in-group while perpetuating its fiction of difference with the homogeneous Other" (2018, p. 943). Hence, whenever mention is made of a particular character's nationality, a number of features are immediately evoked and expected to be confirmed in the construction and description of their personality throughout the narrative. As Hall stated, "we know what it is to be 'British', not only because of certain national characteristics, but also because we can mark its 'difference' from its 'others'—Britishness is not-French, not-American, not-German, not-Pakistani, not-Jamaican and so on" (1997, p. 236).

Paraphrasing Fusco (2017, p. 72) in her approach to gender roles and ideals, I can say that in fiction, as well as in reality, assumptions about national character "are mutually constructed and they continue to dialogue and metamorphose over time". This typical 'dialogue' between masculinity and femininity, which Fusco (2017, p. 73) defines as "a game of alterities," is enriched in our romances with the sociocultural contrast between the Spanishness represented by the hero and the Englishness featured by the heroine, who travels to a remote island to find her true love, thus fulfilling a fantasy that, according to Philips, always involves "a measure of international travel" (2011, p. 114). Interestingly, by using the journey motif, since their plots include a trip to the Canaries and an intercultural encounter in an exotic location, these romances share a lot with travel literature, as proved by González-de la Rosa (2018). Both genres provide readers with escapism and with "the pleasure that comes from imaginative traveling" (Pérez-Gil, 2018, p. 944); besides, their authors inevitably tend to adopt an ethnocentric perspective that assesses the Other's merits and faults by contrasting them with those of their own. This is not in the least surprising since, as Mill (1991, p. 86) explained, travel writing is an 'implicit quest for anomaly,' as if the travel writer were searching for something as strange to describe. And yet, [...] this is only because in describing the anomaly the writer is affirming the societal norms of England [...]. One of the striking features in all the descriptions of other countries is that objects are presented only in terms of their difference to objects in Britain. And this difference is portrayed as 'strange.'

Definitely, the ideas offered about Spanishness in these romances are "far from being 'objective' descriptions of the way the nation is." Rather, they are as biased as those typically found in travel writing, not only for being "largely determined by the socio-historical context within which they are written" (Mills, 1991, p. 89) but also because of the writers' attitudes, beliefs, and abuse of stereotypes, as shown below:

(1) He was so utterly English that she could almost hear Big Ben strike. (Britt 1977, p. 12)
(2) Suddenly feeling very English indeed and glad of it, she disengaged her clasp of Raquel's hands and stood up. (Arbor 1967, p. 86)
(3) ...perhaps it was the Spanish way—a little romance here and there, a little loving to pass away the warmth of a summer's afternoon! (MacLeod 1982, p. 94)
(4) ...everything about the apartment was as English as both men could make it. (Arbor 1967, p. 33)
(5) Catherine found that her 'English tea' was strictly a Spanish affair. (MacLeod 1982, p. 15)

As Quiroga (2013, p. 191) put it, "[s]tereotypes strengthen the idea that national identities are immutable and promote the myth of the existence of quintessential national features," thus hampering critical thinking. Besides, as Pérez-Gil denounces, "the ideology of Englishness runs through" many of these texts, which oftentimes "betray [the authors'] decided defense of the ethical mores of [their] country over the failures and lacks of the enticing South" (2018, pp. 945–946).

40.3 Spanishness and the Image of Spain and Spaniards

A look at the way Spaniards, Spain and Spanishness are perceived in the romances studied reveals its connection with the dominant stereotypes historically created. As Leerssen (2000, pp. 287–88) notes, "national characterization develops and changes over the centuries." Thus, although "Spain as a world power in the seventeenth century provoked, throughout Europe, fear and disgust" and a number of "allegations of cruelty," it is also true that later on, "the Spanish decline from world power [...] made it possible for a more romanticized image to emerge." Admittedly, in a first stage "various negative discursive trends denigrated Spain" (O'Sullivan, 2009, p. 337), "charging the monarchy with appalling crimes and the Spaniards with religious fanaticism" (López de Abiada, 2007, p. 244). Their characterization as "evil, deceitful, murderous, ambitious, etc." (244) had its origin "in the Inquisition and the political hegemony" (O'Sullivan, 2009, p. 337) of the Spanish empire, which was diffused firstly in travel narratives. Likewise, playwrights portrayed different popular national types, including "drunken Germans, fickle French, or arrogant and proud Spanish" (2009, p. 337). In fact, pride was the most stable feature attributed to Spaniards. More recently, the modern Media has reproduced and perpetuated unfavourable views of the country and its people in the international imaginary, particularly in the Anglo-Saxon world. Actually, when dealing here with the notion of Spanishness, I will refer to the representations of Spain and Spaniards (as members of the imagined Spanish community) mostly offered by one of its most "significant Others, namely the British imagined community" (Prieto-Arranz, 2012, p. 1), widely acknowledged as the travellers *par excellence*, and thus, as prolific travel writers.

As underlined elsewhere (González-Cruz & González-de la Rosa, 1998), British visitors in Spain did not really abound until the end of the eighteenth century. In fact, before the Peninsular War (1808–1814) little was heard of Spain, which was virtually unknown to the Europeans. Because of its geographical situation, not in the way to any of the countries which attracted travellers, Spain found itself marginalised at the far end of Europe. Therefore, it was not included, at least initially, in the paths of the Grand Tour. Whereas countries such as Switzerland, Italy, France, or The Netherlands were visited by many travellers during the XVIIth century, the idea of going on a journey to Spain at that time was regarded as preposterous. Cultural conditions and political decadence added to this sense of isolation and to its relegation to the fringes of Europe. Set apart from the European spirit of the Enlightenment, Spain was a thoroughly backward place in both social and political terms. Oddly, however, it is the emergence of Romanticism, with its exaltation of the primitive and the remote in time and space, what elicits interest and attraction for Spain. In addition to the fascination for its landscape, Spain's romantic myth was enhanced by other complex factors related to its genuine cultural traditions: its combination of Moorish, Jewish and later Catholic influences symbolizes the mixed cultural heritage of Spain. In fact, with its profile of orientalism, primitivism and medievalism, Spain came to be known as the romantic country par excellence. In short, the absolute indifference for Spain which had prevailed throughout the foregoing centuries sharply contrasted with the trend of 'hispanophily' that was felt during the first decades of the XIXth century in a large part of the globe. Many travel writers, mostly British, wrote accounts on Spain conveying their experiences and feelings, and contributed to the shaping and propagation of this romantic view of the country, whose typical traits (bullfighting, *flamenco*, gypsies, castanets and *bandoleros*) would become universally known, colouring "the contemporary English perception of Spain" (O'Sullivan, 2009, p. 338).

In light of this historical background, Noya (2013, p. 18) has identified two archetypes in the construction of the image of Spain in Europe throughout history. One derives from the Black Legend that emerged after the decline of the Spanish empire, featuring Spain as a badly governed and inefficient European country. Under this degrading view, propagated by Kant, Montesquieu and Voltaire during the Enlightenment, Spaniards are defined as arrogant, intolerant, deeply religious and radical, conservative people. The other archetype derives from Romanticism and its focus on new ways of life and vivid local colour. This romantic spirit highlights the cultural differences and conceives Spain as an exotic country whose men and women are authentic, freedom lovers, passionate and totally unable of behaving rationally, in a cold civilized way. Thus, Spain becomes a victim of the ethnocentrism of northern Europeans, who tend to Orientalize this country and its people, finding them to be simply "different."

Likewise, when studying the changes in Spain after dictator Franco's era, Hooper (1986, pp. 18–19) refers to the reputation of the people and the place in those days as "forbidding" to the foreigner, "a difficult country to come to grips with from almost any angle." He explains the reasons behind these ideas in the following terms:

> For a start, it [Spain] contains several different cultures. What is true of most of Spain need not be true of the Basque country, or of Catalonia or Galicia. [...] a lot of the popular culture derives from traditions—Arab, Jewish and Gypsy—that are alien to the experience of the majority of Europeans. [...] people's ideas about Spain are still based to a great extent on what was written during or about the period leading up to Franco's takeover. [...] That Spain has gone forever. There is a new Spain and, I believe, a new kind of Spaniard very different from the intolerant, intemperate figure of legend and history.

In his opinion, individualism is the most obvious trait of this new Spaniard; but not in the British or American sense of 'something bordering on eccentricity.' What Hooper means by Spanish individualism is "self-centredness [...] their traditionally egotistical outlook on life" and he remarks how they still "talk loudly and emphatically, shoot the lights and dress beyond their means" (1986, p. 266). Similarly, in her fun-filled guide to the do's and don'ts for visitors in Spain, Graff (1993) concurs that, "to this day, Spaniards retain this extreme individualism" (11) underlining the fact that "although proud, [they] are by nature polite and corteous [and] usually kind to foreigners" (7). In her view, "No land in Europe, possibly no land in the Western world, has such a forceful personality, such a strong flavour as Spain, nor such a proud history." It is precisely this history that helps to explain not only "the customs and traditions enriching the daily lives of the Spanish people" but also "their characters and mannerisms." In addition to various landscapes and climates, the country offers "a fascinating mixture of people with different cultural backgrounds" in such a way that "no one area nor any one Spaniard can be said to be 'typically Spanish'" (1993, p. 10).

Significantly, the representation of Spain in the foreign media has been "heavily based on negative stereotypes," particularly in recent football reportings, which "constantly reinforce rather than challenge notions of national identity" (Quiroga, 2013, p. 191). In fact, Spaniards have been "more often described as backwards, corrupt, authoritarian, lazy and chaotic than as friendly, passionate, hardworking, modern and well-organised" (190).

The discoursive strategies used in these romances for representing Spanishness and Spaniards will be examined in the following sections, focusing on the special features the Spanish hero is given, his physical appearance, character and behaviour. This will confirm Leerssen's claim that "actors in literary texts are often characterized, both in their appearance and in their narrative role, according to conventions and indeed stereotypes regarding their national background" (2000, p. 268).

40.4 The Multiple Faces of Spanishness

Remarks underlining, both directly or indirectly, the differences between the English and the Spanish abound in the texts. For instance, Joanna, the heroine in *Villa Faustino* tells her lover, "You Spaniards do things differently from us" (Britt, 1977, p. 27), making "a gesture which swept away Spanish inhibitions in favour of English fun (65)." Besides, when the Marqués Ramón de Orlerón y Faustino is introduced, another character wonders, "Why do Spaniards always have such long names?" (14). Joanna eventually admits "he really was an incredible man, for he had survived many of her English ways and customs so alien to his aristocratic Spanish upbringing" (113)

The reality of Spain in the 1970s justifies the emphasis placed by many authors on the cultural differences and contrasting mentalities and customs. Thus, in Thorpe's romance, the hero's brother asks Eve whether she is "reconciled to the idea of a Spanish brother-in-law" as she gives the impression at times that she finds "the family overwhelming;" and he notices "Our ways are not your ways" (1973, p. 90). Later on, when Ramón, the hero, complains to Eve, "No Spanish girl would think of acting in the way you did!" she replies with some heat, 'But I'm not Spanish [...] I'm English" and flashes back, "Your ways are not our ways' (110). Similarly, in *Island fiesta* (1980) Juan Martel admits, 'Naturally, you do not know a great deal about Spanish customs—or how a Spaniard expects his wife to behave. I realise it is different in England, and for that reason only shall I grant you a little leeway in your behavior" (112) And he predicts, "Before very long you will know that you have married a Spaniard, and will adapt yourself to the Spanish way of life"'(114), remarking that "Spanish marriage contracts are not easily broken" (185).

It is worth-noticing that the adjective 'Spanish' is not only applied in the novels to the nationality or the language spoken by certain characters. Some writers seem to suggest there is something special about someone's voice, blood, gestures, behaviour and even feelings, posture, beauty or outlooks that qualify as Spanish. For instance, we read:

(6) ...high-pitched Spanish voices appeared to be raised in argument. (MacLeod, 1990, p. 21)
(7) His Spanish voice was loud and angry (Mayo, 1988, p. 5)
(8) The man's shrug was very Spanish. (Britt, 1977, p. 46)
(9) ...he had a grandchild of Spanish blood... (Arbor, 1967, p. 13)
(10) ...taking her hand again to bow over it in a typical Spanish gesture of farewell. (MacLeod, 1990, pp. 14–15)
(11) ...a typical Spanish beauty (Airlie, 1955, p. 130)

(12) …a conventional Spanish beauty. (MacLeod, 1990, p. 21)
(13) Francesca's politeness was wholly Spanish (Britt, 1977, p. 76)
(14) …an inbred Spanish politeness which demanded patience and at least a show of courtesy. (Airlie, 1958, p. 8)
(15) You have become quite Spanish in your outlook' (Airlie, 1955, p. 122)
(16) …an excellent carriage and disciplined grace inherited from Spanish nobility (Britt, 1977, p. 87)

Mention is frequently made in these romances of different Spanish customs, such as the late lunch and dinner-hour, different times of business opening and closing, and the usual *siesta*. An "attractive Spanish name" was chosen for the female protagonist in Arbor's romance (1967, p. 32) who is trained in "Spanish domesticity" (128). While in *Red lotus* Felicity is aware that she is "in a strange country" and needs advice because she has "no knowledge of the Spanish ways," (Airlie, 1958, p. 23) she feels certain from the start that in the weeks ahead she would come "to understand the Spanish character and delight in it" (2). Likewise, oftentimes references are found in the narrative to a variety of items, such as food, architecture, furniture, or clothes, whose style appears to be overtly Spanish:

(17) '…let me introduce you to Spanish food' (Airlie, 1958, p. 11)
(18) …delicious omelettes, Spanish style, (Britt, 1977, p. 31)
(19) …ordered a typical Spanish meal… (Airlie, 1955, p. 163)
(20) …even a light supper would be prepared with Spanish gusto (MacLeod, 1990, p. 26)
(21) The room itself was full of fine old Spanish furniture in the style of a century ago… (MacLeod, 1982, p. 11)
(22) A traditional stately home, Spanish style. (Arbor, 1967, p. 24)
(23) …the town lined with houses of Spanish architecture with wooden carvings and small balconies (Britt, 1977, p. 154)
(24) …a huge rambling mansion-type house came into full view, built, […] in the Spanish style (Corrie, 1980, p. 96)
(25) She could see the beautiful Spanish villa (Britt, 1977, p. 4)
(26) … traditional Spanish furniture […] I'd like it kept in the old Spanish style. (Mayo, 1988, pp. 82–84).

Occasionally, even elements of nature, like the sun, are categorized as Spanish, as the following quotations illustrate:

(27) …his skin glowing and tanned by the Spanish sun (Britt, 1977, p. 188)
(28) He still radiated that dynamic vitality like a kind of miraculous manifestation resulting from the heat of the Spanish sun. (Britt, 1977, p. 200)

Several tropes or motifs tend to appear in almost all the romances, featuring a Spanish hero. These range from certain physical characteristics and character traits, often derived from those of literary or historical figures, patterns of behaviour (including the idea of *mañana* and *machismo*), not to mention Spanish vocabulary and expressions which sprinkle the English texts, providing local colour to the narrative and functioning as identity markers. In the following sections each of these clichés will be illustrated.

40.4.1 Physical Features

Comments on the physical appearance of Spanish men abound in these texts, often depicting attractive males, as when Eve, the heroine in *An apple in Eden* notices that "all waiters in Spain seemed to be young and exuberant" (Thorpe, 1973, p. 150). Typical Spanish heroes tend to be tall, dark-haired and dark-eyed, looking tough and self-confident. Similarly, in Corrie's romance Juan Martel's dark hair gave Corinne "the distinct impression that he was not English. Spanish or Italian perhaps". And we read:

> His features were strong and rather forbidding, and there was an autocratic look about him that many women would find fascinating. Corinne had to admit that he was what could be termed 'good-looking' in a ruthless way, for there was a hardness about him (1980, p. 20)

In turn, Ramón, the Canarian hero in Ashe's *The surgeon from San Agustin*, "had dark eyes, dark as the night, brooding and angry in the olive face. He was lean—almost thin, though the muscles in his shoulders and arms were strong and wiry. He walked with the sensual grace of a mountain lion" (1987, p. 5). In *Flame of Avila* Richard Copeland is of mixed origins, born in Tenerife from a Spanish mother and an English father. When Judith, the heroine, meets him at the airport on arrival, he is described as "a tall man with a strong, hard face and a direct gaze" (MacLeod, 1990, p. 7). In the car, she turns in her seat to look at him, appraising his "eagle profile" as he drives "fast, sure of his own skill." The narrator adds, "A tall man, commanding figure with piercing blue eyes, she could better imagine him on the back of a horse riding about an estate where his word will be the law" (10). Once by the house, she stands looking at the man and wondering again about him, "measuring him up in the faint starlight—his strong, almost arrogant profile and his air of belonging" (21).

The few exceptions to the rule of dark complexion appear when the Canarian aborigines are mentioned. Thus, in *Savage affair* (Mayo, 1988) Rhiannon encounters the Spanish hero on a deserted beach at sunset, a stranger "fiercely and determinedly carving his way through the water." Described as a tall man, he had "wide shoulders and narrow hips [...] a flat taut stomach and muscular chest" (5). She observes "an arrogant lift to his chin [...] a high noble forehead [...] and a statue-like body" (5). Then, studying "the straight nose, the jutting brows, the expressive eyes which looked black in this light but could be any colour," (9) she realizes "he looked hard and untouchable, ruthless even [...] he was all man, for one thing, mature, self-confident, arrogant even" (9). Interestingly, she comments: "He spoke Spanish with the typical sing-song accent of a Canarian, and yet he hadn't looked a typical Spaniard. Or was it the half-light that had played tricks on her?" (9–10). Later on, Pasqual confirms that his ancestors were Guanches, "the fair-haired, blue-eyed Guanches who had inhabited the islands more than two thousand years ago. They were actually little more than cave men who mummified their dead the same as the Egyptians." She realizes that "instead of the usual black hair of the Spaniards they had fair hair and blue eyes—the same as Pasqual!" (158).

40.4.2 Character and Behaviour

The personality of the Spanish heroes in the novels seems to be based on the stereotypes mentioned in Sect. 40.2.2. Admittedly, they also follow the patterns established for the Alphaman hero, whose traits Kamblé (2014, p. 91) describes as follows:

> A man who is physically superior to all men in the novel, never shows a weakness, and is always the dominant sexual partner in an opposite-sex couple. His remoteness, named 'glamorous unapproachability,' keeps the heroine in a state of suspense about his feelings almost till the end, when he declares his love. [...] the hero's arrogance and highhandedness reasserts masculine dominance and the eventual declaration of love sets to rest the fear that he is indifferent to the heroine.

Sometimes it is the narrator, or the very Spanish character that gives details about their national idiosyncrasies, making reference, for instance, to "the spontaneous gaiety of the average Spaniard" (Airlie, 1958, p. 5), "the traditional Castilian values of reserve and austerity" (MacLeod, 1982, p. 14), or other typical features, as the following excerpts reveal:

(29) 'We Spaniards are passionate people.' (Britt, 1977, p. 70)
(30) 'You wouldn't understand the close sense of family we Spaniards have.' (Arbor, 1967, p. 13)
(31) 'We Spaniards don't think a story worth telling if we don't doll it up in drama...' (Arbor, 1967, p. 81)
(32) 'A Spaniard feels more deeply about... the freedom of women to make fools of themselves.' (Britt, 1977, p. 105)
(33) 'I'm a true Spaniard and proud of it.' (Mayo, 1988, p. 158)

Definitely, Spaniards possess two key features which are constantly highlighted by narrators and characters alike: they are passionate and proud, even arrogant. Thus, in Mayo's romance, Pasqual's "savage passion both alarmed and excited" Rhiannon (1988, p. 32). Often, the narrator informs that the hero's "eyes are suddenly lit with passion" (MacLeod, 1977, p. 175) or that "his voice was suddenly vibrant with passion" (180). Sometimes the passion is transferred both to "the fiery execution of flamenco" (87) dancers and to music. Hence, when hearing the melody "played with dramatic vibrancy" nearby in the summer night, Dr. Hannah Day captures the "Iberian passion in that guitar [making] her heart quicken" (Ashe, 1987, p. 37).

In Lane's romance, when nurse Trudy leaves England, her boyfriend feels a wild desperation thinking of the "rich and wonderful sun-bronzed young men" she will find "on the lidos of Tenerife, to say nothing of passionate young Spaniards who would pursue her volubly" (1978, p. 13). Indeed, once there, she meets Miguel, who insistently describes himself as "an *hombre total*—a real full-blooded Spaniard" (29). The narrator reveals Trudy's thoughts after reading the "absolutely absurd" letter Miguel sends her: "Only a man with a Latin temperament could have written it. No Englishman would have penned such words. So Miguel, as well as being a man of passion, was also a great romantic!" (63). She feels overwhelmed by the "Spanish fire" in his gallantry and refers to him as "that Iberian caveman," (35) telling herself: "I'm a liberated woman, and live in a liberated age, thank goodness. And I hate chauvinistic men like Miguel—and Carlos, too. I expect Spain is full of them. How wonderful it would be if somehow, some day, I could teach them both a lesson. A British nurse besting the pair of them—two hot-blooded Spaniards" (97).

In *Villa Faustino*, Joanna tells the hero's English antagonist that "Ramón is Spanish and reserved" (Britt, 1977, p. 47), while Ramón declares "We Spanish value our dignity, a dignity which is extended to the poorest in the land. I do not think it is a bad thing." In *Red lotus*, Felicity describes the hero as "an old man, yet his bearing was upright and proud, like so many of the Spaniards she had seen..." (Airlie, 1958, p. 60). In turn, the hero states, "Julio was all Spanish, from the crown of his black, curly head to the soles of his gaily-shod feet [...]. He is all Spanish, and a Spaniard believes that a woman exists for love" (36/135).

Interestingly, when Richard, the mixed hero in *Flame of Avila*, fails to return the passion in female antagonist Cybele's kiss, the narrator justifies, "but Richard was only half Spanish and not given to dramatic displays of emotions in public" (96–97). Previously, he had confessed Judith: "My mother was a proud Castilian, you see, never willing to give up" (59). In much the same fashion, the heroine in *Island fiesta* refers to Juan Martel's "tall proud figure" (Corrie, 1980, p. 189) whereas Niculoso Meléndez, the hero in Baird's romance, is described twice as a proud man, who "wasn't called the Spanish Stud for nothing..." (2003, p. 6).

Among the recurrent tropes in these novels, I will underline that of "*Mañana*, or the inconsequential disregard for time proverbial to the Spanish character" (Airlie, 1955, p. 170). Thus, a narrator remarks how "she was prepared to wait, already accepting in essence the meaning of the Spanish mañana" (Airlie, 1958, 14). This is related to the reputation of Spaniards as lazy persons, highlighted in *The valley of palms* by Barnard's complaint: "...those Spaniards haven't the guts of the yeoman breed! Lazy as sin, most of them! *Mañana!* Leave till tomorrow all you should have done today!" (MacLeod, 1977, p. 44). Elsewhere Don Rafael admits "No Spaniard would ever work as he has done—for so little return" (Airlie, 1958, 12), whereas in Ashe's novel we read: "All Spanish people believe in *mañana*, you know? ... but *Conquistadores* came from Spain" (1987, p. 75) as if the two ideas were contradictory. Several comments in this same text (and others) show the effects of *machismo*, since "Spanish men can use foreign women but they do not marry them" (80). Hence, "Spanish men can be cruel" (101), and they "may do as they please when it comes to choosing a wife" (Airlie, 1955, p. 68). In contrast, the strong sense of family mentioned above is reinforced by another narrator's comment, revealing the heroine's thoughts: "There was no photograph of her about the *hacienda*, which was strange, since the Spaniards were prone to collect such mementoes of their children from earliest infancy onwards" (Airlie, 1958, p. 164).

40.4.3 Literary and Historical Figures

In some novels, the features and behaviour of the Spanish hero are compared to those of well-known historical or literary figures, such as *Don Quixote, Don Juan* or *El Conquistador*. Thus, in *The surgeon from San Agustin*, one of the female employees in the heroine's small hospital describes the Spanish hero saying: "...he is a Don Quixote, tilting at windmills but doing no harm to the real enemy" (Ashe, 1987, p. 100); whereas in *Beware a lover's lie* (Howard, 1994, p. 11) the hero is depicted as "a regular Don Juan".

One case in point appears in *Meeting in Madrid* (MacLeod, 1982, p. 111), when Catherine Royce travels to Spain to work as the tutor of a willful teenager. On the plane, she browses the beautifully illustrated book her father had given her as a parting gift, a brief record of Spain's colourful history, "written in blood and gold," which will provide "a truer insight into the Spanish character" as well as "a guide which might help her to understand the people she was about to meet and the land in which they lived" (9–10). Suddenly the book slips from her fingers and when she hands it back it happens to be open at one of the central illustrations: a man on horseback with the caption, '*Jaime I de Aragón, El Conquistador*.' Interestingly, the picture is described as follows:

> It was a statue in bronze, the man's face finely chiselled to suggest strength of character and purpose, his firm hand clenched on the shaft of the tall lance he carried, yet there was a hint of cruelty about the mouth and a suggested arrogance in the proud carriage of the head which she did not like. These were the men who had gone out to conquer a whole new world, men of ambition and a fierce, inherited pride to whom ruthlessness was a way of life, yet she tried to imagine a look of compassion as well as purpose in the forward-gazing eyes (10–11).

On arrival, when trying to identify the person meeting her at the airport, Catherine is shocked to find that her employer's son, Don Jaime de Berceo Madroza, actually

> was the man on the bronze horse whose proud face and concentrated gaze had disconcerted her as he had sprung to life from the printed page. He wore a plain grey suit and white shirt, with a striped silk tie in grey and maroon, nothing to connect him with a knight or a conquistador king, but there was the same look in his eyes, the same autocratic turn of the head as he surveyed her fellow-travellers one by one (11–12).

Throughout this novel, references and comparisons between the hero and the Castilian king abound, with the coincidence in their names, Jaime, metaphorically reinforcing his stereotypical characterization. When driving from the airport to the *hacienda* where the Madroza family lives in Madrid, the hero is described as follows:

> Catherine stole a quick glance at the chiselled profile silhouetted against the sudden green of trees as they glided along: the high forehead surmounted by thick black hair, the finely-pencilled brows drawn over the commanding dark eyes, the long, aquiline nose and hard mouth all culminating in a strong chin which gave the face its true character. A man of iron, used to command, who would brook no disobedience from anyone who served him just as he would hold himself on a tight rein where his own responsibilities were concerned. The fact that he was here, in an expensive limousine, driving rapidly towards the heart of one of the liveliest capitals in the world, seemed incongruous in the extreme, completely out of

character, in fact, when she could see him so clearly pictured on a bronze horse with a lance in his gauntleted hand and all the hard purpose of a conquistador king in his eyes. He should have been far from Madrid making his mark on the wider world, riding over vast estates, but perhaps that was no more than her over-active imagination at work (13–14).

Once in the heart of the city, they come to "a wide plaza where high fountains sparkled in the sunshine and the unmistakable likenesses of Don Quixote and his faithful Sancho rode in deathless stone" (15). Again, while conversing once installed in the family house, the recurrent thought emerges:

> A fleeting memory of the equestrian statue pictured in her father's book flashed across her mind, the man on horseback with the look of conquest in his eyes, a man so like Don Jaime de Berceo Madroza as to seem uncannily the same. Yet she had never seen him seated on a horse. On the contrary, he still wore the immaculate light grey suit which made him look every inch the conventional Spanish business man, and his thick dark hair was sleeked back closely against his head. No helmet, no plume, no lance grasped firmly in those shapely hands! (26)

40.4.4 The Spanish Language

Last but not least, the discoursive construction of the Spanish hero in this sample draws largely from the Spanish language employed with a variety of aims, but mainly performing an affiliative function (González-Cruz, 2018). As Clark (2007, p. 126) explains, the use of speech representation is a common feature of fiction and plays different roles in the narrative. What the characters say is not only useful to reveal their personality but also to develop and bring out relationships between them, providing "a sense of social background." This should not be surprising since the central role language plays in individual, social and national identity has been widely recognized (Holmes & Wilson, 2017; Joseph, 2004). Furthermore, identity construction is viewed "as inseparably and dynamically linked to language" (Kleinke, Hernández, & Böss, 2018, p. 1). Undoubtedly, the use of Spanish as a literary strategy in these romances deserves closer attention, which lack of space does not allow here. Elsewhere (González-Cruz, 2017a, 2017b, 2018, 2020) the different ways Spanish words and expressions contribute to the construction of Spanishness have been shown. The following are a few examples:

(34) She's nice but *mucho tímida*. [...] You got a new *medico*?' (Ashe, 1987, p. 30)
(35) 'Plain loco.' [...] it was sheer reckless, macho bravado... (Baird, 2003, p. 148)
(36) The *niebla arenisca* hangs low... (Arbor, 1967, p. 168)
(37) Round the corner strode a *policia* [...] 'We'll have *café con leche* on San Telmo...' (Lane, 1978, p. 43)
(38) In the quiet *siesta* hour the *patio* lay peacefully... She thought of [...] the man in the enveloping *poncho*... (MacLeod, 1982, p. 68)
(39) *Dios!* He was an unfeeling brute. (Baird, 2003, p. 127)
(40) '*Esta* bien,' he said softly. (Howard, 1994, p. 53)

40.5 Conclusion

This chapter has examined the discoursive strategies employed to construct the Spanish identity of the male protagonists in 15 Harlequin/Mills & Boon romances which narrate the love-stories of intercultural/bilingual couples, invariably a Spanish hero and an English-speaking heroine. The national image of Spain and the idea of Spanishness portrayed in these texts have been built through centuries and could be neatly summarized with a few expressions: "*fiesta*, good food, lovely weather, *siesta* and laziness, *machismo* and pride" (Vera-Cazorla, 2020, p. 37). These and other stereotypes regarding the hero's physical features, character and behaviour, together with Spanish vocabulary and references to legendary figures in Spanish history and literature, all help create the identity of a typical Spaniard. It is the Spanish way which, according to popular belief, seems to remain unaltered in the collective imaginary over the course of time, despite the new social values of contemporary Spain.

Admittedly, our sample of romances covers a limited timespan; thus, further research is needed to confirm Tapper's claim that, despite the genre's enduring reputation as inherently conventional and change resistant, contemporary romance writers and publishers have proved to be "consistently forward thinking and progressive, utilising industry innovations in content, technology, branding and business practice to cement their genre's status as an exemplary model for twenty-first century book publishing" (2014, p. 249). A future study of romances published more recently in this digital era would be useful to evaluate possible changes regarding their specific dynamics in the depiction of Spanish heroes.

References

Altenbernd, L. (1979). The idea of national character: Inspiration or fallacy? In S. E. Kagle (Ed.), *America: Exploration and travel* (pp. 9–17). Ohio: Bowling Green University Popular Press.

Anderson, B. (1991). *Imagined communities: Reflections on the origin and spread of nationalism*. London: Verso.

Auchmuty, R. (1999). *Foreword to the romance fiction of Mills & Boon, 1909–1990s* (pp. ix–xii). London and Philadelphia: UCL Press.

Clark, U. (2007). *Studying language. English in action*. Basingstoke, Hampshire/New York: Palgrave Macmillan.

Clark, U. (2013). *Language and identity in Englishes*. London/New York: Routledge.

Dixon, J. (1999). *The romance fiction of Mills & Boon, 1909–1990s*. London and Philadelphia: UCL Press.

Edwards, J. (2009). *Language and identity*. Cambridge: Cambridge University Press.

Fusco, V. (2017). Narrative representations of masculinity. The hard werewolf and the androgynous vampire in Anita Blake: Vampire hunter series. *Journal of English Studies, 15*, 71–88.

González-Cruz, M. I. (2015). Love in paradise: Visions of the Canaries in a corpus of popular romance fiction novels. *Oceánide. Journal of the Spanish Society for the Study of Popular Culture, 7*. http://oceanide.netne.net/articulos/art7-4.pdf.

González-Cruz, M. I. (2017a). Exploring the dynamics of English/Spanish codeswitching in a written corpus. *Alicante Journal of English Studies, 30*, 331–355.

González-Cruz, M. I. (2017b). Conciencia sociolingüística e hispanismos en un corpus de novela rosa inglesa. *SOPRAG, 5*(2), 125–149.

González-Cruz, M. I. (2018). Hispanismos en el discurso romántico de *Harlequin* y *Mills & Boon*. Ámbitos temáticos y funciones socio-pragmáticas. *Moderna Sprak, 1*, 157–178.

González-Cruz, M. I. (2020). Hacia un glosario de hispanismos en un corpus de novela rosa inglesa contemporánea.. *Revista Onomázein, 48*(2), 1–25, 178–201.

González-Cruz, M. I. (Forthcoming). Constructing the exotic Other: Paradise discourse and environmental awareness in a corpus of popular romance fiction novels. In I. Pérez-Fernández & M.C. Pérez-Riu (Eds.), *Romantic escapes: Post-millennial trends in contemporary popular romance fiction.* Peter Lang.

González-Cruz, M. I., & González-de la Rosa, M. P. (1998). Dimensions of the intercultural within travel literature: British images of Spain. In S. Henríquez (Ed.), *Travel essentials* (pp. 43–61). Las Palmas de Gran Canaria: Chandlon in Press.

González-de la Rosa, M. P. (2018). Intersections of inner and outer journeys in contemporary popular romance fiction novels. In M.B Hernández, M. Brito & T.Monterrey (Eds.), *Broadening horizons: A peak panorama of English studies* (pp. 153–160). Servicio de Publicaciones Universidad de La Laguna.

Graff, M. L. (1993). *Culture shock! Spain.* London: Kuperard.

Gratzke, M. (2017). Love is what people say it is: Performativity and narrativity in critical love studies. *Journal of Popular Romance Studies, 4*, 1–20.

Griffith, J. (2011). What is love? In *The book of real answers to everything*. Australia: WTM Publishing and Communications.

Hall, S. (1997). The spectacle of the 'Other'. In S. Hall (Ed.), *Representation: Cultural representations and signifying practices* (pp. 225–239). London/Thousand Oaks, CA/New Delhi: Sage.

Harders, R. (2012). Borderlands of desire: Captivity, romance and the revolutionary power of love. In S. S. Frantz & E. M. Selinger (Eds.), *New approaches to popular romance fiction. Critical essays* (pp. 133–152). Jefferson, North Carolina/London: McFarland & Company.

Holmes, J., & Wilson, N. (2017). *An introduction to sociolinguistics* (5th ed.). London/New York: Routledge.

Hoonselaars, T., & Leerssen, J. (2009). The rhetoric of national character: Introduction. *European Journal of English Studies, 13*(3), 251–255.

Hooper, J. (1986). *The Spaniards. A portrait of the new Spain.* Harmondsworth, Middlesex: Viking, Penguin Books.

Joseph, J. E. (2004). *Language and identity. National, ethnic, religious.* New York: Palgrave Macmillan.

Kamblé, J. (2014). *Making meaning in popular romance fiction. An epistemology.* New York: Palgrave Macmillan.

Kleinke, S., Hernández, N., & Böss, B. (2018). Introduction. In B. Böss, S. Kleinke, S. Mollin, & N. Hernández (Eds.), *The discursive construction of identities on- and offline. Personal, group, collective* (pp. 1–12). Amsterdam/Philadelphia: John Benjamins.

Leerssen, J. (2000). The rhetoric of national character. A programmatic survey. *Poetics Today, 21* (2), 267–292.

Leerssen, J. (2016). Imagology: On using ethnicity to make sense of the world. *Imagology, 10*, 13–31.

Lindsay, I. (2015). The uses and abuses of national stereotypes. *Scottish Affairs, 20*(1), 133–148.

López de Abiada, J. M. (2007). Spaniards. In M. Beller & J. Leerssen (Eds.), *Imagology. The cultural construction and literary representation of national characters. A critical survey* (pp. 242–247). Amsterdam/New York: Rodopi.

Mills, S. (1991). *Discourses of difference. An analysis of women's travel writing and colonialism.* London: Routledge.

Noya, J. (2013). *La imagen de España en el mundo. Visiones del exterior* (Vol. 1). Madrid: Editorial Tecnos.

O'Sullivan, E. (2009). S is for Spaniard. *European Journal of English Studies, 13*(3), 333–349.
Pérez-Gil, M. M. (2018). Exoticism, ethnocentrism, and Englishness in popular romance fiction: Constructing the European Other. *The Journal of Popular Culture, 51*(4), 940–955.
Pérez-Gil, M. M. (2019). Representations of nation and Spanish masculinity in popular romance novels: The Alpha male as 'Other'. *Journal of Men's Studies, 27*(2), 169–182.
Philips, D. (2011). The empire of romance: Love in a postcolonial climate. In R. Gilmour & B. Schwarz (Eds.), *End of empire and the English novel since 1945* (pp. 114–133). Manchester: Manchester University Press.
Prieto-Arranz, J. (2012). España vista desde dentro y desde fuera. Una aproximación sociohistórica y cultural a los discursos de identidad nacional. *Oceánide, 4*, 1–11.
Quiroga, A. (2013). *Football and national identities in Spain: The strange death of Don Quixote*. London: Palgrave Macmillan.
Regis, P. (2003). *A natural history of the romance novel*. Philadelphia: University of Pennsylvania Press.
Sánchez-Palencia Carazo, C. (1997). *El discurso femenino de la novela rosa en lengua inglesa*. Cádiz: Publicaciones de la Universidad de Cádiz.
Selinger, E. M., & Frantz, S. S. (2012). Introduction. In S. S. Frantz & E. M. Selinger (Eds.), *New approaches to popular romance fiction. Critical essays* (pp. 1–9). Jefferson, North Carolina/London: McFarland & Company.
Tapper, O. (2014). Romance and innovation in twenty-first century publishing. *Publishing Research Quarterly, 30*(2), 249–259.
Vera-Cazorla, M. J. (2020). 'And they drive on the wrong side of the road': The Anglo-centric vision of the Canary Islands in Mills & Boon romance novels (1955–1987). In M. Ramos-García & L. Vivanco (Eds.), *Essays on love, language, place and identity in popular culture. Romancing the other*. Lanham: Lexington Books.
Vivanco, L. (2011). *For love and money. The literary art of the Harlequin Mills & Boon romance*. Penrith: Humanities-Ebooks.
Vivanco, L. (2016). *Pursuing happiness. Reading American romance as political fiction*. Tirril Hall, Penrith: Humanities-Ebooks.
Weisser, S. O. (Ed.). (2001). *Women and romance. A reader*. New York/London: New York University Press.
Wodak, R., de Cillia, R., Reisigl, M., & Liebhart, K. (Eds.). (2009). *The discursive construction of national identity*. Edinburgh: Edinburgh University Press.

Primary Sources

Airlie, C. (1955). *The valley of desire*. London: Mills & Boon.
Airlie, C. (1958). *Red lotus*. London: Mills & Boon.
Arbor, J. (1967). *Golden apple island*. Toronto: Harlequin Books.
Ashe, J. (1987). *The surgeon from San Agustin*. London: Mills & Boon.
Baird, J. (2003). *At the Spaniard's pleasure*. London: Mills & Boon.
Britt, K. (1977). *The Villa Faustino*. Toronto: Harlequin Books.
Corrie, J. (1980). *Island fiesta*. London: Mills & Boon.
Howard, S. (1994). *Beware a lover's lie*. London: Mills & Boon.
Lane, P. (1978). *Nurse in Tenerife*. London: Mills & Boon.
MacLeod, J. S. (1977). *The valley of palms*. London: Mills & Boon.
MacLeod, J. S. (1982). *Meeting in Madrid*. London: Mills & Boon.
MacLeod, J. S. (1990). *Flame of Avila*. London: Mills & Boon.
Mayo, M. (1988). *Savage affair*. Toronto: Harlequin Books.
Thorpe, K. (1973). *An apple in Eden*. London: Mills & Boon.

María-Isabel González-Cruz is Full Professor in English Studies at the University of Las Palmas de Gran Canaria (Canary Islands, Spain), where she teaches *Pragmatics* in the Degree in Modern Languages. Her research interests include various issues related to Sociolinguistics and Pragmatics, particularly Anglicisms and Hispanicisms in English. She has also published widely on the Anglo-Canarian socio-cultural and linguistic contact and its bibliographical production. Leader of the ULPGC Research Team *Sociolinguistic and Sociocultural Studies* since 2004, she coordinated the interdisciplinary research project FFI2014–53962-P, "Discourses, gender and identity in a corpus of popular romance fiction novels set in the Canaries and other Atlantic islands", developed between 2015 and 2018 with funding from the Spanish Government. She co-edited the *Revista de Lenguas para Fines Específicos* between 2009 and 1015 and was the Head of the ULPGC Modern Languages Department from July 2011 to June 2016. In addition to several books and international chapters, she has published research articles in academic journals such as *English Today, Lexis, Pragmatics, Intercultural Pragmatics, The European Journal of Humour Research, Sociocultural Pragmatics, Moderna Sprak,Onomazein*, etc.

Chapter 41
Passion Love, Masculine Rivalry and Arabic Poetry in Mauritania

Corinne Fortier

Abstract Love was not born in the West during the twelfth century: the pre-Islamic Arabic poetry of the sixth century testifies to its existence in the ancient Arab world. These poems are well-known among Moors—the population in Mauritania who speaks an Arabic dialect called *Ḥassāniyya*—and inspire the local poetic forms. Unlike numerous traditions, poetic inspiration of Moorish poets is not spiritual but carnal because it takes root in the desire for a woman, who taste like Baudelaire's *Fleurs du Mal*. Love poems in Mauritania are not the privilege of a handful, they are primaly composed with the aim of reaching the woman's heart, like bedouin pre-islamic poetry. So her first name, her body, her qualities and defects, from erotized become poetized.

In the Moorish society of Mauritania, the sphere of seduction and passion, very often poetized, coexists in parallel with the marital sphere. It is thus never his wife to whom the poet addresses his poetry but another woman that he desires. The lover's figure is a feminized figure, because he can no longer control himself and is subject to a passion that is annihilating him. However, even when the man is in this state in the seduction phase, marked negatively with passivity and suffering, it is only a temporary situation that represents minor harm on the way to conquering the woman and gaining a dominant position over other men. Courtship has commonly been a male prerogative, while women are often not supposed to manifest their desires except in an indirect way. The fact that the man is considered the desiring subject and the woman the desired object is a major cross-cultural gendered element which justifies men's appropriation of women's bodies.

Keywords Love · Mauritania · Baudelaire · Passion · Courtship · Gender · Poetry · Arabic pre-islamic poetry

---

C. Fortier (✉)
French National Center of Scientific Research (CNRS), Social Anthropology Lab (Collège de France), Paris, France
e-mail: corinne.fortier@college-de-france.fr

41.1 Introduction: Love Beyond the West

Love and especially passion love was not born in the West during the twelfth century, as Denis de Rougemont (1972) contends: the pre-Islamic Arabic poetry of the sixth century testifies to its existence in the ancient Arab World. These poems are known among Moors of Mauritania and inspire the local poetic forms. They are well-known because most Moors can understand their literal Arabic. These poems of Bedouins in the Arabian desert find a particular echo among the nomads of the Sahara, as they evoke the tent, the encampment, the desert, the tribe, the veiled women[1] wearing henna and ankle bracelets (*khalkhāl*); all Bedouin *realia* which are familiar to Moors. Moors population of Mauritania speaks an Arabic dialect, *Ḥassāniyya*, and self-identifies as *bidān* or 'white people', to distinguish themselves from *sūdān* or 'black people'. In Mauritania, alongside the arabophone Moorish society, one finds Halpulaaren, Soninke and Wolof communities.

Moorish society in Mauritania is well known in the Arab world as a society of a million poets (Taleb-Khyar, 2001). Poetry is very common in this society because poetry is inseparable from love affairs. Unlike numerous traditions, poetic inspiration of Moorish poets is not spiritual but carnal because it takes root in the desire for a woman, who taste like Baudelaire's *Fleurs du Mal* (*Flowers of Evil*). Indeed this poetry, through the archetypal situations it describes, of which I give account in this chapter, reveals the models that shape the gender roles when it comes to love relations.

However, the topic of love, is often neglected in anthropological research, especially on Arab countries. For instance, there is much research on male domination, female agency, and their relation to religious and social norms, but despite its importance in the performance of gender, little has been written on the complex role of love. This absence is especially striking given the fact that in both the present and the past love has been a major preoccupation in the lives of people of the region, as elsewhere, and is well-documented in poetry. Anthropology seems particularly suited to the study of intimate experiences through its focus on practice and everyday discourse.

Indeed, this anthropological research is based on intensive fieldwork in different regions of Mauritania, in the desert (*bādiyya*) and in the capital city Nouakchott, from 1996 to 2018, living with families and interacting with both men and women of different ages, social statuses, and tribal origins. The love poems quoted in this article were collected during this long fieldwork and translated by the author. They were selected because they afford deep insights into intimacy of Moorish society regarding passion love, and gender relations.

---

[1] On the topic of veil in Islam and in Muslims societies, see Corinne Fortier (2017c).

41.2 History of Love in Anthropology

For a long time, the study of kinship in anthropology overshadowed interest in personal sentiment. As long as the study of structures and functions prevailed, individual feelings such as love had only a minor role in research. A few exceptions concern the Pacific islands, which are places that nourished Western love fantasies since the start of their exploration by Europeans in the eighteenth century. The most prominent example in this regard is Margaret Mead's work on the Samoa Islands (1966) from the 1920s (Tcherkézoff, 2004).

If we consider larger trends in anthropology, it is possible to broadly distinguish three main approaches to contemporary studies of love. The first, based mostly on comparative surveys of cultures and rooting its understanding of emotions in biology, emphasizes the universality of the feelings associated with love. William Jankowiak is probably the most famous proponent of this approach. In a study that he coauthored, he argues for instance that the basic emotions related to love are universal, mostly due to hormonal reactions, but shows that the romantic kiss is recorded in less than half of his global sample of cultures (Jankowiak & Fischer, 1992; Jankowiak, Volsche, & Garcia, 2015, see Jankowiak's chapters in this book).

The second trend, among whose main proponents in anthropology is Charles Lindholm, studies love as an outcome of structural features in the organisation of societies (Lindholm, 1988, 2006). Similarly basing his research on a comparative survey of cultures, Lindholm argues that there are three types of society that favour romantic love: hierarchically rigid societies with a strong kinship system, in which people see love relations as an escape from social constraints and as such, incompatible with marriage; fluid societies, in which people try to combine passion love with marriage; and societies in which young people are given the freedom to experiment with romantic love until they reach a certain age, but are sooner or later pulled back into a rigid kinship system. Lindholm's notion of fluidity is reminiscent of sociological theories that consider love an outcome of systemic features of European and North American capitalism (Giddens, 1992; Illouz, 1997).

The third trend considers love in its current shape as primarily a European and North-American cultural product and studies the circulation of this model around the world. A large body of research addresses the impact of love on kinship arrangements (Cole & Lynn, 2009; Hirsch & Wardlow, 2006; Lipset, 2004; Padilla, 2007; Pettier, 2016; Stacey, 2011; Zavoretti, 2013). In her pioneering research on love letters in a rural area of Nepal Laura Ahearn contends, for instance, that romantic feelings, earlier related to shame, had become a symbol of modernity for the villagers she studied (Ahearn, 2003, 2004). They started to dream of love affairs resembling those they saw in Indian and Nepali films, textbooks and magazines, and to conceive marriage as successful if based on a companionate relationship in accordance with the model promoted by development programs.

The three approaches that we analytically distinguish here have their strengths and downsides. The approach based on the universality of certain biological reactions, while acknowledging the importance of love outside Europe and North

America, falls short of explaining the diversity of discourses and practices concerning attraction and desire that can be found around the world.

41.3 Two Kinds of Love

Among Moors in Mauritania the sphere of seduction and passion, very often poetized, coexists in parallel with the marital sphere governed by Muslim jurisprudence (*fiqh*). Masculine love poetry arises from a man's unsatisfied desire of for a woman. It is thus never his wife to whom he addresses his poetry but another woman that he desires. As elsewhere, Moorish men initiate extramarital affairs more frequently that women because expressing their desires freely is socially much more acceptable for them than it is for women. As for feminine love poetry (*tabraʿ*), it circulates only among women, modesty preventing them publicly displaying their desire for men.

Among Moors two kinds of love coexist: love for wives and love for mistresses. The first is a marital feeling which develops within the framework of conjugal relationships; the second, passionate love, is exclusive to mistresses. Passion is forbidden, while marital love is licit. The first belongs to the domain of pleasure and immediacy, while the second involves a sense of duty and its duration over time. These two kinds of love are evoked in a poem using the metaphor of water, which is particularly significant in a desert region where it is an invaluable resource. The poem refers to a married man who goes on a journey with goatskins full of water. On his way, as a flash of lightning announces torrential rain he pours the water out of his goatskins. The flash of lightning represents love for a woman at a first sight, and the rain falling is the image of the passion which makes the man abandon his reserves of water, symbolic of the marital relationship. It shows that the idea of love at first sight is not only a Western idea, as some historians such as Jean-Claude Bologne claim, because we can track it in classical Arabic poetry.

For a long time, it was rather unusual for anthropologists to reveal the *hors champ* of passionate love especially in the "Muslim word" (Fortier, 2018a). They preferred to focus on the alliance system, neglecting extramarital relationships occurring before, during or after married life. Until the 1980s, anthropologists of the Middle East were interested mainly in kinship, with a special focus on the specificities of the so called 'Arab marriage' between parallel patrilateral cousins, in many cases without taking into consideration the sentiments involved (Fortier, 2018b). Research on kinship explore also the concepts of 'honor and shame' as a key to the social and cultural systems in the Mediterranean area. Another important line of inquiry into topics related to love in the Arab world was that of Islamic law (Fortier, Kreil, & Maffi, 2018).

In the 1980s scholarly interest in emotions, personal agency and later the transnational circulation of imaginaries began to grow. Starting in the 1980s, new developments in anthropology paved the way for the integration of love into the study of Arab countries (Fortier, Kreil, & Maffi, 2016). The anthropology of emotions gained increased significance in the United States (Lutz & Abu-Lughod, 1990; Lutz & White, 1986). This attention to subjective experience set the conditions for the anthropology of love to take off in the first decade of the twenty-first century.

Concerning the Arab world, Lila Abu-Lughod's 1986 book played an important role in anchoring the topic in research. In her analysis of poetic genres among the Awlād Alī Bedouins of North-Western Egypt, she shows how poetry praising honour was used in parallel with poetry expressing desire and torment, sometimes contradicting kinship rules (Abu-Lughod, 1986).

However, even if they are rarely an object of study, extramarital relationships are not uncommon in many societies, at least among Moors (Fortier, 2004a). Pastoral nomadism, as well as men's frequent travel for commercial or political purposes, favour them. Nowadays the relative anonymity of contemporary cities also provides a perfect setting for such affairs. Such relations are not even taboo among Moors, as they are in other places around the Mediterranean area and North Africa. These meetings, while illicit from a religious point of view, are socially tolerated as long as they remain discreet.

41.3.1 Courtly Love

Moors have inherited a specific Arabic dialect, *Ḥassāniyya*, from the Arab populations (*Banī Ḥassān*) present in the country since the fourteenth century, and a courtesy code inspired by ancient Arab chivalry or *futūwwa*.[2] Some historians (Von Hammer-Purgstall, 1849) even hypothesize that Arab chivalry pre-existed European chivalry and influenced it. This courtesy code is very similar to that which appeared in the West during the Middle Ages. The similarity is in the 'common medieval cultures which can be found, in broad terms in both the Christian West and the Muslim East' (Zakeri, 1996, 32). The courtesy code does not contradict Islamic values, which have been present in the region for a long time.[3]

As in the thirteenth century in France, the courtesy code represents a social distinction which differentiates the 'courteous' or the 'courtier', from the villain (Duby, 1981). The courtesy code is still alive among Moors, despite the rise of the individualism and the influence of a certain Islamist discourse (Ould Ahmed Salem, 2013), and a man cannot diverge from this code without losing his honour.

The noble man devotes himself to the 'game' of love as he devotes himself to the 'game' of war, both being a form of challenge. The means used to conquer the woman are similar to techniques of hunting and borrow their vocabulary from warriors' and hunters' language. The woman is prey, a gazelle, according to the classical Moorish and Arabic poetic image which is still contemporary, an object of

---

[2]See Farès (1932) and Vadet (1968) on the Arabic notion of *futūwwa*.
[3]In West and North Africa Islam was present even before the Maliki Islamic school of jurisprudence introduced during the eleventh century by the Almoravids (Berbers).

envy which men try to capture as a precious trophy. Thus, women are not much considered for themselves but appear rather as assets in the competition between men. The courtesy context which seems to glorify women in fact essentially highlights the rivalry between men. Seduction represents more than the courting of women: it is a way to perfect male qualities, as in the *fin amor* (Duby, 1988, 47; Baladier, 1999, 82). Thus the 'game of love' is an initiation process, because it is through mastering it that young men acquire self-control (*ḥkam rāsu*), a virtue also known in the Medieval West under the name of *mezura* (Wettstein, 1945).

41.3.2 Night Meetings

Seduction is a rite of passage in which young men compete with other pretenders. One of their favourite settings is late meetings, when in the cool of the night they improvise poems in honour of the attending girls. Men engage in night meetings from puberty, or, according to the local expression, as soon '[the boy] has worn sarouel trousers and fasted for Ramadan' (*rbaṭ sarwāl u ṣām ramaḍān*) at around 12 years of age. For girls it can start very young, at around the age of nine (Fortier, 1998). This type of courtly meeting, similar to that known to Tuaregs by the name *ahal*, is locally given the Arabic term 'night assembly' (*jamāʿat al-layl*). They begin after the night prayers and go on until very late. They generally take place far from houses, on moonlit sand dunes. Such an atmosphere can stimulate the participants' poetic inspiration. These evenings are always accompanied by music (*hawl*) which resounds in the night's silence. It usually consists of a rhythm on a small hand drum (*ṭbal*) played by one of the girls and the sound of a griot's lute (*tidinīt*) or the harp (*ardīn*) of a griotte.

The rivalry between young men appears in the declamation of the most beautiful quatrain (*gāf*), to the woman they wants to court. *Ghazal* refers to a straightforward type of poetry related to flirting. The *ghazal* is an arabic form of poetry from the sixth century (Blachère, 1975). The word *ghazal* itself derives from the verb *ghazala*, meaning 'courting' (*ibid*). The *ghazal*, the more popular form of poetry among Moors, generally takes the shape of a quatrain (*gāf*), and is essentially composed with the aim of reaching the heart of the beloved.

The competitor will increase the difficulty by composing on the same rhyme as its predecessor a longer poem that will become a septan called *ṭalʿa*. This term, which means to climb, refers to the fact that the poet develops the quatrain: *ṭalʿa al-gāf*. A poem always begins with a *gāf*, which is developed in *ṭalʿa*. This poetic rivalry may lead to a satirical poetic game called *gṭāʿ*. This Arabic term means to cut and in this case refers to rivalry, although it is only a verbal duel. Whoever turns out to be the strongest at this poetic tournament has a good chance of gaining the attention of the beloved woman. In love, the poetic duel is similar to the Western Middle Ages tournament since it aims to reach the heart of a woman by means of verses similar to arrows.

To please the young women the men do not spare their poetic eloquence, as shown in this quatrain (*gāf*):

> It is my seventh verse (*gāf*) since the beginning of the evening, and when my beloved deigns to smile/I shall improvise the eighth and the ninth, the tenth and the eleventh (...).

Women who have been honoured with poems can acquire a reputation beyond the assembled circle. Among those who 'arouse the duel' (*labrāz*) at the night meetings, some will become '*shabībāt*'. This term, built on the same Arabic root as *shabāb*, youth, is used for a woman whose name is praised by all; in this respect being quoted in poems which will remain in the oral memory is a great acknowledgment for a woman.

41.4 Nostalgic Poetry

Men appear in Moorish poetry as devoted admirers of women in a tone similar to that of Arabic pre-Islamic poetry and Medieval Occitan madrigals, which mostly describe the woman as a mistress of whom the poet is the devoted slave (Lavaud & Nelli, 2000). There has been a strong link between Mauritanian courtly love and the Arab Bedouin tradition since pre-Islamic times. Two types of love poetry circulating among Moorish men are inspired by two types of Arabic love poetry: the *nasīb* and the *ghazal*. The first traces of these two styles go back to the sixth or seventh century.

Some link the term *nasīb* to the Arabic verb *nasaba*, meaning 'to sing of a lady's beauty and the trouble she inspires' (Blachère, 1975). The *nasīb* has a nostalgic style, evoking places haunted by women and the delicious pangs they provoke. The poet sings of the absence of his beloved, identifying her with the place where he met her. The nostalgique tone of Bedouin poetry, in which the poet depicts the vestiges (dune, tree) of the past, is suggested in Arabic by the periphrase: 'To stop or to cry on the remains of the past' (*al-wuqūf 'ala' al-aṭlāl* or *al-buk' al-aṭlāl*).

The definition of gratitude (1995: 186) of the french philosopher André Compte-Sponville applies perfectly to this specific form of poetry:

> It is this joy of memory, the love of the past or the suffering of whas does not longer exist, not the regret of what did not happen, but the joyful memory of what happened.

The soul of Moorish poetry would hold in this adage of Epicure: 'Sweet is the memory of the disappeared friend', a bittersweet feeling found in many poetic and musical traditions throughout the world.

An archetypal phrase expresses the suffering provoked by the beloved's absence: 'I am languishing with love for you' (*mitwaḥashak*). This expression derives from the Arabic term *waḥsha*, which means to languish, commonly used in *Ḥassāniyya*. This notion which refers to nostalgia is similar to the Baudelairian spleen, an English term wich refers to the organ of spleen. It is also close to the Portuguese *saudade*, an expression first used by the troubadour D. Sancho, and which was probably inspired by the courteous Arab ideal (Demeuldre, 2004, 10) as indicated by the Arabic etymology of this term, *sawdā'*, which designates the atrabile. The term of melancholy in French, derived from the Latin *melancholia* which derives itself from the Greek *mélas khôlé*: black bile. These various expressions have in common to establish a relation between a particular psychological state marked by languor and one of the moods of the body, in this case the black or atrabile mood, in conformity with the humoral theory of hippocratic origin well-known in the West but also in Arabic and Moorish medicine (Fortier, 2017a, b, c).

41.5 The Landscape of Love

The decisive moment of the meeting is fatal for a man. As Gilles Deleuze affirms:

> I do not desire a woman, I also desire a landscape that is enveloped in this woman, a landscape that, if necessary, I do not know and I feel and until I have unrolled the landscape that she envelops, I will not be happy, that my desire will not be fulfilled, my desire will remain dissatisfied.[4]

A Moorish poet was charmed by a beautiful woman despite, and perhaps because of, the dangerous omens that surround the circumstances of her meeting. To speak of the fig-tree of hell with which he noticed it at the hottest hour of the day, is ready to give way to his perishment which he fears and hopes. It is an indirect process, sometimes used in Moorish poetry, to say the ardour of the passion by a detour that evokes its circumstantial aspects, time and space:

> Yesterday at the time of the nap/I saw the one I was dreaming of
> under a shrub of $ātil$[5]/next to a fig-tree of hell.

The landscape of love is also important in the poem of Charles Baudelaire, 'To a Creole Lady' (1975, 62), where the evocation of the atmosphere of Port-Saint-Louis on Mauritius island is merged with the languorous souvenir of Madame Autard de Bragard:

> In the perfumed country which the sun caresses, I knew, under a canopy of crimson trees, And palms from which indolence rains into your eyes, A Creole lady whose charms were unknown.

---

[4]Deleuze-Abécédaire-D Comme désir: https://www.youtube.com/watch?v=03YWWrKoI5A

[5]The scientific name of this tree is *Maerua crassifolia*.

41.6 The Uniqueness of the Beloved Woman

In anti-Islamic Arab romantic poetry the name of the beloved woman is often quoted. The poet Qays ibn al-Mullawah is more well-known under the name 'the fool of Layla' (*majnūn Layla*) by reference for the woman for who he composed poems. This association between the name of the poet and the first name of his muse is also found in some French poets: Aragon is inseparable from Elsa, Lou from Apollinaire.

The woman's name is also the object of love in Moorish poetry. A Moorish poet, obsessed with the souvenir of Mana, cannot hear a word beginning with the initial of her first name, without thinking of her:

> Every time I hear a word beginning with M/I immediately think of Mana.

The poet's inspiration comes from his attraction to a woman whose beauty is usually praised in his poems. According to the sublimation process inherent to creation, the erotic parts of the woman's body are described in the poems. This Moorish poetry is similar to the west form of poetry named 'blazon', from the Middle Age and codified during the Renaissance, which praises some elements of woman body. If the charms of the beloved are honored by the poets, they have also glorified her defects in an affective way.

It is the most beautiful declaration of love that a man can make to a woman that to express his love to her in spite of her defects. It shows that the woman is not considered as an ideal or a perfect woman, or an object of 'crystallization'. The concept of crystallization was created by the French novelist Stendhal (1783–1842): 'What I call crystallization is the operation of the mind, which draws from all that is presented the discovery that the loved object has new perfections' (Dictionnaire Petit Robert 1990, 425). The poet is in love with a singular and imperfect woman, loving her the way she is, whatever her imperfections. As this Moorish poem summarizes, it is a matter of gaze:

> They saw the ugliness of the woman who is at the origin of my pains
> We have all the same pupil but not the same gaze.

41.7 The Pain of Love

Love poems express the pathos of the passion with its distress, suffering and fury. For example, a poet describes the beloved as well as the pains and the joys which she arouses in him in the following verse:

> When she was tinged with henna, the one that I love
> Suffering appears which was not in me.

In the Moorish society, the man is enthralled by the woman: he becomes blind, he loses his mind or his heart (*galb*),[6] she cuts his heart to pieces (*qṭa'ti galbī*), he is possessed by her (*māla' bihā*), she drives him crazy, he wastes away (*mitmumi*), she is killing him (*qatlatnī*), he is dying for her (*muta 'alik*). In anti-Islamic Arabic poetry, especially in one of the Imru'l-Qays b. H'ujr al-Kindî's Mu'allaqâ, he speaks about the woman like: 'The one who throws the arrows of death' (*matānta lahalāk*) (Berque, 1995, 24). In a Moorish poem the lover exclaims like:

> Oh! My friends she knew to show herself so weak, fragile and vulnerable
> Yet it was me she murdered without worrying about the loss.

The beloved woman is an enchantress who has 'tied [the man's] head' (*marbūṭ rāsi*). The expression '*rbīṭ rās*' is generally used for lost cattle which, when found, must be immobilized with a magic spell (*ḥijāb*). This phrase, which belongs to the pastoral register, is used in matters of love to evoke the apathy of the lover bewitched by his beloved. And if the beloved woman's presence makes him suffer, her absence is far more painful. Today in Mauritania young people use an expression derived from French, *fanatique*, which refers to obsession and madness: 'You have made me fanatic about you' (*fanatisaytini*).

Far from hiding his flame, the lover tries to inspire the same passion in the woman by revealing it through his poetry in an attempt to disturb her through the expression of his feelings. It is not until the woman is touched by the man's vibrant appeal that she can give him her favours in response to this love. The lover's tears are intended for the one who causes them, with the intention that she will soothe them. In love poetry the woman is often called 'the reason for my sorrow' (*sabab at-tulāḥ*), or 'the reason for my death' (*sabab qatlī*). The pain of love is known in Ḥassāniyya as *saqam*, a classic Arabic term that refers to physical disease. This kind of love is close to the *pharmakon* (Derrida, 2006) which is the cause of the pain and also its remedy.

The lover's figure is a feminized figure, because he no can longer control himself and is subject to a passion that is annihilating him. Paradoxically, a man whose virility is characterized by self-control can be nevertheless possessed by passion, because for a man, being in the grip of such agony and confessing it to the one who has caused such disorder is the unavoidable preliminary step to the conquest of his beloved. The lover occupies a feminized position as a victim of passion; he seems to have lost the self-control expected of men, and furthermore his submissive attitude towards the object of his love testifies that he is in a situation of dependency, which among Moors and in other societies is usually characteristic of the feminine position. More generally, the feminine position is a fundamental characteristic of a person in a state of passion.

Thus, he has to show himself to be both extremely patient towards the woman he loves as well as profoundly disturbed. However, even when the man is in this state in the seduction phase, marked negatively with passivity and suffering, it is only a

---

[6]On the symbolic meaning of the heart in Arabic and in Islam, see Corinne Fortier (2007: 17). About the memorization process of the Koran in Moorish society related to the heart, see Corinne Fortier (2016a).

temporary situation that represents minor harm on the way to conquering the woman and gaining a dominant position over other men.

From this perspective, poetry, which until recently was exclusively a masculine domain among Moors, constitutes a weapon of choice in the same way that it was a weapon for troubadours in the Medieval West (Roubaud, 1971). Like courteous love, the means used to conquer the woman are similar to techniques of hunting and borrow their vocabulary from warriors and hunters' lexicons.

41.8 Secret Visits

A man who, after a hard fight, wins a girl's favour at a night assembly continues to show her his affection by trying to meet her privately. Among Moors, especially in the desert, moments of intimacy between young people of the opposite sex are rare. It is only at night, when the woman's parents are sleeping, that the young man can try to approach her more closely. The clandestine character of these night visits appears in the term used in this context, which is directly related to the notion of 'secret' (*sarriyya*). By making this visit, which is attended by many risks, the young man shows his beloved that he is ready to die for her.

In the past, young men might travel very long distances to join their beloved. If a man owned a camel he would harness it in the middle of the night in such a way that the camel could not grunt, so that he could travel unnoticed. If he was too young to own a camel he travelled on foot, and moving forward in total darkness he risked getting bitten by a scorpion or a snake. Having arrived at the woman's encampment, the visitor would make sure her parents were sleeping. When he had entered the tent he would awake his beloved by gently pinching her nose.

Then they would converse in low voices. This act of conversing with people of the opposite sex is connected in thought and vocabulary to the act of making love. Thus the term most usually employed to designate intimacy between a man and a woman is *titwannas*, which means 'talking with,' from which the word for lover, *wanīs*, and mistress, *wanīsa*, are derived. In this Muslim society where the prohibition against men and women touching each other is important, conversation between lovers is laden with carnal overtones, close to Roland Barthes' (1977, 87) description:

> The language is a skin: I rub my language against the other.
> It is as if I had words by way of fingers, or fingers at the end of my words.

The young man would lie down behind the girl, who would turn her back on her parents so that they would not perceive the visitor if they woke up. He might be cautious enough to prefer to court her through the thin fabric enclosing the back of the tent (*ukhar kurar*). Seeking her company was perilous, because if he was discovered her father would not hesitate to chase him away with a stick or a rifle.

The visit could go on until late, and the lover would have to fight sleep so as not to be found asleep beside the girl. He would leave as discreetly as he had come to be back in his own encampment before dawn in order not to be discovered. The night visit was a test for the lover who, having defied the dangers of the desert (scorpions, snakes, thorns and cold) and overcome the fear of divine punishment for illicit contact between unmarried men and women, exposed himself to the risk of being discovered. These dangers were the price he had to pay in order to join his beloved. By this visit marked out by risks, he showed his beloved that he was capable of dying for her. Moreover, such proof of love was also an initiatory test whereby the young man proved his bravery to the woman he loved on the one hand, and to friends of his own age on the other (Fortier, 2003). After this visit he would inform his friends in great detail about his perilous adventures.

One of young men's favourite pastimes is hunting women in the evenings. This practice is legitimized by the common assertion that 'a young man is always in search of an adventure'. Young men roam through the city in groups, often by car, in search of women. New expressions inspired by the French language have appeared: '*tantī*', from *tenter*, to try, and '*tdrāgī*', from *draguer*, to hit on someone. This new behaviour is typical of city-dwellers, especially in the capital. In Nouakchott one type of entertainment consists of going out of the city at the weekend (Thursday and Friday), to drink milk, hunt bustards, and conquer country girls, whom which these rich city-dwellers describe as 'good meat'. The men arrive at isolated encampments with their big cars and their expensive presents from the city to try to impress the 'country women' and seduce them.

41.9 The Expenses of Love

Young men who visited their beloved in the night generally brought her a present, for example a perfume bottle (*bush min musk*). Today, young men offer women a henna (*ḥanna*) or hairstyling (*ẓhvir*) session, or another object of feminine finery such as a veil, a handbag or a jewel. These presents are given to pay tribute to the woman and her beauty, and as such are called 'gifts to beauty' (*hadiyāt al-jamāl*). They are necessary proofs of love, and a man trying to seduce a woman cannot avoid making these offerings. The lover has to show himself generous to the woman he loves, sparing no effort, because spending his time and money without stint is like giving himself to her. In the love relationship the man must show his generosity, which is part of his honour. This poem gives an account of the necessary spending for love:

> I want to be with her/I do not wish to distance myself from her,
> I saw her/yesterday while I was crossing a deserted place,
> For her, I lost/so much wealth, oh misfortune,
> For her, I lost/so many quatrains (*givān*) and poems (*ṭal'a*).

Women are not expected to show gratitude when accepting poems and presents. For example, a poet deplores the losses provoked by an unhappy love affair, due in particular to the gifts (*ṭamʿa*) given to griots to sing the poems he had composed for her to his beloved. However, in spite of the poet's bitterness about the disproportion between what he says he gave her and what he has received from her, he tells us that he continues to love her and still dedicates his poems to her.

This sort of feeling (Fortier, 2004b) resembles the *joi* of troubadours, which combines enjoyment, suffering and the game (Roubaud, 1994). Likewise, the woman's refusals, far from repelling the lover, arouse his desire. It is considered part of the game of seduction and explains why women are affectionately called 'traitress' (*khawwāna*) in some poems, an expression found in Baudelaire's poem: 'The invitation to travel' (1975, 53) addressed to Mrs. Sabatier: 'of your treacherous eyes'.

Furthermore, the lover's disappointment not only shows his beloved's indifference but also reveals the level of his love, as this Moorish poem shows:

> You never gave me even a little of your love, /a little of your laugh
> But someone who has never seen you angry/doesn't know the taste of love.

The poems, like the numerous presents and services offered to the beloved woman, thus all participate in what Roland Barthes (1977, 99) broadly calls 'the expenses of love'.

41.10 The Objets of Love

Through these ordeals young men learn to control their desires. As the medieval *cortezia* rules characterized by secrecy, patience and measure (De Rougemont, 1972, 79), the woman's caprice is answered by the constancy of the lover. Like in the medieval *fin amor* (Baladier, 1999, 82), Moorish women give themselves gradually to their lovers to test them, and the man is called a 'sufferer' (*sofridor*) (Dragonetti, 1960: 78). Likewise, Moorish women grant concessions to men only progressively: at first a smile, then a wink, and so on. . . To test their pretenders' patience (*ṣabr*), women refuse any physical contact for a long time. However, they sometimes let the lover steal an object that she is carrying. The lover preserves this object affectedly next to his heart, putting it in the pocket of his boubou (*darāʿa*).[7]

The stolen object is archetypally a toothpick (*miswāk*), an erotic object because the woman has held it between her lips and chewed it sensually. Through the mediation of this metonymical object, the lover kisses her indirectly. Other objects that she has touched can play the same mediating role, such as a rosary (*tasbīḥ*), a ring (*khatma*), or a watch (*waqqāta*), which the lover wears to be closer to the beloved. This 'souvenir'—the French word has been borrowed in *Ḥassāniyya*—also supports him in the absence of the beloved, sometimes even after his death, as

---

[7] The boubou refers in French to the long loose-fitting garment worn by men in Mauritania.

described in a poem where the lover remains faithful to the woman he loved even in the grave, keeping objects that she had carried with him in the tomb.

The fetish object represents not only the beloved woman but also the love relationship itself. By showing it, the young man makes the relationship public. More recently a photograph of the beloved has fulfilled this role; the lover carries it in the pocket of his boubou and shows it proudly to his friends. Women are the object of men's desire; a desire that they learn to discipline through the courtship itself. Proof of love is also proof of virility.

41.10.1 Inaccessible Married Women

In Moorish society seduction aims for the conquest of the desired woman, who is divorced (Fortier, 2012, 2016b) or even married. The desire for these categories of women reveals the challenge that motivates such courtship. Seduction is a test for the man, who must show his virile virtues by being patient, generous, attentive and brave. Like medieval Western courtly love, the supreme test is to win the heart of a married woman, who is by definition inaccessible. The transgression is social but also religious, as according to the Koran (IV, 24, transl. Arberry, 1980), the wife is a forbidden woman. A man's desire for a married woman is enhanced by the illicit character of the relationship. The furtive night meeting suits this type of relationship, which is marked with the seal of secrecy. The man's visit to his beloved is not without risk, and the transgression is always accompanied by fear. The attractiveness of this transgression motivates men to try and visit married women frequently.

The clandestine character of the extramarital relationship forces the lover to use subterfuge to meet the woman. The husband and the lover have to be, according to the *Ḥassāniyya* expression, 'like cow's horns', suggesting that they must not meet. The lover's ingenuity consists of seizing convenient moments when the husband is away. Generally there are many occasions to visit her, the husband being absent from home most of the time; during the day he attends to his work taking care of his cattle, his shop, or his office, and in the evening he usually meets up with friends.

41.10.2 Husbands Who Are Not Jealous

It is believed that Moorish husbands grant a certain amount of freedom to their wives to receive men in their tents or houses and to circulate in the public sphere as they wish. Husbands consider their wives precious goods which grant them social prestige, thanks to their power of seduction. Often flattered by the idea that they have married a woman whom numerous men desire, men allow their wives to play their mundane role by receiving admirers at home. A husband should not be jealous of this assembly of lovers as long as he keeps his exclusive right to the possession of his wife. She should grant only 'a jaw' to lovers, meaning a polite smile and a friendly word.

The Arabic traveller Ibn Battûta (1982, 403), describing the life of people in the old city of Walata in the fourteenth century, was surprised by the freedom in the Moors' customs:

> In this country, the women take friends and companions among foreign and unrelated men. The men, for their part, have partners whom they take among their non-relatives. It often happens that a man enters his home and he finds his wife with her companion: he does not disapprove of this conduct, and does not take offence at it.

If a wife's extramarital affairs are discreet, the husband should not try to catch her out. Jealousy is considered a base feeling that a married man should not show, because the nobility of his behaviour requires that he controls his emotions. In such a situation, again men must visit their beloved furtively: everything is possible as long as it remains discreet.

From this viewpoint, the fault is less adultery than a lack of discretion when committing it, so that when a husband surprises his wife in an unacceptable situation he is forced to defend his honour. He chases away the lover with his rifle or with insults, and then has an argument with his wife. It is one of the few reasons that men beat their wives. However, although adultery is condemned, violence towards a woman is condemned even more. A woman who suffers from such violence may dramatize her misfortune by shouting and tearing her clothes to reverse the opprobrium to her husband.

41.10.3 Jealous Wives

Men are more actively involved in extramarital relationships than women. Adultery is more socially acceptable when committed by men, as it fits their supposed need for conquest (Fortier, 2013a). Moorish women compare men with camels who eat the leaves of a tree while casting their eyes over the foliage of another branch: always in search of a new affair.

However, when a Moorish woman suspects her husband of infidelity, as a sign of her disapproval she may return to her parents' home (Fortier, 2011). Some women leave their husband with their children after learning that he has composed a quatrain about his love for another woman. In such cases the husband usually sends a delegation of respectable men to his wife to ask her to forgive his faults and come back. Furthermore, to redeem himself and as proof of his love, he should offer her valuable presents.

Among Moors, as in many societies, the marital relationship has a main purpose: the creation of a family. The wife has several duties towards her husband, one of which is to give him children. For a woman, extramarital relationships seek not procreation but pleasure—pleasure which can also be pursued in the marital relationship. In parallel, for a man the extramarital relationship aims to secure the desired woman, challenging his rivals and asserting his virile qualities. Some husbands can gain prestige from having an attractive wife, but this does not necessarily suffice to calm their thirst for conquest outside the marital relationship. A wife gives her husband progeny, enabling him to fulfil his social role as a father. A mistress, on the other hand, stimulates his taste for a challenge because she does not belong to him legally. Whether a mistress or a wife, the woman provides the man with the opportunity to demonstrate his virile qualities, in each case related to conquest and to fathering.[8]

41.11 Conclusion: Masculine Desire

For Moors, seduction and poems aim at the conquest of the desired woman. For a man, conquering the courted woman is also a way of defying his rivals. This approach is similar to what Sigmund Freud (1987, 49) describes as the conditions of masculine desire in certain cases:

> [...] the lover shows no desire to possess the woman for himself only, and seems to be fully at ease in the triangular relation [with other men].

It shows that Sigmund Freud analysis on this matter is not only relevant from an occidental point of view but for an universal one.

Women are assets to what is in fact masculine rivalry. The lover's rivalry concerns all the woman' other suitors as if they themselves were objects of desire. In this respect, Freud showed that sexual rivalry implies more interest in the rival than in the woman, an observation confirmed by Roland Barthes (1977: 80):

> Jealousy is an equation involving three permutable (indeterminable) terms: one is always jealous of two persons at once: I am jealous of the one I love and of the one who loves the one I love. The odiosamato (as the Italians call the 'rival') is also loved by me: he interests me, intrigues me, appeals to me.

However, such a feeling is inadmissible because it implies that other men are thought of as objects of desire. Thus, men express themselves through the fight for a woman, who is presented as the sole target of their desire.

In the game of love women are seen as objects of desire for men and their own desires are never acknowledged. The woman who is courted draws some material advantage from seduction relationships, knowing that most of these will be temporary. The man supports the cost because it flatters his virility, of which generosity is part. It also stimulates his taste for conquest associated with challenge. A woman has a more difficult game to play to win respect, because by immediately granting her favours she may appear to be too easy, endangering her dignity, which is closely socially related to modesty. She must defend her image of the inaccessible woman

---

[8]On the importance of becoming a father in this and other societies, see Corinne Fortier (2013b, 2017a).

who will admit the lover to intimacy with her only through patient effort and prodigality. His relationships with women reveal to the man what creates his virility: generosity, courage and self-control.

As in most societies, Moorish men are mainly the initiators of sexual relations, as if the free expression of their desire is authorized more than that of women. In this society sentimental and sexual attraction are a man's privilege. The right to express one's desires is an element of domination in so far as women are deprived of it. The fact that men are considered the subjects of desire and women its object is a major cross-cultural element which ensures men's appropriation of women's bodies and structures relations between people of the opposite sex.[9]

References

Abu-Lughod, L. (1986). *Veiled sentiments: Honor and poetry in a Bedouin society*. Berkeley: University of California Press.
Ahearn, L.-M. (2003). Writing desire in Nepali love letters. *Language & Communication, 23*(2), 107–122.
Ahearn, L.-M. (2004). Literacy, power, and agency: Love letters and development in Nepal. *Language & Education, 18*(4), 305–316.
Arberry, A. J. (1980). *The Koran interpreted* (Trans.) London: George Allen/Unwin.
Baladier, C. (1999). *Eros au Moyen Âge*. Paris: Cerf.
Barthes, R. (1977). *Fragments d'un discours amoureux*. Paris: Seuil.
Baṭṭuṭa, I. (1982). *Voyages. t. 3, Inde, Extrême Orient, Espagne et Soudan, 1858* (Le voyage au Soudan) (Vol. 5, pp. 393–446). Paris: La Découverte.
Baudelaire, C. (1975). *Oeuvres Complètes, t.1*. Paris: La Pléiade.
Berque, J. (1995). Transl., *Les dix grandes odes arabes de l'anté-islam*. Paris: Actes Sud/Sindbad (La bibliothèque arabe).
Blachère, R. (1975). *Analecta*. Damas: Institut Français de Damas.
Cole, J., & Lynn, T. (2009). *Love in Africa*. Chicago: University of Chicago Press.
Comte Sponville, A. (1995). *Petit traité des grandes vertus*. Paris: PUF (Perspectives critiques).
De Rougemont, D. (1972). *L'amour et l'Occident*. Paris: Plon (10/18).
Demeuldre, M. (2004). Introduction. In M. Demeuldre (Ed.), *Sentiments doux-amers dans les musiques du monde. Délectations moroses dans les blues, fado, tango, flamenco, rebetico, p'ansori, ghazal* (pp. 5–23). Paris: L'Harmattan (Logiques sociales, musique et champ social).
Derrida, J. (2006). *La pharmacie de Platon*. Paris: Flammarion-Gallimard (Poche).
Dictionnaire le petit Robert. (1990). *Dictionnaire alphabétique et analogique de la langue française, rédaction dirigée par A Rey & Rey-Debove, J*. Paris: Dictionnaires Le Robert.
Dragonetti, R. (1960). *La technique poétique des trouvères dans la chanson courtoise*. Bruges: De Tempel.
Duby, G. (1981). *Le chevalier, la femme et le prêtre*. Paris: Hachette.
Duby, G. (1988). *Mâle Moyen Âge. De l'amour et autres essais*. Paris: Flammarion.
Farès, B. (1932). *L'Honneur chez les Arabes avant l'Islam*. Paris: Maisonneuve.
Fortier, C. (1998). Le corps comme mémoire: Du giron maternel à la férule du maître coranique. *Journal des Africanistes, 68*(1–2), 199–223.

---

[9]On this subject, see also Corinne Fortier (2019).

Fortier, C. (2003). Épreuves d'amour en Mauritanie. *L'Autre. Cliniques, cultures et sociétés, 4*(2), 239–252.

Fortier, C. (2004a). Séduction, jalousie et défi entre hommes: Chorégraphie des affects et des corps dans la société maure. In F. Héritier & M. Xanthakou (Eds.), *Corps et affects* (pp. 237–254). Paris: Odile Jacob.

Fortier, C. (2004b). "Ô langoureuses douleurs de l'amour". Poétique du désir en Mauritanie. In M. Demeuldre (Ed.), *Sentiments doux-amers dans les musiques du monde* (pp. 15–25). Paris: L'Harmattan.

Fortier, C. (2007). Blood, sperm and the embryo in Sunni Islam and in Mauritania: Milk kinship, descent and medically assisted procreation. *Body and Society, 13*(3), 15–36.

Fortier, C. (2011). Women and men put Islamic law to their own use: Monogamy versus secret marriage in Mauritania. In M. Badran (Ed.), *Gender and Islam in Africa: Rights, sexuality and law* (pp. 213–232). Washington: Woodrow Wilson Press.

Fortier, C. (2012). The right to divorce for women (*khulʿ*) in Islam: Comparative practices in Mauritania and Egypt. In R. Mehdi, W. Menski, & J. S. Nielsen (Eds.), *Interpreting divorce laws in Islam* (pp. 155–175). Copenhagen: DJOF Publishing.

Fortier, C. (2013a). Les ruses de la paternité en islam malékite: L'adultère dans la société maure de Mauritanie. In A.-M. Moulin (Ed.), *Islam et révolutions médicales. Le labyrinthe du corps* (pp. 157–181). IRD/Karthala: Marseille/Paris.

Fortier, C. (2013b). Genre, sexualité et techniques reproductives en islam. In F. Rochefort & M. E. Sanna (Eds.), *Normes religieuses et genre. Mutations, Résistances et Reconfigurations XIXe– XXIe siècle* (pp. 173–187). Paris: Armand Colin (Recherches).

Fortier, C. (2016a). Orality and the transmission of Qur'anic knowledge. In R. G. Launay (Ed.), *Writing boards and blackboards: Islamic education in Africa* (pp. 62–78). Bloomington & Indianopolis: Indiana University Press.

Fortier, C. (2016b). Divorce and custody. Contemporary practices: Mauritania and Egypt. In J. Suad (Ed.), *Encyclopedia of women and Islamic cultures*. Leiden: Brill. Accessed August 8, 2018, from https://doi.org/10.1163/1872-5309_ewic_COM_00203008.

Fortier, C. (2017a). Les procréations médicalement assistées en contexte musulman au prisme du genre. In C. Fortier & S. Monqid (Eds.), *Corps des femmes et espaces genrés arabo-musulmans* (pp. 241–256). Paris: Karthala.

Fortier, C. (2017b). Les maux du médecin: savoir, expérience et dévouement. In V. Barras, C. Fortier, B. Graz, & A.-M. Moulin (Eds.), *Le Recueil des vertus de la médecine ancienne de Maqâri. La médecine gréco-arabe en Mauritanie contemporaine* (pp. 25–36). Lausanne: BHMS éditions (Sources en perspective).

Fortier, C. (2017c). Derrière le 'voile islamique', de multiples visages. Voile, harem, chevelure: identité, genre et colonialisme. In A. Castaing & É. Gaden (Eds.), *Écrire et penser le genre en contextes postcoloniaux* (Comparatisme et société) (pp. 233–258). Berne: Peter Lang.

Fortier, C. (2018a). The expences of love: Seduction, poetry and jealousy in Mauritania. In C. Fortier, A. Kreil, & I. Maffi (Eds.), *Reinventing love? Gender, intimacy and romance in the Arab world* (Middle East, social and cultural studies) (pp. 47–69). Berne: Peter Lang.

Fortier, C. (2018b). Milk, breast. In H. Callan (Ed.), *The international encyclopedia of anthropology*. Oxford: John Wiley. https://doi.org/10.1002/9781118924396.wbiea1433. https://onlinelibrary.wiley.com/doi/abs/10.1002/9781118924396.wbiea1433.

Fortier, C. (2019). Sexualities: Transexualities: Middle East, North Africa, West Africa. In S. Joseph (Ed.), *Encyclopedia of women and Islamic cultures (EWIC)*, Supplement 20. Leiden: Brill. https://doi.org/10.1163/1872-5309_ewic_COM_002185.

Fortier, C., Kreil, A., & Maffi, I. (2016). The trouble of love in the Arab world: Romance, marriage, and the shapping of intimate lives. *The Arab Studies Journal, Special Section: Love in the Arab World, 24*(2), 96–101.

Fortier, C., Kreil, A., & Maffi, I. (2018). Introduction. In C. Fortier, A. Kreil, & I. Maffi (Eds.), *Reinventing love? Gender, intimacy and romance in the Arab world* (Middle East, social and cultural studies) (pp. 9–32). Berne: Peter Lang.
Freud, S. (1987). *Trois essais sur la théorie sexuelle*. Paris: Gallimard.
Giddens, A. (1992). *The transformation of intimacy: Sexuality, love and eroticism in modern societies*. Cambridge: Polity Press.
Hirsch, J. S., & Wardlow, H. (Eds.). (2006). *Modern loves: The anthropology of romantic courtship & companionate marriage*. Ann Arbor: University of Michigan Press.
Illouz, E. (1997). *Consuming the romantic utopia: Love and the cultural contradictions of capitalism*. Berkeley: University of California Press.
Jankowiak, W. R., & Fischer, E. F. (1992). A cross-cultural perspective on romantic love. *Ethnology, 31*(2), 149–155.
Jankowiak, W. R., Volsche, S. L., & Garcia, J. R. (2015). Is the romantic-sexual kiss a near human universal? *American Anthropologist, 117*(3), 535–539.
Lavaud, R., & Nelli, R. (2000). *Les Troubadours. T. II: L'œuvre poétique*. Paris: Desclée de Brouwer.
Lindholm, C. (1988). Lovers and leaders: A comparison of social and psychological models of romance and charisma. *Social Science Information, 27*(1), 3–45.
Lindholm, C. (2006). Romantic love and anthropology. *Etnofoor, 19*(1), 5–21.
Lipset, D. (2004). Modernity without romance? Masculinity and desire in courtship stories told by young Papua new Guinean men. *American Ethnologist, 31*(2), 205–224.
Lutz, C., & Abu-Lughod, L. (1990). *Language and the politics of emotion*. Cambridge/Paris: Cambridge University Press/Éditions de la Maison des sciences de l'Homme.
Lutz, C., & White, G. (1986). The anthropology of emotions. *Annual Review of Anthropology, 15*(1), 405–436.
Mead, M. (1966). *Coming of age in Samoa. A psychological study of primitive youth for Western civilisation*. Harmondsworth: Penguin.
Ould Ahmed Salem, Z. (2013). *Prêcher dans le désert*. Paris: Karthala.
Padilla, M. (Ed.). (2007). *Love and globalization: Transformations of intimacy in the contemporary world*. Nashville, TN: Vanderbilt University Press.
Pettier, J. B. (2016). The affective scope: Entering China's urban moral and economic world through its emotional disturbances. *Anthropology of Consciousness, 27*(1), 75–96.
Roubaud, J. (1971). *Les troubadours. Anthologie bilingue*. Paris: Seghers.
Roubaud, J. (1994). *La Fleur inverse: L'art des troubadours*. Paris: Les Belles Lettres.
Stacey, J. (2011). *Unhitched: Love, marriage, and family values from West Hollywood to Western China*. New York: New York University Press.
Taleb-Khyar, M. B. (2001). *La Mauritanie: le pays au million de poètes*. Paris: L'Harmattan.
Tcherkézoff, S. (2004). *'First contacts' in Polynesia: The Samoan case (1722–1848). Western misunderstandings about sexuality and divinity*. Canberra/Christchurch: Macmillan Brown Centre for Pacific Studies, The Journal of Pacific History Monographs.
Vadet, J.-C. (1968). La futuwwa, morale professionnelle ou morale mystique. *Revue des études islamiques, 66*, 57–90.
Von Hammer-Purgstall, J. (1849). *La Chevalerie des Arabes antérieure à celle d'Europe: De l'influence de la première sur la seconde* (pp. 4–14). Janvier: Journal Asiatique.
Wettstein, J. (1945). *Mezura. L'idéal des troubadours: Son essence et ses aspects*. Genève: Slatkine Reprints.
Zakeri, M. (1996). Muslim 'chivalry' at the time of the crusaders. *Hallesche Beiträge zur Orientwissenschaft, 22*, 29–50.
Zavoretti, R. (2013). *Be my valentine: Bouquets, marriage, and middle class hegemony in urban China*. Halle/Saale: Max Planck Institute for Social Anthropology.

Corinne Fortier is a cultural anthropologist and a researcher at the French National Center of Scientific Research (CNRS). She is also a member of the Social Anthropology Lab (LAS) from the Collège de France (CNRS-EHESS-Collège de France-PSL University, Paris). Bronze Medal 2005 of the French National Center of Scientific Research (CNRS). She conducted research in Mauritania and in Egypt as well as on Islamic scriptural sources related to gender, body, love, and family law.

Chapter 42
"How Do You Spell Love?"—"You Don't Spell It. You Feel It."

Willie van Peer and Anna Chesnokova

Abstract This famous quote from *Winnie-the-Pooh* reveals something fundamental about the role love stories play in the lives of people. That they do, is beyond doubt, as the theme of love pervades all of literature. And this interest in the topic of love has not waned. Publishing love stories is a multi-billion business. Apparently humans are not content with loving and being loved; they also want to read about other people's love. Why?

In this chapter we propose several motifs for reading about love in fiction, based on insights from sexology and expert relation therapy. Love stories apparently *transfer* experiences through the written word into meaningful experiences that, although knowingly fictional, nevertheless are of the utmost importance to readers. After presenting some data on love literature and basic impediments to human love relations, we offer some escape routes from desire (through death, divorce, and extramarital affairs), arguing that the road to desire in relations is hardly represented in fictional literature, with one exception, what we call "the magic of love". With this we mean that in reading literature words have to be pronounced *ad verbatim* so that, similarly to magical practices, they produce the desired effect on the reader.

In a final section we reflect on the urgent need to investigate reading about love through more rigorous, empirical, research methods than the speculative ones employed so far in literary studies.

Keywords Love · Rationale for love stories · Effects of reading · Love stories · Evolutionary perspective on love · Relation therapy

W. van Peer (✉)
Faculty of Languages and Literatures, Ludwig Maximilian University, Munich, Germany
e-mail: w.vanpeer@gmail.com

A. Chesnokova
Department of English Philology and Translation, Borys Grinchenko Kyiv University, Kiev, Ukraine
e-mail: chesnokova2510@gmail.com

© Springer Nature Switzerland AG 2021
C.-H. Mayer, E. Vanderheiden (eds.), *International Handbook of Love*,
https://doi.org/10.1007/978-3-030-45996-3_42

42.1 Introduction: Love?

Winnie the Pooh (a fictional teddy-bear character from the 1926 book by A.A. Milne) may count as a light-hearted yet profound philosopher about daily problems, including, apparently, problems of love. But is love problematic? It no doubt is. One of the clearest specifications of the problem has been offered by Jared Diamond (2015) in his booklet *Why Is Sex Fun?*. It opens with a view on human sexuality through the eyes of a dog:

> Those disgusting humans have sex any day of the month! Barbara proposes sex even when she knows perfectly well that she isn't fertile (...) John is eager for sex all the time, without caring whether his efforts could result in a baby or not.
>
> But if you want to hear something really gross — (...) when John's parents come for a visit, (...) I can hear them too having sex, although John's mother went through this thing they call menopause years ago.
>
> Now she can't have babies anymore, but she still wants sex, and John's father obliges her. What a waste of effort! Here's the weirdest thing of all: Barbara and John, and John's parents, close the bedroom door and have sex in private, instead of doing it in front of their friends like any self-respecting dog! (Diamond, 2015, 3)

Your dog confirms: humans have the most bizarre love life among all mammals. But what do we mean by the word "love"? While there are many aspects to it (for instance, in a religious or filial sense, or in the sense of true companionship or friendship), in this chapter we follow definition **4a** from the Oxford English Dictionary as a standard reference source in the English language:

> An intense feeling of romantic attachment based on an attraction felt by one person for another; intense liking and concern for another person, typically combined with sexual passion.

It will be clear from this definition immediately that only humans dedicate themselves to love. Following Perel (2007, 217), "[a]nimals have sex; eroticism is exclusively human". But then, at other moments, people seem to agree with Diamond's dog, when they appear to rely on an instinctual view of sexuality, as confirmed by Schnarch (1991):

> The notion that sex should not involve work continues to claim its own casualties. It coincides with common views of sex as an "automatic" function. (...) One such belief is the idealized, romantic view of sex (171).

42.2 Popularity of Reading About Love: Some Numbers

Human dedication to love may already be strange in itself, but there is more to it: this bizarre love life of people gets documented in zillions of stories, both written and oral. Also in paintings and sculpture, in movies, soaps and television series—but in the first place in literature. A few figures may be in place here. Regular "literary" publishing houses turn out an ever-growing mass of fiction. Matthew Wilkens

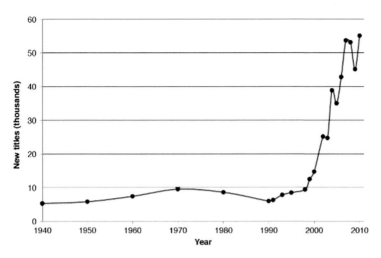

Graph 42.1 Number of new fiction titles published annually in the United States between 1940 and 2010

(2011) of the University of Notre Dame is one of the few scholars who keeps track of this, summarized in the graph above (Graph 42.1). As can be seen from the graph, the development is neither a gradual nor a slow one, but has all the characteristics of an exponential curve, starting around 1990, but accelerating increasingly since the year 2000: between 1990 and 2010 the production of novels multiplied almost tenfold. In 2010, 50,000 new novels appeared in the US alone. No later data are available, but we should not assume that the situation has changed dramatically—even with the advancement of digital reading. Wilkens (2011) suspects that for worldwide figures in the English language the number has to be multiplied by two. Hence some 100,000 new literary works appear annually in the English language. We believe that this is a very conservative estimate. We think so because in the relatively small language area of Dutch (roughly 25 million speakers) there are, as indicated by *Cultuurindex Nederland* (2017), approximately 35,000 new literary titles published every year.

Unfortunately, there is no statistics available on how many of these works deal with the theme of love. Our personal experience as readers is that it will be a fair part of the total number. By the most modest estimate, we are dealing with some 30,000 new literary novels about love *a year* in the English language—with established literary publishing houses. Fortunately for our research, however, we do have figures for novels about love in the more popular genres. Romance is no doubt the largest group in this category. The numbers are staggering. In 2004, 2,285 titles were published in this genre in the US alone (Romance Writers of America, 2008). The sales are equally daunting: in the US romantic fiction generated $1.37 billion in 2008, with more than 7,000 novels published, which equals 13.5% of the book market, with some 75 million readers. Of the entire US population, a quarter read one romance novel or more in 2008 (Ménard & Cabrera, 2011). The stereotype that this is an exclusively female readership is not wholly correct: 16% of men actually are romance readers (*idem*).

On the international market, a Toronto-based company Harlequin Enterprises Limited is the leading publisher of romance novels series and women's fiction, selling more than four books every second (Harlequin Enterprises Limited, 2019)! Most novels are translations from English, but often with alterations to fit the local taste and historical circumstances. Be that as it may, the numbers are quite persuasive: reading about love is not just popular. It is rampant.

Then there are not merely the numbers of titles, but also the numbers of copies being sold. Of the three erotic romance novels by E.L. James *Fifty Shades of Grey* (2011–2017), for instance, as many as 125 million copies were sold worldwide in just a few years. We will refrain from further statistics here, as we believe the numbers speak for themselves. Of all themes in fiction publications, love seems to be one of the most attractive. But why? We will offer some of our considerations in the following section.

42.3 Unfulfillment

One of the deep reasons for our hunger for love stories may be unflattering for our own love relationships. This is what David Schnarch (1991), one of the leading sexologists in the world, observes about the fundamental shortcomings of most love relationships, which are experienced as unfulfilling—or "convenient" rather than profound. Love fiction may cater for this feeling of insufficiency. Schnarch (1991) explains this lack of fulfilment in the following words:

> Not wanting to want sometimes surfaces as an attempt at maintenance of ego boundaries; inhibited sexual desire can be created (and maintained) when wanting becomes integrated into either partner's difficulty accepting emotional boundaries. Some individuals would rather be frustrated with a tolerable level of deprivation than cope with the vulnerability of valuing and the hunger of longing (273).

His conclusion, based on an extensive review of the literature, and his experience as a therapist with hundreds of couples (who are actually the courageous ones, who are prepared to invest energy in developing their relationship to a deeper level) is this: "Human sexuality *can* be beautiful and wonderful but this is the exception rather than the rule" (59).[1]

Many people in surveys declare that they are satisfied with their relationship. Satisfied we may be, yes, content, yes, but deep in our hearts we may venture that we are very far from reaching a complete fulfilment of what a relationship could be. But because of the challenge awaiting us and the fear that such a deep commitment

---

[1] With full awareness of the fact that love and sexuality are different though interrelated concepts, we, due to the limitations of the volume of this chapter, will further on treat them as two facets of one whole.

involves, we renounce this search, and allow ourselves to be content with a *utilitarian* relationship. So let us not deceive ourselves by taking the current ubiquity picture of "happy" couples for granted.

This constellation may explain the enormous (commercial) success of popular romance—and the staggering number of love stories being voraciously devoured by millions. Harlequin Enterprises, which we mentioned above, has an annual revenue of half a billion dollars. This search for intimate experiences which are missed (for a variety of reasons) may as well explain the enormous success of *Fifty Shades of Grey* published by Vintage Books in 2011–2017.

Reading love stories in this sense creates a *compensatory* dimension to life. This could be called escapism, as some scholars have done—Nell (1988) sees this as one of the possible functions of literature. The question should be, however, why readers *need* this escapism in the realm of love. Again Schnarch (1991) provides an intriguing answer:

> There are too few individuals capable of intense eroticism and intimacy to affect social conventions in a meaningful way; conventional cultural norms support utilitarian levels of sexual intensity (60).

When love becomes utilitarian, the longing for intense intimacy will from time to time override the social conventions, and romance literature then provides an escape valve: "When the goal is to be seen as you want, but not known as you are, marriage can never compete with part-time romance" (371).

But do people really read love stories out of unfulfillment? We do not know. Despite an extensive body of research on reading in a cultural aspect (see, for example, Hasebe-Ludt, Chambers, & Leggo, 2009; Zhou, Paul, & Sherman, 2018), they provide no answers to the questions we have put earlier in this chapter, as the issues are themselves not culture-specific, but universal. There is hardly any research on this topic, and what ideas we have ventilated above rest on our intuitions and on anecdotal observations, not on systematic investigation. That there is a need for such research, may by now be obvious.

42.4 A Female Existential Dilemma: In the Real World and in Literature

In a pathbreaking research by Johnston, Hagel, Franklin, Fink, and Grammer (2001)[2] two (manipulated) pictures of a male face are presented. One (a) is a very virile face, with square head, sharp stubbled chin and pronounced cheekbones. The other (b) is the same face, but now manipulated to a more boyish, even a little effeminate contour, exactly the opposite of all the characteristics of face (a). Female

---

[2]For the sake of clarity, the present chapter simplifies the much more complex experimental design. For further details, see Johnston et al. (2001). Recently, the insights of this study have been corroborated by Urszula M. Marcinkoiwska et al. (2019) in the prestigious journal *Nature*.

readers are then requested to choose one of both faces in terms of what they find most attractive in the face of the male *as a lover*.

There is, of course, no room for comparison of different reactions of our female readers in a written chapter in this book. But we can tell them that—unbeknownst to them—their preference for one of the faces will depend on their menstrual cycle. To summarize the results of the study: (on average) female readers will prefer face (b) for most of their cycle, but will have a pronounced preference for face (a) if they are in the time window of their cycle with the highest conception risk (defined as 9 days prior to ovulation). Hence preference for male faces by females is driven by the hormonal cycle. This is perhaps not so strange, as hormones doubtlessly play a role in sexual attraction. More important for our considerations here is that the preferences reveal a fundamental dilemma in females' partner choice. Why would females prefer face (a) over (b) at a time when they are most likely to conceive in intercourse? The standard theory here is that "the masculinity of the face is a reliable physical marker of immunocompetence. (...) The end result is that somewhat masculinized faces signal heritable fitness—a healthy immune system that can be passed down to children. In essence, women's preference for 'good genes' that are sometimes better secured from affair partners than from regular mates. Women judge the less masculine faces, preferred during their least fertile days of the month, as a signal of cooperativeness, honesty, and good parenting qualities" (Buss, 2003, 242). Here we have, in a nutshell, and clearly illustrated in an experiment, the dilemma women face in love: in order to secure the careful upbringing of their children, they need a reliable and devoted partner, who is trustworthy, helpful, supportive and child-oriented. Hence their overall preference for "average" male faces (and personalities). On the other hand, they wish their children to be healthy, with a strong immune system, so that their chances of survival are high, the highest possible. And extreme male faces betray such good genes.

This picture of female attraction is further corroborated in the research by Johnston et al. (2001) by tracing females' emotional reaction to the two faces in terms of seeing them as those of a friend or enemy (and lover). And, clearly, face (a) elicits by far the strongest associations with "enemy", and the (b) face scores highest on "friend".

The interesting aspect of this dilemma for our present essay is that this hard choice (whether to go for a "good" though average man or a really virile male type) is amply reflected in literary works. Think, for instance, of the extremely popular—the movie perhaps more than the novel—*The Bridges of Madison County*. Or Alice Munro's story "What is Remembered", Tolstoy's *Anna Karenina*, or the then enormously popular (novels and movies) of *Captain Blood* by Rafael Sabatini. In the popular genres, the prototype is the "gypsy" passing through the village or the small provincial town. To name only a few of the dozens of titles: *Gypsy Lover* by Connie Mason, *Gypsy Lord* by Kat Martin, *The Heart of a Gypsy* by Robera Kagan, *Mine till Midnight* by Lisa Kleypas, and so forth. The site Goodreads even has a special list with titles on this topic: https://www.goodreads.com/list/show/17755. Gypsies_In_Romance. But THE prototypical example of the dilemma is found in the notorious novel *Lady Chatterley's Lover* (1928). When D.H. Lawrence highlighted this female dilemma—with its concomitant sexual indulgences—society rose up in fury. The fact that we are no longer upset by such stories or scenes is a direct consequence of the power of literature: its contribution to the liberation of female sexuality that has been first imagined and made acceptable to society as a whole by authors such as Lawrence, Flaubert, Tolstoy and Fontane.

This "power" of literature works, however, silently, surreptitiously, as if it were mere entertainment. This force of literature in society uses a ruse, Hegel's *Cunning of Reason* (die List der Vernunft): by acting humbly and outside the great important matters on the world stage and in plain everyday life, and by pretending that in fact it does not have much to do with all that, literature influences world history. In Hegel's *Vorlesungenüber die Philosophie der Geschichte* (1837), Reason moves in the background and lets the human passions work for her own cause and, in comparison with the great (and violent) events on the world stage, takes on the form of a somewhat insignificant and unworldly servant: "This may be called the *cunning of reason*—that it sets the passions to work for itself, while that which develops its existence through such impulsion pays the penalty, and suffers loss"[3] (Hegel, 2008, 129). And scholars who negate this role of literature in world history are simply one of the cogwheels in the mechanisms that the Cunning of Reason employs.

If the above holds, then female readers should be especially attracted to this dilemma of choice for two types of partners. The sales of such subgenres of love stories seem to corroborate this. But what kind of satisfaction do female readers derive from that reading? And what effects do such readings create? We do not know—because there is no research investigating such questions.

42.5 A Universal Love Predicament

The preceding section outlined a fundamental dilemma facing females in the *choice* of a love partner. Now suppose a choice has been made, and a new couple is formed, to the satisfaction of both partners. Maybe this satisfaction may last some time. But after the turbulent first weeks and months, in which desire dictates all thoughts, emotions and actions, couples face a problem: habituation. There is, indeed, a — this time universal — dilemma facing all lovers. But we won't know as outsiders, because no one tells you that desire is waning. Did you ever hear a young couple complain that after their initial infatuation, life became much less pleasant than they had anticipated? Not very likely. But descriptions of this process exist, if we resort . . . yes, to literature! Let us look at one such revelation, in Leo Tolstoy's *Kreutzer Sonata*:

---

[3]"Das ist die List der Vernunft zu nennen, dass sie die Leidenschaften für sich wirken lässt, wobei das, durch was sie sich in Existenz setzt, einbüsst und Schaden leidet" (Hegel, 1980/1823, 78).

Love was exhausted with the satisfaction of sensuality. We stood face to face in our true light, like two egoists trying to procure the greatest possible enjoyment, like two individuals trying to mutually exploit each other.

So what I called our quarrel was our actual situation as it appeared after the satisfaction of sensual desire. I did not realize that this cold hostility was our normal state, and that this first quarrel would soon be drowned under a new flood of the intensest sensuality. I thought that we had disputed with each other, and had become reconciled, and that it would not happen again. But in this same honeymoon there came a period of satiety, in which we ceased to be necessary to each other, and a new quarrel broke out (Tolstoy, 1889/2012, 41).

Presumably all couples in long-term relationships, regardless of their culture, will recognize this creeping decline in mutual attraction as "partners' satisfaction tends to be high around the time of the wedding, after which it begins a slow but steady decline" (Hirschberger, Srivastava, Marsh, Cowan, & Cowan, 2009). The fact is that such processes are a universal and inevitable challenge for all long-lasting relationships. It involves yet another dilemma for partners, one that no couple can escape. There are, however, some escape routes.

42.5.1 Escape Through Death

One possibility to avoid the dilemma is death. And the examples from literature are legion: Romeo and Juliet, Troilus and Cressida, Tristan and Isolde, Hugo's *The Hunchback of Notre Dame*, Brontë's *Wuthering Heights*, Goethe's *The Sorrows of Young Werther* and quite a few others.

De Rougemont (1983) has shown how love in western literature is defined by obstacles that often are impossible to overcome, thus leading to the downfall of the lovers: the story-teller "betrays a hankering after love for its own sake, which implies a secret quest of the obstruction that shall foster love. But this quest is only the disguise of a love for obstruction *per se*. Now it turns out that the ultimate obstacle is death, and at the close of the tale death is revealed as having been the real end, what passion has yearned after from the beginning" (54).

The danger of the relationship ending in death may easily spill over into didactic and moralising literature. The pendant of *Romeo and Juliet* exhibiting such moral traffic rules for young couples is Arthur Brooke's *The Tragicall Historye of Romeus and Juliet*, which antedates Shakespeare's work with some 30 years, and which Shakespeare may well have known while preparing his own production. The moral and poetic differences between both works are glaringly exposed in van Peer (2008). There is even a whole genre dedicated to moralizing through literature, i.e., the *exemplum*, but one may also think of the parables in the gospels. As the example shows, the use of literature to convey established, usually middle-class or religious, values is more or less a matter of the past. Novels of the type *East Lynne* (1861) by Ellen Wood, warning against infidelity, have little appeal for present-day audiences. A rearguard area where moralistic ideas may still be part of story plots is children's literature, but then such stories are rarely about erotic love.

42.5.2 Escape Through Divorce

Or, nowadays, one may escape the dilemma by ending the relationship in divorce. And numbers should not betray us: the divorce rates in Western countries are pretty high: according to the best research, almost half of first marriages in the US end in divorce; see Bramlett and Mosher (2002).

But divorce is a relatively new phenomenon in history. Prior to the nineteenth century, few literary works deal with it. Nowadays echoes of this monumental change in relationships are all over the place in popular literature. We would like to draw attention, however, to the role literature has played in forging this historical change. One of the first to acknowledge the monumental importance of choice in marriage was the poet of *Paradise Lost*. In four different pamphlets, written between 1643 and 1645, Milton argues for the necessity of choosing a partner—but choice inevitably involves the possibility of privately refusing the choice—and that is where divorce comes in. We may not fully appreciate nowadays the revolutionary nature of this proposal, but the religious authorities tried to ban the pamphlets with all their might, and with all the instruments of power that they had at their disposal. Nevertheless, the net result of the polemics involved was that divorce was allowed in specific conditions. It will be clear that Milton owed this success because of his fame as a poet. We also find reminiscences of his argument in his description of the relationship between Adam and Eve in his *Paradise Lost*.

The change in law did mitigate the suffering of incompatible couples in reality, but divorce still remained something not to be spoken of. In fact, it was again in literature that the taboo was broken. Notably the idea that marriage can be terminated by free will of one of the partners is raised in Nathaniel Hawthorne's *The Scarlet Letter* (1850). Its protagonist, Hester Prynne, is chastised by the community for bearing a child during a prolonged absence of her husband, and for refusing to reveal the father's identity. She remains adamant and encourages her lover to elope with her to Europe, where they can live outside the laws they are subject to in America. Her lover can bring himself neither to execute this plan nor to publicly admit his relation to her, until he dies in her arms years later as a broken man. Thereupon Hester leaves the United States for Europe with her daughter, where she starts a new life, free from the social stigma she endured at home. Like Milton, Hawthorne takes the (for his time) radical position that any rigidity on the inseparability of marriage runs counter to human happiness. It was not long after Hawthorne that divorce became a fruitful topic in American literature, as witnessed by the novels by Henry James, such as *The Portrait of a Lady* (1881) and *What Maisie Knew* (1897).

42.5.3 Escape Through Extramarital Affair(s)

While escape from this dilemma by death is no doubt the rarest, and divorce is nowadays the most common, there is another escape road, one that is known to all:

that of extramarital affairs. Monogamy, defined as sexual and emotional exclusivity to one romantic partner, "is the standard adopted by the majority of those in committed romantic relationships in Western societies. It is a relationship form that is viewed as optimal and conferred with many social, financial, and legal benefits" (Lee & O'Sullivan, 2019, 1735). But transgression of this standard is profuse. Almost half of college-aged individuals (46.8%) reported lifetime infidelity (Thompson & O'Sullivan, 2016), and almost one in five individuals (23% of men and 19% of women) reported sexual cheating in their current romantic relationships (Mark, Janssen, & Milhausen, 2011). According to Barker (2011), the rate of lifetime infidelity for men over 60 increased from 20% in 1991 to 28% in 2006. The same tendency holds for women over 60 as the statistics went up from 5% in 1991 to 15% in 2006.

Given these figures, it will not come as a surprise that extramarital affairs are well represented in literature. As a matter of fact such works of fiction are legion. *Anna Karenina* and *Madame Bovary* come to mind immediately, as do others, notably[4]

- *Lady Chatterley's Lover* (1928) by D.H. Lawrence;
- *The Awakening* (1899) by K. Chopin;
- *Adultery* (2012) by P. Coelho;
- *The Great Gatsby* (1925) by F.S. Fitzgerald;
- *The Painted Veil* (1925) and *Theatre* (1937) by W.S. Maugham;
- *Lucy Crown* (1956) by I. Shaw;
- *The Red and the Black* (1830) by Stendhal;
- *The Little Lady of the Big House* (1915) by J. London;
- *And Quiet Flows the Don* (1925–1940) by M. Sholokhov (1965 Nobel prize winner);
- "The Lady with the Dog" (1899) by A. Chekhov;
- *The Forsyte Saga* (1922) by J. Galsworthy.

And many, many others may be added.

> To judge by literature, adultery would seem to be one of the most remarkable of occupations in both Europe and America. Few are the novels that fail to allude to it; and the vogue of the others, how we make allowances for these, the very passion with which we sometimes denounce them—all that shows well enough what couples dream about in the grip of a rule that has turned marriage into a duty and convenience (de Rougemont, 1983, 16).

42.5.4 The Cauldron

But if these escape routes are not taken, the couple is in a cauldron of a terrible strain, trying to reconcile the conflicting prescriptions dictated by the universal predicament

---

[4]We hope it is clear to our readers that all titles referred to are not necessarily our favourites, nor are they in any sense reading "recommendations"—they are merely examples of particular types of love stories. We are engaged in a descriptive effort here, that should in no way be seen as normative.

of long-term relations. The outcome is often decided in accordance with societal norms, and these are imposed by one of the imperatives: the one representing security, associated in most cultures with having a stable partner next to you. If the couple does not take any escape road, only two possibilities are left, and the choice is often easy for many couples. The choice is between *indifference* and going through the *cauldron*. By the former we do not mean indifference toward the partner. In fact, quite the contrary is the case if this path is taken. We are then in a predicament in which everything is geared toward stability, security, certainty, durability and so forth. The indifference is to a deeper level of emotion, and it entails a rejection of desire. The result is usually also immobility: the couple does no longer evolve, but rests assured in self-contained gratification. Nothing new, let alone spectacular, is expected any more. These are the stable partnerships of which our society is largely composed.

It is clear why this road of "indifference" is so often and so easily taken: the alternative is rather frightening—which is why we have chosen the metaphor of the "cauldron": living through the demands of family care and at the same time keeping the mutual attraction awake—and live—is neither easy nor mollifying. It is disturbing instead—something we already hinted at in Sect. 42.3 of this chapter.

No one has described the fundamental trial so succinctly and so eloquently as Esther Perel in her 2019 TED talk, which we would like to quote here:

> the reconciliation of two fundamental human needs: on the one hand, our need for security, for predictability, for safety, for dependability, for reliability, for permanence—all these anchoring, grounding experiences in our lives that we call "home". But we also have an equally strong need, men and women, for adventure, for novelty, for mystery, for risk, for adventure, for danger, for the unknown, for the unexpected, for surprise — for journey, for travel. So reconciling our need for security and our need for adventure into one relationship — or what we today like to call a "passionate marriage" used to be a contradiction in terms. Marriage was an economic institution. (...)
>
> But now we want our partner to still give us all these things, but in addition I want you to be my best friend, and my trusted confidante, and my passionate lover to boot. And we live twice as long (https://www.youtube.com/watch?v=sa0RUmGTCYY, accessed June 5, 2020).

The cauldron then is the place where these two forces collide. If the outcome is not indifference (the solution previously outlined), then the partners face a continuous renewal of their desire. This is a rather frightening (and arduous) prospect, which is why most couples say "No thanks" to it. Not surprisingly, therefore, is the fact that we find little about the cauldron in literature. Maybe *Middlemarch* might qualify, or *Pride and Prejudice*, or—doubtlessly a courageous endeavour—A. de Botton's *The Course of Love* (2017). But in general love literature is more about the spectacular things, like death, or adultery. The day-to-day trouble of keeping the relationship passionate is awesome. As Schnarch (1997, 404) remarks: "[l]oving is not for the weak, nor for those who have to be carefully kept, nor for the faint of heart. That's why there is so little of it in the world. Love requires being steadfast through many difficulties." Or: "for possession is often the death of love. (...) I condemn love without enjoyment as severely as I do enjoyment without love. I leave you to draw the inference" (Casanova, 2006, 756).

Perhaps the most important reason why people avoid intensely pleasurable sex is also the least mentioned: *it hurts* (Schnarch, 1991, 467).

42.6 The Magic of Love

The previous sections have outlined a number of aims and ways to read about love. In this section we will deal with one of the rarest, but also one of the most profound modes of treating love in literature: living through the literature of love as magic. What do we mean by this? A good example is provided by Lisa Appignanesi (2011). She begins her book *All about Love* with a personal confession—when she first became aware of the word "love". She must have been about 7 years old, and the awareness came through a traditional French song, "A la claire fontaine" ("by the clear fountain"). It tells the story of unfulfilled love: a lover finds the water of a spring so clear that he bathes in it. Then follows the refrain:

Il y a longtemps que je t'aime
Jamais je ne t'oublierai.

(I've loved you for so long,
I will never forget you.)

Áppignanesi (2011) writes that the song haunted her during childhood, and released emotions in her of sufficient weight to stay, even while its meaning remained opaque, though realizing that the word "love" harboured a multiplicity of profound significance. She then cites a number of other memories that meant an encounter with love: *Á la Recherche du Temps Perdu*, *Gone with the Wind*, *Romeo and Juliet*, *West Side Story*, and so forth, to make the point that our image of love is intimately linked to individual life stories.

Similarly, the partner of one of us used to sing a ditty for her father:

Alle dagen komt ze vragen of dat ik haar gaarne zie.
  (All days she comes asking me whether I love her.)

And, like Appignanesi (2011), also not grasping the scope of the meaning contained in the words, she nevertheless revelled in singing it to her father. Maybe many readers of this chapter cherish such memories, or (parts of) texts that are intimately linked to love. How many, we do not know—there is no research. What *kind* of scraps of songs, poems, movie dialogues are remembered, we do not know either—there is no research. We are equally ignorant of the influence of such memories on people's actual love life—there is no research.

We do know that this form of confrontation with love started by the Provençal "troubadours" in the eleventh to twelfth century, notably by William IX of Aquitaine, Jaufré Rudel, Bernard de Ventadour, Arnaud Daniel, Bertrand de Born, with poems celebrating *Amor de lonh* ("love at a distance"). Presumably the apex of this kind of amorous involvement is Dante's *Vita Nova* (1294). The lovers only exchanged looks three times, and before they were even in their teens, but this was the beginning of a life-long devotion to the beloved, culminating in the ultimate union in the third volume of the *Divine Comedy*. The *Canzoniere* by Petrarcha (1374) is another example, but the examples quickly multiply when one starts thinking of it—some fictional, like *Tristan and Isolde*, some real, like the love of Abelard and Héloïse. The stories need not even be about sexual love; much of the poetry by the mystics is of the same orientation, that of Hildegard von Bingen (1098–1179), Meister Eckhart (1260–1328), Ruusbroec (1293–1381), San Juan de la Cruz (1542–1591), and many others. The longing is now for a union with the Deity, but framed in erotic terms, not uncommonly borrowed from the Provençal troubadours, as is the case with the Flemish mystic Hadewijch (thirteenth century).

Such are the narratives about love that, as we hope to have demonstrated in previous sections of this chapter, permeate literary history. But what about the readers of such stories? Are they also ready to pick up the magic of love? The short answer to the question is: yes, they are. Casanova regularly, in his *L'histoire de ma vie*, quotes from *Orlando Furioso*, mainly from passages to do with erotic love. He knew the poem by heart—but one should realize that it is a rather long poem: it spans almost 40,000 verse lines! Why would anyone go to the trouble of memorizing such a horrendously long text? The answer shimmers through when one reads his comments: it is because he is in love with the poem—basically he is *in love with love*. It is the magic of the text that attracts him, and Casanova, one of the key figures in the art of love, is enchanted with the magic of love, sung to its apex in poetry. What is the ultimate attraction of this fascination? Maybe it is that "phantasies—sexual and other—also have nearly magical powers to heal and renew" (Perel, 2007, 155).

The word "magic" in the title of this section has therefore to be taken seriously. We indeed propose that this kind of reading literature is akin to magical practice: the words of the magic charm have to be pronounced *ad verbatim*, or the spell will not work.[5] It is a behaviour that is already present early in life: witness small children's vehement protests when an adult deviates from the wording of a well-known story or fairy-tale: to the child, the "magic" of the tale is destroyed when the formula is not pronounced correctly. Parents often wonder why this is so important for the children—we believe this is the reason: the self-soothing through the story can only take place if the magical formula is adhered to literally.

---

[5]As a literary motif it is also well known through Goethe's *Der Zauberlehrling*, popularized first through Paul Dukas' symphonic poem "The Sorcerer's Apprentice" and later through Walt Disney's "Fantasia".

42.7 Conclusions and Recommendations for the Theory and Practice: Research into Love Reading

All previous sections of this chapter have ended with the admission that we hardly know why people read about love—because of the lack of research. Nor are we informed about the effects of reading about love, again because of the lack of serious research. In the face of our ignorance we should ask ourselves in earnest whether we should not leave our armchairs (or libraries, for that matter) and start investigating the place that literature on love has in the lives of people. We are still massively unaware of what literature *does* to readers: why they read (about love in the first place), what emotions are evoked by such kinds of literary pieces, or how such poems, stories, or theatre plays influence people's lives. In order to find answers to such questions one will have to look at *real* readers "in the flesh", and about the only way to address such issues is through empirical research, following the established standards of using the methodology in the Humanities, literary studies in particular (van Peer, Hakemulder, & Zyngier, 2012). This leads us to reflect on the state of art in the area and the ways to improve it in this final section that follows.

Until recently, most of what went on under the name of "research" in literary studies was either anecdotal or speculative (with the exception of some thorough historical research). Thus we have an enormous mass of subjective opinions, views and interpretations of literature mostly by professional academics, but we have hardly any empirical data on how real readers outside the academy deal with literary texts. By "empirical" we mean that data are collected independently as a means of openly verifying the correctness of claims about literary experiences in the reading act. Fortunately there is now an international society that professionally caters for such research: the International Society for the Empirical Study of Literature[6] (see the website: https://sites.google.com/igelassoc.org/igel2018/home), which also publishes the high quality international journal *Scientific Study of Literature* with John Benjamins (see: https://benjamins.com/catalog/ssol).

When it comes to such empirical research there are basically two types of investigation: qualitative and quantitative studies. To start with *qualitative* studies, they are generally used to *explore* issues about which not much is known, usually done through observations that may lead to the formulation of more accurate hypotheses, which are then often checked in *quantitative* research, which aims at the establishment of valid and reliable knowledge about reality. Methods used in qualitative studies are mostly interviews, protocol analysis, focus groups and the like. There is some such research concerning the reading of love stories, especially with respect to romance novels. A central figure in this area is Radway (2009), who observed women reading such romance stories and tried to come to some insights into their reading habits and motivations. Unfortunately, (and this seems symptomatic for this approach) few of the gained insights are formulated as testable

---

[6]Its acronym, IGEL, is short for the society's original, German, name: **I**nternationale **G**esellschaft für **E**mpirische **L**iteraturwissenschaft.

Fig. 42.1 Theory testing model

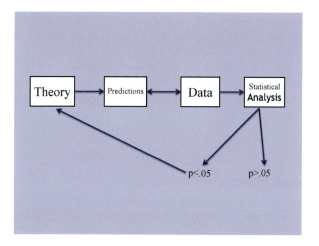

hypotheses. Why is this so important? Basically the reason is that qualitative studies are done with a limited number of participants without the data being transformed into numerical form, thus preventing any (statistical) generalization. Without such inference statistics, it is impossible to say to what extent the observations may be generalized. How crucial that is, turns out when some of the conclusions of qualitative research *are* actually more strictly examined in a quantitative investigation. And how necessary that is becomes evident from the scientific literature. Iqbal (2014), after a review of this literature, concludes that "it remains unclear whether romance novels influence readers' attitudes and beliefs or whether they preferentially attract readers with particular attitudes towards sexuality" (302).

In general, such research follows a model of testing claims by confronting them with observations, somewhat in the following form (see Fig. 42.1).

The original claims are cast in the form of predictions, which are then matched to independently collected data. These data are subjected to a statistical analysis, first of all to see whether they are in the predicted direction and whether they are convincing enough to be accepted and generalized. This is expressed in a p-value, which stands for error probability, which should, naturally, be as low as possible, in any case lower than .05 (which equals roughly 5%). The procedure and rationale for doing so is explained in detail in van Peer et al. (2012). Results in the predicted direction that have error probabilities lower than 5% (p-values lower than .05) are then taken as support for the claim(s) in question. What one has to realize in this kind of research, is that the results may contradict one's own opinions—which can be painful in a certain sense for the investigator(s). With the qualitative approach, it is much easier for the researcher to beat about the bush.

An investigation of some claims about romance novels has been carried out by Bun (2007). She extracted several hypotheses about romance reading from the existing literature and tested them to data collected. The important result from this study was that most hypotheses advanced in the qualitative studies were not confirmed in a more rigorous study. For instance, Radway's claim that women choose romance stories that support the beliefs and values they currently hold, was negated by the data: "Choice of romance novel genre was not shown to correlate to reader's [*sic*] already held beliefs" (Bun, 2007, 59).

As a conclusion, it must now dawn on us that a lot of work awaits us, work that requires another way of looking at literature (and maybe also about love) than we have hitherto been used to. We hope some of us will be ready for this change of perspective.

References

Appignanesi, L. (2011). *All about love: Anatomy of an unruly emotion*. London: Virago.
Barker, M. (2011). Monogamies and non-monogamies: A response to "The challenge of monogamy: bringing it out of the closet and into the treatment room" by Marianne Brandon. *Sexual and Relationship Therapy, 26*(3), 281–287. https://doi.org/10.1080/14681994.2011.595401
Bramlett, M.D., & Mosher, W.D. (2002). *Cohabitation, marriage, divorce, and remarriage in the United States* (Vital Health Statistics, Series 23, No. 22). Hyattsville, MD: National Center for Health Statistics.
Bun, J. (2007). *The effects of romance novel readership on relationship beliefs, romantic ideals, and relational satisfaction*. Honor Thesis, Boston College.
Buss, D. (2003). *The evolution of desire: Strategies of human mating*. New York: Basic Books.
Casanova, G. (2006). *History of my life*. New York: Alfred A Knopf. [Orig. ed. 1822, written 1789–1798].
de Botton, A. (2017). *The course of love*. London: Penguin.
de Rougemont, D. (1983). *Love in the western world*. Princeton, NJ: Princeton University Press.
Diamond, J. (2015). *Why is sex fun? The Evolution of human sexuality*. London: Weidenfeld & Nicolson.
Harlequin Enterprises Limited. (2019). *A global success story*. Accessed June 5, 2020, from https://www.harlequin.com/shop/pages/harlequin-enterprises-limited-a-global-success-story.html
Hasebe-Ludt, E., Chambers, C., & Leggo, C. D. (2009). *Life writing and literary métissage as an ethos for our times*. New York: Peter Lang.
Hegel, G.W.F. (1980). *Vorlesungen über die Philosophie der Geschichte*. Stuttgart: Reclam. [Orig. ed. 1823].
Hegel, G.W.F. (2008). In A. Singh & R. Mohapatra (Eds.), *Reading Hegel. The introductions*. Melbourne: RePress.
Hirschberger, G., Srivastava, S., Marsh, P., Cowan, C. P., & Cowan, P. A. (2009). Attachment, marital satisfaction, and divorce during the first fifteen years of parenthood. *Personal Relationships, 16*(3), 401–420. https://doi.org/10.1111/j.1475-6811.2009.01230.x
Iqbal, K. (2014). The impact of romance novels on women's sexual and reproductive health. *Journal of Family Planning and Reproductive Health Care, 40*, 300–302. https://doi.org/10.1136/jfprhc-2014-100995
Johnston, V. S., Hagel, R., Franklin, M., Fink, B., & Grammer, K. (2001). Male facial attractiveness: evidence for hormone-mediated adaptive design. *Evolution and Human Behavior, 22*(4), 251–267. https://doi.org/10.1016/S1090-5138(01)00066-6
Lee, B. H., & O'Sullivan, L. F. (2019). Walk the line: How successful are efforts to maintain monogamy in intimate relationships? *Archives of Sexual Behavior, 48*(6), 1735–1748. https://doi.org/10.1007/s10508-018-1376-3

Marcinkoiwska, U. M., et al. (2019). Women's preferences for men's facial masculinity are strongest under favorable ecological conditions. *Nature Scientific Reports, 9*, 3387.

Mark, K. P., Janssen, E., & Milhausen, R. R. (2011). Infidelity in heterosexual couples: Demographic, interpersonal, and personality-related predictors of extradyadic sex. *Archives of Sexual Behavior, 40*, 971–982. https://doi.org/10.1007/s10508-011-9771-z

Ménard, D. A., & Cabrera, C. (2011). Whatever the approach, tab B still fits into slot A: Twenty years of sex scripts in romance novels. *Sexuality and Culture, 15*(3), 240–255.

Nell, V. (1988). *Lost in a book. The psychology of reading for pleasure*. Yale, CT: Yale University Press.

Perel, E. (2007). *Mating in captivity. Unlocking erotic intelligence*. New York: Harper.

Radway, J. A. (2009). *Reading the romance: Women, patriarchy and popular literature*. Chapel Hill: University of North Carolina Press.

Romance Writers of America. (2008). *Romance literature statistics: Readership statistics*.

Schnarch, D. M. (1991). *Constructing the sexual crucible. An integration of sexual and marital therapy*. New York: Norton.

Schnarch, D. M. (1997). *Passionate marriage. Keeping love and intimacy alive in committed relationships*. New York: Holt and Company.

Thompson, A. E., & O'Sullivan, L. F. (2016). I can but you can't: Inconsistencies in judgments of and experiences with infidelity. *Journal of Relationships Research, 7*, 1–13. https://doi.org/10.1017/jrr.2016.1

Tolstoy, L. (1889/2012). *The Kreutzer sonata: And other stories*. Auckland: The Floating Press.

van Peer, W. (2008). Canon formation: Ideology or aesthetic quality? In W. van Peer (Ed.), *The quality of literature. Linguistic studies in literary evaluation* (pp. 17–29). Amsterdam: John Benjamins. https://doi.org/10.1075/lal.4.03pee

van Peer, W., Hakemulder, F., & Zyngier, S. (2012). *Scientific methods for the Humanities*. Amsterdam: John Benjamins.

Wilkens, M. (2011). Contemporary fiction by the numbers. *Post45. Contemporaries*. Accessed June 5, 2020, from http://post45.research.yale.edu/2011/03/contemporary-fiction-by-the-numbers

Zhou, Y., Paul, B., & Sherman, R. (2018). Still a hetero-gendered world: A content analysis of gender stereotypes and romantic ideals in Chinese boy love stories. *Sex Roles, 78*(1–2), 107–118. https://doi.org/10.1007/s11199-017-0762-y

Willie van Peer is Professor of Intercultural Hermeneutics at Ludwig Maximilian University, Germany. He is the author of several books and many articles on poetics and the epistemological foundations of literary studies, vice-president of the International Association of Empirical Aesthetics (1996–1998), chair of the international Poetics and Linguistics Association (PALA, 2000–2003), president of the International Society for Empirical Study of Literature (IGEL, 2004–2006), co-founder of the international REDES project (2001–2009), co-editor of the book series *Linguistic Approaches to Literature* (LAL, John Benjamins, 2000–2010), founding editor of the *Scientific Study of Literature* journal series (SSOL, John Benjamins). Willie van Peer has been Visiting Scholar in the Departments of Comparative Literature at Stanford and at Princeton University, and in the Department of (Cognitive) Psychology at the University of Memphis. He is also a Fellow of Clare Hall of Cambridge University.

Anna Chesnokova is Professor at the English Philology (Kyiv National Linguistic University, 1991) and a PhD in Comparative Literary Studies (Taras Shevchenko Kyiv National University, 1999). She is Professor at the English Philology and Translation Department of Borys Grinchenko Kyiv University, Ukraine. She has published on Stylistics and Empirical Studies of Literature. Her publications include *Acting & Connecting. Cultural Approaches to Language and Literature* (co-edited with S. Zyngier and V. Viana, LIT Verlag, 2007), *Directions in Empirical Literary Studies* (co-edited with S. Zyngier, M. Bortolussi, and J. Auracher, John Benjamins, 2008), chapters for *The International Reception of Emily Dickinson* (Continuum Press, 2009), *Cases on Distance Delivery and Learning Outcomes: Emerging Trends and Programs* (with V. Viana, S. Zyngier and W. van Peer, IGI Global, 2009), *Teaching Stylistics* (with W. van Peer and S. Zyngier, Palgrave Macmillan, 2011) and *Scientific Approaches to Literature in Learning Environments* (John Benjamins, 2016).

Chapter 43
"There Are as Many Kinds of Love as There Are Hearts": Age-Gap Relationships in Literature and Cultural Attitudes

Anna Chesnokova and Willie van Peer

Abstract Love comes in many forms, as we all know and as the quote from *Anna Karenina* by Tolstoy holds. Some forms are more frequent than others. As a consequence, less frequent forms may be either tolerated or dismissed as deviant, and therefore socially sanctioned. And different cultures may deal with such forms very differently. In this chapter we look at one form that is less frequent, namely age-gap relations: love relations between either an older man and a considerably younger woman, or vice versa: an older woman and a considerably younger man.

Since it may be expected that nations differ in their attitudes toward such relationships, we investigated two that are (geographically and culturally) wide apart: Brazil and Ukraine.

We offer some examples of empirical methods (Empirical methods aim at knowledge that comes from observation and experience, i.e., evidence gathered through the senses that can be analyzed independently by anyone wishing to re-analyze the data gathered.) with which to investigate short time and longitudinal effects of confronting fictional love stories.

We report a case study, in which we checked how social views on intimate relationships involving a substantial age difference between partners were influenced by reading literary passages from canonical literature, focusing on age-gap relationships. The results cast light on the views on age-gap relations in these respective cultures and thereby highlight their national mentality. Additionally, the findings lend support to the idea that reading literature influences human attitudes.

Keywords Love · Age-gap relationships · Empirical research · Cultural attitudes · Literary reading · Effects of reading on perceptions of love

---

A. Chesnokova (✉)
Department of English Philology and Translation, Borys Grinchenko Kyiv University, Kiev, Ukraine
e-mail: chesnokova2510@gmail.com

W. van Peer
Faculty of Languages and Literatures, Ludwig Maximilian University, Munich, Germany
e-mail: w.vanpeer@gmail.com

43.1 Introduction: Age-Gap Relationships in Real and Fictional Worlds

We will start this chapter with a couple of question to you as a reader.[1] In your circle of friends there are no doubt several (heterosexual) couples, people having a steady relationship, irrespective of whether they happen to be formally married or not. We guess that in many cases you will (more or less) know the relative ages of the partners. So here is our *first* question: how many of the couples that you know are the same age (i.e., born in the same year)?

We think we know the answer that you will give: *none*. It is quite rare for long-term relationships to have both partners of the same age. But if that is the case, then our *second* question is: how large is the age difference between the partners of the couples you know? Again, we think we know the answer: on average it is about 2–3 years. Which leads us to our *third* question: who is the elder in the partnership? And you know the answer as well as we do: it is the male partner.

Before you utter the objection that this may be just a western phenomenon: no, it is not. As far as we know, there is a worldwide pattern according to which females prefer their partners to be a bit older than themselves, and "[t]he worldwide average age difference between actual brides and grooms is three years" (Buss, 2003, 28). True, there are regional and cultural variations[2] (see also Vanderheiden's chapter in this book). For instance, in France the average age difference between partners is less than 2 years, while in Iran it is more than 5 years (*ibid, idem*). So you will find few couples in which both partners have the same age. Isn't that strange? You would expect young people forming relationships either to people of approximately the same age, or to have the difference split evenly across the sexes, so that sometimes the male is the elder, and sometimes the female. Again it is not so.

Why is that the case? Jokingly, one could cast the image of men as a bit behind mentally, so that in a partnership with a female they need a bit of a headstart, in order to be on the same intellectual level with women a couple of years younger than they are themselves. Be that as it may, there are very good evolutionary reasons why females prefer men who are a bit older. One motive pertains to income and economic resources, which rise with age, so if your husband is a bit older, a female's position will be more secure. A second explanation relates to physical prowess, which increases in men until their early 30s. Maybe in present-day urban life bodily strength may not be that important, but the mechanisms for mate choice are deeply engrained in our ancestral brains, which evolved at a time when hunting, fishing, or

---

[1]Empirical methods aim at knowledge that comes from observation and experience, i.e., evidence gathered through the senses that can be analyzed independently by anyone wishing to re-analyze the data gathered.

[2]For the sake of clarity—and for simplicity's sake—when speaking of "culture" in this chapter we mean "national culture". It is intuitively clear that there are considerable differences between Brazilian and Ukrainian, or between German and Chinese "cultures". We are less concerned here with differences between sub-cultures within one nation.

tilling the earth provided the important nutritional ingredients to keep yourself alive, and more importantly still: to keep your children alive. A third reason for the age difference has to do with the emotional balance in men, which indeed increases with age: within the United States, for instance, "men become somewhat more emotionally stable, more conscious, and more dependable as they grow older" (Buss, 2003, 28); see also McCrae and Costa Jr. (1990), Gough (1980).

At the same time, the twenty-first century has brought certain fairly counterintuitive and in a way counter-evolutionary trends, which you can see not only in Hollywood couples, but also in families of top politicians (Karantzas, 2018). Thus recent research reported by *Psychology Today* (Patrick, 2019) has found that

> despite potential stereotyping and stigma, age-gap relationships between younger men and older women continue to survive, and thrive,

and women in such relationships are more satisfied and more committed compared to younger women or to similarly aged partners.

Now let us turn from real world to that of literature—be it the life of writers themselves, or the characters they depict in their works. But before doing so, let us spell out what we understand by "love". In what follows we shall consider love, following Fisher (1995) and Jankowiak (see his chapters in this book) and Fisher (Jankowiak & Fischer, 1992), as an emotion of mutual attraction and attachment, as "primary, panhuman emotions much like fear, anger, joy, sadness, and surprise" (Fisher, 1995, 24).

Literary authors living in happy long-lasting (i.e., decades-long) relationships in which they, the males, were considerably older, are easy to find. Henry Miller and Anaïs Nin (age difference of 12 years), Mark Twain and Olivia Langdon (a difference of 10 years), or Fyodor Dostoevsky and Anna Snitkina (25 years of difference) are the names that occur to us first. Similarly, Edgar Poe was twice as old as his wife, Virginia—who was just 13 at the time of their marriage.

The opposite pattern can be found too. The towering figure of Samuel Johnson comes to mind: at the age of 25, he married Elizabeth Porter, then 21 years older than him. She is said to have told her daughter that he was "the most sensible man [she] ever met", and he, calling her tenderly "Tetty" or "Tetsy", continued to recall her affectionately after her death at the age of 63. Elizabeth's gravestone has the inscription in Latin: *Formosae, cultae, ingeniosae, piae* (meaning: *dedicated to the beautiful, elegant, talented, dutiful*).

More examples can be given. Balzac was only 26 when Madame de Bernay took him as her lover when she was 49, after she had borne nine children. In the same way, Agatha Christie married her second husband, Sir Max Mallowan, when she was 40 while he was just 26, and their marriage lasted for 45 years till the author's death.

The relationship when a woman is older seems not to be always smooth for literary authors. Just think of George Sand's transient affairs with Jules Sandeau, Alfred de Musset, or Frederic Chopin (all from 6 to 7 years her junior). Shakespeare may also come to one's mind: Anne Hathaway was 8 years his senior when they married in 1582. We do not know for sure, but there is little, indeed very little, in the works of Shakespeare, showing affection for his wife. None of the 154 sonnets even obliquely refers to her, and his testament only leaves her his second-best bed.

With inspiration gained from the real world, age-gap couples when the male partner is older are often enough depicted in literature, and the relationships, just like in life, can work well—or not. The happy examples range from Charlotte Brontë's and Jane Austin's characters to a romance of a middle-aged teacher Bill Mor and a young artist Rain Carter in *The Sandcastle* by Iris Murdoch.

Equally numerous are the sad stories that can be recalled. Leo Tolstoy's Anna Karenina is about 20 years younger than her husband Alexei, and the unhappy marriage triggers her involvement with a young officer Vronsky. In Nabokov's *Lolita*, Humbert, the adult protagonist, is trapped in a disastrous love affair with Dolores who is just 12. Similarly, in Hugo's *The Hunchback of Notre-Dame* a beautiful Gypsy dancer Esmeralda is only 16 years old, while Claude Frollo, who is dramatically obsessed with her, is in his late 30s.

The opposite case, when a woman is considerably older than the man she is involved with, is rarer in fiction, and there are social reasons to that. Yet, we do read about happy moments like love affairs of a young man and a 79-year-old woman in Higgins' *Harold and Maude*, or a single mother in McMillan's *How Stella Got Her Groove Back*, who, while on an island vacation, falls for a man half her age. Likewise, Mario Vargas Llosa's semi-autobiographical *Aunt Julia and the Scriptwriter* features an 18-year-old Mario falling in love with a 32-year-old divorcée Julia while Colette's *Cheri* focuses on the affair between the novel's title character and Lea, who is 24 years older than he is. Interestingly enough, the author herself had a (bad) first marriage to a man 14 years her senior and a (good) third marriage to a man 16 years her junior. And there is a sweet section of Bradbury's *Dandelion Wine* in which a young man and a woman over 90 have a series of deep conversations that are essentially a verbal love affair.

Quite predictably the unhappy narratives in literature dominate, so we have stories about Julien Sorel (19) and Louise de Rênal (30) in *The Red and the Black* by Stendhal, or more contemporary characters, like 39-year old Paule and 25-year old Simon in Sagan's *Aimez-vous Brahms?*, and Paul Roberts (19) and Susan MacLeod (48) in *The Only Story* by Julian Barnes.

43.2 Theoretical Background: How Fiction Can Shape Your Views

One's personality is partly genetically predetermined and firmly shaped by the age you are 30 (Whitbourne, 2015). Of course, next to genetics, cultural environment also plays a significant role. Does that mean that after one has entered the fourth decade of one's life, worldviews become rigid, and any alteration from now on is impossible? Fortunately, not, and fiction is found to be an important mechanism to change attitudes and beliefs. Djikic and Oatley (2014) show that fiction can engage readers in ways that enhance their personality qualities. Among other influences, they argue, reading literary texts augments one's social expertise by putting readers inside the minds of others. Being some kind of a "moral laboratory" (Hakemulder, 2000), fiction gives them the opportunity to explore the subjective world of its characters and take or reject their viewpoints (Frankman, 2017):

> When you read fiction, you can be someone you'd never otherwise have the chance to become—another gender, another age, someone of another nationality or another circumstance. You can be an explorer, a scientist, an artist, a young and single mother or an orphaned cabin boy or a soldier.
> When you take off the guise again—set down the book—you walk away changed. You understood things you didn't understand before, and that shapes your worldview.

As a result, as a reader you may develop openness and tolerance by way of empathy, and

> it may also be possible to find the fulfillment you seek in your own long-term relationships (Whitbourne, 2015).

The idea that reading fiction enhances the feeling of empathy is, one may think controversially, applicable less to romantic novels, but rather to realistic ones, like Dickens's or Obreht's (Bury, 2013). Kidd and Castano (2013) have found powerful experimental support for the hypothesis that literary fiction (though not popular fiction) enhances readers' ability to detect and understand other people's emotions, and this skill, usually termed Theory of Mind, in its turn, is vital in navigating complex social relationships. As the *Guardian* reports (8 October 2013), "[f]iction", they claim, "is not just a simulator of a social experience, it is a social experience". At the same time, Kidd counterparts that

> [n]either do we argue that people should only read literary fiction; it's just that only literary fiction seems to improve Theory of Mind in the short-term. There are likely benefits of reading popular fiction—certainly entertainment. We just did not measure them.

Out of various literary genres, in this chapter we focus on those that depict love relationships between characters. Though some psychologists claim that reading romantic novels may be harmful for female readers, as it puts their expectation to the level that does not correspond to everyday reality (Deshpande, 2018), such narratives, according to others, among other psychological and social influences, are able to deepen understanding of people and relationships (Vargas, 2017):

> When written with some care and insight, romance novels can provide lessons in love for people of any age. Protagonists in romance novels are not all bright-eyed teens who have fallen in love for the first time. In fact, some of the greatest romance novels involve people who have been in love too many times to count, or characters who haven't figured out how to navigate the dating world at all. Whether you're 20 or 50, there are always lessons to be learned about understanding others, communicating with them, and strengthening the relationships we have with people.

43.3 Context: Literature and Social Norms

Research shows that social context can influence our dealings with people, as we all have expectations of others that might be based on our personal experience, or on stereotypes we associate with certain contexts (Snyder & Stukas Jr., 1990). Besides, social norms, which are "generally accepted ways of thinking, feeling, or behaving that people in a group agree and endorse as right and proper" (Smith & Mackie, 2000, 594), also direct our perceptions of situations that surround us. Individuals look to social norms to gain an accurate understanding of and effectively respond to social circumstances, especially during times of uncertainty (Cialdini, 2000). Therefore, when we are not confident enough to make our own judgments, we may accept or condemn a person or an action by means of how we believe others in our community would react. This fact shows the greater importance of awareness to society's influence upon us.

Social norms are usually referred to when thinking of community-related issues, such as littering, pollution, political discussions, or economic questions. When dealing with prejudice (see, for example, Brown, 1995), there are studies concerning racial, religious, and sexist issues. In this chapter, we intend to investigate whether such norms are also present in our cultures, concerning a specific form of love relation. This research deals with a more subtle prejudice, one that is not commonly referred to, as it supposedly does not affect society as much as the ones mentioned above.

Love affairs characterized by an explicit age gap may not be treated equally by different societies. Besides, people's attitudes might differ according to who is older or younger in the relationship, as in some cultures it is common to see alliances between much older men and younger women, while the opposite is socially rejected and criticised.

There is a concern whether moral judgments and behavior can be triggered by an exterior stimulus (van Peer, Chesnokova, & Springer, 2017) and whether emotions play a role (Menninghaus et al., 2017). One of our inquiries is whether these emotions, when fostered by an outside factor, might influence people's responses towards age-gap relationships. We intended to create an environment in which participants would be stimulated to feel such emotions, possibly being led to reflect upon the situation. As Miall and Kuiken (2002) claim, reading literature evokes various feelings in readers, and these might contribute to a change in their perception of a situation. Therefore, literature could be the proper trigger we were looking for. We supposed readers would be emotionally engaged with the literary texts provided (for narrative absorption, see Hakemulder et al., 2017), and might, consequently, shift their attitudes. Moreover, as literary texts mirror to a certain extent cultural backgrounds or critically reflect on them, they might push readers towards accepting or condemning certain kinds of behavior.

43.4 Research Methodology: Reading Literary Texts About Age-Gap Relationships

The reported research aims at investigating readers' reactions towards age-gap relationships in real and fictional worlds. In addition, it aims to investigate whether readers' worldviews are influenced by literary texts and whether their attitudes change through reading. Additionally, as the project was carried out in two countries different in their ethnic make-up, their language, and their traditions, the results will also cast light on cultural differences and/or similarities in relation to this issue (for the research outline, see Chesnokova & Mendes, 2005).

We hypothesised that literature shapes readers' attitudes to moral issues. We also expected to find significant differences between Brazilians' and Ukrainians' responses. Besides, we anticipated that in both cultures the case of a woman being older (henceforth—OW) would be treated with less social tolerance than the case when the older partner is a man (henceforth—OM).

The research was carried out among 240 Humanities students (120 per national condition) from three public universities in two countries: Brazil and Ukraine. The study was run in a conventional academic setting. Respondents' age ranged from 17 to 53 in Brazil (with a mean of 24.9 and $SD = 8.1$) and from 19 to 25 in Ukraine (with a mean of 20.7 and $SD = 1.3$). The proportionally small number of male respondents (15 out of 120 in Brazil and 21 out of 120 in Ukraine) can be explained by the dominating presence of female students in the Humanities. The investigation of age and gender influence on the responses was beyond the scope of this project.

We opted for a five-point semantic differential scale as a research tool (van Peer, Hakemulder, & Zyngier, 2012; Viana et al., 2009) as it allowed measuring both the directionality of the response and its intensity. As a first stage, a pilot was run to select the adjectives to be subsequently used in the investigation. In order to obtain them, 26 randomly chosen respondents (16 Ukrainians and 10 Brazilians, all Humanities students, their age ranging from 20 to 26 in Brazil and from 17 to 25 in Ukraine) gave their free evaluation of age-gap love affairs as such.

As a result, 17 adjectives and adjective equivalents were chosen as the most frequently mentioned ones in both countries, and the opposites were selected:

- normal/abnormal;
- loyal/disloyal;
- predictable/unpredictable;
- interesting/boring;
- mature/immature;
- attractive/unattractive;
- reasonable/unreasonable;
- stable/unstable;
- exhibitionist/secretive;
- respectful/disrespectful;
- responsible/irresponsible;

- paternal (maternal)/equal;
- negative/positive;
- sexually driven/heart-driven;
- socially rejected/socially accepted;
- financially driven/disinterested;
- raising the social status/not influencing the social status.

The next stage consisted in selecting the appropriate design of the questionnaire. As we wanted to probe the influence of literary texts on social attitudes toward age-gap love, we needed passages from fiction in which such affiliations would be depicted. On top of that, in order to check the difference between the social acceptance of relationships involving an older man and the ones involving an older woman, we had to select fragments focusing on these two kinds of ties. As we did not want to guide respondents towards evaluating the age-gap relationships as either positive or negative, the texts had to contain descriptions of both happy and frustrating moments of such alliances. Finally, since we did not want any influence from respondents' own cultures, we opted for not using Brazilian or Ukrainian texts.

There was no major difficulty in finding a text for an OM case, as it is quite common to picture an older man falling in love or feeling sexually attracted to a woman who has just blossomed. However, it was harder to find an appropriate text for an OW case. Besides, the narratives had to have been translated into Portuguese and Ukrainian or Russian (on bilingualism in Ukraine see Sergeyeva & Chesnokova, 2008) since we wanted to use respondents' native languages in the questionnaires to avoid any possible misunderstandings.

After a thorough search, we opted for *Gone with the Wind* by Margaret Mitchell (1936/1993) and *Theatre* by W. Somerset Maugham (1937/2001). In the former novel, Scarlett O'Hara, a teenager at the beginning of the book, is involved with Rhett Butler, who is in his 30s. In the second narrative, the middle-aged Julia Lambert plunges into an affair with Tom, who is younger than her son. Both novels focus on ups and downs of such alliances with the age gap factor being one of the key issues of oscillations in the emotional confrontations.

We selected four extracts from these novels: two of them describing happiness, one per case, and the other two describing frustration. The length of the passages ranged from 157 to 385 words in the Russian translation and from 126 to 216 words in the Portuguese one. For the full text of the passages see the Appendix.

The research design involved 12 groups (20 participants each) (Table 43.1):

In the main part of the experiment, participants ranked their emotional attitudes toward age-gap relations as such, separately for the two options (OM and OW), on a five-point scale. In the introductory part of the questionnaire, respondents indicated their gender and age. Room for free commentary was also provided. At the end of the questionnaire, the respondents gave their formal consent to participate in the study.

Control group participants evaluated age-gap relationships without having read any text, while the experimental groups did the same after being exposed to literary passages where such emotions were depicted as demonstrating: (1) happiness (OM); (2) frustration (OM); (3) happiness (OW); and (4) frustration (OW).

Table 43.1 Participant grouping

Group	Nationality	Text	Number of participants
1	Brazilian	OM no text (control group)	20
2		OW no text (control group)	20
3		OM happiness	20
4		OM frustration	20
5		OW happiness	20
6		OW frustration	20
7	Ukrainian	OM no text (control group)	20
8		OW no text (control group)	20
9		OM happiness	20
10		OM frustration	20
11		OW happiness	20
12		OW frustration	20

The data collected were analysed statistically in line with the tenets of using the empirical methodology in the Humanities (van Peer et al., 2012). The following section reports the results of this study.

43.5 Findings: Does Reading Fiction Shape Your Views?

For the control groups' data, an ANOVA test was run in order to check whether respondents within each national sample treated OM and OW relationships in the same way. The Ukrainian control groups' data yielded statistically significant differences between the two conditions (OM and OW) for roughly one-third of the variables: "normal" ($p = 0.000$), "mature" ($p = 0.023$), "respectful" ($p = 0.008$), "responsible" ($p = 0.008$), "positive" ($p = 0.026$), and "socially accepted" ($p = 0.004$). The differences in the Brazilian control groups appeared to be not statistically significant.

Figure 43.1 below shows the mean responses of the Ukrainian control groups (straight line for the OM case and dashed line for the OW case). The variables with the statistically significant results reported above are marked with asterisks. As can be seen in the graph, in the Ukrainian sample OM relationships are, on the whole, considered much more positive than OW ones: the latter are evaluated as less normal, less mature, less respectful, less responsible, less positive and by far less socially acceptable.

Figure 43.2 below, showing the responses of the Brazilian control groups, demonstrates *no* statistically significant differences between the evaluations of the two cases: Brazilian respondents rated the OM and OW relationships almost equally, and somewhere in the middle of the scale.

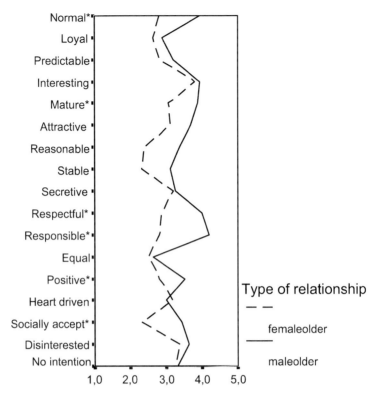

Fig. 43.1 Mean responses of Ukrainian control groups: the OM and OW cases (authors' own construction)

After we analysed the control groups' data and obtained the information about general attitudes to age-gap relationships in the two cultures, we set to the second stage of the experiment. As we aimed at checking whether reading literature influences attitudes towards age-gap relationships, we compared (within each national group) evaluations of such alliances by respondents who

1. read the passage about happy moments;
2. read the passage about frustrating moments, and
3. the control group who read no literary fragment.

Statistically significant differences between the evaluation of Ukrainian respondents of the OM case were found on three variables: "normal" ($p = 0.007$), "mature" ($p = 0.019$) and "socially accepted" ($p = 0.015$). Figure 43.3 below demonstrates the means for the three variables across three conditions: reading the "happy" text, reading the "frustration" text and reading no text (control group).

As can be seen from the figure, for the OM case, there is a difference between the responses of the control group and the group who read the literary passage about

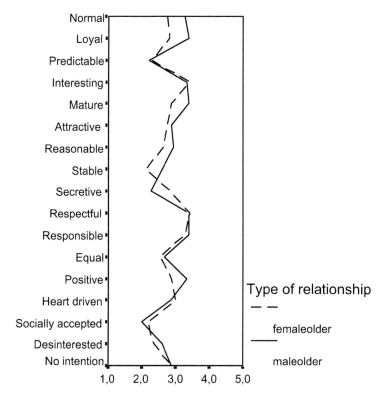

Fig. 43.2 Mean responses of Brazilian control groups: the OM and OW cases (authors' own construction)

frustration in the relationship: the evaluations of the experimental group are lower and tend to be more neutral, approaching 3 on a scale of 5.

The group that read the "happy" passage evaluated the OM case as more normal, more mature, but, unexpectedly, less socially acceptable than the group that read the "frustrated" passage.

The comparison between the reactions of Ukrainian respondents of the control groups and the experimental ones towards the OW case yielded statistically significant differences for only two variables: "normal" ($p = 0.042$) and (tendentially) "positive" ($p = 0.060$). Figure 43.4 below gives the means for the two variables across the same three conditions: reading the "happy" text, reading the "frustration" text and reading no text (control group).

As the figure clearly illustrates, for the OW case, there is a significant increase in the ratings of the variables "normal" and "positive" in comparison with the control group. Both the group who read the "happy" and the one that was exposed to the "sad" text evaluated the OW case as more normal and more positive, thus supporting the idea that literature indeed softens socially controversial issues. It is remarkable that the evaluations became more positive irrespective of whether the passage the

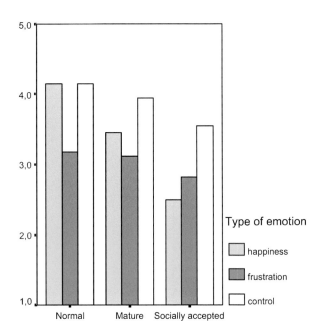

Fig. 43.3 Mean responses of Ukrainian groups: the OM case (authors' own construction)

readers were exposed to focused on happy or frustrating moments in the relationship, and this pattern is very different from that of the OM case demonstrated in Fig. 43.3.

For the Brazilian participants who read the OM text, the values with statistic significance appeared to be higher for just 2 variables out of a list of 17 adjectives: "secretive" ($p = 0.040$) and (tendentially) "positive" ($p = 0.057$). The difference is illustrated in Fig. 43.5 below.

Finally, Fig. 43.6 below demonstrates mean evaluations Brazilian participants attributed to the OW case.

The respondents of this national sample who had read the literary passages showed a much more positive attitude in comparison to the control group in the variables "mature" ($p = 0.009$) and "attractive" ($p = 0.010$)—again irrespective of whether the "happy" or "sad" text was read. The respondents who were exposed to literary passages evaluated the OW relationships as significantly more mature and more attractive in comparison to the control group.

43.6 Discussion

The reported results indicate that literary texts change people's beliefs towards certain controversial social issues, attitudes to age-gap relationships in particular. The experimental groups, who read the literary texts, indeed showed a difference from the control groups, both Ukrainian and Brazilian ones. It seems that literature does affect participants' attitudes in cases in which the original response was rather

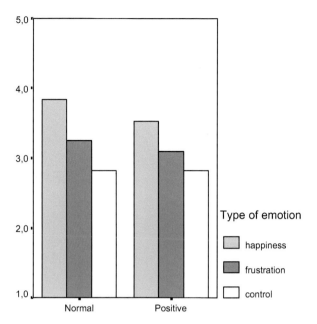

Fig. 43.4 Mean responses of Ukrainian groups: the OW case (authors' own construction)

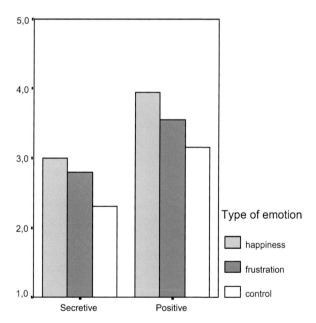

Fig. 43.5 Mean responses of Brazilian groups: the OM case (authors' own construction)

negative. For instance, in the Ukrainian sample, participants of the control group reacted quite negatively to the OW case. Readers' evaluation of this type of relationship became more positive when participants were exposed to a literary text (be it happy or frustrating). This might be an indication that reading literature

Fig. 43.6 Mean responses of Brazilian groups: the OW case (authors' own construction)

softens people's attitudes towards issues that are not accepted by society. The influence of reading the literary texts in Brazil is less outspoken, due to the fact that cultural attitudes in this country were more subtle, and this is what the control groups' response to both OM and OW cases in this sample demonstrated.

Additionally, the results lend support to our hypothesis of cultural differences between Brazil and Ukraine in treating age-gap relationships *per se*. Our initial anticipation that the OW case would get more negative evaluation in both countries was not borne out for Brazil. Brazilian respondents evaluated both OM and OW cases almost equally, with values around the neutral point. At the same time, Ukrainian participants attributed more negative values to the OW case. This could be the influence of mass media and popular culture, as in Brazil many examples of such relationships have been commented on, either in real life or in fictional works, such as soap operas. In spite of being equally popular with the Ukrainian audience, Brazilian soap operas obviously do not have that much effect on local stereotypes: screened mostly in South America, they seem distant and fairytale-like.

Further research should investigate differences between the gender and age of participants and their attitudes to age-gap relationships. Moreover, as both novels we used in this study are third-person narratives, it seems worthwhile to verify whether narrative perspective plays a role and whether results would be different with the first-person texts. Finally, both texts are written from a female perspective, which might also be taken into consideration in further studies of the topic.

43.7 Conclusion

This chapter has investigated, in the first place, social attitudes toward age-gap relations, and we found considerable cultural differences in this respect, though research shows that love in such relationship is not different from more "standard" relationships. More importantly for literary studies, however, was our investigation of the influence exerted by reading literary fragments narrating happy or frustrating episodes in the story of age-gap couples. Although significant differences with the control group were found on only a few variables, the results nevertheless showed that reading (brief fragments) about such relations changed people's attitudes toward them. We believe this is yet another illustration of the power of literature, which is completely in line with the findings of Kidd and Castano (2013). While not being a replication of their study, the results point in the same direction: reading literary texts does exert an influence on readers' cognition, emotion, attitudes, and sometimes also on behaviour (for more research, see Hakemulder, 2000; Gibbs, 2013; Koopman, 2016; Kuijpers, 2014).

Yet many scholars in literary studies and philosophy—less so in history (see, for instance, Darnton, 1996), deny such an influence. No matter how strange this is, the denial is widespread, and the prototypical essay in this respect is the one by Stollnitz (1991)—who never replied to the criticism voiced over it by van Peer (1995). It is irrational to disagree with this affect of literature because the general assumption in the social sciences is that everything people do and encounter has an influence of its own—even chewing chewing-gum has cognitive effects (see the very persuasive overview by Weijenberg, Scherder, and Lobbezoo (2011)). But if this has an influence, then being immersed for days or weeks in gruesome, exhilarating, or heartbreaking stories should definitely have an impact, of which we hope to have persuaded the dissenters.

Thus we would urge our literary colleagues to reflect on their position of dissent by instead joining the empirical branch of literary studies, and engage in research about the *real* effects of reading—effects about which we still know far too little.

Appendix

Though in the research the languages of the questionnaires were Portuguese and Russian, here we append the original versions of the passages read in the experiment.

A.1 The OM Case ("Happiness" Passage)

...she awoke, cold with sweat, sobbing brokenly...

Rhett was leaning over her when she woke, and without a word he picked her up in his arms like a child and held her close, his hard muscles comforting, his wordless murmuring soothing, until her sobbing ceased.

"Oh, Rhett, I was so cold and so hungry and so tired and I couldn't find it. I ran through the mist and I ran but I couldn't find it."

"Find what, honey?"

"I don't know. I wish I did know."

"Is it your old dream?"

"Oh, yes!"

He gently placed her on the bed, fumbled in the darkness and lit a candle. In the light his face with blood-shot eyes and harsh lines was as unreadable as stone. His shirt, opened to the waist, showed a brown chest covered with thick black hair. Scarlett, still shaking with fright, thought how strong and unyielding that chest was, and she whispered: "Hold me, Rhett."

"Darling!" he said swiftly, and picking her up he sat down in a large chair, cradling her body against him.

"Oh, Rhett, it's awful to be hungry."

"It must be awful to dream of starvation after a seven-course dinner including that enormous crawfish." He smiled but his eyes were kind.

"Oh, Rhett, I just ran and ran and hunt and I can't ever find what it is I am hunting for. It's always hidden in the mist. I know if I could find it, I'd be safe forever and ever and never be cold or hungry again."

"Is it a person or a thing you're hunting?"

"I don't know. I never thought about it. Rhett, do you think I'll ever dream that I get there to safety?"

"No," he said, smoothing her tumbling hair. "I don't. Dreams aren't like that. But I do think that if you get used to being safe and warm and well fed in your everyday life, you'll stop dreaming that dream. And, Scarlett, I am going to see that you are safe."

"Rhett, you are so nice."

"Thanks for the crumbs from your table, Mrs. Dives. Scarlett, I want you to say to yourself every morning when you wake up: 'I can't ever be hungry again and nothing can ever touch me so long as Rhett is here and the United States government holds out.'"

A.2 The OM Case ("Frustration" Passage)

...he annoyed her. And he annoyed her frequently.

He was in his mid-thirties, older than any beau she had ever had, and she was as helpless as a child to control and handle him as she had handled beaux nearer her own age. He always looked as if nothing had ever surprised him and much had amused him and, when he had gotten her into a speechless temper, she felt that she amused him more than anything in the world. Frequently she flared into open wrath under his expert baiting, for she had Gerald's Irish temper along with the deceptive sweetness of face she had inherited from Ellen. Heretofore she had never bothered to control her temper except in Ellen's presence. Now it was painful to have to choke back words for fear of his amused grin. If only he would ever lose his temper too, then she would not feel at such a disadvantage.

A.3 The OW Case ("Happiness" Passage)

She had decided how she was going to treat him. She would be amiable, but distant. She would take a friendly interest in his work and ask him about his examination. Then she would talk to him about Roger. Roger was seventeen now and in a year would be going to Cambridge. She would insinuate the fact that she was old enough to be his mother. She would act as if there had never been anything between them and he would go away, never to see her again except across the footlights, half convinced that the whole thing had been a figment of his fancy. But when she saw him, so slight, with this hectic flush and his blue eyes, so charmingly boyish, she felt a sudden pang. Evie closed the door behind him. She was lying on the sofa and she stretched out her arm to give him her hand, the gracious smile of Madame Récamier on her lips, but he flung himself on his knees and passionately kissed her mouth. She could not help herself, she put her arms round his neck and kissed him as passionately.

A.4 The OW Case ("Frustration" Passage)

It was like a knife in her heart. He had never spoken to her in that tone before. But she laughed lightly and getting up took the whisky he had poured out for her and sat down in a chair opposite him. The movement he had made, the words he had spoken, were instinctive and he was a trifle abashed. He avoided her glance and his face once more bore a sulky look. The moment was decisive. For a while they were silent. Julia's heart beat painfully...

"My dear, I'm so terribly fond of you."

"I know, and I'm terribly fond of you. You're great fun to go about with and you're always so well turned out, you're a credit to any woman. I've liked going to bed with you and I've a sort of notion you've liked going to bed with me. But let's face it, I've never been in love with you any more than you've been in love with me. I knew it couldn't last. Sooner or later you were bound to fall in love and that would end it..."

The moment he had gone she turned out the lights and went to the window. She peered cautiously through the curtains... Tears, tears that nobody could see, rolled down her cheeks. She was miserably unhappy.

References

Brown, R. (1995). *Prejudice. Its social psychology*. Oxford: Blackwell.

Bury, L. (2013, October 8). Reading literary fiction improves empathy, study finds. *The Guardian*. Accessed May 31, 2020, from https://www.theguardian.com/books/booksblog/2013/oct/08/literary-fiction-improves-empathy-study

Buss, D. M. (2003). *The evolution of desire: Strategies of human mating*. New York: Basic Books.

Chesnokova, A., & Mendes, M. (2005). Intimate relationships and age gap: The influence of fiction [in Ukrainian]. *Вісник КНЛУ, 8*(2), 135–142.

Cialdini, R. B. (2000). *Influence: Science and practice*. Boston, MA: Allyn & Bacon.

Darnton, R. (1996). *The forbidden bestsellers of pre-revolutionary France*. New York: W.W. Norton.

Deshpande, N. B. (2018, February 24). You won't believe how romance novels affect the psychology of women. *PsycholoGenie*. Accessed May 31, 2020, from https://psychologenie.com/how-romance-novels-affect-psychology-of-women

Djikic, M., & Oatley, K. (2014). The art in fiction: From indirect communication to changes of the self. *Psychology of Aesthetics, Creativity, and the Arts, 8*(4), 498–505. https://doi.org/10.1037/a0037999

Fisher, H. (1995). The nature and evolution of romantic love. In W. Jankowiak (Ed.), *Romantic passion. A universal experience* (pp. 103–134). New York: Columbia University Press.

Frankman, H. (2017, October 18). The importance of reading fiction. *The Mission*. Accessed May 31, 2020, from https://medium.com/the-mission/the-importance-of-reading-fiction-7f57546a229b

Gibbs, R. W. (2013). Walking the walk while thinking about the talk: Embodied interpretation of metaphorical narratives. *Journal of Psycholinguistic Research, 42*(4), 363–373. https://doi.org/10.1007/s10936-012-9222-6

Gough, H. G. (1980). *Manual for the California Psychological Inventory*. Palo Alto, CA: Consulting Psychologists Press.

Hakemulder, F. (2000). *The moral laboratory. Experiments examining the effects of reading literature on social perception and moral self-concept*. Amsterdam: John Benjamins.

Hakemulder, F., Kuijpers, M., Tan, E., Balint, K., & Doicaru, M. (Eds.). (2017). *Narrative absorption*. Amsterdam: John Benjamins.

Jankowiak, W., & Fischer, E. (1992). A cross-cultural perspective on romantic love. *Ethnology, 31*(2), 149–155. https://doi.org/10.2307/3773618

Karantzas, G. (2018, April 20). Why couples with big age gaps are happier, despite the social disapproval. *ABC*. Accessed May 31, 2020, from https://www.abc.net.au/news/2018-04-20/couple-with-a-larger-age-gap-happier/9680764

Kidd, D. C., & Castano, E. (2013). Reading literary fiction improves Theory of Mind. *Science, 342*(6156), 377–380. https://doi.org/10.1126/science.1239918

Koopman, E. (2016). *Reading suffering. An empirical inquiry into empathic and reflexive responses to literary narratives*. Rotterdam: Erasmus University Rotterdam.

Kuijpers, M. (2014). *Absorbing stories. The effects of textual devices on absorption and evaluative responses*. Ridderkerk: Ridderkerk BV.

Maugham, W. S. (1937/2001). *Theatre*. New York: Vintage Books.

McCrae, R. R., & Costa Jr., P. T. (1990). *Personality in adulthood*. New York: Guilford Press.

Menninghaus, W., Wagner, V., Hanich, J., Wassiliwizky, E., Jacobsen, T., & Koelsch, S. (2017). The distancing-embracing model of the enjoyment of negative emotions in art reception. *Behavioral and Brain Sciences, 40*. https://doi.org/10.1017/S0140525X17000309

Miall, D., & Kuiken, D. (2002). A feeling for fiction: Becoming what we behold. *Poetics, 30*, 221–241.

Mitchell, M. (1936/1993). *Gone with the wind*. New York: Warner Books.

Patrick, W. L. (2019, August 19). Why men like to date older women. Research reveals the truth behind the typecasting. *Psychology Today*. Accessed May 31, 2020, from https://www.psychologytoday.com/us/blog/why-bad-looks-good/201908/why-men-date-older-women

Sergeyeva, M., & Chesnokova, A. (2008). Language allergy: Myth or reality? In S. Zyngier, M. Bortolussi, A. Chesnokova, & J. Auracher (Eds.), *Directions in empirical literary studies: In honor of Willie van Peer* (pp. 283–295). Amsterdam: John Benjamins. https://doi.org/10.1075/lal.5.23ser

Smith, E. R., & Mackie, D. M. (2000). *Social psychology* (2nd ed.). Philadelphia, PA: Psychology Press.

Snyder, M., & Stukas Jr., A. A. (1990). Interpersonal processes: The interplay of cognitive, motivational, and behavioural activities in social interaction. *Annual Review of Psychology, 50*, 273–303.

Stollnitz, J. (1991). On the historical triviality of art. *The British Journal of Aesthetics, 31*(3), 195–202. https://doi.org/10.1093/bjaesthetics/31.3.195

van Peer, W. (1995). The historical non-triviality of art and literature. A rejoinder to Jerome Stolnitz. *The British Journal of Aesthetics, 35*(2), 168–172. https://doi.org/10.1093/bjaesthetics/35.2.168

van Peer, W., Chesnokova, A., & Springer, M. (2017). Distressful empathy in reading literature: The case for terror management theory. *Science and Education, 1*, 33–42. https://doi.org/10.24195/2414-4665-2017-1-6

van Peer, W., Hakemulder, F., & Zyngier, S. (2012). *Scientific methods for the humanities*. Amsterdam: John Benjamins. https://doi.org/10.1075/lal.13

Vargas, C. (2017, October 3). 7 amazing benefits you unknowingly get from reading romance novels. *Elitedaily*. Accessed May 31, 2020, from https://www.elitedaily.com/p/7-amazing-benefits-you-unknowingly-get-from-reading-romance-novels-2755616

Viana, V., Zyngier, S., Chesnokova, A., Jandre, J., & Nero, S. (2009). Quantitative research in practice: Applying a differential scale questionnaire to literature. *Вісник Сумського державного університету, 1*(3–4), 67–77.

Weijenberg, R. A. F., Scherder, E., & Lobbezoo, F. (2011). Mastication for the mind – The relationship between mastication and cognition in ageing and dementia. *Neuroscience & Biobehavioral Reviews, 35*(3), 483–497. https://doi.org/10.1016/j.neubiorev.2010.06.002

Whitbourne, S. K. (2015, January 6). How reading can change you in a major way. *Psychology Today*. Accessed May 31, 2020, from https://www.psychologytoday.com/us/blog/fulfillment-any-age/201501/how-reading-can-change-you-in-major-way

Anna Chesnokova holds an MA in English and French Philology (Kyiv National Linguistic University, 1991) and a PhD in Comparative Literary Studies (Taras Shevchenko Kyiv National University, 1999). She is Professor at the English Philology and Translation Department of Borys Grinchenko Kyiv University, Ukraine. She has published on Stylistics and Empirical Studies of Literature. Her publications include *Acting & Connecting. Cultural Approaches to Language and Literature* (co-edited with S. Zyngier and V. Viana, LIT Verlag, 2007), *Directions in Empirical Literary Studies* (co-edited with S. Zyngier, M. Bortolussi, and J. Auracher, John Benjamins, 2008), chapters for *The International Reception of Emily Dickinson* (Continuum Press, 2009), *Cases on Distance Delivery and Learning Outcomes: Emerging Trends and Programs* (with V. Viana, S. Zyngier and W. van Peer, IGI Global, 2009), *Teaching Stylistics* (with W. van Peer and S. Zyngier, Palgrave Macmillan, 2011) and *Scientific Approaches to Literature in Learning Environments* (John Benjamins, 2016).

Willie van Peer is Professor of Intercultural Hermeneutics at Ludwig Maximilian University, Germany. He is the author of several books and many articles on poetics and the epistemological foundations of literary studies, vice-president of the International Association of Empirical Aesthetics (1996–1998), chair of the international Poetics and Linguistics Association (PALA,

2000–2003), president of the International Society for Empirical Study of Literature and Media (IGEL, 2004–2006), co-founder of the international REDES project (2001–2009), co-editor of book series *Linguistic Approaches to Literature* (LAL, John Benjamins, 2000–2010), executive editor of the *Scientific Study of Literature* journal series (SSOL, John Benjamins). Willie van Peer has been Visiting Scholar in the Departments of Comparative Literature at Stanford and at Princeton Universities, and in the Department of (Cognitive) Psychology at the University of Memphis. He is also a Fellow of Clare Hall of Cambridge University.

Chapter 44
Imagining Love: Teen Romance Novels and American Teen Relational Capacity

Estella Carolye Kuchta

Abstract Psychologists and social critics have sounded the alarm that the relational capacity of American youth is decreasing with each generation because of unsupportive cultural practices. However, relational capacity hampered in early childhood, may be fostered by relationally-focused literature in later childhood.

Teen romance novels engage readers in relational processes and potentially advance relational capacity through the biopsychosocial processes of reading. The imaginative work that occurs while reading literature stimulates intellectual, and psychological processes potentially priming youth for actual experience. In this way, teen novels may enable teen readers to imagine possible future selves. Vygotsky emphasized that learning occurs within and because of the relational space between individuals and their sociocultural environment. He asserted that cultural tools—such as books—assist in mediating that space.

Using general theories of attachment, this chapter explains how the novels, *The Fault in Our Stars* (2012) and *Aristotle and Dante Discover the Secrets of the Universe* (2012), draw teen readers into a potent shared space wherein love is defined, witnessed, and imaginatively experienced. However, another teen romance, *Always and Forever, Lara Jean* (2017) amplifies reader anxiety by prioritizing materialistic and extrinsic values, providing illogical trajectories for love, and rewarding its protagonist for manipulative behavior.

Keywords Love · Teen romance · Relational capacity · North American youth · Literature · Reading process

44.1 Introduction

Despite immense popularity, the genre of romance fiction evokes divisive reactions in academic and public spheres. Some psychologists, for example, call the genre an "enabling fiction" (Barreca, 2012) that "portray[s] idealized love" and has been

E. C. Kuchta (✉)
Department of English, Langara College, Vancouver, BC, Canada
e-mail: estellakuchta@gmail.com

designed for those who wish "to avoid having to face the cracks in the façade of their false sense of security" (np). Susan Quilliam (2011), a psychologist and relationship therapist, suggests that a "deep strand of perfectionism, escapism, and idealisation runs through the genre" (p. 180), which undermines healthy values and relationship expectations. On the other hand, Janice Radway (1984) argued that romance fiction offers important social benefits, such as providing emotional nurturance to female readers who receive little emotional nourishment from real-life husbands and children. Tania Modleski (1984) has furthered this idea by suggesting that romance fiction "not only fulfill[s] wishes but also allay[s] fears and anxieties, clear[s] up confusion, and provide[s] outlets for women's repressed rage at their subordination" (p. xvii). Sarah Frantz Lyons (2015) concludes that "we need new approaches to romance fiction" since the fundamental stances of these debates have remained essentially unchanged during the genre's 250-year timeline (np).

This paper answers the call for a new approach to the genre by examining the biopsychosocial experience of reading in relation to the patterns of messages in three teen romance novels. Reading engages individuals in overlapping neurological, biological, psychological, and cultural experiences. These experiences occur within and because of the relational spaces cocreated by authors and readers. Vadeboncoeur (2017) explains that Vygotsky's "general genetic law of cultural development" posits "the idea that the development of mind is a social process and that the social and cultural practices that a child is mentored into, as well as the meaning the child constructs of participation in these practices, form the foundation for individual consciousness" (p. 15). For all of us, but for young people in particular whose identities are at a crucial developmental stage, reading fiction is a process of shared imagining about being and becoming. Fundamentally, reading fiction engages readers in notions of possibility.

This paper asks: What biopsychosocial imaginings are stimulated by reading romance and how might those stimulations develop or thwart relational capacity? Radway (1984) rightly argued that critical investigation of romance fiction "must shift from the text itself, taken in isolation, to the complex social event of reading" (p. 8). Here, I shift the investigation of literature from the page to the shared spaces of the reader's body, the novel, and the cultural environment.

44.2 Teen Relational Capacity Is Decreasing

Psychologists (Twenge, Joiner, Rogers, & Martin, 2018; Gerhardt, 2004, 2010; Narvaez, 2014) and social critics (Maté, 2015; Verny, 2002) have been sounding the alarm that the relational capacity of youth in the dominant North American culture is increasingly atrophying because of a wide range of unsupportive cultural practices. Contemporary North Americans are experiencing unprecedented levels of social disconnection (Gerhardt, 2010; Maté, 2015; Turkle, 2011; Verny, 2002; Zimbardo, 2011), evidenced in high levels of loneliness (Cacioppo & Patrick, 2008) and social awkwardness (Twenge, 2000; Zimbardo, 2011) and in falling levels of empathy, trust, and quality friendships (Gerhardt, 2010; Konrath, O'Brien & Hsing, 2011; Turkle, 2011; Zimbardo, 2011). Narvaez (2014) argues that on a neurobiological level, the relational capacity of American children has become increasingly underdeveloped from one generation to the next due to childrearing norms that overemphasize independence. Twenge et al. (2018) have suggested that burgeoning social media use may be thwarting the kinds of social interactions necessary for sound emotional wellbeing. While psychologists continue to evaluate the causes of relational disfunction, other researchers search for solutions. Because reading romance fiction draws readers into relational processes and relational topics, it likely impacts relational capacity.

44.3 The Experience of Reading

Stories serve an important social purpose. People on every continent and throughout time have told stories. Humans are hardwired to tune in to stories. And, as evolutionary scientists will point out, no trait—whether physical or social—persists with tenacity in a species unless it benefits survival. Thus, the individual's development within the relational space of a story exists within the wider context of the collective cultural imagination and evolutionary process. From a Vygotskian perspective, stories are cultural tools which develop social futures.

Mar and Oatley (2008) compare the function of stories to that of math. They explain that mathematical equations provide a simplified formula that "enables a mode of thinking about the physical world that is both more abstract and more generalizable than intuitive everyday thinking" (p. 175). Equations, they clarify, can be creatively applied to the world to broaden understanding, enable predictions, and improve strategies within in the physical realm. Reality offers us thousands of sensory data points every second. Stories, like mathematical equations, express a pared-down, simplified version of reality. These stories then offer a template that can clarify general principles about life and human experiences (Mar & Oatley, 2008, p. 175). Similar to the function of math, they enable us to make predictions about human behavior and show us ways to reach complex social goals. Thus, those who read are better able to conceptualize social worlds in general, their actual and potential roles within them, and to think creatively about their relationships. As Greene (2000) explained, "Having accepted 'unreality,' we can turn back to the variegated social realities we share and, perhaps, find them enhanced, expanded, corrigible" (p. 187).

Stories impact beingness and identity formation in potentially transformative ways. As Ursula Le Guin (1977) articulates:

> As you read a book word by word and page by page, you participate in its creation, just as a cellist playing a Bach suite participates, note by note, in the creation, the coming-to-be, the existence, of the music. And, as you read and re-read, the book of course participates in the creation of you, your thoughts and feelings, the size and temper of your soul. (p. 127)

Cognitive scientists and literary theorists are still determining the ways books participation in this "creation of you." Mar, Oatley, Djikic, and Mullin (2011) assert, "Novels can act as a powerful emotional prime and once an emotional state has been induced we would expect to see differences in cognitive processing associated with this new emotional state" (p. 829).

Nearly everyone has had the experience of being transported by reading fiction, and of having our mood and our worldview change as a result. Indeed, this is the role of fiction: to change us. We enter into a novel with a willingness—a hope—to be altered by its contents, to have hearts lifted, to be stimulated, to feel the comfort of being understood, or to be exposed to new ideas. Whereas nonfiction engages us in *what is*, fiction draws us into the realm of *what is possible*.

This realm of the possible is experienced both imaginatively and physically as reading fiction triggers both cognitive and physiological processes. Heart rates rise in response to suspense or relax in response to comfort. Hormones associated with anxiety (cortisol), social bonding (oxytocin), and physical arousal (testosterone, estrogen) may increase or decrease in response to the book's events. Cognition too is physical. Preliminary studies suggest reading fiction stimulates the formation and dissolution of "assemblies of neurons, establishing patterns that through repeated firing become our habitual ways of engaging the world" (Armstrong, 2013, p. X). In other words, the reading experience neurologically primes us for particular experiences of the world. This neurological process partly results from "mentalizing" (Oatley, Dunbar & Budlemann, 2018, p. 121), a process which requires readers to create mental pictures of people, places, and events in a story. Reading also requires one to imagine how characters feel and think and to predict their actions. Unsurprisingly then, readers of fiction have increased levels of empathy (Bal & Veltkamp, 2013), which forms the foundation for positive social connection.

Reading fiction also prompts sensory-imaginative experience. Paivio (2008) explains, "Deep (meaningful) comprehension during reading entails activation of visual, auditory, haptic, and motor neural images, movements, or verbal association. The meanings can include affective reactions associated with memory images of emotional events" (p. 103). To put it another way, when we read fiction, we use our own experiences and memories to help us *stretch* to imagine characters' experiences. In this way, reading fiction engages young people in the zone of proximal development (ZPD). In this situation, the ZPD is the space where reader imagination, author imagination, and reader identity meaningfully comingle, expanding young readers' fields of social knowing beyond what they could achieve on their own.

44.4 Reading Love

For multiple reasons, reading high quality, fictional stories about love can potentially enhance relational capacity (Mar, Oatley, Hirsh, dela Paz, & Peterson, 2006). Firstly, love stories are one of the most common story themes worldwide (Hogan, 2003), and immersion in any subject enhances understanding about that subject. Lillard (2013) notes that on a neurological level, imagined experience closely mirrors actual experience. Secondly, the process of mentalizing requires readers to activate empathy; that is, readers must imagine the feelings, thoughts, and experiences of characters in order to make predictions. Indeed, much of the joy of reading involves making predictions about what will happen next. We cannot attempt these predictions without sympathizing or empathizing with characters—and empathy constitutes a centrepiece of social skills. Thirdly, reading fiction evokes emotion (Mar et al., 2011) which contributes to the awareness and management of emotion. Fourthly, fictional love stories expand our knowledge of the possible actions, reactions, and experiences available within the realm of love. Lastly, all the above aspects of fiction reading have a neurobiological basis. Meaning, they cause the repeated firing of neural networks, and as the field of neuroplasticity has illuminated, neurons that fire together, wire together (Hebb as cited in Doidge, 2007). In sum, fictional love stories activate empathy, promote emotional self-awareness, immerse readers in the topic of love, and create neurological pathways linked to love experience.

Of course, reading fiction isn't the same as experiencing social situations in real life. Indeed, researchers have identified nuanced but important differences (Nichols, 2006; Galgut, 2014). Even those researchers who argue that storytelling plays an important social role (Mar et al., 2011) acknowledge that the cognitive process of imagining social moments does not equate exactly to the cognitive process of lived social experience. However, the biological experience of reading stories does not need to mirror real life absolutely to foster relational capacity. After all, knowing the mathematical equations required for launching an aircraft is not the same as launching one. Yet, learning about the social possibilities of love through reading fiction can foster crucial neurological capacity from which to launch actual love experiences.

If fictional love stories potentially alter us cognitively, imaginatively, and neurobiologically, we shouldn't assume those changes are automatically positive. Greene (2000) reminds us that culture "may give rise to tastes, values, even prejudices" (p. 163). Novels within the romance genre—as within any genre—vary significantly in style, content, theme, and quality. The criticism that the genre presents an overly-idealized and narrow view of love is quite justified—in the case of *some* romance novels. Thus, a rough framework for assessing romance quality is required. Clearly quality romance fiction should generally promote prosocial behaviour and healthy emotional attachment. Bowlby's theory of attachment (e.g. Levine & Heller, 2010) provides a helpful starting point. Quality love stories should draw readers into an emotional space that ultimately increases feelings of secure rather than anxious or detached attachment. Using this rough framework, this chapter explains how two teen novels are likely to positively enhance actual love possibilities, while a third novel is likely to reduce them.

44.5 Teen Romance Novels and the Fostering of Love

Critics of romance fiction argue that the genre presents a 'cookie cutter' version of love that narrows, rather than expands, real-world love potentials. They suggest that this genre overly idealizes love by concocting fairy tales and tiptoeing around the muddy complexity of actual love stories. Real life love stories are woven with disappointments, less-than-heroic acts, boredom, and liberating variances from able-bodied, heteronormative expectations. To find emotional security within real-life love stories, individuals must understand that navigation of these features is possible. High quality romance novels illustrate pathways for overcoming challenges and/or for transgressing restrictive social norms.

Thus, the starting point for high quality romance stories is that they must engage realistically flawed characters in real-world obstacles. Since boring literature reduces empathy (Bal & Veltkamp, 2013), high quality romance must contain the kind of the sensory detail and emotional resonance that deeply engages readers in imaginative and transportive experiences. Quality love stories are not one-size-fits all, but unique to specific personalities, circumstances, time periods, and sociocultural conditions. For romance novels to function as a social tool in the development of love—rather than an object merely *branded* with love—they need to illustrate the *actions and emotions of love*. In other words, it is not enough for characters to simply pronounce that they "love" someone; the story must illustrate the feelings and gestures of genuine love, such as: kindness, generosity of spirit, devotion, forgiveness, and willingness to overlook character flaws and moments of ugliness and weakness. By illustrating the actions of love, high quality teen romance novels actively define and extend the possibilities of love for young readers.

John Green's *The Fault in Our Stars* (2012) offers a compelling example of high quality teen romance, though it arguable straddles the genres of 'literature' and 'romance.' Set in an ordinary, contemporary American city, Indianapolis, the novel begins with depressed, socially-isolated, 17-year-old Hazel. These initial contexts are familiar and recognizable to most contemporary, American teens; even if they themselves are not depressed and socially isolated, they surely know someone who is. This initial familiarity quickly diverts into more gripping and suspenseful context. (Spoiler alert.) The two main characters, Hazel and Augustus, meet at a cancer support group for youth. This novel does not contain fluffy, superficial romance or childish, make-believe love. Love here carries the emotional weight and physical nastiness of cancer from start to end. Hazel, the protagonist, cannot be separated from her oxygen tank. Augustus's leg has been amputated.

Readers watch Hazel and Augustus navigate the real possibility that she might die, underscored by her bouts of depression, occasional emotional distancing, and persistent skepticism about her desirability. She makes reference to her own corpse (p. 118) and he wears his death outfit—the suit he will be buried in—on a date (p. 167). They are not deterred by the physical realities of each other no matter how disqualifying they might seem to themselves. Before their first and last act of love-making, she describes:

> We were lying on our backs next to each other, everything hidden by the covers, and after a second I reached over for his thigh and let my hand trail downward to the stump, the thick scarred skin. I held the stump for a second. He flinched. (p. 207)

He flinches, but she doesn't. Readers see that she has already accepted these flaws in his physicality and loves him regardless. Reader and characters shift together from discomfort and inhibition to acceptance and the continuation of love. From the rapidly matured perspective of a teen cancer patient, Hazel understands and readily accepts that love—like life—is an imperfect affair. Augustus is more likeable to her because he understands suffering—her suffering—and he is made wiser because of his own. Although most of the story, Hazel and Augustus focus on her mortality, his cancer returns and rapidly deteriorates body and mind. At one point, Hazel describes:

> I found him mumbling in a language of his own creation. He'd pissed the bed. It was awful. I couldn't even look, really. I just shouted for his parents and they came down, and I went upstairs while they cleaned him up. (p. 239)

When Hazel calls the scene "awful," she is not just commenting on an aversion to "piss" and delirium. She is acknowledging his torment, the humiliation he will surely feel later, and the horror of seeing him slip closer and closer to death's door.

Readers witness the actions of love in this story. In their daily interactions, Hazel and Augustus share inside-jokes, secret words, phrases, and codes that are special to them alone (e.g. p. 208, 210, 231). They actively create special shared moments, such as sipping champagne out of plastic cups and holding a living eulogy for him. Hazel stays by Augustus's side when he unglamorously blurts that he hates himself (p. 245) and, more significantly, when he vomits on himself in a car and when he deteriorates in hospital prior to his death. They feel a deep connection that transcends their frequent inability to physically be together. Love endures. Love survives even his death because he is gone, but *their* love continues. She continues to love him and feel his love for her. In a moment imbued with memory, shared jokes, and forgiveness, she tucks cigarettes into the coffin holding his corpse and whispers, "You can light these ... I won't mind" (p. 270). Her greatest act of love is her eventual willingness to let him go. Despite the overwhelming emotional devastation his death brings her, she is willing to suffer and still go on loving him.

Like Hazel and Augustus, the main characters in Benjamin Alire Sáenz's young adult novel, *Aristotle and Dante Discover the Secrets of the Universe* (2012), also overcome profound obstacles to love. Readers learn that Dante is a gay teen living in Texas, deeply in love with his best friend, Ari, who is "not the same" (p. 151). Quiet, reserved Ari does not *want* to be gay. But this desire and other desires are at odds. In stories, as in life, sudden events can cause the truth to pierce through accepted realities. When Dante is about to be struck by a car, Ari hears "screams" (p. 107) from inside himself and launches into the street. His heroism saves Dante's life, but Ari breaks both legs and an arm in the process. The moment is a turning point, but a slow-moving one; readers journey with Ari over the course of a year as he finally overcomes the societal impediments to love and accepts what his parents, Dante's parents, and perhaps even Dante have suspected: He is in love with Dante.

Saving Dante's life is one of many actions that enact love. The novel demonstrates how personality differences can complement one another—with one character talkative, expressive, emotional, and the other a good listener, restrained, emotionally subdued. Ari is in real pain after enduring surgeries and casts from his car accident, yet he later comforts sobbing Dante after Dante is beaten up for being gay. Meanwhile, Ari feels fully seen by Dante—recognized for his true nature. He reveals, "somehow it felt like it was Dante who had saved my life and not the other way around" (p. 308). Ari opens up to Dante and reveals parts of himself he has been too afraid to talk to anyone about except his mother (p. 308). In this way, the novel frames two kinds of courage: physical courage and emotional courage.

The two also experience deeply sensory (sensual) moments together that are important in engaging readers in transporting experiences. Before the car accident, the two share a moment of vivid, sensual play: "We ran around the truck, naked and laughing, the rain beating against our bodies" (p. 273). With intimate clarity, Ari recalls, "I stretched my arms out toward the sky. And closed my eyes. Dante was standing next to me. I could feel his breath" (p. 273). Later, when Ari is at home recovering from the car accident, Dante gives him a sponge bath. Ari vividly notes, "I felt Dante's hands on my shoulders, the warm water, the soap, the washcloth. Dante's hands were bigger than my mother's. And softer. He was slow, methodical, careful. He made me feel as fragile as porcelain" (p. 144).

Not only do these two novels enable teen readers to envision ways beyond horrific obstacles and witness the actions of love, they also help *define* love. Love inhabits paradox; it is always ever changing and constant, unique and universal. Young people reading these books may have had few opportunities to hear the words of love, the descriptions of love, and the definitions of love's emotions. Ari explains, "Even though we hadn't wanted that kiss to be a big thing, it had been a big thing. It took a while for the ghost of that kiss to disappear" (p. 258). Love lingers. Upon realizing she is falling in love, Hazel describes, "It felt like everything was rising up in me, like I was drowning in this weirdly painful joy" (p. 154). Love can feel frighteningly powerful. Courageously, Augustus announces his love to Hazel:

> I'm in love with you, and I'm not in the business of denying myself the simple pleasure of saying true things. I'm in love with you, and I know that love is just a shout into the void, and that oblivion is inevitable, and that we're all doomed and that there will come a day when all our labor has been returned to dust, and I know the sun will swallow the only earth we'll ever have, and I'm in love with you. (p. 153)

Love is always an act of courage. And as Augustus's words convey, love matters most. In the shared space between novel and reader, teens engage in the work of imagining how for Augustus and Hazel, and Ari and Dante, love overcomes all obstacles. This experiential witnessing builds emotional security and shows teen readers how one might love despite seemingly impossible barriers.

44.6 Teen Romance Novels and the Thwarting of Love

Importantly, not all teen romance is worthy of recommendation. Some teen romance novels may have the power to shrink as much as expand teen relational capacity. A poor quality romance novel directly and/or indirectly emphasizes problematic values. Characters may openly express desire for constricting gender norms, for example. More subtly, the novel may draw repeated attention to particular kinds of objects, thereby elevating their value. It matters whether a novel highlights the familiar objects of 'home' versus the exterior appearance of a house, whether it promotes relationships with trees and sunlight, or with boob enhancements and soda. Functioning as a cultural tool, a novel normalizes situations, priorities, and values. Poor quality teen romance will also animate unoriginal or shallow characters who will do little to touch the deeper concerns, insecurities, and realities of its readers. That is, instead of illuminating pathways to overcome obstacles to love, "love" may be unearned and thus inexplicable. The story may be *branded* as a love story because of the cover art and because words like "love" and "boyfriend" and "kiss" appear with regularity. Yet the actions of love—acts of devotion, selflessness, forgiveness, acceptance, generosity—may be wholly lacking or entirely dependent on the reader's imagination. Lastly, poor quality teen romance does not expand relational awareness by providing meaningful definitions of love which teens can identify with and learn from.

Jenny Han's novel, *Always and Forever, Lara Jean* (2017), may be precisely what critics of romance have in mind when they suggest the genre harms real-life love opportunities. This book is the last in a trilogy about Lara Jean, and as such, higher quality love may or may not exist in the earlier two novels. However, authors know that novels in a series must be designed to also stand alone since readers often don't start at the beginning. Thus, this analysis assesses the novel for its own merits, rather than the broader context of the series. The American protagonist of supposedly Asian descent, Lara Jean, is in a relationship with Peter from the beginning to the end of the novel, with a brief break-up comprising part of the book's climax. Although promoted as a love story, the primary angst in this novel centres around Lara Jean's failure to be accepted into her first choice university. To her utter devastation, she is instead accepted in her second-choice university, a higher ranking school.

Han's novel begins with surface appearances. In the opening lines of the first page, Lara Jean admires her boyfriend, Peter, because of the innocent appearance of his sleeping face: "his jaw, the curve of his cheekbone," and what she vaguely refers to as "a certain kind of niceness" (p. 1). Peter evidences genuine devotion to Lara Jean through small and large gestures throughout the novel. At her request, he dies his hair and, on another occasion, sings part of a song. He even offers to switch universities to be closer to her. But these actions do little or nothing to increase her attraction, admiration, or appreciation of him. Instead, she rests her head on his shoulder when thinking about how "handsome" he is (p. 27). She looks at his profile and comments that she "likes how smooth" he is (p. 139). She loves "the smell of his detergent, his soap, everything" (p. 235). Thus, readers may note that his physical appearance inspires her feelings in a way that his kindness and devotion do not.

Her "love" is also enhanced by their many kisses, which he performs with directness and aggression—stereotypical characteristics of masculinity. Peter "pulls [her] face closer to him" (p. 29), he "pulls [her] toward him, and kisses [her], all in one fast motion" (p. 3), and he "surges up and kisses [her] harder" (p. 238). At one point, harbouring hurt feelings by one of her callous comments, he "plants a chaste peck" on her forehead (p. 45). Her eyes "fly open," and she snaps, "That's all I get?" In doing so, she holds him to her expectations of direct, aggressive passion. These passages clarify that her feelings toward him are predominantly connected to physical passion and his external appearance.

In a similarly disturbing vein, one of the qualities Lara Jean likes best about Peter is the feeling of owning and manipulating him. She admits to being "covetous" of him, noting, "I want his eyes only on me; I want to talk only to him, to be just him and me for this little while longer" (p. 323). When Peter submits to her bizarre desire that he ask her to prom *twice*, she muses, "And grumbling, he does it, in front of everybody, which is how I know he is utterly and completely mine" (p. 55). When Peter asks if she can bring some of her delicious cookies to school the next day, she responds, "We'll see," because she "want[s] to see him make that pouty face [she] loves so much" (p. 21). After Peter does "two romantic things in a row," she figures she "should praise him accordingly" because like a dog, "the boy responds well to positive reinforcement" (p. 58). By caressing his hair and asking sweetly, she manipulates him into dying his hair for the Halloween party so his costume will better match hers. When she's upset with him, he "keeps texting" her, but she is "petty enough to be glad he's not enjoying himself anymore," and she "make[s] him wait longer" before she texts him back (p. 216).

In a psychologically healthy love relationship, these selfish and immature attempts to control would be put in check. The protagonist would be made to reconcile, heal, and make amends for these illustrations of insecure attachment. But here, Han does the opposite; Lara Jean celebrates her manipulations. Giddily, she claps her hands "in delight," and reflects, "Is there anything more intoxicating than making a boy bend to your will?" (p. 188). Notably, Lara Jean reduces Peter to the blank identity of "boy" in two of these moments. His personal identity has been erased; what matters is not *Peter*, but his identity as a *boy*. Near the end of the book, after Lara Jean has been experienced a degree of grief and anxiety, she articulates her desire for control stripped of pomp; she tells Peter simply, "I want you to do what you're supposed to do and I want to do what I'm supposed to do" (p. 300).

What *are* they "supposed" to do? The framework of "supposed to" may be disconcertingly unclear to the reader, but it guides most of the protagonist's actions. She lauds perfection and extrinsic goals. She is "on a quest to perfect [her] chocolate chip cookie recipe" (p. 20). She is "ready to throw out" an entire batch "for not being perfect" (p. 20, 21). Her first choice university has the "perfect storybook campus, the perfect everything" (p. 10). This focus on the "perfect" shifts the character and reader's gaze to externalities. She bubbles, "I think couples costumes might be my favourite part of being in a couple" (p. 37). One can reasonably question the depth and meaning of her relationship if once-a-year dress-up constitutes the best part. Maintaining the focus on externalities, she laments to Peter, "It's too bad we don't have a meet-cute" (p. 21). Her regret stems from her inclination to craft the perfect love story. Felt realities matter less than outward appearances, even if the latter are artificial constructs. In a discussion about going off to different universities, she scolds her friend, "The least you can do is *pretend* you'll miss me!" (emphasis mine, p. 46).

The climax of the novel does force Lara Jean to adjust notions of perfection. Although she is eventually accepted into her first-choice university after all, she briefly grapples with the disappointment of attending her second-choice university. Despite her consistent lack of kindness toward Peter, he remains devoted to her and the novel concludes with the implication that the two will marry. But even this seemingly extraordinary and joyful moment carries some disappointment for her. To her, the perfectly-crafted love story involves older characters. She believes 27 "sounds like" a right age to meet, fall in love, and marry whereas she is only 18 (p. 323).

Why Peter *wants* to marry her remains a mystery, although it could be that author, like protagonist, is busily crafting an outwardly 'perfect' love story. Many of Lara Jean's acts of love, can most generously be interpreted as deeply immature. More worryingly, they may evidence a serious attachment disorder or even psychopathology. In addition to her manipulations, Lara Jean regularly insults and physically pushes Peter. With little or no provocation, she gives him "a dirty look" (p. 224). She insults the smell of his feet, admitting privately that she loves "the way he smells after a lacrosse game" but she "love[s] to tease, to see that unsure look cross his face for just half a beat" (p. 40). When he says he could grow a beard, she remarks, "No, you can't. But maybe one day, when you're a man" (p. 139). When he protests, she ridicules him, "You don't even pack your own lunches. Do you even know how to do laundry?" (p. 140). Although a psychologist may recognize the anxious attachment style in her behaviour, she is aware that she is "testing him" but does not know why. Later, she snaps that he is "being unfair" when he astutely notices her ambivalence that they will soon be living in different places (p. 282). Gesturing to normative models of masculinity where men are expected to exhibit only confidence, she tells him pointedly, "You acted like a jerk tonight. Insecurity is not a good look on you, Peter" (p. 273).

Reminiscent of a pre-teen, rather than the 18-year-old, she yells and "shove [s] him in the chest" for hinting about their French kiss in front of Lara Jean's sister (p. 43). Lara Jean disparages him, "you're not *that* good at French kissing" (p. 43). Later, the two are counting how many people she has kissed, and she shoves him again when he claims one of her kisses didn't count because she "technically cheated on" him (p. 44). Soon after, he suggests that they practice their own kiss. She reports, "I run back to his car, I pull him toward me by his shirt, and angle my face against his—and then I push him away and run backward, laughing" (p. 46). She also "pushes him away" for kissing her in a pool because "there are kids around!" (p. 187). Like her manipulations and penchant for extrinsic rewards, the protagonist is never made to confront these minor physical confrontations nor to recognize that perhaps she should not push, shove, and insult the man she claims to love.

For Lara Jean, love is all about surfaces and outward appearances. Although her and Peter do have some tender moments of tickling, kissing, and giving gifts, and she does eventually apologize when she figures out from his facial expression that she devastated him, these more tender moments are vastly overshadowed by her efforts to control him and their "love" story. In the crafting of this novel, these character flaws are not obstacles to overcome, but celebrated quirks of character. The success of their "love" story is not in their ability to grow as characters, but in her luck at having landed a boyfriend who doesn't challenge her emotionally unhealthy reactions. Essentially, the story develops outwardly through plot developments, but not inwardly through character development.

These direct messages prioritizing externalities are underscored by the persistent attention drawn to material objects and consumerism. Many lines of text are devoted to boob jobs, dresses, and cookies. The teen protagonist is remarkably familiar with the lingo of wedding ring designs. When she is just about to lose her virginity to Peter, she leaps out of bed to go change out of her "normal every day cappuccino-colored bra" and into her "special bra," thereby destroying the moment and thwarting the event (p. 280).

More concerning than these arguably typical consumer tendencies are the repeated instances of brand name identification. Characters read *Teen Vogue*, drink Vitaminwater, and eat at Starbucks and Applebee's. "Fresca," one character describes, is a "delicious grapefruit soda. Zero calories! You have to try it!" (p. 88). When the character does try it, she smiles, agreeing that it is "Very refreshing" (p. 89). Lara Jean's kind and soon-to-be stepmother "loves" Fresca (p. 91), so Lara Jean buys "a case" whenever she goes to the store, adding, "It's actually very refreshing" (p. 91). Can these repeated messages be interpreted as anything other than product placement?

One may wonder just how many teens can relate to this consumerist tale of manipulative love. Yet the book has received four and half stars out of 545 reviews on Amazon.com and is soon going to be made into a movie. As authors know, the success of a book is as much about marketing as about content. Though it's unknown whether Han received endorsements for product placement, it is known that some books that are written with consumerist goals in mind, promote consumerism within their pages, are funded by consumer industries, and thus, fan the flames of consumerism for their readers. Books such as these are not designed to enable readers to navigate complex social worlds; they are deliberately or unwittingly designed to promote consumerism. These books do not offer hope to lovelorn youth. Rather, they pick at and exacerbate low-grade insecurities about attractiveness, success, and luck, for example. Content, hopeful, intrinsically-motivated teen readers do not make good future consumers.

44.7 Conclusion

Teen romance novels meaningfully impact teen relational capacity. Many of today's North American teens lack role models for enduring, deep, and genuine love—whether romantic, platonic, or familial. They suffer unprecedented levels of anxiety, depression, and loneliness. Having underdeveloped critical thinking skills, young readers are particularly susceptible to the overt and covert messaging of novels. The teenage years present the height of identity formation and its twin: insecurity about belonging. Where most adults discard a novel if its values uncomfortably differ from their own, many teen readers do not yet have the self-awareness. Consequently, they may linger longer in novels that cause discomforting gaps between their (still developing) value systems and identities and those presented by the novel. They may wrongly interpret this discomfort as a failure on their part to 'fit in' and 'be part of' the social world around them. If they already feel disconnected socially, they may see the novel as offering an explanation why, as identifying the values that need to shift if they want to belong. Thus, reading low-quality romance novels might be damaging mentally, emotionally, and socially for teens.

Low quality love stories may magnify teen insecurities and isolation and—with a sleight of hand—offer materialistic and other questionable solutions to their angst. *Always and Forever, Lara Jean* evidences a shallow, materialistic, and manipulative teen protagonist whose bad behavior is ultimately rewarded by hints of marriage. Some young readers may be mature enough to accurately identify the attachment issues and materialistic values of this book. Nonetheless, this story likely thwarts relational capacity of its teen readers by provoking perfectionist anxieties and failing to illustrate the prosocial actions of love.

Since reading requires active daydreaming, high-quality romance novels can provide neurobiological experiences of love that may establish cognitive frameworks for teens to understand and, thus, foster meaningful love in their own lives. *The Fault in Our Stars* and *Aristotle and Dante Discover the Secrets of the Universe* show young readers that they can overcome even the most egregious obstacles to love. These novels illustrate that true love is profoundly accepting, generous, kind, and enduring. True love requires authenticity, courage, and action.

Research on the neurological processes involved with reading is still in early stages. Aubry (2011) suggests that contemporary Americans use fiction as a form of therapy or a place from which to gleam life advice, rather than as an aesthetic experience (1). He writes, "They choose books that will offer strategies for confronting, understanding, and managing their personal problems" (1). He coins this "pejorative" category of mostly middle-brow literature: "contemporary therapeutic fiction" (1). It is possible that some readers—or readers some of the time—achieve a feeling of social satisfaction from reading that reduces the need for real-world social contact. More research is needed to determine the point at which the expansiveness of imagining turns into demotivating satiation.

Novels are, in themselves, creating relationship. Meaning, an author is writing for an audience. That audience is tuned in to the author. Together the two create something that may not be completely mirrored by any other reader-novel combination. Just as quality romance fiction resists pressing romantic love stories into flat, predictable shapes, romance fiction develops a unique relationship with individual readers and should encourage development of individual selves, not predetermined, artificial identities. At Augustus's living eulogy, Hazel tells him:

> I cannot tell you how thankful I am for our little infinity. I wouldn't trade it for the world. You gave me a forever within the numbered days, and I am so grateful. (Green, p. 260).

A novel is its own "little infinity," a temporary relational space between author and reader and sociocultural environment. Given the right conditions, a young reader may begin to conceive a better future for themselves.

References

Armstrong, P. B. (2013). *How literature plays with the brain: The neuroscience of reading and art.* Johns Hopkins University Press.

Aubry, T. R. (2011; 2006). *Reading as therapy: What contemporary fiction does for middle-class Americans.* Iowa City: University of Iowa Press. Project Muse University Press eBooks.

Bal, P. M., & Veltkamp, M. (2013). How does fiction reading influence empathy? An experimental investigation on the role of emotional transportation. *PLoS ONE, 8*(1), 1–12. https://doi.org/10.1371/journal.pone.0055341

Barreca, G. (2012). Romance can hurt rather than help real partners. *Psychology Today.* Retrieved from https://www.psychologytoday.com/intl/blog/snow-white-doesnt-live-here-anymore/201210/romance-can-hurt-rather-help-real-partners

Cacioppo, J. T., & Patrick, W. (2008). *Loneliness: Human nature and the Need for Social Connection* (1st ed.). Norton.

Doidge, N. (2007). *The brain that changes itself: Stories of personal triumph from the frontiers of brain science.* New York: Penguin Books.

Galgut, E. (2014). Harnessing the imagination: The asymmetry of belief and make-believe. *Contemporary Aesthetics, 12.*

Gerhardt, S. (2004). *Why love matters: How affection shapes a baby's brain.* Brunner-Routledge.

Gerhardt, S. (2010). *The selfish society.* London: Simon & Schuster.

Green, J. (2012). *The fault in our stars* (1st ed.). New York: Dutton Books.

Greene, M. (2000). *Releasing the imagination: Essays on education, the arts, and social change.* San Francisco: Jossey-Bass Publishers.

Han, J. (2017). *Always and forever, Lara Jean.* New York: Simon & Schuster.

Hogan, P. C. (2003). *The mind and its stories: Narrative universals and human emotion.* New York: Cambridge University Press. Retrieved from https://doi-org.ezproxy.langara.ca/10.1017/CBO9780511499951

Konrath, S., O'Brien, E., & Hsing, C. (2011). Changes in dispositional empathy in American college students over time: A meta-analysis. *Personality and Social Psychology Review, 15*(2), 180–198. https://doi.org/10.1177/1088868310377395

Le Guin, U. (1977). The book is what is real. In U. Le Guin & S. Wood (Eds.), *The language of the night: Essays on fantasy and science fiction* (pp. 127–128). New York: G.P. Putnam.

Levine, A., & Heller, R. (2010). *Attached: The new science of adult attachment and how it can help you find—and keep—love.* New York: TarcherPerigee.

Lillard, A. (2013). Fictional worlds, the neuroscience of the imagination, and childhood education. In M. Taylor (Ed.), *The Oxford handbook of the development of imagination.* New York: Oxford UP.

Lyons, S. F. (2015). From Emma Pearse author. Why can't romance novels get any love? *Smithsonian.* Retrieved from https://www.smithsonianmag.com/arts-culture/why-cant-romance-novels-get-any-love-180954548/

Mar, R. A., & Oatley, K. (2008). The function of fiction is the abstraction and simulation of social experience. *Perspectives on Psychological Science, 3*(3), 173–192. Retrieved from https://doi-org.ezproxy.langara.ca/10.1111/j.1745-6924.2008.00073.x

Mar, R. A., Oatley, K., Djikic, M., & Mullin, J. (2011). Emotion and narrative fiction: Interactive influences before, during, and after reading. *Cognition & Emotion, 25*(5), 818–833. Retrieved from https://doi-org.ezproxy.langara.ca/10.1080/02699931.2010.515151

Mar, R. A., Oatley, K., Hirsh, J., dela Paz, J., & Peterson, J. B. (2006). Bookworms versus nerds: Exposure to fiction versus non-fiction, divergent associations with social ability, and the simulation of fictional social worlds. *Journal of Research in Personality, 40*(5), 694–712. Retrieved from https://doi-org.ezproxy.langara.ca/10.1016/j.jrp.2005.08.002

Maté, G. (2015). *The destruction of childhood.* N.d. TS. Gabor Mate research notes, Vancouver, BC.

Modleski, T. (1984). Loving with a Vengeance: Mass-Produced Fantasies for Women. Metheun.

Narvaez, D. (2014). *Neurobiology and the development of human morality.* New York: Norton.

Nichols, S. (2006). Just the imagination: Why imagining doesn't behave like believing. *Mind Language, 21*(4), 459–474. https://doi.org/10.1111/j.1468-0017.2006.00286.x

Oatley, K., Dunbar, R., & Budelmann, F. (2018). Imagining possible worlds. *Review of General Psychology, 22*(2), 121–124. https://doi-org.ezproxy.langara.ca/10.1037/gpr0000149

Paivio, A. (2008). Looking at reading comprehension through the lens of neuroscience. In C. C. Block & S. R. Parris (Eds.), *Comprehension instruction: Research-based best practices,* 2nd ed. (pp. 101–113). New York: The Guilford Press. Retrieved from https://search-ebscohost-com.ezproxy.langara.ca/login.aspx?direct=true&db=psyh&AN=2008-06649-007&site=eds-live&scope=site

Quilliam, S. (2011). "He seized her in his manly arms and bent his lips to hers...". The surprising impact that romantic novels have on our work. *The Journal of Family Planning and Reproductive Health Care, 37*(3), 179–181. Retrieved from https://doi-org.ezproxy.langara.ca/10.1136/jfprhc-2011-100152

Radway, J. A. (1984). *Reading the romance: Women, patriarchy, and popular literature.* University of North Carolina Press. Retrieved from https://search-ebscohost-direct=true&db=cat05664a&AN=lang.b1008789&site=eds-live&scope=site

Sáenz, B. (2012). *Aristotle and Dante discover the secrets of the universe* (1st ed.). Foglia, C. Simon Schuster Books for Young Readers.

Turkle, S. (2011). *Alone together: Why we expect more from technology and less from each other.* Basic Books.

Twenge, J. M. (2000). The age of anxiety? Birth cohort change in anxiety and neuroticism, 1952–1993. *Journal of Personality and Social Psychology, 79*(6), 1007–1021. https://doi.org/10.1037/0022-3514.79.6.1007

Twenge, J. M., Joiner, T. E., Rogers, M. L., & Martin, G. N. (2018). Increases in depressive symptoms, suicide-related outcomes, and suicide rates among U.S. adolescents after 2010 and links to increased new media screen time. *Clinical Psychological Science, 6*(1), 3–17. https://doi.org/10.1177/2167702617723376

Vadeboncoeur, J. A. (2017). *Vygotsky and the promise of public education.* Peter Lang. https://www.lcjgroup.org

Verny, T. (2002). *Pre-parenting.* London: Simon & Schuster.

Zimbardo, P. G. (Speaker). (2011, March). The demise of guys. *TED Talks.* TED Conferences. Retrieved from https://www.ted.com/talks/zimchallenge?language=en

Estella Carolye Kuchta is the author of *Finding the Daydreamer* (Elm Books, 2020). She teaches English literature at Langara College and worked as a research assistant to Medical Doctor Gabor Maté for 4 years. Her ecocritical love research at the University of British Columbia earned several awards, including the Social Sciences and Humanities Research Council Grant (SSHRC). She holds a BFA in Creative Writing and an MA in Literature and is a member of the Love Research Network. Her journalism and creative writing projects have been published in newspapers, magazines, and literary journals in Canada and the U.S.

Part IX
Love in Workplaces and Business Contexts

Time to Rethink: Leading with Love (Photo: Elisabeth Vanderheiden)

Chapter 45
Compassionate Love in Leaders: Leadership Solutions in the Fourth Industrial Revolution

Claude-Hélène Mayer

Abstract Leaders need many competencies to drive diverse and transcultural workforces by building strong work and positive intergroup relationships. This is particularly true for running organisations which grow in social, cultural and technological diversity. Love, defined as a *compassion* (Schopenhauer), is a form of caring, a form of altruism which emphasises concern for the self and the other person's well-being.

In contemporary globalising work environments, while technologising and digitalisation are at the forefront of the approaching fourth industrial revolution, love, compassion, peace and sustainability are advancing as key components in the art of collaboration for a sustainable, future world.

This chapter presents findings from a qualitative research study in which 22 leaders were interviewed on their views of love and leadership. Leaders explain how they define and interrelate the two concepts, and how love impacts on their leadership in theory and practice. Findings show that love is split into concepts of interpersonal, intra-personal, object-related and toxic or non-existent love in a work environment. Leaders know how to express and detect love at work. They understand love as an emotion which connects people across cultural group membership and supports individuals in finding solutions and working together respectfully and openly. Additionally, love can help employees to transform negative emotions into neutral or positive ones. Finally, extraordinary leaders are defined by the respondents as those who go beyond the regular and customary, and are driven by concepts such as a loving attitude, love for humanity, inclusiveness and unconditional love.

Keywords Love · Leadership · Compassion · Global work places · Fourth revolution · Sustainability · Peace

---

C.-H. Mayer (✉)
Department of Industrial Psychology and People Management, University of Johannesburg, Johannesburg, South Africa

Institut für Therapeutische Kommunikation und Sprachgebrauch, Europa Universität Viadrina, Frankfurt (Oder), Germany
e-mail: claudemayer@gmx.net

© Springer Nature Switzerland AG 2021
C.-H. Mayer, E. Vanderheiden (eds.), *International Handbook of Love*,
https://doi.org/10.1007/978-3-030-45996-3_45

45.1 Introduction: The World of Work During the Fourth Industrial Revolution

The change towards global fourth industrial revolution (4IR) workplaces is in full swing and organisations have to deal with internal and external challenges to manage the turn towards new technologies, new individual and organisational processes of digitalisation, new frameworks of work, and new meanings of work as well as workplaces (Bag et al., 2018). It is argued here that rapid changes in work and organisational culture, new action plans, information trade and upgraded technological applications (Spath et al., 2013) will have a major influence on employee relations, meaning creation and leadership (Mayer, 2019). Automated, flexible and self-controlling production systems will call for new and original ideas and concepts of leadership and meaning of work. Leadership will not only require a deep knowledge of human interactions, but also of human–machine interactions (Stubbings, 2018). Thereby, it is argued that human abilities will play an increasingly important role within work processes and will need to be dealt with and managed constantly. The World Economic Forum (2016) stresses that the skills that are required to be successful in the workplace are changing drastically. It has been highlighted that the ten top skills needed will include, in chronological order, complex problem-solving, critical thinking, creativity, people management, coordination with others, emotional intelligence, judgement and decision-making, service orientation, negotiation and cognitive flexibility. It appears that extraordinary leadership—defined as "going beyond what is usual, regular, or customary. Exceptional to a very marked extent. Rare. Uncommon. Unique" (Catron, 2015, p. xiv)—is needed to drive the contemporary changes.

Changes, according to the World Economic Forum (2016) will mainly be seen in terms of drivers of change in socio-demographics, such as in working environments (44%)[1] (new technologies, remote working, teleconferencing, smaller pool or core time employees with fixed functions and a diverse, global workforce and external consultants), the rise of middle-class emerging markets (23%), climate change and natural resources constraints (23%), rising geopolitical volatility (21%), new consumer concerns (16%), longevity and ageing societies (14%), young demographics in emerging markets (13%), women's rising aspirations and economic power (12%), and rapid urbanisation (8%).

According to Schwab and Samans (2016), the question is how will individuals in workplaces deal with the changes? The Search Inside Yourself Leadership Institute (SIYLI, 2017) argues that the 4IR is actually "the Emotional Intelligence Revolution": in this revolution, one key competence is the trustful and sympathetic collaboration and the conscious way of "human engineering".

In the context of the 4IR, it is suggested that leadership skills need to include the following:

---

[1]The percentages refer to the rating as a "top trend".

1. An awareness of and competence to transform negative emotions into positive emotions, such as love (based on the emotional intelligence model of Goleman, 1995);
2. An increasing awareness of the importance of love in leadership and the ability to define and live love in the workplace and in leadership in a way that influences humane development of human and human–machine interactions, care for the other in diverse work forces, trust in working in remote workplaces and long-distance interrelationships, and ethical behaviour in terms of human rights and the protection of natural resources.

It is assumed that the concept of love in leadership can support transformation of emotions and also create awareness, particularly in leaders, to empower previously marginalised groups in leadership, and women's leadership aspirations in these rapidly changing times of the 4IR.

Larson and Murthadha (2005) have pointed out that love can steer the 4IR and promote leadership values such as social justice, as described in concepts of servant leadership (Patterson, 2003; Dennis, Kinzler-Norheim, & Bocarnea, 2010). This research focuses on concepts of love in leaders who are in the process of transforming organisations and preparing employees to gear up for the 4IR. The aim is to explore what leaders in 4IR organisations think about love and leadership.

In the following, concepts of love in the leadership literature in contemporary workplaces are reviewed and reflected upon with regard to the cultural research context influencing the research.

45.2 Concepts of Love in Leadership in Contemporary Workplaces

Within the concepts of leadership, organisational studies and organisational behaviour, the concept of love and its study has been neglected for many years (Hoyle, 2001). It is argued in this chapter that, for a successful transformation of global and local organisations into the 4IR, love is a key factor for successful organisations, enterprises and leaders.

Only about one decade ago, Barsade and Gibson (2007) observed that emotions play an extraordinary role in workplaces, influencing employee attitudes, performances, the organisational culture and interpersonal relationships at work. Since then, emotions have been researched in the management and organisational literature and it has been noted that positive emotions can impact positively on employees and their effectiveness (see Barsade, Brief, & Spataro, 2003; Hareli & Rafaeli, 2008; Robinson, Watkins, & Harmon-Jones, 2013).

Research usually differentiates between "romantic love" and "love" in general which is often associated with compassionate love (see, for example, Patterson, 2010) or companionate love (O'Neill, 2018). Thereby, romantic love in work places has been evaluated with regard to positive, as well as negative effects and outcomes from different perspectives of employees, co-workers and leaders (Chory & Hoke, 2019; Cowan & Horan, 2014; Malachowski, Chory, & Claus, 2012).

Greenleaf (1977) highlighted that love is indefinable and complex, also with regard to its effect on others, while Lazarus (1991) has emphasised that love—when defined in a broad sense—can be viewed as including compassion, but also affection, tenderness for the other and caring. Several researchers (such as Eldor, 2017; Underwood 2002) have pointed out that compassionate love is connected to caring for others and working towards the prosperity of others. Eldor (2017) emphasises that not only compassionate love is needed, but rather a compassionate workplace in which employees receive compassion from their superiors and supervisors, which is expressed through affection, generosity, caring and tenderness.

Van Dierendonck and Patterson (2014) highlight within the context of servant leadership that compassionate love is a virtue which can encourage an attitude of humility, gratitude, forgiveness and altruism in leaders and in the workplace as such. Patterson (2010) proposes that the concept of love in leadership and organisational contexts needs to be defined in detail, and that leading with love, its potential for transformation and positive impact on leadership in terms of organisational life and culture needs to be explored. Patterson (2010) points out that leaders who abide by the concept of love present their perspectives. Five years after their publication on love and servant leadership, van Dierendonck and Patterson (2014) describe compassionate love as a cornerstone of servant leadership which encourages meaningful and optimal human functioning in organisations. Furthermore, love in servant leadership can impact positively on empowerment, authenticity, stewardship and providing direction (van Dierendonck & Patterson, 2014).[2]

Barsade and O'Neill (2014) report a pervasive belief that work relationships do not include enough depth to be called "love" relationships. However, several researchers counter-argue that organisations and interpersonal relationships at work often carry in-depth emotional experiences and are full of meaning (Fineman, 2000). In 1991, Savickas concluded that love at work can significantly influence careers and work satisfaction. Almost three decades later, O'Neill (2018) points out that companionate love is an important factor in work relationships, referring to fondness, affection, caring, compassion and tenderness (abbreviated as "FACCT"). Further, Barsade and O'Neill (2014) note that emotions in the work context play an outstanding role and that companionate love buffers negatively experienced emotions, such as anxiety. Robinson et al. (2013) affirm that cognition and emotions can affect organisational and workplace behaviour in different ways. Accordingly, scholars agree that love can be seen as a positive emotion which falls into the domain of positive psychology and/or positive organisational behaviour (Rynes, Bartunek, Dutton, & Margolis, 2012). In a study by Kempster and Parry (2013), when love for leaders and leadership was studied not from the leader's perspective, but from that of the follower, most of the participants referred to love stories when talking about charismatic leadership. Only a few participants experienced negative

---

[2]For another leading discussion on compassionate love see Chap. 31.

effects of love and some experienced both positive and negative emotions. Coming from a leader's perspective, Winston (2002), emphasises that a loving leader would be "doing good" for the follower without hidden agendas and particularly for the benefit of the follower.

This perspective is supported by Rapport's (2019) view that love in the workplace can be described as a form of ethical engagement which goes beyond culture and represents a kind of universal culture of ethics.

Frey and Matherly (2006) have found that in organisations which lead from a spiritual perspective, leadership is usually based on values which foster intrinsic motivation, such as spiritual well-being through the experience of membership and a calling, compassion and joy, creating meaning, sense-making, hope, faith and altruistic love (including care, concern, and appreciation for both organisational and employee needs) which leads to the removal of fears related to anger, failure, selfishness, guilt or worry. Additionally, Daft (2002) points out that leading with love in the workplace reduces anxiety and fear in followers and encourages connection, energy and the feeling of being alive in the workplace. Several approaches have been developed to foster compassionate love in workplaces and leadership to reduce stress, promote well-being and relaxation (Cooper, 2013; Gilbert, 2009).

45.3 Love and Leadership in the Fourth Industrial Revolution

With regard to cultural perspectives on love and leadership, it has been previously noted that cultural context plays an important role in the understanding of emotions and at the same time, emotions carry cultural clues (Matsumoto & Hwang, 2012; Smith, Davidson, Cameron, & Bondi, 2016). Geertz (1973), for example, states that emotions are cultural artefacts and therefore immanent and inherent in any cultural context. This is also true for leadership and organisational contexts.

Magubane (2019) recently published a book on love within the 4IR, where he provides examples of the difficulty of dividing love and the 4IR. He describes, for example, algorithms which explore the truth of a message sent by a closely related person and applications which support dating and close relationship-building.

Illouz (2007) expresses a critical view of love and leadership in the capitalist cultures of the world, which strongly impact on love and on love's associations. She disagrees with the commonly held view that capitalism has created a culture of non-emotionality and bureaucratic rationality, indicating that capitalism has changed the workplace culture into an intensely emotional space. Further, Illouz (2007) contends that close and intimate relationships, as well as economic-based relationships are affected by equity, exchange and bargaining, as well as love: this process Illouz (2007) names "emotional economy". In later writings, Illouz (2011, 2019) suggests that love in the 4IR takes on new forms which are mediated by smart technology; these may change the way individuals love, how deeply and intensely they love, and how they create new ways to build and manage relationships. She maintains that love in future will not only happen between humans, highlighting the possibility that relationships with robotics might transform human relationships (see Edirisinghe in this book).

Chandsoda and Salsing (2018) point out that the 4IR requires individuals to consciously integrate compassion and cooperation into human relations, workplaces and leadership. Schwab (2017) agrees, because smart technologies might reduce individuals' time to pause, reflect and engage in meaningful and in-depth conversation. Van der Hoven (2017) emphasises that individuals need to re-learn how to disconnect from the digital world and how to reconnect compassionately with self, others and nature, to live a meaningful life. Compassionate love in leaders aims at letting go of experienced limitations and fears, and at reconnecting with the "true self", collaborating with others, reconnecting with nature, disconnecting from the digital world, listening to the inner voice and getting into a state of flow and creativity (Van der Hoven, 2017). Tu and Thien (2019) suggest that the basic principles of Buddhism might help leaders through the 4IR, including right mindfulness and the right meditation as part of the Buddhist noble eightfold path which defines cooperation of businesses and organisations as needing to be based on trust and love.

Sun (2018) recommends that within the fourth revolution, entrepreneurship and entrepreneurs should use an attitude of "love competition" to develop entrepreneurial competition which is based on a loving attitude, as well as theoretical innovation which takes intelligence, wisdom and market-orientated social demands into account. Sun (2018) advises that these kinds of 4IR principles in business can be seen in the "sharing enterprises" such as Uber, peer-to-peer ride-sharing, or JD.com, the largest online–offline retailer in China. The author promotes the idea that everyone in the 4IR can be successful and innovative as leaders when applying an innovative, entrepreneurial mindset. Sisodia, Sheth, and Wolfe (2003) observe that the most successful organisations bring love, but also joy, empathy, authenticity and soulfulness into their businesses. They thereby create a new quality of connection which is based on experiential, social and emotional value and not just on financial value (Sisodia et al., 2003).

Fabritius (2017) argues for a better society through the fourth industrial and entrepreneurial revolution, and through a purpose-driven entrepreneurial attitude. The author refers to *Ikigai* (Fig. 45.1), a Japanese concept which promotes the idea that each life needs a clear reason to exist. Thereby, the basis for a fulfilling life and work is, according to Ikigai, a combination of "what you love with skills (what you are good at), money (what you can be paid for), and genuine demand (what the world needs)" (Fabritius, 2017, p. 14).

Fabritius (2017) contends that an entrepreneur or leader who is purpose-driven has a competitive advantage at the edge of the 4IR. Consequently, "what I love" creates the basis in Ikigai, and it is argued here that the concept of love plays an important role as the foundation of leadership and the deeper intention. Therefore, it will be taken into account in this chapter and explored in terms of its deeper meaning. According to Fournier (1998), strong and stable relationships build

Fig. 45.1 Ikigai. Source: Edukasyon (2018)

strength against mistakes and errors, and the relationship's quality is based on the intensity of love, but also on other aspects, such as self-connection and commitment, as well as interdependency. Sanders (2002) concurs, highlighting that in creating positive relationships, love is of immense importance and contributes to success.

Literature on love, leadership, workplace management and transformation with regard to the changes of the 4IR is still rare across disciplines. However, it is noteworthy that several authors already conclude that love, and particularly compassionate love, will be inevitable in future workplaces and in leadership to cooperate effectively, based on networks with a deep human connection.

45.4 Research Methodology

According to Creswell (2013), reality is constructed according to its anchoring in time, space, and socio-cultural interaction. This research design is based on the postmodernist premise, assuming reality is defined by subjective measures of perceptions and experiences. The study follows a qualitative research approach within hermeneutics and thereby aims at studying and exploring the viewpoints of individuals with regard to their social worlds (Hassan & Ghauri, 2014) and the hermeneutical understanding of their subjective experiences (Dilthey, 2002) which are assumed to construct socio-cultural meaning (Ellingson, 2013).

45.4.1 Sampling, Data Collection and Analysis

As explained in Chap. 47, CHM love stories, purposeful sampling as well as snowball sampling was used (Naderifar, Golo, & Ghaljaie, 2017). Twenty-two individuals agreed to participate in the research. Of these participants, ten spoke German as their first language, five English, two Afrikaans, and single participants each spoke Japanese, Tswana, Hebrew and Romanian. The nationalities of the participants included eight Germans, five US, two Japanese, two South Africana, and one participant each with White, German-Iranian, Israeli, Romanian and Bavarian background, as indicated by the participants themselves.

Data was collected through an online questionnaire in which qualitative data was collected and 21 in-depth questions were responded to. The participants took an average of 90 minutes to respond to the questionnaire, as described in chap. 47. Date was analysed through a holistic, thematic approach, using the five-step-model of Terre Blanche, Durrheim & kelley (2006). (see Chap. 47).

45.4.2 Ethical Considerations, Quality Criteria and Limitations of the Study

The study was conducted by referring to ethical considerations which included the informed consent of each participant, the participants' rights to confidentiality, anonymity and transparency (Roth & Unger, 2018). A German university provided the approval of the ethics of the research study.

The ethical conduct was supported through the quality criteria applied (see Mayer's Chap. 47). Limitations of this study are bound to the relatively small number of participants, the specific purposeful and snowball sampling technique, the bias of a relatively high number of German-first-language speakers and the overall high educational background.

45.5 Findings

Findings are presented with regard to concepts of love and leadership, leadership expressions and love, love and its impact on work relationships, the transformation of negative emotion and the concept of love in extraordinary leaders.

Generally, findings show that love is seen as an emotion which can support individuals of different cultural and social backgrounds to work together and cooperate successfully for a better world. It is assumed that love is a key concept in transformational times and provides meaning in terms of caring for self and others and having a positive, compassionate impact through leadership in the world.

45.5.1 Concepts of Love in Leadership

Love is viewed by the leaders interviewed as an important emotion in the workplace which is interrelated with other complex emotions, thought processes and value-based concepts (Fig. 45.2).

Leaders differentiate love at work by relating it to a) other individuals at work (interpersonal love), b) to the work itself (object-related love), c) to toxic or non-existent love, or d) to the self (intra-personal love). Interpersonal love concepts seem to be the most focused, because they are the most frequently mentioned and connected to categories such as supportive caring or true teamwork. Interpersonal love also includes the aspects of respect for self and others, a loving attitude, solidarity, empathy, compassion, dignity and kindness, happy communication and negotiation, finding similarities in differences and the building of long-term relationships. In the interviews, we identified 64 statements on interpersonal love in leadership and what it means for the participants. Table 45.1 provides an overview of the four themes and the categories feeding into the themes.

With regard to interpersonal love, a male US participant (P2) explained his concept of love in the workplace as follows:

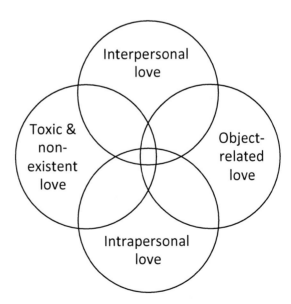

Fig. 45.2 Overview of concepts of love (author's own construction)

Table 45.1 Concepts of love in leadership in detail

Theme	Frequency	Category	Participants
Interpersonal love (64)	11	Supportive caring	P2, P6, P7, P8, P9, P10, P11, P14, P18, P19, P21
	10	True teamwork	P2, P6, P7, P8, P9, P10, P14, P16, P19, P21
	9	Respect for self and others	P4, P7, P11, P12, P13, P16, P17, P19, P22
	8	A loving attitude	P1, P4, P5, P6, P7, P10, P14, P21
	6	Solidarity	P4, P7, P8, P11, P14, P19
	5	Empathy, compassion	P4, P8, P13, P14, P20
	4	Dignity	P4, P7, P11, P16
	4	Kindness	P7, P11, P19, P22
	3	Happy communication and negotiation	P1, P6, P8, P9
	2	Finding similarities in differences	P4, P7
	2	Long-term work relationships	P6, P8
Object-related love (11)	6	Appreciation and gratitude for work	P3, P6, P7, P9, P16, P22
	3	Passion for a common project	P9, P16, P21
	2	Conscious decision-making and wisdom	P1, P13
Toxic or non-existent love (6)	5	No love at work	P1, P6, P17, P20, P21
	1	Romantic love in workplace irritates; love belongs in private context	P4
Intra-personal love (4)	2	Mental health	P4, P14
	2	Freedom of mind and speech	P7, P21

Author's own construction

> Regarding love ... in the delegation of opportunities and second chances, one can show supportive caring and love for another's potential growth. In the excursion of true teamwork, members can feel love for each other, ... in enablement and empowerment, in respectful and trusting interactions, in delegations and second chances.

Altogether, 11 statements refer to love and work and are defined as object-related love, in the sense that leaders love and appreciate their work and feel gratitude for their work. Additionally, love is experienced when leaders have a passion for a common project, and when they make conscious and wise decisions.

P9 narrated:

> Love can be seen in the passion I have for my work and in my gratitude ... for this work.

In total, six statements refer to the idea that there is no love in the workplace, that love does not belong in the work context, and one person (P4) mentioned that "romantic love at work is irritating".

45.5.2 Which Leadership Expressions Do You Associate with Love?

Participants responded to the question, "When is love expressed and used in leadership?" by highlighting the differences between love expression towards the follower, towards the world in general, towards the self, and the avoidance or rejection of expression of love.

With regard to the expression to love for followers, leaders feel that love in leadership is expressed when leaders enable and empower others based on their needs (12 statements), when they act proactively for the greater good (ten statements), when they express care and trust through their interventions, for example by giving advice or examples (ten statements). Leaders further on express love in particular to their followers (eight statements) and through constructing balanced relationships (seven statements). Four participants highlight that love is expressed through a kind of democratic leadership where joint decisions are a foundation and where individuals are given second chances to make up for mistakes or misbehaviour (four statements). Finally love for leaders is expressed in the respecting of boundaries. Love is expressed for the world by acting proactively for a greater good (11 statements), showing respectful and peaceful behaviour (11 statements) and loving consciously and mindfully (six statements). Leaders also mention the expression of love for the self (four statements) and the non-expression of love through its avoidance or through rejection in leadership (three statements). The details of the four categories are shown in Table 45.2.

Love is expressed in careful and trustful interventions, consciously, through the conduct of balanced and equal relationships, democratic leadership styles with joint decision-making processes and offering second chances, but also by showing and respecting boundaries.

Participant P9 pointed out:

> At work, love can be expressed through being on an equal footing with somebody else, ... for example, when a superior speaks to the employees, as if they were the same.

Connection by speaking on the same level and overcoming boundaries seems to be an expression of love between leaders and employees. At the same time, P12 commented that love can only be shown when the leader has love for the follower, as well as for him/herself:

> For one to influence, there are roles that will catch the follower's attention and that puts a leader in a vulnerable position of expressing or exchanging emotions to lead by example and for one to be a leader she/he needs self-love. And to me that's a display of love and leadership.

Table 45.2 Leadership love expressions (author's own construction)

Overall category	Frequency	Subcategory	Participants
Love expression for followers (39)	12	Enable and empower others based on their needs	P2, P4, P6, P7, P9, P10, P12, P14, P16, P18, P19, P20
	10	Careful and trustful interventions (advice, give example)	P2, P6, P7, P10, P12, P14, P16, P17, P18, P21
	8	Love the followers	P5, P6, P7, P12, P14, P16, P18, P19
	7	Balanced relationships	P1, P9, P14, P16, P19, P21, P22
	4	Democratic leadership with joint decisions and second chances	P2, P3, P9, P21
	3	Respect boundaries	P4, P6, P18
Love expression for the world (24)	11	Act proactively for the greater good	P5, P6, P7, P10, P13, P14, P15, P16, P17, P18, P19
	11	Respectful and peaceful behaviour	P2, P4, P6, P7, P8, P9, P10, P12, P13, P14, P19
	6	Conscious love	P1, P6, P8, P12, P20, P21
Love expression for self (4)	4	Have self-love	P11, P12, P18, P20
Avoid or reject love expression in leadership (4)	3	Love and leadership are not connected	P17, P20, P21
	1	Avoid romantic love at work	P4

Four participants' statements highlight that love and leadership are not connected and that romantic love should be avoided.

45.5.3 How Does Love Impact on Work Relationships?

According to the participants, love can impact very positively on relationships. Data from this study show that leaders differentiate between love's positive impact on general relationships, and love's impact particularly on transcultural relationships. Interestingly, love can act as a transcultural experience and can connect people of different origins and across various cultures. The general positive impact, however, frequently precedes the transcultural positive impact. Love is therefore a positive force in all human relationships and particularly in transcultural relationships.

P10, a German entrepreneur living in Sweden, declared:

> Each love story between two cultures can be a stepping stone for more people to follow.

Eight participants each stated that love can help people to find transcultural solutions and to promote respectful, open and trusting behaviour, as well as to

Table 45.3 Love's impact on work relations

Frequency	Overall category	Subcategory: Love ...	Participants
11	General positive impact (52)	promotes respectful, open and trusting behaviour	P1, P2, P3, P6, P7, P9, P10, P14, P17, P18, P22
8		increases acceptance and appreciation	P2, P3, P8, P14, P16, P18, P20, P22
7		fosters a positive attitude	P2, P5, P9, P10, P14, P16, P19
7		steers interest to learn about others	P4, P5, P8, P11, P14, P18, P19
6		increases compassion	P2, P9, P15, P16, P21, P22,
5		fosters love for humanity	P5, P7, P16, P19, P21
3		creates positive relationships	P3, P10, P19
3		motivates patience and kindness	P2, P17, P22
2		motivates to sacrifice own life for others	P5, P21
10	Transcultural impact (40)	is a transcultural experience and connects people	P1, P7, P9, P10, P13, P16, P18, P19, P20, P21
8		helps to find transcultural solutions	P1, P7, P8, P9, P14, P18, P19, P20
6		helps to see the person in his/her context	P4, P5, P6, P11, P13, P18
6		helps to understand other people's values	P4, P5, P8, P10, P18, P22
5		challenges prejudices and racism	P3, P5, P6, P11, P20
3		uses culture-specific expressions	P1, P6, P18
2		creates synergies and contradictions	P12, P20

Author's own construction

increase general acceptance and appreciation. Additionally, seven participants explained that love fosters a positive attitude and that love steers the desire to learn about others. Six statements indicate that love also increases compassion, helps to see people in their context and supports the understanding of other people's values. This shows that love does not require a person to focus on the individual only, but aims at taking the context and the influencing factors into account, which provides a broader view of a person or a situation.

The following Table 45.3 shows the impact of love in work relations.

As shown in this table, five statements each emphasise that love fosters a love for humanity and helps to challenge prejudices and racism. Three statements each point out that love creates positive relationships, uses culture-specific expressions, motivates patience and kindness. Finally, two individuals stated that love motivates individuals to sacrifice their own lives for others and that it creates synergies and contradictions.

P5 mentioned several of the described aspects in his interview:

> I think love can support positive transcultural interaction in at least two ways. Firstly, love between two specific individuals of different cultures can be a powerful way to challenge prejudice and racism when they make an effort to understand each other's cultural world view and accept that world view as valid, though I suspect there are many intercultural relationships in which individuals don't make the effort to fully understand each other or challenge their stereotypes and biases, but if love can't get someone to challenge their prejudices, I'm not sure what would.
>
> Secondly, I think promoting a love for humanity itself, promoting in our cultures the idea that we should respect and value other human lives no matter how different they are from our own, that developing such an ideology would improve transcultural relations. I am thinking of those feelings that encourage one to sacrifice for strangers who are persecuted, such as Europeans who protected Jews during the holocaust, or Americans running the underground railroad to free slaves in the South.

In this case, the participant highlights that love brings the potential energy needed to deal with one's own shadow, for example in working with internal stereotypes and prejudices. Further, love brings meaningfulness and the courage and energy to stand up for a certain idea or to help others, even when this can lead ultimately to death. Love becomes an eternal force.

45.5.4 How Does Love in Leadership Support the Transformation of Negative Emotions?

It has been pointed out that emotions impact on leaders, followers and workplaces. Participants also specified that leadership needs to work on an emotional level and be able to transform negative emotions into neutral or positive emotions.

Seven participants explained how love can transform negative emotions in the self and others in the workplace, by highlighting that individuals are human beings.

A German-Iranian male participant (P8) offered this example:

> The leader can see that we are all human beings and therefore accept the emotions and circumstances which lead to the emotions. A leader needs to see the whole person and accept the feelings and emotions which are displayed and help to transform them, if necessary, for the better of the organisation.

Emotions can also be transformed through acting professionally (according to seven statements). Six statements each pointed out that emotions can be transformed through loving unconditionally, that love helps people to respect others and their negative emotions, and that love transforms negative emotions and feelings. P7, a German female leader, stated:

> When a leader acts with unconditional love, negative feelings and emotions in the workplace can be transformed. A real leader does not only influence the concepts of the follower, but also how this person feels. Leadership goes beyond cognitive aspects and needs to "touch"

Table 45.4 Transformation of negative emotions through leadership

Frequency	Category	Participants
7	Communicate that we are all human beings and accept	P6, P8, P9, P10, P16, P18, P21
7	Act professionally (stick to word, honest, adapt, authentic)	P4, P5, P7, P12, P14, P16; P22
6	Love unconditionally	P5, P7. P10, P13, P19, P21
6	Helps to respect/accept negative emotions	P1, P3, P6, P14, P16, P18
6	Transform negative feelings and thoughts	P1, P7, P8, P9, P12, P13
5	Displays dignity	P3, P10, P11, P14, P16
5	Provide opportunities	P4, P13, P16, P18, P21
5	Communicate irritations openly	P11, P13, P14, P21, P22
5	Communicate positively (listen, show care, ask, balance)	P9, P13, P14, P18, P21
4	Show commitment	P6, P11, P16, P19
4	Connect to greater good	P7, P8, P16, P18
4	Self-reflect and internalise	P7, P16, P18, P22
4	Value every person	P10, P13, P16, P22
3	Invite the other out (coffee, ice-cream)	P11, P14, P21

Author's own construction

the other person to move her/him. The best is when the leader can pick up negative feelings and emotions and transform them for the better, see them as a resource and use the energy to work for the best while feeling happy, motivated and relaxed.

Additionally, five participants each made one of the following observations: love displays dignity and thereby transforms negative emotions, provides opportunities, communicates irritations openly, and helps to communicate positively (Table 45.4).

Four statements each highlight that love shows commitment and thereby transforms negative emotions, connects people to the greater good, supports self-reflection and internalisation, and emphasises the value of a person. By doing all of this, love helps to transform emotions towards the positive. Finally, three participants stated that love contributes to inviting others out and thereby diffuses negative emotions with a positive impact.

45.5.5 Extraordinary Leaders and Love

The findings show that extraordinary leaders are associated with love in one or another way. Altogether, ten statements reflected the loving and charismatic attitude that an extraordinary leader has. A German female participant commented:

> To be really successful, I believe, a leader needs a love attitude, but also charisma—to move people and have influence.

Table 45.5 Extraordinary leaders and love

Frequency	Category	Participants
10	An open, loving attitude with charisma	P1, P3, P4, P6, P8, P11, P12, P15, P18, P19
10	Love and humanity in leading competently	P2, P4, P5, P8, P10, P11, P12, P14, P15, P21
4	Inclusive	P2, P4, P12, P22
4	Leads with the heart	P14, P18, P19, P20
4	Unconditional love	P9, P12, P14, P18
4	Supportive, caring, benevolent	P6, P10, P13, P14
3	Loves the followers	P5, P6, P14
3	Transforms shadow on all levels	P7, P9, P18
3	Creates meaning and identity	P4, P8, P18

Author's own construction

Ten participants recommended that love and humanity need to be seen within the leader. Attributes of a loving extraordinary leader are that the leader acts inclusively (four statements), leads with the heart (four statements), has unconditional love (four statements) and is supportive, caring and benevolent (four statements). P10, a Japanese female participant, explained that:

> In our leadership culture, jintokku (benevolence) is valued. Leaders should be competent, but competence only does not necessarily serve as a requirement for a great leader. Of course, leaders should be competent. But at the same time, they have to be kind and considerate towards others.

A US female participant pointed out:

> By letting love lead, the extraordinary leader seeks what is best in their subordinates at the same time that she is firm with them—love needs boundaries, after all.

Another three participants each mentioned that loving leaders can recognise and transform their shadow aspects on all levels (emotional, cognitive) and create meaning and identity. These results are displayed in Table 45.5.

In the following section, the findings of this research are discussed with regard to the literature on love and the concept of the 4IR. The discussion section further reflects on the importance of love in leaders in the 4IR and highlights the contributing aspects of love concerning the rapid and challenging changes in 4IR workplaces.

45.6 Discussion: Love in Leaders in the Context of the Fourth Industrial Revolution

Findings suggest that the concept love could be particularly important in the transformation towards accepting new work challenges and organisational transformation processes which the 4IR brings, along with regard to relationship-building (interpersonal love), individual perspectives (intra-personal love) and attitudes towards work (object-related love).

New work-related influences and organisational techniques will impact on meaning-making within the organisation and on the employees and leadership (Mayer, 2019), and it is argued here that a loving attitude in leading can support and strengthen the employee relationship in a world which is increasingly technologised. For loving leaders, the ability to accept and handle changes might be easier than for leaders without a loving attitude. The treatment of employees and work will be different coming from leaders with a strong love concept as opposed to leaders with a weak love concept, particularly in terms of how relationships are built and created in face-to-face, as well as in technologised interactions (Spath et al., 2013) and with regard to the self-positioning within the new requirements of work (self-love).

Love, as a positive emotion, is viewed as a key factor in organisations, impacting positively on employees and their work performance and work relationships (see Barsade et al., 2003; Hareli & Rafaeli, 2008; Robinson et al., 2013). Therefore, it is argued that in a world of work which is increasingly changing in terms of meaning construction, technological use and organisational processes (Schwab, 2017; Schwab & Samans, 2016), love as a positive emotion can overcome potentially disruptive changes in relationship-building and work tasks. This is possible because of its strengths-based, positive and compassionate approach to caring for others and self, and acting compassionately and caringly in teams, even in a virtual and digitalised world in which long-distance working relationship connections are the norm.

Leaders who support caring and teamwork as well as other interpersonal love aspects will always, whether technologised or not, care for the employees and keep the building of relationships in mind, which is a key aspect of the 4IR. A question which arises is how these love concepts will affect human–machine interactions (Stubbings, 2018) and how a loving attitude in leaders will relate not only to human, but also to machine-based followers. It might be assumed that leaders who follow a love-based leadership concept will work to integrate all changes by using teamwork and supportive caring with a positive attitude.

The positive love concepts of leaders in this study are similar to those mentioned in the literature as positively impacting on work relationships (Eldor, 2017; Underwood, 2002). As in the study, the love concepts are connected to compassion, caring, empathy and respect which are all aspects of love which will increase in importance in 4IR leadership settings. The concept presented by van Dierendonck and Patterson (2014) of compassionate love as a virtue which can encourage an attitude of humility, gratitude, forgiveness and altruism in leaders and in the workplace, is clearly supported in this study according to the leaders interviewed.

As described in the literature and noted in this study, romantic love and toxic love are seen as having the potential to be negative in the work context (Chory and Hoke, 2019; Cowan & Horan, 2014; Malachowski et al., 2012).

Figure 45.3 presents an overview of love concepts, expressions of love and love's relationship impact in this study from the participants' viewpoints.

Fig. 45.3 Love concepts, expressions and impacts (author's own construction)

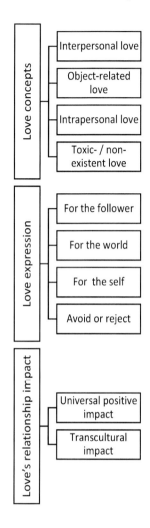

Several of the concepts viewed as being leadership love expressions in this study, fall into the category of servant leadership promoted by Patterson (2010) and by van Dierendonck and Patterson (2014) who see compassionate love as a cornerstone of servant leadership in which the leader enables and empowers others based on their needs, and in which leaders act proactively for the greater good in a respectful and peaceful manner, by using careful and trustful interventions. Leadership is thereby about the love of others and the love of self for the greater good of optimal functioning. In the 4IR empowerment of minorities, it is the previously marginalised groups and women leaders as well as geopolitical shifts of power which will increasingly rely on positive emotion-based concepts of motivation, decision-making and performance. These will foster creativity, innovation, solution-focus and meaning for employees all over the world to connect and work in a highly effective and functioning team. This team will be based on the establishment of long-distance virtual relationships, connection and empathic boundary management across cultures.

O'Neill's (2018) concept of companionate love has been established as an important factor in work relationships, referring to fondness, affection, caring, compassion and tenderness. Even in this study, leaders refer to work relationships and their importance. They mention that work relationships can be established through love. Thereby, love is viewed as a force which helps to overcome voids and gaps, as well as transcultural misunderstandings and irritating situations with a loving attitude. Almost two-thirds of the study participants believe that people can easily connect across cultures and find solutions. Since love is further believed to foster a positive attitude in general and reduces fear in organisations (Barsade & O'Neill, 2014; Rynes et al., 2012; Robinson et al., 2013) it is seen as a positive force in work relationships by reducing stereotypes and prejudices, fostering trust and working for the benefit of the other and not necessarily for the self (Rapport, 2019).

Love not only stimulates positive attitudes and emotions, but can—according to the leaders—even transform negative attitudes and emotions towards positive and resource-orientated emotions. This can happen particularly through connecting on a human basis, act professionally and unconditionally. When followers feel accepted the way they are, and compassionately understood and loved in the way they express themselves, then stress is reduced and well-being fostered (see Cooper, 2013; Gilbert, 2009).

Kempster and Parry (2013) have described love in the workplace as often being associated with charismatic leadership. Also in this study, participants affirmed that the combination of an open, loving attitude in a charismatic leader makes that person a loving and extraordinary leader. When leaders can show love and humanity in their words and actions, such leaders are viewed as extraordinary within a loving embeddedness. Leadership in extraordinary leaders is experienced as something beyond professional leadership which impacts holistically on the person. It is viewed as being an unconditional and loving leadership which is led particularly by the heart, in a supportive, caring and benevolent way. Thereby, the love for the follower is of great importance and the leadership has the strength to transform negative aspects, emotions, feelings, influences on all levels towards the positive. Finally, this leadership impacts on the meaning-making of followers and employees and might even spill over into society, creating an overall meaning and purpose. Such leadership is even seen as identity-creating.

As indicated in the very limited literature on love in the 4IR work and leadership context, it can be supported that love and 4IR can scarcely be divided (see Magubane, 2019), not necessarily for the reasons mentioned by the author, but rather because love is viewed here as an emotional foundation which will help to contain 4IR virtual and distance relationships, as well as ongoing and increasing fears, anxieties, insecurities regarding 4IR rapid workplace changes. Love can further support contributive coping strategies as well as initiate the transformation of negative into positive emotions, thereby fostering highly needed skills, such as solution-orientation, emotional intelligence, and creativity, as predicted and anticipated by the World Economic Forum (2016). Love seems to be a positive emotional concept in terms of compassionate love (Gilbert, 2009) for leaders to act mindfully to guide followers through the anticipated changes (Schwab, 2017; Schwab & Samans, 2016). Love could therefore become a highly transformative emotional force in this 4IR which has been termed "the Emotional Intelligence Revolution" (SIYLI, 2017). It might be assumed that a 4IR based on compassionate love concepts of leaders might even foster marginalised groups such as women leaders and also increase shifts not only geo-politically, but also socio-economically and organisationally by supporting the leadership of previously disadvantaged groups, based on gender, age, cultural or racial belonging. In this way, the 4IR, based on compassionate love, may not only bring power shifts, but could also balance out previous inequalities and might turn around global leadership concepts towards the greater good of humanity. In this way, compassion and cooperation might be integrated (as described in Chandsoda & Salsing, 2018). Love might therefore be the connecting emotion to consciously retract from the virtual world and re-engage in the natural, real world (Van der Hoven, 2017). This study agrees with Tu and Thien (2019) that concepts of love, such as in Buddhism, might support the development of certain skills and basic principles in leaders to steer cooperation in the 4IR and drive competition with a loving leadership attitude (Sun, 2018) which will then bring about an increase of concepts based on sharing and peer cooperation in future. This concept might fit well with the approach of Fabritius (2017) to a purpose-driven, rather than a consumption-driven entrepreneurship in which love for self and other is a critical aspect (Fournier, 1998; Sanders, 2002), all of which was supported by the leaders who participated in this study.

45.7 Conclusions and Recommendations

The concept of love in leaders and particularly the compassionate love concepts will definitely play a key role in the directions taken during the 4IR. They can contribute positively to changing organisational and work concepts, power, radical shifts in employment and work conditions, technologisation, virtual and digital relationship-building and core concepts of human interaction, even when processes change or structures of organisations, power and world order are reconstructed. The power of love of leaders can proactively support humanity within workplaces, societies and beyond, and can support care for each other and the environment, based on emotional intelligence. These concepts will certainly be core aspects in the 4IR to promote sustainable, peaceful and transcultural work and living conditions.

Figure 45.4 provides an overview of the three levels on which the concept of love in leaders of the 4IR can be effective.

Figure 45.4 shows the micro-, meso- and macro-levels on which love in 4IR leaders can operate, particularly the transdisciplinary and transcultural perspectives on individual, organisational and human culture with anchoring in philosophical, organisational and technological as well as psychological discourses. In terms of

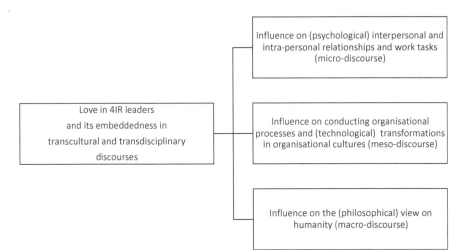

Fig. 45.4 Love in leaders and discourses (author's own construction)

how love influences 4IR leaders and how it is embedded in transcultural and transdisciplinary discourses.

Future research should definitely delve into the question of how love and leadership can support the transformation into the 4IR in detail, and how love can influence the fostering of skills needed in the 4IR to lead humankind in a positive way. Thereby, different cultural and transcultural models of "love" and their interlinkages to other aspects of leadership need to be taken into account. Further questions to be considered might include how love will change in the workplaces which are increasingly automated and digitalised in specific cultural, but also in global contexts. Also, if love will be projected onto machines, robots, virtual characters, and information technology programmes, what kind of influence will this have on leadership, workplaces and organisations and on what leaders love? How will the concepts of love change with regard to human–robot interaction in the workplace and leadership? How can love be expressed in virtual leadership contexts, in global teams and which possibilities of leadership will extraordinary leaders take into account to lead in a real, and at the same time, in a virtual world? And how does it influence purpose, vocation and leadership? Will the expression of love need to be adjusted between these two concepts? Or can love be felt by followers through digitalised leading, automated leadership and when mediated through artificial intelligence?

Studies need to explore the impact of love in leaders in real and virtual world scenarios and develop training courses and educational contexts in which new cultural and transcultural concepts of meaningfulness, love, purpose and leadership are discussed and developed to lead with new forms of technology and with a compassionate and loving attitude, to work consciously for a better, sustainable world and a common good, based on peace and sustainability.

Acknowledgements I would like to thank the following friends and colleagues for their compassionate leadership: Elisabeth Vanderheiden, Freddie Crous, Rudi Oosthuizen, and Lynette Louw. I also would like to thank all the interviewed leaders for sharing their views, opinions and actions. Last but not least, I thank Ruth Coetzee for the leadership in language and technical editing, done with love and patience.

References

Bag, S., Telukdarie, A., Pretorius, A. J. C., & Gupta, S. (2018). *Industry 4.0 and supply chain sustainability: Framework and future research directions.* Benchmarking: An International Journal. https://doi.org/10.1108/BIJ-03-2018-0056

Barsade, S., Brief, A. P., & Spataro, S. E. (2003). The affective revolution in organizational behavior: The emergence of a paradigm. In J. Greenberg & N. J. Mahwah (Eds.), *Organizational behavior: The state of the science* (pp. 3–52). London: Lawrence Erlbaum.

Barsade, S. G., & Gibson, D. E. (2007). Why does affect matter in organizations? *Academy of Management Perspectives, 21*, 36–59.

Barsade, S. G., & O'Neill, O. A. (2014). What's love got to do with it? A longitudinal study of the culture of companionate love and employee and client outcomes in a long-term care setting. *Administrative Science Quarterly, 59*(4), 551–598. https://doi.org/10.1177/0001839214538636

Catron, J. (2015). *The four dimensions of extraordinary leadership: The power of leading from your heart, soul, mind, & strengths.* New York: Nelson Books.

Chandsoda, S., & Salsing, P. S. (2018). Compassion and cooperation: The two challenging ethical perspectives in the Fourth Industrial Revolution. *Journal of International Business Studies, 9*(1).

Chory, R. M., & Hoke, H. G. G. (2019). Young love at work: Perceived effects of workplace romance among millennial generation organizational members. *The Journal of Psychology, Interdisciplinary and Applied.* https://doi.org/10.1080/00223980.2019.1581722

Cooper, M. (2013). *The compassionate mind approach to reducing stress.* London: Constable & Robinson.

Cowan, R. L., & Horan, S. M. (2014). Love at the Office? Understanding workplace romance disclosures and reactions from the coworker perspective. *Western Journal of Communication, 78*(2), 238–253.

Creswell, J. W. (2013). *Qualitative Inquiry & Research: Choosing among five approaches* (3rd ed.). Sage Publications: London.

Daft, R. L. (2002). *The leadership experience.* Mason, OH: South-Western.

Dennis, R. S., Kinzler-Norheim, L., & Bocarnea, M. (2010). Servant leadership theory. Development of the servant leadership assessment instrument. In D. van Dierendonck & K. Patterson (Eds.), *Servant leadership* (pp. 169–179). London: Palgrave Macmillan.

Dilthey, W. (2002). The formation of the historical world in the human sciences. In *Wilhelm Dilthey selected works* (Vol. III). Princeton, NJ: Princeton University Press.

Edukasyon. (2018). *Ikigai.* https://blog.edukasyon.ph/generation-zen/get-your-life-together-how-to-find-your-ikigai/attachment/ikigai-02/

Eldor, L. (2017). Public Service Sector: The compassionate workplace – the effect of compassion and stress on employee engagement, burnout, and performance. *Journal of Public Administration Research and Theory, 28*(1), 86–103.

Ellingson, L. L. (2013). Analysis and representation across the continuum. In N. K. Denzin & Y. S. Lincoln (Eds.), *Collecting and interpreting qualitative materials* (4th ed.). London: Sage.

Fabritius, S. (2017). *Ventures for a better society; 4th entrepreneurial revolution.* Master thesis, Aalto University School of Science, Aalto, Finland. https://aaltodoc.aalto.fi/bitstream/handle/123456789/29251/master_Fabritius_Sampsa_2017.pdf?sequence=1

Fineman, S. (2000). *Emotions in organizations.* New York: Sage.

Fournier, S. (1998). Consumers and their brands: Developing relationship theory in consumer research. *Journal of Consumer Research, 24*(4), 343–373.
Fry, L. W., & Matherly, L. L. (2006). *Spiritual leadership and organizational performance: An explorative study*. Presentation at the Academy of Management meeting, Atlanta, GA. https://www.iispiritualleadership.com/wp-content/uploads/docs/SLTOrgPerfAOM2006.pdf
Geertz, C. (1973). *The interpretation of cultures*. New York: Basic Books.
Gilbert, P. (2009). *The compassionate mind: A new approach to life's challenges*. Maryland, CA: New Harbinger Publications.
Goleman, D. (1995). *Emotional Intelligence. Why it can matter more than IQ*. New York: Bantam.
Greenleaf, R. K. (1977). *Servant leadership: A journey into the nature of legitimate power and greatness*. New York: Paulist Press.
Hareli, S., & Rafaeli, A. (2008). Emotion cycles: On the social influence of emotion in organizations. In A. P. Brief & B. M. Staw (Eds.), *Research in organizational behaviour* (pp. 35–59). New York: Elsevier.
Hassan, I., & Ghauri, P. N. (2014). Evaluating companies for mergers and acquisitions. *International Business and Management, 40*, 75–89.
Hoyle, J. R. (2001). *Leadership and the force of love. Six keys to motivating with love*. Thousand Oaks, CA: Corwin Press.
Illouz, E. (2007). *Cold Intimacies: The making of emotional capitalism*. Cambridge: Polity Press.
Illouz, E. (2011). *Warum Liebe weh tut*. Berlin: Suhrkamp.
Illouz, E. (2019, March 29). *Warum endet die Liebe? Sternstunde Philosophie SRF Kultur*. https://www.youtube.com/watch?v=3HT3c0rawI0
Kempster, S., & Parry, K. (2013). Charismatic leadership through the eyes of followers. *Strategic HR Review, 13*(1), 20–23.
Larson, C. L., & Murtadha, K. (2005). Leadership for social justice. *Yearbook of the National Society for the Study of Education, 101*(1).
Magubane, K. (2019). *This love thing: A new age love story*. Cape Town: umSinsi Press.
Malachowski, C. C., Chory, R. M., & Claus, C. J. (2012). Mixing pleasure with work: employee perceptions of and responses to workplace romance. *Western Journal of Communication, 76*(4), 358–379.
Matsumoto, D., & Hwang, H. S. (2012). Culture and emotion: The integration of biological and cultural contributions. *Journal of Cross-Cultural Psychology, 43*(19), 91–118.
Mayer, C.-H. (2019). Key factors of creativity and the art of collaboration in twenty-first-century workplaces. In M. Coetzee (Ed.), *Thriving in digital workplaces: Innovations in theory, research and practice* (pp. 147–166). Cham, Switzerland: Springer Nature.
Naderifar, M., Goli, H., & Ghaljaie, F. (2017). Snowball sampling: A purposeful method of sampling in qualitative research. *Strides in Development of Medical Education, 14*(3), e67670.
O'Neill, O. M. (2018). The FACCTs of (work) life: How relationships (and returns) are linked to the emotional culture of companionate love. *American Journal for Health Promotion, 32*(5), 1312–1315.
Patterson, K. (2003). *Servant leadership: A theoretical model*. Doctoral dissertation, Regent University.
Patterson, K. (2010). Servant leadership and love. In D. van Dierendonck & K. Patterson (Eds.), *Servant leadership* (pp. 67–76). London: Palgrave Macmillan.
Rapport, N. (2019). *Cosmopolitan love and individuality: Ethical engagement beyond culture*. Lanham: Lexington Books.
Robinson, M. D., Watkins, E. R., & Harmon-Jones, E. (2013). *Handbook of cognition and emotion*. New York: Guilford Press.
Roth, W.-M., & Unger, H. v. (2018). Current perspectives on research ethics in qualitative research. *Forum Qualitative Sozialforschung/Forum: Qualitative Social Research, 19*(3), 1–12. https://doi.org/10.17169/fqs-19.3.3155

Rynes, S. I., Bartunek, J. M., Dutton, J. E., & Margolis, J. D. (2012). Care and compassion through an organizational lens: Opening up new possibilities. *Academy of Management Review, 37*, 503–523.

Sanders, T. (2002). *Love is the killer app*. New York: Crown Business.

Savickas, M. L. (1991). The meaning for work and love: career issues and interventions. *The Career Development Quarterly, 39*(4), 291–379.

Schwab, K. (2017). *The fourth industrial revolution*. Crown Business.

Schwab, K., & Samans, R. (2016). Preface. Global Challenge Insight Report. In World Economic Forum (Eds.), *The future of jobs: Employment, skills and workforce strategy for the Fourth Industrial Revolution*. http://www3.weforum.org/docs/WEF_Future_of_Jobs.pdf

Sisodia, R., Sheth, J., & Wolfe, D. (2003). *Firms of endearment: How world-class companies profit from passion and purpose* (2nd ed.). Upper Saddle River, NJ: Pearson FT Press.

SIYLI Search Inside Yourself Leadership Institute. (2017, April 15). *The emotional intelligence revolution*. https://siyli.org/resources/the-emotional-intelligence-revolution

Smith, M., Davidson, J., Cameron, L., & Bondi, L. (2016). *Emotion, place and culture*. London: Routledge.

Spath, D., Ganschar, O., Gerlach, S., Hämmerle, M., Krause, T., & Schlund, S. (2013). *Produktionsarbeit der Zukunft – Industrie 4.0*. Stuttgart: Fraunhofer Verlag.

Stubbings, C. (2018). Workforce of the future: The competing forces shaping 2030. *PwC*. https://www.pwc.com/gx/en/services/peopleorganisation/publications/workforce-of-the-future.html.

Sun, Z. (2018, July 18). *Innovation and entrepreneurship in the 4th Industrial Revolution*. Joint workshop on entrepreneurship, Lae, PNG. https://www.researchgate.net/profile/Zhaohao_Sun/publication/326475360_Innovation_and_Entrepreneurship_in_the_4th_Industrial_Revolution/links/5b4fdb890f7e9b240fec107e/Innovation-and-Entrepreneurship-in-the-4th-Industrial-Revolution.pdf

Terre Blanche, M., Durrheim, K., & Kelly, K. (2006). First steps in qualitative data analysis. In M. Terre Blanche, K. Durrheim, & D. Painter (Eds.), *Research in practice: Applied methods for the social sciences* (pp. 321–344). Cape Town, SA: University of Cape Town.

Tu, T. N., & Thien, T. D. (2019). *Buddhism and the Fourth Industrial Revolution*. Vietnam Buddhist University Press, Hong Duc Publishing House.

Underwood, L. G. (2002). The human experience of compassionate love. In S. G. Post, L. G. Underwood, J. Schloss, & W. B. Hurlbut (Eds.), *Altruism and altruistic love* (pp. 72–88). Oxford: Oxford University Press.

Van der Hoven, J. (2017, October 22). *Using flow to create meaningful work in the Fourth Industrial Revolution*. https://leaderless.co/blog/2017/10/22/the-flow-of-the-fourth-industrial-revolution/

Van Dierendonck, D., & Patterson, K. (2014). Compassionate love as a cornerstone in servant leadership: An integration of previous theorizing and research. *Journal of Business Ethics, 128*(1), 119–131.

Winston, B. E. (2002). *Be a leader for god's sake*. Virginia Beach, VA: Regent University School of Leadership Studies.

World Economic Forum. (2016). *The future of jobs. Employment, skills and workforce strategy for the Fourth Industrial Revolution*. Global Challenge Insight Report. http://www3.weforum.org/docs/WEF_Future_of_Jobs.pdf

Claude-Hélène Mayer is a Full Professor in Industrial and Organisational Psychology at the Department of Industrial Psychology and People Management at the University of Johannesburg, an Adjunct Professor at the European University Viadrina in Frankfurt (Oder), Germany and a Senior Research Associate at Rhodes University, Grahamstown, South Africa. She holds a Ph.D. in Psychology (University of Pretoria, South Africa), a Ph.D. in Management (Rhodes University, South Africa), a Doctorate (Georg-August University, Germany) in Political Sciences (sociocultural anthropology and intercultural didactics) and Master degrees in Ethnology, Intercultural Didactics and Socio-economics (Georg-August University, Germany) as well as in Crime Science, Investigation and Intelligence (University of Portsmouth, UK). Her Venia Legendi is in Psychology with focus on work, organizational, and cultural psychology (Europa Universität Viadrina, Germany). She has published numerous monographs, text collections, accredited journal articles, and special issues on transcultural mental health and well-being, salutogenesis, transforming shame, transcultural conflict management and mediation, women in leadership in culturally diverse work contexts, coaching, culture and crime and psychobiography.

Chapter 46
Love Is a Many-Splendoured Thing: Brand Love in a Consumer Culture

Leona M. Ungerer

Abstract In a consumer culture, people make sense of their everyday existence based on meanings generated during the consumption process. These meanings feature in establishing human identities and communicating them to others. Brands fulfil a pivotal role in conveying the images associated with particular products in a consumer culture context, and consumers use these brand images to express themselves and delineate their position in the world. Considering the importance of brands during the social meaning-making process, consumers often from strong attachments with brands and might "fall in love" with brands that meet their needs.

Brand love represents the most emotionally powerful consumer-brand relationship and therefore is a primary goal in brand management. The complexity of the concept of love, however, may limit directly applying it to brands and products, explaining the lack of consensus on what brand love is. This lack of agreement about the conceptualisation of brand love may result from the trend that the construct's foundations, boundaries and contents were not clarified sufficiently initially, instead building on the premise of theories on interpersonal love and/or attachment. Brand love, however, is not identical to interpersonal love and when theories on interpersonal love guide brand love research, some of the construct's elements may be overlooked.

Although consensus about the conceptualisation of brand love seems to be elusive, there appears to be some agreement about its outcomes, including brand loyalty, brand commitment, positive word-of-mouth and active participation in a brand community. The antecedents of brand love have not received the same degree of research interest yet. Some antecedents identified include hedonic brands (brands primarily associated with fun, pleasure, or enjoyment), self-expressive brands (brands enhancing a person's social self or reflecting their inner self), brand identification and brand anthropomorphism.

L. M. Ungerer (✉)
Department of Industrial and Organisational Psychology, University of South Africa (Unisa), Pretoria, South Africa
e-mail: ungerlm@unisa.ac.za

Keywords Love · Brand love · Brand relationship management · Consumer culture · Emotions · Interpersonal love

46.1 Introduction

The role of love in consumption is gaining interest in the field of marketing because it may hold the key to sustained consumer-brand relationships (Chew, 2017). Consumers deal with countless brands during their lives, but develop powerful emotional bonds with only a few (Sarkar, 2014). Some of these bonds are so strong that they are equated to love, termed brand love. Brand love still is a fairly new concept in consumer-brand relationship research (Kaufmann, Loureiro, & Manarioti, 2016; Palusuk, Koles, & Hasan, 2019), a field that focuses on how consumers think and feel about brands (Albert & Merunka, 2013). A focus on consumer-brand relationships acknowledges consumers' role as equal partners in generating a brand's value with its owners and managers (Lebar & Blackston, 2015).

Researchers generally relate brand love to interpersonal love, applying terms and definitions from interpersonal love to brand love because of underlying similarities between the concepts (Ahuvia, 2005; Langner, Bruns, Fischer, & Rossiter, 2016). Despite divergent views among scholars in the field of brand love, for instance about its conceptualisation, the construct generates significant interest considering the outcomes associated with it, such as consumers repeatedly purchasing the brand (Batra, Ahuvia, & Bagozzi, 2012; Carroll & Ahuvia, 2006), reduced price-sensitivity (Batra et al., 2012), resisting negative information about a brand (Batra et al., 2012), spreading positive word-of-mouth about the brand (Batra et al., 2012; Carroll & Ahuvia, 2006) and establishing brand loyalty (Albert, Merunka, & Valette-Florence, 2009).

In the remainder of this chapter consumer culture is firstly introduced because brands play an essential role in establishing consumers' identities in this type of culture. A number of definitions of brand love follow, as well as a discussion of the conceptualisation of the construct. The chapter concludes with a section on the empirical investigation and measurement of brand love.

46.2 Consumer Culture

Consumer culture theory (CCT) is an overarching term representing various socio-cultural approaches to consumer behaviour and market research (Arnould & Thompson, 2005). CCT focuses on issues of practical significance originating from the field of consumption and aims at understanding the intricacies involved in consumer culture (Arnould, Press, Salminen, & Tillotson, 2019). CCT approaches the concept of culture completely differently from regular consumer research where culture typically refers to a system of shared meanings, values and ways of life among members of a society (Arnould & Thompson, as cited in Arnould et al., 2019). Consumer culture rather focuses on consumers' actions and their beliefs. CCT posits that consumers' real-world experiences are not completely rational or cohesive (Arnould & Thompson, 2005). Brand love relates to the irrational element of consumption, where consumers create a number of their own realities around consumption experiences (Sarkar, 2014).

The impact of consumer culture is felt globally (Burns, as cited in Burns & Fawcett, 2012). A particularly strong impact is evident in the importance of products in establishing and reflecting people's identities (Gabriel & Lang, as cited in Burns & Fawcett, 2012). Products in themselves, however, do not provide the basis on which people construe their selves; they rather carry the images for guiding this process (Miller, as cited in Burns & Fawcett, 2012).

A brand is a distinctive factor such as a name or symbol that distinguishes a particular company's products or services from competitors (Aaker, 1997), enhancing their value and attractiveness to potential buyers (Garg, Mukherjee, Biswas, & Kataria, 2016). Brands fulfil an essential role in portraying the images associated with products and consumers define themselves and their place in the world through these images (Batey, as cited in Burns & Fawcett, 2012). Brands therefore do not merely communicate information about a product in a consumer culture (Burns & Fawcett, 2012), they serve as crucial collections of meaning (Shery, as cited in Burns & Fawcett, 2012).

A brand is based on perceptions held in consumers' minds (Kotler & Keller, 2006). Consumers encode brands in memory both on cognitive and emotional bases, but the emotional make-up of a brand primarily determines whether consumers use a product to construe their selves (Burns & Fawcett, 2012). Consumers in a consumer culture typically purchase products to incorporate the meaning linked to these products with their selves, particularly their desired selves and marketers aim to generate images for their products that their target markets would find attractive (Batey, as cited in Burns & Fawcett, 2012).

Human beings are inherently social in nature and tend to establish and maintain social relationships. When social relationships lose their significance in a consumer culture, consumers may develop alternative relationships, for instance, around items that they regard as important such as brands (Muñiz & O'Gwinn, as cited in Burns & Fawcett, 2012). Brand communities, for instance, those for Harley Davidson (Fournier & Lee, as cited in Burns & Fawcett, 2012), and Zara clothing stores (Royo-Vela & Casamassima, as cited in Burns & Fawcett, 2012) are acknowledged in consumer culture. These relationships often correspond to human relationships (Lastovick & Sirianni, as cited in Burns & Fawcett, 2012). Finally, Kaufmann et al. (2016) suggest that when the values associated with a brand correspond to consumers' belief systems, when the brand reflects attributes that promote consumers' self-image and social standing and when it established robust, expressive images in consumers' minds, the resulting brand-consumer relationship may resemble compelling, lasting love.

46.3 Definitions of Brand Love

Various definitions of brand love are found in the literature, for instance, that it refers to, "a product, service, or entity that inspires loyalty beyond reason" (Pawle & Cooper, 2006, p. 39). Carroll and Ahuvia (2006, p. 81) define brand love as

> the degree of passionate emotional attachment a satisfied consumer has for a particular trade name,

while Batra et al. (2012, p. 2) describe it as

> a higher-order construct including multiple cognitions, emotions, and behaviors, which consumers organize into a mental prototype.

Bergkvist and Bech-Larsen (2010, p. 509) describe brand love as "deeply felt affection for a brand", and Fetscherin and Conway (2011, p. 3) define it as

> a multidimensional construct consisting of a satisfied consumer's history with a brand, which not only leads to brand loyalty (a predecessor of brand love) but to a deeply emotional relationship.

Definitions such as those by Bergkvist and Bech-Larsen (2010) and Carroll and Ahuvia (2006) position brand love as an emotional, irrational relationship concept (Sarkar, 2014).

46.3.1 Conceptualising Brand Love

According to Broadbent (2012), the lack of consensus about suitably defining brand love extends to its conceptualisation, where considerable divergence is evident. Existing research mainly investigates brand love from interpersonal, parasocial and experiential theoretical perspectives (Palusuk et al., 2019). More recently, researchers suggested a developmental approach to investigating brand love (Langner et al., 2016; Palusuk et al., 2019). Most existing research, however, positions the concept of brand love within the overarching theoretical field of interpersonal relationships (Sarkar, 2014).

46.3.2 Conceptualising Brand Love from an Interpersonal Perspective

Shimp and Madden (1988) coined the term brand love in a conceptual paper and set the scene for research in this field. They posited that the concept of love presents in situations where consumers experience intense enthusiasm towards products or brands (Shimp & Madden, as cited in Broadbent, 2012). Shimp and Madden (1988) applied the concept of interpersonal love to the consumer-object relationships, based on Sternberg's (1986) Triangular Theory of Love. Sternberg (1986) highlighted three components of love, namely intimacy, passion and decision/commitment, as well as eight types of interpersonal love, based on combinations of these three components. Shimp and Madden (1988) replaced intimacy with liking in consumer-object relationships, indicating that it represents an emotional or psychological process. They equated passion to yearning in consumer-object relationships, indicating that it represents motivation as a psychological process, and kept commitment or decision, indicating that it represents cognition or a psychological process. Shimp and Madden (1988) identified eight types of loves from non-liking to loyalty to explain the consumer-object relationship.

Ahuvia (1992, 1993) undertook the first empirical research on the construct, brand love. Ahuvia (1993, p. v) coined the term "philopragia" to describe love in close personal relationships with anything else than a human being. Ahuvia (1993) found that although people's love for an object or brand corresponded to interpersonal love, they were not identical. Interpersonal love and philopragia mainly differed in terms of the extent of the integrity and reciprocity of the relationships involved.

Fournier's (1998) research on consumer-brand relationships followed. She did not elaborate on brand love as such, but included it as a relationship type in her typology of consumer-brand relationships. Fournier (1998) posited that a combination of love-based and experience-based dimensions determine the quality of consumer-brand relationships, including intimacy, love/passion, interdependence, self-connection, commitment and brand partner quality.

In 2005, Ahuvia proposed a brand love prototype that involved passionate feelings, positive emotions, attachment, positively evaluating the brand and sincere declarations of love for the brand (Ahuvia, 2005). Carroll and Ahuvia (2006) further identified emotional attachment and passion as the main components of brand love. Emotional attachment involves an intense bond and psychological closeness between a consumer and a brand. According to Batra et al. (2012), passion involves consumers' longing for a brand, including emotions of excitement, while Albert and Valette-Florence (2010) associate separation anxiety with the term, and Albert et al. (2009) describe it as a comprehensive sense of pleasure generated by owning a brand.

Researchers who rely on interpersonal love theories in guiding their investigations of brand love explain that interpersonal relationship norms often guide people's brand relationships (Aggarwal, as cited in Palusuk et al., 2019). Some researchers, however, believe that love is too complex a construct to apply to consumer behaviour (Albert et al., 2009; Batra et al., 2012). Consumers' experiences with a brand should firstly be investigated, whereafter it would be possible to establish connections to interpersonal theory (Batra et al., 2012). According to Batra et al. (2012), existing research often firstly focused on a particular interpersonal theory, after which researchers developed scales to measure brand love based on the theory involved, instead of first exploring brand love as a construct itself. Notwithstanding these concerns, Batra et al. (2012) did not advise researchers to exclude interpersonal theory completely in investigating brand love but to rather guard against including irrelevant elements from this field in their research on brand love.

Romaniuk (2013) expressed her reservations about the importance of investigating brand love in response to Batra et al.'s (2012) research, explaining that consumers typically are not particularly committed to the brands they purchase. Moussa (2015) also was sceptical about focusing on brand love, suggesting that brand love actually refers to brand attachment. Pedeliento (2018) also equates brand love to brand attachment, suggesting that a focus on distinguishing between brand attachment and brand love may be driven by increasing publication rates and not necessarily augmenting an understanding of brand love. Moussa (2015) further cautions brand managers against investing in brand love because a focus on brand love will not necessarily improve sales and a company's market share.

As is evident above, it is not generally agreed that interpersonal love theory is suitable for describing consumer-brand relationships (Palusuk et al., 2019; Skoog & Söderström, 2015). Sternberg's (as cited in Broadbent, 2012) framework served as foundation for investigating the role of brand love in consumer-object relations and guided a number of empirical studies that investigated brand love (Heinrich, Bauer, & Muhl, 2008; Shimp & Madden, 1988). Skoog and Söderström (2015), however, explain that although Sternberg's (1986) triangular love theory is well-established in the domains of psychology and interpersonal love, some of its terms and components may not be relevant to consumer-brand relationships. The interpersonal love theory does not suitably conceptualise brand love because it does not consider brand love elements such as consumers' rational decisions and the benefits they look for in brands (Langner, Schmidt, & Fischer, 2015). Brand love further has a strong cognitive element and it cannot be said that this type of love is blind (Sarkar, 2014).

46.3.3 Conceptualising Brand Love from a Parasocial Perspective

Some researchers posit that brand love should rather be studied as a unidirectional or parasocial type of relationship (Palusuk et al., 2019). Parasocial relationships involve one-sided relationships where one partner does not experience the same level of emotion than the other (Fetscherin, 2014). In terms of brand love, this would mean that consumers form one-sided relationship with brands and brands are not expected to reciprocate the relationship.

The parasocial perspective corresponds to the concept of brand anthropomorphism (Palusuk et al., 2019). Anthropomorphism refers to "the tendency to imbue the real or imagined behaviour of nonhuman agents with humanlike characteristics, motivations, intentions, or emotions" (Epley, Waytz, & Cacioppo, 2007, p. 100). In ascribing human characteristics to a brand, consumers look beyond its functions and make assumptions about the brand's personality, meaning, and motives (Alvarez & Fournier, 2012). The idea that consumers ascribe human traits to brands is well-established in academic research (Bennet & Hill, 2012). Findings from the field of cognitive psychology, namely that people process brand and interpersonal relationships in different parts of the brain add further support for the parasocial perspective (Yoon, Gutchess, Feinberg, & Polk, as cited in Palusuk et al., 2019).

46.3.4 Conceptualising Brand Love from a Grounded Theory Perspective

Batra et al. (as cited in Palusuk et al., 2019) added a third theoretical perspective by suggesting a grounded theoretical approach to studying brand love, investigating how consumers experience brand love as a phenomenon. Batra et al. (2012) established that although consumers often refer to brand love by using terms related to interpersonal love, they believe that interpersonal love carries more weight, and involves strong elements of both selfless concern for the loved one, as well as reciprocity. These two characteristics do not feature in a brand love context (Batra et al., 2012). Kaufman et al. (2016), however, highlights a debate in literature about whether customers expect some type of mutual exchange from the brands that they use. Consumers form relationships with brands, based on the intrinsic and extrinsic rewards that they offer, but consumers also want to be heard and considered, as evident in co-creation literature (Ind, Iglesias & Schultz, as cited in Kaufman et al., 2016). During the process of co-creation, consumers, managers, and employees collaborate to develop brands and create new products and services (Ind, Iglesias, & Schultz, 2013). Consumers find it gratifying when they belong to a compatible community where they can express themselves, suggesting the importance of meeting consumers' need for belonging in addition to the functional, self-expressive and emotional benefits already established as essential (Ind et al., as cited in Kaufman et al., 2016).

Figure 46.1 presents a summary of the components of brand love that Ahuvia (2016) compiled, based on his own research in the field of brand love, as well as with his co-workers, Rajeev Batra and Richard Bagozzi. Ahuvia (2016, p. 1) explain that brand love simply is "non-interpersonal love when the thing someone loves is a brand, product or possession".

Ahuvia (2016) describes the components presented in Fig. 46.1 as follows,

1. **Consumers rated their loved brand highly**

   Consumer felt that their loved brands would last and were made properly. They rated their loved brands highest on the essential feature or benefit of the particular product category under investigation, but could indicate numerous further benefits.

2. **Consumers had a passionate desire for their loved brands**

   Consumers reported a powerful, passionate longing for their loved brands.

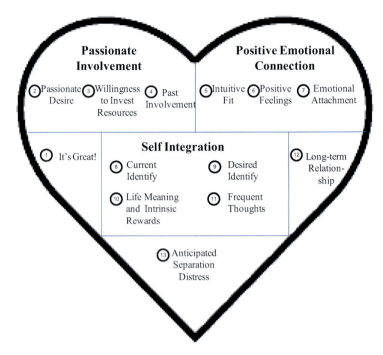

Fig. 46.1 Components of brand love. Source: Ahuvia (2016, p. 1)

3. **Consumers were willing to invest resources in their loved brands**

    Consumers spent considerable amounts of time, energy and finances on their loved brands. In terms of affordable items, consumers often mentioned that they felt that their loved brands were bargains, a positive attribute. If they particularly loved an expensive brand, they felt that it was worth its price. The price may even have increased the brand's specialness for consumers.

4. **Consumers had previous experience or past involvement with their loved brand**

    Consumers indicated that they loved a particular brand more than another, mainly because they used it more often, even if they were reminded that they use a particular brand or product more often than another because of an "exogenous factor" that had no bearing on the merits of the two products.

5. **Consumers experienced an intuitive fit with their loved brands**

    Consumers reported an effortless fit and harmony between themselves and their loved brands. They sometimes equated this experience of a natural compatibility with a brand to love at first sight.

6. **Loved brands generated positive feelings**

   Consumers loved brands that made them feel good.

7. **Consumers experienced a sense of emotional attachment to their loved brands**

   Experiencing a bond with or a sense of emotional attachment to a brand contributed significantly to experiences of brand love.

8. **Loved brands supported consumers' current identity**

   The brands that consumers loved fulfilled a self-expressive role; they enabled consumers to express who they were.

9. **Loved brands supported consumers' desired identity**

   Loved brands fulfilled an aspirational role; they allowed consumers to express who they would like to become.

10. **Loved brands contributed to making consumers' life meaningful and let them experience intrinsic rewards**

    Life meaning and intrinsic rewards initially appeared to be distinct components of brand love, but Ahuvia (2016) and his colleagues later determined through structural equation modelling that they present a single phenomenon. Loved brands may offer various benefits such as entertainment and comfort, but they also related to something meaningful at a higher level, such as self-actualisation or cultural identity.

11. **Consumers frequently thought about their loved brands**

    It was initially thought that frequent thoughts about a loved brand combined with frequent use of a brand formed one component of brand love, namely "frequent thought and use". Structural equation modelling, however, showed that frequent thoughts and use were two distinct aspects of brand love.

12. **Consumers have been using loved brand for some time**

    Although people may love items that they recently experienced for the first time, an established history with a brand typically results in deeper brand love. When sharing a history, the loved brand often featured in consumers' life events and they typically remained loyal to it over time.

13. **Anticipated separation distress**

    Consumers indicated that they would be upset if their loved brand were unavailable. To determine whether they loved a brand they estimated how much they would miss it if it were unavailable and often indicated that they only really truly loved a brand if they could not foresee a life without it.

The components as identified by Ahuvia (2016) are evident in a higher-order brand love factor model, compiled by Bagozzi, Batra, and Ahuvia (2014) based on their research at the time, as evident in Fig. 46.2.

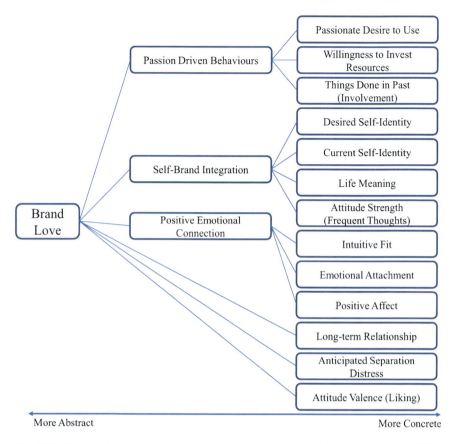

Fig. 46.2 Higher-order factor model of brand love. Source: Bagozzi, Batra, and Ahuvia (2014, p. 4)

Existing research on brand love presents the construct in a static, cross-sectional manner, limiting an understanding of the paths shaping the course of its development (Palusuk et al., 2019). A more recent development is investigating it from a developmental, dynamic perspective and not as a static construct.

46.3.5 Conceptualising Brand Love from a Developmental Perspective

Palusuk et al. (2019) could identify only one study, namely that by Langner et al. (2016) that investigated brand love from a developmental perspective. It is implausible that a basic feature, namely how consumers' love for brands develop has not yet been investigated in depth. This area requires investigation before the outcomes

Fig. 46.3 The proposed consumer brand love relationship stages of progression. Source: Chew (2017, p. 26)

of brand love can be measured (Chew, 2017). Figure 46.3 presents Chew's (2017) proposed conceptual model of the stages of progression in consumer brand-love relationships.

Visualising how consumers progress through the stages of a brand-love relationship as in the above model among others enable companies to identify suitable communication strategies for each stage (Chew, 2017). This model serves to introduce the idea of approaching brand love from a developmental perspective, but a more in-depth approach appears warranted. Investigating brand love from a developmental perspective enables highlighting factors that both support and hinder the development of brand love. There further is scope for investigating negative consumer-brand relationships too, for instance, exploring the relationship between brand love and brand hate (Palusuk et al., 2019). If love serves as the most intense from of devotion to an item, hate serves as its opposite (Pedeliento, 2018). Palusuk et al. (2019), however, highlight research by Zarantonello, Romani, Grappi, and Bagozzi (2016) suggesting that it not a given that brand hate is positioned on a continuum opposite brand love, but that brand love may turn into brand hate through various intricate, cyclic processes. Palusuk et al. (2019) present a conceptual model for brand love that incorporates various relationship paths, based on the aforementioned considerations.

46.3.6 Relational Typologies of Brand Love and Brand Hate

Palusuk et al.'s (2019) conceptual framework, presented in Fig. 46.4, combines the three primary theoretical lenses that are mainly used in conceptualising brand love and incorporates a developmental perspective, suggesting various paths to brand love by applying the analogies of love marriage, experience-based relationships and arranged marriage. In explaining each of the three relationship types, they rely on four types of theoretical framework.

1. They point out links between their framework and the current leading typologies used to investigate consumers' love towards brand (Sternberg, 1986) or the form and strength of consumers' relationships with brands (Fournier, 1998).
2. They expand on a stream of research by Sampedro (2017) and Reimann, Castaño, Zaichkowsky, and Bechara (2012), who identified various consumer-brand relationship types, based on the degree of correspondence between consumer-brand identities. These researchers position consumer-brand relationships on a

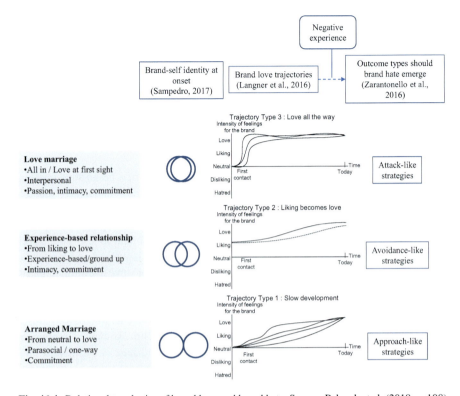

Fig. 46.4 Relational typologies of brand love and brand hate. Source: Palusuk et al. (2019, p. 108)

continuum. At one end of the continuum, the parties' identities do not correspond at all and are presented by two free-standing circles. When parties' identities overlap completely, the consumer-brand relationship will be positioned on the furthest end of the continuum, and the circles representing the parties' identities will overlap largely.

3. They incorporate Langner et al. (2016)'s research on five possible paths to brand love that differ in terms of when they start and how they develop over time, acknowledging differences in consumers' experiences and their relationships with the brands they love. Langner et al.'s (2016) framework identifies various starting points, illustrating that some brand relationships start off at a higher level such as being in love, while some may start at a lower level, where consumers merely like a brand or have neutral feelings towards it. Langner et al. (2016) further acknowledge that some relationships move in a positive direction over time, while some may take on a negative nature or reflect a combination of experiences. Palusuk et al. (2019) only incorporate the first three of five paths that Langner et al. (2016) identified in their model as they believe the final two have not yet been clarified completely.

4. Finally, they integrate brand hate as a potential component in their three relationship paths, based on the work of Zarantonello, Romani, et al. (2016) because of the potential harmful impact on brands when brand hate emerge. Palusuk et al. (2019) apply Zarantonello, Romani, et al.'s (2016) brand hate strategies in the three forms of relationship that they propose in their model, namely avoidance-like, attack-like and approach-like strategies.

Palusuk et al. (2019) address a further important limitation in existing literature in their model, namely distinguishing brand love from related concepts such as brand liking, satisfaction, brand affection, brand trust, brand commitment and brand attachment.

46.3.7 Love Marriage Between Consumers and Brands

In situations where consumers immediately fall in love with brands, they experience ardent emotions from the outset (Palusuk et al., 2019). Their developmental paths to brand love start at a high point and will probably remain high throughout. The interpersonal love perspective is probably most suitable for understanding these immediate experiences of brand love because there is an obvious mutual relationship between consumers and their brands. Consumers will expect delight in their experiences with brands and will continue doing so over time. In terms of Sternberg (1986)'s love theory, this first path to brand love should reflect high levels of intimacy, passion and long-term commitment. The relationship will be characterised by passion, affection and connection (Thomson, MacInnis, & Whan Park, 2005), while the dimensions of passion, love intimacy and interdependence from Fournier's (1998)'s framework will be most relevant to this type of relationship.

In terms of brand outcomes, consumers will probably "rave" about their loved brands, be committed to them and interact with them in a positive manner, being forgiving of sporadic brand failures (Donovan, Priester, MacInnis, & Park, 2012) and remaining loyal to them (Carroll & Ahuvia, 2006). In terms of related constructs, brand affection, trust, passion and attachment probably are most relevant to a love marriage type of brand love. Palusuk et al. (2019) substantiate this suggestion thoroughly by firstly describing each construct and then pointing out how it may relate to brand love.

Consumers in this relationship type are deeply committed to the brand, feel passionately about it and share important values with their brand. There would probably be a strong similarity between consumer-brand identities and they will be committed to their loved brands. Brand transgressions therefore may impact severely on the consumers who love them. In the case of corporate wrongdoing, consumers may experience anger, betrayal and frustration and resort to attack-like strategies such as expressing their dissatisfaction and actively taking part in negative word-of-mouth (Zarantonello et al., as cited in Palusuk et al., 2019).

Consumers in a love-marriage relationship with brands are typically quite forgiving in cases of brand failure, but if the situation becomes severe and consumers' sense of fairness has been violated, it may have severe consequences for brands (Gregoire & Fisher, as cited in Palusuk et al., 2019). In such cases, brands should act proactively and respond to consumer complaints as soon as possible, similar to romantic relationships that involve open communication, trust and sharing (Zarantonello et al., as cited in Palusuk et al., 2019).

46.3.8 Experience-Based Relationships Between Consumers and Brands

The second path presented in Fig. 46.4 reflects conditions where brand love evolves gradually, building on consumers' experiences with a brand over time. The path's direction will be positive if consumer experiences remain positive. Initially consumer and brand identities are fairly similar, as evident in the overlap between the two circles representing the two types of identity. Consumers will probably investigate a number of alternatives before staying with one brand and brand love develop gradually because of, for instance, appealing brand characteristics, frequently using a brand and doing so over an extended period. Consumers may like the brand and have positive attitudes towards it during the initial investigation and choice process, and therefore display a generally positive attitude towards the brand. With increased experiences over time, their liking for the brand increases (Langner et al., as cited in Palusuk et al., 2019).

Consumers from this typology do not show the same degree of initial fervour as consumers from the first typology and would therefore maintain some distance from the brand, especially early in the relationship. They investigate various features and may be hesitant about staying with the brand in the long term. According to Sternberg (1986)'s typology, people's levels of intimacy and commitment are higher than their levels of passion in experience-based relationships, suggesting that rational choice and deliberation will feature in the experience-based typology. This type of relationship further corresponds to Thomson et al.'s (2005) elements of low passion, average affection, and high connection, as well as the elements of medium self-connection and high partner quality in Fournier (1998)'s theory.

Brand satisfaction and brand liking are the most relevant related constructs in guiding experience-based brand love. Brand love stems from appealing brand features that attract consumers both at cognitive and affective level. Tempting features may create positive consumer experiences such as engagement and entertainment which could nurture brand love. Brand satisfaction is beneficial because it results from a cognitive judgement but also generates sustained emotional attachment (Thomson et al., as cited in Palusuk et al., 2019). Brand love and brand satisfaction, however, are not identical. Consumers typically incorporate their loved brands into their identity, but this does not apply to brand satisfaction (Fournier, as cited in Palusuk et al., 2019).

If brand hates emerges in this type of consumer-brand relationship, consumers will probably apply avoidance-like strategies such as purchasing the loved brand less or stop doing so altogether. They would forgive some brand transgressions, but if it occurs often, they would dissociate themselves from the brand, and eventually divorce themselves from it, resembling an avoidance-like coping strategy. To counteract these negative experiences, brands should involve consumers actively, provide them with incentives to compensate for unpleasant experiences and coax them into returning to the brand.

46.3.9 Arranged Marriage Between Consumers and Brands

The third path in Fig. 46.4 involves conditions where consumers do not have previous experience with brands and are neutral toward them initially, gradually developing a liking or even love for a brand. Consumer-brand identities therefore do not overlap at the outset of their relationship. Palusuk et al. (2019) apply the analogy of arranged marriages to describe these conditions because of the brand and consumers' unfamiliarity with each other. In terms of Sternberg (1986)'s typology, this brand-love relationship would involve low levels of passion and intimacy and high levels of commitment, described as "empty love". It further corresponds to Thomson et al.'s (2005) description of low levels of passion and affection, but high levels of connection. Commitment would be the most relevant dimension as identified by Fournier (1998). The consumer may develop closer ties with the brand if the relationship functions well and they may gradually incorporate it in their identities, possibly generating brand love. Brand love in this types of relationship, especially at its onset, corresponds to a one-sided or parasocial relationship type (Fetscherin, as cited in Palusuk et al., 2019). These relationships would probably not be reciprocal and the terms used to describe interpersonal love may not be appropriate in such conditions.

Palusuk et al. (2019) believe that brand commitment is a particularly significant related construct for this typology. Brand commitment is acknowledged as a brand love antecedent in most conceptualisations (Albert & Merunka, 2013). After entering the relationship, consumers enter a stage of exploration and establish a history with the brand, for instance, investigating its applications and benefits. If their trajectory is positive, they may eventually grow to like or even love the brand.

Consumers may develop brand hate if their expectations are violated. In case of continual negative experiences, they may show approach-like coping strategies involving disputes and campaigns. Since the relationship did not involve passion and intimacy from the outset, consumers may be less forgiving of brand failures than those from earlier typologies. They may, however, merely express their dissatisfaction and remain fairly passive because of limited alternatives and having to switch to other brands. Brands aiming to address these consequences should be as open as possible with their consumers (Zarantonello et al., as cited in Palusuk et al., 2019).

Finally, Palusuk et al. (2019) suggest a definition of brand love that reflects its complex, dynamic nature, namely that brand love is "an intensive emotional connection characterised by intimacy, passion and commitment, which may emerge at the initial consumer-brand encounter, but may also develop over time, based on delightful experiences and/or shared history" (Palusuk et al., 2019, p. 116).

46.4 Measurement and Empirical Investigation of Brand Love

Broadbent (2012) could identify only a few empirical studies on the measurement of brand love up until 2012, but Palusuk et al. (2019) identified a few more since then. Shrimp and Madden (1988) did not present their own scale for measuring brand love in their conceptual paper, but rather incorporated Sternberg's (1986) scale and adapted its items to a consumption context. Their research was criticised for merely incorporating Sternberg's (1986) scale in their conceptualisation of brand love, without investigating its psychometric properties (Albert, Merunka, & Valette-Florence, 2008). A further criticism was that they replaced the term "intimacy" with "liking". By doing so, they distorted the construct of love because love is a conceptual construct in its own right and not just an extreme form of interpersonal liking (Carroll & Ahuvia, 2006).

As mentioned earlier, Ahuvia's (1993) research was the first to investigate brand love empirically. Furthering his earlier work, Ahuvia (2005) investigated the role of the possessions that consumers love and how they feature in narratives about their identity. He found that consumers used their loved items to represent their selves to others or to reflect a desirable self-image. Ahuvia (1993, 2005) found that consumers form strong emotional bonds similar to love with objects and brands. The term, love, however, tends to be subjective and people meant different things when using the term (Ahuvia, 1993).

Carroll and Ahuvia (2006) developed a unidimensional, multi-item measure of brand love. They posited that satisfaction can be positioned on a continuum ranging from cognitive experiences where consumers are neutral and do not have any feelings toward a brand to strong brand love that is established gradually. Table 46.1 presents Carroll and Ahuvia's (2006) unidimensional brand love scale consisting of 10 items, measured on a 5-point Likert scale.

Kim, Kim, Jolly, and Fairhurst (2008) built on Carroll and Ahuvia's (2006) research by also conceptualising brand love as a type of satisfaction. They, however, suggest that satisfaction may result from a single transaction while brand love typically develops over several transactions. When brand love is conceptualised as a type of satisfaction, negative feelings such as hate, dislike and negative emotions, including situations where consumers are dissatisfied with a brand, but still experience strong feelings of love for the brand are disregarded.

Heinrich et al. (2008) built on Shimp and Madden's (1988) research by empirically investigating and validating the scale they proposed. Shrimp and Madden (1988) applied Sternberg's (1986) love triangle as an analogy in their conceptual paper, but Heinrich et al. (2008) retained Sternberg's (1986) original terminology in

Table 46.1 Caroll and Ahuvia's unidimensional brand love scale

Items	Cronbach alpha
This is a wonderful brand.	0.91
This brand makes me feel good.	
This brand is totally awesome.	
I have neutral feelings about this brand. (−)	
This brand makes me very happy.	
I love this brand!	
I have no particular feelings about this brand. (−)	
This brand is a pure delight.	
I am passionate about this brand.	
I'm very attached to this brand.	

Source: Palusuk et al. (2019, p. 126)

their research, highlighting brand intimacy, brand passion, and brand commitment as first order factors of brand love. In an online survey, Heinrich et al. (2008) requested respondents to identify a brand that they loved, or felt particular strong feelings of love for and then respond to the items, based on their experience with the particular brand. They concluded that Sternberg's triangular love theory is relevant to a marketing context and that all three factors independently and combined were related to the brand love construct. Heinrich et al.'s (2008) work contributed significantly to the field of brand love measurement (Skoog & Söderström, 2015). They, however, also did not undertake an initial exploratory investigation of the brand love construct from a consumer perspective (Batra et al., as cited in Skoog & Söderström, 2015). Their research further reflects a concern raised about existing brand love research, namely that participants could choose their preferred brand or object in certain studies (Palusuk et al., 2019). This approach does not generate a representative sample from the population of users or buyers of the specific brand or product. It may be advisable to, for instance, rather focus on a particular product category when investigating brand love (Broadbent, 2012).

Albert et al. (2009) developed two brand love scales and suggested that brand love has three positive outcomes, namely trust, positive word-of-mouth, and loyalty. Although Albert et al. (2009) did not initially support the application of theories of interpersonal of love in investigating brand love they concluded that brand love corresponds to interpersonal love.

Batra et al. (2012) developed the most detailed brand love scale, consisting of 56 items measuring seven dimensions (self-brand integration, passion-driven behaviours, positive emotional connection, long-term relationship, positive overall attitude valence, attitude strength and anticipated separation distress). They suggest that identifying these elements makes it possible to determine which of them strengthen or weaken consumers' experience of brand love in a particular situation. Although Batra et al. (as cited in Skoog & Söderström, 2015) aimed at investigating consumers' experiences in depth, they acknowledged that their scale was too long to be used in research. Sajtos, Cao, Espinosac, Phaud, Rossie, Sungd and Voyerg (2020) validated Batra et al.'s (2012) complete scale and its underlying model across five countries (Australia, China, France, the United Kingdom, and the USA). They highlight two important conclusions from a measurement perspective, based on their research. They investigated the existing structure of brand love from the outset, instead of gradually building up the model and found that the conceptualisations of brand love in the new contexts differed considerably from Batra et al's (2012) initial conceptualisation, based on a 'ground up, prototype' approach. The prototype conceptualisation of brand love may reflect cultural influences, limiting its generalisability beyond the context in which it was developed. It further was evident that the scale items should be meticulously adapted for a particular cultural context. Some of the translated scale items in their study, for instance, contained terms that Chinese consumers do not typically use in portraying their beliefs and perceptions of brands.

Albert and Merunka (2013) developed a complex, multidimensional scale to measure brand love, based on interpersonal love theory, measuring the dimensions intimacy, dreams, pleasure, memories, unicity, affection and passion, and consisting of 32 items measured by means of a 10-point Likert scale. Rossiter (2012) focused on developing a brand love measure that did not include the term "love" because of his conviction that it is unacceptable to use the term "love" in such measures, because its meaning may vary across people and situations. Palusuk et al. (2019), however, point out that despite Rossiter's (2012) disapproval of using the word "love" in brand love measures, his rating scale includes the term "love".

Bagozzi, Batra, and Ahuvia (2017) added three further concise scales for measuring brand love. They also developed a single-factor scale consisting of 13 items and a brief scale consisting of 6 items. Zarantonello, Formisano, and Grappi (2016) developed a scale focusing on consumer experience, measuring the dimensions of fantasies and thoughts, attachment, self-expression, pleasure and identification. A number of further studies on brand love were reported in the meantime, but these studies adapted previously validated measures and did not develop new scales for measuring brand love (Palusuk et al., 2019).

In summary, various scales differing in length and the number of dimensions they measure have been developed (Palusuk et al., 2019). The number of dimensions incorporated in brand love scales range between 1 and 11 (Batra et al., 2012). Existing brand love research further is criticised for incorporating the term "love" in brand love measures because of the inherent ambiguity of the term (Palusuk et al., 2019).

Palusuk et al. (2019) highlight disparities in approaches and definitions of brand love in existing research. Although researchers acknowledge that brand love is a conceptually complex construct, they often do not provide their own definitions of brand love. Researchers applying interpersonal love theories in their research further often isolate shared characteristics between brand love and interpersonal love, but also suggest that brand love do not generate the same levels of excitement and emotion as interpersonal love. Brand love further involves stronger rational considerations than interpersonal love (Langner et al., 2015) and consumers do not expect the same level of goodwill and altruism from brands, compared to interpersonal love (Albert & Merunka, 2013). Brand love, therefore, cannot be regarded as corresponding completely to interpersonal love (Carroll & Ahuvia, 2006).

46.5 Conclusion

The allure of the brand love construct lies in the tendency that some brands evoke such strong consumer reactions that it may indeed resemble experiences of love. It therefore appears that brand love will remain of research interest for some time to come, especially considering its probable positive outcomes such as consumers remaining with a brand over an extended period of time. Companies may be particularly interested in generating brand love among consumers and all brands should ideally focus on nurturing brand love among consumers. This process however may not be clear-cut, because brand love may be constantly evolving. Only certain product categories may generate brand love among consumers and it may be necessary to determine where brand love resorts, for instance, in a particular brand, a particular type of consumer, or in the relationship between them. Further investigation of the psychological mechanisms such as personality traits that lead to brand love appears warranted.

There, however, are divergent views about whether it is appropriate to apply love, an interpersonal construct, to brands and consumer behaviour. It is essential that future research on brand love focus on understanding how consumers experience brand love in order to reduce the ambiguity in its definitions and conceptualisations. Investigating the brand love construct across cultures may further enhance its understanding, especially its relation to cultural dimensions. Finally, more elaborate conceptualisations of brand love such as the developmental perspective may enhance an understanding of the construct and its components.

References

Aaker, J. (1997). Dimensions of brand personality. *Journal of Marketing Research, 34*(3), 347–356.
Ahuvia, A. C. (1992). For the love of money: Materialism and product love. In F. Rudman & M. L. Richins (Eds.), *Meaning, measure, and morality of materialism*. Provo, UT: Association for Consumer Research.
Ahuvia, A. C. (1993). *I love it! Towards a unifying theory of love across diverse love objects*. PhD Dissertation, Northwestern University. UMI Dissertation Services, Ann Arbor, MI.
Ahuvia, A. C. (2005). Beyond the extended self: Loved objects and consumers' identity narratives. *Journal of Consumer Research, 32*(1), 171–184.
Ahuvia, A. (2016). What is our love for things made of? In *The brand love components*. Retrieved from http://thethingswelove.com/wp-content/uploads/2016/10/Brand-love-components.pdf
Albert, N., & Merunka, D. (2013). The role of brand love in consumer-brand relationships. *Journal of Consumer Marketing, 30*(3), 258–266.
Albert, N., Merunka, D., & Valette-Florence, P. (2008). *Brand love: Conceptualization and measurement*. Sydney: ANZMAC.
Albert, N., Merunka, D., & Valette-Florence, P. (2009). *The feeling of love toward a brand: Concept and measurement*. ACR North American Advances.
Albert, N., & Valette-Florence, P. (2010). Measuring the love feeling for a brand using interpersonal love items. *Journal of Marketing Development & Competitiveness, 5*(1), 57–63.

Alvarez, C., & Fournier, S. (2012). Brand flings: When great brand relationships are not made to last. In S. Fournier, M. Breazeale, & M. Fetscherin (Eds.), *Consumer-brand relationships: Theory and practice* (pp. 74–96). London: Routledge.

Arnould, E. J., Press, M., Salminen, E., & Tillotson, J. S. (2019). Consumer culture theory: Development, critique, application and prospects. *Foundations and Trends® in Marketing, 12*(2), 80–166.

Arnould, E. J., & Thompson, C. J. (2005). Consumer culture theory (CCT): Twenty years of research. *Journal of Consumer Research, 31*(4), 868–882.

Bagozzi, R. P., Batra, R., & Ahuvia, A. C. (2014). *Brand love: Construct validity, managerial utility, and new conceptual insights*. Working Paper, University of Michigan, Ann Arbor, MI.

Bagozzi, R. P., Batra, R., & Ahuvia, A. (2017). Brand love: Development and validation of a practical scale. *Marketing Letters, 28*(1), 1–14.

Batra, R., Ahuvia, A., & Bagozzi, R. P. (2012). Brand love. *Journal of Marketing, 76*(2), 1–16.

Bennett, A. M., & Hill, R. P. (2012). The universality of warmth and competence: A response to brands as intentional agents. *Journal of Consumer Psychology, 22*(2), 199–204.

Bergkvist, L., & Bech-Larsen, T. (2010). Two studies of consequences and actionable antecedents of brand love. *Journal of Brand Management, 17*(7), 504–518.

Broadbent, S. (2012). *Brand love in sport: Antecedents and consequences* (No. PhD). Deakin University.

Burns, D. J., & Fawcett, J. K. (2012). The role of brand in a consumer culture: Can strong brands serve as a substitute for a relationship with god? *Journal of Biblical Integration in Business, 15*(2).

Carroll, B. A., & Ahuvia, A. C. (2006). Some antecedents and outcomes of brand love. *Marketing letters, 17*(2), 79–89.

Chew, D. J. (2017). From brand awareness to brand love: A conceptual discussion of brand love progression. *Journal of Arts & Social Sciences, 1*(1), 21–29.

Donovan, L. A. N., Priester, J. R., MacInnis, D. J., & Park, C. W. (2012). Brand forgiveness: How close brand relationships influence forgiveness. In S. Fournier, M. Breazeale, & M. Fetscherin (Eds.), *Consumer-brand relationships: Theory and applications* (pp. 184–203). New York: Routledge.

Epley, N., Waytz, A., & Cacioppo, J. T. (2007). On seeing human: A three-factor theory of anthropomorphism. *Psychological Review, 114*(4), 864–886.

Fetscherin, M. (2014). What type of relationship do we have with loved brands? *Journal of Consumer Marketing, 31*(6/7), 430–440.

Fetscherin, M., & Conway, M. (2011). *Brand love: Interpersonal or parasocial love relationship*. Harvard University.

Fournier, S. (1998). Consumers and their brands: Developing relationship theory in consumer research. *The Journal of Consumer Research, 24*(4), 343–373.

Garg, R., Mukherjee, J., Biswas, S., & Kataria, A. (2016). An investigation into the concept of brand love and its proximal and distal covariates. *Journal of Relationship Marketing, 15*(3), 135–153.

Heinrich, D., Bauer, H. H., & Muhl, J. C. M. (2008). *Measuring brand love: Applying Sternberg's triangular theory of love in consumer-brand relations.*. Paper presented at the ANZMAC.

Ind, N., Iglesias, O., & Schultz, M. (2013). Building brands together. *CA Management Review, 55*(3), 5–26.

Kaufmann, H. R., Loureiro, S. M. C., & Manarioti, A. (2016). Exploring behavioural branding, brand love and brand co-creation. *Journal of Product & Brand Management, 25*(6), 516–526.

Kim, H.-Y., Kim, Y.-K., Jolly, L., & Fairhurst, A. (2008). Satisfied customers' love toward retailers: A cross-product exploration. *Advances in Consumer Research – North American Conference Proceedings, 35*, 507–515.

Kotler, P., & Keller, K. L. (2006). *Marketing management* (12th ed.). Upper Saddle River, NJ: Prentice Hall.

Langner, T., Bruns, D., Fischer, A., & Rossiter, J. R. (2016). Falling in love with brands: A dynamic analysis of the trajectories of brand love. *Marketing Letters, 27*(1), 15–26.

Langner, T., Schmidt, J., & Fischer, A. (2015). Is it really love? A comparative investigation of the emotional nature of brand and interpersonal love. *Psychology & Marketing, 32*(6), 624–634.

Lebar, E., & Blackston, M. (2015). Foreword. In M. Fetscherin & T. Heilmann (Eds.), *Consumer brand relationships: Meaning, measuring, managing* (pp. xii–xiii). Springer.

Moussa, S. (2015). I may be a twin but I'm one of a kind. *Qualitative Market Research: An International Journal, 18*(1), 69–85.

Palusuk, N., Koles, B., & Hasan, R. (2019). 'All you need is brand love': A critical review and comprehensive conceptual framework for brand love. *Journal of Marketing Management, 35*(1–2), 97–129.

Pawle, J., & Cooper, P. (2006). Measuring emotion—lovemarks, the future beyond brands. *Journal of Advertising Research, 46*(1), 38–48.

Pedeliento, G. (Ed.). (2018). *Analyzing attachment and consumers' emotions: Emerging research and opportunities*. IGI Global. Emerging trends in attachment studies, Chapter 5.

Reimann, M., Castaño, R., Zaichkowsky, J., & Bechara, A. (2012). How we relate to brands: Psychological and neurophysiological insights into consumer-brand relationships. *Journal of Consumer Psychology, 22*(1), 128–142.

Romaniuk, J. (2013). What's (brand) love got to do with it? *International Journal of Market Research, 55*(2), 185–186.

Rossiter, J. R. (2012). A new C-OAR-SE-based content-valid and predictively valid measure that distinguishes brand love from brand liking. *Marketing Letters, 23*(3), 905–916.

Sajtos, L., Cao, J. T., Espinosa, J. A., Phau, I., Rossi, P., Sung, B., et al. (2020). Brand love: Corroborating evidence across four continents. *Journal of Business Research*.

Sampedro, A. (2017). *Brand hate and brand forgiveness – A dynamic analysis*. Honors Program Theses, Rollins College, FL.

Sarkar, A. (2014). Brand love in emerging market: A qualitative investigation. *Qualitative Market Research: An International Journal, 17*(4), 481–494.

Shimp, T. A., & Madden, T. J. (1988). Consumer-object relations: A conceptual framework based analogously on Sternberg's triangular theory of love. *Advances in Consumer Research, 15*(1), 163–168.

Skoog, M., & Söderström, M. (2015). *Antecedents and outcomes of brand love: A qualitative study within the Swedish clothing industry*. Retrieved from https://www.diva-portal.org/smash/get/diva2:841971/FULLTEXT01.pdf

Sternberg, R. J. (1986). A triangular theory of love. *Psychological Review, 93*(2), 119–135.

Thomson, M., MacInnis, D. J., & Whan Park, C. (2005). The ties that bind: Measuring the strength of consumers' emotional attachments to brands. *Journal of Consumer Psychology, 15*(1), 77–91.

Zarantonello, L., Formisano, M., & Grappi, S. (2016). The relationship between brand love and actual brand performance: Evidence from an international study. *International Marketing Review, 33*(6), 806–824.

Zarantonello, L., Romani, S., Grappi, S., & Bagozzi, R. P. (2016). Brand hate. *Journal of Product & Brand Management, 25*(1), 11–25.

Leona Ungerer is an associate professor in the Department of Industrial and Organisational Psychology at the University of South Africa. Her areas of interest are consumer psychology and technology-enhanced teaching and learning.

Part X
Love in Different Cultural Contexts

"抛绣球" Ceremony or "Embroidered Balls Throwing" (Photo: JJ Ying)

Chapter 47
Meaning-making Through Love Stories in Cultural Perspectives: Expressions, Rituals and Symbols

Claude-Hélène Mayer

> *I am not a poet, but life and love are art.*
> *Erich Fromm*

Abstract The meaning of love differs across social and cultural contexts. These meanings are often constructed and reconstructed through narrations. Love narrations impact strongly on the identity of individuals across their life span and can include different concepts of love, descriptions of love expressions, symbols and meanings.

This chapter presents love narrations from individuals in Japan, the US, South Africa, Israel and Germany. The aim of this chapter is to explore and compare love concepts and narrations of individuals of different cultural, gender, religious and language contexts.

The research design followed a qualitative study design, using semi-structured interviews with 21 questions, exploring narrations on love and culture. The chapter presents findings from a study of 22 individuals of different cultural origin.

Findings provide new insight into concepts of love, feelings associated with love, expressions of love, rituals of love, love symbols and stories of love. Love contributes strongly to meaning-making in connection with the personal and cultural, as well as the environmental context. Conclusions are drawn and recommendations for future research are given.

Keywords Love · Love concepts · Love stories · Narrations · Culture · Meaning-making · Love expression · Symbols of love · Rituals of love · Feelings

---

C.-H. Mayer (✉)
Department of Industrial Psychology and People Management, University of Johannesburg, Johannesburg, South Africa

Institut für therapeutische Kommunikation und Sprachgebrauch, Europa Universität Viadrina, Frankfurt (Oder), Germany
e-mail: claudemayer@gmx.net

47.1 Introduction

Love and its meaning varies across time, space and culture[1]—it is socially, culturally and historically constructed and differs across cultures and languages (Beall & Sternberg, 1995; Dewaele, 2012, 2013; Jahoda & Lewis, 2015; Javaid, 2018; Pavlenko, 2014; Sternberg, 1998). Numerous researchers have explored the concept of love in cultural contexts and explored perspectives across social strata (Barsade & O'Neill, 2014; Beichen & Murshed, 2015; Jankowiak, 2008; Javaid, 2018; Swidler, 2001), and in various historical contexts (Holloway, 2018). Additionally, how individuals communicate about love and what meaning they ascribe to it is influenced by their gender and gender roles (Carter, 2012, 2013; Langford, 1999).

Love is influenced by the language individuals speak and how they can express their emotions (Dewaele, 2017). It has been consistently observed that love is not easy to live, and that individuals frequently get caught up in the complexities of experiencing the highlights of love and dealing with the chaos and trouble it causes (Langford, 1999). Bauman (2003) goes further, in pointing out that love is mainly defined by "liquid modern times" and by the frailty of human bonds, insecurities and conflicting desires. Shumway (2003) argues similarly, that love is in crisis in the Western world, as a consequence of changes in the meaning and experience of marriage as an institution. Changes in love concepts across the centuries are clearly bound to changes in culture and to the stories about love which are connected with culture (Shumway, 2003).

In linguistic terms, love is a concept that strongly relates to attachment, desire, preference, taking pleasure in something, and to physical acts (Gratzke, 2017). Gratzke (2017) emphasises the importance of the role language plays in experiencing, telling and expressing love, noting that the way people experience love is connected to how they express it. Although people use similar words for emotions, the meaning of the words varies (Twamley, 2014). To define and understand what love means from different cultural and language perspectives, a qualitative approach is needed to explore and understand the implicit and often hidden aspects of love.

The talk about love can provide clues about how humans shape their relationships, expectations and behaviours, which are all influenced by social and cultural contexts and by narratives of love (Shumway, 2003; Tamboukou, 2013). Therefore, love itself is a "perfect place to study love in action" (Swidler, 2001, p. 2) and to study contradictory aspects of culture and love within the context of societies, politics and socio-cultural value contexts (Illouz, 1997, 2011, 2019). Love talk is also gendered: Cancian (1990) suggests that the concept of love in the US is feminised and is therefore identified with women and with qualities defined as

---

[1] Culture is defined as "the coordination of meaning and action within a bounded group" (Bennett, 2017). Transculture is viewed as the crossing over of the group's boundaries in terms of coordination of meaning and action.

feminine, such as the ability to express feelings and tenderness. Regan (2016) agrees, highlighting that love is associated with female qualities, the expression of nurturance and emotional warmth. However, still it seems that science does not know a great deal about love and culture (Berscheid, 2006; Sun & Yang, 2019; Swidler, 2001). Feelings and emotions defined as "love" should be studied further in their cultural and transcultural context.

In the following pages, various understandings of these love concepts and related aspects are outlined. Meaning-making through narrations and stories of love is discussed, and the contribution of the chapter clarified. The research methodology is introduced and the findings of the research presented. In the findings section, this chapter takes into account concepts of love from different cultural contexts. It responds to questions such as: What is love? How do you feel when you feel love? How do you express love? What are rituals of love? What are love symbols? The chapter presents love stories from individuals of different cultural backgrounds, and concludes with recommendations for further research.

47.2 Concepts of Love and Culture

In this book chapter, it is argued that love, as a socio-cultural construct, needs contextualisation to be understood in depth and to create meaning with regard to its definition and its emotional experience, as described by Beall and Sternberg (1995). Different forms of love, conceptions, experiences and expressions have been distinguished across cultures and contexts so far (Shumway, 2003). Beall and Sternberg (1995) conclude that love needs a context to be comprehended. This contextualisation needs to take into account: (a) the beloved person, (b) the feelings which accompany love, (c) the thoughts that accompany love, and (d) the actions or the relations which a person has with the beloved person. Therefore, a love concept is never independent of the individuals involved, the feelings connected to love, or the cognitions and the behaviours related to it. Sternberg (1998) proposes that love relationships are usually built on three pillars, namely intimacy, passion, and decision or commitment. He terms this the "triangle of love" and suggests that these three components might be differently weighted across cultures; however, they will be visible in any culture to a certain degree when it comes to love (Sternberg, 1998, p. 5).

In contemporary Western societies, talking about love is common and is often present in daily interactions (Swidler, 2001). Researchers accordingly refer to different love concepts. Often, love is differentiated into romantic love, compassionate love or parental love (Barsade & O'Neill, 2014).

Romantic love relationships have been defined as profound, meaningful and exhilarating (Tomlinson & Aron, 2013). Illouz (1997) contends that romantic moments and the romantic love concept are significantly influenced by the portrayal of love in American film and TV shows, and that the current concepts of love are anchored in the overlap of conceptions of love and a "romantic utopia" which is based on cultural clichés and consumer capitalism (see Chap. 46). Often, love concepts and the clichés in Western and US contexts relate to this romance, but also to dating. Lovemaking, marriage and broader concepts of romantic relationships.

Compassionate love is presented as a humanistic concept of love which is usually associated with compassion, caring, and tenderness for others (Barsade & O'Neill, 2014). Evans (2003) does not call it compassionate love, but points out that love cannot be reduced to only romantic love. It is an emotional concept which depends on reasoned care and commitment. Campbell-Barr, Georgeson, and Varga (2015) observe that in early childhood education, for example, love plays an important and culture-related role. In Hungary, educators speak freely about love, mention love as part of the educational concept, relating to compassionate love, and see it as a key to education, while educators in England speak of care, support and empathy rather than love. Compassionate love concepts are culturally defined.

Parental love, defined as the love between parents and children, is explained differently to compassionate love which one might find in leadership studies, or to romantic love between couples and lovers. Li and Meyer (2017) point out that the love of both parents, mother and father, is very important in child development. These authors highlight that worldwide, parental love which relates to acceptance is particularly important for children and their development and seems to relate to a universal need.

47.2.1 Love Expression in Cultures

The way love is expressed differs across cultures and languages (Dewaele, 2008). Dewaele (2008) explains that verbal expressions of love, such as "I love you", carry different emotional weights in various cultures and languages. "I love you" will have the strongest meaning when it is expressed in the speaker's first language; it weighs emotionally less when it is expressed in a foreign language (Dewaele, 2008). In studying a wide range of emotionally diverse relationships, Lomas (2018) has identified 14 different concepts and expressions of love, which suggests that the nuances of love expressions are culturally and linguistically determined. The expression of feelings and emotions are closely related to the self and the cultural identity (Ye, 2004). In her Chinese upbringing and culture, Ye (2004) explains that emotions such as love are expressed privately, in comparison to the public expression of emotions and feelings in Western contexts. Love in Chinese contexts is shown in gestures and non-verbally, as well as through embodied care and concern for the beloved.

Similarly, it has been found in Japanese culture that feelings are more restrained in verbal expression, in comparison to Western cultures such as the US (Ting-Toomey, 1991; Ting-Toomey & Dorjee, 2018). Further, Sugiyama (2015) finds that in Japanese communication, it is important to "read the air" to grasp the emotional atmosphere and communication climate, and to read between the lines rather than expressing oneself verbally and directly.

Osei-Tutu, Dzokoto, Hanke, Adams and Belgrave (2018) found that Ghanaian Christians express their love in three particular ways: through meeting material needs of the family (children, spouse, parents, and close relatives), by helping people in need (such as the elderly, and friends as well as strangers) and in showing affectionate care for people around them. Love seems to be expressed more readily through maintenance and communal orientation than through anything else. Mokuku (2017) highlights that in African contexts, love is expressed in harmonious co-existence with others, while in the South African context, Bhana (2017) emphasises that money and gifts are expressions of love which are deeply entangled with African cultural norms.

Research on German–English couples by Piller (2002) indicates the importance of intercultural couples developing their own private language and expressions of love which extend beyond national, cultural and language origins. Aleksic and Magali (2018) point out that language and culture affect love, its expression and the affection in love relationships, and that differences in the expression of romantic belief, cultural and linguistic approaches to love, religion, different perspectives of homosexuality and barriers in communication can lead to conflicts in couples with different cultural origins. These examples provide insight into differences in conception and expression of love and accordingly into the different rituals and symbols[2] of love with culture-specific meaning (Swidler, 2001).

47.3 Meaning-Making Through Narrations and Stories of Love

Narrations are present in daily acts and interactions and include the feelings, thoughts and ideas individuals have, to create identity for self and others (Mayer & Flotman, 2017). Through narrative acts, the self, society and socio-cultural acts are created in a dynamic interplay. McAdams et al. (2004) confirm that life narratives often include themes of interpersonal communion, such as love and friendship.

According to Andrews, Day Sclater, Squire and Treacher (2009), "stories involve the narration of a series of events" in a plotted sequence which unfold in time. Thereby, it is assumed that each person is able to tell stories about their life and their experiences, such as love experiences (Leskela-Kärki, 2008). Hardy (1968) points out that people dream in narratives, they remember, anticipate, learn, think and

---

[2]Symbols are defined as tangible signs and are placeholders of certain ideas with specific meaning. They are "signs of recognition", but also allow for different interpretations of meaning (Mayer, 2005, p. 157) which are culture-bound and often socially and politically embedded. Rituals are defined as specific actions which are culture-bound as well and which are procedural expressions of meaning. They often express value orientations and are strongly culturally embedded (Mayer, 2005). Thinking about love often evokes thoughts about love rituals and symbols (Swidler, 2001).

daydream in narratives which create parts of their life and meaning. Through narrations, humans make sense of their world (Wood, 2001).

Love stories usually include an aim which individuals try to fulfil during their life and contribute to building their socio-cultural world. Love narrations are extremely important for teachers in early childhood education, in the context of demonstrating care and compassion in culturally diverse educational settings (Jokikokko & Karikoski, 2016). Love narrations are comparable to a spiritual and social act which emphasises dynamic and social life aspects through stories or other textual material (Erol-Isik, 2015). According to Schnell and Keenan (2011), meaning-making through love and community becomes particularly important for female atheists, while male atheists are instead committed to knowledge, self-knowledge and reason. Sternberg (1996) describes love as a story which is created through personal interaction and environmental attributes, as explored in this chapter.

47.4 The Contribution of this Chapter

This chapter aims to increase the understanding of narrations and stories of love across individuals of different cultural origins. The chapter contributes to the existing literature on love in cultural and transcultural contexts by asking individuals from different cultural backgrounds to tell stories of love. In several different ways, these stories respond to the questions: "What is love?", "How does it feel to love?", "How is love expressed?", "What rituals of love do you know and practise?", and "What symbols of love do you use?". By examining the responses to these questions, the chapter provides in-depth insights into love stories of selected individuals from a variety of cultural backgrounds.

47.5 Research Methodology

The study from which this chapter arose is based in the qualitative research realm (Yin, 2009). In terms of the research strategy, this study is grounded in a hermeneutical and interpretative paradigm (Babbie, 2011; Creswell, 2013), focusing on patterns of meaning that are shared by the participants (Denzin & Lincoln, 2011), thereby exploring the deeper meaning and interpretations of love in cultural contexts, while following the call of Sawyer and Norris (2009, 2013) to expand cultural understandings of meaning. The study uses Ricoeur's (1979, p. 253) text reconstruction method, which has four levels: (1) the perception of the experience (of love), (2) the reflection of the experience and its narration, (3) the analysis and interpretation of the narration, and (4) the presentation of the re-categorised concept (of love).

47.5.1 Data Collection, Analysis and Reporting

The study uses primarily the research method of qualitative written interviews to investigate concepts around love and narrations on love. The interviews were conducted based on an online questionnaire, containing 21 in-depth questions on love and love narrations. The participants took an average of 90 min to respond to the questionnaire.

Data was analysed by using the five-step process of content analysis (Terre Blanche, Durrheim, & Painter, 2006, pp. 322–326): Step 1 is familiarisation and immersion; Step 2 involves inducing themes; Step 3 is coding; Step 4 is elaboration; and the final step involves interpretation and checking to ensure the quality of the data.

Findings are reported in a qualitative reporting style, presenting in-depth information and data-rich excerpts of the interview transcriptions.

Quality criteria in this study were conformability, credibility, transferability and dependability. These quality criteria were addressed by drawing transparent internal causal conclusions and providing generalisations within the context of research (credibility) according to Van der Riet (2017).

47.5.2 Sampling

To identify participants, purposeful sampling and snowball sampling was used (Naderifar, Goli, & Ghaljaie, 2017). The sample consisted of 22 individuals whose first language was German (ten participants), English (five participants), Afrikaans (two participants), as well as one participant each with a first language of Japanese, Tswana, Hebrew and Romanian. In terms of self-stated nationality, the sample consisted of: eight Germans, five US citizens, two Japanese, two South Africans, and one participant each with White, German-Iranian, Israeli, Romanian and Bavarian[3] origin.[4]

The sample further comprised nine female and 13 male participants between the ages of 33 and 80 years. Altogether seven individuals described themselves as Christians, four as Roman Catholics, two as Protestants, and one each as atheist, agnostic, atheist/agnostic, Buddhist, Muslim, Jew, Jesuit, and one without religious affiliation.

In terms of educational background, the participants held nine doctoral degrees, six masters' degrees, three "Diplom" degrees[5], two habilitations (post doctoral degree), one national diploma, and one high school certificate. The sample further included seven professors, three academics, three directors, two consultants, one

---

[3]*Bundesland* (provincial state) in Germany.
[4]All information is based on participants' self-descriptions.
[5]Diplom degrees are equivalent with Master degree levels in Germany.

Table 47.1 Biographical data of participants (Author's own construction)

No.	Sex	Age	First language	Nationality	Religion	Education	Profession
P1	F	58	German	German	Catholic	Master	Director
P2	M	78	English	US	Christian	Master	Consultant
P3	M	47	Afrikaans	White	Christian	Doctorate	Academic
P4	M	67	German	German	None	Doctorate	Academic
P5	M	34	English	US	Atheist & agnostic, raised Roman Catholic	Master	Academic
P6	M	80	English	US	Atheist	Doctorate	Professor emeritus
P7	F	43	German	German	Roman Catholic	Habilitation	Professor & entrepreneur
P8	M	45	German	German–Iranian	Christian	Doctorate	Professor
P9	M	61	German	German	Catholic	Diplom	Director
P10	F	59	Japanese	Japanese	Buddhism (not practising); Christian school education	Doctorate	Professor
P11	M	63	German	German	Roman Catholic	Diplom	Educational officer
P12	M	30	Setswana	South African	Narcissistic	National diploma	Entrepreneur
P13	M	46	German	German	Christianity/ Muslim	High school certificate	Consultant
P14	M	65	Afrikaans	South African	Christian	Doctorate	Professor emeritus
P15	F	54	Hebrew	Israel	Jewish	Doctorate	Professor
P16	M	49	German	Germany	Protestant (not practising)	Diplom	Director
P17	F	81	English	US	Humanist	Doctorate	Psychologist
P18	F	33	English	US	Christianity	Doctorate	Professor
P19	F	44	Romanian	Romanian	Christianity	Master	Teacher
P20	M	49	Japanese	Japanese	Agnostic	Habilitation	Professor
P21	F	42	German	German	Protestant	Master	Project manager
P22	F	60	German	Bavarian	Jesuit	Master	Executive manager

professor/entrepreneur, one entrepreneur, one executive manager, one project manager, one teacher, one psychologist, and one educational officer. Table 47.1 provides an overview of the biographical details of the participants.

47.5.3 Ethical Considerations and Limitations of the Study

The participants consented to the study. Ethical considerations included the rights of the participant, respect afforded to the participant, the creation of informed consent, confidentiality, anonymity and transparency (Roth & Unger, 2018). Ethical approval for this research study was given by the German university.

This research study comes with certain limitations. It is limited to primary and secondary source analyses and triangulation of theories, methods and data. The findings it provides, in terms of qualitative, in-depth information on love, are not generalisable. However, selected aspects of this study could be applicable to other studies and might provide detailed insights which can be used to provide direction for future studies and for the conduct of follow-up studies.

The study is further limited to a qualitative perspective on love and is restricted by the narrow and limited research questions presented. Additionally, only individuals of selected nationalities participated. With regard to the social strata, participants were mainly drawn from a middle- and upper-class social and educational background. There is also a bias present in the data, in that a majority of participants are culturally rooted in German as their first language and hold high educational degrees.

47.6 Findings and Discussion

In the following sub-chapters, findings from the study are presented and discussed.

47.6.1 What Is Love?

Almost half of the participants responded that love means to "have a deep connection" (see Table 47.2) to a person, to a higher power, to the world or to life. It is an emotionally deep connection which, for several participants, has a spiritual depth. P1, for example, commented:

> Now, I would say that love means to have this deep and unique connection deep between two individuals or more.

For not less than ten participants,[6] love was connected to "unconditional acceptance", for six participants to trust and intimacy, and for another six participants, to mental and physical attraction. Caring and responsibility were further associated with love by six individuals, as well as six individuals who defined love as being associated with "meaning in life".

In total, five individuals each stated that love is related to belonging and attachment, compassion, self-sacrifice, freedom and growth. Altogether, four participants

---
[6]Please refer to Table 47.1 for more detailed information with regard to participants.

Table 47.2 What is love? (Author's own construction)

Frequency	Category	Participants
10	Deep connection	P1, P5, P7, P9, P11, P16, P17, P19, P21, P22
10	Unconditional acceptance	P2, P4, P6, P7, P9, P11, P13, P16, P20, P22
6	Trust/intimacy	P1, P2, P4, P7, P17, P18
6	Mental and physical attraction	P1, P5, P7, P8, P17, P20
6	Caring and responsibility	P4, P5, P8, P15, P16, P19
6	Meaning	P5, P7, P10, P14, P21, P22
5	Belonging/attachment	P4, P6, P8, P9, P16
5	Compassion	P2, P4, P9, P12, P17
5	Self-sacrifice	P2, P4, P5, P7, P9
5	Growth	P4, P7, P10, P15, P18
5	Freedom	P4, P7, P9, P13, 15
4	Eternal commitment	P2, P4, P7, P15
4	Respect	P2, P4, P15, P22
3	Miracle	P11, P15, P22
1	Manipulation and power	P7

connected love with eternal commitment and respect, while three participants saw it as a "miracle". Only one person (P7) highlighted negative aspects when responding to what love is. For this individual, love also connected to manipulation and power within the family:

> ... things were said to be done in the name of love, however, there was a lot of power struggle and manipulation involved and not everything that was done in the name of love was done in the name of love.

Generally, people associate love with very positive attributes, with an inner attitude of bonding, and with a deep connection which is usually described in the context of spirituality (Erol-Isik, 2015). Love is further referred to as accepting others for who and what they are (Li & Meier, 2017). The concept of love is connected to trust and intimacy, to taking responsibility for others and being committed to others on a long-term basis. This refers to Sternberg's (1998) triangle of love. With love, individuals are willing to sacrifice and grow, and to balance the compassion for self and others (Barsade & O'Neill, 2014). Love is even described as a "miracle", as something that is almost unbelievable, beyond reason.

The findings of this study expand on Sternberg's (1998) triangle of love, suggesting that, for the participants, love goes beyond the human experiences of intimacy, commitment and passion, to include that which is transcendental, spiritual and universal (see Fig. 47.1). This expanded concept is based on a deep (transhumanist) connection and unconditional acceptance of the given. Transhumanism is here defined as a concept which includes spiritual transcendence, referring to transhumanist philosophies (Manoj, 2008). Part of the transhumanist movement is the idea that new values need to be developed along with human enhancement of options, such as the augmentation of emotional capacities by encompassing socio-economic designs and cultural and psychological skills and

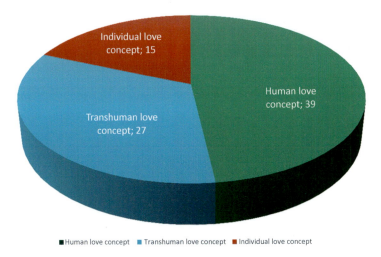

Fig. 47.1 Concepts of love (Author's own construction)

techniques (Bostrom, 2005). It is a view which takes a proactive approach to refining emotional experiences and creating meaningful human relationships, also through increased emotional sensitivity which can enhance the well-being and peacefulness of humans (Bostrom, 2005), not least on a transcendental level. Those values which contribute to love as an emotion relate strongly to spiritual and life enhancing values which contribute to this state of human well-being. This is, for example, reflected in transcendental love being like a deep connection (transcending human emotions), including unconditional acceptance (beyond limiting judgements), being an eternal commitment (beyond human life) and a miracle (beyond rational concepts).

It might be assumed that particularly in transcultural contexts, the definition of love needs to be manifested not only in cultural, intra- and inter-psychological concepts, but also in transhuman concepts which are placed beyond culture and are instead anchored in a more spiritual and transhuman dimension, reaching into the spiritual realm. Besides the transhuman dimension, love is also defined in an individual and in a human way, referring to the personal intra- and inter-psychological principles of growth and freedom. The transhuman concept, however, is viewed here as a more spiritual way, being defined as relating to the human spirit or soul, a soulful connection which connects with transhuman values and beliefs, enhancing human social relations on a spiritual basis.

Table 47.3 details the categories which correspond with each of the three described concepts of love.

Table 47.3 Concepts of love (Author's own construction)

Concept of love	Categories
Human love (39)	Trust, intimacy, mental and physical attraction, caring and responsibility, meaning, belonging, attachment, compassion, respect, manipulation and power
Transhuman love (27)	Deep connection, unconditional acceptance and love, eternal commitment, miracle
Individual love (15)	Self-sacrifice, personal freedom and growth

The number in brackets represents the number of statements made by participants referring to the defined concepts of love

47.6.2 How Do You Feel When You Love?

The concept of love is defined in mainly positive ways; accordingly, it connects to many other positive feelings and emotions. More than half of the participants relate love to feelings of joy and happiness, while in the majority of statements, the participants mentioned several feelings which they simultaneously associate with love. P14, for example, said:

> Love is happiness and well-being. I feel accepted and content. And a feeling of belonging and comfort. This adds up to feeling meaningfulness in my existence here on earth.

Eight individuals experience love as energising, and seven participants described love relating to having a "warm feeling", to "feel complete, passionate and strong", "special" and "accepted when being loved". Five people each said they feel secure or fascinated when experiencing love, but another five reported that love is often connected to negatively classified feelings such as fear and anxiety based on fear of loss, being left, or loving someone who does not love back. P4 pointed out:

> I feel the wish that I can contribute to the other's person well-being and corresponding to this, I am also worried that I will not manage to do so. When I love I also feel the wish that it will go on like this forever and at the same time I fear the possibility of the loss of this love and of shame of losing or being left.

Love is further associated with feeling peaceful and calm, concern about the other, and feeling enriched (according to each of four participants). Three described feeling comfortable, blessed and proud, attraction and desire, devotion, belonging, and pain. Two individuals each felt committed, they feel eternity, while a final two participants connected love with feelings of inadequacy. Table 47.4 illustrates these categories.

47.6.3 How Do You Express Your Love?

For almost half of the participants, love is expressed through words and talking (ten individuals). This is particularly true for individuals of German and US backgrounds

Table 47.4 How do you feel when you feel love? (Author's own construction)

Frequency	Category: accompanying feelings	Participants
12	Joyous, happy	P2, P5, P6, P7, P10, P11, P12, P14, P19, P20, P21, P22
8	Energetic	P1, P7, P9, P10, P11, P18, P21, P22
7	Warm	P1, P10, P11, P16, P18, P21, P22
7	Passionate	P5, P9, P12, P14, P17, P21, P22
7	Complete	P1, P4, P7, P8, P9, P10, P11
7	Strong	P1, P7, P8, P9, P10, P11, P21
7	Accepted and special	P2, P3, P8, P9, P13, P14, P15
5	Secure	P2, P10, P15, P16, P22
5	Fascinated	P4, P5, P7, P9, P11
5 Neg*	Fearful and anxious	P4, P5, P9, P12, P17
4	Peaceful and calm	P7, P11, P16, P21
4	Concerned (positively)	P1, P5, P9, P19
4	Enriched	P1, P7, P9, P21
3	Comforted	P14, P15, P16
3	Blessed and proud	P1, P4, P6
3	Attracted & desired	P4, P5, P9
3	Devoted	P1, P4, P7
3	Belonging	P3, P14, P22
3 Neg	Pain	P7, P9, P20
2	Committed	P6, P15
2	Eternal	P4, P7
2 Neg	Inadequate	P4, P5

*Neg stands for negatively attributed feelings and/or emotions

in this study, because this expression of love is mentioned only by members of this cultural origin. The finding is further supported by the findings of Ye (2004) and (Ting-Toomey, 1991), and by Pillar's (2002) observation that for German–English-speaking couples, the development of a private language is extremely important.

For nine individuals, love is expressed through caring and spending quality time. These two characteristics were mentioned by individuals across all different cultural backgrounds, as was the expression of love through actions (for eight individuals). All participants with Afrikaans or Japanese cultural backgrounds (a total of four) explained that it is specifically the case in their culture to express love through action. This corresponds again with Ye's (2004) findings that love is expressed far more readily through actions than through words (in Chinese and East-Asian cultures), as well as with Ting-Toomey's (1991) study findings in Japan regarding the preference for "reading the air" (Sugiyama, 2015). Another eight participants express love by being present and available. Five participants express love through physical touch, giving support, doing things that make others happy and showing emotional affection. The only Black African participant in this study (P12),

Table 47.5 Expressions of love (Author's own construction)

Frequency	Category	Participants
12	Words and talking	P2, P4, P5, P6, P9, P13, P16, P17, P18, P19, P20, P21
12	Actions	P2, P3, P4, P5, P7, P9, P10, P12, P13, P14, P19, P21
9	Caring	P1, P3, P5, P6, P8, P9, P15, P16, P17
9	Spending quality time	P3, P5, P6, P7, P10, P14, P16, P20, P21
9	Doing things to make others happy	P3, P4, P5, P6, P8, P10, P14, P15, P17
8	Being present and available	P4, P6, P7, P8, P10, P11, P14, P16
6	Support	P1, P8, P10, P14, P17, P22
6	Showing affection and emotions	P7, P12, P14, P16, P19, P22
5	Physical touch	P3, P4, P5, P11, P18
3	Sharing	P1, P6, P7
3	Listening	P1, P6, P10
3	Creative act: writing, poems, music	P7, P11, P20
2	Guide and protect	P3. P10
2	Let somebody grow	P1, P7
2	Seeking the other out	P6, P16
2	Walking together	P4, P13

emphasised that he expresses love by showing emotions and affection, as well as through actions. He explained:

> In our Tswana culture, we believe love goes with works, for example: if you love a woman as a man and you are willing to marry her, as a man who is dedicated, you need to provide livestock (cows or money—and this form is called "lobola") to her family as a result of expressing that you will love, protect and provide for her. And to us, as Tswana, that's a sign of love.

This expression of love from a male participant in South Africa correlates with the findings of Osei-Tutu et al. (2018) who found that love expression in Ghana (West Africa) was in terms of providing for material needs (money, cows), helping people in need and showing affection—which is also mentioned by P12 as expressing affection and emotions in different life situations. Showing affection for others also supports Mokuku's (2017) view that harmony is important in relationships. Bhana's (2017) South African findings corroborate the findings of this study that love and its expression is connected to money and gifts. Besides the Tswana participant, only three German females and one Romanian female, one male German and one male Afrikaans speaker highlight affection. None of the US English-speaking and Asian participants mention "showing affection" as love expression (see Table 47.5).

Table 47.6 Rituals of love (Author's own construction)

Frequency	Category	Participants
8	Care: doing things for and with each other, e.g., listening, talking, small acts of love, praying	P2, P3, P5, P6, P8, P9, P13, P19
6	Gifts	P4 P6, P9, P19, P20, P21
6	Cook and share meals	P1, P2, P5, P7, P9, P13
4	Invitations	P4, P8, P9, P21
4	Marriage/wedding	P13, P15, P18, P21
3	Birthday celebrations	P3, P6, P8
2	Social media declarations	P18, P21
2	Cleaning	P2, P5
2	Compliments	P4, P9
1	Bride price	P12
1	Matching and blind-dating (omiai)	P2

Three people each show love through sharing and listening, while two people each express it through guiding and protecting, letting somebody grow, seeking the other out, by acting creatively and by taking walks together.

47.6.4 What Are the Rituals of Love?

Participants referred to rituals of love, as presented in Table 47.6 and described below.

For eight individuals, love rituals are connected to "doing things for and with each other". Six people commented that "giving gifts" is a ritual of love. For another six individuals, rituals of love include cooking and sharing meals. Four people each stated that invitations are a ritual of love, as are marriage or wedding ceremonials. Three individuals emphasised that particularly birthday celebrations are rituals to show love. Two female individuals considered social media declarations of love as rituals of love. Two male US individuals highlighted that "cleaning the home" is a ritual of love; "giving compliments" was mentioned by another two male German individuals. One South African male individual interpreted the bride price (*lobola*) as a sign of love and one US male individual considered matching and blind-dating (*omiai*) as a Japanese love ritual. Participant P15 provided an example of a Jewish wedding ceremonial as an extraordinary love ritual:

> A Jewish wedding ceremony has a very wide range of local customs and traditions, different countries of origin, streams and courts, and even family customs. Before starting: The bride sits on a chair and receives guests. The groom signs the ketuba—defines the obligations of husband and woman's rights. The groom covers the bride with a veil. The walk to the wedding canopy—a hint of the bride's procession from her home to the bridegroom's house. And when everyone is under the wedding canopy ... you can start.

"Irises is Kiddushim": The ceremony editor takes a glass of wine and blesses: "Blessed are you, our God is the king of the world, seeing the body of the stone. Blessed is our God the king of the world, who sanctified his commandments, and commanded the cities, and forbade the bride. And let us give the wives to us, by the hands of Chupah and Kedushin. Blessed are the Lord, sanctified with the people of Israel by the hands of Chupah and Kedushin." And gives the groom a drink and the mother of the bride who drinks for the bride. [Wearing the ring:] The ceremony leader makes sure that the witnesses are kosher, and that the groom's property is stamped. The bridegroom is wearing the ring on the right finger of the bride, and he blesses: "See, you are sanctified to me, in this patch, as Moses and Israel." [Breaking the glass:] And the groom says: "If I forget you, I will forget my right hand. Catching my tongue, if I do not remember you, if I do not put Jerusalem on the head of my joy."

This Jewish wedding ceremony clearly shows the interlinkages of individual love and ritual within the socio-cultural context of the State of Israel, the religion of Judaism and the interconnectedness to certain ritual and symbolic places in the holy land. It provides an example of the interlinkages of love, rituals, and the environment (Sternberg, 1998).

47.6.5 *What Are Symbols for Love?*

Altogether, half of the participants across different cultures mentioned the heart as a symbol of love (see Table 47.7). Further, hugs were viewed as a symbol of love (ten participants), and giving gifts and rings was mentioned by eight people as signs of love. Seven people considered caressing to be a symbol of love while six individuals each mentioned picking and giving flowers, roses and kisses as being love symbols. Four people each associated the colour red and jewellery with love symbols, while three people each referred to chocolates and smiles. Further on, two people each highlighted creative acts, sex, a flame and religious symbols. Only one person in each case mentioned cows and money (South African male), balloons (Israeli female), a couple of swans (German female) and Japanese symbols (US male) as love symbols.

The symbols of love mentioned can be viewed in eight overall symbolic themes, as shown in Fig. 47.2:

47.6.6 *Stories of Love*

Participants narrated love experiences and told stories of love which can be classified as follows: Seven stories refer to love with regard to *family relationships*, while six deal with *romantic love*. Five stories relate to *spiritual aspects of love*, two stories are about *love experienced in work contexts* and one story is about *love in close friendships*. Six people did not share any story. Four of these stories of love were chosen to

Table 47.7 Symbols of love (Author's own construction)

Theme	Frequency	Category	Participants
Physical and bodily expression as symbol (28)	10	Hugs	P1, P4, P5, P6, P10, P14, P16, P17, P18, P21
	7	Caressing	P1, P5, P9, P10, P14, P18, P21
	6	Kisses	P1, P4, P5, P6, P8, P10
	3	Smile	P6, P10, P17
	2	Sex	P1, P5
Material gift symbols (22)	8	General gift-giving	P2, P3, P4, P5, P9, P14, P17, P21
	8	Rings	P1, P3, P4, P5, P7, P8, P11, P16
	4	Jewellery	P3, P4, P7, P9
	1	Cows and money	P12
	1	Balloons	P15
Natural symbols (16)	6	Picking/giving flowers	P3, P4, P6, P9, P15, P18
	6	Roses	P4, P6, P8, P16, P20, P22
	2	Flame	P21, P22
	1	Couple of swans	P22
	1	Japanese: Ai, Suki, Koi Fishes	P2
Body part symbol (11)	11	Heart	P4, P5, P6, P7, P8, P10, P13, P18, P19, P20, P21
Colour (4)	4	The colour red	P5, P8, P16, P22
Food (3)	3	Chocolates	P6, P15, P21
Creative acts (2)	2	Creative acts: music, love songs, texts	P9, P11
Religious symbols (2)	2	Religious symbols: the cross, bells, Eucharisty	P9, P11

Total number of statements within the theme based on categories

be presented in this chapter to provide the reader with a representative sample of the love concept pursued by the participants in this study (Fig. 47.3).

Table 47.8 provides an overview of the categories of love stories narrated and the titles of those stories. Stories highlighted with an asterisk * are presented and analysed in the next section of this chapter.

The following excerpts of the stories presented could indicate the complexity of love stories and their anchoring in the individual as well as in the cultural and spiritual context of the narrator. It could be assumed that the narrators chose love stories to narrate which were considered "suitable" to be shared with the researcher. If so, the story-tellers may have chosen their stories based on a subjective bias.

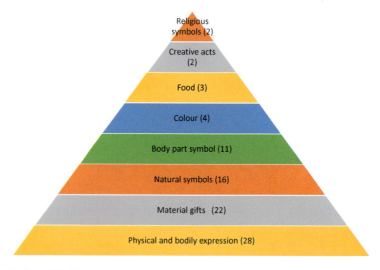

Fig. 47.2 Pyramid of love symbols (Author's own construction)

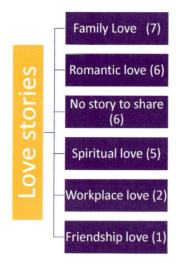

Fig. 47.3 Love story categories (Author's own construction)

47.6.6.1 Love and Family Relationships

A female participant who was 33 years old, Southern American and single (P18), told a story of love in her family about her grandmother and her grandfather:

47 Meaning-making Through Love Stories in Cultural Perspectives: Expressions,...

Table 47.8 Love stories in detail (Author's own construction)

Frequency	Category	Love story	Participants
7	Family love	Loving my niece	P1
		Family love over generations	P3
		Adopting a child	P7
		Grandma's positive attitude*	P16
		Praise of a husband	P17
		Fifty-three years of marriage*	P18
		The tale of the seven brothers	P21
6	Romantic love	Love at two ends of the world	P5
		Story of unhappy couples	P7
		Unexpected love*	P7
		First touch	P7
		Love and the newspaper	P9
		Loss of a big love	P20
6	No story to share		P4, P10, P13, P14, P15, P22
5	Spiritual love	Spiritual love	P7
		The soul in the eyes*	P7
		Erotic love act in bible	P11
		The returning son*	P12
		Prodigal son's story	P19
2	Workplace love	Love expression in team	P1
		Death of a co-worker*	P8
1	Friendship	Be selective with friendship	P2

The "Story of unhappy couples" is described in full in Chap. 34
*Indicate the stories which are going to be described below

> My grandparents were married fifty-three years. My grandmother claims she married my grandfather because he was the smartest man she'd ever met and she wanted smart children. They fought every day (one was a Democrat and one a Republican) but loved each other, never went to bed angry, and when he got sick with dementia, she cared for him as long as she could. When he had to be moved to a home she visited every day for eight months. His last words were telling her he loved her and the day he died he still recognised her. . . . She always says that sex is great, but you really have to like the person you're with.

This love concept relates closely to family bonds which are acknowledged across the family generations. It shows the fascination of the narrator with the long-term relationship of her grandparents for over half a century. The story encompasses the start of the grandparents' relationship, including the idea that the grandmother's choice of husband was based on him being perceived as "smart" and her wish to also have clever children. The narrator describes the dynamics within the love relationship, a "love and fight" dynamic, due to differences in political ideas (Democrat and Republican). She describes further that although they differed in their political views, they always managed to transform negatively perceived emotions such as anger, which led to transforming their (emotional) differences in perspective into synergies. The story refers to the care of the one for the other in times of crises (dementia), the direct verbalising of the love ("I love you"), even on the day of the grandfather's death. The story also describes how the grandfather recognised his wife until his dying day, meaning that their love overcame even the symptoms of the disease of dementia. The importance of sex is finally mentioned, but weighted by the idea that "liking" the other on a deep level is the core of love, not sex.

This story of the couple is told by the granddaughter, described as though this relationship is viewed as an ideal love relationship which could be witnessed within the family of origin. It is therefore also a story of love within the family and between the grandparents and the granddaughter, since it shows the bond of love and appreciation of the granddaughter for her grandparents.

The story further seems to offer advice concerning what should be valued in love relationships, and is associated with aspects of love, such as a long-term relationship which includes a future direction (children), the dynamics of dealing with differences in thought, and the ability to transform negative emotions, care for each other, the verbalisation of their love, great sex, recognition of the other person, and finally the overcoming of a disease's symptoms.

47.6.6.2 Love and Romantic Relationships

A female German participant aged 43 (P7) narrates a story of *romantic love*:

> I once, by a very strange coincidence, ended up in a place I actually did never plan to go to. When I had to leave the place, I started crying. I cried throughout the way home, which was about ten thousand kilometres away. I did not even have a proper explanation for this strong sadness and it was only a few days later that I realised that I had fallen in love with the place I had left behind. And it took me another few weeks to become aware that it was not only the place I was missing and dreaming of, but that it was the person who owned it. I realised how happy I was when I saw him and how I longed to be with him.

The romantic love is not consciously realised in the beginning of this love story. It rather shows the process of the individual realisation of the narrator's love for another person. This love for the other is described in a stepwise process through

1. unconscious sadness about the loss,
2. ascription of the sadness to the place left behind (object relation),
3. realisation of the sadness being connected to the loss of the person met in the left place (subject relation), and
4. becoming aware of the happiness and longing for the person left behind through the remembering of the happiness and closeness experienced in the presence of the other.

The realisation of the romantic love for the other is described over a period of several weeks and is presented as an individual intra-personal process of becoming aware of the love. The narrator seems in the beginning to be in unconscious denial of the love for the other person and only describes the highly unconscious reaction to the loss of the place visited. It takes her days to realise the reason for her sadness about the loss of being in the space and even later about the loss of being with the person in the space. Further, this romantic love story only provides the narrator's perspective of realising the love through the unconscious experience of strong emotional pain and sadness. The love for the other is then identified through the memory of happiness and joy in the presence of the other.

This story narrates the intra-psychological process of growing awareness of love for another person, but does not provide the reader with any information about interpersonal love. The story gives the reader with an idea of the narrator not being prepared to realise and accept the love for quite some time.

Connected to the story of realising the love for the other, are two further implicit themes: the idea of "ending up in the place unintentionally" and the story of travelling between "home and exile". The experience and finding of this romantic love is tacitly related to the idea that the narrator "by fate" or "by coincidence" met this love, providing the love with an embedded quality of "the love that was meant to be". There is also a sense that the loved object was meant to be found, this possibly being the implicitly ascribed reason for the narrator "ending up in this place". This romantic love is therefore placed within a larger dimension of romance where two people seem to be destined for each other, and the love becomes part of the romanticising concept of "finding each other".

Further, the story is embedded in a personal journey of leaving home, being in exile, finding a new "inner home" and returning "home" which has now become "exile". This story of romantic love plays with concepts of belonging, placement and displacement of home/place and the idea of finding a "new home", while having left home. By having found this "new home", the concept of "home" has changed and becomes a place of sadness, since the new home becomes the place of the beloved person, the place where happiness is experienced.

47.6.6.3 Love and Spiritual Relationships

In terms of *spiritual love*, P7 tells a very short story of love which relates to the idea that love is momentous, and that it can occur and be felt in a very short space of time:

> Once, I looked deep into someone's eyes and I could see the soul. That is love. That was a story of love.

This love concept is based on the idea that love is a feeling that can occur between two individuals and that can occur in an instant space of time. Love is described as the "seeing of the soul" in another person when the looks meet. The eyes of the other become the gateway to the soul of the other, and thereby to eternity. The love concept beholds the deep connection that can occur between humans and which goes beyond the outer appearance, referring instead to another kind of spiritual dimension which connects one person to the spiritual world and to the core of the other person, the soul, which in many cultures and religions is viewed as being eternal. Love thereby becomes a concept that opens the door to eternity and a life beyond the contemporary moment.

P12 is a 30-year old Black (Motswana) male from South Africa, who retells a spiritual story of love from the Bible:

> Once upon time, there was a rich man with two sons. The other son decides to have his inheritance while the father was still alive and in their small village it was curse and disrespectful for one to do that but his father didn't refuse, although the other son was not pleased with such. After years and years the father heard that the son is suffering at the near nearby village, but the other son who was home with the father wasn't happy about the fact that his father is planning to take back his son home. And the father end up bring the son home with a good loving welcome despite what he did to the family.

The concept of love in this Christian biblical story is based on the idea that love can overcome disrespectful behaviour between parents and children. The father, as a parental figure, is giving what the child demands, although it is not in the father's own interest or value set. When he hears of the suffering of his child, the father behaves compassionately and allows the disrespectful son to return to his home. Love is shown through forgiving, respectful treatment, compassion and reconciliation, as well as in a welcoming attitude. It is also anchored in a strong fatherly figure who does not adhere to the voice of his other son, but does what he feels is right, to forgive the disrespectful son and treat him respectfully and equally with love. The loving attitude becomes an expression of compassionate love with goes beyond the judgement of the behaviour of the other.

47.6.6.4 Love in the Workplace

P8, a male 45-year-old German–Iranian, president of a professional association, tells this story of love in the workplace:

> After the sudden and surprising death of a very young employee (thirty-five years old), one of his close co-workers was very upset. A colleague called me and asked for permission to go for a walk and support him emotionally. Of course, I consented to her request and was very touched by the consideration everyone had for [one] another: a co-worker being so upset and a colleague taking care of him. It made me proud to work in the organisation.

The love which is described in this story contains the idea of compassion, of caring for and supporting each other in the work context in response to a crisis, the death of a colleague. The storyteller shows his own appreciation of the strength of care and compassion inside the work culture of the organisation. He seems to be surprised at this experience of love within the work context which might, in his view, be seen as a place of task orientation rather than a place of compassion.

47.7 Discussion

The concepts of love which arise in the different categories of love stories told here are multifold and relate to the socio-cultural context of embeddedness, as well as to the individual's subjective experiences of love, to the gender of the narrator and the historical placement of the individual (Barsade & O'Neill, 2014; Beall & Sternberg,

1995; Beichen & Murshed, 2015; Carter, 2012, 2013; Dewaele, 2012, 2013; Jahoda & Lewis, 2015; Jankowiak, 2008; Javaid, 2018; Langford, 1999; Pavlenko, 2014; Sternberg, 1998; Swidler, 2001). The stories provide an idea of the construction of love under the influence of cultural belonging and embeddedness as described above.

The love concepts are influenced by language and culture (Dewaele, 2017) and represent the frailty of human bonds, insecurities and conflicting desires (e.g., being unconscious, becoming conscious of love) which are "tightened to these loose bonds", as described by Baumann (2003). Love concepts provide insight into the meaning of life defined by the narrator (e.g., living to do good, as the father to the lost son) and the culture embedding the constructs (Shumway, 2003; Twamley, 2014).

As indicated by Beall and Sternberg (1995), love needs contextualisation to be comprehended. The contexts for the stories of love narrated in this study refer to (a) the beloved person (family members, strangers who become lovers), (b) the feelings which accompany love (joy, happiness, sadness, jealousy), (c) the questions and thoughts that accompany love (e.g., how do I behave, where do I belong, what do I see?) and (d) the actions or the relations which a person has with the beloved (e.g., transforming negative emotions, welcoming someone home). Consequently, the triangle of love (Sternberg, 1998) has been expanded through this study, in which participants not only refer to interpersonal human concepts of love, but also to its transhuman and individual dimensions.

The often-described concepts of romantic love (Tomlinson & Aron, 2013; Illouz, 1997), compassionate love (Barsade & O'Neill, 2014; Evans, 2003) and parental love (Li & Meier, 2017) are also core concepts of love narrated in this study. Expressions, feelings accompanying love, symbols and rituals—which depend on the construction of culture, and individual and socio-cultural worlds—are all part of the meaning-making processes of the individual participants and contribute to the development of coherent identities of the narrator (see Mayer & Flotman, 2017), to create a sense of life and the world individuals live in (Wood, 2001). As shown in prior studies by Erol-Isik (2015) and Sternberg (1998), these stories show the dynamics of love, aspects of social life and the environment in which the narrators are embedded.

The study contributes to new insights by supporting the previous literature cited.

47.8 Conclusions and Recommendations

The aim of this research was to gain deeper insight into love concepts and stories of individuals from different cultural, gender and religious backgrounds. The conclusions drawn from this study are now presented.

Love, as described and experienced by the participants, has human, transhuman and individual aspects. Concepts of human love can have interpersonal qualities such as trust, intimacy, mental and physical attraction, caring and responsibility, meaning and interpersonal belonging, attachment, compassion, respect, manipulation and power. Love's transhuman concepts are associated with deep connection, unconditional love, eternal commitment and a miracle. Finally, individual love concepts have self-related aspects such as self-sacrifice, personal freedom and growth. These findings thereby exceed Sternberg's (1998) triangle of love and provide dimensions which go beyond love's interpersonal aspects.

The feeling of love has mainly positively connotations such as joy, happiness, feeling energised, warm, passionate, complete, strong, accepted and special, secure, fascinated, peaceful and calm, blessed, proud, attracted, desired, devoted, belonging, committed, and eternal. Negatively connoted feelings relating to love are fear and anxiety, pain and the fear of being inadequate. Negative feelings are narrated in the context of the fear of loss of love, of being left, feeling the pain of the loss, or having to accept the fear of being inadequate. Based on these feelings described, it is suggested that feelings experienced when in love (or with the awareness of loving) could generally have the potential to contribute to an experience of individual growth, positive self-esteem and self-worth, as well as strength, enrichment and increase in energy and passion. The positively associated feelings seem to significantly outrange the negatively perceived feelings.

The findings support the findings reported in the literature, particularly with regard to people of Western cultures (here German, US and English-speaking participants) expressing love through words and talking, as well as Asian participants (here Japanese) expressing love through actions, and one Black African participant expressing love through materials and showing emotions and affect.

Across members of all cultural groups, physical and bodily expression is the mostly frequently mentioned symbol of love, ranging from very close physical contact to more distanced and less intimate contact. Interestingly, material gifts are particularly important as symbols of love, followed by natural symbols and the heart as one of the most important organs of the body. The colour "red" is associated with love; however, this was only mentioned by three Germans and one US participant. Food in terms of sweets (chocolates) is mentioned by members of different cultures, while creative and religious acts are only mentioned by two German Catholic men beyond the age of 60 as symbols of love.

The rituals of love, as described, vary—from caring, gift-giving, inviting, offering compliments, going through marriage rituals and organising birthday celebrations—to stating love via social media, blind-dating, cleaning, cooking, and providing a bride price.

Finally, with regard to the love stories told, seven of these refer to love with regard to family relationships, while six deal with romantic love. Five stories relate to spiritual aspects of love, two stories are about love experienced in work contexts and one story is about love in friendship. Love is told in many different ways, contributing to the creation of a coherent socio-cultural world and meaning-making of the narrator. The majority of the stories relate to family bonds with the family of origin and with romantic love aspects.

It is recommended that future research focuses in depth on the intra-psychological experience of different forms of love and analysis the interplay of human, transhuman and individual concepts of love within family, romantic, spiritual, workplace and friendship love experiences. Further, culture-specific and transcultural concepts might be taken into account by conducting mixed-method studies within same-culture love relationships and transculture love relationships, to take the influence of individual personality, culture and transculture into consideration and explore it in more depth.

Acknowledgements I would like to express my sincere thanks to Ruth Coetzee for the language and technical proof reading of this chapter. Thanks to the interviewees for the wonderful stories of love.

References

Aleksic, G., & Maagali, M. (2018). *Love in intercultural relationships: Affection, commitment, romantic beliefs and conflicts*. Charlotte, NC: Information Age Publisher.
Andrews, M., Day Slater, S., Squire, C., & Treacher, A. (2009). *The uses of narrative: Explorations in sociology, psychology, and cultural studies*. New Jersey: Transaction Publication.
Babbie, E. (2011). *The basics of social research*. Belmont, CA: Wadsworth Publishing.
Barsade, S. G., & O'Neill, O. A. (2014). What's love got to do with it? A longitudinal study of the culture of companionate love and employee and client outcomes in a long-term care setting. *Administrative Science Quarterly, 59*, 1–48. https://doi.org/10.1177/0001839214538636
Bauman, Z. (2003). *Liquid love: On the frailty of human bonds*. New York: Wiley.
Beall, A. E., & Sternberg, R. J. (1995). The social construction of love. *Journal of Social and Personal Relationships, 12*(3), 417–438.
Beichen, L., & Murshed, F. (2015). Culture, expressions of romantic love, and gift-giving. *Journal of International Business Research, 14*(1), 75–91.
Bennett, M. (2017). Online debate on the definition of culture. *Personal email communication*. April 30, 2017.
Berscheid, E. (2006). Searching for the meaning of "love". In R. J. Sternberg & K. Weis (Eds.), *The new psychology of love* (pp. 171–183). New Haven: Yale University Press.
Bhana, D. (2017). *Love, sex and teenage sexual cultures in South Africa*. London: Routledge.
Bostrom, N. (2005). *Transhumanist values. Ethical issues for the twenty-first century* (pp. 3–4). http://citeseerx.ist.psu.edu/viewdoc/download?doi=10.1.1.635.6455&rep=rep1&type=pdf
Campbell-Barr, V., Georgeson, J., & Varga, A. N. (2015). Developing professional early childhood education in England and Hungary: Where has all the love gone? *European Education, 47*, 311–330.
Cancian, F. M. (1990). *Love in America: Gender and self-development*. Cambridge: Cambridge University Press.
Carter, J. (2012). What is commitment? Women's accounts of intimate attachment. *Families, Relationships and Societies, 1*(2), 137–153.
Carter, J. (2013). The curious absence of love stories in women's talk. *The Sociological Review, 61* (4), 728–744.
Creswell, J. W. (2013). *Qualitative inquiry and research design: Choosing among five approaches* (4th ed.). Thousand Oaks, CA: Sage.
Denzin, N. K., & Lincoln, Y. S. (2011). *Handbook of qualitative research* (2nd ed.). Thousand Oaks, CA: Sage.
Dewaele, J.-M. (2008). The emotional weight of I love you in multilinguals' languages. *Journal of Pragmatics, 40*(10), 1753–1780.

Dewaele, J.-M. (2012). L'acquisitionetl'usage descripts dans les différentes langues de multilingues adultes. In N. Auger, C. Béal, & F. Demougin (Eds.), *Interactions et interculturalité: variété des corpus et des approches* (pp. 195–122). Berlin: Peter Lang.

Dewaele, J.-M. (2013). *Emotions in multiple languages* (2nd ed.). Basingstoke: Palgrave Macmillan.

Dewaele, J.-M. (2017). Loving a partner in a foreign language. *Journal of Pragmatics, 108*, 116–130.

Erol-Isik, N. (2015). The role of narrative methods in sociology: Stories as a powerful tool to understand individual and society. *Journal of Sociological Research, 18*(1), 103–125.

Evans, M. (2003). *Love: An unromantic discussion*. Cambridge: Polity Press.

Gratzke, M. (2017). Love is what people say it is: Performativity and narrativity in critical love stories. *Journal of Popular Romance Studies, 6*. http://jprstudies.org/wp-content/uploads/2017/04/LIWPSII.4.2017.pdf

Hardy, B. (1968). Towards a poetics of fiction: An approach through narrative. *Novel: A Forum on Fiction, 2*(1), 5–14.

Holloway, S. (2018). *The game of love in Georgian England: Courtship, emotions, and material culture*. Oxford: Oxford University Press.

Illouz, E. (1997). *Consuming the romantic utopia: Love and the cultural contradictions of capitalism*. California: University of California Press.

Illouz, E. (2011). *Warum Liebe weh tut*. Berlin: Suhrkamp.

Illouz, E. (2019). *Warum endet die Liebe?* Sternstunde Philosophie SRF Kultur. March 29, 2019. https://www.youtube.com/watch?v=3HT3c0rawI0

Jahoda, G., & Lewis, I. M. (2015). *Acquiring culture: Cross cultural studies in child development* (3rd ed.). New York: Psychology Press.

Jankowiak, W. R. (2008). *Intimacies. Love and sex across cultures*. New York: Columbia University Press.

Javaid, A. (2018). *Masculinities, sexualities and love*. London: Routledge.

Jokikokko, K., & Karikoski, H. (2016). Exploring the narrative of a Finnish early childhood education teacher on her professional intercultural learning. *Journal of Early Childhood Education Research, 5*(1), 92–114.

Langford, W. (1999). *Revolutions of the heart: Gender, power and the delusions of love*. London: Routledge.

Leskela-Kärki, M. (2008). Narrating life stories in between the fictional and the autobiographical. *Qualitative Research, 8*(3), 325–332.

Li, X., & Meier, J. (2017). Father love and mother love: Contributions of parental acceptance to children's psychological adjustment. *Journal of Family Theory & Review, 9*(4), 459–490.

Lomas, T. (2018). The flavours of love: A cross-cultural lexical analysis. *Journal for the Theory of Social Behaviour, 48*(1), 134–152. https://doi.org/10.1111/jtsb.12158

Manoj, V. R. (2008). Spiritual transcendence in transhumanism. *Journal of Evolution & Technology, 17*(1), 1–10.

Mayer, C.-H. (2005). *Artificial walls. South African narratives on conflict, difference and identity. An explorative study in post-apartheid South Africa*. Stuttgart: Ibidem.

Mayer, C.-H., & Flotman, A.-P. (2017). The organisational and psychological impact of organisational diagnosis. In N. Martins, E. C. Martin, & R. Viljoen (Eds.), *Organisational diagnosis. Tools and applications for practitioners and researchers* (pp. 257–272). Randburg, SA: KR Publishing.

McAdams, D. P., Anyidoho, N. A., Brown, C., Huang, Y. T., Kaplan, B., & Machado, M. A. (2004). Traits and stories: Links between dispositional and narrative features of personality. *Journal of Personality, 72*(4), 761–784.

Mokuku, T. (2017). The connotation of both philosophy and its potential contribution towards environmental conservation: The case of Tlokoeng community in Lesotho. *Environmental Education Research, 23*(9), 1230–1248.

Naderifar, M., Goli, H., & Ghaljaie, F. (2017). Snowball sampling: A purposeful method of sampling in qualitative research. *Strides in Development of Medical Education, 14*(3), e67670.

Osei-Tutu, A., Dzokoto, V. A., Hanke, K., Adams, G., & Belgrave, F. Z. (2018). Conceptions of love in Ghana: An exploration amongst Chanaian Christians. *Journal of Psychology in Africa, 28*(2), 83–88.

Pavlenko, A. (2014). *The bilingual mind: And what it tells us about language and thought.* New York: Cambridge University Press.

Piller, I. (2002). *Bilingual couples talk: The discursive construction of hybridity.* Amsterdam: John Benjamins.

Regan, P. C. (2016). *The mating game. A primer on love, sex and marriage* (3rd ed.). London: Sage.

Ricoeur, P. (1979). Der Text als Modell: hermeneutisches Verstehen. In W. L. Bruehl (Ed.), *Verstehende Soziologie. Grundzuege und Entwicklungstendenzen.* München: Nymphenburger.

Roth, W.-M., & Unger, H. V. (2018). Current perspectives on research ethics in qualitative research. Forum qualitative Sozialforschung. *Forum: Qualitative Social Research, 19*(3), 1–12. https://doi.org/10.17169/fqs-19.3.3155

Sawyer, R. D., & Norris, J. (2009). Duoethnography: Articulations/(re)creation of meaning in the making. In W. Gershon (Ed.), *Working together in qualitative research: A turn towards the collaborative* (pp. 127–140). Rotterdam: Sense Publishers.

Sawyer, R. D., & Norris, J. (2013). *Understanding qualitative research: Duoethnography.* New York, NY: Oxford University Press.

Schnell, T., & Keenan, W. J. F. (2011). Meaning-making in an atheist world. *Archive for the Psychology of Religion, 33,* 55–78.

Shumway, D. (2003). *Modern love: Romance, intimacy, and the marriage crisis.* New York: New York University Press.

Sternberg, R. J. (1996). Love stories. *Personal relationship, 3*(1), 59–79.

Sternberg, R. J. (1998). *Cupid's arrow: The course of love through time.* Cambridge: Cambridge University Press.

Sugiyama, S. (2015). Kawaii meiru and Maroyaka neko: Mobile for relationship maintenance and aesthetic expressions among Japanese teens. *First Monday, 20*(10). https://journals.uic.edu/ojs/index.php/fm/article/view/5826/4997

Sun, W., & Yang, L. (2019). *Love stories in China. The politics of intimacy in the twenty-first century.* London: Routledge.

Swidler, A. (2001). *Talk of love. How culture matters.* Chicago: The University of Chicago Press.

Tamboukou, M. (2013). Love, narratives, politics: Encounters between Hannah Arendt and Rosa Luxemburg. *Theory, Culture & Society, 30*(1), 35–56.

Terre Blanche, M. T., Durrheim, K., & Painter, D. (Eds.). (2006). *Research in practice. Applied methods for the social sciences.* Cape Town: University of Cape Town Press.

Ting-Toomey, S. (1991). Intimacy expressions in three cultures: France, Japan, and the United States. *International Journal of Intercultural Relations, 15*(1), 29–46.

Ting-Toomey, S., & Dorjee, T. (2018). *Communicating across cultures* (2nd ed.). New York: Guilford Press.

Tomlinson, J. M., & Aron, A. (2013). The path to closeness: a mediational model for overcoming the risks of increasing closeness. *Journal of Social and Personal Relationships, 30,* 805–812. https://doi.org/10.1177/0265407512469137

Twamley, K. (2014). *Love and marriage amongst middle class Guajaratis in India and the UK: A suitable match.* London: Palgrave Macmillan.

Van der Riet, M. (2017). Developmental work research: A theory-informed method for collective analysis and transformation. *Mind, Culture and Activity, 24*(1), 85–88.

Wood, J. T. (2001). The normalization of violence in heterosexual romantic relationships: women's narratives of love and violence. *Journal of Social and Personal Relationships, 18*(2), 239–261.

Ye, V. Z. (2004). La Double Vie de Veronica: Reflections on my life as a Chinese migrant in Australia. *Life Writing, 1,* 133–146.

Yin, R. K. (2009). *Case study research: Design and methods.* London: Sage.

Claude-Hélène Mayer is a Full Professor in Industrial and Organisational Psychology at the Department of Industrial Psychology and People Management at the University of Johannesburg, an Adjunct Professor at the European University Viadrina in Frankfurt (Oder), Germany and a Senior Research Associate at Rhodes University, Grahamstown, South Africa. She holds a Ph.D. in Psychology (University of Pretoria, South Africa), a Ph.D. in Management (Rhodes University, South Africa), a Doctorate (Georg-August University, Germany) in Political Sciences (socio-cultural anthropology and intercultural didactics) and Master degrees in Ethnology, Intercultural Didactics and Socio-economics (Georg-August University, Germany) as well as in Crime Science, Investigation and Intelligence (University of Portsmouth, UK). Her Venia Legendi is in Psychology with focus on work, organizational, and cultural psychology (Europa Universität Viadrina, Germany). She has published numerous monographs, text collections, accredited journal articles, and special issues on transcultural mental health and well-being, salutogenesis, transforming shame, transcultural conflict management and mediation, women in leadership in culturally diverse work contexts, coaching, culture and crime and psychobiography.

Chapter 48
Forbidden Love: Controlling Partnerships Across Ethnoracial Boundaries

Dan Rodríguez-García

Abstract The freedom to love is something most of us take for granted. The reality is that partnerships across racial, cultural or religious lines have historically been problematized around the world. Laws prohibiting mixed unions were present in countless nations until very recently. This preoccupation with intermarriage is why it has been a leitmotiv in literature over the centuries and later on in cinema, from Shakespeare's *Othello* and *Romeo and Juliet*, to Stanley Kramer's *Guess Who's Coming to Dinner*. This chapter will provide a historical and anthropological analysis of state control over partnership formation, offering a number of cases around the world where nations have implemented anti-mixing laws. In these contexts, miscegenation (the mixing of people through marriage who were considered to be of different racial groups) was abhorred and treated as a deviance, as devoid of love, and, above all, as a threat to national integrity and the status quo. This exploration can help us to better understand the social, cultural, and political contexts in which restrictive views of coupling, family, and love have emerged, and to critically reflect on continued prejudices towards mixed unions that still exist in current times.

Keywords Love · Hybridity · Miscegenation · Intermarriage · Discrimination · Social exclusion

48.1 Introduction

Contemporary globalization processes (Friedman, 1995), in parallel with the increase of international mobility (Castles, de Haas, & Miller, 2014), the internationalization of intimacy (Beck & Beck-Gernsheim, 2013), and mounting superdiversity (Vertovec, 2007), have expanded the possibilities for individuals to

---

D. Rodríguez-García (✉)
Department of Social and Cultural Anthropology, Autonomous University of Barcelona, Bellaterra, Spain
e-mail: dan.rodriguez@uab.es

meet and partner across national, ethnocultural, racial, religious, and class borders (Alba, Beck, & Basaran Sahin, 2018; Hull, Meier, & Ortyl, 2010; Rodríguez-García, 2015, Spickard, 1989). Sociocultural hybridization (García Canclini, 1995)[1] is a characteristic of contemporary times.

This increasing tendency, however, has not always been the case. In the not very remote past, the reality was quite the opposite, as miscegenation (the mixing of people through marriage who were considered to be of different racial groups) was abhorred by most nations; it was treated as a deviance and as devoid of love (Moran, 2001).

This phenomenon is relevant because intermarriage is one of the most important tests for determining societal structure and for exposing social boundaries (Davis, 1941; Merton, 1941; Rodríguez-García, 2015). Indeed, the crossing of racial, ethnocultural, religious, or class boundaries through partnering tells us not only about individual choices but also reveals the scope of social divisions and the relationships between groups within a society. For this same reason, the subject of love across boundaries has been a leitmotiv in literature over the centuries and later in cinema: Shakespeare's *Othello* and *Romeo and Juliet*, Jane Austen's *Pride and Prejudice*, D.W. Griffith's *Broken Blossoms*, Robert Wise and Jerome Robbins's *West Side Story*, Stanley Kramer's *Guess Who's Coming to Dinner*, Mira Nair's *Mississippi Masala*, Ken Loach's *Ae Fond Kiss*, and Gurinder Chadha's *Bride and Prejudice*, to name a few examples. All these cultural artefacts remind us that endogamous unions (i.e., partnerships within the same group, whether in terms of race, ethnicity, nationality, religion, or social class) have historically been the ones promoted socially and institutionally, whereas mixed (or exogamous) unions have traditionally been unconventional and even forbidden partnerships.

History has provided too many examples of nations that, guided by an ideology of "mixophobia" (i.e., fear of mixing), have enacted anti-miscegenation laws: from colonial America to Nazi Germany. This chapter will present a historical-anthropological study of six paradigmatic cases in order to better understand and critically reflect on social, political, and economic contexts in which reductionist views on hybridity emerged and were used to legitimize exclusion.

48.2 Methodology

In accordance with the subject of enquiry, this study follows a qualitative anthropological-historical and comparative critical analysis approach, based on content analysis, and fundamentally descriptive and interpretative.

---

[1] It must be acknowledged that categorizations of hybridity, including the term "intermarriage" itself, are contested, context-dependent notions (see, for instance, Brah & Coombes, 2000; Olumide, 2002; Rodríguez-García, 2012, 2015; Spickard, 1989).

Documentary sources of various types have been used: general treaties, historical archives, monographs, national and international specialized magazines, press, historical statistics and visual documents.

Six cases (analysis units) have been chosen for this analysis, all concerning nations that in the past have implemented anti-mixing regulations, namely: Spain and Colonial America, the United States in the nineteenth and twentieth centuries, England in the colonial and post-colonial era, Australia in the English colonial era, Nazi Germany, and South Africa during the Apartheid era. These specific space/time contexts have been selected considering two variables: historical (paradigmatic) relevance, and degree of common knowledge and connections with other contexts. For instance, the case of anti-miscegenation regulations in South Africa during the Apartheid is an interesting and not very well-known case, with remarkable connections with the case of Germany during the Nazi period.

I have tried to generate highly contextualized information for each case, providing as much analytical depth as possible within the space constraints for the chapter. More space is dedicated to some cases than to others, depending on their relevance in the global context.

48.3 Case Studies

48.3.1 Spain and Colonial America

From the very beginning of Spain's conquest of America, this colonial society was characterized by the intermingling of different ethnic groups that coexisted in the territory. However, this miscegenation did not give rise to a socially egalitarian system, but rather to a colonial society with a hierarchical structure inspired by aristocratic criteria with feudal roots from the European metropole. A caste system was created, at the top of which was the white population, either of Spanish-peninsula origin (called *gachupines* and *chapetones*) or American-born *(criollos)*, these two groups being in constant conflict of interest. Below these two groups were the Indians, Blacks, Chinese, Jews, and finally, the *mestizos* (Pitt-Rivers, 1992). But it was not until the end of the sixteenth century that mixing with Native Americans had severe social repercussions, nor were there any special measures taken to limit these unions. Miscegenation between American natives and Spaniards was common, and the mestizos, and especially the native population, played a crucial role in the conquest (Lipschutz, 1975).

In the seventeenth and eighteenth centuries, as the share of both sexes in the white population group (*criollos* and of Spanish-peninsula origin) evened out (given that at the beginning of colonization, there were very few white women), interracial marriages became less and less frequent among the upper class. During the same period, as the Black African slave population started to arrive at the Spanish-conquered territories, the idea was put forward that the "stain of slavery" was transmitted by blood. It was thus over this period, in which miscegenation grew steadily, when a mixophobic or anti-hybridization ideology was fueled, which would further develop and become increasingly strict. As a consequence, in an effort to draw lines of separation between the classes in terms of moral and theological principles, categories were created in the form of fixed social classes or *castes*. The possibilities of crossing these lines were infinite, and administrative adjustments to this reality turned rhetorical as well as absurd.[2] As Jorge Juan y Antonio de Ulloa himself pointed out in his 1748 report *Relación histórica*: "the castes (...) that emerge from unions of some people with other people (...) are creating so many species, and so abundantly, that they do not even know how to differentiate them."

As explained by Caillavet and Minchom (1992), in the first years of colonization, among the new phenomena of the period, the usage of the term *mestizo* appeared. Originally, the term *mestizo* was used back in the metropole to refer to the "mixture of two different animal breeds", but from the sixteenth century onwards, it was also applied to those born from the union of Spanish immigrants and Native American women. This particular type of parentage (white father and Indian mother) outlined the "ideal mestizo". However, in this context of disproportionate race mixing and of a desire to preserve the social, political, and economic order and the *status quo,* this term would soon begin to lose its meaning, as the exact match between the order's *representation* (symbolic structure) and *reality* became increasingly superfluous.

Significantly, in 1776, under the "liberalizing reforms of the Bourbon era", the Spanish king Charles III issued a *Pragmatic Sanction to prevent the overuse of unequal marriages* which was imposed in the Spanish kingdoms and dominions. In 1778, this royal pragmatic sanction on marriage was extended to Spain's overseas possessions. Initially, it aimed at preventing marriages considered as "unequal" in the metropole. Men under the age of 25 and women under the age of 23, and every person who did not live under parental guardianship had to obtain parental consent to get married. This royal edict that excluded black people, mulattos, and other castes (people of mixed blood) was based on the assumption that, since so many of them were illegitimate children, it would be impossible for them to obtain parental consent. In this sense, the ideal theoretical framework that served as a model for the American colonial society was actually a transposition of rigid ideas from the Spanish metropole, where the obsessive concern with the purity of blood and an underlying belief in racial separation did not allow for miscegenation to take place. It was a post-feudal society composed of aristocrats (noblemen) and plebeians, in which only "old Christians", i.e., those who could prove Christian ancestry, were socially accepted. The individual's honor or reputation, which was the pillar on which the recognition of social status rested, depended upon that Christian condition. Nobility was attained by both being a gentleman (having a noble title) and being of a "pure race" (having Christian ancestry), and this criterion was applied to the entire population (Caillavet and Minchom, 1992: 118; Méchoulan, 1981). From the second half of the sixteenth century onwards, purity of blood, a Catholic doctrine

---

[2]For a painting displaying the castes in colonial America in the 18th century, see https://es.m.wikipedia.org/wiki/Archivo:Casta_painting_all.jpg

that distinguished Christians from non-Christians (Muslims and Jews) and that went back as far as the thirteenth century, turned into an obsession towards racial classification. This categorization was defined in biological and moral terms, insofar as traits transmitted by blood from generation to generation were spoken of; and it was even thought that impurity (scab, mange, defects) was transmitted through close proximity. Furthermore, there was an obsession with securing endogamous forms of marriage and the legitimacy of births, which conferred social distinction, as well as with avoiding the opposite: hybridity, which "stained" the individual and its offspring forever. Moreover, apart from it all being regulated by law, this ideology was also firmly rooted in society. Parents expressed their disapproval in terms of the family's integrity and "purity of blood" (lineage), and self-proclaimed themselves as pure of blood and honest citizens that served the community, etc., as opposed to Blacks, Mulattos, Jews, Moors, or newly converted Christians. And regarding illegitimate descendants, their ambiguous ancestry made them untrustworthy.

It should be added that not only marriage but also fornication, concubinage, and false promises of marriage—all transgressions from the Church's perspective of spiritual purity—were considered as acts of adultery. These sorts of situations happened frequently among married men and unmarried women, who often came from a different social class or "racial" group, especially among slave women and plantation owners (see Lavrin, 1992: 219–223).

Hence, the spectre of potential race mixing led to the *Statutes of blood purity (Estatutos de limpieza de sangre)*, whose purpose was to prevent the intermingling of those "pure of blood" with converts and their descendants. Public (honorable) positions could only be held by the first, and blood purity was based on an old belief of fidelity to the Catholic faith.

In sum, in colonial America, marriage legislation, which was enacted to put a limit to miscegenation, evolved into a tool to protect the sociopolitical and economic power interests since it enabled lines of social differentiation to be drawn and, in short, maintained the *status quo*. The Spanish implementation of the Blood Purity Laws in the fifteenth century, served to ensure that only people of Christian ancestry (interpreted as 'racially pure') were able to advance socially and maintain positions of power over converts of Muslim or Jewish descent in Spain or over First Nations/indigenous and African peoples within the context of the colonies. Anti-miscegenation laws in the colonial Americas helped maintain a hierarchical caste system, with 'Old Christians' (considered racially pure whites, and not suspected of secretly practising another religion) at the top. In this way, race, religion, and class were entirely intertwined in Spain and its colonies, and in this context ethnoracial mixing was a synonym for moral/social degradation. Racial purity standards were only completely abolished in 1870. Importantly, Spanish identity has also been created in opposition to the (Moroccan) Muslim world. The Arab Muslim population in Spain, who are chiefly from Morocco (the largest foreign-born population group in the country), have historically been stigmatized as perpetual foreigners (Cebolla & Requena, 2009; Zapata-Barrero, 2006). Islamophobia and Moorphobia in Spain have historical roots dating back to the *Reconquista*, the centuries-long violent conflict in the Iberian Peninsula between Christians and Muslims ('the Moors,' from the Maghreb) that predated the era of the Spanish Empire and related colonization. Later, during the Franco dictatorship (1939–1975), the ruling regime's preoccupation was to morally regenerate what was referred to as 'the Spanish race' through a project of national Catholicism and a revival of 'authentic' Spanish tradition; the notion of 'Spanishness' promulgated was not defined by racial categories per se, but it was highly insular, defined by Catholicism, and deeply antagonistic to 'foreign' elements (Campos, 2016). Given this history, the fact of being Muslim or even just being from a Muslim-majority country becomes a negatively valued attribute in Spain and tends to elicit social distancing and discriminatory reactions from the mainstream society. Significantly, being of Moroccan nationality or heritage is usually conflated with being a Muslim in the Spanish context, and becomes a signifier of the 'ultimate otherness'. This ideology of islamophobia and Moorphobia, is reflected in the negative collective imaginary directed towards the Moroccan (Muslim) community and the fact that people from the Maghreb are the ones that people express the strongest rejection towards intermarrying (Rodríguez-García, Solana, & Lubbers, 2016).

48.3.2 United States in the Nineteenth and Twentieth Centuries

Laws banning interracial couples were implemented in forty-two states over the course of American history. These regulations did not only apply to partnerships between black and white people, but also restricted relationships with Asians, Native Americans, Indians, Hispanics, and other ethnoracial groups.

The first anti-miscegenation law prohibiting marriage between Blacks and Whites was passed in Maryland in 1661 (Sickels, 1972; Sollors, 2000). Most anti-miscegenation laws introduced later on generally coincided with the arrival of migratory flows of great magnitude, especially since the middle of the nineteenth century. As it happened, three significant waves of migration took place: the first between 1841 and 1890, with fifteen million immigrants, mainly Germans, Irish, British, and Scandinavians; the second between 1891 and 1920, with eighteen million incomers, most of them Italians, Austro-Hungarians, and Russians; and the third wave from 1965 onwards, with sixteen million immigrants coming from Mexico, Asia, and the Caribbean. Already in 1790, not counting the Native American, 19% of the US population was of African descent, 12% of Scottish or Irish origin, 10% German, 48% English, and the rest were French and Welsh descendants, amongst others. In other words, it was a highly multi-ethnic society, with groups often having conflicting interests. It is significant to highlight that at the time of the drafting of the Declaration of Independence in 1787, the US Constitution did not define citizenship in a precise way: citizens and naturalized people only distinguished themselves because the latter were not eligible for presidency. A few years later, in 1790, a law regulating naturalization was enacted that set the following requirements: 2 years of residence and having a good reputation and respect for the Constitution. But it was also specified that nationality would only be granted if the foreigner was white and free. This meant that all immigrants of color were excluded. Furthermore, the Protestant crusade against Catholic immigration culminated in 1854 with the creation of the American Party (or the Know-Nothing movement), whose famous motto was "America for the Americans". This attitude, criticized by Abraham Lincoln, was against the Black and foreign people as well as against Catholics (see Todd, 1994: 77–80).

During the period between the Revolution and the American Civil War, anti-miscegenation treaties and caricatures were frequent, illustrating anti-abolitionists' fears of Black and White mixing, i.e., of social equity (Lemire, 2009).[3]

Slavery was abolished in the US in 1863, and both African immigrants and descendants were allowed naturalization in 1870. But another law was passed in 1872 explicitly excluding the Chinese: the Chinese Exclusion Act. This anti-immigration policy was directly linked to the racialist discourse and to the fear of the "death" of the American national character, given the high fertility rates of African immigrants compared to those of the white population (see Teitelbaum & Winter, 1985: 50). It is in this context that movements of Teutonic tradition, or the Ku Klux Klan, arose.

At the time of the First World War, during Roosevelt's mandate, Americanism was at its height. Anti-immigration policies were embodied in the 1921 and 1924 laws, which established a quota system that limited the number of European immigrants entering the States and excluded Asian migrants. Eugenic arguments had great weight, spreading the idea that these "inferior races" contaminated the plasma of the American blood as well as corrupted the American society with their radical ideologies. These arguments served as a basis for the practical application of eugenics in the US, where it has had a long tradition (Ludmerer, 1972).

The restrictive immigration laws of the mid-1920s were maintained until the 1940s. Thus, during World War II, most states still enforced anti-miscegenation laws, mostly focused on prohibiting or limiting marriages between Whites and Blacks. Moreover, some states extended this prohibition to other nationalities (e.g., the State of California prohibited marriage between Whites and Malays or Mongols, a law that ceased to be constitutional in 1948) (Crester & Leon, 1982). Here again, decisions as to which particular "race" a person belonged to were arbitrary. Many states established that people with an eighth of their blood (three generations) of a specific "race" were to be considered as belonging to that "race". Furthermore, in states such as Arkansas, it was laid down that individuals with any trace of black blood in their veins were not allowed to marry a white person (Barnett, 1964; Weinberger, 1966). Indeed, the "one-drop rule" of hypodescent (Daniel,

---

[3]For an illustration of a treaty against miscegenation and abolitionism in 1864 entitled "What Miscegenation Is!", by LL. D. Seaman, see https://archive.org/details/whatmiscegenatio00seam/page/n7/mode/2up See also the anti-miscegenation and anti-abolitionist caricature also date 1864, entitled "Miscegenation or the Millennium of Abolitionism", at https://picryl.com/media/political-caricature-no-2-miscegenation-or-the-millennium-of-abolitionism

2000), by which even having one drop of black blood (i.e., even one ancestor of African ancestry) was considered being black, was also implemented to preclude partnering with whites and from having access to the same rights and privileges as whites.

As late as in 1967, up to sixteen states still had laws banning interracial couples. That was also the year they ended, thanks to the Loving vs. Virginia case, a landmark decision of the U.S. Supreme Court that struck down laws banning interracial marriage in the U.S. (Pratt, 1997). The case involved Mildred (Jeter) Loving, a woman of color, and her white husband Richard Loving, who in 1958 were sentenced to a year in prison for marrying each other.[4] Their marriage violated Virginia's Racial Integrity Act of 1924, which criminalized marriage between people classified as "white" and people classified as "colored". On June 12, 1967, the Court issued a unanimous decision in the Lovings' favor, and struck down Virginia's anti-miscegenation law, ending all race-based legal restrictions on marriage in the United States. The Loving's case (which was the subject of the 2016 film *Loving*) ended a long era of laws that were enforced in forty-two states over the course of American history.

The election in 2008 of U.S. president Barack Obama (a "mixed-race" individual born to a white American woman and a black Kenyan student, reared in Hawaii) was a landmark in the celebration of mixed roots.

48.3.3 England's Colonial and Post-colonial Era

In England, mixophobic policies that were carried out in African and Asian colonies were closely linked to the Victorian ideology which pitted "civilization" against "barbarism". This dichotomy was built upon the image of the Darkest Africa, which was thought of as a place of savagery, brutality, and ignorance, in contrast to English society's rationalism and progress during that period (Chamberlain, 1976). This ideology began with the first voyages of English adventurers to the West African coast around 1550, the involvement of the English in the slave trade to the New World, and the development of plantation societies in America, as well as the importation of the first black slaves into England in 1555 (see Benson, 1981: 2).

The relationships between colonizers and colonized in English settlements were shaped by the hierarchical features of the nation-state: territoriality, sovereignty, and national character (Young, 1985). Hence, in British colonies, restrictions on intimate interracial relations, particularly marital relationships, became essential to the extent that anti-miscegenation laws were dictated by the motherland. And regulations concerning sexual and marital relations, in terms of "degeneracy/survival", increased in a context of growing imperialism and patriotism. Race mixing was considered a

---

[4]For a picture of Mildred and Richard Loving, see http://www.hooverlibrary.org/blog/loving-vs-virginia

"great danger" to English "racial purity" and cultural identity, which, once again, linked *race* and *class* (see Stoler, 1989: 634).

However, at the same time, sexual exploitation, and concubinage (mainly between white men and black women) was a common practice in the colonies (see Benson, 1981: 2). In this respect, the coexistence of the rejection of mixed marriages together with a tolerance for sexual relations was a constant in colonial exploitation; the same occurred in the slave system of southern United States between white owners and black slaves (see Nkweto Simmonds, 1992: 214), and in South Africa between the Dutch settlers and native women (see Van der Berghe, 1967).

At a later stage, a "code of breeding" was laid down that became central to Anglo-Saxon racism (see Cohen, 1988: 64). The transfer of the concept of *selective breeding*, which had been taken from livestock practice, to a code that regulated interracial human relations, legitimized the hierarchical class system and perpetuated the aristocratic status in the late nineteenth century when the first eugenic movements appeared. In this period also, disease was used as a metaphor for contamination and degeneration, which according to the society, was represented by the immigrant ethnic minorities which were perceived as a "social antibody", and this way, immigration control became justified. The same happened in France, where eugenics established a direct relationship between race/ethnicity and social class. It was argued that the poor classes, which were also mainly immigrants, had higher fertility rates and that this would affect the conservation of racial purity (Soloway, 1990). Consequently, pro-natality as well as anti-immigrant and mixophobic programs were carried out simultaneously, a tendency that has predominated in Europe, in general, since the beginning of the twentieth century (Taguieff, 1991). We will return to this subject later, when we analyze the case of Nazi Germany.

Over the nineteenth century, a significant number of English people migrated to the US, Canada, and Australia, and governments thought that this emigration would strengthen the ties between the colonies and the motherland, and that this in turn would also contribute to strengthening the British Empire (see The Runnymede Trust and The Radical Statistics Race Group, 1980: 1). But with the depression between the two World Wars, many emigrants returned. During that period, and until the 1950s, there were virtually no restrictions on immigration. The British Nationality Act of 1948 allowed British Commonwealth citizens to enter the country freely with their families and settle down. Up to the 1950s, the government promoted immigration, especially of workers who would play a central role in the reconstruction of the country. Most immigrants came from the Caribbean, followed by immigrants from the Indian subcontinent and, to a lesser degree, from Africa and the Far East (see Abercrombie & Ware, 1996: 253). Generally speaking, they were welcome. However, concerning intimate interpersonal relations, relationships between Black and White were problematized, particularly the hybrid offspring of black American soldiers arriving in 1942 (the so-called *GIs*) and white English women (see Layton-Henry, 1992: 26, 36; Phoenix & Owen, 2000). Ideas about the dangers of miscegenation were widespread. As an example, following is an extract from the magazine *Glamour* of November 20, 1951 (as quoted in Banton, 1955: 152, and in Benson, 1981: 11):

Many coloured men are fine people, but they do come from a different race, with a very different background and upbringing. Besides, scientists do not yet know if it is wise for two such very different races as whites and blacks to intermarry, for sometimes the children of mixed marriages seem to inherit the worst characteristics of each race.

But perhaps the best example of anti-miscegenation attitudes is the metaphor expressed by Winston Churchill in a talk with the Governor of Jamaica: "We would have a magpie society: that would never do" (Layton-Henry, 1992: 31).

In the 1950s and 1960s, British conservative policy increasingly exercised a strict immigration control (see Skellington, 1996: 69). Interethnic marriages were considered to be appalling, which problematized the whole realm of interracial relations (see Benson, 1981: 10–13). And then during the 1960s, with Enoch Powell, a major ultraconservative figure, the anti-immigration discourse was no longer based on race but on cultural identity instead (the so-called *culturalist racism* or *culturalism*). In this way, the conservative political discourse would continue to legitimize immigration control through an anti-miscegenation ideology and intermingling between Blacks and Whites was regarded as a threat to the English character or *Britishness*, as well as to national unity and order (see Troyna, 1982: 259). Thus, migrants from the New Commonwealth countries, much fewer than European immigrants who had no restrictions to enter the UK, were no longer seen as allies but rather as enemies, despite being British subjects (citizens of the Empire).

48.3.4 Australia in the English Colonial Era

Although the history of Europe's occupation of South Australia differs in some aspects from the colonization of other world regions, the attitudes towards the native people and how they were treated were similar. A brief review of the first occupation of the southern territories of the continent will help to situate us in the context in which racialist laws regulating procreation were developed.

In 1834, a law was passed proclaiming the status of the English colony in Australia. This law, however, did not recognize the existence of the indigenous population. The Colonial Office was in charge of the administration of the colonies, and in 1842, the Waste Lands Act enabled the Aboriginal Protectorate to create reserves for the aboriginal people, small parcels of land where it was assumed that the natives would feel inclined to "civilize" and live like Europeans. During the 1850s, Christian charity missions were established, especially in southeastern Australia. Up until then, there were very few people of mixed-race (from unions between Europeans and Aborigines). Yet in the early nineteenth century, the number of interracial unions and hybrid descendants grew despite attempts by the government and Catholic missions to prevent miscegenation. As a result, a new racial policy was put in place (see Brock, 1993: 15–20). Similarly to the caste system created during the seventeenth and eighteenth centuries in colonial America, several distinctive categories were established in Australia around mixed-race descendants. These categories were based both on blood descent and evolutionist ideas, and basically distinguished between *full blood* (pure), *half-caste* (mixed-race), *quadroon* (one quarter Aboriginal), and *octoroon* (one eighth Aboriginal).

At the beginning of the century that followed, a set of racialist laws was written down in order to organize procreation. Whereas in the past the administration had made few distinctions between "pure" and "mixed-race" descendants, believing that the aboriginal population would eventually disappear, the Royal Commission now recommended a precise distinction between the different "races". In 1911, a law based on the Queensland Aboriginal Protection Act (1897) established that any Australian native or person of mixed-race married to an Australian native or "regularly associating with them", and any person of mixed-race under the age of 16, should be considered an "Aborigine". The Chief Protector was in charge of dealing with the "hybrid" children of "illegitimate" unions and put them under the responsibility of the State Children's Department. This law of 1911 was extended during the following years. Against this background, different sexual notions and uses of the Aboriginal Australians with the European settlers (such as the practice of lending them their women) helped to stir up negative prejudices against them (e.g., women hypersexuality), and also served to legitimize restrictions upon European and Aboriginal interaction (see Cowlishaw, 1988: 38–41).

Australia's colonial population policy combined a paternalistic behavior with segregationist attitudes, since it promoted segregation between the categorized racial groups, compelling them to live in separate and self-sufficient communities, which formed a precedent for South African apartheid. The Royal Commission went on to administer the missions, and the Aboriginal people were converted to Catholicism, keeping them away from their traditional ways of celebration. All these measures caused not only the separation of mixed-race children from their families but also the disintegration of their entire kinship system.

During the 1930s, and especially since the 1939 Aborigines Amendment Act, the emphasis of politics began to shift from *segregation* to *assimilating* the mixed-race descendants into the general population. "Those inside" had the same rights as the rest of the population, whereas "those outside" had no civil rights at all. The policy of separating the mixed-race from the rest continued, thereby ignoring existing family and social ties, as well as the right of people to belong to an ethnic minority.

In the 1960s, the *assimilation* legislation was modified, leading to *integration* policies that began to recognize the right of every person to decide their future and left the door open to the right of all Aborigines to citizenship and to hold title over land (Aboriginal Lands Trust Act). This new policy was embodied in the Aboriginal Affairs Acts of 1962, 1966, and 1968 (see Hunter, 1993: 218 et seq).

48.3.5 Nazi Germany

Inspired by the German romanticism of Johann Gottfried Herder (1744–1803) and his idea of the *Volkgeist* ("national genius or spirit"), the racialist theories about the hierarchy of races emerged in the eighteenth century (Todorov, 1989) and the later eugenic movements of the beginning of the century on "the improvement of the races" (Kevles, 1985; Teitelbaum & Winter, 1985), National Socialism in Germany designed the nation-state as a "race community" where the "German Aryan race" was the superior race, and whose mission was to civilize the world in view of the barbarism of "inferior races". Following this logic, the "superior" Aryan race had to be preserved, avoiding any contact and mixture with the considered "inferior races", mainly thought to be the Jewish population (Berding, 1991). It was thought that the latter not only carried all the imperfections but also transmitted them, through miscegenation, to all other groups with which they intermingled. During the 1930s, this ideology, together with the economic and political interests of the time, gave rise to a specific mixophobic legislation which was principally embodied in the Nuremberg Laws. This legislative body prohibited interracial marriage between Jews and Germans, as well as miscegenation between genetically "healthy or pure materials" and genetically "unhealthy or impure materials". Thus, here again, miscegenation posed a danger of destroying the nation (people), i.e., the *status quo*; and consequently, the "mixed-race" or "hybrid", generically called *Mischling*, was proclaimed the nation's ultimate enemy.

National-socialist movements in Germany and Austria tended to see the *nation-state* as a collective entity or "national community" *(Volksgemeinschaft)*, which from the extremist view of this racialist ideology, was perceived as a "people's community" or "racial community" (*Völkische Gemeinschaft*). In other words, it was not only seen as a *national* group but also as a *racial* group that was bound by common blood in a mystical sense (Balibar & Wallerstein, 1991; Burleigh & Wippermann, 1991). According to Herder and the German Romantics, which were the ideological forerunners of contemporary totalitarianism, the "people" (*Volk*) are the fundamental institutional pillar upon which the sociopolitical hierarchy of the nation rests. This totalitarian conception is linked to a dialectic that proclaims that people are an indissoluble, compact, and homogeneous unity, which can only occur under the assumption of there being a divided people. As a consequence, the idea of cultural plurality is excluded, and the cohesion (existence) of people depends on this homogeneous unity—a fallacy already pointed out by Lévi-Strauss in *Race and History* (1952). In this way, a *national culture* is created, and absolute identity can only be achieved by opposition to the "other", the "enemy of the people", or the "anti-people", which the *racial community* has the right to marginalize, exclude and/or eliminate (Conte & Essner, 1996).

The national-socialist population policy was, therefore, firmly embedded in a simple yet compelling biological ideology. Adolf Hitler, leader of the Nazi Party (German National Socialist Workers Party) and dictator of Nazi Germany between 1934 and 1945, as well as members of the Nazi party in general, believed that a hierarchy of racial groups existed, whose individuals could be distinguished by their natural endowments (genetics) and traits/capacities of moral and physical superiority/inferiority that supposedly were inherited. In this hierarchy, the German Aryan race occupied the top level and could be differentiated from the "inferior races" by features such as integrity, intelligence, or beauty (see Conte & Essner, 1995: 347–369). Aryan Germans considered themselves a superior Aryan type and, as such, were destined to dominate a vast empire they called *Das Dritte Reich* or Third Reich. They resorted to an old romantic idea of a perfect, glorious and "pure" past, and the necessity of returning to it to be able to recover the "ideal world", where the Aryan race would be the leader in defending "civilization" and opposing "barbarism". Accordingly, the dominance of this "race" over the rest was justified and, therefore, miscegenation (race mixing) was something to be avoided, as it was believed that it could cause the degeneration and destruction of the German people (Burleigh & Wippermann, 1991; Vasey, 2006). Thus, arguing for a struggle for subsistence (due to finite space and resources), as well as for the survival of the fittest, the Nazis' evolutionist and racist ideology put the need for the continuity of the Aryan race first. And consequently, a war of purification was declared against the elements of "cultural disintegration" and "degeneration". This ideology strongly objected to miscegenation, since it considered that race mixing would weaken the biological qualities of the race and that, for this reason, it would degenerate.

Nazi ideology regarded Jews as being the opposite pole of the Aryan race, i.e., as "the other absolute race", whom Nazis believed possessed every imperfection and even transmitted all these defects, through miscegenation, to all racial groups with which they had contact. The preservation of Aryan superiority and its supremacy in the world could, therefore, only be achieved by avoiding "crossbreeding with impure races" (which were mainly the Jews), and by favoring mixture between pure Aryans in order to "improve the race".

Moreover, state mixophobia was extended to other non-Jewish peoples, such as Gypsies, Slavs, or Africans (Campt, 2004). To this respect, Hitler also described in *Mein Kampf* the emergence of an African power in the heart of Europe, in rather apocalyptic terms. Hitler even claimed in *Mein Kampf* that Jews had brought the Blacks to the Rhineland (Germany) with the secret intention of destroying the "white race" through bastardization resulting from a biological mixture, an idea still held by American supremacist organizations (see Daniels, 1997: 126–128). And in this manner, through the myth of the "half-breed", the ruling power in Nazi Germany successfully conveyed its ideology (Conte & Essner, 1999).

In 1933, the year Hitler was appointed Chancellor, Alfred Ploetz (founder of the Society for Racial Hygiene) enforced the Eugenic Sterilization Law, which affected all people suffering from hereditary diseases, including epilepsy, blindness, alcoholism, and physical defects. And in September 1935, the Nuremberg Laws were passed (formulated by Wilhelm Frick, Reich Minister of the Interior, and approved by Adolf Hitler and Julius Streicher) whereby the population was split into two exclusive categories, Aryan, and non-Aryan or Jewish, in accordance with a regulation on sexual and matrimonial relations. This legislation was also conveyed by means of informative posters disseminated by the regime.[5]

---

[5]See the chart illustrating the forbidden marriages according to the Nuremberg Laws of 1935, at https://encyclopedia.ushmm.org/content/en/photo/chart-illustrating-the-nuremberg-laws See also the propaganda material from the Reich Committee on Public Health at the Reich Ministry of the Interior in 1940 entitled "The right choice of spouse", which highlights the importance of finding

Only individuals of pure Aryan descent were recognized by the first statute of the Reich's Citizenship Law as German citizens, i.e., as individuals entitled to enjoy all civil and political rights. This law turned Jews into second-class citizens. The second body of law, the Law for the Protection of German Blood, prohibited marriage and also sexual relations between Germans and Jews, and contemplated offenses which, in 1939, led to the death penalty (Gutman, 1990).

Interracial marriage legislation in Nazi Germany reached a climax at the Wannsee Conference (Berlin, January 20, 1942) when fourteen leaders of the SS party and the ministries were called by the Reich's Chief of Security to discuss and decide on the so-called *final solution* for Jews. The treatment of *Mischlinge* ("half-Jews" or "first-degree mixed-race" individuals) was one of the main points addressed at the meeting. The first issue that was raised regarding mixed marriages was to change the Nuremberg regulation by which "half-Jews" (half German-half Jewish) were equated with Germans and, therefore, excluded from all special measures regarding Jews. It was, however, decided that the measures applied to the "pure Jews" would also be applied to them.

Only the end of Nazism put an end to a long period of abominable anti-miscegenation laws affecting this regime's population.

48.3.6 South Africa's Apartheid

The ideological context of South Africa's apartheid was very similar to that of Nazi Germany. As in the German case, the Afrikaner idea of nation was also based on filiation by blood, i.e., belonging to the nation depended upon one's ancestors, and not upon the territory or culture. The main idea behind this ideology was the inferiority of the "black race" ("Coloured") and the superiority of the "white race", Afrikaners or Boers that were descendants of the Dutch peasants who, since the sixteenth century, had settled on the Cape of Good Hope coast and later on also colonized the inland areas.

During apartheid, racial mixing was also demonized in terms of loss of racial purity (race degeneration), as advocated by the Mendelian eugenic theories. This again responded to underlying sociopolitical and economic causes. In this regard, Hyslop (1995) pointed out that proletarianization and the consequent increase of the socioeconomic status of white women (Afrikaners) posed a threat to the Afrikaner patriarchal organization, which translated into a widespread anxiety about sexually controlling the young women of Afrikaner families, the central idea being to "save" the working class from the dangers of racial mixing and disintegrating the traditional family. The belief that hypergamic marriages of black men (non-Afrikaners) with white women (Afrikaners) could indeed overthrow the dominant socioeconomic

---

out about the racial heritage of potential spouses: https://encyclopedia.ushmm.org/content/en/photo/chart-with-the-title-die-nuernberger-gesetze-nuremberg-race-laws

order (for instance, through the appropriation of property and other goods) led to the development of a restrictive segregationist and mixophobic legislation that drew on an eugenic and racial imagery, which also provided politicians with a material to be manipulated in consonance with their socioeconomic interests (see Dubow, 1995: 128–132). Already from the beginning of the century (the Afrikaner Party was founded in 1910), legislation regarding the administration of the colonies pointed to strict racial separation (Beinart & Dubow, 1995). The Immorality Act that prevented extramarital sex between Whites and Blacks was passed in 1927.[6] This law was amended in 1950 (Immorality Amendment Act) in order to extend the prohibition also to sexual relations between white Europeans and non-Europeans, which affected mixed-race people and Asians. During the same period, the Prohibition of Mixed Marriages Act was passed in 1949. This law forbade marriage between individuals of different "race" and was not repealed until 1985.

Eighty percent of the South African population was Bantu, a majority which, nonetheless, was subject to racist state jurisdiction. In the case of the mixed-race, they were a differentiated and oppressed national minority. But neither the definition of the term "Coloured" nor its social use came from the subjects themselves: it was created and imposed by the state administration with laws referring to the different groups (Balibar & Wallerstein, 1991: 116):

In 1983, while Nelson Mandela was still imprisoned, Prime Minister Botha drafted a new constitution that no longer spoke of "races" but of "minorities". However, the same structure of inequality remained. The Indian and "Coloured" (mixed-race) minorities were granted the right to vote, and Parliament was divided into three separate chambers: White, Indian, and "Coloured". But twenty-eight million Blacks were excluded from the right to vote and, therefore, from the national community. Further on, in 1989, De Klerk replaced Botha, and a year later Mandela was released, and the country began its transition to a multi-ethnic democracy. Multi-ethnic elections were held in April 1994 with the victory of the African National Congress party, and Mandela's presidency, with a widely supported government, took place between 1994 and 1999. Nevertheless, racist and segregationist attitudes in the country have not yet disappeared. Recently, there have been reports of illegal neo-Nazi parties in South Africa. At the beginning of the 1990s, a group of journalists interviewed leaders and members of one of the Afrikaner nationalist parties. Their article shows how the same mixophobic ideology from the past was adapted to the present, since one of the leaders said: "We shall all die because of the Blacks... Blacks carry AIDS. We should not mix".

---

[6]See https://commons.wikimedia.org/wiki/File:Immorality_Act_1927.djvu

48.4 Conclusion

In his discussion of caste and class systems, anthropologist Edmund Leach stated, "In a very fundamental way, we all of us distinguish those who are of our kind from those who are not of our kind by asking ourselves the question: 'Do we intermarry with them?'" (1967, 19). A follow-up question would be, Can we?

Historically, mixed partnerships and people of mixed descent have been socially problematized. Mandatory or prescribed endogamous marriages have had the function of perpetuating social, religious, or ethnic groups, especially in highly segmented or socio-ethnically stratified contexts, such as colonial racialized hierarchical contexts, where marriage control was a fundamental element for maintaining the status quo.

This chapter has shown how loving across borders has been problematized in the past through analyzing six paradigmatic cases of nations that developed anti-miscegenation laws in keeping with a logic of "state mixophobia." In all these cases, anti-miscegenation laws prevented mixed couples and their descendants from fully belonging to society. In these contexts, the category of "mixed-race" or "hybrid" became an instrument of social exclusion. As pointed out by Stoler (2000: 20), with reference to the case of French colonization in Southeast Asia, miscegenation in colonial contexts was seen as a danger that could cause the disappearance of internal barriers—as a potential threat to national integrity and the status quo, or to what Fichte defined as "the essence of the nation" (Balibar, 1990). There are many other cases of nations that in the past had regulations controlling marital unions across ethnic and racial lines, or that at least problematized mixedness in their social discourse: for instance, Portugal in its colonial empire period (see Ferraz de Matos, 2019), Japan (see Okamura, 2017), and the Netherlands starting in the Dutch colonial period (see de Hart, 2015). However, because of space constraints, only selected cases could be examined here.

Anti-miscegenation laws of the type discussed in this chapter belong to the past, and clearly intermarriage is on the rise worldwide. Despite this growing normalization of mixing and mixedness, social concerns about mixing and about the transgression of certain racial boundaries still persist, anchored in historically rooted stereotypes and prejudices (Lee & Bean, 2012; Rodríguez-García, 2015, Rodríguez-García et al., 2016; Song, 2014). In fact, both endogamy (marriage within the same group) and homogamy (marriage between individuals of similar socio-economic and educational status) seem to still be the predominant trends globally, owing to a variety of preferential, normative, and structural reasons (Kalmijn, 1998; Rodríguez-García, 2012, 2018). Endogamous preferences have been proven to occur even in online dating (Lin & Lundquist, 2013; Potârcă & Mills, 2015).

This comparative historical and anthropological analysis on the control over romantic partnerships across racial, religious, or ethnic lines can tell us not only about the socially transformative value of mixedness, but also it can shed light on the disheartening persistence of the boundaries hindering love and social unity. Such an exploration can help us today to better understand the social, cultural, and political contexts in which reductionist visions of hybridization have emerged and may emerge, and to critically reflect on continued prejudices towards mixed unions that still exist in current times.

References

Abercrombie, N., & Ware, A. (1996). *Contemporary British society*. Cambridge: Polity Press.
Alba, R., Beck, B., & Basaran Sahin, D. (2018). The rise of mixed parentage: A sociological and demographic phenomenon to be reckoned with. *The Annals of the American Academy of Political and Social Science, 677*(1), 26–38.
Balibar, E. (1990). Fichte et la frontière intérieure: A propos des Discours à la nation allemande. *Les Cahiers de Fontenay, 58/59* (June), 57–81.
Balibar, E., & Wallerstein, I. (1991). *Raza, Nación y Clase*. Madrid: Iepala.
Banton, M. (1955). *The coloured quarter: Negro immigrants in an English city*. London: Jonathan Cape.
Barnett, L. D. (1964). Anti-miscegenation laws. *Family Life Coordinator, 13*, 95–97.
Beck, U., & Beck-Gernsheim, E. (2013). *Distant love: Personal life in the global age*. Malden, MA: Polity Press.
Beinart, W., & Dubow, S. (Eds.). (1995). *Segregation and apartheid in twentieth-century South Africa*. London: Routledge.
Benson, S. (1981). *Ambiguous ethnicity. Interracial families in London*. Cambridge: Cambridge University Press.
Berding, H. (1991). *Histoire de l'antisemitisme en Allemagne* (Vol. II). Paris: Maison des Sciences de L'homme.
Brah, A., & Coombes, A. (Eds.). (2000). *Hybridity and its discontents. politics, science, culture*. London: Routledge.
Brock, P. (1993). *Outback Ghettos. A history of aboriginal institutionalisation and survival*. Cambridge: Cambridge University Press.
Burleigh, M., & Wippermann, W. (1991). *The racial state: Germany: 1933-1945* (Vol. II). Cambridge: Cambridge University Press.
Caillavet, C., Minchom, M. (1992). Le Métis imaginaire: ideaux classificatoires et stratégies socio-raciales en Amérique latine (XVIe-XXe siècle). *L'Homme, 122–124* (La redécouverte de l'Amérique), avr.-déc., *XXXII* (2-3-4), 115–132.
Campos, R. (2016). Authoritarianism and punitive eugenics: Racial hygiene and national Catholicism during Francoism, 1936–1945. *História, Ciências, Saúde-Manguinhos, 23*(1), 131–148.
Campt, T. (2004). *Other Germans: Black Germans and the politics of race, gender, and memory in the third Reich*. Ann Arbor, MI: University of Michigan Press.
Castles, S., de Haas, H., & Miller, M. J. (2014). *The age of migration: International population movements in the modern world* (5th ed.). Hampshire: Palgrave-Macmillan.
Cebolla, H., & Requena, M. (2009). Los inmigrantes marroquíes en España. In D. Reher & M. Requena (Eds.), *Las Múltiples Caras de la Inmigración en España* (pp. 251–287). Madrid: Alianza Editorial.
Chamberlain, M. E. (1976). The Victorian image of Africa. In M. E. Chamberlain (Ed.), *The scramble for Africa* (pp. 17–29). London: Longman.
Cohen, A.P. (1988) "The perversions of inheritance: Studies in the making of multi-racist Britain". In P. Cohen y H.S. Bains (eds.) Multi-racist Britain: New directions in theory and practice, London: Macmillan, 63-86.
Conte, E., & Essner, C. (1995). *La Quête de la Race. Une Anthropologie du nazisme*. Paris: Hachete.

Conte, E., & Essner, C. (1996). L'obsession de la race. Eugénisme, antisémitisme et euthanasie en Allemagne hitlérienne. *L'Information psychiatrique, 8*, 793–802.

Conte, E., & Essner, C. (1999) Der Mythos des 'Mischlings'. Nationalsozialistische Rassenpolitik im 'Altreich' und in den 'eingegliederten Ostgebieten. *Forschungen zur westeuropäischen Geschichte (19./20. Jahrhundert), 26/39*, 129–145.

Cowlishaw, G. (1988). *Black, White or brindle. Race in rural Australia*. Cambridge: Cambridge University Press.

Crester, G., & Leon, J. (1982). Intermarriages in the U.S: An overview of theory and research. *Marriage and Family Review, 5*, 3–15.

Daniel, G. R. (2000). The one-drop rule. In Salem Press (Ed.), *African American encyclopedia*. New York: Marshall Cavendish.

Daniels, J. (1997) *White lies. Race, class, gender, and sexuality in white supremacist discourse*. New York: Routledge.

Davis, K. (1941). Intermarriage in caste societies. *American Anthropologist, 43*, 388–395.

de Hart, B. (2015). Regulating mixed marriages through acquisition and loss of citizenship. *The Annals of the American Academy of Political and Social Science, 662*(1), 170–187.

Dubow, S. (1995). *Scientific racism in modern South Africa*. Cambridge: Cambridge University Press.

Ferraz de Matos, P. (2019). Racial and social prejudice in the colonial empire: Issues raised by miscegenation in Portugal (late nineteenth to mid-twentieth centuries). *Anthropological Journal of European Cultures, 28*(2), 23–44.

Friedman, J. (1995). Global system, globalisation and the parameters of modernity. In M. Featherstone & S. Lash (Eds.), *Global modernities* (pp. 69–90). London: Sage.

García Canclini, N. (1995). *Hybrid cultures: Strategies for entering and leaving modernity*. Minneapolis, MN: University of Minnesota Press.

Gutman, I. (Ed.). (1990). *Encyclopedia of the Holocaust*. New York: Macmillan.

Hull, K. E., Meier, A, & Ortyl, T. (2010). The changing landscape of love and marriage. *Contexts, 9*(2), 32–37.

Hunter, E. (1993). *Aboriginal health and history. Power and prejudice in remote Australia*. Cambridge: Cambridge University Press.

Hyslop, J. (1995). White working-class women and the invention of Apartheid: 'Purified' Afrikaner nationalist agitation for legalisation against 'mixed' marriages, 1934-9. *Journal of African History, 36*, 57–81.

Kalmijn, M. (1998). Intermarriage and homogamy: Causes, patterns and trends. *Annual Review of Sociology, 24*, 395–421.

Kevles, D. (1985). *In the name of eugenics. Genetics and the uses of human heredity*. Berkley, CA: University of California Press.

Lavrin, A. (Ed.). (1992). *Sexuality & marriage in colonial Latin America*. Lincoln, NE: University of Nebraska Press.

Layton-Henry, Z. (1992) *The politics of immigration. Immigration, 'race' and 'race' relations in post-war Britain*. Oxford: Blackwell.

Leach, E.R. (1967). Characterization of caste and race systems. In A. de Reuck & J. Knight (Eds.), *Caste and race: Comparative approach* (pp. 17–27). London: Ciba Foundation Symposia

Lee, J., & Bean, F. D. (2012). A postracial society or a diversity paradox? Race, immigration, and multiraciality in the twenty-first century. *Du Bois Review, 9*(2), 419–437.

Lemire, E. (2009). *"Miscegenation": Making race in America*. Philadelphia, PA: University of Pennsylvania Press.

Lévi-Strauss, C. (1952). *Race et Histoire*. Paris: UNESCO.

Lin, K. H., & Lundquist, J. (2013). Mate selection in cyberspace: The intersection of race, gender, and education. *American Journal of Sociology, 119*(1), 183–215.

Lipschutz, A. (1975). *El problema racial en la Conquista de América*. Madrid: Siglo XXI.

Ludmerer, K. (1972). Genetics, eugenics, and the immigration restriction act of 1924. *Bulletin of the History Medicine, 46*, 59–81.

Méchoulan, H. (1981) [1979]. *El honor de Dios. Indios, judíos y moriscos en el Siglo de Oro*. Madrid: Argos Vergara.

Merton, R. K. (1941). Intermarriage and the social structure: Fact and theory. *Psychiatry, 4*, 361–374.

Moran, R. (2001). *Interracial intimacy: The regulation of race and romance*. Chicago, IL: University of Chicago Press.

Nkweto Simmonds, F. (1992) She's gotta have it: The representation of black female sexuality on film. In F. Bonner et al. (Eds.), *Imagining women. Cultural representations and gender* (pp. 210–220). London: Polity Press & The Open University.

Okamura, H. (2017). The language of 'racial mixture' in Japan: How Ainoko became Haafu, and the Haafu-gao makeup Fad. *Asia Pacific Perspectives, XIV*, 2.

Olumide, J. (2002). *Raiding the gene pool. The social construction of mixed race*. London: Pluto Press.

Phoenix, A., & Owen, C. (2000). From miscegenation to hybridity: Mixed relationships and mixed parentage in profile. In A. Brah, & A.E. Coombes (Eds.), *Hybridity and its discontents. Politics, science, culture* (pp. 72–95). London: Routledge

Pitt-Rivers, J. (1992). La Culture métisse: dynamique du statut ethnique. *L'Homme*, 122–124, avr./ déc., *XXXII* (2-3-4), 133–148.

Potârcă, G., & Mills, M. (2015). Racial preferences in online dating across European countries. *European Sociological Review, 31*(3), 326–341.

Pratt, R. A. (1997). Crossing the color line: A historical assessment and personal narrative of Loving v. Virginia. *Howard Law Journal, 41*, 229.

Rodríguez-García, D. (2012). Considérations théoricométhodologiques autour de la mixité. *Enfances, Familles, Générations, 17*, 41–58.

Rodríguez-García, D. (2015). Introduction: Intermarriage and integration revisited: International experiences and cross-disciplinary approaches. *The Annals of the American Academy of Political and Social Science, 662*(1), 8–36.

Rodríguez-García, D. (2018). Endo/Exogamia. In A. Aguirre Baztán (Ed.), *Diccionario Temático de Antropología Cultural* (pp. 154–160). Madrid: Delta.

Rodríguez-García, D., Solana, M., & Lubbers, M. (2016). Preference and prejudice: Does intermarriage erode negative ethno-racial attitudes between groups in Spain? *Ethnicities, 16*(4), 521–546.

Sickels, R. J. (1972). *Race, marriage, and the law*. Albuquerque, NM: University of New Mexico Press.

Skellington, R. (1996). *'Race' in Britain today*. London: SAGE.

Sollors, W. (2000). *Interracialism: Black-White intermarriage in American history, literature, and law*. Oxford: Oxford University Press.

Soloway, A. (1990). *Demography and degeneration. Eugenics and the declining birthrate in twentieth century Britain*. Chapel Hill, NC: The University of Carolina Press.

Song, M. (2014). Does a recognition of mixed race move us toward post-race? In K. Murji & J. Solomos (Eds.), *Theories of race and ethnicity: Contemporary debates and perspectives* (pp. 74–93). Cambridge: Cambridge University Press.

Spickard, P. R. (1989). *Mixed blood: Intermarriage and ethnic identity in twentieth-century America*. Madison, WI: University of Wisconsin Press.

Stoler, A. L. (1989). Making empire respectable: The politics of race and sexual morality in 20th-century colonial cultures. *American Ethnologist, 16*(4), 634–660.

Stoler, A. L. (2000). Sexual affronts and racial frontiers: European identities and the cultural politics of exclusion in colonial Southeast Asia. In A. Brah & A. Coombes (Eds.), *Hybridity and its discontents. Politics, science, culture* (pp. 19–55). London: Routledge.

Taguieff, P. A. (1991). Doctrines de la race et hantise du métissage. Fragments d'une histoire de la mixophobie savante, Métissages. *Nouvelle Revue d'Ethnopsychiatrie, 17*, 53–100.

Teitelbaum, M., & Winter, J. M. (1985). *The fear of population decline*. London: Academic Press.

The Runnymede Trust and The Radical Statistics Race Group. (1980). *Britain's Black population*. London: Heinemann.
Todd, E. (1994). *Le Destin des Immigrés. Assimilation et ségrégation dans les démocraties occidentales*. Paris: Seuil.
Todorov, T. (1989). *Nous et les autres. La réflexion française sur la diversité humaine*. Paris: Seuil.
Troyna, B. (1982). Reporting the national front: British values observed. In C. Husband (Ed.), *"Race" in Britain. Continuity and change* (pp. 259–278). London: Hutchinson.
Van Der Berghe, P. (1967) South Africa. In P. Van Der Berghe (Ed.), *Race and racism. A comparative perspective* (pp. 96–111). Washington: University of Washington.
Vasey, C. M. (2006). *Nazi ideology*. London: University Press of America.
Vertovec, S. (2007). Super-diversity and its implications. *Ethnic and Racial Studies, 29*(6), 1024–1054.
Weinberger, D. (1966). Interracial intimacy: Interracial marriage, its statutory import and incidence. *Journal of Sex Research, 2*, 158.
Young, C. (1985). Ethnicity and the colonial and post-colonial State in Africa. In P. Brass (Ed.), *Ethnic groups and the state* (pp. 59–93). London: Cromm Helm.
Zapata-Barrero, R. (2006). The Muslim Community and Spanish tradition: Maurophobia as a fact and impartiality as a desideratum. In T. Modood, A. Triandafyllidou, & R. Zapata-Barrero (Eds.), *Multiculturalism, Muslims and citizenship: A European approach* (pp. 143–161). Routlegde: Londres.

Dan Rodríguez-García (Prof. Dr.) is *Serra Hunter* Associate Professor of Social and Cultural Anthropology and Director of the Research Group on Immigration, Mixedness, and Social Cohesion (INMIX) at the Autonomous University of Barcelona (UAB), Spain. He has been a Visiting Professor at the Université Paris-Sorbonne, the Institut National d'Études Démographiques (INED), the University of Vienna, the University of Toronto, and Malmö University. He was the Guest Editor for *The ANNALS*' 2015 Special Issue "Intermarriage and Integration Revisited: International Experiences and Cross-disciplinary Approaches" and co-Guest Editor for the Journal of Ethnic and Migration Studies' 2020 Special Issue "Re-constructing ways of belonging: Crosscountry experiences of multiethnic and multiracial people." He is also the author of "Exploring the Meaning of Intermarriage" (*The SIETAR Europa Magazine*, 2006), "Mixed Marriages and Transnational Families in the Intercultural Context" (*JEMS* 2006), "Contextualizing Transnational Kinship: Theoretical and Methodological Considerations" (*AIBR* 2014), and "Preference and Prejudice: Does Intermarriage Erode Negative Ethno-racial Attitudes Between Groups in Spain?" (*Ethnicities* 2016). https://www.researchgate.net/profile/Dan_Rodriguez-Garcia

Chapter 49
The Triangular Theory of Love Scale Used in a South African Context: A Research Study

Kathryn Anne Nel and Saraswathie Govender

Abstract Sternberg's triangular theory of love utilises the notions of intimacy, passion and commitment as a theoretical underpinning for what we define as 'love.' The Love Scale based on the theory uses specific definitions associated with 'love' which try to ascertain if an individual loves another person or persons in terms of the theoretical construct. Overall, it also refers to an individual's commitment to sustain (or maintain) their commitment to love in terms of the three notions which underpin the theory. The scale derived from the theory has not often been used in an African context. We decided to investigate how Black undergraduate South African students self-reported these notions of love on the scale and discover if any of the participants scored highly in the three components, indicating consummate love. A quantitative approach utilising a cross-sectional survey design and a random sample of undergraduate students (N = 216) was used (113 females and 103 males—Mean Age = M: 19.5 years: SD: 1.23). Inferential statistics were used to analyse data which included an Independent t-test and Pearson Product Moment Correlation. Cross Tabulations and a Chi-Square Test were also used. There were significant differences between males and females on all three components of 'love' namely: intimacy ($p = 0.00$); passion ($p = 0.000$) and commitment ($p = 0.001$). Females were somewhat to significantly above average as compared to males on all three components. Consummate love was significantly more likely to found amongst the female participants.

Keywords Love · African · Black · Commitment · Consummate · Passion · Intimacy

K. A. Nel (✉)
Research, Administration and Development, University of Limpopo, Polokwane, South Africa
e-mail: kathynel53@gmail.com

S. Govender
Department of Psychological Sciences, University of Limpopo, Polokwane, South Africa

49.1 Introduction

Love has been much researched and is multi-faceted. There are several broad theories relating to love for instance, Kephart as early as 1967 found that females conceptualised love more romantically than males. Lee (1973) explored the primary types of love which he related to primary and secondary colour types. Psychologists and social researchers have thus tried to explain love and characterise its different types. This has proved difficult and often controversial however, Sternberg's (1986) Theory of Love Scale has been widely used in Westernised settings (Acker & Davis, 2015; Cassepp-Borges & Pasquali, 2012; Overbeek, Stattin, Ad, Ha, & Engels 2007). It was also used to look at intimacy, passion and commitment between American and Chinese couples. Findings included that passion was found to be higher (significantly so) in American (United States [US]) couples but commitment and intimacy was the same across cultures (Gao, 2001). Sumter, Valkenberg and Peter (2013) also established that the three-factors of the theory were found in both adults and adolescents (that is intimacy, passion and commitment). Older adults were found to have lower levels of intimacy and passion as compared to younger and middle-aged adults, but commitment remained the same. Differences between males and females were also found in terms of the three factors.

In South Africa Sternberg's (1986) scale has not been used widely and finding examples of research has been difficult. Adams & Jones, (1999) looked at how intimacy was constructed amongst a heterosexual farmworker community in the country. However, this was a small qualitative study. Sternberg's (1986) theory was referred to in the literature component and the study findings did not address elements of the scale quantitatively. Pavlou (2009) explored conceptualisations of romantic love amongst the four main cultural groups in South Africa. The research was underpinned by eight (including Sternberg's) theories. Consequently, the authors decided to use the Sternberg's (1986) Love Scale only and test its applicability in a multi-cultural context in South Africa.

49.2 Sternberg's Triangular Love Theory

49.2.1 Properties of the Theory

Sternberg's (1986) Triangular Theory of Love defines love as the interplay of three components: intimacy, commitment and passion which together can be viewed as forming the vertices of the triangle. According to Sternberg (1986) the three components are intimacy (the top vertex of a triangle); passion (the left-hand vertex of a triangle), and decision/commitment (the right-hand vertex of a triangle). Intimacy represents the emotional component and is characterised by feelings of closeness, emotional support and connectedness. Commitment embodies the cognitive aspect of love and is characterised by decisions to be in, and to maintain, a relationship.

Passion refers to the motivational aspect of a relationship and is characterised by arousal and emotional, physical and sexual consummation.

Sternberg (1986) posited that that the three love components are closely interrelated and, when combined in different permutations, may present in eight different styles of love ranging from non-love (that is, absence of all three components) to consummate love (which is presence of all three components). The triangular conceptualisation of love is useful as it creates a rubric which enables researchers' to examine how different relationships arise and why they maintain or dissolve over time (Sternberg & Weis, 2006). Furthermore, these components may be used independently to examine their association to individual love components for instance, psychological well-being, satisfaction and quality relationship outcomes (Bauermeister et al., 2011).

49.2.2 Types of Love

The three components of love interact in a systematic manner and can be described as Sternberg's (1986) eight manifestations of love.

1. **Nonlove**: refers merely to the *absence of all three components*. This (remove word basically) characterises most of our personal relationships which are simply casual interactions. It could apply to acquaintances or someone that an individual is not particularly attached to.
2. **Friendship**: This refers to the set of feelings one experiences in relationships that can be truly considered as friendship and is characterised when **intimacy is present**. An individual feels closeness, bondedness, and warmth towards another, without feelings of intense passion or long-term commitment.
3. **Infatuated love**: It is called infatuation when *passion is present*, and both liking and commitment is absent, Crushes on people known or unknown (for instance, celebrity crushes) fall into this category. People with nothing but a sexual relationship with each other also manifest in this category, as they are only bound by sexual desires. This is the most common root of romantic love as it is believed that intimacy develops over time. But if neither intimacy nor commitment develops infatuation usually (unless there is some form of psychopathy) disappears over-time.
4. **Empty Love**: Empty love is characterised by the absence of passion and intimacy despite the *presence of commitment*. An example of this is an unhappy marriage, where the intimacy or liking for the spouse has gone and passion has died, nothing is left but the contract of marriage itself. A strong love may deteriorate into empty love (an empty shell).
5. **Romantic Love**: This form of love is a *combination between intimacy and passion*. Lovers who are in this category are said to not only be drawn and bonded physically, but emotionally as well. This is one of the most common

stepping-stones to married life. However, romantic love can consist of long-term relationships which lack legal commitment to the union.

6. **Companionate Love**: it is characterised by the *combination of intimacy and commitment and the absence of passion*. This is stronger than the friendship form of love because of elements of commitment. Companionate love is observed in long-term marriages, where passion no longer plays a role (or major role) to stay in love with one's partner, because affection remains. It can also be observed amongst family members and close friends who have platonic, strong relationships.
7. **Fatuous Love**: This type of love is a *combination of commitment and passion without intimacy*. Fatuous love is typified by a whirlwind courtships and marriage in which passion motivates a commitment without the stabilising influence of intimacy. Regrettably, such marriages often end up in divorce.
8. **Consummate Love**: This type of love is at the centre of the triangle because Sternberg (1986) regarded it as the perfect and ideal type of love. *All three components are present* that is, passion, intimacy and commitment, in this type of love. This is the so-called overall goal for people who are in a relationship. According to Sternberg (1986), couples who have consummate love have a great sex life for 15 years or more in their relationship; they cannot imagine their lives with anyone else; they overcome their difficulties and have great joy in their relationships. However, Sternberg cautioned that maintaining this type of love-relationship is harder than achieving it.

49.3 Critique of Sternberg's Triadic Love Theory

The triangular theory of love has been critically examined by researchers for almost three decades (Berscheid; 2010; Graham & Christiansen, 2009). Initially, Sternberg (1986) garnered support for this theory using the Triadic Love Scale (TLS). He used exploratory factor analysis and proposed a three-factor structure that corresponded to the three love components. There were adequate scale reliability estimates for each subscale (Cronbachs's $\alpha \geq .90$). Consistent with his theory, Sternberg (1986) also found that all three factors, while measured independently, were strongly correlated with each other (Pearson's r ranging from .70 to .90). While theoretically meaningful, high correlation coefficients prohibit the simultaneous inclusion of all three TLS constructs in multivariate analyses such as multi-collinearity. Based on these critiques Sternberg (1986) subsequently proposed and tested a revised TLS that minimised, though did not fully eliminate, these measurement concerns as cross-loadings still occurred in the revised scale (Berscheid, 2010).

Conversely, scholars have offered new found support for the TLS. In a meta-analysis, Graham and Christiansen (2009) examined the TLS together with other love measures and concluded that the higher correlations between the TLS scores "suggest the presence of a shared higher order factor, in this case love. Given this evidence, the TLS might prove to be a useful measure of romantic love in a general sense; certainly, it is likely to be a reliable measure that the available psychometric data support" (Graham & Christiansen, 2009, p. 60).

Although love is accepted as a near universal experience, it is said to vary as a function of culture. South Africa's multicultural rainbow nation seems to exhibit both an individualistic as well as a collectivistic mode of loving amongst its four broad cultural groups (Pavlou, 2009). International cross-cultural researchers agree that homogenous results across cultures are emerging and that these may be accounted for by the effect of acculturation (Arnett, 2002; Jensen, 2003). These authors concur that young adults, particularly university students are Westernising and developing multicultural identities. Arnett (2002) claims that adolescents in today's world of globalisation develop a 'local identity' based on their indigenous traditions as well as a 'global identity' based on their exposure to global culture that is conveyed through social media.

49.4 Research Method for the Study

Participants and setting The population consisted of all first-year psychology students at an emerging South African University in a semi-rural setting. The number of male and female first entering psychology students was 500.

Research design The research approach was quantitative in nature using a cross sectional survey design to obtain data for this exploratory research. Colman (2009) indicates that exploratory studies are appropriate in finding out preliminary information and in expanding on existing knowledge.

Instrument Sternberg's (1986) Love Scale—The scale was used to measure intimacy, passion and commitment. It was found reliable when used by Askarpour and Mohammadipour (2016) = Cronbachs's $\alpha \geq .90$, 0.86, 0.87 and 0.91 respectively); Sternberg (1986) = Cronbachs's $\alpha \geq .90$ over the three sub-scales and Cronbachs's $\alpha \geq .80$ on the three sub-scales of this study. It was reported by Sternberg (1986) that if individual's have high scores in all three components it is indicative of the ideal type of love that is, consummate love. He further postulated that low scores do not always mean a relationship is broken down as all relationships are subject to change and can go through 'bad' patches.

Sampling technique Stratified random sampling was employed in order to provide every first-year psychology student with a chance of being selected to participate in this study. According to Babbie (2016), this method uses a procedure that provides respondents with an equal chance of selection. In stratified sampling populations should be organised into homogenous subgroups called strata before sampling, from there a random sample within each subset is drawn.

The researchers developed a random number generator from subgroups to make sure that there was representivity in stratum (males and females). This method helped prevent respondent under-representation or respondents not represented at all (Gravetter & Forzano, 2011). Stratified random sampling utilises specific information known about the respondents in making the sampling process efficient.

In this regard, a random sample of two hundred and sixteen (216) first-year psychology students was drawn from the total first-year psychology population of 500. In the sample, females were 52% (which is 113 students) and males 48% (which is 103 students).

Research hypotheses The following research hypothesis were formulated:

- There are gender differences related to Intimacy between male and female first year psychology students.
- There are gender differences related to Passion between male and female first year psychology students.
- There are gender differences related to Commitment between first year male and female psychology students
- Consummate love is more likely to be found in females than in males.

Process To collect data Stenberg's (1986) self-report, Love Scale Survey was used. Respondents were required to fill in the survey questionnaire by following the instructions at the top of the protocols. The researchers, during first year lectures related to gender issues, asked the designated students to complete the questionnaires. On the first page of the questionnaire there was information about the study, ethics pertaining to the research and voluntary participation. This included the consent form which the respondents signed. The questionnaires were checked for accuracy and inaccurate ones, that were not filled in properly, were discarded.

Data analysis An independent t-test was used to see if there were any statistically significant differences amongst the means in the two unrelated groups (in this case males and females). The use of the Pearson r statistic was also used to determine the strength of the relationship between variables. Cross tabulation tables and a chi-square test were also used to look at the results in their entirety and to examine relationships within the dataset. In this case p was significant at $p > 0.01$, which is the level of significance that represents probability (chance). Moonstats (Terre Blanche, Durrheim, & Painter, 2006) was used to analyse data and reproduce figures.

49.5 Results of the Study

The study had a population of 500 multi-cultural African students (different ethnic groups) registered in Psychology 1 at an emerging university. There were 103 males and 113 females in the final sample (N = 216). Their Mean Age = M: 19.5 years (SD: 1.23).

A t-test for independent groups indicates if there is a significant difference between the means of the groups, in this case males and females, in terms of intimacy. The $p = 0.000$ which suggests that there was a statistically significant difference between the groups with females being more likely to experience feelings

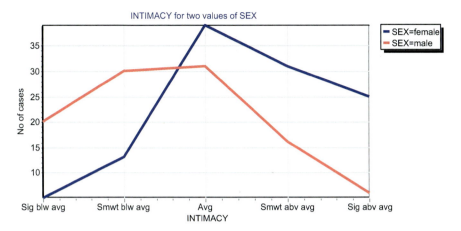

Fig. 49.1 Independent t-test for sex (female and male) and intimacy

of intimacy. The Pearson Product Moment correlation for sex and intimacy showed a moderately strong correlation (Fig. 49.1).

r(x,y) = 0.38
n = 216
p = 0.000

These results were supported by a cross-tabulation showing a broad description of the data and a chi-square test which indicated that sex (female and male) and intimacy are statistically significantly related at the 1% level (chi-square = 32.67; df = 4; p = 0.000) (Table 49.1).

Additionally, a t-test for independent groups was used to see if there was any significant difference in passion between males and females. In this case males and females were statistically different in terms of their mean scores (t = 5.06; df = 214; p = 0.000). Results suggest that females are more likely to experience higher passion than males. A difference of 0.754 between the two means was seen. The Pearson Product Moment correlation for sex and passion showed a moderately strong correlation (Fig. 49.2).

r(x,y) = 0.33
n = 216
p = 0.000

These results were underpinned by a cross-tabulation showing a comprehensive description of the data and a chi-square test which indicated that sex (female and male) and passion are statistically significantly related at the 1% level (chi-square = 24.35; df = 4; p = 0.000) (Table 49.2).

In terms of commitment an independent t-test indicated that there was a significant difference between males and females on the love scale. Overall, results suggest that females were likely to show higher commitment in relationships than

Table 49.1 Cross tabulation table sex by intimacy

Intimacy	Male	Female	Total respondents
Significantly below average	20	5	25
Somewhat below average	30	13	43
Average	31	39	70
Somewhat above average	16	31	47
Significantly above average	6	25	31
Total	103	113	216

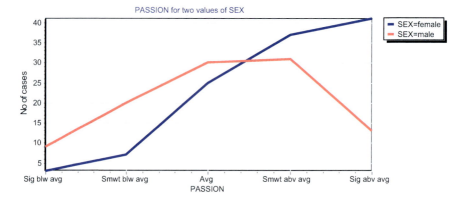

Fig. 49.2 Independent t-test for sex (female and male) and passion

males. There is a statistically significant difference, on an independent t-test, between the groups at a 1% level in terms of their mean scores (t = 5.02; df = 214; p = 0.000). A difference of 0.787 is seen between the means. The Pearson Product Moment correlation for sex and commitment which showed a moderately strong correlation, underpins this result (Fig. 49.3).

r(x,y) = 0.32
n = 216
p = 0.000

A cross-tabulation which indicates a comprehensive description of the data and a chi-square indicated that sex (female and male) and commitment are statistically significantly related at the 1% level (chi-square = 24.58; df = 4; p = 0.000) (Table 49.3).

To test if there was any significant difference between males and females on consummate love, which is the 'ideal' kind of love according to Sternberg (1986), an independent t-test was used. (The levels of intimacy, passion and commitment of the two groups were added and then entered into a spreadsheet). It was found that consummate love is significantly higher in females than males. The two groups

Table 49.2 Cross tabulation table sex by passion

Passion	Male	Female	Total respondents
Significantly below average	9	3	12
Somewhat below average	20	7	27
Average	30	25	55
Somewhat above average	31	37	68
Significantly above average	13	41	54
Total	103	113	216

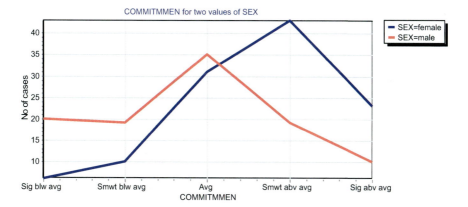

Fig. 49.3 Independent t-test for sex (females and males) by commitment

Table 49.3 Cross tabulation table sex by commitment

Commitment	Male	Female	Total respondents
Significantly below average	20	6	26
Somewhat below average	19	10	29
Average	35	31	66
Somewhat above average	19	43	62
Significantly above average	10	23	33
Total	103	113	216

were statistically significantly different at the 1% level in terms of their mean scores on Consummate love (t = 7.03; df = 214; p = 0.000). I this case there is a difference of 1.047 between the two means.

49.6 Discussion

The first three hypotheses namely (1) There are gender differences related to year Intimacy between male and female first year psychology students; (2) There are gender differences related to Passion between male and female first year psychology students and (3) There are gender differences related to Commitment between first male and female psychology students are all upheld by the results. The fourth hypotheses (4) Consummate love is more likely to be found in females than in males was also upheld.

The findings of this study about intimacy are in line with those of Arnett (2002) who postulated that in many cultures around the world, women are considered intimacy experts. In the past women were considered as emotional, irrational and lovesick, traits that were noted as 'deficient' as compared to the so-called 'rational' male. Today these traits are interpreted as strengths that make women more sensitive and caring and consequently more likely to achieve consummate love than males. One thing that is commonly found in Western culture is that men show their love differently than women which leads to different gender expectations about love and caring. Most men think that love means 'action' for example, doing housework or paying bills. However, women expect men to express their love through talking about their feelings and processing the relationship in intimate terms (Schoenfeld, Bredow, & Huston, 2012).

In Sternberg's (1986) model the related presence of passion, intimacy and commitment are explained as a type of full or consummate love. The results of the study demonstrated a higher importance for female first year psychology students in terms of this type of love as compared to males in the sample. Sternberg and Weis, (2006) pointed out that aspects of passion have different configurations in short duration relationships, in such cases the evaluations on the love scale are more elevated than in long term involvement. As this study used a student sample it is likely that the high elevations on passion, intimacy and commitment (as well as consummate love) particularly on the female sample are associated with short-term relationships. As most of the sample can be defined as young adults and adolescents the study findings are in line with those of Sumter, Valkenberg and Peter (2013) who posited that the triarchic love theory factors were found in both adults and adolescents.

Findings related to gender differences in this research may be useful to university counselling centres in order to help students' expectations of their idealised love (such as consummate love) within their actual relationships (for instance, passionate love) in order to improve the quality of their relationship or, conversely, to provide strategies to reduce the negative effects which can arise when a relationship ends.

Sternberg (1986) also indicated that cultural dimensions are variables that mediate emotions and feelings. Thus, a deeper understanding of Sternberg's (1986) theory and inter-related love styles (intimacy, passion and commitment which together make-up consummate love) may allow scholars to determine if these types of love explain why some relationships endure while others collapse or are not as passionate (Gao, 2001) in multi-cultural environments.

International cross-cultural researchers agree that homogenous results across cultures are emerging and that these may be accounted for by the effect of acculturation (Arnett, 2002; Jensen, 2003). These authors concur that young adults, particularly university students are Westernising and developing multicultural identities. Arnett (2002) claims that adolescents in today's world of globalisation develop a 'local identity' based on their indigenous tradition as well as a 'global identity' based on their exposure to global culture conveyed through social media. The results of this study, using an African sample in a South African context, support these notions.

References

Acker, M., & Davis, H. M. (2015). Intimacy, passion and commitment in adult romantic relationships: A test of the triangular theory of love. *Journal of Social and Personal Relationships, 9*(1), 21–50.

Adams, J. M., & Jones, W. H. (1999). Interpersonal commitment in historical perspective. In J. M. Adams & W. H. Jones (Eds.), *Handbook of interpersonal commitment and relationship stability* (pp. 3–33). New York: Kluwer Academic/Plenum.

Arnett, J. J. (2002). The psychology of globalisation. *American Psychologist, 57*(10), 774–783.

Askarpour, A., & Mohammadipour, M. (2016). Psychometric properties of Sternberg love scale. *Journal of Fundamental and Applied Sciences, 8*(4), 2037–2046.

Bauermeister, J. A., Johns, M. M., Pingel, E., Eisenberg, A., Santana, M. L., & Zimmerman, M. (2011). Measuring love: Sexual minority male youths' ideal romantic characteristics. *Journal of LGBT issues in Counselling, 5*(2), 102–121.

Babbie, E. R. (2016). *The practice of social research*. Boston: Oxford University Press.

Berscheid, E. (2010). Love in the fourth dimension. *Annual Review of Psychology, 61*, 785–799.

Cassepp-Borges, V., & Pasquali, L. (2012). Sternberg's triangular love scale national study of psychometric attributes. Retrieved from http://www.scielo.br/pdf/paideia/v22n51/en_04.pdf

Colman, A. M. (2009). *Oxford dictionary of psychology* (3rd ed.). New York: Oxford University Press.

Gao, G. (2001). Intimacy, passion and commitment in Chinese and US American romantic relationships. *International Journal of Cultural Relations, 25*, 329–342.

Graham, J. M., & Christiansen, K. (2009). The reliability of romantic love: A reliability generalization meta-analysis. *Personal Relationships, 16*(1), 49–66.

Gravetter, F. J., & Forzano, L. B. (2011). *Research methods for the behavioural sciences* (3rd ed.). Belmont, CA: Cengage Learning.

Jensen, L. A. (2003). Coming of age in a multicultural world: Adolescent cultural identity formation. *Applied Developmental Science, 7*(3), 189–196.

Kephart, W. M. (1967). Some correlates of romantic love. *Journal of Marriage and the Family, 29* (3), 470–474.

Lee, J. A. (1973). *Colours of love: An exploration of the ways of loving*. Toronto: New Press.

Overbeek, G. S., Stattin, H., Ad, V., Ha, T., & Engels, R. C. M. (2007). Parent child relationships, and emotional adjustment: A birth to maturity prospective study. *Developmental Psychology, 43* (2), 429–437.

Pavlou, K. (2009). An investigation of the conceptualisation of romantic love across South Africa. In *A cross-cultural study*. Retrieved from https://ujcontent.uj.ac.za/vital/access/manager/Repository/uj:6878?site_name=GlobalView

Schoenfeld, E. A., Bredow, C. A., & Huston, T. L. (2012). Do men and women show love differently in marriage? *Personality and Social Psychology Bulletin, 38*(11), 1396–1409.

Sternberg, R .J. (1986). A triangular theory of love. *Psychological Bulletin, 93*(2), 119–135.

Sternberg, R. J., & Weis, K. (Eds.). (2006). *The new psychology of love*. New Haven, CT: Yale University Press.

Sumter, S. R., Valkenberg, P. M., & Peter, J. (2013). Perceptions of love across the lifespan: Differences in passion, intimacy, and commitment. *International Journal of Behavioral Development, 37*(5), 417–427.

Terre Blanche, M., Durrheim, K., & Painter, D. (2006). *Moonstats 2 license to the owner of Research in practice* (92nd ed.). Cape Town: UCT/Juta Press.

Kathryn Anne Nel (Prof. PhD), University of Limpopo (Turfloop Campus), Sovenga, Limpopo Province South Africa. She acted as HOD Industrial Psychology at the University of Zululand for a period of 3 years before moving to the University of Limpopo in 2009. She has a National Research Foundation (South Africa) rating and broad research interests including gender issues, neuropsychology, social psychology, sport psychology and community psychology.

Associate Professor Saraswathie Govender (Prof. Dr.) University of Limpopo (Turfloop Campus), Sovenga, Limpopo Province, South Africa. She has acted as HOD Psychology in the Department of Psychology at the University of Limpopo (Turfloop Campus). She is Head of Research in the Department and serves on many of the institutions research committees. Her main areas of interest are neuropsychology, social psychology and Indigenous Knowledge Systems (IKS).

Chapter 50
Love in China (1950–Now)

Pan Wang

Abstract This chapter explores love in China through three principal historical stages—The Maoist era, the Opening-up and economic reform period and the new millennium. Although the People's Republic of China established its first marriage law during the Mao era, aiming to promote freedom of marriage and divorce, this did not, however, translate to freedom of love and romance. Love remained bound within a nationalistic framework and was subjected to political revolution. The Economic reform allowed businesses to flourish and allowed China to re-engage with the world and build new international links. This paved the way for the rising popularity of transnational love and marriage in China. However, love appeared to fall into 'crisis' in the new millennium due to the growing level of single individuals resulting from the gender imbalance, rising marriage dissolution, strengthened love censorship and commercialised love practice. This chapter argues that with its strong communist imprint and shaped by commercial forces, love in China has now become a pluralistic and contested product of a hybrid system composed of political socialism and market economy capitalism.

Keywords Love · China · Marriage law · Transnational intimacy · Leftover (wo)men

50.1 Introduction

The chapter examines love in China from the 1950s to the present. The first section introduces the methodology used in the research. The second section explores love during the Maoist era. It shows that although China's first marriage law guaranteed citizens freedom of marriage and divorce, this did not translate to freedom of love and romance. Love remained bound within a nationalistic framework and was subjected to political revolution. In this section, I unpack love under Mao through

P. Wang (✉)
School of Humanities and Languages, Faculty of Arts and Social Sciences, The University of New South Wales, Sydney, NSW, Australia
e-mail: Pan.wang@unsw.edu.au

the theoretical lens of 'class' and explain how the concept of 'class' shaped the pattern of people's mate selection together with the role of socialist institutions in love-control and the class-making process. The third section focuses on transnational love in post-socialist China. Under the new CCP leadership, the adoption of the Opening-up and Economic Reform policy not only ushered in optimistic foreign investments but also created opportunities for love between Chinese and foreigners. Chinese-foreign love, in contrast to domestic love, is an amalgamation of gender and identity politics, simultaneously condemned and romanticized by the PRC media. The fourth section analyses love in the new millennium. Love appeared to fall into 'crisis' in this era evidenced by the growing number of 'left-over' men and women struggling to find love, the rising number of marriage breakdowns, commercialised love practice, and strengthened censorship on Chinese-foreign intimacy. Some of this crisis has already evolved into a social crisis that requires urgent government intervention/mediation. The chapter concludes that with its strong communist imprint and shaped by commercial forces, love in China has become a pluralistic and contested product of a hybrid system comprised of political socialism and market economy capitalism.

50.2 Research Methodology

The research uses both quantitative and qualitative methods to reveal the changing landscape of love in China from the Maoist era to the present. It analyses the marriage statistics compiled by the Chinese Ministry of Civil affairs (MCA) from 1979 to now. This helps to map out the trend of marriage rates in China throughout the decades. This is supplemented with analysis of the Chinese marriage law, marriage registration policies, and the relevant regulations. It reveals how love, intimacy and marriage are governed by the state and a degree of autonomy in love in China. The chapter also examines representations of love in the media and popular culture, including newspaper reports, documentary films, talk shows and government propaganda posters. These representations of love reveal people's everyday love experiences and official love ideologies. In addition, the research draws on the data collected from my ethnographic fieldwork on marriage matchmaking parks in Beijing and Shanghai in 2019. The data is analysed with reference to the theories of exchange and assortative mating and contributes to revealing the current love practices in China's gendered marriage market.

50.3 Revolutionary Love and the Repercussions of 'Class' (1950s–1970s)

After the Chinese Communist Party took power in 1949, it launched a series of campaigns and reforms to rebuild the nation. One of its strategic priorities was to establish a new socialist order by reconstructing China's marriage and family system. This gave birth to the 1950 Marriage Law, which abolished polygamy, along with arranged marriages, mercenary marriages and child betrothals. It also legislated for monogamy, freedom of marriage (Article 3, 17), and recognized equality between men and women (Article 1, 2, Central Government, 1950a). The law was also committed to protecting the interests of women and children, and designated rights and obligations in family and conjugal relations (Article 7, 8). To promote the law, the government organized various campaigns and activities to encourage citizens to study the law, propaganda posters were also distributed around the nation to garner support for the law. Meanwhile, the media were full of optimistic stories/ statistics of free-choice marriages to highlight the significance of the law (Wang, 2014; Wolf, 1974: 170). As a result, many Chinese (women) fought to end their unhappy marriages. This led to a surge in divorce rates in the early 1950s (MCA, 1993), evidence of the success of the law in liberating Chinese women from feudal constraints and awakening them to defending their legal rights. Undeniably, the Marriage Law became an essential force in transforming Chinese women's position both in and outside the family. This became fundamental to facilitating the construction of a new socialist society (Central Government, 1950a, b).

However, in practice, many Chinese women faced enormous difficulties when choosing their own mates and filing for divorce. This was especially evident in rural China where patriarchal culture was deeply entrenched (Diamant, 2000: 171–72). Arranged marriage practices persisted, parents' interference remained strong, and poor rural households had to exchange their daughters in return for their sons' marriages (Zhang, 2013: 446). Moreover, many young adults lacked the resources necessary for mate selection and had to rely on their parents to look for their marriage prospects. In terms of filing for divorce, women faced strong resistance from their husbands, parents, in-laws and local officials, as many households were reluctant to accept the law (Wolf, 1974: 171, 181). Some women were beaten by their husbands over disputes of property rights. Many parents-in-laws were unhappy when they lost control/authority over their sons' brides. Some local officials were more interested in 'ensuring stability and protecting the interests of their male peasant constituency' than helping women to fight their husbands. Other officials, although supporting the provisions of the law, found it difficult to implement it due to lack of guidelines from the central government. Despite some women managing to divorce in the end, they suffered throughout the divorce process. In extreme cases, some divorce initiators were murdered or committed suicide (Wolf, 1974: 171, 179). Some had no luck in terminating their marriage contracts and had to live with the consequences for the rest of their life. Some illiterate women did not know how to file for divorce due to lack of assistance from the state institutions. Some families still held conservative views against divorce as it remained a strong social stigma during the early years. All of these doomed the short lifespan of the 1950 marriage law.

These problems cannot be underestimated as they suggest patriarchal traditions remained strong in (rural) China and rendered the modern state mechanism ineffective. The law did give its citizens freedom of marriage and divorce, albeit limited. The partial success of marriage freedom did not translate into freedom of love and romance as the traditional kinship network, gender relations, social institutions, and old mentality co-existed and were closely intertwined in curbing the growth of a dating culture. Young people also lacked a fundamental understanding of how to find romance by themselves and both the difficulty of divorce and social perceptions towards divorce inhibited them from looking for new love. Hence it can be concluded that the marriage law in line with the national priority in the early 1950s was to establish a modern socialist society by reconstructing family/gender relations through marriage reform rather than creating a democratic atmosphere in which individuals could love, marry and divorce freely.

Another nation-building project conducted by the CCP at this time was the land reform campaign in rural China, during which love was heavily shaped by an imposed class identity, the result of conflicts between the peasantry and landlords in earlier decades (Parish & Whyte, 1978). Such conflicts had escalated since the beginning of the land reform campaign in June 1950 when peasants mobilized to condemn landlords and urge them to return stolen land. When engaged in the class struggle, people were grouped into different class categories based on their possession of land and labour relations (Zhang, 2013: 440). Each individual was assigned a class label based on his/her family origin, and this was inherited along patriarchal lines (fathers' class designation) (Kraus, 1981). The class labels can be grouped into the following categories: The 'exploiting class' or the 'bad' class (Landlords and rich peasants), the 'exploited class' or the 'good class' (poor peasants and lower middle peasants), and the class in between the two (middle peasants and upper middle peasants) (Zhang, 2013: 440). Such labelling explicitly differentiated between sections of the population and pre-defined their political identities. It created a hierarchy in mate selection and marriage: 'good classes' were pursued by people, as 'marrying up' to good classes could improve the social status of individuals and their families whereas 'bad' classes were not favored and struggled to find love. Particularly, people with good class labels had ample opportunities in mate choice in the love market and were not willing to marry down into a lower political category. However, those with bad class labels had limited opportunity and needed to compromise in various ways to be married. For example, 'lower class' (upper middle peasants) marrying 'higher class' (poor peasants) sometimes involved compromises by the former of the latter in terms of age, educational attainment, and even health (Zhang, 2013: 446). However, heterosexual class endogamy was the norm, meaning people were likely to marry within the same class category and were less likely to marry interclass, especially when crossing two opposite classes (Parish & Whyte, 1978).

The concept of 'class' appeared to become less significant in mate selection following the land reform. To achieve the goal of its first 5-year-plan (1953–57), China followed the Soviet model of economic development by focusing on the growth of heavy industry. To fuel the needs of rapid industrialisation, the government also encouraged collective farming. Peasants were mobilized to return the land they had earlier received to the state. Their lands together with associated resources were then pooled together in various combinations so as to boost agricultural output. Both men and women were assigned to work in brigades and cooperative teams to achieve the set economic goals. These cooperatives were then amalgamated to form big communes. This gave villagers greater opportunity to meet, court and form close relationships (Blake, 1979: 43–4). In turn, the engagement between different sexes further increased productivity as evidenced by the popular love songs ('Agrarian Songs') during this time (Blake, 1979). According to Blake's (1979) research, the CCP mobilized the writers, teachers and students to compose these songs for the purpose of conveying the 'values and goals of collectivization' during that time (Blake, 1979: 42). Most of these songs joined the erotic interests of young people with the goals of China's second 5-year-plan (1958–62)—the Great Leap Forward (hereafter 'GLF') (Blake, 1979: 44). For example, 'Little sister carries mud, big brother digs the pond (digging reservoir), pearls of sweat mix with muddy water...big brother and little sister want to be heroes, they dig until the stars set and the sun rises' (Blake, 1979: 46; Guo & Zhou, 1959: 120). Other love songs combined courting with the anticipated 'correct' political motives. For example, one song went 'If big brother becomes a model worker and joins the Party; Little sister will take him a red flag as dowry' (Blake, 1979: 45; Guo & Zhou, 1959: 140). At this juncture, the communists also pinpointed the importance of looking for spouses in 'stress-provoking' situations like the GLF as undertaking hard work and conquering difficulties together can help to build a solid foundation for marriage (Blake, 1979: 43). Love and personal intimacy were thus entangled with revolutionary collectivisation and functioned as a catalyst for socialist development.

As in the countryside, love in the city could also not be separated from the influence of the government. This was achieved via Danwei, the bureaucratic work organization established in the early 1950s. Danwei was a powerful social institution in charge of production tasks and maintained communist political and social order by providing housing, education, medical care, social facilities and other entitlements to its employees. It also functioned to ensure the practices of its employees were in line with the socialist ethos proposed by the Party. It thus found it legitimate to monitor people's recreational activities, private lives and intimate relations to both show care and enact control. For example, work unit leaders (communist party members) were sometimes involved in arranging a marriage partner for an employee (Liu, 2007: 66). Unsurprisingly, their recommended candidates were often revolutionary army men or Communist Party members. Such voluntary acts were often gendered and placed pressure on employees, as women in their 20s started to receive matchmaking offers and to not follow the supervisor's advice could have negative implications on their work performance.

In conjunction with Danwei, the establishment of the Hukou system (household registration system) in 1958 enhanced the division between rural and urban areas. Urban citizens were entitled to various social benefits including education, health care, and other goods and services whereas rural citizens received limited support from the state. It was also difficult for them to seek upward mobility or change residential status, rendering rural citizens 'second-class' citizens. This created a split identity between the urban and rural, confining love within its respective realm—urban citizens were reluctant to date/marry rural citizens unless they had difficulty finding a partner in the city (Zhao & Ding, 2015: 97). Rural citizens tended to look for love in rural areas, as it was difficult to migrate to the city. This did not change until the 1960s, when millions of urban youths were sent to the countryside by the state to study from poor peasants.

Thanks to the 'down to the countryside' movement, an effort to alleviate urban employment pressures and boost agricultural production (Yao, 2010), love became mobile and began to cross the city-rural boundary. Scattered statistics and oral histories from sent-down-youths showed that as these youths were away from their parents, they found the freedom to indulge in 'undisciplined' love, evidenced by the high level of cohabitation and pregnancy among these people and the handwritten copies of pornographic stories circulated by them (Honig, 2003: 161; Jeffreys & Yu, 2015: 5). However, such 'love' was not totally free as the government discouraged 'sent-down-youths' from dating and encouraged them to postpone their marriages and devote their time and youthful energy to the socialist revolution and production. This was partly an effort to tackle teenage marriages and help to solve the housing issues for 'sent-down-youths' in rural China (Zhao & Ding, 2015: 98). This simultaneously suggests that love and marriage were state-led and driven by national interests.

Love was further complicated by the notion of class during the Cultural Revolution (1966–76) as the 'capitalist Class' became a new enemy to struggle against. The Capitalist class, or 'the bourgeoisie', according to Marxist theory, refers to the group of people who control the means/resources of production. Love, romance and intimacy were perceived as tarnished by the capitalist lifestyle and henceforth incompatible with China's socialist ethos. People from different classes who fell in love were unable to marry freely, instead, they had to marry 'politically correct' persons. Moreover, married couples with compatible backgrounds intending to divorce were unable to end their marriages (Chen & Ran, 2009: 45). Overseas relations (haiwai guanxi) were considered to be dangerous and Chinese-foreign intimacy was discouraged. It was considered imperative for China to develop from the purity of socialist soil without being polluted by foreign culture and to carry forward the collective mission of class struggle without being distracted by 'personal matters'. Unsurprisingly, cultural productions, such as short stories, films and literature that featured romantic themes largely disappeared due to information censorship. Instead, the media landscape was dominated by revolutionary stories molded by Maoist political ideologies. Moreover, formal rules were established in different educational institutions to prohibit people from talking about romance. Students who violated these bans risked being criticized in public (Whyte, 1995: 60).

Romantic love was like a 'hot potato' as everyone who attempted to take a bite was also afraid of being burned. However, there were circumstances where love did cross class boundaries. This occurred when parents renounced the relationship with their adult children or vice versa, as it helped to destigmatize love between the 'good' and 'bad' classes as attached to family origin (Friedman, Pickowicz, & Selden, 2005: 98; Zhang, 2013: 463–64).

Class labels had strong implications for individuals' love values throughout the 1950s and 1960s. It wasn't until 1979 that the CCP eliminated class labels as a political category (Zhang, 2013: 38).

50.4   Gendered Implications of International Intimacy (Late 1970s–2000s)

China shifted its ideology from political struggle to a market economy during the 1970s. It launched the Opening-up and Economic Reform policy in 1978. This brought dramatic changes to Chinese society along with personal relations. Politically, China resumed and built new diplomatic ties with several countries, and 'overseas relations' (haiwai guanxi) regained public confidence. This restored communication between China and the outside world on multiple levels. Economically, China opened 14 coastal cities to overseas investments and established five Special Economic Zones (SEZs) in coastal cities in the provinces of Guangdong and Fujian, as well as Hainan. This allowed China to receive growing foreign investments and encouraged domestic companies to 'go out' (zou zhuqu). Chinese people started to have access to western food, cafés, bars, clubs and foreign-invested hotels. Legally, the state revised the Marriage Law (NPC, 1980, 2001), simplified marriage and divorce procedures, and included foreign nationals in marriage registrations (MCA, 1983a, b, 1986, 1994, 2003). In addition, it issued new laws to facilitate travelling, these included The Law of the People's Republic of China on Control of Exit and Entry of Citizens (SCNPC, 1986a) and The Law of the PRC on Control of Entry and Exist of Aliens (SCNPC, 1986b). Despite strong travel restrictions at this time, the laws indirectly triggered the number of inbound and outbound visitors (MPS, 2013), by significantly increasing individual mobility. Culturally, love literature blossomed (Louie, 1989), and the media industry re-opened. This enabled the Chinese to consume diverse popular cultural products featuring 'western' love and romance. This resonated with the younger generation of youths (in contrast to their parents who grew up during the Maoist era), and kindled their aspiration for/imagination of romantic love. All of these changes paved the way for a rising number of intimate relationships between the Chinese and the 'foreigners',[1] evidenced by the marriage data collated by China's Ministry of Civil Affairs (MCA). Figure 50.1 shows that

---

[1] 'Foreigners' refer to citizens from Hong Kong, Macau and Taiwan, foreign nationals, and overseas Chinese in this context. Hong Kong was a British colony until it was placed under the PRC's

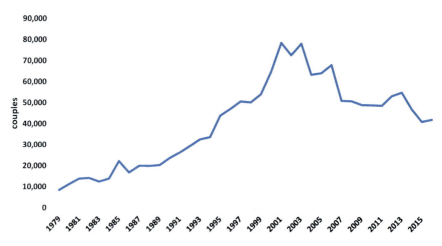

Fig. 50.1 Chinese-foreign marriages (1979–2016). Source: MCA (2017) jiehun dengji. Zhongguo minzheng tongji nianjian [China civil affairs statistical yearbook] (pp.168–69). Wang based on the data released in the official yearbook by the PRC government

over 8400 couples registered a Chinese-foreign marriage in 1979, the figure exceeded 11,300 couples within a year before reaching its climax at 78,600 couples in 2001. The figure then fluctuated and followed a decreased trend throughout the 2000s (MCA, 2017a).

Most of these international couples are located on China's eastern seaboard, including the cosmopolitan cities of Beijing, Shanghai and provinces of Fujian, Guangdong and Zhejiang. These places are also popular trading ports adjacent to Hong Kong, Macau and Taiwan, with which earlier commercial links were formed. Provinces in Northeast China, particularly Hei Longjiang, Jilin and Liaoning also became popular destinations for international marriages. Many marriages in these areas are between mainland Chinese citizens and citizens from the neighbouring countries of Japan and Korea (Jiang, 1999; Wang, 2015: 30–1). Similarly, a number of ethnic minorities residing in China's Southwest provinces of Guangxi and Yun'nan married people from Vietnam, Laos and Burma (Gao, Zhang, & Zhu, 2003: 28; Li & Long, 2008: 34; Luo, 2006: 52). This indicates that geographic, cultural and ethnic proximities are important factors in the formation of transnational love. Other popular countries were the developed 'Western' nations, such as the U. S., Canada, the U.K., France, Germany, and Australia. A closer look at these marriages shows that the overwhelming majority of unions are between Chinese women and foreign men, with the former accounting for more than 85% and the latter less than 15% (Jeffreys & Wang, 2013: 356–57; MCA, 1979–2010).

The gendered composition alludes to the perceived 'upward' socioeconomic mobility of Chinese women in pursuing foreigners during the earlier years. This

---

sovereignty in 1997. Macau was a Portuguese colony from the sixteenth century, and was returned to the PRC in 1999.

group of women were usually much younger than their foreign partners, many with an age gap of over 10 years (Ding et al., 2004: 69). They tended to be portrayed as victims of Chinese-foreign intimacy in the PRC media due to their naivety and motivation to 'marry up' for social and economic gain. As such, their love stories were reported as ending in tragedy. These reports were cautionary tales functioning to warn Chinese women of the potential danger of love and marriage to a foreigner especially when moving overseas (Wang, 2015: 54–5). At this time, many Chinese female celebrities who travelled overseas with their foreign partners attracted negative commentaries and were condemned as lacking patriotism—a sign of rejecting their fans and Chinese men (Wang, 2015: 96–7). Simultaneously, the group of women, dubbed 'mainland sisters' (dalumei) in Hong Kong and Taiwan, tend to be demonized by the local media as hypergamous 'gold-diggers' and 'prostitutes' for marrying men from Hong Kong and Taiwan (Hsia, 2007: 55–62; Shih, 1998: 295–303; Tsai, 2011: 245). This created stereotypes of this group of women and rendered them as 'second-class' citizens inferior to the local citizens of Hong Kong and Taiwan. Such portrayals somehow mirrored the economic disparity between China and the developed countries/regions during the earlier decades. However, they could be distorted and at times misrepresented the group of young women looking for love.

The growing number of women dating and marrying foreign men was concurrent with the phenomenon 'Craze for going aboard' (chuguore) associated with the discourses of 'frowning on everything foreign' (chongyang meiwai) and 'yinsheng yaoshuai' (femininity overpowering masculinity) between the late 1980s and 1990s. Many Chinese citizens who travelled abroad intended to obtain an academic qualification and then return to China (Zhao, 1996). However, the PRC Government observed a 'brain-drain' trend before and after the 1989 Tian'anmen Square incident, and China's media was embroiled in a national campaign against perceived negative western influences such as 'spiritual pollution' and 'bourgeois liberalization' (Wang, 2015: 56). In this context, Chinese citizens who travelled overseas or dated/married foreigners risked being blamed for being 'insufficiently patriotic', 'blindly idealizing everything foreign', or 'marrying up' for socioeconomic gain (Brady, 2003: 28; Fang, Wang, & Ma, 2002: 14–5). Meanwhile, the growing number of women dating/ marrying foreigners also echoed a 'crisis of Chinese masculinity', in which Chinese men were criticized by intellectuals as 'lacking in manliness' vis-à-vis foreign men (Song, 2010: 408–9). This echoes Tang Ying's book Meiguo laide qizi [My wife from America] which interprets Shanghai women's strategies of emigration via international marriages as a sign of crisis in Chinese masculinity (Farrer, 2008: 10; Tang, 1995). This triggered a trend of 'searching for the real man' in China, one who neither falls within western gender standards nor fits into the communist proletarian gender ideology (Song, 2010: 408). This was also the period when China began to witness the return of a feminised type of manhood influenced by 'flower-like' men (huayang meinan) propagated in K-pop and J-pop (Louie, 2014: 24). It further complicated Chinese masculinity and evoked the nation's self-reflection on gender with reference to national identity. All of these discourses show that international love became a contested subject intertwined with gender and nationalism in the 1980 and 1990s. It also reflects China's struggle to integrate into the world economy while maintaining its socialist legacy in the earlier transitional period.

Entering into the new millennium, despite a declining number of international marriages, international love stories proliferated. Numerous newspaper reports underscore the growing educational level, social status and economic independence of Chinese women in concert with their shifting motivations in intercultural intimacy from hypergamy to love (Chen, 2003; 'Shanghai shewai hunyin', 2002; Xin & Ye, 2008). This reversed the earlier logic of international love as being driven by hypergamy. It also indicates China's modernity and increased position in the world that emanated from the Opening-up and economic reform policy. Television programs including talk shows, dating shows, documentaries and dramas produced stories that demonstrate love can conquer all boundaries, including geographical, cultural, class, ethnic or age boundaries (Guan & Yang, 2006; Li, 2005; Wang, 2017a; Zeng & Piao, 2002). Many reports also delivered 'Chinese Cinderella' stories, in most cases, Chinese women with poor backgrounds from rural China met their foreign 'princes' by accident and the couple fell in love at first sight. For example, as the newspaper title suggests 'Henan girl marries Polish presidential candidate, she will bring him to her native home' (Henan meizi jiagei Bolan zhun zongtong, yiding hui daizhe zhangfu hui niangjia) (Gao, 2005). The story highlights love can transcend the formidable boundaries of nation, race, as well as social and political status. Simultaneously, Chinese-foreign love predominantly featured foreign nationals pursuing Chinese, as suggested by titles such as 'An American guy finds love in Anqing city' (Yiwei Meiguo xiaohuo zai Anqing de aiqing) (Li, 2007); 'Russian airhostess chases after Chinese man for thousands of miles' (Eguo kongjie wanly chizhui Zhongguo xiaohuo) ('Eguo kongjie', 2008), and 'British business man falls for migrant worker' (Ying'guo shangren aishang dagongmei) (Yang, 2008). In many of these accounts, traditional Chinese feminine attributes such as women being 'slim, small and tender' (jiaoxiao wenwan), 'gentle' (wenrou de), 'mild and virtuous' (xianliang shude) are celebrated and favoured by foreign men while masculine attributes such as being 'diligent' (qinfen de), 'reliable' (kekao de), 'considerate' (titie de), and 'caring for the family' (gujia de) are reported as culturally attractive to foreign women. Moreover, such cultural attractions in international love are reportedly connected with foreign nationals' 'love of China'. Specifically, their appreciation of Chinese culture, including food, poems, their commitment to learning Mandarin Chinese, and their vision of raising families and advancing personal professions in China thanks to the growing living standard and business opportunities in the country (Liang, 2002; Meng, 2001; Yu & Du, 2008). This also echoes the reversed migration pattern of foreign nationals traveling to China and the relocation of Chinese-foreign couples from overseas to China since the 2000s (Wang, 2015: 182). Moreover, a number of foreign spouses were Sinicized as 'foreign Chinese', demonstrated by their native-level Chinese-speaking capacity, 'Chinese' talents (knowledge about China and artistic Chinese skills), and their self-claimed Chinese identity ('Deguo yang xifu', 2009; 'Jianadaren', 2008; dir. Lu, Wang, & Liu, 2000).

The popular discourses of intercultural love during the 2000s further demonstrate love is a gendered and nationalized product, subject to political, social and economic changes.

50.5 Love 'in Crisis' (Late 2000s to the Present)

Love in China entered a stage of 'crisis' from the late 2000s to the present, evidenced by the rising number of single individuals struggling to find a partner, an increasing number of registered divorces nationwide, and tightened control over love in line with China's new political ideology. First, a substantial number of men and women of marriageable age are having difficulty finding a partner in China mainly due to the imbalanced gender ratio in the marriage market. This can be attributed to the One Child Policy launched in 1979, the cultural tradition of preference for a son in China and the availability of ultrasound and sex-selective abortion technologies from the 1980s. Since the birth planning policy, many families chose to have sons over daughters, and this subsequently resulted in an oversupply of males who were destined to be 'squeezed out' of the marriage market when they grew up. According to the statistics compiled by China's Population Census Office, the male to female ratio at birth has been around 120 males per 100 females since 2000 (Jiang, Yu, Yang, & Jesus, 2016). It is estimated that China can expect 30 million more men than women next year, and the figure may reach 50 million by 2030 (Gaetano, 2017: 125; Ji & Yeung, 2014: 1679). The situation is particularly dire in the countryside as a large number of rural men cannot find a wife, with many remaining single for their entire life. This is exacerbated by poverty, the surging 'bride price' and the inflow of rural women to the city in pursuit of employment opportunities. The oversupply of single males in rural China may potentially revive the abolished feudal practices such as 'arranged marriages', 'exchange marriages' and 'child/mercenary marriages'. It may also give rise to extramarital affairs, sexual crimes, and associated offences. Meanwhile, a number of single men in the countryside are looking for wives from outside China. This has triggered a growing black market of international bride trafficking in which young women are being smuggled to China from countries such as Burma, Thailand, Vietnam, Laos, Mongolia and North Korea (Fetterly, 2014). Either forced or on a voluntary basis, these women were transported to China via marriage brokers and individual traffickers, with some being forced into prostitution or illegal labour (Fetterly, 2014). It can be concluded that the 'love crisis' of rural Chinese men is not simply a gender issue but has evolved into an international complication.

In tandem with the 'love crisis' in rural China, a rising number of single men and women are looking for love in the city, however, without luck. Parents of these 'leftover' men and women have voluntarily organized love matchmaking corners (xiangqin jiao) in parks across various cities and provinces since the mid-2000s. The corners have become immensely popular since the late 2000s and attract hundreds of thousands of visitors, including parents, marriage seekers and tourists. In the matchmaking corners, parents exhibit advertisements of their children and exchange information with one another aiming to find a compatible son/daughter-in-law. A closer look at these advertisements shows that the majority of parents are looking for love for their daughters. Their daughters are mostly in their mid-20s to late 30s, have a good family background, and are well-educated and economically independent. While there are fewer parents advertising for sons, these parents receive most of their inquiries from those who have daughters. The common queries between parents include 'Which city do you come from?' 'Do you have a (local) Beijing Hukou (household registration)?' and 'Does he own an apartment (duli zhufang)?'.

The location of Hukou (birthplace registration) determines the types of social entitlements one receives from the state. For example, having a Hukou in first-tier cities like Beijing, Shanghai and Guangzhou means greater opportunities for education, employment, and easier access to property purchase, healthcare, as well as various types of social services. However, having a rural Hukou or Hukou from lower-tier cities means less access to the designated social resources, despite the government's recent effort to reform the system by expanding urban Hukou and residency permits to migrant workers to rebalance the economy (Sheehan, 2017). Such division is reflected and augmented at the matchmaking corners. For example, in Bejing, both the parents and their children who have a local Hukou are pursued the most. Parents who have a local Hukou but whose children do not are preferred less, and the least favoured are those where neither parents nor their children have a local Hukou . This validates the theory of 'assortative mating' in which people tend to choose partners with whom they share similar cultural and educational backgrounds (Spickard, 1989 ; Wang, 2017b: 90). However, in the matchmaking corners, 'assortative mating' is showcased by parents rather than their children, and similarities are primarily forged through Hukou rather than other factors.

To attract potential marriage candidates, parents who have sons commonly advertise their houses, cars and job professions (tied to level of income) when 'selling' their boys whereas parents who have daughters tend to brag about their youth and beauty, cooking skills and sometimes their profession. While the 'marketing strategies' adopted by parents differ based on traditional gender preference, they also intersect in terms of occupation as both men and women's economic independence are highly valued in the market economy. Most parents uphold the principle of 'matching doors and windows' (mendang hudui) and it's not unusual to see that such compatibility is manifested by social exchange (Blau, 1964; Thibaut & Kelley, 1959). That is parents are trying to maximize the social and economic benefits of themselves and their children while minimizing the potential costs during the matchmaking process. Single young adults are like commodities being promoted, compared, exchanged, and bargained by their parents in the marriage market.

Overall, love mediated by parents is grounded in pragmatism and fertilised by growing commercialism under the market economy. On the one hand, the matchmaking corners reveal the strong desire of Chinese parents to protect their children (most are the Only Child in the family) and their anxieties about their children's marriages caused by the One-Child Policy. On the other hand, it mirrors the enormous challenges faced by the younger generation, such as rising living costs,

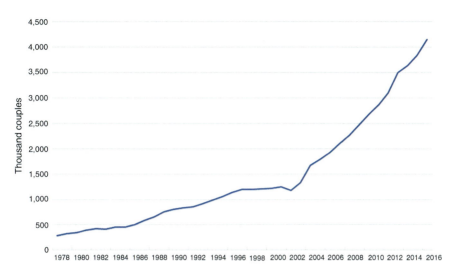

Fig. 50.2 Registered number of divorces in China (1979–2016). Source: MCA (2017). *Lihun dengji, Zhongguo minzheng tongji nianjian* [China Civil Affairs Statistical Yearbook] (p. 170). Wang based on the data released in the official yearbook by the PRC government

unaffordable housing prices, increased job competition, and the current inequalities attributed to the Hukou system.

The second type of 'love crisis' is evidenced by the rising number of divorces in China, particularly in cosmopolitan cities like Beijing, Shanghai, Shenzhen and Guangzhou (Jones, 2015; MCA, 1979–2010). Since the PRC government made 'breakdown in mutual affection' (ganqing polie) grounds for divorce in 1980 (NPC, 1980), the number of couples filing for divorces began to rise. Figure 50.2 outlines the trend of divorces registered in China from 1978 to 2016; it shows that the number of divorces grew steadily from 285,000 couples in 1978 to 982,000 couples in 1994. It exceeded one million in 1995, doubled to two million in 2007, before surging to 3.1 million in 2012 (MCA, 2017b: 170). It was from 2012 that the growth of the divorce rate accelerated and began to outpace that of the marriage rate (MCA, 2013). The divorce figure then maintained a strong momentum and reached nearly 4.2 million in 2016 (MCA, 2017b: 170), that is an increase of 14 times from 1978.

The reasons for the breakdown of marital unions are multifaceted, and most can be attributed to the growing incidences of deception, bigamy, domestic violence and extramarital affairs (Jones, 2015; Wang, 2015). These social problems are part and parcel of China's 'moral crisis (daode weiji)' that emerged from the late 1990s, when society began to witness rising materialism and egoism and declining social responsibility (Liu, 1999; Wang, 2002). This can be traced to the mismatch between the moral code propagated by the CCP and the prevailing social and economic realities in a growing capitalist market economy (Wang, 2002: 4). Meanwhile, the clarification of domestic violence as grounds for divorce in the 2001 Marriage Law and the simplification of divorce procedures in 2003 made divorce rules clearer and easier for the public and this subsequently facilitated the growing trend of divorces (MCA,

2003). Furthermore, inspired by western culture/ideas, Chinese people's perceptions toward marriage and divorce changed. Marriages are no longer perceived as a means for reproduction but rather the culmination of love and romance. Divorces and remarriages are increasingly de-stigmatised and accepted by the society. An increasing number of women have become divorce initiators, pursing new love post-marriage dissolution.

The third type of 'crisis' is censored love against the background of a tightened ideology. While the Chinese government is committed to building a nation that flags the freedom of love, it has simultaneously set up boundaries around such freedom. Specifically, individual love and intimacy must come second to the interests of the country at all times. This can be seen from the propaganda poster campaign called 'dangerous love' (weixian de aiqing) launched by the state in 2016. It constitutes China's National Security Education Day ('quanmin guojia anquan jiaoyuri') on 16 April 2016, and aims to promote the significance of China's national security among the public following the implementation of the new National Security Law of the PRC in 2015.

The poster consists of 16 comic pictures and narrates the love story between a female Chinese civil servant called 'Xiao Li' and a handsome foreign spy disguised as a visiting scholar named 'David'. The poster shows David met Xiao Li at a friend's gathering party and learnt she was working for the state publicity department. He then pursued her afterwards by sending flowers and expressing his affection to her, until Xiao Li was moved. While the couple was having a romantic walk, David found Xiao Li was working on the internal documents for the Central Government. He then persuaded her to lend him the documents for 'research' purposes. 'David' disappeared immediately after he obtained the documents from Xiao Li. As a result, both of them were arrested by China's national security officials for violating national laws. Sitting with handcuffs, Xiao Li burst into tears when she realised that she had been taken advantage of by her boyfriend 'David'. The poster ends with a policeman emphasizing the consequences and penalties for violating the criminal and counterespionage laws of the PRC (A.P., 2016).

The propaganda cartoons are problematic as it enmeshed national security with international intimacy. Love between Chinese citizens (especially state employees) and foreigners have become a political target subjects to state censorship and public scrutiny. This is in line with the government policy that precludes state personnel in charge of confidential work or 'state secrets' to date or marry foreigners (Article 4, MCA, 1983a). The poster thus reinforces the notion of national consciousness and mandates the people's political loyalty to the CCP. However, the dichotomous construction of innocent Chinese woman vis-à-vis evil foreign man is (unintentionally) tainted with 'anti-foreign sentiment' because foreigners are suspected of taking advantage of Chinese women and spying on China. It coincides with the romanticised and demonized images of foreign males in the PRC media coverage of international marriage (Wang, 2015). By putting foreigners and Chinese-foreign intimacy 'in the spotlight', these popular discourses serve to enhance China's national identity and evoke patriotism among the population. It also indicates that love for the nation can be portrayed through the construction of dangerous love.

50.6 Conclusion

In summary, the changing love landscape in China shows that love was freed from its feudalist constraints by the CCP in the earlier years, although it retained a strong communist imprint. It was subjugated to class struggle and was being mobilized as a catalyst for socialist revolution. The socialist institutions like Hukou and Danwei not only confined love within a divided space based on one's birthplace but also created new class divisions. Such divisions remain and have strong implications for mate selection in China today. Love went international with the advent of China's economic reform. However, the increasing number of Chinese women forming intimate relations with foreign men caused controversy and elicited nationalist sentiment. This was replaced by a romanticized discourse of Chinese-foreign love in the new era, when China regained economic vitality. Yet Chinese-foreign love became a target of censorship in the new revolutionary era due to the tightening political ideology and social control by the PRC government. While the free market provided ample opportunities for love, it simultaneously put love at risk. Love has become increasingly commercialised and being 'traded' for personal gain. True Love seekers are becoming lost in gendered demographics. Divorce is on the rise and appears to be increasing more rapidly than marriage due to growing materialism and the rising infidelity of couples. Love in China is entangled in a web of socialist politics, market economy and cultural globalisation, battling for an unknown future.

References

A.P. [Associated Press]. (2016, April 19). *China warns of foreign spies with "dangerous love" campaign*. https://www.foxnews.com/world/china-warns-of-foreign-spies-with-dangerous-love-campaign. Accessed 30 March 2019.

Blake, F. (1979). Love songs and the Great Leap: The role of a youth culture in the revolutionary phase of China's economic development. *American Ethnologist, 6*(1), 41–54.

Blau, P. M. (1964). *Exchange and power in social life*. New York: John Wiley.

Brady, A. -M. (2003). *Making the foreign serve China: Managing foreigners in the People's Republic*. Lanham, MD: Rowman and Littlefield.

Central Government of the PRC. (1950a, May 1). *Zhonghua renmin gongheguo hunyinfa [marriage law of the People's Republic of China]*. https://zhidao.baidu.com/question/3757923. Accessed 7 February 2019.

Central Government of the PRC. (1950b, April 14). *Guanyu Zhonghua renmin gongheguo hunyinfa qicao qingguo he qicao liyou de baogao* [Report on the drafting reasons and process of the marriage law of the PRC].

Chen, L.Y. (2003, June 11). *Hu shewai hunyin jiankang fazhan wanli yinyuan qianshou ge dazhou* [Shanghai–foreign marriage maintains healthy growth, love links all continents]. Renmin ribao.

Chen, W., & Ran, Q. Y. (2009). Goujian hexie de hunyin jiating guanxi [The construction of harmonious marriage and family relationship (sic.)]. *Hebei Law Science, 27*(8), 43–49.

Deguo yangxifu de Zhongguo shenghuo [The life of a German bride in China]. (2009, November 13). Jiating yanboshi, Shanghai Oriental TV, Shanghai.

Diamant, N. (2000). *Revolutionizing the family: Politics, love, and divorce in urban and rural China*. Berkeley, CA: University of California Press.

Ding, J. H., Yang, H. Y., Zhou, S. Y., Zhou, J. X., Lin, K. W., & Zhang, Y. Z. (2004). Lun xinshiqi Zhongguo shewai hunyin de tezheng yu zouxiang [Characteristics and trends of cross-nation marriage in modern Shanghai (sic)]. *Chinese Journal of Population Science, 3,* 66–80.

Eguo kongjie wanly chizhui Zhongguo xiaohuo [Russian airhostess chases after Chinese man for thousands of miles]. (2008, January 16) Wujin ribao.

Fang, N., Wang, B. Q., & Ma, L. J. (2002). *Chengzhang de Zhongguo [Growing China]*. Beijing: Renmin chubanshe.

Farrer, J. (2008). From "passports" to "joint ventures": Intermarriage between Chinese nationals and western expatriates residing in Shanghai. *Asian Studies Review, 32*(1), 7–29.

Fetterly, M. (2014, November 6). Sex trafficking and China's one child policy. https://thediplomat.com/2014/11/sex-trafficking-and-chinas-one-child-policy/. Accessed 20 March 2019.

Friedman, E., Pickowicz, P., & Selden, M. (2005). *Revolution, resistance, and reform in village China*. New Haven, CT: Yale University press.

Gaetano, A. (2017). China's 'leftover women': Myths and realities. In X. W. Zang & X. Zhao (Eds.), *Handbook on the family and marriage in China, UK and USA*. London: Edward Elgar.

Gao, Y. (2005, July 10). *Henan meizi jiagei Bolan zhunzongtong yidinghui daizhe zhangfu hui niangjia [Henan girl marries Polish presidential candidate, she will bring him to her native home]*. Dahe bao.

Gao, Y., Zhang, X. L., & Zhu, W. L. (2003). Beijing jinnian shewai hunyin zhuangkuang yanjiu [A study on cross-nation marriage of Beijing in recent years (sic.)]. *Population and Economics, 1*(196), 27–36.

Guan, H. Y., & Yang, H. (Dir.) (2006). *Yuanfen [Predestined love]*. CCTV-4, Beijing.

Guo M. R., & Zhou, Y. (1959). *Hongqi geyao [Song of the red flag]*. Red Flag Journal Press.

Honig, E. (2003). Socialist sex: The cultural revolution revisited. *Modern China, 29*(2), 143–175.

Hsia, H.-C. (2007). Imaged and imagined threat to the nation: The media construction of the foreign brides phenomenon' as social problems in Taiwan. *Inter-Asia Cultural Studies, 8*(1), 55–85.

Jeffreys, E., & Wang, P. (2013). The rise of Chinese-foreign marriage in mainland China, 1979-2010. *China Information, 27*(3), 347–369.

Jeffreys, E., & Yu, H. Q. (2015). *Sex in China*. Cambridge: Polity Press.

Ji, Y., & Yeung, W. J. J. (2014). Heterogeneity in contemporary Chinese marriage. *Journal of Family Issues, 35*(12), 1662–1682.

Jianadaren Dashan. (2008, July 10). *shi waiguoren que bushi wairen* [Canadian Da Shan—A foreign national but not an outsider]. Wenhui bao.

Jiang, H. S. (1999). Dui Zhong Han shewai hunyin ruogan wenti de tantao [Discussion on Chinese–Korean marriages]. *Journal of Yanbian University, 32*(3), 128–131.

Jiang, Q. B., Yu, Q., Yang, S. C., & Jesus, S. -B. (2016). Changes in sex ratio at birth in China: A decomposition by birth order. https://www.ncbi.nlm.nih.gov/pmc/articles/PMC5533650/. Accessed 17 March 2019.

Jones, P. (2015). What is causing China's divorce rate to skyrocket? https://gbtimes.com/what-causing-chinas-divorce-rate-skyrocket. Accessed 17 March 2019.

Kraus, C. (1981). *Class conflict in Chinese socialism*. New York: Columbia University Press.

Li, W. (Dir.) (2005). *Qingxi Xixili [Love in Sicily]*, television series, CCTV-8, Beijing.

Li, H. (2007, October 24). *Yiwei Meiguo xiaohuo zai Anqing de aiqing* [An American guy finds love in Anqing city]. Anqing ribao.

Li, J., & Long, Y. (2008). Zhong Yue bianjing kuaguo hunyin wenti yanjiu—yi Guangxi Daxin xian Aijiang cun weili [A Study of cross border marriage in the Sino-Vietnamese border regions: A case of Aijing village, Daxin county, Guangxi province (sic.)]. *South China Population, 23*(89), 34–41.

Liang, H. Y. (2002, July 1). *Shewai hunyin laofushaoqi xianxiang jianshao ['Old husband–young wife' phenomenon decreases in Chinese–foreign marriages]* (8th edn.). Wenhuibao.

Liu, Z. F. (Ed.). (1999). *Daode Zhongguo*. Beijing: Zhongguo shehui kexue chubanshe.

Liu, J (2007). The Danwei: Gender at work, gender and work in urban China: Women workers of the unlucky generation (pp. 41–86). London: Routledge.

Louie, K. (1989). *Between fact and fiction: Essays on Post-Mao Chinese literature & society.* Sydney: Wild Peony.

Louie, K. (2014). Chinese masculinity studies in the twenty-first century: Westernizing, easternizing and globalizaing wen and wu. *International Journal for Masculinity Studies, 9* (1), 18–29.

Lu, X. G., Wang, G., Liu, W. P., & Yang, J. N. (Dir.) (2000). Wailai xifu bendi lang [Local men and foreign brides], television series, Guangdong TV, Guangdong.

Luo, W. (2006). Heping yu jiaowang: Guangxi bianjing diqu kuaguo hunyin wenti chutan [Peace and communication: Exploration of transnational marriage in the frontiers of Guangxi province (sic.)]. *Journal of Guangxi Normal University: Philosophy and Social Sciences, 42*(1), 52–56.

MCA. (1979–2010). *Shewai hunyin dengji qingkuang, Zhongguo minzheng tongji nianjian* [China civil affairs statistical yearbook]. Zhongguo tongji chubanshe.

MCA. (1983a, August 26). *Zhongguo gongmin tong waiguoren banli jiehun dengji de jixiang guiding* [The provisions for the registration of marriage between Chinese citizens and foreigners]. http://www.gqb.gov.cn/node2/node3/node5/node9/node101/userobject7ai1288.html. Accessed 13 March 2019.

MCA. (1983b, March 10). *Huaqiao tong guonei gongmin, Gang Ao tongbao tong neidi gongmin zhijian banli jiehun dengji de jixiang guiding* [Rules on marriage registration between Chinese citizens and overseas Chinese and Hong Kong and Macau compatriots]. http://www.oklawyer.cn/fghy08.htm. Accessed 13 March 2019.

MCA. (1986, March 15). *Hunyin dengji banfa* [Marriage registration procedures].

MCA. (1993). 1953-55 nian quanguo jiehun, lihun qingkuang [Chinese marriages and divorces (1953-55)]. In R. S. Li (Ed.), *Minzheng tongji lishi ziliang huibian 1949-92 [Compilation of historical statistical data of civil affairs (1949–92)]* (p. 456). Zhongguo shehui chubanshe.

MCA. (1994, February 1). *Hunyin dengji guanli tiaoli* [The regulations on marriage registration]. http://www.people.com.cn/GB/shehui/212/3576/3577/3593/20020318/689673.html. Accessed 14 March 2019.

MCA. (2003, October 1). *Hunyin dengji tiaoli* [The regulation on administration of marriage registration] General Office of the State Council. http://www.gov.cn/banshi/2005-08/21/content_25042.htm. Accessed 14 March 2019.

MCA. (2013). *2012 nian shehui fuwu fazhan tongji gongbao* [2012 social services development statistical bulletin]. http://www.npc.gov.cn/npc/ztxw/tctjcxsbtxjs/2014-05/20/content_1863756.htm. Accessed 17 March 2019.

MCA. (2017a). *Jiehun dengji, Zhongguo minzheng tongji nianjian* [China civil affairs statistical yearbook] (pp. 168–169). Zhongguo tongji chubanshe.

MCA. (2017b). *Lihun dengji, Zhongguo minzheng tongji nianjian* [China Civil Affairs Statistical Yearbook] (p.170). Zhongguo tongji chubanshe

Meng, X. (2001, February 6). *Yang xifu, yang nüxu: Zhongguo ren kuaguo hunyin yipie* [Foreign sons and daughters-in-law: A glimpse of Chinese–foreign marriages]. Renmin ribao.

MPS [Ministry of Public Security], PRC. (2013). *"1978–2012 nian rujing lüyou renshu" [annual visitor arrivals 1978–2012], Zhongguo lüyou tongji nianjian [China tourism statistical yearbook].* Beijing: Zhongugo lüyou chubanshe.

NPC [National People's Congress]. (1980, September 10). *Zhonghua renmin gongheguo hunyinfa* [Marriage law of the People's Republic of China].

NPC [National People's Congress]. (2001, April 28). *Zhonghua renmin gongheguo hunyinfa* [Marriage law of the People's Republic of China].

Parish, L., & Whyte, M. (1978). *Village and family in contemporary China.* Chicago: University of Chicago.

SCNPC [Standing Committee of the National People's Congress]. (1986a, February 1). *Zhonghua renmin gongheguo gongmin chujing rujing guanli fa* [Law of the People's Republic of China on the control of the entry and exit of citizens]. http://www.china.org.cn/english/travel/40340.htm. Accessed 14 March 2019.

SCNPC. (1986b, February 1). *Zhonghua renmin gongheguo waiguoren rujing chujing guanli fa* [Law of the People's Republic of China on the control of the entry and exit of aliens]. http://www.china.org.cn/english/travel/40340.htm. Accessed 14 March 2019.

Shanghai shewai hunyin danhua gongli secai [Utilitarianism fades in intercultural marriage in Shanghai]. (2002, November 29). Liaoning ribao.

Sheehan, S. (2017, February 22). China's Hukou reforms and the urbanization challenge. https://thediplomat.com/2017/02/chinas-hukou-reforms-and-the-urbanization-challenge/. Accessed 24 March 2019.

Shih, S. M. (1998). Gender and new geopolitics of desire: The seduction of Mainland women in Taiwan and Hong Kong media. *Signs, 23*(2), 287–319.

Song, G. (2010). Chinese masculinities revisited: Male images in contemporary television drama serials. *Modern China, 36*(4), 404–434.

Spickard, R. (1989). *Mixed blood: Intermarriage and mixed identity in twentieth-century America*. Madison, WI: University of Wisconsin Press.

Tang, Y. (1995). *Meiguo laide qizi [wife from America]*. Shanghai: Shanghai yuandong chubanshe.

Thibaut, J. W., & Kelley, H. H. (1959). *The social psychology of groups*. New York: Wiley.

Tsai, M.-C. (2011). "Foreign brides" meet ethnic politics in Taiwan. *International Migration Review, 45*(2), 243–268.

Wang, X. Y. (2002). The Post-communist personality: The spectre of China's capitalist market reforms. *The China Journal, 47*, 1–17.

Wang, W. H. (2014, May 4). *Liu Shaoqi yu Xin Zhongguo diyibu Hunyinfa* [Liu Shaoqi and China's first marriage law]. http://dangshi.people.cn/n/2014/0504/c384616-24971680.html. Accessed 7 February 2019.

Wang, P. (2015). *Love and marriage in globalizing China*. Abingdon: Routledge.

Wang, P. (2017a). Inventing traditions: Television dating shows in the People's Republic of China. *Media, Culture and Society, 39*(4), 504–519.

Wang, P. (2017b). Foreign-related marriages in contemporary China, 1979-2013. In X. W. Zang & X. Zhao (Eds.), *Handbook on the family and marriage in China* (pp. 89–107). London: Edward Elgar.

Whyte, K. M. (1995). From arranged marriages to love matches in urban China. In C.-C. Yi (Ed.), *Family formation and dissolution: Perspectives from East and West* (Sun Yat-Sen Institute for Social Sciences and Philosophy, Book Series 36) (pp. 33–83). Taipei: Academia Sinica.

Wolf, M. (1974). Chinese women: Old skills in a new context. In M. Rosaldo & L. Lamphere (Eds.), *Woman, culture and society* (pp. 157–172). Stanford, CA: Stanford University Press.

Xin, K., & Ye, X. C. (2008, January 10). *Meishan xin'niang Meiguolang shangyan Zhongguoshi jiehun* [Meishan woman and American man stage Chinese–style wedding]. Sichuan Meishan ribao.

Yang, Y. (2008, June 1). *Guge "yi" chu yiduan kuaguo lianqing* [Google 'translates' cross-cultural love]. Jinri zaobao.

Yao, L. H. (2010). *Zhishi qingnian shangshan xiaxiang yundong jianshi* [A brief history of down to the countryside movement]. http://www.people.com.cn/GB/198221/198819/204159/12909768.html. Accessed 30 April 2019.

Yu, X. Y., & Du, Z. F. (2008, December 20). *Qingdao yinian 360 li shewai hunyin waiguoren cheng zai Qing hen shufu* [Qingdao registers 360 Chinese–foreign marriages each year, foreigners enjoy living in Qingdao]. Qingdao chenbao.

Zeng, L. Z., & Piao, L. Z. (2002). *Modeng Jiating* [Modern family]. Television series, CCTV-8, Beijing.

Zhang, W. G. (2013). Class categories and marriage patterns in rural China in the Mao era. *Modern China, 39*(4), 438–471.

Zhao, D. X. (1996). Foreign study as a safety-valve: The experience of China's university students going abroad in the eighties. *Higher Education, 31*(145), 145–163.

Zhao, Y. Q., & Ding, J. H. (2015). Jiqing chongbai yu guojia jieru: 1930-70niandai Zhongguo chengxiang tonghunshi kaocha [Passion, adoration and the involvement of the state: An investigation of the history of rural-urban marriages from 1930 to 1970]. *Journal of East China Normal University, 5*, 94–100.

Pan Wang (Prof. Dr.) is Senior Lecturer in Chinese and Asian Studies, University of New South Wales. She is the author of Love and Marriage in Globalizing China (Abingdon: Routledge 2015). Recent publications include: (2020) International romance: changing discourses of Chinese-foreign intimacy in the decades of economic reforms, Love Stories in China, in Sun W.N. and Yang L. (eds), Routledge; (2018) Foreign-related marriages in contemporary China (1979–2013), Handbook of the Family and Marriage in China, in Zang X.W. (ed.), Edward Elgar; (2018) Pathways to legalizing same-sex marriage in China and Taiwan: globalization and 'Chinese' values (with Elaine Jeffreys), in B. Winter et al. (eds), Global Perspectives on Same-Sex Marriage: A Neo-Institutional Approach, Cham: Palgrave Macmillan; and (2016) 'Inventing Traditions: Television Dating Shows in the People's Republic of China', Media, Culture and Society, 39 (4): 504–19.

Chapter 51
Sustaining Love and Building Bicultural Marriages Between Japanese and Americans in Japan

Clifford H. Clarke and Naomi Takashiro

Abstract The purpose of this chapter is to review the key issues and reveal the cultural assumptions underlying the issues and intercultural competencies for building sustaining loving relationships between Americans and Japanese in bicultural marriages. Transforming bicultural misunderstandings into trusting relationships in bicultural relationships is the ultimate goal of the authors. There is power in empathy, in building shared goals, in a mutual appreciation for diversity, and in continual efforts toward resolving misunderstandings through utilizing intercultural competencies. Cultural interpretations and intercultural competencies applied to the issues most commonly identified in bicultural marriages can be utilized to strengthen and sustain loving relationships between Japanese and Americans. Educators, counselors, friends, and families who strive to support struggling partners in bicultural marriages may find these thoughts and practices applicable.

Keywords Handbook of Love · Japanese bicultural marriages · Love marriages in Japan · Intercultural communication competency · Bicultural counseling and coaching

51.1 Introduction

The latest statistics from 2016 indicate that of 21,180 intercultural marriages, 1309 were between Japanese and Americans, 19.4% of those were American wives and 80.6% were American husbands, which is nearly four times more men than women who married Japanese. The year-by-year data in 2016 showed that new

---

C. H. Clarke (✉)
School of Communications, University of Hawaii at Manoa, Honolulu, Hawaii
e-mail: chclarke@me.com; cclarke@hawaii.edu

N. Takashiro
Department of Global Tourism, Kyoto University of Foreign Studies, Kyoto, Japan
e-mail: takashiron@mac.com

U.S. wives increased by 27% and new U.S. husbands decreased by 6.2% compared to the previous year (Ministry of Health, Labor and Welfare, 2018).

51.1.1 Background

Based on Clarke's fifty years of counseling and coaching bicultural couples in the U.S. and Japan, American and Japanese marriages in Japan are challenged by intercultural conflicts. The purpose of this chapter is to analyze intercultural interaction issues within Japanese–U.S. bicultural marriages in order to clarify some conflicting perceptions, communication styles, and their underlying cultural values that provide the gist for the hard work of constructing satisfying bicultural marriages. Differences in expectations and outcomes for U.S.–Japan couples involved in bicultural marriages depend upon the societal contexts, changing marriage gender roles, legal regulations, changing workforce norms, religious practices, language usage, and the culture's slow movement from interdependency to independency vis-à-vis self-identities and cultural norms. Each imposes limitations upon a bicultural couple's interactions.

Adjusting to the bicultural marriage in a context in which one is a member is quite a different matter from adjusting in a cultural context in which one is not a member and is judged by others to be a foreigner. From the literature it is abundantly clear that the challenges of the adjustment of Japanese wives living with American husbands in the U.S. presents a culturally different set of challenges than those made upon American spouses of Japanese living in Japan (Forgash, 2009; Hayashi, 2019; Okada, 2011, Ono & Berg, 2010).

Therefore, bicultural marriages are best analyzed within their contexts because location, position, time, persons, and occasion heavily influence Japanese interactions. *Basho* or, *toki* or, *hito ni otte* is used by Japanese managers to help American managers in Japan understand contextual conditionality. It shows the dependency on the place, *basho*, the time, *toki,* and the person, *hito,* being right for the occasion (Nitschke, 2018; Nonaka & Konno, 1998). Japanese interpersonal interactions are highly context-based or even context-determined as Hall (1981) suggested.

51.1.2 Cultures Affect Bicultural Marriages

As anthropologists have not been able to agree on a definition of culture for decades (Spencer-Oatey 2012), Clarke's own compilation from many sources has evolved into the following practical definition: Culture is the assumptions, beliefs, values, attitudes, perceptions, and behaviors shared and practiced as norms by a particular group of people distinguished by those characteristics. Cultures are traditionally associated with nations, ethnicities, religions, gender and age groups, language groups, and socioeconomic status groups. Subcultures exist within families, schools, clubs, companies, and physically or mentally challenged groups among others. Each of these environments influences the thinking, feeling, and action of each individual in diverse ways we recognize as culture, which shapes our identity, our view of the world, and our intercultural interactions. These elements of our cultures are sustaining throughout life, yet are also in constant change through continual exposure to differences in others. Those differences create challenges that require adapting to others in various contexts, particularly in the intimacy of bicultural marriages. The extent to which individuals share these influences is the extent to which they share a culture. To the extent that couples do not share these ways of thinking, feeling, and acting they interact with intercultural communications, which is the interpersonal interaction between persons of dissimilar cultures. Most people pay little attention to, or are unaware of, how cultures have influenced them. Many people feel uncomfortable asking another person questions about his/her culture. Awareness of how our cultural identity and experiences bias our perceptions can be the first step in expanding our viewpoints and becoming more effective intercultural communicators.

51.1.3 Model of Intercultural Interactions

In the course of analyzing the communication issues under study we applied a model for understanding the components of our search for meaning in interpersonal dialogue from Barnlund (1976). This model can be applied to dialogue between Japanese and Americans to highlight the differences in thinking, feeling, and acting in dialogue. The model suggests that interpersonal meaning (IpM) is a function of perception orientations (PO), a system of values (SV) underlying those perceptions, and communication styles that reflect them (CS). The course of intercultural interactions is determined by these three factors that are all influenced by one's cultural experiences and identity. This model can be represented by the formula: *IpM=f (PO + SV + CS)* and can guide our integrated analysis of intercultural interactions. These three elements of intercultural meanings as formed from childhood onward are shared within cultures.

51.2 Method

51.2.1 Analysis

We employed an autoethnographic method of analysis that is relatively new to researchers and perhaps needs some clarification as a relatively new approach. Proponents of the method define autoethnography as a qualitative method that uses the researcher's autobiographical experiences as primary data to analyze and interpret sociocultural and social-psychological meanings of experiences (Chang,

2016, p. 444). To clarify, in the word, autoethnographic, 'auto' refers to describing and interpreting, 'graphy' are the cultural texts, experiences, beliefs, and practices, and 'ethno' (Adams, Ellis, & Holman Jones, 2017).

We chose this autoethnographic method to account for personal experiences that complement, or fill gaps in, existing research. The use of everyday personal experience permits descriptions and interpretations of the ways in which communicators make mistakes, errors, and failures in bicultural marriages. In this autobiographic method we relied upon our memory to reflect on past personal experiences and earlier interviews and focus groups with other bicultural couples about their experiences, thoughts, and feelings. We found that we shared the understandings that many other bicultural couples in Japan have, i.e. issues that focused not on external factors but rather on the interpersonal communication issues wherein shared meaning is hard to find and communication mistakes, errors, and failures arise. These summaries were what we wrote as our key issues. Then we searched the research literature for more information about these experiences with which to explain our issues. We wrote about these issues using the storytelling method Hawaiians call Talk Story, and used Japanese kotowaza or sayings and proverbs to represent sources of the cultural values or explain cultural perceptions and communication styles in order to create in readers "a sense of how being there in the experience feels" and how others approach the challenges they face daily (Adams et al., 2017).

Clarke began analyzing and interpreting the cultural differences of perceptions, values, and behavioral causes and consequences of these broken interactions with others who lived in bicultural marriages. With a the actual dialogical interactions between bicultural couples he explored the images, assumptions, expectations, and judgments held between such partners. Thus, intercultural interaction analysis became the approach of this study within the context of American–Japanese bicultural marriages in Japan.

In order to clarify what the authors' bring to this task from their personal experiences, an explanation of their backgrounds, training, and professional experiences related to the subject of sustaining love in American Japanese bicultural marriages in Japan is required.

51.2.2 Subjects Other than Ourselves

The actual intercultural interactions and events between bicultural American and Japanese partners dealing with multiple communication issues were recalled from memory of interviews, counseling, and group discussions largely with two groups. Some were alumni of JET (Japan Exchange and Teaching Program) and alumni of academic exchange programs in Japan, who married a Japanese and remained in Japan. The others were consultants, business or U.S. government workers who married Japanese women and remained in Japan. The members of these two groups of Japanese and Americans have taught us about the issues that challenge bicultural marriages in Japan through minimally structured interviews, focus groups, and ongoing interactions over the past 40 years. These couples were in their late 20s through their 50s and were 27 in number.

51.2.3 The Authors' Backgrounds

Cliff's (the first author) background has been split between Japan and the United States starting with all formative childhood years in Japan. He was stoned at the age of ten by a neighborhood gang of boys and ever since has been studying Japanese–American human relationships. His academic training in Japanese religions, philosophies, anthropology and psychology have given him insight to the origins of the values and perceptions of Japanese and Americans. His academic training and 12 years in intercultural counseling at Stanford and Cornell Universities has informed him of the challenges of bicultural relationships and bicultural identities. His 13 years of teaching in multicultural classrooms has taught him about different culturally influenced learning and teaching styles. His academic training and 30 years of researching and consulting American and Japanese managers in over 300 global bicultural organizations with Clarke Consulting Group has enabled him to understand the struggles between individual and organizational goals and norms of behavior Clarke & Hammer, 1995; Clarke & Lipp, 1998). But, his 20-year immersion into a bicultural marriage with a Japanese woman has been the most personally challenging and rewarding simultaneously.

The second author, Naomi, was born and raised in Japan through university and studied for her master's in intercultural communication and her doctorate in educational psychology. After working in the tourism industry for 13 years and teaching for 5 years in Hawai'i, she currently teaches Japanese university students in Japan and publishes research articles. She contributed to this work from her deep cultural insight and research skills.

51.3 Results of Key Issues

The results are the most salient five intercultural communication style issues that reflected hidden assumptions, expectations, and values that were found to be conflicting in bicultural marriages.

51.3.1 Listening and Accepting

There are many barriers to couples listening to each other that can be avoided but a perpetual other-mindfulness can cause stress. It is difficult to be sure when the other is 'speaking to one's self', especially if there is some physical distance in the home between the two. Another is being unfamiliar with each other's paralinguistic expressions or utterances, which are habits hard to change. Another has to do with lack of clarity if a question was asked or perhaps there were sounds of water running that interfered with hearing the other. Perhaps the volume of speech was too soft or too loud and the other was frightened or really didn't hear. Sometimes an expression in either language was incomplete or incorrect grammar delayed one's response. Often it is the speech that allows for no interruption, or even for one to pause long enough for the other to think through a desired response that causes problems.

In bicultural small group workshop interactions Japanese required 30% more time for pauses than Americans in order to take a turn without feeling interruptive (Clarke & Kanatani, 1979). Incessant talking, extra long pauses, the absence of questions that focus the intended respondent, the use of too many pronouns without reference to the specific subject, and so many other perceived intercultural idiosyncrasies can cause misperceptions of intentions that result in broken communications, including when intended observations are taken as judgments and defenses rise suddenly without expectation. Japanese practice *aizuchi* which is interactive listening frequently uncomfortable particularly to U.S. men who need no other's support for continuing their speech. Japanese enjoy very frequent confirmations of enthusiastic listeners without it being interruptive. These *aizuchi* are very short utterances, some of which are paralinguistic or phatic expressions.

For Japanese, *ishin denshin* is an idiom for understanding another through unspoken mutual sensitivity—'what the mind thinks, the heart transmits'. Such an assumption inherent in the practice of *sasshi* or a noun can be defined as conjecture, surmise, or guessing what one means (Miike, 2003). *Sasshi* is predicated by the act of hesitation—*enryo*—during which time *sasshi* is sought, perceived, and felt. From *sasshi*, the verb form *sassuru* expands the meaning to include imagining, supposing, empathizing with, and making allowances for others (Miike, 2003). This ability is something that takes years, if not decades, to develop between U.S. married spouses. The Japanese have been trained in it since birth and find it unnatural in its absence interculturally.

The *ichi o kiite ju o shiru* or 'hear one, understand ten' *kotowaza* frequently causes misperceptions across cultures where an American 'means what he or she says'—'just listen to my words!' or the famous statement 'read my lips'. Too often for bicultural couples the Japanese partner expects too much from the American whose skill of reading between the lines is under developed by comparison. For Japanese it is a natural skill that helps to avoid conflict when opinions or feelings are expressed too directly and strongly. In such a case, how would it be possible to offer an alternative perspective once the other has expressed such a position with such forcefulness if one's goal was to avoid confrontation? Through the mutuality of indirect expressions, a couple gradually comes to a shared understanding...which may take some time. *Ishi no ue ni mo sannen* or 'sitting on a stone for as long as 3 years' as a Japanese kotowaza expresses the value of perseverance. Patience or *nintai* is a personal characteristic in both cultures but in Japanese the concept includes fortitude, perseverance, and stoicism on occasion.

A long-term U.S. male professor complained often of his Japanese partner never having an opinion of her own, even about where to take a weekend trip or what to eat. The American wanted her honest feeling regardless of potentially having her opinion overruled. Having "no opinion" created comfort in the Japanese woman but not in the U.S. man. It may limit the scope and depth of the bicultural marriage relationship. The man did not value *awaseru*, to adjust, adapt, or match, as did the woman because without 'the truth' how could he know that he was pleasing her? She on the other hand was practicing *enryo*, hesitation, in order to let him choose. Whatever his decision, she was sure that she was happier to *awasu*, to adjust, to his preferences and would easily *gaman*, endure, the consequences. The Japanese wife chose *enryo*, hesitation, and *awasu*, to adapt, to allow him to express his wishes. The husband chose to act in a way that could have conveyed what she may have perceived as *ki ga tsuyoi*, strong mindedness, and *jikoshuchō*, self-assertiveness, not characteristics admired in Japan.

The art of *nemawashi* or 'root binding' that is necessary before transplanting, plays an important role as a distinctly Japanese communication processes wherein each member listens to the other patiently in order to reach a shared understanding and construct a mutually satisfying resolution of issues together rather than entering into a debate mode to convince the other of one's perspective (Fetters, 1995; Kopp, 2019b). As in everything Japanese, successful *nemawashi* depends on the time, the place, and the occasion (TPO), and it also depends on patience and listening to the words and the simultaneous nonverbal communication with appreciation.

Differences across these two cultures due to assumptions about integrity, honesty, persuasion, and adjustment too often result in dissatisfaction within the marriage. However, just deeper understanding is inadequate without changing attitudes, accepting the conflicting values, and experimenting with new behaviors. There are two social paths by which to display integrity. One is by being honest; the other is by being harmonious. In Japan, the predominance of *tatemae,* public speech, rather than *honne,* private speech, in the language enables the construction of greater harmony in large part due to *enryo*, hesitation, *and nintai,* patience. One *kotowaza* shows the necessity in Japan of what Americans call lying; *Uso mo hoben*, similarly, 'a white lie is a necessary evil' teaches us that sometimes lying is expedient in order to save face and build harmony. The professor's wife did have opinions. She was just missing adequate listening, patience, and appreciation from her partner.

51.3.2 Complaining and Complimenting

These are used in each culture in different ways and evoke different psychological emotions of 'get off my back' or 'give me a break!' and *oseji,* flattery or compliment. As *oseji* is primarily flattery, compliments from Americans can be perceived as insincere. Or, perhaps the one receiving it wants to convey humility by saying that the compliment is only *oseji*. The ambiguity is intentional allowing the receiver to attempt 'reading' its true intention. It also allows the recipient to conceal the pride that would belie one's humility. Nomura and Barnlund (1983) found that the American is more likely to express compliments and the Japanese more likely to express complaints. Therefore, in a bicultural marriage it appears that offering compliments creates a good deal of mistaken perceptions and an array of interpretations that must confuse both.

The same could be said for complaints because they often conceal true feelings about somehow being wronged or attacked or disrespected in a relationship. An American husband often perceives a complaint by his Japanese wife as an expression of considerable displeasure, which results in his wondering what her true feelings are. He may get lost in his own feelings of being somehow wronged or attacked or disrespected in the relationship. Such an issue suggests that exploring each other's feelings might aid a couple in furthering their understanding and acceptance of the other. The alternatives are for each to stew in the bowl of confusion and painful disengagement, if not mutual anger and a lack of forgiving that comes from holding a grudge. However, the need for communication processes to resolve this issue through open, patient, and non-judgmental dialogue often is not bicultural in that it clashes with the Japanese culture that does not appreciate so much interpersonal analytical processes in oral communication. Role flexibility and face-saving respectively function for or against such processing.

The cultural norms regarding the scope and depth of comfortable communication in Japan and the U.S. (Asai & Barnlund, 1998; Barnlund, 1975, 1989) come into play with unwritten rules in both cultures regarding dialogue. In American intracultural dialogue the findings were that there was greater scope of discussants and depth of disclosure in the subjects chosen, but the subjects chosen were similar across cultures. Hence, discussion of these kinds of differences as they apply within a bicultural marriage can become the cause for confrontations and judgments that stop the discussion. Self-revelation that goes too deeply into self-analysis is not a comfortable objective, much less a process that is welcomed by members of either culture, perhaps less so in Japan than in the U.S.

However, in bicultural marriages some negotiation of level of comfort for such discussions would be necessary in order to reveal the assumptions that could cause significant confrontations in which partners initiate blaming the other for violations of privacy or worse. Once the blame game starts, it may become increasingly disastrous for the longevity of the relationship. There is no need to create such pain if it can be avoided by finding a better time or place to engage at deeper levels of dialogue with the shared norms of being non-judgmental. In bicultural marriages complaining and complimenting are usually both given without knowledge of the standards each other holds. Without shared standards such judgments are only words that are left to each other's interpretation. In order to build trust it is necessary to create commonly agreed upon standards, which give more significance to any intercultural judgment. With trust, both complaints and compliments can contribute to greater understanding and interdependency. Trust can help soften the suspicion of words implied in the *kotowaza*, 'honey in the mouth, a sword in the belly'.

51.3.3 Apologizing and Forgiving

Rather than holding a grudge after conflicts apologizing and forgiving may be influenced by the cultural norms and possibly the religious backgrounds of each culture in the case of forgiving. Bicultural couples spend a lot of time apologizing but less time forgiving of perceived errors because of misinterpreted intentions. Apologies also differ in meaning, context, and follow-up (Barnlund & Yoshioka, 1990; Kopp, 2019a). The *kotowaza, shitashiki naka ni mo reigi ari*, applies here. In English that is, 'There are formalities between the closest of friends.' A culture that nourishes public speech that maintains harmony would naturally depend heavily upon formality. This key value regarding allegiance to forms for behavior in public transactions is most enthusiastically supported if not generated by the government that is ultimately responsible for harmony as well as the Buddhist and Shinto religions.

Apologies are offered freely amongst Japanese for many and various violations, such as driving errors that cause traffic accidents. But they must be offered very sincerely and show reflection upon how such a mistake can be and will be avoided in the future, an act of *hansei* (Barnlund & Yoshioka, 1990; Kopp, 2019a). In bicultural couples each commit *faux pas* in each other's worldview daily, given all of the form, *kata*, consciousness in the society. Since American husbands in Japan commit most of these violations of *kata* it is essential that they understand the value of speed and sincerity in the act of apologizing. In the home it is beneficial to make a list so as to learn the *kata* of a partner and follow them. Compromising the *kata* may be acceptable in liberal societies but not in one that adheres en masse to the unwritten rules of Japan.

The home is the Japanese woman's kingdom where she makes the rules and they must be followed to bring happiness in the relationship. But, if one makes an honest mistake, evidence suggests that the U.S. husband apologize immediately. If an apology is delayed it is not received as a sincere act. If it is conveyed as a routine, it is not received as a sincere act. And, if there is not some act to follow that demonstrates that *hansei* was considered and demonstrated by evidence of a change in behavior, it is not received as a sincere act. Hence, only by *hansei,* acknowledgement of one's own mistake and pledging or showing improvement, one can apologize sincerely and respectfully (Kopp, 2019a). *Majime* (seriousness, diligence, earnestness) is an attitude that must be conveyed through an apology so it is nothing to joke about. Humor will not solve many problems so one must express sincere humility to convey an effective apology. Apologies show that a partner accepts responsibility and avoids blaming the other. With this skill set of earnestly apologizing and *hansei*, many Japanese will be forgiving even if they do not express it. It will be demonstrated in other behaviors rather than in words.

Couples could learn from discussing their respective feelings and thoughts about apologies, because it would benefit their relationship. Even if his wife develops a degree of flexibility in the home for the health of the bicultural marriage, she will very reluctantly violate Japanese public *kata* (unless she's bursting with anger at a *kata* that she feels is ridiculous, which is a feeling shared by some Japanese who have lived abroad for a number of years) but in her home she more likely feels that it is her right to set the *kata* and for him to follow it. Trying to make this a negotiation for 'home rules' is an effort that has reaped little benefit in Japan's bicultural marriages due to the context and communication style differences.

Forgiveness, on the other hand, has room for intercultural discussion around the meaning it has in each of our cultures. The term *yurushi,* forgiveness, actually means to pardon, exempt or release one, which may imply the sense of responsibility that the partner has for the violation of *kata* has been accepted. It is an act that benefits both parties concerned in that there is enough ambiguity in the term to perceive that the one who offers forgiveness is thereby including one's self in the event and is able to exercise that responsibility to express kindness toward the other regardless of the mistaken behavior. This would make her forgiveness similar to an apology of the driver who apologizes for 'being involved' in the accident thereby forgiveness can mean an apology for the event that occurred. After all the heat cools down, the virtue in Japan is *majime,* seriousness, and not the act of blaming. Ironically, in the American culture that grew out of Christianity, the gift of forgiveness generated from God and as such a marriage partner has the opportunity of offering forgiveness as a blessing that is shared with others genuinely and sincerely. It is actually very similar to the Japanese act of kindness in releasing another from feelings of shame or guilt, whichever one prefers to label the feeling. The difference is whether the inspiration of forgiveness comes from family or society or is divinely given from God. Both acts seem to heal the violator and accept the violator back into the home (church) or one's *uchi.*

51.3.4 Laughing and Seriousness

The role of humor in Japan and the U.S. is different. Private time and shared time in the home is also considered differently. Humor could either increase or reduce stress depending on its nature and style, i.e. sarcasm (utilized in U.S. male relationships) and satire (used extensively in the U.S. late night TV shows) are not as appreciated in Japan where word play results in more laughter. Both *rakugo*, where one person plays two in dialogue, and *manzai*, with two persons where one is the fall guy similar to the Three Stooges in the U.S., are both enjoyed with lots of laughter. Intercultural humor is risky behavior but with proper adaptations it can be effective for *funikizukuri* or setting a proper atmosphere for more open or unreserved communications, which can be in a different location, *basho*, hence the importance on the *basho* being right for different kinds of occasions. Humor about others not present can be shared but not at the expense of each other. Each couple has to find their own way to bringing humor into their lives. This is highly valued by Japanese women in Japan who chose 'fun to be with' as the top characteristic of their ideal husband. That includes sharing in humor. Those marriages in which humor is not present tend to be excessively serious and create tensions in the relationship. Another applicable cultural distinction is found in the differences between American relative spontaneity and Japanese relative seriousness. Japanese often think before they speak, especially in expressing humor. Japanese value humility, *kenson,* and seriousness, *majime,* by usually considering the perceived consequences before speaking.

Reflecting may be evident in hesitation, *enryo,* and public speech—*tatemae,* in Japan is present in any newly developing relationship, including a marriage. The challenge once married when communication slowly turns to more direct communication—*honne,* is to enjoy the humor in life as frequently and as naturally as possible to prevent the stresses of life from overwhelm the relationship. The partners who do not hesitate to share humorous moments in laughter and share their cultural interpretation of why something is so humorous bring joy to their relationship. If successful, they may be surprised at the positive receptivity. Imagine the big smile on your partner's face when she or he says to you, 'You're the funniest person I've ever known.' If the jokes are not clear, laugh with your eyes, and express real curiosity about the joke's intent. Think of the *kotowaza, me wa kuchi hodo ni mono o yuu,* 'the eyes speak as much as the mouth'.

According to Takeo Doi in a lecture at Stanford University some time ago, the U.S. and Japan differ in that 75% of communication in America is oral and 25% is non-verbal communication whereas in Japan it is the exact opposite. This reliance on non-verbal communication in Japan is confirmed in the ancient *kotowaza* about not trusting words, 'honey in the mouth, a sword in the belly'. The American in Japan will benefit by paying more attention to nonverbal communication while reading between the lines of the oral communication. The goal in the U.S. for speaking English is to decipher and distinguish every word articulated with its unique meaning so as to present the truth and attempt to persuade the listener to agree with one's own perspective. An assumption of independence is that one is ultimately alone and is constantly reaching out to connect our thoughts and feelings with others seeking companionship. One wants the unknown to become known. In contrast, many Japanese prefer their true feelings to remain hidden so as not to offend or lose face, which explains the *tatemae,* public expression, and *enryo,* hesitation.

In Japan the Japanese language enables maintenance of a degree of ambiguity that creates an escape route, *nigemichi,* in order to avoid direct confrontation of contrary opinions or feelings and protect everyone's face in ways that maintain harmony. This is why there are 16 ways of saying 'no' (Imai, 1981) and more than a half dozen ways of avoiding a conflict within a relationship. The assumption that informs this interdependent hesitancy to confront is that individuals are known and accepted already within an *uchi* (one's group or home) and therefore must rely on *ishin denshin,* 'what the mind thinks, the heart will transmit'. But, can we read between the lines across cultures? In time, it is possible. Thoughts are revealed through nonverbal communication, nuance and indirectness, hesitation, and even silence, which are all laden with meaning. In a bicultural marriage this communication style creates a great deal of stress and confusion in both partners when communication styles are not in sync. Intercultural couples from different countries exhibit greater internal stress than do intracultural partners in the same country (Holzapfel, Randall, Tao, & Iida, 2018).

Demonstrations of stress are evident when tempers start to flare as communication breaks down. Accusations of ineptitude are may be made against each other. Another *kotowaza* reveals what both partners must remember in the moment: *Tanki wa sonki,* 'short temper causes loss', conveys the value of patience. Patience, *nintai,* is a virtue in both cultures and is a primary resource to rely upon in times of stress rather than spontaneously igniting into rapid-fire blaming and shaming efforts to establish superiority or to protect face. Since Japanese require 30% more pause time between taking turns (Clarke & Kanatani, 1979), Americans seem to do most of the talking because they run out of patience before the Japanese. Several bicultural foreign companies in Japan actually measured this and found that in management meetings Americans did 80% of the taking despite being there in equal numbers to the Japanese. In such serious times between bicultural couples some silence may be useful and later, a dose of humor or happiness that can be shared from past experiences together would help to restore peace. Best would be an apology that would be helpful to convey humility, i.e. *saru mo ki kara ochiru,* meaning 'even masters make mistakes' and perhaps we are the monkeys in situations of intercultural conflict (Galef & Hashimoto, 1987).

51.3.5 Trusting and Reciprocating

The nature of trust (loyalty, cooperation) and love may be differently defined in ways that are initially incompatible within bicultural relationships. Trust can be a product of *wa,* harmony, in which the *amae,* dependence, fostered in teamwork prevails as an agent in building and sustaining harmony (Dalsky, 2018; Doi, 1971; Wierzbicka 1991). Harmony, *wa,* or honesty, *shōjiki,* are respectively the primary value in Japan and in U.S. societies (Clarke, 1992; Nawano, Annakis, and Mizuno, 2006; Oosterling, 2005; Pilgrim, 1986; Prince Shotoku Taishi, 604). Trust within interdependent relationships and trust between independent identities can be motivated by quite different goals. For example, one positive concept of trust is to count on the other's intentions always to be in my best interest, which assures an integrity that is dependable. A negative concept of trust is to have faith that the other's actions will never betray one's self-interest. Each of these 'trust' concepts seem to co-exist within Japan-U.S. bicultural marriages. It becomes complex when the partners' understanding of 'integrity' varies due to the visceral conflict between honesty and harmony.

In Japan there are three ways of being included in maturity, which expresses itself as a context-based balancing of the thoughts and behaviors of the child, the parent, and the adult. It is OK to play the parent of an adult who displays child-like behavior, as it is to play the child in adulthood in order to receive indulgences from other adults playing the parental role. Adult-to-adult behavior is not the only norm due to the Japanese sense of integrity, which is 'above all, there is harmony' (Prince Shotoku Taishi, 604). Participating in indulgences in multiple roles while maintaining harmony within all relationships is the purist form of integrity. While 'staying true to oneself' with a unitary adult identity based on honesty in one's thoughts and feelings despite the context is the American perspective on integrity. The 'healthy' concept of maturity is in being the adult. The concept of "*amae*" (Doi, 1971) literally means the anatomy of dependence but for the Western reader he thought it better to convey the structure of interdependence because of the American psychological orientation to dependency as a mental weakness, encased in the concept of an unhealthy 'co-dependency'. Interdependence in Japan incorporates the reciprocity between parties with obligations, *on,* and duties, *giri,* as ideals of complementary social behavior that maintain harmony, *wa.* These are the reasons and values underlying so much indulgence and sensitivity in relationships in Japan, which are rooted in the parent–child relationship and extend throughout adolescence and adulthood. Others suggest that harmony may be fading in society (Saito & Ohbuchi, 2013) but do not assume that it should also be fading in bicultural marriages.

The interdependency in *amae* relationships allows anyone to act with a "presumed acceptance of one's inappropriate behavior or request" (Yamaguchi & Ariizumi, 2006, p. 164). For an American this behavior may result in a feeing of receiving requests for assistance without an epectation of reciprocity because an independent American does not need such assistance in return. In these changing times in Japan, such assumptions are practiced by an increasing number of people. It can be experienced positively but to most Americans in bicultural marriages it can also create problems, such as, feeling disrespected as an adult or excessively burdened by a perception of the non-reciprocal nature of requests from a partner. It significantly affects the quality of a married couple to engage on frequent clarifications of the expectations they may share about reciprocity of *amae* since they are living in Japan where *amae* is pervasive.

A final critical element in U.S.–Japanese bicultural marriages that supports interdependency is 'responsive (distributed) mindfulness' to all contextual matters (Hall, 1981; Hall & Hall, 1987). It is necessary because context has a strong influence on personal thoughts, feelings, and behaviors in the Japanese society grounded in interdependency as opposed to independence. In Japan mindfulness is inseparable from acting responsively to one's context because it is appropriate to have interdependent thoughts, feelings, and actions.

A Japanese concept that illustrates this integrated perspective is "*kikubari,*" which means 'distributed attention or sensitivity' (Kopp, 2013; Maki & Aoyama, 2012). The key to understanding this concept is the word 'distributed' or responsive to the other in one's environment. A Japanese flight attendant walking down an aisle may demonstrate "*kikubari*" by recognizing a passenger's nonverbal behavior of creating friction for warmth by rubbing each hand on the other arm and then respond by giving the passenger a blanket from the storage rack above the seat. *Kikubari* requires attentiveness, kindness—*shinsetsu,* and compassion to understand and feel such interdependency and is an illustration of distributed or responsive mindfulness.

51.4 Discussion

We have attempted to clarify the cultural interaction issues that can perhaps illuminate some of the chaos that attends the effort of building a marriage together. We have depended on the studies that have strained to create coherent guidance based on etic approaches to discovering cultural differences. We have suggested a process approach to interaction that can facilitate a bicultural married couple's efforts to construct a structure and process through which they can evolve into a sustainable happy relationship. Such a process relies upon each partner's willingness to communicate by sharing their own experiences, perspectives, and feelings with each other continually. It is an emic approach to discovering what together they prefer in communication styles and values that enable them to pull together and stay together in happiness.

Intercultural communication competencies may sound like attitudes in part, i.e. empathy, role flexibility, respect, patience, tolerance, and others, but the demonstration of each in behavioral action is the only way for them to have an impact in bicultural situations, particularly in constructing a bicultural marriage. In approaching models for resolving issues in bicultural marriages between Japanese and Americans, we suggest beginning with the incorporation of oriental and occidental worldviews together. In order to do this we must not only depend on Eastern psychologists who have learned and adopted Western researchers' quantitative scientific methods but also upon those who have found value in their indigenous approaches to investigating phenomena qualitatively and holistically. We all would gain from listening to each other and working together to discover that we have fundamentally different perceptions of ways to structure chaos. With a view that fully accepts diversity in values, allows the existence of alternative perceptions, and enjoys differences in communication style, we would be more able to work together to construct such structure and systems that would bring healing and peace to partners in bicultural marriages.

If we as Americans could release our dependence on words as the ultimate and best way to communicate, and if we as Japanese could release our dependency on the nuance, ambiguity, and indirectness of nonverbals as the safest way to communicate, then perhaps we Americans could learn to enjoy deeper sensitivities to feelings and contexts with longer silences and we Japanese could learn to enjoy the clarity and security in the shared understanding that is possible through the articulate expression of words that reveal rather than hide. Such a reversal of natural communication style tendencies if attempted would reveal a whole new world to enjoy and challenge us with a new system of values that would truly expand our perceptual horizons, our values, and our behavioral repertoires or capabilities such as to potentially become bicultural persons.

There is no better resource today found in our searching for understanding the merger of opposites than the Chinese Yin Yang construct wherein opposites unite in one whole.

The two opposites of Yin and Yang attract and complement each other and as their symbol illustrates, each side has at its core an element of the other (represented by the small dots). Neither pole is superior to the other and, as an increase in one brings a corresponding decrease in the other, a correct balance between the two poles must be reached in order to achieve harmony (Cartwright, 2018, paragraph 1).

It would be constructive to recognize that our allegiance to communicating either by the articulate use of words or by nonverbal nuances (paralinguistic sounds, signs, body language, facial expressions) is a significant cause for the frequent chaos that exists in bicultural marriages, or any Japanese and American effort to communicate. A more Yin Yang approach is appearing in the last two decades in the research of the perceptions of independence and interdependence in cognition, emotion, and motivation. These are studies of culture and the self, identity and self-concepts, that contribute a new paradigm for the subject of constructing bicultural marriages.

Writings from scholars are keys to these concepts (Bond & Smith, 1996; Heine, Lehman, Markus, & Kitayama, 1999; Kitayama & Markus, 1995; Kitayama, Markus, Matsumoto, & Norasakkunkit, 1997; Markus & Kitayama, 2003; Lu, 2010). Lu (2010) in particular explores how the Yin and Yang would be useful in working toward integrating what these researchers understand as not two poles but rather as complementary perspectives that collaborate in creating self-concepts and social norms, even for creating what we call a third culture marriage. Much more collaborative research teams with members contributing equally toward research designs and first-language observation and interviews in order to have validity in a number of different cultural settings (Bond & Smith, 1996) would be exciting. Fortunately since the early 1990s much more of this has been evident in the literature, as in Lu's (2010) study on happiness and Wang, Wiley, and Chiu's (2008) study on praise, from both perspectives of independence and interdependence.

51.5 Conclusion

In this chapter we have sought to analyze intercultural interaction issues within Japanese–U.S. bicultural marriages in order to clarify some conflicting perceptions, communication styles, and their underlying cultural values that provide the gist for the hard work of constructing a more satisfying bicultural marriage in Japan. Within the chosen events and circumstances that cause friction and confusion for so many such partners in Japan, we offered interpretations based upon U.S. and Japanese hidden assumptions, perceptions, values, and styles utilizing Barnlund's (1976) model through which we see the primary foci when searching for meaning. Within these interpretations and recommendations for understanding more deeply we have applied some *kotowaza* that can help to illuminate the sources of values and hidden assumptions.

Intercultural communication competencies can help if behaviorally localized. Although these skills were intended to be universally applicable, we stressed the importance of first discovering from one's Japanese or American partner exactly how such skills might be demonstrated interculturally in the other's culture because such universals must always be demonstrated locally in different ways that are appropriate to the interaction's cultural context. We referenced current research on the issues of cultural identity perception around the current independence–interdependence discussion. These studies offer us an opportunity to explore a new approach of seeing both cultures as equal parts of a whole in a way that is complementary and unifying.

There are limitations to our study in that autoethnography methods are not yet accepted by many researchers due to the focus on personal perceptions revealed by the authors and the absence of quantitative data for analysis (Méndez, 2013). The method depends upon readers who are open to benefitting from others' experiences. These findings are therefore not generalisable except perhaps to others engaged in American and Japanese bicultural marriages and those who counsel and support them. Despite these limitations, our chapter extended the previous studies examining the issues of bicultural marriages by focusing on the intercultural communication issues within American–Japanese bicultural marriages from an evocative autoethnographic approach. This more focused analysis of bicultural partners' internal communications adds to the studies of external trends in democratic variables, the internationally comparative challenge couples face, the laws that create issues between them, the external causes of stress comparatively, the gender roles that differ, the meaning of marriage in each country, conflict resolution approaches in each country, and other culture-specific and cultural comparative studies. This study highlights the opportunities from cultural-interactive analyses of actual people engaged in intercultural interactions within bicultural marriages between Americans and Japanese living in Japan.

Our challenge still remains to experiment with how these two cultures can engage each other within a bicultural marriage in real interaction that honors and respects communication styles that remain far from balanced on their use of verbal and nonverbal modes of interacting. Also, applications of findings from independence and interdependence studies (Kitayama & Markus, 1995; Lu, 2010; Kitayama, Markus, Matsumoto, & Norasakkunkit, 1997; Bond & Smith, 1996) need to be studied in contexts of bicultural marriages. And, of course, this interaction autoethnographic approach could be applied to studies of bicultural marriages between many other cultures. Efforts to approach these interactions are limited, but if the Japanese spouse is not typical because of extensive experience maturing in a western country or if the American spouse is not typical because of extensive experience maturing from an early age in Japan, working through the imbalances is a possibility.

In summary, our approach to discussing the key issues of intercultural communications in bicultural marriages was to integrate the elements of Barnlund's model in that in the lives of such couples they do not generally separate these elements. It may be effective to do so in counseling situations however. We chose here to write about them in a more flowing style, akin to talking story in Hawai'i. The personal experiences and those with others referred to as subjects were also integrated in the discussions because they were common experiences to us all. In applying *kotowaza* (sayings and proverbs) in each issue we clarified some of the sources of values in the Japanese culture. Americans have similar sayings and a more complete writing on the subject could explain those as well. We chose to state their values straightforwardly as is the custom in English communication style. Finally, we indicated the areas of deeper inquiry that would assist couples in exploring their thoughts, feelings, and alternative behaviors that create the challenges that they experience.

References

Adams, T. E., Ellis, C., & Holman Jones, S. (2017). Autoethnography. In J. Matthes (Ed.), *The international encyclopedia of communication research methods*. New York: Wiley.

Asai, A., & Barnlund, D. C. (1998). Boundaries of the unconscious, private and public self in Japan and America—A cross-cultural comparison. *International Journal of Intercultural Relations, 22*(4), 431–452.

Barnlund, D. C. (1975). *Public and private self in Japan and the United States: Communicative styles of two cultures*. Tokyo: Simul Press.

Barnlund, D. C. (1976, July). *Multileveled, multidimensional, multidirectional, multi-coded intercultural communication*. Paper presented at the 1st Stanford Institute for Intercultural Communication, Stanford University, Palo Alto, CA.

Barnlund, D. C. (1989). Public and private self in communicating with Japan. *Business Horizons, 32*(2), 32–40.

Barnlund, D. C., & Yoshioka, M. (1990). Apologies—Japanese and American styles. *International Journal of Intercultural Relations, 14*(2), 193–206.

Bond, M. H., & Smith, P. B. (1996). Cross-cultural social and organizational psychology. *Annual Review of Psychology, 47*, 205–235.

Cartwright, M. (2018). Yin and Yang—Definition. Ancient history encyclopedia. Retrieved on May 16 from: https://www.ancient.eu/Yin_and_Yang/(paragraph 1).

Chang, H. (2016). Autoethnography in health research: Growing pains? *Sage Qualitative Health Research, 26*(4), 443–451.

Clarke, C. H. (1992). Communicating benefits to a culturally diverse employee population. *Employees Benefits Journal, 17*(1), 26–32.

Clarke, C. H. & Hammer, M. R. (1995). Predictors of Japanese and American managers job success, personal adjustment, and intercultural interaction effectiveness. *Management International Review, 35*(2), 153–170.

Clarke, C. H., & Kanatani, K. (1979). Structure of turn taking. *Education and Technology 17*, 12–24 (Japanese).

Clarke, C. H., & Lipp, G. D. (1998). *Danger and opportunity—Resolving conflict in U-S-based Japanese subsidiaries*. Yarmouth: ME. Intercultural Press.

Dalsky, D. (2018, July 18). 甘え: Amae. Retrieved November 28, 2019, from https://www.interculturallab.com/⬚2997612360-amae.html.

Doi, T. (1971). *The anatomy of dependence* (in Japanese, 1973 in English by John Bester, Translator). Tokyo: Kodansha.

Fetters, M. D. (1995). Nemawashi essential for conducting research in Japan. *Social Science & Medicine, 41*(3), 375–381.

Forgash, R. (2009). Negotiating marriage—Cultural citizenship and the reproduction of American empire in Okinawa. *Ethnology, 48*(3), 215–237.

Galef, D., & Hashimoto, J. (1987). *Even Monkeys Fall from Trees*. Tokyo: Charles E. Tuttle.

Hall, E. T. (1981). *Beyond culture*. New York: Anchor Books, Doubleday.

Hall, E. T., & Hall, M. R. (1987). *Hidden dimensions*. New York: Anchor Books, Doubleday.

Hayashi, I. (2019, November 18). On international marriage. In Okinawa Hai–.Okinawa's English Community, Okinawahai.com. Retrieved November 18, from https://okinawahai.com/on-international-marriage/

Heine, S. J., Lehman, D. R., Markus, H. R., & Kitayama, S. (1999). Is there a universal need for positive self-regard? *Psychological Review, 106*(4), 766–794.

Holzapfel, J., Randall, A. K., Tao, C., & Iida, M. (2018). Intercultural couples' internal stress, relationship satisfaction, and dyadic coping. *Interpersona, 12*(2), 145–163.

Imai, M. (1981). *16 Ways of saying no—An invitation to experience Japanese management from the inside.* Tokyo: Nihon Keisai Shimbun.

Kitayama, S. & Markus, H. R. (1995). Culture and self-implications for internationalizing psychology, Chapter 16. In N. R. Goldberger & J. B. Veroff (Eds.), *The culture and psychology reader* (pp. 366–383). New York: New York University Press.

Kitayama, S., Markus, H. R., & Matsumoto, H., Norasakkunkit, V. (1997). Individual & collective processes in the construction of the self—Self-enhancement in the U.S. & self-criticism in Japan. *Journal of Personality and Social Psychology, 72*(6), 1245–1267.

Kopp, R. (2013). Kikubari—The Japanese art of paying attention to others. Retrieved November 28, 2019, from www.japanintercultural.com

Kopp, R. (2019a, April 24). Nobody's perfect, but an apology really helps at a Japanese company. *The Japan Times.*

Kopp, R. (2019b). Ditch the debate tactics when it comes to persuading Japanese colleagues on a course of action. *The Japan Times.* Retrieved November 14, from https://www.japantimes.co.jp/community/2019/04/24/how-tos/nobodys-perfect-apology-really-helps-japanese-company/

Lu, L. (2010). Chinese well-being. Chapter 20. In Bond, M. H. (Ed.), *The Oxford handbook of Chinese psychology.* Oxford: Oxford University Press.

Maki, K., & Aoyama, M. (2012, October). Kikubari—A model for provisioning dynamic context-aware services based on the intentions. In *2012 Conference consumer electronics (GCCE).*

Markus, H. R. & Kitayama, S. (2003). Culture, self, and the reality of the social. *Psychological Inquiry, 14*(3,4), 277–283.

Méndez, M. (2013). Autoethnography as a research method: Advantages, limitations and criticisms. *Colombian Applied Linguistics Journal, 15*(2). Bogotá, July/Dec.

Miike, Y. (2003). Japanese Enryo-Sasshi communication and the psychology of amae—Reconsideration and reconceptualization. Keio Communication Review, No. 25.

Ministry of Health, Labor and Welfare, Statistics and Information Policy. (2018). Intercultural marriages in Japan in 1995–2015. Retrieved November 15, from https://www.nippon.com/en/features/h00096/a-look-at-international-marriage-in-japan.html

Nawano, T., Annakis, J., & Mizuno, T. (2006). The evolution of Wa (Group Harmony) in Japanese Society and the nature of work. *The International Journal of Learning—Annual Review.* https://doi.org/10.18848/1447-9494/cgp/v11/45730

Nitschke, G. (2018, May 16). MA—Place, space, void. Hidden Japan, Kyoto Journal. Retrieved from kyotojournal.org/culture-arts/ma-place-space-void/

Nomura, N., & Barnlund, D. C. (1983). Patterns of interpersonal criticism in Japan and the United States. *International Journal of Intercultural Relations, 7*(1), 1–18.

Nonaka, I., & Konno, N. (1998). The Concept of "BA"—Building a foundation for knowledge creation. *California Management Review, 40*(3), 40–54.

Okada, Y. (2011). Race, masculinity, and military occupation—African American soldiers' encounters with the Japanese at Camp Gifu, 1947-1951. *The Journal of African American History, 96*(2), 179–203.

Ono, H., & Berg, J. (2010). Homogamy and intermarriage of Japanese and Japanese Americans with Whites surrounding World War II. *Journal of Marriage and the Family, 72*(5), 1249–1262.

Oosterling, H. (2005). MA or sensing time-space—Towards a culture of the inter. Internet reprint of lecture. Retrieved from http://www.henkoosterling.nl/pdfs/lect_berlin_ma_2005 .

Pilgrim, R. B. (1986). Intervals ("Ma") in space and time—Foundations for a religio-aesthetic paradigm in Japan. *History of Religions, 25*(3), 255–277.

Prince Shotoku Taishi (604). 1st constitution of Japan. Retrieved July 15, 2019, from http://afe.easia.columbia.edu/ps/japan/shotoku.pdf

Saito, T., & Ohbuchi, K. (2013). Individual differences in the value of social harmony. *International Journal of Conflict Management, 24*(2), 112–125.

Spencer-Oatey, H. (2012). What is culture? A compilation of quotations. GlobalPAD Core Concepts. Retrieved from, http://www.warwick.ac.uk/globalpadintercultural

Wang, Y. Z., Wiley, A. R., & Chiu, C.-Y. (2008). Independence-supportive praise versus interdependence-promoting praise. *International Journal of Behavioral Development, 32*(1), 13–20.

Wierzbicka, A. (1991). Japanese key words and core cultural values. *Language in Society, 20*(3), 333–385.

Yamaguchi, S., & Ariizumi, Y. (2006). Close interpersonal relationships among Japanese. In U. Kim, G. Yang, & K. Hwang (Eds.), *Indigenous and cultural psychology: Understanding people in context* (pp. 163–174). New York: Springer.

Clifford H. Clarke, (ABD), was raised in Japan by second-generation expatriate parents, whose own parents first moved to Japan in 1898 when the U.S. forced the Queen to abdicate her crown in the Kingdom of Hawai'i. Since arriving in Japan at the age of 7, his favorite pastime has been exploring cultural assumptions and at the age of 10 he was asked to become a bridge-between-cultures in Kyoto.

His higher education focused on the goal of becoming an effective "bridge person" by studying world religions and philosophies (B.A.), counseling across cultures (M.Div.), and interdisciplinary studies in the social sciences (ABD) at Stanford University's Graduate School of Education.

His four careers have evolved through 11 years of counseling foreign students at Cornell and Stanford universities, 8 years of teaching intercultural communication at Stanford, 5 years teaching at the University of Hawai'i at Manoa, 30 years of intercultural management consulting in 13 countries in Asia, Europe, and North America, and 6 years of educational program design and evaluation in the State of Hawai'i public and charter schools. He also founded the Stanford Institute for Intercultural Communication (SIIC–1975), Clarke Consulting Group (CCG–1980), and cofounded SIETAR (1971) and SIETAR Japan (1984). Clarke has published 28 papers, chapters, or books in all of these areas, given 45 presentations at professional societies and universities, and been quoted by 25 newspapers and magazines in Japan, the USA, and Europe. Clarke retired from his Affiliated Graduate Faculty position in Hawai'i to return home to Kyoto, Japan in 2016.

Naomi Takashiro, (PhD), received her Ph.D. in Educational Psychology and her M.A. in Communication with an emphasis on Intercultural Communication. She has been teaching English classes as adjunct faculty at the Kyoto University of Foreign Studies and its junior college in Kyoto, Japan. Growing up in a low socioeconomic family, her academic interests are socioeconomic status and inequality in education. She has been publishing articles in this area. She has lived in Hawaii for 20 years and has worked in multicultural organizations before coming back to Kyoto 4 years ago. She has been looking for a full-time job at a university. In her spare time, she likes to cook, walk, swim, and read. She remains grateful to God for his guidance in writing this book chapter.

Chapter 52
Agape Love in Indigenous Women's Memoir: A Quest for Justice and Unity

Helen Fordham

Abstract Contemporary conversations of love tend to be dominated by romance but it is only one experience of attachment, and the personal stories of care, kindness and sacrifice contained in a sample of Indigenous women's memoir published during the 1980s in Australia express an agape form of love. This is a social bond most commonly associated with the western Christian ideal of universal love and explicates humankind's capacity to love selflessly and sacrifice for others. Agape love also recognises the interdependency of social life and thus invokes a moral code that sustains the conditions, attitudes and behaviours that preserve social unity (Beshai. Humanistic Psychologist 45(4):408–421, 2017). In understanding agape love as a quest for unity, the memoirs published during a decade of intensified racial conflict in Australia can be seen as both critiques of the colonial legacies that had created the systemic injustice and which destroyed the unity of Indigenous communities and excluded them from the national story; and calls to social action to address these injustices. In expressing forgiveness towards their oppressors, and in communicating a hope that Indigenous and non-Indigenous Australians could find a way to coexist beyond the nation's racist past, the authors challenged dominant discourses, which portrayed Indigenous Australians as without humanity and unable to care for themselves or others (Bennett. White politics and Black Australians. St. Leonards, NSW: Allen and Unwin, 1999) and radically reimagined the possibility of a more inclusive Australian community.

Keywords Love · Power · Justice–Indigenous Memoir · Australia

H. Fordham (✉)
Department of Media and Communications, University of Western Australia, Crawley, WA, Australia
e-mail: helen.fordham@uwa.edu.au

52.1 Introduction

The 1980s was a period of intensified racial division in Australia and Indigenous women's memoirs published during this decade functioned ostensibly as critiques of power (Fordham, 2018). The memoirs expose the devastating impact of British colonization on Indigenous Australians, at a time when persistent negative media coverage of Indigenous protests had re-animated anxieties about race in the broader non-Indigenous community (Bongiorno, 2015; McCausland, 2004). Yet, in the midst of the Indigenous authors' recollections of oppression, neglect and injustice, there are also narratives in these memoirs of love, sacrifice and forgiveness for each other; for families and for communities. The authors even express love for their oppressors and share their hopes that as non-Indigenous Australians come to understand Indigenous Australians it would possible to create a more inclusive future for all (Langford, 1988; Simon, 1987; Walker & Coutts, 1989). In writing of their sacrifice for others; and in expressing forgiveness and care for all Australians it is argued the authors communicate an agape sense of love, which is akin to the western Christian concept of universal or selfless love associated with God. This form of love recognizes the "social character of existence" and the "inter-related nature of reality" (Beshai, 2017, 411) and as such asserts a moral order that valorizes justice, equality and forgiveness as the necessary conditions and actions for the preservation of community. In writing for mostly urban readers — who had little knowledge of the nation's Indigenous past — (Pettman, 1988, 7) the authors expose the historical injustice and systemic racism that impedes reconciliation. Moreover, in demonstrating through their stories a commitment to the shared moral values of the national community, the author's memoirs emerge as both "a force capable of generating social bonds, of transforming and or revising human relationships" (Iorio, 2014, 14) and an illustration of Martin Luther King's (1963) assertion that agape love is justice in action.

52.2 Love and Power

Many contemporary conversations about love tend to focus upon the discourse of romance, which is a form of love associated with intense emotional and physical attraction, and described as "an irresistible and inexhaustible passion" that can overcome "suffering and even death" (Yalom, 2001, 66). Romance is found in all cultures in various forms (Jankowiak & Fischer, 1992) (see Chaps. 2 and 3 in this book) and it is both a potent fantasy that maintains the ideal that a passionate physical connection and emotional and sacred union with another human being is possible, as well as a generally accepted cultural expectation in the West for a legally binding marriage commitment (Coontz, 2005; Parker, 2005; Shumway, 2003). Indeed, romance, which was once considered separate to marriage, was refashioned in the eighteen century as an ideology that serves to reconcile the modern subjective self and notions of attachment, sexuality and individualism with the economies associated with marriage (Fordham & Milech, 2014, 360). However, despite the media popularity of romance it is just one kind of experience of love (Shumway, 2003, 32).

Other types and conditions of love have also been extensively explored. The role, nature, function and quality of love has been conceptualised in various social contexts, and distinctions made between sexual (erotic), friendship (philia), self-love, love of family (storge), and universal or selfless love (agape). Also considered is the degree to which these different forms of love are exclusive from each other (Tillich, 1954); whether love is altruistic and intentional (Konstan, 2008) and the extent to which love can disinterested and unconnected to any personal interest or advantage (Frankfurt, 2009; Helm, 2010). Love has also been theorised as an emotion (Solomon, 1981, 34); and as actions (Iorio, 2014, 14). It has also been expressed as a response to dignity and loving the subject for its own properties (Velleman, 1999); as an ethic linked to the expression of an individual's subjectivity; and a social evaluation that recognizes value in the subject/object of the love (Helm, 2010). Central to many of these conceptualizations of love are tensions between love as an individual quest to satisfy physical and emotional needs and love as a means of social exchange and inclusion.

In considering the function of love in social contexts (Iorio, 2014; King, 1963; Tillich, 1954) it is necessary to examine agape love, which expresses love as universal and altruistic. Indeed, Martin Luther King explicitly describes agape love as "understanding, creative, redemptive, good will for all men (and women)" (Pinto, 2015, 78). It is a love not based on utilitarianism but upon the grounds that the person is loved by God. Agape love is also understood as a quest for unity and thus invokes justice, equality and forgiveness as the necessary conditions for the preservation of the social bonds that create and sustain community. For King the fate of the individual subject and the other are bound together; one cannot flourish without the other. Similarly, for Paul Tillich (1954) the ontological nature of love is grounded in a sense of belonging and for this reason he theorized love as not just a consideration of others but as a "drive toward the unity of the separated" because it is in the "reunion of the estranged" that "love manifests its greatest power" (1954, 25). It is the will to unity that calls for social action to overcome the inherited injustice and uncritical institutionalized attitudes that can create impediments to reconciliation. It is for this reason that King also defines agape love as justice in action (qtd. in Nwonye, 2009, vi) and an expression of a "willingness to go to any lengths to restore love (and unity) between members of a community" (qtd. in Beshai, 2017, 412). Action, however, requires the exercise of power, which is often conceived of as dominance and therefore incompatible with love. In elaborating this point Tillich argues that "love and power are often contrasted in such a way that love is identified with a resignation of power and power with a denial of love" (1954, 11). Power, however, is not dominance over others but rather the "drive of everything to realise itself with increasing intensity and extensity" (Tillich, 1954, 36). For Tillich power is "self-transcending dynamics" that "overcome internal and external resistance" (1954, 37) and the personal and public impediments to reunification. King similarly theorises power as a striving for reunification and he argues that it is love and its associated goodwill, forgiveness and sacrifice that can best restore communities fragmented by injustice and inequality. Thus for King reconciliation has to be achieved through peaceful non-violent social action because violence excludes love, denies God and the ideal of universal love; and erodes the morality and goodwill that inspires the social action necessary to restore justice (Garber, 1973, 94).

52.3 Justice in Action

Adam Kahane (2009) applied Tillich and Kings's idea of love as justice in action to the complex social issues that divide communities and he argues that this approach is particularly necessary for problems that are dynamically, socially and generatively complex. For Kahane problems are dynamically complex when the cause and effect are interdependent and acerbated by actions over time; socially complex when the individuals come from different perspectives; and generatively complex in the sense that there are no clear solutions and thus approaches must be invented.

Certainly Australia's race relations during the 1980s conform to these problem parameters. Growing international awareness of Indigenous conditions during the decade exposed the deeply entrenched racist attitudes that continued to justify the control and regulation of Indigenous Australians despite political enfranchisement and the growth in Indigenous activism (Foley, 2010). Indeed, it was the international scrutiny that accompanied the growth in Australian tourism and the celebrations associated with Australia's bicentennial during the late 1980s that began the process of rupturing the nation's silence about its Indigenous past; a silence that had bred ignorance of the nation's racist past (Burgmann, 2003; Reynolds, 1984; Stanner, 1969). Indigenous protests exposed the impact of colonization on Indigenous citizens including the destruction of Indigenous culture and language (Heiss, 2003) the dispossession and appropriation of tribal land and the systematized inequality through the categorization of Indigenous identity based upon skin colour (Bennett, 1999; Burgmann, 2003; Morris, 2013; Pettman, 1988; Reynolds, 1984). Colonisation had also fostered fear between Indigenous and non-Indigenous Australians and instilled a sense of shame among Indigenous Australians (Morris, 2013). Colonization had also shaped relationship formation among Indigenous Australians themselves who were traditionally governed by strict tribal and kinship rules. These rules conceive of life as an interconnected web of relationships within and outside the human subject (Morgan, 2008) and in which the health of individual and community relationships are connected to the health of land and culture. For many Indigenous Australians land is not only property but also the site of history and spirituality, constituting a form of metaphorical map of Indigenous knowledge, culture and law (Korff, 2019). Thus the displacement of Indigenous Australians meant more than the loss of their land, it also signaled the destruction of culture, community and tribal and kinship laws which had arranged and regulated Indigenous life (Maddock, 1986).

Social divisions were further complicated during this decade by the government's adoption of welfare as a way of addressing economic and social disadvantage. This led to a decade of what Aboriginal activist and administrator Charles Perkins (1994) recalled as a period characterized by a 'withering away of effort and commitment' to Aboriginal economic independence (38) as Indigenous Australians came to rely upon welfare and competed with each other for government funding. At the same time ongoing negative media coverage of land rights demonstrations saw non-Indigenous Australians become 'quietly unsympathetic' (Bongiorno, 2015, 74) to the early Aboriginal rights agenda and Aboriginal activist unity increasingly 'unraveled' (Morris, 2013, 46) as different groups entered into their own agreements with various State and Federal governments.

52.4 Representations of Love

This was the social and political context in which Indigenous women's memoir began to proliferate in the 1980s, and an examination of these texts demonstrate how representations of love were a part of the discursive practices that can create the conditions for non-violent social change and restorative justice. Interestingly, Indigenous Australians have oral story-telling traditions, thus the memoirs and autobiographies produced in the 1980s were a part of expanding Indigenous discourse and can be considered the 'history and text books of Aboriginal Australia' (Heiss, 2003, 35). Memoirs, however, are not objective perceptions of reality but 'highly selective reconstructions' of experiences that are always mediated by the 'situation in which they are recalled' and by 'the needs and interests of the person or group doing the remembering in the present' (Erll, 2011, 8). Thus the memoirs produced in the context of the 1980s were assembled in response to the individual authors' experiences of the growing conflict between Indigenous and non-Indigenous Australians, and the stories illuminate the nature of love in several ways. First, the memoirs can be seen as acts of self-love as individual authors reclaim their Indigenous identity from the dominant colonial discourse that perpetuated the racist attitudes that denied Indigenous Australians their rights (Morris, 2013). Second, the authors also express love as actions of care and sacrifice for individuals who have been separated from the support structures of family, land and country. Third, in explaining Indigenous Australians connections to land and culture and role in the survival of Indigenous communities, love is a term used to denote social value. Fourth, in retelling the many ways in which Indigenous Australians affiliate and bond with others in different contexts and within the constraints of discrimination, the authors produce an alternative discourse elaborating Indigenous humanity, which had been erased by colonial stereotypes of Indigenous Australians as violent, dangerous and "deficient" (Morris, 2013, 15). Moreover, in expressing love, care and sacrifice for others, the authors both communicate a moral code of universal love that functions to change reader's 'perceptions of reality and in the end—through the reader's actions ... reality itself' (Erll, 2011, 155) and demonstrate that the characteristics associated with agape love —sacrifice, benevolence, and forgiveness — are not only a part of different categories of love but also different cultures. Finally, in identifying the past injustices that caused the social divisions in the 1980s the authors opened up the possibility for social change and reconciliation.

In Anna Heiss' catalogue of Aboriginal literature thirteen Indigenous autobiographies were published in the 1980s and six were examined for representations of love. The sample includes: *Born a Half Caste* (1985) by Marnie Kennedy; *Through My Eyes* (1987) by Ella Simon; *Don't Take Your Love to Town* by Ruby Langford (1988); *Wandering Girl* (1987) by Glenyse Ward; *Somebody Now* (1989) by Ellie Gaffney; and *Me and You* (1989) by Della Walker and Tina Coutts. Textual analysis is a method of investigation that makes it possible to identify how

> meanings are embedded in history, in a sense of who we are and in a network of other texts, contexts and meanings (Hartley & McKee, 2000, 19).

A textual analysis of these memoirs therefore enables;

1. A description of the nature and forms of love discursively produced by Indigenous Australians and an evaluation of how these renderings accord with the different categories of love; and
2. An analysis of the degree to which these representations illustrate Tillich's theory that love is justice in action.

52.5 Love of Family

The Australian and State government's forcible removal of children from their families across the twentieth century as a part of its assimilationist policies— particularly in relation to children of both Indigenous and European heritage— makes it unsurprising that love of family is central to all the memoirs.[1] Marnie Kennedy (1985) expresses her love of family as a yearning for her mother from whom she is separated as a small child. A tribal Indigenous woman, Kennedy's mother is taken advantage of by a non-Indigenous man and after falling pregnant is sent to the Aboriginal settlement at Palm Island as punishment. This was a part of the Queensland government's efforts to criminalize relationships between the races and discourage miscegenation. Later Kennedy's mother and her brother are sent away to work on stations in Queensland and Kennedy is raised on the Island before she too is sent to work. It is a separation from family from which she never recovers and Kennedy's grief over the loss of her family sets up a life of isolation and disconnection.

---

[1] The Bringing Them Home Report (1997) estimates that up to 33% of all children were removed from their families between 1911 and 1970.

Ella Simon (1987) expresses a similar love for family. She, too, is of mixed heritage and is raised by her grandmother because that was:

> the Aboriginal way, to be responsible for all of the family, not just your nearest (2).

This statement directly challenges the dominant non-Indigenous view that Aboriginal people didn't know how to care for themselves. Simon's grandmother raises her in the Christian faith and teaches her not to feel sorry for herself and to meet hatred and bigotry with "love and forgiveness" (Simon, 1987, 1). Simon also expresses love for her non-Indigenous father who had taken advantage of Simon's mother when she worked as a domestic in his home. Initially reluctant to meet him, Simon begins to visit her father and over time she comes to care for him deeply. Later in life after his white family refuses to help him when he is ailing, Simon and her husband take him to live with them on the Purfleet Aboriginal Reserve. His white family, however, doesn't like these arrangements and so they organise for the manager of the Reserve to deny Simon's father permission to stay. As a result he dies alone and Simon is heartbroken. She recalls that his death was one of the saddest moments of her life.

> I was so sad in my heart for so long that I thought it was going to burst. All of us—my husband, my children, and myself—felt a deep sense of grief for a long time. Each of us had grown to love him. (24).

Love of family is also expressed in the memoir of Torres Strait Islander Ellie Gaffney (1989) who was one of the first Indigenous women to qualify as a nurse. She writes of both the love for her close knit family but also an agape love when she describes how her family moved to Australia to carry out God's work of caring for malnourished and neglected Aborigines in Cape York. She, herself, explains that she became a nurse because it gave her great satisfaction to care for people. Gaffney works hard and finally achieves her goal of becoming a nurse but the Thursday Island Hospital Board refuses to hire her after she demonstrates a disregard for the rules of segregation at the hospital. As a result, Gaffney is forced to find work as a kitchen maid in order to support her two children and stay on the Island to care for her ailing father; sacrifices and compromises many women, regardless of race, make.

Ruby Langford (1988) also dedicated her book to her family. Raised by her father after her mother abandons them, he is a source of constant support and love. His health fails, however, from all the hard work he does to feed his children and he eventually dies of a heart attack leaving Langford to mourn her "best friend" (71). Langford too, despite personal and financial instability, is a dedicated mother. She teaches her children to read and write even as they live an impecunious and itinerant life, and she prays for God to save the life of her eldest son when he contracts meningitis. Langford recounts similar pain when her daughter Pearl is suddenly killed by a careless driver and she expresses her shock when her son Nobby is goaled for 10 years for shooting at a police car. Like any parent, Langford's heart breaks for her son as she watches his struggles and she begins to pay attention to the reports of deaths in custody, fearful that his life will end this way.

In contrast to the Indigenous Australians who were taken into care, Della Walker & Coutts (1989) is raised by her family and she expresses love as both a privilege and a duty. She sees her mother as a "precious jewel" who is always there for her and she expresses her desire to always care for her. Walker also writes about the importance of love to families.

> We know that love is everything in the family, in the family home. When you've got that love, you've got everything. (23).

This observation serves to disrupt the colonisers' view that Indigenous Australians did not feel love or miss their children when they were taken into care.[2]

52.6 Romantic Love

Traditionally early non-Indigenous Australian literature depicted Indigenous romantic love as a "ritual of dominance and surrender" (Sheridan, 1988, 82) and the most common representation was that of "romantic elopement in defiance of tribal law" (82). Aboriginal divisions of labour based upon gender, and arranged marriages between old men and young women, were disparaged in the literature as barbaric, and the underlying implication, according to Sheridan (1988), was that the non-Indigenous did not oppress their women in the same way. However, the stories of romantic love in the memoirs do not conform to these non-Indigenous depictions. Indeed, the authors express the same romantic sentiments common to non-Indigenous romance even though the marriage and relationship choices may have been affected by either Indigenous kinship laws or the *Aboriginal Protection Act*. Kennedy (1985) writes of becoming infatuated with a "tall, blond and blue-eyed" staff member on Palm Island (18) before meeting a boy she was "crazy" about. "It's magic," she writes. "When you are in love you see only see love" (18). Kennedy describes how she thought one day they would marry, however, she is sent off the Island to work and she never sees him again. Kennedy eventually marries but not for love. The owner of the station where she works suggests to her that if she married the head stockman it would enable both of them to be released from the *Aboriginal Protection Act*. She writes of many of the girls making the same decision in order to escape the intrusive regulation by the State. Kennedy marries and they have a child but eventually she moves on from the marriage.

> We never fought, we were just not suited and did not love each other (25).

Kennedy sees herself as independent from her husband. She raises her children by herself and she writes that

---

[2]This was the view of WA's Aboriginal Protector at Turkey Creek James Isdell 1910–1915 (Wilson, 2004, 3).

what he earned was his and what I earned was mine. I never thought it was a husband's place to provide for his wife (33).

Later Kennedy meets Sam a man she lives with for many years. Kennedy does not speak of her emotions for Sam but she exposes her feelings for him by describing the actions they take on behalf of each other. He shows her what to do when she gets a job as a cook and she cares for him when he has asthma attacks.

Simon (1987) also writes of love and marriage and she confides that she didn't initially believe that Indigenous and non-Indigenous Australians should marry. Once again this statement contradicts dominant views that Indigenous Australians were keen to marry non-Indigenous Australians because it would denote an improvement in social status (172). Simon admits, however, that after seeing many happy mixed marriages that she has changed her mind.

> I've come down to thinking that a marriage will last only if the couple love one another enough to withstand the pressures of the prejudices they are going to experience (105).

She described how the elders of the tribes would make the marriages and ensured they lasted and she writes that she and her husband were from different tribes and should not have married but they got around the kinship prohibition by having a Christian ceremony instead of a tribal one. Simon describes how she and her husband had their ups and downs but they stuck with their commitment and she writes that trust is the "secret of a happy married life" (117). When he becomes ill after 33 year of marriage she expresses her anguish at watching him slowly die in pain.

> You know, I still love my Joe as much as I did the day we met (160).

Gaffney (1989) also writes of her love for Tony the non-Indigenous law clerk on Thursday Island. The magistrate disapproves of the relationship and has Tony transferred back to Brisbane where he is advised that if he married Gaffney it would interfere with his ability to administer justice to the Aborigines and Islanders. Tony resigns his job and marries Gaffney but such is the prejudice that Tony is unable to obtain clerical law work and ends up working in a fertilizer factory.

Della Walker & Coutts (1989) describes a similar loving and committed relationship in which both partners make sacrifices for the other. Walker loved her husband "deep down inside" (51) from the moment she met him. He was a "humble man, quiet and good" and he worked hard in the asbestos mines and took on additional work on the weekends just to put food on the table.

In comparison to Simon, Gaffney and Walker, Langford's (1988) relationships are more complex. When she is only 17 she falls in love with Sam and despite her father's concerns and her relative's warnings she goes off with him and soon has a baby. However, he begins to beat her so she leaves him and takes up with Gordon who is kind, a hard worker and wants to take care of her. They have children together and, like Kennedy, she writes of how they work together as parents.

> I loved him for being a hardworking man as I was a hard working woman myself, but he was a worrier and didn't show much affection to the kids. By this time matters were practical and not romantic and we adapted (77).

Gordon begins to drink and he eventually leaves Langford who comes to see love as unstable and insecure:

> it seemed like the men loved you for a while and then more kids came along and the men drank and gambled and disappeared. One day they'd had enough and they just didn't come back (96).

52.7 Love of Friends

Friendship is central to survival for all these women and it is a relationship that in the context of alienation from relatives and culture serves as a replacement for family (see Chap. 8 in this book). The friendships are facilitated by the shared experience of being discriminated against, and there is an expectation that friends will help each other during the ordeal of their lives. Indeed, Langford explicitly recalls how her joy at finally receiving state housing turned to disappointment when she discovers her extended family and friends cannot come and stay with her; a policy that renders her housing 'useless in our culture where survival often depended on being able to stay with friends and relatives' (Langford, 1988, 174). Kennedy also speaks of the way in which Indigenous Australians all knew and helped each other and Walker writes of how after her husband's death it was her friends who helped her to raise her 14 children. Yet, friendships were difficult and Kennedy, Langford and Walker write of arguing and physical fighting among friends but this is represented as something that is routine and in no way diminishes their affection for each other. Indeed, almost all the authors write of how Indigenous Australians, despite all that has happened to them, can still laugh and play and tell stories and find community. Ward's friends at the mission where she was raised become her family and she yearns to return to them when she finds herself in service to an unkind employer. It is the friendship of Bill the old Scottish handyman who helps to sustain Ward. Bill helps her in practical ways with her monstrous list of daily chores and his kindness, sympathy and gentle humor helps her to keep a perspective on the unreasonable and cruel behavior of her boss, which is destroying her confidence and self-esteem. Bill tells her not to feel shame about herself, and his gentle encouragement gives her the courage to finally look her boss in the face.

Kennedy (1985) acknowledges how discrimination has made her wary of making friends with non-Indigenous Australians. "The fear of rejection was always there," she explained (34).

> Always a black person would know if white didn't like you because they would give you a certain look. No words need be spoken: we knew we were not welcome and we know that look only too well (53).

Kennedy does have non-Indigenous friends like Sid and Peggy Price and she loves them for all the help they give her, but when she goes out with them she is in a constant state of worry that she will spoil social gatherings, if she is asked to leave because she is Aboriginal.

52.8 Love of Community

All of these authors identify as Indigenous and their love of their land, culture and community helps them to survive the oppression of their lives. Simon (1987), following the example set by her grandmother, cares for tribal Aborigines on reserves who are dying in squalor and isolation. She supports and encourages young people to go to school and to get an education; and she encourages community members to exercise their political rights and vote. It is also love of community and her efforts to help her people deal with the problems of colonisation that leads her to write her memoir. Simon expresses indignation about the non-Indigenous belief that Aborigines can't hold their liquor and she disputes the view that Aborigines are lazy and stupid. She is also critical of non-Indigenous Australians who could have been kinder without much cost to themselves and who would not acknowledge her in the street in case others "saw that you knew an Abo" (167).

Gaffney (1989) was similarly committed to her community and it was the support and kindness that she received from Aboriginal Australians that drives her to become politically active on their behalf. She praises them for their incredible generosity

> with love, materialistically and spiritually. I love them for being what they are. Their friendship and the help they gave my children and I made our stays at Yarrabah wonderful and memorable (69).

Community extended to include non-Indigenous Australians and Kennedy (1985) considers the owners of Blue Range Station as a part of her family. She writes that Mac Core was a good friend and

> if he couldn't do you a good turn he wouldn't do you a dirty one (25).

Kennedy also writes of her love for "Daddy Illin" a white Russian married to an Aboriginal woman.

> Daddy Illin fought for many Aborigines whenever they got into strife with the police and they went to him with their problems and it was through this grand old man that we Aborigines learned a lot. (27).

Langford (1988) recalls the community that formed in Sydney's suburb of Redfern after Indigenous Australians in NSW were taken off the reserves. She also describes her growing political awareness as she sees the unjust treatment meted out to her son and his friends by the police and her activism extends to caring for her community by teaching sewing classes and cooking lunches for pensioners and for the medical service staff. Langford begins to more strongly identify with her Indigenous culture and she writes of her pride in being a member of the Aboriginal race.

All the authors speak of their love of land and culture as a part of their communities and these references express agape love as spiritual. Simon (1987) reconciles her Indigenous spirituality with a Christian God and this helps her to make sense of the cruelty of discrimination, forgive her oppressor and motivates her to help her community. Simon writes that if Aboriginal people believe in something bigger than themselves they can overcome the brokenness that comes with racism and discrimination and break the hold of alcohol on the communities and regain their dignity. She believes things will change for Indigenous Australians

> if we all pull together and work hard and unselfishly to help each other to get back the dignity . . . we have lost (143).

She writes that culture gives life meaning and purpose and that Aboriginal people need to learn to identify with their culture.

52.9 Humanism

For women who lived in a variety of settings ranging from missions to Aboriginal reserves and urban state housing, the authors write of love similar ways. They describe love as a feeling of attachment and affection for families, communities and land. They recount both romantic love, characterised by a sense of excitement and deep connection with their partners, and companionate love in which they see their partners as physical and emotional support and a part of survival. The authors also write of love as altruistic and a set of attitudes and actions that protects the wellbeing of the beloved even at the expense of the individual. Langford's father works himself to death to feed the children he is left with after his wife leaves; Walker and Simon's husbands work until their health is broken in order to give their children a better life; Gaffney's husband gives up practicing the law that he loves rather than surrender the woman he loves; and Simon continues to work within the humiliating administrative structures of the mission settlement because she wants to help others.

The authors expose how the colonial policies of separation, assimilation and discriminatory practices normalised hatred of Indigenous Australians and this intensified the feelings of love for family and country among Indigenous Australians. All the authors see family, community and culture as the mechanisms of survival of Aborigines in the face of institutionalized discrimination and social rejection. Indeed, this is made explicitly clear when Langford tells her children to always stand up for each other because "united we stand, divided we fall" (175). It was the company of those who suffered in the same way and understood the fear, loneliness and alienation that came from the persistent rejection by non-Indigenous people that helped to make lives bearable.

The authors also speak about love in the context of their roles as mothers, daughters, wives and sisters' and these universalising social identities go beyond racialized divisions that hold discrimination in place. Indeed, while non-Indigenous readers, many of whom lived in urban setting and had little to no exposure to Indigenous Australians may not understand Indigenous culture or be suspicious of demands for land rights, they could relate to mothers who anxiously stand watch over ill children, or care for aging parents or work to ensure their children go to school and have a better life. Thus these social roles, which had been collapsed into the racialized narratives, became visible and offered sites of unity with readers which enabled the understanding and sympathy among the non-Indigenous reading public necessary for the political solidarity required for social change. Susan Sheridan (1988) made a similar point in her analysis of representations of Aborigines in Australian literature. She concluded that it was appeals to female roles like motherhood which is "constitutive of shared femininity" that disrupted the nation's colonial discourse that constructs "racial difference as absolute" (80).

The representations of Indigenous love contained in the memoirs also became a part of a discourse in which Indigenous Australians explicitly assert their humanity. Kennedy wonders how it is that non-Indigenous Australians don't think Aborigines are human when

> we know how to feel love, passion, anger, hurt and every feeling there is (19)

and she speaks of the oppressive nature of colonisation in which whites pounded every bit of our lifestyle, culture and language and our identity out of us, which left us a mass of bruised and broken humanity. (24).

Walker & Coutts (1989) makes the same point when she writes that it is important that Indigenous Australians should never think

> they are nothing and nobody. We are all human beings, we are the people (76)

and Simon (1987) protests that she is a human and resents the discrimination that reduces her to just a "thing" who comes from the "Black's camp" (169).

The authors all see unity between Indigenous and non-Indigenous Australians as the solution to the survival of Indigenous Australians. Simon writes that the Aboriginal has to be a part of the

> changing world; not to be beaten by it; to take the best of both cultures(143).

Walker & Coutts (1989) also writes of the need for Indigenous and non-Indigenous Australians to mix and to understand each other and she sees expresses an agape version of love when she describes it as the flow that can bridge the gap between the races. She believes Australia has to be shared between Indigenous and non-Indigenous Australians;

> When this land is so big and beautiful, let us all live together in it and share our love with one another (55).

She writes that she doesn't know what is going to happen to her people in the future but

> we mustn't row and fight one another. Let's share Australia together. There's plenty of room for everyone... let us all live together in it and share our love with one another, just mixing together. (55).

It is racist attitudes that prevent this unity and Kennedy (1985) dedicates her book to her children, her grandchildren and her people in the hope that

> "white people will come to know and understand the plight of my people" and the "terrible injustice and humiliation done over hundreds of years (1)."

Langford (1988) also explains that she has written her book in the hope that Australians will be less racist. In this way the authors express Tillich's self-love, which he describes as affirming and loving another as you would yourself (1954; 34) and which Aristotle saw as a necessary precondition for loving others. Self-love for the Indigenous authors was the rejection of the sense of shame instilled in Indigenous Australians by the colonisers, and in understanding the memoirs as acts of self-love they can also be seen as acts of power when viewed through the lens of Foucault's self-fashioning ethics. Foucault (1994) theorized self-fashioning ethics as a response to institutionalized power and universalized knowledge which seek to create and control the human subject. Foucault believed the modern subject is not fixed and unchanging, but an entity that is constantly refashioned in response to changing circumstances and in relationships with others. It is this idea that subjects can be discursively programmed that underpins the view that literature can operate as a form of social activism and shape reality. It is also this idea that enables the individual subject to resist oppression by consciously choosing how they will assemble and disassemble themselves in relation to particular contingent conditions. In other words, by writing their memoirs Indigenous Australians exercised the freedom to consciously decide who they would be in the world beyond the stereotypes imposed by colonization. It is this decision by the individual authors to self-fashion that produced a competing discourse of Indigeneity which changed attitudes to Indigenous Australians and enabled the solidarity with non-Indigenous Australians necessary for social change and justice.

52.10 Conclusion

Representations of love are shaped by social contexts and in the racially divided Australian communities of the 1980s the Indigenous authors and their love stories emerged as a corrective to the colonial discourses that perpetuated racist stereotypes of Indigenous Australians that limited their agency, denied their humanity, and provided the grounds for ongoing social division and exclusion. Against the backdrop of the nation's excision of its Indigenous past from official history, the memoirs communicated how long-term inequality and injustice had damaged the Australian community, and in expressly identifying as a part of a moral community through actions of love, sacrifice and forgiveness for others, the memoirs served as a prompt to the non-violent social action necessary to address the injustice that eroded unity. Moreover, in recasting Indigenous Australians as loving wives, husbands, parents and community members able to act altruistically for others the authors construct a discourse beyond racialized identities, and reconstruct ideas about community and create new modes of engagement that enable restorative justice. Indeed, these memoirs have been described as an early version of the testimonials and first-hand accounts of abuse collected in the *Bringing Them Home Report (1997)* by Justice

Ronald Wilson. This document served as the basis for the Australian Prime Minister's apology to Indigenous Australians for past wrongs in 2008 (Attwood, 2011; 180). These memoirs can therefore be said to illustrate how agape love existed in Indigenous communities, and the retelling of individual sacrifice and selflessness operated to facilitate justice by restoring Indigenous Australians to the national story and opening up public conversations about what it means to be Australian.

References

Attwood, B. (2011). Aboriginal history, minority histories and historical wounds: The postcolonial condition, historical knowledge and the public life of history in Australia. *Postcolonial Studies, 14*(2), 1171–1186.

Bennett, S. (1999). *White politics and Black Australians*. St. Leonards, NSW: Allen and Unwin.

Beshai, J. A. (2017). Martin Luther King Jr.—On love and justice. *The Humanistic Psychologist, 45* (4), 408–421. Web.

Bongiorno, F. (2015). *The eighties: The decade that transformed Australia*. Collingwood, VIC: Black Ink.

Burgmann, V. (2003). *Power, profit, protest: Australian social movements and globalisation*. Crows Nest, NSW: Allen and Unwin.

Coontz, S. (2005). *Marriage: A history. How love conquered marriage*. New York: Viking Press.

Erll, A. (2011). *Memory in culture*. Basingstoke: Palgrave Macmillan.

Foley, G. (2010). *A short history of the Australian indigenous resistance 1950–1990. The Koori History Website Project*. Accessed October 13, 2017, from http://www.kooriweb.org/foley/resources/pdfs/229.pdf.

Fordham, H. (2018). Remediating Australia's cultural memory: Aboriginal memoir as social activism. *Continuum: Journal of Media and Cultural Studies, 32*(1), 42–51. Web.

Fordham, H., & Milech, B. (2014). Romance, romantic love and the 'want of a fortune.' *Australasian Journal of Popular Culture, 3*(3), 351–362. Web.

Foucault, M. (1994). *Ethics, subjectivity and truth. Essential works of Foucault 1954-1984* (Vol. 1). Ed Paul Rabinow. Trans. Robert Hurley. New York: The New Press.

Frankfurt, H. G. (2009). *The reasons of love*. Princeton, NJ: Princeton University Press.

Gaffney, E. (1989). *Somebody now: The autobiography of Ellie Gaffney, a woman of Torres Strait*. Canberra, ACT: Aboriginal Studies Press.

Garber, P. R. (1973). *Martin Luther King, Jr.: Theologian and precursor of black theology* (Order No. 7418033). Available from ProQuest Dissertations & Theses Global (288064414). Retrieved from https://search-proquest.com.ezproxy.library.uwa.edu.au/docview/288064414?accountid=14681

Hartley, J., & McKee, A. (2000). *The indigenous public sphere*. Oxford: Oxford University Press.

Heiss, A. M. (2003). *Dhuuluu-yala to talk straight*. Canberra, ACT: Aboriginal Studies Press.

Helm, B. W. (2010). *Love, friendship, and the self: Intimacy, identification, and the social nature of persons*. Oxford University Press USA—OSO. ProQuest Ebook Central. https://ebookcentral-proquest-com.ezproxy.library.uwa.edu.au/lib/UWA/detail.action?docID=472290

Iorio, G. (2014). *Sociology of love: The agapic dimension of societal life*. Vernon Press, ProQuest Ebook Central. https://ebookcentral-proquest-com.ezproxy.library.uwa.edu.au/lib/uwa/detail.action?docID=4647860

Jankowiak, W. and Fischer, T. (1992). A cross cultural perspective on romantic love. *Ethnology, 31*, 149–155.

Kahane, A. (2009). *Power and love: A theory and practice of social change*. Berrett-Koehler. ProQuest Ebook Central. https://ebookcentral-proquest-com.ezproxy.library.uwa.edu.au/lib/uwa/detail.action?docID=479225

Kennedy, M. (1985). *Born a half caste*. Canberra, ACT: Aboriginal Studies Press.

King, M. L. (1963). *Strength to love*. New York: Harper & Row. Print.

Konstan, D. (2008). Aristotle on love and friendship. *SCHOLE, 2*(2), 207–212. Web.

Korff, J. (2019). *Meaning of land to aboriginal people*. https://www.creativespirits.info/aboriginalculture/land/meaning-of-land-to-aboriginal-people

Langford, R. (1988). *Don't take your love to town*. Ringwood, VIC: Penguin Books.

Maddock, K. (1986). *The Australian aborigines*. Ringwood, VIC: Penguin Books.

McCausland, R. (2004). Special Treatment - The Representation of Aboriginal and Torres Strait Islander People in the Media. Journal of *Indigenous Policy 4*, 4–98.

Morgan, S. (Ed.) (2008) *Heartsick for country: Stories of love, spirit, and creation*. Fremantle Press. ProQuest Ebook Central. https://ebookcentral-proquest-com.ezproxy.library.uwa.edu.au/lib/uwa/detail.action?docID=576427

Morris, B. (2013). *Protest, land rights and riots: Postcolonial struggles in Australia in the 1980s*. Canberra: Aboriginal Studies Press.

Nwonye, J., and Stassen, G. H. (2009). *The role of agape in the ethics of Martin Luther King, Jr. and the Pursuit of Justice*. ProQuest Dissertations Publishing. Web.

Parker, R. (2005). Perspectives on the future of marriage. *Family Matters, 72*, 78–82. Print.

Perkins, C. (1994). Self-determination and managing the future. In C. Fletcher (Ed.), *Aboriginal Self-determination* (Australian Institute of Aboriginal and Torres Strait Islander Studies Report Series) (pp. 33–46). Canberra, ACT: Aboriginal Studies Press.

Pettman, J. (1988). *Whose country is it anyway? Cultural politics, racism and the construction of being Australian* (Working Paper Series). Canberra: Peace Research Centre, Research School of Pacific Studies, ANU.

Pinto, S. O. (2015). *The ontology of love: A framework for re-indigenizing community* (Order No. 10020266). Available from ProQuest Dissertations & Theses Global. (1771287937). Retrieved from http://journal.media-culture.org.au/index.php/mcjournal/article/view/585

Reynolds, H. (1984). *The Breaking of the Great Australian Silence. Aborigines in Australian Historiography 1955–1983*. London: Australian Studies Centre, Institute of Commonwealth Studies, University of London.

Sheridan, S. (1988). Wives and mothers like ourselves, poor remnants of a dying race: Aborigines in colonial women's writing. In A. Rutherford (Ed.), *Aboriginal culture today* (pp. 59–76). Sydney: Dangaroo Press.

Shumway, D. R. (2003). *Modern love: Romance, intimacy, and the marriage crisis*. New York University Press. ProQuest Ebook Central. https://ebookcentral-proquest-com.ezproxy.library.uwa.edu.au/lib/uwa/detail.action?docID=865918

Simon, E. (1987). *Through my eyes*. Blackburn, VIC: Collins Dove.

Solomon, R. C. (1981). *Love: Emotion, myth, and metaphor*. Garden City, NY: Anchor Press / Doubleday.

Stanner, W. E. H. (1969). *After the dreaming. Black and White Australians. An Anthropologist's View*. Sydney: ABC.

Tillich, P. (1954). *Love, power and justice*. London: Oxford University Press.

Velleman, J. (1999). Love as a moral emotion. *Ethics, 109*(2), 338–374. https://doi.org/10.1086/233898

Walker, D., & Coutts, T. (1989). *Me and you: The life of Della Walker*. Canberra: Aboriginal Studies Press.

Ward, G. (1987). *Wandering girl*. Broome, WA: Magabala Books.

Wilson, R. D. (1997). *Bringing them home : Report of the national inquiry into the separation of aboriginal and Torres Strait Islander children from their families*. Sydney: Human Rights and Equal Opportunity Commission. Print.

Wilson, T. (2004). Racism, moral community and Australian aboriginal autobiographical testimony. *Biography, 27*(1), 78–103.

Yalom, M. (2001). *A history of the wife*. New York: Perennial.

Assoc. Professor Dr. Helen Fordham lectures in media and communications at the University of Western Australia.

Chapter 53
Sacrifice and the Agapic Love Gender Gap in South Korean Romantic Relationships

Alex J. Nelson

Abstract Altruistically re-ordering one's priorities in favor of one's beloved is a core feature of the experience of romantic love cross-culturally. However, Young women in East Asian societies stand out in ethnological studies of love for expressing less agapic (altruistic) attitudes towards their romantic partners than their male counterparts. Drawing on 18 months of ethnographic fieldwork and interviews with 75 Korean adults, this chapter examines South Koreans' cultural logics of sacrifice in the context of romantic love in order to shed light on the agapic love gender gap found in cross-cultural studies of love. Interviewees' responses suggest sacrifices are an integral part of the South Korean constructions of romantic love. Koreans willingly sacrifice for a partner's benefit and for the sake of maintaining romantic love relationships, which ought to be in both lovers' ultimate mutual interest. However, sacrifices should not compromise a person's major life goals or sense of self and should be reciprocated in ways perceived as fair. The sacrifices Koreans describe making for love often conform to gender norms considered "traditional" and often reinforce patriarchy and gender inequality. Korean women's perceptions that they are likely to be asked to make sacrifices that are contrary to their life goals and sense of self are a probable source of the agapic love gender gap in South Korea.

Keywords Love · Romantic love · Agapic love · Gender relations · South Korea · East Asia

53.1 Introduction

Willingness to put the interests of one's beloved before one's own is widely considered a key characteristic of romantic love. Summarizing the American psychological literature, Helen Fisher, Aron, Mashek, Li, & Brown (2002) found a

---
A. J. Nelson (✉)
Department of Anthropology, University of Nevada, Las Vegas, Las Vegas, NV, USA
e-mail: nelson26@unlv.nevada.edu

© Springer Nature Switzerland AG 2021
C.-H. Mayer, E. Vanderheiden (eds.), *International Handbook of Love*,
https://doi.org/10.1007/978-3-030-45996-3_53

"willingness to sacrifice" for a partner, stemming from intense empathy, and a "reordering" of one's priorities to be among the psychological characteristics "associated with romantic attraction" (Fisher et al., 2002, 415–16). Congruently, Charles Lindholm (1998), in his summation of the social and cultural contexts that give rise to elaborated traditions of romantic love, points to cases of lovers willing to make the "ultimate self-sacrifice" (i.e. love suicide) or pursue dangerous covert liaisons, as an unambiguous indicator that a culture conceives of romantic love as an exultant good in and of itself, rather than a means to an end (i.e. sexual gratification, status, alliance) (225). However, it remains an open empirical question whether prioritizing one's beloved over one's self constitutes an essential feature of romantic love that distinguishes love from other complex relational sentiments (i.e.. intimacy, attachment, liking) or if such a bearing is a mere style of loving, as in the "agapic love style" John Alan Lee (1973) typologized.

To investigate the question of romantic love's cross-culturally universal features Victor de Munck and his collaborators initiated a research program where a combination of open and closed ended survey questions were combined with focus groups and ethnographic knowledge to determine what beliefs about romantic love's attributes were culturally salient in the U.S. Russia, and Lithuania (de Munck, Korotayev, de Munck, & Khaltourina, 2011; de Munck, Korotayev, & Khaltourina, 2009). Subsequent studies building on de Munck's measures in China (Jankowiak, Shen, Yao, Wang, & Volsche, 2015) and South Korea (Nelson & Yon, 2019) found support for agapic love and four other components as a prospective core universal feature of romantic love cross-culturally. Despite this coherence, the East Asian studies revealed a gender gap in men's and women's attitudes towards agapic love. When asked whether they agreed with the statement "I will do anything for the person I love" Korean and Chinese female respondents were divided while their male counterparts largely asserted their agreement. Psychologists comparing love styles in the U.S., Russia and Japan found a similar gender gap among their Japanese respondents to measures of agapic love, suggesting this phenomenon is not a unique artifact of de Munck's survey measure (Nelson & Yon, 2019; Sprecher et al., 1994).

The above studies raise two key questions for our understanding of the centrality of agapic (i.e. altruistic, sacrificial) attitudes to romantic love. First, if a willingness to prioritize one's beloved over one's self, to sacrifice for them, is an essential measure of love, are there limits on their extent or must love be unconditional to be considered "true"? Second, how might love attitudes be shaped by gender relations so as to give rise to an agapic love gender gap like that documented in East Asia? In this chapter I utilize interview and ethnographic data from South Korea to examine these questions. Specifically, I will compare the ways in which South Korean men and women discuss sacrifice in the context of romantic relationships and bring a critical feminist perspective to bare on ways South Korean social structures likely reinforce hegemonic gender norms in beliefs about romantic love and how the shifting field of gender relations in Korea encourages many contemporaries to question, and sometimes reject, gendered cultural expectations that have grown incongruent with their personal desires and senses of self, thereby giving rise to the apparent agapic love gender gap. In the next section I will briefly introduce anthropological and feminist theoretical perspectives on the relationships between romantic love and gendered reciprocity.

53.1.1 Theorizing Love and Gendered Reciprocity

Romantic love is not primarily a means to an end, but a highly valued experience in its own right (Lindholm, 1998). Social theorists have thus expressed skepticism at the authenticity of cultural constructions of love that appear expressly conditional. For example, Frederick Engels (1884) asserted that true passionate love cannot be realized where capitalist production shapes property relations since in any such union one's choice of lover inevitably holds economic consequences that will inherently influence an individual's decisions within that cultural system. Indeed, contemporary ethnographers studying love in capitalist and post-socialist societies do find their informants' experiences of love are often entangled with desires for material, emotional, and erotic care and support (See Chap. 3, Sect. 3.4). Rather than concluding that these discrepancies between the theoretical ideal and the ethnographic reality reveal the loves observed to be mere pragmatic discourses or spurious mimicries of "true" unconditional love, anthropologists and sociologists find the cultural ideal of completely separating utility from sentiment is a fantasy divorced from reality. Now the objective of contemporary ethnographic inquiries into love is not to parse "real" cultural constructions of love from "false" ones, but to consider the ways experiences of love are culturally constructed, shaped by social structures, and negotiated by the ethnographers' interlocutors.

Once we abandon the expectation that love ought to be unburdened by pragmatic considerations, we see that love relationships are governed by principles of exchange and reciprocity (Venkatesan, Edwards, Willerslev, Povinelli, & Mody, 2011). The ideal that acts of love are given unconditionally, as free gifts, does not reflect the lived experiences of most ethnographic subjects. Rather, the everyday affection and aid exchanged between couples, like gifts in general, prompt expectations of reciprocation and generate debt, and thereby power, when the receiver cannot reciprocate the giver (Mauss, 1925). Anthony Giddens (1992) observes that western couples are increasingly products of this exchange to the point of approaching an ideal of "pure relationships" that are based on explicit negotiation of terms that fulfill both partners' utilitarian needs. Despite these trends, the reciprocity central to maintaining love relationships is often naturalized and gendered, reinforcing unequal gender norms and perpetuating patriarchy and inequality. This tendency for love to be culturally constructed and enacted in ways that subjugate women and reinforce monogamy and heteronormativity have fueled feminist and queer critiques of romantic love which this chapter empirically engages in order to explain South Korea's agapic love gender gap.

Feminist theorists have persistently critiqued both ideologies of love and the institutions supporting them, particularly marriage. However, many feminist love scholars maintain that love nonetheless offers potential for the radical betterment of society (See Grossi & West, 2017). Summarizing feminist critiques of love, Renata Grossi (2018) notes that to most critics "romantic love is not itself oppressive but often becomes so via marriage, procreation and family" (61). Most relevant for this study, Ann Fergusson (2018) argues that within the affective economy of marriages, women's care and labor are undervalued by the larger society and the benefits of that care accrue to men, who are already favored by the capitalist labor market. Examining how Americans and Europeans navigate markets for romance and marriage, Eva Illouz (2012) observes how concerns over commitment are structured by gendered concerns ranging from the biological realities of fertility, cultural idealization of hypergamy (women marrying men of higher status than themselves) and the psychological effects of access to massive pools of prospective partners via internet matchmaking sites. By highlighting how love relationships are shaped by exchange of capital and power, be they economic, emotional, symbolic, or erotic, these perspectives help us identify the social forces that shape individuals' negotiations of their own love ideals within romantic relationships.

Although the above critiques originate in western feminists' observations of love in western cultural contexts, I find their insights resonate with many of the accounts of my South Korean informants as they grapple with the repercussions of rapid social changes stemming from Korea's industrialization, urbanization, democratization, and, subsequently, women's improved access to education and employment, and the nuclearization of families. In the following sections I will turn to Korea, first briefly reviewing the history of romantic love as it pertains to sacrifice and gendered exchange before proceeding to present my own ethnographic research findings on contemporary South Koreans' beliefs and experiences of agapic love in the context of romantic relationships. In the discussion section I will return to the above critiques and consider how they apply to my Korean findings. I will conclude the paper by suggesting a direction for future empirical, theoretical, and applied work on agapic love.

53.2 The South Korean Cultural Context: A Brief History of Romantic Love and Sacrifice

South Korea is a highly industrialized country, touting the world's 12th largest economy by GDP and a population of 51.2 million, approximately half of which live within the Seoul metropolitan area (World Bank, 2019). South Korea's population is rapidly shrinking and aging, with a fertility rate of 0.98 for the year 2018 (Kwon & Yeung, 8/29/2019). Domestic and international media discourses problematize this fertility rate and attribute it to a combination of social concerns including: a work culture resulting in poor work-family balance, high youth unemployment, a highly competitive job market, extremely high housing costs relative to salaries, high demand for educational attainment, and high education costs, all of which are thought to contribute to delayed marriage and periods of intentional abstention from dating and marriage markets. For many of my unmarried informants these concerns do lead them to postpone dating or marriage. Other's merely struggle to find the right partner despite actively searching for one. For the past three generations in South Korea, romantic love has increasingly come to be considered a marital prerequisite and an essential element for maintaining a happy marriage. However, young women worry that marriage will open them to pressure to leave careers they have come to value as a means of independence, security and esteem, by employers, husbands, or in-laws, as was the norm for their mothers' generation.

I will argue below that because romantic love is now largely merged with the pursuit and maintenance of marital relationships for Koreans, the compromises and sacrifices of marriage have become entangled with romantic love as well. As Engels and later feminist theorists warned, the entanglement of love and marriage further subjects love relationships to social structures shaping families, which often have gendered effects. Foremost among these effects is the gendered division of labor, whereby the reciprocal support and care within romantic relationships is shaped by internal and external pressures to conform to hegemonic gendered expectations that may be contrary to individuals' desires and thus be perceived as alienating sacrifices, even if done for the sake of love and one's relationship. In this next section I review how Korean ideals of love's relation to sacrifice have evolved in response to shifting social and cultural conditions to set the stage for understanding the beliefs and experiences of my South Korean informants in their contemporary historical and cultural context.

53.2.1 Ancient and Medieval Korea: Love and Sacrifice in Folklore

The Korean peninsula has been home to hierarchical agrarian state societies for 5000 years according to the *Samguk Yusa*, a collection of myths and folklore compiled by a thirteenth century Buddhist monk of the Goryeo dynasty (918 AD–1392 AD) but ascribed to Korea's Three Kingdoms period (57 BC to 668 AD) (Grayson, 2001). This text includes one of the earliest accounts of romantic love in Korea and centers on a lover's sacrifice of her own life for her beloved and her kin. The tale of *The Love of a Tigress and a Man* describes a young man and a woman (who is also a tiger) who fall passionately in love and ends with the tigress killing herself in her lover's arms in order to protect her brothers from vengeful townsfolk the brothers had terrorized and to see that credit for saving the villagers went to her lover, who would receive esteem for his supposed courage (Grayson, 2001, 202). This story, presuming it reflects cultural logics salient of the time, suggests that love did not supersede obligations to natal kin, but did encourage sacrifice and a willingness to put one's lover before one's self, if not one's natal kin.

A more recent folktale, the *Tale of Chunhyang*, similarly valorizes a women's self-sacrificial behavior for the sake of her lover. Set during the neo-Confucian

Choson Dynasty (1392 AD–1897 AD) during which Korean society became increasingly patriarchal and patrilineal, limiting women's claims to property and freedom of movement in public as marital patterns became predominantly patrilocal (Deuchler, 1992), the *Tale of Chunhyang* is well known to this day, having been repeatedly immortalized in novels, films and television series in the modern era. Chunhyang was the daughter of a *kisaeng* (the Korean equivalent of a geisha) who becomes the love object of the governor's son. The couple fall in love and elope but Chunhyang is temporarily abandoned and, in her lover's absence, is sentenced to death for refusing to become the concubine of the villainous new governor, only to be rescued from that fate at the eleventh hour by her husband, whose parents consequently accept their elopement out of admiration for Chunhyang's willingness to endure torture, imprisonment, and a death sentence to remain faithful to her absentee husband (Kim et al., 1976/2016).

These folktales illustrate that Korea has not only had conceptions of romantic love for centuries but that these constructions idealized the prioritization of others over one's self to the extent of making the ultimate self-sacrifice. Importantly, in both tales it is the female partner who sacrifices and does so after marriage, even if the marriage is an elopement. The two tales differ in who the heroine sacrifices for, and this may reflect cultural differences between the two time periods. The tigress primarily sacrifices herself for her siblings, although she does so in such a way that it benefits her lover. This may reflect the fact that during the Goryeo period women retained inheritance claims from their parents, and thus maintained close natal ties after marriage and were relatively free to divorce compared to the Choson period that followed (Deuchler, 1992). By the late Choson period, where wives ideally left their natal families for good upon marriage and had no claims to inheritance from parents, the tigress might have been viewed as an unruly daughter-in-law to act against her husband's wishes for the sake of her natal family. In the *Tale of Chunhyang* the principle benefactor of Chunhyang's sacrifice was her husband and her in-laws, whose reputations would have been tarnished had she become a concubine. The neo-Confucian ideals of the Choson dynasty continue to be a primary reference for contemporary Korean beliefs about what is "traditional" Korean culture even for some customs that actually have modern origins (Kendall, 1996). Although conceptions and practices of love and marriage diversified in the twentieth century with Korea's opening to the world and subsequent industrialization, norms of patriarchy, patriliny, patrilocality and primogeniture that became entrenched during the Choson period have a persistent influence today.

53.2.2 Colonial and Post-Colonial Korea: Love, Sacrifice and Modernity

At the beginning of the twentieth century Korea was colonized by Japan and forced to open to the world. That opening exposed Koreans to accounts of foreign conceptions of romantic love and courtship. Concurrently, urbanization, expansion of wage labor and increased access to education created opportunities for experimentation with alternative romantic and gender practices enabled by the new opportunities that schools, cities, postal services, literacy, and factories opened for interactions between the sexes, including discussion of love marriage, free love, gender equality and exposure to Protestant Christian constructions of agape (Kim, 2013; Kwon, 2014; Yoo, 2008). However, the pluralized discourses that attracted debate among the intelligentsia of the colonial period (1910–1945) met with conservative backlash that derided the calls for gender equality and pre-marital romance as selfish at a time when freedom from colonial rule and national development were seen as the top priority towards which social change should be directed (Kim, 2013; Yoo, 2008).

After Japan's defeat in World War II, Korea was divided into north and south at the 38th parallel. Following a bloody civil war, South Koreans were compelled by their authoritarian military regime to put the nation's need for development before their own, encouraging thrift, fertility, and intensive labor for minimal pay until the 1980s when the economy achieved a relatively high level of prosperity. Beginning in the colonial period and gradually becoming more common throughout the development era, Koreans began shifting from arranged marriages, where the couple might not see one another before their wedding day, to developing a culture of courtship. This transition favored grooms' interests as they increasingly insisted on the right to see their prospective brides before the wedding night, a privilege that put the reputation of prospective brides at risk since rejection could tarnish their standing with other prospective suitors (Kendall, 1996).

By the 1980s and 1990s, the era of democratization, South Koreans began to enjoy a level of economic prosperity, women made significant gains in educational attainment and the government began to promote family planning, encouraging couples to have only two children (Kim, E.S., 1993). With this newfound prosperity, the ideal of the male salaryman breadwinner and educated professional stay-at-home housewife peaked, and women, despite their credentials, were largely relegated to career trajectories with little prospect for advancement and were encouraged, if not forced, to leave their positions upon marriage, a sacrifice for their husbands and children that some would later lament and many daughters would reject for themselves (Cho, 2002; Janelli & Yim, 2002). Choosing a spouse for one's self and dating for a period of time to get to better know one another became the norm and the ideal by the early 90s (Kendall, 1996; Kim, M.H., 1993). By the 1990s and 2000s pursuing romance without necessarily having an eye towards marriage, such as through group dates between underclassmen, called "*meeting*", were a customary part of youth culture (Baldacchino, 2008; Lett, 1998). For the young men and women in their 20s and 30s at the time of my fieldwork, experiencing love in the context of a romantic relationship is one of the greatest sources of happiness in their lives, but the desirability of marriage is less certain. Nonetheless, pressure from parents to marry, and to do so within one's social class, or hypergamously, continue to be a major stressor for many young Koreans who are now caught between desires for love, independence, and self-fulfillment at a time when the trappings of the middle class, such as home ownership, are difficult to obtain even for duel income households (Baldacchino, 2008; Yang, 2018). Within the context of this historical shift in the social and cultural forces shaping Koreans' pursuit of romantic love, I will now detail how Koreans' discourses and experiences of romantic love's relationship to sacrifice converge and diverge along gendered and generational lines based on my fieldwork and interviews in South Korea.

53.3 Research Methods

The analysis presented in this paper is based primarily on interviews I conducted throughout South Korea, but principally in Seoul, over the course of 18 months of ethnographic fieldwork between September 2016 and June 2018. Throughout my fieldwork I lived with Korean families in order to observe the rhythms of daily life within Korean households and to better understand the schedules and relationships of Korean couples. Over the course of my fieldwork I conducted formal interviews with 75 Korean adults. These semi-structured interviews lasted from 30 min to 10 h (longer interviews occurred over multiple meetings), with an average length of two hours, and included life history questions focused on the individuals' romantic relationships as well as questions about the meanings they ascribe to romantic love and their love attitudes. I conducted the interviews in Korean, English or a combination of the two.

Although my interviewees were a convenience sample of those I came into contact with throughout the course of my fieldwork and those I had known from previous fieldwork, they are sufficiently diverse to offer insights from a wide range of perspectives and experiences. They largely considered themselves to be part of the middle class. However, they reflect a range of upbringings, from born and bred Seoulites and the children of CEOs to remote villagers who moved to the city in adulthood. Their occupations ranged from housewives, teachers, pastors, small business owners, office workers, middle managers, nurses, musicians, students and the unemployed. Their ages ranged from 18 to 75 years old, with 49% being under the age of 36. Twenty percent of the sample was over the age of 50 and a third of the sample was married, 9% was divorced and 52% had not yet married. Twenty-four percent of the sample identified as Protestant Christians while a small number were Catholic or Buddhist. Some interviewees I lived with for a month or more or met with regularly throughout my fieldwork, having an opportunity to see how they interacted with their partner in public and semi-private spaces. Others I knew only for the length of the interview.

After translating and transcribing the interviews, I used MAXQDA 2018 qualitative analysis software to thematically code interviewees' responses. I did this by creating codes that summarized concepts, connections or examples in their responses and then later identifying themes connecting the various codes and grouping them into a hierarchical structure of increasingly specific categorizations of code sets. The findings I present below reflect the patterns in responses that this process revealed in my interviewees' statements about love and sacrifice, including examples of sacrifices they believe they have made, or are afraid of being asked to make, and those they refuse to make even for someone they love, and the expectations, preconditions and limits they place on what they will do for those they love. I paid particular attention to gendered patterns in responses and interviewees' explicit thoughts of how expectations and experiences of agapic love are gendered.

53.4 Findings: Love, Sacrifice and Reciprocity in Contemporary South Korea

There is broad consensus among my South Korean interviewees and the survey participants of Nelson and Yon's (2019) study that love can, and often does lead one to behave in irrational, uncalculating ways towards one's beloved. Some assert that one is not in love if they behave otherwise. Sacrificing one's own interests in favor of their beloved is one such outcome and sign of love's apparent irrationality. However, even those who professed a willingness to sacrifice usually qualified their responses, noting exceptions or preconditions. As their qualifications demonstrate, love may be one of the most important experiences in a person's life, but for most it is not the only matter of importance to achieving happiness and fulfillment.

53.4.1 The Limits of Love: Uncompromisable Desires and the Need for Reciprocity

When asked what they would be unwilling to do for a romantic partner, both male and female interviewees were most reluctant to give up their career for love. They asserted that the right partner for them would not ask them to do so and that their career was too important to their sense of identity and self-worth.

> I cannot do that (quit their job and become a homemaker). I think if you really like someone, really love someone, you have to be able to support their life's big picture, big wishes. If you think you'll be in a situation where one or the other has to sacrifice their big picture then clearly you aren't really right for each other.—25-year-old male, single, salaried office worker

> So, in the first marriage I realized that I have to do my work. My own profession, that makes me really happy. I can do some housework, but I am not good at full time (homemaking).—36-year-old female, divorced, corporate English instructor and graduate student

Those who thought they could give up their careers usually qualified that their partner would need to be making more money than them or be better able to achieve more in their career than themselves. Some men appeared to fantasize about this possibility, though none asserted they would likely ever become stay-at-home fathers.

> Yeah! *Right, of course. Because... If the person's job is more* visionary *and more likely to develop, I can do it. I would prepare food, wash the clothes and ... [...]* I will be bored, but I (would have) my own time ... probably a hobby. After I did chores, I would go swimming, go out to exercise or go bowling, go to the market to prepare food, clean the rooms and sometimes I'd go on vacation and work together. Probably possible.—36-year-old male, single, insurance salesmen and aspiring entrepreneur (Italics: Translated from Korean)

Nearly all my married female interviewees were engaged in some form of work. Those without professional careers as teachers, counselors or salaried office workers often had left the workforce after becoming pregnant and a number of these wives returned to the workforce doing part-time work in the service industry, a common career trajectory for older generations of Korean women (Cho, 2002).

Whether willing or unwilling to sacrifice their career for a romantic partner, the underlying logic does involve a rational estimation of cost and benefit. Although my interviewees often framed their position as one of personality, that they either were or weren't the "type of person" that could be a homemaker, someone who didn't need a career, those expressing a willingness to give up their careers usually had not achieved a position they desired and that offered them little esteem or certainty for the future. They also indicated that their willingness was dependent on their partner's ability to earn or achieve more than themselves, thus they would receive a net gain, even if it meant compromising on their own opportunities for prestige and autonomy. In other words, when lovers think of sacrificing for their partner, they imagine a compromise that may benefit their partner more than themselves, but which does not completely violate their own self-interest. They ultimately hope the scales will balance and they expect their partner to reciprocate.

> I think that is what you do as a partner. So, not only me, but sometimes discuss and choose something instead of something (else). So, (we weigh) the options and sometimes I can sacrifice and sometimes she can sacrifice, but it has to be a result of the discussion.—36-year-old male, divorced, entrepreneur

> I think he wouldn't let me sacrifice my own wishes either. Same, I don't like this kind of thing. No! I am going to support him for the sake of my husband. For sure, but I cannot say that 'I will endure anything.'—40-year-old female, married, salaried office worker

Both the ideal that love begets sacrifice, or at least compromise, and that said compromises are negotiated to the couples' mutual benefit, were shared by my male and female interviewees. However, for a number of my married informants, patriarchal gender norms, the interference of extended family members, and "personality differences" interfered with realizing a mutually satisfactory reciprocal romantic relationship, a fate that young Korean women are highly cognizant of, and keen to avoid.

53.4.2 The Things We Do for Love: Agapic Love and Gender Relations

The sacrifices Koreans described making for their romantic partners, as opposed to their hypothetical estimations, often reflected and reinforced hegemonic norms of masculinity and femininity. Men described (or were described) traveling long distances to meet or escort their partners, sometimes daily, as a display of affection, interest and capitulation in accordance with ideals of male initiative, protection, and chivalry. The sacrifice men most commonly described making was to provide financial support to their partner through their work, whether in the form of paying the majority of expenses for dating activities or providing for a spouse and children. Women less often framed their financial contributions or work outside the home as making a sacrifice unless they were the primary financial contributor to the relationship. When Korean men assert that their work and financial contributions are sacrifices out of love, they are also asserting their achievement as breadwinners, a central ideal of Korean masculinity which hegemonically contributes to, and is reflected in, Korea's gender pay gap, the largest among OECD countries (Moon, 2002; OECD, 2019).

Korean women, especially those of the elder generation, likewise emphasized sacrifices that conformed to culturally exalted virtues for their gender. Examples of women's gender conforming sacrifices included the provision of domestic support and endurance of hardship springing from inadequate financial resources, conflict with their husbands or in-laws, and husband's attempts to unilaterally exert their will over them, such as by preventing them from going out to socialize. For my informants of the elder generation, sacrifices made to maintain a marriage were not solely framed in terms of love for a spouse but concern for one's children and natal kin, as these quotes illustrate:

> She (mother-in-law) lived with us for 17 years. So, I wanted to get divorced because I was so distressed by her, but at those times, I remembered the love between my husband and me and I didn't get divorced with my strong will (laugh). We should be responsible if we love each other. I have three kids and probably didn't get divorced more because of my kids than my husband.—65-year-old female, married, retired English teacher

> *If men lose against women they believe the household will collapse and so they believe women should always let them win. So, I am my children's mother and I moved to this (my husband's) house from my (maternal) house, [...] and my (natal) family should not get a bad reputation as a result of my behavior. If I sacrifice and treat them well I would hear "she learned well (the lessons from her parents) and came here and did well (towards my affines)" [...] in this way they would praise my (natal) house. But if I do whatever I want they will say "she did not learn well, what did her parents teach her in that house before she came here?"*—61-year-old female, married, service worker

My informants largely frame such patriarchal structuring of domestic hierarchies as holdovers from the neo-Confucianism of the Choson period. The ideal of the male family head is also promoted in Korean Evangelical churches (Chong, 2008; Kim & Pyke, 2015), to which both the above informants belonged, despite Christianity's association in Korea with modernity (Harkness, 2014).

Younger women I interviewed often expressed discomfort with the idea of sacrificing or enduring problems out of love. They expressed a willingness to put up with temporarily uncomfortable or sub-optimal situations for the sake of maintaining a relationship but suggested that a partner who asks them to sacrifice too much would be revealing themselves to be an inadequate partner. While both men's and women's sacrifices for romantic partners often conform to hegemonic gender norms of masculinity and femininity, for younger women accustomed to small families, a greater degree of independence from kin, and who have invested years into schooling with the expectation of pursuing a career, the sacrifices of their mothers appear untenable. In contrast, men rarely problematized the ideal that they ought to be the primary breadwinner, though many feel that their partners should have pursuits beyond homemaking to keep them active and stimulated, acknowledging that housework and childrearing may leave them insufficiently fulfilled. They often frame a prospective partner's ability to contribute to the household economically as of secondary importance to their staying engaged with a meaningful pursuit. This attitude contrasts sharply with accounts in past ethnographies where working class Korean men strongly objected to their wives working outside the household after marriage (Freeman, 2011; Kim, 1997) and likely reflects both a combination of generational shifts in attitudes towards the gendered division of labor, the largely middle class identities and circumstances of my informants, and the shifting economic realities in Seoul that make attaining the trappings of middle class life difficult to obtain even for duel income families with middle class upbringings (Yang, 2018).

53.5 Discussion: Origin and Future of the Agapic Love Gender Gap

South Koreans' discourses of love and sacrifice illustrate that romantic love is associated with a willingness to make compromises for the sake of one's beloved and the maintenance of that relationship. However, lovers are not expected to continually defer their interests for their partner's sake. When they are, they tend to frame their acquiescence as for their children or their natal kin, rather than their lover. Generally, women, and not men, were asked to endure such continual sacrifices. The agapic love gender gap described by Nelson and Yon (2019) likely reflects young women's concern that they may be asked to make the types of continual sacrifices they saw their mothers' generation make as well as the unwillingness of many to give up their career goals in order to stay with a particular partner. The agapic love gender gap may be exacerbated in urban areas where the pool of prospective partners is larger, especially with the aid of internet-based matchmaking platforms, which may make singles less willing to settle for partners who appear potentially problematic, as has been observed in the U.S. (Illouz, 2012).

The feminist critique of romantic love for reinforcing patriarchy and gender inequality is especially apt in the case of agapic love. The agapic aspects of romantic love are particularly susceptible to co-opting by patriarchal gender norms as lovers' expectations of how reciprocity will be achieved are shaped by cultural ideals of "hegemonic masculinity" and "emphasized femininity" (Connell, 1995). If boys and girls are conditioned from youth to see housework and childcare as girls' and women's work, they will likely grow to believe that a loving female partner should show her affection and feminine virtues through housework and childrearing as complimentary reciprocation for men's economic provisioning. In South Korea the conditioning of this gendered division of labor is particularly apparent at family holidays where extended families meet and share large meals prepared exclusively by female family members while the men and boys lounge and socialize. Among couples living in nuclear families, I observed greater, though rarely equal, participation of husbands in cooking and cleaning. In contrast, among those in extended households, such as the 65-year-old teacher quoted in the previous section, parents-in-law may enforce gender norms that couples themselves might be willing to challenge. Thus, the nuclearizing and shrinking of Korean families will likely lead to greater negotiation of how love is reciprocated through forms of economic, caring and erotic support, perhaps eventually growing to resemble Giddens' (1992) "pure relationships". Until then, young Korean women appear increasingly unwilling to accept love as an excuse for what they see as incompatible arrangements for reciprocal care and support. For these women, love may be one of life's greatest goods, but not if it comes at the expense of enduring an unhappy marriage and a complete loss of independence.

53.6 Conclusion

Love, by definition, requires that lovers at times put their beloved before themselves. For South Koreans, a lover who does otherwise would not be believed to be in love. Although some Koreans assert that this reordering of priorities should have few limits and be purely altruistic, the larger consensus is that sacrifices are necessary and done willingly for a partner's benefit and for the sake of maintaining the relationship, which ought to be to both lovers' ultimate mutual interest. These sacrifices should not compromise a person's major life goals or sense of self and should be reciprocated in ways perceived as fair. The sacrifices Koreans report making often conform to gender norms considered "traditional" and reinforce patriarchy and gender inequality. Korean women's perceptions that they are likely to be asked to make sacrifices that are contrary to their life goals are the probable source of the agapic love gender gap in South Korea and other East Asian countries experiencing similar social and cultural transformations documented in survey studies of cultural constructions of love and love attitudes, and may contribute to youth's increasingly tepid attitudes towards marriage in those cultural contexts.

53.7 Recommendations in Theory and Practice

In theorizing romantic love, we ought to examine the gap between the social ideal and empirically documented behavior. Specifically, future research should explore whether holding unattainable ideals, such as unconditional love, serves a useful social function or merely creates cognitive dissonance when individuals find they or their partner are unable to live up to those unrealistic standards. Such projects could eventually lead to the development of measures and recommendations for counseling psychologists' clinical practices and help dispel moralizing discourses blaming "selfish" and "frivolous" youth for East Asia's fertility crises.

References

Baldacchino, J. (2008). Eros and modernity: Convulsions of the heart in modern Korea. *Asian Studies Review, 32*, 99–122.

Cho, H. J. (2002). Living with conflicting subjectivities: Mother, motherly wife, and sexy woman in the transition from colonial-modern to postmodern Korea. In L. Kendall (Ed.), *Under construction: The gendering of modernity, class, and consumption in the Republic of Korea* (pp. 165–196). Honolulu, HI: University of Hawaii Press.

Chong, K. (2008). *Deliverance and submission: Evangelical women and the negotiation of patriarchy in South Korea*. Cambridge: Harvard University Asia Center.

Connell, R. W. (1995). *Masculinities*. Berkley, CA: University of California Press.

de Munck, V., Korotayev, A., de Munck, J., & Khaltourina, D. (2011). Cross-cultural analysis of models of romantic love among U.S. residents, Russians, and Lithuanians. *Cross-Cultural Research, 45*(2), 128–154.

de Munck, V., Korotayev, A., & Khaltourina, D. (2009). A comparative study of the structure of love in the US and Russia: Finding a common core of characteristics and national and gender difference. *Ethnology, 45*(4), 337–357.

Deuchler, M. (1992). *The Confucian transformation of Korea: A study of society and ideology*. Cambridge: Council on East Asian Studies, Harvard University.

Engels, F. (1884). *The origins of the family, private property and the state*. London: Penguin Books.

Fergusson, A. (2018). Alienation in love: Is mutual love the solution? In A. Garcia-Andrade, L. Gunnarsson, & A. G. Jonasdottir (Eds.), *Feminism and the power of love: Interdisciplinary interventions* (pp. 36–54). New York, NY: Routledge.

Fisher, H. E., Aron, A., Mashek, D., Li, H., & Brown, L. L. (2002). Defining the brain systems of lust, romantic attraction, and attachment. *Archives of Sexual Behavior, 31*(5), 413–419.

Freeman, C. (2011). *Making and faking kinship: Marriage and labor migration between China and South Korea*. Ithaca, CT: Cornell University Press.

Giddens, A. (1992). *The transformation of intimacy: Sexuality, love, and eroticism in modern societies*. Stanford, CA: Stanford University Press.

Grayson, J. (2001). *Myths and legends from Korea: An annotated compendium of ancient and modern materials*. London, UK: Routledge.

Grossi, R. (2018). What has happened to the feminist critique of romantic love in the same-sex marriage debate? In A. Garcia-Andrade, L. Gunnarsson, & A. G. Jonasdottir (Eds.), *Feminism and the power of love: Interdisciplinary interventions* (pp. 55–72). New York, NY: Routledge.

Grossi, R., & West, D. (Eds.). (2017). *The radicalism of romantic love: Critical perspectives*. New York, NY: Routledge.

Harkness, N. (2014). *Songs of Seoul: An ethnography of voice and voicing in Christian South Korea*. Berkley: University of California Press.

Illouz, E. (2012). *Why love hurts: A sociological explanation*. Oxford, UK: Polity Press.

Janelli, R. L., & Yim, D. (2002). Gender construction in the offices of a south Korean conglomerate. In L. Kendall (Ed.), *Under construction: The gendering of modernity, class, and consumption in the Republic of Korea* (pp. 115–140). Honolulu, HI: University of Hawaii Press.

Jankowiak, W., Shen, Y., Yao, S., Wang, C., & Volsche, S. (2015). Investigating love's universal attributes: A research report from China. *Cross-Cultural Research, 49*(4), 422–436.

Kendall, L. (1996). *Getting married in Korea: Of gender, morality, and modernity*. Berkley: University of California Press.

Kim, M. C. et al. (1976/2016). *Virtuous women: Three classic Korean novels (a nine cloud dream, Queen Inhyun, Chun-hyang)*. Seoul, ROK: Literature Translation Institute of Korea. Kindle Edition.

Kim, E.S. (1993). The making of the modern female gender: The politics of gender in reproductive practices in Korea. Dissertation, University of California, San Francisco.

Kim, M. H. (1993). Transformations of family ideology in upper-middle class families in urban South Korea. *Ethnology, 32*(1), 69–86.

Kim, S. K. (1997). *Class struggle or family struggle? The lives of women factory workers in South Korea*. Cambridge: Cambridge University Press.

Kim, C. Y. (2013). The conceptual history of 'yonae' (love) in the Korean colonial period. *Acta Koreana, 16*(1), 113–140.

Kim, A., & Pyke, K. (2015). Taming tiger dads: Hegemonic American masculinity and South Korea's father school. *Gender & Society, 29*(4), 509–533.

Kwon, B. (2014). The world in a love letter. In K. H. Kim & Y. M. Choe (Eds.), *The Korean popular culture reader* (Kindle ed.). Durham, NC: Duke University Press.

Kwon, J., & Yeung, J. (2019, August 29). South Korea's fertility rate falls to record low. *CNN*. Retrieved 8 September, 2019, from https://www.cnn.com/2019/08/29/asia/south-korea-fertility-intl-hnk-trnd/index.html

Lee, J. A. (1973). *The colors of love: An exploration of the ways of loving*. Don Mills, ON: New Press.

Lett, D. P. (1998). *In pursuit of status: The making of South Korea's 'new' urban middle class*. Cambridge: Harvard University Asia Center.

Lindholm, C. (1998). Love and structure. *Theory, Culture & Society, 15*(3–4), 243–263.

Mauss, M. (1925/2016). *The gift*. Chicago, IL: Hau Books.

Moon, S. S. (2002). The production and subversion of hegemonic masculinity: Reconfiguring gender hierarchy in contemporary South Korea. In L. Kendall (Ed.), *Under construction: The gendering of modernity, class, and consumption in the Republic of Korea* (pp. 79–114). Honolulu, HI: University of Hawaii Press.

Nelson, A. J., & Yon, K. J. (2019). Core and peripheral features of the cross-cultural model of romantic love. *Cross-Cultural Research, 53*(5), 447–482. https://doi.org/10.1177/1069397118813306.

OECD. (2019). *Gender wage gap* (indicator). https://doi.org/10.1787/7cee77aa-en. Retrieved 8 September 2019, from https://www.oecd-ilibrary.org/employment/gender-wage-gap/indicator/english_7cee77aa-en

Sprecher, S., Aron, A., Hatfield, E., Cortese, A., Potapova, E., & Levitskaya, A. (1994). Love: American style, Russian style, and Japanese style. *Personal Relationships, 1*, 349–369.

Venkatesan, S., Edwards, J., Willerslev, R., Povinelli, E., & Mody, P. (2011). The anthropological fixation with reciprocity leaves no room for love: 2009 meeting of the group for debates in anthropological theory. *Critique of Anthropology, 31*(3), 210–250.

World Bank Group. (2019). *GDP ranking 2018*. Retrieved 8 September 2019, from https://datacatalog.worldbank.org/dataset/gdp-ranking

Yang, M. J. (2018). *From miracle to mirage: The making and unmaking of the Korean middle class, 1960–2015*. Ithaca, CT: Cornell University Press.

Yoo, T. J. (2008). *The politics of gender in colonial Korea: Education, labor and health, 1910–1945*. Berkeley, CA: University of California Press.

Alex J. Nelson earned his Ph.D. in Anthropology at the University of Nevada, Las Vegas and is writing an ethnography of romantic love in South Korea. His work explores how historical/intergenerational changes in Korean expectations and experiences of love and romantic relationships reflect changes in Korean gender relations and the social and economic structures shaping them. He is also a researcher with the Erotic Entrepreneurs Project (www.eroticentrepreneurs.com), an interdisciplinary participatory action study of the business practices and strategies of independent erotic escorts in USA.

Chapter 54
Contestations and Complexities of Love In Contemporary Cuba

Heidi Härkönen

Abstract While love is something deeply personal, people's intimate experiences of love are simultaneously shaped by large-scale cultural and historical processes. Anthropologists have shown how such far-reaching changes as modernization and globalization may introduce people into new ideas of affectionate relationships and transform more long-standing, social and cultural understandings of love. Often such changes bring along novel desires that disrupt traditional marital practices or create new tensions centered on contesting understandings of love.

Drawing on long-term ethnographic research in Havana, this chapter explores ordinary people's understandings and experiences of love in the midst of Cuba's contemporary political and economic changes. Since the 1990s, Cuba has transformed from a socialist country into a new society marked by economic liberalizations, international mass-tourism and heightened inequalities of wealth. The findings show that these structural changes have created intensified complexities and contestations in individuals' love relationships in ways that are emblematic of the emergence of sharpened social inequalities in contemporary Cuba. These results can be applied to understand the consequences that large-scale changes may have for individuals' experiences of love in contexts undergoing drastic structural developments. The chapter concludes by arguing that the troubles that Cubans experience in their relationships differ significantly from the socialist definitions of love publicly promoted by state authorities but they are still not characterized by commodified conceptualizations. On a more general level, this chapter recommends careful ethnographic research as a fertile way for understanding cultural and historical variations in love.

Keywords Love · Cuba · Anthropology · Social change · Inequality · Socialism

H. Härkönen (✉)
Gender Studies, University of Helsinki, Helsinki, Finland
e-mail: hkharkonen@gmail.com

54.1 Introduction

Even though persons experience love as something deeply personal, love is simultaneously shaped by historical and sociocultural developments that go beyond the individual. Anthropologists have shown that far-reaching political, economic and social processes such as modernization, (neoliberal) globalization and postsocialism can transform how people experience and understand intimate relations (Hirsch & Wardlow, 2006; Padilla, Hirsch, Muñoz-Laboy, Sember, & Parker, 2007; Bloch, 2017). Large-scale processes of change may introduce people to new personal desires or ideas about commitment that create shifts in earlier love relations (Ahearn, 2001; Tran, 2018). Such changes may create gendered and generational tensions and transformations in social hierarchies and power relations if, for example, they create disagreements about the role of material dependencies in love relations (Cole, 2009). To understand how large-scale developments interact with individuals' experiences of love, we need empirical accounts of ordinary people's relationships in contexts experiencing significant structural shifts.

Drawing on long-term ethnographic research in Cuba, this chapter explores the complexities and contestations that emerge in individuals' love relations in the context of structural developments. Cuba represents a well-suited place to explore how large-scale processes of change shape individuals' experiences of love. Since the 1990s, Cuba has experienced extensive political, economic and social shifts, as it has transformed from a fairly closed socialist island into a new society significantly shaped by global capitalism. These state-level changes have introduced new complexities and tensions into Cubans' love relations.

This chapter aims to show how large-scale changes may introduce shifts into individuals' experiences of love and to explore the contestations and complexities that persons encounter in such situations. The chapter will introduce the readers to some of the troubles that low-income, racially mixed, heterosexual Havana residents face in their relationships amidst Cuba's contemporary changes. On a more theoretical level, as a detailed, empirical analysis of love, this ethnographic account allows for the examination of historical and sociocultural variations in persons' experiences and conceptualizations of love. The chapter first introduces the theoretical background of the research. It will then discuss Cuba as a research context and the ethnographic methodology of the study. After that, the research findings and their meanings will be discussed on a more theoretical level. Finally, the conclusion returns to the main question of the article regarding the interplay between large-scale developments and ordinary people's personal experiences of love.

54.2 Theoretical Background

While issues related to gender and marital relations have been central to anthropology since the pioneers of the field (e.g. Morgan, 1877/1985), early anthropological studies focused on kinship at the expense of people's subjective experiences. However, in late 1960s, due to its emphasis on the interpretation of cultural meanings, symbolic anthropology raised more interest towards the study of emotions (Peletz, 1995). In particular, David Schneider's (1968) approach on love (defined as diffuse, enduring solidarity) as the characterizing feature of American kinship, surged interest into emotions as cultural systems of meaning. In 1970s, feminist researchers, drawing simultaneously on symbolic anthropology and Marxist influences, turned their gaze to love and sexuality as political sites of gendered power (e.g. Firestone, 1970). Since the 1980s, studies of the cultural meanings of emotions started to gain more ground in anthropology (Abu-Lughoud, 1986; Besnier, 1990; Rosaldo, 1980) and in the 1990s, romantic love began to attract attention as the prime example of an emotion as a subjective experience (Jankowiak & Fischer, 1992; Lindholm, 1998).

Jankowiak (see his chapters in this book) and Fischer (1992) were among the first researchers to highlight romantic love as an object of cross-cultural study, criticizing such historians (e.g. Ariès, 1962) who perceived romantic love as a uniquely Euro-American experience. More recently, some anthropologists have rejected the term "romantic love" because they see it as being too connected to its Euro-American history and thereby ill-fitted to describe other understandings of love (Padilla et al., 2007; Cole & Thomas, 2009; Zigon, 2013). Nevertheless, the rejection of the term "romantic" does not mean that relationships outside Euro-American contexts are devoid of passion, desire and intense attachments (Cole & Thomas, 2009). Love, as a broader concept, has retained its analytical appeal amongst anthropologists. Padilla et al. (2007, p. ix) argue that

> love is a particularly useful tool for social analysis, providing as it does a glimpse onto the complex interconnections between cultural, economic, interpersonal and emotional realms of experience.

Since the 1990s, anthropologists have explored love primarily from the perspective of social change and the interplay between extensive transformations and ordinary people's intimate experiences. In various parts of the world, researchers have drawn attention to how large-scale changes brought about by modernization (Collier Fishburne, 1997; Hirsch & Wardlow, 2006), economic development (Rebhun, 1999; Cole, 2009; Jordan Smith, 2017) and the influx of global migrations and tourism (Brennan, 2004; Hannaford, 2017; Fernandez, 2019) have created new understandings of love and intimacy in ways that provide opportunities for social mobility but also generate challenges in individuals' gender relations. Feminist anthropologists have shown that such shifts in understandings of love have repercussions for people's wider networks of kinship relations, as changed expectations create gendered and generational tensions (Ahearn, 2001; Wardlow, 2006; Cole,

2014; Shakuto, 2019). These studies highlight the diverse ways in which large-scale changes may transform individuals' experiences of love.

In Cuba, the political and economic changes that have since the 1990s gradually dismantled the country's socialism, have created intensified tensions in individuals' love relations. Recently, scholars have shown how in contemporary Cuba, economic inequalities, material insecurities and the struggle for day-to-day survival, threaten more established forms of love, intimacy and sexuality (Härkönen, 2017, 2019; Stout, 2014). Researchers have paid particular attention to the rapid growth of sex work and the central role that material resources play in sexual-affective relations both amongst Cubans and between Cubans and foreign tourists (Allen, 2007; Berg, 2004; Cabezas, 2009; Daigle, 2015). These changes in love relations are connected to larger historical transformations in Cuban society.

54.3 Context

The 1959 Cuban revolution was a modernization project aimed at creating a new industrial, scientific and egalitarian society without discrimination based on gender, race, age, class, wealth or geographical location. State ideology emphasized personal commitment to socialism and collective sacrifices (Guevara 1965/ 2005). As in other socialist states (Verdery, 1996), the government aimed to undermine distinct mediating structures (such as religious institutions) to generate a direct relationship between the state and the individual (Hamilton, 2012, p. 31). The purpose was to create a revolution "outside of which there is no life" (Guevara 1965/2005, p. 30). The state would nurture individuals from cradle to grave, providing basic services such as food, residence, jobs, commodities, child care, education and health care. Everyone would have a state-guaranteed access to goods and services and disparities of wealth would cease to exist.

In pre-revolutionary Cuba, as a legacy of Spanish colonialism, plantation slavery, and the United States governed republican period, racialized inequalities of wealth and status were blatant (Martinez-Alier, 1974). Material wealth was largely concentrated in the hands of a white minority while the Afro-Cuban parts of the population suffered multiple forms of discrimination and poverty (de la Fuente, 2001c). In Havana, white, middle-class persons were able to embrace a desirable life-style but in the slums and in rural Cuba, many people lived in disease-ridden, miserable conditions (Butterworth, 1980; Lewis, Lewis, & Rigdon, 1977a, 1977b). With its policies of social justice, the Cuban revolution sought to equalize such differences and many of its policies benefitted especially the poorest parts of the population (Eckstein, 1994, pp. 149–157).

A part of this endeavor was to create egalitarian gender and love relations. State policy sought to promote relationships and intermarriage across divisions of race, age, wealth and geographical origin as a part of erasing all social differences (Díaz Tenorio, 1993). In colonial Cuba, legal marriage was a significant status symbol in the society controlled by a class and color endogamy (Martinez-Alier, 1974).

Marriage had great value amongst all classes but it was most common amongst the white elite classes, whilst both consensual unions and mother-centered kin relations (matrifocality) were widely practiced amongst the Afro-Cuban population (Martinez-Alier, 1974, pp. 104, 117). Soon after its entry into power, the revolutionary government sought to equalize Cubans' access into legal marriage as a way to promote greater stability in the family relations of the poorer section of the population. Later, in 1975, the new family law granted long-term consensual unions the same legal standing as marriage in terms of children and inheritance (Randall, 1981/2003). However, in practice the value of legal marriage rather eroded during the years of the revolution at the expense of consensual unions and matrifocal kin relations (Safa, 2005).

Nevertheless, the government was more successful in balancing the gendered material dependencies in Cubans' love relations. In an 'Engelsian' (1884/2004) spirit, in a socialist society, love relations were to be free of material dependencies. With the help of the Cuban Women's Federation and by transferring nurturing work such as childcare from individuals to state institutions, women's participation in wage labor was supposed to eradicate *machismo* and create full gender equality (Rosendahl, 1997, pp. 51–77; Safa, 2005, pp. 324–328).[1] As salaried income brought women economic independence, they "could 'marry for love' instead of economic security" (Smith & Padula, 1996, p. 147). In her description of Cuban women in the 1970s, Randall (2003, p. 403) writes:

> Speaking with young people, you won't find many who see their futures dependent on marriage or a future husband's career. Their central goal in life is their own development and their potential contribution to society.

Similarly, in her account of eastern Cuba during the 1980s, Rosendahl (1997, p. 69) states that even though women expected material contributions from their partners, a man's wealth was not overly significant in terms of his attractiveness to women. Instead, women stressed the importance of finding a "good" man who takes care of them and respects them (Rosendahl, 1997, p. 69). However, such relationships changed in the 1990s, when Cuba's position in the global economic order was radically transformed.

In 1960, when the Cuban revolution turned openly socialist and started to nationalize foreign businesses, the United States government isolated Cuba politically and economically through an embargo. Cuba found support in the European socialist block, with 70% of its foreign trade taking place with the Soviet Union (Eckstein, 1994, pp. 88–91). In the 1990s, after the disintegration of Soviet Union, Cuba was plunged into a severe crisis that brought significant changes to the country. Deprived of its most important allies and with its citizens suffering, the government was forced to cut down many of its earlier contributions to the population. Heightened monetization, increased economic liberalism and intensified globalization started to shape life on the island. The opening of the country to tourism, the

---

[1] However, in practice, views drawing on machismo continued to play a role in Cubans' understandings of love, sexuality and domestic relationships throughout the revolution (Rosendahl, 1997; Hamilton, 2012; Härkönen, 2016).

increasing importance of private commerce, widespread black markets and the heightened role of remittances all played a role in accentuating pre-revolutionary divides along wealth and race lines (de la Fuente, 2001a, 2001b; Martinez, 2013). These changes transformed Cubans' love relations in many ways, creating new tensions and complications, many of which characterized life in Havana in the 2000s, when the fieldwork trips for this research were conducted.

54.4 Research Methodology

This chapter draws on a total of 23 months of ethnographic research in Havana since 2003. The research has continually taken place among the same community of people: low-income, racially mixed Havana residents linked to each other by ties of kinship, love, sexuality, friendship or as neighbors. To understand everyday life in Havana, participant observation, interviews, media analysis and archival research were used. Most of the data comes from spending time with men and women of all ages in their daily life and talking with them about their hopes, troubles, joys, fears and dreams. However, close attention was also paid to observing people's day-to-day interactions, exchanges and practices, following Bourdieu's (1990) insights that many fundamental aspects of everyday life are often not verbalized. As this research relies on long-term close relationships with the same people (Härkönen, 2005, 2014), it provides an empirically situated perspective on love from the point of view of low-income, racially mixed Havana residents. It is likely that relationships differ amongst wealthier or white Cubans or in the countryside. As ethnographic research relies on personal relationships and creates an in-depth perspective on life amongst particular people in a specific time, it resists making broad generalizations. At the same time, ethnography engages in a constant interplay between exploring local understandings on their own terms and relating them to wider theoretical discussions for comparison. Whilst ethnography's attachment to a particular place and perspective can be seen as a limitation, it also allows us to explore large-scale global events that have significant consequences at the local level (cf. Besnier, 2011).

54.5 Findings

Drawing on long-term ethnographic research in Cuba, this chapter focuses on a particular love relationship that took place in Havana over several months in 2017 and 2018. This relationship exemplifies many of the complexities that characterize individuals' love relations in post-Soviet Cuba, in particular, the material dependencies that the contemporary inequalities of wealth, race and class create in Cubans' relationships and the tensions they cause amongst people used to socialist egalitarianism.

Yankiel, a 34-year-old *mulato* man, met Gisela, a white woman in her late forties, in a state-owned recreational beach venue, where he worked as a handyman.[2] Gisela, a private entrepreneur, worked as a party decorator and ran a children's clothes shop. They had both recently separated from their partners and the time was right for their romance. During my fieldwork in Havana in 2017, Yankiel's mother explained to me:

> She separated from her partner and they were both alone so [they got together].

As *Habaneros* were of the opinion that it is not good for anyone to live alone, it is not surprising that Yankiel and Gisela were so quick to start a new relationship after their previous separations.[3]

For Yankiel, entering into a relationship with Gisela was an attractive option for various reasons. Yankiel quickly moved in with Gisela to her spacious apartment in a desirable, middle-class suburb, where she had air conditioning, running water and plenty of food, luxuries that he lacked at home. Before living with Gisela, Yankiel had lived with his mother in a small inner-city apartment owned by his stepfather, with whom he did not get along. As a state-employed, low-salaried man from a humble background, entering a relationship with Gisela offered Yankiel the opportunity to taste of some of the pleasures that life had to offer in the new Cuba. Gisela cooked and cleaned and gave Yankiel small amounts of money for his daily needs. She fed Yankiel's enthusiasm for information technology, arranging for him to have computer access at home.[4] With her contacts, Gisela arranged for Yankiel to have eye surgery so that he no longer needed to wear glasses for his myopia. Gisela took Yankiel out to eat in restaurants and organized holidays at the beach several times a year. Gisela's generosity also extended to Yankiel's kin: she regularly gave his mother and his two children by different mothers gifts of food. Yankiel, in turn, helped Gisela around the house and with her business and took a fatherly stance towards her ten-year-old daughter by another father.[5] Materially, Yankiel was very comfortable with Gisela.

However, their relationship was not without problems. Yankiel felt that Gisela was overly jealous and watched his every move:

> Gisela is very jealous [...] When I'm working she calls me six, seven, even ten times; 'where are you, what are you doing?'

---

[2] All the names of my interlocutors are pseudonyms. I use local racial categorizations (see Fernandez, 2010, pp. 20–21).

[3] This idea relates to Habaneros' relational understandings of personhood that emphasize the social embeddedness of human existence (Härkönen, 2016).

[4] Cubans have been allowed to possess computers and cell phones since the change in law in 2008 (Reardon, 2008) but access to both is still relatively limited.

[5] Habanero interlocutors often had children with different partners. Many people's relationships were in practice matrifocal in the sense that mother-child relations were strongly valued whilst father-child relationships could be more sporadic (Härkönen, 2016). Few people were legally married. The historical roots of Caribbean matrifocality lie in the colonial relationships and hierarchies of class, race and gender.

Yankiel explained to me how Gisela was particularly suspicious of his cell phone. Gisela, for her part, had a good reason to be suspicious of Yankiel's phone, as he showed me how he had installed a dating application for meeting other women. Yankiel also showed me that he had installed a spyware application, displaying how Gisela had tried to break into his phone one night when he was a sleep. Yankiel tried to resist Gisela's intrusiveness by not charging his prepaid phone line:

> I don't buy credit on my cell phone because if I have credit, Gisela says to me: 'why didn't you call me?'. This way I don't need to call her all the time. I always leave a bit of credit for emergencies [...], but I don't buy credit so that I don't have to call her.

Before starting a relationship with Gisela, Yankiel had a short relationship with another work colleague, Rosa, a white woman in her mid-twenties. Soon after the start of their relationship, Rosa had fallen pregnant and Yankiel and she had tried to set up life together. However, as neither of them had housing of their own or money to rent a place, they drifted from one kin member's home to another and tried to get by on their small state wages. Rosa quickly became annoyed with the situation and she terminated their relationship when their son was only few months old. They separated in hostile terms and after starting a relationship with Gisela, Yankiel contracted a lawyer to gain more time with his son. However, Yankiel's sister Yadira was of the opinion that he is really only interested in getting back together with Rosa:

> Yankiel is still in love with Rosa, the mother of his son. He says the lawyer is to get to the child, but it is to get to the mother.

In the following months, Yankiel kept on living with Gisela, but he was getting increasingly uncomfortable in the relationship. Gisela's jealousy grew even more after Rosa called her and stated that Yankiel has been trying to constantly harass her. Yadira told me about the conflict:

> On Monday, Yankiel slept at his mother's because Gisela threw him out. The son's mother (Rosa) had sent Gisela a message saying that he should stop harassing her, [...] that he is chasing after her all the time and he should stop it because she (Rosa) has a [new] husband and she doesn't want anything to do with Yankiel.[6] Gisela got furious and said quite a few things to Yankiel and he just stayed silent because it is true, he does it because he is in love with the mother of his son. Gisela threw him out, she took the house key off him and everything. I don't know if she has already picked him up again. Because she throws him out and then she takes him back again. She has already thrown him out three times.

While Gisela's and Yankiel's relationship was stormy, Gisela eventually calmed down this time as well and took Yankiel back. However, she became even more suspicious of Yankiel's every move. Yankiel, on the other hand, growing tired of Gisela's constant jealousy, began to contemplate terminating their relationship:

---

[6]Interlocutors frequently referred to their partners as their "husband" or "wife" (*marido/mujer*) regardless of whether they were legally married. This tendency shows the low importance of legal marriage as a status distinction (see Härkönen, 2016, pp. 12–13).

> Gisela is very possessive, she is very good; she is good to my family and I'm comfortable at her home, but she holds me like this [in a strangle hold]. [...] We'll see if when you come back [to Cuba next time], it is possible that I will be living in Centro Habana [at his stepfather's apartment] again.

Yankiel's kin members, whilst pleased with Gisela's kindness towards them, were also getting annoyed with the situation. His mother stated:

> Gisela is very good to me but it is only to get to Yankiel. [...] She has helped me a lot but I prefer to be left without anything than to live like this; she can't suffocate him like that. Here [at Yankiel's step-father's apartment] he has his room, his things [...]. There [at Gisela's] he is comfortable but one can't live like this, no way.

The relationship came to a turning point in August 2018, when Gisela wanted Yankiel to accompany her on a holiday trip to rural Cuba on a time when Yankiel should have been at work. As Yankiel had already been getting remarks from his boss for his too frequent absences, he was reluctant to go in fear of losing his job. He also wanted to stay in Havana to keep seeing his son, and via him, Rosa. Growing tired of Yankiel's lack of commitment, Gisela gave Yankiel an ultimatum of either going with her or facing the end of their relationship. Yankiel still refused to go and Gisela threw him out for good.

The consequences of their separation were different for the two parties. Gisela was upset and hurt, but she quickly found herself a new, young lover and forgot about Yankiel. Yankiel's sister told me that:

> Gisela took advantage of the situation when she went to the countryside for two weeks, when Yankiel didn't want to go with her, [...] it seems that Gisela said 'there, that's it, it's over' and she found herself another man and when she came back, she wanted nothing to do with Yankiel anymore.

Yankiel, on the other hand, only had himself to blame, but he started to quickly regret the loss of the relationship and the comfortable lifestyle he had been experiencing with Gisela. Yankiel had to move back to his stepfather's home where he was not welcome and had to get again used to a life without luxuries. He kept on hoping to get back together with Rosa, but without money and housing to offer her and their son, his chances were slim. In the months following their separation, Yankiel's body came to bear the testimonial of his suffering:

> I've lost five kilos already in this mess with Gisela and the separation.

Whilst Yankiel and Gisela's stormy love story eventually ended up in separation, their relationship was plagued by insecurities throughout. Gisela, consumed by jealousy, repeatedly threw Yankiel out but later, compelled by her emotional dependency on him, took him back again. Yankiel, on the other hand, drifted from one household to another as a consequence of his messy relationships. Lacking a proper home of his own and unwanted at his stepfather's, he was in a difficult situation and at a material disadvantage, trying to balance his desire for personal and practical autonomy with his economic and emotional dependencies on two women, Gisela and Rosa. Nevertheless, Gisela eventually had the agency to decide that she had had enough.

54.6 Discussion

These tensions and turns in the relations amongst Yankiel, Gisela and Rosa exemplify the complexities and contestations of love in contemporary Cuba. Recently, several researchers have pointed out that as the island's growing inequalities intensify insecurities in relationships both amongst Cubans (Härkönen, 2015, 2019; Stout, 2014) and between locals and tourists (Cabezas, 2009), doubts about material interests disguised as declarations of love run rife. Moreover, during the post-Soviet era, Cuba has become an international center for sex tourism, which further colors relationships on the island with suspicions of commodification. Cabezas (2009, p. 168) describes Cuban sex workers' relationships with foreigners as involving "some commodified aspects blended with intimacy" whilst Roland (2011, p. 72) sees such relationships as forming a continuum from straight out sex workers to more affective engagements. Others reject such classifications altogether, highlighting how material and emotional aspects intertwine and overlap in relationships (Andaya, 2013; Härkönen, 2015, 2016, 2019; Stout, 2014; cf. Illouz, 2017; Zelizer, 2005).

Material issues played a prominent role in the love relations amongst Yankiel, Rosa and Gisela and the same was true for other interlocutors. Whilst in practice, love and material issues were usually intertwined amongst Habaneros, the ways in which people talked about love and material issues were gendered (Härkönen, 2019). Female interlocutors often described their views of a desirable partner by referring to his material possessions. For example, when Yadira explained why she had left her old boyfriend for a new partner, she said:

> Yes, but Roidel did not have money, this one has money!

This idea fits traditional views of masculinity, where the man is supposed to be the breadwinner. In such views, a man's material wealth becomes an aspect of his attractiveness: all female interlocutors rejected a man whom they described as a *muerto-de-hambre* (starving-to-death) as a potential partner. Such ideas show a significant break from earlier, socialist ideals of gender equality, which highlighted the importance of egalitarian relationships and women's independent income and engagement in wage labor (see Castro Ruz, 2006).

For men, love and material issues were more complexly intertwined. My male friends rarely described their attraction to a woman by referring to her material possessions but highlighted instead their love for her. Osdel, a white man in his thirties, said about his girlfriend:

> I love her with all my life! [Last night] I couldn't sleep because I missed her.

On the other hand, some men explicitly rejected the idea of depending emotionally on a woman, considering it a threat to their proper masculinity. Livian, a thirty-year-old *mulato* man, rejected a woman who in his opinion was "very *metalizada*". Yadira explained the term *metalizada* as such:

a woman who doesn't need a man for anything, who has her house, [and] has money.

Being economically dependent on Gisela risked questioning an aspect of Yankiel's masculinity. However, he compensated for this economic dependency by avoiding her and keeping secrets from her, restricting in this way Gisela's access to a level of emotional intimacy with himself. This way he was able to keep up an image of himself as an autonomous, womanizing *macho*.

The fact that material issues played such a prominent role in Habaneros' love relations is most likely a reflection of their low-income position. Wealthier and more middle-class Cubans are likely to experience fewer material tensions in their relationships, although they are unlikely to be completely devoid of them (cf. Lundgren, 2011, p. 64.). Whilst socialist Cuba was officially deemed a classless society, in practice some class inequalities, which are also racialized, have persisted throughout the revolution (de la Fuente, 2001c; Drake & Davidow, 2017). In particular, class differences have increased since the 1990s economic liberalizations, when new sources of income, such as foreign remittances and access to official jobs in the lucrative tourist industry, have disproportionately benefitted white, upper- and middle-class Cubans with access to family resources of housing, money and contacts (de la Fuente, 2011; Bastian, 2018; Hansing & Hoffmann, 2019). Although all Cubans could rely on their state salaries and on the monthly state contributions that they received through the rationing system before the 1990s, in post-Soviet Cuba, both of these have lost their value. State salaries are far too small for anyone to survive on them alone in the new Cuba, creating notable inequalities between state-employed Cubans and those employed in the private sector.

Gisela exemplifies some of these new inequalities of wealth in contemporary Cuba. She lives in a desirable, safe neighborhood in a comfortable, spacious apartment that she inherited from her parents. She is a private entrepreneur and in addition to her decorating business, Gisela owns a popular baby clothes shop in a middle-class suburb. She is able to run her relatively lucrative business thanks to her transnational contacts. Her sister lives in Miami and supplies her with access to many desirable items not found in the Cuban market. In contrast, Yankiel lives in a crowded, dilapidated little flat owned by his mother's partner in a high-crime inner city neighborhood. As the son of poor migrants from east Cuba, he does not have access to remittances, inheritance or housing of his own, making him greatly dependent on his small state salary and forcing him to find new sources of income. At the same time, Yankiel is torn between his economic dependency on Gisela and his affective attachment towards Rosa, who rejects him. His love for Rosa becomes a luxury he can ill afford, as neither of them have money. On the other hand, Gisela, despite her economic stability, experiences constant emotional insecurity, doubting Yankiel's sincerity and commitment, and with good reason.

In Habaneros' love relations, expressions of jealousy play an important role in affirming the union and confirming a person's gendered, heterosexual desirability (Lundgren, 2011, pp. 51–62; Härkönen, 2016, pp. 76–78). Nevertheless, the replacement of the earlier socialist egalitarianism by new material inequalities in contemporary Cuba fosters heightened jealousy and suspicions of material interests in relationships (Härkönen, 2013).

In the time before the 1990s, material dependencies such as those between Yankiel and Gisela would not have existed between Cubans to the same degree because, in the words of Yankiel's mother:

In that era there was no money.

One interlocutor described life before Cuba's 1990s crisis in more detail:

In the 1980s, the society was more homogenous. The state rationing book gave you everything you needed: food, clothes, it was a basic level but a good one, and everybody had the same level.[7] There were festivals, theaters; it was a more civilized way of living. There were no luxuries but everybody had enough to eat, everybody used to go out, there was none of the segregation that exists now, because everybody used to invite each other: you buy me a beer today and tomorrow I'll invite you to have chicken.[8] Now, there exists a structural level of mercantilism.

Here, an interlocutor describes how, in his view, relationships in Cuba before the 1990s crisis were devoid of material dependencies between people. In contemporary Cuba, social relations are different because material inequalities separate people.

Still, the contemporary "mercantilism" and the intertwining of love and money is a complex question. Whilst Yankiel easily comes across as being attracted only to Gisela's wealth, the practical interlinking of material and affective aspects in Habaneros' everyday life rejects such interpretations. Although Yankiel may seem like a selfish climber, he was conscious of the important role that Gisela's generosity played in improving not just his own life, but also the lives of his kin members. Yankiel never said that he was interested only in Gisela's wealth. Although Gisela was older than him, he had a history of dating older women, to such a degree that his sister stated: "Yankiel likes old women (*tembas*)."[9] (cf. Vanderheiden et al.; Chesnokova & van Peer in this book). Moreover, Yankiel suffered visibly after their separation, making it difficult to interpret what aspect of his relationship with Gisela he missed the most. Such ambiguities in Cubans' love relations have definitely intensified along with the growth of income differences in their society.

These tensions that my interlocutors' experience in their love relations indicate a complex relationship with the socialist concept of love promoted by the Cuban revolutionary government. In the Cuban state discourse, love was supposed to be egalitarian and free of material dependencies. Since the 1960s, the government has also tried to promote stability in love relationships, as exemplified by the various state promotion campaigns for legal marriage (see Blanco, 1960). However, my interlocutors' relationships differ significantly from these socialist conceptualizations of love, as they are often unstable and shaped by material dependencies.

---

[7]The rationing system was established in 1962 to ensure that all Cubans had access to the same material contributions from the state (Anonymous, 2013). In 2017, Habanero interlocutors gossiped about state plans to abolish the rationing book system but in 2019, they were still in use.

[8]See Härkönen (2016, 2019) on the importance of reciprocity in social relations in Havana.

[9]Amongst my interlocutors, it was quite common for younger men to date older women. In Cuba, part of socialist ideas of love was to reject relationships defined by differences of age, race and class and foster relations across categorizations instead.

Nevertheless, there are aspects in my friends' relationships that reflect Cuba's socialist legacies. The data from my interlocutors shows that Cubans are critical and uncomfortable of capitalist ideas intruding their relationships. The contemporary inequalities create problems for my interlocutors, as they try to negotiate their relationships amongst complex emotional and economic dependencies. These results resonate with the findings of Stout (2014), who argues that Cubans criticize and seek to resist market logics in their love relations, although in practice such logics often threaten their understandings of intimacy.

Ethnographic data from Habanero interlocutors shows that large-scale transformations in state policies, like the dismantling of many aspects of Cuba's socialism that have taken place since the 1990s, create shifts in ordinary people's intimate relations, but as Friedman (2005) argues, such changes often happen in unexpected ways. As Friedman (2005) points out for China, in Cuba, shifts in individuals' love relations have not taken place as a result of direct state policies seeking to transform people's relationships into socialist gender relations. Instead, Cuba's recent economic and political developments, which have liberalized the economy and intensified inequalities of wealth on the island, have caused individuals to experience significant insecurities and doubts in their relationships, transforming how they experience and understand love.

54.7 Conclusion

Large-scale historical changes may introduce transformations into individuals' experiences of love. In contemporary Cuba, extensive political and economic changes, which have intensified since Fidel Castro officially stepped down from power in 2008, have brought new complications and tensions in ordinary people's love relationships. In the past, relationships were relatively equal: material dependencies were not of the same degree; now material interests are intruding into relationships. As Cuba has transformed from a relatively closed socialist island into a new society characterized by emerging strands of global capitalism, the emerging inequalities of wealth, race, gender and age have become complexly mapped to people's day-do-day experiences of intimacy and affect. In particular, they challenge earlier ideas of socialist, egalitarian gender relations, as love has become ambiguously anchored to material resources and plagued by fears of commodification. At the same time, Habaneros reject the ideas of outright commodification of relationships. Instead, they try to negotiate their love relations amidst emotional and economic dependencies, and simultaneous desires for affective intimacy and personal autonomy. Cubans thus live their love relations as gendered, relational beings torn between multiple social commitments, intimacies and affections. These tensions in Cubans' relationships in contemporary Havana show that people's ideas, practices and experiences of love are historically changing and shaped by sociocultural factors. Ethnography provides a fertile way to understand love and its variations because it pays detailed attention to ordinary people's perspectives in the context of their everyday lives.

54.8 Recommendations in Theory and Practice

Love is historically and culturally contingent. How love is experienced, expressed and understood varies from one context and person to another. Ethnographic research engages in a double movement between locally specific and wide theoretical discussions, as a way to understand both micro-level and large-scale processes in a comparative framework. Ethnographic research shows that to understand love, we should listen carefully to people's own views and accounts of love and life in their full sociocultural, historical, political and economic context. Long-term ethnographic research, which pays close attention to social relations, cultural meanings and values, but also to structural factors, provides fertile insights into something as complicated as love. As a slow research method that takes place over time and relies greatly on trust and the relationships that the researcher is able to create with her interlocutors, ethnographic research approaches love by prioritizing people's on-the ground experiences and relationships over detached theoretical abstractions. Therefore, in ethnography and, more widely, in all research involving human interaction, close attention should be paid to reflexivity (Gould & Uusihakala, 2016); the kinds of social relationships on which the research is based and on the role played by the researcher in the knowledge production.

References

Abu-Lughoud, L. (1986). *Veiled sentiments: Honor and poetry in a Bedouin Society*. Berkeley, CA: University of California Press.
Ahearn, L. M. (2001). *Invitations to love: Literacy, love letters and social change in Nepal*. Ann Arbor, MI: University of Michigan Press.
Allen, J. S. (2007). Means of desire's production: Male sex labor in Cuba. *Identities: Global Studies in Culture and Power, 14*, 183–202.
Andaya, E. (2013). "Relationships and money, money and relationships": Anxieties around partner choice and changing economies in Post-Soviet Cuba. *Feminist Studies, 39*, 728–755.
Anonymous. (2013, July, 11). La Libreta de Racionamiento Cumple ya mas de Medio Siglo en Cuba. *Cubanet*. Retrieved from https://www.cubanet.org/otros/la-libreta-de-racionamiento-cumple-medio-siglo-en-cuba/
Ariès, P. (1962). *Centuries of childhood: A social history of family life*. New York: Random House.
Bastian, H. (2018). *Everyday adjustments in Havana: Economic reforms, mobility, and emerging inequalities*. Lanham, MD: Lexington Books.
Berg, M. L. (2004). Tourism and the revolutionary new man: The specter of Jineterismo in late 'Special Period' Cuba. *Focaal: European Journal of Anthropology, 43*, 46–56.
Besnier, N. (1990). Language and affect. *Annual Review of Anthropology, 19*, 419–451.
Besnier, N. (2011). *On the edge of global: Modern anxieties in a Pacific Island Nation*. Stanford, CA: Stanford University Press.

Blanco, L. (1960, February 7). ¿Lograra la Revolución Poner Fin a las Uniones Ilegales? *Bohemia, 52*(6), 30, 98–30, 99.

Bloch, A. (2017). *Sex, love, and migration: Postsocialism, modernity, and intimacy from Istanbul to the Arctic*. Ithaca, NY: Cornell University Press.

Bourdieu, P. (1990). *The logic of practice*. Cambridge: Polity Press.

Brennan, D. (2004). *What's love got to do with it? Transnational desires and sex tourism in the Dominican Republic*. Durham, NC: Duke University Press.

Butterworth, D. (1980). *The people of Buena Ventura: Relocation of slum dwellers in Post-Revolutionary Cuba*. Urbana, IL: University of Illinois Press.

Cabezas, A. L. (2009). *Economies of desire: Sex and tourism in Cuba and the Dominican Republic*. Philadelphia, PA: Temple University Press.

Castro Ruz, F. (2006). *Mujeres y Revolución*. Havana, Cuba: Federación de Mujeres Cubanas.

Cole, J. (2009). Love, money, and economies of intimacy in Tamatave, Madagascar. In J. Cole & L. M. Thomas (Eds.), *Love in Africa* (pp. 109–134). Chicago: University of Chicago Press.

Cole, J. (2014). The Téléphone Malgache: Transnational Gossip and Social Transformation among Malagasy Marriage Migrants in France. *American Ethnologist, 41*(2), 276–289.

Cole, J., & Thomas, L. M. (Eds.). (2009). *Love in Africa*. Chicago, IL: University of Chicago Press.

Collier Fishburne, J. (1997). *From duty to desire: Remaking families in a Spanish Village*. Princeton, NJ: Princeton University Press.

Daigle, M. (2015). *From Cuba with love: Sex and money in the twenty-first century*. Oakland, CA: University of California Press.

de la Fuente, A. (2001a). Recreating racism: Race and discrimination in Cuba's "Special Period". *Socialism and Democracy, 15*(1), 65–91.

de la Fuente, A. (2001b). The resurgence of racism in Cuba. *NACLA Report on the Americas, 34*(6), 29–34.

de la Fuente, A. (2001c). *A nation for all: Race, inequality and politics in twentieth century Cuba*. Chapel Hill, NC: University of North Carolina Press.

de la Fuente, A. (2011, August 16). Race and income inequality in contemporary Cuba. NACLA. Retrieved August 22, 2019, from https://nacla.org/article/race-and-income-inequality-contemporary-cuba

Díaz Tenorio, M. (1993). *Uniones Consensuales de Cuba*. Havana, Cuba: Ministerio de la Ciencia, Tecnología y Medio Ambiente.

Drake, E. L., & Davidow, J. C. (2017). Old history in the "New" Cuba: Exploring the legacy of race and economic inequality on the Island Today. *Cornell International Affairs Review, 11*(1), 1/1. Retrieved from http://www.inquiriesjournal.com/a?id=1722

Eckstein, S. E. (1994). *Back from the future: Cuba under Castro*. Princeton, NJ: Princeton University Press.

Engels, F. (2004). *The origin of the family, private property and the state: In the light of researches of Lewis H. Morgan*. Newtown, CT: Resistance Books. (Original work published in 1884).

Fernandez, N. (2010). *Revolutionizing romance: Interracial couples in contemporary Cuba*. New Brunswick, NJ: Rutgers University Press.

Fernandez, N. (2019). Tourist brides and migrant grooms: Cuban-Danish couples and family-reunification policies. *Journal of Ethnic and Migration Studies, 45*, 3141–3156. https://doi.org/10.1080/1369183X.2018.1547025

Firestone, S. (1970). *The dialectic of sex: The case for a feminist revolution*. New York, NY: Farrar, Straus and Giroux.

Friedman, S. L. (2005). The intimacy of state power: Marriage, liberation, and socialist subjects in Southeastern China. *American Ethnologist, 32*(2), 312–327.

Gould, J., & Uusihakala, K. (Eds.). (2016). *Tutkija Peilin Edessä: Refleksiivisyys ja Etnografinen Tieto. [Researcher in front of a Mirror: Reflexivity and Ethnographic Knowledge]*. Gaudeamus: Helsinki.

Guevara, E. C. (2005). *El Socialismo y el Hombre en Cuba*. Melbourne: Ocean Press. (Original work published 1965).

Hamilton, C. (2012). *Sexual revolutions in Cuba: Passion, politics and memory*. Chapel Hill, NC: University of North Carolina Press.

Hannaford, D. (2017). *Marriage without borders: Transnational spouses in neoliberal Senegal*. Philadelphia, PA: University of Pennsylvania Press.

Hansing, K. & Hoffmann, B. (2019). Cuba's new social structure: Assessing the re-stratification of Cuban Society 60 years after revolution. *GIGA Working Paper* 315. Hamburg: GIGA. Retrieved from https://www.giga-hamburg.de/en/publication/cubas-new-social-structure-assessing-the-re-stratification-of-cuban-society-60-years

Härkönen, H. (2005). *Quince Primaveras: Tyttöjen 15-vuotisjuhlat ja matrifokaalisuus Kuubassa*. [Quince Primaveras: Girls' Fifteenth Year Birthday Celebration and Matrifocality in Cuba] (unpublished Master's Thesis). Social and Cultural Anthropology, University of Helsinki, Finland.

Härkönen, H. (2013). Love, jealousy and gender in Post-Soviet Havana. *Suomen Antropologi: Journal of the Finnish Anthropological Society, 38*(3), 24–32.

Härkönen, H. (2014). *"To Not Die Alone": Kinship, love and life cycle in contemporary Havana, Cuba*. Helsinki: Helsinki University Press.

Härkönen, H. (2015). Negotiating wealth and desirability: Changing expectations on men in Post-Soviet Havana. *Etnográfica, 19*(2), 367–388.

Härkönen, H. (2016). *Kinship, love, and life cycle in contemporary Havana, Cuba: To not die alone*. New York, NY: Palgrave Macmillan.

Härkönen, H. (2017). Havana's new wedding planners. *Cuba Counterpoints*. Retrieved from https://cubacounterpoints.com

Härkönen, H. (2019). Money, love and fragile reciprocity in contemporary Havana, Cuba. *The Journal of Latin American and Caribbean Anthropology, 24*(2), 370–387.

Hirsch, J. S., & Wardlow, H. (Eds.). (2006). *Modern loves: The anthropology of romantic courtship and companionate marriage*. Ann Arbor, MI: University of Michigan Press.

Illouz, E. (Ed.). (2017). *Emotions as commodities: Capitalism, consumption and authenticity*. London: Routledge.

Jankowiak, W. R., & Fischer, E. F. (1992). Cross-cultural perspective on romantic love. *Ethnology, 31*(2), 149–155.

Jordan Smith, D. (2017). *To be a man is not a one-day job: Masculinity, money and intimacy in Nigeria*. Chicago, IL: University of Chicago Press.

Lewis, O., Lewis, R. M., & Rigdon, S. M. (1977a). *Four men: Living the revolution: An oral history of contemporary Cuba*. Chicago, IL: University of Illinois Press.

Lewis, O., Lewis, R. M., & Rigdon, S. M. (1977b). *Four women: Living the revolution: An oral history of contemporary Cuba*. Chicago, IL: University of Illinois Press.

Lindholm, C. (1998). Love and structure. *Theory, Culture & Society, 15*(3), 243–263.

Lundgren, S. (2011). *Heterosexual Havana: Ideals and hierarchies of gender and sexuality in contemporary Cuba*. Uppsala: Uppsala University Press.

Martinez, H. (2013). From social good to commodity, reproducing economic inequalities. *Anthropology News, 54*, 11–37.

Martinez-Alier, V. (1974). *Marriage, class and colour in 19th century Cuba: A study of racial attitudes and sexual values in a slave society*. Oxford, UK: Cambridge University Press.

Morgan, L. H. (1985). *Ancient Society*. Tucson, AZ: University of Arizona Press. (Original work published in 1877).

Padilla, M. B., Hirsch, J. S., Muñoz-Laboy, M., Sember, R. E., & Parker, R. G. (Eds.). (2007). *Love and globalization: Transformations of intimacy in the contemporary world*. Nashville, TN: Vanderbilt University Press.

Peletz, M. (1995). Kinship studies in late twentieth-century anthropology. *Annual Review of Anthropology, 24*, 343–372.

Randall, M. (2003). The family code. In A. Chomsky, B. Carr, & P. M. Smorkaloff (Eds.), *The Cuba reader: History, culture, politics* (pp. 399–405). Durham, NC: Duke University Press. (Original work published in 1981).

Reardon, M. (2008, March 28). *Ban on cell phones lifted in Cuba*. Retrieved from https://www.cnet.com/news/ban-on-cell-phones-lifted-in-cuba/.

Rebhun, L. A. (1999). *The heart is unknown country: Love in the changing economy of Northeast Brazil*. Stanford, CA: Stanford University Press.

Roland, K. L. (2011). *Cuban color in tourism and La Lucha: An ethnography of racial meanings*. New York, NY: Oxford University Press.

Rosaldo, M. Z. (1980). *Knowledge and passion: Ilongot notions of self & social life*. Cambridge, UK: Cambridge University Press.

Rosendahl, M. (1997). *Inside the revolution: Everyday life in socialist Cuba*. Ithaca, NY: Cornell University Press.

Safa, H. (2005). The matrifocal family and patriarchal ideology in Cuba and the Caribbean. *Journal of Latin American Anthropology, 10*(2), 314–338.

Schneider, D. M. (1968). *American kinship*. Chicago, IL: University of Chicago Press.

Shakuto, S. (2019). Postwork intimacy: Negotiating romantic partnerships among Japanese retired couples in Malaysia. *American Ethnologist, 46*(3), 302–312.

Smith, L. M., & Padula, A. (1996). *Sex and revolution: Women in socialist Cuba*. Oxford, UK: Oxford University Press.

Stout, N. (2014). *After love: Queer intimacy and erotic economies in Post-Soviet Cuba*. Durham, NC: Duke University Press.

Tran, A. L. (2018). The anxiety of romantic love in Ho Chi Minh City, Vietnam. *Journal of the Royal Anthropological Institute, 24*, 512–531.

Verdery, K. (1996). *What was socialism and what comes next?* Princeton, NJ: Princeton University Press.

Wardlow, H. (2006). *Wayward women: Sexuality and agency in a New Guinea Society*. Berkeley, CA: University of California Press.

Zelizer, V. A. (2005). *The purchase of intimacy*. Princeton, NJ: Princeton University Press.

Zigon, J. (2013). On love: Remaking moral subjectivity in postrehabilitation Russia. *American Ethnologist, 40*(1), 201–215.

Heidi Härkönen (Dr.) is a Post-Doctoral Researcher in Gender Studies at the University of Helsinki. She gained her PhD at the University of Helsinki in Social and Cultural Anthropology in 2014 and has been a visiting research scholar at the City University of New York Graduate Center, a visiting post-doctoral researcher at the University of Amsterdam and a visiting anthropology lecturer at the University of Havana. She has been conducting ethnographic research in Cuba since 2003 and is the author of 'Kinship, Love and Life Cycle in Contemporary Havana, Cuba: To Not Die Alone (Palgrave Macmillan, 2016). Her current research interests include gender, kinship, love, life cycle, well-being, care, body, personhood, social change, digitalisation, socialism and post-socialism.

Chapter 55
"If Any Man Loveth Not His Father": Søren Kierkegaard's Psychology of Love

James L. Kelley

Abstract In Søren Kierkegaard's (1813–1855) philosophical psychology, love is not a feeling or a shared mental state per sé; instead, love is a self-relation that is grounded in a unified and transcendent principle beyond self and society. This chapter seeks, through a Kleinian psychobiography of Kierkegaard, to sketch an outline of a psychology of love beyond the paradigm of persons-in-relation, which is dominant in social science research today. We will draw upon Søren Kierkegaard's troubled relationship with his father Michael Kierkegaard to illustrate just how the transcendent function of the superego in Freud, which was taken over somewhat by the overarching concept of phantasy in Kleinian thought, can be seen as a gesture toward radical transcendence. In our concluding remarks, we will touch upon Donald W. Winnicott's "non-communicating self" as a perhaps unconscious elaboration of Freud's transcendent primal father.

Keywords Love · Psychology of love · Søren Kierkegaard · Melanie Klein · Intersubjectivity theory · Philosophy of love · Psychobiography · Continental philosophy

55.1 Introduction

Love has been center-stage in social theory ever since Scottish Enlightenment thinkers such as David Hume and Adam Smith made "sympathy" and "sentiment" the key concepts for understanding the how and why of human beings as social animals (Broadie, 2009). For Hume and Smith, sympathy "connects one sensorium with another by enabling us to face one another, adopt one another's points of view, and modify passion into sentiment by means of virtual circulation" (Chandler, 2013, xvii). The like-minded Alexander Gerard, in the same year that Smith published his *Theory of Moral Sentiments*, spoke of "a sensibility of heart" as a bridge concept

---

J. L. Kelley (✉)
Independent Scholar, Norman, OK, USA
e-mail: romeosyne@gmail.com

between individual feelings of love and their enmeshment, on the societal level, into a system that can be managed by the most morally-advanced elites (Gerard, 1764, p. 81; as cited in Brewer, 2009, p. 25). August Comte, who coined the term "sociology" in 1838, drew upon this Scottish Enlightenment philosophy of persons-in-relation when formulating positivism (Pickering, 2011). For Comte, the French Enlightenment's attempt to found a theory of society on rationality failed because

> universal love…is certainly more important than the intellect itself in…our individual or social existence (Comte, 1975: p. 2.362; as cited in Pickering, 2011, p. 36).

A prominent strand of today's social science research follows classical social theory in presupposing that love is an affect that results from comforting self-conversations and trusting, relatively non-ambivalent interpersonal relationships. Love is a more-or-less smooth internal operation that finds its analogue in a functionally static social interchange. In this social-relational vision of love each individual's desire is met by an engaged other's corresponding need; human society is thus "an economy of love [wherein] the desire of each evokes the desire of the other: mutual recognition, mutual yielding/receiving, mutual delighting, mutual empowering" (Olthuis, 1996, p. 146). As we have suggested, the origin of this now-dominant view of love as the reciprocity of persons-in-relation coincided with the birth of critical social science itself in early nineteenth century France and Germany, where the modified Spinozism of the Romantics marked the first attempt at a scientific theory of social relations (Kelley, 2018, pp. 2–3). The persons-in-relation version of love, though, reaches most psychologists today through numerous intermediaries, through studies indebted to post-Freudian developments in psychoanalysis (on the Continental and British fronts) and to post-behaviorist developments in humanistic psychology (on the American front).

The persons-in-relation concept of love as a circulatory system of desire-flows runs into a snag, however, whenever it encounters thinkers who have been influenced by what might be termed a counter-Romantic current in Western thought. One such counter-Romantic, Emmanuel Levinas, denies the easy symmetry of persons-in-relation by emphasizing the kenotic or radically self-denying aspect of the ethical relation: "I must always demand more of myself than of the other," says Levinas (Levinas & Kearney, 1986, p. 31; cited in Olthuis, 1996, p. 462). Søren Kierkegaard (1813–1855) can be seen as a founding father of counter-Romanticism in that he viewed love, not as a feeling or a shared mental state per sé, but rather as a self-relation grounded in a unified and transcendent principle beyond self and society. Along with Levinas' notion of the Other who takes us hostage through her ineluctable ethical demand (Levinas, 1997, p. 59), we can number William James' "will to believe" (James, 1896) and Carl Schmitt's "Wille zur Realität" (Schmitt, 1919, p. 74) among the many prominent concepts in today's social theory whose lineage we can trace to Kierkegaard's anti-Romanticism.

The present chapter seeks, through a Kleinian psychobiography of Kierkegaard, to sketch an outline of a psychology of love beyond the persons-in-relation paradigm. Søren Kierkegaard's troubled relation to his father Michael Kierkegaard will be used to illustrate just how the transcendent function of the superego in Freud, which was taken over somewhat by the overarching concept of phantasy in Kleinian thought, can be seen as a gesture toward radical transcendence. In our concluding remarks, we will touch upon Donald W. Winnicott's "non-communicating self" (Winnicott, 1963, p. 181) as it relates to Freud's locus of transcendence: the primal father. For Winnicott, there is an inviolable core of subjectivity, a self that remains unseen even when "found," a self that resists any familial, cultural, or cosmic mediation (Winnicott, 1963, p. 185). Kierkegaard, within the bounds of his own clearly-delineated self, discovers the ultimate "highly exalted father" (Freud, 1927, p. 74) in the Christian Holy Trinity; but he also finds, in the Incarnation of God in Christ, the outward, world-directed counterpart of the inviolable self. Today, the latter may be taken as a challenge to Freud's notion that the conscience of the religious or highly moral person precludes her from effective action in the world (Hall, 1954, p. 46). And yet, Kierkegaard's life as a reclusive writer and harsh critic of Danish society may suggest to some the perhaps inevitable limitations of adhering to such an anti-Romantic radical superego. Must one give up all of the mutually-supporting pleasures of family and society in order to become a transparent self in relation to one's heavenly Father? If so, is this indeed a form of "madness" (Kierkegaard qtd. in Thompson, 1973, p. 201), as Kierkegaard himself once suggested?

55.2 Theoretical Background

Melanie Klein's transformations of Freudian theory have been extremely influential for world psychoanalysis (Mitchell & Black, 1995, p. 85) ever since they were first encountered by members of the British Psychoanalytic Society such as Donald Winnicott (Winnicott, 1935) and John Rickman (Rickman, 1937). Klein's most significant contribution, though, may be her refinement of Freud's thoughts on love or Eros. All three of Freud's theories of love are combined by Klein into a single overarching schema of self-object phantasy. First, Freud's notion of love as a "refinding" (Freud, 1905, 1910, 1912) of the oedipal parent appears as Klein's "reparation" (Klein, 1956, 1957) of previous destructive phantasies directed toward a significant other; second, Freud's notion of love as originally narcissistic (Freud, 1914) is reflected in Klein's "splitting," according to which the ego divides itself into good and bad fragments that correspond to an analogous division in the loved object (Klein, 1955, 1956); finally, Freud's notion of love as an orientation of the ego to the beloved based upon the latter's satisfaction of the self's total (not merely sexual) needs (Freud, 1915; Bergmann, 1980; Perlman, 1999) is the basis of Klein's notion of a balancing of love and hate toward the primary loved object (Klein, 1952a, p. 54, 1952b: pp. 67–68).

However, Klein's version of psychoanalysis is more than a mere synthesis of Freudian theoretical strands; indeed, it could be argued that Klein's entire approach to theorizing differed fundamentally from that of psychoanalysis' founder. Freud's theory featured time-bound developmental stages, traumas that were specific to each individual, and an unconscious that obeyed its own idiosyncratic laws (Mitchell &

Black, 1995). Klein's theory, by contrast, has only one decisive category: phantasy (Mitchell, 1986, pp. 22–23). Kleinian phantasy [the "ph" spelling indicating its unconscious origin as opposed to mere conscious reverie (Isaacs, 1948)] is the unconscious depth of all conscious thought. Like Loewald's notion of a bottom layer of human experience as a "primordial density" (Loewald, 1977, p. 186; as cited in Mitchell, 2000, p. 8) that can be overlaid with semantic and abstract-cognitive strata without ever effacing the original formation, Klein's phantasy remains the bedrock of human experience from the womb until death (Klein, 1932, 1940).

But how exactly does Klein reduce all of human existence to an origin in phantasy? In order to function in the world, a human being must grow to tolerate a painful paradox: The self is only made real through trusting interaction with the not-self. First the consciousness or ego must split itself, not into the more familiar subject-object binary of Descartes and Coleridge, but rather into an angst-ridden, self-divided quaternity of (1) good self, (2) bad self, (3) good breast, and (4) bad breast. The primary object for Klein (and for Freud) is the mother's breast, but because the child, rather than getting a perfect feed, inevitably experiences frustration, she phantasizes about devouring the breast, the latter first having been split so that only its hateful, unloving qualities are present. This phantasy leads to a fear of being annihilated by the bad breast, which is introjected or taken into a split-off fragment of the child's "bad self" (Spillius, 1988, p. 198).

Splitting leads the child to experience more deeply the anxious need for both connection to the outside world and isolation from the outside via a durable ego-shell. Since the child finds herself dependent upon, and thus persecuted by, a mother whose less-than-ideal nurturance threatens her life, Klein named this earliest orientation the "paranoid position." However, following Fairbairn, she later revised this to "paranoid-schizoid position" (Klein, 1946; Roth, 2001). In this latter formulation, Klein saw the paranoia brought on by annihilation anxiety suspended by a schiziod process of self-object fragmentation, which turns out to be the aforementioned splitting. The destructive hate of the paranoid is contained, diffused and diverted by the schiziod splitting of the self and its objects into part-objects (Segal, 1973, pp. 19–20).

Splitting is not a direct route from hatred to love, though, and this is why Klein brings in the concept of "depressive position," which is founded on the self's stultifying realization she has, at least in phantasy, attempted to annihilate the primary good object (Klein, 1935). Splitting forges a firm boundary between trusting, loving and vital aspects of object relations, and those aspects that relate more to destruction, hate, and death (Klein, 1963, p. 300). Ironically, the splitting self's newly-strengthened reality principle cross cuts this love-hate dichotomy by imposing on the phantasizing ego the realization that a more fundamental psychic split exists between the self and the other, both sides of which contain love and hate (Klein, 1957). The self has sharpened its definition of love and hate only to discover both qualities present in its more clearly-defined self; the result is replacement of the paranoid-schiziod position by the depressive position, the latter manifesting in a sudden upsurge of guilt over one's own responsibility for the unloving phantasies that have persisted throughout the whole process (Klein, 1948). Reparation is now the self's one and only recourse: amends must be made to the beloved through acts of trust and self-sacrifice, gestures that affirm the inviolable, irreplaceable status of the loved one.

The reparative self gains the ability to tolerate the anxiety of the interplay between love and hate through making herself dependent upon a lover or parent who is in some sense recognized as, if not her creator, then at least one who has a claim of authority that exceeds her own claim. This is an idea not unlike Levinas' notion of the self as the Other's hostage, since human subjectivity itself, as created by God, is structured so that the needs of the Other come before those of the self (Marion, 1998).

55.3 Methodology

The present work is a single-case study that utilizes themes from psychobiography, Kleinian psychoanalytic theory, and various interpersonal psychoanalytic theories that fall outside of the Kleinian rubric to develop insights about the subject over his entire lifespan. Ethical research practice and historical accuracy have been safeguarded by a judicious use of primary and secondary sources that maintains a critical stance toward the evaluative statements of the subject's previous biographers. Without such a conscientious sifting of fact from legend, we risk reducing psychobiography to quasi-historical gossip. In view of McAdams's good insight that psychobiographers are historico-psychological commentators, and not armchair diagnosticians (McAdams, 2016), this study strives to base its evaluations on well-established facts filtered through a historiographical lens shaped by contemporary trends in history and psychology (Brundage, 2018; Sternberg & Sternberg, 2010).

55.4 Findings: Life and Loves

55.4.1 "A Strange Family": Søren at Home (1813–1830)

On 5 May, 1813, Søren Aabye Kierkegaard was born at his family home, a town house at 2 Nytorv in Copenhagen, Denmark (Watts, 2003, p. 14). His father, Michael Pedersen Kierkegaard, was a troubled soul who believed that, owing to his belief that he had abandoned God in a time of youthful hardship, he would live to see all of his children die. Michael later revealed that he had "cursed God" (Kierkegaard, 1959a, p. 556) while working as a shepherd in the harsh Jutland hillside, freezing, hungry, and at his wit's end. In the days following this moment of weakness, Michael's luck turned around miraculously, and he was given a position in his wealthy uncle's hosiery business, a concern that Michael inherited upon his relative's death in 1798 (Watkin, 2010, p. 138). Michael's first wife died before having any children, but Michael committed what he later considered a mortal sin by impregnating his maid, Ane Sørensdatter Lund. The situation was resolved when Michael took Ane as his second wife in 1797 (Hannay, 2018, p. 13). This marriage produced many children, including Søren, all of whom were made to feel that, though they were loved and cherished, God's overarching plan was to punish the Kierkegaard patriarch by taking them away from him. It is no wonder Søren was obsessed with God's difficult-to-fathom love for Job and Abraham, both of whom were faced with the possibility (and in Job's case, the reality) of seeing their sons die (Kierkegaard, 2009b, 2013).

In 1821, when Søren was eight years of age, he began studies at Copenhagen's Borgerdydskolen, where he became known for his impishness (Watkin, 2010, p. 1). He played tricks on anyone who seemed to be more powerful or more authoritative than himself. In this, he seemed to be striking out against proxies of his father. Kierkegaard felt that he had been unduly burdened with the cosmic melancholy of his father Michael (Ostenfeld, 1978, p. 2), but he found it difficult to confront the patriarch directly, especially since Søren, at some level, believed in the authority that his father represented (Kierkegaard, 1959a, p. 214). Thus, Søren sought out those of his schoolmates who were as large and brawny as he was diminutive and frail, and wasted no opportunity in humiliating them with his capacious and mordant wit (Garff, 2005, pp. 19–20; Darrow, 2005, p. 9). Not only students, but also instructors had something to fear from the stooped-shouldered, long-stockinged lad (Hannay, 2001, p. 21). One of Søren's teachers had the misfortune of threatening the class with punishment when the young Kierkegaard set up a picnic in the classroom, replete with bread, meat, and alcoholic drink (Backhouse, 2016). Søren, certainly knowing that his own father Michael would side with him over any authority outside the home, threatened a daily repeat of the untimely repast should the bewildered instructor report the incident to his superiors.

There were two divisions or schisms in Søren's early life that were to make an impact on his later articulations of both God's love for man, and man's possible response to this love. First, there was the pedagogic schism. Kierkegaard's first teacher was his father Michael, and his first school was the Kierkegaard home at 2 Nytorv. Michael experienced God as both an infinitely distant Father, and a tangible, suffering human being that was somehow more present to the mind and heart than to the outer senses. On the other hand, the Kierkegaard patriarch had steeped himself in the official German philosophy of the day, that of Christian Wolfe, and his sons were directed to read Wolfe and other secular thinkers alongside more devotional writings. When Michael sent Søren off to school, it must have seemed an existential continuation of this bifurcation between sacred and secular worlds of learning. Next we find Søren acting-out at the Borgerdydskolen, treating the proceedings as little more than a theater for his pranks and put-downs. Is this because Michael presented his son with two incompatible conceptions of love, one hidden beyond the visible world in Christ and the other an all-too-human, all-too-conventional philosophy of social conformism?

We get a more definite picture once we consider the second schism in Søren's upbringing, that between the Danish Lutheran Church and the Moravian Brethren (Rae, 2010, p. 8). Michael Kierkegaard was a patron of both churches, and he took his family to the former on Sunday mornings and to the latter for evening services (Hughes, 2017, p. 47). Throughout Søren's life he and his brother Peter expressed their strained relationship with their father (and with each other) by periodically withdrawing from Holy Communion to avoid taking the sacrament with the offending family member or members. It seems that this mixing-together of family dynamics with liturgical expression had some connection to Søren's later engagement to Regine Olsen, for the Olsen family attended the Moravian Church, and the latter presented itself as a less rationalistic Christianity, one less focused on externals such as Holy Communion, and instead more centered on the inner life of the Christian, on her moment-to-moment affective connection to Christ (De Schweinitz, 1869, p. 97). Søren must have seen his father's forcing him to shuttle back-and-forth between churches almost as a transmission of original sin from father to son; that is, Michael Pedersen's own tortured inner division between sackcloth-and-ashes repentance before God and a desire for a position in Copenhagen high society via its official Church was reflected in his need to supplement his family's sacramental membership in the official Danish Church with a more personal, intimate experience among the Moravians. After all, the Brethren presented themselves as offering the love that mainstream Christianity often seemed to lack (Atwood, 2009).

55.4.2 Student, Disciple, Public Speaker (1830–1838)

In 1830, Søren Kierkegaard began at the University of Copenhagen, where he studied to become a Lutheran minister (Darrow, 2005, pp. 9–10). However, his wide reading in philosophy, law and theology only underscored his need to, in his words, "get clear about *what I must do*, not what I must know…" (Kierkegaard, 1978, p. 34). As a college student, Kierkegaard had spent the lion's share of his time socializing and drinking with friends and acquaintances, all in an attempt to gain firsthand experience of the outside world from which his father had hitherto sheltered him (Carlisle, 2006, pp. 8–9). By decade's end, Kierkegaard had passed his oral examination for a degree in theology, and a year later, in 1841, his dissertation was accepted, thereby completing Kierkegaard's education.

However, the 1830s were a period of struggle and turmoil for Søren: between 1832 and 1838, both of Kierkegaard's parents died, as well as two of his siblings and his sister-in-law (Watkin, 1990, p. xiii). What is more, Michael Kierkegaard, who had already lost two other children before 1832, continued to intimate to his two sons that his early sexual indiscretions had brought a curse upon the family. It was when Peter's wife Elise Marie died 1837 that Michael Kierkegaard revealed to his sons that the real cause of the family's fate was his cursing of God on the Jutland heath when he was a young shepherd (Garff, 2005, pp. 135–136). This blight, Michael now averred, would result in him living beyond all of his children, both Søren and Peter being fated not to live past Christ's age of thirty-three (Hannay, 2001, p. 123).

In the midst of the 1830s, the decade that saw the young Kierkegaard attempting to define his own place in the world outside the stultifying walls of 2 Nytorv, Søren found a foster father of sorts in J. L. Heiberg (1791–1860), in whose literary journal, *Flyveposten*, Kierkegaard wrote diatribes against the liberal-progressive contributors to several other Copenhagen periodicals (Kierkegaard, 1990, pp. 3–52). Heiberg's home stood as a kind of opposite to Kierkegaard's childhood milieu. In place of the insularity of Michael Kierkegaard's gloomy Pietist enclave, there was Heiberg's salon, in which Søren heard high-society gossip dovetailed with talk of beauty's potential to transform society in the image of Christ (Kirmmse, 1990, pp. 140–141).

Man's love was simply equated with Christ's love in Heiberg's version of Hegelian aesthetics, but this seeming victory for man's freedom in love was bought at a price, since Heiberg's Christ did not Himself will to become Incarnate; rather, for Heiberg, Christ was the instrument of His Father's decision to save mankind. The Incarnation, in Heiberg's hands, becomes a mere metaphor for what some social theorists and theologians would later call persons-in-relation, that is, for humans' striving after social harmony as the highest good (Heiberg, 1861–1862, p. 1390); accordingly, mankind's effort to achieve justice and order in this world becomes nothing more than a fulfillment of Christ's loving example (Kirmmse, 1990, p. 141). Just as there was no father-son relationship in the Heiberg household, only Heiberg, his wife, and his mother, so there was a denial of the tension between man and God in Heiberg's thinking. Projecting the filial tension between God and man into Trinitarian interrelations allowed Heiberg to see the Son of God as a passive instrument that accomplished the greatest act of love while being somehow exempt from the divine decision that He become Incarnate.

Søren soon broke away from this sonless family, replacing Heiberg's humanistic notion that man, by divesting his thoughts of every particular determination, can guide himself toward absolute truth, with a more traditional Christian conception that man's being is grounded in the united and singular will of the Holy Trinity, whose acts of creation are always co-decisions of Father, Son and Holy Spirit (Stewart, 2009, pp. 47–48). On a more personal level, Kierkegaard realized that Heiberg's philosophy, and the fashionable Copenhagen salon that served as its milieu, failed to solve the problem of how both earthly and divine sons related to their fathers. In place of Heiberg's self-grounded human subject, who finds Christ within himself through a process of dialectical thinking, the young Kierkegaard posited man as grounded in the divine will through an ineluctable self-division that forces him to constantly recollect himself from moment to moment, lest he lose his self-transparency and become deluded about who he is. Kierkegaard's journals sum up the whole situation by offering the following answer to the false patriarch Heiberg's self-fathering version of subjectivity: "...I can abstract from everything but not from myself" (Kierkegaard, 1959a, p. 51).

55.4.3 Author, Theologian, Man of the World: Søren at Home and Abroad (1838–1845)

On 9 August, 1838, Michael Kierkegaard died (Geni, 2016, 16 September), leaving Søren, who had been living again at 2 Nytorv after a short period living in his own apartment, free to establish his own home as a bachelor (Garff, 2017, pp. 117, 147). It was two years later that Søren proposed marriage to 18 year old Regine Olsen (1823–1904), whom he had met at his friend Peter Rørdam's home in 1837 (Hannay, 2018, p. 56). It seems that the contingent, real fact of the engagement, which threatened to lead to sex and thus to Søren's transformation from son to father, brought on a psychological crisis: Søren broke off the engagement to Regine on 11 October, 1841 and fled Copenhagen to study at Berlin (Pattison, 2002, p. 172).

In Berlin, Søren began writing several extended works, the most significant being *Either/Or* (Kierkegaard, 1959b) and *Fear and Trembling* (Kierkegaard, 2013). The former created an immediate sensation, and as a result, the term "either or" entered Danish common parlance (Mehl, 2005, p. 13). These two books can be seen as Kierkegaard's first (and some would argue, definitive) presentation of his three stages or spheres of human life. The first stage is the aesthetic, in which the self indulges in its ability to "produce" new mental objects out of sensations and situations from real life. The aesthete can affirm or negate any aspect of any possible experience, especially by dramatizing moral choices into a synthetic mood that evades anything decisive. The author of the "seducer's diary" in *Either/Or*, and the young man who corresponds with Constantine Constantius in *Repetiton* (Kierkegaard, 2009b) are prime examples of the aesthetic sphere. The next stage in Kierkegaard's scheme is the ethical, in which the individual is integrated into human universality through societal norms that express its conventional wisdom. Even though the ethical stage is superior to the aesthetic, it contains the most deadly temptation of all, that of mistaking the "respect of persons" (James 2, 2 King James Version) for the doing of God's will. Marriage is the gate through which the ethical is entered, and though one can ascend to the third stage, the religious, while being married, Kierkegaard felt that this was a rare occurrence. More commonly, the married person mistakes integration into a community with fulfilling God's commandments. Since "God is love" (I John 4, 8 King James Version), Kierkegaard insists that love cannot be reduced to mores that do no more than blend individuals into a collective; in fact, such a confusion of the ethical with the religious is a loss of freedom, selfhood, and love, since the goal of a perfect Christian life is not domestic bliss, but rather a repetition of Christ's self-sacrifice, a crucifixion that is the only true universality, and thus is the only love worth the name (Kierkegaard, 1998, pp. 5–6). Abraham and Job achieved a level of trust in God that rendered their lives a paradox from any perspective that declined from their own absolute God-centeredness.

55.4.4 The Corsair Affair: Søren in the Press and Against the Kirk (1845–1855)

With the engagement to Regine broken off, Kierkegaard separated himself for good from the conventional roles of pastor, son, father, and husband, instead becoming an author whose life became visible to others more through his works and less through his sociality. Two years after the engagement was ended, Regine married J.F. Schlegel, and Kierkegaard

> withdrew more and more from Copenhagen society, partly because of the time and energy consumed by [his] writing and partly because his broken engagement had made him unwelcome in some quarters (Darrow, 2005, p. 12).

In 1846 Kierkegaard published his *Concluding Unscientific Postscript* (Kierkegaard, 2009a), which the author may have intended as his last work, but which was soon followed by *Stages on Life's Way* (Kierkegaard, 1988). The latter work focuses on the third, religious phase of human life at which *Either/Or* had hinted. Therein Kierkegaard explains that a married man's faithfulness cannot be comprehended in mere social or familial terms, but rather is hidden in the hearts of the couple, who believe in the miracle of salvation that the sacrament of marital union points toward (Kierkegaard, 1988, pp. 87–184; cf. 2009a, pp. 47–48, pp. 151–153). This interpretation of true marriage as existing only in terms of God's saving love for man and not within the categories of bourgeois life was seen by Kierkegaard's contemporary Paul Ludvig Møller (1814–1865) as a "dissecting" and a "torturing" of Regine Olsen's soul, as he wrote in a disapproving review of *Stages on Life's Way* at the close of 1845 (Hong & Hong, 1982, pp. xi–xiii). Kierkegaard at once published a pointed reply to Møller's review in a Copenhagen newspaper. He felt that Møller had defamed him, and so Kirekegaard's riposte returned the favor by exposing Møller's heretofore unknown role as a contributor to the academically disreputable paper *The Corsair*, a revelation that helped to bar Møller from a university position in the Danish capital (Collins, 1983, p. 12). Møller and an associated *Corsair* writer next unleashed a stream of articles that ridiculed Kierkegaard's words and physical appearance, including his stooped posture and his spinal condition, which made one of his legs seem shorter than the other (Pattison, 2013, p. 54).

It was not long after the *Corsair* affair broke out that Kierkegaard withdrew from public debate. He became more isolated from Copenhagen society for several years, and his volume of publications decreased considerably. But then the death of Bishop Jacob Peter Mynster (1775–1854), who had been the Kierkegaard family's minister, provoked a final outburst of writings from the melancholy Dane that would end only with his death on 11 November, 1855 (Lowrie, 1942, p. 255). Kierkegaard on his deathbed made two refusals and one affirmation that, together, explain much about his life and his love. First, Søren refused to admit his brother Peter Christian into his hospital room for a final visit. Peter, the well-heeled, respected Danish clergyman, represented to Søren the deification of the merely ethical, the hallowing of an official Danish Church that confused middle-class comfort and all of its niceties with martyrdom, the latter being the only true display of love according to Kierkegaard. Second, Kierkegaard refused the Last Rites of the Danish Church, thus rejecting anything that, in his mind, mistook a mere finite institution as covering the need for a *salto mortale* into love as an infinite relation with Jesus Christ. Finally, the expiring Søren made one affirmation: he bequeathed all of his possessions to Regine Olsen, a motion that was refused by Regine's husband to avoid any hint of scandal (Hannay, 2001, p. 436).

55.5 Conclusions and Recommendations for Further Research

For both Søren Kierkegaard and Melanie Klein love is a fundamental component of the human psyche. Both, however, were sensitive to the ineluctable limitations that nature and nurture, constitution and environment, place on love. Klein followed Freud in professing atheism and reducing love to a primal instinct for survival that has undergone innumerable differentiations since the first protozoan flung its pseudopodia around some obscure object of desire (Beit-Hallahmi, 2007, p. 310; Sulloway, 1979). However, Freud's combination of awe and fear vis-à-vis the Christian notion of God the Father has been put forward as a reason for the quasi-religious overtones of his superego concept (Freud, 1933, pp. 162–163; Vitz, 1988). The superego is an ego object that contains judgments and expectations that "when internalized, retain their otherness" (Church, 1991, p. 217). Human life begins with the child expressing the Lebenstrieb by trusting, not only in the persistent reality of her self, but also in the reality of the breast as the conduit of life-substance. Freud himself recognized, though, that the child may have an even more unmediated relation to the father, with whom the child, in some ways, more directly identifies (Freud, 1925, p. 250, 1921, p. 105). The father may be seen by the developing child as the ultimate "conversation-stopper" (Dennett, 1995, p. 506), the wedge-like chisel that writes the law on stone, or the lightning that strikes without warning (Kelley, 2018), but whose voice floats above the more basic and concrete sustenance provided by the mother. In the Christian tradition, this voice of the Father preempts any doubts about the divinity of his son by proclaiming "Thou art my beloved Son: in thee I am well pleased" (Lk 3, 22 King James Version).

How did Søren Kierkegaard bridge creatively this gap between the messy, inconclusive, groping love of earthly sons and fathers with this impassible, unchanging love that emanates from God the Father and Christ His Son? In Kierkegaard's childhood, his primary love relationship with his mother was undercut by his father's domination of the home, even to the extent that household shopping was done by Michael Kierkegaard (Watkin, 2010, p. 156). The Kierkegaard patriarch was even known to sit with his sons throughout the night, talking to them about religious topics in an intense manner while Søren and Peter, like analysands on couches, reposed in their beds (Garff, 2005, p. 108). Later, Michael's traumatic revelation that he received wealth, and thus his possibility of having sons at all, as a result of his youthful blasphemy, must have greatly confused Søren, who was expected to love two diametrically opposite fathers: an earthly father who burdened him by being too close to him (by being too sinful), and a heavenly Father who burdened him by being too remote (by being too sinless). We can surmise that Søren's superego formation was fraught with more than the usual oedipal ambivalence, especially if we think of Loewald's notion of the superego as the "atonement" for desiring the death of the father (Loewald, 1979; Ogden, 2006).

When Michael Kierkegaard died, his son interpreted the event as something willed by his father. Indeed, Søren saw Michael's death as a repetition and extension of the divine Incarnation. Here we see Søren's creativity in writing his own life narrative: he interpreted his flawed father's life as a parable teaching him that love, in the full sense of the word, is a freely-willed sacrifice that effects a shift which, though cosmic in import, remains nonetheless verifiable only through an unremitting experiential initiation that can end only in death. Michael's demise was, for Søren, the ultimate act of reparation in that it placed love beyond aesthetic narratives of self-creation, beyond ethical narratives of social conformity, even beyond mere family or clan ties. Love as a complete self-emptying could only be conceived in paradox; love, the end of all Christian striving, is "madness," "terror" (Kierkegaard qtd. in Thompson, 1973, p. 201), martyrdom, deifying ravishment. In short, love is as inscrutable and necessary as the Incarnation of God in Christ, which allows sinful men to become "sons of God" (Rom 8:14 King James Version). The break with Regine Olsen was in keeping with Søren's ambivalent relationship with his mother, which followed the Kierkegaard family's pattern of separating sexuality and even tender relations with female family members from intellectual and theological concerns. Søren could love women from afar, but sexuality and the familial threatened to cut the dutiful son off from the religious form of love. At best, Regine turns Søren into another Heiberg, a "father" in a sonless salon; at worst, Søren's marriage transforms him into another tragic father like Michael Kierkegaard, who would entangle his progeny in love paradoxes only solvable through absolute transcendence of any earthly standard. In Kleinian terms, Søren was able to integrate the good and bad aspects of Michael Kierkegaard through an ongoing reparation that used the absence of the flawed though saintly father as a model for Søren's own retreat from family and community ties.

Future research could be done to extend these insights concerning Kierkegaard's psychology of love into Winnicottian territory. Specifically, Kierkegaard's key decision to become a bachelor, author, and cultural critic could be examined in terms of Winnicott's notion of three lines of communication in the healthy individual (Winnicott, 1963, p. 187). If the Danish philosopher's self-narration was an attempt to position himself as a dutiful son in relation to three parents, (1) a divine father, (2) an earthly father, and (3) a chaste and thus matronly fiance, then further psychobiographical research could attempt to relate Kierkegaard's ambivalence to post-Freudian theories of the superego (Harding, 2019). Winnicott's notion of the isolate self that resists being known by other finite selves certainly leaves a space open for a transcendent parent whose will is the only true relation, the only love worth the name.

References

Atwood, C. D. (2009). *The theology of the Czech Brethren from Hus to Comenius*. University Park, PA: The Pennsylvania State University Press.
Backhouse, S. (2016). *Kierkegaard: A single life*. Grand Rapids, MI: Zondervan.
Beit-Hallahmi, B. (2007). Atheists: A psychological profile. In M. Martin (Ed.), *Cambridge companion to atheism* (pp. 300–317). New York: Cambridge University Press.
Bergmann, M. S. (1980). On the intrapsychic function of falling in love. *The Psychoanalytic Quarterly, 49*, 56–77.
Brewer, J. (2009). Sentiment and sensibility. In J. Chandler (Ed.), *The Cambridge history of English romantic literature* (pp. 21–44). Cambridge: Cambridge University Press.
Broadie, A. (2009). *A history of Scottish philosophy*. Edinburgh: Edinburgh University Press.
Brundage, A. (2018). *Going to the sources: A guide to historical research and writing* (6th ed.). Hoboken, NJ: Wiley.
Carlisle, C. (2006). *Kierkegaard: A guide for the perplexed*. London and New York: Continuum.
Chandler, J. (2013). *An archaeology of sympathy: The sentimental mode in literature and cinema*. Chicago & London: University of Chicago Press.
Church, J. (1991). Morality and the internalized other. In J. Neu (Ed.), *The Cambridge companion to Freud* (pp. 209–223). Cambridge: Cambridge University Press.
Collins, J. D. (1983). *The mind of Kierkegaard*. Princeton, NJ: Princeton University Press.
Comte, A. (1975). *Cours de philosophie positive* (Vol. 2 vols). Paris: Hermann. (Work originally appeared in 1830–42).
Darrow, R. A. (2005). *Kierkegaard, Kafka, and the strength of "the absurd" in Abraham's sacrifice of Isaac*. M.A. thesis. Wright State University.
De Schweinitz, E. (1869). *The Moravian manual: Containing an account of the Moravian Church or Unitas Fratrum*. Bethlehem: Moravian Publication Office.
Dennett, D. C. (1995). *Darwin's dangerous idea: Evolution and the meanings of life*. New York: Simon & Schuster.
Freud, S. (1905). Three essays on the theory of sexuality. *S.E., 7*, 125–243.
Freud, S. (1910). A special type of object choice made by men. *S.E., 11*, 165–175.
Freud, S. (1912). On the tendency to degradation in the sphere of love. *S.E., 11*, 178–190.
Freud, S. (1914). On narcissism: An introduction. *S.E., 14*, 69–102.
Freud, S. (1915). Instincts and their vicissitudes. *S.E., 14*, 111–140.
Freud, S. (1921). Group psychology and the analysis of the ego. *S.E., 18*, 67–143.
Freud, S. (1925). Some psychical consequences of the anatomical distinction between the sexes. *S. E., 19*, 243–258.
Freud, S. (1927). The future of an illusion. *S.E., 21*, 3–56.
Freud, S. (1933). New introductory lectures on psycho-analysis. *S.E., 21*, 3–182.
Garff, J. (2005). *Søren Kierkegaard: A biography*. Princeton and Oxford: Princeton University Press.
Garff, J. (2017). *Kierkegaard's muse: The mystery of Regine Olsen*. Princeton, NJ: Princeton University Press.
Geni. (2016, 16 September). *Michael Pedersen Kierkegaard*. Retrieved from https://www.geni.com/people/Michael-Kierkegaard/4976513953430126612
Gerard, A. (1764). *An essay on taste*. Edinburgh: Printed for A. Miller, London & A. Kincaid/J. Bell, Edinburgh.
Hall, C. S. (1954). *A primer of Freudian psychology*. New York: New American Library.

Hannay, A. (2001). *Kierkegaard: A biography*. Cambridge: Cambridge University Press.
Hannay, A. (2018). *Søren Kierkegaard*. London: Reaktion.
Harding, C. (2019). *Dissecting the superego: Moralities under the psychoanalytic microscope*. Abingdon, Oxon, UK and New York: Routledge.
Heiberg, J. H. (1861–1862). *Johan Ludvig Heibergs posaiske skrifter*. 11 vols. Kjøbenhavn: C. A. Reitzel.
Hong, H. V., & Hong, E. H. (1982). Historical introduction. In S. Kierkegaard (Ed.), *The Corsair affair and articles related to the writings* (pp. vii–xxxviii). Princeton: Princeton University Press.
Hughes, C. S. (2017). Søren Kierkegaard: Protesting the Lutheran establishment. In J. A. Mahn (Ed.), *Radical Lutherans/Lutheran radicals* (pp. 43–69). Eugene, OR: Cascade.
Isaacs, S. (1948). The nature and function of phantasy. *The International Journal of Psycho-Analysis, 29*, 73–97.
James, W. (1896). The will to believe. *The New World: A quarterly review of religion, ethics and theology, 5*, 327–337.
Kelley, J. L. (2018). Jim Jones and Romantic socialism. *The Jonestown Report*, 20. Retrieved from https://jonestown.sdsu.edu/?page_id=80804
Kierkegaard, S. (1959a). *The journals of Kierkegaard*. New York: Harper.
Kierkegaard, S. (1959b). *Either/or*. Garden City, NY: Doubleday. (Work originally appeared in 1843).
Kierkegaard, S. (1978). *Søren Kierkegaard's journals and papers, Vol. 5, Autobiographical. Part One, 1829–1848*. Bloomington and London: Indiana University Press.
Kierkegaard, S. (1988). *Stages on life's way*. Princeton: Princeton University Press. (Work originally appeared in 1845).
Kierkegaard, S. (1990). *Early polemical writings*. Princeton: Princeton University Press.
Kierkegaard, S. (1998). *The moment and late writings*. Princeton: Princeton University Press.
Kierkegaard, S. (2009a). *Concluding unscientific postscript to the philosophical crumbs*. Cambridge: Cambridge University Press. (Work originally appeared in 1846).
Kierkegaard, S. (2009b). Repetition: An experiment in experimental psychology. In S. Kierkegaard (Ed.), *Repetition and philosophical crumbs* (pp. 1–81). Oxford and New York: Oxford University Press. (Work originally appeared in 1843).
Kierkegaard, S. (2013). Fear and trembling: A dialectical lyric. In S. Kierkegaard (Ed.), *Fear and trembling and the sickness unto death* (pp. 29–221). Princeton and Oxford: Princeton University Press. (Work originally appeared in 1843).
Kirmmse, B. (1990). *Kierkegaard in golden age Denmark*. Bloomington: Indiana University Press.
Klein, M. (1932). *The psychoanalysis of children*. London: Hogarth Press. (1975).
Klein, M. (1935). A contribution to the psychogenesis of manic-depressive states. *The International Journal of Psycho-Analysis, 16*, 145–174.
Klein, M. (1940). Mourning and its relation to manic-depressive states. *The International Journal of Psycho-Analysis, 21*, 125–153.
Klein, M. (1946). Noes on some schizoid mechanisms. *The International Journal of Psycho-Analysis, 27*, 99–110.
Klein, M. (1948). A contribution to the theory of anxiety and guilt. *The International Journal of Psycho-Analysis, 29*, 114–123.
Klein, M. (1952a). Some theoretical conclusions regarding the emotional life of the infant. In M. Klein, P. Heimann, S. Isaacs, & J. Riviere (Eds.), *Developments in psycho-analysis* (pp. 198–236). London: Hogarth.
Klein, M. (1952b). On observing the behaviour of young infants. In M. Klein et al. (Eds.), *Developments in psycho-analysis* (pp. 237–270). London: Hogarth.
Klein, M. (1955). The psycho-analytic play technique: Its history and significance. In M. Klein, P. Heimann, & R. E. Money-Kyrle (Eds.), *New directions in psycho-analysis: The significance of infant conflict in the pattern of adult behaviour* (pp. 3–22). London: Tavistock.

Klein, M. (1956). A study of envy and gratitude. In J. Mitchell (Ed.), *The selected Melanie Klein* (pp. 211–229). New York: Free Press. (1986).
Klein, M. (1957). *Envy and gratitude: A study of unconscious sources*. London: Tavistock.
Klein, M. (1963). On the sense of loneliness. In M. Klein (Ed.), *Envy and gratitude and other works, 1946–1963* (pp. 300–313). New York: Free Press. (1975).
Levinas, E. (1997). *Otherwise than being, or beyond essence*. Pittsburgh: Duquesne University Press.
Levinas, E., & Kearney, R. (1986). Dialogue with Emmanuel Levinas. In R. A. Cohen (Ed.), *Face to face with Levinas* (pp. 13–33). Albany: SUNY Press.
Loewald, H. (1977). Primary process, secondary process and language. In *Papers on psychoanalysis* (pp. 178–206). New Haven, CT: Yale University Press.
Loewald, H. (1979). The waning of the Oedipus complex. In *The language of psycho-analysis* (pp. 384–404). New Haven, CT: Yale University Press.
Lowrie, W. (1942). *A short life of Kierkegaard*. Princeton: Princeton University Press.
Marion, J.-L. (1998). A note concerning the ontological indifference. *Graduate Faculty Philosophy Journal, 20/21*(2/1), 25–40. https://doi.org/10.5840/gfpj199820/212/15
McAdams, D. (2016, June). The mind of Donald Trump. *The Atlantic*. Retrieved from https://www.theatlantic.com/magazine/archive/2016/06/the-mind-of-donald-trump/480771/
Mehl, P. J. (2005). *Thinking through Kierkegaard: Existential identity in a pluralistic world*. Urbana and Chicago: University of Illinois Press.
Mitchell, J. (1986). Introduction. In J. Mitchell (Ed.), *The selected Melanie Klein* (pp. 9–32). New York: Free Press.
Mitchell, S. A. (2000). *Relationality: From attachment to intersubjectivity* (p. 2014). New York: Psychology Press.
Mitchell, S. A., & Black, M. J. (1995). *Freud and beyond: A history of modern psychoanalytic thought*. New York: Basic Books.
Ogden, T. H. (2006). Reading Loewald: Oedipus reconceived. *The International Journal of Psycho-Analysis, 87*, 651–666.
Olthuis, J. H. (1996). Face-to-face: Ethical asymmetry or the symmetry of mutuality? *Studies in Religion/Sciences Religieuses, 25*(4), 459–479.
Ostenfeld, I. (1978). *Søren Kierkegaard's psychology*. Waterloo, ON: Wilfrid Laurier University Press.
Pattison, G. (2002). *Kierkegaard's upbuilding discourses: Philosophy, literature and theology*. Abingdon, UK: Routledge.
Pattison, G. (2013). *Kierkegaard and the quest for unambiguous life*. Oxford: Oxford University Press.
Perlman, F. T. (1999). Love and its objects: On the contributions to psychoanalysis of Martin S. Bergmann. *The Psychoanalytic Review, 86*(6), 915–963.
Pickering, M. (2011). August Comte. In G. Ritzer & J. Stepnisky (Eds.), *The Wiley-Blackwell companion to major social theorists* (*Classical social theorists*) (Vol. I, pp. 30–60). Chichester, West Sussex, UK: Wiley-Blackwell.
Rae, M. (2010). *Kierkegaard and theology*. London and New York: Continuum.
Rickman, J. (1937). On "unbearable" ideas and impulses. *The American Journal of Psychology, 50*, 248–253.
Roth, P. (2001). The paranoid-schizoid position. In C. Bronstein (Ed.), *Kleinian theory: A contemporary perspective* (pp. 32–46). London: Whurr.
Schmitt, C. (1919). *Politische Romantik*. Munich and Leipzig: Duncker & Humblot.
Segal, H. (1973). *Introduction to the work of Melanie Klein*. (New, enlarged ed.). London: Hogarth.
Spillius, E. B. (1988). *Melanie Klein today: Developments in theory and practice* (*Mainly theory*) (Vol. 1). London: Routledge.
Sternberg, R. J., & Sternberg, K. (2010). *The psychologist's companion: A guide to writing scientific papers for students and researchers* (5th ed.). Cambridge: Cambridge University Press.

Stewart, J. (2009). Johan Ludvig Heiberg: Kierkegaard's criticism of Hegel's Danish apologist. In J. Stewart (Ed.), *Kierkegaard and his Danish Contemporaries. Tome I: Philosophy, politics and social theory* (pp. 35–76). Surrey, UK & Burlington, VT: Ashgate.

Sulloway, F. J. (1979). *Freud, biologist of the mind: Beyond the psychoanalytic legend*. New York: Basic Books.

Thompson, J. (1973). *Kierkegaard*. New York: Borzoi-Knopf.

Vitz, P. C. (1988). *Sigmund Freud's Christian unconscious*. Grand Rapids, MI: William B. Eerdman's.

Watkin, J. (1990). Historical introduction. In S. Kierkegaard (Ed.), *Early polemical writings* (pp. vii–xxxvi). Princeton, NJ: Princeton University Press.

Watkin, J. (2010). *The A to Z of Kierkegaard's philosophy*. Lanham, MD: Scarecrow Press.

Watts, M. (2003). *Kierkegaard*. Oxford: Oneworld.

Winnicott, D. W. (1935). The manic defence. In *Through paediatrics to psycho-analysis* (pp. 129–144). London: Hogarth Press. (1958).

Winnicott, D. W. (1963). Communicating and not communicating leading to a study of certain opposites. In *The maturational processes and the facilitating environment: Studies in the theory of emotional development* (pp. 179–191). London: Hogarth Press and the Institute of Psycho-Analysis. (1965).

James L. Kelley After receiving his education at three American universities, scholar James L. Kelley settled in to a life of researching and writing about, among other things, the fascinating lives of creative people. His first two books are *A Realism of Glory: Lectures on Christology in the Works of Protopresbyter John Romanides* (Rollinsford, NH: Orthodox Research Institute), published in 2009, and *Anatomyzing Divinity: Studies in Science, Esotericism and Political Theology* (Walterville, OR: TrineDay), published in 2011. His third book, *Orthodoxy, History, and Esotericism: New Studies* (Dewdney, B.C.: Synaxis Press, 2016), is a history of esoteric influences on Western religious culture.

Chapter 56
Focus on Cross-Cultural Models of Love

Barbara Lewandowska-Tomaszczyk and P. A. Wilson

Abstract Our paper is part of a larger research project on cross—cultural analyses of emotions. It focuses on a comparison between the concepts of *love* in English and its Polish equivalent *miłość* as well as LOVE cluster emotions as they are used in both languages. Analyses were performed with the use of the GRID instrument, online emotions sorting task as well as the British National Corpus and National Corpus of Polish language materials, particularly with reference to collocational patterns in both languages. Reference to figurative language, mainly metaphor and metonymy, is also discussed. In the conclusions we propose a typology of love emotion models in both cultures and observe differences in the dimension of NOVELTY as well as the clustering structure in Polish and British English love, which can be considered to be associated with a more collectivistic versus individualistic profile in these respective cultures.

Keywords Collocations · Culture · Emotion models · Figurative language · Language corpora · Love · Miłość

56.1 Introduction

Within the context of our larger research project on cross—cultural analyses of emotions, the overarching aim of the present chapter is to present a comparative analysis between the concepts of *love* in British English and its Polish equivalent

---

B. Lewandowska-Tomaszczyk (✉)
Department of Language and Communication, State University of Applied Sciences, Konin, Poland
e-mail: barbara.lewandowska-tomaszczyk@konin.edu.pl

P. A. Wilson (✉)
Institute of English Studies, University of Lodz, Pomorska, Lodz, Poland
e-mail: paul.wilson@uni.lodz.pl

© Springer Nature Switzerland AG 2021
C.-H. Mayer, E. Vanderheiden (eds.), *International Handbook of Love*,
https://doi.org/10.1007/978-3-030-45996-3_56

miłość.[1] One of the major influences on how love is conceptualised is the relative degree of individualism and collectivism. Kim and Hatfield (2004) observe that passionate love is more salient in individualistic cultures such as Britain. This type of love, as Hatfield and Rapson (1996) highlight, is both associated with fulfilment and ecstasy when one is engrossed in such a relationship with a partner, but can also be related to sadness, distress and despair if the relationship flounders or the love is unrequited. In contrast, Kim and Hatfield (2004) refer to the tenderness and warmth that are more likely to be present in intimate relationships in relatively more collectivistic cultures that are based on commitment over time, shared values and intimacy. As opposed to the passionate love that appears to be relatively more prominent in individualistic cultures, such love is often referred to as companionate love.

There is evidence that happiness is particularly salient in experiencing love in collectivistic cultures. Lu and Gilmour (2004) showed that Chinese students conceptualised happiness in terms of both their love for their lover/spouse as well as for friends and family. The derivation of happiness from romantic love can also be seen in young, relatively more collectivistic Bangladeshi women who describe how crucial their marital relationships are for their happiness (Camfield, Choudhury, & Devine, 2009). The importance of good family relationships, including those between romantic partners, is also at the heart of happiness for the Inuit (Kral & Idlout, 2012), a people who have been identified as highly collectivistic (Beckstein, 2014).

It is further proposed that the concept of love is not crisp or universal across cultures. Although ingredients or properties of love can be found in many culture-specific concepts of what could be considered emotions close to love, their cognitive-semantic profiles display unique characteristics both in the configurations of the properties as well as the dominant structure of the most frequent types of love. Each of the types—passionate, erotic, companionate, etc. and other categories of this emotion—are type- and culture-specific.

Connected with this sensitivity of concept formation to cultural impact are the phenomena of *meaning approximation* in interaction and *semantic reconceptualization* of the content of messages conveyed in communicative contexts (Lewandowska-Tomaszczyk, 2012). These phenomena are pertinent to intra- and inter-linguistic comparisons not only of emotion concepts, but of a totality of notions conceived of by humans. What one can identify then in conceptual-semantic comparison contexts are not instances of equivalence between single terms in one language and unique terms in another language but rather instances of cluster equivalence patterns between the systems.

---

[1]The main theses of the present paper were presented at *Love & Time* conference, Galilee (Lewandowska-Tomaszczyk & Wilson, 2015). We very much appreciate comments from the conference participants and the invitation from Professor Aaron Ben-Ze'ev of Haifa University (see his chapter in this book).

Emotion clusters are groups of emotion concepts exhibiting (degrees of) *similarity* along a number of dimensions, such as AROUSAL (e.g., the *fervency of love*), VALENCE and CONTROL as well as particular sets of physiological, behavioural and mental properties, characterised with similar ex-bodied expression as well as results and consequences. The properties can be grouped around one or more basic emotions within an *intra-cluster* setting (e.g., FEAR cluster), while clusters are typically linked by *inter-cluster* relations (e.g., disgust is connected to ANGER and FEAR clusters—Lewandowska-Tomaszczyk & Wilson, 2016). Each individual emotion space on the other hand is inhabited by *polysemous* concepts, that is a range of different, although related, senses of an emotion concept as, for example, in the case of different types of love, further discussed in the present paper.

In the light of the comparison between love in British English and Polish in the present study it is important to narrow our focus on these two cultures. In cross-cultural research, Poland is often described as a collectivistic culture (e.g., Szarota, Cantarero, & Matsumoto, 2015). However, despite a score of 60 on the individualism–collectivism scale, which shows that Poland is clearly more collectivistic in relative terms than individualistic Britain, which has a score of 89, it can be questioned whether Poland can be deemed to have a collectivistic status that is on a par with countries typically considered in such terms, such as China with an individualism–collectivism score of 20 (Hofstede Insights). However, the point to note here is that the individualism–collectivism scale allows the relative comparison of countries on this dimension and Poland is clearly more collectivistic in comparison to Britain on this scale. Therefore, it is predicted that Polish *miłość* and British English *love* will conform to what one would expect on the basis of their relatively more collectivistic and individualistic status, respectively.

Three complementary methods are used [GRID instrument, online emotions sorting task, and a corpus-based cognitive linguistic methodology (Lewandowska-Tomaszczyk & Wilson, 2013)] to test specific hypotheses. On the basis of the commitment over time that characterises companionate *love* (Kim & Hatfield, 2004), it is hypothesised that *miłość* will be conceptualised as having a longer duration than *love*. With respect to the greater salience of happiness in love in collectivistic cultures it is further predicted that there will be a relatively greater association between *miłość* and happiness emotions than between *love* and happiness emotions.

The corpus data, particularly collocational patterns, that is recurring combinations of lexical items which are used in language with a frequency higher than chance occurrence, are further analysed to show the preferred clustering of the senses of love that are characteristic of Polish and British English.

56.2 Emotion Events

Emotions, as proposed in Lewandowska-Tomaszczyk and Wilson (2013), arise in the context of particular Emotion Events. We posit the following structure of a prototypical Emotion Event scenario:

Prototypical Emotion Event Scenario EES: Context (*Biological* predispositions of Experiencer, *Social* and *Cultural* conditioning, *On-line* contextual properties of Event) [Stimulus > Experiencer{(internally experienced) Emotion [**EMBODIED mind—META-PHOR**] + (internally and externally manifested) physiological and physical symptoms} > possible external reaction(s) of Experiencer (approach/avoidance, language) **i.e., EXBODIED mind**

Extended Emotion Event Scenarios involve cases of experiencing more than one emotion of the same valence, namely *emotion clusters*, at the same time, on the one hand, and so-called *mixed feelings*, experienced as two *contradictory emotions* at the same time, on the other.

Both *love* and *miłość* arise in a conceptual space inhabited by a cluster of related emotions: Pol. *radość, szczęście, bliskość* and Eng. *joy, happiness, warmth*, etc. They are situated either within the same cluster or connected to other emotions and emotion clusters of the same positive polarity. Such chains of senses, engaging either *intra-* or *inter-cluster members*, have a significant frequency of occurrence in the analysed corpus data. Inter-cluster members sometimes involve concepts of an opposite polarity such as *love-hate* and, in other cases, more frequently in some cultures, a combination with the concepts of the *sadness* cluster such as *regret, longing*, and *pain* in English and the polysemous emotions of *żal* and *tęsknota* in Polish. While *tęsknota* corresponds roughly to English *longing, yearning*, frequently in terms of the event context of *missing* somebody or something in the sense of 'no longer being close with somebody/something one values, and feeling sad about this', *żal* is a particularly language- and culture- bound term in Polish. It presents a range of meanings and clusters of possible English equivalents such as *sorrow, pity, regret, remorse, compassion, penitence, resentment*, and their various combinations.

56.3 Materials and Methods

56.3.1 Online Emotions Sorting Methodology

In the emotions sorting methodology, emotion terms are typically presented simultaneously on a desk in front of participants who are free to categorise them into as many or as few groups as they wish. In the online version the sorting takes place on the computer desktop. In the only study employing the category sorting task in a cross-cultural perspective (to our knowledge), the conceptual structure of Dutch vs. Indonesian was investigated by Fontaine, Poortinga, Setiadi, and Markham (2002). The category sorting task has also been used to determine the conceptual structure of a specific emotion feature—pleasure (Dubé & Le Bel, 2003).

In the present study we adapted the NodeXL tool to provide information pertaining to the LOVE cluster in British English and Polish and the relationship between each of these to happiness. Although the most common use of NodeXL is to analyse relationships between individuals using online social media networks, we employ NodeXL to create graphical representations of the Polish and British English co-occurrence emotion matrices. The graphs created are similar to those produced by the synonyms rating methodology employed by Heider (1991) to compare and contrast emotion terms across three Indonesian languages. In Heider's (1991) study participants provided a synonym emotion for each target emotion term and in the maps of the emotion domains the nodes are represented by the individual emotion terms. For the sake of consistency, we adopt the same terminology as Heider (1991) where possible. The main difference is in the terms used to refer to the links that show the relationships between the nodes; whereas for Heider connection strength refers to the between-subjects frequency with which an emotion term is given as the synonym for another, the connection strength in our NodeXL graphs represent the co-occurring frequency of the emotion terms in the online emotions sorting data, and are hence sometimes referred to as co-occurrence values or interconnections.

56.3.1.1 Procedure

Participants volunteered to take part in the study either through direct contact by one of the authors or in response to adverts placed on Internet forums. Each volunteer was sent a link to the experimental platform and were allowed to take part in the experiment at a time and location of their choosing, with the request that they do the experiment in seclusion. The first page presented the British and Polish flags and the participants clicked on these according to their nationality. Then the instructions page appeared in the appropriate language. Initially, there was a brief introduction outlining that the study was concerned with finding out about how people think some emotions "go together" and other emotions belong in different categories. More detailed instructions regarding the specific sorting task were as follows:

> You will be presented with 135 emotions on the computer screen. We'd like you to sort these emotions into categories representing your best judgement about which emotions are similar to each other and which are different from each other. There is no one correct way to sort the emotions—make as few or as many categories as you wish and put as few or as many emotions in each group as you see fit. This study requires careful thought and you therefore need to carefully think about which category each emotion belongs rather than just quickly putting emotions in categories without much thought.

Following this, participants were told they would watch a video (about 8 min) that would demonstrate the procedure. They were told that this would be followed by a practice session that involved the categorisation of food items, and once this had been completed the proper experiment with emotion terms would begin. The following message appeared in a central window on the experimental page:

> You need to click on the "New Emotions Group" button and drag emotions to create your emotion groups. When you have finished creating your emotion groups, click on the orange "DONE" button and the experiment has been completed.

56.3.1.2 Participants

There were 58 British English participants (27 females, mean age = 42.7 years) and 58 Polish participants (27 females, mean age = 35.8 years).

56.3.2 Language Corpora

Language corpora are large collections of language materials, combining representative samples of all genres and varieties of authentic spoken and written language (100-million unit British National Corpus and 300-million unit National Corpus of Polish). As has been mentioned in the introduction, the materials have been researched for *collocations*, that is steady combinations of words, which co-occur in the language materials more frequently than by chance (≤ 5). Reference to figurative language, mainly metaphor and metonymy, has also been made.

56.3.3 GRID

The GRID instrument (Fontaine, Scherer, & Soriano, 2013; Scherer, 2005) employs a system of dimensions and components, which bring about insight into the nature of emotion prototypical structures. The GRID project is coordinated by the Swiss Center for Affective Sciences at the University of Geneva in collaboration with Ghent University and is a worldwide study of emotional patterning across 23 languages and 27 countries. The GRID instrument comprises a Web-based questionnaire in which 24 prototypical emotion terms are evaluated on 144 emotion features. These features represent activity in all six of the major components of emotion. Thirty-one features relate to appraisals of events, eighteen to psychophysiological changes, twenty-six to facial, vocal or gestural expressions, forty to action tendencies, twenty-two to subjective experiences and four to emotion regulation. An additional three features refer to other qualities, such as frequency and social acceptability of the emotion. Participants are asked to rate the likelihood of these features for the various emotions. This methodology is comprehensive in its scope as it allows the multicultural comparison of emotion conceptualisations on all six of the emotion categories recognised by emotion theorists (Ellsworth & Scherer, 2003; Niedenthal, Krauth-Gruber, & Ric, 2006; Scherer, 2005).

56.3.3.1 Procedure

Participants completed the GRID instrument in a controlled Web study (Reips, 2002), in which each participant was presented with four emotion terms randomly chosen from the set of 24 and asked to rate each in terms of the 144 emotion features. They rated the likelihood that each of the 144 emotion features can be inferred when a person from their cultural group uses the emotion term to describe an emotional experience. A 9-point scale was employed that ranged from extremely unlikely (1) to extremely likely (9)—the numbers 2–8 were placed at equidistant intervals between the two ends of the scale, with 5 'neither unlikely, nor likely' in the middle and participants typed their ratings on the keyboard. It was clearly stated that the participants needed to rate the likelihood of occurrence of each of the features when somebody who speaks their language describes an emotional experience with the emotion terms presented. Each of the 144 emotion features was presented separately, and participants rated all four emotion terms for that feature before proceeding to the next feature.

56.3.3.2 Participants

The mean ages and gender ratios of the participants for each of the emotion terms were as follows: *love* (32 British English-speaking participants; mean age 20.7 years, 21 females); *miłość* (18 Polish-speaking participants; mean age 22.8 years, 12 females).

56.4 Results

56.4.1 Online Emotions Sorting Study

56.4.1.1 LOVE and HAPPINESS Cluster

Figure 56.1 shows the comparison between *happiness* and British English LOVE cluster emotion co-occurrence values and the corresponding values between *szczęście* and Polish LOVE cluster emotions. It can be see seen that these interconnections are higher for Polish than British English. For example, the higher co-occurrence values between *szszęście* and *miłość* 'love, affection' (36), *troska* 'caring, consideration' (17) and *pożądania* 'desire, lust' (24) can be contrasted with the relatively lower corresponding interconnections between *happiness* and *love* (11), *caring* (10) and *lust* (7).

56.5 LOVE Cluster in Corpora

The LOVE cluster combines closely with happiness as in the following authentic English examples:

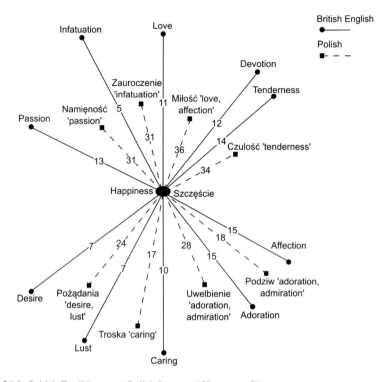

Fig. 56.1 British English versus Polish LOVE and HAPPINESS Cluster

1. all the love and happiness we can get from the women in the family
2. she strikes a dramatic pose of complete withdrawal from love and happiness
3. the bridal night she had dreamed of, that uninhibited leap into love and happiness

In this section we also examine a number of intra-cluster members of the LOVE cluster: *desire*, *passion* and *lust* in English and their approximate equivalents *pasja*, *namiętność*, *pożądanie* and *żądza* in Polish.

Other cluster members also co-occur with love in English:

4. our volunteers provided much love and care to many hurt and lonely people
5. let there be something rich about her to love and desire
6. Their love was founded on love and mutual respect
7. To my dearest grandmother, with love and gratitude
8. providing hours of pleasure, love, and immense fulfilment

Combinations of love, pain (*ból*) and death (*śmierć*) are identified both in the Polish and English materials in similar frequencies:

9. doznałem niepowtarzalnych uczuć, poznałem i zrozumiałem cały wszechświat: miłość i ból 'I got to experience unique feelings, I got to know and understand the whole universe: love and pain'

10. na kartach powieści splatają się nieustannie w namiętnym uścisku miłość i śmierć 'on the pages of the novel there are love and death continuously interweaving in a passionate embrace'
11. wkraczał zatem w okres, kiedy miłość i śmierć stają się nieodłącznymi przyjaciółkami mężczyzny 'he was then entering the period in which love and death become an inseparable part of a man'
12. He takes us right to the complex mixture of love and pain
13. He felt a wave of almost painful love for her
14. A romantic programme, whereby love and death converge, and dying young is the thing to do.

56.5.1 Love Scenarios in Collocations

The materials which are used to propose more detailed LOVE emotion event scenarios, in which cross-cultural differences in AROUSAL, VALENCE and RECOGNITION are evident, are the language data generated from large corpora, together with the results of the online emotions sorting task and GRID questionnaire (Sect. 56.6).

56.5.2 Collocational patterns

Collocates of words, namely words that are neighbours in utterances and which co-occur more frequently than by chance, signal properties of emotions such as their duration, depth and VALENCE (Adjectival collocates), and emotion objects functioning as stimuli and causes (Nominal collocates). Verbal collocates signify properties of *construal* (Langacker, 1987/1991), that is the way that an emotion is conceptualised. In other words, such language materials make it possible for discourse interactants to identify the *construal of emotions* (Langacker, 1987/1991) and their conceptualisations within particular cultures.

Contrasts within intra-cluster emotion members, in this case *love—miłość* (Lists 1, 4, 5 and 2, 3, 6) and *passion* (8)—*pożądanie* (7), provide additional information both in terms of these love types as well as uncovering cross-cultural similarities and differences in this respect.

A number of *association scores* are computed for each collocational combination; in this case t-score (TTEST) and mutual information (MI). The symbol A stands for raw frequencies of collocates, TTEST for probability of statistical significance, while the MI score of two random variables is a measure of the variables' mutual dependence (MI3 signifies a multivariate analysis, i.e., mutual-information for degrees higher than 2 (3 in this case)).

List (1) Eng. *love*

Adjectival Collocates

#	Collocate	POS	A	TTEST	MI3
1	true	AJ%	152.0	10.40	17.17
2	great	AJ%	142.0	7.06	15.59
3	romantic	AJ%	51.0	6.76	15.60
4	passionate	AJ%	48.0	6.75	16.48
5	brotherly	AJ%	36.0	5.98	18.71
6	unrequited	AJ%	33.0	5.73	18.79
7	wonderful	AJ%	41.0	5.42	13.42
8	real	AJ%	72.0	4.97	13.61
9	divine	AJ%	27.0	4.87	13.52
10	mutual	AJ%	29.0	4.83	13.00
11	deep	AJ%	37.0	4.40	12.28
12	undying	AJ%	19.0	4.34	16.42
13	courtly	AJ%	19.0	4.32	15.36
14	sorry	AJ%	42.0	4.25	12.32
15	lose	AJ%	22.0	4.21	12.23
16	eternal	AJ%	19.0	4.10	12.57
17	sexual	AJ%	32.0	4.04	11.81
18	erotic	AJ%	17.0	3.98	13.05
19	lost	AJ%	18.0	3.96	12.27
20	married	AJ%	22.0	3.96	11.60
21	human	AJ%	52.0	3.85	12.50
22	genuine	AJ%	22.0	3.75	11.24
23	unconditional	AJ%	14.0	3.61	12.49
24	perfect	AJ%	25.0	3.53	11.05
25	young	AJ%	70.0	3.51	13.04

List (2) Pol. *miłość* 'love'

Adjectival Collocates

#	Collocate	POS	A	TTEST	MI3	English equivalents
1	prawdziwy	Adj	834.0	26.36	22.92	true
2	wielki	Adj	1249.0	22.97	22.08	great
3	boski	Adj	478.0	21.18	22.81	divine, godly
4	Boży	Adj	429.0	19.68	21.81	God's
5	mój	Adj	986.0	18.00	21.11	my
6	wzajemny	Adj	315.0	16.79	20.82	reciprocal
7	małżeński	Adj	270.0	15.88	21.05	marital
8	pełny	Adj	385.0	14.83	19.21	full
9	twój	Adj	362.0	14.57	19.09	your
10	swój	Adj	1324.0	14.26	21.45	one's
11	wasz	Adj	243.0	13.96	19.11	your (Plural)
12	nieszczęśliwy	Adj	164.0	12.20	19.13	unhappy

(continued)

Adjectival Collocates

#	Collocate	POS	A	TTEST	MI3	English equivalents
13	pierwszy	Adj	817.0	11.83	20.11	first
14	ludzki	Adj	232.0	11.40	17.707	human
15	romantyczny	Adj	141.0	11.31	18.69	romantic
16	czysty	Adj	167.0	11.04	17.54	pure
17	rodzicielski	Adj	125.0	10.91	19.33	parental
18	bezwarunkowy	Adj	102.0	9.98	19.83	unconditional
19	dojrzały	Adj	102.0	9.39	17.19	mature
20	matczyny	Adj	85.0	9.10	19.15	motherly, maternal
21	piękny	Adj	185.0	9.08	16.65	beautiful
22	braterski	Adj	82.0	8.95	19.20	brotherly
23	ojcowski	Adj	82.0	8.85	18.21	paternal
24	bezinteresowny	Adj	79.0	8.68	18.03	selfless, disinterested
25	miłosierny	Adj	77.0	8.58	18.06	merciful
26	wieczny	Adj	95.0	8.52	16.13	eternal
27	chrześcijański	Adj	97.0	8.35	15.92	Christian
28	zmysłowy	Adj	69.0	8.03	17.16	sensual
29	macierzyński	Adj	66.0	7.75	16.55	maternal, maternity

It is worth noting that the significant Adjectival collocates of *love* include *passionate*, *sexual* and *erotic* as significant occurrences in English, while in the comparable list in Polish it is *boży, boski* 'related to God, godly', *małżeński* 'marital', *chrześcijański* 'Christian' and *czysty* 'pure' that are significantly more frequent than sex-related love, and *zmysłowy* 'sensual' appears only at the 28th position in the frequency of occurrence.

The Verbal collocates point to a higher degree of tranquility and lower arousal in the way in which love is construed in Polish. This is also marked by more frequent imperfective and durative senses of the Verbs:

List (3) Pol. *miłość*

Verbal Collocates

#	Collocate	POS	A	TTEST	MI3	English equivalents
1	być	verb	6813.0	30.26	26.12	be
2	kochać	verb	254.0	14.19	19.16	love
3	spełnić	verb	161.0	11.63	18.24	fulfil
4	boży	adj	133.0	11.29	19.68	of God[a]
5	okazywać	verb	166.0	11.28	17.75	show
6	odwzajemnić	verb	127.0	11.22	21.82	reciprocate
7	wyznawać	verb	120.0	10.61	18.84	confess
8	szukać	verb	192.0	10.58	17.25	look for
9	uczyć	verb	165.0	10.30	17.07	teach
10	łączyć	verb	146.0	10.06	16.96	join
11	dawać	verb	214.0	9.913	17.11	give
12	potrzebować	verb	138.0	9.81	16.81	need

(continued)

Verbal Collocates						
#	Collocate	POS	A	TTEST	MI3	English equivalents
13	darzyć	verb	94.0	9.51	18.86	bestow
14	wyrażać	verb	116.0	9.35	16.64	express
15	wyznać	verb	89.0	9.10	17.81	confess perf.
16	pragnąć	verb	118.0	8.97	16.28	desire
17	obdarzać	verb	82.0	8.93	18.96	gift
18	nazywać	verb	132.0	8.62	16.09	call
19	wierzyć	verb	135.0	8.58	16.09	believe
20	przeżywać	verb	92.0	8.51	16.20	experience

[a]This lexical item was erroneously annotated as a verb in the system

List (4) Eng. *love*

Verbal Collocates					
#	Collocate	POS	A	TTEST	MI3
1	fall	V%	901.0	29.01	24.53
2	make	V%	976.0	23.50	21.87
3	hurt	V%	27.0	4.21	11.91
4	is	V%	16.0	3.74	11.97
5	lose	V%	59.0	3.66	12.70
6	hate	V%	22.0	3.53	10.94
7	declare	V%	24.0	3.46	10.93
8	share	V%	31.0	3.37	11.25
9	express	V%	31.0	3.09	11.07
10	inspire	V%	11.0	2.61	9.14
11	profess	V%	6.0	2.31	9.34
12	send	V%	43.0	2.30	11.47
13	anger	V%	7.0	2.27	8.44
14	care	V%	18.0	2.18	9.38
15	understanding	V%	6.0	2.17	8.30
16	conquer	V%	6.0	2.16	8.28
17	blossom	V%	5.0	2.11	8.79
18	triumph	V%	5.0	2.06	8.35
19	sing	V%	14.0	2.01	8.73
20	blind	V%	5.0	1.98	7.80

List (5) Eng. *love*

Nominal Collocates					
#	Collocate	POS	A	TTEST	MI3
1	affair	N%	231.0	13.26	18.68
2	song	N%	76.0	5.86	14.10
3	bite	N%	29.0	4.73	12.77
4	story	N%	107.0	3.96	14.18

(continued)

Nominal Collocates

#	Collocate	POS	A	TTEST	MI3
5	scene	N%	63.0	3.89	12.92
6	triangle	N%	11.0	2.15	8.43
7	potion	N%	5.0	1.98	7.82
8	nest	N%	14.0	1.97	8.69
9	poetry	N%	18.0	1.86	9.17
10	feast	N%	9.0	1.81	7.67
11	philtre	N%	3.0	1.71	9.49
12	tryst	N%	3.0	1.65	7.57
13	songs	N%	3.0	1.63	7.26
14	token	N%	7.0	1.58	6.92
15	shack	N%	3.0	1.37	5.45
16	rolle	N%	3.0	1.35	5.36
17	cheat	N%	3.0	1.31	5.23
18	hearts	N%	3.0	1.06	4.55
19	lyric	N%	4.0	1.00	5.00

List (6) Pol. *miłość*

Nominal Collocates

#	Collocate	A	TTEST	MI3	English equivalents
1	bliźni	425.0	20.35	23.74	fellow human being
2	Bóg	529.0	13.48	19.36	God
3	ojczyzna	157.0	9.58	16.68	fatherland
4	polak	17.0	4.04	13.96	Pole, Polish
5	nieprzyjaciel	20.0	3.11	10.36	enemy
6	bliźnia	10.0	2.37	8.65	fellow human being
7	stwórca	12.0	2.00	8.41	creator
8	niejedno	12.0	1.82	8.24	not one, many
9	wierna	26.0	1.59	9.94	faithful
10	małżonkowie	15.0	0.48	8.00	married couple, spouses
11	kochana	7.0	−1.42	4.99	loved, dear
12	ludzkość	8.0	−3.67	4.79	humanity
13	lud	11.0	−5.80	5.45	people
14	rodzice	90.0	−7.53	12.14	parents
15	spojrzenie	11.0	−11.38	4.77	look
16	poeta	8.0	−13.40	3.47	poet
17	dusza	11.0	−14.59	4.48	soul
18	matka	74.0	−15.40	10.93	mother
19	para	7.0	−18.15	2.64	couple
20	mąż	18.0	−23.92	5.60	husband
21	ojciec	66.0	−24.44	10.08	father
22	król	8.0	−25.17	2.69	king

(continued)

Nominal Collocates

#	Collocate	A	TTEST	MI3	English equivalents
23	serce	19.0	−26.35	5.67	heart
24	bohater	7.0	−26.88	2.13	hero
25	córka	8.0	−28.50	2.53	daughter
26	mężczyzna	45.0	−28.73	8.58	man
27	naród	7.0	−29.36	2.01	nation, people
28	miłość	13.0	−35.56	3.95	love
29	dziewczyna	10.0	−36.58	2.99	girl
30	żona	10.0	−42.14	2.80	wife

The Polish language data in the lists of Nominal Collocates present significant differences in love conceptualisations when contrasted with English. Polish culture involves an alternative conceptualisation of what can be considered a prototypical meaning of love. The most characteristic properties are a high number and frequency of non-erotic love collocates such as both religion-related concepts of *miłość*, (e.g., love of God,—human being/neighbour in the sense of 'Love thy neighbour';—enemy, −Creator, −soul), nation-based notions (e.g., love of fatherland,—Polish), as well as a family-linked type of love (between married couples, of and from −mother, −husband, −daughter, −wife, etc.). On the other hand, what is observed is the scarcity of Nominal collocates linked with romantic/erotic love (apart from possibly 'girl'—at the 29th position).

The collocational analysis of love in both languages is contrasted with that of *desire* (Pol. *pożądanie* (7)). Both Polish and English emphasise its physical and sexual aspects but it is only in Polish that *pożądanie* collocates with the Adjective *sinful* as one of the top twenty collocations. In English, on the other hand, *insatiable* and *unfulfilled* are two of the top twenty collocates. Religious links are thus clearly salient again in Polish, while in English elements of the *sadness* cluster (8) are visible.

List (7) Pol. *pożądanie* 'desire'

Adjectival Collocates

#	Collocate	POS	A	TTEST	MI3	English equivalents
1	seksualny	Adj	43.0	6.43	16.55	sexual
2	godny	Adj	35.0	5.84	16.55	worth(y)
3	mroczny	Adj	25.0	4.95	16.00	gloomy
4	silny	Adj	19.0	3.85	11.60	strong
5	gwałtowny	Adj	14.0	3.62	12.56	violent
6	męski	Adj	11.0	3.10	10.86	masculine
7	kobiecy	Adj	10.0	3.01	11.04	feminine
8	nagły	Adj	10.0	2.99	10.91	sudden
9	erotyczny	Adj	9.0	2.92	11.68	erotic
10	zmysłowy	Adj	8.0	2.79	12.39	sensual
11	cielesny	Adj	7.0	2.60	11.52	carnal, bodily

(continued)

Adjectival Collocates

#	Collocate	POS	A	TTEST	MI3	English equivalents
12	fizyczny	Adj	10.0	2.60	9.13	physical
13	grzeszny	Adj	6.0	2.42	11.61	sinful
14	wasz	Adj	7.0	2.23	8.31	your
15	wzajemny	Adj	6.0	2.15	8.23	mutual
16	pełny	Adj	10.0	1.89	7.96	full
17	dziki	Adj	4.0	1.82	7.50	wild
18	prawdziwy	Adj	8.0	1.73	7.36	real
19	perwersyjny	Adj	3.0	1.71	9.91	perverse
20	oszalały	Adj	3.0	1.71	9.70	mad
21	nienasycony	Adj	3.0	1.71	9.65	insatiable
22	nieodparty	Adj	3.0	1.70	9.41	compelling, irresistable
23	miłosny	Adj	3.0	1.70	9.09	amorous, love
24	namiętny	Adj	3.0	1.69	8.53	passionate
25	homoseksualny	Adj	3.0	1.67	8.16	homosexual

List (8) Eng. *desire*

Adjectival Collocates

#	Collocate	POS	A	TTEST	MI3
1	sexual	AJ%	77.0	7.87	15.8
2	overwhelming	AJ%	32.0	5.38	14.36
3	genuine	AJ%	25.0	4.24	12.00
4	burning	AJ%	19.0	4.04	12.29
5	homosexual	AJ%	16.0	3.81	12.41
6	strong	AJ%	43.0	3.77	12.08
7	insatiable	AJ%	12.0	3.41	13.21
8	unconscious	AJ%	13.0	3.23	10.70
9	urgent	AJ%	14.0	3.09	10.14
10	unfulfilled	AJ%	9.0	2.95	12.44
11	earnest	AJ%	8.0	2.66	10.08
12	passionate	AJ%	9.0	2.65	9.44
13	deviant	AJ%	7.0	2.51	9.96
14	insane	AJ%	6.0	2.27	8.99
15	perverse	AJ%	6.0	2.25	8.80
16	irresistible	AJ%	6.0	2.21	8.56
17	unsatisfied	AJ%	5.0	2.18	10.20
18	repressed	AJ%	5.0	2.16	9.59
19	hidden	AJ%	7.0	2.11	7.92
20	ardent	AJ%	5.0	2.11	8.79
21	understandable	AJ%	6.0	2.05	7.80
22	innate	AJ%	5.0	2.02	8.01
23	frustrated	AJ%	5.0	2.00	7.90

(continued)

Adjectival Collocates

#	Collocate	POS	A	TTEST	MI3
24	carnal	AJ%	4.0	1.94	9.31
25	selfish	AJ%	5.0	1.89	7.35
26	intense	AJ%	8.0	1.88	7.58
27	sensual	AJ%	4.0	1.80	7.37
28	slightest	AJ%	5.0	1.79	6.97
29	romantic	AJ%	7.0	1.77	7.21

The collocates of *desire* and Pol. *pożądanie* are interesting due to the significant frequency of use of *grzeszny* 'sinful' in Polish and the absence of its equivalence in the English data. The frequency of the collocate *homosexual* in the English data is also worth noting, which is significantly more frequent than in Polish (*homoseksualny*). While the equivalent of sinful can be related to the important role of (Catholic) religion in Polish culture, the form *homosexual* might be interpreted as a symbol of greater openness of British culture with respect to discourse related to public morality. This type of classification of love has direct relevance to its temporal properties, arousal, durability and permanence.

56.6 Types of Love

The construal of prototypical love is not entirely identical in British English and Polish. More data on this relationship is presented below in the sections to follow.

56.6.1 Language Corpora and Love Typology

The language corpus data provide evidence to identify five basic categories of love in both languages:

(i) Sex-related love (and desire)

(15) as someone evolved or emerged from a tribal love which is liberating narrowness to an *experience of sexual love.*

Example (15) juxtaposes romantic (*sexual*) love, occurring in the contexts of 'sinful love' in Polish, to the experience of storge (*tribal love* in (15)) and friendship love as in (iv) below, more salient in collectivistic cultures.

(ii) Religion- and God-related love (agape love) as evidenced in Polish *love* collocations, which have religious conditioning and connotations of high frequencies in texts, often co-occurring with other religion-inspired emotion terms:

(16) poprzez kontemplację, *miłość* i uwielbienie 'through contemplation, *love* and admiration'.

(17) zwycięstwo przez miłość, wiarę i nadzieję (religious) 'victory by love, faith and hope'.
(18) Łączyła ich głęboka *miłość* i porozumienie 'They were bound by deep love and understanding'.
(19) Boża miłość, sprawiedliwość i miłosierdzie 'God's love, justice and mercy'.
(20) And thou shalt love the Lord with all thy heart, and with all thy soul, and with all thy might.
(21) his peace upon us, bring us the good news of salvation and always fill us with love for all people.

(iii) Love of country, nation, king/queen (patriotism)
(22) all the people *love the King* so much

(iv) Family love (storge), friendship
(23) I would be surrounded today by love and wives and children and the rest.
(24) and I love the family feeling of a company.
(25) is this why my parents brought me up with so much love and care?

Furthermore, it can be observed that this conceptualisation of love occurs in the context of *pastoral love*, that is pastors' love for their people, present in the English corpus materials, although less frequently than parallel Polish data, which focus on the church, religion, and love of God.

(v) Love for animals, love for objects, etc. (pleasantness/appreciation)
(26) Ronald Fraser had no love for horses.
(27) The reader with a love of art is not always at the front of a publisher's attention.

56.6.2 Bodily and Reistic Expressions of Love: Metaphor

As exemplified below, bodily and physiological reactions (pulse racing, heart clenching) can be extended to focus on facial expression (eyes sparkling, lips moist and parted), bodily gestures (leaning), and behaviour (kissing, running towards the person who is loved), and are frequently described in metaphoric terms (Lakoff & Johnson, 1980). Metaphor *Source Domains* are the conceptual, reistic, domains with pools relating to, frequently physical, objects and events (*res* Latin 'object, thing, matter, property'), in terms of which an emotion scenario is conceptualised and expressed. The Source Domains of love embrace conceptual metaphors such as LOVE IS FIRE, LOVE IS LIGHT, LOVE IS WATER, LOVE IS ENERGY (EXPLOSION), LOVE IS DISEASE, LOVE IS SUFFERING, LOVE IS DEATH, LOVE IS PAIN, LOVE IS WEAKNESS, LOVE IS WAR, LOVE IS COOPERATION, LOVE IS HUNGER, LOVE IS MADNESS, LOVE IS WILDNESS, LOVE IS EXPERIENCER'S HEART GROWING BIGGER, and the metaphor characterising all emotions EXPERIENCER AND THEIR BODY (HEART) ARE CONTAINERS. Each of the emotion types relates to varying sets of bodily sensations and behavioural traits. Properties of Source Domain (physical) objects and scenarios function as models for expressing (more abstract) concepts as can be observed in the examples below. *Love of God* is often conceptualised in terms of the metaphor LOVE

IS LIFE and LOVE IS A VALUABLE COMMODITY and GOD IS A GIVER OF A VALUABLE COMMODITY. Apart from the conventional pool of metaphorical expressions in any language, there appear unconventional figurative descriptions of love, identified particularly in poetry and artistic prose, which are sensitive both to linguistic and cultural influences. They are novel and mostly unpredictable conceptualisations of love phenomena, created and developed beyond a fixed metaphoric pool of expressions as, for example, an unexpected love metaphor in the influential *A Little Book in C Major* (Mencken, 1916; para 16, p. 76): "Happiness is the china shop; love is the bull."

The conventional physical and bodily expression of love in Polish and English as well as the inventory of their metaphorical Source Domains are similar in both languages. Both cultures also consider the heart to be the metonymic location of love and a number of other emotions. Nevertheless, the frequencies of use of particular figurative expressions and metaphoric Source Domains differ in the two cultures, as they are sensitive to the type of the love emotion metaphorised and used in language.

Furthermore, most of the metaphors relating to erotic love first of all have direct relevance to time. 'Bursting' signifies suddenness and a short duration, while 'hunger' points to love completion - (sensual) satisfaction. 'Pain' and 'suffering' tell us about the permanence of love in its more negative context, while life can be considered positive - a valuable God-given quality.

We identify the following Source Domains for *love* in our English data:

LOVE IS LIGHT
(28) Claudia shook her head, her eyes sparkling with love
LOVE IS LIQUID OR SUBSTANCE IN A CONTAINER [BODY/HEART] THAT CAN EXPLODE AND BURST UNDER PRESSURE
(29) As she walked down the aisle her heart brimmed over with love and adoration for Charles
(30) Filled with love
(31) a burst of love and energy
LOVE IS INSANITY/MADNESS
(32) I am mad with love for you!
(33) I'm struck dumb with love
LOVE IS UNTAMED WILDNESS
(34) I was wild with love and jealousy, so I married him!
LOVE IS PAIN
(35) It was in the pain that she found their love
LOVE IS INFLAMATION [SEE DISEASE]
(36) My heart's inflamed with love's alarm
LOVE IS FIRE
(37) she returned home, and was so on fire with love
(38) You're burning up with love for me
(39) her face still flushed but glowing with love

(continued)

LOVE IS BURDEN	
(40) I feel that I could overwhelm her with love now	
LOVE IS DISROBING	
(41) she too could be naked with joy and love	
LOVE IS DISEASE / DYING	
(42) I would be sick/dying with love now	
LOVE IS GATE/KEY	
(43) He turned to smile at her as he answered, making her heart slam with love and helpless grief	
LOVE MAKES THE HEART GROW	
(44) I am, Ronni thought, glancing across at him, feeling her heart swell inside her with love and longing	
Love for God and people:	
LOVE IS LIFE	
(45) though the surroundings were drab, the people were alive with love for God and love for us	

The Polish materials provide additional data on the Source Domains as used in love metaphoricity in Polish. For example, the verbal concept *zaszczepić* has the basic sense of English 'vaccinate, immunise'. However, the English equivalent is applied with the negative meaning to the prepositional object (*to vaccinate/immunize against something*) such as, for example, *children vaccinated against rabies*. This sense is also present in Polish; however, the verb *zaszczepić* (followed by a direct object) can also be used in the positive context with the multiple—cluster—meaning of 'infuse, make aware of, encourage, inspire, spread, instill' and is most frequent in the context of grammatical objects denoting positive emotions (love, hope) and habits as in: *Możemy zaszczepić w młodych ludziach miłość do kraju i rodziny* 'We can inspire young people to love their country and family', lit. 'vaccinate/instill in these young people love'. This sense of love is typically not spontaneous or uncontrolled like romantic love—it is rather an emotion that can be implanted into another person, nourished and bred.

56.7 GRID Results

56.7.1 Novelty

The hypothesis that *miłość* has a longer duration than *love* was tested in a comparison of the low novelty GRID features versus the high novelty GRID features as these features characterise longer versus shorter duration, respectively. A 2 × 2 ANOVA was performed on the means of the low vs. high novelty GRID features (see Table 56.1), which comprised the within-subjects variable of *novelty*. The between-subjects variable was *language group*: English *love* vs. Polish *miłość*.

There was a main effect of *novelty* for the analysis on the novelty features, $F(1, 48) = 16.74$, $p < 0.05$, with the low novelty features rated as more likely to occur than the high novelty features (means of 6.19 and 5.06, respectively). There

Table 56.1 GRID features that characterise the NOVELTY dimension

Low Novelty GRID Features	High Novelty GRID Features
Experienced the emotional state for a long time	Unpredictable
Will be changed in a lasting way	Suddenly
Enough resources to avoid or modify consequences	Had the jaw drop
	Caused by chance
	Opened his or her eyes widely
	Had eyebrows go up
	Caused by supernatural power
	Required an immediate response
	Caused by somebody else's behaviour

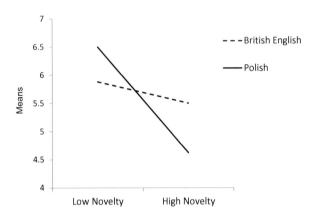

Fig. 56.2 *Love* vs. *Miłość* on the NOVELTY Dimension

was no significant difference in terms of *language group*, $F(1, 48) = 0.23, p > 0.05$. There was significant interaction between *novelty* and *language group*, $F(1, 48) = 16.74, p < 0.01$. Contrasts were performed to break down this interaction. There was a significant difference between low and high novelty features for *miłość*, $F(1, 48) = 18.11, p < 0.01$. Figure 56.2 shows that low novelty was rated higher than high novelty (means of 6.5 and 4.62, respectively). By contrast, there was no significant difference between low and high novelty features for *love*, $F(1, 48) = 1.31, p > 0.05$. There was a significant difference between *love* and *miłość* on the high novelty features $F(1, 48) = 4.74, p < 0.05$. It can be seen in Fig. 56.2 that *love* had a higher score on the high novelty features than *miłość* (means of 5.5 and 4.62, respectively). By contrast, there was no significant difference between *love* and *miłość* on the low novelty features, $F(1, 48) = 3.0, p > 0.05$.

56.7.1.1 Duration

The results of the ANOVA showing that *love* had higher ratings in terms of novelty than *miłość* is directly relevant to how these two variants are conceptualised with respect to duration. It can be concluded that in comparison with the unpredictability that characterises *love*, *miłość* is conceptualised more as expected and having a greater longevity. The latter is consistent with an independent *t*-test conducted on the GRID feature *will be changed in a lasting way*, in which *miłość* scored significantly higher than *love*, $t(46.45) = 7.81$, $p < 0.01$ (means of 8.17 and 7.13, respectively). Overall, the results support the hypotheses that *love* is conceptualised as more novel than *miłość* and that *miłość* is conceptualised as a longer-lasting emotion than *love*.

56.8 Conclusions

It is initially important to note that the differences shown between the models of *miłość* and *love* pertain to a matter of degree rather than polar distinctions. The online emotions sorting results reveal relatively stronger interconnections between the HAPPINESS and the LOVE cluster in Polish compared with relatively weaker corresponding co-occurrences in British English. It can therefore be concluded that the hypothesis that *miłość* has a closer conceptual proximity to its respective HAPPINESS cluster than *love* is supported. It is also consistent with other studies showing that happiness is relatively more salient in love in more collectivistic cultures (e.g., Lu and Gilmour (2004), Camfield et al. (2009), and Kral and Idlout (2012)).

The GRID results support the hypotheses that *love* is conceptualised as a more novel emotion than *miłość* and *miłość* as a longer-lasting emotion than *love*. This is consistent with the unpredictable, sudden nature of passionate love being more salient in the relatively more individualistic concept of *love* and a more stable, long-lasting companionate type of love being relatively more characteristic of the relatively more collectivistic *miłość* and is therefore in accordance with the observations of Kim and Hatfield (2004).

56.8.1 Typology of Love

There are numerous classifications of love in psychological and linguistic literature (e.g., Lewis, 1960; Kövecses, 1986). Our collocation analysis of the Polish collocates of *miłość* shows that they most frequently involve forms with *religious* and *family* connotations of the emotion of love such as *boski* and *boży* 'divine, God's' on the one hand, and *małżeński* 'married', etc., on the other. The next type of love, *passionate* (romantic, erotic) *love*, is the most frequently referred to in English and much less strongly represented in Polish. It is this type of love that refers mainly to unhappy love, involving, for example, the passing of love over time, unfulfilled love, etc. Erotic love and sex-related concepts appear significantly less often in the Polish data; however, in both languages the bodily, physical symptoms of this emotion are similar, particularly from the perspective of facial gestures. It is also worth noting that in both cultures the typology of metaphoric language, particularly with reference to physical/erotic love, is similar. A special type of love discourse in Polish, which is much less conspicuous in English, concerns references to nationalist sentiments and love of one's country (*patriotism*).

The collocational analysis of love in both languages is contrasted with that of *desire* (Pol. *pożądanie*). Both Polish and British English emphasise its physical and sexual aspects but it is only in Polish that *pożądanie* collocates with the Adjective *grzeszny* 'sinful' as one of the top twenty collocations. In contrast, *insatiable* and *unfulfilled* are two of the top twenty collocates in English. The religious links are thus clearly salient again in Polish, while in English elements of the *sadness* cluster are visible.

A combination of emotions of opposing valence such as love and regret, love and pain, and love and longing in the SADNESS cluster is present in both English and Polish corpus data. However, in Polish, more often than in English, stronger links are identified between love with pity, regret and longing, particularly salient in Polish as the polysemous emotion forms *żal* and *tęsknota*. It is also worth noting that there is a fairly strong relation between Polish excessive passionate, erotic love, that is *żądza* 'lust' and *zazdrość* 'jealousy', and the absence of such a link in the analysed English corpus data.

(46) Love Emotion Event scenarios

1. **Romance (amorous, erotic)** > passion > enthusiasm, desire [*wanting the person = wanting good for Experiencer*]
2. **Storge (family love)** > commitment, devotion, closeness [*wanting good for the Experiencer's family*]
3. **Agape (love of God)** > passion, devotion [*wanting good for Experiencer (salvation)*]
4. **Companionship (friendship)** > commitment [*wanting good for friends and Experiencer*]
5. **Patriotism (love for/of country/nation)** > devotion, sacrifice [*wanting good for Experiencer's country/nation*]
6. **Liking (pleasures)** > Love for objects/events: doing something/some properties of people > delight > passion, desire [*wanting good for Experiencer by the presence of particular people, animals, objects, events, etc.*)]

The typology of prototypical Love Event scenarios proposed above (52), forms a complex *radial* category (Lakoff, 1987) of love. It is hypothesised that what all the scenarios have in common is an intrinsic inclusion relationship between the emotion of love in the cluster sense of caring, consideration, etc., and that of wanting (desire) in some of its polysemous meanings. The scenarios also constitute a family resemblance categorisation type (Wittgenstein, 1953) with *romance love* most frequently mentioned, described and talked about in the corpus data, particularly in English. The LIKING scenario on the other hand can be considered rather a peripheral member of the LOVE cluster, which also includes so-called *politeness love cases* such as *I'd love to see you again* in some languages, including English, although not necessarily in others like Polish, which would employ a straightforward CHCIEĆ 'want' scenario in those cases that can be rendered as a prototypical LIKE meaning in English (*Chciałbym cię znów zobaczyć* 'I'd like to see you again').

References

Beckstein, A. (2014). Native American subjective happiness: An overview. *Indigenous Policy Journal, XXV* (2). Retrieved 10 September, from http://indigenouspolicy.org/index.php/ipj/article/view/251/0
Camfield, L., Choudhury, K., & Devine, J. (2009). Well-being, happiness and why relationships matter: Evidence from Bangladesh. *Journal of Happiness Studies, 10*(1), 71–91.
Dubé, L., & Le Bel, J. (2003). The content and structure of laypeople's concept of pleasure. *Cognition and Emotion, 17*(2), 263–295.
Ellsworth, P. C., & Scherer, K. R. (2003). Appraisal processes in emotion. In R. J. Davidson, K. R. Scherer, & H. Goldsmith (Eds.), *Handbook of affective sciences* (pp. 572–595). New York: Oxford University Press.
Fontaine, J. J. R., Poortinga, Y. H., Setiadi, B., & Markham, S. S. (2002). Cognitive structure of emotion terms in Indonesia and The Netherlands. *Cognition and Emotion, 16*(1), 61–86.
Fontaine, J. J. R., Scherer, K. R., & Soriano, C. (2013). *Components of emotional meaning: A sourcebook*. Oxford: Oxford University Press.
Hatfield, E., & Rapson, R. (1996). *Love and sex: Cross-cultural perspectives*. New York: Allyn and Bacon.
Heider, K. G. (1991). *Landscapes of emotion: Mapping three cultures of emotion in Indonesia*. Cambridge: Cambridge University Press.
Hofstede Insights. Accessed on 26 April, 2019. https://www.hofstede-insights.com/product/compare-countries/
Kim, J., & Hatfield, E. (2004). Love types and subjective well-being: A cross-cultural study. *Social Behavior and Personality, 32*(2), 173–182.
Kövecses, Z. (1986). *Metaphors of anger, pride and love: A lexical approach to the structure of concepts* (Pragmatics and Beyond, VII:8). Amsterdam & Philadelphia: John Benjamins.
Kral, M. J., & Idlout, L. (2012). It's all in the family: Well-being among Inuit in Artic Canada. In S. Helaine & G. Davey (Eds.), *Happiness across cultures: Views of happiness and quality of life in non-western cultures* (pp. 387–398). Springer.
Lakoff, G. (1987). *Women, fire, and dangerous things: What categories reveal about the mind*. Chicago: The University of Chicago Press.
Lakoff, G., & Johnson, M. (1980). *Metaphors we live by*. Chicago: Chicago University Press.
Langacker, R. W. (1987/1991). *Foundations of cognitive grammar* (Vol. 1 and 2). Stanford: Stanford University Press.
Lewandowska-Tomaszczyk, B. (2012). Approximative spaces and the tolerance threshold in communication. *International Journal of Cognitive Linguistics, 2*(2), 2–19.
Lewandowska-Tomaszczyk, B., & Wilson, P. A. (2013). English 'fear' and Polish 'strach' in contrast: GRID approach and cognitive corpus linguistic methodology. In J. J. R. Fontaine, K. R. Scherer, & C. Soriano (Eds.), *Components of emotional meaning: A sourcebook* (pp. 425–436). Oxford: Oxford University Press.

Lewandowska-Tomaszczyk, B., & Wilson, P. A. (2015). *It's a date: Love and romance in time and space*. Paper presented at an international workshop "Love and Time", University of Haifa. March 2015.
Lewandowska-Tomaszczyk, B., & Wilson, P. A. (2016). Physical and moral disgust in socially believable behaving systems in different cultures. In: A. Esposito, & L. C. Jain (Eds.), *Toward robotic socially believable behaving systems—Vol. I. Intelligent systems reference library, vol 105* (pp. 105–132). Switzerland: Springer.
Lewis, S. S. (1960). *The four loves*. Ireland: Geoffrey Bles.
Lu, L., & Gilmour, R. (2004). Culture and conceptions of happiness: Individual oriented and social oriented SWB. *Journal of Happiness Studies, 5*(3), 269–291.
Mencken, H. L. (1916). *A little book in C Major*. New York: John Lane.
Niedenthal, P. M., Krauth-Gruber, S., & Ric, F. (2006). *Psychology of emotion: Interpersonal, experiential, and cognitive approaches*. New York: Psychology Press.
Reips, U.-D. (2002). Standards for Internet-based experimenting. *Experimental Psychology, 49*, 243–256.
Scherer, K. R. (2005). What are emotions? And how can they be measured? *Social Science Information, 44*, 693–727.
Szarota, P., Cantarero, K., & Matsumoto, D. (2015). Emotional frankness and friendship in Polish culture. *Polish Psychological Bulletin, 46*(2), 181–185.
Wittgenstein, L. (1953). *Linguistic investigations*. G. E. M. Anscombe & R. Rhees (Eds.), G. E. M. Anscombe (transl.). Oxford: Blackwell.

Barbara Lewandowska-Tomaszczyk, Dr. habil., Full Professor of English and Applied Linguistics at the State University of Applied Sciences in Konin, Poland; Head of the Department of Research in Language and Communication in Konin. Author and editor of numerous books and papers in cognitive and corpus linguistics, emotion studies and translation, invited to read papers at conferences and give workshops at European, American and Asian universities.

Paul A. Wilson holds the post of professor in the Department of Department of Corpus and Computational Linguistics at the University of Lodz, Poland. He completed his PhD on the interplay between cognition and emotion at Birkbeck (University of London) in 2000. His main research interests include the conceptual representation of emotions from a cross-cultural perspective.

Chapter 57
Could Trump Be His Own Valentine? *On Narcissism and Selfless Self-Love*

Jan Bransen

Abstract In this chapter, I aim to contribute to the philosophy of love by arguing for a conceptual distinction between two varieties of self-love. One is the narcissistic variety that seems exemplified by Donald Trump's egoistic and impulsive tendency to satisfy merely his own desires. The other is the selfless variety that is morally respectable and that can be modeled on the ordinary love relation between two persons. The distinction is explored and analysed to make a case against the assumption that self-regarding people neglect their moral concerns. The analysis involves a conceptual exploration of the different roles played by people in love relationships, roles that can best be identified and understood when we focus on reciprocal relations, for which I use, as an illustration, the relation between Donald and Melania Trump. A crucial feature of roles in a reciprocal relationship is that they comprise both passivity and activity. Understanding how the active and the passive are interrelated is key to understanding the morally respectable variety of self-love, which involves, as I argue, the self-lover's capacity to *actively receive* their own love.

Keywords Love · Self-love · Morality · Self-regarding reasons · Receptivity · Egoism

57.1 Trumpmania

Donald Trump's election as president of the United States has given the world a paradigm of narcissistic self-love well beyond compare. There doesn't seem to be another person showing off such incredibly high self-esteem. Trump is special, really, really special, and he wants the world to know this, to recognize this, to *confirm* this. He deserves to be admired, he deserves to be adored. If we would love

J. Bransen (✉)
Department of Philosophy of Behavioural Science, Radboud University, Nijmegen, The Netherlands
e-mail: j.bransen@pwo.ru.nl

him as much as *he* loves himself, the world would be a better place. At least for the USA and for their citizens. But one may wonder whether, or why, such an exceptional champion of self-conceit would limit his successes merely to the country he is now making great again. If only we would let him, he could really run the world and make it the best of all possible worlds...for everyone! Such is his limitless self-confidence. And he can prove it! It is not just because he loves himself that much. No, he *earns* it. We owe him our love. He just *is* the paradigm of success, of what we all aspire, what we all love. And so does he: he loves himself, the greatest, the one beyond compare!

This picture definitely rings an alarm bell too. For the self-love displayed by Trump obviously exemplifies an egotistic attitude that seems the paradigm counterpart of what morality requires. After all, morality requires us to be prosocial, that is, to serve and protect other people's entitlement to well-being and respect. Morality requires us to act not merely for reasons of self-interest, and is therefore an indispensable feature of any viable society. Morality rightly seems to oblige us to resist our apparently natural egoistic inclination to be interested merely in satisfying our own desires. Does this mean that morality would require Trump to give up his self-love? Should we all give up our tendency to love ourselves? Is that moral duty's message?

Whether or not we are inclined to love Trump, or are inclined to hate him for his excessive self-love, or for his indifference to harming others, or his neglect of our needs and our entitlement to well-being and respect—Trump's case, or so I claim, most of all invites us to rethink and clarify our conception of self-love and its relation to morality. This is so for at least two reasons.

Firstly, to assume that the opposition between morality and self-love is evident supports a bizarre schism in human motivation. It should seem weird to each of us, that other people have moral reasons to care for our well-being but that we ourselves don't have such reasons. Why would morality give everybody else a reason not to harm Donald Trump but not Donald himself? What the heck is wrong with him that he is excluded by morality to take care of himself? Why would morality be picking on him? Is this an elitist conspiracy? What is so special about morality anyway that it allows itself to be blind to the fact that no-one could take care of Trump better than Donald himself? Something similar applies to each one of us, and this should at least raise some concern. For apparently, your friends, parents, children, neighbours, and even anonymous strangers in the street, have moral reasons to take care of your needs and to refrain from harming you. So, if everybody is acting morally when they take *your* interests into account, then why can't *you* be acting morally when you take your own interests into account? How could everybody have a moral reason not to harm you, except you? Why is prudence not morally praiseworthy? There is something puzzling about this apparent bifurcation.

There is unsuspected support for this line of reasoning, as it were, from the other side of the same coin. This support comes from Jesus, who proclaims in the Bible that "thou shalt love thy neighbour as thyself".[1] This surely seems to imply that there is something good, something *morally* good, about self-love. For Jesus obviously does not say that we should love others *instead of* ourselves.[2] Loving ourselves apparently provides us with an energetic motivational force that we could apply equally well to love our neighbours and make them flourish as we would wish to flourish ourselves. And no doubt Donald Trump will be the first to claim that this is definitely true in his case: *his* power and energy will suffice to ascertain that he will make all our lives as prosperous as his own.

This does not of course amount to an argument in favour of the claim that moral reasons and reasons of self-interest have one and the same source and might be applied for one and the same cause. But it does suggest that the presupposition that self-love and morality stand in a natural opposition needs further critical scrutiny. We may be wrong to think that moral reasons do not allow us to care for ourselves, as we may be wrong to think that loving ourselves impedes caring for others.

Secondly, we might imagine Donald Trump's self-love to be so grandiose that it comes close to what we may call the "Leviathan promise". In Hobbes' philosophy,[3] the Leviathan is the body politic, representatively actualized in one supreme ruling individual, the absolutely authoritative sovereign. This monarch can be said to need only one motive, one inclination and one aspiration: to love himself, to see to it that he will flourish, that he prospers as an absolute legislator whose will is everybody's law. For if he does, if he loves himself and succeeds in making all his subordinates love him too, this will be good for everybody. And it will be good because his supreme self-love *as an absolute legislator* will create the very possibility of *moral* reasons. That is, the Leviathan's existence will give everybody a reason to care not merely for himself but to act prosocially instead. The Leviathan will make everybody refrain from harming others, because such harm will harm the monarch's absolute authority. And, obviously, the Leviathan will not be pleased by such potentially undermining threats, and will make sure to demolish any insubordinate opponent he comes across. We have seen this corrective power, over the years, in Trump's unscrupulous reactions to those who dare to go against his will.

I agree that the language of the Leviathan does not seem to fit the current democratic constitution, but those who voted for Trump often voice their choice by emphasizing that they adore Trump and adore him for his ruthless and determined self-love, a love they trust will be good for them. Trump's voters seem to believe, as Trump himself does, that he knows what the American people want and need. *To make America great again!* The rhetoric of this phrase nicely captures the notion of American exceptionalism: the idea that America is entitled to think of itself as the most important and best country in the world because it is the only country in the world that fosters the American dream. This dream is precisely what Trump loves in loving himself. For he obviously is the supreme exemplar. He made the American

---

[1] Matthew 22:39; Mark 12:31.
[2] Harry Frankfurt makes this observation in his *The Reasons of Love*, p. 77.
[3] Thomas Hobbes, *Leviathan*. C.B. Macpherson (ed.), London: Penguin Books, 1968.

dream come true. *All by himself!* And actually, just by loving himself. By loving himself in this unprecedented and invincible way. This is why Trump, in loving himself loves the American people, each and every one of them, in quite a similar fashion—if I'm allowed to make this comparison—as when God in loving His Son loves each one of His children.

To be sure, this reasoning does not amount to an argument that by loving oneself one loves other people, not even the people one identifies with. But it does suggest that we should critically scrutinize the distinction between self and other that we presuppose in thinking that self-love implies an egoistic bias and is therefore opposed to morality.

I shall contribute to this much-needed critical reflection on self-love in this paper. I shall argue that there is a variety of self-love that definitely deserves morality's support. I shall argue that for this a person needs to relate to himself in a *selfless* way. This will require a person to distinguish the lover within themselves from the object of their love that, to be sure, they themselves are too. I shall use the name *Valentine* for this alternative of oneself that is one's object of love.

To make sense of this selfless way of lovingly relating to oneself—that is, to make sense of the question of whether Donald Trump can be his own *Valentine*—I need to explain how the ordinary love relation between two persons, a lover and a beloved, can be a useful and informative model for the way in which to think about self-love. I will do so in three steps.

The first step is to give a rather general survey of the characteristic features of love as a relation between a lover and a beloved, explaining what this means for the *lover* as well as for the *beloved*. Step two will zoom in on the role of the beloved, the *Valentine*, which will involve some elucidation of what it means to be active in being passive, of what it means to *receive actively*. The final step will be to spell out how a person might be able to take up both roles in an exercise of self-love. What then is required and what will it mean for someone to be their own Valentine?

Bringing this back to my engagement with the self-love of the president of the United States, the question then will be whether Donald Trump can love himself for letting him be loved by himself. This may be a dazzling question for now. But I hope this will turn out to be a rather straightforward and clear question at the end of my argument. I don't know whether the answer for Donald Trump will be that clear and straightforward. Despite the picture I have been painting in this first section, I actually shall prefer to remain silent about whether or not Trump's self-love is an instance of the *selfless* variety. I cannot look into the man's heart, certainly not from the other side of the Atlantic and through the distorting glasses of the media. But then again, my conclusion is not about Trump. Trump merely provided the occasion and is (*pace* Trump) not all that important. The aim of this paper is to paint a picture of *selfless self-love*, a variety that is morally most respectable and that deserves to beat narcissistic egomania.

57.2 The Roles of Love

One of the most interesting features of human life is the fascinatingly myriad ways in which *activity* and *passivity* involve, evoke, merge, exclude, imply, contradict and require one another. This is particularly clear in love. From the early beginnings of Western culture this has been recognized, as we can clearly see in that phenomenal image the Greeks gave us of their god of love, *Eros*. Depicted with a bow and an arrow with which he can strike us at our heart, Eros both weakens our mind and strengthens our heart, making us hopelessly fall in love. Even though we know *eros* as the linguistic root of 'erotic', there is nothing specifically sexual about *eros*. For the Greeks *eros* implied arousal, to be sure, a strong, resolute motivation, a somewhat dangerous mode of losing control, a kind of madness, which is erotic and corporeal but not necessarily sexual. Those who fall in love are in the grip of a force that is much larger than them, that captivates them, that blinds them, *willingly*. Eros comes with an interesting set of features: a lot of energy and inspiration, an overwhelming sense of urgency, a rather narrow focus, an unusual blend of fearlessness and helplessness, an indifference to more reasoned courses of action, a sense of invincibility, a certain mode of folly and of lightness, of enthusiasm and vitality.

Contemporary neurophysiology offers some kind of explanation of what binds these features under one heading, a story that seems to suggest that a human being in love is neurophysiologically speaking quite similar to an addict: focused, captivated, in the grip of an *accumbens* activated by high levels of *dopamine*.[4] Dopamine fuels our desire; it devotes us to *wanting*. It directs our attention, so that there is not much else we can think of, except our beloved, the one we want to be with, for whom we will move the earth. There is some evidence that this focused craving is distinct from our libido or sex drive, which is fuelled by a different hormone: testosterone. No doubt dopamine and testosterone often work in tandem, but both from the neurophysiological as from the ancient Greek point of view there is no need to jump to the simple idea that the vitality of love is to be understood merely in terms of the urge to procreate. Erotic love is much more than that and does play a role in such diverse activities as loving the Chicago Cubs, loving one's children, loving one's country, loving sex or even loving one's stamp collection. It is the energetic craving for satisfaction, even though its relationship to the satisfaction itself is rather ambiguous. Erotic love is the devotion to wanting, it is the active *loving* itself that makes it worthwhile, much more than the reward it strives for.

As an agent we are definitely active when love in its erotic guise motivates us. But at the same time we feel passive in some sense, captivated, unable to do otherwise. This rather paradoxical state has been at the center of the work of one of the most

---

[4]Marc Lewis, *The Biology of Desire. Why Addiction Is Not a Disease*, Philadelphia: Public Affairs, 2015.

influential contemporary philosophers working on love, Harry Frankfurt.[5] He has tried to account for this phenomenon by analyzing the concept of *volitional necessity*, something that we just *need* to do in virtue of the determination of our own *will*. Frankfurt doesn't use the ancient Greek words for love—*eros, agapè* and *philia*—and is not specifically interested in the erotic nor in the romantic variety of love. His main examples—loving one's children and loving an ideal—for that matter, seem to fit *agapè* better than *eros*. When your child wakes up in the night, hopelessly crying, you get out of bed. You just *have to*—whether or not it is cold, whether or not you're tired and whether or not you seriously would just prefer to sleep on. You *have to* get out of bed to care for your child. And even though you *cannot* do otherwise, you *wouldn't want* to do otherwise. You have to care for your child because you *want to*. You're captivated, Frankfurt admits, but by the commands of your own will.

To understand the depth of this apparently paradoxical state of both being active and passive, and to begin to appreciate what this means for the *roles* of love, it may be useful to leave Frankfurt's analysis to one side and to say a little bit more about the other two Greek words for love. The word *agapè* has made a glorious career of more than two thousand years through the Christian world. Characteristic of agapè is the awe for the object of one's love, the profound dedication it receives and the infinite selflessness it evokes. The adjectives used seem to fit a transcendent, sublime, otherworldly, and divine object of love much more than a merely human and mundane beloved. Agapè is used in the Bible to refer to the love Jesus has for his Father: an unconditional, self-sacrificing love that is taken to be perfectly similar to God's and Jesus' immeasurable love for each and every human being.

Crucially, agapè is selfless; it motivates the lover to completely forget about themselves just to care for the beloved's well-being. Agapè is absolutely unconditional, immersing the lover in a totally disinterested dedication to the beloved object. Agapè is not about the lover's satisfaction. Not at all. It implies the lover's willingness to dedicate their life to the beloved object's flourishing, to provide all their resources, unconditionally, to praise and celebrate the beloved's glorious existence, *for its own sake*. The Christian connection with loving the 'humanity' encountered in another human being, in an unconditional and disinterested way, whether or not this other person is of one's own kin, fits the Greek idea that in agapè it is the universal Idea or Form of our *Valentine* that we love, rather than its actual, material, temporal instantiation. That is why I emphasized above that Frankfurt's main example of a parent loving their child fits agapè so well: in loving your child you love it for what it is now, to be sure, but even in what it is now you will be aware of the fact that your child is full of promises, full of potentiality, that it is a person that deserves to flourish, to express its *telos*, its full-blown potentiality as a precious, lovely human being.

There are some important lessons to be drawn from agapè about the relation between passivity and activity in love. And in a significant sense one lesson is the

---

[5]See, in particular, his collection of essays *Necessity, Volition, and Love*, Cambridge: Cambridge University Press, 1999, and his *The Reasons of Love*, Princeton: Princeton University Press, 2004.

same as the one to be drawn from eros. Love in the guise of agapè motivates the lover to actively spend all their energy and effort for the better cause of the beloved object, but, importantly, the activity is not motivated from within. That is, just as in the case of eros, the motivation comes from without. The lover is not active in making themselves moved to care for their beloved. This willingness to care comes from without. In the case of eros it is *Eros'* arrow that hits you in virtue of which the beloved object, your *Valentine*, strikes you as absolutely worthy of your adoration. In the case of agapè a similar kind of external source motivates you. But whereas in eros it is specifically the actual and material mode of your *Valentine* that triggers you, in agapè it is explicitly not the beloved object as it stands that merits your dedication, but rather its potential perfection.

A further important lesson is that both in eros and in agapè the lover and the beloved are passive in getting the love off the ground. That is, neither you nor your *Valentine* need to do anything to activate your love. For the Greeks there was an easy way to make sense of this. *Eros* is a god, one of the many that were around in Greek life, and it is Eros' activity, his hitting you with his arrow, that triggers your love. In agapè the situation is slightly more complicated, but the motivating force comes from the universal Idea, not from your own local and contingent impulses. Either way, whatever your *Valentine* is doing is neither here nor there when it comes to your love for them. Your love has an entirely different source.

This seems different in the third variety of love the Greeks had a word for: *philia*, usually translated as friendship, apparently involving a crucial reciprocity, requiring both friends to be active in having the love flow. Philia involves a lot of *sharing*. Philia is about joint attention, joint intention and joint evaluation. Philia evolves around intimacy, the sharing of joint existential experience. It includes mutual care, the sharing of responsibility for one another's well-being. And it creates commonality, the sharing of schemes of orientation, interpretation and evaluation. A paradigm of philia for the ancient Greeks is the intimacy among soldiers, side by side facing death, rejoicing in victory, sharing the deepest encounter with their human lethal vulnerability, and taking care, together, for each one's—and thus their *shared*—survival. The depth of philia is obviously significant on the battlefield, where survival is literally a matter of life and death. But also in the more common lives we live today there is ample room for philia and for its depth. The existential experience of communal endurance takes many forms, such as for instance sharing the experience of moving homes, of refurbishing and remodeling one's home together, or of watching the Cubs win the World Series, or even of something as small as singing 'Happy Birthday' to your 5-year-old child.

It seems pretty commonsensical to think of friendship as involving very similar roles to both lover and beloved. Neither friend is supposed to carry more weight in keeping the friendship alive. Neither one is merely the lover or merely the beloved. Both play a similar role, the role of *friend*. This might seem to suggest that there are three distinct roles involved in love: lover, beloved, and friend. This is right, as I shall take for granted. But we will make a mistake, as I shall argue, if we would understand this as implying that passivity and activity in friendship (i.e. in *philia*) neatly lines up with the roles of lover and beloved.

To make my case I will need a special occasion of friendship in which the lover and the beloved come apart. There are many such situations (think, especially, of life's bad times), but one of the more glorious and lighthearted occasions obviously takes center stage on Valentine's Day. Valentine's Day invites each one of us to disregard for a day the reciprocal sharing of orientation, intention and evaluation. On Valentine's Day you are encouraged to take up the sole role of lover. On Valentine's Day you think of your friend as your *Valentine*, assigning them the exclusive role of beloved object. On Valentine's Day Donald Trump is encouraged to think not of himself, but merely of his wife, Melania, his *Valentine*, for whom he will move the earth.

How are we to understand Trump's activity and passivity on Valentine's Day? What does it mean to take up the role of lover in an ongoing reciprocal friendship? Two models seem to suggest themselves, related to the other guises of love the Greeks distinguished. The first would be for Trump to remind himself of the initial erotic inspiration that brought him in this relationship with his beloved Melania in the first place. Trump might remember the enthusiasm and the vitality he experienced in the beginning. He remembers Eros. He uses his emotional imagination. He feels the strength of his heart, the blend of fearlessness and helplessness, the indifference to more reasoned courses of action, and his wish to write his *Valentine* a love poem, trusting the accompanying sense of invincibility. He will resist the thought that Melania will love him for this poem! It's Valentine's Day; it's not about what Trump will receive in return. Valentine's Day is about giving.

The other model might help. Trump might practice agapè. He may look at his *Valentine*, in this sincerely disinterested and unconditional way. He will see Melania's potential perfection—not, obviously, as a faraway ideal, that will require her to improve her character, her behaviour, her looks, but as a delightful reality that is clearly visible for everyone who knows how to look at Melania. If this would be difficult for Trump, he might be inspired by Melania's example, who seems capable of seeing the perfection in what would otherwise seem to be flaws: the political incorrectness, the grandiloquent language, the sandy hair, the wide, belittling smile, the small hands.

Importantly, in both the erotic and the agapic model it is obvious that as a lover one has to be disinterested. Love is not about oneself, not about satisfying one's own desires or needs, not about what is in there for oneself. When someone takes up their role as a lover in a friendship one is dedicated to let one's friend flourish. Whatever the effort this requires, taking up one's role as a lover implies that one gains access to the motivation that comes from without. This will necessitate the lover volitionally, to use Frankfurt's phrase: a lover will *love* to do whatever is required for their *Valentine* to flourish in their life, and selflessly so.

I hope this sketch suffices to explain the role of the lover, both in its passivity and its activity, with respect to their actions, attitudes and motivations, again both passively and actively. But what is the role of the *Valentine*? What do we ask in a loving relationship of the beloved? Is the *Valentine* merely an object, a purely passive entity that is being acted upon? These are easily neglected questions despite their vital importance. I shall spend the next section on the *Valentine's* role, arguing that it is a mistake to overlook its relevance in understanding love, particularly self-love.

57.3 Being Valentine: Lovingly Receptive

Valentine's Day is celebrated all over the world, and obviously local practices will vary greatly. As a Dutch person I may fail to understand and appreciate what Valentine's Day really is like in America, but let me focus for convenience on serious romantic friendships and the custom of giving heart-shaped gifts to one's friend. I take the symbolism to be clear: the lover wholeheartedly gives their heart to their beloved.

So, what is in it for the beloved? Are they merely receptive, the object of attention, care and love of their friend? Well, no. "To receive" is a verb. As with every verb, there are better and worse ways of doing whatever is required for an appropriate execution of the intended activity. And as with every verb, there are even instances that are arguably so far off the mark that they cannot actually be called an instance of suitable activity at all. We can all recall, or imagine, bitter instances or occasions when we gave our heart away to someone who crushed it in response. Giving your heart away, *wholeheartedly*, is a precious, vulnerable deed. Part of the undertaking is of course that you will have to do it unconditionally and selflessly. That is clearly what makes it such a courageous venture. The lover gives, cares, loves *without expecting anything back*. From the point of view of the lover, the beloved does not play a part in making the act of loving successful or not. Loving is the *lover's* activity, merely, purely, wholeheartedly, unconditionally and selflessly.

Yet even though the lover is not expecting anything back, receiving someone's love is still an activity on its own that can, as such, be done in better or worse ways. Not better or worse merely for the lover, but also for the beloved themselves, and, moreover, for the act of receiving itself. This may sound a bit strange, but it is relevant to note that activities have their own internal standards of appropriateness and success. As a social and communicative act, part of what makes receiving a success or not is a function of the assessment of the activity by the interacting persons. If the giver does not consider the receiving a success this matters to the quality of the performance of the receiver, and so does the receiver's judgement. But in addition to this there are also internal standards. Both people may be wrong in their assessment, after all. As a math student you may for instance learn the rules of multiplication, but your teacher may be so crude and uninstructive that we will all abhor and be right to conclude that this was a very bad instance of *"teaching"*, or perhaps even that it wasn't *"teaching"* at all. This is a well-known distinction: it is not always the case that something *is* what it *looks like*.[6]

So, how should the beloved receive the lover's love? What activity do we expect from a *Valentine*? How do you receive your lover's heart? There seem to be good reasons to do this *lovingly*, even though it will be clear too that these reasons do not necessitate you. Love, after all, is presumed to be a free and unconditional exchange between autonomous persons. Yet, it seems obvious that in the case of *philia*, of *reciprocal* love, we may expect a *Valentine* to receive in a loving way. We should, nevertheless, be careful with the reciprocity, as it might interfere with and blur the disinterestedness that is crucial to love. These complications are known at least since Marcel Mauss published his famous book on gift giving in 1925.[7] Mauss showed convincingly that gift giving requires complicated sets of interlocking social norms. In some obvious sense a *gift* is an invitation to give something comparable back in return, which seems to imply the expectation that the gift will be reciprocated, and, within a big enough time frame, this expectation seems to entail something close to an obligation. But of course a *Valentine* should not return the gift immediately and neither should they do so merely out of duty, or of calculation. Sharing love is not a business, not an exchange of commodities of comparable value, not a social contract. Love is a much more subtle adventure.[8]

The gift should first be received, obviously. Moreover, that might seem to be all a *Valentine* is supposed to do. After all, to acknowledge and endorse the essentially *disinterested* character of the lover's gift—which is actually their *love* itself, symbolized in the heart-shape—a *Valentine* could best receive this love as if this receipt is the final move in the transaction between the lover and their beloved. The love of the lover, as a disinterested gift, realizes itself to its full potential by just being this: a disinterested engagement of the lover with the flourishing of their beloved *for the beloved's own sake*.

Intriguingly, however, it is precisely in the receipt of the lover's love as the final realisation of this love, that the beloved's act of receiving this love itself takes on a wonderful *loving* character. Let me explain. Suppose Melania receives a heart-shaped gift from Donald Trump. It is *Valentine's Day*. Melania is Donald's *Valentine*. What should she do? Well, she receives the gift, which may strike her as a mere event. A terrific event, to be sure, but an event all the same, something that happens,

---

[6]These are complicated issues, to be sure, and I'm not in the business of defending realism here. I'm merely reminding us of the layered nature of the criteria of appropriateness and success of categorizing activities. This should open up a lot of dialogical space for critical thinking about facts and their so-called "alternatives". I should like to defend this space as providing room for an honest and seriously open-ended conversation on contested concepts that we do need to overcome the confused and confusing war on the media the Trump Administration seems to wage.

[7]Marcel Mauss, *The Gift. Forms and Functions of Exchange in Archaic Societies*. Originally published in *L'Année Sociologique*, 1925. English Translation, 1966. See: https://archive.org/details/giftformsfunctio00maus

[8]It may even be the kind of extraordinary social interaction that goes beyond Mauss's sociological interpretation.

that takes place without any interference or activity on her part. Literally, though, Melania will know this to be a misleading and incorrect description. She will have to do *something*: open her hands, look at Donald, listen to him, accept the heart-shaped gift he puts in her hands, thank him. And all this she will do in a certain mode: surprised, affected, flattered, excited, uplifted; or perhaps—this is possible too—disappointed, ashamed, annoyed.

The mode of one's receipt reflects one's attitude towards the gift, towards one's friend's giving of their love. This attitude of the recipient will co-determine the character of the giving, in virtue of the giving being a social, communicative act directed at the recipient. If one would refuse to receive the gift, the action could not properly be categorized as a giving. It wouldn't be a gift at all. This is one of the fascinating peculiarities of the metaphysics of social reality: *other* people co-determine what one does.[9]

Trump's giving Melania his love is, as we saw above, a disinterested, selfless act. Trump just cares for Melania and wants her to flourish. So there is *truly* no need at all for Melania to give anything back. All she needs to do is let this gift of love *be. Let it be!* Let it be what it is: *a gift of love*. That is all. That is what Melania's receipt of Trump's love should underscore. In terms of the role she performs as Trump's *Valentine* this requires her to strike a delicate balance. She may be grateful, sure, and express her gratitude. But she should not overdo it. She shouldn't let her gratitude degrade Trump's gift by being too abundant. On the other hand, she shouldn't receive the heart-shaped gift with indifference, either. And neither with too much self-conceit, as if it was only to be expected that she should receive Trump's love. That would be a bad way of receiving a gift. So, what are we to make of this?

Actually, the best reply, simple but also demanding, would be to say that Melania should receive the gift in a *loving* way. This will mean that as a *Valentine* she will receive the gift, Trump's love, in a disinterested and selfless way, moved to care for Trump, volitionally necessitated to let him flourish *as her lover*. There is no contradiction in this, and no paradox, if you would carefully discern what is at stake here. It is because Melania loves Trump that she will be most happy to *receive* his love, a love that itself intends to accomplish nothing but her own flourishing. This means Melania can just flourish, relax in Trump's hands, feeling on top of the world. She can just enjoy her own existence as beautiful and worthwhile, touched by Trump's love that uncovers the full potential of her life as good in itself, for its own sake.

Two features strike out in this loving receipt of someone's love. Firstly, Melania is not doing something for herself in receiving this love. She receives it, in this loving way, because she cares for Trump, her lover who is flourishing now, realizing his full potential *by being Melania's lover*. Melania is not satisfying any of her own

---

[9]There is an awful lot written on this. I'm particularly charmed by Rom Harré, *Social Being*, Oxford: Blackwell, 1979; and Ian Hacking *The Social Construction of What*, Harvard: Harvard University Press, 1999.

desires, even though she might obviously feel fulfilled, more than ever, by being loved by Trump. But it is Trump's love that fulfills her, and that is a love she cannot arrange or bring about. It is a gift, a true gift that she can only receive.

Secondly, Melania has no interest, fundamentally, in *loving* Trump for being her lover. She doesn't love Trump in order to receive his love. She just loves him. Period. As it happens, though, Trump turns out to love Melania. It is his own volitional necessity, not a necessity that she brought about, nor a necessity that she would have intended to bring about if she *could* bring it about. This is the difficult part, but it is crucial. Receiving Trump's love in a truly *loving* way means that Melania's interests do not play a role at all. It is the deep truth that echoes in one of Uriah Heep's songs: "I just want you to be happy, even if it is not with me." Melania will be thrilled and exhilarated, grateful for the wonderful coincidence that the universe offered her and Trump the opportunity to share their love together. But if Melania would have been able to guarantee that Trump would love her (by some act of magic), his love would have lost its most precious and most essential quality. What makes it the love that it is, after all, is that it is *Trump's* love for Melania, a love that comes from without, and truly so.

This, then, is the role of the *Valentine* in a love story: just to be happy in celebrating their own life, lovingly receiving their lover's love, as a true gift from without in which they have no interest. As a loving *Valentine* they feel volitionally necessitated to receive their lover's love in a disinterested way. They do, because they love to see their lover's flourishing, for its own sake.

57.4 Selfless Self-love Without Narcisissm

In each of the roles that I have distinguished in the previous sections passivity and activity play their part. In interesting and subtle ways these attitudes intertwine, but strikingly the satisfaction of someone's own desires is not a motivation in either role. Love is not about one's own satisfaction. Love is selfless. Love is about giving and caring. Love is about letting be, about letting go. The lover cares for their *Valentine*, wishing them to flourish, in the grip of the wonderful view of their *Valentine's* full potential that they discern clearly and love for what it is. And the *Valentine* cares for their lover, wishing *them* to flourish, as their lover, grateful and touched by the gift of their lover's love that encourages the *Valentine* to let themselves be what they are.

The selflessness of both lover and *Valentine* can perhaps best be characterised as the radical motivational silence of any occurring self-interested inclination. Of course we are all limited human beings, all too human, no doubt, and so we can easily imagine that all kinds of inclinations might pop up impulsively, even when we receive a *Valentine's* gift, or when we want to give one ourselves. These inclinations could potentially allure us, making us dramatize our gratitude, or fake indifference, or indulge in self-conceit. But when we are in a loving state, wholeheartedly, firmly in the grip of *Eros*, moved by *agapè* or in the flow of *philia*, these alluring, distracting impulses just go by unheard, in silence, motivationally inert. When we are in love, we can just let it be. We will just care for our beloved's flourishing. It will shine for us as the only thing that matters.

How could this relational view of the roles of love help us understand the case of self-love? How could self-love be selfless? Isn't that an oxymoron? Well, no. At least, that is what I argue. The view of the roles of love I developed in the previous sections can be used to model the self-relation at play in self-love as a relation that is complex, but that is significant, intelligible and viable too. The basic move, both for playing the role of one's own lover and for playing that of one's own *Valentine*, is to view oneself from without. And the basic endeavor then is to see whether you can be moved by the full potential of yourself anticipated from without. This may sound like a dazzling and artificial undertaking, at first, a complicated intellectual operation. But once you get the hang of it, you will begin to appreciate that it is not a cognitively demanding task. It requires you to be mindful, sure, but it is mainly a matter of feeling, of feeling at home in this world, and especially in this life, for the opportunity it offers you to embrace your own peace of mind, being just what you are, living *with* your limits.[10]

So let's return to Donald Trump and imagine what it would be like for Trump to love himself in the selfless way that I've sketched in the preceding sections. First, we'll have to imagine a second Trump, an alternative of the man, and wonder whether this alternative can be selflessly loved by the first, or, conversely, can himself selflessly love the first. Let's call them "Donald" and "Trump" and my question now is whether either one can be the other's *Valentine*, and if so, whether each of them can play the roles I sketched in the previous sections?

A first concern might be whether the world, or better *Trump's* world, can be big enough to include both. Could Trump bear Donald's presence if he were another man? Could the world harbour two men of such megalomaniac proportions? This is relevant, metaphorically, because in the selfless self-love that I'm trying to make sense of, the lover is supposed to love their beloved without thereby satisfying their own interest. So, there is a sense in which the question of selfless self-love is the question of whether the lover, call him Trump, would be capable of loving his beloved, call him Donald, if Donald would not be Trump. We may be reminded of Uriah Heep's lyrics: "I just want you to be happy", the lover sings, "even if it is not with me." If Trump could love Donald for what *he*—that is, Donald—is, and not for the immediate satisfaction this would give Trump, then this implies that Trump would be happy to stand in Donald's shadow, that he could bear the thought of himself—that is, Trump—merely being the stem that feeds the blooming rose he supports. For Trump to love himself, he needs to be able *to love*; that is, he needs to be able to be volitionally necessitated to care about something else, something that is worthy of his love, something that deserves to flourish *for its own sake*. Even though this something is Trump himself, it is not in order to satisfy his own desires that he does what he does when he takes up the role of the lover. When he takes up that role,

---

[10]The phrase is Valerie Tiberius's. See her *The Reflective Life. Living Wisely With Our Limits*. Oxford: Oxford University Press, 2008.

whatever it is that he loves, he starts out with a motivationally silenced self-interest. He is in love, so it is not about him, but about his beloved. In the metaphor of duplication: when Trump loves Donald, Trump's motivational structure is such that Trump does not care about himself. He only cares for Donald.

The *erotic* variant would look a lot like Narcissus' fate in Greek mythology: Trump would be captivated by Donald's image, unaware of the fact that it is merely his own reflection in the water. Helplessly and fearlessly overwhelmed by the infatuation, narrowed down by the dopamine to sheer wanting, Trump would forget about himself, would neglect his own well-being, would be indifferent to more reasoned courses of action, and would chase Donald's image—a fool in love. The *agapic* variant would be self-sacrificing too, but not in this reckless and destructive way. It would be like an enlightened Narcissus, full of admiration for the glorious reflection in the water, but without any inclination to grasp at the image. Agapè is full of awe, but without brash imprudence. It is full of devotion, aimed at seeing the full potential of the beloved, aware of the fact that the object of one's love is glorious in themselves, and can do without one's love, yet deserves this love unconditionally. In the agapic variant Trump would unconditionally devote his care to Donald, completely independent of the efforts this would require and without any attention to whether or not he—that is, Trump—would be rewarded for his dedication.

So far, the picture I'm painting of selfless self-love merely covers what it means for someone to take up the role of lover. The picture may confirm what is almost taken for granted in the diagnosis of narcissism. The pathological narcissist is typically unable to have intimate relationships. For the narcissist relationships merely seem to exist to serve the regulation of their own self-esteem. The narcissist cannot really love. This might seem to imply that the narcissist also cannot really love himself. I'm inclined to believe this is a correct observation. But, of course, one may now object that this conclusion hinges on the assumption that love and self-love are similar kinds of volitional attitudes. That assumption, however, goes unsupported so far and might simply be false. My artificial duplication, separating Trump from Donald, might not only be deeply inconceivable, but also fundamentally misleading. It might suggest that love is essentially a prosocial attitude. This could be the case, and perhaps trivially so, when one loves another person, but it seems quite absurd in case of self-love. Why should Trump need to silence his own interests when he imagines himself to love himself? My sketch may have been suggestive—if it is, as I hope. But that all depended on the duplication I proposed, on modeling Trump's love for Donald on Trump's love for Melania. But is that fair? Shouldn't you need to object to such rhetoric?

I think, however, I can strengthen my case by discussing the role of the beloved in the case of self-love. What would it mean for Trump, or Donald, to be his own *Valentine*? The duplication will help, but I shall be able to discard it in my conclusion, showing that we have good reason to think there are three distinct volitional attitudes: (1) loving another person, (2) loving oneself, (3) being narcissistic. With respect to these three attitudes the import of this essay is that we may have been inclined but do not need to take (2) and (3) together as morally disrespectable attitudes. Loving oneself is not necessarily an egoistic and narcissistic attitude. I have argued instead that we have good reason to take (1) and (2) together. Both are varieties of love, fundamentally selfless, and morally respectable. Both should, therefore, be distinguished from (3), the egoistic tendency to be moved merely by the urge to satisfy one's own desires. Self-love is not intrinsically narcissistic; it can be selfless.

So, how does Donald perform, being Trump's *Valentine*? As we have seen above the easy bit for the *Valentine* is that they are just invited to be what they are, to be happy with themselves, to celebrate their own life. They are lovely, just the way they are. This seems an easy bit for Donald too, being the self-conceited person that he is. Of course, he is lovely the way he is. Sure! No-one needed to tell him that. So there he goes, celebrating his own life, in glory. But there is more to being a *Valentine*. This is so in the case of being another person's *Valentine*, but similarly in the case of being one's own *Valentine*. In both cases part of the performance is in the receptive bit. The *Valentine* has to *receive* the gift of the lover's love. That's a true gift, from without, a gift that only means what it means because it *is* a gift, not something ordered, arranged or otherwise brought about by the *Valentine*. Donald doesn't need the gift. He *knows* he is marvelous. The best there is. Huge. So he could do without the gift. Donald doesn't need to be loved for him to be great. He just *is* great!

This is compatible, to be sure, with both the absence and the presence of the gift of love. Someone can be happily celebrating their own life in the absence of anyone loving them. But once the gift of love comes their way, a *Valentine* should receive it. And we have seen above that receiving a gift is a delicate affair that is best done lovingly. Since we are imagining that Trump loves Donald, and that this is actually a matter of self-love, we need to imagine whether Donald can *receive* Trump's love lovingly. That is the bit where, I argue, self-love will clearly show its potential for being a *selfless* accomplishment, a selfless volitional attitude. So, Donald, in being loved by Trump (appreciating that Donald *is* Trump and that his is a case of self-love), realizes that he—that is, Donald—doesn't need Trump's love to be completely satisfied with himself. Yet, if Trump *would* love Donald, Donald should have to receive this love lovingly. That is, Donald should have to appreciate that Trump gives himself his love, which means that he, Donald, should *receive* his own love in a way that sincerely reflects his gratefulness for the gift of his love being a true gift.

But in so receiving his own love Donald would display, and realize, two layers of disinterestedness. The first is that the acknowledgment of Trump's love as a gift that Donald doesn't need, shows that Donald does not do what he does—namely celebrating his life as a glorious *Valentine*—*in order to* satisfy any of his needs. As a *Valentine* he is not directed by his own desires. Donald is not depending on the gift of Trump's love. The love he receives is not needed to meet an urge. Donald is satisfied with the way he is and he doesn't need Trump's confirmation to feel happy with himself. This is not because Donald is so great and that Trump's love would be insignificantly small compared to Donald's grandiosity, but because Donald's contentment allows him to live happily with himself *whatever he is*. Here we can see a glimmer of what self-love would be for ordinary people. When you can acknowledge that a gift of love is *a gift*, you will realize that you are not craving for love. You can be grateful for the gift, definitely, because it comes from without. But receiving it in this loving way, shows that you feel that what you are is enough for you to be you. In an important sense this is independent of your wealth, looks, character, successes or limits. It is a matter of contentment, of peace of mind. Being capable of receiving love in this selfless way is fundamentally a matter of accepting yourself for what you are, whether or not you are as rich, brilliant, powerful, arrogant and complacent as Donald Trump.

And secondly, receiving Trump's love lovingly requires Donald being sincerely touched by the appearance of Trump *as a lover*, as a person capable of caring in this unconditional and selfless way. Donald loves to see this guise of Trump. Donald loves to see him—that is, Trump—as a loving person. And he loves this guise of Trump *for its own sake*. That is what Donald shows in lovingly receiving Trump's love. Donald receives this love not for Donald himself, but for the opportunity his receipt entails for Trump to exist, *and flourish*, as a lover. In receiving one's own love in this selfless way, a person really shows that he loves himself selflessly.

57.5 Taking Stock

The academic world is in an atrocious shock since Donald Trump's election as president of the United States. There are more than enough convincing reasons to justify this repulsion. Yet, I have tried another approach, gratefully receiving Trump's blatant self-conceit as an opportunity to elucidate an important distinction between two varieties of self-love: an egoistic and narcissistic variety on the one hand and a selfless and morally respectable one on the other.

I warmly recommend all of you, and Donald Trump in particular, to practice the selfless variety. It may require quite an effort, in the beginning. Being one's own *Valentine* may feel alienating, artificial and inappropriate. But it will entail a continued exercise in *receiving*—in *lovingly* receiving—love. That will allow love to grow. And if Donald Trump could be the cause of such a growth... Well, shouldn't that be a reason to welcome him in our world?

Jan Bransen (Prof. Dr.) is Professor of Philosophy of Behavioural Science at Radboud University in the Netherlands. He is the founder of Philosophical Explorations and has written scholarly work on practical identity, autonomy, narrative agency and love. Besides that, he publishes accessible books on the importance of cultivating a philosophical attitude to science, politics, media, mental health, and modern life in general.

His award-winning book on common sense, written in Dutch, was translated and published in by Routledge in 2017: Don't Be Fooled. A Philosophy of Common Sense.

Part XI
Emic Perspectives on Love

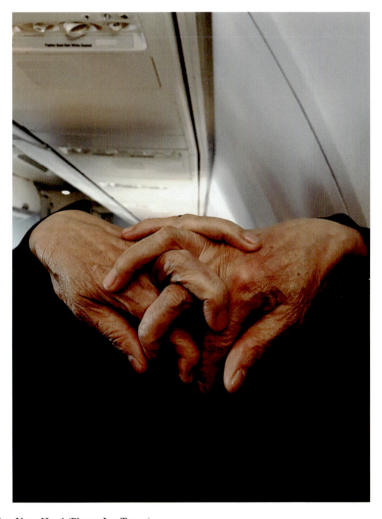

Holding Your Hand (Photo: Jon Tyson)

Chapter 58
Love, Dementia and Intimate Citizenship

Catherine Barrett, Anne Tudor, John Quinn, and Glenys Petrie

Abstract This chapter begins by outlining the myth that people living with dementia are less than human, and therefore incapable of love. The myth emerges from a dominant medical paradigm focused on dementia pathology, treatment and cure for the 50 million people around the world living with dementia.

In contrast to the medical paradigm, the human experience of living with dementia is a much richer story that is gaining recognition. Underpinning stories of the art of living with dementia is the importance of love and how it is experienced with an intimate partner, children, grandchildren, parents, siblings, friends and community.

This chapter explores the meaning of love in the lives of people with dementia and the shift from romanticised notions of love—to love as caring. It builds on Fromm's seminal work, The Art of Love, to show how love is a skill that can be developed and must be studied. It presents a framework called Small Acts of Love to show the ways in which reciprocity is sought and love is enacted.

The chapter then examines how expressions of love have become a means for people with dementia to assert their right to full citizenship. Drawing on Plummer's Intimate Citizenship, the chapter explores how narratives about love are creating cultural shifts for marginalised people living with dementia. Love has become a catalyst for the emergence of a new set of cultural norms that recognise the human rights and human potential of people living with dementia.

Keywords Love · Dementia · Loveless · Enacted · Reciprocity · Citizenship · Rights

58.1   Introduction

There is a widely held myth that people living with dementia are less than human, and therefore incapable of love. This fiction emerges from a medical paradigm focused on dementia pathology—or—the 'dementia patient's diseased brain'. In

---

C. Barrett (✉) · A. Tudor · J. Quinn · G. Petrie
Museum of Love, St. Kilda, VIC, Australia
e-mail: director@celebrateageing.com

© Springer Nature Switzerland AG 2021
C.-H. Mayer, E. Vanderheiden (eds.), *International Handbook of Love*,
https://doi.org/10.1007/978-3-030-45996-3_58

reality the human experience of living with dementia is a much richer story—with love as its central plot.

This chapter challenges the myth that people living with dementia are loveless, by documenting lessons in love from people with dementia and their families. These teachings have been collected as part of the Museum of Love, an Australian based social enterprise utlising art and narrative based approaches to celebrate the importance of love in the lives of people living with dementia (see Barrett, 2017). The Museum is currently the only project in the world providing a platform for people with dementia and their families to build a love library. This focus on love is strategic—it positions people with dementia as human beings and educators and in doing so it challenges dementia stigma.

The chapter begins by defining dementia and then outlining problematic medical discourses as evidence of the need for change. The work of the Museum is presented as shifting the focus from the head to the heart; or from brain pathology to the lived experience of people living with dementia. By doing so, this work addresses the stigma that strips people with dementia of social connections and a sense of belonging.

Drawing on the Museum collections and the published literature, we describe the meaning of love in the lives of people with dementia—particularly in relation to a sense of belonging. Belonging is presented as a consequence of feeling loved and strategies to promote a sense of belonging are outlined.

Having established the importance of love, we describe barriers to loving relationships that people with dementia and their family members may experience. The problems of timely diagnosis, stigma, changes in roles and personality/behaviour, and reduced capacity for reciprocity in relationships can all create love complexities. But rather than see these as insurmountable barriers to love, they are presented as evidence that service providers must recognise the importance of love and understand these challenges in order to support people with dementia and their families to overcome these.

In this context we critique romanticised notions of love and suggest that what matters is how love is enacted. We draw on philosopher Alain de Botton's (2016a, 2016b, 2017) expansion of Fromm's (1954) seminal work, The Art of Love, to present love as a skill that must to be studied. People with dementia and their families need to be offered support to develop the love skills that enable them to overcome the challenges that dementia can bring to interpersonal relationships. Achieving this support requires a paradigm shift in the perspectives of health practitioners—we must recognise people with dementia as interested in, capable of and worthy of love.

In writing this chapter, we draw on our broad expertise as academics, clinicians, a person living with dementia, partners of people living with dementia and Curators of the Museum of Love. We also draw on our sexualities and genders and embrace this traversing of the personal and the professional as an opportunity to develop a resource that is embedded in the real worlds of people whose lives we are exploring.

58.2 Demographics and Discourses of Dementia

Dementia is defined by The World Health Organisation (2017) as a syndrome in which there is deterioration in cognitive function, generally accompanied by declining emotional control, social behaviour, and motivation. Dementia results from a range of diseases and injuries that affect the brain, such as Alzheimer's disease or stroke. There are close to 50 million people around the world living with dementia and the number is increasing by about 10 million new diagnoses each year (WHO, 2017).

Dementia is one of the major causes of disability and dependency among older people worldwide and it also effects younger people. It can be overwhelming for the person living with the disease and for their families. While devastation can be caused by the disease itself, the lack of awareness and understanding of dementia results in stigmatization and barriers that exacerbate the challenges that people with dementia experience (WHO, 2017) and consequently their quality of life. The problem of dementia stigma is so significant that the Global Action Plan on the Public Health Response to Dementia outlines the need for awareness programs to foster an accurate understanding of dementia and reduce stigmatisation and discrimination (World Health Organisation, 2017).

Dementia stigma has been fuelled by medical discourses focused on the diseased brains of people living with dementia. In these approaches, interpersonal interactions are devalued (Heap & Wolverson, 2018) and very little attention is given to the importance of love and how it is enacted. What is particularly problematic is that these medical discourses have become societal discourses; leading to a myth that people with dementia are 'gone' or incapable of interpersonal relationships and love. The effects of this myth on people with dementia is that their family members and friends may avoid spending time with them because of their diagnosis (Alzheimer's Australia, 2014). This is problematic in the face of evidence showing that what people living with dementia want is to have more social contact after diagnosis to enable them to continue doing the things that matter—but what they get is less contact (Alzheimer's Australia, 2014).

In response to this problem, the World Health Organisation (2017) has developed a framework for dementia friendly communities and links are being made to the UN Convention on the Rights of Persons with Disabilities (2006); which promotes respect for dignity and autonomy and full participation in society (Dementia Alliance International, 2016). While initiatives to build dementia friendly communities are being rolling out across the globe—the Museum of Love is currently the only project focusing on love as a strategy to build momentum for change.

58.3 Learning from the Museum of Love

The Museum of Love hosts place-based festivals of love and dementia to engage local communities in learning about love and developing collections for the Museum. Each festival, or LoveFest, is co-produced by people with dementia and their families who share their love skills and make art. The Festivals attract local media who help to challenge stigma through news articles about dementia and love. Each LoveFest results in a Collection that pulls local stories and art together into a resource to educate greater numbers of people. Evaluation of the Festivals shows that the approach is warmly welcomed (Barrett, 2018).

The insights gained from love Festivals are shared in the following section of this chapter. We begin by presenting feedback on the importance of love, particularly in relation to belonging.

58.3.1 Love as Belonging

In strategic planning for the Museum, people with dementia and their families described the importance of focusing on belonging. A sense of belonging was defined as feeling loved and not being an outsider because of dementia diagnosis. This is not surprising given that belonging and love are components of Maslow's (1954) Hierarchy of Human Needs and motivate much human behaviour (Baumeister & Leary, 1995). Our sense of self is built through belonging (May, 2011) and is reached through collective understandings with others (Bottero, 2009). In other words, our sense of belonging is built through our interactions with others.

To explore how a sense of belonging is experienced by people living with dementia, the Museum established a collection entitled Dance. This collection focuses on a series of portraits of people with dementia moving or dancing with others alongside their narratives about belonging. The stories are shared at belonging workshops by people with dementia and then workshop participants are invited to discuss how a sense of belonging can be consolidated. In following quotes from the Dance collection, Kerin Glennen, Ann Pietsch and Tom Harmon describe what belonging means to them.

For Kerin, who lives with younger onset dementia, a sense of belonging was about continuing to be part of his family. Kerin reflected:

> I feel belonging most with family, my brother, my children. I think this is good. We sit in the back area of the house, where we can sit down and just talk. Sometimes I don't talk much, but just listen to them, it's good. . . . I feel belonging when I walk with my wife Karen. . . .on Saturday mornings when we go down and have coffee, have breakfast—it's just good, it's good for my soul. (Barrett, 2017)

Kerin was aware that dementia could limit his capacity to contribute actively to conversations, but he still enjoyed being included and felt a sense of belonging when this occurred. Similarly, being able to continue his weekly breakfast ritual with his wife helped Kerin to feel loved. The consequences of not having these connections were described by Ann who she said:

> Belonging means you fit in, you have a peace that people round you accept you, that you are accepted, ... If you don't feel like you belong, or don't feel accepted for who you are, then you are more likely to withdraw within yourself, and that's probably not as healthy. To be treated as if you have a brain—that's important. (Barrett, 2017)

Ann's reflections highlight how people with dementia are very aware of stigma and want to be accepted as human beings capable of love and belonging. That people with dementia are stigmatised in this way was particularly apparent in reflections shared by Tom, who lived with Parkinson's Disease and dementia. Tom reflected on the differing responses he experienced to the symptoms of each disease and his sense of belonging in this way:

> I feel like I belong. It is very important to me. If I didn't have that sense, I would stay alienated. ... My family is where I belong. I got some close friends and I got some regular friends and sometimes I got people who don't even know me, who come and help because they can see I got Parkinson's Disease and mostly they step up and help. So, I see the good side of people. But they can't tell what you got with dementia and if they don't know—they avoid you. (Barrett, 2017)

While the physical symptoms of Parkinson's Disease drew in support, Tom reported that the stigma related dementia resulted in people withdrawing contact. Tom was able to navigate this rejection because he had the support of family and friends. However, as Tom also noted, rejection—or the fear of rejection—could result in people with dementia withdrawing:

> I know a guy who was told he had dementia and he went home and shut himself away. He didn't want to know anything about dementia. He was angry and in denial. He rejected he had dementia. He needed to find the right group to realize that he did fit in.

The impacts of not feeling a sense of belonging can be devastating for people living with dementia. Those who don't experience belonging have poorer mental wellbeing including depression, anxiety and grief (Baumeister & Leary, 1995). While the feeling of not belonging is generally described as unease (May, 2011) or an emotional pain so intense it can feel physical (MacDonald & Leary, 2005); people with dementia described it as a sense of not fitting in, feeling alienated, disconnected, an outsider and unloved. A sense of belonging was a consequence of feeling loved beyond the dementia disease; and promoted the dignity and personal worth of people living with dementia (Tranvåg, Petersen, & Nåden, 2016).

In workshops to explore the barriers and enablers to belonging for people with dementia, the mostly commonly cited obstacle was the lack of community knowledge about dementia and the resultant stigma (Barrett, 2018). As Tom articulated earlier, people with dementia felt they were being avoided by those who did not understand dementia. This also resulted in a lack of compassion and patience when interacting with people living with dementia.

A further barrier to belonging was the internalisation of dementia stigma by people living with dementia, resulting in the social withdrawal described by Ann and Tom. This could be particularly problematic for people who did not have a strong sense of self-worth prior to dementia diagnosis (Barrett, 2018).

The acceptance of people with dementia by family members, friends and the broader community was not only critical to people living with dementia; it was also a fundamental factor in the wellbeing of their family care givers. Where a person with dementia was rejected by family members or friends—the subsequent isolation meant that intimate partners or other care givers, were also at risk of social isolation and poorer wellbeing. Just as people with dementia need more support after diagnosis, so too do their family care givers (Barrett, 2018).

A sense of belonging epitomised the importance of love and also highlighted the love challenges that can arise for people living with dementia and those they love. These challenges need to be understood by service providers, family members and the broader community if people living with dementia and their families are to be supported to overcome challenges.

58.3.2 Love Challenges

While attention elsewhere has been given to managing 'problem behaviour' displayed by people with dementia—we sought to understand more broadly what challenges exist relating to love. In our exploration of the importance of love we identified problems relating to delayed diagnosis, stigma, changing roles and interests, and the capacity for reciprocity. These challenges are outlined in the following section as prompts for service providers to ensure these issues are addressed.

58.3.2.1 Timely Diagnosis

Delays in diagnosing dementia can occur as a consequence of health practitioner's lack of knowledge. For example, some practitioners assume dementia diagnosis is futile because they believe there are no treatment options, and others may be baffled by the insidious onset of symptoms and a tendency of those yet undiagnosed to compensate for or deny their symptoms (Robinson, Tang, & Taylor, 2015). Additionally, some health practitioners are reluctant to raise such a stigmatised disease with clients (Robinson et al., 2015); because of their own existential anxiety about living with advanced dementia (Gove, Downs, Vernooij-Dassen, & Small, 2016).

The consequences of these delays in diagnosis on interpersonal relationship can be damaging. Family members may notice changes to mood, personality or behaviour (Robinson et al., 2015) years before a formal diagnosis is achieved. This may result in significant difficulties for family members who attribute such changes to a decline in the health of their relationship. By the time a diagnosis is given there may be considerable dissonance and grief around the behaviour of the undiagnosed person. Consequently, diagnosis can bring relief as it shifts the responsibility for such difficulties to the disease, rather than the relationship. Service providers need to understand these difficulties for couples and families and provide support through this difficult period.

58.3.2.2 Stigma

Dementia stigma impacts on the interpersonal relationships of people living with dementia and their families in a multitude of ways. Perhaps the most commonly recognised is the withdrawal of contact by family and friends. This withdrawal can deprive a person with dementia of opportunities for loving relationships and may also rob their intimate partners of contact. The impacts on partners of people living with dementia was noted in interviews by Crameri, Barrett, Lambourne, and Latham (2015), and summarised by one carer who reflected on the experiences of a friend who was dying of cancer and how much support this friend and her partner received:

> ...they get incredible support. People are always dropping round meals and contacting them—but we don't get that. Dementia is a terminal illness but you don't have to take steroids so you don't have that really awful [cancer] look. It's more what's going on in your brain. I've found at times people sort of don't know what to do or they don't know what to say ... (Crameri et al., 2015, p. 10)

As this quote demonstrates, the problem of social isolation may also be exacerbated for couples in same sex relationships who face the dual stigma of dementia and homophobia (Crameri et al., 2015). The relationship privacy sought to survive in an LGBTIphobic world may no longer be possible as services are accessed, relationship status is questioned (Barrett, Crameri, Latham, Lambourne, & Whyte, 2016) and heteronormative services enter an LGBTI person's world. As the risk of contact with LGBTIphobic service providers increases, so too does the risk of further feelings of rejection and isolation.

Dementia stigma is also particularly harmful when it is internalised by people with dementia. The stigma may be grounded in unhelpful myth about dementia and exacerbated by the ways in which diagnosis is delivered. For example, those learning about their diagnosis for the first time may not be given any information about support services or any hope for their future. The difficulties of such insensitive communication may be compounded for people diagnosed with familial type dementia who are concerned about the difficulties their children and grandchildren now face.

The stigma experienced by those receiving news of dementia diagnosis is particularly apparent in what Swaffer (2014) calls Prescribed Dis-engagement™, or health practitioners directing those newly diagnosed to give up their pre-diagnosis life in order to prepare for their death. Some people with dementia are instructed to immediately surrender their driver's license and paid employment. This approach disempowers, devalues and lowers a person's self-esteem and their capacity to be positive, resilient and proactive (Swaffer, 2014). It can also shatter their self-respect and belief that they are capable of love. It can lead to social and emotional withdrawal and strip people with dementia of their dignity and full citizenship.

In another symptom of stigma, people with dementia may be isolated or hidden by family members because of dementia shame or the potential for behavioural or psychological symptoms to be seen by others (WHO, 2012). Such stigma and discrimination can be amplified for trans and gender diverse (TGD) people who are diagnosed with dementia (Barrett et al., 2016). Transphobic family members may take the opportunity presented by the reduced autonomy of the TGD person living with dementia, to place restrictions on expression of gender identity (Barrett et al., 2016). This violation of human rights may be missed by service providers who incorrectly assume that changes to gender expression by TGD people are a consequence of dementia, rather than family pressure to 'straighten up' (Latham & Barrett, 2015).

Dementia is highly stigmatized and universally feared and this stigma not only impacts on people with dementia but also their families, presenting a significant public health challenge (WHO, 2012). The ways in which stigma restricts the capacity of people with dementia and their families to enjoy loving relationships must be understood and addressed by service providers and the broader community.

58.3.3 Changing Roles, Interests and Behaviour

For people who are diagnosed with dementia, the problem of not being able to drive or work or continue to do the things they loved to do prior to diagnosis can adversely effect their self-esteem. For example, men who are the main source of family income can experience a crisis of masculinity or loss of identity when they are forced to give up paid employment. Reduced self-acceptance and self-love can result in people with dementia feeling less worthy of love and withdrawing emotionally from loving relationship.

Other changes can include the progressive reliance on an intimate partner (Molyneaux, Butchard, Simpson, & Murray, 2011) resulting in further compromises to self-worth, particularly where independence is valued (Fletcher, 2018). Over time there may be a degradation in the quality of some relationships with a shift from intimacy to relationships based around care giving (Fletcher, 2018). These changes may result in decreased interest in sexual contact by an intimate partner and this shift may be exacerbated if the person with dementia becomes sexually disinhibited or loses the capacity to negotiate sexual consent. The lack of discussion around intimate relationships has been identified as a barrier to preventing unwanted sexual contact for older women whose male partners have dementia (Mann, Horsley, Barrett, & Tinney, 2014).

There may also be a period of adjustment in intimate relationships where shared interests and activities that form the basis of couplehood are no longer possible (Molyneaux et al., 2011). Dementia may result in the couple being less able to manage crowded or noisy spaces including social functions with family or friends. However, people with dementia and their families may form special bonds with others living with dementia—who understand and accommodate their needs. These new relationships are often cherished as stigma free spaces of mutual respect.

There are a considerable number of changes experienced by people living with dementia that can impact on their capacity to engage in loving relationships. These changes may result in grief, depression or anxiety and require the development of new skills by the person with dementia and their family members. Despite these challenges, intimacy continues to be important (Roelofs, Luijkx, & Embregts, 2019) and this must be acknowledged in the responses of service providers.

58.3.4 Reciprocity

In many cultures, loving relationships are contingent on reciprocity—or equal giving and receiving. Fromm (1954) suggests that there is an aspect of narcissism or self-centredness to relationships; or that our giving of love may be motivated by the love we receive in return. Participation in such conditional exchanges may no longer be possible for people living with dementia. On the contrary, people with advanced dementia may be completely reliant on their intimate partner for physical care and may no longer be able to verbally communicate or otherwise demonstrate their love in return.

In reflecting on the capacity for equal giving, de Botton offers hope that: Love is also, and equally, about weakness, about being touched by another's fragilities and sorrows, adding that the realisation that our partner needs support: draws us closer to each other around a shared experience of pain (de Botton, 2016a, pp. 17–18). Indeed Todorova, Turner, Castaneda-Sceppa, Young, and Bonner (2016) note that in relationships where one partner had dementia, couples can find new ways of being together. It is possible to achieve a shift to mutuality—or sharedness—to a point where caring for someone with dementia felt like acts of love (Todorova et al., 2016). This may be contingent on the relationship having a strong foundation and being guided by service providers.

To help promote a sense of reciprocity, the Museum of Love has developed a collection entitled Letters of Love and Dementia. The collection includes letters written by people with dementia to those they love, as reminders of the love they share. The letters are love artefacts that can be read again and again and again by family and friends, when people with dementia are no longer able to communicate their love. One letter written by John Quinn, who lives with younger onset dementia, for his wife Glenys reads:

> When I look back on all we have come through—the events of our life together—it's hard to believe that we have found ourselves in this place of belonging. There is an ongoing sense of remaining connected to each other. . . . My love for you is bursting at the seams. . . . you are able to overlook my foibles, my annoying personality traits. You see me for the person that I am. I love you even more for that. That's the essence of real love—you don't overlook my weaknesses, you don't ignore them, you look beyond them. I love knowing that there are many things about me you love and that no amount of annoying traits will drive us apart.

Glenys, I pledge my undying love for you—for eternity. Your love has given me a sense of belonging and meaning. In the future, as my dementia progresses I want you to know this: even though you may not think I know you are there—I will know that you are there because my heart remembers. (Barrett, 2017)

John's letter validates the importance of love to creating a sense of belonging and to people with dementia and their family members developing skills to encounter the difficulties that dementia can present. The letter also provides a testament for John's wife Glenys to remember his love—even when he is not able to verbally communicate it.

Reciprocity is not just an issue for intimate partners—it is also something that people with dementia must face. The degenerative nature of the disease means that people with dementia need to recognise the importance of allowing themselves to be loved. This may not be an easy task, as de Botton eloquently suggests:

One of the reasons why love is so tricky for us is that it requires us to do something we really don't want to do, which is to approach another human being and say "I need you. I wouldn't really survive without you; I am vulnerable before you." And there is a very strong impulse in all of us to be strong and to be well defended and not to reveal our vulnerability to another person (de Botton, 2017)

This call could be applied to the experiences of people with dementia who may need to allow themselves to be vulnerable and acknowledge how much they need their partner and family. But if this mutuality is to be achieved then caring for people with dementia cannot be the sole responsibility of partners or other family members. Service providers have a role to play in the provision of physical support that enables family care givers to feel that someone is helping them. Service providers also need to give people with dementia and their families information on reciprocity and how it can be negotiated. The needs of the carer cannot be subjugated to the point of their own health and wellbeing. Yet, family caregivers of people living with dementia are more likely to develop major depression, anxiety and physical health disorders and they have a higher mortality rate than the general population (WHO and Alzheimer's Disease International, 2015).

Caregivers must be provided with support such as resources, education, respite services and financial assistance (WHO and Alzheimer's Disease International, 2015) and increased community connections. These resources and education need to include information about developing the skills that enable improved understanding and adjustments to the changes that love brings.

58.4 Love as a Skill

In the earlier sections of this chapter we explored the importance of love in the lives of people living with dementia. We outlined how medical discourses limit the focus to the diseased brain of a person with dementia and how a broader focus on love can assist in recognising people with dementia as fully human. We described the ways in which love creates a sense of belonging that counterbalances the outsider status that can accompany dementia diagnosis.

The chapter also explored the love challenges that arise for people with dementia. While these challenges are significant—what makes them particularly problematic is that they are seldom acknowledged. The failure to address love challenges robs people with dementia and their families of the opportunity to build love skills that enhance interpersonal relationships.

The proposition that love is a skill that can be learned, was highlighted by Fromm (1954), who contested the myth that love is easy, instead he proposed that love is "a constant challenge, it is not a resting place, but a moving, growing, working together" (p. 118) and that "care and concern for a person we love also brings responsibility [for] ... another person's needs".

These ideas resonate for people living with dementia and their families who encounter significant changes and responsibilities that require couples and families to work together. Fromm's work has been expanded by philosopher Alain de Botton who notes how romanticised ideals of love have created an illusion that difficulties in intimate relationships are unusual and a reflection that our relationships are inadequate (de Botton, 2016b). He suggests that we don't know enough about love and need to understand that love is not an instinct, rather it is a skill:

> ...and it's a skill that needs to be learned. And it's a skill that our society refuses to consider as a skill. We are always just meant to follow our feelings. If you keep following your feelings, you will almost certainly make a big mistake in your life. (de Botton, 2017)

These insights communicate to people with dementia and their families that the romantic hopes of love will most likely be dashed in the very real and challenging experience of living with dementia. De Botton adds that there is no perfect relationship that will meet all our needs and satisfy our every yearning and that we need to need to swap this romantic view for a more realistic awareness that: every human will frustrate, anger, annoy, madden and disappoint us—and we will (without any malice) do the same to them. (de Botton, 2016b).

Acknowledging these difficulties of love are pivotal to normalising the challenges of love for a person living with dementia. It does not require letting go of romantic expectations of connection and passion, rather it's about knowing that when these expectations are not met we may experience lower levels of satisfaction and relationship commitment (Vannier & O'Sullivan, 2017). This can mean that the changes dementia can impose on a loving relationship result in difficulties or fractured relationships. However, resourcing with people with dementia and their families with love skills can assist in ensuring that adjustments are made and that relationships are given the best opportunity to evolve alongside the progression of the disease of dementia. These skills include Small Acts of Love, or small enactments of love in response to the challenges dementia can bring.

58.4.1 Small Acts of Love

In stories about love shared at LoveFest events, people with dementia and their families described the love challenges they experienced and their strategies to overcome these. Their strategies were referred to as Small Acts of Love (Barrett, 2018) and the exchanging of these challenges and strategies by people with dementia and their family members had powerful impacts on their peers. Talking about love challenges gave others permission to acknowledge the difficulties they were experiencing and feel better connected to a community of people who understood their needs. The exchange provided people with dementia and their families with tools to address the challenges they were experiencing—and built the capacity of service providers to assist others.

This exchange of love skills provides evidence that love really is a skill that must be acknowledged if we are to support people with dementia and their families. And we must do this because love matters in the lives of people living with dementia. The leadership taken at LoveFest by people with dementia and their families needs to be recognised by service providers, who have enormous capacity to step in and ask people with dementia and their families about their experiences, and provide support in response. Service providers also have a pivotal role to play in bringing people with dementia together for group work and fun activities for couples and families. There is enormous power in building these connections so that people with dementia and their families are supporting each other.

The other thing to note here is that service providers have much to learn from people with dementia about a sense of belonging and how that can be fostered in services. People with dementia need to feel equal in their interactions with service providers (Ericsson, Kjellström, & Hellström, 2011) if a sense of belonging is to be fostered.

58.5 Conclusion: A Call to Action

In this chapter we highlighted the ways in which love matters in the lives of people with dementia. We hope others will build on the insights outlined in this chapter. More work in needed to document love skills in different cultural contexts and across sexualities, genders and other intersectionalities.

In could be argued that this chapter does not present an innovation, because people with dementia are capable of love. But it seems we are on the cusp of a revolution in awareness of people with dementia as human beings, and that is a very good thing. News of innovations such as people with dementia responding to music or art or animals are all stories about service providers engaging people with dementia—and these initiatives are very worthwhile and to be encouraged. However, it is also important to stop and reflect on why these initiatives are news worthy.

People with dementia are human beings, they are capable of responding to art and nature and love—and that is not news.

Our chapter calls for service providers to understand the importance of love in the lives of people living with dementia. We also call for service providers to assist people with dementia and their family members to develop the love skills they need to continue loving relationships in the context of dementia. Achieving this requires that service providers recognise love as a fundamental human right—rather than an innovation. Exploring the importance of love, or love skills can be an innovative way of addressing stigma—but love itself is not new. Love has always been there in the lives of people living with dementia, we are just beginning to notice.

References

Alzheimer's Australia. (2014). *Living with dementia in the community: Challenges & opportunities a report of national survey findings*. Alzheimer's Australia. Retrieved from https://www.dementia.org.au/sites/default/files/DementiaFriendlySurvey_Final_web.pdf

Barrett, C. (2017). *Museum of love*. Retrieved from https://www.museumoflove.com.au/

Barrett, C. (2018). *The LoveFest Perth collection. Museum of Love*. Melbourne. Retrieved from https://www.museumoflove.com.au/uploads/1/5/3/9/15399992/lovefestperthcollection.pdf

Barrett, C., Crameri, P., Latham, J., Lambourne, S., & Whyte, C. (2016). Person centred care and cultural safety: The perspectives of lesbian, gay and trans (LGT) people and their partners on living with dementia. In S. Westwood & E. Price (Eds.), *Lesbian, gay, bisexual and trans* individuals living with dementia: Concepts, practice and rights*. London: Routledge.

Baumeister, R. F., & Leary, M. R. (1995). The need to belong: Desire for interpersonal attachments as a fundamental human motivation. *Psychological Bulletin, 117*(3), 497–529. https://doi.org/10.1037/0033-2909.117.3.49

Bottero, W. (2009). Relationality and social interaction. *British Journal of Sociology, 60*(2), 399–420. 376 *Sociology, 45*(3).

Crameri, P., Barrett, C., Lambourne, S., & Latham, J. (2015). *We are still gay ... An evidence based resource exploring the experiences and needs of lesbian, gay, bisexual and trans people living with dementia*. Melbourne: Australian Research Centre in Sex, Health and Society, La Trobe University.

de Botton, A. (2016a). *The course of love*. London: Hamish Hamilton.

de Botton, A. (2016b). Why you will marry the wrong person. Opinion. *New York Times*. Retrieved from https://www.nytimes.com/2016/05/29/opinion/sunday/why-you-will-marry-the-wrong-person.html

de Botton, A. (2017). Why you will marry the wrong person. *YouTube*. Retrieved from https://www.youtube.com/watch?v=DCS6t6NUAGQ

Dementia Alliance International. (2016). *The human rights of people living with dementia: From rhetoric to reality*. Retrieved from https://www.dementiaallianceinternational.org/wp-content/uploads/2016/10/The-Human-Rights-of-People-Living-with-Dementia-from-Rhetoric-to-Reality_2nd-Edition_July-2016_English.pdf

Ericsson, I., Kjellström, S., & Hellström, I. (2011). Creating relationships with persons with moderate to severe dementia. *Dementia, 12*(1), 63–79. https://doi.org/10.1177/1471301211418161

Fletcher, J. (2018). Renegotiating relationships: Theorising shared experiences of dementia within the dyadic career. *Dementia, 3*(1), 1–13. https://doi.org/10.1177/1471301218785511

Fromm, E. (1954). *The art of loving*. New York, NY: Harper and Row.

Gove, D., Downs, M., Vernooij-Dassen, M., & Small, N. (2016). Stigma and GPs' perceptions of dementia. *Aging & Mental Health, 20*(4), 391–400. https://doi.org/10.1080/13607863.2015.1015962

Heap, C., & Wolverson, E. (2018). Intensive interaction and discourses of personhood: A focus group study with dementia caregivers. *Dementia*, 1–20. https://doi.org/10.1177/1471301218814389

Latham, J. R., & Barrett, C. (2015). *Gender is just a part of who I am: Stories from trans Australians—Exploring the experiences and needs of trans people for health and aged care services*. Melbourne: La Trobe University.

MacDonald, G., & Leary, M. R. (2005). Why does social exclusion hurt? The relationship between social and physical pain. *Psychological Bulletin, 131*, 202–223. https://doi.org/10.1037/0033-2909.131.2.202

Mann, R., Horsley, P., Barrett, C., & Tinney, J. (2014). *Norma's project. A research study into the sexual assault of older women in Australia* (ARCSHS Monograph Series No. 98). Melbourne: Australian Research Centre in Sex, Health and Society, La Trobe University.

Maslow, A. H. (1954). *Motivation and personality*. New York, NY: Harper and Row.

May, V. (2011). Self, belonging and social change. *Sociology, 45*(3), 363–378. https://doi.org/10.1177/0038038511399624

Molyneaux, V., Butchard, S., Simpson, J., & Murray, C. (2011). The co-construction of couplehood in dementia. *Dementia, 11*(4), 483–502. https://doi.org/10.1177/1471301211421070

Robinson, L., Tang, E., & Taylor, J. (2015). Dementia: Timely diagnosis and early intervention. *BMJ, 350*, h3029. https://doi.org/10.1136/bmj.h3029

Roelofs, T., Luijkx, K., & Embregts, P. (2019). Love, intimacy and sexuality in residential dementia care: A spousal perspective. *Dementia, 18*(3), 936–950. The author(s) 2017 article reuse guidelines: sagepub.com/journals-permissions. https://doi.org/10.1177/1471301217697467

Swaffer, K. (2014). Dementia and prescribed disengagement™. *Editorial, 14*(1), 3–6. https://doi.org/10.1177/1471301214548136

Todorova, I., Turner, H., Castaneda-Sceppa, C., Young, D., & Bonner, A. (2016). I do it with love: Engagement in caring for people with dementia. *Global Qualitative Nursing Research, 3*, 1–14.

Tranvåg, O., Petersen, K., & Nåden, D. (2016). Crucial dimensions constituting dignity experience in persons living with dementia. *Dementia, 15*(4), 578–595. https://doi.org/10.1177/1471301214529783

United Nations. (2006). *Convention on the right of people with disabilities*. Retrieved from https://www.un.org/development/desa/disabilities/convention-on-the-rights-of-persons-with-disabilities.html

Vannier, S. A., & O'Sullivan, L. F. (2017). Passion, connection, and destiny: How romantic expectations help predict satisfaction and commitment in young adults' dating relationships. *Journal of Social and Personal Relationships, 34*, 235–257. https://doi.org/10.1177/0265407516631156

World Health Organisation. (2017). *Global action plan on the public health response to dementia 2017–2025*. Geneva. Retrieved from https://apps.who.int/iris/bitstream/handle/10665/259615/9789241513487-eng.pdf;jsessionid=8A8219AEA9938F31AAAA11463FC590E3?sequence=1

World Health Organisation, Alzheimer's Disease International. (2015). *Supporting informal caregivers of people living with dementia*. Retrieved from https://www.who.int/mental_health/neurology/dementia/dementia_thematicbrief_informal_care.pdf

World Health Organistion. (2012). *Dementia a public health priority*. Retrieved from https://apps.who.int/iris/bitstream/handle/10665/75263/9789241564458_eng.pdf?sequence=1

Catherine Barrett is the Curator of the Museum of Love, an Australian based project that collects, develops and preserves art and narratives that celebrate the importance of love in the lives of people living with dementia. Catherine is also the Director of the OPAL Institute, which promotes recognition of the sexual rights of older people. In 2018 Catherine coedited a book on the Sexual Rights of Older people for Routledge.

Anne Tudor brings clinical psychology and psychanalytical training to contribution to the field of dementia. Anne co-led the successful implementation of Bigger Hearts, Australia's first art based initiative to build a dementia friendly community and has developed a suite of resources on dementia and love. Anne's psychological framework for dementia friendly communities and services invites people to open their hearts and build human connections. She is the foundation chair of Bigger Hearts for Dementia Alliance, Ballarat, a member of Dementia Australia's Dementia Friendly Communities Steering Committee, involved in five National Advisory Committees, and presented nationally and internationally at dementia conferences.

John Quinn is a member of Dementia Alliance International. John presents at National and International conference of his experiences of living with Younger Onset Dementia and masculine plasticity. John is a consumer representative on the National Institute of Dementia Research, the State Dementia Clinical Network and primary health networks. John is on Dementia Training Australia's selection panel for PhD candidates and is currently working with Federal Government's Dept of Health on their Dementia Policy Road Map.

Glenys Petrie is the coordinator of a Brisbane Younger Onset Dementia Support group for people with dementia and their family and friends. She delivers education to undergraduate medical and allied health practitioners and is an advisor with Dementia Training Australia. Glenys is a member of the Dementia Australia's Dementia Friendly Communities Steering Committee and has presented at National and International Conferences on building connections in intimate relationships. She is a member of a dozen research committees exploring nonpharmalogical interventions to improve the lives of people living with dementia.

Chapter 59
Enlisting Positive Psychologies to Challenge Love Within SAD's Culture of Maladaptive Self-Beliefs

Robert F. Mullen

Abstract Social anxiety disorder (SAD) is one of the most common psychophysiological malfunctions, affecting the emotional and mental well being of over 15 million U.S. adults who find themselves caught up in a densely interconnected network of fear and avoidance of social situations. These observations provide insight into the relationship deficits experienced by people with SAD. Their innate need-for-intimacy is no less dynamic than that of any individual, but their impairment disrupts the ability (*means-of-acquisition*) to establish affectional bonds in almost any capacity. The spirit is willing, but competence insubstantial. It is the means-of-acquisition and how they are symptomatically challenged by SAD that is the context of this research.

Notwithstanding overwhelming evidence of social incompatibility, there is hope for the startlingly few SAD persons who commit to recovery. A psychobiographical approach integrating positive psychology's optimum human functioning with CBT's behavior modification, neuroscience's network restructuring, and other supported and non-traditional approaches can establish a working platform for discovery, opening the bridge to the procurement of forms of intimacy previously inaccessible. It is an arduous and measured crossing that only 5% of the afflicted will even attempt in the first year of onset.

Keywords Love · Social anxiety disorder · Intimacy · Philautia · Means-of-acquisition

59.1 Social Anxiety Disorder

Social anxiety disorder (SAD) is the second most commonly diagnosed form of anxiety in the United States (MHA, 2019). The Anxiety and Depression Association of America (ADAA, 2019a) estimate nearly 15 million (7%) American adults currently experience its symptoms. Ritchie and Roser (2018) report 284 million

R. F. Mullen (✉)
ReChanneling Inc, San Francisco, CA, USA
e-mail: robertmullenca@yahoo.com

SAD persons, worldwide, and the National Institute of Mental Health (NIMH, 2017) report 31.1% of U.S. adults experience some anxiety disorder at some time in their lives. Global statistics are subject to "differences in the classification criteria, culture, and gender" (Tsitsas & Paschali, 2014), and "in the instruments used to ascertain diagnosis" (NCCMH, 2013).

> Studies in other western nations (e.g., Australia, Canada, Sweden) note similar prevalence rates as in the USA, as do those in culturally westernized nations such as Israel. Even countries with strikingly different cultures (e.g., Iran) note evidence of social anxiety disorder (albeit at lower rates) among their populace. (Stein & Stein, 2008)

SAD is the most common psychiatric disorder in the U.S. after major depression and alcohol abuse (Heshmat, 2014). It is also arguably the most underrated and misunderstood. A "debilitating and chronic" psychophysiological affliction (Castella et al., 2014), SAD "wreaks havoc on the lives of those who suffer from it" (ADAA, 2019a). SAD attacks all fronts, negatively affecting the entire body complex, delivering mental confusion (Mayoclinic, 2017b), emotional instability (Castella et al., 2014; Yeilding, 2017), physical dysfunction (NIMH, 2017; Richards, 2019), and spiritual malaise (Mullen, 2018). Emotionally, persons experiencing SAD feel depressed and lonely (Jazaieri, Morrison, & Gross, 2015). Physically, they are subject to unwarranted sweating and trembling, hyperventilation, nausea, cramps, dizziness, and muscle spasms (ADAA, 2019a; NIMH, 2017). Mentally, thoughts are discordant and irrational (Felman, 2018; Richards, 2014). Spiritually, they define themselves as inadequate and insignificant (Mullen, 2018).

The National Institute of Mental Health estimates that 9.1% of adolescents experience social anxiety disorder, and 1.3% have severe impairment (NIMH, 2017). The onset of SAD is generally considered "to take place between the middle and late teens" (Tsitsas & Paschali, 2014). Like other *pathogens*, SAD can remain dormant for years before symptoms materialize. Any number of situations or events trigger the initial contact; it could be hereditary, environmental, or the result of some traumatic experience. The LGBTQ community is 1.5–2.5 times as susceptible to SAD "than that of their straight or gender-conforming counterparts" (Brenner, 2019). 39.5% of general anxiety sufferers pursue recovery compared to "5% of SAD persons in the first year of experiencing the malfunction" (Shelton, 2018).

SAD is randomly misdiagnosed (Richards, 2019), and the low commitment-to-recovery (Shelton, 2018) suggests a reticence by those infected to recognize and or challenge their malfunction. Approximately 5% of SAD persons commit to early recovery, reflective of symptoms that manifest maladaptive self-beliefs of insignificance and futility. Grant et al. (2005) state, "about half of adults with the disorder seek treatment," but that is after 15–20 years of suffering from the malfunction (Ades & Dias, 2013). Resistance to new ideas and concepts transcends those of other mental complications and is justified by,

1. general public cynicism,
2. self-contempt by the afflicted, generated by maladaptive self-beliefs,
3. ignorance or ineptitude of mental health professionals,
4. real or perceived social stigma, and
5. the natural physiological aversion to change.

Many motivated towards recovery are unable to afford treatment due to SAD induced "impairments in financial and employment stability" (Gregory, Wong, Craig, Marker, & Peters, 2018). The high percentage of jobless people experiencing social anxiety disorder in the U.S. is related to "to job inefficiency and instability" (Felman, 2018), greater absenteeism, job dissatisfaction, and or frequent job changes. "More than 70% of social anxiety disorder patients are in the lowest economic group" (Nardi, 2003).

According to leading experts, the high percentage of SAD misdiagnoses are due to "substantial discrepancies and variation in definition, epidemiology, assessment, and treatment" (Nagata, Suzuki, & Teo, 2015). The Social Anxiety Institute (Richards, 2019) reports, among patients with generalized anxiety, an estimated 8.2% had the condition, but just 0.5% were correctly diagnosed. A recent Canadian study by Chapdelaine, Carrier, Fournier, Duhoux, and Roberge (2018) reported, of 289 participants in 67 clinics meeting criteria for social anxiety disorder outlined in the Diagnostic and Statistical Manual of Mental Disorders, 4th Edition (*DSM-IV*), 76.4% were improperly diagnosed.

Social anxiety disorder is a pathological form of everyday anxiety. The clinical term "disorder" identifies extreme or excessive impairment that negatively affects functionality. Feeling anxious or apprehensive in certain situations is normal; most individuals are nervous speaking in front of a group and anxious when pulled over on the freeway. The typical individual recognizes the ordinariness of a situation and accords it appropriate attention. The SAD person anticipates it, takes it personally, dramatizes it, and obsesses on its negative implications (Richards, 2014).

SAD's culture of maladaptive self-beliefs (Ritter, Ertel, Beil, Steffens, & Stangier, 2013) and negative self-evaluations (Castella et al., 2014) aggravate anxiety and impede social performance (Hulme, Hirsch, & Stopa, 2012). "Patients with SAD often believe they lack the necessary social skills to interact normally with others" (Gaudiano & Herbert, 2003). Maladaptive self-beliefs are distorted reflections of a situation, often accepted as accurate. The cofounder of CBT, Aaron Beck provides three types of maladaptive self-beliefs responsible for persistent social anxiety. Core beliefs are enduring fundamental understandings, often formed in childhood and solidified over time. Because SAD persons "tend to store information consistent with negative beliefs but ignore evidence that contradicts them, [their] core beliefs tend to be rigid and pervasive" (Beck, 2011). Core beliefs influence the development of intermediate beliefs—attitudes, rules, and assumptions that influence one's overall perspective which, in turn, influences thought and behavior. Automatic thoughts and behaviors (ANTs) are real-time manifestations of maladaptive self-beliefs, dysfunctional in their irrationality (Richards, 2014; Wong, Moulds, & Rapee, 2013).

> Negative self-images reported by patients with social anxiety disorder reflect a working self that is retrieved in response to social threat and which is characterised by low self-esteem, uncertainty about the self, and fear of negative evaluation by others. (Hulme et al., 2012)

Halloran and Kashima (2006) define culture as "an interrelated set of values, tools, and practices that is shared among a group of people who possess a common social identity." As the third-largest mental health care problem in the world (Richards, 2019), social anxiety disorder is culturally identifiable by the victims' "marked and persistent fear of social and performance situations in which embarrassment may occur," and the anticipation "others will judge [them] to be anxious, weak, crazy, or stupid" (APA, 2017). Although studies evidence "culture-specific expression of social anxiety" (Hoffman, Asnaani, & Hinton, 2010), SAD "is a pervasive disorder and causes anxiety and fear in almost all areas of a person's life" (Richards, 2019). SAD affects the "perceptual, cognitive, personality, and social processes" of the afflicted who find themselves caught up in "a densely interconnected network of fear and avoidance of social situations" (Heeren & McNally, 2018).

The superficial overview of SAD is intense apprehension—the fear of being judged, negatively evaluated, and ridiculed (Bosche, 2019). There is persistent anxiety or fear of social situations such as dating, interviewing for a position, answering a question in class, or dealing with authority (ADAA, 2019a; Castella et al., 2014). Often, mere functionality in perfunctory situations—eating in front of others, riding a bus, using a public restroom—can be unduly stressful (ADAA, 2019a; Mayoclinic, 2017b). This overriding fear of being found *wanting* manifests in perspectives of incompetence and worthlessness (Richards, 2019). SAD persons are unduly concerned they will say something that will reveal their ignorance, real or otherwise (Ades & Dias, 2013). They walk on eggshells, supremely conscious of their awkwardness, surrendering to the GAZE—the anxious state of mind that comes with the maladaptive self-belief they are the center of attention (Felman, 2018; Lacan, 1978). Their movements can appear hesitant and awkward, small talk clumsy, attempts at humor embarrassing, and every situation reactive to negative self-evaluation (ADAA, 2019a; Bosche, 2019). They are apprehensive of potential "negative evaluation by others" (Hulme et al., 2012), concerned about "the visibility of anxiety, and preoccupation with performance or arousal" (Tsitsas & Paschali, 2014). SAD persons frequently generate images of themselves performing poorly in feared social situations (Hirsch & Clark, 2004; Hulme et al., 2012) and their anticipation of repudiation motivates them to dismiss overtures to offset any possibility of rejection (Tsitsas & Paschali, 2014). SAD is repressive and intractable, imposing irrational thought and behavior (Richards, 2014; Zimmerman, Dalrymple, Chelminski, Young, & Galione, 2010). It establishes its authority through its subjects' defeatist measures produced by distorted and unsound interpretations of actuality that govern perspectives of personal attractiveness, intelligence, competence, and other errant beliefs (Ades & Dias, 2013).

We are all familiar with the free-association test. The person in the white coat tosses out seemingly random words and the recipient responds with the first word that comes to mind. Consider the following reactions: *boring, stupid, worthless, incompetent, disliked, ridiculous, inferior* (Hulme et al., 2012). Most people use personal pejoratives daily, but few personalize and take them to heart like a SAD person. These maladaptive self-beliefs, over time, become automatic negative thoughts (Amen, 1998) implanted on the neural network (Richards, 2014). They determine initial reactions to situations or circumstances. They inform how to think and feel and act. The ANT voice exaggerates, catastrophizes, and distorts. SAD persons

> crave the company of others but shun social situations for fear of being found out as unlikeable, stupid, or annoying. Accordingly, they avoid speaking in public, expressing opinions, or even fraternizing with peers ... People with social anxiety disorder are typified by low self-esteem and high self-criticism. (Stein & Stein, 2008)

Anxiety and other personality disorders are branches of the same tree. "There is a significant degree of comorbidity between social anxiety disorder and other mental health problems, most notably depression (19%), substance-abuse disorder (17%), GAD [generalized anxiety disorder] (5%), panic disorder (6%), and PTSD (3%)" (Tsitsas & Paschali, 2014). The Anxiety and Depression Association of America (ADAA, 2019a) includes many emotional and mental disorders related to, components of, or a consequence of social anxiety disorder including avoidant personality disorder, panic disorder, generalized anxiety disorder, depression, substance abuse, eating disorders, OCD, and schizophrenia.

> Personality disorders are a group of mental illnesses. They involve long-term patterns of thoughts and behaviors that are unhealthy and inflexible. The behaviors cause serious problems with relationships and work. People with personality disorders have trouble dealing with everyday stresses and problems. (UNLM, 2018)

Personality reflects deep-seated patterns of behavior affecting how individuals "perceive, relate to, and think about themselves and their world" (HPD, 2019). A personality disorder denotes "rigid and unhealthy pattern[s] of thinking, functioning and behaving," which potentially leads to "significant problems and limitations in relationships, social activities, work and school" (Castella et al., 2014). A recent article in Scientific American speculates that "mental illnesses are so common that almost everyone will develop at least one diagnosable mental disorder at some point in their life" (Reuben & Schaefer, 2017).

59.1.1 SAD and Interpersonal Love

In unambiguous terms, the desire-for-love is at the heart of social anxiety disorder (Alden, Buhr, Robichaud, Trew, & Plasencia, 2018). Interpersonal love relates to communications or relationships of love between or among people. The diagnostic criteria for SAD, outlined in the DSM-V (APA, 2017), includes: "Marked fear or anxiety about one or more social situations in which the individual is exposed to possible scrutiny by others." SAD persons find it inordinately difficult to establish close, productive relationships (Castella et al., 2014; Fatima, Naizi, & Gayas, 2018). Their avoidance of social activities limits the potential for comradeship (Desnoyers, Kocovski, Fleming, & Antony, 2017; Tsitsas & Paschali, 2014), and their inability to interact rationally and productively (Richards, 2014; Zimmerman et al., 2010) makes long-term, healthy relationships unlikely. SAD persons frequently demonstrate significant impairments in friendships and intimate relationships (Castella et al., 2014). According to Whitbourne (2018), SAD persons'

> avoidance of other people puts them at risk for feeling lonely, having fewer friendships, and being unable to take advantage of the enjoyment of being with people who share their hobbies and interests.

There is a death of research directly investigating the relationship between SAD and interpersonal love (Montesi, Conner, Gordon, & Fauber, 2013; Read, Clark, Rock, & Coventry, 2018). A study on friendship quality and social anxiety by Rodebaugh, Lim, Shumaker, Levinson, and Thompson (2015) notes the lack of relative quality studies, and Alden et al. (2018) report on the lack of attention paid to the SAD person's inability or refusal to function in close relationships. The few studies that do exist report that the SAD person exhibits inhibited social behavior, shyness, lack of assertion in group conversations, and feelings of inadequacy while in social situations (Darcy, Davila, & Beck, 2005). This dominant culture of maladaptive self-beliefs results in the tendency to avoid new people and experiences, making the development of "adequate and close relationships (e.g., family, friends, and romantic relationships)" extremely challenging (Cuming & Rapee, 2010). Experiencing social anxiety disorder translates to less trust and perceived support from close interpersonal relationships (Topaz, 2018).

Although intimately related, the desire-for-love and the means-of-acquisition are binary operations. Most forms of interpersonal love require the successful collaboration of *wanting* and *obtaining*. The desire-for-love is the non-consummatory component of Freud's *eros* life instinct (Abel-Hirsch, 2010). The means-of-acquisition are the methods and skills required to complete the transaction—techniques that vary depending upon the type of love in the offing. Let us visualize love as a bridge, with desire (thought) at one end and acquisition at the other; the span is the means-of-acquisition (behavior). The SAD person cannot get from one side to the other because the means-of-acquisition are structurally deficient (Desnoyers et al., 2017; Tsitsas & Paschali, 2014). They grasp the fundamental concepts of interpersonal love and are presented with opportunities but lack the skills to close-the-deal. Painfully aware of the tools of acquisition, they cannot seem to operate them.

59.2 Cognitive Behavioral Therapy

CBT purposed for SAD is typically conceptualized as a short-term, skills-oriented approach aimed at exploring relationships among a person's thoughts, feelings, and behaviors while changing the culture of maladaptive self-beliefs into productive, rational thought and behavior (Richards, 2019). CBT focuses on "developing more helpful and balanced perspectives of oneself and social interactions while learning and practicing approaching one's feared and avoided social situations over time" (Yeilding, 2017). Almost 90% of the approaches empirically supported by the "American Psychological Association's Division 12 Task Force on Psychological

Interventions" involve cognitive-behavioral treatments, according to Lyford (2017). "Individuals who undergo CBT show changes in brain activity, suggesting that this therapy improves your brain functioning as well" (NAMI, 2019).

Recent meta-analytic evidence suggests that CBT as an effective treatment for SAD compares favorably with other psychological and pharmacological treatment programs (Cuijpers, Cristea, Karyotaki, Reijnders, & Huibers, 2016). There is no guarantee of success, however, and standard CBT is imperfect (David, Cristea, & Hoffman, 2018; Mullen, 2018). The best outcome a SAD sufferer can hope for is mitigation of symptoms through thought and behavior modification and the simultaneous restructuring of the neural network, along with other supported and non-traditional treatments.

> "[M]any patients, although being under drug therapy, remain symptomatic and have recurrence of symptoms," according to the Brazilian Journal of Psychiatry. "40–50% are better, but still symptomatic, and 20–30% remain the same or worse." (Manfro, Heldt, Cordiol, & Otto, 2008)

Behavioral and cognitive treatments are globally proven methodologies. There are multiple associations worldwide, "devoted to research, education, and training in cognitive and behavioral therapies" (McGinn, 2019). CBT Conferences (2019) are offered across the globe, "where knowledge transfer takes place through debates, round table discussions, poster presentations, workshops, symposia, and exhibitions." David et al. (2018) credit CBT

> as the best standard we have in the field currently available—for the following reasons: (1) CBT is the most researched form of psychotherapy. (2) No other form of psychotherapy is systematically superior to CBT in the treatment of anxiety, depression, and other disorders; if there are systematic differences between psychotherapies, they typically favor CBT. (3) Moreover, the CBT theoretical models/mechanisms of change have been the most researched and are in line with the current mainstream paradigms of the human mind and behavior (e.g., information processing).

The Association for Behavioral and Cognitive Therapies (ABCT) is "a worldwide humanitarian organization," fostering the "dissemination of evidence-based prevention and treatments through collaborations with the World Health Organization (WHO) and the United Nations Educational, Scientific and Cultural Organization (UNESCO)" (McGinn, 2019). The World Confederation of Cognitive and Behavioural Therapies (WCCBT) is a global multidisciplinary organization promoting health and well-being through the scientific development and implementation of "evidence-based cognitive-behavioral strategies designed to evaluate, prevent, and treat mental conditions and illnesses" (ACBT, 2019).

Cognitive-behavioral therapy is arguably the *gold standard* of the psychotherapy field. David et al. (2018)) maintain, "there are no other psychological treatments with more research support to validate." Studies of CBT have shown it to be an effective treatment for a wide variety of mental illnesses including depression, SAD, generalized anxiety disorders, bipolar disorder, eating disorders, PTSD, OCD, panic disorder, and schizophrenia (Kaczkurkin & Foa, 2015; NAMI, 2019). However, David et al. (2018) suggest if *the gold standard* of psychotherapy defines itself as the best in the field, then CBT is not the *gold standard*. There is clearly room for further improvement, "both in terms of CBT's efficacy/effectiveness and its underlying theories/mechanisms of change."

Lyford (2017) provides two examples of criticism. A 2013 meta-analysis published in *Clinical Psychology Review* comparing CBT to other therapies, failed to "provide corroborative evidence for the conjecture that CBT is superior to bona fide non-CBT treatments." An 8-week clinical study by Sweden's Lund University in 2013, concluded that "CBT was no more effective than mindfulness-based therapy for those suffering from depression and anxiety."

Another meta-analysis conducted by psychologists Johnsen and Friborg (2015) tracked 70 CBT outcome studies conducted between 1977 and 2014 and concluded that "the effects of CBT have declined linearly and steadily since its introduction, as measured by patients' self-reports, clinicians' ratings, and rates of remission." According to the authors, "Just seeing a decrease in symptoms," he says, "doesn't translate into greater well-being." This is reflective of most one-size-fits-all approaches.

While this study recognizes CBT as the best foundation for addressing the SAD culture of maladaptive self-beliefs, it makes the point standard CBT alone is not necessarily the most productive course of treatment. New and innovative methodologies supported by a collaboration of theoretical construct and integrated scientific psychotherapy are needed to address mental illness as represented in this era of advanced complexity. A SAD person subsisting on paranoia sustained by negative self-evaluation is better served by multiple non-traditional and supported approaches, including those defined as new (third) wave (generation) therapies, developed through client trust, cultural assimilation, and therapeutic innovation with CBT and positive psychology serving as the foundational platform for integration.

59.3 Categories of Interpersonal Love

In *Nicomachean Ethics*, Aristotle (1999) encapsulates love as "a sort of excess of feeling." Utilizing the classic Greek categories of interpersonal love is vital to this study; each classification illustrates how SAD symptoms thwart the subject's means-of-acquisition in seven of eight categories (with the notable exception of healthy *philautia*). The three primary categories: (1) *philia* (comradeship), (2) *eros* (sexual), and (3) *agape* (selfless and unconditional), are followed by (4) *storge* (family), (5) *ludus* (provocative), (6) *pragma* (practical), and the two extremes of *philautia*: (7) narcissistic and, (8) positive self-qualities. Forms of inanimate love are excluded from this study, "including love for experiences (*meraki*), objects (*érōs*), and places (*chōros*)" (Lomas, 2017).

1. Aristotle called *philia* "one of the most indispensable requirements of life" (Grewal, 2016). *Philia* is a bonding of individuals with mutual experiences—a

"warm affection in intimate friendship" (Helm, 2017). This platonic love subsists on shared experience and personal disclosure. A core symptom of a SAD person is the fear of revealing something that will make them appear "boring, stupid or incompetent" (Ades & Dias, 2013). Even the anticipation of interaction causes "significant anxiety, fear, self-consciousness, and embarrassment" (Richards, 2014) because of the fear of being scrutinized or judged by others (Mayoclinic, 2017b).

2. *Eros* is reciprocal feelings of shared arousal between people physically attracted to each other, the fulfillment declared by the sexual act. The SAD person's self-image of unlikability (Stein & Stein, 2008) coupled with the fear of intimacy (Montesi et al., 2013) and rejection (Tsitsas & Paschali, 2014) has significant consequences in terms of acquiring a sexual partner, and satisfaction of the sexual act (Montesi et al., 2013). SAD's culture of maladaptive self-beliefs poses severe challenges to their ability to establish, develop, and maintain romantic relationships (Cuncic, 2018; Topaz, 2018). A study by Montesi et al. (2013), examining the SAD person's symptomatic fear of intimacy and sexual communication concluded, "socially anxious individuals experience less sexual satisfaction in their intimate partnerships than nonanxious individuals, a relationship that has been well documented in previous research." The study reported a lacuna of literature, however, examining the sexual communication of SAD persons.

3. Through the universal mandate to love thy neighbor, the concept of *agape* embraces unconditional love that transcends and persists regardless of circumstance (Helm, 2017). SAD generally infects adolescents who have experienced detachment, exploitation, and or neglect (Steele, 1995). This form of love characterizes itself through unselfish giving; the SAD person's maladaptive self-belief she or he is the constant focus-of-attention is a form of self-centeredness bordering on narcissism (Mayoclinic, 2017a).

4. Again, the primary cause of SAD stems from childhood hereditary, environmental (Felman, 2018; NAMI, 2019), or traumatic events (Mayoclinic, 2017b). In each case, the SAD person is exploited (unconsciously or otherwise) in the formative stages of human motivational development: those of *physiological safety* and *belongingness and love* (Maslow, 1943). As a result, *storge* or familial love and protection, vital to the healthy development of the family unit, is severely affected. The exploited adolescent (Steele, 1995) faces serious challenges recognizing or embracing familial love as an adolescent or adult.

5. SAD persons' conflict with the provocative playfulness of *ludus* is evident by the fear of being judged and negatively evaluated by others (Mayoclinic, 2017b) as well as themselves (Hulme et al., 2012; Ritter et al., 2013). Persons experiencing SAD do not find social interaction pleasurable (Richards, 2019) and have limited expectation things will work out advantageously (Mayoclinic, 2017b). Finally, SAD persons' maladaptive self-beliefs generally result in inappropriate behavior in social situations (Kampmann, Emmelkamp, & Morina, 2019).

6. The obvious synonym for *pragma* is practicality—a balanced and constructive quality counterintuitive to someone whose modus operandi is discordant thought and behavior (Richards, 2014; Zimmerman et al., 2010). *Pragma* is mutual

interests and goals securing a working and endurable partnership, facilitated by rational behavior and expectation. The SAD personality sustains itself though irrationality (Felman, 2018) and maladaptive self-beliefs (Hulme et al., 2012; Ritter et al., 2013). The pragmatic individual deals with relationships sensibly and realistically, conforming to standards considered typical. The overriding objective of a SAD person is to "avoid situations that most people consider 'normal' " (WebMD, 2019).

The onset of SAD is a consequence of early psychophysiological disturbance (Felman, 2018; Mayoclinic, 2017a). The receptive juvenile might be the product of bullying (Felman, 2018), abuse (NAMI, 2019), or a broken home. Perhaps parental behaviors are overprotective or controlling or do not provide emotional validation (Cuncic, 2018). Subsequently, the SAD person finds it difficult to let his or her guard down and express vulnerability, even with someone they love and trust (Cuncic, 2018). Alden et al. (2018) note that SAD persons "find it difficult, in their intimate relationships, to be able to self-disclose, to reciprocate the affection others show toward them."

There is a large body of research linking love with positive mental and physical health outcomes (Rodebaugh et al., 2015). Relationships, love, and associations with others lead one to recognition of their value to society "and motivates them towards building communities, culture and work for the welfare of others" (Capon & Blakely, 2007). Love is developed through social connectedness. Social connectedness, essential to personal development, is one of the central psychological needs "required for better psychological development and well-being" (Deci & Ryan, 2000). Social connectedness plays a significant role as mediator in the relationship between SAD and interpersonal love (Lee, Dean, & Jung, 2008) and is strongly associated with the level of self-esteem (Fatima et al., 2018).

59.4 Philautia

The seventh and eighth categories of interpersonal love are the two extremes of *philautia*: narcissism and positive self-qualities. To Aristotle, healthy *philautia* is vigorous "in both its orientation to self and to others" due to its inherent virtue (Grewal, 2016). "By contrast, its darker variant encompasses notions such as narcissism, arrogance and egotism" (Lomas, 2017). In its positive aspect, any interactivity "has beneficial consequences, whereas in the latter case, *philautia* will have disastrous consequences" (Fialho, 2007).

> The good man should be a lover of self (for he will both himself profit by doing noble acts, and will benefit his fellows), but the wicked man should not; for he will hurt both himself and his neighbours, following as he does evil passions. (Grewal, 2016)

59.4.1 Unhealthy Philautia

Unhealthy *philautia* is akin to clinical narcissism—a mental condition in which people function with an "inflated sense of their own importance [and a] deep need for excessive attention and admiration." Behind this mask of extreme confidence, the Mayoclinic report (2017a) states, "lies a fragile self-esteem that's vulnerable to the slightest criticism." SAD persons live on the periphery of morbid self-absorption through their self-centeredness. Their obsession with excessive attention (ADAA, 2019b) mirrors that of unhealthy *philautia*. In Classical Greece, persons could be accused of unhealthy *philautia* if they placed themselves above the greater good. Today, hubris has come to mean "an inflated sense of one's status, abilities, or accomplishments, especially when accompanied by haughtiness or arrogance" (Burton, 2016). The self-centeredness and self-absorption of a SAD person often present themselves as arrogance; in fact, the words are synonymous. The critical difference is that SAD persons do not possess an inflated sense of their own importance but one of insignificance.

59.4.2 Healthy Philautia

Aquinas' (1981) response to demons and disorder states, "evil cannot exist without good." The Greeks believed that the narcissism of unhealthy *philautia* would not exist without its complementary opposition of healthy *philautia*, which is commonly interpreted as the self-esteeming virtue—an unfortunate and wholly incomplete definition. Rather than self-esteem only, *philautia* incorporates the broader spectrum of all positive self-qualities.

> Rather, we are concerned here with various positive qualities prefixed by the term self, including -esteem, -efficacy, -reliance, -compassion, and -resliance. Aristotle argued in Nichomachean Ethics that self-love is a precondition for all other forms of love. (Lomas, 2017)

Positive self-qualities determine one's relation to self, to others, and the world. They provide the recognition that one is of value, consequential, and worthy of love. "*Philautia* is important in every sphere of life and can be considered a basic human need" (Sharma, 2014). To the Greeks, *philautia* "is the root of the heart of all the other loves" (Jericho, 2015). Gadamer (2009) writes of *philautia*: "Thus it is; in self-love one becomes aware of the true ground and the condition for all possible bonds with others and commitment to oneself." Healthy *philautia* is the love that is within oneself. It is not, explains Jericho (2015) "the desire for self and the root of selfishness." Ethicist John Deigh (2001) writes:

> Accordingly, when Aristotle remarks that a man's friendly relations with others come from his relations with himself ... he is making the point that self-love (*philautia*), as the best exemplar of love ... is the standard by which to judge the friendliness of the man's relations with others.

Positive self-qualities are obscured by SAD's culture of maladaptive self-beliefs and the interruption of the normal course of natural motivational development. Positive psychology embraces "a variety of beliefs about yourself, such as the appraisal of your own appearance, beliefs, emotions, and behaviors" Cherry, 2019). It points to measures "of how much a person values, approves of, appreciates, prizes, or likes him or herself" (Blascovich & Tomaka, 1991). Ritter et al. (2013) conducted a study on the relationship of SAD and self-esteem. The research concluded that SAD persons have significantly lower implicit and explicit self-esteem relative to healthy controls, which manifest in maladaptive self-beliefs of incompetence, unattractiveness, unworthiness, and other irrational self-evaluations.

Healthy *philautia* is essential for any relationship; it is easy to recognize how the continuous infusion of healthy *philautia* into a SAD person supports self-positivity and interconnectedness with all aspects of interpersonal love. "One sees in self-love the defining marks of friendship, which one then extends to a man's friendships with others" (Deigh, 2001). Self-worthiness and self-respect improve self-confidence, which allows the individual to overcome fears of criticism and rejection. Risk becomes less potentially consequential, and the playful aspects of *ludus* less threatening. Self-assuredness opens the door to traits commonly associated with successful interpersonal connectivity—persistence and persuasiveness, optimism of engagement, a willingness to vulnerability. A SAD person's recognition of her or his inherent value generates the realization that they "are a good person who deserves to be treated with respect" (Ackerman, 2019). A good person is, spiritually, one that is loved by God; reciprocation is instinctive and effortless. "To feel joy and fulfillment at being you is the experience of *philautia*" (Jericho, 2015). The *philautia* described by Aristotle, "is a necessary condition to achieve happiness" (Arreguín, 2009) which, as we continue down the classical Greek path, is *eudemonic*. In the words of positive psychologist Stephen (2019), *eudaimonia*

> describes the notion that living in accordance with one's *daimon*, which we take to mean 'character and virtue,' leads to the renewed awareness of one's 'meaning and purpose in life'.

Aristotle touted the striving for excellence as humanity's inherent aspiration (Kraut, 2018). He described *eudaimonia* as "activity in accordance with virtue" (Shields, 2015). *Eudaimonia* reflects the best activities of which man is capable. The word *eudaimonia* reflects personal and societal well-being as the chief good for man. "The eudaimonic approach ... focuses on meaning and self-realization and defines well-being in terms of the degree to which a person is fully functioning" (Ryan & Deci, 2001). It is through recognition of one's positive self-qualities and their potential productive contribution to the general welfare that one rediscovers the intrinsic capacity for love. Let us view this through the symbolism of Socrates' tale of the Cave (Plato, 1992). In it, we discover SAD persons chained to the wall. Their perspectives generate from the shadows projected by the unapproachable light outside the cave. They name these maladaptive self-beliefs: *useless, incompetent, timid, ineffectual, ugly, insignificant, stupid*. The prisoners have formed a subordinate dependency with their surroundings and resist any other reality until, one day, they find themselves loosed from their bondage and emerge into the light. Like the cave dwellers, the SAD person breaks away from maladaptive self-beliefs into healthy *philautia's* positive self-qualities, which encourage and support connectivity to all forms of interpersonal love.

A study published in *Cognitive Behaviour Therapy* (Hulme et al., 2012) looked at the effect of positive self-images on self-esteem in the SAD person. Eighty-eight students were screened with the Social Interaction Anxiety Scale (SIAS) and divided between the low self-esteem group or the high self-esteem group. The study had two visions. The first was to study the effect of positive and negative self-beliefs on implicit and explicit self-esteem. The second was to investigate how positive self-beliefs would affect the negative impact of social exclusion on explicit self-esteem, and whether high socially anxious participants would benefit as much as low socially anxious participants. The researchers used a variety of measures and instruments. The Social Interaction Anxiety Scale is standard in SAD therapy and CBT workshops; the Implicit Association Test (IAT) reveals the strength of the association between two different concepts. The Rosenberg Self-Esteem Scale (RSES) is a 10-item self-report measure of explicit self-esteem; the State-Trait Anxiety Inventory-Trait (STAI-T) is a 20-item scale that measures trait anxiety; and the Depression Anxiety Stress Scale-21 (DASS-21) is a self-report scale measuring depression, anxiety, and general distress.

> Social exclusion is inherently aversive and reduces explicit self-esteem in healthy individuals ... the effect of exclusion has been measured in terms of its impact on positive affect and on four fundamental need scores (self-esteem, control, belonging, and meaningful existence) which contribute to psychological well-being. (Hulme et al., 2012)

The study's results were consistent with evidence based on implicit self-esteem in other disorders; it found that negative self-imagery reduces positive implicit self-esteem in both high and low socially anxious participants. It provided supporting evidence of the effectiveness of promoting positive self-beliefs over negative ones, "because these techniques help patients to access a more positive working self" (Hulme et al., 2012). It also demonstrated that positive self-imagery maintained explicit self-esteem even in the face of social exclusion.

59.5 Conclusion

For 25 years, since the appearance of SAD in *DSM-IV*, the cognitive-behavioral approach has reportedly been effective in addressing social anxiety disorder. It is structurally sound and would conceivably remain the foundation for future programs, however it is not the therapeutic gestalt it claims to be. Productive cognitive-behavioral approaches emphasize the replacement of SAD's automatic negative thoughts and behaviors (ANT's) with automatic rational ones (ARTs). As defined by UCLA psychologists Hazlett-Stevens and Craske (2002), CBT approaches treatment with the assumption that a specific central or core feature is responsible for the observed symptoms and behavior patterns experienced (i.e., lawful relationships exist between this core feature and the maladaptive symptoms that result). Therefore, once the central feature is identified, targeted in treatment, and changed, the resulting maladaptive thoughts, symptoms, and behaviors will also change.

Clinicians and researchers have reported the lack of clear diagnostic definition for social anxiety disorder; features overlap and are comorbid with other mental health problems (ADAA, 2019a; Tsitsas & Paschali, 2014). Experts cite substantial discrepancies and disparity in the definition, epidemiology, assessment, and treatment of SAD (Nagata et al., 2015). More specifically, according to a study published in the *Journal of Consulting and Clinical Psychology* (Alden et al., 2018), "there is not enough attention paid in the literature to the ability to function in the close relationships" required for interpersonal love.

Standard CBT also lacks methodological clarity. Johnsen and Friborg (2015) cite the varying forms of CBT used in study and therapy over the years. Experts point to two predominant types of CBT: "the unadulterated CBT created by Beck and Ellis, which reflects the protocol-driven, highly goal-oriented, more standardized approach they first popularized," and the more integrative and collaborative approaches of "modern" CBT (Wong et al., 2013). This study maintains neither faction should be ignored if we are to effectively address the complexities of positive self-qualities and their importance to the individual's psychological well-being.

The deficit of positive self-qualities in individuals impaired by SAD's symptomatic culture of maladaptive self-beliefs combined with the interruption of the natural course of human motivational development is a new psychological concept in our evolving conscious complexity. Cognitive-behavioral therapies focus on resolving negative self-imaging and irrationality through programs of thought and behavioral modification. Positive self-qualities in healthy *philautia* is not a new concept; it was being discussed in symposia almost two-and-a-half centuries ago. The psychological ramifications and methods to address it, however, are in their formative stages. There is a need for innovative psychological and philosophical research to address the broader implications of healthy *philautia's* positive self-qualities, which could deliver the potential for self-love and societal concern to the SAD person, opening the bridge to the procurement of all forms of interpersonal love.

Kashdan, Weeks, & Savostyanova (2011) cite the "evidence that social anxiety is associated with diminished positive experiences, infrequent positive events, an absence of positive inferential biases in social situations, fear responses to overtly positive events, and poor quality of life." Models of CBT that attempt only to reduce the individual's avoidance behaviors would benefit from addressing more specifically the relational deficits that such people experience, as well as positive psychological measures to counter SAD's culture of maladaptive self-beliefs. Non-traditional and supported approaches, including those defined as new (third) wave (generation) therapies, with CBT serving as the foundational platform for integration, would widen the scope and perspective in comprehending SAD's evolving intricacies.

One such step is the integration of positive psychology within the cognitive behavioral therapy model which, "despite recent scientific attention to the positive spectrum of psychological functioning and social anxiety/SAD ... has yet to be integrated into mainstream accounts of assessment, theory, phenomenology, course, and treatment" (Kashdan et al., 2011). CBT would continue to modify automatic maladaptive self-beliefs, thoughts, and behaviors, and positive psychology would replace them with positive self-qualities.

Training in prosocial behavior and emotional literacy might be useful supplements to typical interventions. Behavioral exercises can be used to practice the execution of considerate and generous social skills. Positive affirmations have enormous subjective value as well. Data provide evidence for mindfulness and acceptance-based interventions, where the goal is not only to respond to the negativity of maladaptive self-beliefs but to pursue positive self-qualities despite the presence of unwanted negative thoughts, feelings, images, or memories. Castella et al. (2014) suggest motivational enhancement strategies to help clients overcome their resistance to new ideas and concepts. Ritter et al. (2013) tout the benefits of positive autobiography to counter SAD's association with negative experiences, and self-monitoring helps SAD persons to recognize and anticipate their maladaptive self-beliefs (Tsitsas & Paschali, 2014). Finally, the importance of considering the "nuanced and unique dynamics inherent in the relationships among emotional expression, intimacy, and overall relationship satisfaction for socially anxious individuals" should be thoroughly considered (Montesi et al., 2013). As positive psychology turns its attention to the broader spectrum of *philautia's* positive self-qualities, integration with CBT's behavior modification, neuroscience's network restructuring, and other non-traditional and supported approaches would establish a working platform for discovery.

References

Abel-Hirsch, N. (2010). The life instinct. *The International Journal of Psycho-Analysis, 91*(5), 1055–1071. https://doi.org/10.1111/j.1745-8315.2010.00304.x

ACBT (Association for Behavioral and Cognitive Therapies). (2019). *The world confederation of cognitive and behavioral therapies (WCCBT)*. Retrieved September 22, 2019, from http://www.abct.org/docs/Members/WCCBT_2019.pdf

Ackerman, C. (2019). What is self-esteem? A psychologist explains. *Positive Psychology*. Retrieved August 10, 2019, from http://www.positivepsychology.com/self-esteem/

ADAA (Anxiety and Depression Association of America). (2019a). *Facts and statistics*. Retrieved June 7, 2019, from https://adaa.org/learn-from-us/from-the-experts/blog-posts/consumer/understanding-anxiety-and-depression-lgbtq

ADAA (Anxiety and Depression Association of America). (2019b). *What's normal and what's not?* Retrieved August 12, 2019, from https://adaa.org/understanding-anxiety/obsessive-compulsive-disorder/just-for-teens/whats-normal-whats-not

Ades, T., & Dias, S. (2013). *Social anxiety disorder: Recognition, assessment and treatment*. NICE Clinical Guidelines, No. 159. Retrieved October 17, 2019, from https://www.ncbi.nlm.nih.gov/books/NBK327649/

Alden, L. E., Buhr, K., Robichaud, M., Trew, J. L., & Plasencia, M. L. (2018). Treatment of social approach processes in adults with social anxiety disorder. *Journal of Consulting and Clinical Psychology, 86*(6), 505–517. https://doi.org/10.1037/ccp0000306

Amen, D. G. (1998). *Change your brain, change your life: The breakthrough program for conquering anxiety, depression, oppressiveness, anger, and impulsiveness.* New York City: Three Rivers Press.

APA (American Psychiatric Association). (2017). Social anxiety disorder. In *Diagnostic and statistical manual of mental disorders: Fifth edition.* Washington, DC: American Psychiatric Association.

Aquinas, T. (1981). *St. Thomas Aquinas Summa theologica.* Chicago: Thomas More Publishing.

Aristotle. (1999). *Nicomachean ethics* (2nd ed.). Indianapolis, IN: Hackett Publishing.

Arreguín, H. Z. (2009, November 18). The role of philautia in Aristotle's ethics. *Acta Philosophica,* I381–390. Retrieved August 17, 2019, from http://www.actaphilosophica.it/sites/default/files/pdf/2_2009_arreguin.pdf

Beck, J. S. (2011). *Cognitive behavior therapy, second edition: Basics and beyond.* New York City: Guilford Press.

Blascovich, J., & Tomaka, J. (1991). *Measures of self-esteem. Measures of personality and social psychological attitudes.* San Diego, CA: Academic.

Bosche, M. (2019). *Social anxiety disorder and social phobia.* Anxiety.org. Retrieved from https://anxiety.org/social-anxiety-disorder-sad

Brenner, B. (2019). *Understanding anxiety and depression for LGBTQ people.* Anxiety and Depression Association of America. Retrieved April 7, 2019, from https://adaa.org/learn-from-us/from-the-experts/blog-posts/consumer/understanding-anxiety-and-depression-lgbtq

Burton, N. (2016). These are the 7 types of love. *Psychology Today.* Retrieved July 7, 2019, from https://www.psychologytoday.com/us/blog/hide-and-seek/201606/these-are-the-7-types-love

Capon, A. G., & Blakely, E. J. (2007). Checklist for healthy and sustainable communities. *New South Wales Public Health Bulletin, 18,* 51–54. https://doi.org/10.1071/nb07066

Castella, K. D., Goldin, P., Jazaieri, H., Ziv, M., Heimberg, R. G., & Gross, J. L. (2014). Emotion beliefs in social anxiety disorder: Associations with stress, anxiety, and well-being. *Australian Journal of Psychology, 66,* 139–148. https://doi.org/10.1111/ajpy.12053

CBT Conferences. (2019). *Conference series. Psychology health conference series.* Retrieved September 15, 2019, from https://psychologyhealth.conferenceseries.com/events-list/cognitive-behavioral-therapy

Chapdelaine, A., Carrier, J.-D., Fournier, L., Duhoux, A., & Roberge, P. (2018). Treatment adequacy for social anxiety disorder in primary care patients. *PLoS ONE, 13*(11). https://doi.org/10.1371/journal.pone.0206357

Cherry, K. (2019). What exactly is self-esteem? *Verywellmind.* Retrieved September 17, 2019, from https://www.verywellmind.com/what-is-self-esteem-2795868

Cuijpers, P., Cristea, L. A., Karyotaki, E., Reijnders, M., & Huibers, M. J. H. (2016). How effective are cognitive behavior therapies for major depression and anxiety disorders? A meta-analytic update of the evidence. *World Psychiatry, 15,* 245–258. https://doi.org/10.1002/wps.20346

Cuming, P., & Rapee, S. (2010). Social anxiety and self-protective communication style in close relationships. *Journal of Behaviour Research and Therapy, 48*(2), 87–96. https://doi.org/10.1016/j.brat.2009.09.010

Cuncic, A. (2018). How social anxiety affects dating and intimate relationships. *Verywellmind.* Retrieved September, 17, 2019, from https://www.verywellmind.com/adaa-survey-results-romantic-relationships-3024769

Darcy, K., Davila, J., & Beck, G. (2005). Is social anxiety associated with both interpersonal avoidance and interpersonal dependence? *Cognitive Therapy and Research, 29*(2), 171–186. https://doi.org/10.1007/s10608-005-3163-4

David, D., Cristea, I., & Hoffman, S. G. (2018). Why cognitive behavioral therapy is the current gold standard of psychotherapy. *Frontiers in Psychiatry, 9*(4). https://doi.org/10.3389/fpsyt.2018.00004

Deci, E. L., & Ryan, R. M. (2000). The "what" and "why" of goal pursuits: Human needs and the self-determination of behavior. *Psychological Inquiry, 11*(4), 227–268. https://doi.org/10.1207/s15327965pli1104_01

Deigh, J. (2001). *The moral self. Pauline Chazan. Mind.* London: Oxford University Press. https://doi.org/10.1093/mind/110.440.1069.

Desnoyers, A. J., Kocovski, N. L., Fleming, J. E., & Antony, M. M. (2017). Self-focused attention and safety behaviors across group therapies for social anxiety disorder. *Anxiety Stress & Coping, 30*(4), 441–455. https://doi.org/10.1080/10615806.2016.1239083

Fatima, M., Naizi, S., & Gayas, S. (2018). Relationship between self-esteem and social anxiety: Role of social connectedness as a mediator. *Pakistan Journal of Social and Clinical Psychology, 15*(2), 12–17. Retrieved from http://www.gcu.edu.pk/FullTextJour/PJSCS/2017b/2.%20%20Saba%20Ghayas%20(1).pdf

Felman, A. (2018). What's to know about social anxiety disorder? *Medical News Today.* Retrieved August 22, 2019, from https://www.medicalnewstoday.com/articles/176891.php

do Céu Fialho, M. (2007). "Philanthrôpia" and "Philautia" in Plutarch's "Theseus". *Hermathena, 182,* 71–83. Retrieved from https://www-jstor-org.ezproxy.sfpl.org/stable/23041719?seq=1#metadata_info_tab_contents

Gadamer, H.-G. (2009). Friendship and solidarity. *Research in Phenomenology, 39,* 3–12. https://doi.org/10.1163/156916408X389604

Gaudiano, B. A., & Herbert, J. D. (2003). Preliminary psychometric evaluation of a new self-efficacy scale and its relationship to treatment outcome in social anxiety disorder. *Cognitive Therapy and Research, 27*(5), 537–555. https://doi.org/10.1023/A:1026355004548

Grant, B., Hasin, D., Blanco, C., Stinson, F., Chou, S., & Goldstein, R. B. (2005). The epidemiology of social anxiety disorder in the United States: Results from the national epidemiologic survey on alcohol and related conditions. *Journal of Clinical Psychiatry, 66*(11), 1351–1361. https://doi.org/10.4088/jcp.v66n1102

Gregory, B., Wong, Q. J. J., Craig, D., Marker, C. D., & Peters, L. (2018). Maladaptive self-beliefs during cognitive behavioural therapy for social anxiety disorder: A test of temporal precedence. *Cognitive Therapy and Research, 42*(3), 261–272. https://doi.org/10.1007/s10608-017-9882-5

Grewal, D. S. (2016). The political theology of laissez-faire: From philia to self-love in commercial society. *Political Theology, 17*(5), 417–433. https://doi.org/10.1080/1462317X.2016.1211287

Halloran, M., & Kashima, E. (2006). Culture, social identity, and the individual. In *Individuality and the group: Advances in social identity.* London: Sage. https://doi.org/10.4135/9781446211946.n8

Hazlett-Stevens, H., & Craske, M. G. (2002). Brief cognitive-behavioral therapy: Definition and scientific foundations. In F. W. Bond & W. Dryden (Eds.), *Handbook of brief cognitive behaviour therapy* (pp. 1–20). New York: Wiley.

Heeren, A., & McNally, R. J. (2018). Social anxiety disorder as a densely interconnected network of fear and avoidance for social situations. *Cognitive Therapy and Research, 42*(6), 103–113. https://doi.org/10.1007/s10608-018-9952-3

Helm, B. (2017). Love. In *Stanford encyclopedia of philosophy.* Retrieved from https://plato.stanford.edu/entries/love/

Heshmat, S. (2014). Social anxiety disorder (SAD). SAD is a risk factor for addiction. *Psychology Today.* https://www.psychologytoday.com/us/blog/science-choice/201410/social-anxiety-disorder-sad. Accessed 17 August 2019.

Hirsch, C. R., & Clark, D. (2004). Information-processing bias in social phobia. *Clinical Psychology Review, 24*(7), 799–825. https://doi.org/10.1016/j.cpr.2004.07.005

Hoffman, S. G., Asnaani, M. A. U., & Hinton, D. E. (2010). Cultural aspects in social anxiety and social anxiety disorder. *Depression and Anxiety, 27*(12), 1117–1127. https://doi.org/10.1002/da.20759

HPD (Histrionic Personality Disorder). (2019). *Psychology Today.* Retrieved September 12, 2019, from https://www.psychology today.com/us/conditions/histrionic-personality-disorder

Hulme, N., Hirsch, C., & Stopa, L. (2012). Images of the self and self-esteem: Do positive self-images improve self-esteem in social anxiety? *Cognitive Behaviour Therapy, 41*(2), 163–173. https://doi.org/10.1080/16506073.2012.664557

Jazaieri, H., Morrison, A. S., & Gross, J. J. (2015). The role of emotion and emotion regulation in social anxiety disorder current. *Psychiatry Reports, 17*(1), 531. https://doi.org/10.1007/s11920-014-0531-3

Jericho, L. (2015). Inner spring: Eros, agape, and the six forms of loving. *Lilipoh, 20*(79), 38–39.

Johnsen, T. J., & Friborg, O. (2015). The effects of cognitive behavioral therapy as an anti-depressive treatment is falling. *Psychological Bulletin, 141*(4), 747–768. https://doi.org/10.1037/bul0000015

Kaczkurkin, A. N., & Foa, E. B. (2015). Cognitive-behavioral therapy. *Dialogues in Clinical Neuroscience, 17*(3), 337–346. Cognitive-behavioral therapy for anxiety disorders: An update on the empirical evidence.

Kampmann, I. L., Emmelkamp, P. M. G., & Morina, N. (2019). Cognitive predictors of treatment outcome for exposure therapy: Do changes in self-efficacy, self-focused attention, and estimated social costs predict symptom improvement in social anxiety disorder? *BMC Psychiatry, 19*(80). https://doi.org/10.1186/s12888-019-2054-2

Kashdan, T. B., Weeks, J. W., & Savostyanova, A. A. (2011). Whether, how, and when social anxiety shapes positive experiences and events: A self-regulatory framework and treatment implications. *Clinical Psychology Review, 31*, 786–799. https://doi.org/10.1016/j.cpr.2011.03.012

Kraut, R. (2018). Aristotle's ethics. In *The Stanford encyclopedia of philosophy*. Retrieved September 27, 2019, from https://plato.stanford.edu/cgi-bin/encyclopedia/archinfo.cgi?entry=aristotle-ethics

Lacan, J. (1978). *Seminar XI: The four fundamental concepts of psychoanalysis*. London: W.W. Norton.

Lee, R. M., Dean, B. L., & Jung, K. R. (2008). Social connectedness, extraversion, and subjective well-being: Testing a mediation model. *Personality and Individual Differences, 45*(5), 414–419. https://doi.org/10.1016/j.paid.2008.05.017

Lomas, T. (2017). The flavours of love: A cross-cultural lexical analysis. *Journal for the Theory of Social Behaviour, 48*(1), 134–152. https://doi.org/10.1111/jtsb.12158

Lyford, C. (2017). Is cognitive behavioral therapy as effective as clinicians believe? Despite longstanding authority, new research questions CBT's reliability. *Psychotherapy Networker*. Retrieved August 27, 2019, from https://www.psychotherapynetworker.org/blog/details/705/is-cognitive-behavioral-therapy-as-effective-as-clinicians

Manfro, G. G., Heldt, E., Cordiol, A. V., & Otto, M. W. (2008). Cognitive-behavioral therapy in panic disorder. *Brazilian Journal of Psychiatry, 2*(8), 1–7. Retrieved from https://www.scielo.br/scielo.php?pid=S1516-44462008000600005andscript=sci_arttextandtlng=en

Maslow, A. H. (1943). A theory of human motivation. *Psychological Review, 50*(4), 370–396. https://doi.org/10.1037/h0054346

Mayoclinic. (2017a). *Personality disorders. Mayo Foundation for Medical Education and Research*. Retrieved July 25, 2019, from https://www.mayoclinic.org/diseases-conditions/personality-disorders/symptoms-causes/syc-20354463

Mayoclinic. (2017b). *Social anxiety disorder (social phobia). Mayo Foundation for Medical Education and Research*. Retrieved August 13, 2019, from https://www.mayoclinic.org/diseases-conditions/social-anxiety-disorder/symptoms-causes/syc-20353561

McGinn, L. K. (2019). International associates. Association for behavioral and cognitive therapies. In *53rd Annual Convention*. Retrieved September 14, 2019, from http://www.abct.org/Members/?m=mMembers&fa=InternationalAssociates

MHA (Mental Health America). (2019). *Social anxiety disorder*. Retrieved September 15, 2019, from https://www.mhanational.org/conditions/social-anxiety-disorder

Montesi, J. L., Conner, G. T., Gordon, E. A., & Fauber, R. L. (2013). On the relationship among social anxiety, intimacy, sexual communication, and sexual satisfaction in young couples. *Archives of Sexual Behavior, 42*, 81–91. https://doi.org/10.1007/s10508-012-9929-3

Mullen, R. F. (2018). *What is cognitive-behavioral?* rechanneling.org. Retrieved from https://www.rechanneling.org/page-13.htm.

Nagata, T., Suzuki, F., & Teo, A. R. (2015). Generalized social anxiety disorder: A still-neglected anxiety disorder 3 decades since Liebowitz's review. *Psychiatry and Clinical Neurosciences, 69*(12), 724–740. https://doi.org/10.1111/pcn.12327

NAMI (National Alliance on Mental Illnesses). (2019). *Psychotherapy*. Retrieved September 15, 2019, from https://www.nami.org/learn-more/treatment/psychotherapy

Nardi, A. E. (2003). The social and economic burden of social anxiety disorder. *BMJ, 327*. https://doi.org/10.1136/bmj.327.7414.515

NCCMH (National Collaborating Centre for Mental Health (UK). (2013). *Social anxiety disorder: Recognition, assessment and treatment*. NICE Clinical Guidelines, No. 159. Retrieved September 15, 2019, from https://www.ncbi.nlm.nih.gov/books/NBK266258/

NIMH (National Institute of Mental Health). (2017). *Social anxiety disorder*. Retrieved September 15, 2019, from https://www.nimh.nih.gov/health/statistics/social-anxiety-disorder.shtml

Plato. (1992). *The republic*. Indianapolis, IN: Hackett Publishing.

Read, D. L., Clark, G. I., Rock, A. J., & Coventry, W. L. (2018). Adult attachment and social anxiety: The mediating role of emotion regulation strategies. *PLoS ONE, 13*(12). https://doi.org/10.1371/journal.pone.0207514

Reuben, A., & Schaefer, J. (2017). *Mental illness is far more common than we knew*. Scientific American. Retrieved from https://blogs.scientificamerican.com/observations/mental-illness-is-far-more-common-than-we-knew/

Richards, T. A. (2014). *Overcoming social anxiety disorder: Step by step*. Phoenix, AZ: The Social Anxiety Institute Press.

Richards, T. A. (2019). *What is social anxiety disorder? Symptoms, treatment, prevalence, medications, insight, prognosis*. The Social Anxiety Institute. Retrieved June 14, 2019, from https://socialphobia.org/social-anxiety-disorder-definition-symptoms-treatment-therapy-medications-insight-prognosis

Ritchie, H., & Roser, M. (2018). *Mental health. Our world in data*. Retrieved October 7, 2019, from https://ourworldindata.org/mental-health

Ritter, V., Ertel, C., Beil, K., Steffens, M. C., & Stangier, U. (2013). In the presence of social threat: Implicit and explicit self-esteem in social anxiety disorder. *Cognitive Therapy & Research, 37*(6), *1101–1109*. https://doi.org/10.1007/s10608-013-9553-0

Rodebaugh, T. L., Lim, M. H., Shumaker, E. A., Levinson, C. A., & Thompson, T. (2015). Social anxiety and friendship quality over time. *Cognitive Behaviour Therapy, 44*(6), 502–511. https://doi.org/10.1080/16506073.2015.1062043

Ryan, R. M., & Deci, E. L. (2001). On happiness and human potentials: A review of research on hedonic and eudaimonic well-being. *Annual Review of Psychology, 52*, 141–166. https://doi.org/10.1146/annurev.psych.52.1.141

Sharma, A. (2014). Self-esteem is the sense of personal worth and competence that persona associate with their self—concepts. *IOSR Journal of Nursing and Health Science, 3*(6), Ver.4: 16–20.

Shelton, J. (2018). Social anxiety disorder: Symptoms, causes and treatment. *Psycom*. Retrieved September 7, 2019, from https://www.psycom.net/social-anxiety-disorder-overview

Shields, C. (2015). Aristotle. In *Stanford encyclopedia of philosophy*. Stanford, CA: The Metaphysics Research Lab. Retrieved August 23, 2019, from https://plato.stanford.edu/entries/aristotle/

Steele, B. F. (1995). Psychodynamic and biological factors in child maltreatment. In M. E. Helfer, R. S. Kempe, R. D. Krugman (Eds.), *The battered child* (5th Edn., pp. 73-103) University of Chicago Press. https://doi.org/10.1192/S000712500015041X

Stein, M. B., & Stein, D. J. (2008). Social anxiety disorder. *The Lancet, 371*(9618), 1045–1136. https://doi.org/10.1016/S0140-6736(08)60488-2

Stephen, J. (2019). What is eudaimonic happiness? How and why positive psychologists are learning from Aristotle. *Psychology Today*. Retrieved September 12, 2019, from https://www.psychologytoday.com/us/blog/what-doesnt-kill-us/201901/what-is-eudaimonic-happiness

Topaz, B. (2018). You can stop social anxiety from ruining your relationships. *PsychCentral*. Retrieved August 27, 2019, from https://psychcentral.com/blog/you-can-stop-social-anxiety-from-ruining-your-relationships/

Tsitsas, G. D., & Paschali, A. A. (2014). A cognitive-behavior therapy applied to a social anxiety disorder and a specific phobia, case study. *Health Psychology Research, 2*(3), 1603. https://doi.org/10.4081/hpr.2014.1603

UNLM (U.S. National Library of Medicine). (2018). *Personality disorders*. Retrieved September 27, 2019, from https://medlineplus.gov/personalitydisorders.html

WebMD. (2019). *What is social anxiety disorder?* WebMD Medical Reference. Retrieved August 27, 2019, from https://www.webmd.com/anxiety-panic/guide/mental-health-social-anxiety-disorder#1

Whitbourne, S. K. (2018). Is social anxiety getting in the way of your relationships? *Psychology Today*. Retrieved August 14, 2019, from https://www.psychologytoday.com/us/blog/fulfillment-any-age/201806/is-social-anxiety-getting-in-the-way-your-relationships

Wong, Q. L. L., Moulds, M., & Rapee, R. M. (2013). Validation of the self-beliefs related to social anxiety scale. *Assessment, 21*(3), 300–311. https://doi.org/10.1177/1073191113485120

Yeilding, R. (2017). *Developing the positive in managing social anxiety*. National Social Anxiety Center. Retrieved August 14, 2019, from https://nationalsocialanxietycenter.com/2017/09/18/developing-positive-managing-social-anxiety/

Zimmerman, M., Dalrymple, K., Chelminski, I., Young, D., & Galione, J. H. (2010). Recognition of irrationality of fear and the diagnosis of social anxiety disorder and specific phobia in adults: Implications for criteria revision in DSM-5. *Depression and Anxiety, 27*(11), 1044–1049. https://doi.org/10.1002/da.20716

Robert F. Mullen is director of ReChanneling Inc, an organization focusing on the alleviation of Psychophysiological Malfunctions (neuroses) through research and program development. Finding one-size-fits-all approaches inadequate in addressing the complexities of the individual Personality, *ReChanneling* advocates a psychobiographic approach of individual analysis, integrating positive psychology's optimal human functioning with CBT's behavior modification, neural restructuring, and other supported and non-traditional methods, Psychophysiological Malfunctions are generated by mind, body, spirit, and emotions acting jointly. *ReChanneling* utilizes the emotional retrieval and mastery of Stanislavski's method, and the nine right truths (right choice) of *Abhidharma*. Maslowian hierarchical concerns are addressed by a program-in-development called healthy philautia. Dr. Mullen is a philosophy graduate of California Institute of Integral Studies; his disciplines include contemporary behavior, modified psychobiography, and method psychology.

Chapter 60
"Different Race, Same Cultures": Developing Intercultural Identities

Claude-Hélène Mayer and Lolo Jacques Mayer

Abstract This commentary describes the impact of intercultural narrations and autoethnographic experiences regarding intercultural identity development within the context of building the base for successful intercultural encounters based on a loving view of the person. It refers to the importance to see individuals as a whole, entire arts project, based on intersectionalities. Each individual and each individual's life is seen as a construct of stories, narrations and experiences of intersectionalities and thereby as a work of arts. This chapter needs to be read not as a scientific account, but rather as a commentary, as a pleading, a final speech for intercultural identity development through narrative constructions in the frame of love.

Keywords Love · Intersectionalities · Culture · Race · Narration · Intercultural identity development · Life as a work of arts

---

C.-H. Mayer (✉)
Department of Industrial Psychology and People Management, University of Johannesburg, Johannesburg, South Africa

Institut für therapeutische Kommunikation und Sprachgebrauch, Europa Universität Viadrina, Frankfurt (Oder), Germany
e-mail: claudemayer@gmx.net

L. J. Mayer
Courtney House International School, Pretoria, South Africa
e-mail: lolomayer@gmx.net

60.1 Developing Intercultural Identities Through Narratives[1]

> But couldn't everyone's life become a work of art?
> Why should the lamp or the house be an art object, but not your life?
> Michel Foucault

The Life as a Work of Art: Magnificently Created!

When I started to explore this topic for myself, I felt humbled. I could immediately feel the energy rising within my entire body. The human as an art's object! I felt the world of creativity, of colours, of possibilities and love appearing in front of my inner eye. I could feel the limitlessness of this statement, and I could see the doors opening to new topics, contexts, situations—I could literally see myself taking the paint brush—starting to paint, taking the fountain pen—starting to write, taking the clay, modelling new parts of the stories, putting old ones together. Can you feel this energy of the artist who has just decided to create something new?

Maybe you know this energy from intercultural encounters. All intercultural encounters have the potential of creating something new, something innovative and creative. Often, we do give intercultural encounters specific topics, such as building peace or working together effectively. However, I would like to argue that intercultural encounters are basically about the question "who am I?" and "who are we?" and "how do we define ourselves as human beings?"

In times of diversification and internationalisation in all aspects of life, the questions of "who am I?" and "who are we?" gains in importance and it is unbelievable that often educational systems, such as schools and higher education institutions, do hardly put any effort into responding to this question and making their students find answers for themselves. The topic of creating intercultural identities in human beings all over the world has not yet become part of the curricula—however, the time is overdue to look into this topic more deeply and to develop human beings in the name of holistic growth and a loving frame.

Educational systems, such as schools and higher education institutions, have major influence in creating intercultural identity development from an early age onwards. Besides these formal ways of education, training situations and auto-didactical learning processes can lead to intercultural identity development which fosters human understanding, based on the principle of building loving relationships.

In a globalising world, which grows in diversity and in complexity, educational systems and didactical concepts need to focus on intercultural ways of how to develop young, as well as matured learners, in terms of a complex understanding of themselves and others in a culturally complex and hybrid world.

---

[1]The first draft, of this paper was presented at the SIETAR Europa conference in Dublin, Ireland, on 22–27 May 2017. A revised, extended version was presented in a guest lecture on 11 December 2019 at the Department of Intercultural Communication, University of Passau, Passau, Germany, chaired by Professor Christoph Barmeyer.

I argue here that the work with narratives are one great way to work with learners from various cultures on building their intercultural identities in formal and informal educational settings.

Narratives are stories and stories are as old as humankind—they are universal, too. Humans have always used stories to create meaning, to create a common space, to transfer knowledge and to increase learning of a person, no matter what the content of the story is.

Now, why not use the power of narrations for intercultural identity development? The narrative method has gained popularity interdisciplinary in the sciences of the Western world and researchers have highlighted that narratives do not only stimulate the brain activity, but also touch the heart of a person through its emotional content. They can easily create spaces of love.

Intercultural identity development stories are useful to work in educational settings to connect through exchange of experiences and ideas, reflection on intercultural encounters and multiple cultural perspectives (Mayer & Wolting, 2016). We work with these stories to create awareness of the intra-psychological diversity of a person and the spaces that stories open when used in a positive and constructive way.

In educational settings, we either read the intercultural narrations to the learners, or we tell our own stories, and we inspire them to create their own stories, responding to the question "Who am I?", particularly in a diverse world.

Please feel invited to listen to L.'s story on his autoethnographic intercultural identity development experiences in post-apartheid South Africa and Germany.

60.2 "Different Race, Same Cultures": Autobiographical Experiences on Intercultural Identity Development

> I just wanna be me ... someone who will "go forth and set the world on fire."[2]
> Loyola St. Ignatius

Hi, my name is Lolo and I am here today to talk about the theme "Different race, same cultures".

Let's start of on an easy note... as you might most probably anticipate, looking at me ..., standing here in front of you ... I am ... German. However, let me tell you: there are people in the world who would not immediately see that I am German.

And this is exactly what this talk is all about—this talk is about race and culture and about my personal experiences living and growing up in post-Apartheid South Africa and Germany.

---

[2]The metaphor "setting the world on fire" is understood as a positive image which brings light into the dark through passion, illuminating the world with strengths and warmth in a peaceful way. It is not meant to be understood as a violent or aggressive way of transforming the world and the actions within the world.

Let us focus on South Africa first. I was born in Port Elisabeth, a 2.5 million inhabitants city right at the Indian Ocean. Within South Africa, I lived in many different places, such as PE, Grahamstown, Cape Town, which is predominantly inhabited by people of mixed origin, as well as Jo'burg—a pretty much "Black city", mainly inhabited by Zulu and Sotho-speakers. Finally, I lived in Pretoria, a predominantly Afrikaans-speaking metropolis.

During the past 9 years of my life, I have travelled countries such as the US, Australia, New Zealand, different African countries and a few European ones ... I speak English and German as my first languages, I love reading, technical stuff, people with humour and staying up 'til late. I would further consider myself as a global citizen, as someone who loves to think and as an inventor, as a dancer as well.

During daily life, people do not seem to see all of these things that I am and the things that I like. Although these are the things that make me... who I am. They seem to get stuck with one aspect of my outer appearance—my skin colour. However, I would argue that none of us here, that no person in the world is defined by skin colour. We are all defined by who we are and by who we chose to be. We are all defined by the content of our character, by the content of our heart, as Martin Luther King said many years ago.

To make you understand why I would like to talk about this topic, you need to have an idea about post-Apartheid South Africa. During Apartheid, White colonialists came to South Africa and installed a system which defined the White people as the superior class, followed in hierarchy by the Indians, the Coloured and the Black people. Mind you: the Black people were not completely Black and the White people were not so pale—however, to make it easy, they used terms regarding skin colour to classify people.

Twenty-three years after Apartheid has ended, the South African society has installed a new system which just turned this hierarchy upside down and Blacks now gain preferential treatment—it is now "Blacks First". So, things have changed in a way in which people of different race are being treated. However, what stays seemingly the same is the clarity with which people classify others based on racial features. And this can be pretty annoying when you feel that racial classification does not always match with cultural belonging or global citizenship.

Let me give you a few examples so that you can understand what I mean.

You need to know that I was adopted when I was only a few weeks old. That is how I came to grow up living in various places, getting to know different cultures and speaking German and English as my mother tongues.

So, one day, my mum took us to the German school, thinking that we would maybe enjoy attending it. The principle, straigth away, offered that I could attend the "Black class" which had just been introduced. It was a class for "Black kids from the township" to get access to proper education and German language courses.

My mum, obviously a bit irritated, explained to him that I spoke German fluently and that she would not see any reason to put me into this so called "Black class". However, the school principle did not want to let go of his idea and said that I might feel more integrated in this "Black Class" and—if you knew my mum—you could imagine that this was the end of our talk.

Just a little excursus:

By now you might be aware that my mum is of German origin and ... sometimes some people just do not understand how we belong. So, often in South African public spaces, such as shopping centers or at sport events, people keep on asking her—with a curious and surprised face—how my mum comes to walk around with me. In a German context nobody ever asks this question, because people might just assume that we adopted each other and keep silent.

Now, in a South African context, people ask and wait for an interesting story to evolve—What can we say?

In the beginning, my mum explained that I was adopted. She then got pretty bored with this response and came up with others, such as: "We met in a previous life and can not get rid of each other" or "Can you not see the similarity in the way we smile, how our nose is shaped, in the way we walk?" or "How do you assume we do not belong?" or "We share the same MBTI preferences...." People usually then look and try to see the similarities ... and try even harder ... but just to—in the end—slowly shake their heads and give up.

So, one day, my mum took me to this international school, telling the principle that I am a gifted kid and that I would need to skip a class straight away. You might anticipate how this principle's face froze. The principle looked at me, at her, at me and slowly nodded her head. She looked at me with huge eyes and scanned my entire body from top to bottom, as if she was searching for a sign of giftedness ... as if this did not fit with my face ... or my skin colour?

In other incidences, people classify me as "one of theirs" and this happened many times on the street or at the shops. In Jo'burg or Pretoria, people usually try to talk to me in Zulu, no matter if they know me or not, they just imply their language on me, just because of the fact that I share—maybe in their views—part of their features. However, I do not speak Zulu at all and when people start talking to me in Zulu, I usually tell them that I do not understand their language—soon they realise that there is something "wrong with me".

When my mum then comes in and tells them that I grew up speaking English and German, they usually do not want to believe that I am fluent in German and they even act surprised: how would this be possible? As if humans—or only me?—would not be able to learn any language whatsoever, independently of the colour of their skin.

In South Africa, often people think that race equals culture, that being Black is bound to speaking a Black South African language and being part of a Black South African ethnic group. However, for me it is different.

I experience myself as being in a different space. As if I am "Elmar" in a herd of elephants—I am sure you know Elmar? If not, for your explanation, Elmar is an elephant with coloured checks who looks quite different to his fellow grew elephants.

Because I like to speak both languages, English and German, I feel pretty much okay in Germany, as well as in South Africa. I hate to learn Latin—as many other German kids do—and I hate sunshine and sitting at the beach as many of my black South Africans friends do. I love to eat Italian food and sing French songs ... and I would consider myself a global citizen.

Let me tell you: not only in post-Apartheid South Africa one experiences strange things! In Germany they are just a bit different, but when you think about them, they might file down to the same categories.

One day, on the train the conductor said to me that no matter if I had a valid ticket, I was still a "black rider". I looked at him in surprise, I even had to laugh spontaneously, but in the end, I realised that this is not even funny—this is just racist.

The other day at the sports club, one of the kids brought cake to share and—when my brother asked him if he would also share with us—he said he would not share with "black people", just ignoring all the other aspects of our personalities, reducing us to our skin colour. Although we had just attended the same sports club time—we were not accepted within the group of the cake eaters and ... although we spoke the same language and shared the same metropolis, he—this "blond-haired guy"— would not accept us as one of theirs—because of our skin colour?

My mum was so shocked about the whole incident that she decided to talk with the father of the sportsmate who—since then—always brings extra cake for us to the sports club—which also does not make us feel better, the same or more accepted— but rather different. Now, we are the cake eaters ... and they are not.

It is interesting that—also if you might feel "the same"—some people might only see "the difference". However, this does not always need to turn out negative. It can bring you unexpected gifts!

Just a few weeks ago, I walked through a German town, when a middle-aged friendly lady approached me, stuttering in broken English with a heavy German accent. I was so amazed how hard she tried to communicate with me—obviously not in her mother tongue—that I could not even say a word, and she left me standing with my mouth open, when she took off her gloves, handing them over to me, thinking that I was an unaccompanied refugee.

I was amazed:

- how we actually spoke the same language and did not come to speak the same,
- how we somehow shared the same culture, but did not come to share it though,
- but how our differences brought us together to overcome the gaps she saw in our realities.

I have learned that—sometimes—we think that we are many things, but we are often brought down and limited to only one or two aspects of who we are.

I have seen that people reduce others to what is most obvious to them, like the skin colour or their facial features. I have experienced how it feels when you are limited to a certain group of people and when people then realise that you actually not even fit into this limited group you are reduced to.

So, let me tell you:

I just wanna be me—someone who will make a difference by looking into the heart, by seeing the content of a person's character, thereby creating a new reality. And by doing this, *I will go forth and set the world on fire!*

Acknowledgements We would like to thank SIETAR Europe and the SIETAR Europe conference participants at the conference in Dublin in 2017 for appreciating our talk and for the ongoing discussions around concepts of race and culture. We would also like to express our special thanks to Professor Christoph Barmeyer, Lehrstuhl für Interkulturelle Kommunikation at the University of Passau, Passau, Germany, for inviting us to present a revised version of our talk to students at his institute in December 2019.

Reference

Mayer, C.-H., & Wolting, S. (2016). *Purple Jacaranda. Narrations on transcultural identity development*. Münster: Waxmann.

Claude-Hélène Mayer is a Full Professor in Industrial and Organisational Psychology at the Department of Industrial Psychology and People Management at the University of Johannesburg, an Adjunct Professor at the European University Viadrina in Frankfurt (Oder), Germany and a Senior Research Associate at Rhodes University, Grahamstown, South Africa. She holds a Ph.D. in Psychology (University of Pretoria, South Africa), a Ph.D. in Management (Rhodes University, South Africa), a Doctorate (Georg-August University, Germany) in Political Sciences (sociocultural anthropology and intercultural didactics) and Master degrees in Ethnology, Intercultural Didactics and Socio-economics (Georg-August University, Germany) as well as in Crime Science, Investigation and Intelligence (University of Portsmouth, UK). Her Venia Legendi is in Psychology with focus on work, organizational, and cultural psychology (Europa Universität Viadrina, Germany). She has published numerous monographs, text collections, accredited journal articles, and special issues on transcultural mental health and well-being, salutogenesis, transforming shame, transcultural conflict management and mediation, women in leadership in culturally diverse work contexts, coaching, culture and crime and psychobiography.

Lolo Jacques Mayer is a student at Courtney College International in Pretoria, South Africa. He is an aspiring young author and public speaker. He writes childrens' books and short stories. During the past years he has presented talks on contemporary socio-cultural topics at public events, universities and international conferences. His research interests focus on critical discussions of race, culture and identity. He is a member of Mensa Germany.